DATE DUE

LAW OF BUSINESS ORGANIZATIONS AND SECURITIES REGULATION

ROBERT A. PRENTICE

University of Texas at Austin

PRENTICE-HALL, INC., *Englewood Cliffs, New Jersey 07632*

Library of Congress Cataloging-in-Publication Data

Prentice, Robert A. (Date)
   Law of business organizations and securities
regulation.

   Includes index.
   1. Business enterprises—United States—Cases.
2. Securities—United States—Cases. I. Title.
KF1355.A7P74 1987   346.73′065   86-30673
ISBN   0-13-526336-0   347.30665

Editorial/production supervision and interior design: Marcia Rulfs
Cover design: Edsal Enterprises
Manufacturing buyer: Harry P. Baisley

Printed in the United States of America

10   9   8   7   6   5   4   3   2   1

ISBN   0-13-526336-0   01

Prentice-Hall International (UK) Limited, *London*
Prentice-Hall of Australia Pty. Limited, *Sydney*
Prentice-Hall Canada Inc., *Toronto*
Prentice-Hall Hispanoamericana, S.A., *Mexico*
Prentice-Hall of India Private Limited, *New Delhi*
Prentice-Hall of Japan, Inc., *Tokyo*
Prentice-Hall of Southeast Asia Pte. Ltd., *Singapore*
Editora Prentice-Hall do Brasil, Ltda., *Rio de Janeiro*

CONTENTS

Nontax Factors

Tax Factors
Noncorporate Taxation / Corporate Taxation / Subchapter S Corporations

Miscellaneous Forms of Business
Joint Venture / Joint Stock Company / Business Trust / Real Estate Investment Trust / Professional Corporations

Partnership Law

Corporation Law

Part 2   Law of Securities Regulation

1933 Act

TABLE OF CASES

PREFACE

The subjects of business organizations and securities regulation are closely related. One cannot study business organizations without a knowledge of securities regulation unless the study is confined to the smallest organizations. Even then, to totally ignore securities regulation is risky. Similarly, it is difficult to fully appreciate much of the law of securities regulation without a background in business organizations.

I teach courses in both business organizations and securities regulation. Desiring a textbook which would have sufficient business organizations material for an entire course (and supplemental securities regulation law) *and* sufficient securities regulation material for an entire course (with background business organizations material included), I struck upon writing this text. Its salient feature is that it contains enough business organizations law for one course and enough securities regulation law for a separate course.

The book takes a basically traditional approach. In my classrooms, it will replace the law school casebooks I have been using. Though cases are, of course, critically important, I do not believe that casebooks are the optimum format for business students. I have included several cases per chapter, but also substantially more explanatory text than appears in law school casebooks.

The book is intended for juniors, seniors, MBAs, and MPAs of the type I have been fortunate enough to teach in recent years.

I have tried to make the book as accurate and up-to-date as possible. Unfortunately, securities law, and to a slightly lesser degree, corporate law, change daily. The inevitable but unfortunate time lag between when the typed manuscript leaves my hands and when it shows up as a textbook in the bookstores guarantees that there will be some changes in the law which will have to be explained. Errors due to factors other than passage of time are solely my responsibility.

I hope that most of the readings in the book will be helpful and enlightening. A few of them are from articles I have written in other publications.

The end-of-chapter questions are all based on real cases and quite a few are based on recent cases. Many have been exam questions in past semesters in my courses.

The cases contained in the text have been heavily edited. Citations, footnotes, and irrelevant discussions have been omitted, sometimes without ellipses. The essence and flavor of the opinions have been preserved, however.

The statutory supplement, which is recommended highly, will contain all necessary statutes and rules, though space limitations have required some omissions.

I am grateful to every person who buys this book. I am also grateful to the kind folks at Prentice-Hall, especially David Boelio, and to those long-suffering individuals who served as reviewers, including: Professor Thomas Bowers, Indiana University; Professor James W. Freeman University of Kentucky; Professor A. A. Lee Hegner, University of Denver; Professor James Jackman, Oklahoma State University; Professor Gene A. Marsh, University of Alabama; and Professor Lamont Walton, Michigan State University.

CHOOSING
THE PROPER FORM
OF BUSINESS ORGANIZATION

NONTAX FACTORS

A business enterprise—be it engaged in the manufacture of steel, the marketing of chocolate chip cookies, or the sale of accounting advice—can take any of several forms. The four most important forms in the American economy are the sole proprietorship, the general partnership, the limited partnership, and the corporation. The last three of these raise the most legal problems and questions in the area of business organizations, and they will receive substantial treatment in this text.

The following excerpt will introduce these forms of business organization, set the framework for more detailed discussions that will come later, and address some of the more important nontax factors in choosing a form of business enterprise.

"CHOOSING THE PROPER STRUCTURE FOR YOUR BUSINESS" [1]

Robert A. Prentice

Real Estate Business (Spring 1983)

Does your present organizational structure best fit your needs? Should it be a sole proprietorship? A partnership? A corporation? What type of corporation? Choosing the proper organizational form requires careful consideration of a myriad of factors [sic].

Types of Organizations

Numerically, America's most popular form of business organization is the *sole proprietorship*, or one-owner business. In a sole proprietorship, the founder of the business owns all the assets, hires the employees and is ultimately responsible for all the decisions that are made. He is "the boss" with everything to gain if the business does well, and everything to lose if it does not.

A *general partnership* is frequently used when two or more persons begin a business together. Although the specific operation of a partnership may be varied, generally all partners contribute to the success of the venture (with money, time or both), all have an equal say in partnership decisions, all share profits (or losses) equally and the acts of each one while carrying on partnership business are binding on all the other partners.

The *limited partnership* was devised because there are many persons who have the money to invest in an enterprise, but not the time to participate in its operation. A limited partnership can have any number (from one to thousands) of limited partners, but it must have at least one general partner who controls the business and is ultimately responsible for its liabilities. Though denominated "partners," the limited partners are really little more than passive investors.

Whereas partnerships are, in the eyes of the law, merely aggregations of their individual partners, a *corporation* is an entity unto itself. It can sue, be sued, own and transfer property, etc., all in its own name. Its owners are the shareholders, who may or may not take an active role in the corporation's business by serving on its board of directors, acting as officers, or even serving as employees. The corporate form has sufficient advantages so that many more times the volume of business is carried on through corporations each year than through any other form of business . . .

Liability

One of the most important factors in choosing a form of business organization is the concept of liability. The sole proprietor takes all the profits in a business, but he or she also suffers all the losses. Any contracts made in the name of the business are the

---

proprietor's to pay, as are any tort liabilities sustained by the business. The owner, therefore, has *unlimited* liability.

In a general partnership, each partner also has unlimited liability and is completely liable for *all* the partnership's obligations—tort or contract. As a partner, you are liable not only for the contracts you make and the torts you commit, but also for all the contracts and torts of the other partners and the partnership's employees. If another partner makes a contract on behalf of the partnership, you are responsible even if you did not know of its making or if you had told the partner not to make it. For this reason, you must exercise extreme caution in selecting business partners.

If the partnership incurs staggering debts, the creditors have the right to ask that you pay the total amount. Your liability is unlimited in that, even if you intended to invest only $10,000 in the business, the creditors have the right to satisfy their claims out of all your property. If you have a separate savings account of $100,000 that you had intended to use to buy a retirement home, that can be reached by the creditors. The only things the creditors cannot reach are those items protected by state law—usually your home, car, clothing, and the tools of your trade.

In a limited partnership, there must be at least one general partner who has unlimited liability. The creditors of the limited partnership know they can always look to the general partner, and his or her personal assets, to satisfy their claims. Limited partners, on the other hand, have only limited liability. The most they can lose is the amount they have agreed to invest in the partnership. Creditors may not go beyond that sum. In exchange for limited liability, limited partners forfeit the right to participate in the control of the businesses. But limited partners must be careful.

For example, assume that as a limited partner you invest $10,000 in a business, only to see the enterprise start to fail because of what you believe is poor management. In an attempt to prevent loss of the $10,000, you roll up your sleeves and begin to take an active role in directing the business. You thereby forfeit your limited liability and may ultimately be held responsible for all the limited partnership's debts, which may greatly exceed $10,000.

The primary advantage of the corporate form of business is the limited liability of its stockholders. They are liable only for the sum they invest in the corporation's stock, and no more. The corporation is itself a legal entity. Contract creditors of the corporation, and those tortiously injured by the corporation's officers or employees, may look only to the corporation's assets for satisfaction. These creditors may not reach through the "corporate veil" into the pockets of the individual shareholders. For example, if Chrysler Corporation were to go bankrupt while owing millions of dollars, Chrysler's creditors could not go to its hundreds of thousands of stockholders and collect money to satisfy Chrysler's debts.

Although this advantage would seem to make the corporate form the most favorable of the business organization forms, this is not always the case. While it is perfectly legal to have a corporation owned by only one or a few persons, the corporate veil can be pierced and unlimited liability imposed on the owners if they have inadequately capitalized the venture, have used the corporate form to defraud, or have consistently ignored the corporate formalities demanded by state law. (However, some states, such as Texas, have passed special ''close corporation'' statutes that allow a small corporation to be operated essentially as a partnership without loss of limited liability.)

In tort cases, sole proprietorships and partnerships can achieve much the same effect of limited liability by purchasing liability insurance. Studies show that corporations purchase as much liability insurance as do other forms of business, despite the limited liability of the shareholders. Insurance cannot help against contractual obligations, however, so the corporate form may be advantageous here. But if you and just a few friends form a small corporation, this advantage may be illusory. Banks may refuse to loan money to your corporation, and suppliers may refuse to sell to it on credit unless you and the other owners personally guarantee the loans.

Continuity

When a sole proprietor dies, the business entity dies with him. Of course, the assets may be sold or left to an heir and the business continued in that way. If a general partner dies or becomes incapacitated, the law dissolves the partnership. This can be disastrous for the other partners and the business. But with proper planning, the business can be carried on with a minimum of dislocation. It is not unusual for partners to sign buy-sell agreements stipulating that, upon the death of any partner, his or her interest will be purchased by the remaining partners who agree to continue the venture. A degree of continuity is thereby preserved. Each partner is thus assured that his heirs will be provided for by the agreed purchase price if he dies; all partners are assured that the business can carry on unimpeded. Such agreements are frequently funded by insurance policies with premiums being paid out of partnership funds.

Death of a limited partner does not automatically dissolve a limited partnership. Death of a general partner does. Again, planning is needed to preserve continuity.

As a legal entity, a corporation has perpetual existence. If all five owners of a small corporation are killed in a plane crash, the corporation continues to exist. It simply has new owners (the heirs of the original owners). While the concept of continuity is often listed as an advantage of the corporate form, a distinction must be made between legal continuity and economic continuity. If an important owner of a small corporation dies, the corporation continues to exist in a legal sense, but its economic viability may be severely impaired.

Transferability of Interest

If you are the founder and owner of a sole proprietorship, you probably are not particularly interested in the transferability of your interest in the business. You can always sell the physical assets, client lists, and so on.

However, if your interest in a business enterprise is financial rather than active, you may be very concerned with the transferability of that interest. Assume you are one of five partners in an enterprise that is not going very well, and you decide that you would get a better return if your money were invested elsewhere. You may have a difficult time transferring your interest. Under partnership principles, no one can become a general partner without the consent of all the other partners. Therefore, you cannot transfer your interest to another person, intending that he become a partner in your stead, without the consent of all your partners. Furthermore, if you want to get out of the partnership because it is not doing well, it may be difficult to find someone willing to buy your interest and assume unlimited liability for the partnership.

It's a little easier to transfer a limited partnership interest. Still, unless all the other partners agree, an assignee of a limited partnership interest has few rights.

Generally, a corporation has an advantage in the area of transferability of interest because the indicia of ownership—corporate shares of stock—are normally freely transferable. This is certainly the case with most large corporations. If you decide you no longer wish to own stock in IBM, it is usually easy to find a buyer for your stock.

However, there may not be much of a market for your stock in a small corporation. You may, in effect, be trapped because the only interested buyers will be the other shareholders who realize there are no competing buyers and, therefore, offer you only a minimum price. Occasionally, the owners of a small corporation will by agreement limit the transferability of shares. For example, they may agree that before any shareholder can sell stock to an outsider, he or she must first offer it to the other present shareholders at a specified price. Thus, this advantage of transferability may prove illusory in the small, close corporation.

Flexibility

The sole proprietor may have difficulty raising the funds needed to expand or to get through a tight financial period. When his or her resources and credit are exhausted, the sole proprietor has no place to turn. He or she may bring in partners willing to contribute their own assets and credit to the venture, but when those resources are exhausted, there may again be a problem. When an enterprise is financially strapped, it's often difficult to recruit new general partners because of the unlimited liability they will have.

A limited partnership is more flexible. Obviously, it is easier to recruit limited partners with limited liability than it is to recruit new general partners.

The corporation is the most flexible form when it comes to raising needed funds for business expansion. It can simply print and sell more stock (subject to securities laws, of course) or issue debt instruments, such as bonds and debentures.

Cost and Formality

The sole proprietorship is the cheapest and least formal business structure. It costs nothing to form and has no formal rules to follow.

No formal agreement is needed to form a general partnership, either, although it is a good idea to have one. In fact, two persons who begin doing business together have, in the eyes of the law, formed a partnership whether or not they have a formal agreement and regardless of whether they intend to be partners. No papers need be filed or permissions obtained to form a partnership, although some states require partnerships to file notices in every county in which they do business if the partnership acts under an ''assumed name'' (a name that does not reveal the names of the partners).

A limited partnership is more formal. Most states require that forms listing the general partner(s) and the limited partners be filed with the Secretary of State when a limited partnership is being formed. Also, a limited partnership agreement, the contents of which are specified by state statute, must be filed. The limited partners will not be entitled to limited liability if these filing requirements are not met.

The corporation is the most formal and most expensive business structure. The corporation is a creature of statute and must meet all requirements imposed by state law. A corporate charter must usually be filed with the Secretary of State's office in the state in which the corporation is formed. Many states require that the corporation have a minimum level of capitalization (typically $1,000) before it can begin business. There may be additional filing fees, franchise taxes, and the costs of obtaining a minutes book, printing stock certificates, and getting a corporate seal. Usually, a corporation must also pay a fee and receive permission to do business in any state other than the one in which it was formed, whereas partnerships need no such permission. Certain corporate formalities such as electing officers, holding annual meetings, and the like are also required. All this expense may not be justified for a small enterprise just beginning operation.

Conclusion

It is very difficult to lay down hard and fast rules regarding the choice of a business structure. What are normally regarded as a traditional advantage of one form (e.g., the limited liability of corporations or the pass-through taxation of partnerships) may be gained for one of the other forms by careful planning (e.g., purchase of liability insurance or election of Subchapter S status).

For the small, beginning enterprise, many suggest: When in doubt, don't incorporate. The cost and inconvenience will probably outweigh any advantages. If the business is likely to grow rapidly and require much additional financing, the corporate form may be the most advantageous.

The key is to keep all these factors in mind and to plan. The advice gained from attorneys and tax accountants can more than pay for itself. Even if you've been in business for years, never hesitate to consider the advantages in changing your organizational form. While one form may be appropriate in the initial stages of an enterprise, changes in the business, in personnel, in financial needs, or in tax laws may dictate a change in the form of the business.

TAX FACTORS

Tax considerations frequently play a large and sometimes decisive role in choice of a form of business organization. Because partnerships are taxed differently from corporations, potential tax savings of one form may outweigh all nontax factors. Occasionally, Congress has attempted to minimize differences in tax treatment so as to minimize the role of tax planning in the business organization choice. Usually, however, the tax factor has played an important part in the decision-making process.

Because at any given time significant tax reforms are likely being considered on Capitol Hill, it is perilous to give specific tax advice in a text like this. Indeed, in September 1986, just before this book went to press, Congress passed the Tax Reform Act of 1986—the most comprehensive tax reform legislation of the past 40 years. These changes will no doubt have profound effects on America's individuals and businesses. One of the effects will be to alter the mix of factors that shape the choice of business organization for a particular enterprise.

It is too early to assess the exact impact of the 1986 tax legislation upon the choice of a business organization. Furthermore it is unlikely that the 1986 changes will be the last word in tax legislation. Therefore, while we shall hazard a brief description of tax factors facing business enterprises, the best advice that can be given to a person contemplating a choice of business organization is this: Consult a tax expert. Detailed tax planning can be crucial to the choice of form as well as to the continued success of the enterprise.

Noncorporate Taxation

A sole proprietorship's income is taxable to its owner. The individual income tax rates, deductions, and exemptions that apply to wage earners also apply to the sole proprietor's business profits and losses.

Until the Tax Reform Act of 1986, there were 14 individual income tax brackets ranging from 11% to a maximum of 50%. Indeed, until 1981, the top tax rate on earned income for individuals had been 70%. The 1986 legislation dramatically lowered the tax rates for individual earned income. After a brief phase-in period, a married couple filing jointly will pay 15% on taxable income below $29,750 and 28% on income above that level. However, there is also a 5% surtax on income between $71,900 and $149,250. There is also an alternative minimum tax (21%) designed to ensure that no individual with substantial income can avoid significant tax liability by use of tax exclusions, deductions, and credits. Furthermore, the 1986 tax reforms eliminated the long-standing tax break for long-term capital gains which henceforth will be taxed the same as ordinary income for both individuals and corporations.

Taxation for both general and limited partnerships is pretty much the same as for sole proprietorships—the profits or losses of the partnership are "passed through" to the partners. If, for example, you are an equal partner with another in a partnership that made X amount of taxable income last year, one-half of that sum will be added to your income from other sources and taxed at the going individual rate.

Only the partners pay taxes. The partnership entity pays no taxes, though it must file an informational return with the IRS and it can be audited.

A partnership form is frequently suggested for fledgling businesses that expect losses in their early years. These losses are passed through to the partners and lower their individual tax liability by offsetting income received from other sources.

Limited partnerships especially became popular in recent years as "tax shelters" designed to provide losses that high-income investors could offset against income derived from other sources. However, one major goal of the Tax Reform Act of 1986 was to minimize use of tax shelters. To that end, the legislation provided that an individual taxpayer cannot use "passive losses" to offset income from other sources such as salary or portfolio (interest and dividends) income. "Passive losses" are those which result from rental activity or from limited partnership interests or other business enterprises in which the taxpayer "does not materially participate." Henceforth, the individual taxpayer may use those passive losses only to offset other passive income. This legislation is likely to have a dramatic impact on investment in limited partnerships.

Corporate Taxation

The federal income tax rate for corporations has traditionally been different than that for individuals. For many years, the maximum tax rate for corporations was 46%, whereas the maximum rate for individuals was 70%. This obviously provided an incentive for high-end individual taxpayers to incorporate and leave as much of their income in the corporation as possible. However, the Tax Reform Act of 1986 altered the situation dramatically. After a phase-in period, the maximum corporate tax rate will be higher than the maximum individual rate of 28%. Taxable income less than $50,000 will be taxed at 15%. Taxable corporate income between $50,000 and $75,000 will be taxed at $7,500 plus 25% of the excess over $50,000. If corporate taxable income is over $75,000 but less than $100,000, the tax is $13,750 plus 34% of the excess over $75,000. Taxable income between $100,000 and $335,000 will be taxed $22,250 plus 39% of the excess over $100,000. A flat tax rate of 34% will be paid on all taxable income over $335,000.

    The general thrust of the 1986 Tax Reform Act was to lower tax rates for corporations, but to eliminate many deductions—such as the investment tax credit— which had traditionally been allowed. Furthermore, because Congress wished to end a situation in which some corporations made millions of dollars yet paid no income tax, it also instituted a new alternative minimum income tax. The corporate alternative minimum tax base is equal to (1) regular taxable income, plus (2) certain tax preferences (such as accelerated depreciation, mining exploration and development costs, and amortization of certified pollution control facilities), less (3) certain deductions. The thrust of the alternative tax is to ensure that a corporation pays a tax equal to at least 20% of its economic income above an exemption amount. It is expected that many corporations such as General Electric and W. R. Grace & Co. that have paid little or no taxes in recent profitable years will have difficulty escaping the alternative minimum tax.

    The real key to corporate taxation is the concept of "double taxation." A corporation first pays income tax on its taxable income, if any. Then it may pay dividends out of what income is left, and that dividend income is taxable to the shareholders. While double taxation might appear always to put corporations at a disadvantage, this is not the case. Still, substantial planning goes into minimizing its effects.

    One traditional method of mitigating the impact of corporate double taxation— giving individuals a dividend income deduction ($100 on individual returns and $200 on a joint return)—was eliminated in 1986. A second method, the dividend received deduction (DRD) was slightly changed in 1986. When one corporation owns stock in another, the possibility of triple or even quadruple taxation exists. Under the DRD, 80% (reduced from 85% in 1986) of the dividends received by one corporation from its stock ownership in another is excluded from taxable income.

One way to avoid the second layer of double taxation is to avoid paying dividends. This is not a particularly feasible avenue for major public corporations. For their shareholders, dividends are the major source of return on investment. These corporations will strive to pay dividends even when earnings are down. The notion of allowing corporations to deduct at least a portion of the dividends they pay from taxable income was considered but rejected by Congress in 1986.

Avoidance of double taxation is a particularly great concern in small, closely held corporations. One method is to choose Subchapter S status, which is discussed in the next section. Closely held corporations can also attempt to minimize the second layer of double taxation by minimizing dividend payments. If shareholders have other sources of income, they may not mind if corporate earnings are retained by the corporation. However, there are several limitations on this method of avoiding double taxation. First, a primary incentive of earnings retention had been the fact that retained earnings led to appreciation of the value of stock which, when sold, could be taxed at the lower long-term capital gains rate. However, as noted above, the Tax Reform Act of 1986 changed the law so that long-term capital gains income, for the first time since the 1920s, is now taxed at the same rate as other income for both individuals and corporations.

Second, there are limits to the amount of earnings that can be retained by the corporation. The accumulated earnings tax imposes a surcharge on excessive amounts of earnings retained by the corporation and not paid out as dividends. A second device, the personal holding company tax, also discourages the accumulation of earnings in small corporations by imposing a surtax on undistributed personal holding company income in strictly defined circumstances.

A small corporation might try to avoid the first layer of double taxation by eliminating any corporate profit. One way to do that and still transfer income to shareholders is to have shareholders serve as corporate officers or other employees and to divert potential corporate income to them in the form of salaries, bonuses, and health and pension benefits. Dividend payments are not deductible to the corporation, but ''reasonable'' salary and bonus payments are deductible yet carry the same benefit to shareholders. If the IRS successfully challenges the salaries and bonuses as ''unreasonable,'' excess amounts will be reclassified as dividends and treated accordingly.

Similar results can be gained if the corporation transfers wealth to the shareholders in the form of rental payments, repayments of loans, redemptions, and the like.

Subchapter S Corporations

Recognizing that small, close corporations are functionally equivalent to partnerships, Congress acted to minimize the tax considerations in selecting a form of business by creating Subchapter S Corporations. If the proper criteria are met, a corporation can choose to be taxed basically as if it were a partnership (with all profits and losses passed through to its shareholders) although it is treated as a corporation in all other respects.

The requirements for Subchapter S eligibility have been amended several times. At the moment, almost any domestic corporation can choose Subchapter S status as long as:

1. It has only one class of stock (judged by economic criteria; the same class can include both voting and nonvoting stock).
2. There are no more than 35 shareholders.
3. No more than 25% of the corporation's gross profits over a three-year period comes from "passive" sources (e.g., rents, dividends, or interest payments).
4. All shareholders consent to the election.

Although there remain some important differences between partnership and Subchapter S taxation, the latter is quite attractive for businesses expecting losses that could be passed through to the shareholders yet desiring limited liability for those shareholders.

Given that the Tax Reform Act of 1986 fixed the maximum tax rate for individuals at a lower level than the maximum tax rate for corporations, Subchapter S should become a very popular choice of business organization in the next few years. There is almost no way for a corporation to pay income taxes and later distribute income to shareholders without the cumulative tax paid being higher than that which would be paid with a Subchapter S setup. Furthermore, a Subchapter S corporation can create passive income for shareholders who do not actively take part in the management that can be offset by any passive losses from other sources. However, keep in mind that a few states do not recognize Subchapter S status, and impose state *corporate* taxes on such entities.

MISCELLANEOUS FORMS OF BUSINESS

In addition to the sole proprietorship, general and limited partnerships, and the corporation, there exist several other forms of enterprise that deserve brief mention.

Joint Venture

A joint venture is basically a partnership-type enterprise. The main difference is that, while a partnership contemplates an ongoing business relationship, a joint venture is formed for a single project or transaction. Although courts occasionally distinguish joint ventures from partnerships, they almost always apply general partnership law to such ventures.

Joint Stock Company

A joint stock company or joint stock association is a business enterprise organized under a contract normally called the articles of association. The contract can establish various management structures, but usually the joint stock company's affairs are handled by a group of directors or managers who can bind the firm.

Like a partnership, the members or stockholders of a joint stock company have unlimited liability for the company's debts. However, unlike in a partnership, the owners are not agents for and cannot bind the company—only the directors or managers can.

Unlike a corporation, a joint stock company is a creature of contract, not of statute. However, similar to a corporation, the joint stock company is an entity separate and distinct from its members, its capital ownership is represented by freely transferable shares, it has centralized management and continuity of life, and it does business under an assumed name (e.g., ABC Company).

Most states recognize the validity of joint stock companies. However, they are not particularly popular because they carry unlimited liability for their owners, yet are treated as corporations by the tax laws, federal securities laws, and state securities laws.

Business Trust

Business trusts, also called Massachusetts trusts, were originally formed to evade archaic state restrictions on ownership of real estate by corporations. They are formed by contracts in the form of written declarations. Management is centralized in the hands of trustees who are principals operating the business on behalf of the *cestui que trust* (the shareholders). The goal is to attain the limited liability and free transferability of corporations, yet evade state corporate regulation and corporate taxation.

Today, all states recognize the legality of business trusts, but some regulate them as corporations and others treat them as general partnerships by denying the shareholders limited liability.

The popularity of business trusts declined when the Supreme Court [2] held that business trusts should be taxed as corporations if they resemble corporations. The six key characteristics of a corporation are that it has (1) associates, (2) an objective of carrying on a business and distributing gains, (3) continuity of life, (4) centralized management, (5) limited liability, and (6) free transferability of ownership. Today most ordinary business trusts are taxable as corporations, but can elect Subchapter S status if otherwise eligible.

---

[2] *Morrissey* v. *Commissioner*, 296 U.S. 344 (1935).

Real Estate Investment Trust

In 1960, Congress authorized formation of real estate investment trusts (REITs), which are taxable much as partnerships are because they are allowed to deduct dividends paid. The REIT pays corporate income tax only on the undistributed portion of its income. Most REITs choose the business trust form.

To qualify for this pass-through taxation, an REIT must:

1. be taxable as a domestic corporation;
2. have at least 100 shareholders;
3. not have 50% or more of its stock held by five or fewer individuals;
4. distribute 95% of its taxable income to the beneficial owners in the year it was earned or the succeeding year;
5. hold 75% of its assets in real estate or other passive assets; and
6. derive 75% of its income from such assets.

There were some minor changes in REIT tax provisions in the Tax Reform Act of 1986. The overall thrust of the tax reform package, especially the lower personal tax rates, is expected to be a major boost to the REIT form of organization.

Some states provide limited liability for REIT owners, while others do so only if evidence shows that the REIT is "controlled" by its trustees rather than by the owners themselves.

Professional Corporations

At common law, professionals such as doctors and lawyers could not practice in the corporate form. Such a practice was viewed (and still is by some) as unethical and unseemly. However, around 1960, to take advantage of certain tax breaks granted to corporations, professionals lobbied hard and persuaded all the states to authorize professional corporations or associations. The professions covered vary from state to state, but can include doctors, lawyers, dentists, architects, engineers, veterinarians, accountants, pharmacists, and others.

In most states, professional corporate codes are supplemented by the general corporate law. Usually, stock can be issued only to, and held only by, persons licensed in the particular profession. The owners and the corporation remain bound by the state's ethical regulations for the profession.

One advantage of incorporation deals with liability. A doctor in a general partnership has unlimited liability for the malpractice of his partners. However, a doctor in a corporation has general liability only for his own malpractice (and in some states that of the doctors he supervises). His liability for the malpractice of the other doctor-shareholders is limited to the amount of his investment in most states, but not all.

Because the corporate tax maximum tax rate was 46% as opposed to 50% (and before that 70%) for individuals, professional corporations enjoyed a tax advantage until the 1986 tax reforms. That advantage is now lost, which may significantly reduce the incentive for professionals to incorporate, although there still may be some minor benefits flowing from the ability to the corporation to deduct certain pension and insurance benefits provided employees. To take advantage of these benefits, the professionals must convert themselves into "employees" by forming the corporation and then hiring themselves as its employees.

QUESTIONS AND PROBLEMS

1. Assume that you have substantial personal assets and wish to enter a new line of business that entails a high risk of economic loss. Which form of business organization should you select?

2. Which forms of business organization would you favor if you desired a high degree of flexibility in terms of being able to remove yourself from the venture?

3. Assume that you desire to be an active participant in a business, yet you need limited liability. Which form should you select?

4. Assume that Joe and Sue go into business together. They've never had a course in business organizations and know nothing about the subject. They take no steps to organize their business into any particular form. How will their enterprise be treated?

5. Why is it that corporations, with limited liability for their owners, appear to purchase as much liability insurance as partnerships and sole proprietors?

6. Is continuity of existence truly an advantage in a corporation dominated by a single individual?

7. If a corporation is viewed as an "entity" in and of itself in the eyes of the law, why isn't a partnership so viewed?

8. Why would Congress wish to manipulate the tax laws to encourage or discourage various types of business organization?

2

INTRODUCTION
TO PARTNERSHIPS

INTRODUCTION

By any measure, the partnership is an extremely important form of business organization in America. Hundreds of thousands of businesses, ranging from the smallest two-person firm to large, multistate organizations, have chosen the partnership as the appropriate mode of operation. The partnership is a residual form of organization: if two or more persons join together in a business without taking steps to organize some other form such as a corporation or a limited partnership, they will be deemed general partners. The general partnership will be analyzed in this chapter and the following three. Then limited partnerships will be studied in Chapter 6.

In 48 states and the District of Columbia, partnership law is controlled by the Uniform Partnership Act (UPA).[1] Drafted in 1941, the UPA provides substantial uniformity in partnership law throughout the country. The basic UPA scheme is twofold. First, the act provides a very detailed structure to govern the rights of third parties dealing with a partnership. Second, the act gives great flexibility to the partners in structuring

---

[1] Georgia and Louisiana have not adopted the UPA. Alabama and Nebraska did not officially adopt the UPA either, but their acts are substantially similar to it.

the partnership and varying the rights and duties of the partners as to one another. The partners can tailor the partnership to their own individual needs and desires, so long as they do not prejudice third parties.

The UPA is very comprehensive, governing virtually every aspect of partnership law. Only a few matters such as the capacity of persons to be partners, the propriety of suits by or against the partnership in the firm name, and service of process on the partnership and partners are outside the purview of the UPA. The study of partnership law, then, is largely the study of the UPA and how the courts have interpreted and applied it.

DETERMINING THE EXISTENCE OF A PARTNERSHIP

In a surprising number of situations, a question arises as to whether or not the relationship between persons in business constitutes a partnership. One frequent scenario involves a person who has been involved in a business claiming to be a partner in order to be entitled to more compensation via a share of the profits or a share of the assets of the business on dissolution. Another frequent scenario is a mirror image of the first—a person who has been involved in a business will claim to have *not* been a partner in order to avoid liability to partnership creditors for debts that exceed the partnership's assets. Obviously, in the first scenario, the other persons in the business will have reason to claim that the alleged partner was only an employee or perhaps a creditor. In the second case, creditors will be motivated to claim that the person was a partner so they will have another pocket from which to satisfy a debt.

In these and many other situations, the courts decide, on a case-by-case basis, whether or not a particular business relationship constituted a partnership. This is a legal question that requires careful scrutiny of all the surrounding facts. These facts are then applied to the definition of partnership supplied by the UPA: "A partnership is an association of two or more persons to carry on as co-owners a business for profit." [2]

Although this appears to be a very straightforward definition, numerous questions can arise in applying it to the innumerable fact patterns that can exist. The definition can be clarified somewhat by breaking it down into its component parts.

"Association"

A partnership is an *association* of persons. The term association implies both voluntariness and intent. The notion of voluntariness is important because the law will not force anyone to be a partner against his or her will. At the heart of partnership law is the concept of *delectus personae*, a Latin phrase meaning "choice of the person." We are all entitled to choose with whom we wish to be partners and with whom we do not.

---

[2] §6(1). Unless otherwise indicated, all sections cited in this chapter are provisions of the UPA.

The consent of each and every existing partner, therefore, is required before any person can become a new partner in a general partnership.

The question of intent is also critical to determining existence of a partnership. It is always helpful if the parties have clearly expressed in writing their intent to be or not to be partners. However, in the absence of such an expression, the courts can imply intent from the conduct of the parties.

Where a clear expression does exist, it will be given great, but not controlling, weight by the courts. The determinative factor is the intent to enter into a relationship that the law deems a partnership. If the parties had the intent to enter into such a business relationship, they are partners in the eyes of the law even though they might have expressed in writing that they did *not* intend to be partners. Persons cannot enter into a relationship that effectively constitutes a partnership, and yet avoid the legal implications of that relationship simply by stating that they do not intend to be partners.

"Two or more persons having legal capacity"

A person cannot be a partner with himself or herself. Such a business is a sole proprietorship. It takes two (or more) "persons" to have a partnership. Who can be partners? The UPA defines the term "person" to include individuals, partnerships, corporations, and other associations.[3] Thus, a corporation could go into partnership with an individual. Two partnerships could associate, forming a third partnership.

Because the partnership is a legal relationship requiring intent, the partners must have legal capacity. Minors can be partners, but they are allowed to disaffirm the partnership agreement just as they may disaffirm other contracts. According to most courts, the minors may withdraw all capital contributed to the partnership, reduced by only the minor's share of unpaid partnership debts to third parties. The minor may disaffirm all personal liability for partnership debts that exceed partnership assets.

Basically, the same rules apply to mental incompetents as apply to minors. Additionally, however, a partner's mental incompetence gives the other partners the right to dissolve the partnership if they so desire.[4]

"Business for profit"

To be partners, the parties must be involved in "business," a term that the UPA defines as including "every trade, occupation, or profession."[5] Lawyers, welders, doctors, air-conditioning repairers, and thousands of other types of workers can associate as partners.

The term "business" implies a continuity of relationship. If persons join together for but a single project, intending to go their separate ways when it is completed, their relationship will probably be deemed a "joint venture" rather than a partnership. Still,

---

[3] §2.

[4] §32(1)(a).

[5] §2.

a joint venture is so similar to a partnership that the courts apply the UPA by analogy to govern such ventures.

The requirement that a partnership be a business *for profit* excludes charitable, religious, and fraternal groups. These associations of persons are deemed "unincorporated associations" rather than partnerships. The business does not actually have to make money to be a partnership. The mere expectation of profits is sufficient. The "profit" can even be in the form of beneficial tax deductions derived from engaging in a business where tax-deductible losses are expected.

"Co-ownership"

Co-ownership is the essence of the notion of partnership. Co-ownership of the *business* is the key, not just co-ownership of some property. The UPA explicitly provides that merely being joint tenants, tenants in common, or co-owners of property does not establish a partnership.[6] For example, if A and B own an unimproved tract of land on the outskirts of a city, hoping someday to sell the land at a profit due to its appreciation in value stemming from the city's growth (a factor external to the owners' efforts), A and B are co-owners of property but not partners.

Most courts define co-ownership in terms of a "community of interest" between or among the partners. The three most important aspects of this community of interest relate to a sharing of *capital*, of *control*, and of *profits and losses*.

A community of interest in capital is indicative of a partnership because of the important role that capital plays in most businesses. If a person did not contribute capital in any form (money, property, services), it is unlikely that the person was intended to be a partner.

A sharing of control is also very persuasive, though not conclusive. The right to make important policy decisions is rarely delegated to mere employees. The key, however, is the *right* to control. Even if unexercised, the right to control is indicative of partnership status. Therefore, a partner can delegate actual decision making to other partners or even to employees without losing partnership status.

Finally, a community of interest in profits (and losses) is indicative of co-ownership. While the UPA provides that mere sharing of *gross receipts* does not itself establish a partnership,[7] it also states that receipt of a share of *profits* is *prima facie* evidence that a person is a partner.[8] The presumption of a partnership that arises from a sharing of profits may be rebutted by reference to other factors, but it is persuasive. If a person associated with a business derives a fixed compensation, that compensation is probably a wage, indicating that the person is an employee. However, if the person's compensation varies with the success of the business, the person may well be taking risks indicative of ownership.

---

[6] §7(2).

[7] §7(3).

[8] §7(4).

The UPA's presumption of partnership stemming from a sharing of profits is expressly made inapplicable to five situations, these being where the profits were received in payment (1) as a debt, (2) as wages of an employee or rent to a landlord, (3) as an annuity to a widow or representative of a deceased partner, (4) as interest on a loan, or (5) as consideration for the sale of goodwill of a business or other property by installment.[9] In these five situations, the nature of the relationship of the parties makes it much less likely that the sharing of profits is indicative of partnership status. It has long been the practice of creditors of businesspersons, in certain appropriate circumstances, to take a percentage of the profits of a business in repayment of a debt owed by that business. The drafters of the UPA did not wish to disrupt this practice, so they made it clear that no presumption of partnership would arise therefrom. Similarly, it is not unusual to give employees incentive to work hard by supplementing their salaries with a share of the profits. The nature of the employer-employee relationship makes it unlikely that the sharing of profits in this context is indicative of partnership status.

The burden of proof is always upon the person attempting to establish the existence of a partnership. Courts will make their decisions on a case-by-case basis after looking at all the facts. The four most important factors will usually be (1) the stated intent of the parties (if any) plus the three communities of interest in (2) capital, (3) control, and (4) profits that are indicative of co-ownership. If all four factors (expressed intent plus the three communities of interest) are present, there is a partnership. If all four are absent, there is not. If some are present and some are absent, the court must undertake a weighing process, perhaps supplemented by an examination of such additional factors as record title of real and personal property, tax returns, and attempts to evade statutes or tort liability.

The following cases are illustrative of common situations in which the question of existence of a partnership arise.

MILLER v. CITY BANK & TRUST CO.

82 Mich. App. 120, 266 N.W.2d 687 (1978)

In 1959 Philip Miller asked plaintiff to marry him, to move to Jackson, Michigan, and to help him run his nursery business. She did so until his death in 1974. Although plaintiff did not make any capital contributions to the business, she held a management position, kept the books, hired and fired employees, and did physical labor. She received monthly payments of $50 or $100. Whenever plaintiff received such a check, so did Mr. Miller in the same amount. Money for household expenses was taken out of the same account.

In 1960, a business registration certificate was filed for the nursery which indicated it was

---

[9] §7(4).

operated as a partnership. A similar certificate was filed in 1966 with respect to a project involving subdivision of land owned by Mr. Miller which surrounded the nursery. This certificate expired in 1971. Checking accounts, vehicles, and other equipment were bought and held under the assumed business name. However, annual tax forms and schedules listed the business as a sole proprietorship and plaintiff's occupation as a housewife. Michigan business activity forms indicated a sole proprietorship, as did Mr. Miller's 1968 application for a self-employed pension and profit-sharing plan. There was never a formal written partnership agreement, though plaintiff testified that she considered herself a partner and that Mr. Miller told her that she was "the best partner he ever had."

Plaintiff brought this action to establish the existence of a partnership. The trial court found plaintiff failed to carry her burden of proof. Plaintiff appealed.

DANHOF, CHIEF JUDGE:

The elements of a partnership are generally considered to include a voluntary association of two or more people with legal capacity in order to carry on, via co-ownership, a business for profit. Co-ownership of the business requires more than merely joint ownership of the property and is usually evidenced by joint control and the sharing of profits and losses. With the intentions of the party to form a partnership as our polestar we will review the trial court's finding.

It is not disputed that the parties were involved in a business venture for profit and had the legal capacity to form a partnership. However, the evidence relating to co-ownership does not indicate that a legal partnership was contemplated. Prior to the marriage, Mr. Miller operated the business and owned all the property. Mrs. Miller made no capital contributions except her services. Even though plaintiff worked long

and hard hours, this does not establish that the parties had an agreement to form a partnership. This evidence could also be viewed as consistent with an employee-employer relationship or that of a helpful wife who assisted her husband without them intending a legal partnership.

Co-ownership is also indicated by profit sharing. In fact, profit sharing is prima facie evidence of a partnership. However, the court did not find an agreement to share profits, and we cannot say that this was clearly erroneous. That Mr. and Mrs. Miller each received monthly payments from the nursery checking account does not necessarily establish profit sharing. The payments could also be reasonably viewed as salary or wages. Another possible interpretation would be that Mr. Miller was withdrawing money from his sole proprietorship and was dividing it equally because he felt an obligation to share equally with his wife, as a wife rather than a business partner.

Another indicia [sic] of co-ownership is mutual agency and control. That Mrs. Miller kept the books, wrote checks, and hired and fired does not necessarily establish any control other than that which might be given to a trusted employee. However, it is not necessary that this control be exercised as long as it exists. In view of the absence of the exercise of control or mutual agency, evidence of an agreement in respect to the division of control is about the only way to prove mutual agency and control. However, no evidence of an agreement with respect to mutual control was presented.

The intention of the parties to enter into a partnership comprising the above-mentioned elements is the controlling issue in this case. The filing of the business registration papers listing the business as a partnership gives support to plaintiff's claim. As long as the registration was effective, it raised a presumption of a partnership, but this can be overcome by competent evidence. Since the registration certificate filed for the subdivision operation expired in 1971, it does not raise a presumption of a partnership. The trial court found that there was sufficient, competent evidence to rebut the presumption concerning the nursery business.

The other evidence supporting plaintiff's claim is that plaintiff testified that the parties entered into an oral agreement and that Mr. Miller told her "she was the best partner he ever had." The use of the term partner is one factor to be considered in analyzing whether a partnership exists, but it is not controlling. How heavily that factor weighs varies with the circumstances, and the circumstances in this case make the use of that term ambiguous. Mrs. Miller seemed to consider the whole marriage as a partnership and Mr. Miller could have meant that she was the best partner in marriage rather than in business. Also, Mrs. Miller is an interested party and the trial judge is not bound to accept as true her testimony and the inferences she draws from it.

The evidence introduced against these claims indicated that the deceased did not intend to form a legal partnership with his wife. First,

there is no written agreement and there is only plaintiff's testimony in support of an oral one. The income tax returns and schedules listed the business as a sole proprietorship, listed Mr. Miller's income as wages, and listed Mrs. Miller's occupation as a housewife. In 1964, Mr. Miller applied for a self-employee retirement deduction plan as a sole proprietorship. All the capital contributions came from Mr. Miller and the property remained in his name (or his and his wife's name), and none was transferred to the partnership. Shortly before his death, Mr. Miller deeded his homestead to his wife and himself as tenants by the entirety and this would seem needless if they already owned it as partners. Although none of these facts is conclusive, they are all factors to be weighed in the decision.

After reviewing the entire record, we cannot say that the trial court's findings that the presumption established by the filing of business registration papers was rebutted by competent evidence and that plaintiff failed to carry her burden of proof were clearly erroneous.

Affirmed.

ENDSLEY v. GAME-SHOW PLACEMENTS, LTD.

401 N.E.2d 768 (Ind. App. 1980)

In January 1977 Clifford was doing business as Gemini Systems (Gemini) when Endsley invested $6,000 in the business. In return, Endsley was entitled to 49% of the business proceeds. The agreement relieved Endsley of the details of running the business.

In December 1977 Clifford entered into a contract with Game-Show Placements, Ltd. (Game-Show). Game-Show agreed to advertise Gemini projection television units on 15 network

game show spots. Gemini agreed to pay a $195 per spot fee and to supply a television unit to each designated winner. Game-Show had placed six spots on "Nighttime Hollywood Squares" when it was told by Clifford to stop placing the ads.

Game-Show then sued Clifford and Endsley "d/b/a Gemini Systems" for breach of contract. The trial court found Endsley to have been a general partner in Gemini and therefore liable *for a partnership debt to Game-Show in the amount of $12,495. Endsley appealed.*

STATON, JUDGE:

[*The opinion first quoted the Indiana versions of §§6 and 7 of the UPA.*]

According to IC 1971, 23 4–1–7(4), "[t]he receipt by a person of a share of the profits of a business is prima facie evidence that he is a partner in the business. . . ." The record reveals that Endsley was entitled to a 49% share of the profits of Gemini Systems. This inference of partnership could have been rebutted by Endsley if he had shown this share had been received as a type of payment. See IC 1971, 23–4–1–7(4)(a–3). He failed to present any such evidence.

He argues, instead, that the applicable statute requires the *actual* receipt of money as profits in order for the inference of partnership to arise. Such a constrained reading of IC 1971, 23–4–1–7(4) is incorrect. This section clearly states that "[t]he receipt by a person of a *share* of the profits of a business is prima facie evidence that he is a partner in the business" (emphasis added). To read this section narrowly, as suggested by Endsley, would result in making the partnership statute inapplicable to all business ventures which fail before the profits are realized. His approach is untenable, especially in light of the potential involvement of unpaid third-party creditors.

Endsley also argues that Game-Show must show that he agreed to share the losses as well as the profits before a partnership can be proven. Although such an agreement is, of course, relevant to the existence of a partnership, it is not essential. IC 1971, 23 4–1–7(4) establishes proof of profit sharing alone as prima facie evidence of a partnership relation.

Much of the testimony bearing on the business arrangement in question is oral. Endsley denies the existence of a valid partnership agreement, while Game-Show urges that one existed. We noted that there is little evidence as to Endsley's participation in the day-to-day operations of Gemini. According to Clifford, Endsley had never ordered any television components for Gemini and had never been consulted as to the daily running of the business. Gemini's books of account proved to be a checkbook with only Clifford as the authorized signatory. The company's business cards and stationery were devoid of indices of ownership. Neither Clifford nor Endsley placed their name on any Gemini advertising. Despite Endsley's contention, however, his lack of daily involvement in Gemini is not per se indicative of the absence of a partnership.

The record reveals that, initially, Endsley had little to do with the business affairs of Gemini. On November 10, 1977, however, he acted on behalf of Gemini and borrowed $10,000 from a doctor to be used as capital for its operations. In a document entitled Agreement, Endsley and Clifford represented themselves as "doing business as Gemini Systems." One clause in this agreement stated that the interest "will be computed on the basis of partnership return prepared and filed on behalf of Gemini Systems." Both Endsley and Clifford signed the document. A promissory note, executed by Endsley and Clifford, was then drawn to the order of the doctor as evidence of the $10,000 given to Gemini. On April 3, 1978, in his defense of an action upon this note, Endsley admitted, in writing, that he and Clifford operated Gemini and that they had invested the borrowed capital in the company.

Endsley further acted on behalf of Gemini when he discussed the company's lease with a local attorney. The attorney explained:

Q: Can you tell me what you said and what Mr. Endsley said in the phone conversation of November 16, 1978?
A: At that time, Carmen Good and his father were owners of the building out there. There was a lease that was executed by Gemini

Systems, I believe, is the way it was phrased, and *it was our understanding that Mr. Endsley and others were involved in that and they had possession of the premise* and I was making abandonment on payment of rent.

. . .

A: Well, I was—I asked when we would expect payment and there was discussion concerning his responsibility—this is Mr. Endsley's—concerning responsibility of payment, and there was some conversation about corporation for it that was not formed and Mr. Endsley was in the process of reorganizing and *he had hopes of paying off his bills*

and that if we would give him time, once they got the reorganization production going, he thought they would be in a situation where it would be paid.'' (emphasis added)

. . .

In viewing the evidence before us in the prescribed fashion, we find that it does not lead solely to a conclusion which is contrary to that reached by the trial court. We, therefore, must agree with the court's conclusion that Endsley was a partner with Clifford in Gemini.
Affirmed.

PARTNERSHIP BY ESTOPPEL

On the theory that persons who share in profits should also share in losses, many courts formerly held such persons liable to third parties even though there was no co-ownership. This doctrine of ''partnership as to third persons'' imposed a lower standard for determining partnership as to third persons than for determining partnership among the supposed partners. The UPA has eliminated this doctrine by explicitly providing that ''[e]xcept as provided by section 16 persons who are not partners to each other are not partners to third persons.'' [10] The exception is an important one. Section 16 provides for *partnership by estoppel* where a person who is not truly a partner may be estopped or prevented from denying that status as to third parties.

Partnership by estoppel is not a form of business organization. Rather, it is a method of attaching partnership liability to someone who, though not a partner, held himself or herself out to be a partner or allowed another to do so. If the requisite elements are present, such a person may not only be bound as a partner but may by his or her acts bind the partnership. The requisite elements for application of partnership by estoppel have been said to be ''(1) words or conduct by or attributable to the party to be charged amounting to a representation of partnership; (2) detrimental action taken by the plaintiff in reliance upon the representation; and (3) the reasonableness of the representation.'' [11]

Assume, for example, that in the presence of A, B tells C that he (B) and A are partners to induce C to sell property to B on credit. If A does not wish to be liable for the debt when he is not in fact B's partner, he must speak out. If A remains silent,

---

[10] §7(1).

[11] *Facit-Addo, Inc.* v. *Davis Financial Corp.*, 136 Ariz. 6, 653 P.2d 356 (Ariz. App. 1982).

he is allowing B to hold him out to C as a partner in a situation where C could reasonably rely on the representation.

A number of very sticky problems accompany the doctrine of partnership by estoppel. Although some authorities disagree, generally if a representation of partnership status is made privately, only those persons to whom it was made may rely on it, but if the representation is made publicly, the entire world may rely on it. Another area of disagreement centers on how diligent a person must be in preventing others from holding the person out as a partner. Is there a duty to speak out if you discover that someone is unauthorizedly holding you out as a partner? Most courts say yes. Is there a duty to be diligent in discovering that others are holding you out as a partner? One common viewpoint is expressed in the following case.

COX ENTERPRISES, INC. v. FILIP

538 S.W.2d 836 (Tex. Civ. App. 1976)

Cox Enterprises, Inc. (appellant), which owns a newspaper, sued Filip and Elliott for unpaid newspaper advertising services. The trial court found, on the basis of the evidence presented, that Filip was owner of Trans Texas Properties; that Elliott had no ownership interest therein; that in order to obtain credit for Trans Texas Properties, its employee, Peoples, represented to appellant that Elliott was an owner of the business; that Peoples had no authority from Elliott to make that representation; that appellant relied on that representation without making efforts to verify its accuracy; and that Elliott did not hold himself out as an owner of Trans Texas Properties. Additionally, the trial court found that in the exercise of ordinary care, Elliott should have known that Peoples told appellant that he was an owner of Trans Texas Properties.

The trial court found Elliott not to be liable for the debt. Cox Enterprises appealed.

SHANNON, JUSTICE:

. . .

[Appellant claims that] the court erred in not entering judgment for appellant predicated upon the court's finding of Elliott's failure to exercise ordinary care to discover that he had been held out to appellant as an owner of Trans Texas Properties.

Appellant's argument is bottomed upon the Texas Uniform Partnership Act, Section 16(1), which provides as follows: "§16. Partner by Estoppel."

Sec. 16. (1) When a person, by words spoken or written or by conduct, represents himself, or consents to another representing him to any one, as a partner in an existing partnership or with one or more persons not actual partners, he is liable to any such person to whom such representation has been made, who has, on the faith of such representation, given credit to the actual or apparent partnership, and if he has made such representation or consented to its being made in a public manner he is liable to such person, whether the representation has or has not been made or communicated to such person so giving credit by or with the knowledge of the apparent partner making the representation or consenting to its being made.

Prior to the enactment of the Texas Uniform Partnership Act, the rule in Texas was that for liability to be based upon partnership by estoppel, it must be established that the person held out as a partner knew of, and consented in fact to, the holding out.

Section 16(1) codifies and enlarges upon the common law of partnership by estoppel. That section imposes a duty on a person to deny that he is a partner once he knows that third persons are relying on representations that he is a partner. We do not read §16(1) as creating an affirmative duty upon one to seek out all those who may represent to others that he is a partner.

Appellant argues that §16(1) means that one who negligently holds himself out or permits himself to be held out as a member of a partnership relationship is estopped to deny such partnership relationship as against third persons who in good faith relied on the existence of such apparent partnership and extended credit thereon—*Branscome* v. *Schoneweis*, 361 F.2d 717 (7th Cir. 1966). In *Branscome*, the Seventh Circuit construed Ill. Rev. Sta. ch 106 ½ §16(1) (1952), which is identical to the Uniform Partnership Act. The court held Schoneweis personally liable for debts of the company because *he* negligently held *himself* out to be a partner.

In the case at bar, and in the terms of §16(1), appellant's factual theory was that appellee consented to Peoples' representation to appellant that appellee was a partner in Trans Texas Properties. Appellant, however, failed in its burden to convince the trier of fact that appellee consented for Peoples to represent that appellee was a partner in Trans Texas Properties. Appellant's point of error is overruled.

Affirmed.

NATURE OF THE PARTNERSHIP

Entity or Aggregate?

The historical view was that a partnership was merely an aggregation of its partners. Unlike a corporation that is an entity in and of itself, existing separate and apart from its shareholders, a partnership had no life apart from the individual partners. Some framers of the UPA wished to change the historical view so that the law would treat partnerships as entities. Other framers wished to preserve the aggregate approach. A compromise resulted so that today, the partnership is treated by the UPA, the courts, and even the Internal Revenue Service as an entity for some purposes and as a mere aggregation of its partners for other purposes.

Aspects of the aggregate approach would include the facts that a partnership cannot sue or be sued without enabling legislation, that the profits of the partnership are automatically passed through as taxable income for the individual partners,[12] that

---

[12] §701 of the Internal Revenue Code of 1954.

the debts of the partnership are ultimately the debts of the individual partners, and that the partnership dissolves if any partner leaves.[13] Thus, for many substantial purposes, the partnership remains but an aggregation of its individual partners.

On the other hand, there is a trend toward treating the partnership as an independent entity for more and more purposes. For example, although partnership income is taxable to the individual partners, the partnership as an entity is required to file an informational tax return with the IRS.[14] Although enabling legislation outside the UPA is required before a partnership can sue or be sued in its own name, most states have passed such legislation.

Additionally, the UPA itself has several provisions that treat the partnership as an entity. Property can be owned and transferred in the partnership name.[15] Partnership creditors are given priority over creditors of the individual partners regarding partnership property.[16] Indeed, some courts require a partnership creditor to exhaust partnership assets before pursuing individual partners.[17] The partnership is initially responsible for the actions of the partners because every partner is an agent of the partnership.[18] The UPA also provides that capital contributions are made to the partnership,[19] books are kept for the partnership,[20] and every partner is accountable *to the partnership* as a fiduciary.[21] The UPA even defines the term "person" to include a partnership.[22]

The trend is clearly toward treating partnerships as entities when circumstances dictate. Indeed, this trend comports with the practices of the workaday world where the assets, liabilities, and transactions of the partnership firm are usually considered separate from those of the individual partners. A leading Supreme Court case that adopts the entity theory to achieve what the majority believed a sensible result follows.

BELLIS v. UNITED STATES

417 U.S. 85 (1974)

Until 1969, Bellis was the senior partner in Bellis, Kolsby & Wolf, a law firm with the three named partners and six employees. The firm *dissolved in 1969, and in 1973 Bellis came into possession of the firm's records. On May 1, 1973, a federal grand jury subpoena directed*

---

[13] UPA §13.

[14] §703 of the Internal Revenue Code of 1954.

[15] §10.

[16] §40(h), (i).

[17] *May* v. *McGowan*, 194 F.2d 396 (2d Cir. 1952) (New York law).

[18] §9.

[19] §18.

[20] §19.

[21] §21.

[22] §2.

Bellis to testify and bring with him "all partner-ship records currently in your possession for the partnership of Bellis, Kolsby & Wolf for the years 1968 and 1969." Bellis refused to produce the documents, standing on his Fifth Amendment privilege against self-incrimina-tion. The district court found Bellis in contempt, holding that Bellis's personal privilege against self-incrimination did not extend to partnership records. The court of appeals affirmed, and Bel-lis appealed.

MARSHALL, JUSTICE:

The question presented in this case is whether a partner in a small law firm may invoke his personal privilege against self-incrimination to justify his refusal to comply with a subpoena requiring production of the partnership's finan-cial records.

. . .

It has long been established, of course, that the Fifth Amendment privilege against compul-sory self-incrimination protects an individual from compelled production of his personal pa-pers and effects as well as compelled oral testi-mony.

. . .

On the other hand, an equally long line of cases has established that an individual cannot rely upon the privilege to avoid producing the records of a collective entity which are in his possession in a representative capacity, even if these records might incriminate him person-ally. This doctrine was first announced in a series of cases dealing with corporate records.

. . .

But any thought that the principle formulated in these decisions was limited to corporate records was put to rest in *United States* v. *White*,

322 U.S. 694 (1944). In *White*, it was held that an officer of an unincorporated association, a labor union, could not claim his privilege against compulsory self-incrimination to justify his refusal to produce the union's records pur-suant to a grand jury subpoena. *White* announced the general rule that the privilege could not be employed by an individual to avoid production of the records of an organization, which he holds in a representative capacity as custodian on be-half of the group.

These decisions reflect the Court's consistent view that the privilege against compulsory self-incrimination should be "limited to its historic function of protecting only the natural individual from compulsory incrimination through his own testimony or personal records."

. . .

Since no artificial organization may utilize the personal privilege against compulsory self-incrimination, the Court found that it follows that an individual acting in his official capacity on behalf of the organization may likewise not take advantage of his personal privilege.

. . .

The analysis of the Court in *White*, of course, only makes sense in the context of what the Court described as "organized, institutional ac-tivity"—322 U.S., at 701, 64 S. Ct., at 1252. This analysis presupposes the existence of an organization which is recognized as an indepen-dent entity apart from its individual members. The group must be relatively well organized and structured and not merely a loose, informal association of individuals. It must maintain a distinct set of organizational records and recog-nize rights in its members of control and access to them. And the records subpoenaed must in fact be organizational records held in a represen-tative capacity. In other words, it must be fair to say that the records demanded are the records of the organization rather than those of the individual under *White*.

. . .

We think it is similarly clear that partnerships may and frequently do represent organized institutional activity so as to preclude any claim of Fifth Amendment privilege with respect to the partnership's financial records. Some of the most powerful private institutions in the nation are conducted in the partnership form. Wall Street law firms and stock brokerage firms provide significant examples. These are often large, impersonal, highly structured enterprises of essentially perpetual duration. The personal interest of any individual partner in the financial records of a firm of this scope is obviously highly attenuated.

. . .

In this case, however, we are required to explore the outer limits of the analysis of the Court in *White*. Petitioner argues that in view of the modest size of the partnership involved here, it is unrealistic to consider the firm as an entity independent of its three partners; rather, he claims, the law firm embodies little more than the personal legal practice of the individual partners. Moreover, petitioner argues that he has a substantial and direct ownership interest in the partnership records and does not hold them in a representative capacity.

Despite the force of these arguments, we conclude that the lower courts properly applied the *White* rule in the circumstances of this case. While small, the partnership here did have an established institutional identity independent of its individual partners. This was not an informal association or a temporary arrangement for the undertaking of a few projects of short-lived duration. Rather, the partnership represented a formal institutional arrangement organized for the continuing conduct of the firm's legal practice. The partnership was in existence for nearly 15

years prior to its voluntary dissolution. Although it may not have had a formal constitution or bylaws to govern its internal affairs, state partnership law imposed on the firm a certain organizational structure in the absence of any contrary agreement by the partners; for example, it guaranteed to each of the partners the equal right to participate in the management and control of the firm and prescribed that majority rule governed the conduct of the firm's business.

The firm maintained a bank account in the partnership name, had stationery using the firm name on its letterhead, and, in general, held itself out to third parties as an entity with an independent institutional identity. It employed six persons in addition to its partners, including two other attorneys who practiced law on behalf of the firm, rather than as individuals on their own behalf. It filed separate partnership returns for federal tax purposes.

Equally important, we believe it is fair to say that petitioner is holding the subpoenaed partnership records in a representative capacity. Petitioner is of course accountable to the partnership as a fiduciary §54(1), and his possession of the firm's financial records is especially subject to his fiduciary obligations to the other partners. Indeed, Pennsylvania law specifically provides that ''every partner shall at all times have access to and may inspect and copy any of [the partnership books].'' §52. To facilitate this right of access, petitioner was required to keep these financial books and records at the firm's principal place of business, at least during the active life of the partnership. The other partners in the firm were—and still are—entitled to enforce these rights through legal action by demanding production of the records in a suit for a formal accounting—§55.

. . .

This might be a different case if it involved a small family partnership, see *United States*

v. *Slutsky*, 352 F.Supp. 1105 (S.D. N.Y. 1972); *In re Subpoena Duces Tecum*, 81 F.Supp., at 421; or as the Solicitor General suggests, *Brief for United States* 22–23, if there were some other preexisting relationship of confidentiality among the partners. But in the circumstances of this case, petitioner's possession of the partnership's financial records in what can be fairly said to be a representative capacity compels our holding that his personal privilege against compulsory self-incrimination is inapplicable. *Affirmed.*

Despite widespread acceptance of the entity approach, the courts will continue to use the aggregate theory where it produces the more desirable policy result. This is illustrated in the following case.

HARTFORD ACCIDENT AND INDEMNITY CO. v. HUDDLESTON

514 S.W.2d 676 (Ky. App. 1974)

Clifford Huddleston and Orville Prewitt formed a partnership named "City Motor Sales," which was engaged in the garage business. Hartford Accident and Indemnity Co. (Hartford) issued a garage liability policy to "City Motor Sales," which included protection against uninsured motorists. Carl Huddleston, the son of Clifford Huddleston and resident of his house, was killed by an uninsured motorist while he occupied a vehicle unrelated to the partnership business. Hartford claimed the policy covered only the partnership entity. The trial court held Hartford liable because the policy listed as "Persons Insured (a) the named insured and any designated insured and, while residents of the same household, the spouse and relatives of either." Hartford appealed.

REED, JUSTICE:

. . .

Hartford's policy declarations page lists "City Motor Sales," a partnership, as the "Named Insured," while the uninsured motorist coverage page calls "City Motor Sales" the "Designated Insured." Although not expressed directly, the basic premise of Hartford's contention concerning the identity of the insured raises a problem as old as the law of partnerships. There has always been considerable dispute as to whether a partnership is a legal entity or merely an aggregate of persons acting together.

Kentucky adopted the Uniform Partnership Act in 1954 as KRS Chapter 362. The adoption of the act did not resolve the question as to the true nature of a partnership.

We are persuaded the better view is that, although the Uniform Partnership Act regards the partnership as a legal entity for many purposes, these purposes are, nevertheless, limited and the "entity" concept does not possess such attributes of public policy that it must be invoked to achieve an unjust result. The Uniform Partnership Act applies the "aggregate" concept when it makes partners jointly and severally liable; therefore, what public policy could be violated by knowledgeable parties contracting in a context of partnership liability insurance that they contemplate the partnership as an aggregate of persons rather than as a legal entity? The insurance contract with which we are here concerned plainly contracts for the "aggregate" concept to be applied.

A legal entity has no "spouse" or "relatives" or "household." A legal entity could

not sustain "bodily injury." The uninsured motorist insurance contract plainly embraced partners and their spouses and relatives living in the same household. The insurer framed the language of the contractual undertaking. The trial judge correctly imposed liability upon Hartford under its contract and the undisputed facts.

Affirmed.

Types of Partners

Partnership law is filled with references to numerous types of partners, including the following:

1. *General partner*—any partner in a general partnership or a partner with general liability in a limited partnership.
2. *Limited partner*—a partner who enjoys limited liability, such as that of a corporate shareholder, if proper procedures to form a limited partnership are followed. (See Chapter 6.)
3. *Secret partner*—a partner who is active in management of the business, but whose partnership status is unknown to the general public.
4. *Silent partner*—a partner who is inactive in partnership business, though whose status as a partner is publicly known.
5. *Dormant partner*—a partner who is both secret and silent.
6. *Co-partner*—a fancy term for partner.

FORMATION OF THE PARTNERSHIP

Formalities

As noted earlier, a general partnership is extremely easy to form. No forms need be filed. No government permission is required. In fact, nothing need be in writing at all. The partners need not even think of themselves as such so long as they enter into the type of relationship that the law deems a partnership.

Normally, the only formalities a partnership is legally required to consider relate to licensing requirements of the particular line of partnership business, sales tax licenses, and the like.

Name

So informal is the partnership form that a partnership business need not even have a name. It is customary to have a name, however, and partners can choose any name for the partnership they desire so long as (1) the name is not deceptively similar to an existing business's name, (2) if a fictitious name is chosen (i.e., one that does not contain all the names of the partners) [23] it is registered under the assumed name statute existing in many states, and (3) the name does not indicate that the partnership is incorporated—use of the word "company" is prohibited in some states.

Articles of Partnership

Although it is possible (and is done every day) to form a partnership with little or no planning, this is not a good idea. Matters that the partners have not considered and agreed to will be governed by the UPA, sometimes with unexpected results. For example, if A and B agree to form a partnership with A to contribute $100,000 in cash and B to contribute only $1,000 and services, absent agreement to the contrary all profits will be shared equally, a result possibly unforeseen by A. If the $101,000 in capital is invested in a building and inventory that are destroyed in a fire on the first day of business before any insurance is purchased, B may well owe A $49,500—a result B may not foresee.

Because of the great flexibility the UPA gives partners to adjust their relations as to each other, every partnership has the potential to be what the partners want it to be. To avoid misunderstandings, eliminate statute of frauds problems, and achieve desired goals, every partnership of any size should have a carefully drafted written partnership agreement. The simple drafting of such an agreement will force the prospective partners to consider matters they might not otherwise have contemplated, such as, How will losses be shared? How will a steady stream of income be provided for those partners who need it? What will happen if a partner dies unexpectedly?

Attorneys who regularly advise partnerships have lengthy checklists of matters they recommend that prospective partners consider when drawing articles of partnership. These matters include the nature and scope of the business, the duration of the partnership, capital investment and loan obligations of the partners, sharing of profits and losses, wages and "draws" of partners, accounting procedures, availability of partnership books for inspection, division of management responsibilities, limitations on some partners' authority to bind the partnership, grounds for expulsion of partners, causes and methods of dissolution, distribution of assets on dissolution, and many more.

QUESTIONS AND PROBLEMS

1. Gail and Charles were lovers who, in 1974, moved into an apartment in Manhattan. The lease was executed in Charles's name. In light of his higher salary, Charles agreed to pay two-thirds of the rent and to buy all the furnishings. In 1980, Gail moved out. In early 1981, the owners of the apartment building decided to convert the apartments to cooperatives and gave Charles the opportunity to purchase his at

---

[23] If Smith and Jones are partners, the firm name "Smith & Jones" would not be fictitious. However, these names would be: "Smith & Co.," "Smith, Jones & Baker," or "Nighttime Donuts."

a special "insiders" rate. Soon thereafter, Gail sued for one-third of the difference between the "insiders" purchase price and the fair market value of the apartment, claiming that she and Charles had been "partners" in the apartment. Is Gail correct? See *Neild* v. *Wolfe*, 111 Misc.2d 994, 445 N.Y. Supp.2d 934 (1981).

2. Chilcott obtained tens of millions of dollars from hundreds of investors by representing to them that their money would be pooled in a highly profitable investment fund concentrated in the commodities futures market. Actually, Chilcott was running a giant Ponzi scheme. He induced a constant stream of new investments by lying about the pool's performance and profitability and using some of the incoming funds to pay investors who desired to "cash out." Chilcott made all the investment decisions, as the investors relied on his expertise. He denied investors access to the books and bought out complainers. Ultimately, the scheme lost momentum and crashed. In the litigation that followed, noninvestor creditors of the Chilcott Investment Fund claimed all the investors were partners. Is this correct? Discuss. See *Johnson* v. *Chilcott*, 599 F.Supp. 224 (D. Colo. 1984).

3. The Delaware Unemployment Compensation Commission charged C with failing to make contributions on behalf of "employees" S and P. C claimed that S and P, fellow barbers, were not his employees but were partners. C showed that he had properly registered the partnership name, had filed federal partnership income tax forms, and had duly executed partnership agreements with both S and P. The agreements were nearly identical. ¶1 declared the creation of a partnership and the location of the business. ¶2 said C would provide barber chairs, supplies, and licenses, while the other partner would provide tools of the trade. ¶3 declared that upon dissolution, ownership of the items would revert to the provider. ¶4 declared that the income of the partnership would be divided 30% for C and 70% for S (and the other, 20% for C and 80% for P). ¶5 declared that all partnership policy would be decided by C, whose decision was final. ¶6 forbade assignment of the agreement without C's approval. ¶7 required C to hold and distribute all receipts. ¶8 stated hours of work for S and P and holidays. Has C proved the existence of a partnership? Discuss. See *Chaiken* v. *Employment Security Commission*, 274 A.2d 707 (Del. 1971).

4. Stewart, Wood and Rhone (defendants) entered into an agreement with Happy Wheat Growers, Inc., a feedlot. The feedlot agreed to feed and maintain defendants' cattle at its own expense. Defendants were to be charged the "going price" for these services. If the feedlot made a profit from caring for the cattle, the defendants as a group and the feedlot were to divide the profit equally. If a loss resulted, it was to be borne entirely by the feedlot. Plaintiff sold supplies to the feedlot, but had not been paid. Plaintiff sued defendants on the theory that they were partners with the feedlot. Is plaintiff correct? Discuss. See *Tex-Co Grain Co.* v. *Happy Wheat Growers, Inc.*, 542 S.W.2d 934 (Tex. Civ. App. 1976).

5. James had an established plumbing contractor business that his brother Jon joined. A partnership agreement was drafted, but never signed by James, who maintained control of the operations. No partnership tax return was ever filed. Jon eventually sued James, claiming they had formed a partnership, pointing out that they had advertised under the firm name in the phone directory and on letterheads and had

used the firm name in insurance policies. Was there a partnership? Discuss. See *Garner* v. *Garner*, 358 A.2d 583 (Md. 1976).

6. P sued DP Associates, and its supposed partners, David McNamee and Philip Carroll, for breach of a contract to provide construction advisory services. P's evidence showed that at an early meeting in 1976, McNamee told P "he either had just commenced business, or was going into business with" Carroll. Later, P received letters from McNamee on DP Associates letterhead, and he assumed "DP" was derived from the individual defendants' first names. Prior to the signing of the contract, McNamee introduced P to Carroll, who said "I hope we'll be working together." This occurred at the office of DP Associates, where P saw Carroll several times in 1977. After the signing of the contract, Carroll said "I am happy that we will be working with you." Later, when a problem arose, Carroll told P not to worry because McNamee would take care of it. All money was paid to DP Associates. P never saw Carroll at the construction site, but understood that he was buying Carroll's expertise. Carroll swears he was not a partner in DP Associates. McNamee states he has never been in partnership with Carroll and evidence shows Carroll received no income, profits, salary, or other remuneration from the contract between P and DP Associates. Can Carroll be liable as a partner? Discuss. See *Volkman* v. *DP Associates*, 48 N.C. App. 155, 268 S.E.2d 265 (1980).

7. Scoggins was a partner of Evergreen Lawn Management. The other partners were Scoggins's wife and brother. The partnership employed several laborers. Scoggins was injured while unloading a magnolia tree, and filed a worker's compensation claim against himself et al., d/b/a Evergreen Lawn Management, and against Aetna Casualty and Surety Co., Evergreen's worker's compensation insurer. Aetna denied coverage on grounds that a partner could not be an "employee" within the meaning of the worker's compensation act. The court agreed with Aetna's position. Did the court apply the aggregate or entity theory? See *Scoggins* v. *Aetna Casualty & Surety Co.*, 139 Ga. App. 805, 229 S.E.2d 683 (1976).

8. Several minors formed a partnership to conduct a business. A contract was later formed between plaintiff and the partnership. Later, the minors attempted to rescind the contract with plaintiff because they were all without contractual capacity. The court refused to allow disaffirmance. Did the court apply the aggregate or entity theory? See *Kuehl* v. *Means*, 218 N.W. 907 (Iowa 1928).

3

PARTNERS' RIGHTS AND DUTIES AND PARTNERSHIP PROPERTY

INTRODUCTION

This chapter will address two main subjects. First, it will describe the rights and duties of partners as to one another. Second, it will discuss the nature of partnership property and the rights of partners and creditors in partnership and individual property. However, explanation of the rights and duties of partners and creditors in the context of dissolution of a partnership will be reserved for Chapter 5, where such matters will be examined in greater detail.

Uniform Partnership Act

In most states, of course, the Uniform Partnership Act (UPA) governs matters of partners' rights and duties and the property rights of partners and creditors. However, the rights and duties of the partners *inter se* may be altered by *agreement*, so long as the rights of third parties are not prejudiced. This gives the partnership form of enterprise an advantageous flexibility.

For example, as noted near the end of Chapter 2, sometimes UPA provisions lead to results not contemplated by the partners. The example given was A and B agreeing to form a partnership, with A to contribute $100,000 in cash and B to contribute $1,000 and services. Absent agreement, all profits will be shared equally, a result possibly unforeseen by A. If the $101,000 in capital is invested in a building that burns uninsured, B may well owe A $49,500, a result B may not foresee.

With a written partnership agreement, A and B can make the partnership what they want it to be so long as they do not infringe the rights of third parties. Whereas the UPA contemplates that absent agreement partners will share profits, losses, and control equally, A and B could agree that because A contributed so much more money, she will have a greater share of control, profits, and possibly losses. Because B has little money to risk, A and B might agree that in the event of a fire, the loss will be borne primarily by A. Although B remains unlimitedly liable to third parties for partnership losses, the partnership agreement can provide that any payments he makes shall be reimbursed by A. Because B has little money and is contributing services, the partnership agreement may provide that he is to be paid for the services—a result not contemplated by the UPA.

It bears repeating that a well-planned written partnership agreement can avoid a multitude of problems.

RIGHTS OF PARTNERS

Sections 18 through 22 of the UPA outline most of the rights (and duties) partners have that do not directly involve property. The property rights of partners are set out in §§24–28 and will be discussed later in this chapter.

Right to Choose Associates

Section 18(g) of the UPA provides that "[n]o person can become a member of a partnership without the consent of all partners." This is an expression of the Latin concept *delectus personae*, which provides that a person should have the ability to choose his or her own associates.

Because of the fiduciary nature of the relationship among partners, it is natural that no person should have partners foisted on him against his will. Just as no patient need accept a doctor she does not trust and no client need hire a lawyer he dislikes, partners should not have new co-partners forced upon them against their better judgment. This is all the more important because of the substantial liabilities that a partner can incur from the actions of an incompetent, misbehaving, or dishonest co-partner.

By agreement the partners may, of course, provide for admission by a less than unanimous vote of existing partners. Such agreements may provide that minority partners who are unhappy with the decision to admit new members shall have the right to have their interests purchased at a price set by a predetermined formula. If a new partner is added without any existing partner leaving, technically there should be no dissolution of the firm. However, if an existing partner does leave, there is a technical dissolution.

As shall be seen presently, the assignment or purchase of a partner's interest does not make the assignee or purchaser a partner, absent agreement of all existing co-partners.

Right to Manage

Section 13(c) of the UPA states that "[a]ll partners have equal rights in the management and conduct of partnership business." Thus, absent agreement, each partner has an equal vote in "ordinary matters," which §18(h) provides shall be decided by majority vote of the partners. However, §18(h) also says that "no act in contravention of any agreement between the partners may rightfully be done without the consent of all partners." The general rule, therefore, appears to be that both "extraordinary matters" and actions that would violate prior partnership agreements require a unanimous vote. Any partner has a veto. At least one court has held that a fundamental change in the partnership agreement cannot be made without unanimous consent even if the agreement itself provides that it may be amended by majority vote.[1]

Matters that would be considered "extraordinary" and therefore would require a unanimous vote include changes in the capital of the firm, in the partnership agreement, or in the scope of the business. Furthermore, §9(3) expressly provides that absent authorization by all co-partners, no partner has authority to (1) assign partnership property, (2) dispose of the goodwill of the business, (3) do any act that would make it impossible to carry on the ordinary business of the partnership, (4) confess a judgment, or (5) submit a partnership claim or liability to arbitration.

A partner's right to vote in the management of the partnership is a property right. Absent agreement, each partner has an equal voice. Thus, if Ms. A, Mr. B, and Ms. C agree to be partners, and to contribute $50,000, $10,000, and $1,000, respectively, to launch the enterprise, each has an equal voice in firm affairs, absent agreement. Because Ms. A has contributed so much more to the partnership and thus has more to lose, she may refuse to become a partner unless she is given a greater voice in the management than B and C.

By agreement, the parties may alter the management of the firm in any number of ways. Some partners may be given a greater voice than others. One partner may be appointed the "managing partner," or there may be a committee of partners that will manage. The UPA's majority vote approach envisions a relatively small partnership and may not be appropriate for a large law or accounting partnership with hundreds of partners. Indeed, the partners may agree to appoint a nonpartner to manage the firm.[2]

What if an equal number of partners with equal votes split evenly on a partnership vote? Unless the parties have agreed to a tie-breaking mechanism, problems are sure to arise. In *National Biscuit Co.* v. *Stroud*,[3] one partner, Stroud, in a grocery store no longer wished to buy bread on credit and so informed the National Biscuit Company,

---

[1] *McCallum* v. *Arbury*, 393 P.2d 774 (Or. 1964).

[2] *Wilzig* v. *Sisselman*, 442 A.2d 1021 (N.J. 1982).

[3] 106 S.E.2d 692 (N.C. 1959).

telling it he would no longer be responsible for such purchases. The other partner, Freeman, later bought $171.04 worth of bread on credit for the grocery. The bill went unpaid, and National Biscuit sued Stroud. Concluding that "half of the members are not a majority," the court held that Stroud could not properly restrict Freeman's authority to act for the partnership. Because Stroud supposedly benefited from the supplying of the bread, he was held liable. To avoid liability, Stroud should have dissolved the partnership.

The *Stroud* decision must be contrasted with that in *Summers* v. *Dooley*,[4] where two partners disagreed on a specific change of policy—the hiring of an employee by one partner. Because the other partner did not agree to or acquiesce in the hiring, he was held not liable because "those who forbid a change must have their way," even though the partnership benefited from the hiring.

Obviously, in the case of an even number of partners, all should agree upon a method of breaking a deadlock in voting. Otherwise, dissolution may be the only alternative.

Right to Return of Capital

Section 18(a) of the UPA provides that "[e]ach partner shall be repaid his contributions, whether by way of capital or advances to the partnership property." This right, of course, is subject to the rights of creditors; there may be no funds with which to repay contributions.

The right to repayment is also subject to alteration by agreement. The UPA would provide that upon dissolution partners Ms. A and Mr. B, who contributed $100,000 and $50,000, respectively, are entitled to repayment of those same sums. However, the partners may agree that any excess of assets over obligations left on dissolution will be split equally.[5]

Right to Interest

A partner is not entitled to payment of interest on a capital contribution according to §18(d). The profits of the enterprise are considered the earnings on capital, so no interest is needed. However, interest may be paid if (1) the partners agree that interest is due or (2) the contributions are repaid later than agreed.

On the other hand, §18(c) entitles each partner who loans or advances sums to the partnership in excess of the agreed capital contribution to interest on those sums.

A partner entitled to profits who has not withdrawn them from the partnership usually is not entitled to interest on those profits. However, some courts have under certain circumstances deemed those unwithdrawn profits as loans and therefore subject to interest payments.

[4] 481 P.2d 318 (Idaho 1971).
[5] *Citizens Bank of Clovis* v. *Williams*, 630 P.2d 1228 (N.M. 1981).

Right to Profits

People usually enter into partnerships to make money. Section 18(a) gives each partner the right to "share equally in the profits and surplus remaining after all liabilities." This sharing extends to ordinary profits, nonrecurring gains such as sales of partnership property, and profits derived during the winding up of the partnership.[6]

Partners may, by agreement, share profits in any proportion. However, absent agreement, the UPA provides for an equal sharing of profits even though one partner may have contributed much more capital than the others.

The flip side, of course, is that just as partners must share all profits, they must also share all losses. If the partners have no agreement, the UPA provides they will share profits *and* losses equally. If the partners do have an agreement to share profits in some proportion other than equally, but have no agreement as to sharing of losses, the losses must be shared in the same proportion as the profits. Of course, each partner has unlimited liability to third parties for losses. But actions against other partners for indemnity can prorate the losses properly.

Right to Compensation for Services

Section 18(f) gives a surviving partner the right to "reasonable compensation for his services in winding up the partnership affairs." This right is forfeited, however, if the partner wrongfully refuses to wind up the partnership and continues to run the business.[7]

More important is §18(f)'s provision that, absent agreement, no partner is entitled to compensation for services, *other than winding up*, rendered to the partnership. The rationale for this principle rests on the notion that all partners owe a duty to devote their entire time and energy to the partnership business.

In *Levy* v. *Leavitt*,[8] the court explained:

> In the business of a partnership the services of a partner are rendered for the common benefit in the performance of an obligation created by the partnership agreement, and the resultant benefit is divided pro rata as provided in the partnership contract. These profits constitute, in the absence of other agreement, the stipulated reward for services to be rendered, and there is no right to other compensation based on the reasonable value of the services actually rendered.

It bears emphasizing that the partners may very well agree that one or more partners will receive compensation for their labors. Such a wage will be very important to partners who have no other source of income, especially in the early, frequently unprofitable, years of the enterprise.

Some courts have created an exception to the general rule, allowing compensation

---

[6] J. Crane and A. Bromberg, *Law of Partnership*, 2nd ed. West Pub. Co., St. Paul, MN (1968), p. 366.

[7] *Couri* v. *Couri*, 447 N.E.2d 334 (Ill. 1983).

[8] 178 N.E. 758 (N.Y. 1931).

to a partner who has performed tasks expected to be done by hired help.[9] Another court-created exception is explained in the following case.

ALTMAN v. ALTMAN

653 F.2d 755 (3d Cir. 1981)

Brothers Sydney and Ashley Altman operated a number of real estate construction and management partnerships in southeastern Pennsylvania from 1952 to 1973. They shared equally in management and were very successful. Sydney and Ashley received identical salaries, and each was permitted to charge certain personal expenses to the partnerships. They agreed that the amount of such expenses would be equal, so if one brother charged more personal expenses to the partnerships, he would pay to the other brother one-half the amount by which his personal expenses exceeded those of his brother.

In January 1973, Sydney moved to Florida in order to establish residency to obtain a divorce. At first Sydney commuted from Florida to work two to three days each week; later he returned only once a month. In November 1973 Sydney told Ashley he was considering retirement. Exactly what happened thereafter was subject to dispute, but Sydney had little to do with the business thereafter, and Ashley operated it until 1977.

Subsequent litigation between the parties raised a number of issues, including whether Ashley was entitled to additional compensation for operating the partnership from 1973 to 1977. The trial court concluded that he was not so entitled. Ashley appealed.

SEITZ, CIRCUIT JUDGE:

Ashley challenges the district court's holding that he is not entitled to compensation beyond his share of the partnership profits for managing the partnerships between August 1973 and June 1977. The court found that Ashley breached the partnership agreement by unilaterally paying himself salaries from the partnerships in excess of what the brothers had agreed upon. The court concluded that under Pennsylvania law the services rendered by Ashley did not justify additional compensation.

The Pennsylvania Supreme Court has emphasized that "in the absence of an agreement to the contrary, a partner is not entitled to compensation beyond his share of the profits, for services rendered by him in performing partnership matters. . . . [A] right to compensation arises only where the services rendered extend beyond normal partnership functions"—*Rosenfeld* v. *Rosenfeld*, 390 Pa. 39, 45, 133 A.2d 829, 832 (1957); see also *Kirby* v. *Kalbacher*, 373 Pa. 103, 105, 95 A.2d 535, 540 (1953) (services required only for successful operations of existing partnership not beyond normal partnership functions). Ashley, however, does not expressly contend that the services he performed went beyond normal partnership functions. Instead, he relies on *Greenan* v. *Ernst*, 408 Pa. 495,

---

[9] See, for example, *Montgomery* v. *Burch*, 11 S.W.2d 545 (Tex. Civ. App. 1928) (error dismissed).

508–10, 184 A.2d 570, 577–78 (1962), in which the Pennsylvania Supreme Court concluded that it would be "highly inequitable" to deny compensation to an active partner who had assumed sole responsibility for the management of a partnership when the inactive person either "could not or would not" assume any responsibility. The court noted that the "skill and efforts" of the active partner produced large profits for the partnership and therefore benefited the other partners.

In contending that it would be highly inequitable in this case to deny compensation, Ashley emphasizes that after August 1973 the entire management and supervision of the partnerships were left to him. He asserts that he not only preserved the partnerships' properties but also maximized profits during this period. In addition, Ashley points to expert testimony at the trial, emphasizing the high caliber of his management of the partnerships.

Ashley apparently is contending that compensation is awarded under Pennsylvania law whenever it would be highly inequitable not to do so. However, *Greenan* does not support this contention. The *Greenan* court reaffirmed the *Rosenfeld* rule, and it found that the services in question extended beyond normal partnership functions. Thus, Ashley must show more than the fact that a failure to award compensation would be highly inequitable; he must also show that his services extended beyond normal partnership functions.

In this case, the district court concluded that Ashley's services did not warrant compensation in excess of his share of the partnership profits. In reaching this decision, the court necessarily found that the services performed by Ashley did not extend beyond normal partnership functions. We recognize that in *Greenan* the Pennsylvania Supreme Court appeared to relax the definition of "beyond normal partnership functions" by allowing compensation to a partner who had assumed responsibility for the continued operation of an existing partnership. However, the critical factor in *Greenan* was that the active partner had taken an existing partnership and expanded it substantially beyond its previous size and scope. In contrast, the services rendered by Ashley maintained the operation of existing businesses in the same manner as they had been operated before Sydney's departure. In addition, unlike the situation in *Greenan*, the lack of participation in the partnerships by Sydney was with the consent of Ashley. Thus, the district court's factual finding that Ashley's services did not warrant compensation beyond his share of the partnership profits was not clearly erroneous. Although this result may appear to be harsh to some, we believe that the narrow scope of our review of the district court's factual findings and the relevant principles of Pennsylvania law require this conclusion.

Affirmed.

The *Altman* case discusses one state's exception to the "no compensation" principle, but in most instances in most jurisdictions, the principle prevails, absent agreement. Some courts will imply an agreement to compensate where one partner is entrusted with management of the partnership business and devotes his or her whole time thereto while the other partners attend to their personal affairs.[10] However many courts are quite reluctant to do so.[11]

Right to Reimbursement

A partner's right to reimbursement for expenses and liabilities incurred in "the ordinary and proper conduct" of partnership business and for the "preservation of its business or property" is established in §18(b). Thus, whenever a partner dips into his or her own pocket to pay proper partnership expenses, for example, to hire a truck to make a delivery, to pay a repairperson to repair equipment, or to hire an attorney to retrieve partnership property, that partner is entitled to reimbursement. The partnership is primarily liable for indemnity. If it does not pay, the duty falls to the other partners.

Similarly, if a partner pays more than a pro-rata share of partnership debts and liabilities, reimbursement is due from other partners. For example, if one partner must pay a judgment to a bank because of an overdraft caused by the wrongful withdrawal of another partner, contribution is obviously due from the latter partner.[12] Even if the latter partner had not acted wrongfully, he would be liable for his pro-rata share of any partnership loss. Partners who act wrongfully, on the other hand, may not be entitled to indemnity or contribution. Where a partner's bad faith or negligence causes a partnership loss, indemnity may not be proper.

FLYNN v. REAVES

218 S.E. 2d 661 (Ga. App. 1975)

A husband and wife brought a malpractice action against Dr. Moore (defendant). They could have, but did not, sue Dr. Moore's former co-partners (Drs. Flynn, Fokes and Paulk) who were partners in The Eye, Ear, Nose and Throat Clinic with Dr. Moore at the time of the malpractice. Moore, therefore, brought a third-party action against his co-partners, seeking contribution should the malpractice action succeed.

The co-partners moved to dismiss the third-party complaint for failure to state a claim.

The trial judge refused to dismiss, so the co-partners appealed.

CLARK, JUDGE:

The law of partnership is the law of agency: " 'Each partner being the agent of the firm, the firm is liable for his torts committed within the scope of his agency, on the principle of respondeat superior, in the same way that a master

---

[10] For example, *Kirkpatrick* v. *Christensen*, 206 P.2d 577 (Ariz. 1949).

[11] For example, *Conrad* v. *Johnson*, 465 S.W.2d 819 (Tex. Civ. App. 1971) ref. n.r.e., *cert. denied*, 405 U.S. 1041 (1973).

[12] *Bank of Commerce* v. *De Santis*, 451 N.Y.S.2d 974 (N.Y. City Civ. Cy. 1982).

is responsible for his servant's torts, and for the same reason [that] the firm is liable for the torts of its agents or servants,' 1 Bates Law of Partn. §461''—*Hobbs & Tucker* v. *Chicago Packing, etc., Co.*, 98 Ga. 576, 581, 25 S.E. 584, 587. See also Comment (a) of the Restatement of the Law of Agency, 2d §14A, entitled Agent and Partner, which states, ''the rights and liabilities of partners with respect to each other and to third persons are largely determined by agency principles.'' Thus, ''where several physicians are in partnership, they may be held liable in damages for the professional negligence of one of the firm''—60 Am. Jur. 2d 86 Partnership, §166.

In the case at bar, therefore, the co-partners and defendant would be jointly and severally liable to plaintiffs if it were established that defendant in fact negligently diagnosed and treated plaintiff wife in the course of the partnership business. Therefore, plaintiffs had the choice of suing the defendant individually or all of the partners including defendant jointly. But defendant cannot seek contribution from his co-partners simply because they are jointly liable to plaintiffs. ''[T]here may be cases in which a person who has suffered loss or damage may have the right to sue two persons as if they were joint wrongdoers, without their being, as among themselves, joint wrongdoers. A's servant, B, negligently injures C in the performance of A's work. From C's standpoint, A and B are joint wrongdoers, but as among themselves B is the wrongdoer and A is subjected

to liability merely by the doctrine of respondeat superior, so that, if C sues A alone and compels him to pay the damage, A, in turn, may compel B to indemnify him for the loss. So in this class of cases, it is always relevant to inquire, 'Whose wrong really caused the damage?' . . . Generally speaking, a right of action over in such cases exists only where the negligence of him who has been compelled to satisfy the damages is imputed or constructive only, and the negligence of him against whom the remedy over is asserted was actual or more immediately causal''—*Central of Ga. Ry. Co.* v. *Macon Ry. & Light Co.*, 9 Ga. App. 628, 632, 71 S.E. 1076, 1078.

Here, the co-partners and defendant are not joint tortfeasors as among themselves. For the co-partners are subjected to liability only by the doctrine of respondeat superior. Thus, defendant whose negligence, if any, was actual, cannot seek contribution from his co-partners, who are merely constructively negligent. Of course, had defendant alleged that his co-partners were actual tortfeasors, a third-party action for contribution would lie. But such is not the case.

Therefore, we hold, as other courts have held, that where a partner is sued individually by a plaintiff injured by the partner's sole negligence, the partner cannot seek contribution from his co-partners even though the negligent act occurred in the course of the partnership business.

Reversed.

Right to Use Partnership Property

Subject to agreement, each partner has an equal right to use partnership property for partnership purposes. This right will be discussed in greater detail later in this chapter in the section on partners' property rights.

Right to Inspect

If they are properly kept—an unfortunately rare occurrence—partnership books are a key to protection of each partner's interests. Therefore, §19 of the UPA provides that each "partner shall at all times have access to and may inspect and copy any" of the partnership books.

This right of inspection is very broad, but it is not absolute. For example, no partner will be allowed to inspect firm records for a fraudulent purpose or to gain an unfair advantage over the other partners. Nor will a partner be allowed to remove the books from partnership premises without permission of the other partners.

Still, the right is very broad, continuing after dissolution of the partnership during the winding-up period. Indeed, §20 of the UPA specifically allows a partner to demand information even from the legal representative of a deceased partner.

Right to an Accounting

Every partner has the right to a formal accounting, which is a detailed compilation of partnership transactions and financial records that gives a true picture of the partnership and the rights of its partners. Sections 21 and 22 of the UPA entitle a partner to an accounting whenever (1) he or she has been wrongfully excluded from the partnership business or property, (2) the partnership agreement provides for the right, (3) a co-partner may have improperly profited from dealings with the firm, or (4) finally, "[w]henever other circumstances render it just and reasonable." If the other partners do not voluntarily render an accounting, the demanding partner may apply to a court of equity.

The following excerpt from the leading treatise on partnership law illustrates the types of matters covered by a formal accounting:

LAW OF PARTNERSHIP*

J. Crane and A. Bromberg

Published by West Publishing Company, pp. 409–412 (1968).

An accounting action is designed to produce and evaluate all testimony relevant to the various claims of the partners. It results in a money judgment for or against each partner according to the balance struck. Ancillary relief, like injunction, receivership, and partition, may be granted in appropriate cases. Since all activities related to the partnership are subject to scrutiny, a wide variety of matters may be determined, for example:

1. Questions of conventional accounting, such as cash or accrual method of reporting, application of payments, valuation of inventories, type of depreciation, expenses versus capital expenditures, and other factors in computing profit and loss as well as assets and liabilities.

---

2. Questions of reconstruction of inadequate records.
3. Questions of agreement, such as whether a partner was to have a salary, or was to treat an advance to the partnership as a loan (rather than a contribution).
4. Questions of fiduciary duty, such as whether a partner must account for profits from an outside transaction or holds property in trust for the partnership.
5. Questions of scope of the partnership business, such as whether a particular expenditure was proper, or whether certain profits belong to the partnership or to another business.
6. Questions of ownership of property, e.g., whether individual or partnership.
7. Questions of valuation of assets, such as goodwill.

The character of an accounting is concisely conveyed by the court's compilation in a relatively simple case involving the construction and sale of a motel by partners Hargett and Miller. It is easy to visualize the dispute generated by almost every item.

Sales price of motel		$120,000.00	
Cash in cash drawer (admitted by Hargett)		300.00	
Cash in cash drawer (additional amount found by chancellor from testimony)		2,035.39	
A	Total Assets of partnership		$122,335.39
	Payments from assets:		
	(1) To Lovett in discharge of loan	53,417.75	
	(2) To bank in discharge of loan	11,920.80	
	(3) To Hargett in additional salary	2,219.91	
	(4) To Miller, reimbursement for loan payments and other advances	20,875.00	
	(5) To Miller, interest on advances beyond capital	92.23	
	(6) Cash paid for property improvement by Hargett (capital contribution)	2,398.96	
B	Total obligations		90,924.65
C	Balance to divide		31,410.74
D	Amount due each partner from balance		$ 15,705.37
	Amount due Miller from above calculation:		
	(4) Reimbursement for loan payments and other advances	$ 20,875.00	
	(5) Interest on advances beyond capital	92.23	
	(D) Amount due Miller from balance	15,705.37	
E	Total due Miller		$ 36,672.60
	Amount in Miller's possession	36,912.25	
F	Overpayment to Miller		$ 239.65
	Amount due Hargett from above calculation:		
	(3) Additional salary	$ 2,219.91	
	(6) Cash paid (capital contribution)	2,398.96	
	(D) Amount due Hargett from balance	15,705.37	
G	Total due Hargett		$ 20,324.24
	Amount in Hargett's possession	20,084.59	
H	Balance due Hargett		$ 239.65

Accountings normally occur incident to dissolution of the partnership, for example, when the parties are unable to settle a firm dispute that is so serious that carrying on the business of the partnership is impossible. An action for accounting need not, however, be accompanied by dissolution.

It is important to note that the rights and duties of the partners as to each other normally cannot be litigated until after an accounting has taken place. For example, if one partner believes that another partner has converted partnership property to personal use in violation of the latter's fiduciary duty, most courts require that a formal accounting precede any action for conversion. That accounting might show, for instance, that the converting partner is owed more than he or she owes because of earlier transactions.

A case that not only stresses the usual need for a formal accounting before partners can sue each other, but also mentions relevant exceptions follows.

MITCHELL RESORT ENTERPRISES, INC. v. C & S BUILDERS, INC.

570 S.W.2d 463 (Tex. Civ. App. 1978)

C & S Builders, Inc., sued Mitchell Resort Enterprises, Inc., and Mitchell Development Corporation of the Southwest ("Mitchell entities") and William Canfield seeking recovery of profits of a joint venture it entered with defendants as well as punitive damages. Under the joint venture agreement, C & S was to construct townhouses and the Mitchell entities were to provide land, financing, and marketing. When C & S became dissatisfied with the Mitchell entities' sales efforts, it sued, claiming that defendants were trying to squeeze C & S out of the joint venture.

Canfield was dismissed from the action, but the jury found that the Mitchell entities had intentionally and maliciously failed to use ordinary care to sell the constructed townhouses. The jury found that C & S's 50% of the lost profit was $75,000 and added $200,000 in punitive damages. The Mitchell entities appealed.

BROWN, JUSTICE:

Mitchell entities contend the court erred in rendering judgment for damages because C & S failed to plead, prove, or request jury findings that the partnership between the parties had been dissolved and terminated, which is an essential element of a cause of action for damages between partners. We agree.

The court in *Staggers* v. *Vaughan*, 527 S.W.2d 791 (Tex. Civ. App.—Texarkana 1975, writ ref. n. r. e.), said: "The law is well settled that one partner may not sue another partner on a claim arising out of partnership business until an accounting and settlement of partnership affairs is made."

The court in *Chipley* v. *Smith*, 292 S.W. 209 (Tex. Com. App. 1927), recognized exceptions to the general rule, quoting from 21 A.L.R. (page 22) as follows:

However, this broad general rule is subject to many exceptions—such, for instance, as where the partnership was formed for the carrying out of a single venture or transaction, or the action involves a segregated or single unadjusted item of account, or a personal covenant or transaction entirely independent of the partnership affairs. These exceptions, of course, are based upon the theory that such cases do not necessarily involve an accounting, and, therefore, that resort need not be had to an equity forum. Broadly speaking, it might be said that one partner may maintain an action at law against a co-partner if the relief sought does not involve the taking of an accounting of complicated or numerous partnership transactions, but not if such accounts are involved.

C & S argues the applicability in the instant case of one of the exceptions to the general rule. We disagree.

This is not a case where the cause of action is not connected with partnership accounts and is distinct and separate from partnership dealings—*Schwarz* v. *Lee*, 287 S.W. 519 (Tex. Civ. App.—Fort Worth 1926, writ dism'd). Nor is the case one in which the partnership involves a single venture which is completed—*Mullins* v. *Archer*, 176 S.W.2d 763 (Tex. Civ. App.—Amarillo 1943, no writ). Neither is the instant case one for breach of a contract to form a partnership where the partnership has never existed—*Morgan* v. *Steinberg*, 23 S.W.2d 527 (Tex. Civ. App.—Amarillo 1929, no writ). This partnership was formed to build and sell town-

houses. C & S seeks lost profits to that partnership.

C & S contends that it is not suing for assumpsit or breach of contract, but on breach of a fiduciary duty and negligence. Its claim, however, either in contract or tort, involves partnership affairs and the ultimate purpose of the partnership. C & S's pleadings disclose a partnership relationship existing between it and Mitchell Enterprises; a partnership that has not been terminated; the claim sued upon is not one separate and distinct from partnership affairs; nor does the partnership involve a single completed venture bringing the claim within an exception to the general rule, but to the contrary the claim involves loss of profits to the partnership.

As stated in 44 Tex. Jur.2d Partnership §156, citing *Chipley* v. *Smith*: "An accounting and settlement between partners is generally a condition precedent to an action by one against another based on partnership claims and transactions. For this reason a suit for a share of property or profits or an action for contribution to losses or debts may not be maintained by a partner."

C & S having failed to plead or prove an accounting and settlement of partnership affairs, the court erred in rendering judgment for damages against Mitchell Enterprises. This holding makes it unnecessary for us to consider appellants' other points of error.

Reversed.

DUTIES OF PARTNERS

Most of the rights of partners carry corresponding duties. This section concerns the most important of those obligations, many of which are set out in the same sections of the UPA as partnership rights. Some, such as the obligation to bear a share of partnership losses, have already been discussed.

Duty of Obedience

Each partner is obliged to abide by the partnership agreement and to comply with any properly made partnership decision. If an ordinary business policy is decided by majority vote, the minority partners who were outvoted must follow the policy. For example, if by a 3-to-1 vote, partners A, B, and C strip partner D of the authority to hire and fire partnership employees, partner D should no longer hire and fire. A partner who exceeds the properly established scope of authority will be liable for losses caused thereby. If the partnership agreement requires partner E to make certain monetary contributions, partner E must make those contributions.

Assume that partner E refuses to make the agreed-on contributions. What happens? Some courts hold that E has forfeited any right to share in the profits of the partnership. Others hold that no such forfeiture occurs, but that E's share of the profits must be reduced by the amount of damages caused the partnership by the breach. More on this subject will appear in Chapter 5, on dissolution.

Duty of Reasonable Care

In carrying out partnership business, each partner is responsible to act with reasonable care. However, the standard of conduct imposed upon partners is none too harsh. Partners will not be held liable when their honest mistakes of judgment cause losses to the partnership. A partner will be liable for losses caused by "culpable" negligence, which the courts have generally construed as entailing more carelessness than regular negligence, but less than gross negligence.

Similarly, partners are not held to possess the degree of knowledge and skill of the partnership's paid agents,[13] though they may be held liable for acting hastily when they should have consulted with their co-partners.

Fiduciary Duty

Partners are fiduciaries. They owe one another a duty of highest trust and confidence. Section 21 of the UPA clearly provides that each partner "must account to the partnership for any benefit, and hold as trustee for it any profits derived by him without the consent of the other partners from any transaction" connected with the partnership. But the fiduciary's responsibility is broader than this. The Supreme Court stated long ago in *Latta* v. *Kilbourn*: [14]

> [It is] well settled that one partner cannot, directly or indirectly, use partnership assets for his own benefit; that he cannot, in conducting the business of a partnership, take any profit clandestinely for himself; that he cannot carry on the business of the partnership for his private advantage; that he cannot carry on another business in competition or rivalry with that of the firm, thereby depriving it of the benefit of his time, skill, and

---

[13] Crane and Bromberg, *The Law of Partnership*, p. 395.
[14] 150 U.S. 524, 541 (1893).

fidelity without being accountable to his copartners for any profit that may accrue to him therefrom; that he cannot be permitted to secure for himself that which it is his duty to obtain, if at all, for the firm of which he is a member; nor can he avail himself of knowledge or information which may be properly regarded as the property of the partnership, in the sense that it is available or useful to the firm for any purpose within the scope of the partnership business.

The scope of the fiduciary duty is described in this quotation from the Supreme Court; its tenor is indicated in the following famous passage from *Meinhard* v. *Salmon*,[15] by Justice Cardozo. *Meinhard* involved a joint venture in the management of rental property. Near the end of the lease period, one joint venturer secretly negotiated a second, broader lease for himself without telling his co-adventurer of the opportunity. Cardozo held the co-adventurer entitled to a 49% interest in the second lease, writing:

[Joint adventurers], like copartners, owe to one another, while the enterprise continues, the duty of the finest loyalty. Many forms of conduct permissible in a workaday world for those acting at arm's length, are forbidden to those bound by fiduciary ties. A trustee is held to something stricter than the morals of the market place. Not honesty alone, but the punctilio of an honor the most sensitive, is then the standard of behavior. As to this there has developed a tradition that is unbending and inveterate.

The need for a court-enforced fiduciary duty is quite clearly indicated in this shocking case.

ALEXANDER v. SIMS

249 S.W.2d 832 (Ark. 1952)

Alexander and Sims were partners in a retail business which commenced in 1942 and operated successfully until its dissolution upon Sim's death on April 10, 1950. On September 16, 1949, Sims, aged 48, entered a hospital for diagnosis. On September 23rd, she underwent surgery. On that day, the attending physician informed Sims's mother and Alexander that Sims had a serious case of cancer and would live only a short time. On October 14th, while Sims was still in the hospital, and before she learned of the malignancy, Alexander took to Sims an

agreement which provided "that in the event of the decease of either of the partners, all of the partnership assets shall ipso facto *immediately become the sole and exclusive property of the surviving partner." Sims and Alexander both signed the agreement. The next day Sims for the first time made direct inquiry of her physician and learned of the seriousness of her disease.*

In February 1950, Sims executed her will which bequeathed her entire estate, including her interest in the partnership, to her parents.

---

[15] 164 N.E. 545 (N.Y. 1928).

Sims died in April 1950. The trial court refused to give effect to the October 14th agreement, and Alexander appealed.

MCFADDIN, JUSTICE:

We come to the conclusion then that on October 14, 1949, Mrs. Alexander obtained the execution of the written agreement, when her partner, Miss Sims, was ignorant of her impending death and when Mrs. Alexander, knowing such fact, did not divulge it to Miss Sims. Under these circumstances, we think that Mrs. Alexander failed to observe and obey the rule which requires partners to exercise the utmost good faith in their dealings with each other. In *Drummond v. Batson*, 162 Ark. 407, at page 421, 258 S.W. 616, 620, Mr. Justice Hart said: "Partners are bound to conduct themselves with good faith towards each other." The Uniform Partnership Act recognizes this rule.

In 40 Am. Jur. 217, et seq., the holdings from cases generally are summarized:

> The relationship of partners is fiduciary and imposes upon them the obligation of the utmost good faith and integrity in their dealings with one another with respect to partnership affairs. . . . The partners must not deceive one another by concealment of material facts. . . . The general rule that the utmost good faith is required of partners in their relationship with each other, and that, since each is the confidential agent of the other, each has a right to know all that the others know and each is required to make full disclosure of all material facts within his knowledge in any way relating to partnership affairs, is held almost universally to apply in the case of a sale by one partner to another of his interest in the partnership.

There is an Annotation in Ann. Cas. 1912D, page 1245, in which cases are cited from a score of jurisdictions to sustain this statement: "The relation of partners is such that in a sale of his interest in the partnership by one partner to another, the utmost good faith must be observed, and the concealment of any important fact or the failure fully to disclose all knowledge affecting the value of the partnership, or the interest proposed to be sold, or any fraud of any kind, will operate to defeat the sale."

In the case at bar, the effect of the agreement which Mrs. Alexander caused to be prepared and signed by Miss Sims was the same as a sale of Miss Sims's interest in the partnership. Mrs. Alexander knew that Miss Sims had only a short time to live and that the effect of the instrument was for Miss Sims to give all her interest in the partnership to Mrs. Alexander. Yet, Mrs. Alexander, knowing all these facts, did not disclose them to Miss Sims when the agreement was signed, and Miss Sims did not learn of her serious condition and impending death until the next day. We hold that under these circumstances, the agreement was susceptible of being set aside. That Miss Sims did renounce the agreement is thoroughly shown by her will, in which she bequeathed her interest in the partnership to her parents. The validity of the will is not attacked, and it clearly proclaims that Miss Sims renounced the agreement here relied on by Mrs. Alexander. This suit was to accomplish and complete such renunciation.

Affirmed.

The opportunities for breach of the fiduciary duty are many and varied. No partner should buy partnership property at less than market value, for to do so is a breach of fiduciary duty even if the partner ultimately makes no profit.[16] Nor should a

---

[16] *Slingerland* v. *Hurley*, 388 So.2d 587 (Fla. App. 1980).

partner use partnership resources, such as employee and computer time, for personal purposes without consent of other partners.[17]

While partners can engage in nonpartnership enterprises that do not compete with the partnership so long as those ventures do not require so much time and energy that the partners cannot fulfill their partnership responsibilities,[18] they should never take business away from the partnership or appropriate partnership business opportunities. The most difficult questions in the fiduciary duty realm relate to business opportunities and noncompetition. A typical business opportunity case is the following.

MATHIS v. MEYERES

574 P.2d 447 (Alas. 1978)

In 1970 Mathis and Meyeres agreed to jointly purchase a 574-acre tract of land in Fairbanks, Alaska, for the purpose of subdivision and eventual sale. At the time they orally agreed to be equal partners, but discussed no other terms. In 1971 the partnership, known as Wildview Acres, purchased an adjacent 80-acre tract. Soon thereafter, Kohler was brought into the partnership as a one-third equal partner.

In 1975, Meyeres, Kohler, and New State purchased from the Sisters of Providence a 160-acre tract adjacent to the subdivision. Mathis and Wildview Acres Partnership were not afforded an opportunity to participate in the purchase. Mathis brought this suit to impose a constructive trust on the Sisters property claiming that Meyeres and Kohler had wrongfully appropriated a partnership opportunity.

The trial court found no wrongful appropriation and Mathis appealed.

MATTHEWS, JUSTICE:

The parties are not in disagreement concerning the law governing business opportunities among partners. They correctly acknowledge that what

we said in *Alvest, Inc.* v. *Superior Oil Corporation*, 398 P.2d 213, 215 (Alas. 1965), regarding the fiduciary relationship of corporate officers and directors to their corporation applies to the parallel relationship between partners and their partnership.

A corporate officer or director stands in a fiduciary relationship to his corporation. Out of this relationship arises the duty of reasonably protecting the interests of the corporation. It is inconsistent with and a breach of such duty for an officer or director to take advantage of a business opportunity for his own personal profit when, applying ethical standards of what is fair and equitable in a particular situation, the opportunity should belong to the corporation. Where a business opportunity is one in which the corporation has a legitimate interest, the officer or director may not take the opportunity for himself. If he does, he will hold all resulting benefit and profit in his fiduciary capacity for the use and benefit of the corporation.

Whether a business opportunity is a corporate one or one within the legitimate scope of the individual interests of the officer or director depends upon the facts and circumstances of each case.

Reflective of the fiduciary relationship between partners is UPA §21(a):

---

[17] *Veale* v. *Rose*, 657 S.W.2d 834 (Tex. App. 13 Dist. 1983).

[18] *Truman* v. *Martin*, 321 N.W.2d 420 (Neb. 1982).

Every partner shall account to the partnership for any benefit, and hold as trustee for it any profits derived by him without the consent of the other partners from any transaction connected with the formation, conduct, or liquidation of the partnership or from any use by him of its property.

The question in this case is whether the acquisition of the Sisters property was a transaction connected with the conduct of the partnership. The trial court concluded that it was not, finding that the partnership's "sole and primary purpose was to develop, subdivide and sell" the two tracts acquired by the partnership. The court further found:

> That the partnership was entered into for the limited purpose of developing specific property and was not entered into as a general partnership organized for the purpose of buying any lands which might be profitably developed.

These findings are challenged as clearly erroneous.

We have considered the evidence . . . and conclude that there was no error. Mathis and Meyeres became partners almost casually in the course of acquiring and holding a specifically identified tract of land. The partnership provided a means of sharing the expenses and profits resulting from development and sale of the property. It was not a general investment business. The partners were not pledged to spend any particular portion of their time looking after partnership affairs nor did they agree to refrain from buying land individually or from forming other partnerships to buy land. In fact, the evidence indicates that Meyeres was involved in other land investment entities formed both before and after the partnership was created; Mathis knew of these and made no complaint. The fact that the initial 574-acre tract was once enlarged may be taken as some evidence that the partnership purpose was modified to include the acquisition of adjacent lands that appeared to be sound investments. A question of fact was thus created. However, the court was not clearly erroneous in resolving it against Mathis. There is no testimony that such a modified general purpose was either discussed or agreed upon. In regard to the Sisters property specifically, Mathis testified that he had spoken with Meyeres several times about its acquisition by the partnership. Meyeres, however, testified that he could not recall these discussions and that if they had occurred, he would have remembered them. We are required to take Meyeres' view of this matter on review. Further, Kohler testified that it was his understanding upon joining the partnership that its scope was no broader than the development and sale of the property it then owned.

It is significant that knowledge of the Sisters property did not come to Meyeres as a result of his partnership with Mathis. Meyeres acquired knowledge of the availability of the Sisters property prior to the formation of Wildview Acres partnership. It first came to his attention when he was acting as an agent for the Sisters in 1968; he later expressed his interest in the land to the Sisters and was informed that he would be apprised of any plans to sell the property, understanding that he would have first opportunity to purchase the land.

Affirmed.

Most courts hold that fiduciary duties extend beyond dissolution until the termination of the partnership. For example, in *Bovy* v. *Graham, Cohen & Wampold*,[19] the court noted that "while there may be a relaxation of a partner's duties to his co-partner in matters that look beyond the business of the newly dissolved partnership, the good faith and full disclosure exacted of partners continues during the winding up of the partnership affairs." *Bovy* found a breach of fiduciary duty by a partner who, during the winding up of a law partnership, induced his former partners to sign an agreement giving him compensation greatly disproportionate to his production by concealing the number and value of his contingent fee files in progress.

An example of the relaxation of the fiduciary duty that the *Bovy* court mentioned appeared in *Matter of Silverberg*,[20] where the court held that after dissolution of a law partnership, "each former partner is free to practice law individually, and has the right to accept retainers from persons who had been clients of the firm" even though winding up and termination had not yet occurred.

Use of covenants not to compete can, of course, extend the duty not to compete even beyond the termination of the partnership.

Duty to Render Services

As noted in the earlier section on the right to compensation, a plaintiff is normally obliged to provide services to the firm to assist in accomplishing its business goals.[21] Courts naturally scrutinize the partnership arrangement carefully and impose a lesser duty on partners who were intended to contribute primarily money to the business. Indeed, one court has stressed:

> The basic concept of a partnership is a group of persons having a common business interest, working together in their respective spheres toward the successful operation and conduct of the business interest. It does not connote the idea that each and every working partner must punch a clock at eight o'clock in the morning and work continuously through the day until five o'clock.[22]

A partner who agrees to devote time and energy to the partnership business and fails to do so, even if the failure is due to sickness, may find the cost of hiring substitutes or the value of the work unperformed charged against his or her partnership interest.[23]

Inaction by a partner may be just cause for dissolution. Furthermore, UPA §32(b) specifically provides that disability, if that is the cause of the inaction, may constitute grounds for court-ordered dissolution.

---

[19] 564 P.2d 1175 (Wash. App. 1977).

[20] 438 N.Y.S.2d 143 (1981).

[21] *Condon* v. *Moran*, 78 A.2d 295 (N.J. 1951).

[22] *Ramos* v. *United States*, 260 F.Supp. 479 (N.D. Cal. 1966), *rev'd on other grounds*, 393 F.2d 618 (9th Cir.), *cert. denied*, 393 U.S. 983 (1968).

[23] *Blut* v. *Katz*, 81 A.2d 406 (N.J. Super. 1951), cause remanded 93 A.2d 775 (N.J. Super. 1952), *aff'd*, 99 A.2d 785 (N.J. 1953) (right to charge waived by other partners in this case).

Duty to Render Information

Section 20 of the UPA imposes on each partner a duty to render "true and full information on all things affecting the partnership" to co-partners or their legal representatives. This duty is extremely important because courts normally deem notice to any partner to be notice to the entire firm. For example, in most states, service of process on one partner is effective to sustain a judgment against the partnership itself. Indeed, §12 of the UPA provides that notice to one partner about a matter relating to partnership affairs is tantamount to notice to all partners, except in the case of a fraud committed by or with consent of that partner. Knowledge gained by a partner is imputed to the partnership.

The duty to disclose is part of the partners' fiduciary duty, which imposes "the obligation of each member of the partnership to make full disclosure of all known information that is significant and material to the affairs or property of the partnership." [24] It may be enforced by an action for an accounting.

Duty of Accounting/Bookkeeping

Each partner's right to an accounting, as discussed, entails a corresponding duty on the part of each partner to account to the partnership by keeping records of all partnership transactions and giving those records to the appropriate partnership record keeper.

Section 19 of the UPA provides that the partnership books are, absent agreement to the contrary, to be kept at the partnership's principal place of business. The duty to keep the books will fall to the managing partner, if there is one, or to any other partner who agrees to undertake the task. A partner who agrees to keep the books but does an inadequate job has breached a fiduciary duty and will find that in an accounting, courts will resolve close questions against him or her. [25]

PARTNERSHIP PROPERTY

Introduction

Pre–UPA law generally provided that the partnership itself could not own land. Rather, property was held in the name of and conveyed by all the individual partners. Generally speaking, the partners were tenants in common. The UPA recognition that the partnership entity can own real and personal property created a new legal regime that clears up many pre–UPA problems, but has itself a number of tricky issues.

Partnership versus Individual Property

Now that a partnership can own any type of property, questions frequently arise as to whether certain property should be characterized as partnership property or as the individual property of one of the partners. The resolution of such questions can be quite important

---

[24] *Herring* v. *Offutt*, 295 A.2d 876 (Md. 1972).
[25] *Couri* v. *Couri*, 447 N.E.2d 334 (Ill. 1983).

for partnership and individual creditors, determining such matters as which property they can reach, who will have priority as to the property, and whether homestead and other exemptions are available. Whether, on dissolution, title to specific property goes to surviving partners or to heirs of a deceased partner is also determined by how the property is characterized.

The UPA assists the categorizing of property by providing in §8(1) that "[a]ll property originally brought into the partnership stock or subsequently acquired by purchase or otherwise, on account of the partnership, is partnership property." Therefore, there is a very strong presumption that property, real and personal, that is held in the partnership name or carried on the partnership books is partnership property. It is hoped that the partnership agreement will be specific and settle the matter.

Section 8(2) of the UPA further states that "[u]nless the contrary intention appears, property acquired with partnership funds is partnership property." The opening phrase of this section is quite important, for the courts hold that unless estoppel applies, the intent of the partners will control whether specific property belongs to the partnership or to individual partners. Intent will determine whether a partner has contributed certain property to the partnership or has merely loaned it.

Intent is so controlling that even property with record title in an individual partner, or even in a third party who is not a partner, may be deemed partnership property if other evidence demonstrates that such was the intent.

Usage is an important factor. Whereas courts normally assume that property owned before the partnership was formed remains individual property and that property acquired after the partnership is formed and used by it is partnership property, other factors must be considered. If two persons enter into a partnership agreement and at the same time one conveys to the other a one-half interest in land to be used by the firm, an intent to be tenants in common is possible, but an inference that this is to be partnership property is more logical.

Intent also may be shown to overcome usage. Frequently doctors in a medical partnership will allow their medical equipment to be used for firm business without intending to relinquish personal ownership. The same may be said for lawyers and their books, farmers and their tractors, construction partners and their heavy equipment. Usage is a factor, but not controlling.[26]

Factors other than record title, source of funds, and usage that have been deemed important to determining intent include (1) whether proceeds from use of rental of the property went into partnership or individual accounts, (2) whether taxes, insurance, improvements, and repairs were paid with partnership or individual funds, (3) whether taxes were paid or deductions taken on partnership or individual tax returns, and (4) admissions of the partners.[27]

A case applying some of these factors in an unusual context follows.

---

[26] *Gorger* v. *Gorger*, 555 P.2d 1 (Or. 1976).
[27] *Dotson* v. *Grice*, 647 P.2d 409 (N.M. 1982).

IN RE ESTATE OF RIDER

409 A.2d 397 (Pa. 1979)

Appellant operated a dairy farm partnership with his father, Lester Rider, until the latter's death in 1974. Lester Rider's will left his household goods to his wife and a life estate in his farm to his two sons, Paul and the appellant. A dispute soon arose over the compilation of Lester Rider's estate. At a hearing before a special master, appellant testified, over objection, that he was the sole owner of the dairy herd and some of the farm equipment and machinery which the administrator of the estate had inventoried as partnership assets.

Paul Rider's attorney had objected to appellant's testimony, arguing that Pennsylvania's Dead Man's Statute, which disqualifies interested witnesses from testifying in such proceedings, prevented appellant from testifying. The special master then ruled the testimony incompetent. The Court of Common Pleas adopted the special master's report, and appellant brought an appeal to the Supreme Court of Pennsylvania.

EAGEN, CHIEF JUSTICE:

In order to be disqualified as a witness under the Dead Man's Statute, three conditions must be proved: (1) the deceased must have had an interest in the matter at issue, that is, an interest in the immediate result of the suit; (2) the interest of the witness must be adverse; and (3) a right of the deceased must have passed to a party of record who represents the deceased's interest.

Instantly, appellant does not dispute the proof of the latter two conditions. Appellant contends, however, that testator had no interest in the disputed farm machinery, equipment, and cattle. We cannot agree.

The question of whether specific property is partnership property is largely a question of intention—*Collner* v. *Greig*, 137 Pa. 606, 612, 20 A. 938 (1890). Furthermore, property acquired after the establishment of a partnership is partnership property so long as it is acquired and used in the line of business of the partnership and developed with partnership funds, labor, and material—*Rolshouse* v. *Wally*, 263 Pa. 247, 248, 106 A. 227, 228 (1919). Finally, the Act of March 26, 1915, P.L. 18, part II, §§13(1) and 72(1) (1964), provide, respectively, that property originally brought into the partnership stock or subsequently acquired by purchase on account of the partnership is partnership property and that a partner is considered a co-owner of partnership property.

Instantly, appellant and testator were undisputedly partners. Appellant testified he added his cattle to testator's and, thereafter, conducted a dairy farm in partnership with testator. Appellant does not dispute that income from the dairy farm was distributed on a partnership basis (which includes income produced through use of the disputed property); that he never objected to receiving only 50% of the profits from sales of cattle even though he now claims sole ownership of the cattle; that he claimed only 50% of such profits as income on his individual federal tax returns; that the disputed farm equipment and machinery was depreciated on a partnership basis and not listed on individual federal tax returns; that partnership funds were used to purchase feed for the cattle; and, finally, that both partners worked on the farm. Thus, the record reveals appellant and testator treated the disputed property as partnership property. Partnership funds and labor were used in the dairy farm business. The dairy herd consisted of cattle contributed by both testator and appellant. This evidence is sufficient to establish an interest in the disputed property in favor of testator. The testator has prima facie a partner's interest in partnership property.

However, the case was reversed on other grounds.

Conveyance of Partnership Property

Sections 8 and 10 of the UPA work together clearly to alter the common law rule that partnerships cannot own real property. Utilizing the entity theory of partnerships, §8(3) provides that "real property may be acquired in the partnership name" and, moreover, that "[t]itle so acquired can be conveyed only in the partnership name." Section 8(4) reemphasizes by providing that "[a] conveyance to a partnership in the partnership name, though without words of inheritance, passes the entire estate of the grantor, unless a contrary intent appears."

While §8 governs primarily transfers to the partnership, §10 governs conveyance of partnership real property by the partnership. Subsection (1) begins by establishing that "[w]here title to real property is in the partnership name, any partner may convey title to such property by a conveyance executed in the partnership name." However, §10(1) goes on to provide that the partnership may recover the conveyed property, with two exceptions. First, the partnership may not recover the property if the conveying partner's acts bound the partnership under §9(1), which stipulates that every partner is an agent whose acts bind the partnership unless the partner has no actual authority and that lack of authority is known to the person with whom the partner deals. Second, the partnership may not regain the conveyed property if it has been conveyed by the first grantee or someone claiming through that grantee to a holder for value who had no knowledge that the conveying partner acted without authority. Therefore, if partner A sells partnership land to B, in the partnership name, B now has title to the land. That title may be recovered by the partnership only if A acted without actual authority and B knew it. Even if that is the case, if B has conveyed the land to C who paid fair value for the land without knowledge of A's lack of authority, the partnership may not recover the land from C.

The remaining subsections of §10 provide, in part, that land held in the partnership name can be conveyed only in that name and that, if it is held in the names of individual partners, it may be conveyed in those names. Regardless of how the title is listed, the partnership's equitable interest in real property passes only if the conveying partners act within their scope of authority.

The UPA does not have specific rules for conveying partnership personal property. The courts have simply applied agency rules, keying on whether or not the selling partner was acting within the scope of authority.

Property Rights of Partners

Section 24 of the UPA governs the extent of the property rights of partners, noting that they consist of "(1) his rights in specific partnership property, (2) his interest in the partnership, and (3) his right to participate in management."

Working in reverse order, one aspect of a partner's property rights is the right to participate in the management of the firm business. As we have seen, absent agreement, each partner has an equal voice in management.

Each partner's interest in the partnership is defined in §26 to include, first, a share of the firm profits and, second, a share of the firm's surplus assets on dissolution.

Section 26 also characterizes an interest in the partnership as personal property. That means that if X died, leaving all her real property to Y and all her personal property to Z, her interest in a partnership would go to Z *even if* the only asset owned by the partnership was real estate.

The third aspect of a partner's property rights is the right in specific partnership property. At common law, partners held partnership property mostly as tenants-in-common, with some aspects of joint tenancy. Section 25 of the UPA creates a new estate—the tenancy-in-partnership—the incidents of which are explored in the remainder of this chapter.

Use of Partnership Property

As noted earlier in this chapter, each partner has the right to use partnership property for partnership purposes. Subject to agreement, each partner's right is equal.

Section 25(2)(a) specifically provides that there is no right to use partnership property for nonpartnership purposes without the consent of the other partners. For example, to use partnership property for individual gain without the consent of the other partners would be a breach of fiduciary duty, a conversion, and grounds for an accounting and perhaps even dissolution.

Assume a partnership of A, B, and C with primary partnership assets of three semitrailer truck rigs. Partner A has no right to use one of the rigs to move his cousin's possessions to a new house, unless B and C consent.

Assignability

A partner's right in *specific partnership property* is not assignable unless *all* partners assign their rights in that property.

Assume again the existence of the A, B, C partnership with three semitrailer trucks. If B incurs substantial gambling debts, she has no right to assign to her creditors one of the trucks for them to sell to satisfy the individual gambling debt. If B attempts to convey one of the trucks to the creditor, she is acting outside the scope of her authority. This fact is probably known to the creditor, so the conveyance will be ineffective. If B attempts to assign her one-third interest in each of the trucks, that assignment will also be ineffective. Partnership assets are to be used only for partnership purposes.

Only if A and C consented to also convey their interests in one of the semitrailer rigs could B effectively assign that rig to her creditor. The courts have recognized one narrow exception—a partner can assign an interest in specific partnership property *to a co-partner*.

It is also clear that a partner's right to a voice in the management of a partnership is not assignable.

What is assignable, according to §27, is a partner's interest in the partnership— that is, a share of the profits and the surplus on dissolution. So, in an attempt to satisfy her creditors, B could assign to them her interest in the partnership profits and surplus. Thereafter, whenever partnership profits were divided out, A and C would pay B's share to her assigned creditors. Upon dissolution, the assignee/creditors would be entitled to B's share of the surplus, if any, of assets over liabilities.

The assignee, however, does not become a partner. The concept of *delectus personae* means that A and C do not have to accept B's creditor as a partner, although they are free to do so if they desire. Indeed, §27 clearly limits the rights of the assignee. After stating that an assignment of an interest in the partnership does not of itself cause dissolution, §27 specifies that an assignee, during the continuation of the partnership, has *no right* to interfere in the management of the partnership, to require any information or accounting, or to inspect the partnership books.[28] Even upon dissolution, the assignee can demand an accounting only from the date of the last accounting agreed to by all partners.

Unless the remaining partners dissolve the partnership,[29] the assigning partner remains a partner of the firm with all the rights (except those assigned away) and duties attendant to that status.

Creditors' Rights

Section 25(2)(c) provides that while a partner's right in specific partnership property is subject to attachment or execution on a claim by a *partnership creditor*,[30] it is not subject to attachment on a claim by an *individual* partner's creditor. Just as a partner cannot assign an interest in specific partnership property to an individual creditor, an individual creditor is not allowed to seize such an interest.

Thus, in *Bohonus* v. *Amerco*,[31] Amerco, after it secured a judgment against Bohonus, obtained a court order mandating sale of Bohonus's interest in the assets and property of a partnership of which he was a member. Bohonus successfully challenged the sale, the court holding that specific partnership property could not be seized to satisfy an individual partner's debt. That which is assignable—a partner's interest in a partnership's profits and surplus—may be proceeded against by a creditor. Section 28

---

[28] Because §27 leaves the assignee completely at the mercy of the other partners, some states have amended §27 to grant assignees limited rights to inspection and accounting.

[29] An assignment gives to the nonassigning partners the right, if all agree, to dissolve the partnership even if its agreed term has not yet expired.

[30] No homestead or other personal debt exemption on partnership property may be claimed by partners on a partnership debt.

[31] 602 P.2d 469 (Ariz. 1979).

of the UPA provides a rather vague mechanism for enforcement of an individual creditor's rights against a partner's interest in the partnership. The key to §28 is the *charging order*. A judgment creditor of a partner is entitled to apply to a court for an order charging "the interest of the debtor partner with payment of the unsatisfied amount of such judgment debt with interest thereon." The court may also later appoint a receiver of the debtor partner's share of the profits or any other sums due from the partnership.

The interest may be redeemed before a foreclosure sale by other partners using their individual property or partnership property. The creditor may ask the court for a foreclosure sale.

The charging order is a relatively unique device. As one court has stated:

> [A charging order] is nothing more than a legislative means of providing a creditor some means of getting at a debtor's ill-defined interest in a [partnership]. . . . [T]he charging order is neither fish nor fowl. It is neither an assignment nor an attachment . . . [b]ut . . . it resembles both progenitors in some of their characteristics.[32]

How the charging order and subsequent foreclosure sale may operate is discussed in the following excerpt.

LAW OF PARTNERSHIP*

J. Crane and A. Bromberg

Published by West Publishing Company, pp. 246–248 (1968)

Since partnership property is shielded from the attack of a partner's individual creditor, his natural target is the interest in the firm. This is assignable, and extralegal pressures may induce the partner to assign to the creditor, either absolutely or as security. Or, once he has reduced his claim to judgment, the creditor may employ the charging order, a device derived from the English Partnership Act, and very sketchily presented there and in the American version. It is a judicial proceeding leading to a sort of lien on the interest in the firm. By logical consequence, payments (particularly distributions of earnings or withdrawals of capital) which would otherwise go to the debtor partner should be made to the creditor. However, the Act is not quite so explicit. Undoubtedly the court has power to issue such a payment order. A creditor would be wise to ask for it (and a corresponding order against payments to the debtor partner), as well as for notice to the debtor, his co-partners, and the firm and opportunity for hearing.

While the charge is in effect, the partner presumably continues to be a partner in all respects except distributions and withdrawals from the firm. And the charging creditor is not the owner of the interest. He may become so by foreclosing. The Act is vague about this too, not explicitly authorizing foreclosure sale, much less setting standards for it, but only recognizing it obliquely. But there can be no doubt that the Act gives the court enough general power to cover foreclosure. However, consistency with the Act's general concern for the partnership as a going business and as a group of associates suggests that foreclosure should be decreed only if the charged interest is not likely to

---

[32] *Bank of Bethesda* v. *Koch*, 408 A.2d 767 (Md. 1979).
* Copyright 1968 by Alan R. Bromberg. Reprinted with permission.

pay off the debt within a reasonable time. The advantage to a charging creditor in foreclosing and buying is that he becomes the owner of the interest, gaining psychological leverage as well as the improved position of an owner over a lienor. Moreover, he then acquires the right to dissolve the firm if it is one at will. If he presses this far, he will be able to get his hands on partnership assets: whatever share would have come to his debtor after payment of all partnership creditors and claims of co-partners. It is a roundabout route to partnership assets, and one which may yield little or nothing.

The other partners may not like a partner's individual creditor breathing down their necks, and are authorized to dissolve the firm, or to redeem the charged interest (before foreclosure). If they dissolve, they must account to the charging creditor for the debtor partner's interest. If they want to redeem, there is no express statutory procedure for determining the price at which they can do so. Perhaps the price is the amount of the creditor's claim. This would make redemption uneconomic if the claim were greater than the value of the partner's interest. The court probably has general authority in such a case to value the interest and permit redemption at the value.

Although the U.P.A. nowhere says that a charging order is the exclusive process for a partner's individual creditor, the courts have generally so interpreted it.

It bears emphasizing that the holder of the charging interest does not become the owner of that interest unless he or she actually purchases it at the foreclosure sale. Even then, the creditor does not become a partner, although the right to dissolve a partnership at will is gained.[33]

The judgment creditor whose lien is based on an individual partner's debt will be subordinate even to a *subsequent* lienholder whose claim is based on a partnership debt. If more than one judgment creditor obtains a charging order, they will take on a first-come, first-served rather than a pro-rata basis.

Application of some of these principles is illustrated in the following case.

MYRICK v. SECOND NATIONAL BANK

335 So.2d 343 (Fla. App. 1976)

The plaintiff Second National Bank sued defendants Betty and Donald Myrick on unpaid promissory notes, receiving a judgment of $81,348.24. While that judgment was on appeal, the bank instructed the sheriff to levy on the defendants' interest in a partnership known as Port Richey Shopping Village and to publish a notice of sale. The Myricks asked the trial court to set aside the levy and cancel the notice of sale on grounds that their interests in the partnership cannot properly be reached by levy. Defendants claimed only a charging order would be appropriate. The trial court denied the motion, relying on a 1943 case, Lott v. Padgett, 14 So.2d 609 (Fla. 1943). Defendants appealed.

---

[33] See, generally, E. Axelrod, "The Charging Order-Rights of a Partner's Creditor," *Arkansas Law Review*, vol. 36 (1982), p. 81.

SCHEB, JUDGE:

We think the trial judge's reliance upon *Lott* v. *Padgett* was error. *Lott*, decided by our Supreme Court in 1943, correctly stated the common law that a debtor's interest in a partnership was susceptible to being seized by legal process; however, this doctrine was superseded by adoption of the Uniform Partnership Act (UPA) in 1973—The UPA changed the common law nature of a partnership interest.

Section 620.695(1) of the act [based on UPA §28(1)] provides:

> On application to a court having jurisdiction by any judgment creditor of a partner, the court may charge the interest of the debtor partner with payment of the unsatisfied amount of the judgment with interest, and may then or later appoint a receiver of his share of the profits and of any other money due or to become due to him from the partnership, and make all other orders to take the actions that the debtor partner might have made or that the circumstances of the case may require.

Plaintiff argues that §620.695 merely furnishes a creditor with an additional remedy and that while specific partnership property may be exempted from execution under a claim against the partnership, that nevertheless the UPA does not limit the rights of creditors with respect to a partner's interest in the partnership.

The point is one of first impression in Florida since Florida's adoption of the UPA §620.695 is adopted from §28 of the act and it has been held that its purpose is to protect nondebtor partners—*Evans* v. *El Dorado Improvement Co.*, 1975, 46 Cal. App. 3d 84, 119 Cal. Rptr. 889. The distinction for which plaintiff argues appears inconsistent with the language of §28 as to the proper method for a judgment creditor to reach the interest of a partner in the partnership. While "foreclosure" of the partnership interest is contemplated under the act, we do not think this provision justifies an immediate levy and sale. Rather, the charging order is the essential first step, and all further proceedings must occur under the supervision of the court, which may take all appropriate actions, including the appointment of a receiver, if necessary, to protect the interests of the various parties. The reason for prohibiting a levy on partnership assets for debts of individual partners is to prevent disruption of the partnership business and the consequent injustice to other partners (*Evans*, supra). These same considerations weigh against immediate levy and sale of a partner's share in the partnership when less disruptive measures may afford the same and perhaps even a greater level of protection to a judgment creditor.

Accordingly, the order denying the defendant's motion to set aside levy and cancel notice of sale is vacated and the cause is remanded to the trial court for further proceedings consistent with this opinion.

Inheritability

Section 25(2)(d) provides that upon the death of a partner, the right to specific partnership property vests in the surviving partners who may possess it only for partnership purposes. If the dying partner was the last surviving partner, title vests in that partner's legal representative.

Thus, if in the equal partnership between L and M, L dies, her right to specific partnership assets vests in M, not in L's heirs. The death will cause dissolution of the partnership. M will have to settle up with L's heirs, who now own L's right to share in profits and, more to the point, the surplus upon dissolution. Even this, of course, can be altered by agreement. In *Balafas* v. *Balafas*,[34] for example, the evidence clearly indicated that upon his death Mike Balafas wanted his entire interest in the partnership, including the right to specific property, the right to share in profits, and the right to share in surplus to go to his brother and partner, Chris, rather than to his surviving wife. The intent of the partners, the court held, controls.

Community Property

The eight or so states that have community property have had to add specific provisions to their versions of the UPA. Texas, for example, has added to its version of the UPA §§28-A and B. The former provides that while a partner's interest in the partnership (profits and surplus) may be community property, the rights in specific partnership property and in management cannot be community property. The latter section provides that spouses on divorce and heirs in death stand as "assignees and purchasers" regarding their rights.

In *McKnight* v. *McKnight*,[35] the trial court in a divorce case awarded the wife one-fourth of all cattle owned by the ranch partnership in which her husband owned half interest. She was also awarded one-half of all monies in the partnership bank account. The husband was awarded one-fourth of all partnership cattle and a one-half interest in the partnership and its equipment. The Texas Supreme Court held that rights in specific partnership property could not be community property, so the trial court erred in awarding specific partnership property as part of the divorce settlement.

QUESTIONS AND PROBLEMS

1. Covalt owned 25% of the stock of CSI; High owned the other 75%. As partners, they also owned an office building that leased to CSI. Covalt later resigned his officer's position at CSI and went to work for a competitor. However, Covalt remained High's partner and demanded that the monthly rent being charged CSI for the office building be raised from $1,850 to $2,850. High refused. Covalt sued. The trial judge held that High breached his partnership fiduciary duty to Covalt by refusing to consent to the rent increase. Did the trial judge act correctly? Discuss. See *Covalt* v. *High*, 100 N.M. 700, 675 P.2d 999 (N.M. App. 1984).

2. Five sisters sued their father to establish a partnership between him and them for the management and disposition of community assets of the father and his first wife, mother of the sisters. The community property in question consisted of an oil drilling company that the father had operated for 15 years. The trial court found that a partnership did exist and, in rendering judgment, debited $54,751.05 from the father's

---

[34] 117 N.W.2d 20 (Minn. 1962).
[35] 543 S.W.2d 863 (Tex. 1976).

capital account to compensate for "unauthorized drawings" of funds for his own use. On appeal, the father claimed that these draws were simply compensation for his being the sole manager of the partnership. Discuss the validity of the father's position. See *Conrad* v. *Johnson*, 465 S.W.2d 819 (Tex. Civ. App. 1971), *cert. denied*, 405 U.S. 1041.

3. Johnson agreed to be Franich's undisclosed partner in a real estate deal. Johnson provided $11,000. Franich was to invest the money and manage the property. Defendants Franich and Nielsen purchased on an installment basis certain land from plaintiffs, who did not know of Johnson's interest. When defendants failed to make payments, plaintiffs elected to declare a forfeiture. Defendants did not respond to plaintiffs' notice of forfeiture, so, on August 19, 1981, plaintiffs sued to seek forfeiture and cancellation of the contract. Defendants were both served. On September 15, Franich told Johnson he was leaving town and desired to terminate their partnership. He sold his interest to Johnson for $10,000. On September 23, plaintiffs obtained a default judgment that forfeited the interests of all named defendants in the property. Johnson learned of the default and the judgment two days later, and offered to bring the payments current. Plaintiffs refused. Johnson sued to set aside the default judgment on grounds that he was denied proper notice. Discuss. See *Jenner* v. *Real Estate Services*, 659 P.2d 1072 (Utah 1983).

4. P and D were partners in an oil and gas investment firm that acquired, owned, developed, and operated oil, gas, and mineral leases. D was the managing partner who specialized in raising funds. D learned of an Indonesian oil deal and acquired 10% of it for himself. When P learned of this, he demanded the right to contribute his share and participate in the venture. D refused, so P sued. D claimed that P failed to plead and prove the partnership's financial capability to take advantage of this particular deal. Is this a good defense? Discuss. See *Huffington* v. *Upchurch*, 532 S.W.2d 576 (Tex. 1976).

5. Mary and Claude had a "cohabital relationship" and on January 1, 1975, also agreed to be partners in operating a restaurant known as Pete's Truck Stop. Various problems arose, and on February 5, 1977, Claude ousted Mary from his home and the restaurant. Mary sued, and claimed, among other things, an equal share of the profits not only from the restaurant but also from Claude's operation of a bar, a tree trimming business, and an irrigation supply business. Mary had helped Claude only in operation of the restaurant. Is she entitled to share in the profits from the other ventures? Discuss. See *Truman* v. *Martin*, 212 Neb. 52, 321 N.W.2d 420 (1982).

6. Gauldin and Corn entered into a 50:50 partnership to raise cattle and hogs, the business to be carried out on 25 acres of an 83-acre tract owned first by Corn's parents and later by Corn. Some of the profits were put back into the business, including erection of a barn and Cargill unit, which together were worth $11,500. By agreement, no rent was paid on the land. There was no agreement regarding the permanent improvements. Corn's ill health ultimately led to dissolution of the partnership. Gauldin claimed he was entitled to one-half of the value of the barn and Cargill unit because they were partnership property. The trial judge held that the improvements went with the land, since Gauldin knew they could not be moved once built. Was

the trial judge correct in refusing to allow Gauldin compensation for the improvements? Discuss. See *Gauldin* v. *Corn*, 595 S.W.2d 329 (Mo. App. 1980).

7. The Davis Packing Co. was awarded a judgment against Myles individually and had the sheriff levy upon 10 cows owned by R. A. Myles & Co., a partnership of which Myles was a member. The cows were sold and the money was applied toward the judgment. R. A. Myles & Co. claims the cattle were wrongfully taken. Discuss. See *R. A. Myles & Co.* v. *A. D. Davis Packing Co.*, 17 Ala. App. 85, 81 So. 863 (1919).

8. Fred and Juanita Bailes, husband and wife, began a dog food business in 1958 and operated it until Fred died intestate in 1969. Surviving him were Juanita and a son, Fred, Jr., by a previous marriage. Fred, Jr., claims that all the assets of the business should become part of the estate of his father and should be distributed according to the law of descent and distribution. Is this the correct procedure? Discuss. See *Bailes* v. *Bailes*, 549 S.W.2d 69 (Ark. 1977).

4

RIGHTS AND LIABILITIES
AS TO THIRD PARTIES

INTRODUCTION

Having examined the relationship of general partners to one another, we now turn our focus to the partnership's dealings with nonpartners. The two most important matters we will address are the partnership's liability for (1) contracts entered into by partners and (2) torts committed by partners.

As we have noted, partners have the right, subject to agreement, to participate in the management of the business. In so doing, the partners act as agents for the partnership and bind the partnership, as principal, when they act within the scope of their authority. With some modifications of the Uniform Partnership Act (UPA) therefore, the common law of agency governs the partnership relations with third parties.

Traditionally it has been said that every partner is both an agent and a principal. She is an agent (and all other partners are her principals) when she acts within her scope of authority in carrying out ordinary partnership business. She is a principal whenever any other partner acts on behalf of the partnership, for she ultimately may be bound by that action. Two leading experts [1] suggest that it is more accurate to say,

---

[1] J. Crane and A. Bromberg, *Law of Partnership*, 2nd ed. West Pub. Co., St. Paul, MN (1968), p. 273.

as does §9(1), that each partner is an agent of the partner*ship* for the purpose of executing its business. They argue that it is misleading to say each partner is an agent of all other partners because (1) in making a contract the partner creates in the third party a right to judgment collectible out of partnership property as well as separate property of the individual partners, and (2) unlike an ordinary principal, dissenting partners cannot terminate the power of their agents at will, absent dissolution.

Much of this chapter will concern the common law of agency as it is applied through specific UPA provisions. There are some aspects of this law that do not cause too much trouble. For example, an agent who commits a tort is liable for that act.[2] Our focus will be on the more difficult question of under what circumstances the principal/partnership is also liable. An agent who negotiates a contract on a principal's behalf usually is not bound by that contract, but problems will arise if the agent acted outside the proper scope of authority. Our focus will be on the circumstances under which the principal will be liable.

PARTNERSHIP CONTRACTUAL LIABILITY TO THIRD PARTIES

General Principles

Section 9(1) of the UPA, as noted, states that each "partner is an agent of the partnership for purpose of its business." It goes on to say that each partner's act "for apparently carrying on in the usual way the business of the partnership" binds the partnership. The partnership is bound, according to §9(1), unless both of two factors are present: (1) the partner has no authority to act for the partnership as to the matter at hand and (2) the third party knows it.

Just as an act by a partner that apparently carries on the business of the partnership will bind it, §9(2) provides that the act of a partner that is not apparently for the carrying on of the business of the partnership in the usual way does not bind the partnership unless authorized by the other partners.

Both §§9(1) and (2) are generally consistent with normal rules of agency law. As may be deduced from these provisions, the most difficult questions in deciding whether a partnership is liable on a contract negotiated by a partner relate to whether the partner has "authority" and under what circumstances a partner is carrying on business in the "usual way."

Types of Authority

A partnership will be bound if a partner, acting with *actual* authority, negotiates a contract on the partnership's behalf.

There are two types of actual authority. First, there is *express authority*—authority the partners have specifically agreed to. For example, the partners may have a written

---

[2] *Battista* v. *Lebanon Trotting Ass'n*, 538 F.2d 111 (6th Cir. 1976).

partnership agreement that provides that partner A will do all the hiring and firing of employees at the partnership's furniture store. Express authority can arise from other sources, including a formal vote at a partnership meeting or an informal agreement of the partners as they sit over cups of coffee.

The second type of actual authority is called *implied authority*. Assume that a partnership is formed to operate several shoe stores. The partners informally agree that partner A will be manager of the store on Main Street. The partners may not expressly agree that partner A should hire and fire employees of the store. However, despite the lack of an express agreement on that point, partner A's power to hire and fire may be *implied* by the courts as necessary or incidental to carrying out the task that was expressly assigned—managing the store. If hiring and firing of employees is deemed a part of carrying on in the "usual way" the business of the partnership, partner A has this implied power. The tricky question is deciding what constitutes carrying on business in the "usual way" or, more precisely, determining the proper "scope of authority" for the manager of a shoe store. That is a question we will address in a moment.

One specific type of implied authority that should not be overlooked is that arising out of emergency situations. Assume that the partners of our shoe store business set out in a written partnership agreement that partner A will be the manager of the store on Main Street and will have the powers to hire and fire salespersons, to open a bank account, to purchase supplies on credit, to make minor repairs to the premises, and so on. Assume further that a flash flood occurs and that A has no time to contact the other partners. Although the partnership agreement is silent as to A's powers in this regard, A will be deemed to possess authority to hire people to fill sand bags to keep the store dry. The authority is implied from the emergency situation, so the partnership will be bound on the contracts.

Because the agreement of the partners is supreme regarding the relations with each other, partners may always agree that a particular partner will not possess the powers that normally are implied under the circumstances. Assume, for example, that in our shoe store example, most store managers in the locality have the power to hire and fire employees, and the store managers of our partnership's store on Main Street have always had that power. However, because of partner A's inexperience, the partners vote to withhold from A the express authority to hire and fire. If A puts a sign in the window that says "Salesperson Needed" and B applies, interviews with A, and is told by A, "You're hired," the partnership is bound by this contract. Although A had no actual authority, express or implied, because A was the manager of the store doing what store managers of this business and others normally do—hiring necessary employees—it appeared to B that A was acting for the partnership. Therefore a court would probably conclude that A had *apparent* authority, and the partnership would be bound. Because A has acted improperly, she may have to answer to the other partners, but this will not affect B's right to enforce the contract.

The principles at work here are the same ones that govern the doctrine of partnership by estoppel, discussed in Chapter 2.

A partner who acts within the scope of actual (express or implied) or apparent authority will bind the partnership whether contracting in his own name individually or in the partnership name, and whether or not the other partners even know about the contract.[3]

Knowledge of the Third Party

The UPA makes it clear that a partnership will not be bound by the contract between a partner and a third party if there was no express authority and the other party knew it. Assume that in our earlier example job applicant B knew of the partnership agreement that removed from partner A the power to hire and fire. Section 9(1) would provide that the partnership was not bound on the contract by A to hire B because a partnership is bound by a partner's acts except when (1) the partner has no actual authority and (2) the third party knows it.

Section 9(2) reaches the same result. If B knows of the agreement, B could not argue that it appeared A had the power to hire and fire.

Section 9(4) provides a third basis for the same result, stating, "No act of a partner in contravention of a restriction on authority shall bind the partnership to persons having knowledge of the restriction."

The bottom line is that authority cannot appear to exist in the eyes of a third party who knows it does not. For example, in *C. E. Johnson Co.* v. *Marsh*,[4] Ufford leased his farm to Marsh. By the terms of the lease, the parties were to share income and expenses, "but nothing herein shall authorize the lessee to obligate the lessor or to obtain credit in his name." Marsh bought many supplies from plaintiff on credit, promising that Ufford would see to it the bills were paid. When they were not paid, plaintiff sued Ufford, claiming that he was Marsh's partner and was therefore liable for the unpaid bills.

The court held the Ufford-Marsh relationship to be lessor-lessee, not a partnership. Even if it had been a partnership, the court said:

> knowledge of this provision [quoted above] in the lease would have prevented the plaintiff from holding Ufford liable. . . . The information that there was an agreement of lease between Marsh and Ufford concerning the working of the latter's farm, and the representation of Marsh that Ufford would pay the bills, was sufficient to put the plaintiff, as a prudent man, upon inquiry as to the true nature of the contract and he must be charged with knowledge of what such inquiry would have disclosed.

The *Marsh* case is somewhat harsh in barring plaintiff from recovery because of what plaintiff *should have* known. A more recent case held that the "knowledge" of a third party discussed in §9(1) must be *actual* knowledge, not mere constructive knowledge.[5]

---

[3] See, for example, *Beane* v. *Bowden*, 399 So.2d 1359 (Miss. 1981). Note, conversely, that all partners are liable when a single partner breaches a partnership contract. See, for example, *Nuttall* v. *Dowell*, 639 P.2d 832 (Wash. App. 1982).

[4] 15 A.2d 577 (Vt. 1940).

[5] *Owens* v. *Palos Monaco*, 191 Cal. Rptr. 381 (Cal. App. 1983).

Scope of Authority

The most difficult matter in all this is determining what is within the "scope of authority" of a particular partner in a particular partnership. Any express statement is very helpful, particularly if it is written. A partnership agreement is important not only because it may spell out certain powers and limitations, but also because it may describe the scope of the business, which cannot be altered without the unanimous approval of the partners.

For those situations where actual authority has not been expressed, or if expressed remains unknown to third parties, the courts are frequently faced with the task of deciding what matters are within the "scope of authority" of a partner carrying out business in the "usual way."

As a general rule, most courts hold that partners have the power to hire and fire employees, to borrow money needed to stock the shelves of the partnership store, to execute any proper partnership document, to purchase property and equipment needed by the partnership, to make deliveries of items sold and receive payment therefor, to endorse checks and notes, and to file suit to enforce partnership claims.

We will soon examine a couple of these areas in more detail, but it should be obvious that this partial listing can only begin to address the innumerable factual situations in which such questions can arise. What is needed is a general standard to apply to all cases to determine the "scope of authority." Unfortunately, the courts have been unable to settle on just one such standard.

Many courts look to the past practices of the partnership in question to determine what authority "appears" to exist. The following case illustrates that approach.

SMITH v. DIXON

386 S.W.2d 244 (Ark. 1965)

In 1951 the Smith family acquired certain farmland, and soon formed the E. F. Smith & Sons partnership at the request of financial institutions who were going to finance the farming operations. W. R. Smith was the "predominant" member of the partnership, serving as the managing partner with general powers. Charles Smith was in charge of production, but other members of the partnership did not actively participate.

As agent for the partnership, W. R. Smith had twice sold land and once purchased land before entering into a contract with plaintiff Dixon to sell a 750-acre tract to Dixon for $200,000. The contract was signed by Dixon and "E. F. Smith & Sons, a partnership BY: W. R. Smith."

When other partners of E. F. Smith & Sons refused to convey the land, claiming that they had authorized W. R. Smith to sell the land, *but not for less than $225,000, Dixon sued. The trial court ruled for Dixon, and the balking partners appealed.*

HOLT, JUSTICE:

It appears undisputed that appellant W. R. Smith was authorized by the members of the partnership to negotiate for the sale of the lands in question to the appellee. However, it is claimed that his authorization was based upon different terms of sale, mainly, a price of $225,000.00 instead of $200,000.00. Therefore, it is urged that the contract is unenforceable since it was not signed or ratified by other members of the family.

In the case of *May* v. *Ewan*, 169 Ark. 512, 275 S.W. 754, we held that a partnership is bound by the acts of a partner when he acts within the scope or apparent scope of his authority. There we quoted with approval:

> In order to determine the apparent scope of the authority of a partner, recourse may frequently be had to past transactions indicating a custom or course of dealing peculiar to the firm in question.

In the case at bar, it was customary in past transactions, as in the present one, for the partnership to rely upon the co-partner W. R. Smith, to transact the business affairs of the firm. We agree with the chancellor that appellant W. R. Smith was acting within the apparent scope of his authority as a partner when he signed the contract and that it is binding and enforceable upon the partnership.

Affirmed.

In another leading case, *Burns* v. *Gonzalez*,[6] the court decided to look also at the ordinary practices of other partnerships in the same locality to establish the scope of authority of partners. The following case applies both standards.

WOMACK v. FIRST NATIONAL BANK OF AUGUSTINE

613 S.W.2d 548 (Tex. Civ. App. 1981)

In April 1971, Dr. H. Lane McClanahan sent his financial statement to plaintiff First National Bank of Augustine with the notation: "My brother, Charles McClanahan, wants to do business with you for some of the farming operations." Later, on August 14, 1972, the McClanahan brothers signed a one-half-page partnership agreement for the express purpose of operating a hog farm for profit. They agreed Charles would devote his time to the business, receiving 75% of the profits and sharing 50% of the losses. Lane would receive 25% of the profits and share 50% of the losses. Charles agreed to keep records, subject to inspection

---

[6] 439 S.W.2d 128 (Tex. Civ. App. 1969).

by Lane at any time. The agreement was silent as to the partners' authority, neither defining nor limiting it.

In an eight-month period commencing in September 1972, Charles and Lane signed four notes with the plaintiff bank in order to borrow $30,000 to operate the hog farm. Three of these were repaid and a fourth was renewed by a note signed by both brothers. Thereafter, until May 1, 1975, the partnership continued to borrow funds from the bank on a revolving basis. The partnership would borrow money, buy hogs, and then pay off the loans when the hogs were sold and borrow again. The unpaid notes which serve as the basis for this lawsuit are all renewal notes. The money was borrowed by Charles in the partnership name. The money was used by the partnership. Lane's name was signed to the notes. However, unlike with the first notes, Lane did not sign his own name; Charles signed it.

When these renewal notes went unpaid, the bank sued. Charles admitted liability and claimed these were partnership notes. Lane claimed he was not liable on the notes because he had not signed them. Before trial, Lane died and his estate was substituted as defendant. A jury found these were partnership obligations for which Dr. McClanahan's estate was liable, and the estate appealed.

SUMMERS, CHIEF JUDGE:

In support of his contention that Dr. McClanahan's estate cannot be held liable on the subject notes since he did not sign the notes himself or authorize his signature thereon, appellant refers to Tex. Bus. & Com. Code Annotation §3.404(a) (Vernon 1967). That provision provides:

Any unauthorized signature is wholly inoperative as that of the person whose name is signed unless he ratifies it or is precluded from denying it; but

it operates as the signature of the unauthorized signer in favor of any person who in good faith pays the instrument or takes it for value.

Since it is undisputed that Dr. McClanahan did not sign the notes which are the basis of this suit and since no issue was submitted to the jury concerning ratification or estoppel, we agree with appellant that Dr. McClanahan's alleged signature on the note is wholly inoperative as his own. We have examined the record and have found no evidence that Dr. McClanahan authorized his brother to sign his name to the notes. In this connection, we note that §3.401(a) T.B. & C.C. provides that "No person is liable on an instrument unless his signature appears thereon." However, as we view this case and the evidence before us, it is immaterial that Dr. McClanahan did not personally sign the notes. In full recognition of that rule (that one is not liable on an instrument unless he signs it), our Supreme Court has stated that there are several instances in which a nonsigning partner may be liable upon a note signed by another partner.

A partner's authority to bind the partnership and his partners is governed by the Texas version of the Uniform Partnership Act unless expanded or limited by the partnership agreement. Section 9 of the U.P.A. provides that

(1) Every partner is an agent of the partnership for the purpose of its business, and the act of every partner, including the execution in the partnership name of any instrument, for apparently carrying on in the usual way the business of the partnership of which he is a member binds the partnership, unless the partner so acting has in fact no authority to act for the partnership in the particular matter, and the person with whom he is dealing has knowledge of the fact that he has no such authority.

As we construe this section, Dr. McClanahan may be held liable on the notes as a partner if they were executed for "apparently carrying on in the usual way the business of the partnership." Thus, since the partnership agreement was silent as to Charles McClanahan's authority to issue negotiable paper in the partnership name, he had the actual or express authority to do so under §9 if such act were for the purpose of "apparently carrying on" the business of the partnership in the way other firms engaged in the same business in the locality usually transact business, or in the way in which the particular partnership usually transacts its business— *Burns* v. *Gonzalez*, 439 S.W.2d 128, 131 (Tex. Civ. App.—San Antonio 1969, writ ref'd n.r.e.). Whether Dr. McClanahan was aware that Charles was executing the notes has no effect upon his authority to do so, "for it is familiar law that each member of a partnership has, as agent, power to bind all members of his firm for an indebtedness incurred in the prosecution of his firm's business; and this is true even though members other than the acting one is [sic] without knowledge of the obligatory act"—*Mitchell* v. *City National Bank of Wichita Falls*, 14 S.W.2d 909, 910 (Tex. Civ. App.—Fort Worth 1929, writ ref'd n.r.e.). Stated another way, it has been said that an agent's authority is presumed to be co-extensive with the business entrusted to his care. He is limited in his authority to such acts as are incident to the management of the particular business with which he is entrusted. Thus, the inquiry becomes whether Charles McClanahan executed the notes in order to conduct the business, which Dr. McClanahan testified had been entrusted to his care, in its ordinary and normal manner, there being no evidence in the record as to the normal business transactions of other hog farms in San Augustine County.

We believe that there was ample evidence to support the jury's findings that Charles McClanahan had the authority to execute the notes and bind the partnership thereto. The notes themselves reflect that the monies loaned upon the notes were invested in the partnership business; the farm was initially financed over an eight-month period by the execution and payment of a series of notes; the partnership agreement did not attempt, in any manner, to limit Charles McClanahan's authority. This conclusion is further buttressed by the fact that partners normally have the right to execute negotiable paper for commercial purposes consistent with the object of the partnership and for the benefit of the partnership. Where the partnership business contemplates periodical or continuous or frequent purchasing, not as incidental to an occupation, but for the purpose of selling again the thing purchased, it is usual and customary to purchase on credit and to execute paper evidencing the existence of the partnership debt (*Burns*, supra at 133). Both Charles McClanahan and Ray Neal McEachern testified that Charles would execute a note, buy hogs and feed them on the proceeds thereof, sell them, and pay on the notes. Such was the customary business of the partnership. We must therefore conclude that Charles McClanahan had the actual authority to execute the notes in question as partnership obligations.

Affirmed.

The broader approach of *Womack*, which allows the court to look at partnerships generally and therefore does not require a creditor to investigate in great detail the past practices of each individual partnership to which it loans money, is favored by most modern courts.

These guidelines control most cases, but there are certain areas where problems repeatedly arise that should be addressed.

Borrowing Money

The authority to borrow money and bind the partnership to negotiable instruments is obviously important because of the swift and painful implications unwise borrowing by one partner can have for the other partners.

Traditionally, courts drew a distinction between "trading" and "nontrading" partnerships. Partners in a "trading" partnership—the most salient example being a retail store needing to borrow money to buy goods to keep the shelves stocked—were deemed to have the implied or apparent authority to borrow funds. On the other hand, partners in a "nontrading" partnership, such as a law or medical partnership, were deemed not to have such authority absent express authorization.

The UPA does not mention the trading-nontrading distinction. Although the distinction is on the wane, it still influences many modern court decisions. As we saw in *Womack* v. *First National Bank of Augustine*, where the funds borrowed are necessary to the day-to-day operation of the partnership, the courts will have little difficulty in holding that borrowing was within the scope of the partner's authority. This is reinforced where, as in *Womack*, the usual practice of the particular partnership has involved regular borrowing.

Even in cases where a partner totally lacks authority to borrow funds, if those funds are used by the partnership to the benefit of the other partners, the courts should hold the partnership liable on a quasi-contractual, unjust-enrichment basis.[7]

Sale of Property

Generally it is within the partner's scope of authority to sell that which the partnership usually sells in the ordinary course of business. A partner in a shoe store enterprise has authority to sell shoes. That partner, absent the express agreement of other partners, does not have the authority to sell the building that the shoe store occupies. That would make it impossible to carry on the business and would cause dissolution. However, a partner in a partnership engaged in the purchase, development, and sale of land would have the authority to sell real estate.

In *Ball* v. *Carlson*,[8] for example, Carlson, Ishmael, and Teegardin formed the C.I.T. Construction Company, a partnership engaged in the development and sale of real estate. Carlson, on the partnership's behalf, entered into a contract with the Balls for the sale of a lot and construction of a house. Later the partnership breached the contract and the Balls sued all three partners. Teegardin appealed, arguing that because he had not authorized Carlson in writing to enter into the contract, it was only binding on Carlson individually.

---

[7] Crane and Bromberg, *Law of Partnership*, 2nd ed. West Pub. Co., St. Paul, MN (1968), p. 281.

[8] 641 P.2d 303 (Colo. App. 1981).

The court rejected this contention, holding that the effect of §9(1) of the UPA, making each partner's act binding on the partnership so long as it is within the apparent scope of authority, is to "obviate[ ] the necessity of a specific written authorization from other partners." Because C.I.T. was in the business of real estate development and sale, the court had no difficulty in concluding that Carlson was acting within the scope of authority, effectively binding the partnership.

The *Ball* v. *Carlson* result should be compared to that of the following case.

HODGE v. GARRETT

614 P.2d 420 (Idaho 1980)

Voeller, as managing partner of the Pay-Ont Drive-In Theater partnership, signed a contract to sell a small parcel of partnership land to Hodge. The parcel, though adjacent to the theater, was not used in theater operations except that a 20-foot strip was necessary to operation of the theater's driveway.

When the partnership breached the contract, Hodge sued. The other partners claimed that Voeller did not have authority to sell this land. The trial court ruled for Hodge, and the partners appealed.

BISTLING, JUSTICE:

At common law one partner could not, "without the concurrence of his copartners, convey away the real estate of the partnership, bind his partners by a deed, or transfer the title and interest of his copartners in the firm real estate." 60 Am. Jur. 2d *Partnership* §149 (1972). This rule was changed by the adoption of the Uniform Partnership Act. The relevant provisions are currently embodied in I.C. §§53–309(1) and 53–310(1) as follows:

[*Here the court quoted Idaho's version of §10(1) and 9(1) of the UPA.*]

The meaning of these provisions was stated in one text as follows:

If record title is in the partnership and a partner conveys in the partnership name, legal title passes. But the partnership may recover the property (except from a bona fide purchaser from the grantee) if it can show (A) that the conveying partner was not apparently carrying on business in the usual way or (B) that he had in fact no authority and the grantee had knowledge of that fact. The burden of proof with respect to authority is thus on the partnership. [Crane and Bromberg, *Partnership*, §50A (1968)]

Thus this contract is enforceable if Voeller had the actual authority to sell the property, or, even if Voeller did not have such authority, the contract is still enforceable if the sale was in the usual way of carrying on the business and Hodge did not know that Voeller did not have this authority.

As to the question of actual authority, such authority must affirmatively appear, "for the authority of one partner to make and acknowledge a deed for the firm will not be presumed . . ."—60 Am. Jur. 2d *Partnership* §151 (1972). Although such authority may be implied from the nature of the business, *id.*, or from similar past transactions, *Smith* v. *Dixon*, 386

S.W.2d 244 (Ark. 1965), nothing in the record in this case indicates that Voeller had express or implied authority to sell real property belonging to the partnership. There is no evidence that Voeller had sold property belonging to the partnership in the past, and obviously the partnership was not engaged in the business of buying and selling real estate.

The next question, since actual authority has not been shown, is whether Voeller was conducting the partnership business in the usual way in selling this parcel of land such that the contract is binding under I.C. §§53–310(1) and 309(1), that is, whether Voeller had apparent authority. Here the evidence showed, and the trial court found:

III.

That the defendant, Rex E. Voeller, was one of the original partners of the Pay-Ont Drive-In Theater; that the other defendants obtained their partnership interest by inheritance upon the death of other original partners; that upon the death of a partner, the partnership affairs were not wound up, but instead, the partnership merely continued as before, with the heirs of the deceased partner owning their proportionate share of the partnership interest.

IV.

That at the inception of the partnership, and at all times thereafter, Rex E. Voeller was the exclusive, managing partner of the partnership and had the full authority to make all decisions pertaining to the partnership affairs, including paying the bills, preparing profit and loss statements and income tax returns, and ordering of any goods or services necessary to the operation of the business.

The court made no finding that it was customary for Voeller to sell real property, or even personal property, belonging to the partnership. Nor was there any evidence to this effect. Nor did the court discuss whether it was in the usual course of business for the managing partner of a theater to sell real property. Yet the trial court found that Voeller had apparent authority to sell the property. From this it must be inferred that the trial court believed it to be in the usual course of business for a partner who has exclusive control of the partnership business to sell real property belonging to the partnership, where that property is not being used in the partnership business. We cannot agree with this conclusion. For a theater, "carrying on in the usual way the business of the partnership," I.C. §53–309(1), means running the operations of the theater; it does not mean selling a parcel of property adjacent to the theater. Here the contract of sale stated that the land belonged to the partnership, and, even if Hodge believed that Voeller as the exclusive manager had authority to transact all business for the firm, Voeller still could not bind the partnership through a unilateral act that was not in the usual business of the partnership. We therefore hold that the trial court erred in holding that this contract was binding on the partnership.

Judgment reversed.

Because of difficulties in knowing exactly what apparent authority a court will decide a partner has, any person purchasing real property from a partnership should demand that the conveyance be made in the names of all persons shown on the title records *and*, if possible, obtain written authorization from all partners.

Act Not Apparently Within the Scope of Authority

Because §9(2) and the common law make it clear that a partnership is not bound by the acts of a partner that are not apparently within the scope of authority,[9] it is important to be aware of certain types of acts that the courts consistently place within this category.[10]

Entering into a suretyship contract whereby the partnership guarantees the debt of another is outside the scope of business of most partnerships. The purpose of a partnership is to make a profit for the partners, and they have the right to demand that partnership assets be applied to that purpose and not to benefit a nonpartner.

The same reasoning puts a partner's gratuitous undertaking outside the scope of authority.

The application of partnership assets to an individual partner's debts for the personal benefit of the partner is also outside the scope of partnership business. Third parties who assist individual partners in converting partnership funds for their personal use may discover that they have no recourse against the partnership.

Unanimous Authorization

The UPA, in §9(3), expressly adds to those common law categories just listed certain types of conduct that cannot be undertaken without unanimous authorization.

Assignment to Creditors

Section 9(3)(a) states that less than all the partners, unless authorized by the others, have no authority to "[a]ssign the partnership property in trust for creditors or on the assignee's promise to pay the debts of the partnership." Such an assignment will likely make it impossible to carry on the business of the partnership and, therefore, requires special authorization.

Disposition of Goodwill

Section 9(3)(b) prohibits the disposition of the goodwill of the business by fewer than all the partners. Without its goodwill—the name, reputation, and accompanying expectation of continuing customer return—it again might be impossible to carry on the business of the partnership.

Impossible to Carry on Ordinary Business

If the first two categories are not inclusive, §9(3)(c) adds that it takes all partners to "[d]o any other act which would make it impossible to carry on the ordinary business of the partnership." Examples might include sale of key partnership real estate,[11] sale

---

[9] *Stone-Fox, Inc.* v. *Vandehey Development Co.*, 626 P.2d 1365 (Or. 1981).

[10] See Crane and Bromberg, *Law of Partnership*, 2nd ed. West Pub. Co., St. Paul, MN (1968), p. 291.

[11] For example, *Feingold* v. *Davis*, 282 A.2d 291 (Pa. 1971).

of major partnership assets, and cancellation of a contract that the partnership was formed to perform.

Confession of Judgment

Though defending a lawsuit against a partnership is within the normal scope of authority, §9(3)(d) says that fewer than all partners have no authority to confess a judgment that will bind partnership property or co-partners. A partner who confesses judgment, however, may bind his or her own personal assets. Such a confession is viewed not as void but as voidable by the other partners.[12]

Submission to Arbitration

Finally, §9(3)(e) provides that fewer than all partners have no authority to "[s]ubmit a partnership claim or liability to arbitration or reference." Partners act within the scope of authority when they settle a partnership lawsuit in good faith, but the UPA prohibits them from placing the partnership's fate in the hands of a nonjudicial third party.

This UPA provision was drafted in the days when arbitration was much less popular than it is today. If the UPA were being written today, it is unlikely that it would contain this provision. Indeed some court decisions have mitigated its effect.

For example, in *Wydel Associates* v. *Thermasol Ltd.*,[13] a plaintiff partnership sued in court on various breach of contract and breach of warranty claims. The defendant moved to dismiss on grounds that the contract contained a clause calling for arbitration in New York of any disputes. Although plaintiff argued that the arbitration clause was outside the authority of the partner who signed the contract, the federal district court granted the motion to dismiss for two reasons.

First, the court believed that the Federal Arbitration Act, which encourages arbitration, overrode the state UPA.

Second, the court held that the partnership clearly ratified the arbitration clause by accepting the benefits of the contract and bringing suit for its breach. Parties to a contract cannot pick and choose which parts they wish to enforce and which they wish to discard. All partners accepted the benefits, and all partners supported the lawsuit. That unanimous ratification evaded §9(3)'s bar against arbitration.

The *Wydel Associates* case points out that the unanimity required for confession of judgment, reference to arbitration, and so on can come via consent or ratification of all partners. This consent must be actual, not implied, and clearly proven.

For example, in *Shafer Bros.* v. *Kite*,[14] one partner signed confession of judgment notes. The trial court would not allow the other partners to set the confession aside,

---

[12] *Bethlehem Steel Corp.* v. *TriState Industries, Inc.*, 434 A.2d 1236 (Pa. Super. 1981).

[13] 452 F.Supp. 739 (W.D. Tex. 1978).

[14] 406 A.2d 673 (Md. App. 1979).

holding that it was normal for this partnership to sign such notes, so authority was implied from the nature of the business. The appellate court reversed, holding that §9(3) requires *actual* authorization by all other partners before one can confess judgment and that the authorization must be proved by some positive evidence of consent or ratification. Such authorization cannot be implied as part of the ordinary course of business.

Obviously the partners could expressly agree, perhaps in a written partnership agreement, that one or more, but fewer than all, can do the acts covered by §9(3). That would be the type of express authorization §9(3) contemplates.

Ratification

The previous section's discussion of ratification is important. If a partner enters into a contract lacking express, implied, or even apparent authority, the partnership may still be bound if the other partners *ratify* the contract.

A ratification can be express or implied from conduct. If the other partners learn of the contract and do not repudiate it within a reasonable time, or accept its benefits, or sue on it, as in *Wydel*, they will probably be deemed to have ratified the contract.[15]

Ratification is illustrated in the following case.

STALLINGS v. PURVIS

257 S.E.2d 664 (N.C. App. 1979)

Plaintiff Stallings, looking for a location for a restaurant, was told by a realtor to contact Purvis, a "leg man" for a group of investors who owned a certain building. Purvis's number was on the "for sale" sign in front of the building, so plaintiff called him. Purvis told plaintiff he had "sole custody" of the building and could arrange a lease. On March 25, 1970, plaintiff and Purvis agreed on a one-year lease at $250 per month. Purvis gave plaintiff a key so he could renovate the building during April.

Plaintiff, with Purvis's full knowledge, spent $6,000 renovating the building. Purvis promised plaintiff a written lease at $250 a month.

Problems arose with a septic tank and plaintiff's demand for a written lease. Plaintiff was then told by Purvis to contact Hollowell. Then, for the first time, plaintiff learned there were six owners of the building. Hollowell told plaintiff that Purvis was "custodian" of the building, that the owners could meet soon, and that a lease would be ready by May 1, 1970. Plaintiff tendered and Hollowell accepted the check for the first month's rent less certain deductions approved by Purvis.

Delays resulted, but Purvis kept reassuring plaintiff that a lease in accord with the March 25 agreement would be forthcoming. When the

---

[15] Some courts utilize the concept of estoppel to achieve the same result.

written lease finally arrived, it was for only 90 days at $300 a month. Plaintiff sued for damages resulting from defendant partners' failure to honor his March 25 oral agreement with Purvis.

The trial judge granted defendants' motion for a directed verdict. Plaintiff appealed.

VAUGHN, JUDGE:

It is admitted in the pleadings that the defendant owners were engaged in business as general partners. The acts of Purvis and also of Hollowell as well could therefore, bind the partnership.

> Every partner is an agent of the partnership for the purpose of its business, and the act of every partner including the execution in the partnership name of any instrument, for apparently carrying on in the usual way the business of the partnership of which he is a member binds the partnership, unless the partner so acting has in fact no authority to act for the partnership in the particular matter, and the person with whom he is dealing has knowledge of the fact that he has no such authority. (U.P.A. §9)

The principles of agency law could bind the investors. Principals are liable upon contracts duly made by an agent, with a third person "(1) when the agent acts within the scope of his actual authority; (2) when the contract, although unauthorized, has been ratified; (3) when the agent acts within the scope of his apparent authority, unless the third person has notice that the agent is exceeding his actual authority"— *Investment Properties of Asheville, Inc.* v. *Al-*

len, 283 N.C. 277, 285–86, 196 S.E.2d 262, 267 (1973).

Under agency law principles, even if the evidence in this case does not show that Purvis acted as an agent within the scope of his actual authority, it tends to show that the other defendants *ratified* his actions and could therefore be estopped to now deny his authority and that the other defendants held Purvis out to others, including plaintiff, as having apparent authority to lease the realty. Both implied agency authority or agency by estoppel as it is sometimes known and apparent authority theories could be upheld by the facts in evidence, and the inferences therefrom at the time plaintiff rested his case. Purvis's phone number was on the for sale sign located on the premises. He was referred to as the "leg man" or "custodian" of the property by Rupy and Hollowell, two of the other five owners. A check made to "W. G. Purvis, Agent" for rent tendered to Hollowell was accepted by Hollowell. This acceptance of rent could constitute a ratification. On his dealings with Purvis and Hollowell directly, and Rupy through the realtor, plaintiff was at no time given notice that Purvis did not have the power he claimed to have to deal with the property. No one objected to plaintiff going into possession and making major renovations.

Purvis individually could have made a lease for one year. His statements to plaintiff in front of others seem to indicate he could. One does not have to be the fee owner to make a lease. Although the present case, as well as others at the directed verdict stage, presents thorny problems, we hold plaintiff's evidence sufficient to take the case to the jury.

Reversed and remanded.

TORT LIABILITY

General Torts

Section 13 of the UPA provides that where "by any wrongful act or omission of any partner acting within the ordinary course of the business of the partnership or with the authority of his co-partners, loss or injury is caused to any person," the partnership is liable to the same extent as the acting partner. More simply, a partnership is liable for the torts of its partners committed within their scope of authority.

As with a partnership contract liability, frequently the most difficult matter is to define the scope of authority.

Negligence

Doctors who carelessly diagnose partnership patients, and lawyers who give negligently erroneous advice to partnership clients are liable for their negligence. But they also subject the partnership and their partners to liability according to §13, if the tort is committed within the scope of authority. Obviously, diagnosing patients is within the ordinary course of business of a medical partnership, and counseling clients is within the ordinary course of business of a legal partnership.

Difficult questions frequently arise, however, in the ubiquitous car wreck case. If a partner is driving a personal car on an individual errand when she negligently causes a wreck, obviously the partnership should not be liable for injuries caused to third parties. The same result should obtain if the partner is driving a partnership-owned car for personal purposes, unless the particular state has a special statute imposing broad liability on the owners of automobiles involved in accidents.

If the partner is driving a partnership car for partnership purposes, the partnership will almost certainly be liable for resulting negligence.

In the fourth and final permutation—a partner driving a personally owned car on partnership business—the partnership will probably be liable if its business inherently involves making deliveries of goods or services. But if it is simply a case of a doctor using her own car to travel to the hospital to perform surgery or a lawyer using his own car to go to the courthouse for a trial, partnership liability usually will not result.

Intentional Torts

Section 13 covers partners' intentional torts as well as negligence, making the partnership liable for both. But can a partner be acting within the scope of partnership business in committing an intentional tort? The courts have not been consistent in answering this question, but it is clear that just because a tort is intentional does not necessarily mean that the partner who committed it acted outside the scope of partnership business.

If a partner is simply venting his spleen when committing an assault and battery on a customer, for example, and is not advancing the partnership's interests in any way, the partnership probably will not be liable to the injured customer.[16] However, if the partner is attempting to collect money due the partnership or to protect partnership property, but does so in an improper manner resulting in an assault and battery, the partnership probably will be liable. Similarly, if a partner makes fraudulent representations in trying to sell a partnership product, or slanders an employee who the partner suspects is stealing from the partnership, vicarious liability should result.

The partnership is liable for all its agents—employees and partners—who commit intentional torts within the scope of authority. An interesting case follows.

KELSEY–SEYBOLD CLINIC v. MACLAY

466 S.W.2d 716 (Tex. 1971)

Plaintiff John Maclay sued Dr. Brewer and the Kelsey–Seybold Clinic, a medical partnership, for the tort of alienation of affection. In summary, plaintiff alleged that while treating plaintiff's family, Dr. Brewer had showered attention and gifts on Mrs. Maclay in a scheme to alienate her affections for plaintiff; that various acts of undue familiarity occurred both on and off the partnership property; that these acts occurred in the course and scope of Dr. Brewer's employment as a partner at the Clinic; that the Clinic, through Dr. Mavis Kelsey, a senior partner, had knowledge of Dr. Brewer's actions; and that the partnership approved of, ratified, and consented to Brewer's conduct.

The Clinic moved for summary judgment, arguing that as a matter of law, it could not be responsible for Dr. Brewer's actions. The trial court agreed. The intermediate appellate court reversed and remanded the case for trial. The Clinic appealed.

WALKER, JUSTICE:

The bases of liability alleged in the petition are (1) that Dr. Brewer's wrongful conduct was in the course and scope of the partnership business and was approved, consented to, ratified, and condoned by the Clinic, and (2) that the Clinic, after notice of the alleged relationship between Dr. Brewer and Mrs. Maclay, failed to take any action. Plaintiff is thus relying upon the vicarious or partnership liability of the Clinic for the acts of one of the partners and also its liability for breach of a duty owing by the Clinic when it learned of Dr. Brewer's relationship with Mrs. Maclay.

On the question of vicarious liability, plaintiff argues that the affidavit of the members of the Clinic's executive committee will not support a summary judgment since it comes from interested parties and contains mere conclusions. No attempt will be made to consider this conten-

---

[16] Annotation, 30 A.L.R. 2d 859 (1953).

tion, because the judgment of the Court of Civil Appeals must be affirmed for other reasons that will be discussed below. We are unwilling to believe that plaintiff seriously expects to prove in a conventional trial that the acts alleged to have been committed by Dr. Brewer were in the course and scope of the partnership business or were either authorized or ratified by the Clinic. Rather than concern ourselves about possible deficiencies in the affidavit filed by the Clinic, we assume for the purpose of this opinion that Dr. Brewer was not acting in the ordinary course of the Clinic's business and that his conduct was neither authorized nor ratified by the partnership. This will enable us to reach questions that may well arise at the trial of the case.

The Court of Civil Appeals reasoned that the summary judgment was improper because the Clinic had not conclusively negated consent on its part to the alleged wrongful conduct of Dr. Brewer. In reaching this conclusion, it relied on our opinion in *K & G Oil Tool & Service Co.* v. *G & G Fishing Tool Service*, 158 Tex. 594, 314 S.W.2d 782, where it was stated that:

A non-participating partner is ordinarily not personally liable for the wrongful, tortious or criminal acts of the acting partner unless such acts are within the scope of the partnership's business or were consented to, authorized, ratified or adopted by the non-participating partner.

There was no question of consent in *K & G*, and it was held that the nonparticipating partner was not liable.

Two courts apparently entertain the view that mere tacit consent is enough to make the nonparticipating partner liable for the willful tort of the acting partner outside the scope of the partnership business. See *Polis* v. *Heizmann*, 276 Pa. 315, 120 A. 269, and *Dulchevsky* v. *Solomon*, 136 Wash. 645, 241 P. 19. Their conclusion in this respect appears to be due, at least in part, to an erroneous interpretation of the opinion in *Williams* v. *F. & W. Grant Five, Ten and Twenty-five Cent Stores*, 273 Pa. 131, 116 A. 652. The plaintiff there was accused of stealing a toothbrush. While being interrogated in defendant's store, she was assaulted by the operative of a private detective agency employed by defendant to guard the store. The trial court rendered judgment on the verdict in favor of the plaintiff, and it was contended on appeal that defendant could not be responsible for an assault committed by the employee of an independent detective agency. The appellate court pointed out that the jury had been instructed to find for the plaintiff if they believed that the manager of the store was present and participated in the acts or permitted the operative to insult and assault the plaintiff when he could and should have protected her. It then observed that the defendant was held responsible not for the acts of the operative but for those of its own manager.

Where a partner proposes to do, in the name or for the benefit of the partnership, some act that is not in the ordinary course of the business, consent by the other partners may constitute his authority to do the act for the partnership. See Restatement, Second, Agency, §§7, 27. We also recognize that even a willful or malicious act outside the ordinary scope of the partnership business may be so related to the business that tacit consent of the other partners could fairly be regarded as a grant of authority. In this instance, however, Dr. Brewer was acting solely for his own personal gratification. His conduct could not benefit the Clinic in any way, and no one would have supposed that he was acting for the partnership. It is our opinion that in these circumstances the ''consent'' that might be inferred from the silence or inaction of the Clinic after learning of his conduct does not render the Clinic vicariously liable for the damages claimed by plaintiff.

On the basis of the present record and the

facts we are assuming in this case, the liability of the Clinic must rest, if at all, upon some theory akin to that recognized by the court in *Williams*. The Clinic was under a duty, of course, to exercise ordinary care to protect its patients from harm resulting from tortious conduct of persons upon the premises. A negligent breach of that duty could subject the Clinic to liability without regard to whether the tortious conduct immediately causing the harm was that of an agent or servant or was in the ordinary scope of the partnership business. For example, it might become liable, as a result of its own negligence, for damage done by a vicious employee while acting beyond the scope of his authority. See Restatement, Second, Agency, §213.

We are also of the opinion that the Clinic owed a duty to the families of its patients to exercise ordinary care to prevent a tortious interference with family relations. It was not required to maintain constant surveillance over personnel on duty or to inquire into and regulate the personal conduct of partners and employees while engaged in their private affairs. But if and when the partnership received information from which it knew or should have known that there might be a need to take action, it was under a duty to use reasonable means at its disposal to prevent any partner or employee from improperly using

his position with the Clinic to work a tortious invasion of legally protected family interests. This duty relates only to conduct of a partner or employee on the premises of the Clinic or while purportedly acting as a representative of the Clinic elsewhere. Failure to exercise ordinary care in discharging that duty would subject the Clinic to liability for damages proximately caused by its negligence. See Restatement, Second, Torts, §317.

The rather meager information in the present record does not necessarily indicate that the Clinic was under a duty to act or that it could have done anything to prevent the damage when Dr. Kelsey first learned of the situation. On the other hand, it does not affirmatively and clearly appear that the Clinic could or should have done nothing. Mrs. Maclay's affections may have been alienated from her husband before anyone talked with Dr. Kelsey, but the facts in that respect are not fully developed. In our opinion the Clinic has failed to discharge the heavy, and in a case of this character, virtually impossible, burden of establishing as a matter of law at the summary judgment stage that it is not liable under any theory fairly presented by the allegations of the petition.

The judgment of the Court of Civil Appeals is affirmed.

Thus, the partnership in *Kelsey–Seybold Clinic* was held potentially liable not because a partner committed a tort within the scope of authority—for Dr. Brewer had clearly acted outside the ordinary course of partnership business—but because the partnership itself had been potentially negligent in its supervision. A strong dissent in the case argued that it was improper to extend the tort of alienation of affection, which many states have abolished, beyond those defendants whose acts actually produced the alienation.

If, in committing an intentional tort, a partner acts *solely* for his or her own purpose, the partnership may successfully argue that it should not be liable. But if even part of the partner's motivation was to further partnership business, the partnership will most likely be held liable as well.

Breach of Trust

Section 14 of the UPA specifically addresses breaches of trust. Partnerships are liable when they owe a fiduciary duty to a third party that is breached by a partner. This section has been broadly applied to all sorts of fiduciary breaches, including converting funds, obtaining secret commissions, and receiving kickbacks.

Because law partnerships owe fiduciary duties to their clients, §14 has frequently been applied in cases involving such partnerships. The following case is illustrative.

HUSTED v. McCLOUD

450 N.E.2d 491 (Ind. 1983)

The law partnership of Selwyn and Edgar Husted was hired by Herman McCloud to represent his mother's estate. After the estate, for which Herman was executor, was closed, the IRS demanded an extra estate tax payment of $13,006.73. McCloud prepared a check payable to the IRS; however, Edgar falsely represented that the exact amount of the tax liability was unknown. He took McCloud's check for $18,800 payable to the Husted and Husted Trust account and told McCloud he would pay the liability and keep the remainder as his fee. There was no such trust account. Edgar deposited the entire check into his personal account and converted the funds to his personal use.

Though Edgar devised an elaborate scheme to cover his actions, ultimately he was discovered and entered a plea of guilty to three counts of theft and one count of forgery involving the handling of three other estates. McCloud had to use his own savings and borrow money to pay the IRS tax assessment and penalties.

McCloud sued. The trial court, inter alia, awarded compensatory and punitive damages against the partnership of Husted and Husted

as well as punitive damages against Edgar Husted. The appellate court affirmed and this appeal ensued.

PIVNARIK, JUSTICE:

[The court first set aside the award of punitive damages against Edgar Husted. The public interest in punishing him and deterring such conduct was satisfied by his prison sentence. The court then quoted UPA §§13 and 14.]

The trial court and the Court of Appeals determined that §13 required that the partnership be liable to the same extent as Edgar Husted for any civil penalty imposed in this case. The partnership claims that Edgar's criminal acts were not within the ordinary course of partnership business. Furthermore, the partnership claims that it never had possession of the certain funds converted and therefore the partnership cannot be held liable for Edgar's acts with respect to said funds. There were two partners in the partnership law firm, Edgar Husted and Selwyn Husted, Edgar's father. McCloud clearly was a client of the partnership since McCloud dealt with both Selwyn and Edgar on his estate case. In fact, Selwyn was the partner who first brought McCloud's case into the partnership's office. Edgar was acting within the ordinary course of the partnership's business and with apparent authority since Edgar's request for and acceptance of money from McCloud to pay McCloud's estate tax liability was well within the work parameters of the attorney properly handling a decedent's estate. We therefore find that even though fraud and conversion of a client's funds are not part of the ordinary course of a law partnership's business, the trial court correctly found pursuant to §14 that the partnership was responsible for partner Edgar in taking money entrusted to him and misapplying it. We also find that the trial court was justified in finding that McCloud's money was in the partnership's possession when it was in Edgar's possession since Edgar deviated from McCloud's plan and converted the money to his own use only after he received it in the ordinary course of the partnership's business. Accordingly, the trial court did not err by holding the partnership responsible to McCloud for compensatory damages.

Whether Appellant partnership is liable for punitive damages, however, is another story. Husted & Husted argues that the cases decided under §13 or its counterpart in other jurisdictions as well as the earlier cases decided under the common law of agency and partnership have generally held that where a partnership is sued for a partner's intentional tort, the partnership's liability turns on whether the purpose or effect of the tortious act was to benefit the partnership's business or whether the tort was so removed from the ordinary course of that business that it could not be considered within the implicit authorization of the co-partners. Appellant partnership cites *Riley* v. *LaRocque*, (1937) 163 Misc. 423, 297 N.Y.S. 756, where a plaintiff sued a law partnership for the breach of trust

committed by one of that firm's general partners. The defendant partner and another attorney handled the estate of the plaintiff's father. After the estate's assets were distributed, the defendant partner induced the plaintiff to "invest" his share of said assets with the firm. The defendant partner then signed a demand note against his firm to convert the plaintiff's funds to his own use. The New York court found that the unknowing and innocent partners were not liable for the personal misconduct of their co-partner. That court cited the well-settled principle of agency law that when an agent commits an independent fraud for his own benefit, he ceases to act as an agent for his principal. That court also indicated finding no purpose or intent to advance any partnership interest and that the misdeeds were not in the ordinary course of the partnership's business since a law firm is not in the usual business of investing people's money while handling their legal affairs. Appellant partnership also cites other jurisdictions that have reached the same result in cases dealing with intentional torts other than conversion. Those cases have held innocent co-partners not liable for the intentional torts of a defendant partner when committed out of purely personal motives or with no purpose or effect to benefit the partnership.—*Wheeler* v. *Green* (1979) 286 Or. 99, 593 P.2d 777 (defamation); *Kelsey–Seybold Clinic* v. *Maclay* (Tex. 1971) 466 S.W.2d 716, *reh. denied* (alienation of affections); *Vrabel* v. *Acri* (1952) 156 Ohio St. 467, 103 N.E.2d 564 (battery).

We accept Appellant's contention that §13 is the only section by which punitive damages can be imposed against a partnership since §14 merely limits a partnership's liability to restitution. We further agree with Appellant partnership that the rationale behind punitive damages in Indiana prohibits awarding such damages against an individual who is personally innocent of any wrongdoing. Punitive damages are not intended to compensate a plaintiff but rather are intended to punish the wrongdoer and thereby deter others from engaging in similar conduct in the future. Accordingly, we now hold that the trial court erred by adjudging the innocent partner in this case responsible for punitive damages.

Punitive Damages and Penalties

Husted raised a very interesting question. Should the partnership and other partners be liable for punitive damages or statutory penalties resulting from the acts of a single partner of which the other partners were unaware? Normally persons are liable for such punitive damages and penalties only if they have the requisite mental intent to engage in intentional wrongdoing.

Husted notwithstanding, there is a substantial body of case law holding partnerships liable for such damages.[17] Obviously the courts are split on the proper approach; the law in this area has been summarized like this:

> Generally, the courts have held that a partner who did not authorize, participate in, or ratify the wrongful act of his copartner is not liable for punitive damages awarded in connection with the partner's wrongful act, although there is authority to the contrary, particularly in cases involving fraud. Moreover, a number of cases have held that a partner who did not authorize or participate in the wrongful act of his co-partner will not be liable for punitive damages even if he subsequently ratified the act.[18]

CRIMINAL LIABILITY

Despite the fact that many courts have held the partnership and other partners liable for punitive damages resulting from the wrongful acts of one partner, individual partners will not be held criminally liable unless they assent to or participate in the criminal activity.

Acceptance of the entity theory of partnership has led courts to hold the partnership itself criminally liable in many situations. The Supreme Court approved this development in *United States* v. *A & P Trucking Co.*[19] Two partnerships were charged, as entities, with violating certain federal laws relating to transportation of explosives. One of those statutes made it illegal for any "person" knowingly to violate certain regulations. The act defined "person" to include "co-partnership." The Supreme Court held that Congress had the power to change the common law notion that a partnership is not an entity and that the law is clear that entities can be found criminally liable for knowing and willful legal violations through the doctrine of *respondeat superior*.

---

[17] For example, *Meleski* v. *Pinero Intern. Restaurant, Inc.*, 424 A.2d 784 (Md. App. 1981); *Termeer* v. *Interstate Motors*, Inc., 634 S.W.2d 12 (Tex. App. 1982).

[18] Annotation, 14 A.L.R. 4th 1355 (1982).

[19] 358 U.S. 121 (1958).

PROCEDURAL MATTERS

Joint and Several Liability

Section 15 of the UPA provides that partners are jointly and severally liable for *torts* committed by other partners. It also provides that partners are jointly liable for *contractual* obligations, although (1) it expressly provides that partners may enter into separate agreements to perform contractual obligations and (2) several states have altered their versions of the UPA to provide joint and several liability for contractual obligations as well as torts. The distinction between joint and several liability is largely procedural. At common law, a plaintiff suing persons who were jointly liable on an obligation had to sue *all* the joint obligors. The release of one defendant, perhaps via a settlement of the suit, would release all other defendants. On the other hand, if persons are jointly *and severally* liable, the plaintiff may pick and choose defendants.[20] For example, a plaintiff could sue one of four joint and several obligors rather than all. And, if a settlement or judgment did not satisfy the entire obligation, a plaintiff could sue any one or all of the remaining three obligors.

Service of Process

At common law, plaintiff suing a partnership would have to serve all partners. Today, most states have passed "common name" statutes, "joint debtor" statutes, or the like that allow service upon the partnership via service on any partner. Some even allow the partnership to be sued in its own name. Although provisions in the 50 states vary widely, most states provide that a plaintiff who sues all partners but serves only one partner may obtain a judgment collectible out of all partnership property (notice to one partner is notice to all) and out of the individual property of the partner served and any other partners who voluntarily appear as defendants.

The general rule may be thus stated:

> Service upon a partnership sued in its firm name, when allowable, is expressly covered by local practice provisions, which generally permit the service in such case to be made by leaving a copy of the summons at the usual place of business of the partnership, or with any member of the partnership. In no case, however, will a judgment entered after service on less than all partners be given the effect of a personal judgment against partners not actually served.[21]

A partnership judgment creditor is generally allowed to proceed against partnership assets, individual assets, or both at the same time. However, several states require a partnership judgment creditor to prove that partnership assets are inadequate to satisfy the judgment before that creditor may proceed against the individual assets of the partners.

---

[20] *In re Huckins*, 17 B.R. 620 (D. Me. Bkrtcy 1982).

[21] *Mid-City Materials* v. *Heater-Beaters*, 674 P.2d 1271 (Wash. App. 1984).

Enforcement of Partnership Rights

At common law, the partnership could not sue on partnership obligations in its own name. The proper approach was for one or more partners to bring suit, joining all other partners as plaintiffs. However, a growing number of states, and federal courts in federal question cases, do allow suits in the partnership name.

QUESTIONS AND PROBLEMS

1. MLH was a partnership owning certain real estate. Its three partners were Owens, Fink, and Pearl. Kajima was interested in buying a 57-acre tract of MLH land, and Owens told a real estate agent to pursue the sale and keep him informed. As talks progressed, Fink did almost all the negotiating for MLH. Owens said several times that Fink would be handling things and that Fink spoke for the two of them. Ultimately, Fink negotiated the sale, but at the last minute, Owens tried to block the sale saying that Fink had acted outside the scope of his authority. Owens claims that the agreement of all three partners is required for this sale. Is Owens correct? See *Owens* v. *Palos Verdes Monaco*, 142 Cal. App. 3d 863, 191 Cal. Rptr. 381 (1983).

2. Smith loaned Andrew $10,000. Because they were friends, Smith required no promissory note; she accepted Andrew's word that he would repay it. Andrew used the money to purchase three commercial properties that benefited a business in which both he and his wife were involved. When Andrew did not repay the loan, Smith sued. Andrew claimed that he and his wife share joint liability on the $10,000 debt because the partnership benefited from the loan. Discuss. See *Zack* v. *Smith*, 429 N.E.2d 983 (Ind. App. 1982).

3. Rubin sued A. C. Kluger & Co. and its 12 general partners for $10,000 in attorney's fees. One defendant, Kluger, signed a confession of judgment on the partnership's behalf. The other partners object. What is the effect of the confession of judgment? Discuss. See *Rubin* v. *A. C. Kluger & Co.*, 383 N.Y.S.2d 828 (1976).

4. While handling a divorce for plaintiff, attorney Lyon was asked if he knew who plaintiff could consult about investing $60,000. Lyon told her he was a silent partner in a real estate firm and induced plaintiff to loan money to and later buy stock in the company, which later went bankrupt. Law firm stationery was used in correspondence, but plaintiff's money never went into a law firm account. Checks were made payable to "Warren Lyon as attorney for" plaintiff. Lyon told plaintiff that he had prepared the contract covering the investment and that as her attorney he could assure her that her interests were well protected. Plaintiff sued Lyon's law firm. The firm claims that it is not liable, because Lyon was acting outside the scope of his authority. Discuss. See *Cook* v. *Brundidge, Fountain, Elliott & Churchill*, 533 S.W.2d 751 (Tex. 1976).

5. Partner 1 in an auto repair partnership accepted plaintiff's auto for repair, but then drove it to Houston and into a lake. Plaintiff sued partner 2, who knew nothing of partner 1's acts until after the fact. Plaintiff seeks to recover treble damages under

the Texas Deceptive Trade Practices Act, which requires "knowing" conduct by a defendant. Should plaintiff prevail? Discuss. See *Termeer* v. *Interstate Motors, Inc.*, 634 S.W.2d 12 (Tex. Civ. App. 1982).

6. Reich was the general partner of a limited partnership. He owned over 50% of the business; no limited partner owned more than 6%. Unknown to the other partners, Reich set fire to the partnership's building to obtain the insurance money. The insurance company claims that it should not have to pay *any* amount on the fire insurance policy, which naturally had an arson exclusion. The limited partners would like to receive their proportionate share of the policy proceeds. Discuss. See *Courts of the Phoenix* v. *Charter Oak Fire Ins. Co.*, 560 F.Supp. 858 (N.D. Ill. 1983).

7. Dr. Barbour negligently performed an operation on plaintiff. Plaintiff sued both Barbour and his partner in the medical practice, Dr. Egle. Dr. Egle proved he did not assist or participate in the surgery and never treated plaintiff in any way, though he was Dr. Barbour's partner at the time of the surgery. A jury returned a verdict against Dr. Egle in the sum of $125,000, which the trial judge set aside. Did the trial judge act correctly? Discuss. See *Martin* v. *Barbour*, 558 S.W.2d 200 (Mo. 1977).

8. De Santis and Noonan were partners in a real estate business, D/N Realty. The partnership certificate authorized the Bank of Commerce (plaintiff) to honor, receive, and/or pay all instruments signed by either partner without inquiry into the circumstances of the issuance or use of the instrument. Noonan deposited into the D/N account two $6,000 checks payable to Krauss and endorsed to Noonan. Noonan claims he was acting merely to accommodate a friend by cashing his checks. A few days later, Noonan withdrew $12,000 from the D/N account and deposited it in his personal account. A few days later, the two $6,000 checks came back with "stop payment" orders, creating an overdraft in the D/N Realty account. Plaintiff sued De Santis and Noonan for the overdraft. De Santis claims he is not liable because the transactions were conducted solely by Noonan without knowledge or authority of De Santis and outside the partnership business. Can De Santis's personal assets be used to satisfy the overdraft? See *Bank of Commerce* v. *De Santis*, 114 Misc.2d 491, 451 N.Y.S.2d 974 (1982).

5

PARTNERSHIP DISSOLUTION, WINDING-UP, AND TERMINATION

THREE PHASES

Introduction

The conclusion of a partnership business involves three phases. The first step is "dissolution," which §29 of the Uniform Partnership Act (UPA) defines as "the change in the relation of the partners caused by any partner ceasing to be associated in the carrying on" of the business. Thus, the death of a partner, and several other matters that will be discussed here, dissolves the partnership. However, these acts do *not* end its existence.

The legal existence of a partnership continues after dissolution while partnership affairs are being settled. This "winding-up" period is the second phase of the conclusion of a partnership. Typically, during a winding-up, surviving or continuing partners will

> complete transactions begun but not then finished, . . . collect the accounts receivable, . . . pay the firm debts, . . . convert the remaining firm assets into cash . . . and pay in cash to the partners and the legal representative of the deceased partner the net

amounts shown by the accounts to be owing to each of them in respect of capital contributions and in respect of their shares of profits and surplus.[1]

"Termination" occurs when the winding-up is completed. Although courts sometimes use the terms interchangeably, dissolution should not be confused with termination.

Right to Wind up

Section 37 of the UPA provides that, subject to agreement, the right to wind up a partnership vests in all partners who have not wrongfully dissolved a partnership or in the legal representative of the last surviving partner not bankrupt, should that situation arise. A partner who breaches a partnership agreement by, say, wrongfully ejecting a co-partner, forfeits the right to wind up.[2] However, this forfeiture is subject to one exception. Section 37 provides that *any* partner, apparently even a wrongdoer, may, upon cause shown, obtain a winding-up *by a court*.

Section 35(1)(a) provides that in the period between dissolution and termination, non-wrongdoing partners retain the authority to wind up partnership affairs or to complete transactions begun but not then finished. This means that the other partners (with some limited exceptions that will be discussed) are bound by such acts of a winding-up partner as are necessary to preserve the assets, pay partnership obligations, collect partnership debts, and settle litigation.

STARK v. UTICA SCREW PRODUCTS, INC.

425 N.Y.S.2d 750 (City Ct. of Utica 1980)

Stark and Henning were sales representatives for various firms in upstate New York. To limit travel, they formed a partnership, with Stark taking the eastern half of the state and Henning the western half. The partnership contracted to represent Utica Screw Products, Inc. (Utica), among other firms. When a dispute as to the accounting of commissions occurred, Stark sent a letter dated October 22, 1976, to Henning dissolving the partnership. Upon notice of the dissolution, Utica retained Henning, but not Stark.

Stark sued Utica, claiming there were still commissions due from Utica to the partnership for orders received by the defendant corporation between February 10, 1976, and October 20, 1976. Utica moved to dismiss for the reason that Stark had no standing to sue because he had not received authority from Henning.

[1] *McClennen v. Comm'r of I.R.S.*, 131 F.2d 165, 167 (1st Cir. 1942).
[2] For example, *Miernicki v. Seltzer*, 458 A.2d 566 (Pa. Super. 1983).

.HYMES, JUDGE:

The defendant contends that plaintiff Stark has no standing in this action because he has not received authority from his co-partner to institute this action. This defense is without merit.

Upon dissolution of a partnership, any partner has the right to participate in the winding-up of a partnership. He needs no authority from his co-partners. A unilateral letter of dissolution does not cut off the partnership relationship. On dissolution the partnership continues until the winding-up of the partnership affairs is completed. The only way in which a partnership is wound up is through an accounting—*Toeg v. Margolies*, 280 A.D. 319, 321, 113 N.Y.S.2d 372, 374.

The duty imposed upon the partner who is engaged in winding-up the partnership business is one of agency. The general agency of one partner for his co-partner ceases, but each partner then has the equal duty and power to do whatever is necessary to collect the debts of the partnership—*Gray v. Green*, 142 N.Y. 316, 37 N.E. 124.

After the dissolution of a partnership, a partner may bind the partnership by any appropriate action necessary to wind up the partnership affairs or to complete transactions unfinished at the time of dissolution. While a partner would not be entitled to remuneration for winding-up the partnership affairs, he would be allowed reasonable expenses incurred in performing these services. Such expenses could include the commencement of an action to collect on accounts due and payable to the partnership and the hiring of counsel for that purpose.

A partner cannot bar his co-partner from suing to collect debts due the partnership. Any judgment recovered by Stark would be for the benefit of the partnership and not for himself individually. It would then be up to the partners to wind up the partnership through an accounting.

Judgment for plaintiff.

There are limitations to the authority to wind up. For example, a partner who should be winding-up the business but instead is simply continuing it indefinitely cannot saddle the estate of a deceased partner with expenses of continuing the business.[3]

Compensation for a partner's labor expended in winding-up is available if dissolution was caused by death, or by agreement if dissolution was due to other causes. Only if there is fraud, mismanagement, or waste will a court appoint a receiver to handle the winding-up instead of the partners.[4]

Liquidation Right

Section 38(1) of the UPA gives each partner the right, unless otherwise agreed, "to have the partnership property applied to discharge its liabilities, and the surplus applied to pay in cash the net amount owing to the respective partners." Theoretically, this right to be paid in cash rather than in kind (even if distribution in kind makes more

---

[3] *King v. Stoddard*, 104 Cal. Rptr. 903 (Cal. App. 1972).
[4] For example, *Hankin v. Hankin*, 465 A.2d 1272 (Pa. Super. 1983).

sense) gives each partner an equal opportunity to purchase the assets and continue the business.[5]

In one case, a trial court ordered that the plaintiff partner in a suit for dissolution should have the partnership's sole asset, a bulldozer valued at $20,000. The judge then ordered plaintiff to pay the defendant partner half that sum minus some minor set-offs to settle the matter. On appeal, plaintiff successfully claimed that he should not be required to accept the bulldozer, but was entitled to have it sold and to receive his interest in cash.[6]

The liquidation right of §38 is subject to the right of partners, in certain situations, to continue the partnership business. The continuation right will be discussed later in this chapter.

Continued Existence

The continued existence of the partnership entity during the winding-up process has many implications. It means, for example, that liability may continue on obligations incurred prior to dissolution. Thus, lawyers who dissolve their law partnership cannot simply abandon their clients.[7] Also, the partners who continue to service clients during the winding-up period will be compensated in accord with the partnership agreement, not on a *quantum meruit* basis.[8]

Most important, the fiduciary duty that partners owe one another continues during the postdissolution, pretermination period. Although there are some controversies as to the exact scope of this duty,[9] most courts apply it in a broad fashion even during the winding-up period. As long ago as 1885, a court held it to be "the duty of the surviving or solvent member to take possession of the firm assets and perform its contracts, extinguish its liabilities and close up its business in the manner most advantageous to the interests of *all* the parties concerned." [10]

CAUSES OF DISSOLUTION

Sections 31 and 32 of the UPA address various causes of dissolution, the latter section concentrating on dissolution decrees issued by courts.

---

[5] H. Reuschlein and W. Gregory, *Agency and Partnership*, West Pub. Co., St. Paul, MN (1979), p. 345.

[6] *Taylor* v. *Bryan*, 664 S.W.2d 53 (Mo. App. 1984).

[7] *Vollgraff* v. *Block*, 458 N.Y.S.2d 437 (Supp. 1982).

[8] *Jewel* v. *Boxer*, 199 Cal. Rptr. 273 (Cal. App. 1984).

[9] Compare *Matter of Silverberg*, 438 N.Y.S.2d 143 (App. Div. 1981) with *Bovy, Graham, Cohen & Wampold*, 564 P.2d 1175 (Wash. App. 1977).

[10] *King* v. *Leighton*, 3 N.E. 594 (N.Y. 1885) (emphasis added).

Dissolution Without Violation

Section 31(1) discusses four causes of dissolution that do not violate the agreement of the parties. This is an important distinction because the other partners have a right to continue the business if the dissolving partner violates the partnership agreement.

First, a partnership is dissolved by "termination of the definite term or particular undertaking specified in the agreement." Thus, if partnerships are formed for a period of two years or for the construction and sale of a building, they dissolve upon the expiration of two years or the completion or sale of the building, absent express or implied agreement to the contrary.

Second, dissolution occurs without violation of the agreement "[b]y the express will of any partner when no definitive term or particular undertaking is specified." Thus, an "at-will" partnership is subject to dissolution at any time at the whim of any partner. Many courts, but not all, have been reluctant to impose a "good faith" condition on a partner's right to dissolve an "at-will" partnership.[11] However, courts occasionally find by implication, rather than by express agreement, that a partnership is for a particular term or undertaking.[12]

Third, dissolution occurs without breach "[b]y the express will of all partners who have not assigned their interests." At common law, the assignment of a partnership interest automatically dissolved the partnership. As we have seen in previous chapters, §27(1) changes the common law rule. Still, by assigning her interest, partner A in the ABCD Partnership would be giving partners B, C, and D the right, if all concur, to dissolve the partnership even if it were only in the second year of an agreed five-year term.

Fourth, dissolution occurs without violation of the agreement "[b]y expulsion of any partner from the business bona fide in accordance with such a power conferred by the agreement between the partners." Partnership agreements may provide for expulsion with or without cause, and by vote of a majority or perhaps all of the other partners. A provision for expulsion without cause reduces somewhat the litigation by the excluded partner who will likely believe good cause, if required, was not present. A partner who is expelled in violation of the agreement can recover damages from former partners.

Dissolution in Contravention

No one can be compelled to be a partner. Thus, it is beyond the power of a court to order that a partnership continue in existence against the will of one of its partners, even if it would preserve the going value of the concern to do so. Every partner has the *power* to dissolve a partnership at any time. Thus, §31(2) notes that dissolution is caused "[i]n contravention of the agreement between the partners, where the circumstances do not permit dissolution under any other provision of this section, by the express will

---

[11] Compare *Cude* v. *Couch*, 588 S.W.2d 554 (Tenn. 1979) with *Heath* v. *Spitzmiller*, 663 S.W.2d 351 (Mo. App. 1983).

[12] For example, *Owen* v. *Cohen*, 119 P.2d 713 (Cal. 1941).

of any partner at any time.'' The power to dissolve, however, must be distinguished from the *right* to dissolve.

The distinction between dissolution in contravention of the partnership agreement and dissolution without must be drawn because breach by one partner gives the other partners the right to recover damages that will reduce the dissolving partner's interest.[13] It also gives them the right to continue the business without liquidating.[14] Still, the wrongfully dissolving partner does not forfeit all interest in the partnership, and to continue, the other partners must indemnify the dissolving partner against continuing partnership liabilities.

Illegality, Death, or Bankruptcy

According to UPA §31(3), dissolution is also caused by any event making it unlawful for the members to carry on the business. Therefore a law partnership is automatically dissolved if one of its partners becomes a circuit judge in a state where circuit judges are not allowed to practice law.[15]

Section 31(4) provides that dissolution also occurs "[b]y the death of any partner." This was the common law view. Some states have expressly qualified this rule with a phrase such as "unless the partnership agreement otherwise provides," and courts of other jurisdictions have accepted this notion. The death of a partner in a small partnership will probably dissolve the partnership both technically and practically. But bigger partnerships, such as major law and accounting firms, provide for continuity to avoid disruption of business caused by the inevitable changes of membership brought about by death and other factors.

The bankruptcy of any partner or of the partnership also causes dissolution, according to §31(5).

Dissolution by Decree of Court—Application of Partner

Section 32(1) provides that a court *shall* decree dissolution upon the application of a partner in six circumstances. Despite this mandatory language, courts have frequently denied dissolution on equitable grounds.

Lunacy and Incapacity

Section 32(1)(a) and (b) provide for dissolution whenever a partner is declared a "lunatic" in a judicial proceeding, is shown to be of unsound mind, or becomes "in any other way incapable of performing his part of the partnership contract." It is hoped

---

[13] UPA §38(2) (a) (II). Although liable for damages, the partner who dissolves the partnership in breach of the agreement does not completely forfeit all interest in the partnership. See *Dobson* v. *Dobson*, 594 S.W.2d 177 (Tex. Civ. App. 1980).

[14] Courts have granted the remaining partners the right to continue the business when there was any "wrongful" dissolution, not just one in violation of an express partnership agreement.

[15] *Justice* v. *Lairy*, 49 N.E. 459 (Ind. App. 1898).

that the courts would not dissolve merely due to a temporary incapacity, but if a partner is going to be unable to carry out partnership obligations for a substantial period of time, dissolution is proper.

Prejudicial Conduct or Breach of Agreement

Section 32(1)(c) provides for dissolution whenever a partner's conduct prejudicially affects the carrying on of the business, as does §32(1)(d) whenever a partner "willfully or persistently" breaches the partnership agreement or conducts himself or herself in partnership matters so that "it is not reasonably practicable to carry on the business in partnership with him."

The difficulty for the courts is to distinguish between relatively minor misconduct and breaches of the partnership agreement that will not warrant dissolution, and more substantial misdeeds and breaches that will. A case attempting to draw this distinction follows.

LOGAN v. LOGAN

675 P.2d 1242 (Wash. App. 1984)

On July 29, 1975, plaintiffs Richard and Barbara Logan entered into a partnership agreement with Richard's brother Donald, the defendant. The purpose of the partnership was to acquire and hold four apartment buildings. The initial capital contribution was $70,000. Plaintiffs contributed 10% more than two-thirds of this sum in exchange for defendant's time, effort, and expertise in locating and purchasing the buildings.

Because Richard's job with the Federal Drug Enforcement Administration made him unavailable for months at a time, plaintiffs' financial advisor, David Shymko, was appointed as their attorney-in-fact to represent their interests. Friction between Shymko and the defendant ultimately led plaintiffs to sue for dissolution. The trial court, inter alia, denied plaintiffs' request for dissolution. They appealed.

CALLOW, JUDGE:

The *first* issue presented is whether the trial court properly [dismissed] on grounds that no right to relief was shown to permit judicial dissolution of a partnership under RCW 25.04.320 [Washington's version of UPA §32].

. . .

The plaintiffs first challenge the trial court's findings of fact relevant to the trial court's conclusion of law that "[p]laintiffs have failed to prove that defendant has materially or substantially breached the Partnership Agreement in any manner." However, the plaintiffs' failure to assign error specifically to the trial court's findings of fact causes such findings to become the established facts of the case.

. . .

Plaintiffs next challenge the trial court's conclusion of law that:

> Plaintiffs have failed to prove that defendant has been conducting himself in a manner which would make it not reasonably practicable to carry on the business of the partnership with defendant, and therefore, plaintiffs are not entitled to judicial dissolution under RCW 25.04.320(d).

[The court then quoted Washington's version of UPA §32(1)(d).]

Moreover, in jurisdictions which have adopted the Uniform Partnership Act, judicial dissolution will be allowed only where the alleged breach or misconduct was injurious to the partnership. *Fuller* v. *Brough*, 159 Colo. 147, 411 P.2d 18 (1966) stated:

> Although the general rule is that gross misconduct, want of good faith, willful neglect of partnership obligations, and such other causes as are productive of serious and permanent injury to the partnership, or which render it impracticable to carry on the partnership business, are proper grounds for the dissolution of a partnership by a court of equity at the instance of the innocent partner, nevertheless a court of equity will not dissolve an existing partnership for trifling causes or temporary grievances involving no permanent injury.

Here, the trial court entered the following unchallenged findings of fact:

> 2.2. . . . The partnership, Logan & Logan Investments, has been a successful business and has resulted in substantial economic benefit to all partners in the venture. . . .
>
> 2.6. . . . At all times defendant Donald Logan carried out his responsibilities as manager of the Logan & Logan Investments properties, in a manner which both preserved the partnership assets and enhanced their value. . . .
>
> 2.14. . . . At all times, defendant Donald Logan cooperated with agents of plaintiffs, provided access to the partnership records and books, and made a reasonable attempt to comply with all plaintiffs' requests throughout the term of the partnership. . . .
>
> 2.16. . . . Plaintiffs have failed to allege or prove any fraud or malfeasance on the part of defendant Donald Logan in regard to his management of the Logan & Logan Investments properties.
>
> 2.17. . . . The conduct of the partnership business by defendant has resulted in no damages to plaintiffs, . . . by the defendant.

These findings and the absence of findings to the contrary fully support the trial court's conclusion that the plaintiffs were not entitled to a judicial dissolution.

Affirmed.

Courts have also refused to dissolve partnerships on grounds that a partner was irascible and rude to customers,[16] that a partner had a bona fide dispute regarding whether speculative land held by the partnership should be sold,[17] that a partner briefly withheld one-half of the normal compensation for working partners in a short-lived attempt to convince them to accept an additional partner,[18] and that an error in judgment by a partner had caused a slight loss.[19]

On the other hand, courts have ordered dissolution where a partner withheld

[16] *Gerard* v. *Gateau*, 84 Ill. 121 (1876).
[17] *Fooks* v. *Williams*, 87 A. 692 (Md. 1913).
[18] *Potter* v. *Brown*, 195 A. 901 (Pa. Super. 1938).
[19] *Cash* v. *Earnshaw*, 66 Ill. 402 (1872).

significant business information, failed to call any business meetings, and ran the business solely for his own benefit; [20] where two partners diverted partnership business to a competing entity that they owned; [21] where three partners wrongfully excluded a fourth from the management and benefits of the partnership; [22] and where a partner continually wrote overdrafts on the partnership account.[23] Although courts are reluctant to dissolve partnerships that are profitable, they have done so where an atmosphere of suspicion and distrust stultified partnership affairs.[24]

Losing Enterprise

Section 32(e) provides for dissolution when "[t]he business of the partnership can only be carried on at a loss." The courts have generally taken a long-term view, refusing to dissolve where, if the partner seeking dissolution would perform his contractual obligations, there would be a "reasonable expectation of profit," [25] and where though a partnership had been a losing venture there was "substantial evidence" that it would generate a profit.[26]

On the other hand, where a partnership has lost money in 15 of 17 prior months, with losses averaging $4,100 per day and growing, one court ordered dissolution and brushed aside the claim that the tax deductions provided by the losses benefited the partners individually.[27] The court refused to focus on the individual partners rather than the partnership itself, but in an era when many partnerships were formed as tax shelters, perhaps the courts should have looked at "losses" in context.

Equitable Grounds

Finally, §32(1)(f) provides a catch-all, allowing courts to dissolve partnerships whenever "[o]ther circumstances render a dissolution equitable." Courts have dissolved on such grounds where, for example, both partners were guilty of fiduciary breaches and an air of mistrust and suspicion pervaded the partnership.[28]

Dissolution by Decree of Court—Application of Purchaser of Partner's Interest

Under §32(2), persons who have purchased a partner's interest as the result of a charging order are given the right to dissolve a partnership if it is one at will.

---

[20] *Lau* v. *Wong*, 616 P.2d 1031 (Haw. App. 1980).

[21] *Olivet* v. *Frischling*, 164 Cal. Rptr. 87 (Cal. App. 1980).

[22] *Susman* v. *Venture*, 449 N.E.2d 143 (Ill. App. 1982).

[23] *Darlington* v. *Perry*, 187 N.E. 796 (Ill. 1933).

[24] *Ferrick* v. *Barry*, 68 N.E.2d 690 (Mass. 1946).

[25] *Collins* v. *Lewis*, 283 S.W.2d 258 (Tex. Civ. App. 1955).

[26] *Metro U.S. Construction Corp.* v. *Reilly*, 232 N.W.2d 208 (Minn. 1975).

[27] *Mandell* v. *Centrum Frontier Corp.*, 407 N.E.2d 821 (Ill. App. 1980).

[28] *Stark* v. *Reingold*, 113 A.2d 679 (N.J. 1955).

EFFECT OF DISSOLUTION ON POWERS OF PARTNERS

Authority *Inter Se*

Act of Partner, Death, or Bankruptcy

Section 33 provides that except for the authority to wind up partnership affairs or to complete transactions already begun, "dissolution terminates all authority of any partner to act for the partnership . . . [w]ith respect to other partners." This termination is unqualified if the dissolution is *not* by the act, bankruptcy, or death of a partner. However, if the dissolution is due to one of these causes, the termination of authority is qualified by §34.

Right to Contribution

Section 34 provides that in situations where dissolution was caused by the act, bankruptcy, or termination of a partner, each partner is liable for his or her proportionate share of liability created by a partner acting as though the partnership had not been dissolved, *unless* (1) if the dissolution was by act of any partner, the partner creating the liability had *knowledge* of the dissolution, or (2) if the dissolution was by bankruptcy or death, the partner creating the liability had *knowledge or notice* of the dissolution. This provision is designed to alter the common law rule of agency that an agent is not entitled to indemnity after termination of authority even if the termination is unknown to the agent. But the §34 right to indemnity or contribution is clearly predicated on the existence of factors—lack of knowledge, or (in the case of dissolution caused by death or bankruptcy) lack of knowledge or notice—not relevant to the predissolution right to indemnity or contribution.

Authority as to Third Parties

The lengthy provisions of §35 govern the postdissolution authority of partners to bind the partnership in dealing with third parties. Except as provided in subsection (3), which we shall soon describe, §35 establishes three categories of postdissolution authority vis-à-vis third parties.

Regular Partners

First, as noted earlier, §35(1)(a) provides that all partners have postdissolution authority to wind up the affairs of the partnership and to complete unfinished transactions.

Second, §35(1)(b) states that if a partner acts in a manner that would have bound the partnership before dissolution, it will also bind it though occurring after dissolution, *provided* that the third party either:

(I) [h]ad extended credit to the partnership prior to dissolution and had no knowledge or notice of the dissolution, or (II) [t]hough he had not so extended credit, had nonetheless known of the partnership prior to dissolution, and, having no knowledge or notice of dissolution, the fact of dissolution had not been advertised in a newspaper of general circulation in the place . . . at which the partnership business was regularly carried on.

This provision clearly indicates that upon dissolution, partners not wishing to be held liable for subsequent acts of their former co-partners should give personal notice to all creditors who have previously extended credit to the partnership and should advertise the fact of dissolution in a newspaper of general circulation to give notice to potential creditors.

Questions frequently arise regarding the adequacy of notice. The fact that a bank note was signed by two partners and, then, after dissolution, was extended several times and modified by the signature of only one did not give notice to the bank of dissolution.[29] In another case, actual notice to the sales manager of a creditor that a partnership was "in the process of dissolution" was deemed adequate.[30] The following case presents another interesting scenario.

JENSEN SOUND LABORATORIES v. LONG

447 N.E.2d 464 (Ill. App. 1983)

Plaintiff Jensen Sound Laboratories (Jensen) provided an open-end credit account to Long's Auto Sound, a partnership composed of George and Alice Long, in June 1978. Long's Sound Systems, Inc. incorporated on January 24, 1979, and acquired the business of Long's Auto Sound. Later plaintiff filed suit to collect account balances owed by the corporation. Jensen claimed the Longs were individually liable as partners because it had no knowledge they had incorporated except for the corporate checks that were issued to pay their account balances.

The trial court held the Longs were not individually liable as partners. Plaintiff Jensen appealed.

JONES, JUSTICE:

[T]he plaintiff contends that the defendants had an affirmative duty to notify the plaintiff-creditor of their partnership's incorporation and that notice imparted by corporate checks delivered to the plaintiff was insufficient to relieve the defendants of personal liability. Otherwise stated, the plaintiff's argument is that the defendants should be held liable for the debt in question because of their failure to notify the plaintiff of the dissolution of their partnership.

As a general rule in Illinois, actual notice of the dissolution of a partnership must be given to persons who have dealt with the firm and

---

[29] *Farmers & Merchants Bank of Stuttgart* v. *Harris*, 559 F.2d 466 (8th Cir. 1976).

[30] *Sta-Rite Indus., Inc.* v. *Taylor*, 492 P.2d 726 (Ariz. App. 1972).

who have no knowledge of the dissolution in order to relieve the partners of debts incurred after the dissolution in the name of the partnership. Partnership liability will be incurred under this rule, however, only if, when an existing partnership is incorporated, the firm continues dealing in the same way and the change of name does not convey information of the incorporation. In *Weise* v. *Gray's Harbor Commercial Co.* [111 Ill. App. 647 (1904)], the appellants had been in business as a partnership known as George B. Weise & Son. No notice of dissolution of the partnership was given, and the court, noting that "[t]here was nothing in the outward appearance of things to indicate to the appellee's agent . . . that he was dealing with a corporation, and not with private persons," ruled that the appellee was not chargeable with notice of the dissolution and could hold the appellants liable as partners. Similarly, in *Bredhoff* v. *Lepman* [181 Ill. App. 247 (1913)], where there was no evidence that notice had been given of the dissolution of the partnership "Lepman & Heggie" after it was incorporated under the name of "Lepman & Heggie," the court found partnership liability. In that case letterheads used by the corporation at the time of the transaction

in question contained merely the words "Lepman & Heggie, Commission Merchants," with nothing to indicate that this was the name of a corporation.

In the instant case, the stipulation of evidence upon which the trial court made its ruling indicated that the plaintiff was in receipt of corporate checks for almost two years from the time of the defendants' incorporation until the transaction in question. The name of the corporation, Long's Sound Systems, Inc., was significantly different from that of the partnership, Long's Auto Sound, and contained an appropriate indicium of corporateness. There was no evidence that the defendants continued to deal with the plaintiff as a partnership after their incorporation, as the stipulation did not indicate how the defendants' orders to the plaintiff were sent in and filled or whether the order in question was made in the partnership or corporate name. On this record, then, we cannot say that the trial court erred in finding that the plaintiff was sufficiently notified of the defendants' incorporation to entitle the defendants to individual immunity from corporate debts.

Affirmed.

Secret and Dormant Partners

Secret and dormant partners are not individually liable on these postdissolution liabilities, and therefore the liabilities may not be satisfied out of their individual assets if the partners prior to dissolution are unknown to the third party and sufficiently unknown and inactive that the business reputation of the partnership is not in any degree due to the partners' connection to it.

Qualifying Provisions

Section 35(3) qualifies the potential postdissolution liability of the partnership by stating that it is *in no case* bound by any postdissolution act of a partner (though obviously the acting partner may be personally liable) where the dissolution was due to illegality (unless the act was merely for winding-up), *or* where the partner has become bankrupt, *or* where the partner has no authority to wind up partnership affairs. This last situation could arise, for example, where the partner in question had wrongfully dissolved the partnership and therefore forfeited his or her right to wind up. But this exclusion of authority is qualified by the provision that the partnership will nonetheless be held liable under the concept of *apparent authority* to a creditor who had extended credit before dissolution and had no knowledge or notice of the acting partner's want of authority. The apparent authority could also extend liability to third parties who had not extended predissolution credit but had no knowledge or notice of the want of authority because it had not been advertised in a newspaper of general circulation. Subsection 35(3) means, in essence, that by giving proper notice—actual notice to preexisting creditors and constructive notice by publication to potential creditors—partners can properly limit postdissolution liability except in cases of illegality or bankruptcy. Naturally, notice need not be given to a party already possessing actual knowledge.

Nothing in §35 affects the §16 provisions regarding partnership liability by estoppel.

DISSOLUTION'S EFFECT ON EXISTING LIABILITIES

Section 36(1) of the UPA provides that the dissolution of a partnership does not of itself discharge the existing liability of any partner. If the rule were otherwise, partners could avoid all obligations simply by dissolving the partnership. Of course, if dissolution is due to illegality or to the death of a partner whose personal services are indispensable to the contract, some liabilities may be discharged on those grounds.

What happens to the liabilities of a departing partner upon a dissolution when the business is continued by others? Section 36(2) provides that the departing partner is discharged from any existing liability if the partnership creditor and those continuing the partnership so agree. The agreement may be express or implied from the course of dealing between the creditor who has knowledge of the dissolution and those partners continuing the business. Furthermore, §36(3) states that where a person agrees to assume existing liabilities of a dissolved partnership, the departing partners are discharged from liability to any creditor who, knowing of the agreement, consents to a material alteration in the nature or time of the payment of the debt.

For example, in *United Counties Trust Co.* v. *Podvey*,[31] a law partnership composed of Podvey, Sachs, and Witherington borrowed money from a bank but later dissolved. The partners agreed that Podvey and Sachs would undertake to pay off certain partnership loans and that Witherington would undertake primary responsibility on the bank note. When the bank, knowing of the partnership's dissolution, allowed a renewal note on different terms to be signed only by Witherington, Podvey and Sachs were held discharged from liability.

---

[31] 389 A.2d 515 (N.J. Super. 1978).

CONTINUING THE BUSINESS

Right to Continue the Business

Normally the §38(1) liquidation right discussed earlier stands as an impediment to continuing the partnership business after dissolution. However, such continuation is frequently desirable so that the going-concern value of the firm can be maintained. Therefore, it is important to understand the three main situations in which a departing partner forfeits the right to liquidate the partnership and, concomitantly, the surviving partners gain the right to continue the business.[32]

Breach of Agreement

If a partner dissolves the partnership in breach of an agreement to carry on the business for a fixed term or for a specified undertaking, that partner forfeits the liquidation right. The other partners may choose to liquidate, but they may also choose to use the firm property to continue the business themselves or with new partners. To do so, however, the remaining partners must settle with the dissolving partner who is entitled to receive the value of his interest in the partnership reduced by the damage caused by his breach. The partnership's goodwill (appreciation in assets over book value) need not be considered in evaluating the wrongdoer's interest. Also, the wrongdoer need not be settled with until the end of the agreed term or undertaking. But, as pointed out earlier, the continuing partners must indemnify the departing partner against all future partnership liabilities.

    Keep in mind that this continuation right is inapplicable to dissolutions occurring in partnerships at will and in other partnerships where the dissolution is due to nonwrongful causes such as death or disability.

Expulsion of a Partner

    A partner who is legitimately expelled from a partnership under a partnership agreement also has no liquidation right. Again the remaining partners may continue the business, but to do so must settle seasonably with the departing partner (whose interest should be calculated with consideration given to goodwill).

Agreement

    Partners may give up the liquidation right in the partnership agreement, or by agreement reached at the time of dissolution. Continuation agreements are the most frequent basis for continuing the partnership business. All partners in all partnerships

---

[32] See, generally, J. Crane and A. Bromberg, *Law of Partnership*, 2nd ed. West Pub Co., St. Paul, MN (1968), pp. 474–477.

should give serious consideration to incorporating into their partnership agreements continuation provisions covering such matters as triggering events, disposition of outgoing partners' interests, and valuation and compensation.

Courts will enforce such agreements, which are often funded by life insurance policies paid for by partnership funds and keyed to tax considerations. Among the types of such agreements are

1. Buy-Sell Agreements to Resolve Disputes, which might provide, for example, that in the event of an irreconcilable dispute in the AB Partnership, A could resolve the dispute by offering to sell her interest in the partnership to B for $100,000 with the understanding that if B did not purchase, A would be obligated to buy B's interest for the same sum. This is known as a ''push-pull'' agreement.
2. Option or Obligation to Purchase Interest of a Deceased Partner, an agreement that, if it properly utilizes life insurance, can provide a fair settlement to the estate of a deceased partner while allowing the remaining original partners to keep control and continue the business without undue financial strain.
3. Agreement to Provide Continuity, which, if properly drawn, can avoid the winding-up and termination that usually follow dissolution no matter what the cause.

Obligations of the Continuing Partners

In addition to any obligations specified in a partnership agreement, partners continuing the partnership business have numerous liabilities established in §41 of the UPA. For example, any time a technical dissolution occurs by the adding or subtracting of partners, if the partnership business is continued without liquidation, creditors of the first (dissolved) partnership become creditors of the second (continuing) partnership. Creditors of the original partnership are also creditors of the continuing partnership business *when* dissolution is caused by the retiring (or assigning of interests to the continuing partner) of all but one partner, *when* any partner dies and the business is carried on with the consent of the retired partners but without any assignment of interests to creditors, *when* all partners assign their rights in partnership property to third parties who promise to pay the debts and continue the business of the partnership, and *when* dissolution is caused by wrongful act or expulsion.

Also, any person who joins an existing partnership shall be liable for all its preexisting obligations as though he had been a partner all along. However, that liability, according to both §17 and §41(7), is to be satisfied only out of partnership property. Assume the ABC partnership has assets of $100,000 when A leaves and is replaced by D who makes a $50,000 contribution. By agreement of all concerned, the partnership is not liquidated, and the business continues. If a tort committed by a partner before D joined the firm resulted in a judgment of $500,000, D is liable, but only to the extent of the $50,000 he has contributed. B and C have the unlimited personal liability that characterizes general partners. A probably does also, though he may have some sort of indemnification agreement with B and C.

Rights of the Deceased or Retiring Partner When Business Is Continued

Section 42 provides an election for a retiring partner or the estate of a deceased partner in situations where the business is continued without any settlement of accounts. To encourage the continuing partners to settle up with the departing partner or his or her estate, §42 entitles that partner to the value of his or her interest in the partnership at the time of dissolution *plus either* legal interest *or* profits attributable to the use of his or her right in partnership property accrued until satisfaction. The following case illustrates application of this provision. Note carefully the distinction between calculation of a departing partner's interest when the business is continued and when it is promptly wound up.

CAUBLE v. HANDLER

503 S.W.2d 362 (Tex. Civ. App. 1973)

Handler (defendant/continuing partner) and Cauble (deceased co-partner) were equal partners in a retail furniture and appliance store until the latter's death on May 18, 1971. Some time later, the administratrix of Cauble's estate brought this action for an accounting of partnership assets.

The trial court awarded plaintiff a judgment of $20.95 plus 6% interest from the date of judgment and taxed all costs to her, including a $1,800 auditor's fee incurred in auditing the partnership accounts.

Plaintiff appealed.

BREWSTER, JUSTICE:

[*The court first held that the trial judge had erred in valuing the deceased partner's interest by use of book value, which it viewed as simply "arbitrary" and therefore unusable. Market value should have been used instead.*]

Much of plaintiff's argument . . . is devoted to her contention that the trial court erred in

failing and refusing to allow her a share of the profit made by Handler by continuing the partnership business between date of dissolution and date of judgment.

We sustain this contention.

The undisputed evidence shows that Handler continued to operate and to control the partnership business after the death of Cauble and down to the trial date, and that he used and sold the assets of the partnership during all that period. The record does not show that this was done with the consent of the administratrix of the deceased's estate.

Exhibit E of the court-appointed auditor's report was offered into evidence, and it showed that during the period from May 19, 1971, to May 21, 1972, Handler made a net profit of $40,163.42 out of operating the partnership business after dissolution.

The trial court, in its judgment, refused to allow the plaintiff to recover one-half of the profits that were made by Handler after the dissolution of the partnership by his continued operation of the business.

It is Section 38(1) of [the UPA] that gave the representative of the estate of the deceased partner the right to elect, if she so desired, to have the partnership assets liquidated, the debts paid, and the share of each partner in the surplus paid to him in cash.

The plaintiff in this case did not elect to have this done.

If that election is made, it many times results in the sacrifice of going-concern values.

The following quotation explains the several elections that were open to the plaintiff under the fact situation that we have here. It is from *Law of Partnership* by Crane and Bromberg, Section 86(c), pages 495–496, and is as follows:

> If a partnership is seasonably wound up after dissolution, profits and losses during the liquidation are shared by the partners in proportion to their predissolution ratios, unless they have agreed otherwise. . . .
>
> *The situation changes if the business is not wound up, but continued, whether with or without agreement.* In either case, the noncontinuing partner (or his representative) has a first election between two basic alternatives, either of which can be enforced in an action for an accounting. He can force a liquidation, taking his part of the proceeds and thus sharing in profits and losses after dissolution. Alternatively, he can permit the business to continue (or accept the fact that it has continued) and claim as a creditor (though subordinate to outside creditors) the value of his interest at dissolution. This . . . means he is unaffected by later changes in those values. *If he takes the latter route, he has a second election to receive in addition* either interest . . . *or profits from date of dissolution.* This second election shields him from losses. . . .
>
> The second election may seem one-sided. It serves as "a species of compulsion . . . to those continuing the business . . . to hasten its orderly winding up." In part it is compensation to the outgoing partner for his liability on partnership obligations existing at dissolution; this liability continues until satisfaction, which would normally occur in the process of winding up. . . .
>
> The second election rests partly on the use of the outgoing partner's assets in the conduct of the business . . . his right to profits ends when the value of his interest is properly paid to him. (emphasis added)

Section 42 of the Uniform Partnership Act gives the representative of the estate of a deceased partner a right to share in the profits, if he elects to do so, if the other partner continues to operate the business after dissolution.

The great weight of authority is to the effect that Section 42 giving the option to take profits to the noncontinuing partner is applicable regardless of whether the business is continued with or without the consent of the noncontinuing partner or the representative of his estate.

Although the undisputed evidence showed that Handler made over $40,163.42 by operating the partnership business after dissolution, the Court refused to allow plaintiff to recover from Handler the Cauble estate's share of those profits, which plaintiff had a right to do. In lieu of profits, which plaintiff elected to recover, the Court awarded her 6% interest on what he found to be the cost or book value of the Cauble interest in the partnership at date of dissolution. This interest amounted to $3,764.89, which was considerably less than a one-half interest in the $40,163.42 in profits that Handler made out of his operation of the partnership business after dissolution.

This error was obviously prejudicial to plaintiff.

[*The court also held that the costs of the audit should have been paid out of the partnership estate and not taxed solely to plaintiff.*]

Reversed.

RULES FOR DISTRIBUTION

Assets

In the settling of a dissolved partnership's affairs, the assets of the partnership are deemed by §46 to include not only partnership property but also any contribution that general partners are required to make to close the gap between insufficient assets and excessive liabilities.

Order of Payment

The assets of the partnership shall be applied to partnership liabilities in this order: (1) debts to third parties, (2) loans from partners, (3) partners' capital contributions, and (4) partners' shares of profits. While the last three categories may be adjusted by agreement of the partners, naturally the first may not be.

  If partnership assets are insufficient to satisfy outside creditors' claims, the partners are to contribute the amount necessary to finish the job. If some of the partners are insolvent, not amenable to service of process, or refuse to contribute, §40(d) provides that "the other partners shall contribute their share of the liabilities, and, in the relative proportions in which they share profits, the additional amounts necessary to pay the liabilities." Partners paying these extra amounts have a right of contribution against the partners who did not pay their shares.

  Section 40(h) also provides that when both partnership and individual properties are in the hands of a court for distribution, partnership creditors shall have priority on partnership property, and individual creditors will have priority on individual property. This "jingle" rule of the UPA was formerly also the federal bankruptcy rule. In 1978, however, Congress changed the bankruptcy law to provide that partnership creditors had priority over individual creditors as to partnership property and equal status regarding individual property. Thus, priorities may be determined by the forum in which the matter is decided.

Examples

Assume that the ABCD partnership consists of A, B, C, and, naturally, D. At the time the partnership was formed, A contributed $30,000, B contributed $20,000, C contributed $20,000, and D contributed $10,000. Assume that these contributions have not been repaid and that D has loaned the partnership $10,000. Finally, assume that third-party creditors E and F are owed $20,000 and $30,000, respectively, and that liquidation of partnership assets has produced $170,000. Step 1 in dissolution is to pay off the outside creditors, E and F. That leaves $120,000 ($170,000 − $50,000) for distribution. Step 2 is to pay off D's partnership loan, which leaves $110,000: $120,000 − $10,000. Step 3 is repayment of capital contributions, which leaves $30,000: $110,000 − ($30,000 + $20,000 + $20,000 + $10,000). This $30,000 represents profit. Absent agreement to the contrary, the partners will split this profit equally, each receiving $7,500.

As another example, repeat all the assumptions just given, but reduce the amount produced by liquidation of assets to $110,000. The steps remain the same. First, outside creditors E and F are paid, leaving $60,000 for distribution. Second, D's partnership loan is repaid, leaving $50,000. Third, capital contributions are repaid, but only $50,000 is left to repay $80,000 in contributions. This means that the partnership has suffered a loss of $30,000 that absent agreement the partners will share equally. If each partner receives $7,500 less than his or her original capital contribution, the loss will have been shared equally.

BANKRUPTCY

More than occasionally the winding-up of a partnership occurs under the aegis of a bankruptcy court. A partnership is a ''person'' afforded the same protections from creditors as insolvent individuals. As noted earlier, partnership creditors have priority over individual partners' creditors as to partnership assets and equal standing as to individual partners' assets if the individual partners are bankrupt. If partnership assets are inadequate to satisfy partnership debts, the trustee in bankruptcy may proceed against partners who are not in bankruptcy and, if recovery still is insufficient, then against partners undergoing individual bankruptcy proceedings.[33]

QUESTIONS AND PROBLEMS

1. Susman was a partner with three brothers named Asher. After a disagreement arose, the Ashers treated Susman as if he had no interest in the partnership, telling him he was no longer a partner, altering the partnership tax returns to indicate Susman's interest was zero, excluding Susman from partnership business, denying him information concerning the activities of the partnership, and refusing to account for partnership expenses. Susman claims that these activities are grounds for court-ordered dissolution. Is he correct? Discuss. See *Susman* v. *Venture*, 449 N.E.2d 143 (Ill. App. 1982).

2. Orbin, Henderson, and Ramsey formed a partnership called Stone City Attractions in February 1973 for the purpose of organizing rock 'n roll concerts. Orbin was to be managing partner. Before the end of 1973, Henderson and Ramsey were imprisoned for conspiring to import marijuana. While Henderson and Ramsey were in prison, Orbin incorporated Stone City Attractions, Inc., as an entity to hold his interest in the partnership. Henderson and Ramsey claim that this action gives them the right

---

[33] See, generally, J. Hanley, "Partnership Bankruptcy Under the New Act," *Hastings Law Journal*, Vol. 31 (1979), p. 149; and F. Kennedy, "Partnership and Partners' Estates Under the Bankruptcy Code," *Arizona State Law Journal* (1983), p. 219.

to dissolve the partnership. Are they correct? Discuss. See *Stone City Attractions, Inc.*, v. *Henderson*, 571 S.W.2d 206 (Tex. Civ. App. 1978).

3. Stoutt and Ridgway were partners in a commercial waterslide venture. The trial court held in a suit for dissolution that Stoutt had failed to perform the partners' contract in a satisfactory fashion. It therefore (1) ordered Stoutt to pay Ridgway $10,566 in damages and (2) barred Stoutt from sharing in partnership profits. Stoutt does not appeal the first ruling, but challenges the second. Should Stoutt prevail? Discuss. See *Stoutt* v. *Ridgway*, 658 S.W.2d 420 (Ark. App. 1983).

4. H and D were "at-will" partners in "Gateway Realty." They earned commissions by selling real estate. In January 1973, H told D that the partnership was over, and D left the premises (which were owned by H and her husband). H continued to operate a real estate business after changing the name to Betty Hilgendorf, Realtor. She accounted for and paid to D one-half of all the commissions resulting from listings that were in the office at the time of the dissolution. Eleven months later, D sued, claiming that she was entitled to one-half the value of the assets of the partnership at the time of dissolution (a classified ad and a telephone number) and one-half of all profits H had earned in the intervening period. Discuss D's rights in this regard. See *Hilgendorf* v. *Denson*, 341 So.2d 549 (Fla. App. 1977).

5. Sta-Rite had been selling to a partnership known as Hamilton & Hood, consisting of partners Taylor and Hood. Taylor purchased the partnership business and became its sole proprietor in March 1968. This fact was communicated to the salesman-manager of Sta-Rite. Thereafter, Taylor bought on credit from Sta-Rite and executed a note as the sole maker. Sta-Rite now sues on that note, including Hood as a defendant. Is Hood liable? Discuss. See *Sta-Rite Industries, Inc.* v. *Taylor*, 16 Ariz. App. 230, 492 P.2d 726 (1972).

6. A newspaper was operated by a partnership consisting of Lyman and Alda Stoddard and their son Lyman, Jr. Alda died on January 3, 1963. Lyman, Sr., died on February 13, 1964, and his son John was appointed executor. Lyman, Jr., continued to operate the newspaper. John attempted unsuccessfully to persuade Lyman, Jr., to wind up the business and to sell the newspaper himself. In 1965, John sued to force a liquidation and accounting, and the case was settled on September 6, 1966, with Lyman, Jr., agreeing to be responsible for all debts arising after February 13, 1964. The business was in a weak condition and was soon discontinued. Plaintiff accountants had rendered services to the newspaper for years. They now seek to hold the estates of Lyman, Sr., and Alda liable for bills incurred after their deaths on the theory that these were proper "winding-up" expenses. Discuss. See *King* v. *Stoddard*, 28 Cal. App. 3d 708, 194 Cal. Rptr. 903 (1972).

7. V and S were equal partners in a two-person partnership that was established by purchasing the stock of a corporation. V had contributed $10,000 to the capital of the partnership that was used to pay part of the purchase price of the stock. The balance was paid out of subsequent profits. Neither partner contributed any other capital. In winding-up the partnership, the partners sold its only asset, the stock, for $21,474. There were no liabilities. The trial judge found that the $10,000 capital

contribution had been repaid to V shortly after sale of the stock. He then held V's 50% share of the $21,474 to be $10,737 and subtracted $10,000. Judgment for V in the amount of $737 was rendered. Did the trial judge rule correctly? See *Vassallo* v. *Sexauer*, 177 N.W.2d 470 (Mich. App. 1970).

8. In 1946, Donald joined his father William in a business that William had previously run as a sole proprietorship. William contributed $41,000 in cash, equipment, and inventory; Donald contributed nothing. Donald ran the business until his death in 1964. When William refused to distribute any of the $18,572 worth of partnership property remaining at Donald's death to Donald's estate, the estate sued. William claimed he was entitled to repayment of the entire $41,000 in capital contribution before there would be anything to distribute to the estate. Discuss. See *Petersen* v. *Petersen*, 284 Minn. 61, 169 N.W.2d 228 (1969).

6

LIMITED PARTNERSHIPS

INTRODUCTION

Unknown at common law, the limited partnership, a creature of statute, came to the United States through state laws as early as 1822. In recent years the limited partnership has gained unprecedented popularity as a form of business organization. Limited partnerships are now so significant in terms of numbers, size, and influence that they deserve at least a full chapter of discussion.

Characteristics

A limited partnership, defined in §1 of the Uniform Limited Partnership Act (ULPA) as a partnership composed of at least one general and at least one limited partner, is a blend of corporate and general partnership characteristics. Like a general partnership, a limited partnership has general partners with unlimited personal liability who control the business and receive partnership taxation. Like corporations, limited partnerships are creatures of statute, have centralized management (by general partners), and have investors (the limited partners) who have limited liability in that they can lose only their capital contributions and generally will not be personally liable for partnership debts.

Uses

The combination of partnership taxation and limited liability makes the limited partnership an attractive vehicle for investment. This is particularly so in enterprises that are likely to show losses in their early stages or that show tax losses despite positive cash flows due to deductions such as those for depreciation. These losses are passed through to the general and limited partners who, unlike corporate shareholders, can use the business's losses to offset income from other sources on their individual income tax forms. Wealthy individuals and individuals willing to invest in new, perhaps risky, ventures find the limited partnership especially attractive.

Limited partnerships have recently been quite popular as an investment vehicle in the fields of oil and gas, real estate, and research and development. They have also been used in an infinite variety of other enterprises, including motion pictures, orchards, cattle feedlots, amusement parks, and pecan groves.

No longer confined to relatively small enterprises involving primarily friends and acquaintances, many limited partnerships today are huge, involve thousands of limited partners whose interests are publicly traded, and resemble corporations more than general partnerships.

However, as noted in Chapter 1, the Tax Reform Act of 1986 will decrease the popularity of the limited partnership "tax shelter." After a phase-in period, "passive losses" generated by limited partnership interests can no longer be used by individuals to offset income from salary or portfolio (interest and dividends) income. Rather, "passive losses" can be used to offset only "passive income," such as that produced by other limited partnership interests. Thus, only "income producing" limited partnerships are likely to be enticing to the individual investor.

On the other hand, the 1986 reforms allow non-closely held corporations to use passive losses to offset their income from all sources. And closely held corporations (five or fewer shareholders own more than 50% of the stock) may offset passive business losses against active business income, though not against portfolio income. So, limited partnership tax shelters should still be attractive to corporate investors.

Governing Law

To encourage the formation of limited partnerships whose growth had been stunted by a hodgepodge of restrictive state laws, the National Conference of Commissioners on Uniform State Laws promulgated the Uniform Limited Partnership Act in 1916. The ULPA slowly gained acceptance over the years and by the early 1980s had been adopted by every state but Louisiana.

Experience and litigation over the years exposed a number of weaknesses, omissions, and ambiguities in the ULPA. Therefore, in 1976, a Revised Uniform Limited Partnership Act (RULPA) was promulgated. Although some questions about the tax implications of forming a limited partnership under RULPA slowed its initial acceptance, by late 1985 about 40 states had replaced their versions of ULPA with RULPA. In August 1985, the commissioners approved a superseding version of RULPA (1985 RULPA). Because no state has adopted the 1985 RULPA as of this writing and because its changes in the 1976 RULPA are comparatively minor, our discussion of the 1985 RULPA will be confined to the footnotes. The text will compare primarily RULPA, which is becoming the dominant model, and ULPA, under which most limited partnership litigation has taken place.

As an overview, note that RULPA's main differences from ULPA are, first, a tendency to draw more from corporation law—often treating limited partners much more like shareholders—and, second, an increased flexibility for the partners who are given greater latitude to vary RULPA provisions by agreement.[1]

Several of RULPA's changes, it has been suggested, were aimed at making limited partnerships more satisfactory as vehicles for large-scale tax shelters.[2] Indeed, in an attempt to lure businesses to their states, several legislatures have made wholesale changes even in RULPA. Although this chapter cannot discuss all the individual variations in the 50 states' limited partnership laws, anyone contemplating formation of a large limited partnership would do well to examine the largely unique laws of Delaware and California.

Whether a state has ULPA, RULPA, or some variation thereof, any legal questions that are not covered by those acts will be resolved by reference to the UPA and the common law.

FORMATION OF LIMITED PARTNERSHIPS

Filing Requirements

ULPA

Unlike a general partnership that can be formed simply through agreement of the partners, a limited partnership must be formed in compliance with certain statutory requirements. The limited partnership resembles a corporation in this regard.

Section 2 of ULPA provides that the persons forming a limited partnership shall sign and swear to a certificate that shall be filed in an office designated by the particular state. Some states have chosen the Secretary of State's office; most ULPA states have required filing in the county clerk's office of the county where the limited partnership's principal place of business is located.

The 14 items that must be set out in a §2 certificate include, among others: (1) the name of the partnership, (2) the character and principal location of its business, (3) the duration of its existence, and (4) the names, residences, and contributions of all partners. In addition, the certificate requires disclosure of any additional contributions the partners have agreed to make and under what conditions; the time agreed on (if any) for return of the limited partners' contributions; the share of profits and right to

---

[1] The 1985 RULPA continues both these liberalizing trends.

[2] J. Donnell, "An Analysis of the Revised Uniform Limited Partnership Act," *American Business Law Journal*, vol. 18 (1980), pp. 399, 401.

assign interests of each limited partner; the right to admit additional limited partners; the priorities given (if any) to some limited partners over others as to contributions or compensation; the right to continue the partnership upon the death, retirement, or insanity of the general partner; and the right (if given) of a limited partner to demand and receive property other than cash in return for the contributions.

This extensive disclosure ensures that privacy is not among the advantages of the limited partnership. It does, however, have the advantage of forcing the partners to consider some important aspects of the business before they form it. They will not blindly wander into a partnership without planning, on the basis of only a handshake as members of a general partnership might.

The purpose of this disclosure is to provide a location where those dealing with a limited partnership can go to discover with whom they are dealing, who has general liability and who does not, the initial financial structure of the limited partnership, and other such information. Note that unlike corporations, limited partnerships under ULPA need not inform those with whom they deal of their status as limited partnerships.

The written limited partnership agreement (which, it is hoped, exists) can be, but need not be, attached to the certificate. The agreement provides additional information for potential creditors, but its attachment may increase the frequency of amendments to the certificate, which must be kept updated and accurate.

RULPA

Section 201 of RULPA provides for the filing of a certificate of limited partnership requiring much the same information as §2 of ULPA.[3] RULPA has made some changes in the filing process, however.

First, RULPA follows corporate precedent in requiring that the name of the business shall contain without abbreviation the words "limited partnership" to inform creditors of the nature of the entity with which they are dealing. Section 102, drawing again on corporate practice, states that the name shall not contain any words or phrases that would mislead as to purpose or be "deceptively similar" to the name of an existing limited partnership or corporation.

ULPA's only requirement as to name was the provision of §5 that the name of the partnership should not, except under very limited circumstances, contain the surname of a limited partner. RULPA's §102 continues this prohibition. Both ULPA and RULPA punish violation by forfeiture of the limited partner's limited liability. This prevents paupers such as Prentice from obtaining credit for the firm of "Prentice & Rockefeller" without disclosing that Rockefeller is a limited partner and only Prentice's meager personal assets are available to creditors beyond those of the limited partnership itself.

---

[3] Section 201 of the 1985 RULPA dramatically increases the privacy available to limited partners by substantially decreasing the certificate disclosure requirements. Only the name of the limited partnership, the address of the office and name of the agent for service of process, the name and business address of each general partner, and the latest date upon which the limited partnership is to dissolve need be set forth. Limited partners need not be named and need not sign the certificate.

Second, RULPA eliminates the state option and establishes the Secretary of State's office in each state as the repository for limited partnership certificates. There is no provision for designating county offices as alternatives.

Third, RULPA requires in §104 appointment of a registered agent for purposes of service of process. The name and address of the agent are to be disclosed in the §201 certificate.

Consequences of Defective Formation

ULPA

Under ULPA, the limited partnership is formed if there is "substantial compliance in good faith" with the §2 filing requirement. In cases of defective filing, whether there is "substantial compliance" or "good faith" may determine whether the purported limited partners lose their limited liability status. Unfortunately, the courts have not been completely consistent in interpreting and applying these concepts.

One unsettled area is the definition of "substantial compliance." It is generally held, of course, that failure to file the certificate is not "substantial compliance" and will lead to limited partners being deemed general partners as to third parties. (As to other partners, limited partners may still be limited partners despite the failure to file the certificate if that was their intent.) Displaying a liberal approach, one court held that a delay of 49 days in filing a limited partnership certificate after it was signed constituted "substantial compliance" so that the limited partners did not become generally liable.[4] A stricter approach was taken in the following case.

WISNIEWSKI v. JOHNSON

223 Va. 141, 286 S.E.2d 223 (1982)

Wisniewski, Gearhart, and Walter and Olga Luchaka executed and recorded a certificate of limited partnership in an attempt to comply with Code §50–45, Virginia's enactment of ULPA's §2. Gearhart was to be the general partner and the others limited partners. The

certificate was signed and acknowledged by all the partners before a notary.

Thomas and Suzanne Johnson bought a house from the partnership in 1975. Later they brought this suit claiming breach of warranty. The trial court found for the Johnsons and held the pur-

[4] *Stowe* v. *Merrilees*, 44 P.2d 368 (Cal. App. 1935).

ported limited partners liable as general partners, ruling that since they had not sworn to the statements in the certificate, a limited partnership had not been formed.

The purported limited partners appealed.

STEPHENSON, JUSTICE:

The appellants argue that an acknowledgment is constructively the same as swearing to a document and in any case meets the "substantial compliance" test of §50–45(3). We cannot agree.

There is a marked difference between acknowledging a signature and signing a document under oath. An acknowledgment merely verifies that the person named executed the document in question (Code §55–118.3). By swearing to a document, on the other hand, one vouches that the contents of the writing are true. A person who swears falsely may be guilty of a felony (Code §18.2–434).

Support for our position is found in *Bergeson v. Life Insurance Corp. of America*, 170 F.Supp. 150 (D. Utah 1958), *rev'd on other grounds*, 265 F.2d 227 (10th Cir.), *cert. denied* 360 U.S. 932 (1959). Dealing with the issue before us, the court said:

In order for the liability of partners to be limited there must be substantial compliance with the statute providing for limited partnerships. . . . [The statute] requires that the certificate of partnership be signed and sworn to. This is not a mere formal requirement. There are good reasons why this statement should be sworn to, not least of which is to bring home to the signers the necessity of the certificate's being true and correct—[Id. at 158.]

In 1981, the General Assembly amended Code §50–45 to provide that the signers of the certificate should "acknowledge" rather than "swear to" it. In *Boyd v. Commonwealth*, 216 Va. 16, 20, 215 S.E.2d. 915, 918 (1975), we said: "[I]n the field of statutory construction, a presumption normally arises that a change in law was intended when new provisions are added to prior legislation by an amendatory act." The 1981 amendment strengthens our view that the oath requirement of §50–45 was not equivalent to an acknowledgment. We hold, therefore, that the appellants' failure to "swear to" the certificate was such a noncompliance with the requirements of Code §50–45 as to render the certificate ineffective for the creation of a limited partnership.

Affirmed.

Another area of disagreement concerns whether a third party should have to prove "reliance" before holding a limited partner liable as a general partner, even where no certificate was ever filed. Some courts have rejected a reliance requirement, holding that creditors have the "right to rely upon there being substantial compliance with [§2] before the protection of its provisions would be afforded to any member of the partnership." [5] However, an early Supreme Court case approved a reliance requirement,[6] as did the following case.

---

[5] *Tiburon National Bank* v. *Wagner*, 71 Cal. Rptr. 832 (Cal. App. 1968).
[6] *Giles* v. *Vette*, 263 U.S. 553 (1923).

GARRETT v. KOEPKE

569 S.W.2d 568 (Tex. Civ. App. 1978)

Appellants Garrett and Henson sold a motel to a limited partnership formed in February 1971 for the purpose of operating the motel. The partnership agreed to assume and pay installments on the lease of a sign for the motel. When payments were missed, Garrett and Henson sued.

The limited partnership agreement designated appellees as limited partners. However, neither the agreement nor the limited partnership certificate were ever filed as required by Texas' enactment of the ULPA, art. 6132a. On the other hand, Garrett testified in his deposition that he knew he was dealing with a limited partnership and understood the consequences of dealing with such an entity.

The trial judge granted summary judgment to appellees. Garrett and Henson appealed.

AKIN, JUSTICE:

Appellees admit that they had failed to file a certificate of limited partnership as required by Tex. Rev. Civ. Stat. Annotation art. 6132a (Vernon 1970). Appellants contend, therefore, that appellees are liable for the debt sued upon as general partners. We cannot agree with this contention. We see no logical reason to strip appellees of their limited liability under their partnership agreement merely because they failed to comply with art. 6132a. The purpose of the filing requirements under the act is to provide notice to third persons dealing with the partnership of the essential features of the partnership arrangement—*Hoefer* v. *Hall*, 75 N.M. 751, 411 P.2d 230 (1966); and *Tiburon National*

Bank v. *Wagner*, 265 Cal. App.2d 868, 71 Cal. Rptr. 832 (1968).

Since appellants knew that the entity with which they were dealing was a limited partnership, as well as the consequences of dealing with such an entity, they were in no way prejudiced by the failure to comply with the statute. We see no compelling policy reason here for holding that appellees became general partners by requiring technical compliance with these notice provisions. Indeed, such was not the intent of the legislature in enacting the statute; instead, its intent was to provide notice of limited liability of certain partners to third parties dealing with a partnership—*R. H. Sanders Corp.* v. *Haves*, 541 S.W.2d 262, 265 (Tex. Civ. App.—Dallas 1976, no writ). The nature and legal existence of a partnership does not depend upon any filing required by a statute—*Tracy* v. *Tuffly*, 134 U.S. 206 (1890). We hold, therefore, that where a party has knowledge that the entity with which he is dealing is a limited partnership, that status is not changed by failing to file under art. 6132a.

Appellants rely on *Lowe* v. *Arizona Power & Light Co.*, 5 Ariz. App. 385, 427 P.2d 366 (1967), and *Hoefer* v. *Hall*, supra, for the proposition that in order to obtain protection as a limited partner, there must be compliance with the statutory requirements. In *Lowe*, a certificate of limited partnership had been filed, but after the withdrawal of one of the general partners, the remaining partners executed and filed a certificate of partnership which did not indicate whether a general or limited partnership was intended. The court held that even though the certificate of partnership did not specify a general partnership, it did not refer back to the certificate of limited partnership nor indicate an amendment to it, and, therefore, the second certificate of partnership superseded the limited partnership certificate. Accordingly, that court held Lowe liable as a general partner. *Lowe* is distinguishable on the ground that plaintiffs there did not have actual notice that a limited partnership existed. Thus, we do not consider it controlling. *Hoefer* held that the failure to record a certificate of limited partnership did not preclude the existence of the partnership insofar as the parties to the agreement are concerned. Although *Hoefer* quotes the "rule" requiring compliance with the statute in order to have a limited partnership, that court arrived at the same conclusion as we have here where all parties had knowledge of the nature of the partnership. We do not agree, however, with *Hoefer* insofar as it states that compliance with the statute is necessary to have a limited partnership.

[*Affirmed.*]

Those seeking to form limited partnerships in ULPA states will do well to remember that not all courts are as lenient as the Texas court in *Garrett* v. *Koepke* regarding the filing requirements for forming a limited partnership. Note also that §11 of the ULPA, to be discussed soon, can also provide a method of escaping general liability for limited partners whose certificate is not filed.

RULPA

Section 201 of RULPA continues ULPA's "substantial compliance" language, but eliminates the reference to "good faith." Regarding time for filing, however, there is no such thing as "substantial compliance." Because a major purpose of filing the certificate is to delineate when persons became general and limited partners, the filing of the certificate is apparently a prerequisite to limited partnership status.

False Statements

Another way a limited partner may forfeit limited liability is to sign a certificate containing a statement known to be false. The same result may occur when a limited partner fails to cancel or amend a previously signed certificate that he or she discovers later to contain false statements. Section 6 of ULPA provides that anyone who relies on the false statement and thereby suffers a loss is entitled to hold the limited partner individually liable.

Thus, in *Walraven* v. *Ramsay*,[7] a limited partner who signed a certificate knowing that certain land he had contributed to the partnership was not worth as much as the certificate indicated was held personally liable to a subsequent creditor.

RULPA §207 contains a similar reliance requirement, allowing recovery from any limited partner who knew, and any general partner who knew or should have known

---

[7] 55 N.W.2d 853 (Mich. 1953).

the statement to be false at the time it was executed.[8] The section also imposes liability on general partners who learn of a changed fact that makes the certificate inaccurate but fail to cancel or amend it.

Renunciation

A person who *erroneously* believes that he or she is a limited partner can avoid being treated as a general partner, according to ULPA's §11, "provided that on ascertaining the mistake he promptly renounces his interest in the profits of the business, or other compensation."

The promptness requirement means that an investor who learns in March that the §2 certificate has not been filed, but does not file a proper renunciation until the following September, is properly treated as a general partner.[9] A proper renunciation is described in the following case.

VOUDOURIS v. WALTER E. HELLER & CO.

560 S.W.2d 202 (Tex. Civ. App. 1977)

Plaintiff Walter E. Heller & Co. brought action on a sworn account against Nick Wayne Voudouris and Johnny Voudouris, d/b/a Carpet Gallery of Austin, Ltd. The plaintiff claimed Johnny, a supposed limited partner, should be treated as a general partner because no certificate of limited partnership had ever been filed.

The evidence showed that Nick wanted to start a carpet business, but could not get credit; that Johnny co-signed a promissory note as his capital contribution to the business; that a limited partnership agreement was drawn up naming Johnny as a limited partner with a 20% ownership interest; that Nick was supposed to file the limited partnership certificate but failed to do so; that Johnny took no part in the business and, in fact, knew very little about it; and that as soon as Johnny discovered that Nick was

not paying the business's bills, he secured a list of creditors from Nick and wrote all of them indicating that he had sold his interest to Nick and was no longer liable on any past or future indebtedness of the business. Johnny did repay the original promissory note that he had co-signed.

The trial court held Johnny Voudouris liable as a general partner to plaintiff. Johnny appealed.

COLEMAN, CHIEF JUSTICE:

The limited partnership agreement evidences the fact that Johnny Voudouris agreed to become a limited partner and contributed $9,500.00 to the capital of the business. It further recites that Nick Voudouris is a general partner. While

---

[8] Because §204 of the 1985 RULPA eliminates the requirement that limited partners sign the certificate or its amendments, they would not be potentially liable for false statements in those documents.

[9] *Vidricksen* v. *Grover*, 363 F.2d 372 (9th Cir. 1966).

these recitations are not established to the extent that they cannot be contradicted by other evidence, there is no other evidence to contradict these recitations. While the limited partnership agreement never became effective according to its terms because it was never filed with the Secretary of State, it does illuminate the intent of the parties. Whether a particular association is in fact a partnership depends largely on the intention or understanding of the parties involved. They must ordinarily agree and intend to become partners—*Luling Oil & Gas Co.* v. *Humble Oil & Refining Co.*, 144 Tex. 475, 191 S.W.2d 716 (1945).

An indication of the interpretation to be given [§11 of the ULPA] is found in *United States* v. *Coson*, 286 F.2d 453 (9th Cir. 1961). The court quoted from *Giles* v. *Vette*, 263 U.S. 553, where the Supreme Court said:

> Section 11 is broad and highly remedial. The existence of a partnership—limited or general—is not essential in order that it shall apply. The language is comprehensive, and covers all cases where one has contributed to the capital of a business conducted by a partnership or person erroneously believing that he is a limited partner. It ought to be construed liberally, and with appropriate regard for the legislative purpose to relieve from the strictness of the earliest statutes and decisions.

In a footnote, the court said:

> Of course an intent to become a general partner may be inferred from conduct. In this case no such conduct was shown. Coulson had nothing to do with management of Moulin Rouge, or with its organization. The only conduct shown on his part was consistent solely with his belief that he was dealing with a limited partnership. The ancient rule that failure to comply with statutory provisions renders the association a general partnership, vanished with the enactment of Uniform Limited Partnership Act. As stated in the Commissioners' note on the act: [''']Third: The limited partner not being in any sense a principal in the business, failure to comply with the requirements of the

act in respect to the certificate, while it may result in the nonformation of an association, does not make him a partner or liable as such. The exact nature of his liability in such cases is set forth in Section 11.['']

The 9th Circuit went on to hold that it was not important whether the renunciation operated to relieve Coson from liability *ab initio* or whether it operated to compel a finding that Coson was not a general partner at any time, first, because he never had the necessary intent to join a partnership in that capacity and, second, because his renunciation under Section 11 was fully effective.

Here we find that the limited partnership failed to become effective because it was not filed with the Secretary of State. There is testimony from the defendant that immediately upon learning that the partnership agreement had not been filed he renounced the partnership. This testimony is supported by documentary evidence.

. . .

Nick Voudouris furnished a copy of Johnny Voudouris's financial statement to the plaintiff. The letter which Johnny Voudouris sent to Walter E. Heller & Company informing them that he had sold his interest and limited partnership to Nick Voudouris was mailed in an envelope bearing the logo of Carpet Gallery of Austin. Johnny Voudouris executed an instrument purporting to establish a limited partnership with Nick Voudouris under the name Carpet Gallery of Austin. He co-signed a note with Nick Voudouris to secure funds for the business. These are the only circumstances in evidence which tend to support the finding of the trial court that Johnny Voudouris was a general partner with Nick Voudouris in the business. The failure to file the limited partnership agreement with the Secretary of State did not result in the formation of a general partnership. It was stipulated that there was no basis for a finding of partnership by estoppel. The remaining circumstances are legally insufficient as a basis for a finding that the formation of a general partnership between Johnny and Nick Voudouris was intended by the partners—*Giles* v. *Vette*, supra; *United States* v. *Coson*, supra; and *J. C. Wattenbarger & Sons* v. *Sanders*, 216 Cal. App.2d 495, 30 Cal. Rptr. 910 (5th Dist. Cal. 1963).

Appellant's testimony that he intended to en-

ter a limited partnership, took no part in the management of the enterprise, and gave up his interest therein soon after his discovery that the partnership agreement had never been filed with the Secretary of State was clear and positive. [Section 11 of the UPA] prevents the imposition of liability on Johnny Voudouris for the debts of Carpet Gallery of Austin, Ltd.

Reversed.

RUPLA's §304 is similar to ULPA's §11, providing that a person who erroneously and in good faith believes he is a limited partner will not have general liability if, on ascertaining the mistake, he amends the certificate or "withdraws from future equity participation in the enterprise." [10] RULPA also expressly limits liability to those creditors who transacted business with the enterprise before the limited partner withdrew or amended while believing in good faith that the person was a general partner at the time of the transaction.

A renouncing partner need not, under ULPA or RULPA, return benefits received from the partnership (such as profits) before the mistake was discovered. [11] And under RULPA a renouncing partner who withdraws is entitled to return of capital.

CONTROL

One of the basic concepts underlying the limited partnership is that investors (limited partners) can obtain limited liability in exchange for forfeiting their right to *control* the enterprise. Section 7 of ULPA specifically states: "A limited partner shall not be liable as a general partner unless, in addition to the exercise of his rights and powers as a limited partner, he takes part in the control of the business." This statement presupposes, of course, that the limited partner has not allowed his or her surname to appear in the firm name, that the limited partnership certificate has been filed, that the limited partner knew of no erroneous statements therein, and that the limited partner has not held himself or herself out to be a general partner so as to become one by estoppel under UPA §16.

---

[10] §304 of 1985 RULPA specifies that withdrawal is effected "by executing and filing in the office of the Secretary of State a certificate declaring withdrawal under this section."

[11] *Gilman Paint & Varnish Co.* v. *Legum*, 80 A.2d 906 (Md. App. 1951).

ULPA

The most controversial part of ULPA has been §7 and the attendant question of under what circumstances a limited partner should be deemed to have exercised "control" and under what further circumstances general liability should follow.

Courts have refused to hold limited partners generally liable on grounds they had exercised "control" when they merely served as employees of the limited partnership under the supervision and control of the general partner,[12] participated in the choice of key employees where their nominations were subject to the general partner's veto,[13] rendered advice and consultation to the general partners, especially in times of financial difficulty,[14] brought a derivative action on the limited partnership's behalf,[15] or indicated their desires regarding a partnership decision.[16]

Despite this flexibility, there are limits beyond which limited partners cannot go without being deemed to have exercised the forbidden "control." One case suggested that control is exercised where the limited partners have "decision-making authority that may not be checked or nullified by the general partner." [17] An example of prohibited conduct appears in the following case.

HOLZMAN v. DE ESCAMILLA

86 Cal. App.2d 858, 195 P.2d 833 (1948)

In 1943, Hacienda Farms, Ltd., was organized as a limited partnership with de Escamilla as the general partner and Russell and Andrews as the limited partners. After the partnership went into bankruptcy less than a year later, Holzman was appointed as trustee in bankruptcy. Holzman brought this action seeking a judicial declaration that Russell and Andrews had taken part in control of the business and should therefore be held liable as general partners to partnership creditors.

The trial judge ruled for Holzman. Russell and Andrews appealed.

MARKS, JUSTICE:

De Escamilla was raising beans on farmlands near Escondido at the time the partnership was formed. The partnership continued raising vegetable and truck crops which were marketed principally through a produce concern controlled by Andrews.

---

[12] *Grainger v. Antoyan*, 313 P.2d 848 (Cal. 1957).

[13] *Plasteel Products Corp.* v. *Helman*, 271 F.2d 354 (1st Cir. 1959).

[14] *Trans-Am Builders, Inc.* v. *Woods Mill, Ltd.*, 210 S.E.2d 866 (Ga. App. 1974).

[15] *Smith* v. *Bader*, 458 F.Supp. 1184 (S.D. N.Y. 1978).

[16] *Stone Mountain Properties*, Ltd. v. *Helmer*, 229 S.E.2d 779 (Ga. App. 1976).

[17] *Gast* v. *Petsinger*, 323 A.2d 371 (Pa. Super. 1971).

The record shows the following testimony of de Escamilla:

A. We put in some tomatoes.
Q. Did you have a conversation or conversations with Mr. Andrews or Mr. Russell before planting the tomatoes?
A. We always conferred and agreed as to what crops we would put in. . . .
Q. Who determined that it was advisable to plant watermelons?
A. Mr. Andrews. . . .
Q. Who determined that string beans should be planted?
A. All of us. There was never any planting done—except the first crop that was put into the partnership as an asset by myself, there was never any crop that was planted or contemplated in planting that wasn't thoroughly discussed and agreed upon by the three of us, particularly Andrews and myself.

De Escamilla further testified that Russell and Andrews came to the farms about twice a week and consulted about the crops to be planted. He did not want to plant peppers or eggplant because, as he said, "I don't like that country for peppers or eggplant; no sir," but he was overruled and those crops were planted. The same is true of the watermelons.

Shortly before October 15, 1943, Andrews and Russell requested de Escamilla to resign as manager, which he did, and Harry Miller was appointed in his place.

Hacienda Farms, Ltd., maintained two bank accounts, one in a San Diego bank and another in an Escondido bank. It was provided that checks could be drawn on the signatures of any two of the three partners. It is stated in plaintiff's brief, without any contradiction (the checks are not before us), that money was withdrawn on 20 checks signed by Russell and Andrews and that all other checks except 3 bore the signature of de Escamilla, the general partner, and one of the other defendants. The general partner had no power to withdraw money without the signature of one of the limited partners.

Section 2483 of the Civil Code provides as follows: "A limited partner shall not become liable as a general partner, unless, in addition to the exercise of his rights and powers as a limited partner, he takes part in the control of the business."

The foregoing illustrations sufficiently show that Russell and Andrews both took "part in the control of the business." The manner of withdrawing money from the bank accounts is particularly illuminating. The two men had absolute power to withdraw all the partnership funds in the banks without the knowledge or consent of the general partner. Either Russell or Andrews could take control of the business from de Escamilla by refusing to sign checks for bills contracted by him and thus limit his activities in the management of the business. They required him to resign as manager and selected his successor. They were active in dictating the crops to be planted, some of them against the wishes of de Escamilla. This clearly shows they took part in the control of the business of the partnership and thus became liable as general partners.

Affirmed.

Note that the *Holzman* decision did not address the issue of whether creditors should be required to prove that they *relied* on the limited partners as being general partners before they can hold the purported limited partners personally liable. The courts are divided on whether reliance should be required in such a case, just as they are in disagreement as to whether under ULPA, limited partners should be allowed to control a corporation that is organized to be the limited partnership's sole general partner. Both issues are addressed in the following case.

WESTERN CAMPS, INC. v. RIVERWAY RANCH ENTERPRISES

138 Cal. Rptr. 918 (Cal. App. 1977)

Plaintiff Western Camps, Inc., sued defendants Riverway Ranch Enterprises, a limited partnership, and Wallace McCoy, one of its limited partners, seeking damages for defendant's alleged wrongful termination of their sublease of real property to plaintiff. The trial court found Riverway liable, and found McCoy, an officer and director of CRC—a corporation and Riverway's sole general partner—generally liable.

McCoy appeals claiming, inter alia, *that he should not be held liable as a general partner.*

Dunn, Judge:

A limited partner is not bound by the obligations of the limited partnership, and is not liable as a general partner, unless he takes part in the control of the partnership business. The trial court found that at the time the sublease was negotiated, McCoy, in addition to being a limited partner, also was one of the three officers, directors, and shareholders of CRC, the corporate general partner. The court further found that McCoy exercised complete management and control in the negotiations for the sublease and in its termination, and acted without the advice or guidance of the other officers and directors of CRC. Pointing out that a corporation may be a general partner in a limited partnership (Corp. Code, §§ 15002, 15501) and that a corporation may act only through its agents (*Gardner*

v. *Jonathan Club* (1950) 35 Cal.2d 343, 348 [217 P.2d 961]), McCoy argues that he is not liable as a general partner because, in the transactions regarding the sublease, he was acting in his capacity as agent of the corporate general partner, not in his capacity as a limited partner. The question thus presented is whether a limited partner in a limited partnership becomes liable as a general partner if he takes part in the control of the partnership business while acting as an agent of the corporation which is the sole general partner of the limited partnership.

This question apparently has not been considered in California. In two other jurisdictions, conflicting conclusions have been reached on the point. In *Delaney* v. *Fidelity Lease Limited* (Tex. 1975) 526 S.W.2d 543, 545, it was held that "the personal liability, which attaches to a limited partner when 'he takes part in the control and management of the business,' cannot be evaded merely by acting through a corporation." The court rejected the argument that, for the purpose of fixing personal liability upon a limited partner, the "control" test should be coupled with a determination of whether the limited partner held himself out as being a general partner having personal liability to the extent that the third party (or plaintiff) relied upon the limited partner's general liability. In this regard, the opinion pointed out that Section 7 of the Uniform Limited Partnership Act simply provides that a limited partner who takes part in the control of the business subjects himself to personal liability as a general partner and does not mention any requirement of reliance on the part of the party attempting to hold the limited partner personally liable. The court further expressed concern that the statutory requirement of at least one general partner with general liability in a limited partnership could be circumvented by limited partners operating the partnership through a corporation with minimum capitalization and, therefore, with limited liability.

In *Frigidaire Sales Corp.* v. *Union Properties, Inc.* (1976) 14 Wn.App. 634 (544 P.2d 781), the court rejected the reasoning of the *Delaney* case and concluded that the dominant consideration in determining the personal liability of a limited partner is reliance by the third party, not control by the limited partner. It was there stated that

> If a corporate general partner in a limited partnership is organized without sufficient capital so that it was foreseeable that it would not have sufficient assets to meet its obligations, the corporate entity could be disregarded to avoid injustice. We find no substantive difference between the creditor who does business with a corporation that is the general partner in a limited partnership and a creditor who simply does business with a corporation. In the absence of fraud or other inequitable conduct, the corporate entity should be respected. . . . Here, there was an overt intention to regard the corporate entity and no showing of the violation of any duty owing to the creditor. The creditor dealt with the corporate general partner in full awareness of the corporate status of the general partner. There is no showing of any fraud, wrong, or injustice perpetrated upon the creditor, merely that [Section 7 of the Uniform Limited Partnership Act] provides that a limited partner becomes liable as a general partner if he takes part in the control of the business. When these are the circumstances, we hold that the corporate entity should be upheld rather than the statute applied blindly with no inquiry as to the purpose it seeks to achieve. . . .

A limited partner is made liable as a general partner when he participates in the "control" of the business in order to protect third parties from dealing with the partnership under the mistaken assumption that the limited partner is a general partner with general liability. . . . A third party dealing with a corporation must reasonably rely on the solvency of the corporate entity. It makes little difference if the corporation is or is not the general partner in a limited partnership. In either instance, the third party cannot justifiably rely on the solvency of the individuals who own the corporation.

We agree with the views expressed in the *Frigidaire* case, and accordingly apply the principles there stated to the facts in the instant case. Such facts are: before the sublease was negotiated, [plaintiff's president] Oken was aware of the corporate capacity of CRC, the general partner, and he knew that McCoy was one of its "principals." In June or July 1970, Oken asked Dick Browne, then president of CRC, who would be representing CRC in its negotiations with plaintiff regarding the sublease. Browne replied that McCoy would be "making the decisions." McCoy signed the sublease on behalf of Riverway, adding after his signature the words "for CRC." Moreover, the trial court found, as a fact, that "CRC was organized in good faith and had an adequate capitalization necessary to liquidate its indebtedness." Under these circumstances, no fraud or injustice to plaintiff results from respecting the corporate entity of the general partner. We hold, therefore, that CRC, the corporate general partner, is solely liable for the obligations of the limited partnership under the sublease and that McCoy, a limited partner, has no personal liability for such obligations.

The judgment against defendant Riverway is affirmed. The judgment against defendant McCoy is reversed.

The reliance requirement can be criticized because it would theoretically allow a limited partner who stays in the background to control completely a limited partnership's every move, yet escape general liability because creditors would be unaware of his role. Nonetheless, the trend in ULPA states appears to be generally, though far from unanimously, in favor of imposing a reliance requirement and allowing limited partners to exert some control through corporate general partners.

RULPA

Section 303, RULPA's "control" provision, clarifies a little of ULPA's ambiguity. One change made in §303 is provision of a "safe harbor"—a nonexclusive listing of acts that are deemed not to be participating in control of the partnership. Thus, without forfeiting limited liability, a limited partner may (1) be a contractor, agent, or employee of the limited partnership or of a general partner; (2) consult with and advise general partners; (3) act as a surety for limited partnership loans; (4) approve or disapprove an amendment to the partnership agreement; or (5) vote on any of the following matters: (a) dissolution and winding-up, (b) sale or other transfer of all or substantially all of the partnership assets, (c) incurrence of indebtedness other than in the ordinary course of business, (d) a change in the nature of the business, or (e) removal of a general partner.[18]

For the limited partner who sails beyond the safe harbor, §303 establishes two tiers of liability. If the limited partner's exercise of control is "not substantially the same as the exercise of the powers of a general partner," his general liability will run only "to persons who transact business with the limited partnership with actual knowledge of his participation in control."

On the other hand, if the control exercised by the limited partner *is* substantially the same as that exercised by a general partner, then there is no actual knowledge or reliance predicate to general liability. This should prevent limited partners from controlling the partnership from behind the scenes and yet escaping liability.[19]

---

[18] §303(a) of the 1985 RULPA substantially expands this safe harbor by additionally providing that a limited partner does not take part in control solely by guaranteeing or assuming specific obligations of the limited partnership; by taking action to bring a derivative suit on the limited partnership's behalf; by requesting or attending a meeting of partners; by winding up the limited partnership pursuant to §803; by exercising rights or powers permitted limited partners in the act but not specifically listed in §303; or by voting as to admission or removal of a limited partner, as to a transaction involving a conflict of interest between a general partner and the limited partnership or the limited partners, as to an amendment to the partnership agreement or certificate, or as to matters related to the business of the limited partnership not otherwise enumerated that the partnership agreement states in writing may be subject to the approval or disapproval of limited partners. This last phrase is a dramatic extension.

[19] The 1985 RULPA eliminates this double tier, providing simply that a limited partner who participates in control "is liable only to persons who transact business with the limited partnership reasonably believing, based upon the limited partner's conduct, that the limited partner is a general partner."

RULPA, CORPORATE GENERAL PARTNERS, AND TAXATION ISSUES

Consistent with most ULPA jurisdictions, RULPA §101 allows corporations to be general partners, even the sole general partner. As we have seen before, this gives the limited partner an opportunity to control the limited partnership by controlling the sole general partner and yet retain limited liability by remaining a limited partner and hiding behind the corporate veil of the general partner.

Limited partnership control can also be exercised under the provisions of §303 that allow limited partners, without being deemed to exercise control, to remove the general partner. Arguably, this provision allows limited partners to have the general partner serve at their pleasure.

These provisions slowed initial adoption of RULPA because they threatened a primary benefit of the limited partnership form of organization—partnership taxation. Initially the Internal Revenue Service hesitated to allow limited partnerships organized under RULPA to be taxed as general partnerships. However, with some restrictions,[20] the IRS has agreed to tax RULPA limited partnerships as partnerships, even where the sole general partners are corporations.

Notwithstanding existing IRS rules, some have suggested that modern large, publicly traded limited partnerships so resemble corporations that all limited partnerships with over 100 partners should be taxed as corporations. Supporters of this reform fear that huge multibillion-dollar corporations will liquidate and re-form as limited partnerships for tax advantages. Opponents note that this has not happened and claim that limited partnerships are not a "tax dodge" but an innovative method of attracting capital to risky ventures.[21] In 1986 Congress considered this type of change, but did not enact it.

RIGHTS AND RESPONSIBILITIES OF LIMITED PARTNERS

In addition to the right of limited liability and rights upon dissolution, which will be discussed later, limited partners have several important rights and some attendant responsibilities.

Control and Approval

The limited partners, as discussed, have substantial rights of control and approval under both §7 of ULPA and §303 of RULPA. In addition to what has specifically been mentioned, §2 of ULPA requires a limited partner to sign the limited partnership certificate and its amendments. However, this provision is frequently circumvented by the execution of

---

[20] Note, "Piercing the Veil of the Corporate General Partner in the Hybrid Limited Partnership," *Suffolk University Law Review*, Vol. 17 (1983), p. 949.

[21] See "Hill Effort Begun on Tax Loopholes for Partnership," *Legal Times of Washington*, October 31, 1983, p. 1.

powers of attorney that authorize the general partner to sign these documents on the limited partner's behalf. RULPA's provisions are similar.[22]

Also, §9 of ULPA lists certain "extraordinary" acts that the general partners are forbidden to do without the specific written consent or ratification of all the limited partners, including doing any act contravening the certificate or making it impossible to carry on partnership business; confessing a judgment; possessing partnership property or assigning rights in it for other than a partnership purpose; admitting a person as a general partner; admitting a person as a limited partner; or continuing the partnership business after death, retirement, or insanity of a general partner unless the right to do so is given by the certificate. RULPA eliminates the unanimity requirement of §9(1) of ULPA, thereby facilitating the practical operation of large, publicly traded limited partnerships.

Informational Rights

Section 10 of ULPA gives the limited partner the same rights as a general partner to inspect and copy partnership books, to have those books kept at the principal place of business, to demand full and true information from the general partner at all times, and to demand a formal accounting whenever "circumstances render it just and reasonable." Sections 105 and 305 of RULPA are similar, but are even more specific about the types of records that must be kept and made available to limited partners.

Access to Courts

As noted earlier, although ULPA does not specifically provide for it, many courts have allowed limited partners to file derivative actions on behalf of the limited partnership when the general partners refused to act. RULPA §§1001–1004 specifically grant the derivative action right to limited partners and spell out in detail the prerequisites for its use.

Profits and Return of Capital

Of course limited partners have the right to share in profits in accordance with the provisions of the certificate that may or may not subordinate some limited partners' rights to those of other limited partners. If for some reason there were no agreement, resort would be had to the UPA, and profits would be split equally.

Section 16 of ULPA also entitles a limited partner to return of his or her capital contribution on the date established in the certificate or upon dissolution, subject to payment of creditors. If the certificate does not provide a date for return or dissolution, a limited partner may make a written demand for return of capital and the partnership must meet that demand within six months.

---

[22] The 1985 RULPA eliminates the requirement that limited partners sign the certificate or its amendments.

RULPA also provides for the sharing of profits and losses as agreed in the partnership agreement. In the event of no provision, §503 states that profits and losses will be shared on the basis of contributions paid and not returned. To the apparent detriment of third parties, §606 gives creditor status to partners whenever they are owed a distribution under the partnership agreement and do not receive it.

RULPA §501 gives the right to make a capital contribution in the form of a promissory note or promise of future services. ULPA's §4 had required that a contribution consist of cash or services already performed.

Capital Contribution

The primary responsibility of a limited partner is to make the agreed capital contribution. If a limited partner does not pay as agreed, an obligation arises under §17 of ULPA that may be enforced by either the partnership or unpaid creditors. Similarly, if a limited partner receives repayment of a capital contribution, a contingent liability arises. If at some later point partnership creditors go unpaid, the limited partner is liable to the partnership under ULPA §17(4) "for any sum, not in excess of such return with interest, necessary to discharge its liabilities to all creditors who extended credit or whose claims arose before such return."

RULPA §§502 and 608 are similar, though not identical.[23]

GENERAL PARTNERS' RIGHTS AND RESPONSIBILITIES

Rights and Powers

Under both ULPA and RULPA, the rights and powers of a general partner are similar to the rights and powers of partners of a general partnership under the UPA.

General partners have the right to make the day-to-day decisions necessary to operate the partnership, though, as noted, there are certain "extraordinary" acts that cannot be performed without unanimous limited partner consent or ratification, such as confessing a judgment or admitting a general partner. Large limited partnerships evade the practical difficulties presented by such a unanimity requirement by providing in the partnership agreement—which all limited partners must sign—that consent of a certain percentage of limited partners (e.g., 51%) will be deemed to be the consent of all where these "extraordinary" matters are concerned.

The general partner's "scope of authority" is established in the same manner in a limited partnership as in a general partnership.

Note that under §12 of ULPA and §404 of RULPA, a person may simultaneously be both a general and a limited partner. Therefore, though a general partner will continue

---

[23] §502 of the 1985 RULPA adds that a promise to make a contribution "is not enforceable unless set out in a *writing* signed by the limited partner."

to have unlimited liability, he or she can be treated as a limited partner for purposes of a partnership contribution made in the capacity of a limited partner.

Duties of General Partners

In addition to the duties attendant to general liability, general partners have all the other duties of partners in a general partnership. Most important among these is the fiduciary duty, which, if anything, is heightened by the necessarily passive role of the limited partners.[24]

General partners are liable to limited partners for losses caused by their breach of the duty of due care, and the business judgment defense accorded corporate directors has been held unavailable to them.[25]

ASSIGNMENTS

ULPA

One of the attractive features of a limited partnership is the relatively free transferability of the limited partnership interest. With proper planning, such interests may even be publicly offered and traded, just like corporate stock.

Section 19(1) of ULPA states that a limited partnership interest, which is personal property, is assignable. The assignor remains liable for unpaid contributions, returned contributions, and any false statements in the certificate. A simple assignee receives only the right to share in profits, losses (which the IRS allows to be assigned for tax purposes), and return of capital contributions. No other rights, such as informational rights, go to the mere assignee.

However, the assignee may become a "substitute limited partner" if all other partners consent, or if the assignor is empowered by the certificate to make the assignment without the consent of others. A substitute limited partner receives all the rights of the other limited partners and, at the same time, assumes all the assignee's liabilities except those that were unknown and could not have been detected by an examination of the certificate.

The assignee becomes a substitute limited partner effective when the certificate is amended to reflect the change.

Most publicly traded limited partnerships have very specific language in their partnership agreements governing assignment rights and procedures. Approval of the general partner is frequently a prerequisite. The agreement may also place restrictions on transferability to meet tax or securities exemption requirements.

Maryland's version of ULPA controls the outcome of the next case.

---

[24] *Dixon* v. *Trinity Joint Venture*, 431 A.2d 1364 (Md. App. 1981).

[25] *Roper* v. *Thomas*, 298 S.E.2d 424 (N.C. App. 1981). Compare *Wyler* v. *Feuer*, 85 Cal. App. 3d 392, 149 Cal. Rptr. 626 (1978) (allowing limited partners a business judgment defense).

BANK OF BETHESDA v. KOCH

408 A.2d 767 (Md. App. 1979)

Between April 1, 1975, and November 24, 1976, defendant Koch assigned his 22% interest in Holly Hills Associates Limited Partnership to Vechery and Broderick in exchange for adequate consideration. Until the summer of 1976 when the partnership was notified of the assignments, none but the participants knew of them. Koch was indebted to the plaintiff Bank on April 1, 1975, on a $130,000 confessed judgment note. However, the Bank did not reduce its judgment to a charging order until after Koch had assigned all his rights in the partnership.

The trial court ruled against plaintiff Bank's attempt to charge the assigned interests with the assignor's debts, so the Bank appealed.

LOWE, JUDGE:

There should be noted here the distinction between an assignment of a limited partner's interest and a substitution of a limited partner. The distinction is implicit in [§19(3) of the ULPA]. That section makes it clear that a limited partner's interest is assignable, but unless he becomes a substitute limited partner "he is only entitled to receive the share of the profits or other compensation by way of income or the return of his contribution, to which his assignor would otherwise be entitled." An assignee, to become a limited partner, must first obtain the consent of all the other members of the limited partnership, unless the limited partnership certificate authorizes substitution. However, in either case, the assignee will not secure the rights of a limited partner until the original certificate is appropriately amended to indicate the substitution.

Implicit is a significant feature of limited partnerships, that is, that a mere assignment of partnership interests need not be recorded or notice given publicly or to anyone other than the participants. It is a transaction strictly between assignee and assignor, questionable by others only as to bona fides of the transaction if and when subsequently disclosed. It may very well be that it is this facility of concealment of fiduciary interests which makes limited partnerships so attractive to those who not only wish to limit their liability in investing, but prefer anonymity in doing so.

Secrecy was not necessarily sought in this case, however, but neither were the assignments publicized, perhaps because none of us desire to advertise financial adversity. Koch and his wife had become delinquent in paying the $120,262.50 balance on their note to the Bank, and on January 12, 1976, a judgment was confessed against them in the Bank's favor and, over a year and a half later on September 29, 1977, the Bank sought to satisfy its judgment by obtaining the charging order against what it thought was Koch's interest in the Holly Hills Associates Limited Partnership, and an order to sell that interest. But there was no such interest to sell, and this first became apparent when Vechery and Broderick were permitted to intervene and move to set aside the charging order and the order to sell. [The trial judge], finding Koch had previously assigned his pecuniary interest in Holly Hills, vacated and set aside the order to charge and to sell the limited partnership interest of Koch to satisfy the Bank's judgment debt.

The initial questions raised by the Bank here are predicated upon our deciding "whether a statutory charging order . . . is a form of judicial assignment or a form of attachment.'' Assuming we decide the former, the Bank then contends that its ''assignment'' should be treated as a commercial transaction which would provide priority as to some of the actual assignments by reason of its prior notice.

Neither alternative description is necessary nor particularly desirable. A charging order is nothing more than a legislative means of providing a creditor some means of getting at a debtor's ill-defined interest in a statutory bastard, surnamed ''partnership,'' but corporately protecting participants by limiting their liability as are corporate shareholders. While limited partnerships were not created to assist creditors, but to enable persons to invest their money without being liable for partnership debts for more than their contribution, *Gilman Paint & Varnish Co.* v. *Legum*, 197 Md. 665, 670, 80 A.2d 906 (1951), neither were they intended to protect a partner's interest in the partnership against legitimate personal creditors. Since the statutory offspring is unique, the rights of creditors against partnerships were necessarily peculiar as well; hence, the charging order—which like the limited partner to which it applies—is neither fish nor fowl. It is neither an assignment nor an attachment. But, like many such questionable offspring, it resembles both progenitors in some of their characteristics.

The [charging] order serves only the precise purpose statutorily indicated, that is, to ''charge'' an interest with a debt. Since appellant does not question the bona fides of the prior assignments, there was no interest in Holly Hills held by Koch to be ''charged'' with the debt. We decline appellant's invitation to expand a limited statutory right given creditors by judicial baptism with a pseudonym.

Affirmed.

RULPA

RULPA's assignment procedures are quite similar to ULPA's. Although the term ''substitute limited partner'' is eliminated by RULPA, the concept continues in §§301 and 304.

DISSOLUTION AND DISTRIBUTION

Causes of Dissolution

Much of the law regarding dissolution, its causes and effects, is the same for limited partnerships as it is for general partnerships. This is illustrated by the causes of dissolution of a limited partnership, which include death, retirement or insanity of a *general* partner, expiration of the agreed term, and court decree. However, the death, insanity, or bankruptcy of a *limited* partner will not cause dissolution.

One other change is the provision of §16(4) of ULPA that a limited partner can force dissolution when (1) he or she rightfully but unsuccessfully demands return of his or her capital or (2) other liabilities of the partnership are unpaid or partnership property is insufficient for their repayment.

RULPA provides in §§801 and 802 for dissolution (1) at the time or upon the happening of events specified in the certificate, (2) by written consent of all partners, (3) by judicial order, which may be issued whenever it is not reasonably practicable to carry on the business in conformity with the partnership agreement, and (4) upon an "event of withdrawal" of a general partner unless there are other general partners that the certificate allows to carry on the business. "Events of withdrawal" are defined in §402 and include such things as death, adjudication of incompetency, adjudication of bankruptcy, and the like.

Winding-up

ULPA does not have detailed provisions regarding the winding-up process. Generally, the winding-up of a limited partnership will resemble the winding-up of a general partnership because UPA provisions control where ULPA is silent.

RULPA provides in §803 that winding-up should be done by general partners who have not wrongfully dissolved the partnership or, if none, by the limited partners.

If, after dissolution, limited partners continue the business without winding-up, they may find themselves liable as general partners.[26]

Distribution of Assets

The following discussion outlines the distribution of limited partnership assets upon dissolution.

LIMITED PARTNERSHIPS: LEGAL AND BUSINESS ASPECTS OF ORGANIZATION, OPERATION, AND DISSOLUTION*

Bruce Lane and David Falk

(Bureau of National Affairs 1981)

The U.L.P.A. creates an order of priority in which the assets of a limited partnership are to be distributed upon its dissolution, as follows:

(1) to the creditors of the partnership. Limited partners may be treated as third-party creditors to the extent they have extended credit to the partnership, but general partners are specifically denied treatment as third-party creditors.
(2) to the limited partners with respect to their share of accumulated profits and then the return of their earlier partnership capital contributions.
(3) to the general partners, first, for their claims against the partnership as creditors, second, for their share of accumulated profits, and, third, for the return of their partnership capital contributions.

---

[26] For example, *Downey* v. *Swan*, 454 N.Y.S.2d 895 (App. Div. 1982).

A court would not enforce a provision of a partnership agreement that subordinates the claims of nonconsenting creditors to payments to the general or limited partners. However, the two courts that have considered whether the partnership agreement can alter the statutory order of priority as between the general and limited partners have reached conflicting results [*Dycus* v. *Belco Industries, Inc.*, 569 P.2d 553 (Okla. App. 1977) (deviations not allowed); *Lanier* v. *Bowdoin*, 282 N.Y. 32, 24 N.E.2d 732 (1939) (deviations allowed)]. In practice, most partnership agreements do in some respect vary the statutory order of priority between the general and limited partners. Two frequent variations are allowing loans made by the general partners to the partnership to be repaid, with interest, before the capital contributions of the limited partners are repaid, and reducing the amount of capital contributions of the limited partners to be repaid at the time of dissolution by the sum of prior cash flow distributions to the limited partners.

The Revised U.L.P.A. maintains the first priority for creditors, but it also specifically provides that general and limited partners are to be treated equally with creditors with respect to all partnership debts to them except for those relating to the partners' rights to partnership cash distributions, return of capital, or residual distributions and except as otherwise provided by applicable bankruptcy or other creditors' rights laws. The Revised U.L.P.A. gives specific recognition to the partners' right to establish their own priority of distributions among themselves in the partnership agreement. If the partnership agreement is silent, the Revised U.L.P.A. provides that, after creditors are paid, the partnership must pay to both general and limited partners, including partners who may have withdrawn earlier, all unmet obligations to them that were created and were payable prior to the date of dissolution with respect to partnership profits or, in the case of the previously withdrawn partners, the return of their capital contributions to the partnership.

Finally, but again only if the partnership agreement does not establish a different priority, the Revised U.L.P.A. would distribute the remaining partnership assets to the general and limited partners, without priority between them,

*first, for the return of their capital contributions and,

*second, respecting their partnership interests in the proportions in which the partners share distributions.

If a limited partnership is dissolved and has insufficient assets to return the limited partners' capital contributions, they cannot proceed against the general partners for their unpaid capital contributions unless the partnership agreement specifically provides this right, according to the one decision on this question [*Lanier* v. *Bowdoin, supra*]. Most partnership agreements are drafted on the implicit assumption that the distributions made to the partners following dissolution will be made only to the extent of the partnership's available assets, and that the general partners will not be answerable to the limited partners for any shortfall in the latter's expectations, whether for the return of their capital or for profits. However, the general partners are likely to be held personally liable for the limited partners' claims as partnership creditors, as opposed to their claims as partnership members.

These principles are applied in the following ULPA case.

MATTER OF DUTCH INN OF ORLANDO, LTD.

2 B.R. 268 (Bankruptcy, M.D. Fla. 1980)

Dutch Inn of Orlando, Ltd. (the Debtor), was a limited partnership and now the debtor in this bankruptcy proceeding. The Debtor owes its former general partner, Dutch Inns of America, Inc., $530,000. Dutch Inns of America, in turn, owes American Financial Corporation $640,000. A proposed bankruptcy plan would take $500,000 of the Debtor's funds for pro-rata distribution to its unsecured creditors. The unsecured creditors would still hold unpaid debts exceeding $2 million.

American challenges the proposed plan, claiming, inter alia, *that it has rights as an assignee of Dutch Inns of America's rights against the Debtor.*

PASKAY, BANKRUPTCY JUDGE:

Even assuming, but not admitting that it was, in fact, an assignment made by Dutch Inns of America, Inc., to American of the indebtedness owed to it by this Debtor, it is clear that the assignment could not have granted a greater right than that which was possessed by the assignor itself. This leads us to the question of the precise legal status and character of the claim of Dutch Inns of America, a general partner against the partnership. The rights of the assignor, in this instance Dutch Inns of America, Inc., shall be, of course, determined with reference to the partnership laws of this State.

The Debtor is a limited partnership, and under the laws of this State is an entity, separate and apart from its partners. It is the sole owner of the partnership property originally brought into the partnership and subsequently acquired by purchase or otherwise. The general and limited partners of a Florida limited partnership have no property interest in or to any limited partnership property. Any estate in real property acquired in the name of the partnership is partnership property, and is not property of the partners. The property of a limited partnership constitutes a trust fund for the benefit of its creditors.

A partner's interest in the partnership is his share of the profits and surplus. It is personal property. This rule of law is applicable also to a general partner's interest in a limited partnership, which interest in the partnership is also deemed to be personal property.

Creditors of general partners of a limited partnership have no rights in or to the property of the limited partnership for satisfaction of their claims against such general partners. It is basic law that a creditor of a general partner can only reach a general partner's distributive share of the partnership's profits and surplus after all the limited partnership's debts have been paid. The general partner's creditor does not have any right to participate in any proceeds derived from the sale or liquidation of the limited partnership's property and assets, unless there is surplus or profit derived from the sale or liquidation of the limited partnership assets—*Shirk* v. *Caterbone*, 193 A.2d 664 (Pa. 1963).

Accordingly, the creditor of the general partner for a nonlimited partnership indebtedness, who holds the general partner's claim against the limited partnership, can only be paid out of any distribution available to general partner after all the partnership obligations have been satisfied in full. Under the laws of this State, upon dissolution of the limited partnership and the distribution of its assets, the rights of the general and limited partners are subordinate and inferior to the rights of creditors of the limited partnership.

Applying the foregoing principles to the facts of this case, it is evident that Dutch Inns of America, Inc.'s right against the Debtor was inferior to the claim of the creditors of the Debtor. Thus it has no right to assert its claim against the Debtor's properties [and] neither does American, its assignee, for the following reasons:

[T]he liquidation did not produce a surplus, which would be distributable under the laws of this State to Dutch Inns of America, and in turn there is none available to American, its assignee.

Thus, even assuming but not admitting that the claim filed by American can be allowed, no payment can be made on the claim under the partnership laws of this State until the general unsecured creditors of the Debtor are satisfied in full. Since all creditors of the Debtor are not paid in full, no claim of Dutch Inns of America, Inc., could be paid, and the fact that this claim is assigned and now held by American is of no consequence.

[The claim of American Financial Corporation is disallowed.]

FOREIGN LIMITED PARTNERSHIPS

As limited partnerships become larger and more sophisticated, officials are more concerned with how to deal with limited partnerships formed in other states but doing business in theirs. States have long registered foreign corporations, but ULPA had no such provision. Acting individually, and somewhat haphazardly, many states have enacted some type of foreign registration provision over the years. The lack of uniformity has caused major problems.

RULPA's increased acceptance may solve those problems. Section 902 requires a foreign limited partnership to register with the Secretary of State by filing a sworn application disclosing its name, the state and date of its formation, the general character of its business, the name and address of an agent for service of process, and a few other factors.

Section 907 denies unregistered foreign limited partnerships access to courts, but does not invalidate contracts they have entered into or deny limited partners their limited liability.[27]

MASTER LIMITED PARTNERSHIPS

Normally, limited partnership interests are purchased with the intent of holding them during the life of the enterprise. However, several times, this chapter has referred to the fact that limited partnership interests are "securities" and that they may be traded.

---

[27] The various state registration laws are surveyed in "State Registration Requirements for Limited Partnerships," *Practical Lawyer*, Vol. 30 (July 15, 1984), p. 45.

If the limited partnership agreement is properly drawn, limited partnership interests can have the liquidity of corporate stock.[28]

The most exciting recent development in limited partnerships is creation of Master Limited Partnerships (MLP), mostly in the oil and gas industry. This has been a very effective financing tool for promoters in this industry. The MLP is a hybrid investment form combining the tax advantages of limited partnerships with the marketability of corporate shares.

There are two basic types of MLPs. First is the "roll up," which consolidates existing limited partnerships into one "master" limited partnership. Usually, all the limited partnerships have already been under the control of the general partner. The second type is the "roll-out," in which a company spins off assets to shareholders who become limited partners in the entities that will now own those assets.

The possibility that the venture will have to comply with federal securities laws is a disadvantage, but did not prevent the sale of $5 billion in real estate partnership interests in 1984, or $850 million in oil and gas interests in the first nine months of 1985. By the end of 1985, there were 30 MLPs, mostly in oil and gas, with a combined market value of over $22 billion.[29] The 1986 tax changes are likely to somewhat dampen the activity in MLPs.

QUESTIONS AND PROBLEMS

1. Bentley, Shindler, and Reamer, using the name Eaglewood Associates, Ltd., bought land upon which the "Eaglewood Apartments" were to be built, made application to a savings and loan for an interim loan to finance acquisition of the land, and applied for a first mortgage construction loan secured by the property. Matz, a real estate broker, worked to secure equity financing, which he did by facilitating DSG, Inc.'s entry as a limited partner in Eaglewood Associates, Ltd. On July 19, 1977, Bentley, acting as managing partner of Eaglewood, signed a contract promising to pay Matz $60,000 for his efforts. At closing, Eaglewood refused to pay, claiming that it was not operating as a limited partnership on July 19, 1977, and proving that its limited partnership certificate was not filed with the State until December 5, 1977. Is this a good defense in a ULPA state? Discuss. See *Shindler* v. *Marr & Associates*, 695 S.W.2d 699 (Tex. App. 1985).

2. Mr. Laney bought a $1,000,000 piece of real estate and then sold it to a corporation he controlled that in turn sold it to a limited partnership. The corporation was the sole general partner; the limited partners were Covington who contributed $500 and Mrs. Laney who contributed $1,000. Three months later the articles of limited partner-

---

[28] Sales of publicly offered limited partnerships totaled $2.28 billion in the first three months of 1986. See Peers, "New Types of Limited Partnerships May Not Be Best Investments Now," *Wall Street Journal*, July 1, 1986, p. 25.

[29] L. Cohen and B. Burrough, "Master Limited Partnerships Take Off, But Some May Fall Short of Promises," *The Wall Street Journal*, December 2, 1985, p. 19.

ship were filed. But 16 months thereafter the project collapsed and the corporation had to declare bankruptcy. The Laneys reported losses of over $700,000 to the IRS. But under IRS rules, they could deduct only amounts they were generally liable for, so the IRS disallowed all amounts but $1,000 as loss deductions. Mrs. Laney claimed that because the limited partnership certificate was filed three months late, no limited partnership came into existence, and she did have unlimited liability. Is this true in a ULPA state? See *Laney* v. *Commissioner of Internal Revenue*, 674 F.2d 342 (5th Cir. 1982).

3. On October 25, 1972, Cosmopolitan Chinook Hotel contracted through "Evan Bargman, V.P., R. Powers, President," to buy neon signs from plaintiff. Cosmopolitan's witnesses claim that plaintiff knew Cosmopolitan was a limited partnership at the signing of the contract because the parties signed as officers rather than as general partners. However, as of October 25, 1972, Cosmopolitan had taken no steps to comply with the ULPA's filing requirement. The certificate of limited partnership was not filed until February 1973. When Cosmopolitan defaulted on payments, plaintiff sued, alleging that Cosmopolitan's partners were generally liable. Discuss. See *Dwinell's Central Neon* v. *Cosmopolitan Chinook Hotel*, 587 P.2d 191 (Wash. App. 1978).

4. A and B bought a tavern. They orally agreed that A would manage the business at a stipulated salary and receive 50% of the profits as his share as a limited partner and that he would not be liable for any losses. Subsequently, the IRS assessed a tax deficiency of $46,000 against the business. A claimed that as a limited partner he could not be liable for any part of this deficiency. Discuss. See *Filisi* v. *U.S.*, 352 F.2d 339 (4th Cir. 1965).

5. Defendants were limited partners in a construction project. They held at least two meetings after it became apparent that the project was in financial difficulty. At these meetings the situation was presented by the general partner, discussions were participated in, and additional money was raised to meet financial obligations. At least one of the limited partners went to the project and surveyed it with the superintendent, "obnoxiously" complaining about the manner in which the work was being conducted. There is no evidence that this limited partner gave any directions that were followed, however. Plaintiff creditors, in this ULPA jurisdiction, claim that defendants engaged in "control" and thereby forfeited their limited liability status. Discuss. See *Trans-Am Builders, Inc.* v. *Woods Mill, Ltd.*, 210 S.E.2d 866 (Ga. 1974).

6. Plaintiffs are former limited partners in a limited partnership that was formed to assume a 20-year lease on a mobile home park. They claim that the dissolution and winding up of the partnership was wrongfully accomplished by the lone named general partner, Watkins. Specifically, their theory is that another limited partner, Erickson, occasionally acted as a general partner and, therefore, under §7 of the ULPA, should be reclassified as such. If Erickson is treated as a general partner, then Watkins needed his permission to dissolve the limited partnership but did not get it. Should Watkins have obtained Erickson's permission to dissolve the limited partnership? Discuss. See *Roeschlein* v. *Watkins*, 686 P.2d 1347 (Colo. App. 1983).

7. Kramer, a limited partner in a restaurant franchise, invested $90,000 in the business. To secure his investment, he took a security agreement from the franchisee covering all equipment, inventory, and receivables. When the business failed, another creditor caused a public sale of the assets, which McDonald's bought. Kramer sued McDonald's for conversion of his property in violation of his secured interest. McDonald's claimed that other creditors had the right to force the sale. Discuss. See *Kramer* v. *McDonald's System, Inc.*, 396 N.E.2d 504 (Ill. 1979).

8. The C. L. Barnhouse Company, a publisher of music, was founded in 1886. Since that time it has existed in various forms, including a sole proprietorship, a general partnership, and after 1956, a series of limited partnerships. All partners are lineal descendants of the founder. This suit by limited partners against the general partners claims that after the final limited partnership's dissolution in 1967, which was followed by substantial litigation, the limited partners are entitled to claim a pro-rata share of the profits generated by the general partners who have continued the business. Discuss. See *Porter* v. *Barnhouse*, 354 N.W.2d 227 (Iowa 1984).

7

FORMATION
OF THE CORPORATION

INTRODUCTION

The corporation—from the small enterprise with but a single shareholder to the huge multinational with hundreds of thousands of shareholders—is a dominant form of business enterprise in America today. In 1981, of the nonagricultural business enterprises in the United States, 9,585,000 were sole proprietorships, 1,461,000 were partnerships, and 2,812,000 were corporations.[1] Though outnumbered, corporations transact over 80% of the private business in this country in terms of dollar volume.

This chapter addresses the process by which some 300,000 corporations are formed annually in the United States. It also discusses problems attendant to that process, including the responsibilities and liabilities of the persons who form corporations (''promoters'') and their impact on the corporation's liabilities.

---

[1] U.S. Department of Commerce, *Statistical Abstract of the United States 1985* (Washington, D.C.: U.S. Government Printing Office, 1985), p. 517.

Governing Law

Corporations are creatures of statute. They exist only by legislative act. The bulk of the body of law called "corporation law" is state law. All 50 states have corporate codes that govern the internal affairs of corporations formed in their states and regulate all corporations' relationships with other businesses and with individuals and the government.

There is more state-to-state variety in the law of corporations than exists in the law of partnerships. Nonetheless, in broad outline all states' corporate codes are similar. Although there is no "uniform" corporate code as there is a Uniform Partnership Act (UPA), the Model Business Corporation Act (MBCA) has been substantially adopted in about 35 states. The focus of this book's treatment of corporate law will be on the MBCA as it has been amended over the years. The MBCA was first published in 1950. It was substantially amended in 1960 and 1969, with lesser amendments including some adopted in 1975 and 1980. The 1969 version of the act is the most pervasively adopted, and it will be our focus, with special attention given to the amendments to financial provisions made in 1980.

However, students should be aware that in 1984, the American Bar Association adopted the first comprehensive revision of the MBCA. The Revised Model Business Corporation Act (Revised MBCA or RMBCA) makes many substantive changes in the prior versions of the MBCA. Because as this chapter is written only a few states have adopted the RMBCA,[2] our focus will remain on the more widely adopted 1969 version of the MBCA. In light of the strong possibility that the RMBCA will soon be widely adopted, however, its major alterations in the law will be pointed out—primarily in the footnotes to this text. By the time the next edition of the book is published, the focus of the book may be on the RMBCA, and the older MBCA may be relegated to footnote treatment.

Students should also be aware of the American Law Institute's Corporate Code, presently scheduled for completion in 1988, which has already aroused controversy concerning its approach to directors' responsibilities and liabilities.[3] The American Law Institute has always been a persuasive source of legal pronouncements, but this is its first major venture into corporate law and the potential influence of its code is unclear.

Other influential corporate codes include those of the states of California, New York, and, most of all, Delaware. The laws of California and New York are important because of the size of those states and their economic influence. The corporate law of Delaware is influential because a large percentage of America's largest corporations are incorporated in Delaware and because several states have patterned their corporate laws after the Delaware law. Long established as an inviting haven for incorporation, Delaware has a large, well-developed body of case law and a legislature willing to amend the law to keep pace with modern developments. In areas where Delaware law

---

[2] For example, Virginia and Indiana.

[3] "Corporate Code Gets Stormy ALI Consideration," *Legal Times of Washington*, May 21, 1984, p. 2.

is particularly influential—such as that of mergers, acquisitions, and appraisal rights—
it will receive our special attention.

Over the years many persons have called for a *federal* corporate code or at
least greater federal regulation of state corporation law.[4] Those cries have had little
effect, however. The vast bulk of American corporation law remains state law.

Still, federal law does have a tremendous impact on the operating life of a
corporation, just as it does on the lives of all individuals. Federal securities, antitrust,
labor, civil rights, bankruptcy, social security, and tax laws, among others, have an
overriding influence on what every American corporation can and cannot do. Each
corporation must cope with the Securities and Exchange Commission, the Federal Trade
Commission, The National Labor Relations Board, the Environmental Protection Agency,
the Internal Revenue Service, and many other federal agencies. Federal influence on
corporate life is obvious and perhaps growing, despite recent attempts at "deregulation." [5]

Types of Corporations

There are many types of corporations that can be placed into various categories.

Public, Private, and Quasi-Public

Public corporations, such as municipal corporations (cities), are formed under
the authority of state government to administer public affairs and operate local government.

Private corporations are also established under the authority of state law, but
by private citizens for profitable or charitable purposes.

Public utilities are examples of *quasi-public corporations*, which are formed
by private citizens to provide services critical to the public.

Domestic and Foreign

As to Delaware, a corporation formed in Delaware is a "domestic" corporation.
Any corporation formed under the laws of any other state or nation would be a "foreign"
corporation as to Delaware. Most states have provisions in their corporate codes that
regulate foreign corporations.

Profit and Nonprofit

Although the focus of this text is on corporations formed with the intent of
operating profitable business enterprises, we should not ignore the 800,000 or so charitable
corporations that exist in this country. That most of our hospitals are operated by nonprofit
corporations is reason enough to take note of them. Most states have special corporate

---

[4] See, for example, R. Nader, M. Green, and J. Seligman, *Taming the Corporate Giant*, W. W.
Norton & Co., New York, NY (1976); and Cary, "Federalism and Corporate Law: Reflections upon Delaware,"
Yale Law Journal, Vol. 83 (1974), p. 663.

[5] L. S. Black, "Toward a Federal Law of Corporations," *National Law Journal*, August 6, 1984,
p. 22.

codes governing only nonprofit corporations. There is also a Model Nonprofit Corporation Act.

Others

Most states also have special bodies of law governing corporations involved in the businesses of insurance, banking, savings and loan, and transportation.

Additionally, though it was long deemed unseemly for professionals such as doctors, lawyers, and engineers to incorporate, this is now allowed in most states. Still, all states have professional corporation or professional association codes that impose some restrictions on corporations engaged in the practices of such professions as law and medicine that do not apply to corporations engaged in regular business enterprises. There is also a Model Professional Corporation Supplement to the MBCA.

THE CORPORATE ENTITY

Recognition of the Entity

Unlike in partnership law, there is no argument that a corporation is a mere aggregation of its owners, the shareholders. The legal fiction of a corporate entity is well established. In the words of one court, "A corporation is not in fact or in reality a person, but is created by statute and the law treats it as though it were a person by the process of fiction, or by regarding it as an artificial person distinct and separate from the individual stockholders." [6]

Although H. L. Mencken was no doubt correct when he noted that a corporation has no soul to damn, corporations do have enough substance in the eyes of the law to be able to own property, pay taxes, hire employees, sue and be sued, and, acting through human agents, of course, do just about anything necessary to run a business.

Because of the separate existence of the corporate entity, sale of the stock of a corporation that owns only real estate does not implicate the statute of frauds provision relating to sale of an interest in land.[7] The selling shareholder is not selling the land directly, but is only selling an interest in a corporation—the entity that the law views as owning the land.

The separate existence of the corporate entity was recently recognized in a case involving a corporation that paid a wrongful death judgment rendered against its wholly owned subsidiary. Because the sole shareholder ("parent corporation") is a separate entity from its corporation ("subsidiary"), it is not liable for the corporation's torts. Therefore, the parent was held to be a mere "volunteer" and unable to be reimbursed by the subsidiary's insurance company for the judgment it paid.[8]

---

[6] *Airvator, Inc.* v. *Turtle Mountain Mfg. Co.*, 329 N.W.2d 596 (N.D. 1983).

[7] *Burns* v. *Gould*, 374 A.2d 193 (Conn. 1977).

[8] *Beatrice Foods Co.* v. *Illinois Insurance Guaranty Fund*, 460 N.E.2d 908 (Ill. App. 1984).

The following case is an old but famous illustration of the law's recognition of the corporate entity.

PEOPLE'S PLEASURE PARK CO. v. ROHLEDER

61 S.E. 794 (Va. 1908)

In 1900 Bliss Black and his wife acquired title to 125 acres of land in Virginia. They platted the land into 130 lots with the intention of establishing a "settlement of white persons." Appellee Rohleder and appellant Butts bought lots from the Blacks pursuant to a restrictive covenant (at that time not yet declared unconstitutional by the Supreme Court) which provided that "The title to this land is never to vest in a person or persons of African descent."

At some point later, Butts sold certain portions of the land to Fulton who the same day conveyed the property to appellant People's Pleasure Park Company, Inc. All owners of this corporation were "colored persons" and the land was purchased for the express purpose of converting it into a "park or place of amusement for colored persons."

Appellee sued to annul the conveyance as inconsistent with the restrictive covenant. Appellants appealed from a lower court ruling that in order to have the sale sustained, they must pay appellee the market value of the three lots she purchased.

CARDWELL, JUSTICE:

Aside from the question whether or not appellee could obtain the relief she asks against appellants—that is, an annulment of the conveyance to appellant People's Pleasure Park Company, Incorporated—on the ground that the restriction on the right of alienation of any of the Fulton Park land to "a person or persons of African

descent" or "colored person" had been violated by a sale of a part of the land to said appellant, the bill fails to allege facts showing a violation of the restriction, and should have been dismissed upon the demurrers thereto. Such a conveyance, by no rule of construction, vests the title to the property conveyed in "a person or persons of African descent." Although a copy of the charter of the grantee is filed as an exhibit with the bill and made a part thereof, and which sets out that the object for which the corporation is formed is "to establish and develop a pleasure park for the amusement of colored people," a contemplated sale of the property to "a person or persons of African descent" is not even alleged, but only a contemplated use of the property as a place of amusement for colored persons, which the restriction relied on neither expressly, nor by implication, prohibits.

"A corporation is an artificial person like the state. It is a distinct existence—an existence separate from that of its stockholders and directors"—1 Cook on Corp. (4th ed.) §1.

Prof. Rudolph Sohm, in his *Institutes of Roman Law*, pp. 104–106 says:

In Roman law the property of the corporation is the sole property of the collective whole; and the debts of a corporation are the sole debts of the collective whole. . . . It represents a kind of ideal private person, an independent subject capable of holding property, totally distinct from all previously existing persons, including its own members. It possesses, as such, rights and liabilities of its own. It leads its own life, as it were, quite unaffected by any change of members. It stands apart as a separate subject or proprietary capacity, and, in contemplation of law, as a stranger to its own members. The collective whole, as such, can hold property. Its property, therefore, is, as far as its members are concerned, another's property, its debts another's debts. . . . Roman law contrived to accomplish a veritable masterpiece of juristic ingenuity in discovering the notion of a collective person; in clearly grasping and distinguishing from its members the collective whole as the ideal unity of the members bound together by the corporate constitution; in raising this whole to the rank of a person (a juristic person, namely); and in securing it a place in private law as an independent subject of proprietary capacity standing on the same footing as other private persons.

. . .

For the above reasons, we are of opinion that the decree complained of is erroneous. *Reversed.*

Constitutional Rights of Corporations

The corporate entity is so firmly embedded in American law that corporations have even been extended some, but not all, of the constitutional rights given to individuals. The recognition that corporate political speech is at least partially protected under the Free Speech Clause of the First Amendment is noted in the following excerpt.

CONSOLIDATED EDISON AND BELLOTTI: FIRST AMENDMENT PROTECTION OF CORPORATE POLITICAL SPEECH*
Robert Prentice
16 Tulsa Law Journal 599 (1981)

It is clear that neither the Founding Fathers nor the framers of the fourteenth amendment had the rights of corporations foremost in their minds as they carried out their historic functions. The word "corporation" does not even appear in the Constitution. A scanning of the courts' treatment of corporate constitutional rights reveals, as might be expected due to the dearth of guidance given by the Constitution, a rather spotty development.

The traditional view of corporations is epitomized in an often-quoted passage from Chief Justice Marshall's opinion in *Dartmouth College* v. *Woodward* [17 U.S. 518 (1819)]:

> A corporation is an artificial being, invisible, intangible, and existing only in contemplation of law. Being the mere creature of law, it possesses only those properties which the charter of creation confers upon it, either expressly, or as incidental to its very existence. These are such as are supposed best calculated to effect the object for which it was created.

Consistent with this constricted view of the nature of corporations, the Supreme Court has denied that corporations are "citizens" for purposes of the privileges and immunities clauses of the Constitution and has held that the "liberty" referred to as protected in the fourteenth amendment is that of natural, not artificial, persons. Similarly, the Court has denied corporations the rights of privacy and the privilege against self-incrimination which the Constitution accords individuals.

On the other hand, the Supreme Court has given corporations some significant constitu-

---

tional protections. Most importantly, corporations have been deemed "citizens" protected by the due process clauses of the fifth and fourteenth amendments, and the latter amendment's equal protection clause. Additionally, corporations have been given constitutional protection against double jeopardy and unreasonable searches and seizures. . . .

The first unmistakeable Supreme Court recognition of corporate political speech as a protected form of expression came in *First National Bank of Boston* v. *Bellotti* [435 U.S. 765 (1978)]. At issue was the constitutionality of a state criminal statute which prohibited expenditures by banks and business corporations for the purpose of influencing the vote on state referendum proposals not "materially affecting" any of the property, business, or assets of the corporation. . . .

Justice Powell [speaking for the majority], initially noted that the speech which the plaintiffs sought to undertake was "at the heart of First Amendment protection." Stating that our system of free expression serves not just the interest of self-expression, but also that of self-government, the opinion established a theoretical basis for protecting corporate political speech which parallels the right to receive theory underlying the protection of commercial speech. Because the message itself deserves first amendment protection, Justice Powell wrote, its source was irrelevant to the analysis:

> If the speakers here were not corporations, no one would suggest that the State could silence their proposed speech. It is the type of speech indispensable to decisionmaking in a democracy, and this is no less true because the speech comes from a corporation than from an individual. The inherent worth of the speech in terms of its capacity for informing the public does not depend upon the identity of its source, whether corporation, association, union, or individual.

THE INCORPORATION PROCESS

Planning

Although thousands and perhaps hundreds of thousands of corporations are formed each year without substantial planning, this practice cannot be recommended. Standardized corporation laws, the widespread availability of "canned" forms, and the existence of such corporation service organizations as The C.T. Corporation System, The Prentice-Hall Corporation System, and the United States Corporation Company to which a lawyer may delegate organizational details, all make it relatively easy to form a corporation without much forethought. Formation can be merely a paper-shuffling exercise that can be adequately performed by paralegals or legal secretaries. However, every corporation from the smallest family closely held corporation to much larger publicly held corporations can profit by careful planning. Many aspects of planning that require the most scrupulous attention to detail, such as setting the capital structure of the corporation, will be discussed in later chapters.

State of Incorporation

Once the decision to incorporate has been made, the state in which to incorporate must be chosen. Although all state corporate codes address the same subjects in generally the same manner, there are important variations.

For example, the MBCA is generally regarded as embodying an approach that balances the rights of shareholders with the needs of management for flexibility. Several other approaches, including most notably that of Delaware, have been intentionally drafted to grant wide discretion and flexibility to corporate managers, arguably at the expense of shareholder protection.

States such as Delaware take this approach to present an attractive atmosphere in which to incorporate or reincorporate. Delaware has been so successful—one source lists 35 advantages to Delaware incorporation [9]—that approximately half of the *Fortune* 500 companies are incorporated there. Delaware derives substantial revenue from filing fees and activity related to the incorporation process.

The recent trend across the country, and it is even seen in the Revised Model Business Corporation Act, is in a pro-management direction. Some have decried the "race" among the states to ease legal restrictions on management authority in order to entice incorporations,[10] but the trend continues. Still, Delaware seems destined to win the race for the larger corporations.

> The popularity of the Delaware General Corporation Law is due to that state's sympathetic attitude toward business corporations, demonstrated over an extended period of time by its laws and the decisions of its courts. As long as that attitude continues, Delaware will probably remain the favored domicile for larger corporations. Other states have in past years held and lost that favored position. Delaware has been successful in maintaining its preeminence and at the moment shows no tendency to relinquish it.[11]

For smaller corporations, especially close corporations whose managers tend to also be its major shareholders, the flexibility of the Delaware law is not so important. Smaller corporations are usually best counseled to incorporate in the state where they will do most of their business. A small Iowa firm could incorporate in Delaware, but the advantages of doing so would probably be outweighed by the disadvantages, which include the need to maintain a resident agent in Delaware, being subject to suit in Delaware, and having to qualify as a "foreign" corporation to do business in Iowa.

Certain states do have laws that are particularly favorable for close corporations and should be considered for that reason. Perhaps more states will adopt such laws, such as the Proposed Close Corporation Supplement to the MBCA.[12]

---

[9] H. Henn and R. Alexander, *Law of Corporations* 3rd ed. (West Publishing Co: St. Paul, MN, 1983), p. 186.

[10] See, for example, Cary, "Federalism and Corporate Law," p. 663; and Comment, "Law for Sale: A Study of the Delaware Corporation Law of 1967," *Univ. of Pennsylvania Law Review*, Vol. 117 (1969), p. 861.

[11] G. Seward and W. Nauss, *Basic Corporate Practice*, 2nd ed. (American Law Institute, St. Paul, MN, 1977), p. xi.

[12] See "Proposed Close Corporation Supplement to the Model Business Corporation Act," *Business Lawyer*, Vol. 37 (1970), p. 269.

Choice of Name

Before filing any documents, it is possible in most states to call or write the Secretary of State's office to clear the name chosen for a new corporation and to reserve that name for a time to ensure that it is not taken by another corporation.

Most states have few requirements regarding choice of a corporation's name. Generally, the name must include the words "corporation," "incorporated," or "company," or their abbreviations, to inform those who deal with it of its corporate nature. The name must not mislead as to the corporate purpose. Finally, the name should not be "deceptively similar" to a name already being used.

After incorporating, corporations may also have to comply with "assumed name statutes." In many states this entails filing certain basic information about the corporation in every county where the corporation has an office or intends to do business.

Mere compliance with the provisions of the corporate code and the assumed name statute may not protect the name from infringement by others. Corporate officers should be familiar with the laws regarding use of trade names to protect a corporate name fully.

The Filing Process

Early suspicion of corporations and the power that their large accumulations of capital might generate was responsible for restrictions on the number of corporations and their powers. In early England, corporations could be chartered only with the permission of the king. At the time of America's independence, there were only about 25 corporations in the entire nation. Throughout much of the following century corporations in most states could be formed only by special legislative act and only for limited purposes. Most corporations were formed for public works–type projects—canals, dams, turnpikes, and railroads.

Throughout the nineteenth century, hostility to corporations gradually abated. Most states adopted general corporation laws that established certain procedural and substantive requirements for the formation of a corporation. Any group of promoters which met the standards was entitled to issuance of a corporate charter without having to petition the legislature.

Although they vary from state to state, the general procedures for forming a corporation are much the same nationwide. Generally speaking, this procedure involves, in addition to selection of a jurisdiction and reservation of a name, the drafting of articles of incorporation, filing of those articles, an application for issuance of a certificate of incorporation with the Secretary of State, payment of filing fees and franchise taxes, payment of the statutory minimum capital (if any), recording of the articles in the offices of counties where the principal place of business will be located, drafting of bylaws, and conducting of an initial organizational meeting.

The persons who sign, and in some states verify, the articles of incorporation are called "incorporators." Traditionally each corporation was required to have at least three incorporators, but the trend is toward requiring only one.

Many states, the MBCA as amended and the RMBCA, have eliminated the minimum capital requirement. Other states continue to require that anywhere from $300 to $1,000 be in the corporate treasury before business is conducted. The purpose of such a requirement is to protect creditors, but it is difficult in light of today's inflated standards to conclude that much protection is provided.

Although it is relatively simple to follow the required incorporation procedures in most states, a surprisingly high percentage of applications are rejected at least once because of technical errors. The incorporation services, mentioned earlier, can help to minimize such errors.

Noncorporate matters that must be considered while the incorporation process is being completed include application for a federal employer identification number, securing of unemployment insurance and worker's compensation coverage, hiring legal counsel, selection of a bank, and obtaining liability insurance.[13]

Articles of Incorporation

The articles of incorporation, frequently called the "certificate of incorporation," are at the heart of the incorporation process. They must be filed with the Secretary of State to provide to the government and any party dealing with the corporation, certain key information. Section 54 of the MBCA sets forth ten items that must be in the articles of incorporation, including the corporation's name; its duration (which may be perpetual); its purposes; the number of its authorized shares and a description of them; a designation of classes of stock, if any; the relative rights of preferred stock, if any; preemptive rights of shareholders, if any; address and name of its registered agent; the names and addresses of its initial board of directors; and the names and addresses of its incorporators.[14]

Section 54 also authorizes the articles to contain provisions on such permissive subjects as the direction of the management of the business; limitations on the powers of directors, officers, and shareholders, including restrictions on the transferring of shares; par value of stock; and any matter required or permitted in the bylaws.

The following is a sample certificate of incorporation for a corporation to be formed in Delaware, which is one of the easiest states in which to incorporate. Although the certificate (or articles) of incorporation may be much longer and more complex, they may also be as simple as the following.[15]

[13] Henn and Alexander, *Law of Corporations*, p. 272.

[14] RMBCA §2.02 simplifies the contents of the articles, requiring only the corporate name, the number of authorized shares, the address and name of the registered office and agent, and the name and address of each incorporator. Other information may be included, but need not be.

[15] The source of this sample certificate is D. Drexler and A. Gilbert Sparks, *The Delaware Corporation: Legal Aspects of Organization and Operation* (Bureau of National Affairs: Wash., D.C., 1978), p. B-101. Reprinted by permission from *Corporate Practice* Series, copyright 1978 by The Bureau of National Affairs, Inc., Washington, D.C.

CERTIFICATE OF INCORPORATION OF **XYZ PRODUCTS, INC.**

FIRST: The name of the corporation is XYZ Products, Inc.

SECOND: The address of the registered office of the corporation in the State of Delaware is 25 Central Drive, in the City of Wilmington, County of New Castle. The name of the registered agent of the corporation at such address is Incorporation Company.

THIRD: The purpose of the corporation is to engage in any lawful act or activity for which corporations may be organized under the General Corporation Law of the State of Delaware.

FOURTH: The total number of shares of stock which the corporation is authorized to issue is one thousand (1,000) shares of common stock, having a par value of one dollar ($1.00) per share.

FIFTH: The business and affairs of the corporation shall be managed by the board of directors, and the directors need not be elected by ballot unless required by the by-laws of the corporation.

SIXTH: In furtherance and not in limitation of the powers conferred by the laws of the State of Delaware, the board of directors is expressly authorized to adopt, amend or repeal the by-laws.

SEVENTH: The corporation reserves the right to amend and repeal any provision contained in this Certificate of Incorporation in the manner prescribed by the laws of the State of Delaware. All rights herein conferred are granted subject to this reservation.

EIGHTH: The incorporator is John Doe, whose mailing address is Second and Middle Streets, Wilmington, Delaware 19899.

I, THE UNDERSIGNED, being the incorporator, for the purpose of forming a corporation under the laws of the State of Delaware do make, file and record this Certificate of Incorporation, do certify that the facts herein stated are true, and, accordingly, have hereto set my hand and seal this __day of _____, 197__.

John Doe

If the Secretary of State finds the articles of incorporation to be in good order and the filing fees paid, a certificate of incorporation will be issued. Under MBCA §56, that event begins the legal life of the corporation. Complications that can arise when business is conducted in the corporate name before the certificate is issued are discussed later in this chapter and in the next.[16]

---

[16] To eliminate such complications, the RMBCA's §2.03 commences corporate existence with the *filing* of the articles, unless a delayed effective date is specified.

Organizational Meeting

In most states the issuance of the certificate of incorporation by the Secretary of State should be almost immediately followed by an organizational meeting. The MBCA requires a meeting of the board of directors named in the articles. Other states may require that the meeting be held by the incorporators, or by both the incorporators and the initial board of directors. In some states the corporation does not effectively come into existence until the organizational meeting is held.

The organizational meeting is highly formalized, as its agenda is set to accomplish a series of acts prerequisite to effective corporate activity. The meeting need not actually be held. Rather, the directors or incorporators can agree in writing to handle matters by written consent.

A number of matters must be addressed at the meeting, including election of chairman and secretary of the board of directors, adoption of corporate bylaws, adoption of the corporate seal, appointment of officers, approval of the form of stock certificates,[17] acceptance of share subscriptions and authorization of issuance of stock, adoption or rejection of preincorporation contracts signed by the corporation's promoters, authorization of the opening of bank accounts, and appointment of a resident agent.

In *Bostetter* v. *Freestate Land Corp.*,[18] the court rejected the notion that all corporate acts that occurred between the issuance of a corporate charter on May 3, 1965 and an organizational meeting on July 28, 1972 were ineffectual because such a meeting was prerequisite to a transfer of corporate powers from the original incorporators to the board of directors. Small corporations frequently misplace corporate documents. For that reason, "after the expiration of a long period of time, a presumption of regularity attends corporate proceedings."

Bylaws

Bylaws govern the internal control of the corporation. Although subordinate to the articles of incorporation, which are in turn subordinate to the state's corporate code, the bylaws control many important matters.

Bylaws may be relatively brief documents, but they may also be comprehensive treatises. They usually cover at least such basic matters as the terms and compensation of directors, the time and place of shareholder and director meetings, notice and quorum requirements, and selection procedures for officers and directors.

The following has been suggested as a checklist to guide lawyers in drafting bylaws in an MBCA state.

---

[17] Note that a few states are moving toward a certificateless approach where stock holdings are officially transferred by notations on the corporation's books and not by the changing hands of paper certificates. See RMBCA §6.26.

[18] 440 A.2d 380 (Md. 1982).

§20:163 Checklist—Matters To Be Considered in Drafting Bylaws For Business Corporation

1. Registered office and other offices.
2. Shareholders.
   a. Annual and special meetings.
   b. Time and place of meetings.
   c. Notice of meetings.
   d. Record date for determining shareholders of record.
   e. Waiver of notice.
   f. Adjournment of meetings.
   g. Requirement of more than majority for shareholder action.
   h. Manner of execution, revocation and use of proxies.
   i. Restrictions as to telephone meetings.
3. Directors.
   a. Powers.
   b. Number, tenure, removal and qualifications, compensation and time of annual election.
   c. Classification.
   d. Meetings.
      (1) Regular and special meetings.
      (2) Time and place of meetings.
      (3) Notice of meetings.
      (4) Waiver of notice.
      (5) Quorum, if greater than majority.
      (6) Requirement of action of more than majority to constitute action of board of directors.
      (7) Designation of officer to call meetings, and conditions relative to such meetings.
   e. Action by written consent in lieu of meeting.
   f. Restrictions as to telephone meetings.
4. Authorization of appointment of officers other than directors and specification of duties, compensation, and tenure of office.
5. Authorization to board of directors to appoint executive and other committees.
6. Form of stock certificates and provision for lost, destroyed and stolen certificates.
7. Subscriptions for stock.
8. Provision for issuance and recognition of fractional shares.

Texas Forms §20:163 (Bancroft-Whitney Co: San Francisco, CA, 1981). Copyright 1981 by Bancroft-Whitney Co. All rights reserved. Reprinted with permission.

9. Imposition of restrictions on the transfer or registration of transfer of securities.

10. Penalties for failure to pay installments or calls that may become due.

11. Corporate actions, such as contracts, loans and bank deposits.

12. Requirement that annual reports and financial statements be distributed to shareholders.

13. Inspection of corporate records.

14. Inspection of articles of incorporation, bylaws, etc.

15. Specification of who may vote shares held in other corporations.

16. Fiscal year.

17. Corporate seal.

18. Inclusion of any other proper and lawful regulations not in conflict with the articles of incorporation.

Foreign Qualification

A corporation that has been formed in one state but intends to do business in another will have to comply with the latter's foreign "qualification" or "domestication" statute. This normally entails the filing of an authenticated copy of the certificate of incorporation with some additional information, the selection of a resident agent, and the paying of certain taxes and fees. Indeed, the primary reason most states insist on "domesticating" foreign corporations is to facilitate the payment of taxes.

Section 107 of the MBCA provides that a properly domesticated foreign corporation shall have the same rights as a true domestic corporation. The internal affairs of the foreign corporation are governed by the laws of the state of incorporation, and §107 states that no foreign corporation shall be denied a certificate of authority to transact business merely because the laws of the state of incorporation differ from those of the forum state. Although §107 also states that it does not authorize a state to regulate the organization or internal affairs of a foreign corporation, states occasionally attempt to do just that. For example, California, which required that cumulative voting be made available to shareholders, forced a corporation organized under the laws of Delaware, which did not require such voting, to bend to the public policy of California.[19]

A corporation that transacts business in a foreign jurisdiction without qualifying to transact business, faces a variety of penalties that vary from state to state. Most states provide that although contracts entered into by an unqualified foreign corporation are valid, the foreign corporation can neither sue for breach of those contracts nor defend suits arising from them until the qualification statutes have been complied with. But some states hold the contracts invalid and even hold directors and officers of unqualified corporations to be personally liable on them.

The most difficult question in this area involves the issue of when states can

---

[19] *Western Air Lines, Inc.* v. *Sobieski*, 12 Cal. Rptr. 719 (Cal. App. 1961).

properly regulate foreign corporations under their domestication statutes. The Supreme Court has made it clear that a state cannot apply its law to a foreign corporation engaged in *inter*state commerce without risking running afoul of the Commerce Clause of the Constitution.[20] A state can regulate *intra*state commerce, but §106 of the MBCA lists a number of activities that are not to be considered "transacting business" in a state for purposes of application of that state's foreign qualification requirements. These include suing and being sued, holding directors' and shareholders' meetings, maintaining bank accounts, selling through independent contractors, soliciting orders that require acceptance outside the state, collecting debts, and conducting isolated transactions. Foreign corporations are more likely to be held within the scope of a state's laws if they maintain employees, inventory, or offices in that state.

Some of these matters are discussed in the following case.

JOHNSON v. MPL LEASING CORP.

441 So.2d 904 (Ala. 1983)

Plaintiff MPL Leasing Corp. (MPL) is a California corporation which offers alternative financing plans to dealers of Saxon Business Products. Saxon specializes in the sale of paper copiers distributed through independent dealers, such as defendants Jay Johnson and Jay Johnson Business Products, Inc. (Johnson).

Through mailings and phone calls into Alabama, MPL solicited Johnson's attendance at a sales seminar in Atlanta, Georgia. Johnson attended, and entered into an agreement to lease with the option to buy. MPL shipped the copiers to Alabama and filed a financing statement with the Secretary of State.

Johnson fell behind on his payments, so MPL sued. Johnson moved to dismiss on grounds that MPL had never qualified to do business in Alabama and therefore was not entitled to bring suit. The trial court overruled the motion and entered judgment for MPL. Johnson appealed.

TORBERT, CHIEF JUSTICE:

Section 323 of the Alabama Constitution and §10–2A–247, Code 1975, bar foreign corporations not qualified to do business in this state from enforcing their contracts through our courts. These laws only come into play "when the business conducted in the state by nonqualified corporations is considered 'intrastate' in nature"—*First Inv. Co. v. McLeod*, 363 So.2d 774, 776, 777 (Ala. Civ. App. 1978). MPL's activities within Alabama are limited to (1) delivering copying machines by common carrier and (2) filing this action. This Court has never held previously that contacts as minimal as those of MPL constitute "intrastate" business.

For example, in *Kentucky Galvanizing Co. v. Continental Gas. Co.*, 335 So.2d 649 (Ala. 1976), this Court considered whether the foreign, nonqualifying corporation's contacts were sufficient to constitute "intrastate" business.

---

[20] *Allenberg Cotton Co., Inc. v. Pittman*, 419 U.S. 20 (1974).

The facts in *Kentucky Galvanizing* are indistinguishable from those in this case. The corporation's activities in Alabama were "simply solicitation of orders and delivery incident to that solicitation"—335 So.2d at 651. This Court held that "Galvanizing, conducting business in interstate commerce, is justified and welcomed to use the state courts of Alabama to enforce its claim against those who defaulted on payment of an order which was delivered here"—Id. at 652.

In *First Investment*, the Court of Civil Appeals considered whether a bank, which purchased a promissory note from a foreign, nonqualified corporation, could maintain an action against the maker of the note. The foreign corporation, Great Lakes, solicited franchises for the sale of Christmas trees and delivered Christmas tree seedlings in Alabama. The court found an "absence of facts showing that Great Lakes was doing 'intrastate' business in Alabama."

The appellant cites several cases for the proposition that solicitation of sales constitutes "doing business"—*SAR Manufacturing Co.* v. *Dumas Brothers Manufacturing Co.*, 526 F.2d 1283 (5th Cir. 1976) (applying Alabama law), held that a foreign, nonqualifying corporation (SAR) could not sue on a promissory note against an Alabama co-maker. Unlike MPL, SAR expanded its operation by purchasing a warehouse in Alabama, maintaining two vehicles in Alabama, and employing seven Alabama residents full time. These factors were "localized enough to easily fall under the ambit of a series of transactions which are primarily intrastate and concomitantly the corporation falls under the satrapy of the qualification statutes."

• • •

As the decisions make clear, it is far easier to find that a foreign corporation is "doing business" for service of process than it is to find that the corporation is conducting intrastate business subject to state regulation in view of the Commerce Clause.

Affirmed.

PROMOTERS AND THEIR CONTRACTS

The Promoter

Those who actively take part in organizing the corporation prior to its coming into being in a legal sense are called "promoters." This term, which to some carries a distasteful connotation, includes "those who undertake to form a corporation and to procure for it the rights, instrumentalities and capital by which it is to carry out the purposes set forth in its charter, and to establish it as fully able to do its business." [21]

Promoters may be forming a corporation that they intend to be part of and perhaps control for many years. Or they may be professional promoters who, upon bringing a corporation to fruition move on to their next project. Either way, the promoters will do such things as develop ideas, research markets, select locations, purchase real estate, rent offices, and hire employees—all for the ultimate use of a corporation that

---

[21] *Old Dominion Copper Mining and Smelting Co.* v. *Bigelow*, 89 N.E. 193 (Mass. 1909), *aff'd* 225 U.S. 111 (1912).

does not yet exist. All this activity frequently leads to tangled questions regarding the rights and liabilities of the promoters, third parties with whom they deal, and the corporation should it later come into existence.

Fiduciary Duties

A promoter is in a unique position to profit when a corporation comes into existence. The promoter has controlled everything up to that point. If the promoter has purchased land for the corporation's use, the corporation must now assume the contract to use the land. If the promoter owns the land and sells it to the corporation at a large profit, is the profit illicit? Isn't the promoter entitled to compensation for his or her efforts?

The bottom line is that promoters are, of course, entitled to compensation for their labor. But they are not entitled to secret profits, undisclosed to the corporation's directors or shareholders. Promoters are fiduciaries, owing a duty of trust and good faith to their co-promoters, to the corporation, and to its shareholders. If they derive profits by concealment, promoters may be forced to disgorge those profits.

There are safe ways for a promoter to profit. Full disclosure to and approval by an *independent* board of directors will legitimize a promoter's profit. Promoters who are also directors should abstain from voting on their own contracts. If the promoter is also the majority shareholder who has handpicked the board of directors, its independence will be questioned.

Full disclosure to and approval by all existing shareholders will probably legitimize the profit. This is no doubt true when at the time of the disclosure, no other shareholders are contemplated. But what if the promoter discloses at a time when the only shareholders are the promoter and his or her cronies with the express plan of selling the shares to an unsuspecting public as soon as the profit is approved? Despite the language of one Supreme Court case that appeared to sanction such a scheme,[22] most cases indicate that this would be a breach of fiduciary duty.[23]

If a secret profit is later discovered, and yet subsequently approved by all existing shareholders, the promoter could keep it.

A typical case follows in which a court also had to struggle to find an appropriate remedy.

---

[22] *Old Dominion Copper Mining & Smelting Co.* v. *Lewisohn*, 210 U.S. 206 (1908).

[23] *Old Dominion Copper Mining & Smelting Co.* v. *Bigelow*, 89 N.E. 193 (Mass. 1909), *aff'd* 225 U.S. 111 (1912).

WHALER MOTOR INN, INC. v. PARSONS

363 N.E.2d 493 (Mass. 1977)

Defendants Lipton, Parsons, and David and Louis Freeman were promoters planning to form a corporation to operate a motel near Boston. The promoters met in 1965, but earlier Parsons had brought a parcel of land for $2,000 with the thought of opening a motel by himself. After joining the other defendants, Parsons bought a larger parcel for $35,000 and secured an option on a third parcel. The promoters chose a Holiday Inn franchise and on February 14, 1967 caused plaintiff Whaler Motor Inn, Inc., to be incorporated with 1,000 no par shares authorized.

At an October 19, 1967, meeting, the board of directors, which consisted of the promoters and Lipman, an interested investor, accepted offers by each of the promoters to purchase 130 shares for $100,000 and by Lipman to purchase 120 shares for $100,000. Lipman paid cash for his shares. Unknown to him, the defendant promoters did not.

On October 28, 1967, Parsons, pursuant to an informal agreement with the other promoters, conveyed the two parcels and the option to the corporation for an understood price of $75,000, though their fair market value was $150,000 and the documents executed indicated the price was $37,500.

A bank loan was lined up, but the corporation was first required to deposit $300,000 with the bank, of which $100,000 would be used to make the first payments for construction. Investors were brought in to buy the remaining 360 shares at $833 per share, the price Lipman had paid. Parsons used $75,000 of the proceeds to cover his sale of the land. The motel was built, but business reverses led to investigation by Lipman

and discovery that defendants had never paid for their shares.

This suit followed. The trial judge in Superior Court rendered a verdict against the promoters which was modified by the Appeals Court. This appeal followed.

KAPLAN, JUSTICE:

The nub of the final decrees of the judge of the Superior Court was that there were breaches of duty and that the proper remedy was to restore the shares to the corporation allowing credit only for the unreimbursed out-of-pocket expenditures incurred by the promoters; and with respect to the land, to require the return to the corporation of all consideration received by Parsons above his own costs, that is, $37,500. This was also the view taken by the dissenting Justice of the Appeals Court. The majority of that court agreed there were breaches of duty, but held that credit should be allowed for the value (to be ascertained on remand) of the promotional services as well as for the promoters' unpaid actual expenditures, and that, as to the land, there need be no payment to the corporation since the market value exceeded the price received by Parsons. We agree with the majority and largely for their reasons.

1. We agree that whatever their own understanding of the situation may have been, the defendants must be held to have committed breaches of duty toward the corporation and thus to the outsiders. In transactions with their corporate instrument, promoters are considered to be fiduciaries. To fulfill their responsibilities, the defendants in the present case were bound to make full disclosure

about the two transactions (land and shares) to the outsiders as intending investors. See *Old Dominion Copper Mining & Smelting Co.* v. *Bigelow*, 203 Mass. 159, 178, 89 N.E. 193 (1909), aff'd 225 U.S. 111 (1912). Failing that, the promoters might have exculpated themselves if, after the corporation was firmly established and under sail, they had secured due and knowing ratification of their actions by the shareholders or by an independent management. We need not renew the problem whether or how far a subsequent shareholder may complain of a transaction between promoters and the corporation concluded at a time when the promoters owned all the issued (though not all the authorized) stock. It is not suggested that there is any such complication here.

2. Seeking to delineate remedies for corporations commensurate with promoters' breaches of duty, we can be sure that any rigid rules would soon be shown to be vulnerable, so great is the variety of circumstances likely to arise and beyond our powers to foresee or appreciate. It is well to proceed more modestly, with no hope of finding invariant precepts.

What the Appeals Court did was to treat the cases as appropriate for the remedy of rescission or, in the case of the shares, a remedy on the order of rescission though not quite the usual article. Parsons received $75,000 for his conveyance, but if this transaction were undone (substituting a money value for the land and land interests), the corporation would be a loser, so rescission resulted here in a null recovery for the corporation. The shares issued to the promoters were to be returned to the corporation (or canceled, which is the same thing for present purposes), and the corporation was to return to the promoters, not the price they had paid to the corporation, for they had paid none, but rather the promoters' expenses and the value of their services in launching the venture, which could figure in a sense as that price, or as a reasonable substitute for it.

Similar results typical of rescission or in that mode can be found in promoters' cases decided by this and other courts. Thus for failure to make proper disclosure, sales of property by promoters to their corporations have been undone by requiring return of the thing or its value against return of the price paid by the corporation. See *Old Dominion Copper Mining & Smelting Co.* v. *Bigelow*, supra. So too, promoters required to restore unpaid-for shares to the corporation have been allowed as a credit not only their actual promotional expenditures but also the value of their promotional services as determined.

Much authority can be cited in which harsher measures have been applied to promoters guilty of failure to disclose. Thus in an instance of sale of property to the corporation, the promoter may be deprived of every advantage, as by making him disgorge all that he has received exceeding his own investment in the property, even if such an exaction involves a windfall to the corporation (a result that would follow in the present case if the decrees in the Superior Court were upheld). See *Koppitz-Melchers, Inc.* v. *Koppitz*, 315 Mich. 582, 24 N.W.2d 220 (1946). And there are decisions which, in the process of rescission, would not allow the value of promotional services to count as any part of the "price" for shares issued to the promoter (although they may treat actual promotional expenditures otherwise, a somewhat awkward distinction also may be found in the Superior Court decrees). See *Hayward* v. *Leeson*, 176 Mass. 310, 318, 322, 57 N.E. 656 (1900).

We observe, however, that where corporations have been permitted the more sweeping remedies described, certain features are likely to be present. The promoter, in a case of sale to the corporation, is understood to be acting for the venture rather than himself at the earlier point when he acquired the property, so that he cannot in conscience take any profit for himself. Or the promoter is conspicuously blameworthy, for example, because of his active misrepresentation on which the outsiders relied to their detriment. As already suggested, however, the cases do not fall into clear-cut categories.

We join with the Appeals Court in deploring the behavior of the promoters from the formation of the corporation to the crisis leading to the litigation. They were slipshod and assumed an attitude of proprietorship toward the project without proper regard to the interests of the outsiders. But it is not every sin that suffices to make a party a wolf's head. Thus, despite weighty argument in the dissent, we join also with the Appeals Court in thinking that these cases do not call for measures quite as drastic as those taken by the decrees of the Superior Court. As to the land transaction, Parsons's acquisition in 1964 was surely for himself, and according to the findings his later purchase and other activities in connection with the site occurred before there was solid assurance of a market for the land. Having assumed individual risks, Parsons was entitled to an individual profit on the subsequent sale to the corporation. That profit was small in relation to the benefit obtained by the corporation. As to the shares, with proof of misrepresentations or their consequences at the ambiguous level described, we think promoters' services (including exposure on the guaranty to the banks), so far as valuable to the enterprise, should not be disregarded; they deserve recognition on much the same footing as out-of-pocket expenditures. We would emphasize, however, that the burden of showing value remains on the promoters as wrongdoers and the trier should insist on clear proof.

Remanded.

Some aspects of the promoter's fiduciary problem have been mitigated by state and federal securities laws that require disclosure to potential investors of compensation received by promoters.

Promoter Liability on Contracts

Although the courts are not completely consistent in their approach to the problem, promoters tend to be held personally liable on most contracts they enter into on the corporation's behalf. After all, the corporation is not yet in existence. If the third party intends to have a contract, it must be with the promoter.

Even if the corporation subsequently comes into existence and adopts the contract for itself, the promoter usually continues to be liable. Now the third party has two parties to look to should the contract be breached—the corporation and the promoter.

Should the corporation not come into existence, it is almost a certainty that the promoter who was supposed to form it will be liable for the contracts made on behalf of a nonexistent corporation. The promoter may also be held liable on all contracts made by co-promoters, because courts tend to treat co-promoters as partners or joint venturers who are liable for one another's contracts and torts. Whether co-promoters are to be treated as partners is, however, a question of fact revolving around their intent.

Although courts tend to construe preincorporation contracts to bind promoters, there are certain limited circumstances where liability may not be imposed. For example, occasionally agreements between promoters and third parties are deemed nonbinding "gentlemen's agreements" as to which the promoter has neither rights nor liabilities. The "agreement" is treated as merely an offer to the corporation that becomes binding only if the corporation is formed and adopts the contract before the offer is revoked.

A second situation of promoter nonliability exists where the corporation comes into existence and adopts the promoter's contract with a third party, *and* the third party then agrees to look to the corporation as the sole obligor on the contract. This is a *novation*, where a new party (the corporation) is substituted for the original obligor (the promoter) with the consent of the third party. The third party's agreement to the novation must be clear, for the natural assumption is that the third party would prefer to look to *both* the promoter and the corporation should a breach occur.

A third situation where a promoter might not be liable on a contract exists where it is clear that the third party never considered the promoter bound on the contract but always looked solely to the corporation about to be formed. The intent not to hold the promoter liable should be clearly spelled out in the contract, for close calls tend to go against the promoter.

In *Sherwood & Roberts–Oregon, Inc.* v. *Alexander*,[24] real estate developers applied to a lender for financing. The lender suggested a long-term loan commitment at 12% interest. Because this rate was usurious as to individuals, but not as to corporations, the bank told the developers that they would have to incorporate. The note was signed: "Iron Mountain Investment Co., Inc., By David Alexander." The lender knew that the corporate entity was not yet in existence at the time the note was signed. Given all the circumstances, especially the illegality of lending at this rate to individuals, the court concluded that the bank had agreed to look solely to the corporation.

A more typical result appears in the following recent case.

GOODMAN v. DARDEN, DOMAN & ASSOCIATES

670 P.2d 648 (Wash. 1983)

Goodman, a real estate salesman, sold an apartment building to Darden, Doman & Stafford Associates (DDS), a general partnership. The apartments needed renovation, and Goodman offered to do it. During negotiations, Goodman informed DDS that he would be forming a corporation to limit his personal liability. A contract was executed in August 1979 between DDS and "BUILDING DESIGN AND DEVEL- *OPMENT, INC. (In Formation), John A. Goodman, President." The partners of DDS knew no corporation was yet in existence, and testified at trial that they never agreed to look solely to the corporation for performance of the contract.*

The work was not completed by the required date of October 15, and what work was done was of poor quality. On November 1, Goodman

---

[24] 525 P.2d 135 (Or. 1974).

filed articles of incorporation. On November 2 a corporate license was issued in the name of "Building Renovation and Design Consultants, Inc." The first board of directors meeting was not held until the following February. Between August and December of 1979, DDS made five progress payments. The first check was made out to "Building Design and Development [sic] Inc.—John Goodman." Goodman struck out his name and endorsed the check "Bldg. Design & Dev. Inc., John A. Goodman, Pres." He told DDS to make further payments to the corporation only.

The alleged breaches in performance were never remedied, so in May 1980 DDS demanded arbitration of both the corporation and Goodman. The trial court dismissed Goodman, as an individual, from the arbitration. The Washington Court of Appeals reversed. Goodman appealed.

DIMMICK, JUSTICE:

The issue is whether Goodman, as a promoter, is a party to the preincorporation contract and as such whether he is required to take part in the arbitration. As a general rule,

> where a corporation is contemplated but has not yet been organized at the time when a promoter makes a contract for the benefit of the contemplated corporation, the promoter is personally liable on it, even though the contract will also benefit the future corporation—*Harding* v. *Will*, 81 Wash.2d 132, 139, 500 P.2d 91 (1972).

There is a "strong inference that a person intends to make a contract with an existing person"—*White & Bollard, Inc.* v. *Goodenow*, 58 Wash.2d 180, 184, 361 P.2d 571 (1961).

An exception to the general rule is that if the contracting party knew that the corporation was not in existence at the time of contracting but nevertheless agreed to look solely to the corporation for performance, the promoter is not a party to the contract.

As the proponent of the alleged agreement to look solely to the corporation, Goodman has the burden of proving the agreement. As with any agreement, release of the promoter depends on the intent of the parties. The parties did not manifest their intentions in the contract. Goodman argues that the language indicating that the corporation was "in formation" was an expression by the parties of their intent to make the corporation alone a party to the contract. Some courts do look to such language in the contract and contemporaneous documents to determine intent to release the promoter. See *Stap* v. *Chicago Aces Tennis Team, Inc.*, 63 Ill. App.3d 23, 379 N.E.2d 1293 (1978); *H.F. Philipsborn & Co.* v. *Suson*, 59 Ill.2d 465, 322 N.E.2d 45 (1974); and *Schwedtman* v. *Burns*, 11 S.W.2d 348 (Tex. Civ. App. 1928). Those cases and others cited by Goodman do not analyze the agreements in light of a "strong inference" that one intends to contract with an existing party—an inference we must keep in mind. The mere signing of a contract with a corporation "in formation" does not suffice to show an agreement to look solely to the corporation. It simply begs the question to say that such language in a contract with a promoter in and of itself constitutes an agreement to release the promoter from the contract. Rather, the language raises the question of the parties' intent. Given the "strong inference" that DDS intended to contract with an existing party, the "in formation" language drafted by Goodman is at best ambiguous as to the parties' intentions.

Courts of other jurisdictions differ in their approach as to how specific the agreement must be to release a promoter from a contract and what evidence they will consider in determining the parties' intent. . . . "Some jurisdictions require that the contract show clearly on its face that there is *no* intent to hold the promoter liable before he is released." [Appeals Court in this case, citing *Vodopich* v. *Collier Cy. Developers, Inc.*, 319 So.2d 43, 45 (Fla. App. 1975).]

We do not believe the agreement to release a promoter from liability must say in so many words, "I agree to release." Where the promoter cannot show an express agreement, existence of the agreement to release him from liability may be shown by circumstances. Of course, where circumstantial evidence is relied on, the circumstances must be such as to make it reasonably certain that the parties intended to and did enter into the agreement.

Goodman cites *Quaker Hill, Inc.* v. *Parr*, 148 Colo. 45, 364 P.2d 1056 (1961), and *Sherwood & Roberts–Oregon, Inc.* v. *Alexander*, 525 P.2d 135 (Or. 1974), as cases similar to this one. The courts in those cases found that the promoter had been released from liability. Among the circumstances considered by those courts was the fact that the parties seeking personal liability on the part of the promoter actually urged that the contract be made in the name of the proposed corporation. DDS did not so urge Goodman or even suggest incorporation to him.

From its oral opinion it is clear that the trial court relied on three considerations in holding that the parties agreed to release Goodman from the contract: (1) DDS knew of the corporation's nonexistence; (2) Goodman told Doman that he was forming a corporation to limit his personal liability; and (3) the progress payments were made to the corporation.

The fact that DDS knew of the corporation's nonexistence is not dispositive in any way of its intent. The rule is that the contracting party may know of the nonexistence of the corporation *but nevertheless* may agree to look solely to the corporation. The fact that a contracting party knows that the corporation is nonexistent does not indicate any agreement to release the promoter. To the contrary, such knowledge alone would seem to indicate that the members of DDS intended to make Goodman a party to the contract. They could not hold the corporation, a nonexistent entity, responsible, and of course they would expect to have recourse against someone (Goodman) if default occurred.

The fact that Goodman expressed a desire to form the corporation to limit his liability also is not dispositive of the intentions of the members of DDS. No one from DDS objected to his incorporating but this failure to object does not indicate an affirmative assent to limit Goodman's personal liability. Apparently Goodman believed that incorporation would automatically limit his liability thus misunderstanding the rules regarding promoter liability.

The only other evidence of the parties' intent to make the corporation the sole party to the contract is that the progress payments were made payable to the corporation. However, they were so written only at the instruction of Goodman and in fact the first check written by DDS after the signing of the contract was written to the corporation *and* Goodman as an individual. This evidence does not show by reasonable certainty that DDS intended to contract only with the corporation.

The trial court erred in dismissing Goodman from the arbitration proceedings. We therefore remand.

Corporation's Liability on Promoter's Contracts

A newly formed corporation normally becomes liable on contracts made by its promoter when its board of directors meets and votes to adopt those contracts. Of course, the directors might vote to reject the promoter's contract, in which case the corporation would not be liable on them. Naturally, the corporation cannot obtain the benefits of a rejected contract either.

Adoption, rather than *ratification*, is the proper term because the latter term implies that the principal (corporation) was in existence when the agent (promoter) acted. Courts tend to use the terms interchangeably, which usually causes no problems. Occasionally, however, the distinction can be important.[25]

The corporation's adoption of a promoter's contract need not always be express, such as by a formal board of directors resolution. Adoption may also be implied by the corporation's acts, including a voluntary retention of benefits from a contract. If, for example, a corporation accepted delivery of and used supplies ordered by the promoter before the corporation came into existence, it could be held to have impliedly adopted the contract.

The result may well be different if the retention of benefits is *involuntary*. For example, in *Kridelbaugh* v. *Aldrehn Theatres Co.*,[26] promoters promised an attorney $1,500 if he would investigate, choose the proper state for incorporation, and file the documents to form the corporation. The attorney did so, but was not paid. Regarding the question of whether the corporation was liable for an implied adoption due to its retention of the benefits of the lawyer's work, the court said: "This is not a case in which the corporation can accept or refuse the benefits of a contract. Under the instant record, it had no choice. Like a child at its birth, it must be born in the manner provided. There is no volition on its part."

This does not mean that the attorney in this position will go uncompensated. Many courts will allow recovery not on the contract but on a *quantum meruit* basis for benefits involuntarily received by the newly formed corporation.

Other theories that are occasionally used to bind a corporation to its promoters' contracts include assignment, estoppel, and third-party beneficiary principles. But keep in mind that the corporation's mere coming into existence does not bind it on its promoters' contracts. Only its actions will lead to express or implied adoption.

Corporation's Right to Enforce Promoter's Contracts

When the promoter and a third party intend that the contract be made on behalf of a contemplated corporation, that corporation will, upon expressly or impliedly adopting the contract, have the right to enforce it. It will be no defense to the third party that the corporation did not exist at the time of the agreement between the promoter and the third party.

---

[25] See, for example, *McArthur* v. *Times Printing Co.*, 51 N.W. 216 (Minn. 1892).
[26] 191 N.W. 803 (Iowa 1923).

K & J CLAYTON HOLDING CORP. v. KEUFFEL & ESSER CO.

272 A.2d 565 (N.J. Super. Ct. 1971)

In August 1969, defendant K&J Clayton Holding Corp. (K&J) contracted to sell certain land to plaintiff Keuffel & Esser Co. (K&E) for $750,000. The agreement was signed on plaintiff's behalf by "Benjamin Cohen, President," though no certificate of incorporation was filed by K&E until October 31, 1969.

On November 3, 1969, the scheduled date of the closing, the president of K&J wrote K&E indicating that he had discovered that K&E had not filed incorporation papers and therefore believed the contract of sale was a "nullity" because K&E never existed. K&J returned a $10,000 deposit check.

On November 13, 1969, K&E's attorney wrote K&J indicating that K&E was ready, willing and able to perform the contract by paying $650,000 in cash and delivering a mortgage for the remaining $100,000, as agreed. K&J refused. K&E sued for specific performance. Cross motions for summary judgment were filed.

LYNCH, JUDGE:

The fact is that there *were* two parties to this contract at the time of its execution. The agreement was signed on behalf of the buyer by the purported president of the embryonic or proposed corporation. As such he was a "promoter." Whether or not the corporation were later to "adopt" the contract, a promoter could be held liable thereon. Thus, defendant was not without a fellow contracting party against whom it could have enforced the agreement.

In the context of a promoter having executed the contract, the corporation later coming into existence, the corporation is entitled to all the rights thereunder as well as assuming full liability therefor—1 Fletcher, *Cyclopaedia of Corporations*, §214 at 836–837. Even though the embryo corporation was not able to contract, it could adopt a contract made for its benefit. Having adopted the contract, the corporation may then sue for its enforcement. One mode of adopting the contract is the institution of suit thereon by the corporation.

Defendant's attempt at avoidance of the contract is based, to borrow a phrase, on a "hypothetical horrible," namely, that *if* defendant had attempted to enforce the contract against the plaintiff before the latter's incorporation, it could not have done so. As we have stated above, the contract could have been enforced against the promoter. In any event, plaintiff was in fact incorporated before the date when defendant was entitled to performance.

Plaintiff's motion for summary judgment is granted and that of defendant is denied.

Enforcing Shareholder Subscription Agreements

The traditional method of raising capital for a new corporation was the shareholder subscription agreement. The promoters approached investors who promised to buy certain numbers of shares for certain prices. If there were enough subscribers to meet the contemplated corporation's capital needs, the promoters would cause it to be formed. But what happens if by that time, some subscribers changed their minds and refused to honor their commitments?

Many early cases held subscription agreements to be revocable. Later, courts moved to render them enforceable by finding consideration in the promises of the other subscribers. Section 17 of the MBCA largely solves the problem by making subscription agreements "irrevocable for a period of six months, unless otherwise provided by the terms of the subscription agreement or unless all of the subscribers consent to the revocation of such subscription."

Modern investment banking techniques and the constraints of federal securities laws make subscription agreements impractical for large corporations. They are occasionally used for close corporations today, but more often simple contracts are used.

Tort Liability

Promoters are liable for the torts that they commit while forming a corporation. They also will be liable for the torts of their co-promoters if the court treats them as partners. The corporation, once formed, will not be liable for the preincorporation torts of its promoters unless it in some way ratifies or approves the promoters' actions. For example, if the board of directors adopted a promoter's contract knowing that the promoter had fraudulently induced the other party to sign it, the corporation could be liable in a later fraud suit.

ULTRA VIRES DOCTRINE

The *ultra vires*, literally "beyond its powers," doctrine originally provided that corporations could not stray beyond the powers and purposes specified in their charters. Based on the historic distrust of corporations, the doctrine was intended to protect shareholders and creditors by preventing dissipation of assets through unauthorized ventures. The doctrine was potent in the days when corporate charters were required to spell out precisely the purposes of the corporation. For example, in a famous English case,[27] plaintiff built a railroad for defendant corporation. The defendant managed to breach the contract and yet avoid liability by using the *ultra vires* doctrine as a shield. Because owning a railroad was not listed as a purpose in the corporation's charter, the court held that the contract was *ultra vires*, unenforceable, and could not be saved even if all the shareholders attempted to ratify it.

Later American decisions attempted to limit the doctrine to executory contracts, to uphold *ultra vires* transfers of property that had already occurred, and to hold a corporation liable for the *ultra vires* torts of its agents who were acting to benefit the corporation.

---

[27] *Ashbury Railway Carriage & Iron Co.* v. *Riche*, L.R. 7 H.L. 653 (1875).

The *ultra vires* doctrine has now largely disappeared for two reasons. First, today's general corporation laws usually allow a corporation to incorporate for "any lawful purpose." Specific purposes need not be listed or, if listed, need not be exclusive. By careful drafting, the *ultra vires* problem can be virtually eliminated.

Second, §7 of the MBCA, §3.04 of the RMBCA and similar laws in non-MBCA jurisdictions pretty much eliminate the *ultra vires* doctrine as a shield and as a sword for corporations. Section 7, for example, provides that no act or transaction of a corporation shall be invalid by reason of being outside the capacity or power of the corporation. Only three exceptions are provided. Shareholders may still sue to enjoin a proposed *ultra vires* act. The corporation may sue officers or directors who have injured it by *ultra vires* acts. And the attorney general may use the doctrine to dissolve a corporation or enjoin it from transacting unauthorized business. These three exceptions are seldom invoked.

Section 4 of the MBCA lists numerous powers all corporations shall have, including "to have and exercise all powers necessary or convenient to effect its purposes." Although some courts have noted that corporations are "organized and carried on primarily for the profit of the stockholders" and that the "powers of the directors are to be employed for that end," [28] the more modern view of corporate powers and purposes is discussed in the following case.

THEODORA HOLDING CORPORATION v. HENDERSON

257 A.2d 398 (Del. Ch. 1969)

Plaintiff holding company was formed by Theodora Henderson. Defendants include her former husband, Girard Henderson, and a corporation he controls called Alexander Dawson, Inc. Plaintiff owned shares in defendant corporation and was not happy with the way Girard was running it. Among several other complaints, plaintiff objected to certain contributions defendant corporation made to Alexander Dawson Foundation, an organized charitable trust.

Defendants made various contributions to the trust over the years, averaging around $60,000–70,000 per year from 1960 to 1966.

In 1966 a large tract of land in Colorado worth $467,750 was donated. All the defendant corporation's stockholders, including Theodora, approved of these gifts.

The challenged gift of $528,000 worth of defendant corporation's stock occurred in 1967. It was intended to provide the funds to finance a western camp for underprivileged boys on the aforementioned ranch.

Plaintiff claimed the gift injured the assets and dividends of defendant corporation. On the basis of this and its other complaints, plaintiff sought appointment of a liquidating receiver for Alexander Dawson, Inc.

---

[28] *Dodge* v. *Ford Motor Co.*, 170 N.W. 668 (Mich. 1919).

MARVEL, VICE CHANCELLOR:

Title 8 Del. C. §122 provides as follows:

> Every corporation created under this chapter shall have power to—
>
> . . .
>
> (9) Make donations for the public welfare or for charitable, scientific or educational purposes, and in time of war or other national emergency in aid thereof.

There is no doubt but that the Alexander Dawson Foundation is recognized as a legitimate charitable trust by the Department of Internal Revenue. It is also clear that it is authorized to operate exclusively in the fields of "religious, charitable, scientific, literary, or educational purposes, or for the prevention of cruelty to children or animals." Furthermore, contemporary courts recognize that unless corporations carry an increasing share of the burden of supporting charitable and educational causes, the business advantages now reposed in corporations by law may well prove to be unacceptable to the representatives of an aroused public. The recognized obligation of corporations towards philanthropic, educational, and artistic causes is reflected in the statutory law of all of the states, other than the states of Arizona and Idaho.

In *A. P. Smith Mfg. Co.* v. *Barlow*, 13 N.J. 145, 98 A.2d 681, appeal dismissed, 346 U.S. 861, a case in which the corporate donor had been organized long before the adoption of a statute authorizing corporate gifts to charitable or educational institutions, the Supreme Court of New Jersey upheld a gift of $1,500 by the plaintiff corporation to Princeton University, being of the opinion that the trend towards the transfer of wealth from private industrial entrepreneurs to corporate institutions, the increase of taxes on individual income, coupled with steadily increasing philanthropic needs, necessi-

tate corporate giving for educational needs even were there no statute permitting such gifts, and this was held to be the case apart from the question of the reserved power of the state to amend corporate charters. The court also noted that the gift tended to bolster the free enterprise system and the general social climate in which plaintiff was nurtured. And while the court pointed out that there was no showing that the gift in question was made indiscriminately or to a pet charity in furtherance of personal rather than corporate ends, the actual holding of the opinion appears to be that a corporate charitable or educational gift to be valid must merely be within reasonable limits both as to amount and purpose.

I conclude that the test to be applied in passing on the validity of a gift such as the one here in issue is that of reasonableness, a test in which the provisions of the Internal Revenue Code pertaining to charitable gifts by corporations furnish a helpful guide. The gift here under attack was made from gross income and had a value as of the time of giving of $528,000 in a year in which Alexander Dawson, Inc.'s total income was $19,114,229.06, or well within the federal tax deduction limit of 5% of such income. The contribution under attack can be said to have "cost" all of the stockholders of Alexander Dawson, Inc. including plaintiff, less than $80,000, or some 15 cents per dollar of contributions, taking into consideration the federal tax provisions applicable to holding companies as well as the provisions for compulsory distribution of dividends received by such a corporation. In addition, the gift, by reducing Alexander Dawson, Inc.'s reserve for unrealized capital gains taxes by some $130,000, increased the balance sheet net worth of the stockholders by such amount. It is accordingly obvious, in my opinion, that the relatively small loss of immediate income otherwise payable to plaintiff and the corporate defendant's other stockholders, had it not been for the gift in question, is far outweighed by the overall benefits flowing from the placing of such gift in channels where it serves to benefit those in need of philanthropic or educational support, thus providing justification for large private holdings, thereby benefiting plaintiff in the long run. Finally, the fact that the interests of the Alexander Dawson Foundation appear to be increasingly directed towards the rehabilitation and education of deprived but deserving young people is peculiarly appropriate in an age when a large segment of youth is alienated even from parents who are not entirely satisfied with our present social and economic system.

Plaintiff's application for a liquidating receiver is denied.

Section 3.02 of the RMBCA contains an even more extensive listing of corporate powers than does the MBCA, including the power "to make donations for the public welfare or for charitable, scientific, or educational purposes."

QUESTIONS AND PROBLEMS

1. On March 13, 1979, two children alighting from a school bus were killed when the driver of a truck owned by Fortner LP Gas Company, Inc., was unable to stop his truck in time to avoid running them over. A subsequent inspection of the truck disclosed grossly defective brakes. A grand jury subsequently indicted the corporation, Fortner, for manslaughter in the second degree. Can a corporation be charged with a crime requiring "wantonness" as an element? Discuss. See *Commonwealth* v. *Fortner LP Gas Co.*, 610 S.W.2d 941 (Ky. App. 1981).

2. On September 11, 1973, an inspector from OSHA entered the customer service area of Barlow's, Inc., an electrical and plumbing installation business. The inspector showed his credentials and stated that he wished to conduct a search of the working areas of the business. Because the inspector had no search warrant, the corporation's president refused to allow the inspector entry into the nonpublic areas of the business. The Secretary of Labor then sought a court order compelling Barlow's, Inc., to admit the inspector. Can the corporation claim the protection of the Fourth Amendment's ban on unreasonable searches and seizures? Discuss. See *Marshall* v. *Barlow's, Inc.*, 436 U.S. 307 (1978).

3. Goodwin Brothers Leasing, Inc., was a Kentucky corporation that was not registered to do business as a foreign corporation in Massachusetts. Goodwin had no place of business, employees, or inventory in Massachusetts. It did not solicit lessees of equipment there. Instead, it solicited business from manufacturers who themselves found customers interested in obtaining equipment. To finance the acquisition, Goodwin would buy from the manufacturer and lease to the customer the manufacturer had already found. Goodwin's bills were mailed from Kentucky; customers' payments were mailed to Kentucky. Goodwin leased a Ballantyne pressure fryer to Nousis who operated a pizza business in Massachusetts. When Nousis missed payments,

Goodwin sued. Nousis claimed that Goodwin was disqualified from suing on contracts in Massachusetts courts because of its failure to register as a foreign corporation. Should Goodwin have registered? Discuss. See *Goodwin Bros. Leasing, Inc.* v. *Nousis*, 366 N.E.2d 38 (Sup. Jd. Ct. of Mass. 1977).

4. The Craigs needed $100,000 to start a clothing store. Because they lacked credit, they formed a corporation and sought investors. They prevailed upon four friends to invest $12,000 each, with the understanding that the Craigs would borrow $52,000 to buy their shares, completing the $100,000 capitalization. Instead, the Craigs, with the First National Bank's knowledge, invested only $3,000 of their own money and had the corporation borrow the remaining $49,000. Not knowing about this corporate debt, three of the investors were later induced to sign guaranties covering notes of the corporation. When the business went belly up, the bank sought to enforce the guaranties as covering the $49,000 loan. Can the bank prevail? Discuss. See *First Nat. Bank* v. *One Craig Place, Ltd.*, 303 N.W.2d 688 (Iowa 1981).

5. On November 3, 1978, Central National Bank of Miami (Bank) entered into a merchant's Mastercharge agreement with "The Stereo Corner, Inc., by Joel S. Ratner." Under the agreement, the merchant agreed to be liable for fraudulently accepted sales drafts. The Stereo, Inc., was not incorporated until eight months later, on July 10, 1979. During that period, the Bank was unable to collect from Mastercharge on several sales drafts forged by Stereo Corner employees. Is Ratner individually liable on the Bank's chargeback? See *Ratner* v. *Central Nat. Bank of Miami*, 414 So.2d 210 (Fla. App. 1982).

6. Stap, a professional tennis player, entered into a contract on January 24, 1974 to play with the Chicago Aces Tennis Team. The contract was signed by Stap and "CHICAGO ACES TEAM TENNIS, INC. [Club], By Jordan H. Kaiser, Pres." The contract referred several times to the obligations of the "Player" and the "Club." A June 1, 1974 amendment between "Chicago Aces Tennis Team, Inc., Owner, and Sue Stap, Player," signed by Stap and "Jock A. Miller, General Manager, Chicago Aces," changed plaintiff's bonus provision. The Club was not incorporated until May 1974, with Jordan and Walter Kaiser as its sole shareholders. Later a dispute arose; Stap seeks to hold Jordan Kaiser liable individually on the contract. Is he personally liable as a promoter? Discuss. See *Stap* v. *Chicago Aces Tennis Team, Inc.*, 63 Ill. App.3d 23, 379 N.E.2d 1298 (1978).

7. On September 12, McArthur orally agreed with a promoter of D Corporation to work as an advertising solicitor for a period of one year beginning on October 1. Indeed, McArthur began working on that day and received a regular paycheck until the following April, when he was fired. The directors of D, which was not officially organized until October 16, knew of the contract with McArthur but took no formal action to adopt it. When McArthur sued on the contract, the corporation claimed it was not bound on the contract, and, in any event, the contract was unenforceable as an oral contract not to be performed within one year of the making. Discuss. See *McArthur* v. *Times Printing Co.*, 48 Minn. 319, 51 N.W. 216 (1892).

8. A public utility's board of directors authorized a contribution of $10,000 to an association that advocated the defeat of Proposition T, which, if approved in an election,

would require voter approval for construction of any building more than 72 feet in height. The board concluded Proposition T would (a) cause an increase in the tax rate applicable to the company's facilities and (b) interfere with several present and future building plans of the company. Shareholders challenged the legality and propriety of the contribution. Discuss. See *Marsili* v. *Pacific Gas & Electric Co.*, 51 Cal. App.3d 313, 124 Cal. Rptr. 313 (1975).

8

RECOGNITION
OF THE CORPORATE
ENTITY

INTRODUCTION

One of the prime advantages of the corporate form of enterprise is the limited liability afforded shareholders. This chapter examines two problems that are related to limited liability and to each other. First, are there instances where even though the corporation has been defectively formed, its existence should be recognized to preserve limited liability for its shareholders? Second, are there situations where, although a corporation has been properly formed, its existence should be disregarded so that liability can be imposed on its shareholders? Although these are separate problems, similar considerations affect both.

DEFECTIVE INCORPORATION

De Jure Corporations

A *de jure* corporation exists where there is "substantial compliance" with all steps required for incorporation. Such a corporation will be recognized by the courts for all purposes and as to all parties. It is free from attack on grounds that it was not properly formed. Its shareholders' limited liability is established in the first instance.

As indicated in the previous chapter, the process of incorporation involves myriad major and minor acts. Fortunately, the courts do not require perfect compliance with all steps to recognize a corporation as *de jure*. Rather, they require only "substantial compliance." This has been construed to mean compliance with all "mandatory" provisions of the incorporation process. Failure to complete a minor or "directory" requirement will not prevent a *de jure* corporation from coming into existence.

Courts disagree as to which steps in the incorporation process are mandatory and therefore "conditions precedent" to corporateness, but the following are usually included in this category: filing articles of incorporation in the proper public office(s), payment of incorporation taxes, and payment of required fees. Matters that do not bar *de jure* status but that may lead to revocation of corporate status (and may therefore be viewed as "conditions subsequent" to incorporation) include payment of minimum capital and the filing of certain required reports or statements.[1]

As we shall see, several states have amended their corporation laws to clarify exactly when corporate existence begins. These statutes eliminate much of the confusion arising from the disparate court interpretations in the area.

De Facto Corporations

Failure to achieve *de jure* status through substantial compliance with the statutory requirements for incorporation will not always lead to imposition of personal liability on the shareholders. This is so because the courts developed the doctrine of the *de facto* corporation. Although this status is no defense to a *quo warranto* action by the *state* seeking revocation of the corporate charter, it may bar collateral attack on corporateness by other parties.

There are three generally recognized requirements for recognition of *de facto* status: (1) existence of a statute under which the corporation might have been validly incorporated, (2) a "colorable" attempt at compliance, and (3) some "user" or exercise of corporate status. Courts disagree as to what constitutes a "colorable" attempt at compliance, just as they disagree as to what constitutes "substantial compliance" for purposes of *de jure* status. Still, a *bona fide* or good faith attempt is usually required. Corporate "user" is usually present, because no lawsuit would have arisen if there had not been some attempt to exercise corporate status.

Application of the *de facto* doctrine depends heavily upon the circumstances of the case. *De facto* status may be recognized for some purposes, but not for others. It will frequently be applied in contract cases where parties dealt with what they believed was a properly formed corporation, but later attempted to impose personal liability on the shareholders because of defects in the incorporation process.

The following case contains such a scenario.

---

[1] H. Henn and J. Alexander, *Law of Corporations*, 3rd ed. (West Publishing Co.: St. Paul, MN, 1983), p. 328.

CANTOR v. SUNSHINE GREENERY, INC.

398 A.2d 571 (N.J. Super. 1979)

Plaintiffs prepared a lease for property they owned naming Sunshine Greenery, Inc., as the tenant. The lease was signed by Brunetti, as president of Sunshine. Plaintiffs knew the corporation was to be liable on the contract and not Brunetti individually. On November 11, 1974, Brunetti reserved the corporate name with the Secretary of State's office. On December 3, the certificate of incorporation was signed by the incorporators and forwarded to the Secretary of State. The aforementioned lease was signed on December 16, but the certificate of incorporation for some unexplained reason was not officially filed until two days later on December 18.

The trial court held Brunetti personally liable on the lease, in part because Sunshine was neither a de jure *nor a* de facto *corporation. Brunetti appealed.*

LARNER, JUDGE:

In view of the late filing, Sunshine Greenery, Inc., was not a *de jure* corporation on December 16, 1974, when the lease was signed. See *N.J.S.A.* 14A:2–7(2). Nevertheless, there is ample evidence of the fact that it was a *de facto* corporation in that there was a *bona fide* attempt to organize the corporation some time before the consummation of the contract, and there was an actual exercise of the corporate powers by the negotiation with plaintiffs and the execution of the contract involved in this litigation. When this is considered in the light of the concession that plaintiffs knew that they were dealing with that corporate entity and not with Brunetti individually, it becomes evident that the *de facto* status of the corporation suffices to absolve Brunetti from individual liability. Plaintiffs in effect are estopped from attacking the legal existence of the corporation collaterally because of the nonfiling in order to impose liability on the individual when they have admittedly contracted with a corporate entity which had *de facto* status. . . . In fact, their prosecution of the claim against the corporation to default judgment is indicative of their recognition of the corporation as the true obligor and theoretically inconsistent with the assertion of the claim against the individual.

The trial judge's finding that Sunshine Greenery, Inc., was not a *de facto* corporation is unwarranted under the record facts herein. The mere fact that there were no formal meetings or resolutions or issuance of stock is not determinative of the legal or *de facto* existence of the corporate entity, particularly under the simplified New Jersey Business Corporation Act of 1969, which eliminates the necessity of a meeting of incorporators. See *N.J.S.A.* 14A:2–6 and Commissioners' Comment thereunder. The act of executing the certificate of incorporation, the *bona fide* effort to file it, and the dealings with plaintiffs in the name of that corporation fully satisfy the requisite proof of the existence of a *de facto* corporation. To deny such existence because of a mere technicality caused by administrative delay in filing runs counter to the purpose of the *de facto* concept and would accomplish an unjust and inequitable result in favor of plaintiffs contrary to their own contractual expectations.

Reversed.

In tort cases, the *de facto* doctrine is frequently used on behalf of plaintiff corporations so that defendants cannot escape liability for their wrongdoing by challenging the corporation's existence. When a corporate charter expires for some technical reason, most courts hold that the *de facto* doctrine is available to protect shareholders from personal liability on the enterprise's obligations incurred before revival of the charter. Some courts use the doctrine in the similar situation between suspension and reinstatement of the corporate charter. The following case is instructive in this regard.

PEOPLE v. ZIMBELMAN

572 P.2d 830 (Colo. 1977)

Zimbelman (appellee) and Knox incorporated Balto Industries, Inc., in 1969. Each owned half the stock. Although the corporation was declared defunct by the Secretary of State in 1972 for failure to pay annual taxes and file annual reports, the two owners continued to operate the business in the corporate name.

In 1976, after the death of Knox, evidence came to light that appellee had diverted to his personal account checks made out to the corporation. Mrs. Knox and a court-appointed accountant gave information to the police that led to the filing of felony theft charges against the appellee. The trial judge dismissed the charges for lack of a corporate victim. The prosecution appealed.

CARRIGAN, JUSTICE:

A co-owner of property cannot ordinarily be guilty of theft of that property—*People v. McCain*, Colo., 552 P.2d 20 (1976). Here, therefore, the People were required to establish the existence of a corporate entity. Otherwise the appellee simply would have been a co-owner of his company's funds, and the funds would not have been susceptible to theft by him. The

trial court ruled that, because the corporation had been legally defunct since 1972, the appellee and Knox were doing business as co-owners, and there was no basis for criminal theft charges. We disagree.

The People correctly assert that in criminal cases the prosecution is required to prove only the *de facto* corporate existence of an alleged corporate victim—*Goodfellow* v. *People*, 75 Colo. 243, 224 P.1051 (1942).

For an enterprise to constitute a *de facto* corporation, three elements must coincide: (1) a law under which a corporation may lawfully be formed; (2) a *bona fide* attempt to form the corporation according to that law; and (3) an exercise of, or attempt to exercise, corporate powers. . . . The record clearly indicates that these three requirements were met in this case.

It is clear beyond dispute that Balto Industries, Inc., was validly incorporated under Colorado law. Several witnesses testified that business operations continued under the corporate name even after the corporation was declared defunct in 1972. All business records and books, bank accounts, and the sign on the company headquarters bore the name "Balto Industries,

Inc.,'' clearly evincing an intent to carry on the business as a corporation. Ordinarily, evidence of this nature is sufficient to establish *de facto* corporate status in a criminal case.

The trial court distinguished this case, however, on the basis of the fact that at the time of the alleged thefts, the company had been declared defunct. Thus the ultimate question is whether that defunct status prevented Balto Industries from operating even as a *de facto* corporation. We conclude that it did not.

Generally, a corporation which has been dissolved by judicial decree or statutory forfeiture cannot exist thereafter as a *de facto* corporation. . . . The statute under which Balto Industries was declared defunct, Section 7–10–109, C.R.S. 1973, penalizes a corporation for failing to pay franchise taxes or file annual reports by prohibiting its transacting business *as a corporation* while it is defunct. However, the statute also provides that upon filing the necessary reports and paying the delinquent taxes, plus a penalty, the corporation is "revived" and reinstated to full corporate status.

Thus, the statute does not authorize involuntary dissolution of the corporation, but merely allows the secretary of state to suspend its operations while it is in default. . . . The corporation's shareholders retain the power to hold annual meetings and elect corporate officers and directors, and the corporation may still hold, mortgage, and convey real estate—Section 7–10–109(2) and (3) C.R.S. 1973. A "revived" corporation is regarded as having had continuous existence throughout the period of suspension.

In other words, despite its technically defunct status, Balto Industries, Inc., still retained very real powers and duties *as a corporation*, including the power to hold property in the corporate name. Although its power to transact business had been suspended, the corporation had not totally ceased to exist as a legal entity.

Since Balto Industries' defunct status did not preclude its continued existence as at least a *de facto* corporation, we hold that the People's evidence sufficiently established the existence of a corporate victim of the alleged thefts.

Reversed.

Corporation by Estoppel

Even where there is no *de jure* or *de facto* status, collateral attack on a corporation's existence may be barred if the classic elements of estoppel—holding out and reliance—are present. The party claiming estoppel is arguing that the other party has, by conduct, agreement, or admission, placed himself or herself in a position where it would now be inequitable to allow him or her to deny the corporation's existence.

The doctrine has been used where a corporation was sued and its incorporators denied its existence, where a corporation sued a debtor that had dealt with it on a corporate basis yet denied its existence, and where the owners of a business were sued individually by third parties who had dealt with the business as a corporation.[2]

A recent application of the doctrine of corporation by estoppel follows.

---

[2] Note, "Estoppel to Deny Corporate Existence," *Tennessee Law Review*, Vol. 31 (1964), p. 336.

GOODWYNE v. MOORE

316 S.E.2d 601 (Ga. App. 1984)

Over the period of several years, appellee/ plaintiffs loaned funds to several corporations formed by appellant/defendant Goodwyne. Many promissory notes were executed either by "Mobile Listing & Locator Service, Inc.," or "Budget Homes, Inc.," followed by appellant's name as president. On December 15, 1978, the parties executed a note signed "C & N Industries, Inc., By Charles Goodwyne, Pres." Appellees accepted payments from C & N Industries and issued receipts to it. Following default on the note, appellees filed a complaint against C & N Industries. After it confessed judgment, appellees filed this suit against appellant Goodwyne alleging individual liability.

Appellant raised in defense the doctrine of corporation by estoppel, but the jury found in favor of appellees. Goodwyne appealed.

CARLEY, JUDGE:

The doctrine of corporation by estoppel is viable in this state. "The existence of a corporation claiming a charter under color of law cannot be collaterally attacked by persons who have dealt with it as a corporation. Such persons are estopped from denying its corporate existence"—OCGA §14-5-4. ". . . It is the general rule that a person who has contracted or otherwise dealt with a corporation as such is estopped to deny its corporate existence in any action arising out of or involving such contract. For instance, 'where a person *enters into a contract with a body purporting to be a corporation, and such body is described in the contract by the corporate name* . . . or is otherwise clearly

recognized as an existing corporation, *such person thereby admits the legal existence of the corporation* for the purposes of any action that may be brought to enforce the contract, and in such an action he will not be permitted . . . to deny the legality of its corporate existence' " (emphasis added)—*West v. Flynn Realty Co.*, 53 Ga. App. 594, 595, 186 S.E. 753 (1936). Appellees in the instant case clearly entered into a contract with a body described therein by a corporate name.

Appellees, however, rely upon *Don Swann Sales Corp.* v. *Echols*, 160 Ga. App. 539, 287 S.E.2d 577 (1981), for the proposition that the doctrine of corporation by estoppel is inapplicable to the instant case. In *Don Swann*, this court held that where an individual purports to act for a *nonexistent* corporation, the doctrine of corporation by estoppel will not be applied. " '[O]ne who assumes to act as agent for a nonexistent principal or one having no legal status renders himself individually liable in contracts so made.' Where the evidence supports a finding that the purported corporation is *not* a valid corporate entity, there is no doubt that the agent is bound by his [execution of a promissory note]"—*Don Swann Sales Corp.* v. *Echols*, supra at 541, 287 S.E.2d 577.

However, *Don Swann* is clearly distinguishable from the instant case. In *Don Swann*, the corporation in question was not " 'properly' registered with the Secretary of State" and, therefore, was not in existence until sometime after the occurrence of the transactions at issue between the parties. In the case at bar, the evidence shows that appellant incorporated C & N Bottle Shop, Inc. (C & N Bottle), on October 11, 1978. The articles of incorporation provided that the purpose of the corporation was to operate a retail store selling bottled beverages, "and any other business for profit permitted under the Georgia Business Corporation Code." However, appellant was unable to obtain financing to open a liquor store, and therefore decided instead to establish a salvage operation. On December 11, 1978, a name certificate was obtained for C & N Industries. Four days thereafter, the promissory note at issue was executed by C & N Industries. On February 26, 1979, approximately two months after the execution of the note, C & N Bottle filed articles of amendment with the Secretary of State, "changing its name to C & N Industries, Inc."

Thus, unlike *Don Swann*, a corporate entity was in "existence" at the time the note was executed but was undergoing a name change to C & N Industries. The certificate of incorporation by the Secretary of State is "conclusive evidence of incorporation." See OCGA §14–2–173. The relevant certificate of incorporation was filed on October 11, 1978, well before the execution of the note. Following the issuance of the certificate of incorporation, the corporation merely changed its name from C & N Bottle to C & N Industries.

. . .

Appellees, by accepting the instant promissory note from a "body purporting to be a corporation" and described in the note by a corporate name, have admitted the legal existence of C & N Industries and are estopped from denying its legal existence in a suit to enforce the note. This conclusion is further supported by the evidence that appellees had dealt with appellant exclusively as an agent for a corporation on numerous occasions in the past. Further, appellees issued receipts to the corporation for its payments on the note before its default.

. . .

Reversed.

Statutory Developments

The cases in this whole area have been called "irreconcilable" [3] and worse. Fortunately, in recent years problems have diminished. One reason is that there have been fewer problems with defective formation of corporations because many states have simplified the incorporation process. Simplifications have included eliminating minimum capital requirements, requiring filing only with state authorities thereby ending county filing requirements, and other such changes.

A second reason lies with many new state laws that attempt to clarify with precision exactly when corporate existence begins by clearly establishing certain conditions precedent to corporate existence or by providing that issuance of a formal certificate of incorporation establishes a conclusive presumption of corporateness except as to proceedings by the state.

Although, as some of the earlier cases in this chapter indicated, the doctrines of *de facto* corporation and corporation by estoppel are still alive and well in many

---

[3] Frey, "Legal Analysis and the 'De Facto' Doctrine," *Univ. of Pennsylvania Law Review*, Vol. 100 (1952), p. 1153.

jurisdictions, many other jurisdictions have held that the new statutes have eliminated these doctrines. An influential case is *Robertson* v. *Levy*.

ROBERTSON v. LEVY

197 A.2d 443 (D.C. Ct. App. 1964)

On December 22, 1961, Robertson agreed to sell his business to a corporation, Penn Ave. Record Shack, Inc., to be formed by Levy. Levy submitted articles of incorporation to the Superintendent of Corporations on December 27, but no certificate of incorporation was issued then. The contract of sale was signed on December 29. On January 1, 1962, the articles of incorporation were rejected by the Superintendent, but Levy began operating the business under the corporate name. Robertson executed a bill of sale on January 8. A certificate of incorporation was finally issued on January 17, 1962. The corporation ceased doing business in June 1962.

Robertson later sued Levy individually for the balance due on the December 29 contract. The trial court held Robertson to be estopped to deny the corporate existence and entered judgment for Levy. Robertson appealed.

Hood, Chief Judge:

For a full understanding of the problem raised, some historical grounding is not only illuminative but necessary. In early common law times private corporations were looked upon with distrust and disfavor. This distrust of the corporation form for private enterprise was eventually overcome by the enactment of statutes which set forth certain prerequisites before the status was achieved, and by court decisions which eliminated other stumbling blocks. Problems soon arose, however, where there was substantial compliance with the prerequisites of the

statute, but not complete formal compliance. Thus the concepts of de jure corporations, de facto corporations, and of "corporations by estoppel" came into being.

. . .

One of the reasons for enacting modern corporation statutes was to eliminate problems inherent in the de jure, de facto and estoppel concepts. Thus Sections 29–921c (MBCA §56) and 950 (MBCA §146) were enacted as follows:

§29–921c. Effect of issuance of incorporation

Upon the issuance of the certificate of incorporation, the corporate existence shall begin, and such certificate of incorporation shall be conclusive evidence that all conditions precedent required to be performed by the incorporators have been complied with and that the corporation has been incorporated under this chapter, except as against the District of Columbia in a proceeding to cancel or revoke the certificate of incorporation.

§29–950. Unauthorized assumption of corporate powers

All persons who assume to act as a corporation without authority so to do shall be jointly and severally liable for all debts and liabilities incurred or arising as a result thereof.

The first portion of Section 29–921c sets forth a sine qua non regarding compliance. No longer must the courts inquire into the equities of a case to determine whether there has been "colorable compliance" with the statute. The corporation comes into existence only when the certificate has been issued. Before the certificate issues, there is no corporation de jure or de facto or by estoppel. After the certificate is issued under Section 921c, the de jure corporate existence commences. Only after such existence has begun can the corporation commence business through compliance with Section 29–921d, by paying to the corporation the minimum capital and with Section 921a(f), which requires that the capitalization be no less than $1,000.

. . .

The authorities which have considered the problem are unanimous in their belief that Section 29–921c (similar to Model Business Corporation Act §56) and Section 29–950 (similar to Model Business Corporation Act §146) have put to rest de facto corporations and corporations by estoppel. Thus the Comment to section 56 of the Model Act, after noting that de jure incorporation is complete when the certificate is issued, states that

> Since it is unlikely that any steps short of securing a certificate of incorporation would be held to constitute apparent compliance, the possibility that a de facto corporation could exist under such a provision is remote.

. . .

The portion of §29–921c that states that the certificate of incorporation will be "conclusive evidence" that all conditions precedent have been performed eliminates the problems of estoppel and de facto corporations once the certificate has been issued. The existence of the corporation is conclusive evidence against all who deal with it. Under §29–950, if an individual or group of individuals assumes to act as a corporation before the certificate of incorporation has been issued, joint and several liability attaches. We hold, therefore, that the impact of these sections, when considered together, is to eliminate the concepts of estoppel and de facto corporateness under the Business Corporation Act of the District of Columbia. It is immaterial whether the third person believed he was dealing with a corporation or whether he intended to deal with a corporation. The certificate of incorporation provides the cut-off point; before it is issued, the individuals, and not the corporation, are liable.

Turning to the facts of this case, Penn Ave. Record Shack, Inc., was not a corporation when the original agreement was entered into, when the lease was assigned, when Levy took over Robertson's business, when operations began under the Penn Ave. Record Shack, Inc., name, or when the bill of sale was executed. Only on January 17 did Penn Ave. Record Shack, Inc., become a corporation. Levy is subject to personal liability because, before this date, he assumed to act as a corporation, without any authority to do so. Nor is Robertson estopped from denying the existence of the corporation because after the certificate was issued he accepted one payment on the note. An individual who incurs statutory liability on an obligation under Section 29–950, because he has acted without authority, is not relieved of that liability where, at a later time, the corporation does come into existence by complying with Section 29–921c. Subsequent partial payment by the corporation does not remove this liability.

The judgment appealed from is reversed.

Robertson notwithstanding, the MBCA's attempt in §§56 and 146 to eliminate the *de jure* corporation, *de facto* corporation, and corporation by estoppel doctrines has not been successful in all jurisdictions.[4]

Consequences of Defective Incorporation

Where there is no *de jure* corporation, and where the doctrines of *de facto* corporation and corporation by estoppel are either unavailable or inapplicable, the traditional rule held all shareholders liable as general partners for the debts of the defectively organized corporation. Some courts,[5] basing their reasoning on the language of MBCA §146, impose liability on shareholders actively involved in the corporation, but not on passive shareholders.[6]

PIERCING THE CORPORATE VEIL

Introduction

Related to and sometimes overlapping the problems of defective incorporation are those considerations that accompany what is known as "piercing the corporate veil." Normally, if there are no defects in the incorporation process, the corporate entity will be recognized and the shareholders will be accorded limited liability. Corporate creditors will not be allowed to chase the personal assets of individual shareholders, and creditors of individual shareholders will not be allowed to seize corporate assets.

In some instances, however, policy considerations will dictate that the existence of even a perfectly formed corporation should be ignored. In such cases courts pierce the corporate veil, usually to impose liability upon individual shareholders for the debts of the corporation. The difficulty, of course, is determining exactly when the corporate veil is properly pierced. On the one hand, we wish to encourage development of our economy by allowing persons to invest their money in business enterprises without the risk of unlimited personal liability. On the other hand, we do not wish to allow the corporate entity to be used "to defeat public convenience, to justify wrong, protect fraud, or defend crime."[7]

Unfortunately, the case law has been remarkably inconsistent in this area. Very few firm guidelines regarding when courts will pierce the corporate veil may be stated with certainty. However, the remainder of this chapter will offer at least some guidance

---

[4] The RMBCA's §2.03 goes even farther to eliminate these doctrines by providing that a corporation comes into existence when the articles of incorporation are *filed* with the Secretary of State. Thereafter, only the state can challenge the corporate existence.

[5] For example, *Timberline Equipment Co.* v. *Davenport*, 514 P.2d 1109 (Or. 1973).

[6] RMBCA §2.04 changes the rule slightly, providing that all persons purporting to act on behalf of a corporation *knowing* there was no incorporation are jointly and severally liable for all liabilities created.

[7] *U.S.* v. *Milwaukee Refrig. Transit Co.*, 142 F. 247 (C.C.E.D. Wis. 1905).

by discussing many of the main factors considered by the courts in some of the common circumstances in which the doctrine is asserted.

Despite the absence of a concrete set of rules as to when courts will pierce the corporate veil, perhaps some comfort can be taken in the words of one commentator who concluded that "what the formula comes down to once shorn of verbiage about control, instrumentality, agency, and corporate entity, is that liability is imposed [on individual shareholders] to reach an equitable result." [8]

Factors

Courts have considered innumerable factors in deciding whether to pierce the corporate veil in various cases over the years. Decisions are rendered on a case-by-case basis after a weighing of relevant factors. No single factor is determinative. Still, some are mentioned more than others.

No court has ever pierced the corporate veil of a corporation whose shares were publicly traded or widely held. The doctrine's use is limited to closely held corporations. Even there, the mere fact that a corporation has a single owner does not alone mean that the corporate veil should be pierced. This is true even if the shareholder's main motivation in incorporating was to escape personal liability. Acquisition of limited liability is recognized as a proper benefit of incorporation.

Various courts and commentators list different factors that *will* justify piercing the corporate veil. Their formulations differ, but the fact that a corporation is undercapitalized and that it is merely an "instrumentality" or "alter ego" of its shareholders are two very important considerations. That a corporation is merely an alter ego of its shareholders is shown by such facts as commingling of corporate and individual funds and a failure to observe corporate formalities. Always lurking in the background is the question of whether considerations of equity and fairness mandate a departure from the tendency to observe the existence of the corporate entity.

Although no listing could be inclusive, one author has culled the following factors from court opinions deciding whether or not to pierce the corporate veil. One or more of these factors were present in all cases where the corporate veil was pierced:

1. Commingling of funds and other assets of the corporation with those of the individual shareholders (Corporation XYZ holds no separate bank account but deposits the receipts from its business transactions in the personal account of A, its sole shareholder).
2. Diversion of the corporation's funds or assets to noncorporate uses (to the personal uses of the corporation's shareholders).
3. Failure to maintain the corporate formalities necessary for the issuance or subscription to the corporation's stock, such as formal approval of the stock issue by an independent board of directors.
4. An individual shareholder representing to persons outside the corporation that he or she is personally liable for the debts or other obligations of the corporation.
5. Failure to maintain corporate minutes or adequate corporate records.

---

[8] E. Latty, *Subsidiaries and Affiliated Corporations* (Foundation Press: Chicago, Ill., 1936), p. 191.

6. Identical ownership in two entities (Corporation A is owned by the same shareholders and in the same proportions as Corporation B).

7. Identity of the directors and officers of two entities who are responsible for supervision and management (a partnership or sole proprietorship and a corporation owned and managed by the same parties).

8. Failure to capitalize a corporation adequately for the reasonable risks of the corporate undertaking.

9. Absence of separately held corporate assets.

10. Use of a corporation as a mere shell or conduit to operate a single venture or some particular aspect of the business of an individual or another corporation.

11. Sole ownership of all stock by one individual or members of a single family.

12. Use of the same office or business location by the corporation and its individual shareholders.

13. Employment of the same employees or attorney by the corporation and its shareholder(s).

14. Concealment or misrepresentation of the identity of the ownership, management, or financial interests in the corporation and concealment of personal business activities of the shareholders (sole shareholders do not reveal the association with a corporation, which makes loans to them without adequate security).

15. Disregard of legal formalities and failure to maintain proper arm's-length relationships among related entities.

16. Use of a corporate entity as a conduit to procure labor, services, or merchandise for another person or entity.

17. Diversion of corporate assets from the corporation by or to a stockholder or other person or entity to the detriment of creditors, or the manipulation of assets and liabilities between entities to concentrate the assets in one and the liabilities in another.

18. Contracting by the corporation with another person with the intent to avoid the risk of nonperformance by use of the corporate entity, or the use of a corporation as a subterfuge for illegal transactions.

19. The formation and use of the corporation to assume the existing liabilities of another person or entity.[9]

Different factors are emphasized in different contexts.

Contract Cases

Persons dealing with business enterprises that they believe to be corporations should know that the owners of the corporation normally have limited liability. They have the opportunity, whether or not they exercise it, to investigate the corporation to determine whether it has sufficient assets to cover its obligations. If it does not, these potential creditors have the option of refusing to deal with the corporation unless its owners *personally* guarantee the corporation's performance. Only in that manner can these creditors ensure access to the personal assets of individual shareholders.

Because one who voluntarily deals with a corporation may be characterized as assuming the risk of the corporation's nonperformance, many courts are reluctant to pierce the corporate veil to impose liability on shareholders in contract cases. Therefore,

---

[9] D. Barber, "Piercing the Corporate Veil," *Willamette Law Review*, Vol. 17 (1981), p. 371.

one who deals with a corporation should be wary. For example, in *Bartle* v. *Home Owners Cooperative*,[10] Home Owners Cooperative (HOC) established a wholly owned subsidiary, Westerlea Builders, Inc., to construct housing to be sold to HOC's members *at cost*. The arrangement ensured that Westerlea could not make a profit and that it would probably go broke, which it did. Yet, when unpaid contract creditors of Westerlea attempted to sue HOC, they were unsuccessful. Because the creditors could have investigated the arrangement and Westerlea's financial status before dealing with it, and because the creditors were not misled and there was no fraud, the court refused to pierce Westerlea's corporate veil. The assets of HOC were not available to Westerlea's creditors.

Fraud is a very important factor in contract cases. While some courts clearly state that they do not always require a showing of fraud to pierce in contract cases, other courts just as clearly do require such a showing. But what constitutes fraud?

Usually, inadequate capitalization alone will not be viewed as fraudulent, because potential creditors can always check the corporation's financial position and require personal guarantees by shareholders if necessary. On the other hand, if a shareholder misled a third party as to the amount of capital a corporation had, a court would not be reluctant to pierce the corporate veil. Similarly, someone who misleads a third party into believing that he is dealing with an individual (whose personal assets will be available should a lawsuit ensue) rather than a corporation may be held personally liable. However, merely buying goods on credit on the corporation's behalf, even though the purchasing shareholders know that the corporation probably cannot pay for those goods, is not fraud because the creditor can always check to protect himself or herself.[11]

Courts tend to find fraud or other requisite misconduct in situations where the corporation is a mere "instrumentality" or "alter ego" of its controlling shareholders. If, for example, a controlling shareholder ignored corporate formalities, siphoned off any corporate funds into his individual pocket so that the corporation was perpetually insolvent, and intermixed corporate and personal funds at will, many courts would pierce the corporate veil even in a contract case.[12]

The following case is instructive.

TEXAS INDUSTRIES, INC. v. DUPUY & DUPUY DEVELOPMENT, INC.

227 So.2d 265 (La. App. 1969)

A. J. Dupuy, Sr., was a real estate broker and A. J. Dupuy, Jr., was involved in residential construction. On February 19, 1965, the residential construction business was incorporated with the Dupuys and a local attorney as incorporators. The principal offices in Dupuy & Dupuy

---

[10] 127 N.E.2d 832 (N.Y. App. 1955).

[11] *Hickman* v. *Rawls*, 638 S.W.2d 100 (Tex. Civ. App. 1982).

[12] *DeWitt Truck Brokers* v. *W. Ray Flemming Fruit Co.*, 540 F.2d 681 (4th Cir. 1976).

Development, Inc., were held by the Dupuys. Dupuy, Sr., who advanced the $1,000 statutory minimum capitalization, received 98 of the 100 authorized shares. Dupuy, Jr., and the attorney each received 1 share. Six months later, 60 of Dupuy, Sr.'s shares were transferred to his son.

Dupuy, Jr., controlled the corporation, as he had managed the construction business before its incorporation. Dupuy, Sr., exercised no control except on one occasion when he was instrumental in closing a sale and a loan on behalf of the corporation. When the corporation needed funds, Dupuy, Sr., would advance them or endorse notes at the local bank as he had done for his son's business before it was incorporated.

Texas Industries, Inc., delivered construction materials to the corporation, but it was not paid after the corporation sold the lot on which the materials were used and its improvements to Taylor. A lawsuit followed, and the corporation was held liable as were both Dupuys individually.

Dupuy, Sr., appealed the judgment holding him personally liable.

AYRES, JUDGE:

Corporations are individual beings, separate and distinct from the individuals who compose their membership. The estates and rights of corporations belong exclusively to them. Therefore, the debts and obligations due to a corporation are not due to the individuals who compose its membership. Hence, a creditor of a corporation cannot compel the corporate members or stockholders to individually pay that which is due by the corporation.

A general exception to the rule of nonliability of shareholders and officers for corporate obligations is recognized where the shareholder or officer has practiced fraud upon a person through the corporation or upon the corporation itself.

Other exceptions to these rules of nonliability of a shareholder for corporate debts have been recognized where the stockholder is the alter ego of the corporation. For the doctrine of an alter ego to apply, it must be shown that the stockholder whose individual and personal liability for a corporate debt is sought disregarded the entity of the corporation and, thus, made the corporation a mere agency for the transaction of his own private business. Thus, the separate individualities of the corporation and its stockholders must have ceased to exist—*Brown* v. *Benton Creosoting Co., Inc.*, 147 So.2d 89 (La. App., 2d Cir. 1962—*cert. denied*).

The doctrine of alter ego does not create assets in a corporation, but it simply fastens liability on an individual who uses the corporation merely as an instrumentality in conducting his own personal business. Liability in such instances springs from fraud perpetrated not necessarily on the corporation itself but upon third persons dealing with the corporation—*Shreveport Sash & Door Company* v. *Ray*, 159 So.2d 434, 437 (La. App., 2d Cir. 1963). Though the exception to the principle of nonliability of a stockholder is applicable when an individual stockholder in a corporation has utilized the corporate identity as a screen or cover-up of his individual acts of fraud or deception practiced upon the public or the creditors of a corporation, the record in the instant case is barren of proof that A. J. Dupuy, Sr., used the corporation for the advancement of his personal affairs, that he exercised any control over its affairs or operations, or that he received the smallest benefit therefrom. No evidence has been produced warranting a finding of fraud, deception, or ill practice on the part of A. J. Dupuy, Sr.

Nor can the liability of A. J. Dupuy, Sr., for corporate debts be predicated upon the corporation's limited capitalization. The amount of paid-in capital was in accordance with statutory authorization. The articles of incorporation are matters of public record. All persons contemplating business transactions with the corporation have ready access to the information disclosed by the public records. Included in the information disclosed is the paid-in capital of the corporation. There is no presumption of fraud, deceit, or ill practices on the part of a stockholder because of a corporation's limited capitalization. Inadequate capitalization is not of itself a badge of fraud. A subscription of an incorporator of a corporation limits his liability and such limitation is legitimate.

The general rule is that an individual may incorporate his business for the sole purpose of escaping liability for the corporate debts. As pointed out in *L. L. Ridgeway Company* v. *Marks*, 146 So.2d 61, 63 (La. App., 4th Cir. 1962), limitation of liability is often a primary reason for incorporating; escape of individual liability may be its sole purpose.

The fact that one owns a majority of stock in a corporation does not of itself make him liable for the corporate debts. So long as the corporate existence is maintained, immunity from liability of even a sole stockholder is the same as if there are many stockholders. . . . Except under circumstances whereby a shareholder becomes individually liable for corporate debts through fraud, deceit, or ill practices, the shareholder is within his rights to limit his obligation by the amount of and to the extent of his subscription for capital stock. He may properly say, "Thus far I will go but no farther—I will risk the amount paid for my stock, but no more."

Reversed.

Tort Cases

Although there are many leading tort cases in which courts have refused to pierce the corporate veil, courts are generally more inclined to pierce in tort cases than in contract cases because plaintiffs in tort cases are not readily able to look out for themselves. A potential contract creditor of Corporation X can fully investigate its financial status before dealing with it. However, a pedestrian in a crosswalk who looks up to see a speeding Corporation X truck bearing down on her has no opportunity to inspect a balance sheet before the tort occurs.

Because corporations generally carry as much liability insurance as other forms of business, the need to pierce the corporate veil to compensate an injured tort plaintiff adequately does not arise as often as it otherwise might. When the need does arise, however, the courts pay particular attention to the adequacy of capitalization. If the corporation did not have sufficient capital to meet tort liabilities that might foreseeably arise from the nature of its business, a court will be tempted to reach into the pockets of shareholders to compensate the injured plaintiff fully.

The following case implies that inadequate capitalization alone may be a sufficient reason to pierce the corporate veil in tort cases.

MINTON v. CAVANEY

364 P.2d 473 (Cal. 1961)

Seminole Hot Springs Corporation (Seminole) was incorporated in March 1954 for the purpose of operating a public swimming pool which was leased from the pool's owners. In June 1954, plaintiffs' daughter drowned in the pool, and plaintiffs, the Mintons, subsequently sued Seminole and obtained a $10,000 judgment for wrongful death. When that judgment went unsatisfied, plaintiffs sued to hold Cavaney personally responsible.

Evidence showed, in part, that Cavaney was hired to be Seminole's attorney by its promoters, Kraft and Wettrick; that Cavaney was a director and secretary of Seminole; that Seminole never issued stock because its application to issue three shares, one each to Kraft, Wettrick, and Cavaney, was denied; and that Seminole never had any assets.

The trial court entered judgment for plaintiffs. Cavaney's estate (Cavaney died before trial) appealed. Because Cavaney's estate was held liable on the basis of the judgment against Seminole and was not given an opportunity to contest the merits of the issues raised in that suit, the California Supreme reversed the trial court's decision. The court also had to address the contention that regardless of the merits of the claim against Seminole, the corporate veil should not be pierced to reach Cavaney.

TRAYNOR, JUSTICE:

Defendant contends that the evidence does not support the [trial] court's determination that Cavaney is personally liable for Seminole's debts and that the "alter ego" doctrine is inapplicable because plaintiffs failed to show that there was " '(1) . . . such unity of interest and ownership that the separate personalities of the corporation and the individual no longer exist and (2) that, if the acts are treated as those of the corporation alone, an inequitable result will follow''—*Riddle* v. *Leuschner*, 51 Cal.2d 574, 580, 335 P.2d 107, 110.

The figurative terminology "alter ego" and "disregard of the corporate entity" is generally used to refer to the various situations that are an abuse of the corporate privilege—Ballantine, *Corporations* (rev. ed. 1946) §122, pp. 292–293; . . . The equitable owners of a corporation, for example, are personally liable when they treat the assets of the corporation as their own and add or withdraw capital from the corporation at will; when they hold themselves out as being personally liable for the debts of the corporation; or when they provide inadequate capitalization and actively participate in the conduct of corporate affairs.

In the instant case the evidence is undisputed that there was no attempt to provide adequate capitalization. Seminole never had any substantial assets. It leased the pool that it operated, and the lease was forfeited for failure to pay the rent. Its capital was " 'trifling compared with the business to be done and the risks of loss' ''—*Automotriz Del Golfo De California S.A. De C.V.* v. *Resnick*, 306 P.2d 1, 4. The evidence is also undisputed that Cavaney was not only the secretary and treasurer of the corporation but was also a director. The evidence that Cavaney was to receive one-third of the shares to be issued supports an inference that he was an equitable owner, and the evidence that for a time the records of the corporation were kept in Cavaney's office supports an inference that he actively participated in the conduct of the business. The trial court was not required to believe his statement that he was only a "temporary" director and officer "for accommodation." In any event, it merely raised a conflict in the evidence that was resolved adversely to defendant. It is immaterial whether or not he accepted the office of director as an "accommodation" with the understanding that he would not exercise any of the duties of a director. A person may not in this manner divorce the responsibilities of a director from the statutory duties and powers of that office.

There is no merit in defendant's contention that the "alter ego" doctrine applies only in contractual debts and not to tort claims.

Reversed so that Cavaney's estate may challenge the merits of the judgment against Seminole.

Of course, any corporate principal who is actively involved in commission of a tort will be personally liable, regardless of whether the corporate veil is pierced. Such liability is direct, stemming from the personal commission of a tort. It does not depend on the secondary liability that results from a piercing of the corporate veil.

Undercapitalization

Although undercapitalization is particularly critical in tort cases, it is frequently an important consideration in any case where courts are deciding whether to pierce the corporate veil. Inadequate capitalization may occur because the shareholders put too little money into the corporation or because little of the money they put in is labeled as "capital." Shareholders frequently label much of the money they use to start a corporation as a loan in an attempt to preserve their own status as creditors should things go badly for the corporation's business, or for tax reasons.

Adequacy of capitalization must be gauged in relation to the size and nature of the corporation's business. In *Minton* v. *Cavaney* the court had little difficulty in deciding that zero capitalization was inadequate. In one contract case, $7,700 was viewed as inadequate capitalization for a corporation doing $2 million worth of business annually.[13] Obviously, mere compliance with the minimum capital requirement of the incorporation process will not guarantee that a court will uphold the adequacy of capitalization when asked to pierce the corporate veil.

Because the tort liabilities of corporations engaged in "extrahazardous activities"—such as use of explosives—are potentially quite high, courts are particularly inclined to pierce the veil of such corporations when their assets are insufficient to cover damage judgments.

Adequacy of capitalization is generally judged as of the corporation's inception. That the corporation has suffered business reverses and seen its capital dwindle is no reason to pierce, unless the shareholders have fraudulently siphoned off corporate funds

---

[13] *Remme* v. *Herzog*, 35 Cal. Rptr. 586 (Cal. App. 1963).

for their personal uses. Thus, in a case involving an insufficient funds check written by a corporation, adequate capitalization was found where the corporation was formed with $100,000, and $103,000 was later injected though business reverses resulted in losses exceeding the $203,000 in capital.[14] However, insolvency occurring *soon after* incorporation may indicate that capitalization was inadequate.[15]

Corporate Shareholders

Frequently the shareholders into whose pockets a plaintiff seeking to pierce the corporate veil wishes to reach are other corporations, not individuals. In deciding whether to pierce the veil of a subsidiary to hold the parent corporation liable for the subsidiary's debts, courts use the same factors we have already discussed, though perhaps with some differences in emphasis.

As long ago as 1929 experts suggested that parent corporations could insulate themselves from liability by operating through subsidiaries if they would do four things: (1) establish the subsidiary as a separate financial unit with adequate capitalization, (2) keep separate the day-to-day business of parent and subsidiary, (3) maintain formal barriers between the two management structures, and (4) do nothing to represent the two corporations as a single entity.[16] If this advice is followed, the corporate veil of the subsidiary probably will not be pierced even if the parent owns 100% of the subsidiary's stock; the two corporations have common officers, directors, attorneys, and auditors; and they file consolidated tax returns.[17]

However, if formalities are not followed, or the subsidiary is undercapitalized, or the subsidiary is used simply to funnel profits to the parent, courts may pierce the corporate veil. The courts are particularly sensitive to a parent's use of a subsidiary as a mere instrumentality or alter ego.[18]

A practical application of this test appears in the following case.

U.S. v. JON-T CHEMICALS, INC.

768 F.2d 686 (5th Cir. 1985)

Jon-T Chemicals (Chemicals) was incorporated in 1969 as a fertilizer and chemicals business. From 1970 through 1973, John Thomas *was its president and chairman. In April 1971, Chemicals incorporated Jon-T Farms (Farms) as a wholly owned subsidiary to engage in farm-*

---

[14] *Curtis* v. *Feurhelm*, 335 N.W.2d 575 (S.D. 1983).

[15] *Norris Chemical Co.* v. *Ingram*, 679 P.2d 567 (Ariz. App. 1984).

[16] W. O. Douglas and C. M. Shanks, "Insulation from Liability Through Subsidiary Corporations," *Yale Law Journal*, Vol. 39 (1929), p. 193.

[17] R. Hamilton, "The Corporate Entity," *Texas Law Review*, Vol. 49 (1971), p. 49.

[18] *Moffett* v. *Goodyear Tire & Rubber Co.*, 652 S.W.2d 609 (Tex. App. 1983).

ing and land leasing. Chemicals invested $10,000 in Farms. Chemicals and Farms shared officers and directors. Farms used the offices, computer, and accountant of Chemicals without paying any fee; Chemicals paid the salary of Farm's only regular employee; and Chemicals made ongoing, informal advances to cover Farms's expenses, reaching $1.8 million by the end of 1973 and $7.1 million in January 1975.

In 1972 and 1973, Thomas, along with several other business associates (including directors, officers, and employees of Chemicals and Farms) formed two cotton-farming joint ventures. They leased land from Farms and employed a custom farmer. On behalf of the ventures, Thomas and Farms submitted fraudulent applications for agricultural subsidies totaling $2,263,601.15 and converted five drafts of the Commodity Credit Corporation in the sum of $269,901.90.

After obtaining criminal convictions against Thomas and Farms, the government filed this civil suit against Thomas, Farms, and Chemicals, alleging violations of the False Claims Act and common law conversion. The trial court found Thomas and Farms liable, but both were insolvent. The trial court also found that Farms was a mere appendage of Chemicals and that therefore Chemicals was liable for the illegal acts of Farms. Chemicals appeals from a judgment of $4,787,604.20.

GOLDBERG, CIRCUIT JUDGE:

A

Under the doctrine of limited liability, the owner of a corporation is not liable for the corporation's debts. Creditors of the corporation have recourse only against the corporation itself, not against its parent company or shareholders. See *Baker v. Raymond International*, 656 F.2d 173, 179 (5th Cir.1981), *cert. denied*, 456 U.S. 983

(1982). It is on this assumption that "large undertakings are rested, vast enterprises are launched, and huge sums of capital attracted"— *Anderson v. Abbott*, 321 U.S. 349, 362 (1944).

While limited liability remains the norm in American corporation law, certain equitable exceptions to the doctrine have developed. The most common exception is for fraud. If, for example, a corporation is established for a fraudulent purpose or is used to commit an illegal act, or if its shareholders drain the corporation's assets, limited liability may not apply. Another exception arises where, as here, a parent company totally dominates and controls its subsidiary, operating the subsidiary as its business conduit or agent. See *Nelson v. International Paint Co.*, 734 F.2d 1084, 1091–93 (5th Cir.1984) (applying Texas law).

[T]he control required for liability under the "instrumentality" rule amounts to total domination of the subservient corporation, to the extent that the subservient corporation manifests no separate corporate interests of its own and functions solely to achieve the purposes of the dominant corporation. As Professor Fletcher states, "The control necessary to invoke what is sometimes called the 'instrumentality rule" is not mere majority or complete stock control but such domination of finances, policies and practices that the controlled corporation has, so to speak, no separate mind, will or existence of its own and is but a business conduit for its principal." 1 W. Fletcher [*Cyclopedia of the Law of Private Corporations*] § 43 at 204–05 [rev. perm. ed. 1963]—In such cases, the subsidiary is considered the "alter ego" "agent," or "instrumentality" of the parent company, and the district court, acting in its equitable capacity, is entitled to pierce the corporate veil.

The complementary theories of limited liability and piercing the corporate veil have provoked consternation among courts and legal scholars alike. They have been variously described as a "legal quagmire,"—Ballantine, "Separate

Entity of Parent and Subsidiary Corporations," *California Law Review*, Vol. 14 (1925), pp. 12, 15—and as being "enveloped in the mists of metaphor"—*Berkey* v. *Third Avenue Ry.*, 244 N.Y. 84, 155 N.E. 58, 61 (1926) (Cardozo, J.). Nowhere is this more true than in the case of the alter ego doctrine. In some sense, every subsidiary is the alter ego of its parent company. Where the subsidiary is wholly owned by the parent and has the same directors and officers, operating the subsidiary independently of the parent company not only has little practical meaning, it would also constitute a breach both of the subsidiary's duty to further the interests of its owner, and of the directors' and officers' duty toward the parent company. Nevertheless, our cases are clear that 100% ownership and identity of directors and officers are, even together, an insufficient basis for applying the alter ego theory to pierce the corporate veil. Instead, we maintain the fiction that an officer or director of both corporations can change hats and represent the two corporations separately, despite their common ownership.

In lieu of articulating a coherent doctrinal basis for the alter ego theory, we have instead developed a laundry list of factors to be used in determining whether a subsidiary is the alter ego of its parent. These include whether

(1) the parent and the subsidiary have common stock ownership.

(2) the parent and the subsidiary have common directors or officers.

(3) the parent and the subsidiary have common business departments.

(4) the parent and the subsidiary file consolidated financial statements and tax returns.

(5) the parent finances the subsidiary.

(6) the parent caused the incorporation of the subsidiary.

(7) the subsidiary operates with grossly inadequate capital.

(8) the parent pays the salaries and other expenses of the subsidiary.

(9) the subsidiary receives no business except that given to it by the parent.

(10) the parent uses the subsidiary's property as its own.

(11) the daily operations of the two corporations are not kept separate.

(12) the subsidiary does not observe the basic corporate formalities, such as keeping separate books and records and holding shareholder and board meetings.

Nelson, 734 F.2d at 1093; Additional factors that are sometimes mentioned are (1) "[w]hether the directors and officers of [the subsidiary] act independently in the interest of that company, or whether they take their orders from the [parent] and act in the [parent's] interest," and (2) the "connection of [the] parent's employee, officer or director to [the] subsidiary's tort or contract giving rise to [the] suit." Analytically, however, these last two factors are on a different plane from the other factors. The first is, in essence, the conclusion that we reach through our alter ego analysis and thus depends on the preceding factors. When the directors and officers of the subsidiary are also directors and officers of the parent, it makes little sense to ask whether they take orders from the parent since they themselves constitute the parent's decision-making body and are duty bound to act in the parent's interest. The second factor relates more to the involvement of the parent itself in the acts giving rise to the suit than to its vicarious liability for the subsidiary's acts in general.

Although Chemicals does not directly challenge the legal standard applied by the court below, it implicitly raises two objections. First, Chemicals contends that a finding of fraud is an essential element of any alter ego determination. According to Chemicals, unless a parent intentionally misleads outsiders, uses the corporate form for fraudulent purposes, or milks the subsidiary's assets, then it is entitled to hide behind the corporate veil of its subsidiary.

Chemicals argues that since Farms was established for a proper business purpose—that is, tax advantages—and since neither Chemicals nor Farms misled outsiders regarding their relationship and finances, the district court erred in piercing the corporate veil.

We disagree. Recently, we held that, in contract cases, fraud is an essential element of an alter ego finding. However, we do not require a finding of fraud in tort cases, particularly where the subsidiary is undercapitalized—*Nelson*, 734 F.2d at 1092; cf. *Anderson* v. *Abbott*, 321 U.S. 349 (1944) (''The cases of fraud make up part of that exception [to limited liability]. But they do not exhaust it. An obvious inadequacy of capital . . . has frequently been an important factor in cases denying stockholders their defense of limited liability.'')—*DeWitt Truck Brokers, Inc.* v. *W. Ray Flemming Fruit Co.*, 540 F.2d 681, 684 (4th Cir. 1976) (contract case applying South Carolina law and holding that fraud is not a necessary element of alter ego finding). The reason for this distinction is clear. In a contract case, the creditor has willingly transacted business with the subsidiary. If the creditor wants to be able to hold the parent liable for the subsidiary's debts, it can contract for this. Unless the subsidiary misrepresents its financial condition to the creditor, the creditor should be bound by its decision to deal with the subsidiary; it should not be able to complain later that the subsidiary is unsound. In a tort case, by contrast, the creditor has not voluntarily chosen to deal with the subsidiary; instead, the creditor relationship is forced upon it. Thus, the question of whether the creditor relied on misrepresentations by the subsidiary is irrelevant. Where a parent establishes a subsidiary, undercapitalizes it, and dominates it to such an extent that the subsidiary is a mere conduit for the parent's business, then the parent should not be able to shift the risk of loss due to the subsidiary's tortious acts to innocent third parties.

Here, the government's claims for fraudulent misrepresentation and conversion sound in tort rather than contract. Moreover, the government did not voluntarily enter into the relationship with Farms. It did not have the option of granting or not granting the subsidies to the joint ventures. Under the Upland Cotton Program, it was obligated to subsidize applicants who purportedly qualified. The fact that the government did not rely on any misrepresentations regarding Farms's financial condition or its relationship with Chemicals is thus wholly irrelevant to the question whether Chemicals should be held liable for Farms's misconduct. Unlike the ordinary contracting party, the government was not dilatory in any duty to investigate Farms's finances, since it had no such duty. As long as Chemicals exercised total domination and control over Farms, it was liable for Farms's acts.

Chemicals also contends that the district court gave insufficient weight to the fact that Farms observed all of the formalities required by corporation law, including keeping separate books and records and holding regular meetings of shareholders and of the board of directors.

Our only reply is that Chemicals puts form ahead of substance. We agree with the view expressed by the Fourth Circuit that ''in applying the 'instrumentality' or 'alter ego' doctrine, the courts are concerned with reality and not form, with how the corporation operated and the individual defendant's relationship to that operation''—*DeWitt Truck Brokers*, 540 F.2d at 685. ''[T]he subsidiary must be more than a corporate charter embellished by a few formal niceties. We cannot, as in the case of the Emperor's new clothes, pretend to see something which does not exist''—*Edwards Co.* v. *Monogram Industries*, 700 F.2d 994, 1002, *vacated*, 715 F.2d 157 (1983), *reversed*, 730 F.2d 977 (5th Cir. 1984) (en banc). In determining whether a subsidiary is the alter ego of its parent, we apply a multifactor test. One of these factors is whether the corporate formalities were observed—but this is only one of several factors; it is not determinative. Thus, Chemicals' argument that Farms observed the corporate formalities goes merely to the weight of the evidence, not to the correctness of the legal standard applied by the district court.

B

As we have noted, there is no litmus test for determining whether a subsidiary is the alter ego of its parent. Instead, we must look to the totality of the circumstances.

First, Chemicals challenges the district court's finding that Farms "operated with a grossly inadequate capital." Chemicals claims that although Farms initially had only $10,000 in capital, it subsequently received millions of dollars in advances for working capital from Chemicals. In our view, Chemicals' argument misses the point. The underlying question is whether Farms was an economically viable, independent entity, or whether it operated merely as the adjunct or alter ego of Chemicals. The fact that Farms continually had net operating losses and survived due to massive and ongoing transfusions from Chemicals does not indicate that Farms ever stood on its own two feet. Quite the contrary; it reinforces the district court's conclusion that Farms did not have any separate financial existence. As the district court properly concluded, Farms operated primarily on the capital of Chemicals rather than on its own capital.

Chemicals also claims that the district court erred in finding that Chemicals and Farms jointly used and owned property and that they commingled their assets. In regard to the joint use of property, it is undisputed that Farms used the offices and computer of Chemicals. It is also undisputed, as the district court found, that Chemicals paid the expenses of several tractors used by Farms. Although Chemicals claims that these expenses were carried on its books as

loans to Farms, given the pervasive interconnections between Farms and Chemicals, we do not regard the district court's finding regarding the joint ownership of property to be clearly erroneous.

The district court's finding that there was a commingling of the corporate funds of Chemicals and Farms is similarly supported by the record. It is undisputed that Chemicals made ongoing advances to Farms. Basically, whenever Farms could not pay its bills, Chemicals did so by writing a check. These intercorporate loans were handled informally, without any corporate resolutions authorizing them.

Although Chemicals claims that there was no commingling of funds because records were kept of each advance made by Chemicals to Farms, Chemicals admits that no collateral was posted for the "loans" it made to Farms and does not contest that Farms paid no interest on the loans. While we do not denigrate careful record keeping of corporate transactions, we do not regard mere records as a philosophers' stone capable of transmuting alter egos into distinct corporations. Records are primarily a memorialization of economic reality, not constitutive of that reality.

Having found the district court's subsidiary findings to be supported by the record, we have little trouble in affirming the court's ultimate finding that Farms is the alter ego of Chemicals. To mention just some of the evidence supporting the district court's alter ego holding, all of the directors and officers of Farms served as directors and officers of Chemicals; Farms was wholly owned by Chemicals; Chemicals paid many of the bills, invoices, and expenses of Farms; it covered Farms's overdrafts; it made substantial loans to Farms (at one time amounting to $7 million) without corporate resolutions authorizing the loans and without demanding any collateral or interest; Chemicals and Farms filed consolidated financal statements and tax returns; Farms used the offices and computer of Chemicals without paying any rent; the salary of Farms's one regular employee was paid by Chemicals; and employees of Chemicals performed services for Farms without charging for their time. Chemicals also advanced money and provided services on an informal basis to the joint ventures.

A corporation, unlike Proteus, cannot assume a new form at will. While we generally recognize a corporation's attempt to assume the guise of a subsidiary, even this expedition into fantasyland has its bounds. Here, as in *National Marine Service, Inc.* v. *C. J. Thibodeaux & Co.*, 501 F.2d 940 (5th Cir. 1974), "[t]he corporate veil with which appellants would enrobe [the subsidiary] to give it the semblance of being attired in corporate clothing was so diaphanous that the district court was well able to see through it."

Affirmed.

Courts are also sensitive to attempts to avoid liability by dividing a natural business entity into several insulated units. To allow such unnatural divisions does not further the purpose of limited liability, which is, in the main, to encourage investment by protecting the wealth of individuals. Thus, as one court recently noted,[19]

> The extension of liability for a corporation's obligations beyond the confines of its own separate entity is appropriate in those cases where an essentially single business or economic enterprise is nevertheless conducted through several separate corporations, either in a parent-subsidiary arrangement or under common ownership as in the case of affiliated corporations.
>
> Such a division or fragmentation may take the form of a traditional parent-subsidiary relationship or that of a single individual or group of individuals owning directly the stock of the various corporations which go to make up the single business enterprise. Upon disregard of the separate entity of one of the corporate components, the rights of a creditor of that corporation would be as great against an affiliate with substantial identity of stock interest as against a parent which owns substantially all the stock of a subsidiary. The extent of recovery, however, would properly be limited to the pool of assets of the larger business entity. In other words, only the internal subdivision of the single business entity would be disregarded and the parent or affiliate *stockholders* would nonetheless retain *their* privilege of limited liability.
>
> Dean Latty has identified four factors common to those cases in which courts have allowed recovery from the parent or affiliated corporations: (1) corporations with identity or substantial identity of ownership, that is, ownership of sufficient stock to give actual working control; (2) unified administrative control (which follows almost automatically from such ownership) of corporations whose business functions are similar or supplementary; (3) involuntary as opposed to voluntary creditors; and (4) the insolvency of the corporation against which the claim primarily lies.

Public Policy and Statutory Requirements

Just as shareholders should not be allowed to use the corporate veil to perpetuate fraud, so should they be prevented from using it to violate public policy or statutory law. Whether the corporate veil should be pierced to impose liability on shareholders for an

---

[19] *Glenn* v. *Wagner*, 313 S.E.2d 832 (N.C. App. 1984).

act of the corporation depends, in this context, on the court's view of public policy or legislative intent.

For example, if a statute prohibited rebates by railroads to a certain corporation, shareholders of that company probably should not be allowed to receive such rebates individually or to establish and control a second corporation for the sole purpose of having it receive the rebates.[20] Similarly, in a recent sex discrimination case, a woman sued both her immediate employer, the Terre Haute Regional Hospital, Inc., and its parent corporation, HCA. Considering Congress's intent that the term "employer" in Title VII's prohibition against discrimination in employment be given a liberal interpretation, and considering the interrelationship of operations, common management, centralized control of labor relations, and common financial control, the court held that HCA was a proper defendant.[21]

One area in which courts have had particular trouble is usury. Most states put a ceiling on interest rates that can be charged to individual borrowers, but many have no such ceiling for corporate borrowers. Assume that Mr. X goes to A Bank for a loan. Viewing the risk, A Bank tells Mr. X that it would loan the money only at a usurious interest rate. Mr. X then incorporates and borrows the money in the corporate name, while at the same time signing a personal guaranty on the loan. Has the statute been violated so that the bank is penalized under the usury law? Some jurisdictions say "yes." Others say "no," because the parties have simply taken advantage of a loophole that the legislature meant to leave in the usury statute.

Many states follow the "New York rule," which does not allow the individual guarantor to raise the usury defense if the purpose of the loan is to finance a profit-oriented business, but would allow interposition of the defense if the purpose of the loan is to discharge a personal obligation. Assume, for example, that Ms. X borrowed money to buy a pleasure boat and fell behind on her payments. Assume further that the lender was willing to refinance the loan, but only at an interest rate so high that Ms. X would have to form a corporation to receive it. In such a case, the usury defense could be raised.[22]

Juxtaposition of the following two cases clearly indicates that resolution of cases in this area turns on legislative intent and public policy considerations that must be discerned on a case-by-case basis.

---

[20] *U.S.* v. *Milwaukee Refrig. Transit Co.*, 145 F. 1007 (C.C.E.D. Wis. 1906).

[21] *Burns* v. *Terre Haute Regional Hospital*, 581 F.Supp. 1301 (S.D. Ind. 1983).

[22] *Schneider* v. *Phelps*, 359 N.E.2d 1361 (N.Y. App. 1977).

STARK v. FLEMMING

283 F.2d 410 (9th Cir. 1960)

Appellant Stark seeks review of the decision of the Secretary of Health, Education, and Welfare that she is not entitled to old age benefits under the Social Security laws. The trial judge affirmed the Secretary's decision.

PER CURIAM:

Appellant placed her assets—a farm and a duplex house—in a newly organized corporation. Then she began to draw $400 per month as salary. The Secretary has found the corporation was a sham. There is no doubt that the corporation was set up to qualify appellant in a short time for Social Security payments.

But here there seems to have been proper adherence to the normal corporate routines. And it is difficult to understand how the corporate arrangement would not have to be respected by others than the Secretary. And we think he must respect it, too.

Congress could have provided that the motivation to obtain Social Security by organizing a corporation would defeat the end. It did not.

Reversed.

ROCCOGRANDI v. UNEMPLOYMENT COMPENSATION BOARD OF REVIEW

178 A.2d 786 (Pa. Super. 1962)

Appellants' application for state unemployment benefits was denied by the Board of Review. On appeal, the trial court held that the corporate entity of the family corporation could be ignored for purposes of determining benefit eligibility. This appeal followed.

MONTGOMERY, JUDGE:

The appellants are all members of a family who are involved in the wrecking business together. Each owns 40 shares of stock in the company, which has 205 outstanding shares, and all three are officers of the company. The officers of the company, during periods of insufficient work to employ all the members of the family, hold a meeting and by majority vote decide which members shall be "laid off." It was decided by majority vote of all the stockholders that the appellants would be "laid off" because it was their respective turns. Immediately thereafter claims for unemployment compensation benefits were filed by the three appellants. The Bureau of Employment Security denied the claims on the grounds that the appellants were self-employed. Upon appeal the referee reversed the bureau and held the appellants to be entitled to benefits. The Board of Review reversed the referee's decision, holding that the appellants had sufficient control to lay themselves off and that they did just that. Therefore the appellants were self-employed and must be denied eligibility for benefits under Section 402(h) and Section 402(b) (1) of the law.

The case is ruled by *De Priest Unemployment Compensation* case, 196 Pa. Super. 612, 177 A.2d 20, in which this court held that the corporate entity may be ignored in determining whether the claimants, in fact, were "unemployed" under the act, or were self-employed persons whose business merely proved to be unremunerative during the period for which the claim for benefits was made.

Decisions affirmed.

"Deep Rock" Doctrine

Many times shareholders become creditors of their corporation. Perhaps they loan it money, or sell property to it on credit, or function as officers without collecting pay that the bylaws provide they are entitled to. When a corporation faces bankruptcy or reorganization, and creditors are scrambling after limited corporate assets, a question frequently arises as to the proper priority to be given shareholder/creditors. There are certainly classic cases giving shareholders with secured claims priority over unsecured outside creditors.[23]

In such cases, outside creditors will frequently ask that shareholder-creditors "go to the end of the line." That is, outside creditors seek to have the shareholders' loans treated as investment capital so that their claims are subordinated to those of outside creditors. The "Deep Rock" doctrine, named after a company involved in a seminal Supreme Court case,[24] allows subordination of even a secured shareholder claim to an unsecured claim of a third party where the shareholder has acted inequitably to prejudice the rights of the outsider. This subordination is not as severe a remedy as piercing the corporate veil. The courts who apply it are not forcing shareholders to pay corporate debts from personal funds; they are merely ordering those shareholders to take their own claims against the corporation and "go to the end of the line."

A famous Supreme Court case is *Pepper* v. *Litton*,[25] in which Pepper sued Dixie Splint Coal Company and its dominant shareholder, Litton, for royalties due under a lease. Believing that Pepper had a good claim, Litton set about to thwart recovery. Litton first sued Dixie Splint for alleged accumulated back salary and then had Dixie Splint confess judgment to Litton in the sum of $33,468.89. As soon as Pepper received a judgment against Dixie Splint for $9,000, Litton caused an execution to issue on his confessed judgment. When Pepper took steps to enforce her judgment, Litton in collusion with the sheriff sold all Dixie Splint's property at auction. Litton was the purchaser for

---

[23] See, for example, *Salomon* v. *Salomon & Co.*, Ltd., L.R. [1897] App. Cas. 22.

[24] *Taylor* v. *Standard Gas & Electric Co.*, 306 U.S. 307 (1939).

[25] 308 U.S. 295 (1939).

$3,200. Litton then formed a new corporation and transferred all Dixie Splint's former property to it in exchange for $20,000 in stock. Finally, Litton had Dixie Splint declare bankruptcy and interposed that as a defense to collection of Pepper's judgment. In bankruptcy court, Litton made claim for an unsatisfied portion of his confessed judgment.

Other steps were involved in Litton's scheme, but, in essence, he was trying to defeat Pepper's just claim by transferring all the property of one corporation to a newly formed corporation that he also controlled. The Supreme Court ordered Litton's claim subordinated to Pepper's, recognizing Litton's machinations as a "planned and fraudulent scheme." An insider, said the Court, "cannot manipulate the affairs of his corporation to their [stockholders' and creditors'] detriment and in disregard of the standards of common decency and honesty. . . . He cannot by the use of the corporate device avail himself of privileges normally permitted outsiders in a race of creditors."

A similar case follows.

COSTELLO v. FAZIO

256 F.2d 903 (9th Cir. 1958)

Fazio, Ambrose, and Leonard were partners in Leonard Plumbing and Heating Supply Co. The capital contributions of the three in September 1952 were Fazio, $43,169.61; Ambrose, $6,451.17; and Leonard, $2,000. The partnership lost $22,521.34 during the year ending September 30, 1952 and its sales were rapidly declining. On September 15, 1962, Fazio and Ambrose withdrew all but $2,000 of their capital contributions from the partnership, taking promissory notes in the sums of $41,169.61 and $4,451.17, respectively. They then incorporated the business with Fazio as president and Ambrose as secretary-treasurer. The corporation's capital was $6,000—$2,000 from each of the three principals. The corporation adopted all the partnership liabilities, including the promissory notes to Ambrose and Fazio.

In October 1954, after continued losses, the corporation took bankruptcy. Fazio and Ambrose filed claims based on the unpaid promissory notes. The referee in bankruptcy refused the bankruptcy trustee's request that the claims

of Fazio and Ambrose be subordinated to those of the general creditors of the corporation. The district court affirmed. The trustee appealed.

HAMLEY, JUSTICE:

Recasting the facts in the light of what is said above, the question which appellant presents is this:

> Where, in connection with the incorporation of a partnership, and for their own personal and private benefit, two partners, who are to become officers, directors, and controlling stockholders of the corporation, convert the bulk of their capital contributions into loans, taking promissory notes, thereby leaving the partnership and succeeding corporation grossly undercapitalized, to the detriment of the corporation and its creditors, should their claims against the estate of the subsequently bankrupted corporation be subordinated to the claims of the general unsecured creditors?

The question almost answers itself.

In allowing and disallowing claims, courts of bankruptcy apply the rules and principles of equity jurisprudence—*Pepper* v. *Litton*, 308 U.S. 295, 304. Where the claim is found to be inequitable, it may be set aside or subordinated to the claims of other creditors. As stated in *Taylor* v. *Standard Gas Co.*, supra, 306 U.S. at page 315, the question to be determined when the plan or transaction which gives rise to a claim is challenged as inequitable is "whether, within the bounds of reason and fairness, such a plan can be justified."

Where, as here, the claims are filed by persons standing in a fiduciary relationship to the corporation, another test which equity will apply is "whether or not under all the circumstances the transaction carries the earmarks of an arm's length bargain"—*Pepper* v. *Litton*, supra, 308 U.S. at page 306.

Under either of these tests, the transaction here in question stands condemned.

Appellees argue that more must be shown than mere undercapitalization if the claims are to be subordinated. Much more than mere undercapitalization was shown here. Persons serving in a fiduciary relationship to the corporation actually withdrew capital already committed to the business, in the face of recent adverse financial experience. They stripped the business of 88% of its stated capital at a time when it had a minus working capital and had suffered substantial business losses. This was done for personal gain, under circumstances which charge them with knowledge that the corporation and its creditors would be endangered. Taking advantage of their fiduciary position, they thus sought to gain equality of treatment with general creditors.

In *Taylor* v. *Standard Gas & Electric Co.*, 306 U.S. 307, and some other cases, there was fraud and mismanagement present in addition to undercapitalization. Appellees argue from this that fraud and mismanagement must always be present if claims are to be subordinated in a situation involving undercapitalization.

This is not the rule. The test to be applied, as announced in the Taylor case and quoted above, is whether the transaction can be justified "within the bounds of reason and fairness." In the more recent *Heiser* case, supra, 327 U.S., pages 732–733, the Supreme Court made clear, in these words, that fraud is not an essential ingredient:

> In appropriate cases, acting upon equitable principles it [bankruptcy court] may also subordinate the claim of one creditor to those of others in order to prevent the consummation of a course of conduct by the claimant, which, as to them, would be fraudulent *or otherwise inequitable.* (emphasis added)

The fact that the withdrawal of capital occurred prior to incorporation is immaterial. This transaction occurred in contemplation of incorporation.

Nor is the fact that the business, after being stripped of necessary capital, was able to survive long enough to have a turnover of creditors a mitigating circumstance. The inequitable conduct of appellees consisted not in acting to the detriment of creditors then known, but in acting to the detriment of present or future creditors, whoever they may be.

Reversed.

Piercing at Shareholder's Request

A final point to be made in this chapter is that the corporate veil normally will not be pierced at the request of the very persons who erected it in the first place—the shareholders. That is, shareholders will not be allowed to incorporate and hide behind the corporate veil when it suits their purposes to do so, but then turn around and ask the court to disregard the corporate entity when that suits their interests. Estoppel theory applies here, and many of the cases are analogous to those discussed under the topic of corporation by estoppel earlier in this chapter.

In one case, an engineer who had formed a professional corporation sued for breach of a contract he had performed in the corporation's name. He won, and asked for attorney's fees under a statute that allowed recovery of such fees to individual plaintiffs but not to corporate plaintiffs. The court said:

> Adams, Jr., being the only shareholder, employee, officer and director of Adams, Inc., argues that the corporation is only a "piece of paper" in the office of the Secretary of State and, in effect, urges that the "corporate veil" should be pierced and attorney's fees thereby permitted. We disagree.
>
> It is obvious that Adams, Jr., deliberately chose to operate his business as a corporation, and we are of the opinion that it would be inequitable now to allow him to recover attorney's fees as an individual.[26]

In another case, Lyons, a legal secretary, fell and was injured while employed by Leo J. Barrett, P.A., a professional law corporation. Lyons received worker's compensation benefits from the corporation and was therefore barred from suing it in tort for her injuries. However, the building in which the law office was located was owned by Barrett individually. When Lyon sued Barrett for negligently maintaining the building, he was not allowed to use the corporation's worker's compensation defense even though he was the sole owner of the corporation.[27]

In the words of one court, "one who has gained the advantages of separate incorporation must also be willing to accept the consequences of such incorporation."[28]

QUESTIONS AND PROBLEMS

1. The State of Kansas Corporate Code has a provision stating that "[u]pon the filing with the Secretary of State of the articles of incorporation . . . the incorporators . . . shall be and constitute a body corporate from the date of such filing," subject to filing a certified copy in the office of the register of deeds of the county in which the corporation's registered office is located. The owners of Construction Enterprises, Inc., failed to file a certified copy in the county office. The State of Kansas therefore sought to hold the owners personally liable for unpaid unemployment taxes. The trial judge held that defendants had "substantially complied" with the statute and refused to impose liability because a *de facto* corporation existed. Discuss the validity of this ruling. See *State ex rel. McCain* v. *Construction Enterprises, Inc.*, 6 Kan. App.2d 627, 631 P.2d 1240 (1981).

---

[26] *Adams* v. *Big Three Industries, Inc.*, 549 S.W.2d 411 (Tex. Civ. App. 1977).

[27] *Lyon* v. *Barrett*, 445 A.2d 1153 (N.J. 1982).

[28] *Gregory* v. *Garrett Corp.*, 578 F.Supp. 871 (S.D. N.Y. 1983).

2. Dr. Bennett and two others signed articles of incorporation on January 22, 1970 for Aero-Fabb Co. Because the articles were not in accord with the statutes, no certificate of incorporation was issued until June 12, 1970. In that interim period, the corporation entered into certain leases, and then defaulted. Can Dr. Bennett be held personally liable under MBCA provisions? Discuss. See *Timberline Equipment Co., Inc.* v. *Davenport*, 514 P.2d 1109 (Or. 1973).

3. On December 6, 1978, D signed a "Letter of Agreement" to construct a boat for $1.35 million to sell to Southern-Gulf Marine Co. No. 9, Inc. On May 30, 1979, a vessel construction contract was executed between D and Southern-Gulf, which appeared through its president, Barrett. On February 21, 1980 Southern-Gulf was incorporated in the Cayman Islands and ratified the contract with D. D subsequently defaulted. D claims it cannot be liable because every contract requires two parties, and this one did not because Southern-Gulf did not exist on May 30, 1979. Is this a good defense? Discuss. See *Southern-Gulf Marine Co. No. 9, Inc.* v. *Camcraft, Inc.*, 410 So.2d 1181 (La. App. 1982).

4. Szelc bought a car from H.E.D. Sales, Inc., on a car lot where the corporate name was clearly displayed. His check was made payable to H.E.D. Sales, Inc., and the bill of sale was in the corporation's name. Szelc later sued the corporation and Torregrossa individually for breach of implied warranty of title. Evidence showed Torregrossa was a 50% owner of the business and occupied an office on the property. The other 50% owner was actively involved in the business. The corporation had been capitalized with the state statutory minimum of $1,000. There was no evidence regarding corporate formalities or any unpaid creditors, though the corporation had its own bank account. Should Torregrossa be held personally liable? Discuss. See *Torregrossa* v. *Szelc*, 603 S.W.2d 803 (Tex. 1980).

5. Defendants (Ds) were land developers who owned a tract upon which they wished to have a building. Ds incorporated Mar, Inc., a construction company, and contracted to pay it $680,000 to build the building, though all reasonable estimates were that it would cost at least $900,000. Mar, Inc., then farmed virtually all the work out to subcontractors pursuant to contracts that denied them the right to any recourse to the mechanics lien law. The building was built, but Mar became bankrupt and many subcontractors were unpaid. The trustee in bankruptcy for Mar sought to pierce the corporate veil to hold Ds liable. Discuss. See *Yacker* v. *Weiner*, 109 N.J. Super. 351, 263 A.2d 188 (1970).

6. Iron City sued when two of its barges were damaged due to the negligence of West Fork Towing Corporation's employees. The trial court found defendant Pitrolo personally liable when the evidence showed (1) in 1957, with an authorization of $50,000 in capital, West Fork issued 10 shares for a total of $1,000, with Pitrolo purchasing 8 of them; (2) until his death, Pitrolo was president and general manager of West Fork; (3) almost from its inception, West Fork was insolvent, its funds being supplied by Pitrolo or corporations he controlled; and (4) other than an organizational meeting in 1957, no stockholders' or directors' meetings were ever held. Did the trial court act correctly? See *Iron City Sand & Gravel Div.* v. *West Fork Towing Corp.*, 298 F.Supp. 1091 (N.D. W.Va. 1969).

7. Gannett, a newspaper publisher, feared that a newsprint shortage was imminent, so it purchased all the shares of Berwin Paper Co. for $400,000. Berwin made paper, but not newsprint. Gannett elected three directors to the Berwin board, all of whom were Gannett directors also. The directors hired five officers to run Berwin, four of whom were also Gannett officers. Berwin then converted one of its machines to the manufacture of newsprint. Gannett loaned Berwin over $560,000 to pay its debts and rehabilitate and modernize its plant and for working capital. Berwin sold some newsprint to Gannett, but when the expected shortage did not develop, Gannett lost interest. Berwin became insolvent and went into bankruptcy. Gannett claimed that it was a general unsecured creditor for the money it had loaned to Berwin. Berwin's other creditors claimed Gannett's claim should be subordinated. Discuss. See *Gannett* v. *Larry*, 221 F.2d 269 (2d Cir. 1955).

8. Six wholly owned subsidiaries of Alaska Lumber and Pulp Co. (ALP) were engaged in a maze of corporate enterprises in Alaska, including purchase of timber, operation of a pump mill and two saw mills, acquisition of a seafood company, and formation of a housing development company. The corporations were commonly owned, centrally managed, had interlocking officers and directors, and maintained close business ties. For tax purposes, the corporations argued that their activities functionally constituted a "single business" and that they should be taxed as one unit rather than separately. Should a court accept this argument? Discuss. See *State Dept. of Revenue* v. *Alaska Lumber and Pulp Co.*, 674 P.2d 268 (Alas. 1983).

9

CORPORATE FINANCIAL STRUCTURE AND SHAREHOLDER DISTRIBUTIONS

INTRODUCTION

Creation of the corporate financial structure and its continued maintenance present corporate managers with their most difficult problems. Some of these problems are discussed in other chapters, including the liabilities of promoters, and the vast array of securities laws that impact on the raising of capital by publicly held corporations. This chapter focuses on two areas. First, it analyzes creation of the corporate financial structure. Although the majority of working capital is derived from internal sources such as retained earnings and much of it comes from simple bank borrowing and buying on credit, this section will concentrate on the sale of securities because that is where most legal problems arise.

Second, this chapter addresses the important matter of shareholder distributions. In the eyes of many shareholders, the main purpose of corporate existence is to operate a profitable business that will return money to shareholders as dividends and other types of distributions. These matters can also create complex legal problems.

Types of Securities

There are two basic types of securities, *equity securities* and *debt securities*. There are many categories of equity securities, the most important being *common shares*. The holders of the common shares of stock are the true owners of the corporation. Each share of stock entitles its holder to vote for board of director candidates, to share pro rata in the profits of the corporation when paid out as dividends, and to share pro rata in the surplus of assets over liabilities, if any, when the corporation is liquidated.

Most closely held corporations have only one class of shares, the common shares. Larger and more sophisticated corporations, perhaps to induce investment from those who are not interested in common shares, may create shares with a preference over the common shares as to dividends or as to assets upon dissolution. Obviously, persons may be more willing to invest if they know they will be first in line to receive any earnings that the board of directors decides to pay out as dividends. Thus, many large corporations have one or more classes of *preferred shares*.[1]

Holders of debt securities, like the holders of common shares, have invested money that the corporation will use to run its business. But they are creditors, not owners. They have no vote in how the business is operated. Unlike common shareholders, they have no inspection rights and are not owed a fiduciary duty by the managers. However, they are entitled to receive regular payments at a fixed interest rate, regardless of whether the corporation is profitable. On the other hand, common shareholders are generally entitled to dividends only out of corporate profits and even then at the discretion of the board of directors. Holders of debt securities are also entitled to repayment of the principal sum at a fixed date or in installments. Common shareholders may never have their investments returned if the corporation's debts exceed its liabilities on liquidation. Importantly, payments to debt security holders are deemed *interest* and are deductible expenses for the corporation. This creates an important tax advantage, for payments to common shareholders are usually deemed *dividends*. These are not deductible by the corporation and are taxable to the shareholder, thus creating the well-known "double taxation" of corporations.

As can be seen, preferred shares are hybrids lying somewhere between common shares and debt securities. As with common shares, the dividends on preferred shares are not deductible to the corporation and thus cause double taxation. Unlike common shares, however, preferred shares generally carry no vote. The line between debt and equity securities is further blurred by the fact that preferred stock is frequently *convertible*, at the holder's option, into common stock. Indeed, sometimes even debt securities carry a convertibility feature. This is attractive when the corporation is doing so well in terms of dividends and market value appreciation that the common stock is earning more than the interest rate specified for the preferred stock or debt security.

---

[1] The Model Business Corporation Act (MBCA) §§15 and 16 authorize issuance of preferred shares. However, because it is possible under modern statutes to create classes of "common" stock that have economic preferences, or classes of "preferred" stock that can be economically subordinate to common shares or identical in terms of voting rights, Revised Model Business Corporation Act (RMBCA)§6.01 eliminates the terminology "common" and "preferred."

Additional Terms

Authorized but unissued shares are shares whose issuance has been authorized by the articles of incorporation, but have not yet been sold. All shares must be so authorized, or their issuance will be illegal. There are many reasons to authorize more shares than management intends to sell initially. Having a supply of authorized but unissued shares allows management to act quickly to sell shares without the need for shareholder approval of an amendment to the articles. This ability comes in handy during a financial crisis or a takeover attempt.[2]

Treasury shares are shares that were at one time issued but have been, for one reason or another, repurchased by the corporation.[3] Unless canceled, those shares remain in the corporate treasury. They do not receive dividends and cannot be voted in corporate elections.

Debt securities are given many labels. If we are precise, debt securities that are secured by corporate property are called *bonds*. Unsecured debt securities are called *debentures* if long term and *notes* if short term. Frequently, however, these terms are used interchangeably.

Debt securities, and preferred shares, frequently are *redeemable*. This feature allows the corporation, at its option, to repurchase the securities at a specified price. This is advantageous for the corporation where interest rates have dropped and money may now be borrowed at lower rates than those carried by the outstanding debt securities or preferred stock.

There are a variety of forms for preferred stock. Typically, such shares are *cumulative*. That means that if dividends are not paid on them in one year, the amount owed accumulates and must be satisfied before the common shareholders may be paid any dividends. Assume, for example, that X Corporation has issued $1,000 worth of 10% cumulative preferred stock. Assume further that in 1985, the board of directors determines that the financial condition of X Corporation is such that no dividends of any kind can be paid. Because the shares are cumulative, if the board wishes to pay dividends to common shareholders in 1986, it must first pay the preferred holders both the $100 they were owed for 1985 and the $100 they are owed for 1986. No dividends may be distributed to common shareholders until those sums are paid. When no dividends were paid in 1985, the preferred shares were in ''arrears.'' Preferred shareholders are sometimes given the right to vote in corporate matters during periods when their shares are in arrears.

If the shares in the previous example had been *non*cumulative preferred, no arrearage would have arisen in 1985. Assuming good faith on the part of the directors, the preferred shareholders have no claim for the $100 they might have received. If the

---

[2] RMBCA §6.02 gives directors, if the articles so provide, the power to issue ''blank'' stock. The board is given discretion to set the terms of classes of stock to meet exigencies of the market or facilitate negotiations for acquisitions.

[3] Because most distinctions between treasury shares and authorized but unissued shares are technical and basically meaningless if par value is absent, RMBCA §6.31 follows the 1980 amendments to the MBCA in eliminating the concept of treasury shares.

board wishes to pay a dividend in 1986, it need pay only $100 to the preferred shareholders before paying dividends to the common shareholders.

Sometimes preferred shares are *cumulative if earned*. That means that they do not cumulate in years when the corporation makes no profit, but do cumulate in years when there were sufficient profits from which to pay the preferred dividends but the board elected not to do so.

Typically preferred shares are *nonparticipating*. That term indicates that all they are entitled to receive in any given year is the stipulated interest. Sometimes, however, preferred shares are *participating*. After these shares are paid their stipulated interest, they may participate side-by-side with the common shares in the remaining dividends to be paid. Thus, participating stock shares with the common stock in the bounty of a very good year.

Usually preferred stock carries a preference not only as to payment of dividends, but also as to payment of assets on liquidation.

The similarities between debt securities and participating preferred are such that they are both frequently termed *senior securities*. There are obvious similarities between preferred stock and debt securities. In recent years there has been a trend toward use of the latter. For the creditor, debt securities are preferable to preferred stock because they can be secured and are entitled to interest and principal repayment regardless of the financial condition of the corporation. For the corporation, the deductibility of interest gives debt securities a major tax advantage.

CONSIDERATION FOR SHARES

Shares should only be issued in exchange for consideration that meets both quality and quantity tests.

Quality Tests

MBCA §19 is typical of the provisions of most states in specifying certain types of consideration that are, and other types that are not, acceptable in exchange for the issurance of shares of stock. Section 19 states that proper consideration includes money paid, tangible or intangible property received, and services performed for the corporation.

Impermissible as consideration are promissory notes and mere promises of future services, according to §19. Only a few jurisdictions disagree, though their number is slowly growing.[4]

Most courts will allow securities to be issued in exchange for promissory notes if those notes are fully secured by property the corporation can seize to assure payment

---

[4] RMBCA §6.21 specifically authorizes as legitimate consideration for the issuance of shares promissory notes, contracts for services to be rendered, plus any "benefit" to the corporation—a concept that should be broadly construed to include things such as release of a claim against the corporation. The corporation *may* place such shares in escrow until the note is paid, the services are performed, or the benefit is received.

in full. But if the property used to secure the promissory note is worthless, the issuance is improper. Courts will even sustain use of an unsecured promissory note so long as the corporation retains possession of the securities and the purchaser does not exercise the rights of a shareholder until the notes are paid in full.

While some courts hold it improper to issue shares in exchange for preincorporation services on the theory that those services were not performed *for the corporation* that was not yet in existence, other courts uphold such transactions,[5] especially if they are approved by informed shareholders.[6] A few states' statutes specifically approve preincorporation services as proper consideration.

Some courts have even loosened the requirement regarding promises of future services to allow corporations to induce employees to come to work for them in cases where there was no hint that the corporation had been defrauded.[7] Most courts, however, hold to a stricter interpretation. One way to evade the problem is to compensate employees for future services with treasury stock that, because it is not technically being "issued," is not governed by these restrictions.[8]

Many states have constitutional provisions that parallel the MBCA provision regarding issuance of stock. The laws of one such state are discussed in the following case.

EMCO, INC. v. HEALY

602 S.W.2d 309 (Tex. Civ. App. 1980)

Emco is a small manufacturing company, founded by Zuckerman who hired Manning as president in 1971. Needing more capital, Emco solicited investors, including defendant Healy. Healy agreed to invest but could not obtain financing in Dallas. Therefore, Zuckerman and Manning arranged financing for Healy with the First Trust & Savings Bank of Davenport, Iowa (Bank). Under the agreement, Healy would purchase 3,334 shares of Emco stock, giving his note payable to Emco in the sum of $50,000, together with a collateral

security agreement mortgaging the 3,334 shares to secure the note. The note and security agreement were then assigned to the Bank, which in turn paid the $50,000 note to Emco.

After several interest payments, Healy defaulted on the note. The Bank called upon Emco for performance, whereupon it paid the note and took a reassignment from the Bank. Emco then brought this suit against Healy to collect the note. The trial judge held that Emco should recover nothing. Emco appealed.

---

[5] *Burge* v. *Frey*, 545 F.Supp. 1160 (D. Kan. 1982).
[6] *Fitzpatrick* v. *O'Neill*, 118 P. 273 (Mont. 1911).
[7] *Petrishen* v. *Westmoreland Finance Corp.*, 147 A.2d 392 (Pa. 1959).
[8] *Mills* v. *Esmark, Inc.*, 544 F.Supp. 1275 (N.D. Ill. 1972).

CORNELIUS, CHIEF JUSTICE:

Emco raises six points of error which, for better organization, will be discussed out of numerical sequence. In point 4 it is contended that recovery should be allowed on the note because the constitutional and statutory provisions were intended to insure that a corporation receive money for its shares, and to rule that a note given for stock is unenforceable in the hands of the corporation would defeat, rather than fulfill, that purpose while protecting a stock purchaser who has agreed to pay for his stock but fails to do so. That argument has some support in logic, but it conflicts with the respected public policy principle that the law will not enforce, as between the parties, the payment of a debt growing out of an illegal transaction. That principle has been repeatedly applied to stock transactions, and it is thus well settled that a note given to a corporation for the purchase of shares of stock in that corporation is unenforceable in the hands of the corporation or in the hands of an assignee or holder having, or being charged with, knowledge of the nature of the transaction in which the note was given.

It is also urged, in point 1, that the transaction involved here was legal because money was actually received by the corporation for its stock. The rationale is that because Emco received full value for Healy's note when it was transferred to the Davenport Bank, the constitutional and statutory requirements were met. We do not agree. The assignment of the note to the bank was with full recourse. Even if the assignment had been without recourse, Emco would still have been subject to certain contingent liabilities. In those circumstances, Emco's assignment of the note to the bank amounted to no more than a loan advance by the bank on the collateral of the note. Such an arrangement amounts to nothing more than a sale of stock in consideration of a note from the purchaser to the corporation. It is not the same situation

as found in cases such as *Citizens' Nat. Bank v. Stevenson*, 231 S.W. 364 (Tex. Com. App. 1921, jdgmt adopted); *Ruthart v. First State Bank, Tulia, Texas*, 431 S.W.2d 366 (Tex. Civ. App.—Amarillo 1968, writ ref'd); and *Weichsel v. Jones*, 109 S.W.2d 332 (Tex. Civ. App.—Dallas 1937, no writ). In none of those cases did the corporation stand to lose if the note given for the stock was not paid. In none of those cases was the note in payment of the shares given to the corporation. Those cases correctly held that there is nothing illegal in a prospective shareholder buying shares in a corporation by using money he has borrowed from a third party. In this case, however, the corporation financed the initial sale of the stock and stood to lose all of the consideration if the note was not paid. Indeed, that is exactly what happened. Such an arrangement is clearly a violation of the constitutional and statutory provisions.

Neither are the cases of *Hatcher v. Jack Miller Milling Corporation*, 501 S.W.2d 439 (Tex. Civ. App.—Texarkana 1973, writ ref'd n.r.e.), and *McCarty v. Langdeau*, 337 S.W.2d 407 (Tex. Civ. App.—Austin, 1960, writ ref'd n.r.e.), applicable here. In the *Hatcher* case, no stock was to be issued until the notes were paid in full. In the *McCarty* case, the court, without deciding whether the stock was issued before or was to be issued after the notes were paid, held that the notes would be enforceable in either event because the suit was on behalf of the creditors of the corporation, who stand in the same position as a bona fide holder and can enforce the note even if it was illegally given as payment for stock.

Points 2 and 3 assert that the transaction here did not violate the constitutional and statutory provisions because the stock was neither issued nor delivered to Healy. We overrule these points. The evidence shows that the certificate was issued in the name of Healy, and although it was retained by the corporation and delivered to the bank to secure the note, Healy was treated in all respects as a stockholder. In such circumstances there was an actual issuance, and at least a constructive delivery, of the stock.

Finally, it is asserted that because the note was secured by the stock itself, it constituted "property actually received" as used in the constitutional and statutory provisions. We reject that proposition. A promissory note, although considered property in the general sense, is not "money paid" or "property actually received" for stock as contemplated by the constitution and statutes—Model Business Corporation Act Annotation, Section 19, Paragraph 4.04. And while notes secured by first mortgages on real estate have been held to constitute "property actually received," that is entirely different from what we have here, for as said in *General Bonding & Casualty Ins. Co.* v. *Moseley*, 110 Tex. 529, 222 S.W. 961 (1920), the corporation in those instances has obtained,

> the right to have the land appropriated. . . . This is a valuable right, a property right, as fully so as any contract right, and, in general, as valuable as any such right. The corporation receives it and owns it. It constitutes a distinct asset in its hands;

That is much more than merely having a mortgage on the stock for which the note was given. A mortgage on a corporation's own stock, which has not been paid for, cannot be said to be a distinct asset available for the protection of creditors. If such an arrangement could be construed as constituting property actually received, the constitutional and statutory provisions would be rendered meaningless and their purpose could easily be thwarted.

The judgment of the trial court is affirmed.

Quantity Tests

In addition to meeting qualitative tests, the consideration given for the issuance of stock must meet a quantitative test. In most states this means that the shares must be issued for no less than the sale price fixed by the board, and no less than the par value of the stock. Section 18 of the MBCA so provided until the 1980 amendments eliminated the concept of par value. This requirement demands some explanation of the concept of par value.

Par Value

Par value arose from the requirement of early laws that the capital paid into the corporation be specified. By multiplying the total number of shares outstanding by the "par value" of each share, creditors could supposedly calculate the corporation's total capital. This system worked fine so long as all the shares in a subscription were sold for the specified par value. But par value is a sum set arbitrarily by the board of directors. If the shares are sold at a price below par value, the assumption that par value is an accurate guide to the "cushion" creditors can expect if they lend money to the corporation is destroyed.

Unfortunately, as we shall see, shares were not always issued at par value. If the consideration was less, creditors were not as protected as they might think. Par value remains a completely arbitrary figure established by the board. No longer is it an important guide for the protection of creditors. Indeed, the concept of par value has been abolished in California and in the as yet largely unadopted 1980 amendments to the MBCA.[9]

Still, par value remains an important concept in many states because par value shares are not to be issued for less than the stated par value. Par value is also important in the process of calculating the amount of funds available for dividends and other shareholder distributions as we shall see later in this chapter.

No-Par Stock

When it became clear that par value did not adequately protect creditors of corporations, almost all jurisdictions authorized use of *no-par* stock. Such stock carries no par value. It is sold, as is par value stock today, at a stated value set by the board of directors. It cannot be sold at a price below that stated value, just as par value stock cannot properly be sold for consideration smaller than the stated par value.

No-par stock was intended to add flexibility to corporate finance and to prevent creditors and other shareholders from being misled. It has not been particularly successful. As we shall see in the section on dividends, *low-par* stock is much more popular than is no par.

The qualitative tests for consideration apply equally to par and no-par stock.

Valuation of Consideration Received

When stock is issued in exchange for property received or services performed, the value of the consideration should equal or exceed the par value of par stock and the established consideration set by the board for par value and no-par stock. Unfortunately, it is not always easy to determine accurately the value of services that perhaps were unique to this corporation. And how are we to value property received? Should we use market value? Or book value? Or replacement value? How about liquidation value?

Courts generally lean toward market value if an established market is available. Fortunately, the difficult problem of valuing property and services in most states is eliminated by the "good faith" rule. Formerly many jurisdictions found that shares were improperly issued if, in hindsight, it was determined that they were sold in exchange for property with a smaller value than the par value of the shares. This was known as the "True Value Rule." In most states this rule has been replaced by the "Good Faith Rule," which is typified by MBCA §19, which states that in the absence of fraud, "the judgment of the board of directors or the shareholders, as the case may be, as to the value of the consideration received for shares shall be conclusive."

Occasionally the judgment of the board of directors, the entity that usually values the consideration, is overridden because of concerns about fraud. Such a case follows.

---

[9] RMBCA §6.21 follows the 1980 MBCA amendments in eliminating the concept of par value.

LEWIS v. SCOTTEN DILLON COMPANY

306 A.2d. 755 (Del. Ch. 1973)

On May 15, 1970, the boards of directors of Iroquois Industries, Inc., and Scotten Dillon Company approved a contract providing for the acquisition of all assets of Scotten Dillon in exchange for 450,000 shares of Iroquois common stock. The exchange was related to all outstanding stock of Scotten Dillon and, in effect, involved a 1.5 ratio of Iroquois shares to Scotten Dillon shares (450,000 to 300,000).

On July 6, 1970, plaintiff, an Iroquois shareholder, filed this suit seeking to enjoin the proposed transaction as a waste of Iroquois assets. Seventeen days later Scotten Dillon withdrew from the plan as it had a right to do under the contract.

Plaintiff now seeks attorney's fees. Regardless of whether plaintiff's suit was the reason for termination of the acquisition, a matter not proved, plaintiff is entitled to attorney's fees if he had a "meritorious action." Whether or not plaintiff's action was meritorious is the issue to be resolved.

DUFFY, CHANCELLOR:

Iroquois argues that the complaint is not and cannot be regarded as meritorious because at bottom it is based on a disagreement about the value of the Scotten Dillon assets to be acquired. Relying on 8 Del. Ch. Section 152, defendant says that actual fraud has not been shown and hence the statute makes the judgment of the directors conclusive on the valuation issue.

Actual fraud may, of course, be shown directly, but it may also be inferred from the attendant circumstances, and inadequacy of consideration is a part of such circumstances. However, excessive valuation, standing alone, is not enough unless it is so gross as to lead the court to conclude that it was due, not to an honest error of judgment, but to bad faith or a reckless indifference to the rights of others—*Fidanque v. American Maracaibo Co.*, 33 Del. Ch. 262, 92 A.2d 311 (1952).

In applying these rules to this case, I assume that all Iroquois directors, other than Fox, were independent in all necessary aspects. Indeed that is more than an assumption because there is nothing in the record to show that they are not. But the position of Fox is quite different.

Certainly Fox was the central figure in the transaction. He was president and board chairman of Iroquois. He negotiated the terms of the acquisition with Scotten Dillon. He presented the proposal to the Iroquois Board. Compare *Fidanque* v. *American Maracaibo Co.*, supra. At the time of negotiation and at the time of presentation, Fox owned (or at least had a substantial claim to ownership of) $1,500,000 in value of convertible debentures of Scotten Dillon. How much of this he revealed to the Iroquois Board is not clear from the record. But it is clear that he did not disclose to the Board that he had pledged the debentures to secure three bank loans totaling $475,000. I need not determine what inference should be drawn from these facts. I need note only that one inference which may be drawn is that Fox had a significant personal interest in consummation of the transaction which required the fullest disclosure on his part; and it was not made. By the terms of the contract which he negotiated and recommended Iroquois would have assumed, apparently, the obligation to convert his debentures into its stock at the 1.5 to 1 ratio. I need not decide that Fox would have had an enforceable legal right to conversion at that ratio but certainly he would have been in position to strongly argue a right to do so and that is enough for present purposes.

In terms of market price Iroquois would have been required to pay a substantial premium for Scotten Dillon, as shown by the following comparison between market value of 450,000 Iroquois shares and 300,000 Scotten Dillon shares:

| | MARKET PRICE/SHARE | | TOTAL MARKET VALUE | | |
| | | SCOTTEN | | SCOTTEN | |
DATE	IROQUOIS	DILLON	IROQUOIS	DILLON	EXCESS
5/1/70	9⅝	8¼	$ 4,331,250	$2,475,000	$1,856,250
5/6/70	Purchase approved by the Iroquois Board of Directors				
5/14/70	8¼	9⅛	3,712,500	2,737,500	975,000
7/6/70	6¾	6⅛	3,037,500	1,837,500	1,200,000
7/23/70	7¾	6½	3,487,500	1,950,000	1,537,500
10/29/71	22½	9	10,125,000	2,700,000	7,425,000
10/11/72	14⅛	8⅞	6,356,250	2,662,500	3,693,750

Iroquois argues that the "control" which would accompany its acquisition of all Scotten Dillon assets is a value factor to be weighed. And so it is. And I agree that market price is not necessarily conclusive in these matters, particularly under the statute and because assets, not shares, were to be acquired. But I am unable to find from the record facts which eliminate all reasonable hope of success for plaintiff. Iroquois argues that in *Puma* v. *Mariott*, Del. Ch., 283 A.2d 693 (1971), this court applied the business judgment test to the decision of independent directors who approved a stock-for-stock transaction. There the case went to final hearing and the court found that the plaintiff had not shown fraud. And that points up the critical difference between *Puma* and this case: plaintiff is not obliged to prove fraud at this time in this case. His burden is not "absolute assurance" but only "reasonable hope" of ultimate success. *Puma* is not controlling.

We have, then, a situation in which the chief executive of and negotiator for Iroquois (Fox) apparently stood to gain significantly through his investments in the *other* company, if the deal were consummated. And on the face of things, the difference in market value of the respective shares is significant. Under these circumstances I conclude that Section 152 does not cut off inquiry as a matter of law. In short, plaintiff has demonstrated a triable issue on fraud under Section 152. Given the significant difference in "value" on the respective sides (as shown by the market prices for shares), the key position of Fox in the negotiation and his failure to disclose his special interest, I conclude that plaintiff has shown such reasonable hope of ultimate success that he is entitled to an allowance for compensation.

Applying the usual standards, in my judgment a total allowance for all services and expenses of $25,000 is reasonable under all the circumstances.

"Watered Stock" and Its Consequences

"Watered stock" is sometimes used as an umbrella term to cover all varieties of stock issued for inadequate consideration. More specifically, "bonus stock" frequently denotes stock that is given in exchange for no consideration while "discount stock" refers to shares issued for consideration below par value. "Watered stock" specifically refers to stock issued in exchange for property that is not worth as much as the stock's value. The phrase is derived from the shady practice of some ranchers who, just before taking their cattle to market, would feed the cattle salt to make them thirsty and then lead them to water. A stomach full of water would artificially boost the cow's weight.

There were several watered stock scandals in the late 1800s. Many creditors relying on the par value of issued stock were greatly deceived because corporations had issued the stock for sums below par. The courts responded to this situation in a number of ways.

Many early courts adopted the "trust fund" theory espoused in Justice Story's 1824 holding in *Wood* v. *Dummer* [10] that the assets of a corporation including the amount that should have been paid for shares but was not constitute a trust fund for the benefit of creditors. Though generally rejected today, "trust fund" language still appears in occasional decisions.

The leading approach for many years was the "misrepresentation theory" of *Hospes* v. *Northwestern Manufacturing Car Co.*,[11] which allowed creditors to recover amounts between par value and lesser sums actually paid, but only if they could prove that they relied on the represented par value in making the loan.

Later, many statutes were enacted that specifically required that stock be issued for no less than par value. This development gave rise to the "statutory obligation" theory discussed in the next case.

BING CROSBY MINUTE MAID CORPORATION v. EATON

297 P.2d 5 (Cal. 1956)

Defendant Eaton formed a corporation to acquire his frozen foods business. The California Commissioner of Corporations issued a permit authorizing the corporation to sell not more than 4,500 shares of $10 par value stock to the defendant and others. The permit stipulated that 1,022 of these shares be deposited in escrow and not issued until the Commissioner had ap-

---

[10] 30 F.Cas. 435, No. 17,994 (C.C.D. Me. 1824).

[11] 50 N.W. 1117 (Minn. 1892).

proved and the prospective shareholders agreed to waive certain rights to participate in dividends and liquidation of assets. Although the 1,022 shares were listed on the corporate books as held by defendant, they were never released from escrow.

Plaintiff corporation recovered a judgment against defendant's corporation for $21,246.42. The judgment went unsatisfied because of the corporation's poor financial condition. Plaintiff then brought this action against defendant to recover the alleged difference between the par value of the stock issued to him and the fair value of the consideration he paid.

The trial judge found that the value of the consideration given by the defendant was $34,780.83 and that 4,500 shares of $10 par value stock were issued to defendant who became the owner of them. The trial judge, holding that defendant was liable for the difference between the par value of the 4,500 shares and the value of the consideration he gave, rendered judgment for plaintiff in the sum of $10,219.17, approximately the par value of the shares placed in escrow. Later defendant's motion for a new trial was granted and plaintiff appealed.

SHENK, JUSTICE:

The plaintiff seeks to base its recovery on liability for holding watered stock, which is stock issued in return for properties or services worth less than its par value. Accordingly, this case calls for an analysis of the rights of a creditor of an insolvent corporation against a holder of watered stock. Holders of watered stock are generally held liable to the corporation's creditors for the difference between the par value of the stock and the amount paid in.

The defendant's first contention is that because of the escrow he never became an owner of the 1,022 shares and that he therefore never acquired such title to the 1,022 shares as would

enable a creditor to proceed against him for their par value. The escrow in the present case permitted the defendant to retain some, but not all, of the incidents of ownership in the 1,022 shares. Although he could not transfer the shares, it appears that despite the escrow he was entitled to count them in determining the extent of his rights to vote and to participate in dividends and asset distributions. The critical feature of the escrow for purposes of the present case is the absence of any restriction on representations that the escrowed shares were outstanding and fully paid. Therefore, it would appear that despite the escrow the defendant acquired sufficient title to the 1,022 shares to permit the plaintiff to proceed against him for their par value.

The defendant's second contention is that the trial court failed to make a finding on a material issue raised by his answer.

The liability of a holder of watered stock has been based on one of two theories: the misrepresentation theory or the statutory obligation theory. The misrepresentation theory is the one accepted in most jurisdictions. The courts view the issue of watered stock as a misrepresentation of the corporation's capital. Creditors who rely on this misrepresentation are entitled to recover the "water" from the holders of the watered shares.

Statutes expressly prohibiting watered stock are commonplace today. In some jurisdictions where they have been enacted, the statutory obligation theory has been applied. Under that theory the holder of watered stock is held responsible to creditors whether or not they have relied on an overvaluation of corporate capital.

In his answer the defendant alleged that in extending credit to the corporation, the plaintiff did not rely on the par value of the shares issued, but only on independent investigation and reports as to the corporation's current cash position, its physical assets, and its business experience. At the trial the plaintiff's district manager admitted that during the period when the plaintiff extended credit to the corporation, (1) the district manager believed that the original capital of the corporation amounted to only $25,000, and (2) the only financial statement of the corporation that the plaintiff ever saw showed a capital stock account of less than $33,000. These admissions would be sufficient to support a finding that the plaintiff did not rely on any misrepresentation arising out of the issuance of watered stock. The court made no finding on the issue of reliance. If the misrepresentation theory prevails in California, that issue was material and the defendant was entitled to a finding thereon. If the statutory obligation theory prevails, the fact that the plaintiff did not rely on any misrepresentation arising out of the issuance of watered stock is irrelevant, and accordingly, a finding on the issue of reliance would be surplusage.

It is therefore necessary to determine which theory prevails in this state. The plaintiff concedes that before the enactment of Section 1110 of the Corporations Code in 1931, the misrepresentation theory was the only one available to creditors seeking to recover from holders of watered stock. However, he contends that the enactment of that section reflected a legislative intent to impose on the holders of watered stock a statutory obligation to creditors to make good the "water." Section 1110 provides that "The value of the consideration to be received by a corporation for the issue of shares having par value shall be at least equal to the par value thereof, except that: (a) A corporation may issue par value shares, as fully paid up, at less than par, if the board of directors determines that such shares cannot be sold at par." The statute does not expressly impose an obligation to creditors. Most jurisdictions having similar statutes have applied the misrepresentation theory obviously on the grounds that creditors are sufficiently protected against stock watering schemes under that theory. In view of the cases in this state prior to 1931 adopting the misrepresentation theory, it is reasonable to assume that the Legislature would have used clear language expressing an intent to broaden the basis of liability of holders of watered stock had it entertained such an intention. In this state the liability of a holder of watered stock may only be based on the misrepresentation.

The plaintiff contends that even under the misrepresentation theory a creditor's reliance on the misrepresentation arising out of the issuance of watered stock should be conclusively presumed. This contention is without substantial merit. If it should prevail, the misrepresentation theory and the statutory obligation theory would be essentially identical. This court has held that under the misrepresentation theory a person who extended credit to a corporation (1) before the watered stock was issued, or (2) with full knowledge that watered stock was outstanding, cannot recover from the holders of the watered stock. These decisions indicate that under the misrepresentation theory, reliance by the creditor is a prerequisite to the liability of a holder of watered stock.

The order granting the new trial is affirmed.

The problem of watered stock has diminished because of the advent of no-par and, especially, low-par stock. Today, if a corporation intends to sell stock at $50 per share, it will not set the par value at $50. Rather, it will set the par value at some lesser sum, such as $1 or $10. Then, even if the market for the stock weakens and the shares must sold for less than the originally intended sum, watered stock liability can be avoided. Use of low-par stock also has significant advantages for a management wishing to pay dividends and other distributions, as we shall see later in the chapter.

Today the main problem is not the sale of shares for below par value. Rather, it is the sale of shares, whether par or no par, to a buyer who does not pay the specified purchase price. Section 25 of the MBCA provides that a holder or subscriber of shares has no obligation to the corporation or its creditors regarding those shares "other than the obligation to pay to the corporation the full consideration for which such shares were issued or to be issued." [12]

Implicitly, creditors may sue if obligations due them from the corporation go unpaid because shareholders do not pay what they agreed to pay for their shares. The corporation also has such a cause of action. However, the result of such a suit may depend on who brings it, and under what circumstances.

For example, in *Emco, Inc.* v. *Healy*, presented earlier in this chapter, a clear constitutional provision led the court to declare shares issued for improper consideration to be void. Many courts will hold that shares issued for illegal or inadequate consideration may be deemed only voidable, rather than void, depending on the policy demands of the circumstances. For example, in *Frasier* v. *Trans-Western Land Corporation*,[13] Frasier was a shareholder who believed that under the terms of an agreement with other shareholders he did not have to make a capital contribution in exchange for his shares. The remaining shareholders apparently waived the contribution and allowed Frasier to act as a shareholder. However, at a point when it appeared that the corporation might turn a profit through liquidation, the other shareholders canceled Frasier's shares and refused to allow him to participate.

The court held that the issuance of shares to Frasier in exchange for no consideration rendered the shares merely *voidable*, not void. Because the remaining shareholders had acquiesced in Frasier's status as a shareholder until a profit appeared on the horizon, they were deemed estopped to challenge the validity of his shares. The court stressed that had the challenge been brought by third-party creditors, the result would have been much different. Provisions such as Section 25 of the MBCA are aimed at protecting creditors. They are not meant to protect a solvent corporation where it or its shareholders are attempting to evade prior agreements.

Officers and directors who authorize the issuance of shares for inadequate or illegal compensation are also liable to creditors for the difference between the value of the shares and the consideration received, unless their judgment is upheld under the "good faith" rule.

DEBT-EQUITY RATIO

In forming the corporation's capital structure, one must not forget the advantages of debt. The primary advantage is debt's effect on tax liability. Because interest payments may be deducted by the corporation, unlike payments made in the form of dividends

---

[12] RMBCA §6.22 similarly stipulates that a purchaser of shares is liable only for "the consideration for which the shares were authorized to be issued."

[13] 316 N.W.2d 612 (Neb. 1982).

or stock redemptions, double taxation can be minimized. Furthermore, accumulation of legitimate corporate debt is a defense to the accumulated earnings tax.

Leverage

When funds are obtained from outsiders via borrowing or sale of preferred shares, the common shareholders may gain the advantage of *leverage*. If I need $100,000 to start my corporation's business and expect a first-year profit of $20,000, I can use my $100,000 and receive a return of 20% on the dollar. However, if I can borrow $50,000 at less than 20% and use only $50,000 of my own money, my return per dollar invested will rise dramatically, especially when the tax advantages of the interest deduction are considered. Ideally, leverage involves borrowing money via issuance of debt securities or nonparticipating preferred stock at a cost per dollar in interest that is less than the profit I can make on that dollar. Leverage can magnify the earnings per dollar invested of the common shareholder so long as earnings per dollar exceed interest cost per dollar (adjusted for tax considerations). If earnings fall, however, losses are magnified as the following chart demonstrates.[14]

			VERY POOR YEAR	POOR YEAR	AVERAGE YEAR	GOOD YEAR
A. BONDS	= $1,000,000	LEVERAGE RATIO = 2				
B. SHARES	= 1,000,000	[TOTAL INVESTMENT]:				
C. TOTAL INVESTMENT	= $2,000,000	1 [SHARES]				
D. Earnings after taxes (before bond interest)			($ 30,000)	$150,000	$300,000	$600,000
E. Bond interest (15%)			150,000	150,000	150,000	150,000
F. Net earnings distributable to shareholders (D minus E)			(180,000)	0	150,000	450,000
G. Percentage earned on total investment (D divided by C)			(1.5%)	7.5%	15%	30%
H. Percentage earned on shareholder investment (F divided by B)			(18%)	0	15%	45%
(_____) = deficit						

Thin Capitalization

The advantage of leverage makes it attractive for corporations to borrow from outside sources. The tax advantages of debt and the fact that creditors are at the head of the line in bankruptcy court lead owners of closely-held corporations especially to consider labeling much of the sums they intend to invest in the business as "loans" rather than as "capital investment."

Too much debt and too little capital, however, create a situation of "thin capital-

[14] H. Henn and J. Alexander, *Law of Corporations* 3rd ed. (West Publishing Co.: St. Paul, MN, 1983), p. 414.

ization,'' which may lead the IRS or a court to treat what has been labeled "debt" as capital instead. Generally, capital has not been held to be too thin if the ratio of outside debt to equity does not exceed 10 to 1 and the ratio of inside debt to equity (excluding outside debt) does not exceed 3 to 1. This numerical guideline is a rough one, and not the only factor considered.

TANZI v. FIBERGLASS SWIMMING POOLS, INC.

414 A.2d 484 (R.I. 1980)

In 1968 Richard Tanzi incorporated his swimming pool construction business with a $3,000 capital contribution. His parents were nominal shareholders. Tanzi invested additional personal funds as annual gross sales rose from $35,000 to $238,000 in 1973. Because the pool business was seasonal, Tanzi withdrew his personal funds every spring in order to begin pool installations after the winter shutdown. When additional capital was needed in 1972, Richard again transferred personal funds to the corporation, defendant Fiberglass, in order to buy additional equipment and to construct a model pool for display purposes. Richard's mother, Lucy, also transferred $25,000 of her personal funds to the corporation, allegedly as a loan. On the 1973 financial records these cash transfers were called loans. Richard received $5,000 as repayment in 1973.

The business soon foundered and Richard petitioned the corporation into receivership in March 1976. The receiver wished to sell corporate assets free and clear, but the Tanzis petitioned for reclamation of certain corporate equipment which had allegedly been pledged as security for a corporate $40,818.76 promissory note executed on November 23, 1973. The receiver claimed the advances to the corporation were capital contributions that should be subordinated to creditors' claims.

The trial judge ruled that the so-called loans should be treated as capital contributions. The Tanzis appealed.

KELLEHER, JUSTICE:

In the present controversy, the trial justice at the close of testimony drew certain inferences regarding the structure and management of Fiberglass. Finding that the transactions were "suspect," the trial justice apparently attached great significance to the fact that the promissory note was not executed until over a year after the final cash advance was made to Fiberglass.

Accordingly, the trial justice held that the money represented a "contribution to capital . . . [used] for the operation of this corporation,'' thus rejecting the debtor-creditor theory advanced by the Tanzis. The action of the trial justice released to Fiberglass creditors an additional $21,000 held by the permanent receiver. In our view, the trial justice was correct. Even though a shareholder loan is not per se invalid, obviously the transaction is subject to strict judicial scrutiny. The general rule would also permit corporate directors and officers as well as shareholders to attain creditor status for loans advanced to the corporation—16 Fletcher, *Cyclopedia of the Law of Private Corporations*, Section 7919 at 647 (rev. perm. ed. 1979). It goes without saying that courts are particularly watchful in all these situations because of the fiduciary status that officers and dominant shareholders must observe vis-à-vis the corporation when the individual acts both for himself and for the corporation.

With this background in mind, we now proceed to consider the Tanzis' contention that their claim should have received priority because they were secured creditors of Fiberglass. The issue narrows to whether these transactions by the Tanzis first met the requirements of valid loans in that a debtor-creditor relationship ever existed between them and Fiberglass. The trial justice remained unconvinced, as do we. Clearly, persons making capital contributions are not corporate creditors—*Albert Richards Co.* v. *The Mayfair, Inc.*, 287 Mass. 280, 288, 191 N.E. 430, 434 –35 (1934).

The Court of Appeals of Maryland found that the note of the corporation to its principal stockholder represented a debt and not a contribution to capital; yet we find their reasoning in *Obre* v. *Alban Tractor Co.*, 228 Md. 291, 179 A.2d 861 (1962), helpful to the issue before us. The court in particular considered whether the corporation formed with a risk capital of $40,000 was undercapitalized. In addition, the court took into account that the note was listed on the monthly financial reports of the corporation as a debt and that an interest provision was included although interest was never paid.

In *Weyerhaeuser Co.* v. *Clark's Material Supply Co.*, 90 Idaho 455, 461, 413 P.2d 180, 183 (1966), the Supreme Court of Idaho found that the transaction under review did not meet the requirements of a valid loan and hence the shareholder and his wife could not share in the distribution of the corporate assets. In reaching its decision, the court considered the following factors: the husband and wife were not listed on the corporate records as creditors; no note was executed; and they did not regard the security advanced earlier as a loan until after a decision was reached in litigation concerning the appointment of the corporate receiver.

We also note with approval a recent well-reasoned decision by the Supreme Court of Wisconsin in which it reversed the trial court's decision to subordinate a director-shareholder loan. In *In re Mader's Store for Men*, 77 Wis.2d 578, 254 N.W.2d 171 (1977), the court collected and analyzed cases in which advances to a corporation were subordinated on the capital contribution theory and extracted the following relevant factors: (1) was the claimant in a position to control corporate affairs ''at least to the extent of determining the form of the transaction''; (2) were the advances intended to be repaid in the ordinary course of the corporation's business; and (3) was the paid-in stated capital ''unreasonably small in view of the nature and size of the business in which the corporation was engaged.''

In our view, the *Mader* court correctly indicated that a breach of fiduciary duties was not a prerequisite to treating shareholder advances as capital contributions. Although it reached a contrary result, we would agree with the *Mader* court: ''Inequity enough to justify subordination exists when it is shown that a claim which is in reality a proprietary interest is seeking to compete on an equal basis with true creditors' claims.''

In the bankruptcy context, the following criteria have been considered in determining the treatment of the disputed advances: the adequacy of capital contribution, the ratio of shareholder loans to capital contribution, the amount of shareholder control, the availability of similar loans from outside lenders, and certain relevant questions, such as, whether the ultimate financial failure was caused by undercapitalization, whether the note included repayment provisions and a fixed maturity date, whether a note or debt document was executed, whether proceeds were used to acquire capital assets, and how the debt was treated in the corporate records.

These recurring themes also emerge from the internal revenue cases, although in somewhat distinctive factual context. In the tax situation, the debt or equity distinction resolves the question of whether amounts qualify as bad-debt deductions for internal revenue purposes, for example, *Berkowitz v. United States*, 411 F.2d 818 (5th Cir. 1969).

Applying the criteria enunciated earlier to the facts in this case, we conclude that the trial justice was justified in finding that the cash advances to Fiberglass were contributions to risk capital rather than bona fide loans to the corporation. We feel that the initial risk capital of $3,000 was inadequate to sustain corporate sales in excess of $200,000. Furthermore, Richard Tanzi completely controlled the corporation, a factor to which the trial justice specifically alluded as follows: "As long as it [Fiberglass] was making profits, he was taking the profits out. When he needed money to buy additional assets or run the business, he put money in." On balance, the transaction itself bore very few earmarks of an arm's-length bargain. The note lacked either interest, repayment, or default provisions and had no fixed maturity date. Although an actual repayment of $5,000 was made to Richard Tanzi, this factor is offset by the fact that the proceeds, in reality, were used to acquire capital assets necessary for corporate expansion. Finally, the belated execution of the promissory note strongly suggests that it was an attempt in form rather than in substance to protect the family investment. Surely, under these circumstances, in which repayment safeguards were virtually nonexistent, an outside lender would have been foolhardy to risk its funds. The Tanzis' "loan," therefore, qualified as a contribution to capital that was correctly subordinated to the claims of the general creditors.

Affirmed.

The shareholder who wishes to have part of his or her investment in a corporation treated as debt rather than equity should act like a creditor as to that portion. In deciding whether to treat what was labeled as "debt" as though it were capital, the Tax Court has noted that

> The essential difference between a stockholder and a creditor is that the stockholder's intention is to embark upon the corporate adventure, taking the risks of loss attendant upon it, so that he may enjoy the chances of profit. The creditor, on the other hand, does not intend to take such risks so far as they may be avoided, but merely intends to lend his capital to others who intend to take them.[15]

As the *Tanzi* case indicated, the courts consider many factors in deciding whether to treat a shareholder's supposed loan as a capital contribution. Among these are the following.[16]

First, courts consider whether shareholders' advances are made in roughly the

[15] *Baker Commodities, Inc.* v. *Commissioner*, 48 T.C. 374, 395 (1967).

[16] C. Taylor, "Classifying Shareholder Advances to a Closely Held Corporation as Debt or Stock: Guidelines for the Befuddled Practitioner," *Drake Law Review*, vol. 33 (1983–84), p. 33.

same proportions as their capital contributions. Proportionality indicates that the advance is a contribution rather than a loan.

Second, courts consider how the transaction is labeled in the corporation's financial records. Labels obviously are not conclusive, but if an advance is intended as a loan, it should be so labeled on the books, on tax returns, and so on.

Third, prompt and regular payment of principal and interest strongly indicates debt.

Fourth, a fixed, unconditional maturity date indicates a loan also. Again, this factor is not decisive because preferred stock often carries such a feature.

Fifth, fixed, unconditional interest payments indicate debt. If payments are made only in years when the corporation is profitable, they look more like dividends than interest.

Sixth, the rate of interest is important. It should be a reasonable rate, somewhat close to the market rate.

Seventh, courts frequently go into the facts at great length to determine whether, at the time of the advance, there was a reasonable expectation that it would be repaid.

Eighth, the corporation's overall debt-equity ratio is examined. If that ratio is "excessive," the thin capitalization will tempt the court to treat shareholder "loans" as capital. In one case, for example, a debt-equity ratio of 80 to 1 helped the court decide to treat alleged loans as capital contributions.[17] Again, this factor is not conclusive. In one case a ratio of 692.5 to 1 was upheld where all other factors were consistent with debt treatment.[18]

Ninth, courts sometimes inquire as to whether shareholder advances were used to purchase assets needed for initial operation of the business. Such advances will likely be treated as capital contributions.

Tenth, courts often inquire as to whether upon default by the debtor, the shareholder-creditor attempted to enforce the obligation as a true creditor would.

These factors are not exclusive, but they frequently appear in such cases.

PREEMPTIVE RIGHTS

Stock ownership conveys three major rights to the shareholder: the right to share in control, the right to share in dividends, and the right to share in assets upon dissolution. Normally, a shareholder owning one-tenth of a corporation's shares will have one-tenth of the votes in the election of directors and will receive one-tenth of the dividends and of the assets on dissolution. Assume, however, that the corporation decides to sell additional shares, doubling the number outstanding, to raise new capital. If our shareholder is unable to purchase any of the new issuance, his proportionate voting power is reduced from one-tenth to one-twentieth. The same may be said for his share of dividends,

---

[17] *Fett* v. *Moore*, 438 F.Supp. 726 (E.D. Va. 1977).

[18] *Baker Commodities, Inc.* v. *Commissioner*, 48 T.C. 374 (1967).

though, it is hoped, the infusion of capital will raise the corporation's earning power. Worse still, if the shares were issued in exchange for consideration that is smaller per share than the value of existing shares, our one-tenth owner's share of assets upon liquidation has been diluted.

To protect the proportionate interests of shareholders, most jurisdictions provide for *preemptive rights*. Such a right would require a corporation making any additional issuance of stock to offer it first to existing shareholders who have the right to purchase enough shares to maintain their proportional position in the corporation. Thus, if shareholder Jones owns one-tenth of the 1000 outstanding shares of X Corp., and X Corp. decides to issue an additional 500 shares, Jones would have the preemptive right to purchase 50 of those shares before they could be sold to anyone else.

The MBCA, in §26, follows the modern trend limiting preemptive rights. It states that shareholders shall have no preemptive right "except to the extent, if any, that such right is provided in the articles of incorporation." Thus, §26 provides a presumption against preemptive rights unless they are expressly written into the articles.

However, the MBCA also offers an alternative, §26A, which presumes the existence of preemptive rights, unless they are expressly *denied* in the articles. Even in §26A certain exceptions are provided that are commonly found in the laws of various jurisdictions.[19]

Exceptions

For example, the preemptive right may not exist as to authorized but unissued shares,[20] because at the time the shareholders purchased they should have known of the potential dilution. The fact that the shares were already authorized indicates the intent to issue them eventually. Many jurisdictions also deny preemptive rights as to sale of treasury shares, which are being *re*issued.

Common shareholders normally do not have the preemptive right to purchase preferred shares, unless, perhaps, those shares are convertible to common stock.

Usually there are no preemptive rights to purchase shares issued in exchange for noncash consideration. Thus, if a corporation is issuing shares in exchange for specific property it wishes to buy, or as part of a merger, shareholders have no right to bollix the deal by exercising preemptive rights. Similarly, there are usually no preemptive rights for shares issued in exchange for specified services. This exception allows corporations to set up employee stock option plans without the confusing hindrance of preemptive rights.

Preferred shares normally carry no preemptive rights, nor do nonvoting common shares as to an issuance of voting common.

---

[19] These exceptions generally reflect the court-created exceptions discussed in the following section. RMBCA §6.30 follows MBCA §26 in adopting an "opt-in" provision regarding preemptive rights, but contains §26A's exceptions.

[20] *Yasik* v. *Wachtel*, 17 A.2d 309 (Del. Ch. 1941). But see *Hanny* v. *Sunnyside Ditch Co.*, 353 P.2d 406 (Id. 1960).

Impact

The beneficial impact of preemptive rights is questionable. The many exceptions, coupled with the fact that even if the rights are available the shareholder may not have the financial wherewithal to exercise them, limits the protection afforded by the rights. And, of course, the rights may be eliminated altogether in the articles of incorporation.

Most publicly held corporations do eliminate preemptive rights. These rights are a particular hindrance for the public corporation that frequently issues securities because underwriters may well refuse to handle an offering that is complicated by preemptive rights. Even if underwriters do agree to handle such an offering, they will demand higher compensation, and a favorable ''window'' in the market may be missed because of the delay attendant to exercise of preemptive rights.

Furthermore, preemptive rights are not particularly important in the public corporation. Dilution of control is not a major factor because of the relatively small holdings of most individuals. When AT&T eliminated preemptive rights in 1975, for example, no individual owned more than one-fiftieth of 1% of the company's common shares. Because such shares are almost always issued at or near market price, dilution of share value is not a major problem either.

In closely-held corporations, however, preemptive rights may be much more important. For tax reasons closely-held corporations avoid paying dividends. Funds are frequently withdrawn from the corporation in the form of deductible wages. A shareholder whose control is diluted may also lose his or her job with the corporation, and thereby lose the only chance to benefit financially.

Fiduciary Duty

Where preemptive rights are applicable, shareholders must be given a reasonable time in which to exercise them. A shareholder who does not exercise the right within a reasonable time waives it. Thus, a shareholder in a financially troubled corporation cannot waive the preemptive right being exercised by his fellow investors, yet later seek to exercise that right after their infusion of capital has placed the corporation back on its feet.[21]

A shareholder who does not exercise his or her preemptive rights may avoid dilution by obtaining court-ordered cancellation of the issuance if it appears that the controlling shareholders breached their fiduciary duty by authorizing it. For example, if the main purpose of an issuance of additional stock is to dilute greatly a minority shareholder's interest, the fiduciary duty is breached. This is particularly so where there is no financial reason for issuing more shares and the majority knows that the minority shareholder has no funds with which to exercise his preemptive rights.[22]

A famous case in the area follows.

---

[21] *Fuller* v. *Krogh*, 113 N.W.2d 25 (Wis. 1962).

[22] *Browning* v. *C & C Plywood Corp.*, 434 P.2d 339 (Or. 1967).

KATZOWITZ v. SIDLER

249 N.E.2d 359 (N.Y. Ct. App. 1969)

For twenty-five years plaintiff Katzowitz and defendants Sidler and Lasker were jointly engaged in several corporate ventures. They always shared equally in ownership and compensation. For example, all three were directors and one-third owners of Sulburn Holding Corp., formed in 1955. Each contributed $500 and received 5 shares of stock.

In 1956 disagreements flared and defendants joined forces in an attempt to oust plaintiff Katzowitz from any role in managing the various corporations. Katzowitz sued, and the matter was settled out of court in 1959 with Katzowitz withdrawing from the day-to-day affairs of the corporation. Defendants agreed that Katzowitz could stay on the various boards and would continue to receive equal compensation and benefits and maintain equal ownership. Despite this agreement, Sidler and Lasker still desired to oust plaintiff.

In December 1961 Sulburn owed each shareholder $2,500 for fees and commissions. Sidler and Lasker wished to loan that money to another corporation owned by the three and suggested that additional Sulburn shares be offered at $100 each to substitute for the money owed. Katzowitz objected and at the board meeting payment of cash was authorized.

At a later meeting, attended only by Sidler and Lasker, the board authorized issuance of 75 shares of Sulburn stock at $100 per share, the exact amount of the debt to the directors. Book value of Sulburn stock at that time was $1,800 per share. Sidler and Lasker each purchased their full complement of 25 shares. Katzowitz did not. He did receive a $2,500 check from Sulburn.

In August 1962 the principal asset of Sulburn,

a tractor trailer truck, was destroyed. The directors unanimously voted to dissolve the corporation. Upon dissolution, Sidler and Lasker each received $18,885.52, but Katzowitz received only $3,147.59.

When Katzowitz sued to establish his proportionate rights, the lower courts held that he had waived his preemptive rights and was not entitled to relief. Katzowitz appealed.

KEATING, JUDGE:

The concept of preemptive rights was fashioned by the judiciary to safeguard two distinct interests of stockholders—the right to protection against dilution of the their equity in the corporation and protection against dilution of their proportionate voting control. After early decisions, legislation fixed the right enunciated with respect to proportionate voting but left to the judiciary the role of protecting existing shareholders from the dilution of their equity.

Issuing stock for less than fair value can injure existing shareholders by diluting their interest in the corporation's surplus, in current and future earnings, and in the assets upon liquidation. Normally, a stockholder is protected from the loss of his equity from dilution, even though the stock is being offered at less than fair value, because the shareholder receives rights which he may either exercise or sell. If he exercises, he has protected his interest and, if not, he can sell the rights, thereby compensating himself for the dilution of his remaining shares in the equity of the corporation.

When new shares are issued, however, at prices far below fair value in a close corporation or a corporation with only a limited market for its shares, existing stockholders, who do not want to invest or do not have the capacity to invest additional funds, can have their equity interest in the corporation diluted to the vanishing point.

The protection afforded by stock rights is illusory in close corporations. Even if a buyer could be found for the rights, they would have to be sold at an inadequate price because of the nature of a close corporation. Outsiders are normally discouraged from acquiring minority interests after a close corporation has been organized. Certainly a stockholder in a close corporation is at a total loss to safeguard his equity from dilution if no rights are offered and he does not want to invest additional funds.

Though it is difficult to determine fair value for a corporation's securities and courts are therefore reluctant to get into the thicket, when the issuing price is shown to be markedly below book value in a close corporation and when the remaining shareholder-directors benefit from the issuance, a case for judicial relief has been established. In that instance, the corporation's directors must show that the issuing price falls within some range which can be justified on the basis of valid business reasons. If no such showing is made by the directors, there is no reason for the judiciary to abdicate its function to a majority of the board or stockholders who have not seen fit to come forward and justify the propriety of diverting property from the corporation and allow the issuance of securities to become an oppressive device permitting the dilution of the equity of dissident stockholders.

The defendant directors here make no claim that the price set was a fair one. No business justification is offered to sustain it. Admittedly, the stock was sold at less than book value. The defendants simply contend that, as long as all stockholders were given an equal opportunity to purchase additional shares, no stockholder can complain simply because the offering dilutes his interest in the corporation.

The defendant's argument is fallacious.

A stockholder's right not to purchase is seriously undermined if the stock offered is worth substantially more than the offering price. Any purchase at this price dilutes his interest and impairs the value of his original holding. ''A corporation is not permitted to sell its stock for a legally inadequate price at least where there is objection. Plaintiff has a right to insist upon compliance with the law whether or not he cares to exercise his option. He cannot block a sale for a fair price merely because he disagrees with the wisdom of the plan but he can insist that the sale price be fixed in accordance with legal requirements'' (*Bennett* v. *Breuil Petroleum Corp.*, supra, 34 Del. Ch., pp. 14–15, 99 A.2d p. 241). Judicial review in this area is limited to whether under all the circumstances, including the disparity between issuing price of the stock and its true value, the nature of the corporation, the business necessity for establishing an offering price at a certain amount to facilitate raising new capital, and the ability of stockholders to sell rights, the additional offering of securities should be condemned because the directors in establishing the sale price did not fix it with reference to financial considerations with respect to the ready disposition of securities.

Here the obvious disparity in selling price and book value was calculated to force the dissident stockholder into investing additional sums. No valid business justification was advanced for the disparity in price, and the only beneficiaries of the disparity were the two director-stockholders who were eager to have additional capital in the business.

It is no answer to Katzowitz's action that he was also given a chance to purchase additional shares at this bargain rate. The price was not so much a bargain as it was a tactic, conscious or unconscious on the part of the directors, to place Katzowitz in a compromising situation. The price was so fixed to make the failure to invest costly. However, Katzowitz at the time might not have been aware of the dilution because no notice of the effect of the issuance of the new shares on the already outstanding shares was disclosed. In addition, since the stipulation entitled Katzowitz to the same compensation as Sidler and Lasker, the disparity in equity interest caused by their purchase of additional securities in 1961 did not affect stockholder income from Sulburn and, therefore, Katzowitz possibly was not aware of the effect of the stock issuance on his interest in the corporation until dissolution.

By permitting the defendants to recover their additional investment in Sulburn before the remaining assets of Sulburn are distributed to the stockholders upon dissolution, all the stockholders will be treated equitably. Katzowitz, therefore, should receive his aliquot share of the assets of Sulburn less the amount invested by Sidler and Lasker for their purchase of stock on December 27, 1961.

Accordingly, the order of the Appellate Division should be reversed.

Equitable considerations predominate in cases such as *Katzowitz*. Thus, one plaintiff in a similar position lost his suit, in part it seems, because he was actively competing against the corporation.[23]

Reverse Preemptive Right

A shareholder's proportionate interest can be injured by corporate repurchases of shares as much as by an offering of new shares. If, for example, book value and market value are about $100 per share and the corporation repurchases shares from shareholder White for $200 per share, the value of shareholder Black's shares that are not repurchased are diluted.

While it is generally agreed that there is a fiduciary duty governing both the issuance and repurchase of shares, only a few cases have suggested that there is what might be called a "reverse preemptive right"—a right in shareholder Black to demand that an equal portion of his shares be repurchased at the $200 per share price.[24]

CORPORATE DISTRIBUTIONS

Introduction

The law governing corporate distributions is extremely complex. Numerous competing interests, including those of the managers, the shareholders, and the creditors, must be weighed and balanced. And the context must always be considered. Shareholders of closely-held corporations will generally wish to avoid payment of dividends, which are

---

[23] *Hyman* v. *Velsicol Corp.*, 97 N.E.2d 122 (Ill. App. 1951).

[24] See *Donahue* v. *Rodd Electrotype Co. of New England*, 328 N.E.2d 505 (1975).

taxed as ordinary income, thereby creating the dreaded double taxation. These shareholders will prefer to take their funds from the corporation via wages and other mechanisms creating tax deductions for the corporation.

Most shareholders of larger corporations, on the other hand, will not work for the corporation. They will likely favor payment of a large, regular dividend, for this is the major way they can profit from their investment. To keep shareholders happy and the market price high, directors will frequently authorize payment of a larger dividend though profits have declined.

Because shareholders and corporate managers may well have an incentive to pay dividends or other distributions to the detriment of creditors, much of the law in this area is designed to provide sensible restraints on payment of such distributions. The general goal is to preserve a pool of assets that are for the corporation's use and cannot be siphoned off by the shareholders. Complementing this idea is the notion that dividends and other distributions should be paid from *profits*, if any. As we shall see, in practice this is somewhat more complicated than the basic theory.

Types of Dividends

Cash

The cash dividend is the most common type of dividend. Its size is usually established at a dollar amount per share.

Property

Corporations will occasionally give dividends in the form of property. Frequently the property will be stock of a subsidiary corporation. However, over the years corporations here and in Great Britain have given shareholders dividends in the form of products made by the corporation, including tobacco products, certificates to buy whiskey at cost, and certificates for free cremations!

Shares

Most jurisdictions, and the MBCA in §45 (and the RMBCA in §6.23), provide for dividends in the form of the corporation's own shares. Thus, in a year when no cash is available for dividends, a corporation might authorize distribution of 1 share for every 20 held by its shareholders.

The accounting treatment of share dividends, and their distinction from a stock split, will be discussed later. However, it should be clear at the outset that there is little immediate advantage to the shareholder from a share dividend. Assume that X owns 100 of 1,000 outstanding shares of Y Corp. Y Corp. announces a share dividend of 1 share for every 10 shares outstanding. X will now own 110 shares out of a total of 1,100. Thus, he still owns a one-tenth interest in the corporation. And the corporation's assets have not been increased by the mere paper transaction.

Sources of Dividends

To protect creditors and other shareholders, all states impose restrictions on sources of dividends and other distributions. A creditor that loaned money to X Corporation believing that X Corp. had $100,000 in its corporate treasury and was therefore a substantial entity and a good credit risk would not be pleased to learn that a week after the loan, X Corp. distributed all its capital to its shareholders and was operating solely on the funds obtained from the creditor. If this were done, only the creditor's funds would be at risk.

Most jurisdictions, to provide a "cushion" for creditors, prohibit distributions to shareholders from certain accounts. Although payments to shareholders adversely affect creditors in the same manner, many jurisdictions distinguish between sources of funds for payment of dividends and sources of funds for other distributions. Thus, a corporation might be allowed to repurchase shares from shareholders out of a fund from which it could not pay dividends, even though the practical effect is the same— transfer of corporate funds to shareholders and away from the grasp of corporate creditors.

Definitions

Although considered outmoded by some, concepts such as "par value," "stated capital," and "earned surplus" are critical to evaluation of sources of dividends in most states.

Section 2 of the pre-1980 MBCA contained the following definitions:

> "Stated capital" means, at any particular time, the sum of (1) the par value of all shares of the corporation having a par value that have been issued, (2) the amount of the consideration received by the corporation for all shares of the corporation without par value that have been issued, except such part of the consideration therefor as may have been allocated to capital surplus in a manner permitted by law, and (3) such amounts not included in clauses (1) and (2) of this paragraph as have been transferred to stated capital of the corporation, whether upon the issue of shares as a share dividend or otherwise, minus all reductions from such sum as have been effected in a manner permitted by law.
>
> "Surplus" means the excess of the net assets of a corporation over its stated capital.
>
> "Capital surplus" means the entire surplus of a corporation other than its earned surplus.
>
> "Earned surplus" means the portion of the surplus of a corporation equal to the balance of its net profits, income, gains, and losses from the date of incorporation, or from the latest date when a deficit was eliminated by an application of its capital surplus or stated capital or otherwise, after deducting subsequent distributions to shareholders and transfers to stated capital and capital surplus to the extent such distributions and transfers are made out of earned surplus. Earned surplus shall include also any portion of surplus allocated to earned surplus in mergers, consolidations, or acquisitions of all or substantially all the outstanding shares or of the property and assets of another corporation, domestic or foreign.
>
> "Net assets" means the amount by which the total assets of a corporation exceed the total debts of the corporation.
>
> "Treasury shares" means shares of a corporation that have been issued, have

been subsequently acquired by and belong to the corporation, and have not, either by reason of the acquisition or thereafter, been canceled or restored to the status of authorized but unissued shares. Treasury shares shall be deemed to be "issued" shares, but not "outstanding" shares.

"Insolvent" means inability of a corporation to pay its debts as they become due in the usual course of its business.

Note particularly that stated capital is keyed initially to par value. If 100 shares of stock are issued for $10 each and carry a $10 par value, stated capital will be credited with $1,000 and capital surplus with $0. This is undesirable, for as we shall soon see, some corporate distributions are payable out of capital surplus but not out of stated capital. This explains the popularity of low-par stock. Assume the same issuance of 100 shares in exchange for $10 per share, but assume a par value of $1 each. In such a case stated capital would be credited with $100 and capital surplus with $900. This gives the corporation much more flexibility in payment of dividends and other distributions.

Regarding no-par stock, the board of directors is usually given discretion as to allocation of the consideration received. Some states limit that discretion. Texas, for example, formerly allowed the board of directors to allocate up to one-fourth of the consideration received for no-par stock to capital surplus. Thus, if 100 shares of no-par stock were issued in exchange for $10 each, the board could allocate up to $250 to capital surplus. The rest would go to the stated capital account. However, in 1985 the board's discretion was increased by an amendment allowing it to allocate "any part, but not all" of the consideration to the capital surplus account.[25]

Legal Restrictions on Dividends

The states take a number of different accounting approaches to legal restrictions on dividends and other distributions. In this section we will concentrate on payment of dividends.[26] Later in the chapter we shall address restrictions on distributions through corporate repurchases of stock.

Pre-1980 MBCA

Almost 30 states have adopted the substance of the dividend and other financial provisions of the pre-1980 MBCA. These provisions are anchored in the legal capital concept.

Section 45 begins with an immediate insolvency qualification forbidding payment of dividends (and other distributions) if the corporation is insolvent or would be rendered so by the payment. As noted earlier, insolvency consists of the "equity" notion of being unable to meet obligations as they come due. The MBCA does not adopt the "bankruptcy" definition of insolvency that results when total liabilities exceed total assets.

---

[25] TEX.BUS.CORP.ACT ANN. art. 2.17 (Vernon) West Publishing Co.: St. Paul, MN.

[26] This discussion will draw heavily from R. Kummert, "State Statutory Restrictions on Financial Distributions by Corporations to Shareholders: Part II," *Washington Law Review*, Vol. 59 (1984), p. 187.

Section 45 also prohibits payment of any dividends (or other distributions) in violation of any provision of the articles of incorporation. This would prevent dividends from being paid in violation of the rights of preferred shareholders.

Subject to these two restrictions, §45(a) states that dividends may be declared "only out of the unreserved and unrestricted *earned* surplus of the corporation, except as otherwise provided in this section" (emphasis added). Thus, this approach pays lip service to the notion that dividends should be paid only out of profits. However, §46(3) also allows, if the articles so provide or the shareholders approve by vote, distributions to shareholders of cash or property paid out of capital surplus. Such a distribution is also subject to the insolvency restriction.

In this scheme, the insolvency restriction and the stated capital account stand as the basic protections for the creditor.

Balance Sheet Approach

About sixteen states, including the influential jurisdictions of Delaware and New York, and the District of Columbia key their dividend restrictions to the corporation's balance sheet.

Michigan is typical.[27] Subject to restrictions to prevent insolvency and violation of the articles of incorporation, Michigan's statute allows dividends (and other distributions) to be paid only out of surplus. If paid out of a surplus account other than earned surplus, the dividend must be accompanied by a written notice disclosing how its payment affects stated capital, capital surplus, and earned surplus.

So long as assets exceed liabilities plus capital, balance sheet jurisdictions allow payment of dividends, even in the absence of any earned surplus. To put it another way, these states allow payment only out of surplus, which is defined as the excess of net assets over capital, with net assets determined by subtracting total liabilities from total assets.

Post-1980 MBCA and RMBCA

The 1979 amendments to the MBCA switched to a system not based on the legal capital concept. The RMBCA follows suit. Par value and stated capital are discarded. Unlike the views discussed already, the post-1980 MBCA and the RMBCA make no distinction between dividends and other shareholder distributions. Whether in the form of a dividend, or purchase, redemption, or other acquisition of shares, all distributions are treated the same.

The amended MBCA's test is based on insolvency concepts. The new §45 prohibits a distribution if, after giving it effect, either "(a) the corporation would be unable to pay its debts as they become due in the regular course of business, or (b) the corporation's total assets would be less than the sum of its total liabilities and (unless

---

[27] MICH.COMP.LAWS Sections 450.1351, .1365(1) [MICH.STAT.ANN. Sections 21.200 (351), (365) (1) (Callaghan 1983)].

the articles of incorporation otherwise permit) the maximum amount that then would be payable, in any liquidation, in respect of all outstanding shares having preferential rights in liquidation.'' RMBCA §6.40 is similar.

In determination of total assets and total liabilities, §45 authorizes the board of directors to choose between ''(i) financial statements prepared on the basis of accounting practices and principles that are reasonable and fair in the circumstances, or (ii) a fair valuation or other method that is reasonable in the circumstances.''

Thus, the amended MBCA combines an equity insolvency test in subparagraph (a) with a balance sheet test in subparagraph (b). What is unique about the approach, in addition to its abolition of stated capital and par value concepts, is its emphasis on the future course of the corporation. In calculating insolvency, the board is entitled to consider the firm's ability to generate earnings to satisfy existing or future obligations as they mature. Cash flow analysis, current liquidity, projected earnings, and anticipated debt become more important than whether today's liquidation value exceeds today's liabilities.

The balance sheet test of new MBCA §45 and RMBCA §6.40, concentrating as they do on preserving liquidation preferences rather than stated capital, protect preferred shareholders as well as traditional creditors from excessive distributions to common shareholders.[28]

Although the amended MBCA approach is unlikely to receive wide acceptance in the near future, California has adopted a vaguely similar approach that has in fact rejected the legal capital approach.[29]

Special Dividend Problems

Contractual Limitations

In practice, the most important limitations on payment of dividends tend to be contractual, rather than statutory. Lenders wishing to protect themselves from dissipation of corporate assets via distributions to shareholders may condition a loan to the corporation upon a corporate promise not to pay dividends for a certain period of time. Or the loan might be conditional upon transfer by the board of corporate funds from the capital surplus account where they are subject to being distributed under pre-1980 MBCA §46(e), to the stated capital account where they are not. Such contractual limitations are usually much stricter than the statutory limitations, but they will vary depending on the relative bargaining strengths of the lender and borrower. Underwriters will frequently protect themselves with such provisions when they handle public offerings on a firm commitment basis, and sometimes preferred shareholders will be protected in this manner.

---

[28] See, generally, ''Changes in the Model Business Corporation Act—Amendments to Financial Provisions, A Report of the Committee on Corporate Law, *Business Lawyer*, Vol. 34 (1979), p. 1867.

[29] CAL.CORP.CODE Section 500 (West 1977 & Supp. 1983, West Publishing Co; St. Paul, MN). RMBCA §6.40 is based on the 1980 MBCA amendments.

"Nimble" dividends

Although a basic notion is that dividends should be paid primarily out of profits, around 15 states allow payment of "nimble" dividends. Assume that a young corporation loses $20,000 in its first year of operation and $10,000 in its second. It has no earned surplus from which to pay dividends; it has only a deficit. Assume further that the corporation earns a $5,000 profit in its third year. States permitting "nimble" dividends might allow payment of dividends out of that $5,000 before the income statement for the third year is merged into the balance sheet to show an overall deficit of $25,000. The pre-1980 MBCA §45, for example, contains an alternative provision allowing payment of dividends out of "unreserved and unrestricted net earnings of the current fiscal year and the next preceding fiscal year" even if there is no earned surplus.

Depletion reserves

Section 45(b) of the pre-1980 MBCA allows payment of dividends out of depletion reserves if the corporation is engaged in the business of exploiting natural resources such as mines, oil and gas, and timber. The articles must permit such payments and the shareholders must be notified of the amount and source of the distribution.

Revaluation of Assets

In *Randall* v. *Bailey*,[30] a balance sheet jurisdiction court was faced with the question of whether dividends could be paid out of unrealized appreciation. If only book value based on purchase price were utilized, liabilities exceeded assets. However, if book value were adjusted to reflect unrealized appreciation, assets exceeded total liabilities by an amount exceeding the dividend. The court approved the adjustment and the dividend.

However, most courts do not allow upward revaluation to allow such a payment of dividends.[31] Their hostility can be traced to abuse of revaluation by corporations in financial trouble in the Great Depression. This hostility has abated somewhat in the modern financial and accounting community. This is reflected, perhaps, in the post-1980 MBCA, which, as noted, allows the board of directors in calculating its balance sheet test to use "a fair valuation or other method that is reasonable under the circumstances." This provision could authorize departure from historical cost accounting and use of appraisal methods.[32]

---

[30] 23 N.Y.S.2d 173 (S. Ct. 1940), *aff'd*, 288 N.Y. 280, 43 N.E.2d 43 (1942).

[31] *Berks Broadcasting Co.* v. *Craumer*, 356 Pa. 620, 52 A.2d 571 (1947).

[32] "Current Issues on the Legality of Dividends from a Law and Accounting Perspective: A Task Force Report," *Business Lawyer*, Vol. 39 (1983), p. 289. RMBCA §6.40 is similar to the post-1980 MBCA in this regard.

Liability for Illegal Dividends

Section 48 of the MBCA makes directors who vote for or assent to declaration of any illegal dividend (or other distribution) jointly and severally liable to the corporation for the amount of the illegal distribution. Such directors are entitled to contribution from other directors. Shareholders who knowingly received illegal dividends are also liable to pay contribution in proportion to the amounts received by them.

In practice, directors are usually sheltered from liability if they acted in good faith. Section 35 of the MBCA, for example, explicitly allows directors to rely on information, reports, and financial statements prepared by officers, employees, counsel, public accountants and other persons whom the directors believe to be reliable and competent.

The post-1980 MBCA's §45 undercuts this defense slightly by requiring directors to exercise their business judgment in use of accounting principles and practices that are "reasonable" in the circumstances. However, given the courts' reluctance under the "business judgment rule" to second guess the decisions of directors, it is unlikely that this provision, if adopted, would have much impact on directors' liability for illegal dividends. Besides, illegal dividends are covered by most directors' and officers' (D & O) liability insurance policies.

Board Discretion

Most laws, including §45 of the MBCA, give the board of directors great discretion in deciding whether or not to pay a dividend and, if so, in what amount. Shareholders who are disgruntled because the board will not pay them dividends have a heavy burden to carry if they seek to persuade a court to override the board's decision. It is not enough simply to prove that funds were legally available for payment. Rather, the shareholders must prove that the board was acting in bad faith or from an improper motive.

If the board can show that the funds that could be used for dividends are not being wasted, but are, instead, being used for reinvestment as part of a long expansion plan, it is unlikely that a court will disturb the decision not to pay.

A court would be particularly hesitant to disturb the discretion of the board of a publicly held company. Actually, this should seldom be a problem because the boards of most widely held corporations strive to pay a regular dividend regardless of the vicissitudes of the pattern of earnings. By so doing they can support the market price of the stock.

In one rare and famous case,[33] shareholders of the Ford Motor Company sought to force Henry Ford, who founded and at that point still controlled the company, to pay a larger dividend. The corporation had a yearly profit of $60 million, assets of over $132 million, a surplus of $112 million, cash on hand of $54 million, and total liabilities, including capital stock, of only $20 million. Yet the company was paying

---

[33] *Dodge* v. *Ford Motor Co.*, 170 N.W. 668 (Mich. 1919).

only modest dividends and was plowing the rest back into the company for continued expansion.

Ford announced that his ambition was "to employ still more men; to spread the benefits of this industrial system to the greatest possible number, to help them build up their lives and their homes. To do this we are putting the greatest share of our profits back into the business." Ford also reduced the price of his cars to the public, thus reducing the profits that could have been earned.

The court noted Ford's charitable motives, but held that

> A business corporation is organized and carried on primarily for the profit of the stockholders. The powers of the directors are to be employed for that end. The discretion of directors is to be exercised in the choice of means to attain that end, and does not extend to a change in the end itself, to the reduction of profits, or to the non-distribution of profits among stockholders in order to devote them to other purposes.

The court therefore ordered the payment of a dividend of about $19 million. This, plus the fact that the plaintiff Dodges were using their dividends to finance a competing automobile manufacturing company, so enraged Ford that he bought out all the outside shareholders and took the company private. It remained a family-owned corporation into the 1950s.

Although the *Ford* decision is something of a rarity, the fewer the number of shareholders a corporation has, the more likely it is that the courts will give scrutiny to a decision not to pay dividends. The reason is that the fewer the number of shareholders, the more likely it is that a majority will abuse a minority. By refusing to pay dividends, and by not allowing the minority to be employed by the corporation, the majority can "freeze out" the minority and make them sell their stock. And the majority owners will likely be the only interested buyers, making it a definite "buyer's market."

A typical case follows.

ZIDELL v. ZIDELL, INC.

560 P.2d 1086 (Or. 1977)

The Zidell family business started as a partnership and was later incorporated. Eventually defendant Emery Zidell and plaintiff Arnold Zidell, sons of the founder, came to each own 37.5% of the stock of four closely related family corporations. They were directors; Emery was chief executive officer. In 1972, Rosenfeld sold to Emery's son Jay enough of his stock in the corporation to give Jay and Emery voting control of the corporations.

There had previously been friction between Emery and Arnold and that friction increased after the sale, especially when Emery increased Jay's salary but not Arnold's. Emery was also apparently displeased with Arnold's life-style. At a director's meeting in May 1973, Arnold *demanded that his salary be raised from $30,000 to $50,000 a year, saying that he would resign if his request were not granted. It wasn't and he did. He resigned only his employment, not his directorships, but when his term expired, he was not reelected.*

Prior to Arnold's resignation, the companies had retained their earnings rather than paying dividends. Once he was no longer receiving a salary, Arnold objected to this practice. Thereafter a small dividend was paid on 1973 earnings, but Arnold brought this suit, claiming he was entitled to a larger return on his equity. He pointed out that at about the same time the small dividend was declared, employee salaries and bonuses were raised substantially. Although he did not claim these were excessive, he argued they were evidence of concerted activity against him.

The trial judge declined to find that the defendants (the directors and the corporations) acted in bad faith but did order payment of a larger dividend. Defendants appealed.

HOWELL, JUSTICE:

We have recognized that those in control of corporate affairs have fiduciary duties of good faith and fair dealing toward the minority shareholders. Insofar as dividend policy is concerned, however, that duty is discharged if the decision is made in good faith and reflects legitimate business purposes rather than the private interests of those in control.

In *Gay* v. *Gay's Super Markets, Inc.*, 343 A.2d 577 (Me. 1975), that court analyzed both the duties of corporate directors and the proper role of the courts in overseeing corporate dividend policies in the following terms:

> To justify judicial intervention in cases of this nature, it must, as a general proposition, be shown that the decision not to declare a dividend amounted to fraud, bad faith or an abuse of discretion on the part of the corporate officials authorized to make the determination. . . .

> The burden of demonstrating bad faith, fraud, breach of fiduciary duty or abuse of discretion on the part of the directors of a corporation rests on the party seeking judicial mandatory relief respecting the declaration of dividends. . . .

> Furthermore, judicial review of corporate management decisions must be viewed in the light of this other rule that "it is not the province of the court to act as general manager of a private corporation or to assume the regulation of its internal affairs"—*Bates Street Shirt Company* v. *Waite*, 130 Me. 352, 359, 156 A. 293, 298 (1931).

> *If there are plausible business reasons supportive of the decision of the board of directors, and such reasons can be given credence, a Court will not interfere with a corporate board's right to make that decision. It is not our function to referee every corporate squabble or disagreement.* It is our duty to redress wrongs, not to settle competitive business interests. Absent any bad faith, fraud, breach of fiduciary duty, or abuse of discretion, no wrong cognizable by or correctable in the Courts has occurred"—Id. at 580. (emphasis added)

Plaintiff had the burden of proving bad faith on the part of the directors in determining the amount of corporate dividends. In the present case, plaintiff has shown that the corporations could afford to pay additional dividends, that he has left the corporate payroll, that those stockholders who are working for the corporations are receiving generous salaries and bonuses, and that there is hostility between him and the other major stockholders. We agree with plaintiff that these factors are often present in cases of oppression or attempted squeeze-out by majority shareholders. See, generally, F. H. O'Neal, *Oppression of Minority Stockholders*, 57–103, Sections 3.02–3.03 (1975). They are not, however, invariably signs of improper behavior by the majority (see *Gottfried* v. *Gottfried*, [73 N.Y.S.2d 692 (Sup. 1947)].

There are no infallible distinguishing earmarks of bad faith. The following facts are relevant to the issue of bad faith and are admissible in evidence: Intense hostility of the controlling faction against the minority; exclusion of the minority from employment by the corporation; high salaries, or bonuses or corporate loans made to the officers in control; the fact that the majority group may be subject to high personal income taxes if substantial dividends are paid; the existence of a desire by the controlling directors to acquire the minority stock interests as cheaply as possible. *But if they are not motivating causes they do not constitute "bad faith" as a matter of law.* (emphasis added)

Defendants introduced a considerable amount of credible evidence to explain their conservative dividend policy. There was testimony that the directors took into consideration a future need for expensive physical improvements, and possibly even the relocation of a major plant; the need for cash to pay for large inventory orders; the need for renovation of a nearly obsolescent dock; and the need for continued short-term financing through bank loans which could be "called" if the corporations' financial position became insecure. There was also evidence that earnings for 1973 and 1974 were abnormally high because of unusual economic conditions that could not be expected to continue.

In rebuttal, plaintiff contends that the directors did not really make their decisions on the basis of these factors, pointing to testimony that they did not rely on any documented financial analysis to support their dividend declarations.

This is a matter for consideration, but it is certainly not determinative. All of the directors of these corporations were active in the business on a day-to-day basis and had intimate firsthand knowledge of financial conditions and present and projected business needs. In order to substantiate their testimony that the above factors were taken into consideration, it was not necessary that they provide documentary evidence or show that formal studies were conducted. Their testimony is believable, and the burden of proof on this issue is on the plaintiff, not the defendants.

Nor are we convinced by plaintiff's arguments that we should approve the forced declaration of additional dividends in order to prevent a deliberate squeeze-out. Plaintiff left his corporate employment voluntarily. He was not forced out. Although the dividends he has since received are modest when viewed as a rate of return on his investment, they are not unreasonable in light of the corporations' projected financial needs. Moreover, having considered the evidence presented by both sides, we are not persuaded that the directors are employing starvation tactics to force the sale of plaintiff's stock at an unreasonably low price.

Since we have determined that plaintiff has not carried his burden of proving a lack of good faith, we must conclude that the trial court erred in decreeing the distribution of additional dividends.

Reversed and remanded with directors to enter decrees of dismissal.

The same basic considerations apply in the relatively rare instance where shareholders complain that too much is being paid out in dividends. For example, in *Sinclair Oil Corporation* v. *Levien*,[34] Sinclair decided to expand its business through subsidiaries other than Sinven (Sinclair Venezuelan Oil Corp.). Sinclair, owning 97% of Sinven's

---

[34] 280 A.2d 717 (Del. Supr. 1971).

stock, had it pay dividends of $108 million from 1960 to 1966, $38 million more than it earned. Such payments made expansion of Sinven impossible, and Levien, a minority shareholder in Sinven, complained. The court ruled against plaintiff because he could not show the dividend payments "resulted from improper motives and amounted to waste." The court noted that a proportionate share of the allegedly excessive dividends was received by plaintiff. Note, however, that a court is more likely to intervene in a dividend decision in a close corporation than in a publicly held one.

Preferred Dividends

Problems sometimes arise with payment of preferred dividends. As noted before, because dividend payments are generally discretionary, if a board declines to pay any dividends in a year when legal funds are available, holders of noncumulative preferred stock are generally out of luck.

Sometimes dividends on preferred stock are referred to as "mandatory." Courts disagree as to proper treatment of such provisions. In one case,[35] a corporation amended its certificate of incorporation to provide that holders of preferred stock were entitled to receive and the corporation was bound to pay, but only out of net profits, a yearly dividend of 50 cents per share. This provision was held to be overridden by public policy, state statute, and corporate bylaws, all of which gave discretion to the board of directors. On the other hand, other courts [36] have held that a clear contract between the corporation and preferred shareholders can limit the board's discretion.

Stock Dividends and Stock Splits

Occasionally corporations will distribute dividends in the form of their own shares. For example, each shareholder might be entitled to receive 1 share for each 10 already held. The corporation might issue such a dividend because it has no readily available funds for cash dividends. It might do so to lower slightly the price of its stock. A stock dividend does not reduce the assets in the corporate till. Nor does it transfer anything but paper to the shareholders. Theoretically a 10% share dividend should lead to a 10% reduction in market price. However, if the market does not respond with perfect efficiency, perhaps the price will drop only 5%. The shareholders will then profit because they have 10% more shares to sell.

Theoretically, again, a stock or share dividend only divides the corporation into smaller pieces, with each shareholder maintaining a proportionate position. Assume, for example, that X Corporation has 1,000 shares outstanding. A owns 100, or 10%. B owns 200, or 20%. Assume further that X Corporation pays a 10% share dividend. A is entitled to 10 shares, and B to 20. A still owns 10% (110/1,100) and B still owns 20% (220/1,100) of the outstanding shares.

A stock or share split closely resembles a share dividend. It simply involves a

---

[35] *L. L. Constantin & Co.* v. *R. P. Holding Corp.*, 153 A.2d 379 (N.J. Super. 1959).

[36] *New England Trust Co.* v. *Penobscot Chem. Fibre Co.*, 50 A.2d 188 (Me. 1946).

greater increase in outstanding shares. Assume, for example, that X Corporation has done so well in recent years that its per share market price has rocketed from $20 to $100. The board of directors might believe that the higher price is stifling the market for X Corporation shares because the average investor cannot readily buy the normal "round lot" of 100 shares at $100 each. Therefore, the board might authorize a 5-for-1 split. Each shareholder owning 100 shares will now own 500. Again, this transaction has no effect on the net worth of the corporation. It has no more, and no fewer assets. And nothing but paper is transferred to the shareholders. Their proportionate holdings are unaffected. Instead of owning 100 shares out of 1,000, for example, two shareholders may own 500 out of 5,000.

The only difference other than size, between a share dividend and a share split, is an accounting difference.[37] One court explained it this way:

> A substantial and conclusive difference exists between a "stock split" and a "stock dividend": in the former, a division of the shares of stock, not of the earnings or profits of the corporation, takes place without any change in or impingement upon the then existing status on the corporate books of the earned surplus and capital accounts; in the latter, an addition of shares of stock and a division of, at least, some of the earnings or profits of the corporation take place, such division being reflected on the corporate books by an irreversible allocation of corporate funds from the earned surplus to the capital account.[38]

Occasionally, the practical difference between a stock dividend and stock split will be important, as this case illustrates.

ROGERS WALLA WALLA, INC. v. BALLARD

553 P.2d 1372 (Wash. App. 1976)

Ballard, who along with his wife is a defendant in this suit, joined plaintiff Rogers Walla Walla, Inc. (Rogers) in 1962. In April 1964 Ballard was promoted to executive vice-president in charge of daily operations. To secure his loyal service, the Rogers board allowed Ballard to buy 100 shares of Rogers stock for $10,000. The agreement concluded: "It is mutually agreed that if, at any time within ten years from date hereof, Ballard ceases employment or desires to sell said shares or any portion thereof, they shall be sold only to Rogers, and said Rogers agrees to purchase said shares for $100 per share."*

In 1966 the Rogers board decided to acquire another company. In the transaction by which the acquisition was accomplished, Rogers announced a 24-to-1 stock split. On May 1, 1967,

---

[37] Because the main difference between share splits and share dividends is an accounting treatment of par value—a concept the RMBCA rejects—RMBCA §6.23 eliminates the distinction between share splits and share dividends.

[38] *In re Trust Estate of Penn*, 158 A.2d 552 (Pa. 1960).

Ballard exchanged his 100-share certificate for a certificate showing him and his wife to be owners of 2,400 shares. Total Rogers shares outstanding increased from 29,309 to 703,416 after the split.

In 1971 the Rogers board became unhappy with Ballard's work and asked for his resignation. After Ballard resigned, Rogers sought return of the 1967 stock certificate, tendering $10,000. Ballard refused. Rogers sued for specific performance. The trial judge ordered defendants to return the 2,400 shares upon tender of $10,000. Defendants appealed.

PEARSON, JUDGE:

[W]e must consider the defendants' argument that the court's finding of a stock split of 24 to 1 unsupported by the evidence. This is important because assuming the 1964 agreement remains viable, Ballards argue that the 1967 exchange was a 2,300-share dividend that should be unaffected by the decree of specific performance of the agreement to resell only 100 shares. The defendants contend the capitalization of earnings surplus in the amount of $3,000,000 settles the issue of dividend versus split. While stock dividends are ordinarily paid out of earnings transferred to capital, a capitalization of earnings incident to an increase in the number of outstanding shares is far from conclusive as to whether the transaction is properly designated a dividend or split—11 W. Fletcher, *Cyclopedia of Corporations*, Sections 5359–5362.1 (M. Wolf, rev. ed., 1971). Plaintiff's experts identified and applied several other factors in determining the character of the transaction. We summarize these considerations as follows: (1) It is clear that Rogers's board of directors intended the distribution be treated as a split; (2) the distribution resulted in a pronounced ratio of new shares to old; ordinarily, 25% is viewed as the maximum share increase for a stock dividend, as distinguished from a split; (3) there was no recent history of Rogers stock dividends to minimize this percentage test; and (4) the per share unit value was markedly diluted, from $100 par value to $6 stated value, by the transaction. The court's finding that a split occurred is amply supported by the evidence and must stand on appeal.

The effect of a stock split is merely to change the form of the stockholder's interest in the company, but not the substance of his property. It simply involves a division of the outstanding shares into more units, each with less value. Each stockholder's proportionate share of ownership, his rights on dissolution, and the total value of his investment in the corporation are maintained intact. The only significant changes are the issuance of a new certificate and a reduction in market value of each share unit, which usually increases marketability of the shares— 11 W. Fletcher, *Cyclopedia of Corporations*, supra, Section 5362.1

Here, the effect of the stock split, as the Ballards admitted, was to preserve the percentage of Rogers stock owned by them before the split. They were not required to give any consideration for the new certificate except the former one for 100 shares.

[Affirmed.]

Share Repurchases

When a corporation repurchases shares from its shareholders, the effect is much the same as if a dividend were paid. Money is transferred from the corporation to the shareholder. Formerly, tax treatment of the transaction was a motivation for corporate repurchases because, in some instances, favorable capital gains tax treatment was available to shareholders.[39] However, the 1986 tax legislation eliminated the lower tax rate for capital gains. Nevertheless, there remain other reasons to distribute benefits to shareholders in the form of repurchases.

Other reasons for repurchases might be to cancel fractional shares, to silence troublesome minority shareholders, to stabilize the market price, to eliminate burdensome preferred shares, to eliminate excess corporate cash and drive up the market price to make a tender offer less attractive, to fulfill a buy-sell agreement following a shareholder's death, to honor a redemption provision in a departing employee's contract, to change the capital structure by increasing the debt-equity ratio, or to comply with state appraisal rights.

No matter what the motivation, one consequence of a repurchase is that corporate assets are transferred away from the grasp of corporate creditors. To protect those creditors from shareholders seeking to strip the corporation of assets, limitations are placed on share repurchases that are very similar to restrictions placed on payment of dividends.[40] These limitations also vary from jurisdiction to jurisdiction.

Pre-1980 MBCA

With the overlying prohibition against any repurchase that would render the corporation insolvent, §6 of the pre-1980 MBCA allows such repurchases out of unrestricted and unreserved earned surplus *and*, if the articles permit or the shareholders approve, out of unreserved and unrestricted capital surplus. If earned or capital surplus is used, such surplus is restricted so long as such shares are held as treasury shares. Upon disposition of the shares, the restriction is removed.

Section 6's limitations except from the *surplus limitations* any repurchases made (1) to eliminate fractional shares, (2) to collect or compromise indebtedness, (3) to honor appraisal rights of dissenting shareholders, or (4) to effect the retirement of redeemable shares by redemption or by purchase not to exceed the redemption price. These transactions are not excepted from the insolvency limitation.

Redemption. Redemption is a special type of repurchase pursuant to provisions in the articles or bylaws that may make corporate repurchase at a specified price mandatory upon the occurrence of certain events, or optional with the corporation.[41] If a repurchase is a redemption, rather than another type of reacquisition such as a negotiated purchase or a corporate reorganization, the corporation can even use stated capital to purchase the shares, although §66 reiterates §6's insolvency limitation. Redeemed shares, under §67, are canceled by the act of redemption.

---

[39] I.R.C. Section 302 (exchange of shares may be entitled to capital gains treatment) and Section 346 (partial liquidation).

[40] Shareholders who seek to prejudice corporate creditors in this manner must also reckon with §§3 and 4 of the Uniform Fraudulent Conveyances Act and §548 of the Bankruptcy Reform Act of 1978. Both acts allow for the setting aside of conveyances undertaken to prejudice creditors.

[41] See, generally, D. Murphy, "Redemption of Stock Under the Model Business Corporation Act and the Virginia Stock Corporation Act," *Univ. Richmond Law Review*, Vol. 14 (1980), p. 311.

Insolvency Limitation. A question arises when shares are repurchased on the installment plan. What if the corporation is solvent at the time it agrees to repurchase a shareholder's shares in five annual installments, but due to financial reverses would be rendered insolvent by the time the third annual installment is due? Need the corporation be solvent only at the time the contract is formed? Or must it be solvent at the time each payment is due?

The courts have disagreed,[42] but the majority rule appears to be that such an agreement is unenforceable if any subsequent installment is not covered by adequate surplus, even though the entire purchase price could have properly been paid at the time the agreement was made without causing insolvency.

Balance Sheet Approach

The balance sheet test, as exemplified by Michigan's statute,[43] takes an approach to repurchase that is quite similar to the pre-1980 MBCA's legal capital approach. Repurchases are allowed only out of surplus, unless they are to redeem fractional shares, to collect or compromise an indebtedness to the corporation, or to pay dissenting shareholders entitled to such payment.

Post-1980 MBCA and RMBCA

The recently amended version of the MBCA eliminated §§66 and 67, among others. The post-1980 MBCA and the RMBCA treat share repurchases as being virtually identical to other distributions such as dividends. Therefore, the main constraint on share repurchases is the insolvency test described earlier in the chapter.

Regarding the problem of repurchasing shares on an installment basis, the 1980 amendments to the MBCA altered §45 to measure such a distribution's effect as of the date the debt is incurred or the date the shareholder ceases to be a shareholder, whichever is earlier. If proper funds are available legally to make the distribution at that time, later financial reverses by the corporation will not affect the enforceability of the debt. Indeed, §45 was amended to provide that "[i]ndebtedness of a corporation incurred or issued to a shareholder in accordance with this Section shall be on a parity with the indebtedness of the corporation to its general unsecured creditors" unless subordinated by agreement.[44]

---

[42] Compare *Mountain State Steel Foundries, Inc.* v. *Commissioner*, 284 F.2d 737 (4th Cir. 1960) (if each installment can be paid as it comes due, agreement is enforceable even though at the time it was made it could have rendered corporation insolvent); *McConnell* v. *Estate of Butler*, 402 F.2d 362 (9th Cir. 1968) (corporation must be solvent at time agreement is made and as each payment comes due to be enforceable).

[43] Again, see R. Kummert, "State Statutory Restrictions on Financial Distributions by Corporations to Shareholders: Part II, *Washington Law Review*, Vol. 59 (1984), p. 187.

[44] RMBCA §6.40(c) mirrors the 1980 amendments to the MBCA by establishing insolvency tests as the basic restriction on distributions through repurchases as well as through dividend payments. RMBCA §6.40(e) and (f) follow the 1980 amendments regarding the installment payment problem also.

Fiduciary Duty

Under any statutory scheme, the repurchase of shares implicates the fiduciary duty of the board. Just as the board cannot abuse the minority by withholding dividends or paying excessive dividends without good purpose and with evil motive, so is the board constrained in stock repurchases. The "reverse preemptive rights" discussed earlier in this chapter represent the ultimate extension of the fiduciary concept in this area.[45]

QUESTIONS AND PROBLEMS

1. Plaintiff Arthur Kaiser joined his cousin Jerry in the real estate business in 1955. Jerry Kaiser and Associates, Inc., was incorporated in 1962, though no shares were issued to plaintiff. In June 1963, while on jury duty, plaintiff met a realtor who told him of the availability of some unimproved ground that was subsequently acquired by the corporation and developed. On November 1, 1963, the day a loan commitment for the project was secured, the shareholders voted unanimously to amend the articles of incorporation to authorize the issuance of a new class of nonvoting common stock and to issue 25 of those shares to plaintiff. Plaintiff later left the firm, and subsequently litigation arose. Defendants claimed that plaintiff was not a shareholder because not until December 10, 1963 did the corporation amend its articles of incorporation in the Secretary of State's office to authorize creation of a new class of stock. Was the issuance *ultra vires* and void? Discuss. See *Kaiser* v. *Moulton*, 631 S.W.2d 44 (Mo. App. 1981).

2. D entered into a contract with an insurance company which provided that D was to purchase 19,370 shares of stock of the company for $20 a share, D was to pay $20 in cash as a down payment, and D was to pay the balance of $387,380 in equal monthly installments, not exceeding 30. The company was to have the right to retain the certificates evidencing the stock until the stock was fully paid for by D. Was §19 of the MBCA violated? Discuss. See *McCarty* v. *Langdeau*, 337 S.W.2d 407 (Tex. Civ. App. 1960).

3. LaRue and his brother Larry intended to extract minerals and sell timber from two parcels of land owned by LaRue. In September 1975, the brothers and their wives incorporated. Each brother received 10,000 $0.25-par-value shares and a promissory note for $2,500. Each wife received 5,000 shares and a note for $1,250. LaRue transferred to the corporation title to the two parcels of land worth $68,900. Larry transferred title to his $1,000 car. In 1977 the corporation ran out of money and dissolved. LaRue argued that Larry would be unjustly enriched if the corporation's assets were distributed according to share ownership; he suggested distribution consonant with capital contributions. Discuss. See *Belt* v. *Belt*, 679 P.2d 1144 (Idaho App. 1984).

---

[45] See *Donahue* v. *Rodd Electrotype Co. of New England, Inc.*, 367 Mass. 578, 328 N.E.2d 505 (1974).

4. Fett incorporated his sheet metal business in 1965, transferring to the corporation assets worth $4,914.85 for which he received 25 shares of stock. The stated capital of the corporation never increased thereafter. As the need arose for more capital, Fett would borrow money from the bank, make the funds available to the business, and take back promissory notes. Sums involved in these transactions in 1974, 1975, and 1976 were $7,500, $40,000, and $30,000, respectively. By April 1976, the corporation owed $413,000 to secured creditors alone. In that month, plaintiff recorded three deeds of trust intended to secure his three loans with the realty, inventory, equipment, and receivables of the corporation, which soon took bankruptcy. How should Fett's loans be treated by the bankruptcy court? Discuss. See *In re Fett Roofing and Sheet Metal Co., Inc.*, 438 F.Supp. 726 (E.D. Va. 1977).

5. With the advice of reputable accountants, Obre and Nelson formed a corporation by pooling equipment and cash. Obre transferred approximately $65,000 in value to the corporation; Nelson contributed $10,000. In return, Obre received $20,000 in par value nonvoting preferred stock, an unsecured note for $35,000 payable in five years at 5% interest, and $10,000 in voting common stock. Nelson received $10,000 in voting common. The corporation had financial trouble right away, and Obre started paying debts with his personal funds. No payments were ever made on his note, which was listed on corporate records as a debt. A court eventually took control of the corporation, and the priority of Obre's note versus other creditors came into question. Discuss. See *Obre v. Alban Tractor Co.*, 228 Md. 291, 179 A.2d 861 (Md. App. 1962).

6. P and two Ds each owned one-third of the shares of T.J.'s Big Boy, Inc. Each received 200 shares, and each was to hold an office. No salaries were to be increased without unanimous approval of the shareholders. A dispute arose, and the Ds ousted P from his employment. P now challenges a decision by Ds to offer 600 shares of authorized but unissued stock to the shareholders at $100 per share and to authorize sale of 1,000 additional shares to active employees at 50% of market value. Book value of the shares was $266 and market value between $500 and $575. Should these offerings be enjoined? Discuss. See *Gazda v. Kolinski*, 91 A.D.2d 860, 458 N.Y.S.2d 387 (1982).

7. Gay's Super Market's, Inc. (GSMI), was owned 51% by Hannaford and 49% by Gay and his brother. Gay was manager of GSMI's store in Maine until the board fired him in 1971. The board also voted not to pay a dividend that year. Gay sued over the decision not to declare a dividend. The directors testified that a competitor's new store had placed competitive pressure on the Maine store, that GSMI needed to improve and expand its building in Maine, that $70,000 in corporate funds were allotted to open a new store in Vermont, that the new store's first-year losses would be $25,000, and that therefore the board felt that none of the $125,000 of GSMI corporate surplus should be used for dividends. Do these reasons justify nonpayment of a dividend? Discuss. See *Gay v. Gay's Super Markets, Inc.*, 343 A.2d 577 (Me. 1975).

8. J. Paul Getty controlled Getty Oil, which controlled Mission Development, which in turn controlled Tidewater Oil Co. The only thing Mission did was hold Tidewater

stock. In 1954, Tidewater stopped paying cash dividends, retaining all earnings, leaving Mission Development with no income. Tidewater's capital investment in refineries and oil fields, which had never exceeded $41 million in any year prior to 1953, rose to $111 million in 1961. The market price of Mission stock held steady in the 1950s and early 1960s. In 1960, Tidewater announced that capital expansion would continue and no dividends would be paid for at least 5 years. Minority shareholders of Mission challenged the decision not to pay dividends, claiming that Getty, for whom more income only meant more tax, was trying to depress the price of Mission stock artifically so that he could buy more shares of it. Mission directors claimed that Tidewater's policies were necessary for corporate expansion. Discuss. See *Berwald* v. *Mission Development Corp.*, 40 Del. Ch. 509, 185 A.2d 480 (1962).

10

SHAREHOLDERS AND CORPORATE MANAGEMENT STRUCTURE

INTRODUCTION

Most states' corporate codes are based on what has been denominated the "statutory model" of management, which envisions the shareholders as the ultimate source of corporate authority exercised through their power to elect and remove directors and to approve or disapprove extraordinary corporate transactions. Under this model the directors manage the daily affairs of the corporation and propose significant changes, and the officers carry out the directors' orders. This model leaves shareholders with two major means of control—the vote and their ability to bring derivative lawsuits against misbehaving officers and directors.

The model may have some accuracy as it applies to large publicly held corporations, though it no doubt exaggerates the real power of shareholders and underestimates the influence of the officers. Surely the shareholder vote is important in those corporations. In fact, the entire chapter on proxy regulation appearing later in this book discusses regulation of the shareholder vote in public corporations.

The model described does not fit the closely held corporation very well, however. The average investor in a close corporation expects, and reasonably so, to also exert influence through active participation in the corporation's management. When some public corporations have millions of shareholders, it is clear that an individual shareholder's chances to participate actively in management are nil. But the vast majority of American corporations are owned by but a few shareholders who do reasonably expect to take an active role in the corporation's business.

A large portion of this chapter will be devoted to a study of how courts and legislatures— dealing with corporate codes written with IBM and General Motors in mind—have adapted corporate law to the realities of the American close corporation. It is in those corporations that shareholders exert the most real influence.

The 30 million or so individual shareholders and the numerous institutional investors have many rights and responsibilities worthy of study. Many are covered in other chapters of this book. As noted, voting rights in the public corporation are so heavily influenced by federal proxy regulation that a separate chapter is warranted. Shareholders' rights to dividends and their responsibilities for "watered stock" are described in the chapter on the corporate financial structure. The right of shareholders to approve or disapprove fundamental changes in corporate structure is highlighted in the chapter describing such changes.

This chapter will begin by discussing the very important right to vote. It will then highlight the shareholder inspection and information rights that may be critical to a knowing exercise of the franchise. Then the shareholder right to bring derivative litigation on the corporation's behalf will be described. Finally, shareholder participation in the management of closely held corporations will be emphasized, with analysis of such matters as share transfer restrictions, voting agreements and trusts, and special close corporation statutes.

RIGHT TO VOTE

Overview

Although today most jurisdictions permit issuance of nonvoting stock, most shareholders (unlike most creditors) have the right to vote their shares. They may vote to elect directors and to remove directors. They may vote to approve or disapprove changes in the basic corporate structure, such as mergers, consolidations, and liquidations. They may vote to approve or disapprove transactions as to which the board of directors has a conflict of interest. They may vote on bylaws and amendments to the articles of incorporation. However, on a realistic level all these inputs to management tend to have a smaller impact the larger the corporation involved.

Who Is Entitled to Vote?

Shareholders who hold title in their own names as of the "date of record" are normally entitled to vote their shares. But if they have given a "proxy"—a written authorization to vote the shares—to another, then the proxyholder has the right to vote the shares. And if the shareholder has only the beneficial title to the shares—which normally entails the important right to receive dividends—the right to vote may be in the hands of the holder of legal title such as a legal guardian, a custodian, or a voting trustee. Brokers who hold legal title as a convenience to their principals are obliged to follow the instructions of those principals on voting matters. If a shareholder pledges his shares to a bank as collateral for a loan, normally the shareholder is entitled to vote the shares until title has been transferred to the pledgee.[1]

As a matter of simple logistics, it is impossible for a large corporation with thousands of shareholders to keep an up-to-the minute list of shareholders that will take into account all the purchases and sales of shares that have occurred. Therefore, §30 of the MBCA (Model Business Corporation Act) authorizes the board of directors to establish a fixed "record date" to determine the shareholders entitled to notice of and to vote at a shareholders' meeting. The stock transfer books may be closed for at least 10 days, but no more than 50 days, before the meeting, or if the books are not closed, the record date may be established in the bylaws somewhere during that 40 day period. Thus, if 5 days before an annual shareholders' meeting shareholder X sells all her shares to shareholder Y, shareholder X is entitled to vote the shares.[2] Usually an arrangement can be worked out whereby X will grant a proxy to Y or will vote according to Y's instructions.

Note that a corporation's board of directors cannot vote treasury shares held by the corporation at an annual meeting, nor can a subsidiary corporation (whose policies are determined by the board of directors of its parent) vote any shares it owns of the parent at the parent's annual meeting. These rules help to prevent a board of directors from perpetuating itself.[3]

Proxies

As will be explained in more detail in the chapter on proxy regulation (Chapter 21), a shareholder may vote in person or by a written authorization to another known as a "proxy." The proxyholder acts as the agent of the shareholder. Section 33 of the MBCA and the laws of virtually all jurisdictions require that a proxy be in writing. Section 33 also provides that "[n]o proxy shall be valid after eleven months from its date of execution, unless otherwise provided in the proxy."

A proxy may be revoked orally, in writing, or simply by giving a later, inconsistent proxy. Proxies are not irrevocable, even if they expressly state that they are unless

---

[1] MBCA §33.

[2] RMBCA §7.07 allows the record date to be as much as 70 days before the meeting.

[3] The RMBCA establishes the concept of a "voting group." RMBCA §10.04 entitles holders of a series or class of stock to vote as a separate voting group on proposed amendments to the articles that would adversely or disparately affect their shares by, for example, increasing the number of authorized shares, reclassifying the shares, creating a new class of shares with superior preferences, or denying preemptive rights to the class. RMBCA §11.03 also requires separate voting by groups of shares that are disparately affected by plans of merger or share exchange. The right to vote as a group even extends to shares the articles state are nonvoting. RMBCA §7.25 requires a quorum for each voting group of shares entitled to vote, and §7.26 provides that where action by two or more voting groups is required, "action on that matter is taken only when voted upon by each of those voting groups counted separately."

they are "coupled with an interest" or "given as security." This means that a proxy could be irrevocable, for example, if given to a pledgee, someone who has purchased the stock, a creditor who has loaned money to the corporation in consideration for the proxy, or someone who has agreed to perform services as an officer of the corporation if the proxy were given in consideration for the services.[4]

Types of Voting

In most corporations, no matter what the subject matter of the election, each share carries one vote. This is known as "straight voting" and has almost completely replaced per capita voting, an older practice in which each shareholder had one vote regardless of the number of shares owned.

Straight voting may be altered in a number of ways. As noted earlier, issuance of nonvoting shares is now permitted in most jurisdictions. Sometimes there is class voting where shares are issued in classes, such as A and B, with provisions in the bylaws that any basic change in corporate structure must be approved by a majority vote in each class, or perhaps a provision that Class A shareholders are entitled to elect three directors at the annual meeting and Class B shareholders are entitled to elect four. In this manner the Class B owners, perhaps individuals who contributed an important infusion of capital when the corporation was foundering, can better protect their interests.

Most jurisdictions also allow issuance of shares carrying multiple or fractional votes. Thus, if it suits the corporation's purposes in allocating control, not all shares need be accorded one whole vote. One relatively recent case approved a "sliding scale" voting provision in the articles that allowed 1 vote per share for the first 50 owned by any shareholder, but only 1 vote per 20 shares thereafter.[5] The obvious purpose was to limit the ability of any one shareholder to gain a controlling block of shares.

As is noted in the preceding chapter on financial structure, preferred shares are sometimes accorded contingent voting rights. For example, the shares may carry no vote unless the corporation is in arrears on dividends due those shares.

Cumulative Voting

In straight voting, a majority faction can elect *all* directors and thereby dominate the corporation. Assume that shareholder A owns 51 outstanding shares of X Corporation and that B owns the other 49. Assume there are seven directors. If A and B have a disagreement and each nominates seven director candidates, though A has only two more shares than B, his candidates will be the top seven vote getters— each with 51. Thus, A will be represented by all seven directors—and B by none.

Because of the arguable unfairness of this result, many jurisdictions have instituted *cumulative voting*, which is a method of achieving proportional representation in director

---

[4] *McKinney's N.Y. Business Corporation Law*, §609 (f) (West Publishing Co.: St. Paul, MN, 1963).

[5] *Providence & Worcester Co.* v. *Baker*, 378 A.2d 121 (Del. Supr. 1977).

elections. In cumulative voting, each share is entitled to a number of votes corresponding to the number of directors to be elected. Furthermore, those votes may be cumulated—grouped for one or just a few candidates. Thus if B owns 49 shares and if seven directorships are up for election, B will have a total of 343 votes. If B casts 114 votes for his candidate B_1, and 114 and 115 for B_2 and B_3, all three of those candidates will be elected. There is no way that A can spread his 357 votes (51×7) around so that B's candidates will not be among the top seven vote recipients.

A simple formula has been suggested to determine how many shares must be controlled to elect a given number of directors: [6]

$$\frac{\text{\# needed to elect } X}{\text{\# of directors}} = \frac{\text{\# of shares voting} \times X}{\text{to be elected} + 1} + \begin{array}{l} 1 \text{ (or fraction needed} \\ \text{to produce next} \\ \text{highest whole)} \end{array}$$

Assume that you are a minority shareholder in a corporation with 1000 outstanding shares that will be voted at the upcoming election. All nine of the corporation's director-ships are at stake. You wish to know how many votes you must control to elect four directors. The formula will read

$$\underline{\hspace{5cm}} = \frac{1,000 \times 4}{9 + 1} + 1 \text{ (or fraction)}$$

The answer is 401. That number of shares would give you 3,609 votes (401 $\times$ 9). If you nominate four persons and give three of them 902 votes and the fourth 903, a majority faction controlling the other 599 shares cannot prevent you from electing at least four directors. Indeed, occasionally a majority faction will fail to cumulate its votes properly and will lose control of the corporation to the minority.[7]

The advantages of cumulative voting are thought to include the following: (1) it is more democratic to give the minority a voice in management, (2) minority goals may be different from majority goals and should be represented, (3) the minority faction can serve as a watchdog to keep the board honest, and (4) minority representation makes management more efficient by providing an alternative point of view.

Detractors suggest that cumulative voting carries corresponding disadvantages, including (1) disharmony results from disputes between majority and minority board factions, (2) partisanship reduces efficiency as each faction attempts to promote its own narrow interests, and (3) competitors and corporate raiders can put representatives on the board to further their own selfish interests.

These disadvantages are of sufficiently serious concern that fewer than 20 states now require a corporation to offer a cumulative voting option, and that number is dwindling. Around 30 states follow MBCA §33, which allows corporations to choose whether or not to offer cumulative voting.[8] In those states fewer and fewer corporations are

---

[6] A. Cole, "Legal and Mathematical Aspects of Cumulative Voting," *South Carolina Law Review*, Vol. 2 (1950), p. 225.

[7] For example, *State ex rel. Springs* v. *Ellison*, 106 S.C. 139, 90 S.E. 669 (1916).

[8] RMBCA §7.28 states that no cumulative voting rights exist unless the articles of incorporation so provide.

choosing to allow cumulative voting. Furthermore, even where available, the option to cumulate votes in director elections is seldom exercised.

A majority faction that wishes to avoid the problems attendant to having minority directors can blunt the effect of cumulative voting in a number of ways. Except in the jurisdictions that mandate cumulative voting, the majority can amend the articles of incorporation to eliminate cumulative voting. Even in jurisdictions that require cumulative voting's availability, the majority has many options.

For example, one tactic has been to exercise the shareholders' right to remove directors without cause to eliminate minority directors. However, MBCA's §39 defeats this tactic by stating that if cumulative voting exists, and less than the entire board is to be removed, "no one of the directors may be removed if the votes cast against his removal would be sufficient to elect him if then cumulatively voted at an election of the entire board of directors." Thus, if none of the minority director's support has eroded since the election, the same block of minority votes that elected the director can block his or her removal. RMBCA §808(c) has the same provision.

More effective is to classify the board. Assume that you own 401 shares in a corporation electing nine directors each year. We already know, by use of our formula,[9] that you can elect four-ninths of the directors. But if the board is classified into three classes of directors serving rotating three-year terms, you could elect only one director out of three. Your voting power has been diluted to one-third.

Assume that you owned only 250 of the 1,000 shares. If the corporation elected nine directors, you could place two of your candidates on the board. However, if the board were classified into three classes of three, you could not elect any directors. Some courts have allowed classification for the purpose of defeating cumulative voting;[10] others have not.[11] Section 37 of the MBCA and §8.06 of the RMBCA expressly allow classification, but only of a board with nine or more members and then only into two or three classes.

Other methods of minimizing the effect of cumulative voting include reducing the number of directors, having the board act primarily through committees—authorized by MBCA §42 and RMBCA §8.25, and even changing the state of incorporation to one more hostile to cumulative voting.

Notice and Meetings

Section 28 of the MBCA provides that an annual meeting of shareholders shall be held each year at a specified time and place. If no annual meeting is held during any 13-month period, a court may order one upon the application of any shareholder.[12] If

---

[9] Note that the suggested formula is not perfect and there have been several attempts to improve on it. See, for example, A. Glazer, D. Glazer, and B. Grofman, "Cumulative Voting in Corporate Elections: Introducing Strategy into the Equation," *South Carolina Law Review*, Vol. 35 (1984), p. 295.

[10] *Janney* v. *Philadelphia Transp. Co.*, 387 Pa. 282, 128 A.2d 76 (1956).

[11] *Wolfson* v. *Avery*, 6 Ill.2d 78, 126 N.E.2d 701 (1955).

[12] RMBCA §7.03 allows a court to order a meeting upon shareholder application if an annual meeting "was not held within the earlier of 6 months after the end of the corporation's fiscal year or 15 months after its last annual meeting."

special meetings are needed, for example, to vote on a change of corporate structure or to remove the directors, they may be called by the board of directors or by the holders of one-tenth or more of the shares.

Written notice stating the place, day, and hour of the meeting is to be delivered not more than 50 or fewer than 10 days before the meeting to each shareholder of record, determined as of the fixed record date.[13]

A quorum is needed for effective action. MBCA §32 designates a majority of the shares entitled to vote as a quorum if the articles are silent. However, in the articles, the corporation can raise the percentage needed for a quorum or can lower it—but not below one-third.[14] Usually courts will not order shareholders to attend shareholders' meetings, even if their absence prevents formation of a quorum.[15] However, if a quorum is present at the start of the meeting, in most jurisdictions effective action cannot be thwarted by a subsequent walkout of some shareholders. A majority vote of the shares present and entitled to vote will constitute effective action unless the articles or bylaws require a larger percentage.[16]

MBCA §138 allows shareholder action without a meeting via *unanimous* written consent. Delaware has a relatively unique consent device that allows shareholders to take effective action without a meeting via written consents of holders of a *majority* of shares.[17] The Delaware provision is obviously much more practicable for corporations of substantial size.

Removal of Directors

Shareholders have the inherent power to remove directors and can force a meeting for that purpose.[18] They may remove the directors for cause, such as conviction of a felony, incapacity, or bankruptcy. They may also remove them without cause, subject to the limitation arising from cumulative voting noted earlier. Directors cannot remove each other unless the shareholders have delegated that power via provision in the articles or bylaws.

Section 38 of the MBCA provides that any vacancy on the board may be filled by affirmative vote of a majority of the remaining directors, though less than a

---

[13] MBCA §§29, 30. RMBCA §7.05 sets the parameters at no more than 60 nor fewer than 10 days before the annual meeting. It also provides that a shareholder can waive right to notice in writing or by attendance in certain cases.

[14] RMBCA §7.25, like MBCA §32, provides that a quorum is a majority if the articles are silent on the matter. RMBCA §7.27 allows the articles to provide for a greater quorum (and voting) requirement up to and including unanimity. As noted earlier, the RMBCA requires a quorum for each "voting group" entitled to vote.

[15] *Hall* v. *Hall*, 506 S.W.2d 42 (Mo. App. 1974).

[16] Assume 1,000 shares outstanding and articles silent on a quorum. The MBCA's §32 provides that 501 would be a quorum. It would then take 251 votes to approve an action. If 240 voted for, 220 against, and 41 abstained, the measure would fail. The RMBCA alters this result by providing in §7.25 that in matters other than the election of directors, approval occurs if the votes cast in favor of an action exceed those cast against. Abstentions are disregarded.

[17] Del. Corp. Code §229. See *Calumet Ind., Inc.* v. *McClure*, 464 F.Supp. 19 (N.D. Ill. 1978).

[18] MBCA §§28, 39; RMBCA §808. *Auer* v. *Dressel*, 118 N.E.2d 590 (N.Y. App. 1954).

quorum. The director chosen shall serve only the remainder of the unexpired term. RMBCA §8.10 allows other alternatives and protects the rights of "voting groups."

RIGHT TO INSPECTION AND INFORMATION

The shareholder's right to vote knowingly is impaired and several other valuable rights imperiled if shareholders cannot gain information about their corporations. Many years ago the board of directors could keep shareholders almost completely in the dark about corporate business. But evolving common law and new statutes, such as MBCA §52, and RMBCA §16.01–16.04, have greatly improved the shareholders' position.

Common Law

Under the common law in most jurisdictions, shareholders have a board right to inspect corporate records and documents such as shareholder lists, minutes of meetings, financial statements, and even contracts. They also may inspect the corporation's physical premises. This right is not unqualified. The inspection must occur at proper times and in the proper places and, most important, must be for proper purposes.

If challenged by management, a shareholder asserting common law inspection rights has the burden of proof in a mandamus action to convince the court that a proper purpose underlies the request to inspect.

What is a proper purpose? Generally speaking, the courts have held that it is a purpose germane to the shareholder's business interests in the corporation. It is proper for the shareholders to inspect (1) to ascertain the financial status of the corporation; (2) to detect mismanagement; (3) to ascertain the value of their shares; (4) to aid legitimate litigation against management; and (5) to communicate with other shareholders for such purposes as offering to buy their shares, soliciting support in a proxy fight, and inviting them to join litigation.

Improper purposes have been held to exist where the request to inspect arose out of an intent: (1) merely to harass the corporation; (2) to obtain a shareholder list in order to sell it for personal profit; (3) to learn trade secrets of a competitor; (4) to find technical defects in corporate transactions in order to bring frivolous litigation; and (5) to further the shareholder's political, moral, or religious views.

The proper purpose requirement is important because, as one court put it,

> Considering the huge size of many modern corporations and the necessarily complicated nature of their bookkeeping, it is plain that to permit their thousands of shareholders to roam at will through their records would render impossible not only any attempt to keep their records efficiently, but the proper carrying on of their business.[19]

Some courts have been relatively restrictive in interpreting the idea of a proper purpose. In one leading case, *State ex rel. Pillsbury* v. *Honeywell*,[20] plaintiff learned

---

[19] *Cooke* v. *Outland*, 265 N.C. 601, 144 S.E. 2d 835 (1965).
[20] 291 Minn. 322, 191 N.W.2d 406 (1971).

that Honeywell Corp. manufactured weapons being used in the Vietnam War, which plaintiff opposed. Plaintiff then bought shares in Honeywell (only to discover that he was already beneficiary of a trust owning Honeywell stock) and requested an inspection of Honeywell's shareholder lists and all records dealing with weapons manufacture. When management resisted, plaintiff asked the court for a writ of mandamus.

The court rejected the notion, accepted by many courts, that "a mere desire to communicate with other shareholders is, per se, a proper purpose," concluding that "a better rule would allow inspections only if the shareholder has a proper purpose for such communication." No such proper purpose existed because plaintiff's *sole* goal "was to persuade the company to adopt his social and political concerns irrespective of any economic benefit to himself or Honeywell."

Many other courts have not been so insistent that a proper purpose relate solely to a shareholder's economic interest. Furthermore, most courts hold that so long as the shareholder's primary purpose is proper, the fact that he or she has a secondary purpose that is improper or even illegal is irrelevant.[21]

Statutory Inspection Rights

Most states' corporate codes delineate shareholder inspection rights. In virtually every jurisdiction, these statutory rights supplement, rather than replace, common law inspection rights.[22] There is quite a bit of variation from state to state, but MBCA and RMBCA provisions are representative of the majority approach.

General Inspection

Section 52 of the MBCA provides that any person who has been a shareholder for at least six months, *or* who owns at least 5% of all outstanding shares (regardless of the length of time), "upon written demand stating the purpose thereof," shall have the right to inspect relevant books, records, and minutes.[23]

For persons who do not meet the six-month or 5% threshold, §52 explicitly states that common law rights still exist *if* the shareholder shows a proper purpose. For those who do meet the requirements, the burden shifts to management to prove that a proper purpose does not exist. Any officer, agent, or corporation wrongfully refusing a proper request for inspection is liable to the shareholder for a penalty of 10% of the value of the shareholder's stock in addition to any other damage or remedy afforded by the law. Many states have diluted this rather stringent liability provision, as does RMBCA §16.04.

---

[21] *General Time Corp.* v. *Talley Ind., Inc.*, 43 Del. Ch. 531, 240 A. 2d 755 (S. Ct. 1968).

[22] But see *Caspary* v. *Louisiana Land & Exploration Co.*, 707 F. 2d 785 (4th Cir. 1983).

[23] RMBCA §16.02 eliminates the six-month or 5% requirement, providing that any shareholder is entitled, upon written notice, to inspect and copy minutes and records of board and shareholder meetings, accounting records, and the record of shareholders. But to have this right, a shareholder's demand must be in good faith and for a proper purpose, it must describe with reasonable particularity the purpose and records sought, and the records must be directly connected to the purpose.

Courts have generally been liberal in interpreting the "proper purpose" concept to protect shareholder inspection rights, particularly when a shareholder list was the document sought. However, at the same time courts have tried to prevent inspecting shareholders from unduly disrupting the corporation's business.

The following case illustrates.

SCHWARTZMAN v. SCHWARTZMAN PACKING CO.

659 P.2d 888 (N.M. 1983)

Plaintiffs are minority shareholders in Schwartzman Packing Company (Company). Defendants include the Company and several of its officers. Plaintiffs sued alleging that defendants engaged in various willful acts of oppressive conduct which injured plaintiffs and the Company. The trial court ruled for the defendants. Plaintiffs raised several claims on appeal, including that the trial court unduly limited plaintiffs' inspection rights under §53–11– 50(B), N.M.S.A. 1978 [New Mexico's statute that is identical to MBCA §52].

The record showed that two months before trial, defendants agreed to cooperate with plaintiffs' inspection request. Plaintiffs delayed almost two months before beginning. When plaintiffs sent teams of three to six accountants to inspect the corporation's records during normal business hours, business operations were disrupted. As a result defendants informed plaintiffs they would have to inspect after 5 P.M. Defendants furnished a representative after hours to accommodate plaintiffs' accountants, but those accountants did not always appear.

Plaintiffs then asked the court to order defendants to allow examination during regular business hours. By that time, plaintiffs had spent almost 200 man hours in defendants' offices. The court ordered that plaintiffs have one additional day to use as many accountants as

they wished and work as long as they deemed necessary.

FEDERICI, JUSTICE:

This is a case of first impression in New Mexico on the question of a shareholder's right to inspect a corporation's books and records. There is little doubt that applicable statutes and case law grant to shareholders the right to inspect, at reasonable times and at reasonable places, a corporation's books and records for proper purposes—§53–11–50.

This right was recognized under the common law and exists independently of statute. The New Mexico statute was adopted verbatim from Section 52 of the ABA Model Corporation Act. It is not a limitation or abrogation of the common law rights of inspection and is sometimes described as an extension or even an enlargement of the right as recognized under the common law.

However, the right of a shareholder to examine books and records under Section 53–11–50 is not unlimited. Inspection must be made at "reasonable times," and as the Supreme Court of Pennsylvania said in *Ruby* v. *Penn Fibre Board Corporation*, 326 Pa. 582, 192 A. 914, 916 (1937),

What is reasonable and proper necessarily depends upon the circumstances of each case and must be determined by the exercise of the discretion of the court enforcing the right. The problem is essentially one of the relative convenience of all parties concerned. . . . [T]he examination should not be allowed at a time or place or under conditions which would unduly interfere with the regular course of business of the company.

The case cited by plaintiffs also recognizes that the right of examination must be exercised at reasonable and proper times—*Weigel* v. *O'Connor*, 57 Ill. App.3d 1017, 373 N.E.2d 421 (1978).

A trial court must of necessity have some discretion in determining when and in what manner the right of examination should be exercised. Under the facts in this case, it was not an abuse of discretion for the trial court to limit examination to regular business hours in addition to the 222 hours of examination which had previously been allowed.

Plaintiffs also urge that the statutory penalty provided by Section 53–11–50(B) should be imposed against officers or directors of the corporation. The statute provides for imposition of a penalty upon an officer or agent who "shall refuse to allow" a qualified shareholder to examine books and records of the corporation. Insofar as we can determine from the record, no officer or agent of the corporation refused any plaintiff access to its books and records. The penalty is not applicable here. In any event, the imposition of a penalty under Section 53–11–50(B) is within the discretion of the trial court. Under the facts in this case we find no abuse of discretion in the trial court's refusal to impose a penalty on officers or agents of the corporation.

Affirmed as to this point.

Financial Statements

Section 52 was amended in 1978 to require corporations to furnish shareholders annual financial statements, including at least a balance sheet and income statement prepared in accordance with generally accepted accounting principles. The statements are to be mailed within 120 days after the close of the fiscal year. It remains to be seen how many jurisdictions will adopt this MBCA provision. The requirement would affect mostly close corporations because, as we shall see in later chapters, the larger public companies are already required by federal securities laws to make similar disclosures.[24]

Shareholder List

In addition to the provision of §52, the MBCA aids shareholders by requiring in §31 that the corporation keep an alphabetical list of shareholders (with addresses and number of shares owned) and that the list be kept open at the annual meeting for inspection by *any* shareholder.[25]

---

[24] RMBCA §16.20 follows the 1978 amendments in this regard.

[25] RMBCA §7.20 requires that a shareholders' list be made available for inspection by *any* shareholder starting two business days after notice of the meeting is given and continuing through the meeting. A proper written demand will entitle the shareholder to inspection and copying rights.

DERIVATIVE ACTIONS

Introduction

Shareholders have the right to bring and defend lawsuits in the corporation's behalf. Suits brought in the corporation's behalf are called *derivative suits* because the right to sue derives from wrongs done primarily to the corporation and not to the shareholder individually.

The derivative suit was developed by the courts primarily for the situation where those who have wronged the corporation are the very officers and directors who control the corporation and can refuse to authorize it to sue. However, the suit can also be brought against persons having no connection with the corporation.

The derivative suit has great potential as a device to protect the corporation and its shareholders. A single shareholder can institute the suit and take the wrongdoers to task. However, a potent weapon is also subject to great abuse. In the derivative litigation context, that abuse takes the form of a "strike suit"—a spurious suit brought not to benefit the corporation but to blackmail defendants into a settlement that will personally profit plaintiffs and their attorneys. Plaintiffs have often instituted derivative suits and offered to dismiss them for sums slightly smaller than the amount the corporation would have to spend to defend the suit.

Procedural Overview

To reduce abuses of the derivative suit, a number of procedural requirements that do not apply to most types of suits have been applied. Federal Rule of Civil Procedure 23.1, applicable to derivative suits in federal court, requires, among other things (1) that plaintiff was a shareholder at the time of the transaction of which he complains or that his ownership thereafter devolved upon him by operation of law; (2) that plaintiff be a fair and adequate representative of the interests of the shareholders; (3) that plaintiff allege with particularity the efforts made to seek action from the directors and, if necessary, from the shareholders, and the reason for not being successful, or for not making the effort; and (4) that the action not be dismissed without court approval following notice to shareholders.

MBCA §49 and RMBCA §7.40 mirror Rule 23.1's ownership requirement. Many jurisdictions also require that plaintiff continue to be a shareholder throughout the life of the lawsuit, or face dismissal. These sections also empower courts finding that a derivative suit was instituted "without reasonable cause" to require plaintiffs to pay defendants' costs, including attorney's fees. As we shall see momentarily, some jurisdictions also require some plaintiffs to post a bond to cover such costs.

These procedural matters will be given more attention directly.

Characterization of Suits

Because so many special procedural requirements apply to the derivative suit, and because recovery in such a suit goes into the corporate treasury rather than the shareholder-plaintiff's pocket, it is important to distinguish between suits that shareholders can bring in their own right and suits that must be brought derivatively. If a suit is properly deemed derivative, even the corporation's sole shareholder cannot bring an individual action.

No completely satisfactory test has been developed to distinguish individual from derivative causes of action. The most common test focuses on whether the injury was primarily to the shareholder as an individual or whether the shareholder only suffered incidentally because of an injury to the corporation. This test is applied in the following unusual case.

CUNNINGHAM v. KARTRIDG PAK CO.

332 N.W. 2d 881 (Iowa 1983)

Plaintiff Cunningham, after certain discussions with defendant's representatives, formed and became principal stockholder in Iowa Meat Fabricators Corp. (IMF). The corporation was formed to produce a mechanically processed pork product. Defendant agreed to provide a mechanical processor, the Yieldmaster, which purportedly would produce a product meeting U.S.D.A. standards.

Despite numerous adjustments, the Yieldmaster never produced pork which met U.S.D.A. standards. The calcium content was always too high for the pork to be marketable. Eventually the stock and assets of IMF were sold. The sale transaction did not reserve to plaintiff or to IMF the right to sue defendant.

Thereafter, plaintiff filed this suit in his individual capacity for losses sustained due to Yieldmaster's failure. His suit was based on breach of warranty, negligence, and strict liability theories. The trial court held plaintiff had no right to sue individually. Plaintiff appealed.

McGIVERIN, JUSTICE:

I. *General rule*

We basically are presented with the question of whether plaintiff has a right to sue. Defendant contends that plaintiff was suing in his individual capacity as a shareholder for damages suffered by the corporation. As a matter of general corporate law, shareholders have no claim for injuries to their corporations by third parties unless within the context of a derivative action.

There is, however, a well-recognized exception to the general rule: a shareholder has an individual cause of action if the harm to the corporation also damaged the shareholder in his capacity as an individual rather than as a shareholder. Courts vary in their articulation of the test for showing direct injury to the individual. Some describe the direct injury as a special duty owed to the shareholder. See *Sherman* v. *British Leyland Motors, Inc.*, 601 F.2d 429, 440 n. 13 (9th Cir. 1979).

In other cases the direct injury is said to be an injury to the individual separate and distinct from that suffered by the other shareholders. See *Alario* v. *Miller*, 354 So.2d 925, 926 (Fla. App. 1978).

Recognizing that these two concepts will usually, if not always, overlap, we conclude that the test is best stated in the disjunctive: in order to bring an individual cause of action for direct injuries a shareholder must show that the third-party owed him a special duty *or* that he suffered an injury separate and distinct from that suffered by the other shareholders.

Plaintiff claims that he meets this test. He

alleges that defendant's wrongful conduct injured him in his individual capacity because Kartridg Pak knew that if the Yieldmaster failed to perform, plaintiff, a majority stockholder of IMF, would be injured.

When we view the record in the light most favorable to the plaintiff, it appears that he organized IMF for the purpose of producing a mechanically processed pork product with a Yieldmaster. Our task is to determine whether the trial court correctly ruled that, as a matter of law, plaintiff failed to satisfy the test for the direct injury exception. We conclude that the trial court was right.

The fact that plaintiff was the majority shareholder of IMF is irrelevant. See 13 Fletcher, *Cyclopedia of Corporations*, §5910 ("The fact that a stockholder owns stock does not itself authorize him to sue as an individual."). Plaintiff must satisfy one of the prongs of the test articulated above.

A. *Separate and distinct injury.* The record is barren of any facts which even remotely suggest that Cunningham's injuries were unique in comparison to those of the other shareholders, if any. The unhappy ending of this business venture was caused by the Yieldmaster's failure to function as desired, resulting in the sale of IMF at a loss. Naturally, the loss fell heaviest on those who had invested the most, but that does not make Cunningham's injury separate and distinct from that of any other shareholders.

B. *Special duty.* A closer question is whether organization of IMF to produce a pork product by use of the Yieldmaster created a special duty from Kartridg Pak to Cunningham. As a matter of law, we conclude that it did not.

Plaintiff's only rights must be traced to the lease agreement between IMF and Kartridg Pak which specified that the Yieldmaster would "produce [a pork] product within U.S.D.A. standards for calcium." Plaintiff signed the lease in his capacity as president of IMF; all prior understandings and agreements were merged into the lease agreement. Consequently, plaintiff's only rights arise by virtue of the fact that he was a stockholder; he has failed to establish that he possessed rights extrinsic from the corporation.

In view of the above conclusions, we should distinguish a few cases in which a special duty to the shareholder was found. In *Eden* v. *Miller*, 37 F.2d 8 (2d Cir. 1930), plaintiffs formed a corporation for freight hauling in consideration for defendant's promise to provide the corporation with capital and to secure business for it. Defendant breached the oral contract and plaintiffs were allowed to recover in their individual capacity. In contrast to the present case, in Eden the corporation was *not* a party to the breached contract.

A special duty arising out of a contract was also present in *Sedco International, S.A.* v. *Cary*, 522 F.Supp. 254 (S.D. Ia. 1981). The court recognized that the estate of the shareholder, Roy Carver, had an individual cause of action "when the wrong is both to the stockholder as an individual and to the corporation." In that case the wrong to the individual, Carver, was plaintiff's alleged fraudulent inducement of Carver to make substantial loans of operating capital to the corporation of which Carver was a stockholder and with which plaintiff was doing business.

In sum, plaintiff does not show direct injuries. The injuries alleged are the consequence of being a shareholder of IMF and the cause of action rightfully belongs to the corporation.

II. *Products liability theory*

As an alternative to the direct injury exception, plaintiff advances the novel theory that because he alleges this is a products liability claim he should be allowed to sue the manufacturer directly. Plaintiff bases this theory on our holdings that absence of privity of contract does not preclude one from seeking to recover for strict liability.

The theories behind product liability arose from the legitimate needs of plaintiffs to recover for damages resulting from the manufacture of defective and unreasonably dangerous products.

. . .

Plaintiff is not an injured consumer; he was a shareholder of a corporation whose expectations did not materialize. To allow a shareholder to use products liability law as the vehicle to a direct cause of action otherwise denied by general corporate law would be an injustice to both areas of the law.

The general rule prohibiting shareholders from suing for injuries to the corporation is grounded on sound policy. It is based on the principle that all shareholders suffer in proportion to the number of shares he or she holds. Thus when the corporation brings the cause of action, all shareholders are benefited. A contrary rule would authorize each shareholder to sue and would result in a multiplicity of suits against the wrongdoer. Further, the rule is necessary to prevent impairment of creditors' rights and to retain in the board of directors of the corporation its prerogative to use recovered damages for any legitimate business purpose.

IMF could have sued defendant for breach of warranty, and if it had refused to do so, plaintiff could have sued derivatively. Additionally, when IMF was sold, its rights against Kartridg Pak could have been reserved. In view of these alternatives for holding defendant responsible for the failure of its machine to perform as warranted, we conclude that there is no policy justification to allow plaintiff to use products liability law as a back-door approach to the direct injury exception.

Affirmed.

Although the courts have not been consistent, generally the following types of action have been held to be derivative in nature: (1) suits against third parties who have committed torts against or breached contracts with the corporation; (2) suits against directors and officers for mismanagement, misfeasance, or misappropriation of corporate property; (3) suits against insiders for *ultra vires* acts; and (4) suits to recover improperly paid dividends.

Among the types of suits generally held to be individual in nature are (1) suits to enforce a shareholder's right to inspect, or to vote, or to exercise preemptive rights; (2) suits to recover from insiders who traded on inside information or otherwise fraudulently induced plaintiff to sell his shares; (3) suits against directors and officers for harassment, oppression, or denial of a fair return; (4) suits to force payment of previously declared dividends; and (5) suits to compel dissolution.

Plaintiff Qualifications

As noted, several procedural requirements of derivative suits aim at ensuring that plaintiff will adequately protect the interests of the other shareholders and of the corporation, which is the real party in interest in the litigation.

Ownership Requirements

The requirement that plaintiff shareholder in a derivative suit must have owned shares at the time of the challenged transaction was originally aimed at preventing champerty. It prevents an uninterested third party from learning of a transaction and then purchasing one share to buy into litigation. However, a few jurisdictions do allow subsequent purchasers to sue derivatively on the theory that the right to sue is indivisible and attaches to the shares when they are transferred. Some courts use a "continuing wrong" theory to expand the number of shareholders able to sue.

The requirement that plaintiff remain a shareholder until judgment seeks to ensure that the real party in interest does not become plaintiff's attorney who might pursue the case only to recover the fees that a successful conclusion might bring. Thus, if plaintiff owned shares at the time of the alleged wrong, but sold them almost a year before filing suit, the action will be dismissed in most jurisdictions.[26]

Security for Expenses

Although the owner of a single share is entitled to file a derivative action, a small shareholder may be required by the court, upon a request by management, to post a bond as security for defendants' expenses should the suit fail. The purpose of this requirement is also to prevent strike suits by discouraging shareholders who do not meet the threshold level (typically, 5% ownership or shares worth $25,000, whichever is lower). A shareholder who was not required to post a bond normally will not be required to pay defendants' costs in the event of failure. The requirement is only to discourage suits by those without a significant stake in the corporation.

Almost 20 jurisdictions contain such a bond-posting requirement, although it was eliminated from MBCA §49 in 1982.[27] The Supreme Court held such a requirement constitutional, despite its potential for burdening the rights of small shareholders.[28] The potential impact of the requirement has been mitigated by decisions holding that a plaintiff who alone might have to post a bond is entitled to communicate with other shareholders to determine if they wish to join him so that cumulatively the minimum holding requirement for exemption can be met.[29] To avoid publicizing a plaintiff's charges, many corporate defendants choose not to ask the court to require a bond.

Where security bonds are required, however, sums needed to cover modern attorneys' fees can easily exceed $100,000.

Fair and Adequate Representation

In determining whether a derivative plaintiff meets Rule 23.1's requirement of a "fair and adequate" representative, courts look at such factors as (1) the size of plaintiff's holdings, (2) plaintiff's sophistication, (3) whether plaintiff has a personal ax to grind, and (4) the quality of plaintiff's attorneys.

---

[26] For example, *Keever* v. *Jewelry Mountain Miner, Inc.*, 688 P.2d 317 (Nev. 1984).

[27] RMBCA §7.40 also omits this requirement.

[28] *Cohen* v. *Beneficial Industrial Loan Corp.*, 337 U.S. 541 (1949).

[29] For example, *Baker* v. *MacFadden Publications*, 300 N.Y. 325, 90 N.E.2d 876 (1950).

Demand Requirements

On Directors

Most jurisdictions require that derivative plaintiffs, before filing suit, make written demand on the directors and, if necessary, the shareholders, before bringing suit.[30] These requests allow the corporation, the real party in interest, to decide whether to sue. They also preserve the discretion of the board of directors to operate the company.

If a disinterested, fair-minded board of directors determines that the lawsuit would not be in the best interests of the corporation, the suit is barred. This procedure preserves the "business judgment rule" under which courts will not substitute their judgment for the good faith business decisions of the board of directors. Even if the board cannot be deemed disinterested, a disinterested special litigation committee (SLC) can be appointed. Most courts will honor the decision of an SLC that a suit should not be pursued, even if the claim appears substantively meritorious. The business judgment rule and the SLC are covered in some detail in the chapter on directors, Chapter 11.

However, if the board of directors is not disinterested—perhaps because all members participated in the alleged fraud—the demand requirement may be excused as futile. The following is a leading case in this area.

POGOSTIN v. RICE

480 A.2d 619 (Del. Supr. 1984)

Plaintiffs are shareholders of City Investing Company (City) who bring this derivative action on City's behalf against City and its board of directors (four company officers and ten outsiders). The basic claim arises from City's rejection of a tender offer and the tender offer's effect on a preexisting officer compensation plan.

In June 1980, Tamco Enterprises made a $1.1 billion tender offer for City's stock, bidding $32.50 per share for stock that had been trading on the New York Stock Exchange at $20.00. City's board rejected the offer on July 23, 1980, and City's price immediately tumbled from the high 20s. Plaintiffs claim that the board acted imprudently and improperly in rejecting the offer, that the board breached its fiduciary duty

by depriving City's shareholders of a chance to sell their shares at a profit, and that the board was motivated by an improper purpose of retaining control of the corporation for the four inside directors.

More important, plaintiffs complain of an executive compensation plan called the Share Unit Plan (the Plan), which awards bonuses to executive employees, the amount being set by a preexisting timetable relative to the market price of City stock. The notion is that if the managers do a good job, the price of City's stock will rise and the managers will profit accordingly. However, plaintiffs claim that the amount of the bonus was calculated at $26 per share, the average market price from June to

---

[30] Though the MBCA does not expressly impose such a demand requirement, RMBCA §7.40 does. About 26 jurisdictions have statutes expressly imposing a demand on directors requirement.

September 1970. This, they claim, resulted in abnormally large payments to the four inside directors, based on artificially inflated stock prices caused by heavy trading during the tender offer.

Regarding the substantive complaints, defendants point out that the board appointed a special committee of outside directors to consider the tender offer and that this committee hired two investment banking firms to prepare valuation studies of City. After one month's analysis, the committee concluded that Tamco's price was too low because City's stock was actually worth $48 per share. The board unanimously voted to reject the tender offer, and it is clear that the majority of the board had no personal financial interest in the compensation plan. As to the Plan, defendants argue that compensation arrangements for officers are matters of business judgment and point out that the plan was approved by City shareholders nine years before the tender offer.

Plaintiffs' complaint stated that demand on the City board should be excused as futile because each director participated in the wrongs and could be liable therefor and because the directors could not and would not sue themselves.

The Court of Chancery dismissed the suit for plaintiffs' failure to either make a demand upon City's board for appropriate corrective action or to allege with particularity that demand was futile pursuant to Delaware Chancery Rule 23.1. Plaintiffs appealed.

MOORE, JUSTICE:

· · ·

II.

The bedrock of the General Corporation Law of the State of Delaware is the rule that the business and affairs of a corporation are man-aged by and under the direction of its board. See 8 Del.C. § 141(a). It follows that the existence and exercise of this power carries with it certain fundamental fiduciary obligations to the corporation and its shareholders—*Aronson v. Lewis*, 473 A.2d at 811 [citing *Loft, Inc. v. Guth*, Del. Ch., 2 A.2d 225 (1938), *aff'd*, Del Supr., 5 A.2d 503 (1939)]. Balanced against the managerial power of directors is the derivative action enabling shareholders to sue on behalf of the corporation where those in control of the enterprise refuse to assert a claim belonging to it. The derivative action is one method by which shareholders may obtain redress for the misuse of managerial power.

However, because the derivative action impinges on the managerial freedom of directors, the law imposes certain prerequisites to the exercise of this remedy. Thus, the requirement of Chancery Court Rule 23.1 exists at the threshold to prevent abuse and to promote intracorporate dispute resolution. Inextricably bound to threshold questions of demand futility are issues of business judgment and the standards by which director action is measured.

The test for determining demand futility reflects the interrelationship of business judgment, director independence, and interest. It requires a bifurcated factual analysis based upon a reasonable doubt standard. Under the demand futility test, the facts alleged in the complaint are examined to determine whether they create a reasonable doubt that (1) the directors are disinterested and independent and (2) the challenged transaction otherwise was the product of a valid exercise of business judgment. As to the first *Aronson* inquiry, the court reviews the factual allegations of the complaint to determine whether they create a reasonable doubt as to the disinterestedness and independence of the directors at the time the complaint was filed.

The second, or business judgment inquiry of *Aronson*, focuses on the substantive nature of the challenged transaction and the board's approval thereof. A court does not assume that the transaction was a wrong to the corporation requiring corrective measures by the board. Rather, the transaction is reviewed against the factual background of the complaint to determine whether a reasonable doubt exists at the threshold that the challenged action was a valid exercise of business judgment. If the Court of Chancery in the exercise of its sound discretion is satisfied that a plaintiff has alleged facts with particularity which, taken as true, support a reasonable doubt as to either aspect of the *Aronson* analysis, the futility of demand is established and the court's inquiry ends.

Thus, the *Aronson* test examines the alleged wrong to the corporation in relation to issues of independence, interest, and the exercise of business judgment by the directors. The reasonable doubt standard in conjunction with the particularity requirement of Rule 23.1 strikes the essential balance between avoiding abuse of the derivative action and forcing a plaintiff to plead evidence without the benefit of discovery.

III.

In assessing plaintiffs' attack on the payments made under the Plan we begin with an analysis of the applicable statutory framework relative to matters of executive compensation. Section 141(h) of the General Corporation Law of Delaware expressly authorizes directors to fix their remuneration. Under Section 122(5) a corporation may compensate its officers and agents, and Section 122(15) provides for stock option, incentive, and other compensation plans for directors, officers, and employees. In addition, Section 157 confers broad discretion upon directors in the issuance of stock options and rights. Moreover, it makes clear that absent "actual fraud", the judgment of the directors as to the consideration for such options or rights is conclusive. Section 157 was enacted to "protect directors' business judgment in consideration

inuring to the corporation in exchange for creating and issuing stock options."

The consideration typically involved in stock options, that is, continued and greater efforts by employees, is ephemeral and not susceptible of identification and valuation in dollar terms— *Beard* v. *Elster*, Del. Supr., 160 A.2d 731, 736(1960) (use of term "consideration" to identify benefit corporation receives from stock option plan was "ill-advised" because consideration implies some measurable quid pro quo)— *Lieberman* v. *Becker*, Del. Supr., 155 A.2d 596, 600 (1959).

In this action, the essence of plaintiffs' claim is that the substantial sums which became due under the Plan were materially affected by the unrelated Tamco tender offer, and were not a reward for successful managerial performance. The plaintiffs therefore argue that permitting and accepting the payments were breaches of fiduciary duty.

However, it is undisputed that the Plan was adopted by a majority of disinterested directors and later ratified by City shareholders in 1971. There is no charge of inadequate disclosure in the proxy materials. Under the circumstances plaintiffs have the burden of demonstrating by particularized allegations that the Plan itself is so devoid of a legitimate corporate purpose as to be a waste of assets. They have not done so.

Moreover, the Plan is administered by a committee of four outside directors who are themselves ineligible to participate therein. The Plan, as shown by its terms, represents a legitimate attempt to come within the factual context and legal standards of *Beard* and *Lieberman*. Given the additional fact that the market appreciation aspect of the Plan was entirely disclosed to the City shareholders in 1971 when they approved it, we conclude that the plaintiffs have failed to allege facts under the *Aronson* test which would excuse demand. We also conclude that plaintiffs have failed to allege facts creating a reasonable doubt regarding the independence and disinterestedness of the City board. Only the four officer-directors of the fourteen member City board are beneficiaries of the Plan. Plaintiffs do not allege control by these four insiders, nor do they claim that the remaining ten directors have any financial or other interest whatsoever in the Plan. Given the existing legal principles applicable to matters of executive compensation, and the enumerated voids in the pleadings, we must conclude that demand was not excused.

IV.

Apart from the executive compensation claims, the plaintiffs challenge the rejection of the Tamco tender offer by the City board. They claim that the directors refused to negotiate with Tamco, or to accept the Tamco premium, solely because the four insiders sought to retain control of City and continue to receive their substantial benefits under the Plan. Plaintiffs also argue that the board had no proper business purpose for rejecting the tender offer. According to plaintiffs, the board's action was a breach of fiduciary duty, and therefore, is not a valid exercise of business judgment.

In *Aronson*, we discussed the availability, function and operation of the business judgment rule, including the standards by which director conduct is judged. What we said there is equally applicable here in the context of a takeover. Thus, an informed decision to reject a takeover proposal, hostile or friendly, will not excuse demand absent particularized allegations of a breach of fiduciary duty, such as self-dealing, fraud, overreaching, or lack of good faith. Where, for example, allegations detail the manipulation of corporate machinery by directors for the sole or primary purpose of perpetuating themselves in office, the test of *Aronson* is met and demand is excused. It is the plaintiff's bur-

den to allege with particularity that the improper motive in a given set of circumstances, that is, perpetuation of self in office or otherwise in control, was the sole or primary purpose of the wrongdoer's conduct.

Against this legal background plaintiffs have failed to plead any facts supporting their claim that the City board, or any subgroup thereof, rejected the Tamco offer solely to retain control. Rather, plaintiffs seek to establish a motive or primary purpose to retain control only by showing that the City board opposed a tender offer. Acceptance of such an argument would condemn any board, which successfully avoided a takeover, regardless of whether that board properly determined that it was acting in the best interests of the shareholders.

We are not persuaded by plaintiffs' claim that the City board's refusal to accept the premium offered by Tamco, or to negotiate with Tamco under these circumstances, are prima facie breaches of fiduciary duty and hence, excuse demand. Establishing such a principle would rob corporate boards of all discretion, forcing them to choose between accepting any tender offer or merger proposal above market or facing the likelihood of personal liability if they reject it. To put directors to such a Hobson's choice would be the antithesis of the principles upon which a proper exercise of business judgment is demanded of them. The ultimate loss would, of course, be upon the shareholders. Here, the complaint does not overcome the presumption that the City board properly and prudently exercised its managerial discretion. Valuation studies, carefully prepared by outsiders, were presented to the board prior to its decision. A special committee of independent, outside directors was charged with gathering and analyzing this information. There is nothing in the complaint to suggest that the board's action was other than a carefully considered decision made on an informed basis. Thus, we cannot accept plaintiffs' position, either as applied to these facts, or standing alone, as a per se rule to excuse demand.

Under the standards of *Aronson*, we are satisfied that demand was not excused, and affirm

the trial court's dismissal for plaintiffs' failure to comply with Rule 23.1.

. . .

Affirmed.

Generally, courts have been willing to find that demand on the board could be excused as futile where the majority of the board was dominated by or composed of wrongdoers, where a pervasive conflict of interest existed, or where a majority of the board actively participated in the wrongdoing. The *Pogostin* case's application of the *Aronson* standards indicates a trend to make things more difficult for derivative plaintiffs.

On Shareholders

Rule 23.1 requires not only a written demand on the board, but also demand on shareholders "if necessary." Approximately 15 states have statutes expressly imposing a similar requirement.[31] Again, the courts have not been completely consistent in interpreting this shareholder demand requirement. Most require a derivative plaintiff to have made such a demand if, under law, the shareholders could have ratified the wrongdoing.

However, the demand is excused if futile, as in a case where the sole minority shareholder charged the sole majority shareholder with misappropriation of corporate assets.[32] Some courts find futility where under the law all shareholders could do would be to ask the directors to bring an action against themselves.[33]

Some courts, but not all, excuse demand on shareholders when director fraud is charged on grounds that a majority of shareholders cannot legally ratify fraud.[34] And other courts have waived the demand requirement when the corporation had so many shareholders that the requirement posed an insurmountable obstacle.

Recovery, Settlement, and Fees

The derivative plaintiff is pursuing the corporation's cause of action. Therefore, any judgment recovered usually goes into the corporate treasury to protect its financial condition and to protect its creditors. Plaintiff shareholders' benefit will be indirect—perhaps in the form of higher dividends—though a few courts have allowed derivative judgments to be paid directly to shareholders on a pro-rata basis.

---

[31] Neither MBCA §49 nor RMBCA §7.40 imposes such a requirement.

[32] *Pupecki* v. *James Madison Corp.*, 376 Mass. 212, 382 N.E.2d 1030 (1978).

[33] For example, *Zimmerman* v. *Bell*, 585 F.Supp. 513 (D. Md. 1984) (Maryland law).

[34] For example, *Mayer* v. *Adams*, 37 Del. Ch. 298, 141 A.2d 458 (Sup. Ct. 1958) (cannot ratify). Compare *Claman* v. *Robertson*, 164 Ohio St. 61, 128 N.E.2d 429 (1955) (can ratify).

Studies show that the vast majority of derivative suits are settled. As noted earlier, to ensure that "strike suits" are not settled in a way that benefits only the plaintiff and plaintiff's attorneys, Rule 23.1 requires court approval of settlements following court-ordered notice to other shareholders.

Attorneys' fees are a matter of concern, because corporate derivative litigation can be extremely expensive. In hotly contested cases involving big corporations, attorneys' fees of a million dollars or more on each side of the suit are not unknown. The "American" rule, prevalent in this country, provides that—win, lose, or draw—each side in a lawsuit pays its own attorneys' fees. The courts have developed three exceptions to this general rule in derivative litigation.

First, a winning plaintiff's attorneys' fees can be paid out of the judgment secured for the corporation. Second, a winning defendant may recover costs and fees out of a security bond if the court finds the suit was filed "without reasonable cause." [35] Third, a winning defendant who is not reimbursed from such a bond may be indemnified by the corporation. Rules on indemnity are discussed in detail in Chapter 11.

Assessment

The derivative suit is a controversial device. Supporters believe that it is important to protect shareholder rights, and they stress its deterrent effect on insiders contemplating wrongdoing. Detractors believe that it is an inefficient device because courts and shareholders have no business second-guessing the decisions of management. [36]

Whatever the case, relatively few derivative suits are filed by shareholders of large publicly held corporations. [37] And when they are, the business judgment rule and the shareholder litigation committee, discussed in detail in Chapter 11, limit a plaintiff's chances for success. The derivative suit is relatively more important as a device to protect minority shareholders of close corporations.

SHAREHOLDERS IN THE CLOSE CORPORATION

Introduction

As noted in the *Pogostin* case, state corporation codes envision a system of indirect control by shareholders. Officers are to manage the company under the supervision and control of the directors. Shareholders simply elect and remove directors and approve or disapprove basic changes in corporate structure. Real control lies with the directors.

This statutory model arguably fits large public corporations, but nine out of every ten companies in the United States are owned and controlled by a single family.

---

[35] MBCA §49, RMBCA §7.40.

[36] See Note, "Shareholders' Derivative Suits and Shareholders' Welfare: An Evaluation and a Proposal," *Northwestern University Law Review*, Vol. 77 (1983), p. 856.

[37] T. Jones, "An Empirical Examination of the Incidence of Shareholder Derivative and Class Action Lawsuits," *Boston University Law Review*, Vol. 60 (1980), p. 306.

Many others are formed by friends or associates. In the close corporation, shareholders reasonably expect to take an active role in management. This expectation creates practices and problems not seen in publicly held corporations.

For example, a family of shareholders may wish to limit stock ownership to family members. They may attempt to attain this and other goals by use of share transfer restrictions (STRs) that limit the ability of a shareholder to sell stock to outsiders. Such restrictions serve no useful purpose in a public corporation.

Even if shareholders begin amicably, disagreements among the best of friends and closest of relatives frequently arise in business contexts.[38] As we saw in the chapters on partnerships, such disagreements can lead to bitter battles for control. A majority shareholder or group of shareholders may resort to any number of devices to gain or maintain control that would not be relevant in the public corporation. These devices might include shareholder agreements, irrevocable proxies, and voting trusts.

Publicly held corporations are seldom deadlocked by director or shareholder disagreements. But close corporations frequently have equal numbers of shareholders or directors on opposite sides of a dispute, leaving the corporate ship rudderless. Should dissolution be an option for a deadlocked corporation? Should it be an option for a minority shareholder being abused by the majority in a close corporation but having no market for his shares?

Matters such as STRs, shareholder control devices, and corporate deadlocks—and the legal complications they present—are the subject of the rest of this chapter. Discussion of the evolution of legal rules will show that the courts and legislators have slowly adjusted to the reality that close corporations are functionally more like partnerships than they are like the public corporations for which traditional state corporate codes were written.

While there is no precise definition of the term "close corporation," it implies (1) a small number of shareholders, (2) with no ready market for their shares, and (3) substantial shareholder participation in management.[39]

Share Transfer Restrictions

Corporate law originally favored free transferability of shares consistent with full contract rights for shareholders. Over the years, however, the courts have come to recognize the validity of reasonable STRs adopted for proper purposes. STRs are occasionally utilized in public corporations that might, for example, issue a class of stock to be owned only by employees. However, STRs are primarily a close corporation phenomenon.

Purposes

Proper purposes for STRs include (1) limiting ownership to a desired group such as family members (*delectus personae*), (2) maintaining the existing pattern of control, (3) maintaining Subchapters S status (no more than 35 shareholders allowed),

---

[38] See P. Rosenblatt, "Family, Inc.," *Psychology Today*, Vol. 19 (July 1985), p. 54.

[39] *Donahue* v. *Rodd Electrotype Co.*, 367 Mass. 578, 328 N.E.2d 505 (1975).

(4) estate planning by avoiding locking heirs into an inappropriate investment or keeping out heirs who know nothing of the business, (5) preventing a shareholder or group of shareholders from gaining control, and (6) solving the problem of a lack of a market for shares.

Types of Restrictions

STRs can take a number of forms, but three types predominate: (1) consent restrictions, (2) first options, and (3) buy-sell agreements. Whatever form they take, they must be "reasonable" to be enforceable. Factors considered by courts include (1) the size of the corporation, (2) the stringency and time frame of the restriction, (3) the purpose served, (4) the possibility of injury by hostile shareholders, and (5) the likelihood of a benefit to the corporation as a whole.

Consent Restrictions. A consent restriction exists, for example, where a corporation's bylaws stipulate that no shareholder can sell any shares without the consent of all other shareholders or the board of directors. Although consent restrictions have been enforced in some jurisdictions, the more they act as an absolute bar to alienability, the more likely they are to be invalidated by the courts. Therefore, consent-type restrictions are not favored.

First Options. A first-option provision might stipulate that before a shareholder can sell his or her shares to an outsider, he or she must offer to sell the shares to the existing shareholders and/or to the corporation. The first option can be exercised by meeting the price offered by outsiders.

Buy-Sell Agreements. A third variety of STR is the buy-sell agreement. Such an agreement might provide that upon the death of any shareholder, the corporation will buy his or her shares at a specified price. This device prevents the decedent's heirs from being trapped in an investment that no longer is appropriate, if, for example, the corporation paid no dividends and all the decedent's income had come from wages. The heirs receive a lump sum or periodic cash payments.

Buy-sell agreements for estate planning purposes are frequently funded by insurance policies. They must be carefully structured to minimize tax consequences.

Such agreements can serve other purposes, including deadlock-breaking devices. In a buy-sell agreement, two equal shareholders who have deadlocked on critical corporate matters could, for example, make sealed bids for each other's shares. The high bidder then owns the corporation.

An important concern in most buy-sell and many first-option agreements is the setting of the purchase price. Various agreements have set the price with reference to (1) book value; (2) par value; (3) market price, if any; (4) capital-to-earnings ratio; (5) expert appraisals; and (6) combinations of these and other factors. An established price should be recalculated periodically to take into account changed circumstances.

If the shareholders agree on a purchase price, courts are likely to enforce the buy-sell agreement even though at the time of exercise, it appears to bear little relation to the shares' true value. For example, in *In re Mathes*,[40] the court enforced an agreement to buy a deceased shareholder's shares at one dollar each, even though evidence showed the shares were worth 50 times that much when the agreement was made and perhaps 1,000 times as much when suit was filed.

The discussion of buy-sell agreements in the partnership chapters is quite relevant here.

Conspicuousness

The MBCA and RMBCA are not particularly helpful in providing guidance for drafting an enforceable STR. Section 54(2) does state that the articles of incorporation may contain provisions "including restrictions on the transfer of shares" that are not inconsistent with the law. RMBCA §6.27 is more liberal in authorizing STRs than is the MBCA. STR provisions should also appear in the bylaws and, for purposes of enforceability against third parties, on the shares themselves.

Uniform Commercial Code §8–204 provides that an STR is not binding on a third person *without actual knowledge* of it unless the restriction appears conspicuously on the stock certificate (or, if the corporation has converted to certificateless stock, a notation is contained in the first transaction statement sent to the person). A simple line of print appearing on the face of a share of stock that refers the holder to restrictions printed on the back side has been held not to be sufficiently conspicuous.[41]

Shareholder Control Devices

Introduction

Absent special devices, a majority shareholder can easily dominate a corporation under a state corporate code. Assume that a three-owner corporation is formed, with A owning 55% of the shares, B owning 25%, and C owning 20%. If things start amicably, A, B, and C will likely elect themselves to the board of directors. But if A has a disagreement with B and C, they will rapidly learn how tenuous their position is. Under most corporate codes, A could quickly call a shareholders' meeting and remove B and C without cause, or increase the size of the board and pack it with his relatives, or reduce the size of the board to just one.

This reality led one person, when asked the value of the shares of his corporation to state, "There are 51 shares that are worth $250,000. There are 49 shares that are not worth a _____."

Shareholders, in consultation with attorneys, can utilize special control devices that can help to protect minorities from abuse and accomplish numerous other purposes. The following is an excerpt from a landmark article on the subject.

---

[40] 410 Pa. 361, 189 A.2d 586 (1963).

[41] *Ling and Co. v. Trinity Savings & Loan Ass'n*, 482 S.W.2d 841 (Tex. 1972).

CONTROL DISTRIBUTION DEVICES *

F. Hodge O'Neal
1969 Illinois Law Forum 48

I. Introduction

This Article will discuss the various devices which may be utilized in allocating control and management powers in a close corporation. Specifically, it will analyze the following devices and techniques: (1) classification of stock and allocation of shares of the various classes among the shareholders; (2) class voting for directors; (3) charter or by-law provisions requiring unanimity or high percentage votes for shareholder or director action; (4) miscellaneous special charter or by-law clauses affecting management; (5) voting agreements and other agreements among shareholders; (6) voting trusts; (7) irrevocable proxies; (8) holding companies; and (9) management contracts. . . .

II. Classification of Stock

A useful technique in distributing control is to create two or more classes of shares and carefully allocate shares of the various classes among the participants in the close corporation. Provision can be made in the charter for several classes of shares with different voting power, rights to dividends, rights on liquidation and other qualities. . . . By varying the voting powers, dividend rights, and qualities of the several classes of stock, and by using different combinations in allocating shares of the various classes, almost any desired control arrangement can be achieved. . . .

III. Class Voting for Directors

One of the best techniques for assuring that all or several of the participants in a close corporation will be represented on the board of directors is to create two or more classes of shares and provide that each class shall elect a specified number or a stated percentage of the directors. Thus, class A common stock might be given the power to elect three directors and class B common stock the power to elect two. . . .

IV. Charter or By-law Clauses Requiring High Votes

Businessmen acquiring minority interests in close corporations often seek protection against the broad powers vested in shareholders and directors to determine corporate policies and to make decisions by simple majority vote. In effect, they want the power to veto some or all corporate decisions. One of the most effective ways to provide this veto is by charter or by-law provisions requiring unanimity or concurrence of a high percentage of voting units for shareholder or director action. . . .

Although high vote provisions are very useful in fashioning management patterns for closely held corporations, the limitations and disadvantages of such provisions must not be overlooked. They give a veto and no more. . . . Secondly, they deprive the corporation of the flexibility it may need to adjust to unexpected business situations. . . . Finally, high vote requirements may place one or two shareholders in a position to extort unfair concessions from the other shareholders as a condition to approving beneficial corporate action. . . .

---

* Copyright 1969 by the Board of Trustees of the University of Illinois. Reprinted with permission.

V. Special Charter or By-law Clauses Affecting Control

Special charter or by-law clauses are often very useful in tailoring the control pattern of a corporation. Among the clauses which may be employed are those which: (1) give shareholders the power to remove directors at any time without cause; (2) abolish the board of directors or sharply restrict the board's powers (in jurisdictions where this is permissible); (3) strengthen the shareholders' rights to inspect books and records; (4) strengthen, define, or abolish pre-emptive rights; (5) provide for arbitration or other procedures for settling disputes or resolving deadlocks; (6) authorize directors to fix their own compensation; (7) require an increase in dividends when compensation of executives is increased. . . .

VI. Voting Agreements and Other Shareholder Contracts

. . .

VII. Voting Trusts

. . .

VIII. Irrevocable Proxies

The parties to a shareholders' agreement, instead of merely binding themselves to vote their shares as a unit or in accordance with a predetermined plan, sometimes relinquish their power to vote their own shares and confer that power, in the form of an irrevocable proxy, upon one or more of their number or upon some person not a party to the agreement. Even though a shareholders' agreement does not expressly provide for an irrevocable proxy, such a proxy may be inferred from the content and purposes of the agreement. A proxy may be advantageous in a voting agreement to facilitate implementation of the agreement and to avoid the possibility that a suit for specific performance, with the attendant uncertainties and delays, will be necessary to put into effect decisions reached under the agreement. . . .

IX. Holding Companies

A holding company can be used instead of a shareholders' voting agreement or a voting trust to consolidate the voting power of a group of majority shareholders. The holders of a majority of the voting shares in company A can create another corporation, company B, and transfer their shares to it. Thereafter the shares in company B will be voted as a unit pursuant to direction from B's board of directors. . . .

X. Management Contracts

To be distinguished from control agreements among some or all of the shareholders are agreements executed by the corporation itself under which its management or the control over certain aspects of its operations are entrusted to a creditor or to some other individual or corporation. . . .

A management contract may be subject to attack on two grounds: (1) the contract violates a statute which provides that the affairs of a corporation shall be managed by its board of directors, and (2) the directors of a corporation, in view of their limited term of office, do not have the capacity to enter into long-term contracts which would bind future boards for long or indefinite periods on basic policy or management matters.

Taking the decisions as a whole, the validity of a contract by which a corporation vests control of its affairs in another person or company seems to depend upon the number and importance of the powers that are delegated, the length of time for which the powers are to be held, and perhaps the purpose of the contract or the situation out of which it arose. . . .

Discussion of the voting agreement and voting trust was omitted from this excerpt so that they may be given special attention. They are the most widely used and most controversial of the devices.

Shareholders' Agreements

Shareholder agreements concerning how shareholders will vote or otherwise allocate control are a frequent phenomenon in the close corporation. A few or all shareholders may be parties. The agreements frequently address how the shareholders will vote, who will be officers and directors, what dividend policy should be, and similar matters. Frequently minority shareholders will band together through a shareholder agreement to form a controlling majority faction.

There have been questions as to the legality of shareholder agreements. A leading view came from a line of New York cases [42] which upheld shareholder agreements that merely addressed how the parties would act as shareholders.[43] But if the agreement addressed how they would act as directors, problems arose because of the concept that directors were to have direct control of the corporation. If the agreement only slightly impinged on directors' discretion and did not injure creditors or the public, it would likely be enforced, especially if *all* shareholders were parties. On the other hand, if the agreement severely impinged on directorial discretion, the courts would not enforce it even if all shareholders were parties to it.

These traditional distinctions have slowly diminished in importance, but have not faded completely. Still many courts have approved shareholder agreements that did substantially impinge directors' discretion, including agreements to employ particular persons, to pay dividends in a certain manner, and even to give minority shareholders a veto over corporate actions. Many courts presume validity where *all* shareholders are parties. Clearly, the old views are on the way out, but courts will still refuse to enforce such agreements when the rights of nonconsenting shareholders are violated.[44]

Much of judicial acceptance of shareholder agreements has come through courts' realization that close corporations are functionally similar to partnerships and therefore should not be required to adhere strictly to corporate code provisions more appropriately applied to large public corporations.

A landmark case in this area is *Galler* v. *Galler.*

---

[42] For example, *McQuade* v. *Stoneham*, 263 N.Y. 323, 189 N.E. 234 (1934); *Clark* v. *Dodge*, 269 N.Y. 410, 199 N.E. 641 (1936).

[43] MBCA §34 validates shareholders' agreements concerning how they vote their shares.

[44] Annotation, "Validity of Stockholders' Agreements Allegedly Infringing on Directors' Management Powers—Modern Cases," 15 A.L.R. 4th 1078 (1982).

GALLER v. GALLER

32 Ill. 2d 16, 203 N.E.2d 577 (1964)

In 1924, Benjamin and Isadore Galler incorporated a wholesale drug business, each owning one-half of 220 outstanding shares. In 1945 each contracted to sell 6 shares to an employee, Rosenberg, who was still making payments at the time this suit was filed. In March 1954, Benjamin and Isadore decided to enter into an agreement for the financial protection of their immediate families and to assure their families, after the death of either brother, of equal control. While the agreement was being prepared, Benjamin had a heart attack and his health remained very poor until the agreement was signed in July 1955. Before Benjamin died in 1957, defendants Isadore Galler, his wife Rose, and son Aaron (now president) decided not to abide by the July 1955 agreement. However, they did not inform Benjamin or his wife Emma, the plaintiff.

The agreement recited that Benjamin and Isadore wished to provide income for the support of their immediate families. It included provisions (a) that the by-laws be amended for a board of four directors; (b) that the shareholders would cast their votes for Benjamin, Isadore, Emma, and Rose; (c) that in the event of the death of either brother, his spouse would nominate a replacement director; and (d) that annual dividends of $50,000 payable out of accumulated earned surplus in excess of $500,000 would be paid.

When defendants refused to honor the agreement, Emma filed this suit. During the litigation, defendants bought Rosenberg's 12 shares. Emma also seeks the right to claim 6 of those. The Appellate Court found the agreement void because of its undue duration, stated purpose, *and substantial disregard of the state's corporate code. Plaintiff appealed.*

UNDERWOOD, JUSTICE:

It should be emphasized that we deal here with a so-called close corporation. For our purposes, a close corporation is one in which the stock is held in a few hands, or in a few families; and wherein it is not at all, or only rarely, dealt in by buying or selling. Moreover, it should be recognized that shareholder agreements similar to that in question here are often, as a practical consideration, quite necessary for the protection of those financially interested in the close corporation. While the shareholder of a public issue corporation may readily sell his shares on the open market should management fail to use, in his opinion, sound business judgment, his counterpart of the close corporation often has a large total of his entire capital invested in the business and has no ready market for his shares should he desire to sell. He feels, understandably, that he is more than a mere investor and that his voice should be heard concerning all corporate activity. Without a shareholder agreement, specifically enforceable by the courts, insuring him a modicum of control, a large minority shareholder might find himself at the mercy of an oppressive or unknowledgeable majority. Moreover, as in the case at bar, the shareholders of a close corporation are often also the directors and officers thereof. With substantial shareholding interests abiding in each member of the board of directors, it is often quite impossible to secure, as in the large public issue corporation, independent board judgment free from personal motivations concerning corporate policy. For these and other reasons too voluminous to enumerate here, often the only sound basis for protection is afforded by a lengthy, detailed shareholder agreement securing the rights and obligations of all concerned.

There has been a definite, albeit inarticulate, trend toward eventual judicial treatment of the close corporation as *sui generis*. Several shareholder-director agreements that have technically "violated" the letter of the Business Corporation Act have nevertheless been upheld in the light of the existing practical circumstances, that is, no apparent public injury, the absence of a complaining minority interest, and no apparent prejudice to creditors. However, we have thus far not attempted to limit these decisions as applicable only to close corporations and have seemingly implied that general considerations regarding judicial supervision of all corporate behavior apply.

It would admittedly facilitate judicial supervision of corporate behavior if a strict adherence to the provisions of the Business Corporation Act were required in all cases without regard to the practical exigencies peculiar to the close corporation. However, courts have long ago quite realistically, we feel, relaxed their attitudes concerning statutory compliance when dealing with close corporate behavior, permitting "slight deviation" from corporate "norms" to give legal efficacy to common business practice. This attitude is illustrated by the following language in *Clark* v. *Dodge* 269 N.Y. 410, 199 N.E.641: "Public policy, the intention of the Legislature, detriment to the corporation, are phrases which in this connection [the court was discussing a shareholder-director agreement whereby the directors pledged themselves to vote for certain people as officers of the corporation] mean little. Possible harm to bona fide purchasers of stock or to creditors or to stockholding minorities have more substance; but

such harms are absent in many instances. If the enforcement of a particular contract damages nobody—not even, in any perceptible degree, the public—one sees no reason for holding it illegal, even though it impinges slightly upon the broad provisions of [the relevant statute providing that the business of a corporation shall be managed by its board of directors]."

Again, "As the parties to the action are the complete owners of the corporation, there is no reason why the exercise of the power and discretion of the directors cannot be controlled by valid agreement between themselves, provided that the interests of creditors are not affected."

One article concludes with the following:

New needs compel fresh formulation of corporate "norms." There is no reason why mature men should not be able to adapt the statutory form to the structure they want, so long as they do not endanger other stockholders, creditors, or the public, or violate a clearly mandatory provision of the corporation laws. In a typical close corporation the stockholders' agreement is usually the result of careful deliberation among all initial investors. In the large public-issue corporation, on the other hand, the "agreement" represented by the corporate charter is not consciously agreed to by the investors; they have no voice in its formulation, and very few ever read the certificate of incorporation. Preservation of the corporate norms may therefore be necessary for the protection of the public investors. Hornstein, "Stockholders' Agreements in the Closely Held Corporation," 59 Yale L. Journal, 1040, 1056.

Perhaps, as has been vociferously advanced, a separate comprehensive statutory scheme governing the close corporation would best serve here.

At any rate, however, the courts can no longer fail to expressly distinguish between the close and public-issue corporation when confronted with problems relating to either. What we do here is to illuminate this problem—before the bench, corporate bar, and the legislature, in the context of a particular fact situation. To do less would be to shirk our responsibility; to do more would, perhaps, be to invade the province of the legislative branch.

We now, in the light of the foregoing, turn to specific provisions of the 1955 agreement.

Since the question as to the duration of the agreement is a principal source of controversy, we shall consider it first. The parties provided no specific termination date, and while the agreement concludes with a paragraph that its terms "shall be binding upon and shall inure to the benefits of" the legal representatives, heirs, and assigns of the parties, this clause is, we believe, intended to be operative only as long as one of the parties is living. It further provides that it shall be so construed as to carry out its purposes, and we believe these must be determined from a consideration of the agreement as a whole. Thus viewed, a fair construction is that its purposes were accomplished at the death of the survivor of the parties. While these life spans are not precisely ascertainable, and the Appellate Court noted Emma Galler's life expectancy at her husband's death was 26.9 years, we are aware of no statutory or public policy provision against stockholders' agreements which would invalidate this agreement on that ground. While defendants argue that the public policy evinced by the legislative restrictions upon the duration of voting trust agreements should be applied here, this agreement is not a voting trust, but is a straight contractual voting control agreement which does not divorce voting rights from stock ownership.

The clause that provides for the election of certain persons to specified offices for a period of years likewise does not require invalidation. In *Kantzer* v. *Bensinger*, 214 Ill. 589, 73 N.E. 874, this court upheld an agreement entered into by all the stockholders providing that certain parties would be elected to the offices of the corporation for a fixed period.

We turn next to a consideration of the effect of the stated purpose of the agreement upon its validity. The pertinent provision is: "The said Benjamin A. Galler and Isadore A. Galler desire to provide income for the support and maintenance of their immediate families." Obviously, there is no evil inherent in a contract entered into for the reason that the persons originating the terms desired to so arrange their property as to provide postdeath support for those dependent upon them. Nor does the fact that the subject property is corporate stock alter the situation so long as there exists no detriment to minority stock interests, creditors, or other public injury. It is, however, contended by defendants that the methods provided by the agreement for implementation of the stated purpose are, as a whole, violative of the Business Corporation Act to such an extent as to render it void *in toto*.

The terms of the dividend agreement require a minimum annual dividend of $50,000, but this duty is limited by the subsequent provision that it shall be operative only so long as an earned surplus of $500,000 is maintained. It may be noted that in 1958, the year prior to commencement of this litigation, the corporation's net earnings after taxes amounted to $202,759 while its earned surplus was $1,543,270, and this was increased in 1958 to $1,680,079 while earnings were $172,964. The minimum earned surplus requirement is designed for the protection of the corporation and its creditors, and we take no exception to the contractual dividend requirements as thus restricted.

The salary continuation agreement is a common feature, in one form or another, of corporate executive employment. It requires that the widow should receive a total benefit, payable monthly over a five-year period, aggregating twice the amount paid her deceased husband in one year. This requirement was likewise limited for the protection of the corporation by being contingent upon the payments being income tax–deductible by the corporation. The charge made in those cases which have considered the validity of payments to the widow of an officer and shareholder in a corporation is that a gift of its property by a noncharitable corporation is in violation of the rights of its shareholders and *ultra vires*. Since there are no shareholders here other than the parties to the contract, this objection is not here applicable, and its effect, as limited, upon the corporation is not so prejudicial as to require its invalidation.

We hold defendants must account for all monies received by them from the corporation since September 25, 1956, in excess of that theretofore authorized.

Affirmed in part and reversed in part, and remanded with directions.

The Illinois legislature, along with those of several other jurisdictions, took the advice of the *Galler* court by enacting special close corporation legislation. We shall examine those in more detail presently. Such decisions and statutes have continued a trend toward acceptance of what might be called the "incorporated partnership."

Indicative of the continuation of this trend is the decision in *Zion* v. *Kurtz*,[45] a New York Court of Appeals case also involving a shareholder agreement. Kurtz was sole shareholder of a corporation (known as Group) that wished to acquire another corporation. Because Kurtz did not have sufficient assets to make the acquisition, he turned to Zion who provided them via a loan agreement and guarantee. Zion became a shareholder of Group. Kurtz, Zion, and Group all agreed that Group would not "engage in any business or activities of any kind, directly or indirectly," other than the contemplated acquisition. However, Group did engage in other activities that were approved by its board over the objection of Zion that the shareholders' agreement was being violated.

The court enforced the agreement even though the applicable Delaware statute allowing close corporations to have such agreements was not complied with. Although Group was incorporated as a regular corporation rather than a special close corporation and although the agreement was not incorporated into its certificate as the law required, the court held that it could order Kurtz to file the paperwork necessary to comply with the law and carry out the agreement.

Voting Trusts

A voting trust is a very formal type of shareholder agreement. In a voting trust, shareholders agree to transfer legal title to their shares to a trustee or trustees who will vote those shares for a specified period of time. The trustees become the legal owners of the shares; the shareholders receive voting trust certificates evidencing their beneficial ownership and, hence, their entitlement to dividend payments.

The key features of a voting trust are (1) formal separation of voting rights

---

[45] 50 N.Y. 2d 92, 428 N.Y.S.2d 199, 405 N.E.2d 681 (1980).

from beneficial ownership, (2) irrevocability for a stated period of time, and (3) for the primary purpose of exercising control over the corporation.[46]

Voting trusts were even more slowly accepted than were voting agreements. The same thinking that for many years barred issuance of shares without voting rights also opposed divorcing voting rights from shares that had them. Over the years, however, most jurisdictions have passed statutes that specifically authorized voting trusts. The courts have required such trusts to hew closely to statutory requirements.

Typical of such statutes is MBCA §34. Among other provisions, the MBCA limits the term of a voting trust to ten years or less, requires that it be in writing, and requires that a copy of the agreement be on file at the corporation's registered office and open to inspection by other shareholders.[47]

Voting trusts are not used as much in close corporations as they once were because the same objectives may be accomplished through simpler means. Not only is the voting trust agreement formal, cumbersome, and limited in time frame, but it may also cost shareholders some of their usual rights. In some jurisdictions, shareholders who have assigned their voting rights (becoming mere beneficial owners possessing voting trust certificates) may lose the right to file derivative actions or to inspect corporate records. Some jurisdictions have acted to protect these rights.

Voting trusts are frequently used by creditors, especially in corporate reorganizations, to ensure control by a management in which the creditors have confidence. Perhaps the most famous voting trust was used by creditors who loaned billionaire-recluse Howard Hughes the funds to buy airplanes for his airline, TWA. Because the creditors disapproved of Hughes's management, they conditioned the loan on Hughes's putting his shares in a voting trust. The trustees, appointed by the creditors, substantially changed the TWA management team. Don't feel too sorry for Hughes who soon thereafter sold his interest in TWA for more than $500 million.

Dissolution

A problem peculiar to close corporations is the deadlock. Disagreements between equal shareholders or equal numbers of directors can stalemate a corporation. Escalation of these disputes into physical violence is not unknown.[48] One or more of the parties to such a dispute may wish to dissolve the corporation as a means of breaking the deadlock.

Dissolution may also be the preferred remedy for a minority shareholder in a close corporation who feels abused by the majority. Perhaps the corporation for tax reasons has never paid dividends, and the minority shareholder has recently been removed as an officer, thus ending the sole source of income from the corporation.

---

[46] *Lehrman* v. *Cohen*, 222 A.2d 800 (Del. 1966).

[47] RMBCA §7.30 allows the parties to a voting trust to extend its life for additional terms of not more than ten years each. A written agreement and the trustee's consent are needed.

[48] For example, *Nashville Packet Co.* v. *Neville*, 144 Tenn. 698, 235 S.W. 64 (1921).

Less Drastic Measures

Not every deadlock need lead to dissolution. Solutions for deadlock fall into judicial and nonjudicial categories. It is hoped that the parties have by agreement provided for a means of resolution, such as a buy-sell agreement, appointment of an arbitrator, or appointment of a provisional director. The parties may have even agreed that any shareholder shall have the right to dissolve the corporation under specified circumstances, such as deadlock.

If the shareholders have not planned ahead, deadlock will likely result in resort to the courts. Deadlocked or dissenting factions have sought such remedies as (1) appointment of a receiver, (2) injunctions to restrain directors from acting on the corporation's behalf or paying dividends, (3) appointment of a statutory custodian, (4) declaratory judgment regarding the respective rights of the stockholders and directors, (5) writ of mandamus to compel cooperation, and (6) provisions for an accounting of assets. Notwithstanding a deadlock, courts are reluctant to grant such remedies absent "an 'urgent necessity' with 'present peril' to the stockholders' interests consisting of a suspension of business or a threatened depreciation of corporate assets." [49]

Court-Ordered Dissolution

If judicial and nonjudicial methods short of dissolution do not break the deadlock or produce the desired result, one party or faction may seek court-ordered dissolution. Traditionally, courts have been reluctant to order dissolution solely on grounds of deadlock, especially if the corporation was profitable. In one famous case,[50] the court refused dissolution even though a sister (half-owner) refused to sign the paychecks of her brother (other half-owner) who was operating the business. The court stressed that despite the bitter personal dispute between the two half-owners, the corporation's business was flourishing.

Exceptions to the general reluctance to dissolve have arisen in situations where the deadlock resulted in a spreading corporate paralysis.[51] In *Kolbaum* v. *K & K Chevrolet, Inc.*,[52] for example, the court ordered dissolution where a disagreement resulted in the owners running two separate operations under the same roof.

As for the minority shareholder trapped in the close corporation, again the courts are reluctant to grant dissolution to save the shareholder from an unprofitable investment. Nonetheless, dissolution has been ordered in some cases involving substantial oppression by majority factions.[53]

Whether dissolution is sought to end a deadlock or to end oppression by a majority, it is a matter of court discretion. That discretion derives from laws similar to MBCA §97, which gives a court power to liquidate a corporation upon the application

---

[49] Annotation, 34 A.L.R. 4th 13 (1983).

[50] *In re Radom & Neidorff, Inc.*, 307 N.Y. 1, 119 N.E.2d 563 (1954).

[51] Annotation, 83 A.L.R. 3d 458 (1978).

[52] 196 Neb. 555, 244 N.W.2d 173 (1976).

[53] *E.G.*, *Stumpf* v. *C. E. Stumpf & Sons, Inc.*, 120 Cal. Rptr. 671 (Cal. App. 1975).

of a shareholder when it is shown that (1) corporate management is deadlocked to the irreparable injury of the shareholders; (2) those in control of the corporation are acting illegally, oppressively, or fraudulently; (3) the shareholders are deadlocked in voting power and have failed for at least two consecutive annual meeting dates to elect successors to directors; or (4) the corporation's assets are being wasted.

The MBCA also has provision for involuntary dissolution upon the application of creditors [54] and for voluntary dissolution.[55]

Fiduciary Duty

Cases such as *Galler* v. *Galler* and *Zion* v. *Kurtz* illustrate the judicial trend toward treating close corporations as incorporated partnerships. A small group of entrepreneurs may envision all members actively involved in the business as partners, but may choose the corporate form for its tax treatment and limited liability. A salient feature of partnerships is, of course, the fiduciary duty that partners owe one another. As courts have treated close corporations more like partnerships, they have inevitably extended fiduciary duties beyond directors and officers to shareholders, especially those exercising control or functioning directly in corporate affairs. The following opinion is illustrative, though few cases have gone so far. The opinion should be contrasted with that of *Zidell* v. *Zidell* in the previous chapter.

ORCHARD v. COVELLI

590 F.Supp. 1548 (W.D.Pa. 1984)

Plaintiff Orchard, his brother-in-law, defendant Covelli, and a group of investors (the Chicago group) purchased three McDonald's restaurant franchises in Erie, Pennsylvania, in 1964. Three more franchises were ultimately added, each incorporated separately. By 1975, Covelli was president of the six corporations, drawing a salary of $96,000. Orchard was vice-president of each, receiving a $62,400 salary. The Chicago group owned 45% of each corporation, Covelli owned 40%, and Orchard 15%.

In 1975, McDonald's became interested in

opening a restaurant on Buffalo Road in Erie. Covelli secured the franchise. Orchard again owned 15%, but unknown to him, Covelli had not informed the Chicago group about this deal. Covelli owned 85% of the restaurant. Because Buffalo Road was within the franchise territory of the previous Erie corporations, Covelli and Orchard had to sign a waiver on behalf of those corporations, which they did, again without the knowledge of the Chicago group.

In May 1977, Covelli bought out the Chicago group through a stock redemption plan, raising

---

[54] MBCA §97 (b).

[55] MBCA §§82–92. The RMBCA has dissolution provisions that generally follow the MBCA for both voluntary and court-ordered dissolutions. RMBCA §§14.01–14.33.

his holdings in the six Erie corporations to 73% and Orchard's to 27%. Orchard was by then on bad terms with Covelli and asked to be bought out on the same terms. Covelli offered to do so, but with no compensation for the Buffalo Road restaurant. When Orchard balked, Covelli removed Orchard as an officer and director of the six corporations, replacing him with his own son.

Soon thereafter, franchises for three of the Erie corporations' restaurants expired. Covelli renewed them in his name alone, not exercising the corporations' rights of renewal. The next year, McDonald's learned from Covelli's attorney, Milligan, that Orchard had acquired a franchise in a competing restaurant chain and was therefore in violation of a franchise covenant not to compete. Thereafter, McDonald's would deal only with Covelli. Covelli bought the assets of the corporations holding the expired franchise rights at book value, with the minority interest held by Orchard either dissenting or abstaining from approval of the transactions.

Orchard then filed this suit against Covelli, charging him with (a) misappropriation of corporate assets and opportunities; (b) breach of an oral contract to give Orchard a 50% interest in all the franchises; (c) breach of an oral contract to employ Covelli; and (d) breach of fiduciary duty to minority shareholders.

The trial court denied the first claim because McDonald's had the right and apparently preferred to contract with Covelli alone. Clear proof of the terms of the two alleged oral agreements was missing; those claims were dismissed also. Regarding the claim of breach of fiduciary duty, the court had the following to say.

WEBER, DISTRICT JUDGE:

Tolstoi once wrote that "happy families are all alike; every unhappy family is unhappy in its own way." We sense that Tolstoi was less

familiar with the American modern law of closely held corporations from which we note an alarming similarity in the demise of such entities where the survival of a business association is so perilously tied to the continuing vitality of intimate personal relationships. Many lawsuits arising from disputes among shareholders in closely held corporations are characterized by the inability to separate the business and personal aspects of their relationship. We find ourselves struck by the unavailability or inadequacy of identifiable legal remedies to aid minority shareholders equipped with unfettered power over the management of the close corporation. We bind ourselves to a careful balance of equities in fashioning appropriate relief under the present circumstances.

Courts have consistently recognized that the duty of loyalty owed to the corporation by the controlling interest holders includes a duty of loyalty and fairness to minority shareholders— *David J. Greene and Co.* v. *Dunhill International, Inc.*, 249 A.2d 427 (Del. Ch. 1968). Where a majority shareholder stands to benefit from his decision as a controlling stockholder, the law requires that the majority's action be "intrinsically fair" to the minority interest. A policy of corporate governance which has as its objective the denial of benefits to the minority interest runs afoul of this fairness standard and calls to question the majority's fulfillment of its fiduciary duty to the other shareholders.

Courts have found an abuse of the corporate process in the context of mergers designed to discount or remove the minority interest— *Singer* v. *Magnavox*, 380 A.2d 969 (Del. 1977). The corporate process may not be used legitimately to remove the participation of minority shareholders. Self-dealing is present when the minority shareholder is denied the right to participate in the benefits of the corporation—*Harriman* v. *E. I. Dupont de Nemours & Co.*, 411 F.Supp. 133 (D. Del. 1975). Adherence by the majority interest to a fiduciary duty of strict fairness is particularly critical in the context of the closely held corporation.

The acute vulnerability of minority shareholders in the closely held corporation is well recognized. It stems principally from two factors. Because of its controlling interest, the majority is able to dictate to the minority the manner in which the corporation shall be run. In addition, shares in close corporations are not publicly traded, and a fair market for these shares is seldom available. In contrast, a partner can act to dissolve a partnership and a shareholder in a large public-issue corporation can sell his stock on the market if he is dissatisfied with the way things are run. Dissension within the close corporation tends to make the minority interest even more unattractive to a prospective purchaser. As a consequence, a shareholder challenging the majority in a close corporation finds himself on the horns of a dilemma; he can neither profitably leave nor safely stay with the corporation. In reality, the only prospective buyer turns out to be the majority shareholder. Such is the case here.

Frequently, closed corporations originate in the context of relationships personal in nature, often undertaken by family members or friends. It is ironic that these enterprises become a most frequent setting for the exploitation of minority shareholders when the personal relationship has gone sour. See, for example, *Thrasher* v. *Thrasher*, 103 Cal. Rptr. 618 (Cal. App. 1972) (marital dispute led to withholding of dividends); *Blackman* v. *Las Vegas-Tonopah-Reno Stage Line, Inc.*, 476 P.2d 964 (Nev. 1970) (interfamily dispute sparked wrongful withdrawal and use of family corporation's funds by its officers and directors).

Because of these factors, the law imposes a fiduciary duty upon the majority requiring it to act with the utmost good faith and loyalty in transacting corporate affairs. We note from reported cases that it is a duty frequently honored in the breach.

It follows that any attempt to "squeeze out" a minority shareholder must be viewed as a breach of this fiduciary duty. The reasons for excluding an obstreperous shareholder may often appear compelling to the majority, and the conduct which eventually leads to a "squeeze-out" may not have been undertaken with such intent. Yet such conduct is injurious when the result is the exclusion of minority shareholders without adequate recompense, and it is particularly harmful when carried out with malevolence or indifference. The law recognizes a right to recovery under such circumstances.

Tactics employed against a minority shareholder to effect a squeeze-out can take on many forms, including generally oppressive conduct, the withholding of dividends, restricting or precluding employment in the corporation, paying excessive salaries to majority stockholders, withholding information relating to the operation of the corporation, appropriation of corporate assets, denying dissenting shareholders appraisal rights, failure to hold meetings, and excluding the minority from a meaningful role in the corporate decision making.

In the present case we find that the fiduciary duty owed the minority shareholders was all but ignored by the defendant Covelli. We note a systematic effort to exclude Orchard from any meaningful role in the corporation as well as an effort to deny him benefits therefrom.

[*As evidence for this conclusion, the court noted Covelli's insistence that Orchard forfeit compensation for the Buffalo Road store; Covelli's making known his intention to push Orchard into bankruptcy, remove him from any responsible position in the corporation, and deny him any benefit from the corporation; the subsequent termination of Orchard's positions as officer and director and his replacement with Covelli's son; and the fact that the corporations had not paid a dividend in five years.*]

Second, Covelli's refusal to compensate Orchard for his interest in the seventh restaurant is itself evidence of a breach of the majority shareholders' fiduciary duty. Covelli bought out the Chicago Group but failed to disclose to them the existence of the Buffalo Road Restaurant. A distinct, but related, and perhaps more damaging, harm occurred in the offer to Orchard where the existence of the restaurant was known but compensation for it was deliberately excluded from the buy-out price. After Orchard declined to accept the offer, it was withdrawn and the franchises of the three corporations eventually expired. In the end Orchard was left with an interest in the corporate shells. Covelli's bargaining power in the face of the eventual expiration of the franchises and his ability to forcefully command the buy-out price cannot be overlooked. It was a bargaining position he knowingly exploited to the detriment of the minority shareholder.

Covelli failed to use his best efforts to procure the continued life of the existing franchises in the names of the corporations.

The duty of utmost good faith and loyalty in the context of closely held corporations has been recognized by a number of courts confronting similar fact situations. In *Donahue* v. *Rodd Electrotype*, 367 Mass. 578, 328 N.E.2d 505 (1975), the president and majority shareholder of Rodd Electrotype, a closely held Massachusetts corporation, sold 45 shares of company stock valued at $36,000 to the corporation. Prior to the sale the majority shareholder, Harry Rodd, shifted his controlling interest and management responsibilities to his children. The transaction was negotiated by Rodd's son, the corporation's new president, and authorized by the Board of Directors consisting of Rodd's two sons and the family attorney. The purchase merely served to redistribute the Rodd family interest among family members. Plaintiff was the major nonfamily minority shareholder and refused to ratify the transaction. The sale was consummated and plaintiff then offered her shares to the corporation at the price paid to Harry Rodd. Plaintiff

had previously rejected lesser offers made over a period of several years. Upon refusal of the offer, plaintiff commenced an action in Massachusetts state court to have the purchase of Harry Rodd's shares rescinded. The complaint was dismissed and the intermediate state appellate court affirmed. The Massachusetts Supreme Judicial Court reversed.

The Supreme Court considered several aspects of the close corporation, those characterized by (a) existence of only a small number of shareholders, (b) the fact that no ready market is available to the corporate stock, (c) and the substantial majority stockholder participation in the management, direction, and operation of the corporation. It concluded that because a close corporation resembles a partnership with limited ownership and a high level of mutual dependency, because it requires close cooperation in management, and because the majority can control corporate decision making to the detriment of the minority, Courts must be prepared to fashion special relief in appropriate circumstances. As a result, Chief Justice Tauro concluded, "stockholders in a close corporation owe one another substantially the same fiduciary duty in the operation of the enterprise that partners owe to one another."

The judicial relief fashioned in *Donahue* reflected the Court's concern with the vulnerability of minority shareholders in close corporations particularly where the distribution of assets is involved. The Court concluded that the stock repurchase arrangement between Rodd Electrotype and its majority shareholder made it incumbent upon the majority to "cause the corporation to offer to each stockholder an equal opportunity to sell a ratable number of shares to the corporation at an identical price." The failure to do so, the Court determined, entitled the minority interest to relief either in the form of rescission of the primary sale or a requirement that the corporation purchase the minority interest at a price paid the majority.

We think this is a sound result, one which is applied easily to the present case.

The court ordered defendant to compensate plaintiff for his interest in the Buffalo Road store at a price consistent with the offer for the other six stores, but it refused plaintiff's request that the corporations be dissolved and liquidated.

Close Corporation Statutes

Approximately 15 state legislatures have recognized the need for special treatment of close corporations by enacting either separate chapters of their state corporate codes or sprinkling special provisions throughout them. These states include New York, California, Delaware, Illinois, and Texas.

On the heels of these enactments, the American Bar Association promulgated a Close Corporation Supplement to the MBCA that draws from many of the earlier state statutes.[56] Its stated purpose is to provide model legislation that will "incorporate the best available ideas on the special needs of close corporation shareholders and . . . at the same time provide basic statutory protection to the shareholders even in situations where they are not represented by experienced corporate counsel." The Close Corporation Supplement is based on four principles: "(1) the need for a flexible, useful statutory framework; (2) the desirability of having adequate basic protection against oppression of minority shareholders; (3) the desirability of codifying some of the customary practices used by experienced practitioners to achieve the objectives and expectations of investors in close corporations; and (4) the necessity of integrating the special close corporation statutory provisions in the supplement with all other statutory provisions governing business corporations."

Election

To be a close corporation governed by the Supplement, a corporation must make an affirmative election. But once the decision is made, execution is easy—all that need be done is place a statement in the articles of incorporation that the corporation is a "statutory close corporation." [57]

An existing corporation cannot make that election if it has more than 50 shareholders. However, a new corporation can make the election regardless of how many shareholders it has when formed, and an existing corporation that properly makes the election remains a close corporation even if at some later time it has more than 50 shareholders.

---

[56] "Proposed Statutory Close Corporation Supplement to the Model Business Corporation Act," *Business Lawyer* Vol. 37 (1981), p. 269. In 1983 the Supplement was revised stylistically but not substantively as part of the process leading to promulgation of the RMBCA.

[57] MBCA Close Corporation Supplement §3.

STRs

The Supplement assumes that STRs will be desired by most corporations. Therefore, in §4(a), it bars all transfers of shares. In §4(b) it lists numerous exemptions, including transfers among existing shareholders and to members of an existing shareholder's immediate family. If a shareholder wishes to make a nonexempt transfer, for example, by selling to a nonrelative outsider, §4(c) requires the shareholder to get a cash offer from the outsider and then give the corporation a chance to match it. In essence, §4 contains an automatic first-option STR. However, the shareholders have the option of eliminating this provision in the articles of incorporation.

Shareholder Participation

The Supplement is expressly intended to be a bridge between the MBCA and the UPA. One method of achieving this ''incorporated partnership'' status is contained in §10's provision that ''[a] statutory close corporation may operate without a board of directors if the articles of incorporation contain a statement to that effect.'' [58]

This provision is supplemented by §11, which recognizes the validity of unanimous shareholder agreements, even if they eliminate the board of directors or infringe on its discretion, and even if ''the effect of the agreement is to treat the corporation as if it were a partnership.'' Thus shareholders may agree as to dividend policy, as to employment of officers and others, and as to arbitration of deadlocks. They can even agree that management will be in the hands of a single shareholder or even a nonshareholder, and that any single shareholder will, like a partner, have the right to dissolve the corporation at will.

Dispute Resolution and Dissolution

To aid the heirs of a deceased shareholder, §14 of the Supplement allows them to require the corporation to purchase all the deceased's shares. The articles must so provide for this provision to be operable, and it may be expanded (e.g., to cover situations other than death) or restricted (e.g., to cover only some of the shareholders). If the purchase price is not set by agreement, courts may be required to set the fair value.

To avoid deadlocks, §15 states that the articles may provide that any shareholder, or a given percentage of shareholders, has the right to dissolve the corporation at will or upon the happening of a stated event. This provision is meant to circumvent the traditional reluctance of courts to dissolve corporations and to give close corporation shareholders the same rights as partners in this area.

Finally, §16 of the supplement allows courts to grant relief upon such grounds as illegal, oppressive, or fraudulent conduct or corporate deadlock. Fortunately, §16

---

[58] The RMBCA itself, not just its Close Corporation Supplement, provides in §8.01 (c) that a corporation with 50 or fewer shareholders may eliminate or limit the authority of a board of directors by describing in its articles who will perform some or all of the board's normal functions.

gives the courts a much wider array of relief measures than just liquidation. For example, to break deadlocks, the court is authorized to appoint a custodian to manage the business or to appoint a provisional director to cast a tie-breaking vote. A judge can also order the payment of dividends, remove a director or officer, or cancel provisions in the articles of incorporation.

QUESTIONS AND PROBLEMS

1. There are 1,000 outstanding voting shares of X Corporation stock that will be voted at next month's election of seven directors. Jill, a dissident shareholder, owns 354 shares. If she invokes the right to vote cumulatively in accordance with the provisions of X Corporation's articles of incorporation, how many directors will she probably be able to elect?

2. Plaintiffs, two former pilots of a now-bankrupt airline, demanded inspection of the corporate stock ledger of the airline's parent company, purportedly to communicate with its shareholders about the company's management, operations, and relationship with the airline subsidiary. Plaintiffs are also members of a union engaged in a labor dispute with the parent over the bankruptcy declaration. The union drafted the inspection demands, had plaintiffs sign them, and is paying for the litigation following the company's refusal to grant inspection. Is this demand for a proper purpose? Discuss. See *Carpenter* v. *Texas Air Corp.*, Vol. 17, no. 19 Sec. Reg. & L. Rep. (BNA) 861 (Del. Ch., 4/18/85).

3. A former shareholder of Pabst Brewing Co. sued its directors, alleging that they interfered with the bidding process in a tender offer battle for control of Pabst between Heileman and Jacobs. Plaintiff claims that the settlement agreement, which required payments to secure Jacobs's approval, discouraged additional offers and therefore constituted a waste of corporate assets in violation of the directors' fiduciary duties. May plaintiff properly maintain this action? Discuss. See *Shapiro* v. *Pabst Brewing Co.*, Vol. 17, no. 36 Sec. Reg. & L. Rep. (BNA) 1615 (Del. Ch. 7/30/85).

4. Plaintiff shareholders sued derivatively, alleging that directors of Bally Mfg. Corp. breached their fiduciary duty and wasted corporate assets in a scheme to enrich former president O'Donnell. Plaintiffs alleged, inter alia, that director defendants (a) caused Bally to buy O'Donnell's Bally shares at a 20% premium over market price, though he had already agreed to divest his shares under order of a state gambling commission; (b) extended O'Donnell's employment for five years and raised his salary despite the fact that he was under investigation by gambling authorities; and (c) paid $1.9 million to a partnership in which O'Donnell had an interest for purchase of land it already owned. Plaintiffs claimed they did not have to make a demand on the directors before suing because the directors would have to initiate the suit against themselves, and O'Donnell owned substantial stock and was an officer of the corporation. See *Tabas* v. *Mullane*, 608 F.Supp. 759 (D. N. J. 1985).

5. When Bendix Corporation made a tender offer for control of Martin Marietta Corporation, the directors of Martin undertook a number of defensive moves to prevent

Bendix from buying control. Among these was the granting of "golden parachute" contracts to some of its officers. Plaintiff shareholders filed this derivative action against the directors, claiming they had breached their fiduciary duty to the corporation and engaged in a waste of corporate assets to perpetuate their control over Martin. Under applicable state law, shareholders could only bring suit by demanding that directors bring the action. Does this excuse these shareholders from making demand on other shareholders before suing? Discuss. See *Zimmerman* v. *Bell*, 585 F.Supp. 512 (D. Md. 1984).

6. On February 1, 1983, siblings Cox, Powell, and Thomas, all one-third owners of the shares of two corporations, entered into a stock purchase and restriction agreement to protect "their best interests." Under the agreement, all shares owned by a shareholder at time of death were to be acquired by the corporations through life insurance policies established to fund the transaction. The agreement provided "Each price shall be reviewed at least annually no later than the annual meeting of shareholders" and "The purchase price shall remain in full force and effect until so changed." No annual meeting was held in February 1984. Cox died in an accidental fire on March 14, 1984. The price established in the agreement was $374,976, though Cox's shares were worth perhaps twice that much. The administrator of Cox's estate refused to tender the shares because of the price-value differential and the failure to review the repurchase price in 1984. Discuss. See *Concord Auto Auction, Inc.* v. *Rustin*, 627 F.Supp. 1526 (D. Mass. 1986).

7. In 1956, the late J. D. Jackson executed a trust indenture that set up the J. D. Jackson trust for the benefit of his children. He transferred to the trust virtually all the shares of the Register Publishing Co., giving the trustees title, the power to vote the shares, and full power and authority to hold and manage the assets of the fund, to sell or exchange them, and to invest and reinvest in other types of property. Other stocks were also transferred into the trusts. Plaintiffs, beneficiaries of the trust, sued in the 1970s to have the trust declared an invalid voting trust. If it is a voting trust, it has lasted longer than the ten-year existence permitted voting trusts by Connecticut's voting trust statute. Discuss. See *Jackson* v. *Jackson*, 178 Conn. 42, 420 A.2d 893 (1979).

8. Marr owned 800 of the 11,340 shares of the closely held Gloucester Ice & Cold Storage Co., but had never been an officer or director of the company. On her death, her estate's administrator demanded that Gloucester purchase the shares at a fair price, though there was no agreement among shareholders or between the corporation and Marr or any provision in the articles or bylaws requiring such a repurchase. When Gloucester refused, the administrator sued for breach of fiduciary duty. Discuss. See *Goode* v. *Ryan*, 489 N.E.2d 1001 (Mass. 1986).

11

THE BOARD OF DIRECTORS AND OFFICERS

INTRODUCTION

The board of directors is in many ways the center of power in the corporation. Elected by the shareholders and working through the officers, the board is paramount, at least in theory. Section 35 of the Model Business Corporation Act (MBCA) provides that "All corporate powers shall be exercised by or under the authority of . . . a board of directors." Thus, the directors occupy a unique position, being ultimately responsible not to the wishes of the shareholders who elected them, but to the best interests of the corporation as viewed by the directors. Although they may forfeit reelection or risk immediate removal, the directors may properly ignore the sentiments of a majority of the shareholders.

Selected by the directors, the officers of the corporation are theoretically in charge of the day-to-day corporate affairs. In large corporations the directors cannot hope to have the time to involve themselves in the minute details of daily operations. In smaller corporations, the membership of the board of directors may be coextensive with that of the principal corporate offices. Any description of how American corporations function must note the very real differences between the management of large publicly held corporations and that of smaller close corporations.[1]

Directors and officers play a key role in many areas of corporate and securities law. While this chapter will focus on many duties and obligations of these corporate managers, many others are discussed elsewhere in the book, such as in the areas of insider trading, mergers or consolidations for the benefit of those in control, management's use of corporate funds in proxy contests, purchases of shares with corporate funds to avoid loss of control, and declaring or withholding dividends.

DIRECTORS

Procedures and Powers

Number and Qualification

Although traditionally corporations were required to have a minimum of three directors, §36 of the MBCA allows as few as one, with no maximum being set. Many jurisdictions have followed the MBCA in this regard. A few jurisdictions have age, residency, or other such requirements for directors, but the MBCA and RMBCA reflect the modern trend by eliminating such qualifications.

Election, Tenure, and Removal

The initial directors are named in the articles of incorporation, and their successors are elected at annual shareholders' meetings. According to MBCA §36, each director serves a one-year term unless the board is "classified." Any time a board contains nine or more directors, §37 allows its members to be divided into two or three classes serving rotating terms. For example, a 15-member board could be divided into three classes, with 5 members being elected each year to serve a three-year term.

Shareholders have always had the inherent power to remove directors for cause, subject to court review for fairness.[2] The MBCA's §39 also allows removal *without cause* at any meeting called for that purpose. The vote of the holders of a majority of shares will effect removal, unless the director was elected through cumulative voting. In that case, §39 provides that the director will be retained in office if sufficient votes are cast against removal that, if cumulated, they would have been sufficient to elect the director in the first place. This prevents a majority faction, able to elect only, say, two of three directors at an annual meeting where votes were cumulated, from removing that minority director without cause. If the shares voted for the director in the first instance are voted against removal, the director will be retained.

---

[1] As noted in Chapter 10, the RMBCA recognizes this difference by providing in §8.01 that a corporation with fewer than 50 shareholders can eliminate the board or curtail its powers.

[2] RMBCA §8.09 expressly recognizes this right by authorizing court removal of a director in a suit commenced by the corporation or holders of 10% of its shares if the court finds (1) the director engaged in fraud, dishonesty or gross abuse of discretion or (2) removal is in the corporation's best interest.

If a vacancy occurs on the board due to a resignation or death, for example, a majority of the remaining directors (even though not constituting a quorum) may appoint a replacement to serve until the next annual meeting.[3]

De Facto Directors

A person who is elected as a director occasionally will not attain the legal status of a director because of some irregularity, such as a technical problem with the election or a lack of qualification to serve. Such a person is a *de facto* director whose actions may bind the corporation in its dealings with third parties. Thus, directors who were elected by other directors rather than by shareholders, as required in the articles of incorporation, could bind the corporation in a contract with an employee who was unaware of the irregularity. However, the corporation's shareholders may always launch a direct attack on the *de facto* director's authority. That is, the doctrine may not be invoked to retain an illegally elected or unqualified director whose status is challenged by a shareholder.

Procedural Formalities

Traditionally, directors could act effectively only at a formal board meeting with a quorum present. Section 40 of the MBCA provides that a majority of the directors constitutes a quorum unless the articles or bylaws require a greater number. Thus, in one case a deed signed by all 11 directors of a corporation was deemed invalid because they signed it at different times and places. The court noted that directors "are agents of the corporation only as a board and not individually. Hence it follows that they have no authority to act, save when assembled at a board meeting."[4]

The modern trend in case law affords more flexibility, especially for smaller, closely held corporations. For example, an employment contract negotiated by the sole shareholder of a corporation has been held to bind the corporation although it was not authorized at a formal board of directors meeting.[5] And a promise made to employees by one director and acquiesced in by a second was held binding on the corporation though it was unknown to the third member of the board.[6] To be absolutely safe, one dealing with a single director should still require formal board action for any matter normally requiring board approval.[7]

---

[3] MBCA §38. RMBCA §8.10 also allows the shareholders to fill such a vacancy.

[4] *Baldwin* v. *Canfield*, 1 N.W. 261 (Minn. 1879).

[5] *Rapp* v. *Felsenthal*, 628 S.W.2d 258 (Tex. Civ. App. 1982).

[6] *Mickshaw* v. *Coca-Cola Bottling Co.*, 70 A.2d 467 (Pa. 1950).

[7] For example, *Dowdle* v. *Texas American Oil Corp.*, 503 S.W.2d 647 (Tex. Civ. App. 1973) (alleged understanding among directors regarding severance and vacation pay could not override specific board of directors meeting's minutes which set plaintiff president's compensation without including such items).

Statutory trends also authorize more informality in board action. Section 44 of the MBCA provides that by unanimous written consent, the directors can act without a meeting unless the articles or bylaws prohibit such action. And §45 authorizes the board to meet via conference telephone calls.

Whether a board meeting occurs in the traditional manner or telephonically, §43 of the MBCA has specific notice provisions that must be met, unless waived by directors. The RMBCA makes similar provisions.

Delegation of Authority

Inside Directors, Outside Directors, and Officers

In a small, closely held corporation, there may be a substantial identity of officers and directors. Theoretically, the same person might be the sole shareholder, sole director, and president of the corporation. In a larger corporation, there are more likely to be some directors who are not also officers or other employees of the corporation. These directors are called "outside" directors, in contrast to directors who are also officers, employees, or major shareholders of the corporation who are called "inside" directors.

Selection and removal of officers is in the hands of the board of directors, according to §§50 and 51 of the MBCA. Officers serve at the pleasure of the board, which should exercise supervisory powers. The board will also fix the officers' compensation, as shall be discussed in more detail soon.

Committees

Section 42 of the MBCA authorizes action through committees composed of a portion of the directors. These committees may undertake a number of important functions. However, certain actions may be executed only by the entire board, including (1) authorizing distributions, (2) recommending to the shareholders proposals that require their approval, (3) designating candidates for the office of director for proxy solicitation purposes, (4) amending bylaws, (5) approving mergers not requiring shareholder approval, and (6) authorizing reacquisition of shares.

Corporate Governance Controversy

Corporations do not always operate in practice as they do in the theory underlying state corporate codes, including those patterned on the MBCA. The notion that shareholders elect directors who select and supervise officers is somewhat artificial in the small family corporation where the same individual plays all three roles. For that reason, many states have started to give special attention and broad flexibility to small, closely held corporations. This development was explored in detail in Chapter 10.

At the other end of the spectrum, theory does not comport with reality in the bigger corporations either. The problem is that outside directors tend to become "captives" of the inside officer-directors, so that the board becomes a "rubber stamp" for the officers. The problem, and a proposed solution, are discussed in the following excerpt.

CORPORATE GOVERNANCE[8]

George Dent

61 Boston University Law Review 623 (1981)

A. The Failure of the Old Model

The keystone of the traditional model of corporate governance was the provision once contained in state corporate laws that "[t]he business and affairs of a corporation shall be managed by the board of directors." In fact, boards of directors do not and have never managed public corporations. That task is performed by the executive officers, particularly the chief executive officer. These corporate officers may also be members of the board, but their power to manage derives not from board membership but from corporate office. Outside directors—directors who hold no office with the corporation— play little role in its management. With few exceptions, the board quickly rubberstamps proposals drafted by the true management, the executive officers. As Myles Mace showed in his classic study, *Directors: Myth and Reality*, directors occasionally give advice and counsel at the request of the chief executive officer, provide some limited discipline over management, and replace the chief executive officer in times of crisis. The board does not even plan the corporation's general strategy, as some have argued it could or should do.

The directors' failure to manage springs not from personal negligence but from a basic structural defect in the traditional model of corporate governance; that is, the board could not manage the corporation even if it wanted to do so. First, the chief executive officer dominates the board. Despite the trend toward more outside directors, boards traditionally have been, and in many cases still are, composed largely of insiders— the chief executive officer and his subordinates. The subordinates cannot flout the chief's authority when functioning as directors in his presence. Outside directors, though less subject to the control of the chief executive officer, are still unlikely to be very independent. Many are either quasi-insiders whose autonomy is curbed by economic ties to the corporation and its head, or else friends of the chief executive officer. Moreover, most outside directors are corporate executives who expect outside directors to play a passive role on their own boards and who naturally play a passive role when they themselves are outside directors. Directors who cause trouble may be fired.

Outside directors lack not only the independence but also the intimate knowledge of the corporation, the time, and the information generated by an independent staff that would be necessary to manage. Most outside directors have their primary jobs with corporations in industries different from the corporations on whose boards they sit; indeed, the antitrust laws would generally prevent the use of outside directors from corporations in the same industry. Their contact with the corporation is usually limited to a meeting of a few hours' duration once a month or less frequently, much too little time to learn to manage a public corporation. Information presented to the board is prepared under the chief executive officer's control and usually arrives too late to be digested by the outsiders before they must act on it. The minimal pay given most directors shows how insignificant their role is in corporate governance. Thus, outside directors are neither disposed nor able to play an active role in managing the corporation.

In light of the commentators' recognition that boards cannot manage, it is not surprising that courts have explicitly held on occasion that the directors are not liable for failing to do so. More often, though, courts have maintained the fiction that the board must manage, but in various ways have whittled the duty down almost to nothing. In either case, the board was left, so far as the courts were concerned, with no significant function. Some state corporation laws have been amended to reflect the realization that boards do not manage. The Model Business Corporation Act, for example, was revised to provide that "the business and affairs of a corporation will be managed under the direction of a board of directors," and many state statutes followed suit. Although the amendments relieve the board of the duty to manage, they give no inkling of what the directors are supposed to do.

B. The New Model: The Board as Monitor of Corporate Officers

The old model of corporate governance having been discredited, commentators began to fashion a new model that concedes to the executive officers the authority to manage but retains a useful role for the board. Professor Melvin Eisenberg, the leading advocate of the new model, reviewed proposals intended to enable the board to manage—including ones that called for fully-staffed boards and boards dominated by professional or full-time directors—and concluded that none was likely to succeed. He argued that, rather than make an unrealistic demand that the board manage the corporation, we should try to ascertain what useful functions boards can perform and then conform the model of corporate governance to that reality. Examining those functions that the board can perform, he found none very important except the monitoring function. He therefore proposed a new model of corporate governance that focuses on the board's monitoring function.

· · ·

All agree that monitoring entails selecting, evaluating, and, if necessary, removing and replacing directors and corporate executives. Corollary functions include fixing management's compensation, reviewing transactions between the corporation and its insiders, and overseeing management's compliance with the law. It is an open question whether the board would select corporate accounting procedures. The commentators have not suggested the methods by which the board should discharge its duties—for example, how the board could evaluate management's performance or monitor management's compliance with law, or whether the board should have an independent staff to provide it with information.

· · ·

A key question is to what extent, if any, the board would retain authority to set or to review long range goals and major projects. Professor Eisenberg believes that the board is incompetent to decide these matters. Moreover, assigning these duties to the officers would facilitate development of an effective duty of care. However, whether the courts will permit boards to abdicate completely their traditional authority over major corporate policy is questionable. The revision of the Model Act and of many state statutes to relieve the board of the express duty to manage the corporation's business does not seem to have been intended to deny the board's authority over long range goals and major projects.

If the board does retain some power over long range goals and major projects, the difference between the monitoring model and the traditional model of corporate governance is arguably a difference of emphasis only. Even if this is true, however, the difference of emphasis is significant. The traditional model has tended to view the corporate officers as mere functionaries effectuating the orders of the board. Accordingly, any duty to manage carefully rested with the board. Similarly, the board's duty to monitor the corporate officers was accorded little importance on the theory that the officers were mere functionaries. The monitoring model reverses this approach by placing the duty to manage primarily, if not exclusively, with the corporate officers and by elevating to major significance the board's duty to monitor.

Although the utility of outside directors has hitherto been limited, the monitoring model may change this. The outside directors are not asked to manage, a task for which they are ill-suited, but only to monitor management, a task for which an outsider's perspective is well-suited, perhaps even necessary. Inside directors cannot be expected to evaluate their own performance dispassionately. Moreover, once it is candidly recognized that the board does not itself manage but rather monitors management, arguments for a board dominated by outsiders become much more persuasive. Once outsiders dominate the board and control nominating procedures, they will be in a much better position to act independently of management.

Many commentators have accepted Professor Eisenberg's views or ones similar to them. More important, many corporations are stressing the director's monitoring function, as evidenced by the growing number of both outside directors and oversight committees. The oversight committees are established expressly to perform various monitoring functions. The most common are audit committees, which review the independent accountant's reports on auditing and accounting matters; nominating committees, which review the performance of incumbent directors, suggest the removal of unsatisfactory directors, and recommend replacements for vacancies; and compensation committees, which review compensation of executive officers and may evaluate management's performance as part of this review. Most of these committees are composed primarily or exclusively of outside directors. Acceptance of monitoring by commentators and corporations has led the *Corporate Director's Guidebook* and some other authorities to speak of a duty of monitoring as if it were established fact rather than a remote ideal.

Advocates of the monitoring model hope that it will provide some meaningful check on self-serving behavior, incompetence, or complacency on the part of management, a check not always provided by shareholders or market forces.

The Securities and Exchange Commission has also pushed the large public companies toward reforms it believes would provide more protection for shareholders. Following its investigation of National Telephone Co., Inc., the Commission concluded that the corporation's outside directors had acted tardily in urging the failing company to disclose to the public its dire financial straits. The SEC noted that

> The Commission is not saying that the directors of a company are responsible for approving every line of every press release and periodic filing made by the company; rather, the Commission is saying that, at a time of distress in the company's existence, the directors have an affirmative duty to assure that the marketplace be provided accurate and full disclosures concerning the basic liability of the company and the continuity of its operations. . . . In general, outside directors should be expected to maintain a general familiarity with their company's communications with the public. In this way, they can compare such communications with what they know to be the facts, and if the facts as they know them are inconsistent with those communications, they can see to it, as stewards for the company, that appropriate revisions or additions be made.[9]

---

[9] *Securities and Exchange Commission, Release*, no. 34–14380, January 16, 1978.

When Mattel, Inc., ran afoul of the SEC because its financial statements substantially overstated sales, net income, and accounts receivable, it signed a consent decree agreeing to place a majority of outside directors acceptable to the SEC on its board; to establish and maintain an executive committee, financial controls committee, and a litigation and claims committee, each consisting of a majority of outside directors; and to retain a special counsel and special auditor acceptable to the SEC.[10]

OFFICERS

Introduction

Selected and guided by the board of directors, the corporation's officers are its most important agents in carrying out the corporation's business. Like the directors, officers are bound by agency and fiduciary law.

Most state statutes prescribe the officers a corporation must have. Many parallel MBCA §50, which states that a corporation's officers shall consist of a president, one or more vice-presidents, a secretary, and a treasurer.[11] Section 50 also provides that other officers or assistant officers may be appointed by the board if necessary. Many corporations have a controller or comptroller who keeps financial records and handles funds, complementing the treasurer.

These labels tend to cause confusion, as the duties of a treasurer, for example, may vary from corporation to corporation. Labels also vary. The role filled by a "president" in one corporation might be filled by a "chief executive officer" or a "general manager" in another corporation. What counts is the function served, not the title.

Few statutes impose any legal qualifications on officers. Most allow one person to hold more than one office, though MBCA §50 qualifies this by providing that the same person cannot simultaneously be both president and secretary.[12] But some jurisdictions allow one person to hold all four offices.

Appointment, Tenure, and Removal

Although officers are sometimes selected by the shareholders directly, usually they are chosen by the board of directors. And they serve at the pleasure of the board, being removable with or without cause. An officer with a two-year contract may be removed by the board at the end of one year for no reason, although the corporation may be liable for breach of contract.[13] In a few cases courts have specifically enforced long-term contracts for officers,[14] but normally damages constitute the only remedy.

---

[10] SEC v. Mattel, Inc. [1974–75 Binder], Federal Securities Law Reports (CCH), ¶94,807 (D. D.C. 1974).

[11] RMBCA §8.40 alters the usual pattern by simply providing that a corporation shall have the officers listed in its bylaws or appointed by the board of directors in accordance with the bylaws. No particular number of officers is specified.

[12] The RMBCA eliminates this prohibition in §8.40(d).

[13] MBCA §51; RMBCA §8.44.

[14] Jones v. Williams, 139 Mo. 1, 39 S.W. 486 (1897).

In close corporations, sometimes shareholder or director agreements will bind the parties to keep a certain person in a certain office. Such agreements are frequently enforced if the officer is competent and loyal. The conditions of enforcement of such agreements were examined in detail in Chapter 10.

Just as there are *de facto* directors, there can be *de facto* officers. If such persons exercise the powers of a corporate office under color of title, the corporation may be bound by the person's actions if the elements of estoppel are present.

POWERS OF OFFICERS

Agency Law

Because a corporation is a legal fiction existing only in the minds of men, it must act through its directors, officers, and lesser employees. The principles of agency law, which we have already seen in other contexts, govern the relationships among corporations, their directors, officers and other employees, and third parties. An area of continuing difficulty is the proper authority of corporate officers. Although the corporation should be bound if the officer acts with (1) actual authority, express or implied, (2) apparent authority, or (3) no authority but the action is later ratified by the corporation—it is not always easy to draw the line between what is authorized and what is not.

Express Authority

One type of actual authority is express authority—authority that is put into words, written or otherwise. One source of express authority for officers is the state corporate code. However, such statutes are usually rather vague, and normally describe only officers' powers inside the corporation. The president has the authority to call a special meeting, the secretary has the authority to keep the minutes of the meeting, and so on. The difficult questions arise not in these internal matters, but in dealings with third parties. Does the president have authority to sell corporate land? Does the treasurer have power to endorse corporate checks? Most statutes are not helpful here.

More helpful sources of officers' express authority are (1) articles of incorporation, (2) bylaws, and (3) resolutions of the board of directors. The bylaws especially may be a fruitful source for expressions of authority granted to officers. If the bylaws are stingy in conferring such authority, the officers may frequently have to ask the board of directors to approve resolutions granting authority for particular transactions.

Implied Authority

Implied authority, also known as inherent or presumptive authority, is actual authority that is not expressed in statutes, articles, bylaws, or board resolutions. It is authority that is derived by "reading between the lines" of these other sources.

Under agency law, some courts hold that certain officers carry inherent power by virtue of the office they hold. Other courts imply all authority necessary to carry out the tasks assigned by the bylaws or board resolutions. Some find authority to act flowing from past practices to which the board has acquiesced. Most courts also find that officers have the authority to use their best judgment to act in the corporation's best interests in emergency situations when there is no time to consult the board for advice. This is a slippery area where there are few clear lines. Obviously, a third party dealing with a corporate officer on an important matter should protect himself or herself by demanding that the officer present proof of authority in the form of a bylaw or board resolution.

How much authority will be implied and under what circumstances depends on which office is involved.

President

The courts have taken three main views regarding the powers that may be implied from the nature of the president's office. The more conservative view is that the president has no more presumptive power by virtue of the office than does any other officer or director. A third party attempting to negotiate a contract with a corporate president in such a jurisdiction should always demand a certified board resolution to ensure the president's authority. Many courts place the burden on the third party to prove that the president had authority whenever the corporation attempts to evade a contractual obligation by claiming lack of authority.

The majority view is that the president has inherent authority by virtue of the office to bind the corporation in *ordinary* business transaction. However, "extraordinary" transactions require board of directors authorization. What is "extraordinary"? The cases vary, naturally. Usually the president can hire and fire necessary employees, but the granting of a long-term or lifetime contract is probably extraordinary. The president can usually establish the salaries of employees, but alloting an employee a percentage of the corporate profits is frequently deemed extraordinary. Other actions not usually viewed as within the scope of ordinary corporate business include (1) borrowing large sums of money, (2) selling or mortgaging corporate real estate, (3) settling important litigation (not simple suits to collect sums due on sales of corporate products), and (4) promising to pay large bonuses to employees.

A third view, which represents the modern trend, is that the office of president should be deemed inherently to carry broad powers to act on the corporation's behalf in just about any manner that could be authorized by the board of directors. This view accords with reasonable public expectations, so many courts today hesitate to allow the board of directors to repudiate a president's actions.

A case exemplifying the majority rule follows.

TEMPLETON v. NOCONA HILLS OWNERS ASSN., INC.

555 S.W.2d 534 (Tex. Civ. App. 1977)

Appellee Nocona Hills Owners Assoc., Inc., is a corporation whose shareholders are persons who have purchased lots or homes in the Nocona Hills Subdivision. On July 1, 1975, appellee also took ownership and control of a country club from the subdivision's developer. In June, prior to the take-over, seven directors were elected to appellee's board, effective on July 1. Jameson was elected director and president of the board; Jones was appointed by the board to serve as general manager.

Appellant Templeton had managed the country club under the prior ownership. In late June, Jameson approached her about remaining in her position. Appellant consented but stated that she wanted a contract. They discussed a salary of $1,000 per month. After consulting the board, Jameson told appellant that the salary could not be more than $850 per month. When appellant insisted on a written contract, Jameson suggested that she write one up, and she did. Jameson signed the contract on June 20 as president of appellee's board of governors. The contract was for a term of one year. Jones witnessed the signing.

Jameson testified that he told appellant the contract would not be binding until it was authorized by the board. Appellant denied this. The board rejected the contract, agreeing simply to retain appellant at her previous salary of $750 per month. Jameson testified that he told appellant of the rejection; appellant denied this also. On July 9, 1975, appellant was discharged for disloyalty by Jones. She was paid at a rate of $750 per month until that time.

Appellant sued claiming breach of the June 20 "contract." The jury found for appellant, but the trial court set the verdict aside and entered a take-nothing judgment for the reason, inter alia, *that Jameson did not have the authority to bind appellee.*

Templeton appealed.

CORNELIUS, JUSTICE:

The appellee denied under oath that the contract sued upon had been executed by its authority. Appellant therefore had the burden to establish the authority of the officer to make the contract on behalf of the corporation—*In Re Westec Corporation,* 434 F.2d 195 (5th Cir. 1970).

The authority of an officer to contract for a corporation may be actual or apparent. In Texas, by statute, the board of directors of a corporation, not its president, is charged generally with the duty of managing the corporation's affairs (Tex. Bus. Corp. Act Ann. art. 2.31). Consequently, actual authority of the president to contract on behalf of the corporation must be found either in specific statutes, in the organic law of the corporation, or in a delegation of authority from the board of directors formally expressed, or must be implied from the nature of his position or from custom or habit of doing business.—*Manufacturers' Equipment Co.* v. *Cisco Clay & Coal Co.,* 118 Tex. 370, 15 S.W.2d 609 (1929); Tex. Bus. Corp. Act Ann. art. 2.42. As to express authority, there was no proof in this case of any of the provisions of the corporate charter or bylaws, and there was no attempt to prove that the board of directors or the shareholders had invested the president with any authority to make contracts on its behalf. In fact, the only evidence concerning contracts on behalf of the corporation was Jameson's testimony that only the board could authorize them, and that the board refused to approve the one in question here. As to implied authority, the settled rule in Texas is that a corporation president, merely by virtue of his office, has no inherent power to bind the corporation except as to routine matters arising in the ordinary course of business—*Miles Realty Co.* v. *Dodson*, 8 S.W.2d 516 (Tex. Civ. App.—Amarillo 1928, writ dism'd). The execution of an employment contract binding the corporation to employ a person in a managerial position for a period of one year could not be considered a matter in the ordinary and usual course of appellee's business. Espe-

cially is this true since the power to hire and discharge employees for appellee was vested in a general manager rather than in the president. Indeed, Jameson had not even taken office as president on June 20 when the contract was executed. Under the record in this case, we are impelled to the conclusion that appellant failed in her burden to establish that Mr. Jameson was invested with actual authority to make the contract sued upon.

The court also rejected appellant's claims of apparent authority and ratification. The trial court's judgment was affirmed.

A president's authority can be implied from the practices of the corporation as well as from the office itself. If, for example, the board of directors has repeatedly allowed the president to sell corporate real estate, though no charter provision, bylaw, or board resolution authorized such sales, a court would likely conclude that the board had impliedly given the president that power. However, a court would not imply authority that that board of directors could not legally confer.[15] Corporations are not bound when the president negotiates a contract that is beyond the power of the board to authorize.

General Manager

Many times a corporation will have a general manager—also called a chief executive officer and other such terms. Frequently, the general manager is also the president. Courts tend to take a broad view of the general manager's inherent authority, holding it to be greater than that of the president alone.[16] Many courts hold a general manager to be impliedly authorized to do any act the board of directors could ratify.

If a president has the title of general manager, or even lacks the title but functions as one, he may well exercise near total control over corporate affairs. Where this is the case, courts hesitate to restrict presidential authority. For example, in *Behrstock* v. *Ace Hose & Rubber Co.*,[17] a question arose as to a corporate president's authority to give a written employment contract including a percentage of net profits as compensation. The court noted,

---

[15] For example, *Boston Athletic Ass'n* v. *International Marathons, Inc.*, 392 Mass. 356, 467 N.E.2d 58 (1984).

[16] For example, *Memorial Hospital Ass'n of Stanislaus Co.*, v. *Pacific Grape Products Co.*, 45 Cal.2d 634, 290 P.2d 481 (1955).

[17] 114 Ill. App.3d 1070, 70 Ill. Dec. 607, 449 N.E.2d 954 (1983).

It is well established under Illinois law that a contract to pay as compensation a percentage of the net profits of a corporation is not a usual and ordinary contract, and that under most circumstances the president of the corporation has no authority, absent authorization by the board of directors, to enter into any such unusual or extraordinary contract on behalf of the corporation. However, an exception to this rule may arise when a corporation allows its president to assume ''complete control'' over its affairs. In such situations, the officer exercising such control is said to hold, *prima facie*, the power to bind the corporation to such contracts. A corollary to this exception, however, is that the power may be rebutted where it is affirmatively shown that such contracts were unauthorized.

In *Behrstock*, because the existence of complete control was never established, the contract was held to be unauthorized.

Public corporations seldom deny the authority of their presidents. Disputes as to officers' authority usually arise in the context of close corporations where, for example, an officer has engaged in a self-serving transaction at the corporation's expense, or where a competing faction of shareholders challenges the president's actions. For example, plaintiff and defendant in *Behrstock* were brothers who each owned 50% of five corporations.

Vice-presidents

Vice-presidents come in assorted types and with various functions. Some corporations have more than 100 vice-presidents. There are senior vice-presidents, junior vice-presidents, executive vice-presidents, administrative vice-presidents, and so on.

Most courts hold that vice-presidents have no authority by virtue of their office to deal with third parties. Rather, their inherent powers are mainly internal. Only if a vice-president steps into the president's shoes in an emergency would most courts find broad inherent powers. However, courts might imply broader authority for a vice-president if traditional corporate practice warranted it. The *Kanavos* case, which shall soon be discussed, illustrates this point.

Furthermore, some courts have started to take a more liberal view of vice-presidential authority, holding that by virtue of their offices many vice-presidents have broad authority.[18] This development has paralleled the recent trend toward a broader interpretation of the power of corporate presidents.

Secretary

Most courts hold that secretaries have no power by virtue of their office to bind the corporation in contracts with third parties. Rather, the secretary's duties are usually internal and ministerial—to attend meetings of directors, officers, and shareholders to record minutes, to give notice of meetings, to keep certain corporate records, to certify copies of board resolutions and other corporate documents, and to keep and attest to the application of the corporate seal. Unless the corporation established an

---

[18] For example, *Morrison v. Bank of Mt. Hope*, 124 W. Va. 478, 20 S.E.2d 790 (1942).

unusual practice, a secretary would have no implied powers, for example, to sign a real estate lease on the corporation's behalf.[19]

Treasurer

Like secretaries, treasurers usually have no implied authority arising by virtue of their office to bind the corporation to contracts with third parties. Corporate treasurers' powers are strictly internal, except with regard to collection and disbursement of corporate funds as authorized. Treasurers cannot, by the inherent power of their offices alone, transfer or cash checks payable to the corporation's order without authorization.[20]

Apparent Authority

Even if an officer has no actual authority, either express or implied, he may *appear* to third parties to have authority. If such an officer acts outside actual authority, but inside the appearance of authority, who should lose? Most courts believe that the corporation that put the officer in the position to sign the unauthorized contract should suffer the loss, not the innocent third party who reasonably relied on the appearance.

For example, assume that X is president of A Corporation. Although the bylaws specifically provide that all real estate transactions must be approved by the board of directors, X has been single-handedly carrying out such deals for years, letting the board know only afterward that the deal has been consummated. Assume that Ms. B knows of this practice and buys land from A Corp. solely on X's say-so. Later the corporation attempts to repudiate. It is clear that X had no actual authority to act. The express provision in the bylaws would foreclose any attempt to imply actual authority to act.

However, Ms. B's knowledge of the corporation's past practices and the board's acquiescence in them gives the appearance that X had authority. The corporation is bound under the doctrine of apparent authority. Of course, if we change the facts and assume that Ms. B knew of the bylaw limitation, then she could not claim that it *appeared* X had authority. She knew better.

Keep in mind that the appearance of authority must arise from an act of the purported principal (the corporation), not of the agent. Otherwise, anyone could wander into a car dealership, claim to be president of A Corporation, and bind A on a contract to purchase a car. To be bound, the corporation must in some manner hold the officer out as having authority. If the corporation restricts the normal authority of an officer, that restriction is not binding on a third party without notice of it.

Apparent authority of an officer, or any corporate agent, will be determined from all the facts and circumstances of the case. According to one court,

---

[19] *Hollywyle Assoc., Inc. v. Hollister*, 164 Conn. 389, 324 A.2d 247 (1974).
[20] *Slavin v. Passaic National Bank & Trust Co.*, 114 N.J.L. 341, 176 A. 339 (N.J. Ct. of Errors & Appeals 1935).

The principal's manifestations giving rise to apparent authority may consist of direct statements to the third person, directions to the agent to tell something to the third person, or the granting of permission to the agent to perform acts and conduct negotiations under circumstances which create in him a reputation of authority in the area in which the agent acts and negotiates.[21]

An illustrative case, involving a corporation's vice-president, follows.

KANAVOS v. HANCOCK BANK & TRUST CO.

14 Mass. App. 326, 439 N.E.2d 311 (1982)

In the ten years preceding 1975, Harold Kanavos and his brother borrowed money on at least 20 occasions from Hancock Bank and Trust (the Bank), always dealing with loan officer James M. Brown. At times the loans totaled $800,000.

Between 1965 and 1974, Brown's responsibilities at the Bank grew. He became executive vice-president and chief loan officer for the Bank, which had fourteen or so branch offices in addition to its head office. Brown's office was in the head office, opposite that of the Bank's president, Kelley. Often Brown told Kanavos that he had to check a matter with Kelley, but Kelley always approved Brown's actions.

In 1974 a real estate recession imperiled the Kanavos brothers. The Bank, through Brown, sought to liquidate $300,000 of unsecured loans. The brothers, through a wholly owned corporation called 1025, Inc., owned Executive House, a relatively new apartment building. Their stock in 1025, Inc., had been foreclosed, however, subject to the right to redeem. Brown had loan workout responsibilities and devised a deal whereby the Bank would loan Kanavos an additional $265,000 to repurchase the foreclosed shares. Then the shares

would be sold to the Bank for $522,322.21 to liquidate the Kanavos indebtedness. Kanavos was to have the option to buy back the shares for the same price plus a daily charge (which was in lieu of interest). Any loss sustained by the Bank during the option period was added to the repurchase price.

The Bank board approved the transaction, and Kelley signed the agreement on the Bank's behalf. Soon thereafter Brown, without the involvement of Kelley or the board, amended the agreement to raise the purchase price, the option repurchase price, and the daily charge. Brown took charge of Executive House for the next 17 months. Kanavos met with him monthly because he hoped to repurchase. Kanavos sought to introduce potential financing sources to Kelley, but was always told by him to deal with Brown.

Brown ultimately told Kanavos that he preferred that Kanavos not exercise the repurchase option. Rather, Brown said he would go back to Kelley to see what kind of an offer he could make. On July 16, 1976, on Bank letterhead, Brown wrote Kanavos a letter offering that in return for Kanavos not exercising the option, the Bank would pay $40,000 representing a

---

[21] *Hawaiian Paradise Park Corp.* v. *Friendly Broadcasting Co.*, 414 F.2d 750 (9th Cir. 1969).

commission upon the sale of the property and give Kanavos 60 days to match any offer received. When Kanavos sued to enforce this offer, it was excluded from evidence by the trial judge on grounds that Kanavos had not established Brown's authority to make the offer. Kanavos appealed from a directed verdict for the Bank.

KASS, JUSTICE:

Among the exhibits introduced was a document which Brown identified as his job description. In broad terms he was to manage the commercial and consumer loan division. In furtherance of a duty to develop and maintain "a profitable loan portfolio," he, "personally, or through subordinates," was to "direct the resolution of particularly complex and/or unusual credit, lending or collection problems related to important customers." He was also to "[m]aintain a continuous review of the loan portfolio and oversee the resolution of significant delinquent and workout loans." That language sketches an authority to alter a subsidiary aspect of a loan or workout agreement. Restatement (Second) of Agency §33 (1957) ("An agent is authorized to do, and to do only, what it is reasonable for him to infer that the principal desires him to do in the light of the principal's manifestations and the facts as he knows or should know them at the time he acts"). See also §§34 and 35 relating to circumstances considered in interpreting authority and when incidental authority is inferred. The jury could have believed that the sale of stock with repurchase option was a furtherance of a workout arrangement and Brown's job description would have supported a jury finding that he had authority to amend the repurchase option in a manner that did not fundamentally alter the agreement, that is, to substitute for the price certain in the agreement, as amended, a right of last refusal or a cash payment should the property be sold

to someone else. It was a revision which afforded the Bank a chance to realize more money from the 1025, Inc., stock; it did not commit the Bank to a loan in excess of Brown's lending authority, to a sale or purchase of property of the Bank, or any step which, in the business context, was so major or unusual that a businessman in Brown's position would reasonably expect to require a vote of the board of directors. See *England Bros.* v. *Miller*, 274 Mass. 239, 241, 174 N.E. 483 (1931).

Whether Brown's job description impliedly authorized the right of last refusal or cash payment modification is a question of how, in the circumstances, a person in Brown's position could reasonably interpret his authority. Whether Brown had *apparent authority* to make the July 16, 1976, modification is a question of how, in the circumstances, a third person, for example, a customer of the Bank such as Kanavos, would reasonably interpret Brown's authority in light of the manifestations of his principal, the Bank—Restatement (Second) of Agency §§8, Comment c, 27 and 49, Comment c (1957).

Titles of office generally do not establish apparent authority. *James F. Monaghan Inc.* v. *M. Lowenstein & Sons*, 290 Mass. 331, 333, 195 N.E. 101 (1935) (vice-president had no apparent authority to authorize preparation of plans for a finishing mill). *Kelly* v. *Citizens Fin. Co. of Lowell, Inc.*, 306 Mass. 531, 532–533, 28 N.E.2d 1005 (1940) (president did not, by virtue of the office alone [i.e., in the absence of evidence as to general authority, implied or apparent], have apparent authority to hire a lawyer for his company). Brown's status as executive vice-president was not, therefore, a badge of apparent authority to modify agreements to which the Bank was a party.

Trappings of office, for example, office and furnishings, private secretary, while they may have some tendency to suggest executive responsibility, do not without other evidence provide a basis for finding apparent authority. Apparent authority is drawn from a variety of circumstances. Thus in *Federal Natl. Bank* v. *O'Connell*, 305 Mass. 559, 562, 565–567, 26 N.E.2d 539 (1940), it was held apparent authority could be found because an officer who was a director, vice-president, and treasurer took an active part in directing the affairs of the bank in question and was seen by third parties talking with customers and negotiating with them. In *Costonis* v. *Medford Housing Authy.*, 343 Mass. 108, 114–115, 176 N.E.2d 25 (1961), the executive director of a public housing authority was held to have apparent authority to vary specifications on the basis of the cumulative effect of what he had done and what the authority appeared to permit him to do.

In the instant case there was evidence of the following variety of circumstances: Brown's title of executive vice-president; the location of his office opposite the president; his frequent communications with the president; the long course of dealing and negotiations; the encouragement of Kanavos by the president to deal with Brown; the earlier amendment of the agreement by Brown on behalf of the Bank on material points, namely the price to be paid by the Bank for the shares and the repurchase price; the size of the Bank (fourteen or fifteen branches in addition to the main office); the secondary, rather than fundamental, nature of the change in the terms of the agreement now repudiated by the Bank, measured against the context of the overall transaction; and Brown's broad operating authority over the Executive House—all these added together would support a finding of apparent authority. When a corporate officer, as here, is allowed to exercise general executive responsibilities, the "public expectation is that the corporation should be bound to engagements made on its behalf by those who presume to have, and convincingly appear to have, the power to agree"—Kempin, "The Corporate Officer and the Law of Agency," 44 Va. L. Rev. 1273, 1280 (1958). This principle does not apply, of course, where in the business context, the requirement of specific authority is presumed, e.g., the sale of a major asset by a corporation or a transaction which by its nature commits the corporation to an obligation outside the scope of its usual activity. The modification agreement signed by Brown and dated July 16, 1976, should have been admitted in evidence, and a verdict should not have been directed.

Judgment reversed.

Remember, there is no apparent authority when a corporate officer does an act that the board of directors could not authorize or otherwise acts outside the ordinary scope of corporate business. When that situation arises, the presumption of authority does not exist, and the third party has a duty to inquire as to whether the officer truly has authority. The third party should demand a certified copy of a bylaw or corporate resolution that authorizes the unusual act.

Ratification

Even if an officer has neither actual nor apparent authority, a corporation may be liable on a contract if it *ratifies* an officer's unauthorized actions. Frequently, a corporate president, faced with an unusual opportunity but no time to consult the board of directors, will seize the opportunity for the corporation though lacking authority. The board will usually support the president by ratifying the transaction.

Ratification may come through a formal board resolution, but it can also come through informal means such as a knowing retention of the fruits of an unauthorized transaction. In one case, an unauthorized purchase of season football tickets was deemed ratified by the fact that the corporation paid for the tickets without question.[22] In another case, ratification of an unauthorized real estate transaction was found in the knowing acquiescence of all the stockholders and directors of a close corporation even though there was no formal board resolution.[23]

A board of directors can ratify only actions that it could have authorized in the first place. For example, a board cannot authorize *ultra vires* or illegal acts. Nonetheless, if a corporation knowingly accepts the benefits of such a transaction, it may be held liable for those benefits under an estoppel theory. Even if the acceptance of benefits is without full knowledge, some cases have found *quantum meruit* liability.

MANAGEMENT COMPENSATION

Compensation of officers is established by the board of directors. In addition to a salary, compensation can take the form of cash bonuses, share bonuses or options, share purchase plans, stock appreciation rights, insurance, pension plans, deferred compensation, various "perks," and the like.

In determining the legality of compensation, two major concerns are reasonableness of amount and formal procedural requirements.

Reasonableness

Compensation should be reasonable in amount and bear a reasonable relationship to the services being rendered. In public corporations, "reasonableness" is seldom successfully challenged. Although the courts are fond of stating that compensation of officials should not be so high as to constitute waste or spoilation, they are very reluctant to judge compensation as excessive.[24] Occasionally, a court will strike down a compensation scheme under extreme circumstances—such as where a board agrees to pay a retiring officer for "consulting" that he is not physically capable of doing.

As long as the compensation of officers of public corporations is fully disclosed under federal proxy rules, however, normally it will not be disturbed by the courts. Instead, it becomes a matter of curiosity. In 1984, for example, the average salary and bonuses of the presidents of 259 top corporations was $653,000, with average total compensation of $1.1 million. Topping the list was T. Boone Pickens of Mesa Petroleum, who received annual and long-term compensation of $22,823,000.[25]

---

[22] *State Block, Inc.* v. *Poche*, 444 So.2d 680 (La. App. 1984).
[23] *Lake Motel, Inc.* v. *Lowery*, 299 S.E.2d 496 (Va. 1983).
[24] For example, *Rogers* v. *Hill*, 289 U.S. 582 (1933).
[25] *Business Week*, May 6, 1985, p. 78.

Reasonableness is a more substantial concern in close corporations for two reasons. The first concern is tax related. Because officer compensation is tax deductible, a tax advantage is derived by funneling potential corporate profits away from dividends toward officer salaries. In that manner, "double taxation" is minimized. Section 162 of the Internal Revenue Code allows the deduction of "reasonable" compensation.

The second concern is fairness related. A controlling faction of a corporation can freeze out a minority faction by depriving the minority shareholders of employment and then funneling all corporate profits into salaries and bonuses for themselves.

For example, in *Wilderman* v. *Wilderman*,[26] a husband and wife co-owned a corporate business. The wife drew a modest salary as vice-president, secretary, and treasurer. The husband drew a larger salary as president. At the end of most years, the husband would be paid a large bonus for tax purposes. This procedure worked well until the pair divorced. Thereafter, the ex-wife derived no benefit from the large bonuses paid to her ex-husband, so she sued, claiming that his compensation was unreasonably high. The court partially agreed, and in so doing listed some of the factors to consider in evaluating the reasonableness of officer compensation:

> In *Hall* v. *Isaacs* [37 Del. Ch. 530, 146 A.2d 602, aff'd in part, 39 Del. Ch. 244, 163 A.2d 288 (1960)], the Court was of the view that evidence of what other executives similarly situated received was relevant, and in *Meiselman* v. *Eberstadt* [39 Del. Ch. 563, 170 A.2d 720 (1961)], the ability of the executive was considered. Other factors which have been judicially recognized elsewhere are whether or not the Internal Revenue Service has allowed the corporation to deduct the amount of salary alleged to be unreasonable. Other relevant factors are whether the salary bears a reasonable relation to the success of the corporation, the amount previously received as salary, whether increases in salary are geared to increases in the value of services rendered, and the amount of the challenged salary compared to other salaries paid by the employer.

Procedure

Directors normally establish compensation for officers, and for themselves unless it is otherwise provided in the articles. Procedurally there is nothing wrong with this. Shareholder approval, however, will virtually assure immunity from challenge. If the directors set their own compensation and the amount is challenged as unreasonably high, absent shareholder approval, the directors will have the burden of proof to establish reasonableness.

When compensation takes the form of cash or property bonuses structured on an incentive basis, they should be "qualified" for federal income tax purposes. If the plan is qualified by meeting IRS requirements, all corporate funds set aside are deductible and employees pay no income tax until receipt of payments. Stock options, as a form of executive compensation, are not as attractive now that the 1986 tax reform legislation has eliminated the capital gains tax break; however, their use will no doubt continue because of the incentives they provide to managers.

---

[26] 315 A.2d 610 (Del. Ch. 1974).

RIGHTS OF MANAGEMENT

Directors' Right to Information

To discharge their obligations properly, directors must have access to corporate information. Therefore, the courts have held that directors have a right to inspect corporate books and records that cannot be thwarted by the officers.

In most jurisdictions the right of a director to inspect is deemed absolute. In one case a director was being sued by the corporation that claimed he had breached his fiduciary duties to benefit a competitor that he controlled. Nonetheless, the court ruled for the director in his attempt to inspect the corporate books, stating: "It is of no consequence that [the director] may be hostile to the corporation. His object in seeking the examination is immaterial. His right of inspection is not dependent upon his being able to satisfy other officers of the corporation that his motives are adequate." [27]

Because of the possibility of abuse of the inspection right in situations such as that just described, the courts of many jurisdictions hold that the right to inspect is qualified and may be defeated by a showing of bad faith or ulterior motive. But the courts providing an absolute right to inspect argue that removal is the proper way to deal with a director who seeks to injure the corporation.

Even after removal, a director retains a qualified right to inspect the corporate books relating to the term of the directorship. Such a right is accorded on the theory that the director remains liable for acts taken while a director and inspection may be necessary to protect the director's "personal responsibility interest" that might, in turn, "inure to the benefit of the stockholders by a disclosure to them of any derelictions by other directors or officers." [28]

Rights of Statutory Action

A few states, such as Georgia [29] and New York,[30] statutorily provide that directors and officers have the right to bring an action on the corporation's behalf. Such a right is usually free of many of the procedural restrictions that hamper shareholder derivative actions.

DUTIES OF MANAGEMENT

One study has indicated that the average award against a director or officer of a large public corporation was $407,420 in 1978, entailing attorneys' fees averaging $277,549 per claim.[31] And it has been suggested that corporate directors face at least 133 types

---

[27] *Davis* v. *Keilsohn Offset Co.*, 79 N.Y.S. 2d 540 (App. Div. 1948).

[28] *Matter of Cohen* v. *Cocoline Products, Inc.*, 127 N.E. 2d 906 (N.Y. 1955).

[29] *Georgia Business Corporation Code*, §22–714 (Charlottesville, Va.: The Michie Co.).

[30] *McKinney's New York Business Corporation Laws*, §720(b) (St. Paul, Minn.: West Publishing Co.).

[31] *The 1978 Wyatt Directors and Officers Liability Survey*.

of liability.[32] Therefore, it is obviously important to be familiar with at least the basic legal responsibilities of corporate directors and officers. A discussion will demonstrate that while the positions are not as perilous as these figures might suggest, there are grounds for concern.

Duty of Attention

The courts have been surprisingly reluctant to impose liability on directors who were guilty not of misfeasance, but of simple nonfeasance or inattention. Traditionally, most cases excused directors who had not paid attention to their duties. Even where the courts found inexcusable inattention, they were reluctant to conclude that it *caused* the defalcations or other misconduct of officers or other directors. The cases imposing liability almost always involved banks or other financial institutions requiring the public's trust.

The modern trend rejects the traditional excuses directors have given for failure to carry out their responsibilities—old age, nonresidence, or inexperience. Courts now expect directors to be more than figureheads. Directors who are unwilling or unable to "direct" should resign, or face liability such as that imposed in the following case.

FRANCIS v. UNITED JERSEY BANK

432 A.2d 814 (N.J. 1981)

Pritchard & Baird Intermediaries Corp. (Pritchard & Baird) was a reinsurance broker acting as an intermediary between an insurance company that wished to share a risk (ceding company) and another insurance company (reinsurer) willing to share the risk in exchange for a part of the premium. After 1964 Pritchard & Baird was operated as a close family corporation with Charles Pritchard, Sr., his wife Lillian, and their sons Charles, Jr., and William as the only directors.

Pritchard & Baird violated industry custom by commingling its own funds with those of the reinsurers and ceding companies. Charles, Sr., started the practice of withholding such funds for his own use and labeling them as "loans." He always paid back the money, but following his death the sons took out larger

"loans" which they could not repay. By October 1975, the corporation entered bankruptcy, owing over $12 million.

The bankruptcy trustees brought suit against Lillian Pritchard, who died soon after suit was instigated, to recover for her failure to discharge her responsibilities as a director. The trial court entered a judgment of over $10 million against Mrs. Pritchard, and her estate appealed.

The Appellate Division affirmed, and the estate appealed again.

POLLOCK, JUDGE:

Mrs. Pritchard was not active in the business of Pritchard & Baird and knew virtually nothing of its corporate affairs. She briefly visited the corporate offices in Morristown on only one

---

[32] W. Knepper, *Liability of Corporate Officers and Directors*, 3rd ed. (Indianapolis, Ind.: A. Smith Co., 1978), p. 558.

occasion, and she never read or obtained the annual financial statements. She was unfamiliar with the rudiments of reinsurance and made no effort to assure that the policies and practices of the corporation, particularly pertaining to the withdrawal of funds, complied with industry custom or relevant law. Although her husband had warned her that Charles, Jr., would "take the shirt off my back," Mrs. Pritchard did not pay any attention to her duties as a director or to the affairs of the corporation.

After her husband died in December 1973, Mrs. Pritchard became incapacitated and was bedridden for a six-month period. She became listless at this time and started to drink rather heavily. Her physical condition deteriorated, and in 1978 she died. The trial court rejected testimony seeking to exonerate her because she "was old, was grief-stricken at the loss of her husband, sometimes consumed too much alcohol and was psychologically overborne by her sons." That court found that she was competent to act and that the reason Mrs. Pritchard never knew what her sons "were doing was because she never made the slightest effort to discharge any of her responsibilities as a director of Pritchard & Baird."

Individual liability of a corporate director for acts of the corporation is a prickly problem. Generally directors are accorded broad immunity and are not insurers of corporate activities. The problem is particularly nettlesome when a third party asserts that a director, because of nonfeasance, is liable for losses caused by acts of insiders, who in this case were officers, directors, and shareholders. Determination of the liability of Mrs. Pritchard requires findings that she had a duty to the clients of Pritchard & Baird, that she breached that duty and that her breach was a proximate cause of their losses.

The New Jersey Business Corporation Act, *N.J.S.A.* 14A:6–14, makes it incumbent upon directors to discharge their duties in good faith and with that degree of diligence, care, and skill which ordinarily prudent men would exercise under similar circumstances in like positions.

This provision was based primarily on section 43 of the Model Business Corporation Act.

· · ·

As a general rule, a director should acquire at least a rudimentary understanding of the business of the corporation. Accordingly, a director should become familiar with the fundamentals of the business in which the corporation is engaged. Because directors are bound to exercise ordinary care, they cannot set up as a defense lack of the knowledge needed to exercise the requisite degree of care. If one "feels that he has not had sufficient business experience to qualify him to perform the duties of a director, he should either acquire the knowledge by inquiry, or refuse to act."

Directors are under a continuing obligation to keep informed about the activities of the corporation. Otherwise, they may not be able to participate in the overall management of corporate affairs. *Barnes* v. *Andrews*, 298 F. 614 (S.D. N.Y. 1924) (director guilty of misprision of office for not keeping himself informed about the details of corporate business)—*Atherton* v. *Anderson*, 99 F.2d 883, 889–890 (6 Cir. 1938) (ignorance no defense to director liability because of director's "duty to know the facts"). Directors may not shut their eyes to corporate misconduct and then claim that because they did not see the misconduct, they did not have a duty to look. The sentinel asleep at his post contributes nothing to the enterprise he is charged to protect.

Directorial management does not require a detailed inspection of day-to-day activities, but rather a general monitoring of corporate affairs and policies. Accordingly, a director is well advised to attend board meetings regularly. Indeed, a director who is absent from a board meeting is presumed to concur in action taken on a corporate matter, unless he files a "dissent with the secretary of the corporation within a reasonable time after learning of such action"— *N.J.S.A.* 14A:6–13 (Supp. 1981–1982). Regular attendance does not mean that directors must attend every meeting, but that directors should attend meetings as a matter of practice. That burden is lightened by *N.J.S.A.* 14A:6–7(2) (Supp. 1981–1982), which permits board action without a meeting if all members of the board consent in writing.

While directors are not required to audit corporate books, they should maintain familiarity with the financial status of the corporation by a regular review of financial statements. In some circumstances, directors may be charged with assuring that bookkeeping methods conform to industry custom and usage—*Lippitt* v. *Ashley*, 89 Conn. 451, 464, 94 A. 995, 1000 (Sup. Ct. 1915). The extent of review, as well as the nature and frequency of financial statements, depends not only on the customs of the industry, but also on the nature of the corporation and the business in which it is engaged. Financial statements of some small corporations may be prepared internally and only on an annual basis; in a large publicly held corporation, the statements may be produced monthly or at some other regular interval. Adequate financial review normally would be more informal in a private corporation than in a publicly held corporation.

Of some relevance in this case is the circumstance that the financial records disclose the "shareholders' loans." Generally directors are immune from liability if, in good faith,

> they rely upon the opinion of counsel for the corporation or upon written reports setting forth financial data concerning the corporation and prepared by an independent public accountant or certified public accountant or firm of such accountants or upon financial statements, books of account or reports of the corporation represented to them to be correct by the president, the officer of the corporation having charge of its books of account, or the person presiding at a meeting of the board. (*N.J.S.A.* 14A:6–14)

The review of financial statements, however, may give rise to a duty to inquire further into matters revealed by those statements. *Corsicana Nat'l Bank* v. *Johnson*, 251 U.S. 68, 71 (1919). Upon discovery of an illegal course of action, a director has a duty to object and, if the corporation does not correct the conduct, to resign. *See Dodd* v. *Wilkinson*, 42 N.J.Eq. 647, 651, 9 A. 685 (E. & A. 1887).

In certain circumstances, the fulfillment of the duty of a director may call for more than mere objection and resignation. Sometimes a director may be required to seek the advice of counsel. . . . A director may require legal advice concerning the propriety of his or her own conduct, the conduct of other officers and directors or the conduct of the corporation.

. . .

A director is not an ornament, but an essential component of corporate governance. Consequently, a director cannot protect himself behind a paper shield bearing the motto, "dummy director." . . . The New Jersey Business Corporation Act, in imposing a standard of ordinary care on all directors, confirms that dummy, figurehead and accommodation directors are anachronisms with no place in New Jersey law. See *N.J.S.A.* 14A:6–14.

. . .

In general, the relationship of a corporate director to the corporation and its stockholders is that of a fiduciary. *Whitfield* v. *Kern*, 122 N.J.Eq. 332, 341, 192 A. 48 (E. & A. 1937). Shareholders have a right to expect that directors will exercise reasonable supervision and control over the policies and practices of a corporation. The institutional integrity of a corporation depends upon the proper discharge by directors of those duties.

. . .

Mrs. Pritchard should have obtained and read the annual statements of financial condition of Pritchard & Baird. Although she had a right to rely upon financial statements prepared in accordance with *N.J.S.A.* 14A:6–14, such reliance would not excuse her conduct. The reason is that those statements disclosed on their face the misappropriation of trust funds.

From those statements, she should have realized that, as of January 31, 1970, her sons were withdrawing substantial trust funds under the guise of "Shareholders' Loans." The financial statements for each fiscal year commencing with that of January 31, 1970, disclosed that the working capital deficits and the "loans" were escalating in tandem. Detecting a misappropriation of funds would not have required special expertise or extraordinary diligence; a cursory reading of the financial statements would have revealed the pillage. Thus, if Mrs. Pritchard had read the financial statements, she would have known that her sons were converting trust funds. When financial statements demonstrate that insiders are bleeding a corporation to death, a director should notice and try to stanch the flow of blood.

In summary, Mrs. Pritchard was charged with the obligation of basic knowledge and supervision of the business of Pritchard & Baird. Under the circumstances, this obligation included reading and understanding financial statements, and making reasonable attempts at detection and prevention of the illegal conduct of other officers and directors. She had a duty to protect the clients of Pritchard & Baird against policies and practices that would result in the misappropriation of money they had entrusted to the corporation. She breached that duty.

Nonetheless, the negligence of Mrs. Pritchard does not result in liability unless it is a proximate cause of the loss.

Within Pritchard & Baird, several factors contributed to the loss of the funds: commingling of corporate and client monies, conversion of funds by Charles, Jr., and William and dereliction of her duties by Mrs. Pritchard. The wrongdoing of her sons, although the immediate cause of the loss, should not excuse Mrs. Pritchard from her negligence which also was a substantial factor contributing to the loss—*Restatement (Second) of Torts*, supra, §442B, comment b. Her sons knew that she, the only other director, was not reviewing their conduct; they spawned their fraud in the backwater of her neglect. Her neglect of duty contributed to the climate of corruption; her failure to act contributed to the continuation of that corruption. Consequently, her conduct was a substantial factor contributing to the loss.

Analysis of proximate cause is especially difficult in a corporate context where the allegation is that nonfeasance of a director is a proximate cause of damage to a third party. Where a case involves nonfeasance, no one can say "with absolute certainty what would have occurred if the defendant had acted otherwise"—*Prosser*, supra §41 at 242. Nonetheless, where it is reasonable to conclude that the failure to act would produce a particular result and that result has followed, causation may be inferred.

We conclude that even if Mrs. Pritchard's mere objection had not stopped the depredations of her sons, her consultation with an attorney and the threat of suit would have deterred them. That conclusion flows as a matter of common sense and logic from the record. Whether in other situations a director has a duty to do more than protest and resign is best left to case-by-case determinations. In this case, we are satisfied that there was a duty to do more than object and resign. Consequently, we find that Mrs. Pritchard's negligence was a proximate cause of the misappropriations.

The judgment of the Appellate Division is affirmed.

The *Francis* case teaches that a director should, at the very least, gain a basic understanding of the corporation's business, obtain and read basic financial documents, and attend most board meetings. If something suspicious occurs, investigation is in order. Should that inquiry disclose improper activity by the officers or other directors, a director should object, consult legal counsel, or even resign. A director "does not exempt himself from liability by failing to do more than passively rubberstamp the decisions of the active managers." [33]

In one case where some directors were held liable for their reckless, self-dealing mismanagement of a corporation, one director escaped liability by expressing his concern, protesting, threatening legal action, and finally forming a stockholders protective committee that brought suit. [34] According to MBCA §35, directors wishing to protect themselves from liability arising from improper actions of a majority of the board should dissent *in writing*. If that dissent is not registered in the written minutes of the board meeting, a separate written dissent should be promptly delivered to the corporation's secretary.

Duty of Care

Closely related to the duty of attention is the duty of due care. Just as every driver has a duty of due care in operating an automobile, so do officers and directors have a duty of due care in running the affairs of a corporation. Section 35 of the MBCA, imposes on the director a duty to act "in good faith, in a manner he reasonably believes to be in the best interests of the corporation, and with such care as an ordinarily prudent person in a like position would use under similar circumstances." RMBCA §8.30 is similar. Many courts have stated the director's duty in similar terms by requiring, for example, such care as that an ordinarily prudent person would use in the exercise of his or her own personal affairs.

The courts have imposed similar standards of care on officers who face firing, as well as lawsuits, if they breach those standards. [35]

Right to Rely

The duty of due care has not been applied in a burdensome manner. Part of the reason is that after setting forth the duty of care, §35 of the MBCA immediately provides that directors are entitled to rely on information, reports, opinions, financial statements, and financial data provided by officers, employees, counsel, public auditors, or committees of directors that are reasonably believed to be reliable.

The courts have readily held that, in the absence of suspicious circumstances, directors can rely on the honesty and integrity of the officers running the company. Officers are also entitled to rely on the information they receive from fellow officers and other employees. [36] The following case illustrates this right of reliance.

---

[33] *Barr* v. *Wackman*, 329 N.E.2d 180 (N.Y. 1975).

[34] *Selheimer* v. *Manganese Corp. of America*, 224 A.2d 634 (Pa. 1966).

[35] RMBCA §8.42 imposes a similar standard of conduct for officers.

[36] RMBCA §8.42 expressly extends this right of reliance to officers. Naturally, outside directors will be held to a lesser standard and be granted greater leeway in reliance than will inside directors. *Rowen* v. *Le Mars Mutual Insurance Co.*, 282 N.W.2d 639 (Iowa 1979).

GRAHAM v. ALLIS-CHALMERS MANUFACTURING CORPORATION

188 A.2d 125 (Del. Ch. 1963).

Allis-Chalmers and four of its nondirector employees entered guilty pleas to indictments charging violations of federal antitrust laws. Shareholders brought a derivative action on behalf of Allis-Chalmers against those four nondirector employees and *against its directors. Plaintiffs' initial theory was that the director defendants had actual knowledge of the violations. When hearings and depositions produced no evidence that the directors knew of or had any reason to suspect the violations, plaintiffs switched to a theory that directors are liable as a matter of law for failing to detect and prevent such violations. The trial judge entered a ruling of nonliability on behalf of the director defendants. Plaintiffs appealed.*

WOLCOTT, JUSTICE:

. . .

As we have pointed out, there is no evidence in the record that the defendant directors had actual knowledge of the illegal anti-trust actions of the company's employees. Plaintiffs, however, point to two FTC decrees of 1937 as warning to the directors that antitrust activity by the company's employees had taken place in the past.

Plaintiffs argue that because of the 1937 consent decrees, the directors were put on notice that they should take steps to ensure that no employee of Allis-Chalmers would violate the antitrust laws. The difficulty the argument has is that only three of the present directors knew of the decrees, and all three of them satisfied themselves that Allis-Chalmers had not engaged in the practice enjoined and had consented to the decrees merely to avoid expense and the necessity of defending the company's position. Under the circumstances, we think knowledge by three of the directors that in 1937 the company had consented to the entry of decrees enjoining it from doing something they had satisfied themselves it had never done, did not put the Board on notice of the possibility of future illegal price fixing.

Plaintiffs are thus forced to rely solely upon the legal proposition advanced by them that directors of a corporation, as a matter of law, are liable for losses suffered by their corporations by reason of their gross inattention to the common law duty of actively supervising and managing the corporate affairs. Plaintiffs rely mainly upon *Briggs* v. *Spaulding*, 141 U.S. 132, 11 S. Ct. 924, 35 L.Ed. 662.

From the Briggs case and others cited by plaintiffs, it appears that directors of a corporation in managing the corporate affairs are bound to use that amount of care which ordinarily careful and prudent men would use in similar circumstances. Their duties are those of control, and whether or not by neglect they have made themselves liable for failure to exercise proper control depends on the circumstances and facts of the particular case.

The precise charge made against these director defendants is that, even though they had no knowledge of any suspicion of wrongdoing on the part of the company's employees, they still should have put into effect a system of watchfulness which would have brought such misconduct to their attention in ample time to have brought it to an end. However, the Briggs case expressly rejects such an idea. On the contrary, it appears that directors are entitled to rely on the honesty and integrity of their subordinates until something occurs to put them on suspicion that something is wrong. If such occurs and goes unheeded, then liability of the directors might well follow, but absent cause for suspicion there is no duty upon the directors to install and operate a corporate system of espionage to ferret out wrongdoing which they have no reason to suspect exists.

The duties of the Allis-Chalmers Directors were fixed by the nature of the enterprise which employed in excess of 30,000 persons, and extended over a large geographical area. By force of necessity, the company's Directors could not know personally all the company's employees. The very magnitude of the enterprise required them to confine their control to the broad policy decisions. That they did this is clear from the record. At the meetings of the Board in which all Directors participated, these questions were considered and decided on the basis of summaries, reports and corporate records. These they were entitled to rely on, not only, we think, under general principles of the common law, but by reason of 8 Del. C. §141(f) as well, which in terms fully protects a director who relies on such in the performance of his duties.

In the last analysis, the question of whether a corporate director has become liable for losses to the corporation through neglect of duty is determined by the circumstances. If he has recklessly reposed confidence in an obviously untrustworthy employee, has refused or neglected cavalierly to perform his duty as a director, or has ignored either willfully or through inattention obvious danger signs of employee wrongdoing, the law will cast the burden of liability upon him. This is not the case at bar, however, for as soon as it became evident that there were grounds for suspicion, the Board acted promptly to end it and prevent its recurrence.

Plaintiffs say these steps should have been taken long before, even in the absence of suspicion, but we think not, for we know of no rule of law which requires a corporate director to assume, with no justification whatsoever, that all corporate employees are incipient law violators who, but for a tight checkrein, will give free vent to their unlawful propensities.

We therefore affirm the Vice Chancelor's ruling that the individual director defendants are not liable as a matter of law merely because, unknown to them, some employees of Allis-Chalmers violated the antitrust laws thus subjecting the corporation to loss.

Business Judgment Rule

Courts are reluctant to second-guess businesspersons and will not hold management liable for honest mistakes. So great is this reluctance that liability has been refused "though the errors may be so great that they demonstrate the unfitness of the directors to manage the corporation's affairs." [37]

This shielding of corporate managers from liability for their honest mistakes is embodied in the "business judgment rule," which has been stated as follows:

---

[37] 3A Fletcher, *Cyclopedia of Corporations*, §1039, (Wilmette, Ill.: Callahan & Co., 1975), p. 38.

> In the absence of a showing of bad faith on the part of the directors or of a gross abuse of discretion the business judgment of the directors will not be interfered with by the courts. . . . The acts of directors are presumptively acts taken in good faith and inspired for the best interests of the corporation, and a minority stockholder who challenges their *bona fides* of purpose has the burden of proof.[38]

Two applications of the business judgment rule demonstrate how firmly it has been entrenched in American corporate law.

Takeovers. *Panter* v. *Marshall Field & Co.*[39] is a case that arose out of the tender offer situation that will receive substantial attention in Chapter 22. Carter-Hawley Hale (CHH) wished to buy control of Marshall Field & Co. (MF). To that end, CHH announced that it was prepared to buy a controlling interest in MF by offering the latter's shareholders $42 for each share of Marshall Field stock they held. This seemed like an attractive offer to many MF shareholders, especially since their stock had been trading on the open market at $22 per share. Nonetheless, MF's directors decided to resist the tender offer and forced CHH to reconsider its plans by, *inter alia*, purchasing stores that competed with CHH, thereby creating possible antitrust violations should CHH proceed.

After CHH ceased its plans, MF stock dropped to less than $20 per share. Disgruntled shareholders who had been deprived of a chance to sell at $42 per share sued MF's seven outside and three inside directors. The court invoked the business judgment rule to dismiss plaintiffs' claims that the directors had breached their state law fiduciary duty to the corporation and its shareholders. The court was not impressed by plaintiffs' claims that the business judgment rule should not be applied because the directors were in an inherent conflict-of-interest situation because they stood to lose their positions as officers and directors should CHH purchase control. Nor was the court swayed by the strong dissent of Judge Cudahy, who said:

> Unfortunately, the majority here has moved one giant step closer to shredding whatever constraints still remain upon the ability of corporate directors to place self-interest before shareholder interest in resisting a hostile tender offer for control of the corporation. There is abundant evidence in this case to go to the jury on the state claims of breach of fiduciary duty. I emphatically disagree that the business judgment rule should clothe directors, battling blindly to fend off a threat to their control, with an almost irrebuttable presumption of sound business judgment, prevailing over everything but the hobgoblins of fraud, bad faith, or abuse of discretion.

Panter is representative of the traditional view regarding the application of the business judgment rule to the tender offer context. Chapter 22 will discuss some recent qualifications to the rule in this context.

Special Litigation Committees. Although shareholders have the right to initiate derivative litigation on the corporation's behalf where the board of directors refuses

---

[38] *Warshaw* v. *Calhoun*, 221 A.2d 487 (Del. 1966).

[39] 646 F.2d 271 (7th Cir.), *cert. denied*, 454 U.S. 1092 (1981).

to sue, the business judgment rule has been applied to allow a "shareholder litigation committee" (SLC) to terminate that litigation if it decides dismissal is in the corporation's best interests.

A leading case is *Zapata Corporation* v. *Maldonado*,[40] which arose out of the actions of directors of Zapata Corporation in altering stock options to give to certain officers a tax advantage that otherwise would have gone to the corporation. Maldonado, a shareholder, brought a derivative action against ten officers and directors of the corporation. Two years after the suit was filed, four of the defendants had left the board and the remaining directors appointed two new outside directors. A special litigation committee, composed solely of the two new directors, was then formed to determine whether Maldonado's action should be continued. The committee's decision was to be final and binding.

The committee decided that continued maintenance of the action was inimical to the corporation's best interests, and defendants moved for dismissal on this ground. The Delaware Supreme Court determined that a court could dismiss shareholder litigation upon the recommendation of a shareholder litigation committee, if the proper procedures were followed:

> First, the Court should inquire into the independence and good faith of the committee and the bases supporting its conclusions. Limited discovery may be ordered to facilitate such inquiries. The corporation should have the burden of proving independence, good faith, and a reasonable investigation, rather than presuming independence, good faith, and reasonableness.
>
> If the Court determines either that the committee is not independent or has not shown reasonable bases for its conclusions, or, if the Court is not satisfied for other reasons relating to the process, including but not limited to the good faith of the committee, the Court shall deny the corporation's motion. If, however, the Court is satisfied that the committee was independent and showed reasonable bases for good faith findings and recommendations, the Court may proceed, in its discretion, to the next step.
>
> The second step provides, we believe, the essential key in striking the balance between legitimate corporate claims as expressed in a derivative stockholder suit and a corporation's best interests as expressed by an independent investigating committee. The Court should determine, applying its own independent business judgment, whether the motion should be granted. This means, of course, that instances could arise where a committee can establish its independence and sound bases for its good faith decisions and still have the corporation's motion denied. The second step is intended to thwart instances where corporate actions meet the criteria of step one, but the result does not appear to satisfy its spirit, or where corporate actions would simply prematurely terminate a stockholder grievance deserving of further consideration in the corporation's interest. The Court of Chancery of course must carefully consider and weigh how compelling the corporate interest in dismissal is when faced with a nonfrivolous lawsuit. The Court of Chancery should, when appropriate, give special consideration to matters of law and public policy in addition to the corporation's best interests.
>
> If the Court's independent business judgment is satisfied, the Court may proceed to grant the motion, subject, of course, to any equitable terms or conditions the Court finds necessary or desirable.

---

[40] 430 A.2d 779 (Del. 1981).

In practice, shareholder litigation committees seem almost always to conclude that derivative litigation by shareholders should be terminated. For that reason, they have become very popular with management defendants. Many jurisdictions have accepted their use. Some courts have been even more protective of defendants by holding that the SLC's independence and good faith are the only matters for court review, eliminating the second step review by the court suggested in *Zapata*.[41] Other courts have leaned the other way, holding that an SLC cannot be deemed "independent" when, as in *Zapata*, its members are appointed by directors who are defendants in the litigation.[42]

The reluctance of courts to impose liability for breach of a duty of care as tempered by the business judgment rule has led one commentator to note that there is a "minuscule likelihood of liability [being imposed] on independent directors."[43] Indeed, it has also been said that the search for cases holding directors liable for negligence when self-dealing was not involved is like trying to find "a very small number of needles in a very large haystack."[44]

The chance of imposition of painful liability for a breach of the duty of due care is rendered even more remote by the availability of indemnification from the corporation and of indemnity insurance, both discussed later in this chapter.

Despite these conclusions, which must be heartening for officers and directors, we cannot leave this section without mentioning one major storm cloud on their horizon. The following case surprised many experts by imposing liability in a situation where the business judgment rule would traditionally have been expected to provide a good defense. The case has already had substantial implications for directors' and officers' liability insurance, as we shall see later in this chapter, and for tender offer defenses as we shall see later in the text.[45]

SMITH v. VAN GORKOM

488 A.2d 858 (Del. 1985)

Trans Union Corporation's stock price suffered due to an inability to utilize large investment tax credits by generating additional income. Senior management discussed solutions, including a leveraged buy-out by management in the $50- to $60-per-share range. Trans Union stock was selling at $29–38 per share at that time.

Trans Union's president, Van Gorkom, unilaterally decided to meet with Jay Pritzker, a

---

[41] For example, *Auerbach* v. *Bennett*, 419 N.Y.S.2d 920 (1979).

[42] For example, *Miller* v. *Register and Tribune Syndications, Inc.*, 336 N.W.2d 709 (Iowa 1983).

[43] V. Brudney, "The Independent Director—Heavenly City or Potemkin Village?" *Harvard Law Review*, Vol. 95 (1982), p. 597.

[44] J. Bishop, "Sitting Ducks and Decoy Ducks: New Trends in Indemnification of Corporate Officers and Directors," *Yale Law Journal*, Vol. 77 (1968), p. 1078.

[45] Chapter 22.

person wealthy enough to buy Trans Union. Pritzker was interested, so Van Gorkom suggested a price of $55 per share but said Trans Union should be free to accept a better offer if one arose. After a series of meetings with Van Gorkom, on Thursday, September 18, 1980, Pritzker told him that he intended to make a cash-out merger offer for $55 per share and demanded that Trans Union's board act within three days. On Friday, Van Gorkom retained special legal counsel and called a board meeting for Saturday, September 20. The directors were not told the purpose of the meeting and Trans Union's investment banker was not invited.

Nine of the ten board members, all of whom were familiar with Trans Union's affairs and five of whom were outside directors, were present. During the two-hour meeting the directors received no explanation as to the origin of the $55 per share price, nor did they receive any estimate of the value of the corporation. They did hear a 20-minute summary of the Pritzker offer by Van Gorkom; a statement by Romans (Trans Union's chief financial officer) that he hadn't seen the proposal until that morning and that his studies did not indicate a fair price for the company's stock but that in his opinion $55 was "in the range of a fair price" but "at the beginning of the range"; and a statement by attorney Brennan that the members might be sued if they failed to accept the offer and that a fairness opinion was not required as a matter of law.

The board approved the merger, though the directors had not reviewed the merger documents which Pritzker's attorney was drawing. That night at an opera, Van Gorkom signed the merger documents without reading them. Later the board claimed to have reserved the right to accept a better offer during the 90-day period it would take to close the deal (so-called "curative" action). No such offer was forthcoming.

Shareholders brought this suit against Trans Union and its directors seeking rescission of the merger. The trial court ruled for defendants, concluding that the board had acted in an informed manner and that the shareholder vote which later approved the merger should not be set aside because the stockholders had been "fairly informed." Plaintiffs appealed.

HORSEY, JUSTICE:

Under Delaware law, the business judgment rule is the offspring of the fundamental principle, codified in 8 Del. C. §141(a), that the business and affairs of a Delaware corporation are managed by or under its board of directors. *Pogostin v. Rice*, Del. Supr., 480 A.2d 619, 624 (1984); *Aronson v. Lewis*, Del. Supr., 473 A.2d 805, 811 (1984); *Zapata Corp. v. Maldonado*, Del. Supr., 430 A.2d 779, 782 (1981). In carrying out their managerial roles, directors are charged with an unyielding fiduciary duty to the corporation and its shareholders. *Loft, Inc. v. Guth*, Del. Ch., 2 A.2d 225 (1938), *aff'd*, Del. Supr., 5 A.2d 503 (1939). The business judgment rule exists to protect and promote the full and free exercise of the managerial power granted to Delaware directors. The rule itself "is a presumption that in making a business decision, the directors of a corporation acted on an informed basis, in good faith and in the honest belief that the action taken was in the best interests of the company"—*Aronson*, supra at 812. Thus, the party attacking a board decision as uninformed must rebut the presumption that its business judgment was an informed one—Id.

The determination of whether a business judgment is an informed one turns on whether the directors have informed themselves "prior to making a business decision, of all material information reasonably available to them"—Id.

Under the business judgment rule there is no protection for directors who have made "an unintelligent or unadvised judgment." *Mitchell*

v. *Highland-Western Glass*, Del. Ch., 167 A. 831, 833 (1933). A director's duty to inform himself in preparation for a decision derives from the fiduciary capacity in which he serves the corporation and its stockholders. *Lutz* v. *Boas*, Del. Ch., 171 A.2d 381 (1961). *See Weinberger* v. *UOP, Inc.*, supra; *Guth* v. *Loft*, supra. Since a director is vested with the responsibility for the management of the affairs of the corporation, he must execute that duty with the recognition that he acts on behalf of others. Such obligation does not tolerate faithlessness or selfdealing. But fulfillment of the fiduciary function requires more than the mere absence of bad faith or fraud. Representation of the financial interests of others imposes on a director an affirmative duty to protect those interests and to proceed with a critical eye in assessing information of the type and under the circumstances present here.

Thus, a director's duty to exercise an informed business judgment is in the nature of a duty of care, as distinguished from a duty of loyalty. Here, there were no allegations of fraud, bad faith, or self-dealing, or proof thereof. Hence, it is presumed that the directors reached their business judgment in good faith, *Allaun* v. *Consolidated Oil Co.*, Del. Ch., 147 A. 257 (1929), and considerations of motive are irrelevant to the issue before us.

The standard of care applicable to a director's duty of care has also been recently restated by this Court. In *Aronson*, supra, we stated:

> While the Delaware cases use a variety of terms to describe the applicable standard of care, our analysis satisfies us that under the business judgment rule director liability is predicated upon concepts of gross negligence.

We again confirm that view. We think the concept of gross negligence is also the proper standard for determining whether a business judgment reached by a board of directors was an informed one.

-A-

On the record before us, we must conclude that the Board of Directors did not reach an informed business judgment on September 20, 1980 in voting to "sell" the Company for $55 per share pursuant to the Pritzker cash-out merger proposal. Our reasons, in summary, are as follows:

The directors (1) did not adequately inform themselves as to Van Gorkom's role in forcing the "sale" of the Company and in establishing the per share purchase price; (2) were uninformed as to the intrinsic value of the Company; and (3) given these circumstances, at a minimum, were grossly negligent in approving the "sale" of the Company upon two hours' consideration, without prior notice, and without the exigency of a crisis or emergency.

As has been noted, the Board based its September 20 decision to approve the cash-out merger primarily on Van Gorkom's representations. None of the directors, other than Van Gorkom and Chelberg, had any prior knowledge that the purpose of the meeting was to propose a cash-out merger of Trans Union. No members of Senior Management were present, other than Chelberg, Romans and Peterson; and the latter two had only learned of the proposed sale an hour earlier. Both general counsel Moore and former general counsel Browder attended the meeting, but were equally uninformed as to the purpose of the meeting and the documents to be acted upon.

Without any documents before them concerning the proposed transaction, the members of the Board were required to rely entirely upon Van Gorkom's 20-minute oral presentation of the proposal. No written summary of the terms of the merger was presented: the directors were given no documentation to support the adequacy of $55 price per share for sale of the Company; and the Board had before it nothing more than Van Gorkom's statement of his understanding of the substance of an agreement which he admittedly had never read, nor which any member of the Board had ever seen.

Under 8 Del. C. §141(e), "directors are fully protected in relying in good faith on reports made by officers." *See also Graham* v. *Allis-Chalmers Mfg. Co.*, Del. Supr., 188 A.2d 125, 130 (1963). However, there is no evidence that any "report," as defined under §141(e), concerning the Pritzker proposal, was presented to the Board on September 20. Van Gorkom's oral presentation of his understanding of the terms of the proposed Merger Agreement, which he had not seen, and Romans' brief oral statement of his preliminary study regarding the feasibility of a leveraged buy-out of Trans Union do not qualify as §141(e) "reports" for these reasons: The former lacked substance because Van Gorkom was basically uninformed as to the essential provisions of the very document about which he was talking. Romans' statement was irrelevant to the issues before the Board since it did not purport to be a valuation study.

The defendants rely on the following factors to sustain the Trial Court's finding that the Board's decision was an informed one: (1) the magnitude of the premium or spread between the $55 Pritzker offering price and Trans Union's current market price of $38 per share; (2) the amendment of the Agreement as submitted on September 20 to permit the Board to accept any better offer during the "market test" period: (3) the collective experience and expertise of the Board's "inside" and "outside" directors; and (4) their reliance on Brennan's legal advice that the directors might be sued if they rejected the Pritzker proposal. We discuss each of these grounds *seriatim*:

(1)

A substantial premium may provide one reason to recommend a merger, but in the absence of other sound valuation information, the fact of a premium alone does not provide an adequate basis upon which to assess the fairness of an offering price. Here, the judgment reached as to the adequacy of the premium was based on a comparison between the historically depressed Trans Union market price and the amount of the Pritzker offer. Using market price as a basis for concluding that the premium adequately reflected the true value of the Company was a clearly faulty, indeed fallacious, premise, as the defendants' own evidence demonstrates.

(2)

This brings us to the post–September 20 "market test" upon which the defendants ultimately rely to confirm the reasonableness of their September 20 decision to accept the Pritzker proposal. In this connection, the directors present a two-part argument: (a) that by making a "market test" of Pritzker's $55 per share offer a condition of their September 20 decision to accept his offer, they cannot be found to have acted impulsively or in an uninformed manner on September 20; and (b) that the adequacy of the $17 premium for sale of the Company was conclusively established over the following 90 to 120 days by the most reliable evidence available—the marketplace.

Again, the facts of record do not support the defendants' argument. There is no evidence: (a) that the Merger Agreement was effectively amended to give the Board freedom to put Trans Union up for auction sale to the highest bidder; or (b) that a public auction was in fact permitted to occur.

(3)

The directors' unfounded reliance on both the premium and the market test as the basis for accepting the Pritzker proposal undermines the defendants' remaining contention that the

Board's collective experience and sophistication was a sufficient basis for finding that it reached its September 20 decision with informed, reasonable deliberation.

(4)

Part of the defense is based on a claim that the directors relied on legal advice rendered at the September 20 meeting by James Brennan, Esquire, who was present at Van Gorkom's request.

Several defendants testified that Brennan advised them that Delaware law did not require a fairness opinion or an outside valuation of the Company before the Board could act on the Pritzker proposal. If given, the advice was correct. However, that did not end the matter. Unless the directors had before them adequate information regarding the intrinsic value of the Company, upon which a proper exercise of business judgment could be made, mere advice of this type is meaningless; and, given this record of the defendants' failures, it constitutes no defense here.

A second claim is that counsel advised the Board it would be subject to lawsuits if it rejected the $55 per share offer. It is, of course, a fact of corporate life that today when faced with difficult or sensitive issues, directors often are subject to suit, irrespective of the decisions they make. However, counsel's mere acknowledgement of this circumstance cannot be rationally translated into a justification for a board permitting itself to be stampeded into a patently unadvised act. While suit might result from the rejection of a merger or tender offer, Delaware law makes clear that a board acting within the ambit of the business judgment rule faces no ultimate liability. *Pogostin* v. *Rice*, supra. Thus, we cannot conclude that the mere threat of litigation, acknowledged by counsel, constitutes either legal advice or any valid basis upon which to pursue an uninformed course.

-B-

[The court then concluded that nothing the board had done after September 20, 1981, remedied its mistakes.]

IV.

Whether the directors of Trans Union should be treated as one or individually in terms of invoking the protection of the business judgment rule and the applicability of 8 Del. C. §141(c) are questions which were not originally addressed by the parties in their briefing of this case.

The parties' response, including reargument, has led the majority of the Court to conclude: (1) that since all of the defendant directors, outside as well as inside, take a unified position, we are required to treat all of the directors as one as to whether they are entitled to the protection of the business judgment rule; and (2) that considerations of good faith, including the presumption that the directors acted in good faith, are irrelevant in determining the threshold issue of whether the directors as a Board exercised an informed business judgment. For the same reason, we must reject defense counsel's *ad hominem* argument for affirmance: that reversal may result in a multimillion-dollar class award against the defendants for having made an allegedly uninformed business judgment in a transaction not involving any personal gain, self-dealing or claim of bad faith.

In their brief, the defendants similarly mistake the business judgment rule's application to this case by erroneously invoking presumptions of good faith and ''wide discretion.'' However, plaintiffs have not claimed, nor did the Trial Court decide, that $55 was a grossly inadequate price per share for sale of the Company. That being so, the presumption that a board's judgment as to adequacy of price represents an honest exercise of business judgment (absent proof that the sale price was grossly inadequate) is irrelevant to the threshold question of whether an informed judgment was reached.

[*The court finally concluded that because*

the shareholders had not been adequately informed, their vote approving the merger did not constitute a ratification that would absolve defendants of liability.]

Reversed.

Van Gorkom's main message appears to be that directors and officers had better do their homework if they want the protection of the business judgment rule.[46]

Miscellaneous Statutory Duties

The statutes of many states expressly impose liability on directors and officers for a variety of prohibited acts relating to the running of the corporation. For example, §48 of the MBCA imposes liability on any director who votes for or assents to payment of a dividend or any distribution in violation of the provisions of the MBCA. RMBCA §8.33 is similar. Such a director is entitled to a due care defense, and if found liable, to contribution from any recipient shareholder or fellow director who assented to the violation.

Similar statutes deal with such matters as improper purchases by the corporation of its own shares, issuance of shares without proper consideration, preferential transfers to shareholders during liquidation, and commencement of business without the statutory minimum capitalization.

Loans to directors and other insiders present another problem. Section 47 of the MBCA provides that a corporation shall not lend money to a director or use its credit to assist a director without shareholder authorization, *but* may loan money to an employee, including an employee who is also a director, "if the board of directors decides that such loan or assistance may benefit the corporation." [47] Some states prohibit any loans to directors, but most allow them if there is full disclosure.

There are also various statutes, state and federal, that subject officers and directors to liability for OSHA violations, antitrust violations, overtime due under the Federal Fair Labor Standards Act, failure to withhold federal income tax payments, and a wide variety of other actions or omissions.

---

[46] *See* L. Herzel, S. Davis, D. Colling, " 'Smith' Brings Whip Down on Directors' Backs," *Legal Times*, May 13, 1985, p. 14; and B. Schwartz and J. Wiles, "Business Judgment Rule Clarified by Del.'s Trans Union Decision," *National Law Journal*, July 8, 1985, p. 42.

[47] RMBCA §8.32 provides a second method of approving a loan to a director—approval by holders of a majority of shares. The votes of shares controlled by the interested director are not counted.

Duty of Loyalty

Conflict of Interest

While mere negligence or incompetence seldom leads to manager liability, a number of types of self-dealing will. Directors' and officers' conflicts of interest are a major problem. Section 41 of the MBCA legitimizes contracts between a corporation and its director or between a corporation and another business in which one of its directors is financially interested, if (1) the interest of the director is disclosed to the board or a committee of the board that approves the arrangement without the vote of the interested director, or (2) there is disclosure to the shareholders who approve, or (3) "the contract or transaction is fair and reasonable to the corporation." Use of the conjunction "or" makes it appear that the MBCA authorizes even secret transactions between a director and the corporation *if* upon discovery the transaction proves fair to the corporation.

Still, dealings between a director or officer and the corporation are fraught with possibilities that the corporation's interests will be subordinated. That is why courts place the burden on the manager to prove the fairness of a transactions with the corporation.

To illustrate, a fiduciary breach was found when Smith, a director of Citation Manufacturing Co., failed to warn Citation of the imminent bankruptcy of his wholly owned company that purchased substantial goods from Citation *on credit*.[48] Similarly, an inappropriate conflict of interest was held to exist when Edward, who had formed a real estate development corporation with his stepbrother William, informed William that he wanted to purchase one-half of a double house owned by the corporation to provide security for his mother, but then bought the entire house for himself and his wife at below market price without notifying William.[49]

Yet another improper conflict arose in *Globe Woolen Co.* v. *Utica Gas & Electric Co.*,[50] when Maynard, a director of Utica, negotiated and framed a contract for Utica to sell electricity at bargain prices to Globe Woolen, a corporation owned primarily by Maynard, its president. The appellate court approved the setting aside of the contract, though Maynard had abstained from voting when Utica's board approved it, saying

> [T]he refusal to vote does not nullify as of course the influence and predominance exerted without a vote. We hold that the constant duty rests on a trustee to seek no harsh advantage to the detriment of his trust, but rather to protest and renounce if through blindness of those who treat with him he gains what is unfair.

Interlocking Directorships. The *Globe Woolen* case raises a persistent conflict of interest problem—that of interlocking directorships. Maynard was a director of both

---

[48] *Smith* v. *Citation Mfg. Co., Inc.*, 587 S.W.2d 39 (Ark. 1979).

[49] *Warren* v. *Warren*, 460 A.2d 526 (Del. 1983).

[50] 121 N.E. 378 (N.Y. 1918).

Globe Woolen and Utica. When those two corporations dealt with one another, how could Maynard fairly serve two masters? Certainly the courts carefully scrutinize transactions between corporations with common directors. The test is fairness.

Additionally, the Clayton Act [51] outlaws interlocking directorates between corporations where (1) one has at least $1 million in assets and (2) the corporations are in sufficiently close competition that the antitrust laws would be violated if they cooperated. Note, however, that this prohibition does not apply to parent-subsidiary, or corporation-supplier relationships, nor does it prevent Corporation A from having its directors on the boards of competitors B and C, so long as A does not compete with either B or C.

Corporate Opportunity Doctrine

Favorable business opportunities frequently arise that directors or officers would like to have for themselves. However, if managers appropriate for themselves opportunities that might benefit the corporation and in which the corporation might reasonably be interested, they violate their fiduciary duty of loyalty.

A rather blatant example of such a violation appears in the following case.

MORAD v. COUPOUNAS

361 So.2d 6 (Ala. 1978)

In 1972, Morad, Thomson, Coupounas, and Shaw formed Bio-Lab, Inc., for the purpose of establishing a plasmapheresis business. This involves separating red blood cells from the plasma of paid donors, returning the red blood cells to the donors' circulatory system, and selling the plasma to biological manufacturing companies. Bio-Lab's first office was opened in Montgomery, Alabama, with Morad, who had experience in the business, installed as president. Coupounas, who lived in Massachusetts, was to handle the books. At the outset, the parties expected to expand Bio-Lab's business to other cities, including Tuscaloosa.

Shaw soon sold her interest, leaving Morad
(42%), Thomson (28%), and Coupounas (30%) as the sole owners. Dissension arose, and Coupounas was removed from Bio-Lab's board of directors. In September 1974, Med-Lab, Inc., a corporation formed by Morad, his wife, and Thomson, began operating a plasmapheresis business in Tuscaloosa.

Coupounas, shut out of the Tuscaloosa venture, filed suit. Evidence showed that both corporations were profitable, that the two corporations sold 95% of their products to the same three purchasers, that Morad jointly purchased insurance policies and supplies for both corporations, and that Morad used a car supplied him by Bio-Lab for Med-Lab purposes.

[51] 15 U.S.C. §19.

The trial court ruled for Coupounas, ordering Morad and Thomson to offer him a 30% interest in Med-Lab. Defendants appealed.

FAULKNER, JUSTICE:

In *Lagarde* v. *Anniston Lime & Stone Co.*, 126 Ala. 496, 28 So. 199 (1899), this Court first formulated its doctrine of corporate opportunity. There it was stated:

> It is well settled that directors and other governing members of a corporation are so far agents of the corporation that in their dealings respecting corporate interests, they are subject to the rules which apply generally to persons standing in fiduciary relations and which forbid such persons to secure an advantage for themselves which fidelity to the trust reposed in them would carry to others whose interests they ought to represent.
>
> [I]n general the legal restrictions which rest upon such officers in their acquisitions are generally limited to property wherein the corporation has an interest already existing, or in which it has an expectancy growing out of an existing right, or to cases where the officers' interference will in some degree balk the corporation in effecting the purposes of its creation.

We think that *Lagarde* when properly read establishes responsibilities for the corporate officer or director comparable to those outlined *Guth* v. *Loft, Inc.*, 23 Del. Ch. 255, 5 A.2d 503 (1939), where the Delaware Supreme Court employed the doctrine of corporate opportunity and observed that it

> demands of a corporate officer or director, peremptorily and inexorably, the most scrupulous observance of his duty, not only affirmatively to protect the interests of the corporation committed to his charge, but also to refrain from doing anything that would work injury to the corporation, or to deprive it of profit or advantage which his skill and ability might properly bring to it, or to enable it to make in the reasonable and lawful exercise of its powers. The rule that requires an undivided and unselfish loyalty to the corporation demands that there shall be no conflict between duty and self-interest. The occasions for the determination of honesty, good faith and loyal conduct are many and varied, and no hard and fast rule can be formu-

lated. The standard of loyalty is measured by no fixed scale.

Moreover, the Delaware Supreme Court stated in more practical terms what the law demands of corporate officers or directors:

> [I]f there is presented to a corporate officer or director a business opportunity which the corporation is financially able to undertake, is, from its nature, in the line of the corporation's business and is of practical advantage to it, is one in which the corporation has an interest or a reasonable expectancy, and, by embracing the opportunity, the self-interest of the officer or director will be brought into conflict with that of his corporation, the law will not permit him to seize the opportunity for himself.

We think that this passage provides a workable definition of "balking the corporate purpose." To this definition must be added the caveat that whether or not an officer has misappropriated a corporate opportunity and thereby balked the corporate purpose does not depend on any single factor. On the contrary,

> [n]umerous factors are to be weighed, including the manner in which the offer was communicated to the officer; the good faith of the officer; the use of corporate assets to acquire the opportunity; the financial ability of the corporation to acquire the opportunity; the degree of disclosure made to the corporation; the action taken by the corporation with reference thereto; and the need or interest of the corporation in the opportunity. These, as well as numerous other factors, are weighed in a given case. The presence or absence of any single factor is not determinative of the issue of corporate opportunity—*Paulman* v. *Kritzer*, 74 Ill. App.2d 284, 219 N.E.2d 541 (1966).

Here the trial court specifically found that one of the corporate purposes of Bio-Lab was to expand into specific new areas, including Tuscaloosa. Ample evidence in the record supports this conclusion. Bio-Lab's certificate of incorporation declared that one of the purposes of the business was "to have one or more offices." While this open-ended, boilerplate language standing alone might not be sufficient to support the trial court's findings, testimony and exhibits produced at trial show that expansion to Tuscaloosa was anticipated for Bio-Lab's future.

As pointed out above, one of the factors to be considered by the trial court is the corporation's financial ability to undertake the new enterprise, although financial ability must be carefully considered and will not necessarily be determinative. As observed in *Paulman* v. *Kritzer*,

> The inherent dangers of permitting a corporate officer or director to seize upon an opportunity on the grounds that the corporation is financially unable to do so, at a time when the corporation is solvent, is recognized in *Irving Trust Co.* v. *Deutsch*, 73 F.2d 121, at page 124 (C.A.2, 1934) where the court stated:
> "If directors are permitted to justify their conduct on such a theory, there will be a temptation to refrain from exerting their strongest efforts on behalf of the corporation since, if it does not meet the obligations, an opportunity of profit will be open to them personally."

Testimony on the issue of financial ability was given at trial by Herbert Raburn, a certified public accountant, familiar with the books of both Bio-Lab and Med-Lab. Counsel for Morad sought to have Raburn testify that Bio-Lab could not have obtained a loan to finance expansion to Tuscaloosa. In fact, no one had ever sought a loan for this purpose. Because no loan had been sought, the trial court refused to allow Raburn to testify on this point, and observed that any testimony on what a particular bank would do, would be, under the circumstances, highly speculative. We agree. Raburn admitted that he knew only "in general terms" what banks look for in making loans. Consequently, he was not qualified to testify whether or not Bio-Lab could have gotten a loan.

Furthermore, Raburn's testimony revealed that $44,000 had been required to establish Med-Lab. At the end of 1974 Bio-Lab had only $24,300 available for this purpose. But, Raburn also testified that in 1974 Bio-Lab had paid a "rather high" dividend of $20,000. His testimony indicated that the payment of dividends is often restricted when a corporation wishes to expand. Thus, if the dividend had not been paid, Bio-Lab clearly should have had the financial ability to expand to Tuscaloosa, with or without a loan. In light of this testimony the trial court's finding that defendants improperly formed Med-Lab to the detriment of Bio-Lab is clearly supportable and will not be disturbed by this Court on appeal.

We do not, however, feel that the trial court was justified in ordering defendants to offer 30% of Med-Lab's stock to Coupounas. The traditional remedy in cases of this sort is a constructive trust imposed for the benefit of the corporation. See e.g. *McKinstry* v. *Thomas*, 258 Ala. 690, 64 So.2d 808 (1953); *Guth* v. *Loft, Inc.*, 23 Del. Ch. 255, 5 A.2d 503 (1939); *Legarde* v. *Anniston Lime & Stone Co.*, 126 Ala. 496, 28 So. 199 (1899). In *McKinstry* a constructive trust was precluded because the corporation had been dissolved. But no such justification exists for the remedy imposed here. One purpose for preserving the use of a constructive trust in this sort of situation is to avoid forcing individuals into business together under strained circumstances. Such a situation would only be counterproductive. The policy underlying the use of a constructive trust is well illustrated by this case. Coupounas and defendants were not getting along prior to the formation of Med-Lab. It is hardly likely that their relations have improved through the course of this lawsuit. While the courts should strive to place the parties in their proper financial positions, they should not force individuals into business arrangements they clearly do not want. Here, a constructive trust for the benefit of Bio-Lab was the appropriate remedy.

Affirmed in part, reversed in part, and remanded.

One interesting case held that although a director may have appropriated a corporate opportunity, his action was automatically ratified because he was the corporation's sole shareholder.[52] Absent this unusual situation, however, it is clear that a manager who takes personal advantage of a corporate opportunity bears a heavy burden of demonstrating good faith and fairness.

CONTRACTUAL, TORT, AND CRIMINAL LIABILITIES

Contractual Liabilities

When officers contract on behalf of the corporation, naturally they intend the corporation to be liable on the contract rather than themselves. This is usually the case. However, under standard agency principles an officer may be personally liable on a contract if he or she (1) exceeds the limits of actual authority, (2) fails to sign the contract in a representative capacity, (3) signs a personal guaranty to support the corporate obligation, or (4) appears to be the contracting party while the corporation remains an undisclosed principal.

Tort Liabilities

In addition to being liable in tort to the corporation for breach of the duty of due care and the fiduciary duties already discussed, directors and officers may also be held liable to *third parties* for tortious actions committed by them personally or under their direction that injure employees, creditors, and others. They are personally liable even if their actions are done in the name of the corporation. Standard agency principles apply. The corporation will also be liable if the agent was acting within the scope of authority when committing the tort.

Corporate officers and directors are sometimes sued in tort by third parties when they direct the corporation to breach a contract with that third party. Unless they are bound as parties, such as guarantors, corporate managers are not liable in this manner so long as they believed they were acting in the corporation's best interests.[53] The third party is relegated to a breach of contract suit against the corporation.

Criminal Liabilities

Directors

Directors are fortunate in that criminal prosecutions against them have seldom succeeded absent egregious circumstances. Usually prosecutions have focused on officers rather than directors. Nonetheless, directors face potential criminal liability under federal

---

[52] *Canion* v. *Texas Cycle Supply, Inc.*, 537 S.W.2d 510 (Tex. Civ. App. 1976).

[53] For example, *Maxey* v. *Citizens National Bank of Lubbock*, 507 S.W.2d 722 (Tex. 1974).

antitrust, securities, tax, corrupt practices, environmental, and other laws for violations occurring with their participation or under their authority.

Furthermore, many states also have criminal provisions nominally applicable to the director. New York, for example, makes it a misdemeanor for a director intentionally to falsify business records, issue false financial statements, engage in commercial bribery, advertise falsely, bribe a labor official, authorize improper dividends or distributions, or receive notes in payment for stock.[54]

Officers

An officer who commits a crime, directs a subordinate to commit a crime, or acquiesces in a criminal act committed by a subordinate under his or her supervision is guilty of a crime. The fact that the officer is acting in an official capacity for the purpose of benefiting the corporation is no defense. The officer may be liable as a principal or an aider and abettor. Officers are usually not criminally liable for criminal acts committed by other officers or employees not acting under their supervision or with their permission.[55]

Normally an officer must have criminal intent to be held criminally liable. However, there are a few federal statutes imposing strict criminal liability on corporate officers that have been enforced.[56]

Officers are not often held criminally liable, especially in light of a recent trend to hold the corporate entity itself criminally liable for the acts of its agents.[57] Nonetheless, in a recent case, *People* v. *O'Neil*,[58] three corporate executives were found guilty of *murder* in the deaths of employees exposed to cyanide gas in the workplace.

INDEMNITY AND INSURANCE

Indemnity

As the potential liability of directors and officers has widened, there has been an accompanying tendency to increase corporate indemnification of managers. Indemnification occurs when a corporation reimburses one of its managers from corporate funds for fines, judgments, and expenses incurred by the director in litigation arising out of corporate activity.

---

[54] M. Schultz, *The Board of Directors: Composition, Duties and Liabilities, Meetings and Procedures A-8* (Washington, D.C.: Bureau of National Affairs, Corporate Practice Series, 1980).

[55] *See* Note, ''Limits on Individual Accountability for Corporate Crimes,'' *Marquette Law Review*, Vol. 67 (1984), p. 604.

[56] For example, *U.S.* v. *Park*, 421 U.S. 658 (1975) (Federal Food, Drug and Cosmetics Act).

[57] For example, *Commonwealth of Pennsylvania* v. *McIlwain School Bus Line*, 283 Pa. Super. 1, 423 A.2d 413 (1980).

[58] No. 83C-11091 (Cook County, Ill. Circuit Court 1985).

Three major reasons for allowing corporations to indemnify officers and directors are (1) it encourages innocent managers to defend themselves, (2) it induces quality people to serve as directors, and (3) it deters "strike suits" by shareholders and others.[59] On the other hand, too liberal a policy of indemnification may protect wrongdoing officers and directors and remove any incentive for managers to be law abiding. Despite this controversy, the strong modern trend favors indemnification.

This trend is embodied in the 1980 amendments to MBCA §5 and RMBCA §8.51, which empower a corporation to indemnify a director if (1) he conducted himself in good faith, (2) he reasonably believed his conduct was in the corporation's best interests, and (3) in the case of any criminal proceedings, he had no reasonable cause to believe his conduct was unlawful. This *permissible* indemnity extends to judgments, penalties, fines, settlements, and expenses actually incurred in actions by third parties. However, if the action was brought by or on behalf of the corporation, indemnification extends only to expenses and shall not be paid at all if the director is held liable to the corporation. Obviously, there is an illogical circuity if a director is required to pay a judgment to the corporation, but the corporation then reaches into its treasury to reimburse the director for the judgment and his expenses. Also, no indemnity may be paid if a director is held liable on a claim that he received improper personal benefit.

Section 5 of the MBCA and §8.52 of the RMBCA also provide for *mandatory* indemnification, stating that unless the articles otherwise provide (1) a director shall be indemnified for reasonable expenses if he has been wholly successful in his defense and (2) a court has authority to order indemnification (a) upon application of a wholly successful defendant director who has been denied indemnity by the corporation or (b) if it determines that the director is "fairly and reasonably" entitled to indemnification in light of all relevant circumstances.

No permissive indemnification may be paid unless a determination that the director has met the proper standard of conduct is made by (1) a majority vote of a quorum consisting of nondefendant directors, or (2) a majority of an independent committee of the board, or (3) special legal counsel, or (4) the shareholders.

So, generally speaking, a director who acted in good faith may be reimbursed for judgments, fines, settlements, payments, and expenses incurred in suits by *third parties*. But if the suit is brought *by the corporation* or on its behalf, the director is entitled only to expenses if he or she prevails and if properly approved.

The MBCA's §5 and RMBCA §8.56 accord officers essentially the same rights to indemnification as are given directors and even allow the articles of incorporation or bylaws to extend those rights.

Indemnity Insurance

To cover situations where indemnity is not available, directors' and officers' (D&O) insurance has become quite popular. Section 5 of the MBCA and RMBCA §8.57 specifically authorize corporations to pay for such insurance for their officers and directors.

---

[59] *Solimine* v. *Hollander*, 19 A.2d 344 (N.J. 1941).

D&O policies are very helpful to the director, though they do have some important limitations. For example, most insurance companies refuse to write such insurance for smaller corporations, say, under $2 million in assets. Also, most policies have exclusions for liabilities arising from (1) antitrust violations, (2) §16(b) (1934 Act) insider trading violations, (3) defamation, (4) ERISA violations, (5) violation of environmental laws, and (6) active dishonesty.

Despite these limitations, over 90% of *Fortune* 500 companies, and many smaller corporations, carry D&O insurance. Even the SEC, which generally opposes indemnification for any securities law violation, approves the purchase by the corporation of D&O insurance.

Current "Crisis"

Together, indemnification and D&O insurance provide a substantial shield for officers and directors. However, that shield is weakened if D&O insurance is unavailable or prohibitively costly. Cases such as *Smith* v. *Van Gorkom* and the *Wickes Co.* case, where $25 million was paid in settlements under a D&O policy, have led insurance companies to make drastic changes. Some have quit writing D&O policies. Others have increased their premiums by up to 45 times, while some have drastically reduced coverage. This has made it very difficult for many corporations to procure affordable D&O insurance. Without such coverage, surely many persons will decide that it is not worth the risk to be a corporate director.

Numerous solutions to this liability insurance "crisis" are being considered. Indiana has passed a law eliminating any liability for directors for breach of a duty of care except for willful or reckless misconduct. Delaware authorized charter amendments to achieve the same goal. The American Law Institute's (ALI's) discussion draft No. 1 of its "Principles of Corporate Governance" takes the position that corporations could validly place ceilings on liability for due care violations in the corporate charter.

Substantial reform in this area is almost certain to occur in the very near future.

QUESTIONS AND PROBLEMS

1. Senior Citizens Land and Development Co. was incorporated in October 1960 under the guiding hand of Florence. It originally had nine directors, including Kring. In November 1960, Kring was issued 30,000 shares of stock at $0.50 per share; he paid $2,500 in cash and gave a $12,500 note. The corporation never made money and ceased operation in about a year. In August 1961, a meeting with Kring, Florence, and Mathis, all directors, apparently led to an agreement whereby Kring would return his shares in exchange for cancellation of his note. Plaintiff, suing on behalf of creditors, seeks to enforce the note as an unpaid subscription. Was the August 1961 meeting effective to cancel the note? Discuss. See *Doyle* v. *Chladek*, 401 P.2d 18 (Or. 1965).

2. Carps, Inc., had seven directors: Herbert and Emile Carp (who were also president and vice-president); their uncles I. L., Meyer, and Zola Carp; Stephen Carp; and Herman Willer. Herbert and Emile applied for a personal loan of $267,000 at Lindell Trust, which refused to approve the loan without endorsement. Herbert endorsed the note in the name of Carps, Inc., and convinced Molasky to sign as a second endorser. Molasky did not ask for a corporate resolution authorizing Herbert to make Carps, Inc., an endorser on the note, explaining that he knew it was a closely held family corporation operated in an informal manner. He relied on oral assurances of Herbert and Emile. Lindell Trust did request a board of directors resolution authorizing the endorsement but processed the loan without it. Indeed, the board never took action. Stephen Carp and Herman Willer were never informed of the transaction. The uncles gave, at most, their family approval or "blessing." When neither Herbert and Emile nor Carps, Inc., repaid the loan, Molasky had to. He sued Carps, Inc., as first endorser. Is Carps, Inc., bound by its endorsement? Discuss. See *Molasky Enterprises, Inc.* v. *Carps, Inc.*, 615 S.W.2d 83 (Mo. App. 1981).

3. Shiflett founded, controlled, and owned 100% of Panama, Inc., until he sold it to AOG Co. in 1963. Shiflett remained with Panama as president. In 1965, Shiflett told 14 employees that "if we make some money, well, then, we would follow up on our bonuses just like we had been doing," and "I have no authority to write checks for bonuses unless they gave the authority down here." The employees sued for $71,728 in bonuses they claimed Shiflett promised. The company defended, arguing that Shiflett had no authority. Plaintiffs claim he had apparent authority. Discuss. See *Douglass* v. *Panama, Inc.*, 504 S.W.2d 776 (Tex. 1974).

4. Defendant's president negotiated the purchase of a pickle business by promising long-term employment to the seller. Defendant honored the employment contract for 13 months, but then fired the seller without cause. The seller's trustee in bankruptcy obtained a judgment against defendant's president for breach of contract. Is the defendant corporation also liable? Discuss. See *In re Gross*, 51 B.R. 480 (E.D. Pa. Bkrtcy. 1985).

5. Martin was a director of Illinois Valley Acceptance Corporation (IVAC). He helped to pushed through loans to ISS, Inc., without disclosing that he was a shareholder and director of ISS, Inc. Anderson was also a director of IVAC; he knew of Martin's conflict of interest, but did not inform the other directors of IVAC. After IVAC went into bankruptcy, Martin and Anderson were sued for having breached their fiduciary duty to IVAC in approving loans that were not paid back. Discuss Anderson's liability. See *In re Illinois Valley Acceptance Corp.*, 531 F.Supp. 737 (C.D. Ill. 1982).

6. Klinicki conceived the idea of engaging in the air transportation business in Berlin. In April 1977, he and his friend Lundgren incorporated Berlinair, Inc. Each owned 33% of the stock; each was a director and officer. In November 1977, Klinicki and Lundgren met with Berliner Flug Ring (BFR), a consortium of Berlin travel agents. This would have been a lucrative contract, but it first appeared that Berlinair had no chance to receive it because BFR was satisfied with its present carrier. Then, in

June 1978, Lundgren learned that the BFR contract might be available. He quickly incorporated ABC Co. and was its sole owner. He concealed from Klinicki his negotiations with BFR and his diversion of the contract to ABC even though he used Berlinair working time, staff, money, and facilities. When Klinicki learned of Lundgren's treachery, he sued for appropriation of a corporate business opportunity. Lundgren claimed that Berlinair did not have the financial wherewithal to undertake the contract. Is this a good defense? Discuss. See *Klinicki* v. *Lundgren*, 298 Or. 662, 695 P.2d 906 (1985).

7. Plaintiff is a minority shareholder of Chicago National League Ball Club, Inc., owner of the Chicago Cubs who play at Wrigley Field. He brings a derivative action challenging the defendant directors' decision not to install lights at Wrigley Field. Plaintiff points out that all other major league baseball teams have lights and play at night, that the Cubs have lost money in recent years, and that the Cubs could attract more paying fans by playing games at night. Plaintiff claims that it is defendant Wrigley's (owner of 80% of the shares) personal belief that baseball is a "daytime sport" and that night baseball will have a deteriorating effect on the surrounding neighborhood, rather than the interests of the corporation, that accounts for the decision. Should plaintiff prevail? Discuss. See *Shlensky* v. *Wrigley*, 95 Ill. App. 2d 173, 237 N.E.2d 776 (1968).

8. Kaplan, a shareholder of Coastal Corp., brought a derivative action claiming that Coastal's founder, chairman, and CEO, Wyatt, (1) had interpositioned himself in the Rotterdam Spot Market, profiting from oil trading activity that should have belonged to Coastal, (2) wrongfully caused Coastal to enter on unfair terms into a sale and leaseback of an oil tanker, and (3) received excessive compensation from Coastal for the lease of his personal plane to the corporation. Coastal's board appointed two outside directors, Holliday and Marshall, as a special litigation committee (SLC). Holliday was an attorney, a CPA, and an outside director on several other corporate boards. Marshall had joined the board as an outside director under the aegis of the SEC in an unrelated matter. The SLC interviewed 140 people throughout the world in its investigation, incurring $500,000 in fees due an independent law firm hired to help in the investigation. The SLC concluded that there was no evidence that Wyatt had wrongfully profited in oil trading activity, that the sale and leaseback arrangement was fair to Coastal, and that the only excessive compensation relating to the plane was a $60,000 payment mistakenly made and since paid back by Wyatt. The SLC recommended that the suit be dismissed; the court did so upon application of Coastal. Kaplan challenges the action. Discuss. See *Kaplan* v. *Wyatt*, 499 A.2d 1184 (Del. 1985).

12

ORGANIC CHANGES
IN CORPORATE STRUCTURE

INTRODUCTION

When a corporation sells most of its assets, or amends its articles in an important way, or merges with another corporation, the shareholders' interests are vitally affected. Any of these changes can radically alter the nature of the enterprise in which the shareholders choose to invest. Shareholders, though willing to let directors and officers manage the day-to-day affairs of the corporation, will want a voice in such basic changes.

Indeed, early American corporate law analogized the corporation to a contractual arrangement—alterable only upon the consent of *all* the parties. Thus, if the vast majority of shareholders viewed a particular change as desirable, a few dissenters could block the change, or blackmail the majority. To remedy this situation, corporate law has evolved a method of effecting basic changes through the approval of the board of directors and *most* of the shareholders. A small minority can no longer block such changes. Instead, dissenters' rights are protected in other ways. For example, frequently dissenters can force the corporation that has made a basic organic change to purchase their shares at a fair price. This is known as the ''appraisal right'' or the ''dissenters' right.''

There are many types of basic corporate changes, and they tend to create many complicated problems. This chapter emphasizes changes accomplished through sales of assets, amendments of articles of incorporation, and mergers and acquisitions. Tender offers are covered in Chapter 22. The focus will be on types of changes, reasons for choosing various methods, proper procedures, and results and implications of such changes. Means of protecting the rights of minority shareholders are a matter of constant concern.

The discussion will show that the clear trend in modern corporate law has been toward allowing corporate managers more discretion to effect basic changes through simplified procedures with less opportunity for minority shareholders to block or retard changes.

TYPES OF CHANGES

Sales of Assets

Most nonservice corporations sell assets and property on a daily basis. Inventory, used equipment, unprofitable store locations, and the like may be sold in the ordinary course of business. Such transactions are within the discretion of the corporate managers who usually need not bother the shareholders for approval. But if a furniture manufacturing corporation sells its plant and all its equipment and inventory and invested the proceeds in a chain of bowling alleys or in municipal bonds, there has been a basic change in the nature of the enterprise that dramatically affects the shareholders.

Under the Model Business Corporation Act (MBCA) §78, the board can *sell*, lease, or exchange "all, or substantially all," of the corporation's assets "*in* the regular course of its business" without shareholder approval. It can also *mortgage* "all, or substantially all," of the assets without shareholder approval even though such is *not* within the ordinary course of business.[1] What the board cannot do, according to MBCA §79, is *sell* "all, or substantially all," of the property and assets "if *not* within the usual and regular course of its business."

Determining what actions are within the "ordinary course" of business may be difficult; however, the board of a corporation formed primarily to develop and sell shopping centers could probably sell such a center without shareholder approval.[2] It may also be difficult to define "substantially all" of the assets. In Delaware, a sale of assets is viewed as "quantitatively vital" to the corporation if it "substantially affects the existence and purpose of the corporation."[3]

Procedure

MBCA §79 mandates a three-step procedure for effecting sale of substantially all of a corporation's assets outside the scope of ordinary business. First, the board of

---

[1] RMBCA §12.01 also explicitly recognizes the board's power to transfer any and all corporate property to a wholly owned subsidiary without shareholder approval.

[2] For example, *Western Land Corp.* v. *Lichtenstein*, 361 N.E.2d 730 (Ill. App. 1977).

[3] *Gimbel* v. *Signal Companies, Inc.*, 316 A.2d 599 (Del. Ch.), *aff'd* 316 A.2d 619 (Del. 1974).

directors shall adopt a resolution recommending the sale and directing its submission to a shareholder vote at an annual or special meeting. Second, shareholders shall be given written notice of the meeting and informed that one of its purposes is to consider the resolution of sale. Third, the shareholders shall authorize the sale by the "affirmative vote of the holders of a majority of the shares of the corporation entitled to vote thereon." [4] If some classes of shares carry the independent right of approval of such a transaction, then the affirmative vote of the majority of the shares of each such class will also be required. Some jurisdictions require, as the MBCA once did, the affirmative vote of two-thirds of the shares rather than a simple majority. A corporation's articles could also raise the approval percentage required for effective action.

Even if a resolution of sale is properly approved, the board of directors has discretion, subject to the rights of third parties to the contract, to abandon the transaction. This discretion might be exercised if, for example, so many dissenting shareholders exercised their appraisal rights that it became economically impractical to carry out the sale.[5]

Appraisal Rights

MBCA §80 and RMBCA §13.02 award dissenters' rights to shareholders in the event of a sale of substantially all assets outside the ordinary course of business, unless (1) the sale was court ordered or (2) substantially all net proceeds of the sale will be distributed to the shareholders within a year. This right to have the corporation purchase the dissenters' shares at a "fair value" is discussed in detail later in this chapter. A few jurisdictions, including Delaware, do not provide dissenters' rights in the sale of assets situation.

Amendments to Articles of Incorporation

Corporations are empowered to amend their articles of incorporation in just about any manner so long as unlawful provisions are not added. MBCA §58 contains a lengthy, nonexclusive laundry list of permissible changes, including alterations to the corporation's name, its duration and purposes, its number of shares, par values, dividend rights, board authority, and shareholder preemptive rights.

---

[4] For approval of a sale of assets (and other organic changes discussed in this chapter such as mergers and amendments to articles), the RMBCA also requires the affirmative vote of "a majority of all the votes entitled to be cast." This is a higher standard than RMBCA §7.25 imposes on most matters requiring shareholder approval. RMBCA §7.25 requires only that the votes cast in favor exceed the votes cast in opposition. If abstentions occur, that might produce approval by fewer votes than a majority.

[5] RMBCA §12.02 expressly allows the board to submit the sale of assets to shareholder vote on a conditional basis. One such condition might be that only a certain percentage of shareholders exercise appraisal rights. Other RMBCA sections allow conditional submission of merger, amendment of articles, and other transactions.

Procedure

MBCA §59 now allows the board of a corporation with only one class of shares to amend the articles to effectuate share dividends and share splits without shareholder approval.[6] However, other amendments must follow a procedure resembling that for approval of sale of assets. Board resolution, notice to shareholders, and an affirmative vote of a majority (or in some jurisdictions, two-thirds) of eligible shares are required.[7]

Sometimes amendments might adversely affect a particular class of stock. In such a case, MBCA §60 authorizes those shares, even if normally nonvoting, to vote on the proposed amendment *as a class*. Unless the class approves the change by the necessary majority or two-thirds margin, it is vetoed even if approved by the other classes of stock.

Section 60 confers this right where the proposed amendment would adversely affect the class of shares by, for example, increasing or decreasing its aggregate number of authorized shares; exchanging, reclassifying, or canceling all or part of its shares; changing its preferences or relative rights; creating a new class of shares with superior rights; or canceling dividends on its shares that have accrued but have not been declared.

To be effective, an amendment must be properly executed and filed with the Secretary of State in accordance with state procedural provisions.[8]

Appraisal Rights

State corporate codes are varied regarding appraisal or dissenters' rights in the case of amendments to articles. MBCA §80 accords such rights to dissenters where amendments adversely affect the preferential rights, redemption rights, preemptive rights, or voting rights of their shares.[9] So does RMBCA §13.02.

Mergers and Consolidations

When two corporations combine their assets, a basic structural change occurs for one or both of the corporations. If Corporation A combines with Corporation B with the result that Corporation A survives (now owning the assets and liabilities of both) and

---

[6] RMBCA §10.02 lists a number of housekeeping-type amendments that the board can make without shareholder approval, including extension of duration of the corporation, deletion of names and addresses of initial directors, and minor changes in the corporate name.

[7] RMBCA §10.03(e) requires approval by a majority of votes eligible to be cast by "any voting group with respect to which the amendment would create dissenters' rights." Additional approval must be gained from other groups entitled to vote but without appraisal rights, and their approval must only meet the standard of RMBCA §7.25—more votes cast for than against. Thus, a higher level of approval is required by those shareholders whose interests are adversely affected by the proposed amendment.

[8] For example, MBCA §§61, 62; RMBCA §10.06.

[9] RMBCA §10.03(e) gives the right to vote as a group to shareholders who are accorded dissenters' rights due to amendments under the criteria of RMBCA §13.02. This leads to a symmetry not present in the MBCA, though the types of amendments that lead to group voting rights under MBCA §60 are similar to the types that give rise to dissenters' rights under MBCA §80.

Corporation B disappears, a *merger* has occurred. If Corporation A and Corporation B combine into a new entity C Corporation (which owns the combined assets of A and B), and Corporations A and B disappear, a *consolidation* has occurred. There is little substantive difference between these two transactions and, hence, little reason to retain the term consolidation as a separate concept.[10]

Later in the chapter we will return to mergers to discuss strategies, alternative means of accomplishing the same result, and tax issues.

Procedures

The first step in effectuating a merger, according to MBCA §71 and RMBCA §11.01, is approval of a plan of merger by the boards of both merging corporations. The usual steps of notice to shareholders and affirmative vote of a majority (MBCA §73) or two-thirds (many jurisdictions) of the shares outstanding of *both* corporations to be merged normally follow.[11] Again, the boards of directors have the authority to abort the merger, even after approval by the shareholders if, for example, too many dissenters exercise appraisal rights.

In certain cases a merger plan will not lead to a dramatic change of structure for one of the corporations. In such cases, approval of the shareholders of that corporation will not be needed. Section 73(c) of the MBCA states that approval of the shareholders of the *surviving* corporation in a merger will be unnecessary, if (1) its articles do not change, except for the corporation's name, after the merger; (2) its shareholders before the merger hold the same number of shares with the same rights afterward; (3) the number of voting shares outstanding after the merger (plus the number that could result from conversion of rights and warrants) does not exceed by more than 20% the number outstanding before the merger; and (4) the same 20% cap is met regarding an increase in participating shares. If these four requirements are met, the change for the shareholders of the surviving corporation are deemed so insignificant as to not require its shareholders' assent. Not all jurisdictions have such a provision, however. RMBCA §11.03 is similar.

What has been described thus far is a standard "long-form" merger. However, there are a number of variations to be considered.

Consolidation. As noted earlier, a consolidation is functionally equivalent to a merger. In most jurisdictions, including those following the MBCA, the procedure for effectuating a consolidation is the same as that for a merger.

Exchange of shares. Sometimes corporate combinations take the form of Corporation A exchanging its shares for all the shares or a class of shares of Corporation B. If Corporation A deals directly with the shareholders, usually a tender offer (covered

---

[10] The RMBCA eliminates the term "consolidation."

[11] Both the MBCA and RMBCA allow group voting by classes of shares in a merger if the merger plan contains a provision that, if it were contained in an amendment to the articles, would allow group voting.

in Chapter 22) is taking place. But if Corporation A's and B's boards approve the plan and it is approved by the shareholders of Corporation B, it will be effective.[12] The approval of Corporation A's shareholders is not required.

However, if the consideration given by Corporation A consists of common stock that could increase its total outstanding common stock by 20% or more, corporations with shares listed on the New York Stock Exchange must, under NYSE rules, seek shareholder approval.[13] The American Stock Exchange has similar rules.

"Short-Form" Merger.   Sometimes a merger may be carried out without the approval of the shareholders of either the surviving or the acquired corporation. Under MBCA §75, any corporation (parent) owning at least 90% of the shares of another (subsidiary) may merge the latter into itself without approval of the shareholders of either corporation. Most jurisdictions have such a provision, though the ownership requirement may vary from 80% to almost 100%.

In most jurisdictions, the procedure that must be followed to complete a short-form merger resembles that outlined in MBCA §75 and RMBCA §11.04. First, the parent's board of directors must approve a plan of merger setting forth the names of the corporations, the fact that the parent owns at least 90% of the subsidiary's stock, and the consideration to be paid the subsidiary's minority shareholders. Second, a copy of this plan of merger must be mailed to each of the subsidiary's holders of record. Third, articles of merger shall be executed and verified. Fourth, on the thirtieth day after the merger plan was mailed to the subsidiary shareholders, the articles shall be delivered to the Secretary of State for filing. No shareholder approval is necessary.

The "short-form" merger is a popular method of "going private" or squeezing out the minority shareholders of a corporation. Later in the chapter we shall return to that subject.

Triangular Mergers.   To avoid the necessity of obtaining the approval of its own shareholders, a corporation can effectuate a merger by working through a subsidiary. Assume that Corporation A wishes to acquire the assets of Corporation B. A simple merger would do the trick, but the board of directors can also, without shareholder approval, form a wholly owned subsidiary, Corporation A_1. It can then have Corporation A_1 merge with Corporation B. Corporation B's shareholders will have to approve the merger, but not Corporation A's. Without the approval of its own shareholders, Corporation A now controls the assets of Corporation B through its (A's) subsidiary, Corporation A_1.

A true triangular merger occurs when the consideration received by B's shareholders consists of the shares of A, not A_1. In such a case, A owns 100% of A_1 and thus exercises complete control over B's former assets. Further, B's former liabilities now belong to the subsidiary A_1, not to A itself.

---

[12] MBCA §§72A, 73.

[13] New York Stock Exchange, *Manual* (New York: NYSE, 1977), pp. A-283–284.

Appraisal Rights

MBCA §80 and RMBCA §13.02 afford appraisal rights to the shareholders of all corporations involved in a merger or consolidation except for the shareholders of the surviving corporation in cases where their approval is not needed. For example, in a "short-form" merger the shareholders of the disappearing subsidiary would have appraisal rights, but the shareholders of the surviving parent, whose approval is not necessary, would not.

In an exchange of shares, the shareholders of the corporation whose shares are to be acquired will have appraisal rights.

More states allow appraisal rights for mergers than for any other type of transaction.

Dissolution

Obviously the dissolution of a corporation is a major organic change. Dissolution procedure has been discussed in the close corporation context earlier in the book. We are here concerned with voluntary dissolution, not involuntary dissolution at the behest of shareholders or creditors.[14]

Procedure

Section 83 of the MBCA provides for the voluntary dissolution of a corporation upon the written consent of *all* its shareholders. Larger corporations are unlikely to gain such unanimity, however, so §84 provides an alternative procedure that consists of the familiar three-step process: board resolution, notice to shareholders, and approval of holders of a majority of shares. Many jurisdictions require two-thirds approval. RMBCA §14.02 is similar.

Appraisal Rights

MBCA §80(a)(2) and RMBCA §13.02 accord appraisal rights to any sale of substantially all assets "including a sale in dissolution" unless the sale is pursuant to court order or for cash on terms requiring that the net proceeds be distributed to the shareholders within one year.

ACQUISITION STRATEGIES

If one corporation believes that it would be a wise business move to acquire the assets of another corporation, it might well consider a merger or consolidation with that other corporation. However, the same basic result could be obtained by purchasing the assets

---

[14] MBCA §97; RMBCA §14.30.

of the other corporation, or buying all its stock. Many factors must be considered in determining which avenue of approach to take.[15]

Nontax Considerations

Merger or Consolidation

Assume that Corporation A believes that its overall enterprise would be strengthened by acquiring the assets of Corporation B. A could merge with B under a plan that leaves A as the surviving corporation. There are several advantages to this approach. The merger procedure itself transfers all B's properties to A. There is no need for significant additional paperwork in the form of deeds and assignments to convey B's property and assets. Also, because most shareholders of B become shareholders of A, there is no need to deal with or attempt to acquire a minority interest in a subsidiary.

The disadvantages of this approach include the need to obtain shareholder approval, which can be quite expensive, especially if the corporations are public and subject to the SEC's proxy rules. Federal proxy regulation is so significant that it is accorded an entire chapter (Ch. 21) later in this book. Many of the cases there will discuss attempts to gain shareholder approval for mergers.

Another disadvantage of the merger process is that appraisal rights must be accorded to dissenting shareholders. As noted, if too many shareholders exercise appraisal rights, the entire merger plan may be thwarted if the board has not set aside enough funds to compensate the dissenters for what the court determines is the fair value of their shares.

A third disadvantage of the merger process is that Corporation A, by merging Corporation B into itself, succeeds to all B's liabilities as well as its assets. Some of those liabilities may be "contingent and unknown." For example, B may be defendant in a lawsuit where the jury might ultimately render a verdict for plaintiff of $1 or $1 million. Or B may have manufactured an airplane part that will, in a couple of years, fail and thereby cause a crash killing hundreds. There is no way that A can calculate all these unknown liabilities, so it is difficult to know what to pay B's shareholders in the merger.

These disadvantages not withstanding, there are a sufficient number of advantages to mergers that over $190 billion worth of merger activity occurred in 1985.

Stock Acquisitions

Another way Corporation A can gain control of Corporation B's assets is to swap its stock for shares of B. In that way, B's shareholders become owners of A, and B becomes a subsidiary of A.

---

[15] See, generally, R. Stark, "Non-Income Tax Aspects of Corporate Reorganizations: A Check List of the Issues and Problems Involved," *Proceedings*, 24th *Annual N.Y.U. Institute on Federal Taxation* (1966), p. 1085.

A stock-for-stock swap is the simplest form of transaction unless A must register its shares under the Securities Act of 1933 [16] or unless federal tender offer rules come into play.[17] Paperwork for and local taxes on transfer of assets are avoided. Usually there are no dissenters' rights. Consent of the management of B is not needed, and approval of the shareholders of A is unnecessary so long as there has been previously authorized enough shares of unissued A stock to swap to B shareholders.

Disadvantages of the stock acquisition include the need for approval of A's shareholders if A is covered by NYSE rules, and if the number of A shares issued to B shareholders would increase the total number of outstanding A shares by 20% or more. Also, the problem of unknown and contingent liabilities also arises in the stock acquisition. Finally, it would be rare that all B's shareholders would agree to A's planned swap. Though A may gain control of B, it is left with a troublesome minority faction of B shareholders who must either be accommodated or removed by way of a separate "going private" transaction.

Purchase of Assets

A third way for Corporation A to gain control of Corporation B's assets is to buy them from B. A big advantage of this type of transaction is that the contract can be written and the purchase price adjusted so that A buys B's assets, but is not saddled with B's unknown and contingent liabilities. As we shall see later in the chapter, when we focus on succession to liabilities, the law in this area has been changing rapidly and this advantage is not as certain as it once was. Also, there is no troublesome minority interest to be dealt with following a purchase of assets.

Disadvantages include the need for approval of B's shareholders in most jurisdictions and, in many others, the availability of appraisal rights. Although approval of A's shareholders is usually unnecessary, some states require it, especially if the purchase price includes a substantial increase in the number of A's shares outstanding. Also, substantial paperwork and payment of state and local excise and transfer taxes may be required to switch title to the assets from Corporation B to Corporation A.

Tax Considerations

In the eyes of the IRS, when goods are exchanged for cash or other goods, a taxable gain or loss usually occurs. This is usually the case when corporate stock is sold or otherwise exchanged. However, §368 of the Internal Revenue Code recognizes three primary types of tax-free reorganizations that may be used to effectuate acquisitions. Strict (and complicated) requirements must be met.

The essence of all three types of transactions is a continuity of shareholder interest in that a significant part of the consideration given by the acquiring corporation is its own equity stock (or that of its parent corporation if the parent is working through

---

[16] See Chapter 15.
[17] See Chapter 22.

a subsidiary). In that way, the shareholders of the acquired corporation remain interested in the continuing entity. Also, there must be a legitimate business purpose for the transaction. This requirement is usually met when there is arm's-length bargaining between two corporations.[18]

Type A

A standard merger or consolidation effectuated under state corporation law can be a tax-free reorganization known as a *Type A*. The acquiring corporation can merge the acquired corporation directly into itself or into its subsidiary (triangular merger) or even merge its subsidiary into the acquired corporation (reverse triangular merger). The main requirement is shareholder continuity, which requires that some of the consideration be in the form of the acquirer's equity stock. Unlike other types of tax-free reorganizations, however, the Type A can have "boot" (cash, debentures, or other nonequity consideration) worth up to 50% of the value of all former outstanding stock of the acquired corporation.

Type B

A *Type B* reorganization involves an acquirer swapping its stock for the *stock* of the acquired corporation. To be tax free, the acquirer must pay *solely* with *voting* stock (or the voting stock of its parent in a triangular merger). Except for very limited exceptions, any "boot" included in the purchase price will destroy the tax-free status. Additionally, after the transaction, the acquirer must "control" the acquired corporation by having direct ownership of at least 80% of all its voting classes of stock.

Type C

A *Type C* reorganization occurs where the acquiring corporation swaps its stock for the *assets* of the acquired corporation. Again, the consideration paid by the acquirer must usually consist solely of its voting stock (or that of its parent). If any "boot" is present, its value plus the acquired corporation's liabilities assumed must not exceed 20% of the market value of the gross assets conveyed. Because the liabilities assumed frequently exceed the 20% limitation by themselves, "boot" usually cannot be paid in a Type C transaction.

Consequences

If the requirements of §368 are met, the transaction—except for the "boot" portion—is tax free for both purchaser and seller. Obviously, §368 puts severe limitations on the type of consideration that can be paid in such a transaction. Sometimes sellers might prefer to have a taxable transaction to receive cash as consideration.

---

[18] *See, generally*, D. Kahn and P. Gann, *Corporation Taxation and Taxation of Partners and Partnerships* (St. Paul, Minn.: West Publishing Co., 1979), pp. 704–710.

GOING PRIVATE TRANSACTIONS

Introduction

Later in this book we will discuss the process of "going public," where, for example, a small family-owned corporation with a solid business and a great need of funds to expand will sell shares to the public. Occasionally that process is reversed; a corporation with public shareholders will eliminate them and "go private." Many of the techniques discussed so far in this chapter, such as mergers, are used to implement going private transactions.

Why reduce the number of shareholders? The motivation might be simply to eliminate a troublesome minority shareholder or to clean out a number of very small shareholders who create more paperwork than their investment warrants. The motive might be to reduce ownership to the hands of just a cohesive few to produce a more unified management that could more rapidly respond to business opportunities. If managers are included among the smaller group of owners, they will probably be more highly motivated because they have a bigger piece of the action.

A public corporation can, by dramatically reducing the number of its shareholders, escape the regulatory net of the federal securities laws. Eliminating the effort and expense of disclosure requirements, proxy regulation, and even share transfer and dividend distribution expenses can save hundreds of thousands of dollars a year. The privacy advantage that comes from eliminating federal reporting requirements is also substantial.

Terminology

There are numerous terms used, frequently interchangeably, to describe the going private transaction, including "freeze-out," "squeeze-out," "take-out," "cash-out," and the like. We will use the term "squeeze-out" to describe a *close* corporation's reducing its number of shareholders, perhaps by buying out an unhappy minority shareholder. The term "going private" will be used to describe a public corporation's controllers reducing its number of shareholders sufficiently to evade the web of federal securities regulation. A "take-out" occurs where the controller is a corporation, not a group of individuals. A two-step take-out would occur, for example, where a corporation bought a controlling interest in a target public corporation and then used its voting power to eliminate the minority shareholders of the target in a merger with a wholly owned subsidiary.[19]

Leveraged Buy-outs

Leveraged buy-outs (LBOs) are at present a very popular type of going private transaction. Although there is some variation, the LBO type of going private transaction

---

[19] A. Borden, *Going Private* ¶1.03 (New York: Law Journals Seminar Press, 1984).

usually has several features. First, management of the corporation that is going private is cooperative and, indeed, usually part of the purchasing organization. Second, equity investors provide the capital needed to pay a small portion of the purchase price, frequently only 1% to 10%. Third, the assets of the corporation are used as security to borrow the rest of the purchase price. Most LBOs are highly leveraged indeed.

The ideal LBO candidate is an establish company with a good cash flow (which can be used to service the debt incurred in the purchase), a clean balance sheet, hidden or undervalued assets, and an efficient management team eager to increase its stake in the business. The tax advantages of debt are exploited to the hilt by the LBO, which frequently creates debt-equity ratios of 12:1 or higher, as compared to the 2:1 or 3:1 maximums normally found in public corporations.

Whereas the 1960s and part of the 1970s were characterized by conglomerate mergers, many corporations retrenched in the early and middle 1980s. This deconglomeration trend led many large corporations to spin off unwanted divisions. For example, in January 1982, RCA Corp. sold its Gibson Greeting Card division to Wesray Corp. in an LBO. The purchase price was $81 million. Wesray put up $1 million in cash and covered the rest through bank borrowings and real estate leasebacks. In May 1983, Gibson again went public. The 50% interest owned by Wesray's top two partners, including former U.S. Secretary of the Treasury William Simon, was then valued at $140 million.

Returns of 40% per year for equity investors of LBOs have been commonly reported. No wonder LBO activity increased from 16 corporations going private for $600 million in 1979 to 36 going private in 1983 for $7.1 billion. In the first nine months of 1984, at least five corporations worth $500 million each went private (Wometco, Dr Pepper, Harte-Hanks, Conoco Chemical, and U.S. Industries), and total LBO activity was $27.9 billion.[20]

Many fear the LBO craze will go too far as greedy investors attempt LBOs in corporations that are not really suitable candidates.[21] Others criticize LBOs as unfair to minority shareholders because management is on both sides of the transaction—officers and directors are supposed to be negotiating a good price on behalf of the selling public shareholders, but they themselves are purchasers.[22] Protection of public shareholders in LBOs and minority shareholders in mergers, sales of assets, and the like will be scrutinized in detail presently. For the moment it may be noted that no court has found an illegal conflict of interest from the mere fact that management was on both sides of the transaction.[23] And some believe that going private transactions are generally beneficial for the selling shareholders because of the large premium over market price they usually

---

[20] *See* R. Daitz, C. Kaufman, R. Lang, D. Ley, and R. Messineo, "Leveraged Buy-outs," in *Acquisitions and Mergers* (New York: Practicing Law Institute, 1984), p. 277.

[21] A. Sloan, "Luring Banks Overboard," *Forbes*, April 9, 1984, p. 39.

[22] B. Longstreth, "Management Buy Outs: Are Public Shareholders Getting a Fair Deal?" *Federal Securities Law Reports (CCH)*, ¶83,436, October 6, 1983.

[23] *Field* v. *Allyn*, 457 A.2d 1089 (Del. Ch. 1983).

receive as well as to the buyers who eliminate federal securities law compliance costs and increase incentives to management.[24]

Changes in the tax laws made in late 1986 make high debt loads somewhat less manageable than they were before. This may lead to a reduction in LBO activity. As this text is written in October 1986, LBO and merger activity has accelerated, apparently in an attempt to complete transactions before the less hospitable tax laws enacted in 1986 go into effect.

Techniques

Most going private transactions are carried out through mergers or sales of assets. The buying group might, for example, form a corporation for the specific purpose of merging the target corporation into it or having it purchase the target's assets.

Sometimes these transactions take the form of issuer tender offers. These are covered in more detail in the chapter on tender offers, but the basic notion is that the company itself makes an offer to buy the public shareholders' stock. Management waives any right to participate. The tender offer could also be made directly by the management group or by its wholly owned subsidiary formed for that purpose.

Finally, a corporation can be taken private through a reverse stock split. Just as a corporation can have a 2-for-1 stock split, it can have a reverse stock split of 1-for-2 or 1-for-2,000. Many jurisdictions have provisions, such as §24 of the MBCA, that allow corporations to "clean up" fractional shares by paying fair value for them. If the largest minority shareholder has 10,000 shares, the corporation can have a 1-for-20,000 reverse split. That will reduce every minority shareholder to a mere fraction of a share so that the corporation can cash them out. Appraisal rights seldom apply to reverse stock splits, though they may be voluntarily granted by the purchasers.

PROTECTING MINORITY SHAREHOLDERS

Introduction

The transactions discussed so far in this chapter can be used to abuse the rights of minority shareholders. Advantage can be taken in any number of ways. Those who control the corporation can arrange a sale of assets to, or a merger with, a corporation they control in exchange for inadequate consideration. Articles can be amended to strip preferred shareholders of their preferences, or to issue new shares to the controllers for inadequate consideration. Corporations can be dissolved at the behest of controllers who are the only parties in a position to purchase the corporation's assets at liquidation and continue the business. In a leveraged buy-out, management can negotiate a sale price that is much too low and has the incentive to do so since its members comprise the purchasing group.

---

[24] For example, H. De Angelo, L. De Angelo, and E. Rice, "Going Private: Minority Freezeouts and Shareholder Wealth," *Journal of Law & Economics*, Vol. 27 (1984), p. 367.

Numerous legislative provisions and judicial techniques have been devised over the years to protect the minority shareholders while, at the same time, it is hoped not unduly hindering what can be very beneficial corporate transactions. Some of these devices, as we shall soon see, have been more successful than others.

Voting Rights

One important protection for shareholders is the right to vote in mergers, sales of substantially all assets, and amendments of articles. Majority or two-thirds approval, depending on the jurisdiction, is generally needed. If a bad deal is proposed, the shareholders, theoretically, can reject it.

Sometimes the shareholders' right to vote can be sidetracked. For example, in *Wanvig* v. *Johnson Controls, Inc.*,[25] Johnson Controls wished to merge with Hoover Universal Corporation as part of an attempt to ward off a takeover attempt by Victor Posner. In a direct merger, the shareholders of both corporations would have had the right to vote. That would mean that Posner, who owned 19% of Johnson Controls' stock, and other shareholders who favored Posner's position, could have voted against the merger plan. To thwart this opposition, Johnson Controls' board formed a wholly owned subsidiary, HVU Acquisition Corp., and planned to have it merge with Hoover Universal in a forward triangular merger. Because Johnson Controls would not be a "constitutent party" to the merger, its shareholders would have no right to vote under state law.

The plaintiff stockholders of Johnson Controls sued, claiming breach of fiduciary duty on grounds that Johnson Controls' management was not only trying to entrench itself but also was risking delisting on the New York Stock Exchange, which apparently required shareholder approval for the merger though Wisconsin's corporate law did not. Plaintiffs asked the court to "ignore the plan's 'form' and look to its substance." But the court ruled against plaintiffs, noting that the Wisconsin Business Corporation Law could have imposed voting requirements in three-party triangular mergers, but did not do so. Fiduciary arguments were rejected under the business judgment rule.

Realistically, even where the shareholders are accorded the right to vote they will almost always approve a merger plan proposed by management. One recent study of 71 merger proposals put to a shareholder vote found that *all* passed.[26] Another study found 42 of 44 passing.[27]

Disclosure

So that shareholders at least have the option to cast an informed ballot, those soliciting support for (and opposition to) a merger or other transaction needing shareholder approval

---

[25] No. 663–487, *Securities Regulation and Law Report*, Vol. 17, no. 16 (Wis. Cir. Ct., March 29, 1985), p. 659.

[26] P. Dodd, "Merger Proposals, Management Discretion and Stockholder Wealth," *Journal of Finance & Economics*, Vol. 8 (1980), p. 105.

[27] H. DeAngelo, L. DeAngelo, and E. Rice, "Going Private," p. 367.

must meet certain disclosure requirements. Falsehoods will constitute fraud and create a state law cause of action, but the most demanding disclosure requirements are federal.

Proxy Regulation

The process of proxy regulation in public corporations is covered in detail in Chapter 21. At this point, suffice it to say that there is a very formalized procedure for soliciting shareholder votes in any proxy contest, there are strict disclosure requirements for those who do the soliciting, *and* there are rules for disclosure about the proposed transaction which are tailored to fit mergers, sales of assets, or whatever the transaction might be.

Rule 13e-3

As noted earlier, the potential for abuse of minority shareholders is quite strong in many corporate transactions, particularly those in the going private vein. In *Sante Fe Industries, Inc.* v. *Green*,[28] a corporate take-out case where the minority was bought out in a short-form merger, the U.S. Supreme Court held that no federal securities cause of action arose even if plaintiffs were correct in their argument that the majority was paying them much too little for their shares. Rather, the Court held, this was merely a breach of fiduciary duty remediable under state law.

Despite the *Green* ruling and the fact that minority shareholders in a short-form merger do not even have the right to vote on the transaction, in 1979 the SEC decided the shareholders could benefit from disclosure and promulgated Rule 13e-3.

The rule applies to any public company or its affiliate engaged in going private or take-out transactions that would reduce the number of shareholders below 300 or would result in the corporation being delisted from national securities exchanges or NASDAQ. Matters that must be disclosed under Rule 13e-3 include a description of the plan and its financing, whether alternatives were considered and why they were rejected, any firm offers made by unaffiliated persons during the prior 18 months, a detailed discussion of the fairness of the transaction to the minority shareholders, and the limitations of any expert's opinion relied on to demonstrate the transactions fairness.

Substantive Protections

Much of the law in the area of mergers and going private transactions has been made by corporate attorneys who manipulated and tested the outer limits of the law to fulfill their clients' wishes outside the legal limitations envisioned by the statutes. We have already seen the *Wanvig* case where a triangular merger was used to evade the shareholder approval requirement. But how far can corporate attorneys go?

---

[28] 430 U.S. 462 (1977) (covered in detail in Chapter 18).

Vested Rights

Today courts still refer to "vested rights" of shareholders, though not as much as they did in the past. The question frequently arises as to how far corporate law should be analogized to contract law where changes cannot be made without the assent of all the parties. Can corporations take actions that will injure certain shareholders' rights on the basis of just majority approval?

The high-water mark of the "vested rights" doctrine has been said to be *Keller* v. *Wilson & Co.*,[29] where the court held that preferred shareholders' rights to accumulated dividends must, where the law at the time of their issuance did not provide for their elimination, be regarded as *vested property*.

However, over the years the doctrine of vested rights has clearly suffered. In *Barrett* v. *Denver Tramway Corp.*,[30] for example, cumulative preferred stock arrearages had reached almost $70 per share. Simply to cancel them would have required unanimous shareholder approval. But management proposed a charter amendment that would swap the old preferrred shares for shares of new preferred. The new preferred carried exactly the same preference as the old, but the transaction would forfeit the arrearages. A majority was likely to vote for the plan for fear that absent approval the directors would defer dividends indefinitely. Although the judge believed the plan was unfair to the preferred shareholders, he refused to enjoin it because the Delaware standards for "constructive fraud," "bad faith," and "gross unfairness" were not met.

Mergers are frequently used to similar effect. In *Bove* v. *Community Hotel Corp. of Newport*,[31] for instance, a corporation proposed a merger with its newly formed subsidiary for the sole purpose of obviating the necessity for the unanimous vote that would otherwise be required to cancel priorities of preferred shareholders. The court upheld the transaction, noting that the *Keller* holding had already been overturned in a nearly identical case out of Delaware also involving what has been termed a "phantom merger." [32]

Further guidance as to what is permissible in this area may be derived from the following case.[33]

---

[29] 21 Del. 391, 190 A. 115 (1936).

[30] 53 F.Supp. 198 (D. Del. 1943), *aff'd* 146 F.2d 701 (3d Cir. 1944).

[31] 105 R.I. 36, 249 A.2d 89 (1969).

[32] *Hottenstein* v. *York Ice Machinery Corp.*, 136 F.2d 944 (3d Cir. 1943).

[33] The MBCA attempted to limit the impact of the vested rights doctrine by listing in §58 a number of types of amendments to articles that are clearly permissible. RMBCA §10.01(b) goes further, stating expressly that a shareholder does not have a vested right "resulting from any provision in the articles of incorporation."

B & H WAREHOUSE, INC. v. ATLAS VAN LINES, INC.

490 F.2d 818 (5th Cir. 1974)

In 1943, defendant-appellee Atlas Van Lines was incorporated in Delaware. In its charter's fourteenth paragraph it reserved the right to amend and provided that the rights of shareholders were subject to that reservation. In 1949, B & H Warehouse, plaintiff-appellant, bought 30 shares of Atlas Class A common stock that, at the time, carried no restrictions on sale.

In 1966, the Atlas Charter was amended to provide that Class A common stock could not be sold until first offered in writing to the corporation for book value plus $100. In 1967, Delaware amended its corporate law [§202(b)] to limit the power of corporations to restrict alienability. In 1970, Atlas again amended the charter to require a seller of Class A common to first offer the shares to the corporation for book value of $333.33 per share. Plaintiff sued Atlas for $60,000, the alleged difference between what it could receive on the open market and this book value.

The trial court held that §202(b) invalidated the 1970 amendment because plaintiff B & H was not a party to the agreement and did not vote for it. However, the court held the 1966 restriction to be binding, first, because pre-1967 Delaware law did not require that a shareholder must have indicated its approval of a restriction to be bound by it, and, second, §202(b) was not retroactive in its attempt to impose such a restriction.

B & H appealed.

MORGAN, CIRCUIT JUDGE:

The district court was correct in holding that the 1970 amendment to the charter is not binding on B & H. Because B & H neither entered an agreement containing the restriction nor voted in favor of the restriction, it is protected from the effect of the restriction by §202(b).

We cannot, however, uphold the district court's determination that B & H is bound by the 1966 charter amendment.

It should be noted first that the validity of any restriction is to be determined according to the law of the state of incorporation—in this case, Delaware.

To support the restriction, defendants rely primarily on *Lawson* v. *Household Finance Corporation*, 17 Del. Ch. 343, 152 A. 723 (1930). Lawson was the transferee of 100 shares of Class B common stock. He bought a bill in the Court of Chancery seeking to compel the defendant Delaware corporation to transfer the shares of its books from the transferor to the plaintiff. This the defendant refused to do, basing its refusal on certain provisions of its certificate of incorporation, as amended, and its by-laws.

Existing Delaware corporation law authorized corporations to make bylaws relating to the transfer of their stock, and also provided that a corporation and its directors shall have all the powers granted by its certificate of incorporation "so far as the same are necessary or convenient to the attainment of the objects set forth in such charter or certificate of incorporation." Noting that the defendant corporation was in the small loan business and required competent, honest, and trustworthy employees, the court held that the corporation's practice of providing employees with an interest in the business was a valid means of effectuating its purposes, and the right of first refusal outlined in the certificate of incorporation was a reasonable way of furthering the scheme of employee ownership.

The court, after holding the restriction contained in the bylaw valid under the corporation law of Delaware, went on to hold that the restriction was also valid as part of the contract between the corporation and its shareholders. The shareholders could be held to have agreed to the restriction when they acquired the stock, since the restriction was not only included in the articles of incorporation, but was also printed on the back of the stock certificates. In short, the court upheld the restriction, both as a bylaw and as a contract.

Lawson is important, but it is not directly in point for two reasons. First, the restriction on stock transfer was included in the original articles of incorporation of the Household Finance Corporation, in addition to being printed on all the stock certificates. In this case, the restriction was added to the bylaws after the plaintiff acquired its shares of stock. A second difference is that the corporation in *Lawson* could exercise its right to buy only at the appraised value of the shares. The *Lawson* court clearly indicated that its upholding of the restriction was based on a holding that the restriction was reasonably related to the purposes of the corporation, and the price at which the stock is to be offered clearly relates to the reasonableness of the restriction.

Another line of cases involves restrictions and other disabilities attached to stock after the shareholder challenging the disability acquired his shares.

The wellspring of this line of Delaware cases is *Peters* v. *United States Mortgage Co.*, 13 Del. Ch. 11, 114 A. 598 (1921). The certificate of incorporation of the defendant corporation defined the authorized capital of the corporation and provided that the preferred stock would receive cumulative dividends of 7% per year, that the common stock could receive from the surplus (after the preferred stock had been paid) dividends of 7% per year, and that the remaining surplus would be divided in certain proportions between the surplus account and the preferred and common stockholders. The directors proposed an amendment to the certificate that would deprive the preferred stock of any opportunity to share in the apportionment of surplus and net profits, change the common stock from par to no-par stock, and leave the distribution of surplus in the discretion of the directors.

The court noted:

> A corporation, in the sale and issuance of its stock, assumes a contractual relation to the shareholder. For the terms of the contract, the rights of the stockholder and the duties of the corporation, reference is to be made to the appropriate provisions of the certificate of incorporation and the law of the sovereign conferring the corporate franchise. Unless there be some provision in either the law or the corporate certificate reserving the power to do so, there can be no alteration in the terms of the contract under which the shareholder, as such, possesses his rights, without his consent. If, however, the right to change or alter the stockholder's contract be reserved in proper way, then no shareholder can complain against a proposed change therein, for the very plain reason that one of the terms by which he holds his contract is that the same may be altered.
>
> The only question, therefore, in this case is whether there is power reserved in the defendant company to make the change in question. . . .

The court held that the corporation had properly reserved the power to amend in two ways. First, there was an explicit provision in the articles of incorporation allowing amendments, and second, the General Corporation Law, which is implicitly included in the charter of every Delaware corporation, allowed amendments. Therefore, the court held, the amendments were proper.

The very broad language in *Peters* seems to support the position of the defendants in this case. If the only question is whether the corporation reserved the power to amend its certificate of incorporation and bylaws, the answer is easy: it did so in the fourteenth paragraph of its certificate.

In addition, the Delaware corporation law, 8 Del. C. §242, allows a corporation to amend its certificate of incorporation. As the court in *Peters* stated, "There is impliedly written into every corporate charter in [Delaware], as a constituent part thereof, every pertinent provision of [the Delaware] Constitution and statutes." Thus, just as in *Peters*, the automatic inclusion of the Delaware corporation law in the Atlas certificate of incorporation, if taken literally, gives Atlas the power to include the challenged restriction, or any other provision, in an amendment.

Later Delaware cases, however, make the inquiry more complex.

Thus, the Delaware courts, while following the general rule that any amendment is permissible if it is authorized by the articles of incorporation (and, by implication, the corporation law), have at times vacillated from that position and read into the unrestricted constitutional provisions certain limitations. Exceptions are unusual, but as the *Morris* case demonstrates, they do exist.

The *Lawson* line of cases demonstrates that if the restriction being contested had been included in the original articles of incorporation, or had been a part of the bylaws when B & H acquired its stock, there would be no question that the restriction would be valid. Alternatively, if B & H had specifically agreed to the possibility that its shares might at some future time be encumbered with such a restriction, we would have no trouble in upholding the restriction.

But neither situation confronts us here. In this case, all the plaintiff agreed to was the very general right to amend which is included in virtually every corporate charter and in the Delaware corporation law. What we must decide is whether these provisions provided plaintiff with sufficient notice that it can be held to have assented to such a change.

After a careful consideration of all of the factors in this area of the law, we conclude that the courts of Delaware would rule that the restriction is invalid. Although the restriction would have been valid had it been in effect when B & H obtained its stock, to add it afterwards contravenes two important policy considerations prevalent in the law of Delaware. The first is the rule that restraints on alienation are disfavored generally. The second is that restrictions on alienation are to be allowed only so long as they reasonably relate to a valid corporate purpose. There is a valid purpose involved in this case. That is, Atlas is organized as a cooperative association of transport companies, that and the restriction was obviously intended to retain control of Atlas among its associated moving companies. Nevertheless, we find that the restraint being challenged is too restrictive to be sustained by reference to this purpose. The interest of Atlas in restricting ownership to associated movers could have been accomplished, at least with respect to those obtaining stock before the amendment took effect, by providing that the corporation would have its right of first refusal based on the market price of the shares. We would then have a situation in which only the choice of buyer and not the amount of money to be received for the stock would have been restricted. Such a mechanism would have been much more closely related to the valid corporate purpose. But in forcing shareholders to offer their shares to the corporation at book value, Atlas has imposed a restriction significantly broader than necessary to effectuate its purpose. When this occurs, it cannot be said that the general grant of the power to amend contained in the fourteenth paragraph of the articles of incorporation suffices to validate the amendment. B & H can be held to have assented only to amendments reasonably related to a valid corporate purpose, not to any and all amendments which a majority of shareholders agree upon, regardless of their content. We are unwilling to hold that B & H consented to being bound by the contested restrictions because of the very vague language of the fourteenth paragraph.

Reversed and remanded.

De Facto Mergers

As we have seen, if they are careful, corporate managers can use mergers and other devices to accomplish indirectly what they cannot do directly. They may engage in "phantom mergers" with subsidiaries that have no real purpose related to a traditional merger. But what about the burdens that go along with mergers, such as the need for majority (or two-thirds) shareholder approval and appraisal rights? Can these be avoided by engaging in a mergerlike transaction, but calling it something else? Some cases, including the following one, say "no."

RATH v. RATH PACKING COMPANY

136 N.W. 2d 410 (Iowa 1965)

Plaintiffs own more than 6,000 shares of Rath Packing Co. Rath has 993,185 shares outstanding, held by about 4,000 owners. Its annual sales have recently ranged from $267 million to $296 million. As of January 2, 1965, its balance sheet showed assets of $56.5 million, current liabilities of $20.6 million, and long-term debt of $7 million.

Needham Packing Co. has 787,907 shares held by about 1,000 owners. Its annual sales have been around $80–100 million. Its balance sheet shows assets of $10.3 million, current liabilities of $2.65 million, and long-term debt of $3.1 million.

On April 2, 1965, Rath and Needham entered into an agreement designated, "Plan and Agreement of Reorganization." Rath agreed to (1) amend its articles to double the number of its common shares, create a new class of preferred, and change its name to Rath-Needham; (2) issue to Needham 5.5 shares of Rath common and 2 shares of preferred stock for each 5 shares of Needham stock in exchange for all Needham's assets; (3) assume all Needham's debts and liabilities; and (4) elect two Needham directors to its board. Needham agreed to (1) transfer its assets to Rath, (2) distribute the new Rath-Needham shares to its shareholders, and (3) liquidate.

Under the plan, the 1,000 Needham shareholders would own 54% of Rath-Needham common stock. Needham and the 4,000 Rath shareholders would own 46%. Also, the book value of Rath shares would be reduced from $27.99 to $15.92, while that of Needham shares would increase from $6.61 to $23.90. In addition,

Needham shareholders would have a preference in liquidation by virtue of the preferred shares.

Portions of the plan were approved by 60.1% of the Rath shares voted at an April 26, 1965 meeting.

Plaintiffs challenge the plan. They claim it is a merger that under Iowa statute (496A.68–78) requires two-thirds approval and provision of appraisal rights to dissenters. Defendants claim this is merely an amendment to the articles which under Iowa Statute (496A.56) requires only majority approval and affords no appraisal rights.

The trial court held for defendants, concluding that the transaction could proceed under sections of the law dealing with amendment to articles and issuance of stock. Plaintiffs appealed.

GARFIELD, CHIEF JUSTICE:

The principal point of law defendants asked to have adjudicated is that the provisions of chapter 496A are legally independent of, and of equal dignity with, those relating to mergers and the validity of the action taken by defendants is not dependent upon compliance with the merger sections under which the same result might be attained. The trial court accepted this view.

It is clear the view just expressed emanates from the opinion in *Hariton* v. *Arco Electronics, Inc.*, Del., 188 A.2d 123, the only precedent called to our attention which sustains the decision appealed from. Virtually the only basis for the conclusion Hariton reaches is the statement of the law point these defendants raised. The opinion contains little discussion and cites no authority that supports the decision.

The "Plan and Agreement of Reorganization" clearly provides for what amounts to a merger of Rath and Needham under any definition of merger we know.

"A merger of corporations consists of a combination whereby one of the constituent compa-

nies remains in being—absorbing or merging in itself all the other constituent corporations"—19 Am. Jur. 2d, Corporations, section 1492.

If, as we hold, this agreement provides for what amounts to a merger of Rath and Needham, calling it a Plan and Agreement of Reorganization does not change its essential character. A fundamental maxim of equity, frequently applied, is that equity regards substance rather than form.

The power of a corporation to merge must be derived from the law of the state which created it. There must be some plain enactment authorizing the merger, for legislative authority is just as essential to a merger as to creation of the corporation in the first instance.

At common law no merger could take place without unanimous consent of the stockholders. However, statutes in all jurisdictions now authorize mergers upon a vote of less than all stockholders. A shareholder who dissents to a merger may obtain the value of his stock if the right thereto is provided by statute, if procedure is established therefor and is followed by him. Sections 496A.77 and 496A.78 confer such right and provide such procedure.

In seeking the scope and effect of the two sets of sections relied upon at least one fundamental rule of statutory construction is applicable. As stated, the merger sections specifically provide for a particular thing—mergers. The sections authorizing amendment of articles and issuance of stock apply to all amendments and stock issues, whether or not amending the articles or issuing stock is part of a merger, as they may or may not be. As applied to mergers, the sections on which plaintiffs rely are specific provisions, those on which defendants rely are not.

It is apparent that if the sections pertaining to amending articles and issuing stock are construed to authorize a merger by a majority vote of shareholders, they conflict with the sections specifically dealing with the one matter of mergers which require a two-thirds vote of shareholders. The two sets of sections may be harmonized by holding, as we do, that the merger sections govern the matter of merger and must be regarded as an exception to the sections dealing with amending articles and issuing stock, which may or may not be involved in a merger.

The construction we give these sections is in accord with the cardinal rule that, if reasonably possible, effect will be given to every part of a statute.

The merger sections make it clear the legislature intended to require a two-thirds vote of shareholders and accord so-called appraisal rights to dissenters in case of a merger. It is unreasonable to ascribe to the same legislature an intent to provide in the same act a method of evading the required two-thirds vote and the grant of such appraisal rights. The practical effect of the decision appealed from is to render the requirements of a two-thirds vote and appraisal rights meaningless in virtually all mergers. It is scarcely an exaggeration to say the decision amounts to judicial repeal of the merger sections in most instances of merger.

It is obvious, as defendants' counsel frankly stated in oral argument, that corporate management would naturally choose a method which requires only majority approval of shareholders and does not grant dissenters the right to be paid the fair value of their stock. The legislature could hardly have intended to vest in corporate management the option to comply with the requirements just referred to or to proceed without such compliance, a choice that would invariably be exercised in favor of the easier method.

15 Fletcher, *Cyclopedia of Corporations* (1961, rev. vol. §7165.5), p. 307, contains this: "however, where a particular corporate combination is in legal effect a merger or a consolidation, even though the transaction may be otherwise labeled by the parties, the courts treat the transaction as a de facto merger or consolidation so as to confer upon dissenting stockholders the right to receive cash payment for their shares."

We hold entry of judgment of dismissal on the pleadings was error, that defendants should be enjoined from carrying out the "Plan and Agreement of Reorganization" until such time, if ever, as it is approved by the holders of at least two-thirds of the outstanding shares of Rath and in the event of such approval plaintiffs, if they dissent to such plan and follow the procedure provided by Code section 496A–78, I.C.A., shall be entitled to be paid the fair value of their shares in Rath.

Reversed and remanded.

Despite *Rath*, the de facto merger doctrine has not flourished. The leading case in the area is *Hariton* v. *Arco Electronics, Inc.*,[34] cited by the *Rath* trial court. In a case that also involved an arguable merger framed as a sale of assets, the court rejected the de facto merger doctrine (though the judge showed some sympathy for it), saying:

> There is authority in decisions of courts of this state for the proposition that the various sections of the Delaware Corporation Law conferring authority for corporate action are independent of each other and that a given result may be accomplished by proceeding under one section which is not possible, or is even forbidden under another.

---

[34] 182 A.2d 22 (Del. Ch. 1962), *aff'd* 188 A.2d 123 (Del. 1963).

For example, dividends which have accrued to preferred stockholders may not be eliminated by an amendment to the corporate charter under §242, Title 8—*Keller* v. *Wilson & Co.*, 21 Del. Ch. 391, 190 A. 115. On the other hand, such accrued dividends may be eliminated by a merger between the corporation and a wholly owned subsidiary—*Federal United Corporation* v. *Havender*, 24 Del. Ch. 318, 11 A.2d 331; and *Hottenstein* v. *York Ice Machinery Corp.*, 136 F.2d 944 (3d Cir. 1943). In *Langfelder* v. *Universal Laboratories*, D.C. 68 F.Supp. 209, Judge Leahy commented upon these holdings as follows:

> . . . Havender and Hottenstein hold that in Delaware a parent may merge with a wholly owned subsidiary and thereby cancel old preferred stock and the rights of the holders thereof to the unpaid, accumulated dividends, by substituting in lieu thereof stocks of the surviving corporation. Under Delaware law, accrued dividends after the passage of time mature into a debt and cannot be eliminated by an amendment to the corporate charter under Sec. 26 of the Delaware Corporation Law, Rev. Code 1935, §2058. But the right to be paid in full for such dividends, not withstanding provisions in the charter contract, may be eliminated by means of a merger which meets the standard of fairness. The rationale is that a merger is an act of independent legal significance, and when it meets the requirements of fairness and all other statutory requirements, the merger is valid and not subordinary or dependent upon any other section of the Delaware Corporation Law.

Nonetheless, the de facto merger doctrine is not completely moribund. It was invoked in *Pratt* v. *Ballman-Cummings Furniture Co.*,[35] where two corporations controlled by the same family entered into a partnership agreement to do business under a new name. The result was that the corporation in which plaintiff owned stock went from an active, consistently profitable enterprise to a moribund entity compiling consistent losses. All profits went to the other corporate partner. The court found a de facto merger and awarded plaintiff appraisal rights.

Fairness

As noted in the *Hariton* opinion, mergers will usually be upheld if they meet statutory and *fairness* requirements. But what standard are we to use in merger and going private transactions to gauge fairness? The leading cases have come from the courts of Delaware.

The legal community looked to Delaware especially following the Supreme Court's decision in *Santa Fe Industries, Inc.* v. *Green* that matters of fairness and fiduciary duty were outside the realm of federal concern. The Delaware Supreme Court soon responded with what was perceived to be a very pro-minority shareholder opinion in *Singer* v. *Magnavox Co.*,[36] which involved a take-out of minority shareholders through a long-form merger instigated by the majority (84%) owner. Minority shareholders who did not wish to be cashed out challenged the transaction as violative of the majority's fiduciary duty. The defendants claimed that plaintiff's only remedy was the statutory appraisal right.

---

[35] 549 S.W. 2d 270 (Ark. 1977).
[36] 380 A.2d 969 (Del. 1977).

The Delaware Supreme Court held that (1) a controlling shareholder owed a duty of "entire fairness" to minority shareholders in the exercise of control over corporate powers and properties, (2) this duty is not discharged simply by relegating minority shareholders to the appraisal remedy, (3) shareholders have legally protected rights (vested rights?) in their shares beyond simply the right to be paid fair value, and (4) some "business purpose" beyond merely a desire to be rid of the minority is needed to justify termination of the minority's shareholder status.

A series of Delaware cases then strove to determine exactly what sort of "business purpose" was needed to justify a take-out and what procedures might preserve "entire fairness." Ultimately, most of the *Singer* holding was discarded in the following case, which now stands as the leading case in the area.

WEINBERGER v. UOP, INC.

457 A.2d 701 (Del. 1983)

In 1975, Signal Companies, Inc., through a tender offer and an agreement with UOP's board to buy unissued shares, acquired 50.5% of UOP's outstanding common stock. The tender offer price was $21 per share; UOP's market price had been $14 per share. Signal then placed 6 directors on UOP's 13-director board.

In 1978, Signal decided to acquire the remaining 49.5% of UOP's stock. A study done by Arledge and Chitiea, Signal officers who sat on UOP's board, concluded UOP would be a good investment at any price up to $24 per share. Signal's senior management then decided to pursue a cash-out merger at $20 to $21 per share. They informed Crawford, the former head of a Signal subsidiary whom Signal had recently installed as UOP's CEO. Crawford said he thought the price was "more than fair."

On February 28, 1978, Signal announced its plan. In the next four business days until March 6, Crawford spoke telephonically with other UOP directors and through Glanville (a UOP director and a partner at Lehman Brothers) hired Lehman Brothers to render a fairness opinion. That opinion, rendered in rush fashion

on March 6, concluded that $21 per share would be a fair price. UOP's market price was $14.50 per share.

On March 6, both boards met. Signal authorized the cash merger at $21 per share upon the stipulation that the merger be approved by a majority of the minority UOP shares voted at the meeting and that those shares, when added to Signal's, constitute at least two-thirds of all UOP shares. UOP's board, with Signal's officers abstaining, also approved the plan. They were not told of the $24 per share price discussed in the Arledge-Chitiea study.

At the shareholder meeting, 56% of the minority shares (3,208,652 of 5,688,302) were voted. Of those, 2,953,812 or 51% of the total minority shares voted for the merger. Only 254,840 voted against. When Signal's shares are added, 76.2% of the outstanding shares were voted for the merger and 2.2% against.

Plaintiffs, dissenting minority UOP shareholders, challenged the cash-out. The trial judge (Chancellor) held that the terms of the merger were fair and entered judgment for defendants. Plaintiffs appealed.

MOORE, JUSTICE:

In ruling for the defendants, the Chancellor restated his earlier conclusion that the plaintiff in a suit challenging a cash-out merger must allege specific acts of fraud, misrepresentation, or other items of misconduct to demonstrate the unfairness of the merger terms to the minority. We approve this rule and affirm it.

The Chancellor also held that even though the ultimate burden of proof is on the majority shareholder to show by a preponderance of the evidence that the transaction is fair, it is first the burden of the plaintiff attacking the merger to demonstrate some basis for invoking the fairness obligation. We agree with that principle. However, where corporate action has been approved by an informed vote of a majority of the minority shareholders, we conclude that the burden entirely shifts to the plaintiff to show that the transaction was unfair to the minority. See, for example, *Michelson* v. *Duncan*, Del. Supr., 407 A.2d 211, 224 (1979). But in all this, the burden clearly remains on those relying on the vote to show that they completely disclosed all material facts relevant to the transaction.

Here, the record does not support a conclusion that the minority stockholder vote was an informed one. Material information, necessary to acquaint those shareholders with the bargaining positions of Signal and UOP, was withheld under circumstances amounting to a breach of fiduciary duty. We therefore conclude that this merger does not meet the test of fairness, at least as we address that concept, and no burden thus shifted to the plaintiff by reason of the minority shareholder vote. Accordingly, we reverse and remand for further proceedings consistent herewith.

In considering the nature of the remedy available under our law to minority shareholders in a cash-out merger, we believe that it is, and hereafter should be, an appraisal under 8 Del. C. §262 as hereinafter construed. We therefore

overrule *Lynch* v. *Vickers Energy Corp*, Del. Supr., 429 A.2d 497 (1981) (*Lynch II*) to the extent that it purports to limit a stockholder's monetary relief to a specific damage formula. See *Lynch II*, 429 A.2d at 507–08 (McNeilly and Quillen, *J.J.*, dissenting). But to give full effect to section 262 within the framework of the General Corporation Law we adopt a more liberal, less rigid and stylized, approach to the valuation process than has heretofore been permitted by our courts. While the present state of these proceedings does not admit the plaintiff to the appraisal remedy per se, the practical effect of the remedy we do grant him will be coextensive with the liberalized valuation and appraisal methods we herein approve for cases coming after this decision.

Our treatment of these matters has necessarily led us to a reconsideration of the business purpose rule announced in the trilogy of *Singer* v. *Magnavox Co.*, supra; *Tanzer* v. *International General Industries, Inc.* Del. Supr., 379 A. 2d 1121 (1977); and *Roland International Corp.* v. *Najjar*, Del. Supr., 407 A.2d 1032 (1979). For the reasons hereafter set forth we consider that the business purpose requirement of these cases is no longer the law of Delaware.

[*The court then reviewed the facts in detail with regard to the adequacy of disclosure to the UOP board and to UOP's minority shareholders, who were not told of the $24 per share figure that resulted from a study done by UOP directors (Arledge and Chitiea) using UOP records solely for the benefit of Signal. The court noted that the $24 figure would have reduced Signal's return on investment only two-tenths of 1%, but would have meant an extra $17 million to UOP's minority shareholders.*]

In assessing this situation, the Court of Chancery was required to

examine what information defendants had and to measure it against what they gave to the minority stockholders, in a context in which "complete candor" is required. In other words, the limited function of the Court was to determine whether defendants had disclosed all information in their possession germane to the transaction in issue. And by "germane" we mean, for present purposes, information such as a reasonable shareholder would consider important in deciding whether to sell or retain stock.

. . . Completeness, not adequacy, is both the norm and the mandate under present circumstances—*Lynch* v. *Vickers Energy Corp.*, Del. Supr., 383 A.2d 278, 281 (1977) (*Lynch I*).

This is merely stating in another way the long-existing principle of Delaware law that these Signal designated directors on UOP's board still owed UOP and its shareholders an uncompromising duty of loyalty.

Given the absence of any attempt to structure this transaction on an arm's-length basis, Signal cannot escape the effects of the conflicts it faced, particularly when its designees on UOP's board did not totally abstain from participation in the matter. There is no "safe harbor" for such divided loyalties in Delaware. When directors of a Delaware corporation are on both sides of a transaction, they are required to demonstrate their utmost good faith and the most scrupulous inherent fairness of the bargain. The record demonstrates that Signal has not met this obligation.

The concept of fairness has two basic aspects: fair dealing and fair price. The former embraces questions of when the transaction was timed; how it was initiated, structured, negotiated, and disclosed to the directors; and how the approvals of the directors and the stockholders were obtained. The latter aspect of fairness relates to the economic and financial considerations of the proposed merger, including all relevant factors: assets, market value, earnings, future prospects, and any other elements that affect the intrinsic or inherent value of a company's stock. However, the test for fairness is not a bifurcated one as between fair dealing and price. All aspects of the issue must be examined as a whole since the question is one of entire fairness. However, in a nonfraudulent transaction we recognize that price may be the preponderant

consideration outweighing other features of the merger. Here, we address the two basic aspects of fairness separately because we find reversible error as to both.

Part of fair dealing is the obvious duty of candor required by *Lynch I*, supra. Moreover, one possessing superior knowledge may not mislead any stockholder by use of corporate information to which the latter is not privy. With the well-established Delaware law on the subject, and the Court of Chancery's findings of fact here, it is inevitable that the obvious conflicts posed by Arledge and Chitiea's preparation of their "feasibility study," derived from UOP information, for the sole use and benefit of Signal, cannot pass muster.

The Arledge-Chitiea report is but one aspect of the element of fair dealing. How did this merger evolve? It is clear that it was entirely initiated by Signal. The serious time constraints under which the principals acted were all set by Signal. For whatever reasons, and they were only Signal's, the entire transaction was presented to and approved by UOP's board within four business days.

The structure of the transaction, again, was Signal's doing. So far as negotiations were concerned, it is clear that they were modest at best. Crawford, Signal's man at UOP, never really talked price with Signal, except to accede to its management's statements on the subject, and to convey to Signal the UOP outside directors' view that as between the $20–21 range under consideration, it would have to be $21. The latter is not a surprising outcome, but hardly arm's-length negotiations.

As we have noted, the matter of disclosure to the UOP directors was wholly flawed by the conflicts of interest raised by the Arledge-Chitiea report. All of those conflicts were resolved by Signal in its own favor without divulging any aspect of them to UOP.

This cannot but undermine a conclusion that this merger meets any reasonable test of fairness. The outside UOP directors lacked one material piece of information generated by two of their colleagues, but shared only with Signal. True, the UOP board had the Lehman Brothers' fairness opinion, but that firm has been blamed by the plaintiff for the hurried task it performed, when more properly the responsibility for this lies with Signal. There was no disclosure of the circumstances surrounding the rather cursory preparation of the Lehman Brothers' fairness opinion. Instead, the impression was given UOP's minority that a careful study had been made, when in fact speed was the hallmark.

Finally, the minority stockholders were denied the critical information that Signal considered a price of $24 to be a good investment. Since this would have meant over $17,000,000 more to the minority, we cannot conclude that the shareholder vote was an informed one. Under the circumstances, an approval by a majority of the minority was meaningless.

[*At this point the court turned to the matter of fair price, addressing the proper method of determining the fair value of stock. We shall omit this discussion for now, and return to it when we discuss dissenters' appraisal rights.*]

While a plaintiff's monetary remedy ordinarily should be confined to the more liberalized appraisal proceeding herein established, we do not intend any limitation on the historic powers of the Chancellor to grant such other relief as the facts of a particular case may dictate. The appraisal remedy we approve may not be adequate in certain cases, particularly where fraud, misrepresentation, self-dealing, deliberate waste of corporate assets, or gross and palpable overreaching are involved—*Cole* v. *National Cash Credit Association*, Del. Ch., 156 A. 183, 187 (1931). Under such circumstances, the Chancellor's powers are complete to fashion any form of equitable and monetary relief as may be appropriate, including rescissory damages. Since it is apparent that this long, completed transaction is too involved to undo, and in view of the Chancellor's discretion, the award, if any, should be in the form of monetary damages based upon entire fairness standards, i.e., fair dealing and fair price.

[H]ereafter, the provisions of 8 Del. C. §262, as herein construed, respecting the scope of an appraisal and the means for perfecting the same, shall govern the financial remedy available to minority shareholders in a cash-out merger. Thus, we return to the well-established principles mandating a stockholder's recourse to the basic remedy of an appraisal.

Finally, we address the matter of business purpose. The defendants contend that the purpose of this merger was not a proper subject of inquiry by the trial court. The plaintiff says that no valid purpose existed—the entire transaction was a mere subterfuge designed to eliminate the minority. The Chancellor ruled otherwise, but in so doing he clearly circumscribed the thrust and effect of *Singer*.

The requirement of a business purpose is new to our law of mergers and was a departure from prior case law.

In view of the fairness test which has long been applicable to parent-subsidiary mergers, *Sterling* v. *Mayflower Hotel Corp.*, Del. Supr., 93 A.2d 107, 109–10 (1952), the expanded appraisal remedy now available to shareholders, and the broad discretion of the Chancellor to fashion such relief as the facts of a given case may dictate, we do not believe that any additional meaningful protection is afforded minority shareholders by the business purpose requirement of the trilogy of *Singer, Tanzer, Najjar*, and their progeny. Accordingly, such requirement shall no longer be of any force or effect.

The judgment of the Court of Chancery, finding both the circumstances of the merger and the price paid the minority shareholders to be fair, is reversed.

Although *Weinberger* is a very persuasive case, its holdings are not universally accepted. For example, *Weinberger* appears to torpedo *Singer's* holding that a shareholder has any sort of vested right to own stock in any particular corporation. It assumes that a cashed-out shareholder can take the cash and make an equally good investment elsewhere. However, other jurisdictions still cling to the vested right notion.[37]

Weinberger's elimination of the business purpose test is inconsistent with many other jurisdictions; however, perhaps in response to *Weinberger*, New York recently softened its business purpose test. In *Alpert* v. *28 Williams St. Corp.*,[38] a freeze-out merger had been invalidated by a lower court because defendants could not show a "strong and compelling legitimate business purpose" for it. New York's highest court reversed, holding that the corporate benefit underlying the merger "need not be great."

Also, although many other jurisdictions refuse to hold appraisal rights to be the minority shareholder's exclusive remedy in this context, *Weinberger* pretty much closes the door to other remedies. Although *Weinberger* left the potential for other remedies in cases of fraud and misrepresentation, subsequent Delaware cases have read such allegations narrowly. The clear trend is to hold that a minority shareholder is entitled to "entire fairness," which consists mostly, but not entirely,[39] of a fair price.

DISSENTERS' APPRAISAL RIGHTS

Introduction

The appraisal right—the right to force the corporation to purchase their shares at "fair value"—may be the main protection for shareholders who are squeezed or taken out or who unsuccessfully oppose a merger or sale of substantially all assets.

The availability of the remedy has already been discussed. Virtually all jurisdictions provide it for dissenters in a merger. Most jurisdictions provide it for dissenters in a sale of assets situation, and so on.[40]

Not previously mentioned is the fact that about 20 jurisdictions have enacted a "stock market" exception. The MBCA and RMBCA do not have such an exception, but Delaware, for example, provides no appraisal right for shareholders of corporations listed on a national stock exchange or with more than 2,000 shareholders. The theory is that if such shareholders are upset by a transaction, they can sell their shares in the "efficient marketplace" and be assured of receiving fair value.

Authors not enamored with the efficient market hypothesis have pointed to fluctuations of market prices of NYSE-listed firms of 50% in less than eight months and concluded that "it seems arbitrary, to say the least, to remit an enterprise-oriented

---

[37] For example, *In re Jones & Laughlin Steel Corp.*, 488 Pa. 524, 412 A.2d 1099 (1980).

[38] 63 N.Y. 2d 557, 483 N.Y.S. 2d 667 (Ct. App. 1984).

[39] For example, *Rabkin* v. *Philip A. Hunt Chemical Corp.*, 498 A.2d 1099 (Del. 1985).

[40] See MBCA §80 and RMBCA §13.02, which provide appraisal in a wide range of situations.

shareholder to the market for relief.'' [41] Problems also arise when the dissenters' block of shares is so large that putting it on the market will alone depress the price, or when announcement of the transaction the dissenters oppose adversely affects the market price.

Procedures

The appraisal remedy has been criticized as inadequate on grounds that the procedures that a shareholder must go through are so complicated and expensive as to render the right virtually worthless. Although Delaware law, New York law, and the RMBCA have recently attempted to simplify and streamline the process, in most jurisdictions potential appraisal plaintiffs face difficult obstacles. Failure to comply with all procedural requisites frequently leads to forfeiture of the right.

Section 81 of the MBCA sets out a typical procedure. The notice of a proposed transaction requiring shareholder approval must inform shareholders of their right to dissent and obtain payment for their shares. Shareholders wishing to exercise their appraisal right must so inform the corporation in writing and refrain from voting for the action.

If the transaction is approved, the corporation must notify the shareholders who have given notice, stating where a demand for payment can be sent and where share certificates can be deposited. A deadline of not less than 30 days from the mailing of the notice shall be set. Shareholders who do not meet the deadline forfeit their appraisal right.

Immediately upon effectuation of the transaction, the corporation is to remit to the shareholder the amount it estimates to be the fair value of the shares. If it does not do so, or if the dissenter believes the sum remitted to be inadequate, he shall send the corporation his estimate of the fair value and a demand for the deficiency. Unless the estimate is sent within 30 days of the remittance, the right to receive an additional sum is waived. If the demand remains unsettled, the corporation shall take the matter to court within 60 days or be liable for the amount demanded.

Traditionally, dissenting plaintiffs, even if they prevailed, have had to pay court costs and their own attorney's fees even where their efforts inured to the benefit of other dissenters. MBCA §81 now softens this blow by providing that costs, including fees of court-appointed appraisers, will normally be paid by the corporation. Also, the court has discretion to assess expenses of counsel and other experts against the corporation.

"Fair Value"

The most important question about appraisal rights is how ''fair value'' will be determined. Section 81 of the MBCA is not too helpful, defining it only to be the shares' ''value immediately before the effectuation of the corporation action . . . , excluding any appreciation or depreciation in anticipation of such corporate action unless such exclusion would be inequitable.'' The RMBCA is similarly vague.

---

[41] M. Eisenberg, ''The Legal Roles of Shareholders and Management in Modern Corporate Decision-making,'' *California Law Review*, vol. 57 (1969), p. 1.

The most popular method of determining fair value is known as the "Delaware block." This procedure values shares by evaluating them from three perspectives: asset value, market value, and earnings value. These values are then weighed and factored together.

Asset value is determined by subtracting total liabilities from total assets and then dividing by the total number of shares.

Market value is determined by looking at the price quoted on an exchange or NASDAQ, or if the stock is not publicly traded by determining what a willing buyer would pay a willing seller. Recent sales, if any, may provide evidence of market price.

Calculation of earnings value is a two-step process. First, earnings per share is calculated by dividing average earnings during the previous five years by the total number of outstanding shares. That figure must then be capitalized by use of a price/earnings multiplier derived by comparisons with competing corporations. Assume that Corporation A's average earnings have been $5 per share. Assume that its competitors, Corporation B and C have had, respectively, earnings of $10 per share and $20 per share and market prices of $50 per share and $100 per share. These figures indicate the appropriateness of a price/earnings multiplier of 5, leading to an earnings value of $25 per share.

Appropriate percentages are then assigned to each of the three figures, and they are factored together. For example, in *Gibbons* v. *Schenley Industries*,[42] the court's calculations looked like this:

	VALUE FACTORS	WEIGHT	ASSIGNED VALUE
Market price	$29.00	55%	$15.95
Earnings value	39.79	45	17.91
Asset value	49.83	0	0.00
		"Fair value" =	$33.86

Why was asset value given no weight? The court believed that investors would not consider them because they had little predictive value in determining future income in this case. Schenley's assets consisted largely of an overvalued inventory consisting of many unpopular brands, and most of its 29 distilleries were shut down.

In *Bell* v. *Kirby Lumber Corp.*,[43] the calculations looked like this:

	VALUE FACTORS	WEIGHT	ASSIGNED VALUE
Market price	?	0%	$ 0.00
Earnings value	$120	60	72.00
Asset value	456	40	182.40
		"Fair value" =	$254.40

---

[42] 339 A.2d 460 (Del. Ch. 1975).

[43] 395 A.2d 730 (Del. Ch. 1978), *aff'd, 413 A.2d 137 (Del. 1980)*.

Because no reliable market value could be reconstructed in this case, market value was given no weight. In cases where an active market exists, market value will usually be weighed heavily. The average weight given asset value is about 33%, but this varies greatly from case to case. Asset value was assigned 100% weight in the case of a closely held corporation not operated primarily for profits.[44]

The Delaware block method has been criticized on a number of grounds, including (1) by looking at just the earnings of the past five years, *future* earnings potential is ignored; (2) in most jurisdictions postmerger gains are ignored (including under MBCA §81 "unless such exclusion would be inequitable"); (3) premiums normally paid in similar transactions are ignored; and (4) rescissory damages are not available.

The Delaware Supreme Court took some of these criticisms to heart in the *Weinberger* case. *Weinberger* expressly attempted to liberalize the appraisal remedy to better protect minority shareholders. Here is the relevant portion of the *Weinberger* opinion that was deleted earlier:

WEINBERGER v. UOP, INC.

457 A.2d 701 (Del. 1983)

MOORE, JUSTICE:

Turning to the matter of price, plaintiff also challenges its fairness. His evidence was that on the date the merger was approved the stock was worth at least $26 per share. In support, he offered the testimony of a chartered investment analyst who used two basic approaches to valuation: a comparative analysis of the premium paid over market in ten other tender offer-merger combinations and a discounted cash flow analysis.

In this breach of fiduciary duty case, the Chancellor perceived that the approach to valuation was the same as that in an appraisal proceeding. Consistent with precedent, he rejected plaintiff's method of proof and accepted defendants' evidence of value as being in accord with practice under prior case law. This means that the so-called "Delaware block" or weighted average method was employed wherein the elements of value, that is, assets, market price, earnings, etc., were assigned a particular weight and the resulting amounts added to determine the value per share. This procedure has been in use for decades. However, to the extent it excludes other generally accepted techniques used in the financial community and the courts, it is now clearly outmoded. It is time we recognize this in appraisal and other stock valuation proceedings and bring our law current on the subject.

While the Chancellor rejected plaintiff's discounted cash flow method of valuing UOP's stock, as not corresponding with "either logic or the existing law" (426 A.2d at 1360), it is significant that this was essentially the focus, that is, earnings potential of UOP, of Messrs.

---

[44] *King* v. *Southwestern Cotton Oil Co.*, 585 P.2d 385 (Okla. App. 1978).

Arledge and Chitiea in their evaluation of the merger. Accordingly, the standard "Delaware block" or weighted average method of valuation, formerly employed in appraisal and other stock valuation cases, shall no longer exclusively control such proceedings. We believe that a more liberal approach must include proof of value by any techniques or methods which are generally considered acceptable in the financial community and otherwise admissible in court, subject only to our interpretation of 8 Del. C. §262(h), infra. This will obviate the very structured and mechanistic procedure that has heretofore governed such matters.

Fair price obviously requires consideration of all relevant factors involving the value of a company. This has long been the law of Delaware as stated in *Tri-Continental Corp.*, 74 A.2d at 72:

> The basic concept of value under the appraisal statute is that the stockholder is entitled to be paid for that which has been taken from him, viz., his proportionate interest in a going concern. By value of the stockholder's proportionate interest in the corporate enterprise is meant the true or intrinsic value of his stock which has been taken by the merger. In determining what figure represents this true or intrinsic value, the appraiser and the courts must take into consideration all factors and elements which reasonably might enter into the fixing of value. Thus, market value, asset value, dividends, earning prospects, the nature of the enterprise and any other facts which were throw any light on *future* prospects of the merged corporation are not only pertinent to an inquiry as to the value of the dissenting stockholders' interest, but *must* be considered by the agency fixing the value. (emphasis added)

This is not only in accord with the realities of present-day affairs, but it is thoroughly consonant with the purpose and intent of our statutory law.

It is significant that section 262 now mandates the determination of "fair" value based upon "all relevant factors." Only the speculative elements of value that may arise from the "accomplishment or expectation" of the merger are excluded. We take this to be a very narrow exception to the appraisal process, designed to eliminate use of pro forma data and projections of a speculative variety relating to the completion of a merger. But elements of future value, including the nature of the enterprise, which are known as susceptible of proof as of the date of the merger and not the product of speculation, may be considered. When the trial court deems it appropriate, fair value also includes any damages, resulting from the taking, which the stockholders sustain as a class. If that was not the case, then the obligation to consider "all relevant factors" in the valuation process would be eroded.

It was not until the 1981 amendment to section 262 that the reference to "fair value" was repeatedly emphasized and the statutory mandate that the Court "take into account all relevant factors" appeared [section 262(h)]. Clearly, there is a legislative intent to fully compensate shareholders for whatever their loss may be, subject only to the narrow limitation that one cannot take speculative effects of the merger into account.

Although the Chancellor received the plaintiff's evidence, his opinion indicates that the use of it was precluded because of past Delaware practice. While we do not suggest a monetary result one way or the other, we do think the plaintiff's evidence should be part of the factual mix and weighed as such. Until the $21 price is measured on remand by the valuation standards mandated by Delaware law, there can be no finding at the present stage of these proceedings that the price is fair. Given the lack of any candid disclosure of the material facts surrounding establishment of the $21 price, the majority of the minority vote, approving the merger, is meaningless.

The plaintiff has not sought an appraisal, but rescissory damages of the type contemplated by *Lynch* v. *Vickers Energy Corp.*, Del. Supr., 429 A.2d 497, 505–06 (1981) (*Lynch II*). On remand the plaintiff will be permitted to test the fairness of the $21 price by the standards we herein establish, in conformity with the principle applicable to an appraisal—that fair value be determined by taking "into account all relevant factors" [*see* 8 Del. C. §262(h), supra]. In our view this includes the elements of rescissory damages if the Chancellor considers them susceptible of proof and a remedy appropriate to all the issues of fairness before him.

As the debate over the true utility of appraisal rights continues,[45] perhaps *Weinberger's* liberalized approach will revitalize the remedy. Cases decided since *Weinberger*, however, have hesitated to stray far from the traditional Delaware block.[46]

SALE OF CONTROL

A 52% block of stock is worth more than twice as much as a 26% block of stock. Not only will it entitle the owner to twice as big a share of dividends and other distributions, it will also give control over the direction of the enterprise. Purchasers are willing to pay more per share for a control block than for a noncontrol block. That extra amount is called the control "premium."

Is the control premium the personal property of the controlling shareholders, or is it a corporate asset that must be shared with the minority shareholders? Most courts in most circumstances have held that the control premium belongs to the controlling shareholders and need not be shared.[47] However, some sales of control do cause problems.

First there is the "looting" line of cases. Typical is *DeBaun* v. *First Western Bank & Trust Co.*,[48] in which Mattison bought control of the corporation from defendants and reduced its net worth from a positive $220,000 to a negative $200,000 in just 11 months. Because the seller knew facts that made it likely that Mattison would loot, it was held liable to the minority shareholders for lost net worth, lost going concern value, and unpaid debts.

The key in the looting cases is whether the seller knew or should have known of the likelihood of the looting. Some courts have held that payment of a huge premium alone places upon the seller a duty to investigate, but a recent case disagreed.[49]

Second, and standing somewhat alone, is the well-known *Perlman* v. *Feldmann*.[50]

---

[45] See B. Manning, "The Shareholder's Appraisal Remedy: An Essay for Frank Coker," *Yale Law Journal*, Vol. 72 (1962), p. 223; and D. Fischel, "The Appraisal Remedy in Corporate Law," *American Bar Foundation Research Journal* (1983), p. 875.

[46] For example, *Rosenblatt* v. *Getty Oil Co.*, 493 A.2d 929 (Del. 1985).

[47] For example *McDaniel* v. *Painter*, 418 F.2d 545 (10th Cir. 1969).

[48] 46 Cal. App. 3d 686, 120 Cal. Rptr. 354 (1974).

[49] *Clagett* v. *Hutchinson*, 583 F.2d 1259 (4th Cir. 1978).

[50] 219 F.2d 173 (2d Cir.), *cert. denied*, 349 U.S. 952 (1955).

During the Korean war, steel was in short supply. Potential purchasers wanted to control steel, which Feldmann's corporation made. One purchaser was willing to buy *all* the corporation's shares at a profit to all shareholders, but Feldmann negotiated a deal to sell only his controlling interest at a greater profit to himself. The court held that where a very high premium was paid, primarily for a corporate asset, it should be shared with minority shareholders. The factual situation of *Perlman* has been deemed unique, and few cases have applied its ruling.

Finally, in two recent cases, also involving somewhat unusual factual circumstances, the California courts have indicated an intention to strengthen the fiduciary duty owed by majority sellers.[51] In *Brown* v. *Halbert*, for example, the president and majority shareholder of a savings and loan association was asked whether the association was for sale. He said no, but offered to sell his controlling interest. He did, for $1,500 per share. He also promised to give the purchaser access to the association's books, that all officers and directors would resign, and that no dividends would be paid. He then induced minority shareholders to sell out for only $300 per share by pointing out that no further dividends would be paid. A fiduciary breach was found.

Conventional wisdom today is that a controlling shareholder can keep the control premium. But to be safe, a controller should disclose a purchase offer to the minority shareholders and make at least some effort to induce the purchaser to make a similar offer for the minority shares. The focus of analysis has shifted from whether the seller can keep the control premium to the effect on the corporation and the minority shareholders.[52]

An unusual context for the control premium issue appears in the next case.

DOLEMAN v. MEIJI MUTUAL LIFE INSURANCE CO.

727 F.2d 1480 (9th Cir. 1984)

In 1976 Meiji Mutual Life Insurance Company purchased 62.5% of the outstanding shares of Pacific Guardian Life (PGL) from the pledge-holders of LTH, Ltd., a corporation in liquidation. LTH received $16.06 per share for stock that normally traded for less than $5.00 per share. The price was not publicly announced, and LTH was liquidated immediately.

In 1979, Meiji made a tender offer to purchase all remaining shares at $6.00 each. Plaintiff PGL shareholders sued Meiji directly, not derivatively, claiming, inter alia, that Meiji was liable for not offering the same premium to minority shareholders and for diverting PGL's assets for its own use. The trial court held for Meiji, and plaintiffs appealed.

---

[51] *Brown* v. *Halbert*, 271 Cal. App. 2d 252, 76 Cal. Rptr. 781 (1969); and *Jones* v. *H. F. Ahmanson & Co.*, 1 Cal. 3d 93, 460 P.2d 464, 81 Cal. Rptr 592 (1969).

[52] C. Blackmar, ''Fiduciary Duty to Minority in Sale of Majority Shares,'' *Univ. Missouri–Kansas City Law Review*, Vol. 51 (1982), p. 1.

SNEED, CIRCUIT JUDGE:

The first claim alleges a breach of a purchaser's duty in a sale of control transaction. No claim is made against the seller in this transaction. Appellants seek to recover their share of the premium paid to LTH for the control block, or, alternatively, to force Meiji to offer to all minority shareholders the price paid to LTH in 1976. The complaint embodied the theory that Meiji owed a direct fiduciary duty to the minority shareholders. The district court found that no fiduciary duty existed between a purchaser and the minority shareholders. We agree. The complaint also suggested in general and imprecise terms that Meiji participated in a civil conspiracy with LTH to defraud the minority shareholders. The district court, however, did not address the civil conspiracy theory because that theory was not clearly asserted in the complaint. We also agree. On appeal, the appellants primarily raise arguments based upon the civil conspiracy theory.

The appellants thus appear to acknowledge that, under corporate case law, no direct duty exists between the purchaser of a control block and the minority shareholders. Instead, they argue that their complaint alleged (1) that LTH, the controlling shareholder, breached its fiduciary duty to the minority shareholders by selling an asset of the corporation—the insurance business—to Meiji at a premium, and (2) that the sale of control transaction was part of an overall scheme between LTH and Meiji to loot PGL without compensating the minority shareholders. This is a claim distinct from either Claim A or B. It rests upon the existence of a civil conspiracy between LTH and Meiji.

We acknowledge that a properly pled conspiracy theory would enable the minority shareholders to charge the purchaser of control with any breach of duty by the sellers of control. This, in turn, would focus attention on that body of case law and commentary that has imposed certain duties on sellers of controlling interests of corporations. At one end of the spectrum that these authorities represent is the "equal opportunity" doctrine. *See* Andrews, "The Stockholder's Right to Equal Opportunity in the Sale of Shares," 78 Harv.L.Rev. 505 (1965). Under it, "a controlling stockholder should not be free to sell, at least to an outsider, except pursuant to a purchase offer made equally available to other shareholders." No court has adopted it as a basis for general recovery of the control premium. See *Clagett* v. *Hutchison*, 583 F.2d 1259, 1263–64 (4th Cir. 1978); *McDaniel* v. *Painter*, 418 F.2d 545, 548 (10th Cir. 1969); *Zetlin* v. *Hanson Holdings, Inc.*, 48 N.Y. 2d 684, 421 N.Y.S. 2d 877, 397 N.E.2d 387 (1979). At the other extreme is the view "that those who produce a gain [through transfers of control of corporations in whatever form] should be allowed to keep it, subject to the constraint that other parties to the transaction be at least as well off as before the transaction." Easterbrook & Fischel, *Corporate Control Transactions*, 91 Yale L.J. 698, 698 (1982). As these authors see it, "[a]ny attempt to require sharing simply reduces the likelihood that there will be gains to share."

More centrally located on this spectrum are the "inherent fairness" tests of *Jones* v. *H. F. Ahmanson & Co.*, 1 Cal. 3d 93, 460 P.2d 464, 81 Cal. Rptr. 592 (1969), and the proscription against mergers, having the sole purpose of "freezing out for cash" the minority shareholders, set forth in *Perl* v. *IU International Corp.*—61 Haw. 622, 607 P.2d 1036 (1980). Along this spectrum also lies *Perlman* v. *Feldmann*—219 F.2d 173 (2d Cir.), *cert. denied*, 349 U.S. 952, 75 S. Ct. 880, 99 L.Ed. 1277 (1955). In *Perlman* a derivative action by the minority shareholders against a controlling shareholder was held proper when the sale of control was for the purpose of transferring a corporate asset made valuable by wartime demand. The seller was barred from appropriating the full value of the monopoly gain.

Positioned nearby are the so-called "looting" cases. These cases recognize that there is a duty on the part of a controlling shareholder not to transfer control to those who will "loot" the corporation by withdrawing shortly after the acquisition valuable assets, frequently cash and marketable securities. See, for example, *Insuranshares Corp.* v. *Northern Fiscal Corp.*, 35 F.Supp. 22 (E.D. Pa. 1940); *DeBaun* v. *First Western Bank & Trust Co.*, 46 Cal. App. 3d 686, 120 Cal.Rptr. 354 (1975); and *Gerdes* v. *Reynolds*, 28 N.Y.S.2d 622 (Sup. Ct. 1941).

The only specific reference to the civil conspiracy theory of recovery in the complaint appears in the following sentence:

Defendant Meiji was further aware that under circumstances its willingness to pay a large premium to the majority shareholders alone would induce them to violate their duty to the minority shareholders and that Meiji by its actions was becoming a participant in the breach of duties being perpetrated on the minority and would be liable as such. Plaintiffs' Complaint at 7.

This is too conclusory.

Deprived of conspiracy garments, Claim A, as already indicated, can be disposed of easily. It baldly asserts that a purchaser of control has a duty to purchase all the stock at the same price. Such an "all or nothing" principle has been embraced by no case or commentary of which we are aware. Even "equal opportunity" advocates have not gone so far. Therefore, we have no hesitancy in holding that the law of Hawaii does not embrace it.

[*The court then affirmed dismissal of the diversion of assets claim on grounds that it belonged to the corporation and could only be asserted derivatively.*]

Affirmed.

SUCCESSOR PRODUCTS LIABILITY

As noted earlier, when Corporation A acquires Corporation B via a merger, it acquires all Corporation B's liabilities. However, if Corporation A simply purchases Corporation B's assets, it usually only acquires the liabilities it agrees to assume.

But assume the owners of Corporation B realize their enterprise has manufactured a number of defective products. Can they escape liability in the products liability suits that will eventually be filed by forming Corporation A, having A purchase B's assets under an agreement that leaves all liabilities with B, and then dissolving B? Courts say "no." This is one area where the de facto merger doctrine is alive and well. Most courts would find a de facto merger of A and B, or find that A was a "mere continuation" of B and hold A liable for B's defective products.

But what if Corporation C, completely unrelated to B or its owners, buys B's assets? Corporation C continues to make the same product at the same plant with many of the same employees. A few years later, let's assume, a consumer is injured by a product manufactured when B still owned the assets. But Corporation B no longer exists. Can the consumer sue Corporation C? The courts are split on this question. A leading theory is discussed in the following case:

HALL v. ARMSTRONG

103 Wash. 2d 258, 692 P.2d 787 (Wash. 1984)

Plaintiffs claim that Marvin Hall was injured by exposure to asbestos-containing products while he was in the Navy from 1942 through 1945 and while he worked in a shipyard from 1946 through May 1962. One of the products he was exposed to was Unibestos pipe insulation.

The insulation to which Hall was exposed was manufactured by UNARCO, which made Unibestos pipe insulation from 1936 until July 1962. UNARCO is still in business, but is being reorganized under Chapter 11 of the Bankruptcy Reform Act.

Defendant Pittsburg Corning bought the entire Unibestos product line from UNARCO in July 1962, including all assets related to Unibestos, all real estate and fixtures used in its manufacture, unsold inventory, contracts, trademarks, and, Plaintiff contends, good will. There was no transfer of stock between the companies, and no common directors, officers, or shareholders. The purchase agreement expressly provided that UNARCO was selling only the Unibestos product line and that it would continue to operate separately and distinctly. The agreement also provided that UNARCO retained responsibility for damages resulting from the manufacture and sale of its Unibestos products.

Plaintiffs seek to hold Pittsburgh Corning liable under the "product line" theory of successor liability, though they admit that Hall was never exposed to asbestos manufactured by Pittsburgh Corning. The trial court ruled against plaintiffs, who appealed.

ROSSELLINI, JUSTICE:

The general rule in Washington is that a corporation purchasing the assets of another corporation does not, by reason of the purchase of assets, become liable for the debts and liabilities of the selling corporation, except where: (1) the purchaser expressly or impliedly agrees to assume liability; (2) the purchase is a de facto merger or consolidation; (3) the purchaser is a mere continuation of the seller; or (4) the transfer of assets is for the fraudulent purpose of escaping liability—*Martin v. Abbott Laboratories*, 102 Wash. 2d 581, 689 P.2d 368 at p. 384. The basis of this traditional corporate law doctrine is that a sale of corporate assets transfers an interest separable from the corporate entity and does not result in a transfer of unbargained-for liabilities from the seller to the purchaser. Rather, the purchasing corporation receives the protection traditionally accorded any purchaser of property: the bona fide purchaser who gives adequate consideration and who lacks notice of prior claims against the property acquires no liability for those claims. The four exceptions to the traditional rule were developed to protect the rights of commercial creditors and dissenting shareholders following corporate acquisitions.

In *Abbott Labs.*, we determined that the policies underlying strict liability in tort necessitated the formation of an additional exception or rule to address the particular circumstances of a products liability claimant. Rather than expanding the mere continuation exception founded on corporate law principles, we adopted the "product line rule" of liability as developed by the California Supreme Court in *Ray v. Alad. Corp.*, 19 Cal. 3d 22, 136 Cal. Rptr. 574, 560 P.2d 3 (1977).

Application of the product line rule requires the court: (1) to determine whether the transferee has acquired substantially all the transferor's assets, leaving no more than a mere corporate shell; (2) to determine whether the transferee is holding itself out to the general public as a continuation of the transferor by producing the same product line under a similar name; and (3) to determine whether the transferee is benefiting from the goodwill of the transferor.—*Abbott Labs.*, at 387

The first element, requiring acquisition of all or substantially all of the manufacturing assets of the selling corporation, has not been met. The purchase agreement specifically provides for Pittsburgh Corning to acknowledge UNARCO's continuation of the manufacture and the sale of asbestos-containing products. UNARCO did in fact continue to operate as a going concern and exists to this date despite having filed for reorganization.

Notwithstanding the lack of the first element of product line successor liability, appellants contend that this is an appropriate case to apply successor liability. Appellants maintain that neither the unavailability of the predecessor as a potential defendant, nor the lack of a causal relationship between the transfer of assets and the predecessor's unavailability are appropriate and necessary requisites to successor liability. We disagree.

The product line rule formulated in *Ray*, and adopted by this court in *Abbott Labs.*, has its roots in both corporate law and strict tort liability. Our choice to adopt the product line rule rather than extend the mere continuation exception of corporate law was not an abandonment of traditional rules of corporate succession.

The policy justifications for our adoption of the product line rule require the transfer of substantially all of the predecessor's assets to the successor corporation as a prerequisite to imposing liability on the successor. Two compelling rationales are inherent in this requirement. First, in keeping with the social policies underlying strict product liability, the product line rule is one of necessity. Absent such a rule, the injured plaintiff is left without meaningful remedy. Sec-

ond, elemental fairness demands that there be a causal connection between the successor's acquisition and the unavailability of the predecessor. Thus, the product line rule strikes a balance between the necessity of compensating the injured plaintiff and the fairness of requiring causation on the part of the defendant. When, as here, there has been no complete transfer of assets, the element of necessity is not present as the plaintiff may look to the original manufacturer; and further, the sale of the product line has no connection to UNARCO's present financial condition.

An examination of the competing policies of strict products liability and corporate acquisitions reveals that an essential purpose of the product line exception is to afford a products liability claimant an opportunity to bring an action against the successor corporation when his or her rights against the predecessor corporation have been essentially extinguished either de jure, through dissolution of the predecessor, or de facto, through sale of all or substantially all of the assets of the predecessor. The successor corporation, operating in a like fashion as the predecessor, is in a sense a continuation of the predecessor.

The *Ray* court determined that the strict liability policies of compensation and cost spreading were promoted by imposing liability upon a successor under the circumstances where (1) the plaintiff's remedy against the defective product's manufacturer was virtually destroyed by the successor's acquisition of the business (the predecessor had liquidated its assets and dissolved its corporate evidence in accordance with the terms of the acquisition agreement within 2 months of its acquisition by the successor); (2) the successor, by its acquisition, had virtually the same capacity as its predecessor—the manufacturer of the defective product—to estimate the risks of product defects and to spread the costs of insuring against those risks to the product's consumers; and (3) the court deemed it essentially fair to require the successor to bear the burden of its predecessor's strict liability because such liability was necessarily attached to the benefits of the predecessor's goodwill and trade name now being exploited extensively by the successor. The court ultimately concluded that the policies underlying strict liability were sufficiently promoted so that the policies underlying the traditional rules of corporate successor liability were outweighed.

A key premise of the product line exception is that successor liability is only appropriate when the successor corporation by its acquisition actually played some role in curtailing or destroying the claimants' remedies. In such a way, the product line rule strikes a desirable balance between the competing concerns of products liability and a corporation's need to limit its risk exposure.

Imposing liability upon Pittsburgh Corning would promote the policies of risk spreading and compensation. Indeed, successor liability under any circumstances would promote these policies. It is the element of causation, however, that tips the balance in favor of imposing successor liability. The traditional corporate rule of nonliability is only counterbalanced by the policies of strict liability when acquisition by the successor, and not some later event or act, virtually destroys the ability of the plaintiff to seek redress from the manufacturer of the defective product.

Ray itself distinguishes the transfer or acquisition of a business from other events which might affect a plaintiff's remedy.

Pittsburgh Corning did not hold itself out to the world as a continuation of UNARCO, neither did it purchase nor receive any good will associated with the UNARCO name. Although Pittsburgh Corning did exploit the goodwill associated with the product line, it also informed its Unibestos customers that Pittsburgh Corning was the manufacturing entity. The goodwill transfer contemplated by the product line rule is that associated with the predecessor business entity, not that associated with individual products.

The requirement of a transfer of the substantial assets of the predecessor together with its goodwill is founded on the policy that the successor has benefited from the predecessor's goodwill and has acquired the resources to compensate the victims of the predecessor's manufacturing defects. The destruction of the predecessor by acquisition and the benefits derived by the successor from the predecessor's product line preserves a sense of balance in the rule of successor liability, making it more than an unbalanced assertion of social policy.

The transaction between UNARCO and Pittsburgh Corning contemplated the UNARCO would continue in existence, hence maintaining its separate goodwill and the resources to compensate the victims of its own manufacturing defects.

We can discern no valid reason for extending the product line exception when the predecessor has not been extinguished, in law or fact, by succession or dissolution.

The case involving Pittsburgh Corning and UNARCO fails to satisfy the elements of the product line exception. Subsequent to the acquisition of the Unibestos product line, UNARCO continued to operate as a going concern and still remains in business to date. Further, no evidence in the record indicates that Pittsburgh Corning's acquisition of the one product line caused any of UNARCO's financial difficulties which resulted in Chapter 11 proceedings 20 years later.

Affirmed.

QUESTIONS AND PROBLEMS

1. Mutual owned 85.6% of Nationwide, and decided to "go private" via a merger that would cash out minority shareholders. In its Rule 13e–3 disclosure, Mutual gave four reasons for doing so: (a) to eliminate potential conflict of interest problems when Nationwide dealt with other Mutual affiliates, (b) to increase management flexibility, (c) to simplify management structure in order to reduce duplication of effort, and (d) to eliminate the substantial cost of servicing public shareholders. Mutual also disclosed financial information necessary to compute Nationwide's net book, liquidation, and going concern values, but did not disclose an investment banker's projections regarding future increases in earnings. A dissident minority shareholder challenged these disclosures as inadequate. Discuss. See *Howing Company* v. *Nationwide Corporation*, 625 F.Supp. 146 (S.D. Ohio 1985).

2. Morley Brothers, plaintiff corporation, negotiated a takeover by S&T Industries rather than take bankruptcy. Under the agreement, Morley increased its outstanding stock by over 400%. When these shares were purchased by S&T, it became an 80% holder and defendant minority shareholders' interests shrunk from 9.1% to 2.0%. Defendants claim this was a *de facto* merger that entitled them to claim appraisal rights. Discuss. See *Morley Bros.* v. *Clark*, 361 N.W.2d 763 (Mich. App. 1984).

3. Olin Corp. bought 63.4% of Hunt Chemical Corp.'s stock pursuant to an agreement that if it were to acquire all or substantially all of the Hunt stock within a year, it would pay the equivalent of $25 per share. Olin waited just over a year and proposed a merger to cash out the minority at $20 per share. A special committee of outside directors of the Hunt board (now dominated by Olin) met with investment bankers and was told a fair price would range from $19 to $25. It recommended that Olin consider raising its price, but Olin refused. Minority shareholders sue to stop the merger. Defendants argue that plaintiffs are relegated to the appraisal remedy. Discuss. See *Rabkin* v. *Philip A. Hunt Chemical Corp.*, 498 A.2d 1099 (Del. 1985).

4. The Opatut family owned 75% of the stock and completely controlled Colonial Foods Corp. The Opatut family transacted business with Colonial on a frequent basis, and minority Colonial shareholders ultimately brought a derivative action claiming that the Opatuts had profited unfairly in a large range of business dealings with Colonial. To end the derivative suit, the Opatut family initiated a merger to buy out the minority shareholders. Once the merger was completed, the plaintiffs were no longer shareholders and therefore had no standing to bring the derivative suit. However, they brought an action challenging the motives behind the merger and the $3-per-share price that the Opatuts had selected unilaterally. Are plaintiffs relegated to the appraisal right? Discuss. See *Merritt* v. *Colonial Foods, Inc.*, 505 A.2d 797 (Del. Ch. 1986).

5. A court was required to value the 25% interest Blake owned in the common stock of Blake Agency, Inc., a storefront insurance brokerage firm. Blake believed that he had been "frozen out" of the corporate affairs by his brothers who owned the remaining 75% of the shares. Of the three factors utilized in the "Delaware block" method of valuation, which should be given the most weight: market value? asset

value? earnings value? Discuss. See *Blake* v. *Blake Agency, Inc.*, 486 N.Y.S. 2d 341 (A.D. 1985).

6. Defendants Browne and Shawver (directors) and McGrath (president) agreed to purchase enough shares to increase their substantial holdings in the Boulevard State Bank to a majority position. Once they did, they pooled their interests and sought a buyer. Eventually they negotiated a deal to sell their shares to Hentzen and Lawrence for $80 per share, about a $30-per-share premium. Other directors did not know of the transaction until the day before it was approved. Plaintiff minority shareholders in the bank sued, claiming that the defendants' sale had constituted a sale of a corporate asset. Discuss. See *Ritchie* v. *McGrath*, 1 Kan. App. 2d 481, 571 P.2d 17 (1977).

7. H-E Co. manufactured cotton gins. Continental began buying H-E shares and became a 95% owner by 1975. H-E continued to operate as a separate corporation and in 1977 sold all its assets relating to making cotton gins to Lummus. Pursuant to an agreement with Lummus, H-E changed its name to Sherman Gin Co. Six months later, Sherman dissolved and its assets were distributed to its shareholders, mainly Continental. Two months after that, Suarez was injured by a cotton gin that H-E had made years before Continental ever entered the picture. Can Suarez recover from Continental on a products liability theory? Discuss. See *Suarez* v. *Sherman Gin Co.*, 697 S.W. 2d 17 (Tex. App. 1985).

8. Plaintiff females claim they were injured by their mothers' ingestion of the drug DES during pregnancies in the 1950s. Plaintiffs sued, *inter alia*, Warren-Teed Pharmaceuticals, Inc. (D), which in 1963 bought the assets of Warren-Teed Products Co., an independent corporation. D never existed while its predecessor made or sold DES, and D never made or sold DES itself. Can D be held liable on a product line theory? Discuss. See *Burnside* v. *Abbott Labs et al.*, 505 A.2d 973 (Pa. Sup. 1985).

13

INTRODUCTION
TO PUBLIC CORPORATIONS
AND SECURITIES REGULATION

PUBLIC CORPORATIONS

Transition

Publicly held corporations—those whose shares are offered generally to the public for sale—have many concerns, legal constraints, and problems in common with closely held corporations—those whose shares are not sold to the general public. For example, the provisions of the Model Business Corporation Act, which we have examined in previous chapters, or the Delaware Corporation Code are applicable to all corporations from the smallest single-shareholder business to mighty publicly held corporations such as IBM and General Motors. Only recently have states begun passing supplementary corporate laws recognizing the unique problems of the small, closely held corporation. As another example of shared concerns, some provisions of the Securities Exchange Act of 1934 apply to all closely held corporations as well as to the major public corporations at which they were primarily aimed.

Despite the many legal concerns publicly and closely held corporations have in common, there is certainly a difference in emphasis between the two. In the past several chapters we have concentrated on legal problems of primary concern to the closely held corporation. Most cases we have studied involved the smaller corporations. Now, as we make the transition into the field of securities regulation, we are moving into an area that mostly concerns the large public corporations. Although the small, medium, and giant corporations of America are all incorporated under similar state laws, a corporation changes qualitatively as well as quantitatively when it grows. The securities regulation laws ensure that a growing corporation's legal concerns change qualitatively and quantitatively as well.

Why "Go Public"?

Every year many corporations that have operated, frequently quite successfully, as closely held corporations, decide to "go public" by offering new shares of stock for general public sale in a "primary offering" (or by having existing shareholders sell some of their shares to the general public in what is known as a "secondary offering"). The corporation that "goes public" steps into the prestigious world occupied by America's biggest corporations, and a desire to move into the "big time" may underlie many decisions to go public.

Still, the major motivations to go public are financial in nature. The typical corporation that goes public needs additional funds to modernize equipment, move into new geographical markets, develop new products, expand volume of production, and the like. When these new funds can no longer be raised by the corporation's retained earnings or existing shareholder contributions, and when the credit of both shareholders and corporation is exhausted, the logical solution is to turn to the general public for needed capital infusions. Sales of shares to the general public can range from relatively small amounts (though usually exceeding a million dollars) to over $100 million.

Going public has financial advantages beyond the additional funds raised. For example, the value of the shares held by the original shareholders may well increase in value because there are now so many more potential purchasers for their stock. Before the company went public, shareholders who wished to transfer their investment to other pursuits would normally find potential buyers only among the existing shareholders. After the company went public, the entire investing public becomes a potential market.

This increased transferability of stock also makes feasible the use of stock options to compensate and give incentive to employees. And purchase of other companies is easier because the sellers may be willing to accept the buyer's securities instead of cash. Finally, if a company cannot only raise substantial sums by the sale of shares, but also perform well after going public so that the shares trade well on the open market, the company will find it much easier to borrow or to sell additional securities when more money is needed in the future.

All is not roses in going public. The disadvantages must also be considered.[1] Of immediate concern is the high cost of complying with securities laws that regulate the public sale of securities. These expenses will be detailed in Chapter 15, but typically

---

[1] See, generally, M. Halloran, *Going Public*, 2nd ed. (Sorg Printing Co., Inc., 1979).

run around $100,000 to $200,000 per offering and can go much higher. Obviously, quite a large amount of securities must be sold to make it feasible to spend this much on financing costs.

Once the company goes public, an entire network of securities laws that did not apply before must now be complied with. For example, there are expensive and detailed registration requirements under the 1934 Act that require disclosure of large amounts of corporate information. Additionally, other regulatory provisions of the 1934 Act dealing with such matters as insider trading, tender offers, and proxy regulation apply only to public corporations. These complex regulations will be outlined later in this chapter and detailed in succeeding chapters.

Perhaps most important, those persons who founded the corporation and probably still retain controlling interests, may lose that control when the company goes public. Once the company goes public, there is a whole new constituency of shareholders to whom corporate managers must account. If the new owners are not continuously satisfied, they may oust the original founders from controlling positions. The manner in which going public can affect the lives and jobs of the original managers of a corporation is illustrated in the following essay.

GOING PUBLIC PROVIDES MONEY BUT CHANGES LIVES OF OWNERS *

Sanford L. Jacobs

The Wall Street Journal, November 15, 1982, p. 31

Going public brought tiny Dynatrend, Inc., $1.9 million, money for product development that it couldn't have raised otherwise with so few strings attached. Money it won't have to repay. The public stock sale last December made three Dynatrend owners near-millionaires and enhanced the Woburn, Mass., company's standing with its customers and bankers.

Dynatrend's founder and chief executive, Ronald J. Massa, says selling stock was the best way to get money for product development. However, he has mixed feelings about going public. "It has basically changed my whole world," says the 47-year-old executive.

He had to change his management style. Employees he used to pal around with seldom speak to him now. The company is judged by Wall Street standards that he disagrees with, yet he bends operations to meet them. "I have a new boss," he says, "I don't work for myself anymore." There is a general uneasiness about being a public company at Dynatrend, Mr. Massa says. "We've all become circumspect and a little jittery."

Going public puts owners "through a wringer emotionally," says Michael Schaenen of Schaenen, Jacobs, Etheredge & Co., the New York investment banking firm that took Dynatrend public. "They are living in a goldfish bowl." What used to be no one's business has to be disclosed now. "My wife," says Mr. Massa, "thinks it's terrible that everyone knows my salary," which is $98,000.

Dealing with the public aspect of the company leaves him less time to manage. "Much of what I do is nothing in anyone's interest," he says. As an example he notes that the report for the quarter ended Sept. 27 occupied much of a day recently. Revenue was off, and explaining why was difficult.

Being public costs the company more than $100,000 a year, he estimates. There are transfer agent, legal, auditing, investment banking, financial public relations, printing and mailing costs. "It's very bad to be a small company and a public company. You just don't have the wherewithal the big companies have," says Mr. Massa, who left Avco Corp. in 1971 to start Dynatrend with three other men. He has always been president and chief executive.

He used to manage by consensus but hasn't time for the meetings that collective decision-making requires. A score of brokers, analysts and investors call him most weeks, seeking information, even though securities laws forbid premature disclosure of important information. "Brokers are always looking for an edge," Mr. Massa says, "but I keep my mouth shut." He doesn't talk about the company anymore with a friend in whom he used to confide.

Making the investment community aware of Dynatrend is important because the performance of its stock is the yardstick by which the company is measured. But appearances before Wall Street groups unnerve Mr. Massa. "I'm like a deaf guy playing a violin in concert: I can't tell if I'm doing well or not."

His new role means "it's an absolute necessity to delegate and I am nervous about it," he says. Some employees apparently are perplexed about his new duties. "If you asked some of the people here, they'd tell you that Ron Massa doesn't do anything since the company went public. Some of them know I do weird things like talk to strange people who come here, like you," he tells a reporter.

Dynatrend has always worked for the government. Its 55 employees do systems engineering, program management and security analysis. Most of its revenue—$3.6 million in the year ended July 27—comes from federal contracts. From security work for the military, the company developed an idea for an electronic security system that eliminates the need for a team of guards. But there wasn't money to develop a product.

He rejected a venture-capital deal because it meant giving up control of the company. "I wanted money, not partners," he says. A stock offering looked attractive. So, on Dec. 8, 1981, Dynatrend sold 700,000 shares of common stock, or 43.5% of its equity, to the public at $3.50 a share.

The sale produced $2,450,000. The underwriters took 10%, and legal, accounting and other underwriting costs consumed $350,000, leaving Dynatrend $1,855,000. The money has moved development of the security system along.

Meanwhile, he is in thrall to outside forces that he doesn't believe are entirely good for the company. "Despite what people tell you, investors want to make money tomorrow. They aren't in this for the long run. They aren't willing to wait five years."

Investors like to see earnings rise each quarter. That influences Mr. Massa's decisions, though he says bluntly: "This quarter-quarter pacing is manipulating the company, not managing it." Dynatrend's underwriter owns 16% of the stock. One of its partners is on Dynatrend's board and reminds Mr. Massa of Wall Street's views.

Going public added to the company's prestige with customers and its bank, Mr. Massa says. But now everyone judges the concern by the stock's price, which can change for reasons having nothing to do with the company's performance. One day the price dropped $1.25 a share from the $3.50 offering price, reducing Mr. Massa's fortune, on paper, by nearly $180,000. Investors wanted to know what the company had done—and hadn't disclosed—to cause the decline, which made the stock one of the biggest losers of the day in the over-the-counter market. The drop resulted from someone unconnected with the company selling 5,000 shares to pay brokerage debts.

It's no wonder, then, that Mr. Massa says: "I worry now. I never did before." But running a public company has added a positive dimension. "I have never been so motivated to succeed," he says.

Influence of Public Corporations

In making the transition from the study of corporate law primarily in the context of small private corporations to the study of securities regulation that focuses mainly on large public corporations, we must make mention of the incredible influence that these latter entities have on law, economics, and life in general in the United States.

America's major corporations are not just big; they are mammoth. Some have more than a million shareholders and more than a million employees. Annual profits of a single corporation in excess of a billion dollars are not unknown. Many American corporations command larger economic resources than many of the world's countries. Economic entities with such power will inevitably, for good or evil, exert significant influence over national life, not to mention international affairs. Many view the influence of these major corporations as largely sinister. A more benevolent view of the role of large corporations in America follows.

THE REVOLUTIONARY CORPORATIONS *

John D. Glover

Published by Dow Jones-Irwin (1980)

Our large corporations have been a major source of impetus, of driving force in making America what it is. Forty-some years ago, Adolf Berle and Gardiner Means were struck by how "ubiquitous" were the large corporations of the day, and their products and services. Nowadays, our Largest Corporations and their outputs are far more than merely ubiquitous. Now, they are among those elements of living and producing that are most characteristic of the "American System." In a literal sense, they are of the essence of that System.

Our Largest Corporations have grown in numbers and in mass. They have changed in their character. This expansion and development of our corporate population have gone ahead, interacting in reciprocal relationships with the general growth and evolution of the nation and its economy.

• • •

The whole American system has grown and changed—expanding and evolving as a system, not as unrelated elements, independently following unrelated, isolated trajectories.

Growth is only part of our nation's story of the past forty-odd years. More important by far have been the processes and facts of change. The "American System" is not only much larger than it was. It is very different: not only from what it was; but different, even, from the handful of other leading industrial nations.

We know that. But we are seldom aware of how much of those differences of American life and ways of doing things are due to the workings of our large corporations. Directly, by themselves, and through massive industry systems of which they are nuclei, our large corporations have been leading actors in the transformation of the American System. From these large corporations, interacting with thousands upon thousands of even very small companies, flow the lion's share of what are the most typical tools, products, and services of "modernity."

---

* Copyright 1979 by John D. Glover. Reprinted with permission.

Other institutions, of course, have also had their own effects on growth and change in America: governments, universities, unions, churches, foundations, associations of all sorts, for instances. But their influences, speaking generally, have been of rather intangible and indirect sorts. They have often expressed, and have helped determine "rules of the game," values and priorities, allocations of resources. Occasionally, intervention of government has been paramount, as in World War II.

• • •

But constraints, incentives, knowledge, "demands," aspirations—even visions—are all intangible in their nature. These are forces that shape what happens. Their actual effects, however, if there were—and are—to be any, had to be made manifest, and expressed concretely.

A principal instrumentality through which these forces have achieved realization and concreteness has been the business community, composed, as it is, of the several industry systems. And as we have seen, in many of these industry systems, the nuclei that do so much to condition what they do, and how they do it, are made up of our Largest Corporations. The tangible, concrete America we see, live in, and cope with—the best we can—is, to a very large degree, the joint and cumulating product of the workings of hundreds of thousands of corporations, which have been making and doing—changing—things day after day, all these years.

As one looks about a room—a living room, a classroom, an operating room—about a factory; as one walks or drives through our cities, even the countryside, it requires no great sensitivity or knowledge of history to see how America and its way of life have been literally revolutionized, not merely transformed. We may be a little slower in coming to realize that among the chief "engines of change" in making this revolution a reality have been our large corporations.

Not so obvious, but no less real, is that many of the chief "revolutionaries" have been the thousands upon thousands of managers of these firms who have labored day after day for forty years to bring about change: to introduce new products; to find, mobilize and utilize new inputs, new means of production and distribution, new means of communication, new means of transportation. Managers, in the last four decades, have made innumerable decisions committing billions of dollars of labor-years of human endeavor to bring about such changes. With all that going on, it would be unthinkable that America could have remained as it was. Or that the working out to equilibrium positions of sets of givens, or the attainment of "dynamic stability" could have been, in any sense, historic realities.

Whether these changes have produced a "better" nation is a metaphysical question.

• • •

Until recently, what went on inside corporations and how they were run—as contrasted to what they did—were not widely thought of as matters of community concern. But that is history. In implicit recognition of the important institutional nature, role, and consequence of the corporation, various legal and communal sanctions are now in place that constrain the governance, beyond the behavior, of the corporation.

For instance, the Financial Accounting Standards Board, the American Institute of Public Accountants, and the New York Stock Exchange have joined with the Securities Exchange Commission to prescribe the contents of financial disclosures by corporations and acceptable means of valuing revenue, cost, and balance-sheet items. Pressures are developing to constrain corporations in the design of their management information and control systems, even the organization for designing and operating those systems.

Numerous official and unofficial pressures are operating on boards of directors and managements to nominate and select directors who are utterly independent of the management of the corporation and of each other, and with no actual, and presumably, no potential conflict of interest with the corporation. This sort of pressure is making for committees composed exclusively of "outside" members for dealing with compensation; with nomination of directors and key executives; with supervision of the auditing and publication of the corporation's financial and other material information. More subtle pressures are urging corporations in the direction of obtaining demographically representative boards.

Stockholders' derivative suits and class actions by parties and groups allegedly affected by corporate actions seek, in effect, to impose standards of responsibility upon directors and managers that would go far beyond the traditional norms of what was to be expected of prudent men and women.

Equal-opportunity legislation and administration of such statutes stemming from evolving community sentiments as to individual rights, and very real possibilities of injunctive and punitive litigation, now constrain the freedom of managers to hire, fire, retire, assign, promote, and pay whom they choose and how. Civil rights now follow the individual through the doors, right on to the factory floor and into the offices.

All this is to be expected. More is surely yet to come. And it all follows on from the fact that the corporation has left behind in history its status of private enterprise and now has become an institution. The "letter" of many of these growing constraints is truly suffocating, often offends common sense, and is sometimes scarcely more than hostile and punitive. But their "spirit" can be basically in harmony with the corporation's own interest: if the corporation is to be a moral, democratic force in the political system, of course it will have to operate with due regard for communal values and aspirations. Some corporations, it does seem, need a bit of encouragement of a "stick behind" to help them line themselves up on the side of the angels.

It is really too bad, just the same, that Congress, the President, the courts do not give to bureaucrats and other public custodians and censors the admonition that the old Bishop gave to the newly ordained young priests: "Above all, not too much zeal!"

Corporations, no doubt, are flattered by all the attention; but they will be understood if, like the man in Lincoln's story who was being ridden out of town on a rail, they feel, "If it wasn't for the honor, I'd just as soon walk."

Corporate Controversies

Two aspects of the preceding essay require expansion. First, the managers who run the modern large corporation typically own only a small portion of the corporation's shares. The owners of the vast majority of shares, conversely, take no active role in running the corporation. This separation of ownership and control, first prominently noted by Berle and Means in 1932, has increased over the years. Much of the law of securities regulation that we shall study seeks to protect the large body of passive investors from potential abuse by those few managers who actually operate the corporations. Many persons are much more concerned with the potential for and extent of these abuses than was the author of the preceding essay.

Second, because large public corporations have attained the status of *institutions* in our political and economic system, there has been a fierce debate concerning the social responsibility, if any, of such corporations. Some maintain that despite the size and influence of these corporations, they exist solely to reap profits for their owners, the shareholders. For example, in response to the question of whether corporate officials should voluntarily take action to stop pollution out of a sense of social responsibility when such action is not required by law, Milton Friedman stated:

> I wouldn't buy stock in a company that hired that kind of leadership. A corporate executive's responsibility is to make as much money for the stockholders as possible, as long as he operates within the rules of the game. When an executive decides to take action for reasons of social responsibility, he is taking money from someone else—from the stockholders, in the form of lower dividends; from the employees, in the form of lower wages; or from the consumer, in the form of higher prices. The responsibility of a corporate executive is to fulfill the terms of his contract. If he can't do that in good conscience, then he should quit his job and find another way to do good. He has the right to promote what he regards as desirable moral objectives only with his own money. If, on the other hand, the executives of U.S. Steel undertake to reduce pollution in Gary for the purpose of making the town attractive to employees and thus lowering labor costs, then they are doing the stockholders' bidding. And everybody benefits: The stockholders get higher dividends; the customer gets cheaper steel; the workers get more in return for their labor. That's the beauty of free enterprise.[2]

An opposing point of view, representative of the notion that corporations should not be solely concerned with their profit margins but should be cognizant of the broader interests of society, is presented by Christopher Stone:

> Suppose, for example, that the corporation's plant was emitting a pollutant that caused $200,000 damage annually to the environment, but which the corporation could remedy by the construction of the pollution-abatement device that costs, amortized, $50,000 annually. One can imagine jurisdictions in which the addition of the device is not required by law. In such a case, it would not be in the best interest of the corporation, and it would not be required by law, to add the device. Yet, the imposition on society of a $200,000 social cost which the corporation could remedy by an outlay of $50,000 is the very sort of evil that Friedman specializes in—a clear misallocation of resources.[3]

Although the serious debate about the role of corporations in society continues, as this is written chances seem remote that suggested reforms such as federal chartering of corporations [4] or placing "public interest directors" on the boards of directors of the major corporations [5] will occur.

SECURITIES REGULATION

A Survey

Securities regulation has a long, if somewhat checkered, history. Securities are merely pieces of paper whose value lies solely in the interest they represent in an underlying enterprise. If someone tries to sell a car, the buyer can kick the tires and check under

---

[2] *Playboy Magazine*, February 1973, p. 59.

[3] C. Stone, *Where the Law Ends* (New York: Harper & Row Publishers, Inc., 1975), p. 76.

[4] Ralph Nader, "The Case for Federal Chartering," in R. Nader and M. Green, eds., *Corporate Power in America* (New York: Grossman Publishers, 1973).

[5] Arthur Goldberg, "Debate on Outside Directors," *The New York Times*, October 29, 1972.

the hood to determine if the vehicle is worth the requested price. It is much more difficult to check the health of the underlying business organization when buying a security. Also, anyone with a printing press can produce securities in an unlimited quantity. The expansive contours of human greed and gullibility, therefore, set the main limits on securities fraud, absent government regulation.

As early as 1285, King Edward I of England attempted to exert control over expanding British capital markets by licensing London's stockbrokers. Later, around 1700, British trading companies in the Western Hemisphere were so popular that at one time investment schemes offered stock worth more than the value of all the land in Great Britain. So intense was the speculative fever during the "South Sea Bubble" that people invested in projects for desalinization of water, for a wheel of perpetual motion, and even for "an undertaking which shall in due time be revealed." [6] Finally Parliament passed the so-called Bubble Act of 1720 that held issuers and brokers of securities liable for their dishonesty.

In America securities fraud was controlled only by the inadequate common law fraud rules until Kansas passed the first American securities law in 1911. Most other states soon passed similar laws, but exceptions, exemptions, and weak enforcement provisions limited their effectiveness. More important, companies found it easy to evade regulation simply by operating across state lines since there was no federal agency to police interstate activity.

The 1920s in America were characterized by fevered stock investing and trading. Investor enthusiasm was matched by abuses of the system, including stock price manipulation, trading on secret information by corporate insiders, excessive buying of stocks on credit, and flagrant fraud. Of the $50 billion of new securities offered for sale in the United States during the decade, approximately one-half were worthless.

The great stock market crash of 1929 was symptomatic of the problems produced by the lack of effective regulation. When stock market prices fell 89% between 1929 and 1933, Congress was finally prompted to pass the first comprehensive federal securities legislation. In the following decade Congress created the Securities and Exchange Commission (SEC) and passed six major acts aimed at remedying securities abuses. The SEC and these laws are described in the following excerpt published by the SEC itself.

THE WORK OF THE SECURITIES AND EXCHANGE COMMISSION
Securities and Exchange Commission, 1980

Introduction

"The Securities and Exchange Commission (SEC) was created on July 2, 1934 by an act of Congress entitled the Securities Exchange Act of 1934. It is an independent, bipartisan, quasi-judicial agency of the United States Government.

"The Commission is composed of five members not more than three of whom

---

[6] John K. Galbraith, *The Great Crash* (New York: The Hearst Corp., 1979), pp. 41, 43.

may be members of the same political party. They are appointed by the President, with the advice and consent of the Senate, for five-year terms, the terms being staggered so that one expires on June 5th of each year. The Chairman is designated by the President.

"The Commission's staff is composed of lawyers, accountants, security analysts and examiners, engineers and other professionals, together with administrative and clerical employees. The staff is divided into Divisions and Offices (including nine Regional Offices), each under charge of officials appointed by the Chairman.

"The laws administered by the Commission relate in general to the field of securities and finance, and seek to provide protection for investors and the public in their securities transactions. They include (in addition to the Securities Exchange Act of 1934) the Securities Act of 1933 (administered by the Federal Trade Commission until September 1934), the Public Utility Holding Company Act of 1940, and the Investment Advisers Act of 1940. The Commission also serves as advisor to Federal courts in corporate reorganization proceedings under Chapter 11 of the Bankruptcy Reform Act of 1978 and, in cases commenced prior to October 1, 1979, Chapter X of the National Bankruptcy Act.[7]

"The Commission reports annually to the Congress. These reports contain a review of the Commission's administration of the several laws.

"It should be understood that the securities laws were designed to facilitate informed investment analyses and prudent and discriminating investment decisions by the investing public. It is the investor, not the Commission who must make the ultimate judgment of the worth of securities offered for sale. The Commission is powerless to pass upon the merits of securities; and assuming proper disclosure of the financial and other information essential to informed investment analysis, the Commission cannot bar the sale of securities which such analysis may show to be of questionable value.

"It is hoped that the following description of the nature and scope of the Commission's work and authority will contribute both to a better understanding of the laws and to their objective of investor protection.

SECURITIES ACT OF 1933

"This 'truth in securities' law has two basic objectives: (1) to provide investors with material financial and other information concerning securities offered for public sale and (2) to prohibit misrepresentation, deceit, and other fraudulent acts and practices in the sale of securities generally (whether or not required to be registered).

Registration of Securities

"The first objective applies to securities offered for public sale by an issuing company or any person in a control relationship to such company. Before the public offering of such securities, a registration statement must be filed with the Commission by the issuer, setting forth the required information. When the statement has become effective, the

---

[7] Since passage of the Bankruptcy Reform Act of 1978, the SEC's role in bankruptcy proceedings has diminished, though not disappeared entirely. K. Victor, "SEC Takes Low-Key Approach in Bankruptcy Area," *Legal Times*, January 13, 1986, p. 5.

securities may be sold. The purpose of registration is to provide disclosure of financial and other information on the basis of which investors must be furnished with a prospectus (selling circular) containing the salient data set forth in the registration statement to enable them to evaluate the securities and make informed and discriminating investment decisions.

Exemptions from Registration

"The registration requirement applies to securities of both domestic and foreign private issuers, as well as to securities of foreign governments. . . . The antifraud provisions referred to, however, apply to all sales of securities involving interstate commerce, or the mails, whether or not the securities are exempt from registration.

Purpose of Registration

"Registration of securities does not insure investors against loss in their purchase, nor does the Commission have the power to disapprove securities for lack of merit—and it is unlawful to represent otherwise in the sale of securities. The only standard which must be met in the registration of securities is an adequate and accurate disclosure of the material facts concerning the company and the securities it proposes to sell. The fairness of the terms of securities (whether price, promoters' or underwriters' profits, or otherwise), the issuing company's prospects for successful operation, and other factors affecting the merits of securities, have no bearing on the question whether securities may be registered.

"The purpose of registration is to provide disclosure of these and other important facts so investors may make a realistic appraisal of the merits of the securities and thus exercise an informed judgment in determining whether to purchase them. Assuming proper disclosure, the Commission cannot deny registration or otherwise bar the securities from public sale whether or not the price or other terms of the securities are fair or the issuing company offers reasonable prospects of success. These are factors which the investor must assess for himself in the light of the disclosures provided; and if the facts have been fully and correctly stated, the investor assumes whatever risks may be involved in the purchase of the securities.

"Nor does registration guarantee the accuracy of the facts represented in the registration statement and prospectus. The law does, however, prohibit false and misleading statements under penalty of fine or imprisonment, or both. In addition, if an investor suffers loss in the purchase of a registered security, the law provides him with important recovery rights if he can prove that there was incomplete or inaccurate disclosure of material facts in the registration statement or prospectus. These rights must be asserted in an appropriate Federal or State court (not before the Commission, which has no power to award damages); and if such misstatements are proved, the issuing company, its responsible directors and officers, the underwriters, controlling interests, the sellers of the securities, and others (or one or more of such persons) would be liable to the purchaser of the securities for losses sustained in their purchase.

The Registration Process

"To facilitate the registration of securities by different types of issuing companies, the Commission has prepared special registration forms which vary in their disclosure requirements to provide disclosure of the essential facts pertinent in a given type of offering while at the same time minimizing the burden and expense of compliance with the law. In general, the registration forms call for disclosure of information such as (1) a description of the registrant's properties and business, (2) a description of the significant provisions of the security to be offered for sale and its relationship to the registrant's other capital securities, (3) information about the management of the registrant, and (4) financial statements certified by independent public accountants.

"The registration statement and prospectus become public immediately on filing with the Commission; but it is unlawful to sell the securities until the effective date. After the filing of the registration statement, the securities may be offered orally or by certain summaries of the information in the registration statement as permitted by rules of the Commission. The Act provides that registration statements shall become effective on the 20th day after filing (or on the 20th day after the filing of the last amendment thereto); but the Commission, in its discretion, may advance the effective date if, considering the adequacy of information theretofore publicly available, the ease with which the facts about the new offering can be disseminated and understood, and the interests of investors and the public, such action is deemed appropriate.

"Registration statements are examined by the Division of Corporation Finance for compliance with the disclosure requirements. If a statement appears to be materially incomplete or inaccurate, the registrant usually is informed by letter and given an opportunity to file correcting or clarifying amendments. The Commission however, has authority to refuse or suspend the effectiveness of any registration statement if it finds, after hearing, that material representations are misleading, inaccurate or incomplete.

Interpretations and Rulemaking

"As a part of its activities under this Act, the Division of Corporation Finance also renders administrative interpretations of the law and regulations thereunder to members of the public, prospective registrants and others, to help them decide legal questions about the application of the law and the regulations to particular situations and to aid them in complying with the law. This advice, for example, might include an informal expression of opinion about whether the offering of a particular security is subject to the registration requirements of the law and, if so, advice as to compliance with the disclosure requirements of the applicable registration form. Other Divisions render similar advice and assistance.

Fraud Prohibitions

"Generally speaking, the fraud prohibitions of the Securities Act are similar to those contained in the Securities Exchange Act of 1934, under which topic the Commission's investigation and enforcement activities are discussed.

SECURITIES EXCHANGE ACT OF 1934

"By this Act, Congress extended the "disclosure" doctrine of investor protection to securities listed and registered for public trading on our national securities exchanges; and the enactment in August 1964 of the Securities Acts Amendments of 1964 applied the disclosure and reporting provisions to equity securities of hundreds of companies traded over-the-counter (if their assets exceed $1 million and their shareholders number 500 or more).[8]

Corporate Reporting

"Companies which seek to have their securities listed and registered for public trading on such an exchange must file a registration application with the exchange and the Commission. A similar registration form must be filed by companies whose equity securities are traded over-the-counter if they meet the size test referred to. The Commission's rules prescribe the nature and content of these registration statements, including certified financial statements. These data are generally comparable to, but less extensive than, the disclosures required in Securities Act registration statements.[9] Following the registration of their securities, such companies must file annual and other periodic reports to keep current the information contained in the original filing.

"The law prescribes penalties for filing false statements and reports with the Commission, as well as provision for recovery by investors who suffer losses in the purchase or sale of registered securities in reliance thereon.

Proxy Solicitations

"Another provision of this law governs the solicitation of proxies (votes) from holders of registered securities (both listed and over-the-counter), whether for the election of directors or for approval of other corporate action. In any such solicitation, whether by the management or minority groups, disclosure must be made of all material facts concerning the matters on which such holders are asked to vote; and they must be afforded an opportunity to vote 'Yes' or 'No' on each matter. Where a contest for control of the management of a corporation is involved, the rules require disclosure of the names and interests of all 'participants' in the proxy contest. Holders of such securities thus are enabled to vote intelligently on corporate actions requiring their approval. The Commission's rules require that proposed proxy material be filed in advance for examination by the Commission for compliance with the disclosure requirements.

---

[8] To relieve the burden on smaller companies, the SEC has raised the asset requirement from $1 million to $5 million.

[9] The disclosure requirements of the 1933 and 1934 acts have been substantially coordinated by the "integrated disclosure system" discussed later, in Chapter 15.

Tender Offer Solicitations

"In 1968, Congress amended the Exchange Act to extend its reporting and disclosure provisions to situations where control of a company is sought through a tender offer or other planned stock acquisition of over 10 percent of a company's equity securities. The amount was reduced to 5 percent by an amendment in 1970. These amendments and Commission rules thereunder require disclosure of pertinent information, by the person seeking to acquire over 5 percent of the company's securities by direct purchase or by tender offer, as well as by any persons soliciting shareholders to accept or reject a tender offer. Thus, as with the proxy rules, public investors who hold stock in the subject corporation may now make informed decisions on take-over bids.

Insider Trading

"The protection provided the investing public through disclosure of financial and related information concerning the securities of registered companies is supplemented by provisions of the law designed to curb misuse of corporate information not available to the general public. To that end, each officer and director of such a company, and each beneficial owner of more than 10 percent of its registered equity securities, must file an initial report with the Commission (and with the exchange on which the stock may be listed) showing his holdings of each of the company's equity securities. Thereafter, they must file reports for any month during which there was any change in such holdings. In addition, the law provides that profits obtained by them from purchases and sales (or sales and purchases) of such equity securities within any six months period may be recovered by the company or by any security holder on its behalf. This recovery right must be asserted in the appropriate United States District Court. Such insiders are also prohibited from making short sales of their company's equity securities.

Margin Trading

"The statute also contains provisions governing margin trading in securities. It authorizes the Board of Governors of the Federal Reserve System to set limitations on the amount of credit which may be extended for the purpose of purchasing or carrying the securities. The objective is to restrict the excessive use of the nation's credit in the securities markets. While the credit restrictions are set by the Board, investigation and enforcement are the responsibility of the Commission.

Market Surveillance

"The Securities Exchange Act also provides a system for regulating securities trading practices in both the exchange and the over-the-counter markets. In general, transactions in securities which are effected otherwise than on national securities exchanges are said to take place 'over the counter.' Designed to protect the interests of investors and the public, these provisions seek to curb misrepresentations and deceit, market manipulation and other fraudulent acts and practices and to establish and maintain just and equitable principles of trade conducive to the maintenance of open, fair and orderly markets.

"While these provisions of the law establish the general regulatory pattern, the Commission is responsible for promulgating rules and regulations for their implementation. Thus, the Commission has adopted regulations which, among other things, (1) define acts or practices which constitute a 'manipulative or deceptive device or contrivance' prohibited by the statute, (2) regulate short selling, stabilizing transactions and similar matters, (3) regulate the hypothecation of customers' securities, and (4) provide safeguards with respect to the financial responsibility of brokers and dealers.

Registration of Exchanges and Others

"In addition, the law as amended requires registration with the Commission of (1) 'national securities exchanges' (those having a substantial securities trading volume); (2) brokers and dealers who conduct securities business in interstate commerce; (3) transfer agents; (4) clearing agencies; (5) municipal brokers and dealers; and (6) securities information processors.

"To obtain registration, exchanges must show that they are so organized as to be able to comply with the provisions of the statute and the rules and regulations of the Commission and that their rules contain provisions which are just and adequate to insure fair dealing and to protect investors.

"Each exchange is a self-regulatory organization, and its rules, among other things, must provide for the expulsion, suspension or other disciplining of member broker-dealers for conduct inconsistent with just and equitable principles of trade. While the law contemplates that exchanges shall have full opportunity to establish self-regulatory measures insuring fair dealing and the protection of investors, it empowers the Commission by order, rule or regulation to amend the rules of exchanges with respect to various phases of their activities and trading practices if necessary to effectuate the statutory objective. For the most part, exchange rules and revisions thereof suggested by exchanges or by the Commission reach their final form after discussions between representatives of the exchange and the Commission without resort to formal proceedings.

"By an amendment to the law enacted in 1938, Congress also provided for creation of a self-regulatory organization to prevent fraudulent and manipulative acts and practices, to promote just and equitable principles of trade among over-the-counter brokers and dealers. One such association, the National Association of Securities Dealers, Inc., is registered with the Commission under this provision of the law. The establishment, maintenance and enforcement of a voluntary code of business ethics is one of the principal features of this provision of the law.

Broker-Dealer Registration

"Applications for registration as broker-dealers and amendments thereto are examined by the Office of Reports and Information Services with the assistance of the Division of Market Regulation. The registration of brokers and dealers engaged in an interstate over-the-counter securities business also is an important phase of the regulatory plan of the Act. They must conform their business practices to the standards prescribed in the law and the Commission's regulations for the protection of investors (as well as to the fair trade practice rules of their association); in addition, as will be seen later, they may violate these regulations only at the risk of possible loss of registration with the Commission and the right to continue to conduct an interstate securities business, or of suspension or expulsion from the association and loss of the benefits of such membership.

Investigation and Enforcement

"It is the duty of the Commission under the laws it administers to investigate complaints or other indications of possible law violations in securities transactions, most of which arise under the Securities Act of 1933 and the Securities Exchange Act of 1934. Investigation and enforcement work is conducted by the Commission's Regional Offices and the Division of Enforcement.

"Most of the Commission's investigations are conducted privately, the facts being developed to the fullest extent possible through informal inquiry, interviewing of witnesses, examination of brokerage records and other documents, reviewing and trading data and similar means. The Commission however, is empowered to issue subpoenas requiring sworn testimony and the production of books, records and other documents pertinent to the subject matter under investigation; in the event of refusal to respond to a subpoena, the Commission may apply to a Federal court for an order compelling obedience thereto.

"Inquiries and complaints of investors and the general public provide one of the primary sources of leads for detection of law violations in securities transactions. Another is the surprise inspections by Regional Offices of the books and records of brokers and dealers to determine whether their business practices conform to the prescribed rules. Still another is the conduct of inquiries into market fluctuations in particular stocks which appear not to be the result of known developments affecting the issuing company or of general market trends.

"The more general types of investigations concern the sale without registration of securities subject to the registration requirement of the Securities Act, and misrepresentation or omission of material facts concerning securities offered for sale (whether or not registration is required). The anti-fraud provisions of the law also apply equally to the purchase of securities, whether involving outright misrepresentations or the withholding or omission of pertinent facts to which the seller was entitled.

"Other types of inquiries relate to the manipulation of the market prices of securities; the misappropriation or unlawful hypothecation of customers' funds or securities; the conduct of a securities business while insolvent; the purchase or sale of securities by a broker-dealer, from or to his customers, at prices not reasonably related to the current market prices therefor; and violation by the broker-dealer of his responsibility to treat his customers fairly.

Statutory Sanctions

"It should be understood that Commission investigations (which for the most part are conducted in private) are essentially fact-finding inquiries. The facts so developed by the staff are considered by the Commission only in determining whether there is prima facie evidence of a law violation and whether an action should be commenced to determine whether, in fact, a violation actually occurred and, if so, whether some sanction should be imposed.

"Assuming that the facts show possible fraud or other law violation, the laws provide several courses of action or remedies which the Commission may pursue:

a. *Civil injunction*. The Commission may apply to an appropriate United States District Court for an order enjoining those acts or practices alleged to violate the law or Commission rules.

b. *Criminal prosecution*. If fraud or willful law violation is indicated, the Commission may refer the facts to the Department of Justice with a recommendation for criminal prosecution of the offending persons. That Department, through its local United States Attorneys (who frequently are assisted by Commission attorneys), may present the evidence to a Federal grand jury and seek an indictment.

c. *Administrative remedy*. The Commission may, after hearing, issue orders suspending or expelling members from exchanges or the over-the-counter dealers association; denying, suspending or revoking the registrations of broker-dealers; or censuring individuals for misconduct or barring them (temporarily or permanently) from employment with a registered firm.

Broker-Dealer Revocations

"All of these sanctions may be applied to any person who engages in securities transactions violative of the law, whether or not he is engaged in the securities business. However, the administrative remedy is generally only invoked in the case of exchange or association members, registered brokers or dealers, or individuals who may associate with any such firm. In any such administrative proceeding, the Commission issues an order specifying the acts or practices alleged to have been committed in violation of law and directing that a hearing be held for the purpose of taking evidences thereon. . . . If the Commission in its ultimate decision of the case finds that the respondents violated the law, it may take remedial actions as indicated above. Such action may effectively bar a firm from the conduct of a securities business in interstate commerce or on exchanges, or an individual from association with a registered firm—subject to the respondent's right to seek judicial review of the decision by the appropriate United States Court of Appeals.

"In its investigation and enforcement actions, the Commission cooperates closely with other Federal, State and local law enforcement officials, as well as with such private agencies as the Better Business Bureaus.

"The many instances in which these sanctions of the law have been invoked present a formidable record. However, of perhaps greater significance to the investing public is the deterrent or prophylactic effect of the very existence of the fraud prohibitions of the law and the Commission's powers of investigation and enforcement. These provisions of the law, coupled with the disclosure requirements applicable to new security offerings and to other registered securities, tend to inhibit fraudulent stock promotions and operations. They also increase public confidence in securities as an investment medium, thus facilitating financing through the public sale of securities, which contributes to the industrial growth of the nation.

PUBLIC UTILITY HOLDING COMPANY ACT OF 1935

Purpose of Act

"This statute was enacted by Congress to correct the many abuses which Congressional inquiries had disclosed in the financing and operation of electric and gas public-utility holding-company systems.

"When the Act became law in 1935, some 15 holding company systems controlled 80 percent of all electric energy generation, 98.5 percent of all transmission of electric energy across State lines, and 80 percent of all natural-gas pipeline mileage in the United States. Many of the huge utility empires then in existence controlled subsidiaries operating in many widely-separated States and which had no economic or functional relationship to each other. Holding companies were pyramided layer upon layer, many of them serving no useful or economic purpose, and many systems had very complicated corporate and capital structures, with control often lodged in junior securities having little or no equity. These conditions ranked high among abuses which the Act was designed to correct.

Registration

"Interstate holding companies which are engaged through their subsidiaries in the electric utility business or in the retail distribution of natural or manufactured gas are subject to regulation under the statute. The Act requires that they register with the Commission and file initial and periodic reports containing detailed data about the organization, financial structure and operations of each such holding company and of its subsidiaries. Once the holding companies are registered, they and their subsidiaries become subject to regulation by the Commission in accordance with statutory standards designed for the protection of investors, consumers, and the public interest. If, however, a holding company or a subsidiary thereof meets certain specifications, it may be exempted from part or all the duties and obligations otherwise imposed on it by statute.

Integration and Simplification

"From the standpoint of their impact on the electric and gas utility industries, the most important provisions of the Act are its requirements for the physical integration and corporate simplification of holding systems. The integration standards of the statute restrict a holding company's operations to an 'integrated utility system,' which is defined in the Act as one capable of economical operation as a single coordinated system confined to a single area or region in one or more states and not so large as to impair (considering the state of the art) the advantages of localized management, efficient operation, and effectiveness of local regulation. Additional systems or incidental businesses are retainable only under certain limited conditions. The corporate simplification provisions of the Act require action to insure that the capital structure and the continued existence of any company in a holding-company system do not unduly or unnecessarily complicate the corporate structure of the system or unfairly or inequitably distribute voting power among security holders of the system.

"Since 1938, more than 2,500 companies have been subject to the Act as registered holding companies or subsidiaries thereof at one time or another. Included in this total were over 227 holding companies, 1,046 electric and gas utility companies, and 1,210 other companies engaged in a wide variety of pursuits. Among the latter were brick works, laundries, experimental orchards, motion picture theaters and even a baseball club. Today the picture is strikingly different. Only 14 holding company systems are now registered. They are comprised of 13 registered holding companies which function solely as holding companies, 5 holding companies which also are engaged in utility operations, 60 electric and/or gas subsidiary companies, 70 nonutility subsidiaries and 20 inactive companies, making a total of 168 companies with aggregate assets of $48 billion. Further, these 14 systems now account for only about one-fifth of the aggregate assets of the privately-owned electric and gas utility and gas pipeline industries of the nation. Most electric and gas utility companies, which formerly were associated with registered holding companies, now operate as independent concerns.[10]

TRUST INDENTURE ACT OF 1939

"This Act applies in general to bonds, debentures, notes, and similar debt securities offered for public sale which are issued pursuant to trust indentures under which more than $1 million of securities may be outstanding at any one time. Even though such securities may be registered under the Securities Act, they may not be offered for sale to the public unless the trust indenture conforms to specified statutory standards of this Act designed to safeguard the rights and interests of the purchasers.

"The Act was passed after studies by the Commission had revealed the frequency with which trust indentures failed to provide minimum protections for security holders and absolved so-called trustees from minimum obligations in the discharge of their trusts. It requires that the indenture trustee be free of conflicting interests which might interfere with the faithful exercise of its duties in behalf of the purchases of the securities.

[10] The SEC has been so successful in administering the Public Utility Holding Company Act of 1935 that in 1981 the Commission voted to recommend that Congress repeal the act because it was no longer needed. Congress did not do so, however.

It requires also that the trustee be a corporation with minimum combined capital and surplus; imposes high standards of conduct and responsibility on the trustee; precludes preferential collection of certain claims owing to the trustee by the issuer in the event of default; provides for the issuer's supplying evidence to the trustee of compliance with indenture terms and conditions such as those relating to the release or substitution of mortgaged property, issuance of new securities or satisfaction of the indenture; and provides for the reports and notices by the trustee to security holders. Other provisions of the Act prohibit impairment of the security holders' right to sue individually for principal and interest except under certain circumstances, and require the maintenance of a list of security holders which may be used by them to communicate with each other regarding their rights as security holders.

INVESTMENT COMPANY ACT OF 1940

"This legislation, together with the Investment Advisers Act of 1940, discussed below, resulted from a study of the activities of investment companies and investment advisers conducted by the Commission pursuant to direction of Congress contained in the Holding Company Act. The results of this study were reported to Congress in a series of reports filed in 1938, 1939, and 1940, the legislation being supported both by the Commission and the investment company industry.

"Under this Act, the activities of companies engaged primarily in the business of investing, reinvesting, and trading in securities and whose own securities are offered and sold to and held by the investing public, are subject to certain statutory prohibitions and to Commission regulation in accordance with prescribed standards deemed necessary to protect the interests of investors and the public.

"It is important for investors to understand, however, that the Commission does not supervise the investment activities of these companies and that regulation by the Commission does not imply safety of investment in such companies.

"In addition to a requirement that such companies register with the Commission, the law requires disclosure of their financial condition and investment policies to afford investors full and complete information about their activities; prohibits such companies from changing the nature of their business or their investment policies without the approval of the stockholders; bars persons guilty of security frauds from serving as officers and directors; prevents underwriters, investment bankers or brokers from constituting more than a minority of the directors of such companies; requires management contracts (and material changes therein) to be submitted to security holders for their approval; prohibits transactions between such companies and their directors, officers, or affiliated companies or persons, except on approval by the Commission as being fair and involving no overreaching; forbids the issuance of senior securities by such companies except under specified conditions and upon specified terms; and prohibits pyramiding of such companies and cross-ownership of their securities.

"Other provisions relate to sales and repurchases of securities issued by investment companies, exchange offers, and other activities of investment companies, including special provisions for periodic payment plans and face-amount certificate companies.

"With respect to plans of reorganization of investment companies, the Commission is authorized to prepare advisory reports as to the fairness of their terms and provisions if requested by the company or 25 percent of its stockholders; and it may institute court proceedings to enjoin a plan of reorganization if it appears grossly unfair to security holders. The Commission may also institute court action to remove management officials who may be guilty of gross misconduct or gross abuse of trust.

"The securities of investment companies are also required to be registered under the Securities Act; and the companies must file periodic reports and are subject to the Commission's proxy and 'insider' trading rules.

INVESTMENT ADVISERS ACT OF 1940

"This law establishes a pattern of regulation of investment advisers which is similar in many respects to Securities Exchange Act provisions governing the conduct of brokers and dealers. It requires, with certain exceptions, that persons or firms who engage for compensation in the business of advising others about their securities transactions shall register with the Commission and conform their activities to statutory standards designed to protect the interests of investors.

"The registration of investment advisers may be denied, suspended or revoked by the Commission if, after notice and hearing, it finds that a statutory disqualification exists and that such action is in the public interest. Disqualifications include a conviction for certain financial crimes or securities violations, the existence of injunctions based on such activities, a conviction for violation of the Mail Fraud Statute, the willful filing of false reports with the Commission, and willful violations of this Act, the Securities Act or the Securities Exchange Act. In addition to the administrative sanction of denial, suspension or revocation, the Commission may obtain injunctions restraining violations of this law and may recommend prosecution by the Department of Justice for fraudulent misconduct or willful violation of the law or rules of the Commission thereunder.

"The law contains anti-fraud provisions, and it empowers the Commission to adopt rules defining fraudulent, deceptive or manipulative acts and practices and designed to prevent such activities. It also requires that investment advisers disclose the nature of their interest in transactions executed for their clients, and, in effect, it prevents the assignment of investment advisory contracts without the client's consent. The law imposes on investment advisers subject to the registration requirement the duty to maintain books and records in accordance with such rules as may be prescribed by the Commission, and it authorizes the Commission to conduct inspections of such books and records."

. . .

These are the major federal securities laws. In later chapters, the provisions of the 1933 Securities Act and the 1934 Securities Exchange Act will be examined in detail. These remain the most important securities laws for most businesses.

Three other securities-related laws are also important.

SECURITIES INVESTOR PROTECTION ACT OF 1970

Partially because of insufficient financial controls on securities broker-dealers, many such firms became financially insolvent in the late 1960s. When a securities broker-dealer has financial difficulties, its customers can suffer as cash disappears and securities left in the broker-dealer's hands for safekeeping are frozen when the firm's assets are liquidated.

To protect such customers, Congress in 1970 amended the 1934 Act by passing the Securities Investor Protection Act. Just as Congress created the Federal Deposit Insurance Corporation in the 1930s to protect the depositors in failed banks, this act creates the Securities Investor Protection Corporation (SIPC). The SIPC is a nonprofit, federally chartered corporation. Its members include most of the 6,000 or so brokers and dealers registered under the 1934 Act and all members of the national stock exchanges. The SIPC has a seven-member board of directors. Five members are chosen by the president, and one each by the Secretary of the Treasury and the Federal Reserve Board. Two of the members may not be associated with the securities industry.

By collecting fees from its members, the SIPC creates a fund to compensate the customers of failed broker-dealers. The fund is used to protect investors to a limit of $500,000 per account and a maximum of $100,000 for cash claims in each account. There is also stand-by authority for the SIPC to borrow up to $1 billion from the U.S. Treasury. Thus far the SIPC has kept its fund solvent by raising fees in times of financial stress when many firms fail, and lowering the fees in comparatively good times.

If the SIPC finds that any member broker-dealer has failed or is in danger of failing financially, it may apply to a federal district court for a decree that the member's customers need protection. If the court agrees, an impartial trustee will be appointed to handle liquidation of the firm.

FOREIGN CORRUPT PRACTICES ACT OF 1977

In the wake of the Watergate and other scandals of the early 1970s, it was learned that many U.S. corporations had been paying bribes to foreign politicians and officials to obtain business. In 1976, the SEC documented foreign bribes by over 450 American companies. This discovery was particularly distressing because the financial records of the corporations did not disclose these illicit activities. These inaccuracies cast doubt upon the SEC's disclosure system upon which all federal securities regulation is based.

Accounting Provisions

Responding to these shocking disclosures, Congress overwhelmingly agreed to amend the 1934 Act by passage of the Foreign Corrupt Practices Act of 1977 (FCPA). The FCPA has two primary thrusts. First, it imposes internal accounting requirements for all *reporting* companies. They must keep reasonably detailed records that "accurately and fairly'' reflect the company's financial activities. The company must also devise and maintain a system of internal accounting sufficient to put management in a position to know whether bribes are being paid, directly or indirectly, to foreign officials. Although aimed at foreign bribes, the accounting provisions are not limited to detection of such bribes. The burdensome implications of these broad accounting provisions are illustrated in the following case.

SEC v. WORLD-WIDE COIN INVESTMENTS, LTD.

567 F.Supp. 724 (N.D. Ga. 1983)

World-Wide Coin Investments, Ltd. was a corporation headquartered in Atlanta, engaged primarily in the wholesale and retail sale of rare coins, precious metals, gold and silver coins, and bullion and, until 1979, in the retail of camera equipment. It bought its coins from estates, private individuals, dealers, and major coin shows. World-Wide's stock was registered under the 1934 Act, and until late 1981, its stock was registered on the New York Stock Exchange. Prior to July 1979, the company's assets totaled over $2 million, and it had over 40 employees. When this lawsuit was filed in August, 1981 the company's assets amounted to less than $500,000, and it had only three employees.

Defendant Joseph Hale took over management and control of World-Wide in July 1979 by purchasing 51% of its stock. Previously, Hale had been a national bank examiner and a broker-dealer. After taking control of World-Wide, and becoming chairman of the board of directors, Hale appointed defendant Floyd Seibert as a director and World-Wide's one-man audit committee.

In July 1974, the World-Wide's board of directors issued 300,000 additional shares to Hale at the price of $.75 per share; Hale was to pay for the stock in cash or rare medals.

Hale ultimately transferred to World-Wide certain gold medals that substantial evidence indicated were worth much less than $225,000.

The SEC brought this action in the wake of World-Wide's financial decline, alleging numerous legal violations of tender offer rules, proxy rules, and other disclosure requirements. The SEC also alleged violations of the FCPA provisions relating to internal controls and accounting procedures. The first major problem dealt with inventory controls. Rare coins were left unguarded; employees were allowed to take large quantities of assets off the premises. Appraisals were inadequate, and the company could not even determine how much was paid for coins in the inventory. The second major problem related to separation of duties. One employee could accomplish several transactions without supervision. For example, a salesperson could appraise a particular coin offered for purchase by a customer, purchase that coin with a check that the salesperson alone had drawn, count that same coin into inventory, value the coin for inventory purposes, and sell the coin to another purchaser. None of the employees was bonded, yet they were allowed to take large amounts of inventory off the premises. Documentation requirements were so lax that it could not even be determined if coins had been sold *at a profit or a loss. Poor control of checks caused World-Wide to bounce over 100 checks after Hale took over. Approximately $1.7 million in checks were written to Hale and his affiliates or to cash without supporting documentation or any indication of the purpose of the checks. The third accounting problem related to the books and records. A lack of qualified accounting personnel resulted in totally inaccurate and incomplete books. Lawyers informed World-Wide of a possible FCPA violation. An accounting firm recommended numerous specific changes to improve the record keeping, but little or nothing was ever done.*

Regarding the SEC's allegations of FCPA violations, the court said the following.

VINING, DISTRICT JUDGE:

The Foreign Corrupt Practices Act, 15 U.S.C. §78m(b)(2) (Amend. 1977) ("FCPA") was enacted by Congress as an amendment to the 1934 Securities Exchange Act and was the legislative response to numerous questionable and illegal foreign payments by United States corporations in the 1970's. Although one of the major substantive provisions of the FCPA is to require corporate disclosure of assets as a deterrent to foreign bribes, the more significant addition of the FCPA is the accounting controls or "books and records" provision, which gives the SEC authority over the entire financial management and reporting requirements of publicly held United States corporations.

The FCPA was enacted on the principle that accurate recordkeeping is an essential ingredient in promoting management responsibility and is an affirmative requirement for publicly held American corporations to strengthen the accuracy of corporate books and records, which are "the bedrock elements of our system of corporate disclosure and accountability." A motivating factor in the enactment of the FCPA was a desire to protect the investor, as was the pur-

pose behind the enactment of the Securities Acts. It is apparent that investors are entitled to rely on the implicit representations that corporations will account for their funds properly and will not channel funds out of the corporation or omit to include such funds in the accounting system so that there are no checks possible on how much of the corporation's funds are being expended in the manner management later claims.

Like the anti-fraud provisions of the 1934 Securities Exchange Act, the FCPA's provisions on accounting controls are short and deceptively straightforward. Section 13(b)(2) of the FCPA provides that every issuer having a class of securities registered pursuant to section 12 of the Exchange Act shall

(a) Make and keep books, records, and accounts which, in reasonable detail, accurately and fairly reflect the transactions and dispositions of the assets of the issuer; and

(b) Devise and maintain a system of internal accounting controls sufficient to provide reasonable assurances that

   (i) transactions are executed in accordance with management's general or specific authorization;

   (ii) transactions are recorded as necessary (I) to permit preparation of financial statements in conformity with generally accepted accounting principles or any other criteria applicable to such statements, and (II) to maintain accountability for assets.

   (iii) access to assets is permitted only in accordance with management's general or specific authorization; and

   (iv) the recorded accountability for assets is compared with the existing assets at reasonable intervals and appropriate action is taken with respect to any differences.

· · ·

It is clear that section 13(b)(2) and the rules promulgated thereunder are rules of general application which were enacted to (1) assure that an issuer's books and records accurately and fairly reflect its transactions and the disposition of assets, (2) protect the integrity of the independent audit of issuer financial statements that are required under the Exchange Act, and (3) promote the reliability and completeness of financial information that issuers are required to file with the Commission or disseminate to investors pursuant to the Exchange Act.

Since the FCPA became effective, the SEC has interpreted its authority to enforce the Act's requirements quite broadly, taking the position that "it is important that issuers . . . review their accounting procedures, systems of internal accounting controls and business practices in order that they may take any actions necessary to comply with the requirements contained in the Act." The SEC has three basic tools to enforce the requirements of the FCPA: (1) judicial injunctions to prevent violations pursuant to section 21(d) of the 1934 Securities Exchange Act, (2) the ability to institute administrative proceedings to compel issuer compliance with the provisions of the FCPA or to discipline certain categories of persons who cause violations pursuant to section 15(c)(4) of the 1934 Act, and Rule 2(e) of the SEC's Rules of Practice, and (3) the opportunity to refer the case to the Department of Justice for criminal proceedings.

From 1977 to 1979, the SEC was primarily preoccupied with the prevention of the foreign bribery provisions of the FCPA; however, the thrust of its enforcement proceedings at present are with the section 13(b)(2) violations. The FCPA actions currently being litigated by the SEC indicate that it apparently intends to rely heavily on the Act to address management misfeasance, misuse of corporate assets, and other conduct reflecting adversely on management's integrity.

· · ·

Section 13(b)(2) contains two separate requirements for issuers in complying with the FCPA's accounting provisions: (1) a company must keep accurate books and records reflecting the transactions and dispositions of the assets of the issuer, and (2) a company must maintain a reliable and adequate system of internal accounting controls. In applying these two separate requirements to the instant case, the court will examine the requirements of each provision and the problems inherent in their interpretation.

The "books and records" provision, contained in section 13(b)(2)(A) of the FCPA has three basic objectives: (1) books and records should reflect transactions in conformity with accepted methods of reporting economic events, (2) misrepresentation, concealment, falsification, circumvention, and other deliberate acts resulting in inaccurate financial books and records are unlawful, and (3) transactions should be properly reflected on books and records in such a manner as to permit the preparation of financial statements in conformity with GAAP and other criteria applicable to such statements.

Congress' use of the term "records" suggests that virtually any tangible embodiment of information made or kept by an issuer is within the scope of section 13(b)(2)(A) of the FCPA, such as tape recordings, computer printouts, and similar representations. As indicated, the purpose of this provision is to strengthen the accuracy of records and the reliability of audits.

· · ·

The only express congressional requirement for accuracy is the phrase "in reasonable detail." Although section 13(b)(2) expects management to see that the corporation's record-keeping system is adequate and effectively implemented, how the issuer goes about this task is up [to] the management; the FCPA provides no guidance, and this court cannot issue any kind of advisory opinion.

Just as the degree of error is not relevant to an issuer's responsibility for any inaccuracies, the motivations of those who erred are not relevant. The concept that the books and records provision of the act embodies a scienter requirement would be inconsistent with the language of section 13(b)(2)(A), which contains no words indicating that Congress intended to impose such a requirement. Furthermore, either inadvertent or intentional errors could cause the misapplication or unauthorized use of corporate assets that Congress seeks to prevent. Also, a scienter requirement is inappropriate because the difficulty of proving intent would render enforcement extremely difficult. As a practical matter, the standard of accuracy in records will vary with the nature of the transaction involved.

The second branch of the accounting provisions—the requirement that issuers maintain a system of internal accounting controls—appears in section 13(b)(2)(B). Like the recordkeeping provisions of the act, the internal controls provision is not limited to material transactions or to those above a specific dollar amount. While this requirement is supportive of accuracy and reliability in the auditor's review and financial disclosure process, this provision should not be analyzed solely from that point of view. The internal control requirement is primarily designed to give statutory content to an aspect of management stewardship responsibility, that of providing shareholders with reasonable assurances that the business is adequately controlled.

Internal accounting control is, generally speaking, only one aspect of a company's total control system; in order to maintain accountability for the disposition of its assets, a business must attempt to make it difficult for its assets to be misappropriated. The internal accounting controls element of a company's control system is that which is specifically designed to provide reasonable, cost-effective safeguards against the unauthorized use or disposition of company assets and reasonable assurances that financial records and accounts are sufficiently reliable for purposes of external reporting. "Internal accounting controls" must be distinguished from the accounting system typically found in

a company. Accounting systems process transactions and recognize, calculate, classify, post, summarize, and report transactions. Internal controls safeguard assets and assure the reliability of financial records, one of their main jobs being to prevent and detect errors and irregularities that arise in the accounting systems of the company. Internal accounting controls are basic indicators of the reliability of the financial statements and the accounting system and records from which financial statements are prepared.

. . .

Although not specifically delineated in the Act itself, the following directives can be inferred from the internal controls provisions: (1) Every company should have reliable personnel, which may require that some be bonded, and all should be supervised. (2) Account functions should be segregated and procedures designed to prevent errors or irregularities. The major functions of recordkeeping, custodianship, authorization, and operation should be performed by different people to avoid the temptation for abuse of these incompatible functions. (3) Reasonable assurances should be maintained that transactions are executed as authorized. (4) Transactions should be properly recorded in the firm's accounting records to facilitate control, which would also require standardized procedures for making accounting entries. Exceptional entries should be investigated regularly. (5) Access to assets of the company should be limited to authorized personnel. (6) At reasonable intervals, there should be a comparison of the accounting records with the actual inventory of assets, which would usually involve the physical taking of inventory, the counting of cash, and the reconciliation of accounting records with the actual physical assets. Frequency of these comparisons will usually depend on the cost of the process and upon the materiality of the assets involved.

The defendants in the instant case contend that the SEC has misconstrued the provisions of the FCPA relating to a knowledge requirement, contending that the SEC must show scienter.

This court has already declined to adopt the defense offered by the defendants that the accounting controls provisions of the FCPA require a scienter requirement. The remainder of World-Wide's defense appears to be that such a small operation should not be required to maintain an elaborate and sophisticated internal control system, since the costs of implementing and maintaining it would financially destroy the company. It is true that a cost/benefit analysis is particularly relevant here, but it remains undisputed that it was the lack of any control over the inventory and inadequate accounting procedures that primarily contributed to World-Wide's demise. No organization, no matter how small, should ignore the provisions of the FCPA completely, as World-Wide did. Furthermore, common sense dictates the need for such internal controls and procedures in a business with an inventory as liquid as coins, medals, and bullion.

The evidence in this case reveals that World-Wide, aided and abetted by Hale and Seibert, violated the provisions of section 13(b)(2) of the FCPA. As set forth in the factual background portion of this order, the internal recordkeeping and accounting controls of World-Wide have been sheer chaos since Hale took over control of the company.

. . .

Individually, the acts of these defendants do not appear so egregious as to warrant the full panoply of relief requested by the SEC or to impose complete liability under the FCPA. However, the court cannot ignore the all-pervasive effect of the combined failure to act, failure to keep accurate records, failure to maintain any type of inventory control, material omissions and misrepresentations, and other activities which caused World-Wide to decrease from a company of 40 employees and assets over $2,000,000 to a company of only three employees and assets of less than $500,000. It is evident that World-Wide, Hale, and Seibert violated all provisions contained in Section 13(b)(2)(A) and (B) and the SEC's rules promulgated thereunder.

Antibribery Provisions

As may be gleaned from the *World-Wide Coins* opinion, the second major thrust of the FCPA is a prohibition of foreign bribery. All U.S. concerns and their officers, directors, employees, agents, and shareholders are prohibited from offering "any thing of value," directly or indirectly, to foreign officials, political parties, or candidates for the purpose of obtaining or retaining business.

The FCPA's concept of bribery does not include so-called "grease" payments to lower-level foreign officials whose duties are primarily clerical or ministerial. Thus, a payment to expedite goods through customs or to obtain a license to do business is not prohibited.

The act's penalties are harsh, providing for up to a million-dollar fine for a company's violation and fines of up to $10,000 and/or imprisonment of up to five years for an individual's violations.

While there is strong evidence that the FCPA has helped to reduce bribery in foreign countries, there is also evidence that reduction of this bribery has cost the United States huge amounts of foreign business. For example, the U.S. position in the world construction market dropped from first in 1976 to twelfth in 1979.[11] There are also many unanswered questions about the exact meaning of many of the antibribery and accounting provisions of the FCPA.

As this is written, criticisms of the FCPA have led Congress to consider softening and otherwise amending much of the FCPA, although the antibribery provisions especially have been seldom invoked recently.

RACKETEERING INFLUENCED AND CORRUPT ORGANIZATIONS ACT OF 1970

In an effort to block the entry of organized crime into legitimate business, Congress passed the Racketeering Influenced and Corrupt Organizations Act of 1970 (RICO). RICO provides criminal penalties and civil remedies against defendants who engage in "racketeering activity" to operate or gain control of "business enterprises."

Although Congress' specific goal was to attack organized crime, it neither included a definition of "organized crime" in the act nor expressly required a link between a defendant's activities and organized crime. Because of the loose wording of RICO, it has been more frequently used as a civil tool against legitimate businesses than as a criminal tool against organized crime. Indeed, the act has been applied to many "garden variety" frauds and business torts. Imaginative plaintiffs' attorneys have converted many standard commercial tort cases into RICO actions, and the motivation is obvious: RICO's civil remedies include treble damages, attorney's fees, and costs to the winning plaintiff, who has the use of civil discovery and need only prove the case by a preponderance of the evidence.

Elements

A RICO plaintiff must prove the following: (1) a pattern of *racketeering activity*, (2) the existence of an *enterprise* engaged in or affecting interstate or foreign commerce, (3) a *nexus* between the pattern of racketeering activity and the enterprise, and (4) an *injury* to plaintiff's business or property by reason of the racketeering activity.

Pattern of Racketeering Activity

RICO defines "racketeering activity" as any act or threat involving certain listed crimes "chargeable" under state law, including murder, arson, extortion, gambling, and drug dealing, *or* as any act or threat "indictable" under a long, nonexclusive list

---

[11] "Criminalization of American Extraterritorial Bribery," *New York University Journal of International Law & Politics*, vol. 13 (1980), p. 645.

of federal criminal statutes that prohibit such activities as bribery, counterfeiting, mail fraud, wire fraud, securities fraud, and "white slavery."

A "pattern" of racketeering activity is proved by showing defendant has committed two or more acts of racketeering within a ten-year period. These acts arguably need not be connected to each other, but must be connected to the "enterprise." Separate acts in the same scheme, such as two installment payments of a bribe, can suffice.

Because almost any commercial transaction will involve use of the telephone or mail, wire and mail fraud are easy to allege. If fraud is proved, "racketeering" is also proved. Two letters containing false statements could constitute a "pattern of racketeering activity."

Enterprise

The "enterprise" may be any individual, partnership, corporation, or association. According to the Supreme Court, it can be a legitimate enterprise, or an illegitimate one, such as an association of jockeys and bettors engaged in illegal gambling.[12]

The enterprise must be engaged in or affecting interstate or foreign commerce, but this requirement is liberally construed. Almost any interstate travel by a defendant will meet the test, as will interstate phone calls.

Illegal Activity

The RICO claim must allege that defendant has violated one of the four subdivisions of §1962 of the act. Subsection (a) makes it unlawful for any person who has received any income, directly or indirectly, from a pattern of racketeering activity to *invest* any of that income in an enterprise. Subsection (b) makes it illegal to acquire an interest in or *control* of an enterprise through racketeering activity. Subsection (c) prohibits the actual *conduct* of affairs of an enterprise through racketeering. Finally, subsection (d) makes it unlawful to *conspire* to commit any of the activities prohibited in subsections (a), (b), or (c).

Applications and Limitations

RICO began appearing in so many types of lawsuits that some courts began looking for ways to limit its impact. The lack of a requirement that defendants be connected to actual organized crime had resulted in RICO claims being brought against such prominent entities as investment bankers and brokers Bache Halsey Stuart Shields, Inc., and Dean Witter Reynolds, Inc.; CPA firms Arthur Andersen & Co. and Coopers & Lybrand; banks such as Citibank and Continental Illinois National Bank and Trust Co.; insurance companies such as Allstate and Lloyd's of London; and manufacturing companies such as Boeing, General Motors, and Miller Brewing.

To limit the impact of RICO, some courts began requiring that a plaintiff

---

[12] *U.S.* v. *Turkette,* 452 U.S. 576 (1981).

prove, among other things, (1) that defendant had actually been convicted of the alleged acts of racketeering, (2) that plaintiff suffered a "racketeering" injury beyond that caused by the individual acts of racketeering alleged, and (3) that defendant had a link to actual organized crime. Most courts refused to impose such requirements, as the following case illustrates.

ALFARO v. E. F. HUTTON & COMPANY, INC.

606 F.Supp. 1100 (E.D. Pa. 1985)

Plaintiffs Alfaro and his wholly owned corporation, Araraquara Citrus, Inc., purchased limited partnership interests in Energy Resources 1981-A Ltd. (Energy Resources) after July 8, 1981, as a result of promotion of these interests by defendant E. F. Hutton & Co. Plaintiffs claim that defendant made numerous misrepresentations regarding the nature and riskiness of this investment that caused them to enter into the deal. Among the alleged misrepresentations, which Hutton supposedly made knowingly or recklessly, are that the Energy Resources investment (1) was low risk, (2) would yield a 3-to-1 return on 50% of the proceeds that would be invested in low-risk developmental wells, (3) would call for 50% of the proceeds to be invested in controlled exploratory drilling, and (4) was likely to produce a 6-to-1 return on investment over time.

Plaintiffs bring this as a class action on behalf of themselves and other investors, founding their claim on RICO, among other statutory and common law bases. The case is before the district judge on defendant's motion to dismiss.

POLLAK, DISTRICT JUDGE:

. . .

Count three of the complaint alleges that the defendant's conduct violated the Racketeering Influenced and Corrupt Organizations Act. Spe-

cifically, the complaint alleges that defendant violated subsections (c) and (d) of Section 1962 of RICO and that those violations support civil liability under section 1964 of that statute.

The nature of the activity proscribed by RICO, and the statute's interweaving of criminal and civil liability, were recently discussed by the Court of Appeals for the Third Circuit in *Sevelle Industrial Machinery Corp.* v. *Southmost Machinery Corp.*, 742 F.2d 786, 788–89 (3d Cir. 1984):

[RICO] makes it unlawful, *inter alia*, for any person to acquire or maintain any interest in or control of an "enterprise" through a "pattern of racketeering activity"—18 U.S.C. §1962(b)(1982). RICO also makes it unlawful for any person employed by or associated with any enterprise to conduct the affairs of the enterprise through a pattern of racketeering activity—18 U.S.C. §1962(c)(1982). An "enterprise" is defined to include "any individual, partnership, corporation, association, or other legal entity, and any union or group of individuals associated in fact though not a legal entity"—18 U.S.C. §1961(4)(1982). "Racketeering activity" is defined to include state law claims such as murder, bribery, and extortion, and a specified list of federal crimes that includes mail fraud, wire fraud, and interstate transportation and sale of stolen and fraudulently obtained goods. A "pattern of racketeering activity" requires at least two acts of racketeering activity within a ten-year period—18 U.S.C. §1961(5)(1982). In brief, RICO makes it unlawful to acquire or maintain control of an enterprise—broadly defined to include virtually any *de facto* or *de jure* association—through a pattern of criminal activity—18 U.S.C. §1962(b), (c)(1982). It is also unlawful to conspire to perform these acts—18 U.S.C. §1962(d)(1982). While RICO is primarily a criminal statute, it also provides for civil remedies, including a cause of action for treble damages, available to ''[a]ny person injured in his business or property by reason of a violation of §1962.''

The complaint alleges that the defendant violated subsection (c) of 1962 of RICO by ''knowingly conduct[ing] and participat[ing] in the conduct of the affairs of Energy Resources and Hutton through a pattern of racketeering activity.'' It also avers that defendant violated subsection (d) of section 1962 by conspiring to conduct the affairs of those enterprises through a pattern of racketeering activity.

The pattern of racketeering activity alleged includes securities fraud, mail fraud, and wire fraud, all of which are federal offenses. But the complaint supplies no factual details regarding these alleged ''racketeering activities.''

Defendant challenges the viability of this count on a number of separate grounds. Certain of these arguments focus upon the sufficiency of the pleadings while others are directed to the substantive sufficiency of the claim. I will consider the latter first.

a) *Need to Establish Prior Criminal Convictions*

Defendant asserts that in order to state a claim for civil relief under RICO, it is essential that there have been a prior determination that the civil defendant is criminally liable for the offenses which allegedly constitute the ''pattern of racketeering activity'' upon which RICO liability is based. In support of this position, defendant relies upon the Second Circuit's recent decision in *Sedima, S.P.R.L.* v. *Imrex Co.*, 741 F.2d 482 (1984), *cert.* granted, 53 U.S.L.W. 3506 (1985).

Most of the courts which have addressed this issue have concluded that RICO's civil liability provisions do not incorporate a requirement of prior criminal convictions [citations omitted].

There is much that is compelling in the *Sedima* rationale. As Judge Oakes shows, zealous plaintiffs seem with considerable frequency to be trying to employ RICO in settings far removed from the organized crime context which was in the forefront of congressional awareness when the statute was enacted. Undoubtedly, this threatened distortion of the statute could be significantly restrained by limiting civil RICO liability to those instances in which antecedent criminal liability for predicate acts has already been established. Nonetheless, the text of the statute does not, in terms, contemplate such a restrictive reading, and I see nothing in the legislative history that warrants importing such a limitation into the statute. If Congress feels that RICO is being taken too far afield, Congress has both the responsibility and the competence to fashion suitable narrowing amendments.

Accordingly, I will deny defendant's motion to dismiss count three to the extent that it relies upon the proposition that civil liability under RICO must be preceded by a finding of criminal responsibility.

b) *Need to Establish ''Racketeering Injury''*

Defendant also argues that civil RICO liability must be based upon injury beyond that caused by the individual racketeering activities which are a predicate to liability. Defendant asserts that plaintiffs must plead and prove an injury arising out of the organized nature of the misconduct or an injury from racketeering itself as well as injury from the predicate criminal acts. Defendant again relies upon Judge Oakes's analysis in *Sedima* in support of this position.

. . .

I retain the view [I expressed in *General Accident Insurance Company of America* v. *Fidelity and Deposit Company of Maryland*, 598 F.Supp. 1223 (1984)] that civil RICO liability does not depend upon pleading or proof of a unique injury other than the injury caused by the predicate racketeering acts. For the reasons stated in *General Accident* and the decisions cited therein which have reached the same conclusion, I conclude that a racketeering enterprise injury is not essential to pleading or proof of a civil RICO claim.

c) *Need to Establish a Link to Organized Crime*

Defendant also contends that a civil RICO plaintiff must establish a nexus between the RICO claim and organized crime.

However, as plaintiffs note, every appellate court which has considered this issue to date has concluded that no nexus between the claim and organized crime need be pleaded or proven [citations omitted]. In addition, the great majority of district court decisions on this issue have determined that no such organized crime nexus is necessary [citations omitted].

Upon consideration of the reported decisions on this issue, I decline to adopt this limitation on the availability of the civil RICO remedy. As Judge Giles noted in his thoughtful and thorough analysis of this issue in *Kimmel* v. *Peterson*, 565 F.Supp. 476, 490–93 (E.D. Pa. 1983), the requirement of a nexus to organized crime is inconsistent with the clear terms of the statute and the vast majority of court decisions as well as the legislative history of RICO. Consequently, I conclude that no organized crime nexus must be pleaded or proved to state a claim under RICO's civil liability provisions.

d) *Distinction Between Enterprise and Defendant*

Defendant contends that the complaint fails to identify an "enterprise" apart from the defen-

dant. It asserts that such a distinction between the enterprise and the defendant is essential to RICO liability.

Plaintiffs respond that RICO established no requirement that the defendant and the enterprise be distinct entities. In addition, plaintiffs assert that the complaint identifies both defendant and Energy Resources as "enterprises." Therefore, plaintiffs argue, an enterprise is identified in the complaint which is distinct from the defendant.

[O]n December 31, 1984, the [Third Circuit], speaking through Judge Seitz, held that "a violation of section 1962(c) by a corporate entity requires an association with an enterprise that is not the same corporation"—*B. F. Hirsch* v. *Enright Refining Company*, No. 84-5087 (3d Cir.) at 13. Therefore, it is necessary to look at the complaint to determine whether plaintiffs have identified adequately an enterprise associated with the defendant which is an entity other than the defendant.

The complaint states that "Energy Resources and Hutton are enterprises within the meaning of 18 U.S.C. §1961(4)." Consequently, an enterprise other than the defendant—Energy Resources—is identified in the complaint. The only remaining question is whether the complaint alleges a relationship between defendant and Energy Resources of the type which would form the basis for RICO liability.

RICO requires (a) that the defendant be "employed by or associated with" the enterprise and (b) that the defendant "conduct or participate, directly or indirectly, in the conduct of such enterprise's affairs through a pattern of racketeering activity"—18 U.S.C. §1962(c). Paragraph 35 of the complaint plainly satisfies the second of those requirements by alleging that the "[d]efendant [Hutton] knowingly conducted and participated in the conduct of the affairs of Energy Resources and Hutton through a pattern of racketeering activity." The complaint does not in terms allege that Hutton was "associated with" Energy Resources. Nonetheless, I conclude that the allegation that Hutton "knowingly conducted and participated in the conduct of Energy Resources" sufficiently comprehends the required *association* of Hutton and Energy Resources to satisfy the pleading requirements of RICO. Accordingly, I will deny the motion to dismiss the RICO count on this ground.

[The judge then examined the sufficiency of plaintiffs' conspiracy and fraud allegations, concluding that they were too vague. Accordingly, he dismissed the RICO claim, but specifically gave plaintiffs permission to correct the deficiency by amending the complaint to include more specific allegations.]

Supreme Court

Soon after the *Alfaro* case, the Supreme Court decided *Sedima, S.P.R.L.* v. *Imrex Co.*, Inc.,[13] reversing the Second Circuit's decision discussed in *Alfaro*. *Sedima* was not a securities case, but its rationale is fully applicable to a securities case containing a RICO claim. The Supreme Court acknowledged that RICO was being applied in areas Congress probably had not contemplated. Indeed, the Court noted that only 9% of the civil RICO cases involved allegations to criminal activity generally associated with professional criminals. Nonetheless, the Court concluded that any changes would have to come from Congress.

Sedima specifically rejected the notion that a plaintiff had to prove that a defendant had been convicted of the predicate acts of racketeering or that plaintiff had to show a "RICO-type" injury apart from that caused by the predicate acts. The Supreme Court's language also indicated that the Court would, if given an opportunity, probably reject most of the other limitations the lower courts have tried to read into RICO's broad language.

The *Sedima* decision led to renewed calls for congressional action to limit RICO. If Congress does so act, RICO may be reduced to a mere footnote in the next edition of this book. If Congress does not act, RICO will warrant an entire chapter in the next edition, for its treble damages and attorney's fee provisions make it more attractive than traditional securities law claims.

SELF-REGULATION

As indicated in the earlier essay by the SEC, although the SEC is the primary regulatory force in the securities field, it is not the only one. For example, the New York Stock Exchange has regulated its members for almost 200 years. The existing self-regulatory structure of the NYSE and other stock exchanges was incorporated into the overall scheme of the 1934 Act. The SEC was given power to oversee these self-regulatory bodies to ensure the effectiveness of their control.

---

[13] 105 S. Ct. 3275 (1985).

In 1938, a similar self-regulating organization, the National Association of Securities Dealers (NASD) was organized for the over-the-counter securities markets. The NASD's importance has continually increased over the years. In 1975, Congress created the Municipal Securities Rulemaking Board (MSRB) as a self-regulating body for municipal securities dealers.

Most courts hold that if an exchange fails to enforce one of its own rules, or if an NYSE or NASD member violates the rules of those bodies, no private cause of action accrues to the investor injured by the violation. This somewhat limits the impact of the regulation.

AMERICAN LAW INSTITUTE PROPOSED FEDERAL SECURITIES CODE

Because the body of statutory federal securities law is the product of several different statutes passed for different purposes at different times, it is not as cohesive, consistent, or comprehensive as is desirable. Additionally, most of the major provisions were passed over 40 years ago with little amendment since.

To the end of modernizing and bringing consistency to federal securities laws, the American Law Institute over 20 years ago began drawing up a Proposed Federal Securities Code. Although the proposed code has served as a pattern for sporadic legislative and regulatory reform, and as persuasive authority for some court-initiated changes, at the moment there seems little hope that the code will be fully adopted in the near future.

QUESTIONS AND PROBLEMS

1. Assume that as CEO of X Corporation you learn the following facts from a confidential, internal report: (a) X Corporation's manufacturing processes cause a heretofore unknown risk of cancer to employees; (b) the cancer is unlikely to manifest itself for many years; (c) X Corporation's manufacturing processes meet all legal standards; (d) X Corporation's competitors have not done and do not intend to do anything about the danger; and (e) correcting the problem would require such a large expenditure of funds that when these costs are passed on to the consumer it might price X Corporation's products out of the market, jeopardizing X Corporation's existence and the jobs of all its employees. What action will you take in response to the report?
2. Assume that you are a director of ABC Corporation. Mary, ABC's CEO, gave $100,000 of her personal funds to a local university and is asking the board to vote to have ABC match her contribution. Assuming that ABC hires many graduates of the university, is this expenditure proper? sensible? Assume that although ABC does no business in South Africa, Mary is very concerned with the issue of apartheid. She has personally contributed $100,000 to an antiapartheid organization and would like to have ABC match her contribution. Is this expenditure proper? sensible? Discuss.

3. Assume that your cousin Waldo is a very successful businessperson in the business of fabricating plastic parts. He just opened his third plant, and his personal net income is now well above $1 million per year. Waldo now has the opportunity to obtain some large government contracts that could triple his volume of business. However, to obtain the necessary funds for expansion to handle the business, he would have to "go public." Waldo is torn between his choices. Advise him. Should he go public or pass up the chance to expand?

4. Assume that Tonka Corp., a 1934 Act reporting company, discovers that its former chief financial officer and treasurer had Tonka invest $2 million in a shell corporation. The former officer and his business associates then put much of the money to their personal use. Now Tonka learns that the SEC is investigating it for violating the Foreign Corrupt Practices Act. Given that all the transactions between Tonka and the shell corporation occurred in the United States, does Tonka have anything to worry about? Discuss.

5. Evaluate the following transactions as potential violations of the antibribery provisions of the Foreign Corrupt Practices Act:
   a. Asking the U.S. ambassador in Qatar who could be bribed to renew an oil concession for which a $1.5 million bribe had previously been paid.
   b. Paying a $337,000 bribe to the prime minister of the Cook Islands to keep exclusive rights to distribute the nation's postage stamps.
   c. Paying a $9.9 million bribe to subdirectors of Pemex, the Mexican national oil company, in exchange for a major contract.
   d. Paying a sum well over true value for property owned by a personal adviser to the sultan of Oman in exchange for the adviser's help in obtaining a contract to buy oil from Oman.
   e. Paying a gratuity to a customs agent to speed processing of a customs document.

6. Lewis, a shareholder of NSC Corporation, brought a derivative suit against NSC and its directors and officers after NSC pled guilty to criminal charges of filing false government reports and paid a fine of $1.75 million and paid $3 million to IBM in settling a suit for trade secret misappropriation. Among Lewis's causes of action was a claim that defendants had violated the accounting provisions of the Foreign Corrupt Practices Act. NSC argues that there is no private right of action under the FCPA's accounting provision and therefore only the SEC can bring suit. Discuss. See *Lewis* v. *Sporck*, 612 F.Supp. 1316 (N.D. Cal. 1985).

7. Brant was a stock broker who worked for the firm of Kidder, Peabody. He repeatedly lied to Turner, president of investor Intre Sport, about inside information he was supposedly receiving about American Surgery Centers (ASC). Brant told Turner this was a great investment, even as the price of ASC shares plummeted from $14.25 to $3.125. Brant also completely disregarded "sell" orders made by Intre Sport, causing further losses. Intre Sport sued Brant and Kidder, Peabody under several theories, including a RICO claim. The evidence is clear that Kidder, Peabody knew nothing of Brant's misdeeds. Kidder, Peabody moves to dismiss the RICO claim on grounds that RICO contemplates that a "person" employed by or associated with an "enterprise" will conduct the enterprise's affairs through a pattern of racketeer-

ing activity. Kidder, Peabody argues that it cannot be both the "person" and the "enterprise." Is this a good defense? Discuss. See *Intre Sport Ltd.* v. *Kidder, Peabody & Co.*, 625 F.Supp. 1303 (S.D.N.Y. 1985).

8. Modern Settings, Inc., maintained a securities account at Prudential-Bache Securities, Inc. Modern Settings alleges that in August 1983, Pru-Bache abruptly announced that the account was undermargined and immediately sold all of Modern Settings' holdings. Modern Settings sued on a number of theories, including RICO. Defendants moved to dismiss the RICO claim on grounds that there was no "pattern" of racketeering activity involved in the allegedly precipitous liquidation of Modern Settings' account. Discuss. See *Modern Settings, Inc.* v. *Prudential-Bache Securities, Inc.*, 629 F.Supp. 860 (S.D.N.Y. 1986).

14

THE SCOPE OF FEDERAL SECURITIES REGULATION

INTRODUCTION

The federal securities laws are, in essence, a subdivision of the general body of contract law; they provide specialized rules for a very specialized business area.

By passing the antifraud provisions contained in the federal securities laws, Congress did not intend to cover all fraud. Indeed, the federal securities laws are limited in application by two major factors. First, there is a constitutional limitation—Congress' authority to pass such laws is limited. Second, there is a self-imposed limitation—Congress intended to regulate issuance and transactions in *securities*.

The first section of this chapter will briefly examine the permissible scope of federal securities regulation under the Constitution. The second section will examine in greater detail the intended scope of federal securities regulation by defining the term "securities." The ultimate conclusion will be that the scope of federal securities regulation, though not unlimited, is very broad indeed.

JURISDICTION AND INTERSTATE COMMERCE

The federal securities laws were passed pursuant to Article I, Section 8, of the U.S. Constitution, which grants Congress the authority to regulate commerce with foreign nations and among the several states. For that reason, the Securities Act of 1933 describes itself as an act "[t]o provide full and fair disclosure of the character of securities sold in *interstate and foreign commerce and through the mails*, and to prevent frauds in the sale thereof, and for other purposes" (emphasis added). The 1934 Act contains a similar introduction. The specific provisions of both acts are repeatedly constrained by reference to interstate commerce. For example, the very important §10 of the 1934 Act provides that "[i]t shall be unlawful for any person, directly or indirectly, *by use of any means or instrumentality of interstate commerce or of the mails, or of any facility of any national securities exchange*" (emphasis added) to commit various deceptive acts.

Thus, only those transactions that involve interstate or foreign commerce are within the purview of federal securities laws. However, the 1933 and 1934 acts contain very broad definitions. Section 3(a)(17) of the 1934 Act, for example, defines "interstate commerce" to mean "trade, commerce, transportation, or communication among the several States, or between any foreign country and any State, or between any State and any place or ship outside thereof" and also to include "intrastate use of (A) any facility of a national securities exchange or of a telephone or other interstate means of communication, or (B) any other interstate instrumentality." The 1933 Act definition is not quite so broad, but it has been interpreted comparably.

Therefore, any transactions in securities that involve interstate commerce, or even use of interstate facilities, such as the telephone or the mails, may be within the scope of federal securities laws. Even an *intra*state phone call is sufficient in many instances, because that same telephone could be used to make an interstate call and is therefore an "interstate means of communication."

In *Gower* v. *Cohn*,[1] for example, Robert Cohn was accused of securities fraud in part because he purchased his mother's shares in a corporation for a very cheap price apparently to keep the shares out of the hands of the bankruptcy court when the mother declared bankruptcy. The entire transaction occurred inside Georgia, and the only connection with interstate commerce appeared to be an intrastate phone call from Robert Cohn to his mother telling her he was sending a lawyer with papers for her to sign. The court said

> The telephone call must only be made in connection with a fraudulent scheme. Although a use of interstate commerce facilities totally unrelated to the defendant and the transaction would not support jurisdiction, . . . the "subsequent use of interstate facilities in further-ing the scheme is sufficient to establish federal jurisdiction"—*Myzel* v. *Fields*, 386 F.2d 718, 728 (8th Cir. 1967). The telephone call in this case clearly furthered Robert Cohn's overall scheme and as such it fell within the jurisdictional means requirement as articulated by this Court because it was of "material importance to the consummation of the scheme"—*Hooper* v. *Mountain States Securities Corp.*, 282 F.2d 198, 205 (5th Cir. 1960).

---

[1] 643 F.2d 1146 (5th Cir. 1981).

In summary, very few securities transactions will fall outside the scope of federal regulations because they did not involve interstate commerce. A transaction must be negotiated and executed in a face-to-face meeting to avoid federal jurisdiction. In addition, cash must be paid, because the clearing of a check would probably involve facilities of interstate communication.

DEFINITION OF "SECURITY"

Introduction and History

A share of corporate stock is the prototypical security. Stocks, bonds, and debentures are the types of securities that will be involved in most of the securities cases we study in this book. However, the mind of man is an imaginative one and the investment interest is quite malleable. Early state blue-sky laws were continuously amended to broaden the definition of "security" to cover the new, irregular instruments that promoters conceived as ways to evade securities regulation. The states utilized broad, catch-all terms such as "investment contracts" or "certificates of interest in any profit-sharing agreement" in an attempt to plug any gaps in coverage.

The federal government learned from this experience of the early state blue sky laws. In both the 1933 and 1934 acts, Congress took an enumerative approach, comprehensively listing the many types of investment interests that might be deemed securities. The lists included the same catch-all terms that the states had invented. For example, §2(1) of the 1933 Act defines "security" to mean "any note, stock, treasury stock, bond, debenture, evidence of indebtedness, certificate of interest or participation in any profit-sharing agreement, collateral-trust certificate, preorganization certificate or subscription, transferable share, investment contract, voting-trust certificate, certificate of deposit for a security, fractional undivided interest in oil, gas, or other mineral rights, or, in general, any interest or instrument commonly known as a 'security.' . . ."

The wording of the 1934 Act's definition of security is similar, and the Supreme Court had held that for most purposes, the definitions may be considered identical.[2] The wording is very important, as the Supreme Court has also concluded that any attempt to define a security must begin with the statutory language.[3] These words are to be liberally construed, for the legislative history of the 1933 Act indicates that the statute defines the term "security" in "sufficiently broad and general terms so as to include within that definition the many types of instruments that in our commercial world fall within the ordinary concept of a security." [4]

For most of the past 50 years, the courts have construed the term "security" liberally, finding securities to exist in investment interests involving silver foxes, vending machines, orchards, vineyards, franchises, condominiums, fishing boats, even cemetery plots (when sold in sufficient quantities to bury several generations), and Scotch whiskey

---

[2] *Tcherepnin* v. *Knight*, 389 U.S. 332 (1967).
[3] *Rubin* v. *United States*, 449 U.S. 424 (1981).
[4] H.R. Rep. No. 85, 73d Cong., 1st sess. 11 (1933).

warehouse receipts. Also, for the past 50 years, there has been a raging controversy over how to apply the concept of a "security" to the gray areas that continually arise. In the gray areas, notions about the proper goals and policies of securities regulation will govern whether a "security" will be found to exist. Although the Supreme Court has laid down some general tests for defining securities, special considerations require application of special criteria where specific types of investment interests are considered. The same rules cannot be used when one is investing in a condominium as when one is investing in a commodities account.

That philosophical considerations underlie application of the term "security" is highlighted by the fact that all five cases decided before the conservative philosophy of the Burger Court took hold in the securities law area around 1973 found securities to exist. The first three decided thereafter found securities not to exist.

Unfortunately, despite 50 years of litigation, controversy and uncertainty continue to characterize courts' efforts to chart the outside limits of the definition of "securities."

Investment Contracts

If a particular type of investment interest is clearly listed in the 1933 or 1934 act definitions of a "security," courts will usually have little trouble in concluding the federal securities laws apply. It is the innovative or unusual investment interest that will raise questions. Early on the Supreme Court made it clear that promoters could not evade the securities laws by inventing new labels for investment devices that, in substance, were securities.

For example, in *SEC* v. *C.M. Joiner Leasing Corp.*,[5] defendants sold assignments of oil leases accompanied by an agreement that defendants would drill exploratory wells. In essence, defendants had a very large leasehold and were raising money to drill the wells by selling small portions of the leasehold to a variety of investors. While defendants argued that they were selling mere naked leasehold rights, the Court pointed out that without the drilling of the well, no one's leases had any value. Therefore, the agreement was "a form of *investment contract* in which the purchaser was paying both for a lease and for a development project" (emphasis added). Setting the tone for a liberal construction of the term "security," the Court stressed that "the reach of the Act does not stop with the obvious and commonplace. Novel, uncommon, or irregular devices, whatever they appear to be, are also reached if it be proved as a matter of fact that they were widely offered or dealt in under terms or courses of dealing which established their character in commerce as 'investment contracts,' or as 'any interest or instrument commonly known as a "security."'

It was appropriate that *Joiner* involved an investment contract, as this has become the most litigated of all types of securities. In fact, this catch-all term has been the subject of almost every Supreme Court case involving the definition of a security. It is the investment contract concept that the SEC and plaintiffs have attempted to stretch to cover most unusual investment interests.

---

[5] 320 U.S. 344 (1943).

The leading criteria for establishing the existence of an investment contract were set forth in *SEC* v. *W. J. Howey Co.*[6] Defendants in *Howey* had an orange grove they were interested in expanding. To obtain the funds, they could have incorporated and sold shares of stock. Instead, perhaps to avoid the 1933 Act's requirement of registration before public offering of securities, defendants sold rows of trees to investors who were mostly living out of state. Because it was not feasible for the investors to cultivate the groves themselves, defendants also sold a service contract. Defendants had full discretion and authority over cultivation, harvesting, and marketing, being accountable only for an allocation of the net profits out of a pool of produce.

Stressing that the 1933 Act was meant to afford "broad protection to investors," the Court found the presence of a security in the form of an investment contract, despite defendants' claims that they were only selling trees and land. The test for an investment contract, the court said, "is whether the scheme involves an investment of money in a common enterprise with profits to come solely from the efforts of others."

Howey thus established a four-element test for the presence of an investment contract: (1) an investment of money, (2) in a common enterprise, with (3) an expectation of profits, (4) to come solely from the efforts of others. A true understanding of the present law regarding the definition of an investment contract requires analysis of these four elements.

Investment of Money

This element has been liberally construed. To have an investment contract, the purported investor must have invested money *or* "money's worth." Thus, if the investment takes the form of land, machinery, or other business assets rather than cash, the requirement is still met.

Common Enterprise

The term "security" connotes an interest in a business enterprise of some variety. Application of the common enterprise element is somewhat muddled because the courts are unable to agree on its meaning. One type of commonality, known as "horizontal" commonality, is accepted by all courts. Horizontal commonality focuses on the relationship between investors and requires a pooling of funds among investors before the commonality requirement can be met. Thus, in the *Howey* case, there were a number of purchasers of rows of trees and accompanying service contracts. Defendants would sell the harvest from all the trees, pool the profits, and distribute them proportionately to all investors. Thus, the fates of the investors were inextricably intertwined. With good weather and proper management by defendants, all would profit. Bad weather or bad management would mean that all would lose.

The other type of commonality is called "vertical" commonality. It focuses on the relationship between the investor and the promoter, ignoring the absence of

---

[6] 328 U.S. 293 (1946).

multiple investors, pooling of resources, and sharing of profits. The courts that accept vertical commonality conclude that the commonality element of the *Howey* test is met when the fortunes of the investor and the promoter are intertwined. Connection with other investors is not required. Many courts do not accept vertical commonality as an appropriate way of satisfying the common enterprise requirement. An example of the latter school of thought follows.

SILVERSTEIN v. MERRILL, LYNCH, PIERCE, FENNER & SMITH

618 F.Supp. 436 (S.D.N.Y. 1985)

Early in 1983 plaintiff invested $50,000 in a commodity futures account at the defendant brokerage firm (Merrill Lynch). The account was managed by defendants Leonard and Fisher (the brokers or investment managers) who were in turn supervised by defendant Tabone. Plaintiff alleged that in just a few months the account was so mishandled that he lost $16,541. Plaintiffs sued alleging violations of the federal securities laws.

Defendants moved to dismiss the action on grounds that no "security" was involved and therefore the federal securities laws were inapplicable.

KNAPP, DISTRICT JUDGE:

Defendants contend that plaintiff's claims under the federal securities laws must fall because his discretionary commodity futures account was not a security. There is no question that a commodity future is not included within the statutory definition of a security. . . . However, the definition of a security does encompass an "investment contract," . . . which has been defined by the Supreme Court as having three elements: (1) an investment of money (2) in a common enterprise with (3) the expectation of profits to come solely from the efforts of others.

SEC v. *Howey* (1946), 328 U.S. 293, 298–99. Plaintiff maintains that his account constitutes such an investment contract and that his claim is therefore properly brought. There is little question, and defendants concede, that the first and third prongs of the *Howey* test are here met. We therefore focus our inquiry on the second, or "common enterprise" requirement, a definition of which has not yet been provided by our Court of Appeals.

It is generally agreed by all courts which have considered the question that the common enterprise requirement is met where there has been a showing of "horizontal commonality." Horizontal commonality focuses on the relationship between an individual investor and a pool of other investors. It requires that these investors be "joint participants in the same investment enterprise," *Milnarik* v. *M.S. Commodities, Inc.* (7th Cir.), 457 F.2d 274, 277, *cert. denied* (1972), 409 U.S. 887, and that the success or failure of the other investments have a direct impact on the profitability of the plaintiff investor's account. Id. at 476. In such an arrangement, profits may be shared in proportion to one's contribution to the pool. It is clear that the instant case does not meet that requirement.

A second approach toward finding a common enterprise focuses on the relationship between the investor and the broker. This perspective has been dubbed "vertical commonality" and has been interpreted both broadly and narrowly.

A variety of cases, including some from our own district, have applied a "broad" vertical commonality test to facts not too dissimilar from those before us and have concluded that a common enterprise could be found. See, for example, *Troyer* v. *Karcagi* (S.D. N.Y. 1979), 476 F.Supp. 1142 (discretionary trading account is investment contract); *Berman* v. *Orimex Trading, Inc.* (S.D. N.Y. 1968), 291 F.Supp. 701 (test satisfied by promoter's statement that it would make all investment decisions and could earn profit for investor). . . . Other courts, applying a "narrow" standard, have rejected a finding of common enterprise on facts similar to those before us. See, for example, *Mordaunt* v. *Incomco* (9th Cir. 1982), 686 F.2d 815, *cert. denied* (1985), 105 S.Ct. 801; and *Brodt* v. *Bache* (9th Cir. 1979), 595 F.2d 459.

Without attempting a detailed analysis of the opinions in those cases, it seems to us that no interpretation of the facts in the instant action would meet the *Howey* criterion that plaintiff be engaged in a "common enterprise." An essential element of any common enterprise is that the fortunes of its members be to some degree related to each other. Here, however, it would be perfectly possible, on the one hand, for the defendants to have suggested a few lucky (or wise) investments which would have brought great profit to the plaintiff and practically no revenue to the defendants, and on the other hand—as plaintiff claims here to be the case—defendants to have so poorly managed the account that plaintiff suffered great losses while defendant earned huge commissions. See, for example, *Brodt* v. *Bache*, supra (where defendant brokerage firm earned commissions based not on profitability of transactions, but simply by their frequency, no common enterprise existed).

We conclude that the *Howey* test has not been met and that no "investment contract" is before us. The complaint is accordingly dismissed.

So ordered.

Expectation of Profit

The third element of the Howey test requires that the investor have an expectation of profit arising from the investment. Because of this element, the SEC has concluded that trading stamps, streetcar tokens, and Christmas gift certificates are not securities. Similarly, one entrepreneur who desired to sell, for $9.95, a one-millionth share in a longhorn steer and an illustrated certificate stating the holder is a genuine one-millionth owner of a Texas longhorn steer asked the SEC whether he would have to register under the 1933 Act. The SEC held that since this was obviously a novelty item carrying no expectation of profit for the purchaser, no security was involved.[7]

A key question frequently concerns whether the purchaser of an interest is buying for personal consumption or for investment purposes. If the purchase is for personal consumption, the courts are less likely to find a security. The following Supreme Court decision makes this point, among others.

---

[7] Terlingua Cattle Co., *Federal Securities Law Reports* (CCH), ¶77,026 (Securities Exchange Commission, 1981).

UNITED HOUSING FOUNDATION, INC. v. FORMAN

421 U.S. 837 (1975)

Co-Op City was a massive cooperative housing complex in New York City built with government support and operated on a nonprofit basis. To acquire an apartment, eligible prospective purchasers had to buy 18 shares of "stock" in the cooperative for each room at $25 per share, or $1,800 for a four-room apartment. This purchase was, in effect, a recoverable deposit. The shares were expressly tied to the apartment and could not be pledged, encumbered, or transferred to a nontenant. No voting rights were attached to the shares; each apartment had one vote in management no matter how many rooms or shares were owned. Any tenant leaving the complex had to offer to sell his or her stock back to the corporation at the initial selling price.

When the monthly rental on the apartments rose to almost double the early predictions, several tenants sued, claiming, inter alia, federal securities violations. The trial court found that no security was present; the Court of Appeals reversed. Defendant appealed to the Supreme Court.

POWELL, JUSTICE:

[The Court first rejected the notion that a security was present merely because what plaintiffs purchased was labeled "stock." Rather than blindly accept the labels put on the instruments by the parties, the Court held that the determination of whether a security is present must turn on the "economic realities" underlying the transaction. Admitting that in some instances use of the name "stock" might lead a purchaser to assume justifiably that the federal securities laws applied, the Court held that in this case no such assumption could have been made since the "shares" purchased bore none of the characteristics traditionally associated with true corporate stock (transferability, voting rights in proportion to number of shares, dividend rights, etc.). The Court then turned to the claim that an "investment contract" was present.]

. . .

The touchstone [of the *Howey* test] is the presence of an investment in a common venture premised on a reasonable expectation of profits to be derived from the entrepreneurial or managerial efforts of others. By profits, the Court meant either capital appreciation resulting from the development of the initial investment, as in [*SEC* v.] *Joiner*, supra (sale of oil leases conditioned on promoters' agreement to drill exploratory well), or a participation in earnings resulting from the use of investors' funds, as in *Tcherepnin* v. *Knight*, supra (dividends on the investment based on savings and loan association's profits). In such cases the investor is "attracted solely by the prospects of a return" on his investment—*Howey*, supra, at 300. By contrast, when a purchaser is motivated by a desire to use or consume the item purchased—"to occupy the land or to develop it themselves," as the *Howey* Court put it, ibid.—the securities laws do not apply.

. . .

In the present case there can be no doubt that investors were attracted solely by the prospect of acquiring a place to live, and not by financial returns on their investments. . . . *[The*

*Court then rejected the notion that an expecta-
tion of "profits" could be derived from the fact
that Co-op City offered space at a cost substantially below the going rental charge or that
rental rates were reduced to the extent, if any,
that Co-op City made a profit on rental of commercial offices and parking spaces, and its operation of community washing machines.]*

There is no doubt that purchasers in this housing cooperative sought to obtain a decent home
at an attractive price. But that type of economic

interest characterizes every form of commercial
dealing. What distinguishes a security transaction—and what is absent here—is an investment
where one parts with his money in the hope
of receiving profits from the efforts of others,
and not where he purchases a commodity for
personal consumption or living quarters for personal use.

. . .

Reversed.

The *Forman* decision is as important for its rejection of the "literal" approach
and embracing of the "economic realities" test as it is for its relevance to the "expectation
of profits" element of the *Howey* test. A more recent Supreme Court case that is also
important on several levels is *International Brotherhood of Teamsters* v. *Daniel*.[8] Plaintiff
in *Daniel* was the member of a union that entered into a collective bargaining agreement
with trucking firms. The agreement provided for a mandatory, noncontributory pension
plan. That is, all the contributions were made by the employers; the defendant union
officials administered the fund. When told he was not eligible for benefits, Daniel sued
for securities fraud.

Regarding the first element of the *Howey* test, the Court held that there was
no "investment of money" since the plan was noncontributory. Although Daniel argued
that he was investing his labor, the Court held that "[l]ooking at the economic realities,
it seems clear that an employee is selling his labor primarily to obtain a livelihood, not
making an investment."

Regarding the remaining elements of the *Howey* test, Daniel argued that he
had an expectation of profit derived from the union's successful management of the
pension fund and investment of its assets. But the Court concluded that while the fund
gained some profit from investment of its assets, most of the income came from employer
contributions that had nothing to do with the efforts of the fund's managers. Furthermore,
the principal barrier to a worker's realization of benefits was not the financial health of
the fund, but his or her own ability to meet the eligibility requirements. "When viewed
in light of the total compensation package an employee must receive in order to be
eligible for pension benefits, it becomes clear that the possibility of participating in a
plan's asset earnings 'is far too speculative and insubstantial to bring the entire transaction
within the Securities Acts,' *Forman*, 421 U.S., at 856."

---

[8] 439 U.S. 551 (1979).

Importantly, the Court also noted that the Employee Retirement Income Security Act of 1974 regulated pensions in detail and concluded that "[t]he existence of this comprehensive legislation governing the use and terms of employee pension plans severely undercuts all arguments for extending the Securities Acts to noncontributory compulsory pension plans. . . . Whatever benefits employees might derive from the effect of the Securities Acts are now provided in more definite form through ERISA."

It should be noted that courts have also held compulsory *contributory* plans not to be securities, though the SEC continues to take the position that a *voluntary*, contributory plan would be a security.

Finally, regarding the element of expectation of profit, the California Supreme Court promulgated the "risk capital" test in *Silver Hills* v. *Sobieski*.[9] The "risk capital" test produces the same result as the *Howey* test when there is the traditional expectation of profit present. In addition, it will result in the finding of a security where the investors provide the "risk capital" that gets the venture off the ground. In *Silver Hills*, defendants wished to buy, remodel, and expand a country club, but did not have the cash to do so. Therefore, defendants sold memberships in the club to raise funds. The purchasers of memberships had no rights to use the club's facilities. Thus, there was no "expectation of profit" in the traditional sense. Nonetheless, the California Supreme Court found a security, noting: "We have here nothing like the ordinary sale of a right to use existing facilities. [Defendants] are soliciting the risk capital with which to develop a business for profit. The purchaser's risk is not lessened merely because the interest he purchases is labeled a membership. Only because he risks his capital along with other purchasers can there be any chance that the benefits of club membership will materialize."

The "risk capital" test has gained some support in the lower federal courts, but remains a minority approach.

Efforts of Others

The fourth element of the *Howey* test requires that the expected profits be derived solely from the efforts of persons other than the investor. The notion underlying this requirement is that a party who is actively involved in an enterprise will succeed or fail on his or her own merit and does not need the protection of the securities laws as much as a passive investor.

The word "solely" in the *Howey* formulation is troublesome; if literally applied, it means that defendants in *Howey* could have avoided federal securities regulation simply by having the investors pick a single orange. To avoid this result, most courts have required only that "the efforts made by those other than the investor are the undeniably significant ones, those essential managerial efforts which affect the failure or success of the venture." Under this test, there can even be labor by plaintiff so long as it is not entrepreneurial or managerial. A leading case in this vein involves a very interesting form of enterprise.

---

[9] 361 P.2d 906 (1961).

SEC v. KOSCOT INTERPLANETARY, INC.

497 F.2d 473 (5th Cir. 1974)

This appeal comes from a trial judge order denying an injunction sought by the SEC against Koscot Interplanetary. The SEC maintained that the pyramid promotion scheme operated by Koscot was a "security" and therefore had to be registered under the 1933 Act. The trial judge held that no security was involved.

GEWIN, CIRCUIT JUDGE:

I

A. The Koscot Scheme

The procedure followed by Koscot in the promotion of its enterprise can be synoptically chronicled. A subsidiary of Glen W. Turner Enterprises, Koscot thrives by enticing prospective investors to participate in its enterprise, holding out as a lure the expectation of galactic profits. All too often, the beguiled investors are disappointed by paltry returns.

The vehicle for the lure is a multi-level network of independent distributors, purportedly engaged in the business of selling a line of cosmetics. At the lowest level is a "beauty advisor" whose income is derived solely from retail sales of Koscot products made available at a discount, customarily of 45%. Those desirous of ascending the ladder of Koscot enterprise may also participate on a second level, that of supervisor or retail manager. For an investment of $1,000, a supervisor receives cosmetics at a greater discount from retail price, typically 55%, to be sold either directly to the public or to be held for wholesale distribution to the beauty advisors. In addition, a supervisor who introduces a

prospect to the Koscot program with whom a sale is ultimately consummated receives $600 of the $1,000 paid to Koscot. The loftiest position in the multi-level scheme is that of distributor. An investment of $5,000 with Koscot entitles a distributor to purchase cosmetics at an even greater discount, typically 65%, for distribution to supervisors and retailers. Moreover, fruitful sponsorship of either a supervisor or distributor brings $600 or $3,000 respectively to the sponsor.

. . .

The modus operandi of Koscot and its investors is as follows. Investors solicit prospects to attend Opportunity Meetings at which the latter are introduced to the Koscot scheme. Significantly, the investor is admonished not to mention the details of the business before bringing the prospect to the meeting, a technique euphemistically denominated the "curiosity approach." . . . Thus, in the initial stage, an investor's sole task is to attract individuals to the meeting.

Once a prospect's attendance at a meeting is secured, Koscot employees, frequently in conjunction with investors, undertake to apprise prospects of the "virtues" of enlisting in the Koscot plan. The meeting is conducted in conformity with scripts prepared by Koscot. Indeed, Koscot distributes a bulletin which states: ". . . this program is to be presented by the script. It is strongly recommended that you consider replacing any individual who does not present the program verbatim." The principal design of the meetings is to foster an illusion of affluence. Investors and Koscot employees are instructed to drive to meetings in expensive cars, preferably Cadillacs, to dress expensively, and to flaunt large amounts of money. It is intended that prospects will be galvanized into signing a contract by these ostentatious displays in the evangelical atmosphere of the meetings. Go-Tours, characterized by similar histrionics, are designed to achieve the same goal.

The final stage in the promotional scheme is the consummation of the sale. If a prospect capitulates at either an Opportunity Meeting or a Go-Tour, an investor will not be required to expend any additional effort. Less fortuitous investors whose prospects are not as quickly enticed to invest do have to devote additional effort to consummate a sale, the amount of which is contingent upon the degree of reluctance of the prospect.

B. The District Court

The district court correctly cited *SEC* v. *W. J. Howey Co.*, 328 U.S. 293, 298–299 (1946), as the standard controlling its disposition of the case. . . . This test subsumes within it three elements: first, that there is an investment of money; second, that the scheme in which an investment is made functions as a common enterprise; and third, that under the scheme, profits are derived solely from the efforts of individuals other than the investors.

II

A. The First Two Elements

Since it cannot be disputed that purchasers of supervisorships and distributorships made an investment of money, our initial concern is whether the Koscot scheme functions as a common enterprise. As defined by the Ninth Circuit, "[a] common enterprise is one in which the fortunes of the investor are interwoven with and dependent upon the efforts and success of those seeking the investment or of third par-

ties"—*SEC* v. *Glen W. Turner Enterprises, Inc.*, 474 F.2d 476, 428 n. 7 (9th Cir. 1973). The critical factor is not the similitude or coincidence of investor input, but rather the uniformity of impact of the promoter's efforts.

* * *

[T]he fact that an investor's return is independent of that of other investors in the scheme is not decisive. Rather, the requisite commonality is evidenced by the fact that the fortunes of all investors are inextricably tied to the efficacy of the Koscot meetings and guidelines on recruiting prospects and consummating a sale.

B. The Third Element—Solely from the Efforts of Others

As was noted earlier, the critical issue in this case is whether a literal or functional approach to the "solely from the efforts of others" test should be adopted, that is, whether the exertion of some effort by an investor is inimical to the holding that a promotional scheme falls within the definition of an investment contract.

1. The Legal Standard

We begin our analysis by noting that the 1933 and 1934 acts are remedial in nature and hence are to be broadly construed.

* * *

A literal application of the *Howey* test would frustrate the remedial purposes of the act. As the Ninth Circuit noted in *SEC* v. *Glen W. Turner Enterprises, Inc.*, supra at 482, "[i]t would be easy to evade [the *Howey* test] by adding a requirement that the buyer contribute a modicum of effort." The Supreme Court admonished against such a rigid and quixotic application, noting in *Tcherepnin* v. *Knight*, 389 U.S. 332, 336 (1967), that in searching for the meaning and scope of the word security, form should be disregarded for substance and proclaiming in *SEC* v. *W. J.* Howey Co., 328 U.S. at 301, that "[t]he statutory policy of affording broad protection to investors is not to be thwarted by unrealistic and irrelevant formulae." It would be anomalous to maintain that the Court in *Howey* intended to formulate the type of intractable rule which it had decried. The admitted salutary purposes of the Acts can only be safeguarded by a functional approach to the *Howey* test.

Moreover, a close reading of the language employed in *Howey* and the authority upon which the Court relied suggests that, contrary to the view of the district court, we need not feel compelled to follow the "solely from the efforts of others" test literally. Nowhere in the opinion does the Supreme Court characterize the nature of the "efforts that would render a promotional scheme beyond the pale of the definition of an investment contract. Clearly the facts presented no issue of how to assess a scheme in which an investor performed mere perfunctory tasks. Indeed, just prior to concluding that the sales of units of citrus grove development, coupled with contracts for cultivating, marketing and remitting the net proceeds to investors constituted sales of investment contracts, the Court observed that "the promoters *manage, control* and *operate* the enterprise"—328 U.S. at 300 (emphasis added).

. . .

Moreover, a significant number of federal courts invoking the *Howey* test have either given it a broader, more salutary application or endorsed such an application in principle. Thus, in several cases where the scheme required or envisioned the possibility of participation by an investor in the enterprise, courts nevertheless found an investment contract to exist.

. . .

In view of these developments and our analysis of the import of the language in and the derivation of the *Howey* test, we hold that the proper standard in determining whether a scheme constitutes an investment contract is that explicated by the Ninth Circuit in *SEC* v. *Glen W. Turner Enterprises, Inc.*, supra. In that case, the court announced that the critical inquiry is "whether the efforts made by those other than the investor are the undeniably significant ones, those essential managerial efforts which affect the failure or success of the enterprise."

. . .

2. Application of the Test to the Instant Facts

Having concluded that the district court misperceived the controlling standard, it becomes incumbent upon us to determine whether Koscot's scheme falls with the standard adopted. . . .

Our task is greatly simplified by the Ninth Circuit's decision in *SEC* v. *Glen W. Turner Enterprises, Inc.*, supra. The promotional scheme confronting the Ninth Circuit is largely paralleled by that exposed before this court. Dare to be Great (Dare), which like Koscot, is a subsidiary of Turner Enterprises, offered five plans in its self-improvement program, three of which entitled an investor to earn money for coaxing additional prospects into the Dare fold.

. . .

As in the Koscot scheme, the initial task of a purchaser of a Dare plan was to lure prospects to meetings, denominated Adventure Meetings. These were characterized by the same overzealous and emotionally charged atmosphere at which the illusion of affluence fostered in Opportunity Meetings was created and relied upon in securing sales. The Adventure Meetings were run according to script, but, as the Ninth Circuit noted, "The Dare People, not the purchaser-'salesman,' run the meetings and do the selling."

· · ·

. The recruitment role played by investors in Koscot coincides with that played by investors in Dare to be Great. That investors in the latter did not participate in Adventure Meetings while they do in the Koscot scheme is insignificant. Since Koscot's Opportunity Meetings are run according to preordained script, the deviation from which would occasion disapprobation or perhaps exclusion from the meetings, the role of investors at these meetings can be characterized as little more than a perfunctory one. Nor does the fact that Koscot investors may have devoted more time than did Dare investors to closing sales transmute the essential congruity between the two schemes. The act of consummating a sale is essentially a ministerial not managerial one, one which does not alter the fact that the critical determinant of the success of the Koscot Enterprise lies with the luring effect of the opportunity meetings. As was noted earlier, investors are cautioned to employ the "curiosity approach" in attracting prospects. Once attendance is secured, the sales format devised by Koscot is thrust upon the prospect. An investor's sole contribution in following the script is a nominal one. Without the scenario created by the Opportunity Meetings and Go-Tours, an investor would invariably be powerless to realize any return on his investment.

III

We confine our holding to those schemes in which promoters retain immediate control over the essential managerial conduct of an enterprise and where the investor's realization of profits is inextricably tied to the success of the promotional scheme. Thus, we acknowledge that a conventional franchise arrangement, wherein the promoter exercises merely remote control over an enterprise and the investor operates largely unfettered by promoter mandates presents a different question than the one posed herein. But the Koscot scheme does not qualify as a conventional franchising arrangement.

· · ·

The test we adopt . . . also comports with the observation of the Supreme Court in *SEC v. W. J. Howey Co.*, supra, 328 U.S. at 299, that the definition of securities "embodies a flexible rather than a static principle, one that is capable of adaptation to meet the countless and variable schemes devised by those who seek the use of the money of others on the promise of profits." We merely endorse a test which is resilient enough to encompass the egregious promotional scheme purveyed by Koscot.

· · ·

Reversed.

Additional Factors

While most litigation regarding the definition of a security has focused on the four-part *Howey* test, many other factors have been applied in various factual contexts. For example, the *Forman* case demonstrated that if a buyer is buying for consumption rather than for investment, the court will be less likely to find a security present. *Daniel* indicated that the presence of alternative forms of protection mitigates against finding a security.

The more odious or flagrant a fraudulent scheme, the more willing the court will be to stretch the definition of security to protect victims, as in *Koscot*. Additionally, the more investors involved in a particular enterprise, the more the courts will lean toward finding a security. Further, the extent to which an investment arrangement is a substitute for conventional financing bears on the finding of a security.

Additional considerations appear in this recent Supreme Court decision regarding the definition of securities.

MARINE BANK v. WEAVER

455 U.S. 551 (1982)

The Weavers bought a $50,000 certificate of deposit, insured by the FDIC, from Marine Bank. They then pledged the CD to the bank to guarantee a $65,000 loan made by the bank to the Columbus Packing Co., owned by the Piccirillos. In consideration for guaranteeing the new loan, Columbus agreed to give the Weavers 50% of Columbus' net profits, $100 per month as long as the loan was guaranteed, and right to use Columbus' barn and pasture at the discretion of the Piccirillos.

The Weavers sued, claiming that the bank induced them into the arrangement without disclosing that most of the $65,000 loan would be used not to fortify Columbus' business but to repay the bank for money Columbus already owed. The Weavers sued, inter alia, under federal securities laws claiming both the certificate of deposit and the agreement with the Piccirillos were securities. The trial court held that no securities were involved. The Court of Appeals reversed, and the bank appealed.

BURGER, CHIEF JUSTICE:

The definition of security in the Securities Exchange Act of 1934 is quite broad. The act was adopted to restore investors' confidence in the financial markets, and the term "security" was meant to include "the many types of instruments that in our commercial world would fall within the ordinary concept of a security"—H.R. Rep. No. 85, 73d Cong., 1st sess., 11 (1933). The statutory definition excludes only currency and notes with a maturity of less than nine months. It includes ordinary stocks and bonds, along with the "countless and variable schemes devised by those who seek the use of the money of others on the promise of profits . . ."—*SEC* v. *W. J. Howey, Inc.*, 328 U.S. 293, 299 (1946). Thus, the coverage of the antifraud provisions of the securities laws is not limited to instruments traded at securities exchanges and over-the-counter markets, but extends to uncommon and irregular instruments—*Superintendent of Insurance* v. *Bankers Life & Casualty Co.*, 404 U.S. 6, 10 (1971); and *SEC* v. *C. M. Joiner Leasing Corp.*, 320 U.S. 344, 351 (1943). We have repeatedly held that the test "is what character the instrument is given in commerce by the terms of the offer, the plan of distribution, and the economic inducements held out to the prospect"—*SEC* v. *United Benefit Life Insurance Co.*, 387 U.S. 202, 211 (1967).

The broad statutory definition is preceded, however, by the statement that the terms mentioned are not to be considered securities if "the context otherwise requires. . . ." Moreover, we are satisfied that Congress, in enacting the securities laws, did not intend to provide a broad federal remedy for fraud. *Great Western Bank & Trust* v. *Kotz*, 532 F.2d 1252, 1253 (CA9 1976).

The Court of Appeals concluded that the certificate of deposit purchased by the Weavers might be a security. Examining the statutory definition, the court correctly noted that the certificate of deposit is not expressly excluded from the definition since it is not currency and it has a maturity exceeding nine months. It concluded, however, that the certificate of deposit was the functional equivalent of the withdrawable capital shares of a savings and loan association held to be securities in *Tcherepnin* v. *Knight*, 389 U.S. 332 (1967). The court also reasoned that, from an investor's standpoint, a certificate of deposit is no different from any other long-term debt obligation. Unless distinguishing features were found on remand, the court concluded that the certificate of deposit should be held to be a security.

Tcherepnin is not controlling. The withdrawable capital shares found there to be securities did not pay a fixed rate of interest; instead, purchasers received dividends based on the association's profits. Purchasers also received voting rights. In short, the withdrawable capital shares in *Tcherepnin* were much more like ordinary shares of stock, and "the ordinary concept of a security," than a certificate of deposit.

The Court of Appeals also concluded that a certificate of deposit is similar to any other long-term debt obligation commonly found to be a security. In our view, however, there is an important difference between a bank certificate of deposit and other long-term debt obligations. This certificate of deposit was issued by a federally regulated bank which is subject to the comprehensive set of regulations governing the banking industry. Deposits in federally regulated banks are protected by the reserve, report-ing, and inspection requirements of the federal banking laws; advertising relating to the interest paid on deposits is also regulated. In addition, deposits are insured by the Federal Deposit Insurance Corporation. Since its formation in 1933, nearly all depositors in failing banks insured by the FDIC have received payment in full, even payment for the portions of their deposits above the amount insured—*1980 Annual Report of the Federal Deposit Insurance Corporation*, 18–21 (1981).

We see, therefore, important differences between a certificate of deposit purchased from a federally regulated bank and other long-term debt obligations. The Court of Appeals failed to give appropriate weight to the important fact that the purchaser of a certificate of deposit is virtually guaranteed payment in full, whereas the holder of an ordinary long-term debt obligation assumes the risk of the borrower's insolvency. The definition of security in the 1934 Act provides that an instrument which seems to fall within the broad sweep of the act is not to be considered a security if the context otherwise requires. It is unnecessary to subject issuers of bank certificates of deposit to liability under the antifraud provisions of the federal securities laws since the holders of bank certificates of deposit are abundantly protected under the federal banking laws. We therefore hold that the certificate of deposit purchased by the Weavers is not a security.

The Court of Appeals also held that a finder of fact could conclude that the separate agreement between the Weavers and the Piccirillos is a security. Examining the statutory language, the court found that the agreement might be a "certificate of interest or participation in any profit-sharing agreement" or an "investment contract." It stressed that the agreement gave the Weavers a share in the profits of the slaughterhouse that would result from the efforts of the Piccirillos. Accordingly, in that court's view, the agreement fell within the definition of investment contract.

Congress intended the securities laws to cover those instruments ordinarily and commonly considered to be securities in the commercial world, but the agreement between the Weavers and Piccirillos is not the type of instrument that comes to mind when the term security is used and does not fall within "the ordinary concept of a security."

The unusual instruments found to constitute securities in prior cases involved offers to a number of potential investors, not a private transaction as in this case. In *Howey*, for example, 42 persons purchased interests in a citrus grove during a four-month period—328 U.S., at 295. In *C. M. Joiner Leasing*, offers to sell oil leases were sent to over 1,000 prospects—320 U.S., at 346. In *C. M. Joiner Leasing*, we noted that a security is an instrument in which there is "common trading"—Id., at 351. The instruments involved in *C. M. Joiner Leas-*

ing and *Howey* had equivalent values to most persons and could have been traded publicly.

Here, in contrast, the Piccirillos distributed no prospectus to the Weavers or to other potential investors, and the unique agreement they negotiated was not designed to be traded publicly. The provision that the Weavers could use the barn and pastures of the slaughterhouse at the discretion of the Piccirillos underscores the unique character of the transaction. Similarly, the provision that the Weavers could veto future loans gave them a measure of control over the operation of the slaughterhouse not characteristic of a security. Although the agreement gave the Weavers a share of the Piccirillos' profits, if any, that provision alone is not sufficient to make that agreement a security.

Accordingly, we hold that this unique agreement, negotiated one-on-one by the parties, is not a security.

Marine Bank is a very important case. While the need for protection has traditionally been considered a separate question from that of whether a security was present, *Marine Bank* took the supporting argument in *Daniel* that alternative regulation eliminated the need for securities law coverage and elevated it to a primary consideration. It also apparently added to the four *Howey* factors requirements that (1) offers be made to a number of potential investors, (2) the instruments involved be of equivalent value to most persons and therefore tradeable publicly, and (3) the specific instrument have no important features unique to plaintiff or generally characteristic of the traditional security.[10] The *Marine Bank* ruling adds substantial clarity to a previously controversial area—how to treat promissory notes. Whether the ruling will help to clarify other areas of dispute remains to be seen.

Problem Areas

There are several different areas of enterprise where the question of whether a security exists continually arises. Different factual circumstances, as noted previously, require application of a different set of rules. Some of those problem areas are discussed in this section.

---

[10] Pitt, " 'Weaver' Could Invite New Generations of Litigation," *Legal Times of Washington*, March 15, 1982, p. 11.

Partnerships

If a party is induced to become a partner in a general partnership, the courts will generally hold that no investment contract, and hence no security, has been purchased. Because a general partner, by definition, has the right to take part in control of the venture, his or her profits do not come from the efforts of others. A person taking an active role in the management of the enterprise does not need the protection offered by the securities laws. The same conclusion normally results in joint venture cases.

However, some courts have indicated a willingness to find a general partner's or joint venturer's interest to be a security if, in reality, the investor merely passively relied on the management expertise of another. For example, in *McLish* v. *Harris Farms, Inc.*,[11] a joint venturer's purchase, with partial financing by the promoter/co-joint venturer, of cattle to be fed and sold from the promoter's feedlot was an investment contract. Although the investor had some control over the operation, pervasive control retained by the promoter made his efforts the undeniably significant ones. For example, the promoter had the daily management of the cattle as well as absolute control over their care and custody. Although the investor had the theoretical right to sell the cattle before their feeding period was completed, to exercise the right he had to come up with enough money to free the cattle of the security lien.

A limited partnership interest is considered a classic security. The limited partner, again by definition, cannot take an active role in the management of partnership affairs. Therefore, the limited partner stands in the same position as a corporate shareholder who puts money into the venture but exercises no control. A limited partner who is at the same time a general partner does not hold a security.

Franchises

When someone purchases a franchise, for example, a fast-food hamburger operation, the question of whether that interest is a security depends on the nature of the arrangement. If it is a traditional franchise in which the franchisor provides guidance, assistance, training, and so on, but the franchisee/investor takes an active role in the business, no security exists. Because the important efforts upon which success or failure turn are the franchisee's, the expected profits do not stem primarily from the efforts of others.

However, courts that adopt the "risk capital" test might find a security present if the franchisor sells franchise interests to raise enough capital to get the whole operation off the ground, as did the promoters in *Silver Hills* v. *Sobieski* who sold memberships to raise enough money to open the country club. Additionally, if the franchise happened to be set up so that the franchisor exercised such control as to render the franchisee's efforts of minimal importance, a security in the form of an investment contract might be found.

---

[11] 507 F.Supp. 1075 (E.D. Cal. 1981).

Real Estate Interests

Interests in land, leases, cooperatives, condominiums, and the like may or may not be securities. The sale of land, for example, normally will not constitute a security if the purchaser is buying for his or her own use. The result may be different if the promoter/seller promises to resell the land at a profit. Similarly, if the scheme involves rental pools, or the land is sold in conjunction with services provided by the seller, securities may exist.

An interest in a traditional co-operative is probably not a security. A leasehold is not a security either, even if the landlord gets a percentage of the tenant's profit as a portion of the rent.

Regarding condominiums, the SEC has stated that a typical condominium unit in a metropolitan area is sold for the buyer's occupancy and therefore is not a security. However, if management is provided to the unit owner or units are sold prior to construction and the proceeds used as "risk capital" by the promoter, there may be a security. The SEC has issued guidelines indicating that sales involving the following would be viewed as investment contracts: [12]

1. The condominiums, with any rental arrangement or other similar service, are offered and sold with emphasis on the economic benefits to the purchaser to be derived from the managerial efforts of the promoter, or a third party designated or arranged for by the promoter, from rental of the units.
2. The offering of participation in a rental pool arrangement.
3. The offering of a rental or similar arrangement whereby the purchaser must hold his or her unit available for rental for any part of the year, must use an exclusive rental agent, or is otherwise materially restricted in occupancy or rental of the unit.

Sale of a Business

If A wishes to purchase B's incorporated business, A might simply purchase the business's assets from B. Such a transaction clearly would not involve the sale of "securities." However, A might accomplish the same acquisition by buying 100% of the corporation's stock. Whether the purchase of all (or most) of the stock of an incorporated business constitutes the purchase of a security has recently been a very controversial question.

Most lower courts adopted the "sale of business" doctrine, which provides that such a purchase does not constitute a purchase of securities. Proponents of the doctrine argue that the *Howey* test for an investment contract is not met because the purchaser of the business intends to profit through his or her own efforts, not through the efforts of others, and that there is no common enterprise because the purchaser becomes the sole owner.

The Supreme Court settled a lively controversy among the lower courts in the following case.

---

[12] *Securities Act Release*, No. 5347 (1973).

LANDRETH TIMBER CO. v. LANDRETH

105 S.CT. 2297 (1985)

Respondents father and sons owned all the common stock of an incorporated lumber business. They offered the stock for sale, and purchasers were located. A stock purchase agreement was executed, and the purchasers formed petitioner company to hold the stock. Respondent father agreed to stay on as a consultant to help operate the lumber mill. After the acquisition, the business did not live up to the purchasers' expectations. Petitioner corporation sold the mill at a loss and went into receivership.

Petitioner filed this action alleging respondents were guilty of fraudulent misstatements and material omissions in connection with the sale of the stock in violation of provisions of the 1933 and 1934 Acts. Respondents moved for summary judgment, invoking the "sale of business" doctrine and arguing that the transaction did not involve "securities" within the meaning of the acts. The trial court adopted the "sale of business" doctrine and granted respondents' motion. The Ninth Circuit affirmed. Petitioners applied for certiorari.

POWELL, JUSTICE:

I

[The opinion first recited the facts.]

II

[The statutory definition of "securities in the 1933 Act] is quite broad, *Marine Bank* v. *Weaver*, 455 U.S. 551, 556 (1982), and includes both instruments whose names alone carry well-settled meaning, as well as instruments of "more variable character [that] were necessarily desig-

nated by more descriptive terms," such as "investment contract" and "instrument commonly known as a 'security.' '' *SEC* v. *C. M. Joiner Leasing Corp.*, 320 U.S. 344, 351 (1943). The face of the definition shows that "stock" is considered to be a "security" within the meaning of the Acts. As we observed in *United Housing Foundation, Inc.* v. *Forman*, 421 U.S. 837 (1975), most instruments bearing such a traditional title are likely to be covered by the definition.

As we also recognized in *Forman*, the fact that instruments bear the label "stock" is not of itself sufficient to invoke the coverage of the Acts. Rather, we concluded that we must also determine whether those instruments possess "some of the significant characteristics typically associated with" stock, recognizing that when an instrument is both called "stock" and bears stock's usual characteristics, "a purchaser justifiably [may] assume that the federal securities laws apply." We identified those characteristics usually associated with common stock as (i) the right to receive dividends contingent upon an apportionment of profits; (ii) negotiability; (iii) the ability to be pledged or hypothecated; (iv) the conferring of voting rights in proportion to the number of shares owned; and (v) the capacity to appreciate in value.

Under the facts of *Forman*, we concluded that the instruments at issue there were not "securities" within the meaning of the Acts. That case involved the sale of shares of stock entitling the purchaser to lease an apartment in a housing cooperative. The stock bore none of the characteristics listed above that are usually associated with traditional stock. Moreover, we concluded that under the circumstances, there was no likelihood that the purchasers had been misled by use of the word "stock" into thinking that the federal securities laws governed their purchases. The purchasers had intended to acquire low-cost subsidized living space for their personal use; no one was likely to have believed that he was purchasing investment securities.

In contrast, it is undisputed that the stock involved here possesses all of the characteristics we identified in *Forman* as traditionally associated with common stock. Moreover, unlike in *Forman*, the context of the transaction involved here—the sale of stock in a corporation—is typical of the kind of context to which the Acts normally apply. It is thus much more likely here than in *Forman* that an investor would believe he was covered by the federal securities laws. Under the circumstances of this case, the plain meaning of the statutory definition mandates that the stock be treated as "securities" subject to the coverage of the Acts.

Reading the securities laws to apply to the sale of stock at issue here comports with Congress' remedial purpose in enacting the legislation to protect investors by "compelling full and fair disclosure relative to the issuance of 'the many types of instruments that in our commercial world fall within the ordinary concept of a security.'" *SEC* v. *W. J. Howey Co.*, 328 U.S., at 299 (quoting H. R. Rep. No. 85, 73d Cong., 1st sess., 11 (1933)). Although we recognize that Congress did not intend to provide a comprehensive federal remedy for all fraud, *Marine Bank* v. *Weaver*, 455 U.S. 551, 556 (1982), we think it would improperly narrow Congress' broad definition of "security" to hold that the traditional stock at issue here falls outside the Acts' coverage.

III

Under other circumstances, we might consider the statutory analysis outlined above to be a sufficient answer compelling judgment for

petitioner. Respondents urge, however, that language in our previous opinions, including *Forman*, requires that we look beyond the label "stock" and the characteristics of the instruments involved to determine whether application of the acts is mandated by the economic substance of the transaction. Moreover, the Court of Appeals rejected the view that the plain meaning of the definition would be sufficient to hold this stock covered, because it saw "no principled way" to justify treating notes, bonds, and other of the definitional categories differently. We address these concerns in turn.

A

It is fair to say that our cases have not been entirely clear on the proper method of analysis for determining when an instrument is a "security." This Court has decided a number of cases in which it looked to the economic substance of the transaction, rather than just to its form, to determine whether the Acts applied.

. . .

Respondents contend that *Forman* and the cases on which it was based require us to reject the view that the shares of stock at issue here may be considered "securities" because of their name and characteristics. Instead, they argue that our cases require us in every instance to look to the economic substance of the transaction to determine whether the *Howey* test has been met. According to respondents, it is clear that petitioner sought not to earn profits from the efforts of others, but to buy a company that it could manage and control. Petitioner was not a passive investor of the kind Congress intended the Acts to protect, but an active entrepreneur, who sought to "use or consume" the business purchased just as the purchasers in *Forman* sought to use the apartments they acquired after purchasing shares of stock. Thus, respondents urge that the Acts do not apply.

We disagree with respondents' interpretation of our cases. First, it is important to understand the contexts within which these cases were decided. All of the cases on which respondents rely involved unusual instruments not easily characterized as "securities." Thus, if the Acts were to apply in those cases at all, it would have to have been because the economic reality underlying the transactions indicated that the instruments were actually of a type that falls within the usual concept of a security. In the case at bar, in contrast, the instrument involved is traditional stock, plainly within the statutory definition. There is no need here, as there was in the prior cases, to look beyond the characteristics of the instrument to determine whether the Acts apply.

. . .

Second, we would note that the *Howey* economic reality test was designed to determine whether a particular instrument is an "investment contract," not whether it fits within *any* of the examples listed in the statutory definition of "security." . . . Moreover, applying the *Howey* test to traditional stock and all other types of instruments listed in the statutory definition would make the Acts' enumeration of many types of instruments superfluous.

Finally, we cannot agree with respondents that the Acts were intended to cover only "passive investors" and not privately negotiated transactions involving the transfer of control to "entrepreneurs." The 1934 Act contains several provisions specifically governing tender offers, disclosure of transactions by corporate officers and principal stockholders, and the recovery of short-swing profits gained by such persons. See, *e. g.*, 1934 Act, §§14, 16, 15 U.S.C. §§78n, 78p. Eliminating from the definition of "security" instruments involved in transactions where control passed to the purchaser would contravene the purposes of these provisions.

. . .

B

We now turn to the Court of Appeals' concern that treating stock as a specific category of "security" provable by its characteristics means that other categories listed in the statutory definition, such as notes, must be treated the same way. Although we do not decide whether coverage of notes or other instruments may be provable by their name and characteristics, we do point out several reasons why we think stock may be distinguishable from most if not all of the other categories listed in the acts' definition.

Instruments that bear both the name and all of the usual characteristics of stock seem to us to be the clearest case for coverage by the plain language of the definition. First, traditional stock "represents to many people, both trained and untrained in business matters, the paradigm of a security." Thus persons trading in traditional stock likely have a high expectation that their activities are governed by the acts. Second, as we made clear in *Forman*, "stock" is relatively easy to identify because it lends itself to consistent definition. Unlike some instruments, therefore, traditional stock is more susceptible of a plain meaning approach.

Professor Loss has agreed that stock is different from the other categories of instruments. He observes that it "goes against the grain" to apply the *Howey* test for determining whether an instrument is an "investment contract" to traditional stock. See L. Loss, *Fundamentals of Securities Regulation* (1983), pp. 211–212.

. . .

We here expressly leave until another day the question whether "notes" or "bonds" or some other category of instrument listed in the definition might be shown "by proving [only] the document itself." *SEC* v. *C. M. Joiner Leasing Corp.*, supra, at 355. We hold only that "stock" may be viewed as being in a category by itself for purposes of interpreting the scope of the acts' definition of "security."

IV

We also perceive strong policy reasons for not employing the sale of business doctrine under the circumstances of this case. By respondents' own admission, application of the doctrine depends in each case on whether control has passed to the purchaser. It may be argued that on the facts of this case, the doctrine is easily applied, since the transfer of 100% of a corporation's stock normally transfers control. We think even that assertion is open to some question, however, as [purchasers] had no intention of running the sawmill themselves. [Respondent father] apparently stayed on to manage the daily affairs of the business. Some commentators who support the sale of business doctrine believe that a purchaser who has the ability to exert control but chooses not to do so may deserve the acts' protection if he is simply a passive investor not engaged in the daily management of the business. . . . In this case, the district court was required to undertake extensive fact-finding, and even requested supplemental facts and memoranda on the issue of control, before it was able to decide the case.

More importantly, however, if applied to this case, the sale of business doctrine would also have to be applied to cases in which less than 100% of a company's stock was sold. This inevitably would lead to difficult questions of line-drawing. The acts' coverage would in every case depend not only on the percentage of stock transferred, but also on such factors as the number of purchasers and what provisions for voting and veto rights were agreed upon by the parties. . . . [C]overage by the Acts would in most cases be unknown and unknowable to the parties at the time the stock was sold. These uncertainties attending the applicability of the Acts would hardly be in the best interests of either party to a transaction. Respondents argue that adopting petitioner's approach will increase the work load of the federal courts by converting state and common law fraud claims into federal claims. We find more daunting, however, the prospect that parties to a transaction may never know whether they are covered by the Acts until they engage in extended discovery and litigation over a concept as often elusive as the passage of control.

Reversed.

QUESTIONS AND PROBLEMS

1. Responding to a magazine ad, Mordaunt entered into a discretionary commodities futures contract with respondent Incomco, a commodities broker. Respondent was given full discretion over investment decisions and received a commission on each transaction. Soon Mordaunt's investment of $45,000 was largely depleted, while respondent had earned $20,000 in commissions. Mordaunt sued, alleging securities fraud. Incomco moved to dismiss, arguing that no "security" was involved under the *Howey* investment contract test. Discuss. See *Mordaunt* v. *Incomco*, 686 F.2d 815 (9th Cir. 1982), *cert. denied*, 105 S. Ct. 801 (1985).

2. In 1880 Mark Hopkins died, leaving a fortune that was distributed to heirs by decree of court in 1883. Latta, who claims to be a "double-blood heir" of Hopkins, sued to set aside the distribution and to reclaim the fortune for the "rightful heirs." This suit was terminated by unfavorable court decision in 1949. This result did not deter Latta. In 1963, Latta was offering and selling to alleged heirs of Mark Hopkins a "Contract in Event of Recovery." The contract allowed the payer of $100 to Latta—

to be used in Latta's fight for redistribution of the Hopkins estate—to receive "a sum equal to One Per Cent of one-fifth ($\frac{1}{5}$) of one-sixth ($\frac{1}{6}$) of one-seventh ($\frac{1}{7}$) interest in the estate of Mark Hopkins." The SEC sued Latta for selling unregistered securities. Latta claimed the "Contract in Event of Recovery" was not a "security." Is she right? Discuss. See *SEC* v. *Latta*, 250 F.Supp. 170 (N.D. Cal. 1965).

3. Gross, in a promotional newsletter, solicited persons to raise earthworms to help Gross reach his quota for selling worms to fishermen. Buyers were promised that they could profit, that the time involved would be similar to that of raising a garden, that the earthworms double in quantity every 60 days, and that Gross would buy back all bait-size worms produced at $2.25 a pound. The Smiths, living in Phoenix, invested after being told that they did not need to worry about marketing the worms because Gross would take care of it. The Smiths eventually sued for fraud, claiming that the worms multiplied at one-eighth the promised rate, that they could profit only if the promised rate of multiplication occurred and Gross bought back all worms at $2.25, and that Gross could buy back the worms at that price only if he could sell them to new worm farmers at inflated market rates. The true value of worms was only one-tenth what Gross promised to pay. Did the Smiths purchase an "investment contract"? Discuss. See *Smith* v. *Gross*, 604 F.2d 639 (9th Cir. 1979).

4. Inforex is the representative of actor Sean Connery. In connection with several James Bond films, Connery or his assigns were promised as part of the compensation a guaranteed sum plus an amount equal to 1% of all gross monies in excess of $4,000,000 received by distributors. Inforex sued MGM/UA Entertainment Co. on several grounds, including securities fraud. Was the profit-sharing provision of Connery's contract a "security"? Discuss. See *Inforex Corp.* v. *MGM/UA Entertainment Co.*, 608 F.Supp. 129 (C.D. Cal. 1984).

5. Plaintiff Frazier was one of two active general partners engaged in real estate development through limited partnerships. Frazier sued the other general partner alleging improper sale of limited partnership interests on the theory that certain limited partnership interests he had purchased were securities. Does Frazier's active control of the ventures render his limited partnership interests nonsecurities? See *Frazier* v. *Manson*, 651 F.2d 1078 (5th Cir. 1981).

6. Several investors, as general partners, contributed money for financial investment. All investment decisions were to be made by a single managing partner who was a brokerage firm employee. If all investment decisions were made by the managing partner, could the other general partners characterize their interests as "securities"? Discuss. See *Wagner* v. *Bear, Stearns & Co.*, *Federal Securities Law Reports* (CCH), ¶99,032 (N.D. Ill. 1982).

7. Wolf read an ad in a California newspaper for certificates of deposit, in pesos, offered by Banamex, a Mexican bank. He wrote for information, and received a brochure entitled "Mexico's Other Great Climate . . . Investment." He purchased three separate peso CDs. The deposits, which were converted to pesos at the prevailing rate, were uninsured, nonnegotiable, and nonwithdrawable and carried interest rates of up to 33.9%. When Mexico's central bank ceased supporting the peso, it quickly

lost value in relation to the dollar. Upon maturity of the certificates, Wolf received the same number of pesos he originally deposited, but they were worth $25,000 less in U.S. dollars. He sued alleging that Banamex had sold unregistered securities in violation of the 1933 Act. Were these CDs securities? Discuss. See *Wolf* v. *Banco Nacional de Mexico, S.A.*, 739 F.2d 1458 (9th Cir. 1984).

8. Wayne, a farmer in financial straits, responded to an ad by Stephen, whose organization represented itself as equipped to develop ''creative financing'' to help farmers. Stephen induced Wayne to sign a document that Stephen characterized as a sale and repurchase agreement that would immediately provide large sums of money Wayne could use to operate his farm. Instead, the document was a limited partnership agreement that was extremely favorable to Stephen's company and generated very little cash for Wayne's operational needs. Wayne sued, alleging securities fraud under §10(b) of the 1934 Act. Stephen defended, arguing that the federal securities laws governed only interstate commercial activity and that all his contacts with Wayne took place inside Illinois. Can federal securities jurisdiction be predicated on a single phone call from Stephen to Wayne who were both located in Illinois at the time? Discuss. See *Miller* v. *Affiliated Financial Corp.*, 600 F.Supp. 987 (N.D. Ill. 1984).

15

REGISTRATION
OF PUBLIC OFFERINGS

SECURITIES MARKETS

Trading Markets

The bulk of this chapter concerns the process for and legal rules governing the *issuance* of corporate securities. A major task of the securities markets and of securities dealers is the initial distribution of securities from the issuing corporation to the purchasers. However, every bit as important are the trading markets in which those securities will later be traded by their purchasers. A salient feature of the corporate security is its transferability. The initial goal of this chapter, then, is briefly to describe the markets in which corporate stock and other securities are traded.

Overview

There are approximately 5,000 securities firms scattered around the United States (but concentrated in the larger cities, particularly New York) that assist in the trading of securities. Such firms are frequently referred to as *broker-dealers*. It is important to understand that the same securities firm can act as a broker on one transaction and as a dealer on the next. When a firm acts as a *broker*, it is merely an agent ordering securities on behalf of a purchasing customer or making offers on behalf of a selling customer. A broker is a "go-between" compensated on a commission basis. When a firm acts as a *dealer*, it is buying and selling on its own account and risk. A dealer purchases securities and resells them, making a profit, it is hoped, by selling at a higher price than that at which it bought.

There are two types of trading markets for securities. Securities are bought and sold on stock exchanges, where the securities firms usually act as agents or brokers. There is also the *over-the-counter* (OTC) market, where, as shall be explained, the securities firm might act as either a broker or as a dealer.

New York Stock Exchange

The most famous and prominent of securities trading markets is the New York Stock Exchange, which was created in 1792 when a number of securities traders met under a buttonwood tree on New York's Wall Street to formalize rules for their trading. The basic outline of how the "Big Board" works has remained essentially the same for many years, but technological advances now allow the trading of more than 150 million shares daily (with gusts near 250 million shares daily)—a breathtaking increase from the figures of even a few years ago. Peak days of 400 million shares traded are already being predicted for the 1990s.

The NYSE has stringent requirements that must be met (and a fat fee that must be paid) before a security can be listed on the Big Board. About 1,550 of America's premier stocks are "listed" on the NYSE. The exchange itself is essentially a communications system. It is run by approximately 1,500 "members" who also must meet stringent requirements and buy their seats on the exchange for as much as $500,000 (though usually much less).

These members play various roles. About 400 are *specialists* who *make a market* in the stocks to which they are assigned. The specialists run an auction for other members who acts as brokers, purchasing and selling on behalf of investors. The specialists take the buy and sell orders from the brokers, assess the bids (offers to buy) and offers (to sell), and help to determine the price of the securities for which they are responsible. The specialists are expected to buy and sell stocks on their own accounts if such is necessary to assure a good market. The Exchange expects that specialists will have sufficient capital to handle these responsibilities and sufficient personnel to manage the blizzard of paperwork that can result when trading in a particular stock boom.

The NYSE members who are brokers rather than specialists have varying tasks, but generally speaking they are all part of the chain between the investor and the specialist. They are compensated by commission. Roles of all the principals at the NYSE are slowly evolving as technological changes impact on a very old process.

The New York Stock Exchange is a self-regulating organization that delists the stocks that cease meeting its requirements and disciplines members who violate its rules. Naturally, the Securities and Exchange Commission has a strong influence on the content and enforcement of these rules.

Other Exchanges

The American Stock Exchange (Amex) is a major national stock exchange located in New York City. Although Amex has less stringent listing requirements than does the NYSE, it still carries the stocks of many important corporations.

There are also several regional exchanges scattered around the country, including the Pacific (Los Angeles), the Midwest (Chicago), and the Philadelphia, Boston, and Cincinnati exchanges. These regional exchanges are closely regulated. Along with Amex, they operate on generally the same system used by the NYSE and frequently provide an important market for the securities of regional corporations.

Amex and the regional exchanges are also important because NYSE-listed securities can be traded on these exchanges as well as on the NYSE. In fact, in 1979, 88% of the trading activity on the regional exchanges was in NYSE-listed securities.[1] It is indicative of the stature of the NYSE that even given these figures, only 10% of the trading volume in NYSE-listed shares occurred on the regional exchanges and 10% on Amex. The other 80% were traded on the Big Board itself. In fact, at times in the past, the dollar value of just one NYSE-listed stock, IBM, has exceeded the dollar value of all the securities listed on Amex.

Over-the-Counter Markets

The over-the-counter market is an extremely important securities trading market, one that grows in volume and significance with each passing year. The OTC market has no centralized trading floor filled with bustling activity as does the NYSE. Rather, the OTC market encompasses any securities trade that does not occur on an exchange. Any time two securities traders flick on their computer terminals, call each other on the phone, and decide to trade, an OTC transaction occurs.

As noted earlier, around 6,000 broker-dealers are scattered around the United States. Notably, an occasionally active market in cheap "penny stocks" of oil and mineral companies exists in Denver. But the OTC market is not confined to inferior securities. Of approximately 50,000 securities traded in the United States, only about 3,000 are listed on the various exchanges. The rest are traded OTC. Increasingly, some OTC stocks are traded on exchanges. Many highly successful corporations had their greatest period of growth while their shares were traded OTC. As they grew and met listing requirements, many corporations listed their shares on the NYSE or Amex. But some qualified corporations have remained in the OTC market.

In addition to handling the securities of many young companies, the OTC market also handles the securities of foreign corporations, most insurance companies' and banks' securities, and mutual funds. Also, the OTC handles all municipal bonds (those issued by state, county, and local governments), most U.S. government securities, and most corporate bonds. Although the bond market does not receive significant legal attention because most purchasers are professional and institutional investors who do

---

[1] New York Stock Exchange, *NYSE 1980 Fact Book* (New York: NYSE, 1980).

not need government protection, and because federal and municipal securities are largely exempt from SEC regulation, its size is staggering. In dollar volume, the bond market normally dwarfs the sale of equity securities. The OTC, then, is a very important market.

The OTC market is known as a "negotiated" market rather than an "auction" market like the exchanges. Each security listed OTC may have several market makers, not just one as on the NYSE. If an investor contacts a stock broker about a particular security, that broker will contact the market makers to see where the best price can be obtained. The market makers buy and sell on their own account, thus acting as dealers. Just like the specialists on the NYSE, they "maintain" a market by being willing at all times to buy or sell the particular security at the prices they quote. The market maker profits from the "spread" between bid and ask prices.

In 1938, Congress authorized creation of self-regulating bodies for the OTC market. The National Association of Securities Dealers (NASD), to which some 3,500 securities dealers belong, is the only such organization. The NASD has disciplinary powers to enforce its rules. Those rules require such things as reasonable and nondiscriminatory commissions, disclosure as to whether the firm is acting as a broker or as a dealer, and fair, nonfraudulent conduct.

A major accomplishment of the NASD was the implementation in 1971 of a system of computers and electronic terminals, the Automated Quotation System (NASDAQ). The NASDAQ system allows any broker to glance at a computer terminal to receive the current quotations (highest bid and lowest ask) for about 4,700 securities. More than 2,000 of these have been designated "national market securities" for which not only are current quotations available, but also the more valuable "last sale" price data. About 8,000 NASD securities' quotations are reported only in daily "pink sheets" published by the National Quotations Bureau. To obtain current competitive quotations on these securities, a broker or dealer must telephone one or more dealers.[2]

Recent innovations enable the NASDAQ system to accommodate over 125 million shares per day, and that capacity may soon expand substantially. NASDAQ share volume as a percentage of NYSE volume rose from 30% to 66% between 1975 and 1981.

Third and Fourth Markets

Two other trading markets worth mentioning are the so-called Third and Fourth Markets. The *Third Market* consists of OTC transactions in exchange-listed shares. Before 1975, commissions charged for transactions on the NYSE were fixed by the NYSE itself. To achieve better prices, some investors traded NYSE shares in the OTC market. However, when antitrust considerations led to termination of the NYSE-mandated commission rates, the rates became negotiable. Because better commission rates could be achieved on the NYSE itself, demand for the Third Market diminished. OTC trading of NYSE-listed shares fell from about 8% of the market in 1971 to less than 2% in

---

[2] *See, generally,* J. Seligman, "The Future of the National Market System," *Journal of Corporation Law,* Vol. 9 (1984), p. 790.

1984. Still, the Third Market can be helpful to an investor when the Big Board is closed or when it suspends trading in a particular security.

The *Fourth Market* refers to purchases and sales between investors, usually institutional investors, without the use of a broker or dealer. For example, two life insurance companies might negotiate directly with each other for sale of a large block of securities that one of them owns, thereby avoiding the commission a broker would charge to facilitate the transaction.

The National Market System

It is apparent that the stock exchanges and the OTC market cannot exist independently of one another. The activities of one affect all, and the interrelationship is certain to grow more complete. Still, the history of these markets does not evidence much voluntary cooperation or coordination. Also, in the late 1960s a massive increase in the volume of trading caused a paperwork crisis that nearly crippled the securities industry. Inefficient processing of transactions, poor record keeping, untrained personnel, and other deficiencies contributed to the crisis.

In the wake of this unhealthy situation, Congress held extensive hearings, ultimately enacting the Securities Acts Amendments of 1975.[3] Those amendments called for the utilization of new technologies to improve the clearance and settlement of securities transactions. More important, Congress was concerned with restrictions that hampered competition in the trading of securities. The 1975 Amendments expressly directed the SEC to establish a national market system (NMS) for securities by linking all securities markets in such a way as to "foster efficiency, enhance competition, increase the information available to brokers, dealers, and investors, facilitate the offsetting of investors' orders, and contribute to the best execution of such orders."[4]

Several steps toward creation of a true national market system have been taken. In 1976, the SEC implemented the Consolidated Last Sale Reporting System, which reports on a nationwide basis the trades in all common stocks listed on the NYSE and Amex and some regionally listed securities, wherever these trades occurred. In 1978, the Composite Quotation System—which displays nationwide the prices currently bid and offered on any exchange or OTC for exchange-listed securities—was instituted. Also in 1978, the Intermarket Trading System (ITS), a communication network designed to allow a broker seeing a better quotation on another exchange to route an order to that exchange, was developed. In 1983, the Computer Assisted Execution System (CAES) was begun. It is basically an enhanced NASDAQ system that facilitates direct execution of orders through NASDAQ terminals. A CAES/ITS linkage has attempted to connect most exchanges and the OTC nationwide so that any investor can get the best price wherever offered. However, the system has been limited to certain categories of stock, and trading through it has been modest. As of this writing, the most recent NMS development, occurring in late 1985, was an SEC announcement of conditions under which

---

[3] P.L. 94–29, June 4, 1975, 89 Stat. 97.

[4] Id., Subsection 11A(a)(1).

exchanges were to be allowed to commence trading some OTC securities on an unlisted basis.

Despite all these initiatives, the SEC has been roundly criticized for its timidity in forcing the industry to accept changes, and the NMS remains a long way from the goal of efficiently linking all exchanges and the OTC so that the investing public trading in all securities can get the best price available anywhere in the country in whatever market.

Recent Developments

No picture of the American securities market would be complete without mention of some recent developments that have occupied much of the SEC's time and attention.

Options.   As early as 1972, some exchanges allowed the trading of stock options, as well as options in Treasury bonds and gold. Commodities options have a long history, but only recently has trading in options of OTC stocks been allowed through NASD and the exchanges. An option gives a purchaser the right to buy or sell the underlying contract at a set price within a given period. The options trader, in essence, is betting as to the direction the price of the particular security will take.

Stock Index Futures.   Also increasingly popular is trading in stock index futures, where traders guess the direction an entire group of stocks will take. The Kansas City Board of Trade allows trading on the Valueline Index, the Chicago Mercantile Exchange uses the Standard & Poor's Index, and the New York Futures Exchange uses the NYSE composite index. Stock index futures trading is much more enticing and more dangerous than securities trading. An investor in securities must put down at least 50% of the purchase price. But a trader in futures on the New York Futures Exchange can deposit $3,500 and receive an index contract valued at $44,000. The market is so volatile that a trader can quickly double his or her investment if the market moves in the direction guessed, or can have the entire deposit and more wiped out just as quickly.[5]

Banks.   As this chapter is written, the SEC is giving much thought to the recent trend of commercial banks and savings and loans becoming active as securities brokers and even investment advisers. Before the Great Depression, many commercial banks had investment banking units. The Great Crash of 1929 left these units decimated and contributed to many bank failures. Congress was concerned that a conflict of interest could arise out of difficult market situations, where the investment banking units holding stocks would be tempted to dispose of those stocks through the trust departments of

---

[5] P. Sebastian, ''Index Options Proliferate: A Guide to Calls, Puts and Striking Prices,'' *The Wall Street Journal* (Southwestern edition), March 13, 1985, p. 35.

the bank. Therefore, the 1933 Banking Act (Glass-Steagall) [6] attempted to erect a wall between investment banking and commercial banking.

The Glass-Steagall Act prohibited commercial banks from underwriting corporate securities or owning corporate securities for their own account. Because of the Glass-Steagall Act, securities firms and commercial banks have traditionally been separate, noncompetitive entities. However, in the 1980s, commercial banks have aggressively exploited apparent loopholes in Glass-Steagall. For example, the act does not explicitly prohibit commercial banks from acting as securities brokers, giving advice and buying and selling on behalf of customers. Many banks and thrift institutions have moved into the brokerage business and beyond. The courts are now in the process of trying to determine to what extent the SEC should regulate such activities in light of the traditional notion that such banks are regulated not by the SEC but by such entities as the Comptroller of Currency, the Federal Reserve System, and the Federal Deposit Insurance Corporation. [7]

The securities industry is fighting the potential competition. Every new advance by the commercial banks is challenged in litigation instituted by the Securities Industry Association, Wall Street's trade association. And some brokers are retaliating by slowly moving into traditionally commercial banking activities, such as accepting customer deposits and granting unsecured lines of credit. [8]

INVESTMENT BANKING AND UNDERWRITING

The names of a number of securities firms that engage in investment banking activities are familiar to most: Merrill Lynch, E. F. Hutton, Salomon Brothers, Morgan Stanley, First Boston, and others. These firms engage in a variety of activities that are extremely beneficial to corporations seeking capital.

Investment bankers engage in underwriting, the process of publicly distributing securities that will be explained in detail presently. They also assist in finding large institutional investors and negotiating sales of large blocks of securities by issuers to these investors, a process known as "private placement." In both underwriting and private placement, investment bankers give important financial advice regarding the type of security that should be issued, the timing of the issuance, the price to be asked, and so on.

A "glamour" area for investment bankers is that of mergers and acquisitions. Many investment bankers have made their reputations by finding suitable merger partners or acquisition targets, negotiating friendly mergers and acquisitions, and advising as to tactics when the potential partner or target resists the proposed take-over. The role of investment bankers in unfriendly take-overs will be examined in more detail in Chapter 22, on tender offers. Suffice it to say at this point that investment bankers' advice is

[6] Ch. 89, §16, 48 Stat. 184 (1933).

[7] American Bankers Assoc v. SEC, No. 85–02842 (D.C.Cir. 1986) (invalidating SEC attempt to register bank brokerage business).

[8] S. McMurray, "Banks and Rivals Push into New Businesses as Congress Dawdles," *The Wall Street Journal* (Southwestern edition), March 23, 1984, p. 1.

deemed so important in such matters that fees in the tens of millions of dollars are often paid by the corporations who seek their advice.

Types of Underwriting

Corporations can raise capital by printing and selling securities. When never-before-issued securities are issued, and the cash received in return goes to the issuing corporation, a *primary securities offering* occurs. Sometimes certain parties, such as the founders of a corporation, hold very large blocks of corporate securities that they wish to resell. Because the proceeds of the sale do not go to the issuing corporation, sale of these previously issued shares is termed a *secondary securities offering*.

In either type of offering, the services of an investment banker in an underwriter capacity may be required. The distribution of corporate securities may be analogized to the distribution of any product. The chain of manufacturer-wholesaler-retailer-customer in the distribution of a product is comparable to the chain of issuer–underwriter–broker-dealer–investor in the distribution of a security.

The purpose of underwriting is to ensure that the issuer obtains the necessary funds from the distribution of securities. Several types of underwriting exist.

Firm commitment underwriting is the most prevalent type. The process will be explained in detail soon, but the basic notion is that a syndicate of underwriters purchases the securities from the issuer, thus ensuring the issuer the needed funds, and then sells the securities to broker-dealers and to the public, it is hoped, at a profit.

In *best efforts* underwriting, the underwriter does not buy the securities on its own account and then resell them. Rather, the underwriter merely acts as a broker, attempting to sell the securities on a commission basis. This method is frequently used by small companies that are not well established and therefore are unable to convince any underwriter to undertake a firm commitment. The agreement may be that the underwriter will exert its best efforts to sell whatever percentage of the issuance it is able to sell. Other times the arrangement is that if all or at least a minimum percentage of the shares are not sold, none will be sold. This process is really merchandising, not true underwriting. Ironically, it is occasionally used not by weak companies but by very strong companies who are confident that their shares can be sold and wish to save on the underwriter's fee.

Stand-by underwriting, also known as strict or old-fashioned underwriting, occurs when an underwriter agrees for a fee that it will purchase on its own account whatever portion of an offering is not purchased by investors. This method is infrequently used in the United States with one important exception. It is often used when a corporation makes a "rights" offering, that is, when an issuer gives existing shareholders a chance to purchase additional shares of stock. Invariably some shareholders will be uninterested or unable to exercise their rights, and underwriters can step in to complete the offering, assuring the issuer of the needed cash return.

Competitive bid underwriting occurs when the underwriting agreement is awarded entirely on the basis of sealed bids. This method is infrequently used, being restricted to securities offerings by municipal public utility companies and railroad corporations.

Alternatives to Underwriting

An issuing corporation can sometimes avoid the underwriting process by selling new securities to existing shareholders or to the public without any assistance from an underwriter in any capacity. A direct sale from an issuer to the public is risky and seldom used except by companies with a very strong credit rating and very firm demand for their shares.

Also, an issuing corporation can use the securities firm merely as an agent to find an entity and negotiate a sale privately. Such a sale is called a *private placement*. The purchaser is usually a large institution, such as an insurance company. The investment banker serves merely as a broker working for a commission in a private placement.

Private placements do not always raise as much money as the issuer could have earned by selling to the public. However, private placements are less expensive and less time consuming than are public offerings. Also, they have the advantage of secrecy. Of the 1980 total corporate issuances of $78.1 billion, $11.5 billion were private placements.[9]

The Mechanics of Underwriting

The process of a standard firm commitment underwriting begins when an issuer consults an investment banker for advice regarding a potential issuance. The issuer's financial position, past performance, future prospects, and urgency of need for capital must be considered, as must the general market conditions. In light of these and other factors, a decision must be reached as to the type of security to be issued, the amount of the offering, the unit price, and the timing.

The agreement between the underwriter(s) and the issuer usually takes the form of a nonbinding "letter of intent" that sets out the important terms of the offering and sets a maximum public offering price for purposes of determining the SEC filing fee. After the registration statement is filed with the SEC, the main underwriter or underwriters who will manage the underwriting begin to piece together an underwriting syndicate. Even the wealthiest underwriters can seldom handle a large underwriting by themselves. When a major corporation such as IBM decides to issue as much as a billion dollars worth of securities at one time, it takes a large number of underwriters to handle the distribution. During the waiting period, potential underwriters will test the market and receive indications of buyer interest from investors.

On the basis of these indications of interest, tentative agreement will be reached as to how big a share of the issuance each underwriter will handle. For many issuances, additional securities firms will come in as part of a "selling group" that helps to merchandise the securities. Members of the selling group receive price concessions off the public offering price, but frequently do not buy on their own account and therefore take much less risk than the underwriters.

---

[9] *SEC Monthly Statistical Review*, no. 3 (March 1981), p. 28.

The day before the registration statement becomes effective through SEC approval, the issuer and the managing underwriter or underwriters will agree on the final offering price in light of current market conditions. At the same time, the "agreement among underwriters" will be signed, designating the managing underwriter(s) and setting the fees and obligations of the parties. Because the managing underwriters do the most work, they receive the highest compensation. The syndicate of underwriters receives a smaller cut, and the selling group that takes the least risk receives the least compensation.

The public offering process can be time consuming. It can take up to four months to contact an underwriter, allow the underwriter to investigate fully and advise, and then prepare the paperwork for SEC filings. Once the registration statement is filed, the SEC can then take up to two or three months to allow it to become effective.

A trend worth noting is that toward use of unsyndicated underwritings. Institutional investors now dominate the market. For that reason, several issuers have recently distributed offerings entirely to institutional investors through the managing underwriter alone. In bypassing the country's 70,000 stock brokers and their customers, the issuers save on fees. In 1981, 98% of all issues were syndicated; by 1985, 30% of all issues (by dollar value) were unsyndicated.[10]

A sample time frame for a registered public offering is illustrated in the exhibit on the next two pages.

LEGAL FRAMEWORK

Overview

Much of the 1933 Act revolves around §5. That section is critical because it establishes the registration statement and prospectus as the most important, and nearly exclusive, means of offering and selling securities. Subsection (a) of §5 provides that unless a registration statement has been filed, it is illegal to sell a security. Subsection (b) makes it unlawful to (1) use a prospectus that does not comply with the requirements of §10 or (2) deliver a security unless it was preceded or accompanied by a prospectus. Finally, subsection (c) makes it illegal to *offer* to sell or to buy securities before a registration statement has been filed.

Two critical points in the registration process are the filing of the registration statement and the SEC's allowing the statement to become effective. Section 5, viewed somewhat simplistically, forbids offers or sales before the registration statement is filed ("prefiling period"), allows offers but not sales while the statement is pending ("waiting period"), and allows offers and sales once it becomes effective ("post effective period"). It is very important for every issuing company, underwriter, and broker-dealer to understand exactly what is permissible and what is illegal in each of these three periods.

---

[10] A. Monroe, "Unsyndicated Stock Offerings Are Increasing," *The Wall Street Journal*, February 24, 1986, p. 13.

Illustrative Example of Registration Process*

EVENT	PARTICIPANTS	AGENDA	TIMETABLE
Preliminary meeting to discuss issue	President; VP-Finance, independent accountants, underwriters; counsel	Discuss financial needs; introduce and select type of issue to meet needs.	1 July (Begin)
Form selection	Management, counsel	Select appropriate form for use in registration statement.	3 July (3 days)
Initial meeting of working group	President, VP-Finance, independent accounts, underwriter, counsel for underwriter, company counsel	Assign specific duties to each person in working group; discuss underwriting problems with this issue; discuss accounting problems with the issue.	8 July (8 days)
Second meeting of working group	Same as for initial meeting	Review work assignments; Prepare presentation to board of directors.	22 July (22 days)
Meeting of board of directors	Board of directors, members of working group	Approve proposed issue and increase of debt or equity; Authorize preparation of materials.	26 July (26 days)
Meeting of company counsel with underwriters	Company counsel, counsel for underwriters, underwriters	Discuss underwriting terms and blue sky problems.	30 July (30 days)
Meeting of working group	Members of working group	Review collected material and examine discrepancies.	6 Aug. (37 days)
Prefiling conference with SEC staff	Working group members, SEC staff, other experts as needed	Review proposed registration and associated problems: legal, financial, operative.	9 Aug. (40 days)
Additional meetings of working group	Members of working group	Prepare final registration statement and prospectuses.	12–30 Aug. (61 days)

Meeting with board of directors	Board of directors, members of working group	Approve registration statement and prospectuses; discuss related topics and problems.	6 Sept. (68 days)
Meeting of working group	Members of working group	Draft final corrected registration statement.	10 Sept. (72 days)
Filing registration statement with SEC	Company counsel or representative and SEC staff	File registration statement and pay fee.	12 Sept. (74 days)
Distribution of "red herring" prospectus	Underwriters	Publicize offering.	16 Sept. (78 days)
Receipt of letter of comments	Members of working group	Relate deficiencies in registration statement.	15 Oct. (107 days)
Meeting of working group	Members of working group	Correct deficiencies and submit amendments.	21 Oct. (113 days)
"Due diligence" meeting	Management representatives, independent accountants, company counsel, underwriter's counsel, underwriters, other professionals as needed	Exchange final information and discuss pertinent problems relating to underwriting and issue.	24 Oct. (116 days)
Pricing amendment	Management, underwriters	Add the amounts for the actual price, underwriter's discount or commission, and net proceeds to company to the amended registration statement.	25 Oct. (117 days)
Notice of acceptance	SEC staff	Report from SEC staff on acceptance status of price-amended registration statement	28 Oct. (120 days)
Statement becomes effective			30 Oct. (122 days)

* K. Fred Skousen, AN INTRODUCTION TO THE SEC (3d ed. 1983), pp. 58–59. Copyright 1983 by South-Western Publishing Co. Reprinted with permission.

Prefiling Period

Section 5(c) is very broad in barring *any person* from making an *offer* to buy or sell securities before a registration statement has been filed. However, very practical considerations mandate §2(3)'s provision that the term "offer to buy" does not include preliminary negotiations between an issuer (or a controlling person thereof) and any underwriter. Therefore, before a registration statement is filed, an issuer can negotiate the terms of an issuance with an underwriter. Normally such negotiations culminate in a "memorandum of understanding" or "letter of intent" that addresses such matters as the amount of the issue, the preparation of a registration statement, formation of an underwriting syndicate, allocation of expenses, maximum and minimum offering prices, and so on. Although this agreement is technically nonbinding, it is usually followed by issuers and underwriters alike.

     Section 2(3)'s exception also allows negotiations among underwriters that may result in an "agreement among underwriters" discussing such matters as who will be the lead underwriter, how the issuance will be divided among the various underwriters, and levels of compensation. This agreement normally is not executed until the registration statement is about to become effective.

     Thus, issuer-underwriter negotiations and negotiations among underwriters are the main activities allowed during the prefiling period. Any other "offer" to sell securities would violate §5(c). The term "offer" is defined very broadly and can include just about any publicity that might stir an interest in an issuance that has not yet been registered. The SEC's view of illicit prefiling publicity, so-called "gun jumping," is presented in the following excerpt.

PUBLICATION OF INFORMATION PRIOR TO OR AFTER THE EFFECTIVE DATE OF A REGISTRATION STATEMENT

Securities Act Release No. 3844 (October 8, 1957)

     It follows from the express language and the legislative history of the Securities Act that an issuer, underwriter or dealer may not legally begin a public offering or initiate a public sales campaign prior to the filing of a registration statement. It apparently is not generally understood, however, that the publication of information and statements, and publicity efforts, generally, made in advance of a proposed financing, although not couched in terms of an express offer, may in fact contribute to conditioning the public mind or arousing public interest in the issuer or in the securities of an issuer in a manner which raises a serious question whether the publicity is not in fact part of the selling effort.

     Instances have come to the attention of the Commission in which information of a misleading character, gross exaggeration and outright falsehood have been published by various means for the purpose of conveying to the public a message designed to stimulate an appetite for securities—a message which could not properly have been included in a statutory prospectus in conformity with the standards of integrity demanded by the statute.

     Many of the cases have reflected a deliberate disregard of the provisions and purpose of the law. Others have reflected an unawareness of the problems involved or a failure to exercise a proper control over research and public relations activities in relation to the distribution of an issue of securities.

Example #1

An underwriter-promoter is engaged in arranging for the public financing of a mining venture to explore for a mineral which has certain possible potentialities for use in atomic research and power. While preparing a registration statement for a public offering, the underwriter-promoter distributed several thousand copies of a brochure which described in glowing generalities the future possibilities for use of the mineral and the profit potential to investors who would share in the growth prospects of a new industry. The brochure made no reference to any issuer or any security nor to any particular financing. It was sent out, however, bearing the name of the underwriting firm and obviously was designed to awaken an interest which later would be focused on the specific financing to be presented in the prospectus shortly to be sent to the same mailing list.

The distribution of the brochure under these circumstances clearly was the first step in a sales campaign to effect a public sale of the securities and as such, in the view of the Commission, violated Section 5 of the Securities Act.

• • •

Example #5

Immediately preceding the filing of a registration statement for an issue of securities by a large industrial company, the research department of an investment banking firm distributed to a substantial number of the firm's institutional customers a brochure which referred specifically to the securities and described the business and prospects of the parent company of the prospective issuer. The business of the prospective issuer represented the principal part of the over-all operations of the total enterprise. The investment banking firm had been a principal underwriter of prior issues of securities by the parent and in accordance with policy of the firm from time to time distributed reports to its clients concerning securities of issuers which the firm had financed. It appeared, in this particular case, that the research department of the banking firm had prepared and distributed such a report to its clients without being fully aware of the activities of the underwriting department or the timing of the forthcoming offering.

The Commission advised the representatives of the issuer and the prospective underwriters that under all the circumstances, including the content, timing and distribution given to the brochure, participation of the firm in the distribution of the securities would pose difficulties from the point of view of the enforcement of the provisions of Section 5 of the Securities Act. In order to avoid any question as to violations of this provision of the Act, the banking firm did not participate in the distribution.

Example #6

In recognition of the problems presented, the Commission's staff frequently receives inquiries from company officials or their counsel with respect to circumstances such as the following:

The president of a company accepted, in August, an invitation to address a meeting of a security analysts' society to be held in February of the following year for the purpose of informing the membership concerning the company, its plans, its record and problems. By January a speech had been prepared together with supplemental information and data, all of which was designed to give a fairly comprehensive picture of the company, the industry in which it operates and various factors affecting its future growth. Projections of demand, operations and profits for future periods were included. The speech and the other data had been printed and it was intended that several hundred copies would be available for distribution at the meeting. In addition, since it was believed that stockholders, creditors, and perhaps customers might be interested in the talk, it was intended to mail to such persons and to a list of other selected firms and institutions copies of the material to be used at the analysts' meeting.

Later in January, a public financing by the company was authorized, preparation of a registration statement was begun and negotiation with underwriters was commenced. It soon appeared that the coming meeting of analysts, scheduled many months earlier, would be at or about the time the registration statement was to be filed. This presented the question whether, in the circumstances, delivery and distribution of the speech and the supporting data to the various persons mentioned above would contravene provisions of the Securities Act.

It seemed clear that the scheduling of the speech had not been arranged in contemplation of a public offering by the issuer at or about the time of its delivery. In the circumstances, no objection was raised to the delivery of the speech at the analysts' meeting. However, since printed copies of the speech might be received by a wider audience, it was suggested that printed copies of the speech and the supporting data not be made available at the meeting nor be transmitted to other persons.

Example #7

Two weeks prior to the filing of a registration statement the president of the issuer had delivered, before a society of security analysts, a prepared address which had been booked several months previously. In his speech the president discussed the company's operations and expansion program, its sales and earnings. The speech contained a forecast of sales and referred to the issuer's proposal to file with the Commission later in the month a registration statement with respect to a proposed offering of convertible subordinated debentures. Copies of the speech had been distributed to approximately 4,000 security analysts.

The Commission denied acceleration of the registration statement and requested that the registrant distribute copies of its final prospectus to each member of the group which had received a copy of the speech.

· · ·

Example #9

An issuer was about to file a registration statement for a proposed offering on behalf of a controlling person. The timing of the issue was fixed in accommodation to the controlling person. It appeared, however, that registration would coincide with the time when the company normally distributed its annual report to security holders and others. In recognition of the problem posed, inquiry was made whether such publication and distribution of the report at such time would create any problems. The issuer was advised that, if the annual report was of the character and content normally published by the company and did not contain material designed to assist in the proposed offering, no question would be raised.

A classic example of abusive "gun jumping" occurred in the *Carl M. Loeb, Rhoades & Co.* case,[11] wherein Davis, who owned much property in Florida, decided to place some of it in a new corporation financed primarily through a public offering.

---

[11] 38 S.E.C. 843 (1959).

Before a registration statement was filed, the issuer and the underwriters issued press releases that contained glowing descriptions of the land that the corporation would own, the new enterprise, and Florida in general. Following this publicity, 101 broker-dealers indicated an interest in helping to distribute the offer and investors indicated an interest in purchasing up to $500,000 worth of the contemplated issuance. Only later, when a final prospectus was filed, were many negative facts, such as the undesirable location of the land and certain flood plain problems, disclosed.

The SEC concluded that the broker-dealers who had participated in this prefiling publicity had violated §5(c) and should be sanctioned. The Commission explained the rationale for a very broad definition of the term "offer" in this way:

> Securities are distributed in this country by a complex and sensitive machinery geared to accomplish nationwide distribution of large quantities of securities with great speed. Multi-million dollar issues are often oversubscribed on the day the securities are made available for sale. This result is accomplished by a network of prior informal indications of interest or offers to buy between underwriters and dealers and between dealers and investors based upon mutual expectations that, at the moment when sales may legally be made, many prior indications will immediately materialize as purchases. It is wholly unrealistic to assume in this context that "offers" must take any particular legal form. Legal formalities come at the end to record prior understandings, but it is the procedures by which these prior understandings, embodying investment decisions, are obtained or generated which the Securities Act was intended to reform.
>
> One of the cardinal purposes of the Securities Act is to slow down this process of rapid distribution of corporate securities, at least in its earlier and crucial stages, in order that dealers and investors might have access to, and an opportunity to consider, the disclosures of the material business and financial facts of the issuer provided in registration statements and prospectuses. Under the practices existing prior to the enactment of the statute in 1933, dealers made blind commitments to purchase securities without adequate information, and in turn, resold the securities to an equally uninformed investing public. The entire distribution process was often stimulated by sales literature designed solely to arouse interest in the securities and not to disclose material facts about the issuer and its securities. It was to correct this situation that the Securities Act originally prohibited offers to sell and solicitations of offers to buy as well as sales prior to the effective date of a registration statement and imposed a 20-day waiting period between the filing and the effective date.

In light of this purpose, the SEC established a presumption that prefiling publicity by issuers and underwriters constituted an attempt to condition the public mind or arouse interest in particular securities, even though it might not be couched in the form of an express offer.

Permissible Publicity by Issuers

The desire to avoid premature publicity that might convince investors that they wanted to purchase shares before full disclosure of information via the registration statement and prospectus must be weighed against the need for a continuing flow of information from corporations to the investing public. An efficient market and wise investment decisions are predicated upon an informed market. Realizing this, the SEC has made it clear that §5(c) does not bar "normal" communications between corporations and their shareholders, customers, or potential investors. The SEC has stated that it encourages the flow of factual information to shareholders and the investing public.[12] Therefore, a corporation contemplating an issuance of new securities should

1. Continue to advertise products and services.
2. Continue to send out customary quarterly, annual, and other periodic reports to stockholders.
3. Continue to publish proxy statements and send out dividend notices.
4. Continue to make announcements to the press with respect to factual business and financial developments (i.e., receipt of a contract, the settlement of a strike, the opening of a plant, or similar events of interest to the community in which the business operates).
5. Answer unsolicited telephone inquiries from stockholders, financial analysts, the press, and others concerning factual information.
6. Observe an "open-door" policy in responding to unsolicited inquiries concerning factual matters from securities analysts, financial analysts, security holders, and participants in the communications field who have a legitimate interest in the corporation's affairs.
7. Continue to hold stockholder meetings as scheduled and to answer shareholders' inquiries at stockholder meetings relating to factual matters.

On the other hand, the SEC believes that issuers should avoid

1. Issuance of forecasts, projections, or predictions relating but not limited to revenues, income, or earnings per share.
2. Publishing opinions concerning values.

Additionally, SEC Rule 135 allows an issuer to publish a notice that it proposes to make an offering so long as that notice states that the offering will be made only by means of a prospectus and gives no more information than the name of the issuer, the title, amount, and basic terms of the securities, the anticipated time of the offering, and the purpose of the offering (so long as the underwriters are not named).[13]

Permissible Publicity by Others

The efficient market is fueled not only by information provided by issuers, but also by the financial analysts employed by investment bankers and broker-dealers who might also be involved in underwriting an issuance. While the SEC certainly seeks to avoid a situation where an investment banker "hypes" shares of a proposed issuance it intends to underwrite before a registration statement is filed, it also realizes the importance of the recommendations and opinions of such entities. Three important SEC rules help to resolve this tension.

Rule 137 permits dealers who are not participating in a contemplated or ongoing

---

[12] *Securities Act Release*, no. 5180 (August 16, 1971).

[13] Rule 135 allows disclosure of some small, additional information in the case of rights offerings to shareholders, exchange offers, and offers to employees.

issuance to publish and distribute, in the regular course of their business information, opinions or recommendations concerning the securities of a 1934 Act reporting company that has filed or contemplates filing a registration statement.[14] Such communications will not be deemed prefiling "offers," which would violate §5. However, the privilege of a nonparticipating dealer to publish such information is destroyed if it obtains any compensation from the issuer.

Rule 138 allows even broker-dealers who are participating in an issuance of common stock to publish, in the regular course of business, information, opinions, or recommendations regarding nonconvertible senior securities of the issuer. Conversely, if an offering of nonconvertible senior securities is contemplated or ongoing, participating broker-dealers can publish opinions about the issuer's common stock. Because the markets for common stock and senior nonconvertible securities are substantially different, publicity about one type of security is not likely to precondition the market for the other. However, Rule 138 may be used only as to issuers eligible to use Form S-2, that is, major reporting companies about which substantial information is always public.

Rule 139 allows participating broker-dealers to publish information, opinions, or recommendations as to a company in registration or any of its securities *if* the publication in which the communication is contained is distributed with reasonable regularity in the normal course of business. Rule 139 applies if the issuing company meets (1) the eligibility requirements of Form S-3 (i.e., be a reporting company whose shares are well followed in the marketplace) and (2) certain guidelines relating to the amount of stock that is held in the hands of nonaffiliates [15] and of trading volume.

If issuers do not qualify for the S-3 Form, Rule 139 still allows participating broker-dealers to publish information, opinions, or recommendations in the normal course of business *if* (1) the publication is distributed with reasonable regularity; (2) it includes similar opinions or recommendations regarding a substantial number of companies in the issuer's industry or contains a comprehensive list of securities currently recommended by the broker-dealer; (3) the information, opinion, or recommendation is given no greater prominence than that given to other securities; and (4) an opinion or recommendation at least as favorable as to registrant or its securities appeared in the broker-dealer's last publication prior to commencement of participation in the distribution.

To summarize, the permissible activities during the prefiling period include (1) issuer-underwriter negotiations, (2) negotiations among underwriters, (3) normal communications by the issuer regarding factual matters, (4) Rule 135 announcements of a planned offering, (5) Rule 137 publications by nonparticipating dealers, (6) Rule 138 publications by participating brokers regarding securities of a type not being offered, and (7) Rule 139 information, opinions, or recommendations by participating underwriters under strict circumstances.

---

[14] Generally, a 1934 Act reporting company is one that is required to file periodic reports with the SEC pursuant to §§12(g) or 15(d) of the 1934 Act. This includes companies with shares listed on a stock exchange and companies with over $5 million in assets and more than 500 shareholders in a single class whose shares are traded over the counter.

[15] An "affiliate" of an issuer "is a person that directly, or indirectly, through one or more intermediaries, controls or is controlled by, or is under common control with" the issuer (Rule 405).

Waiting Period

The waiting period is that period existing while the SEC decides whether a registration statement that has been filed should be allowed to become effective. While the law does not allow sales to be completed before a final registration statement and prospectus are approved, it is important that as much information about the issuer be disseminated as possible. The purpose of the waiting period is to slow down the process so that the dealers and through them the potential investors can become familiar with the issuer and the offering so they can make unhurried decisions.

During the waiting period, the communications authorized by Rules 137–139 are still permitted. Additionally, the lead underwriter can organize the "selling group"— that group of dealers that will help sell the securities at the lower echelon of the distribution chain.

Although no sales may be consummated during the waiting period, the underwriters and dealers are allowed to make certain types of offers to gather "indications of interest" by potential investors. These indications of interest, it is hoped, can be quickly turned into sales when the registration statement becomes effective.

Oral offers, such as over the telephone, are permitted during the waiting period, although television and radio advertisements are not. Written offers to sell are permitted, however, only if they comply with the proper rules.

Rule 134 authorizes one type of written offer—the so-called "tombstone advertisement." An advertisement shall not be deemed an illegal prospectus if it contains only that information authorized by Rule 134: (1) the name of the issuer, (2) the full title of the security and the amount being offered, (3) a brief description of the company's business, (4) the price range of the security, (5) the name of the managing underwriter, (6) the contemplated date of issuance, and (7) a few other minor items. Furthermore, the ad must specifically state that

> No offer to buy the securities can be accepted and no part of the purchase price can be received until the registration statement has become effective, and any such offer may be withdrawn or revoked, without obligation or commitment of any kind, at any time prior to notice of its acceptance given after the effective date. An indication of interest in response to this advertisement will involve no obligation or commitment of any kind.

Rule 134 communications are called "tombstone ads" because they appear in the pages of publications such as *The Wall Street Journal* surrounded by a black border. Also called an "identifying statement," the Rule 134 communication is sometimes used to test the strength of the market during the waiting period, but more commonly is published more as a matter of record after the effective date and frequently after all the securities have been sold.

A second type of written offering permitted during the waiting period is the "preliminary prospectus" authorized by Rule 430. It is through this device that the SEC hopes to transmit most of the information that will reach investors before they decide to purchase. The preliminary prospectus must contain substantially the same information that will be contained in the final prospectus that will meet the requirements of §10(a). Because the offering price of the securities will not be determined until the registration statement becomes effective, it is permissible for the preliminary prospectus to omit such items as the offering price, underwriting discounts or commissions, amount of proceeds, and other matters dependent on the offering price.

The preliminary prospectus is called a "red herring" prospectus because on its cover will appear the following statement in red ink:

> A registration statement relating to these securities has been filed with the Securities and Exchange Commission but has not yet become effective. Information contained herein is subject to completion or amendment. These securities may not be sold nor may offers to buy be accepted prior to the time the registration statement becomes effective. This prospectus shall not constitute an offer to sell or the solicitation of an offer to buy nor shall there be any sale of these securities in any State in which such offer, solicitation or sale would be unlawful prior to registration or qualification under the securities laws of any such State.

The final type of written offer permitted during the waiting period is the Rule 431 "summary prospectus," which, though seldom used, is authorized for the more substantial issuing corporations.

Any written offer that does not comply with Rules 134, 430, or 431 is illegal if it occurs during the waiting period. Furthermore, an illegal offer is not cured by a following legal sale.

DISKIN v. LOMASNEY & CO.

452 F.2d 871 (2d Cir. 1971)

Plaintiff Diskin conversed with defendant/underwriter Lomasney regarding the securities of two companies, Ski Park City West and Continental Travel, Ltd. On September 17, 1968, defendant sent plaintiff a final prospectus as to Ski Park City West. That company's registration statement had become effective. Included with the prospectus was a letter that indicated that if plaintiff took 1,000 shares of Ski Park City West, Lomasney would "commit to you the sale at the public offering price when, and if issued, 5,000 shares of Continental Travel, Ltd," for which a registration statement had been filed but was not yet effective.

After the Continental Travel registration statement became effective, defendant sent plaintiff a confirmation of sale of 5,000 shares at $12 each. Later plaintiff received a final prospectus for these Continental shares. Only then did plaintiff pay for and receive the shares.

Later plaintiff sued to rescind the sale of Continental Travel shares on grounds that the September 17, 1968 letter constituted an illegal written offer in violation of §5(b)(1). The trial court dismissed the complaint, so plaintiff appealed.

FRIENDLY, CHIEF JUDGE:

. . .

[T]he mere filing of a registration statement does not ensure the legality of *any* written offer made during the post-filing, pre-effective period; to be lawful, such written offers must be made by way of a "prospectus" which meets the requirements of §10.

. . . .

[Defendants argue] that the violation was cured by Diskin's receipt of a prospectus prior to the actual purchase.

. . .

[However, we] agree with Professor Loss that "[w]hatever doubt there may once have been as to the applicability of §12(1) to illegal offers [followed by legal sales] was resolved when the original definition of sale was split into separate definitions of 'sale' and 'offer' in 1954, with the incidental amendment of §12(1) to refer to any person 'who offers or sells a security in violation of section 5' so as 'to preserve the effect of the present law' by not excluding the newly permissible pre-effective offers from liabilities under §12"—III Loss, *Securities Regulation 1695–96*, 2d ed., 1961.

The result here reached may appear to be harsh, since Diskin had an opportunity to read the final prospectus before he paid for the shares. But the 1954 Congress quite obviously meant to allow rescission or damages in the case of illegal offers as well as illegal sales. Very likely Congress thought that, when it had done so much to broaden the methods of making legal offers during the "waiting period" between the filing and the taking effect of a registration statement [1954 Congressional amendments authorized use of the "red herring" preliminary prospectus], it should make sure that still other methods were not attempted. Here all Lomasney needed to have done was to accompany the September 17, 1968 letter with any one of the [legal] types of prospectus for the Continental shares. Very likely Congress thought a better time for meaningful prospectus reading was at the time of the offer rather than in the context of confirmation and demand for payment. In any event, it made altogether clear that an offeror of a security who had failed to follow one of the allowed paths could not achieve absolution simply by returning to the road of virtue before receiving payment.

The judgment dismissing the complaint is reversed, with instructions to enter judgment for the plaintiff that, upon delivery of 5,000 shares of Continental Travel, Ltd., he shall receive $60,000 with interest.

Encouraging Dissemination

As noted earlier, the preliminary prospectus is the primary means of conveying information to potential investors during the waiting period. To encourage dissemination of the information contained in these "red herring" prospectuses, the SEC has issued Rule 460. As will be explained in the next section of this chapter, generally there is a 20-day waiting period between the filing of a registration statement and when it becomes effective. A number of SEC actions may slow down the review process, but 20 days is the minimum waiting period unless the SEC grants acceleration. Importantly, any amendment to a registration statement restarts the running of the 20-day period. Because most registrations that are reviewed take much longer than 20 days, the initial filing cannot contain the final price of the securities. Only after SEC objections have been satisfied will the issuer amend the registration statement, in light of current market conditions, to fix the final price.

Once that final price is fixed, most issuers will wish to sell as soon as possible before the market changes again. Therefore, the amendment will be accompanied by a request that the SEC exercise its discretion to "accelerate" the effective date of the offering to allow sales to begin immediately. Under Rule 460 the SEC conditions such acceleration upon written assurances from the lead underwriter that reasonable steps have been taken to provide each underwriter and each dealer with sufficient copies of the preliminary prospectus so that they and their offerees may become fully acquainted with the issuer in advance of the anticipated effective date of the registration statement.

Additionally, Rule 15c2–8 of the 1934 Act makes it an illegal "deceptive act or practice" for broker-dealers to fail to take reasonable steps to provide preliminary prospectuses to any investor who requests one in writing. Furthermore, lead underwriters must take reasonable steps to assure that other underwriters and all broker-dealers participating in the issuance have sufficient copies of the preliminary prospectus to meet their needs.

Posteffective Period

Once the registration statement has become effective, the "indications of interest" that were solicited during the waiting period can be converted into concrete sales. Oral offers to sell may still be made, but the preliminary prospectus can no longer be used.

Section 5(b)(1) provides that during the posteffective period, only final statutory prospectuses meeting the requirements of §10 can be used. This means that *any* written offer made during the posteffective period must be a final prospectus or be preceded or accompanied by one. Use of supplemental sales literature, so-called "free writing" that was illegal during the waiting period is authorized during the posteffective period, but *only* if preceded or accompanied by a final prospectus.

Many times, for reasons of convenience or safekeeping, the securities themselves will not be delivered to the investor, but for statute of frauds purposes, written confirmations of sales will be. Section 2(10) of the 1933 Act defines the term "prospectus" so broadly that it includes such written confirmations that, therefore, must also be preceded or accompanied by a final prospectus.

Prospectus Delivery Requirements

Section 5(b)(2) does not allow delivery of a security unless it is preceded or accompanied by a final prospectus. That accompanying the security with a final prospectus can satisfy the statute creates a bit of a loophole. An offer that is made and accepted over the telephone, for example, can be consummated by mailing the purchaser the security and the final prospectus in the same envelope. In this circumstance, the prospectus does the purchaser precious little good and is therefore sometimes referred to as a "retrospectus." [16]

The prospectus delivery requirements must be observed by participating underwriters and dealers as long as they are selling part of their original allotment of securities from the issuance. Problems arise, however, when securities are resold by their initial purchasers. Although §5(b)(2)'s prospectus delivery requirements apply to "any person," §4(1) exempts from the provisions of §5 any "transactions by any person other than an issuer, underwriter, or dealer." Therefore, a normal investor can resell without worrying about delivering a final prospectus.

Because a purchaser of an issuing company's stock a week after the effective date might be purchasing a never-before issued share or might be purchasing a share that has been purchased and resold, §4(3) requires any dealer, participating or otherwise, to deliver a prospectus with the sale of any registered security. In this manner, the fortuity of whether an investor is buying shares sold for the first time or shares being resold will not determine entitlement to a final prospectus. In either case, a final prospectus must be delivered. However, this burdensome obligation is limited. It runs for the first 40 days of the issuance of shares of a company that has previously sold through a registration statement and for the first 90 days of the issuance of a "first-time" company.

Rule 174 refines these requirements by eliminating the prospectus delivery requirement for the resale of securities of companies which must report under §§13 or 15(d) of the 1934 Act. Also, in a "shelf registration" (which shall soon be explained), the 40- and 90-day periods run only from the initial prospectus delivery period following the first *bona fide* offering of securities under the registration statement.

Prospectus Update Requirements

Ideally an offering will sell out very soon after the registration statement becomes effective. But occasionally an offering will be extended. Although a registration statement and prospectus may be accurate at the effective date, events occurring during the posteffective period may render them inaccurate. If that occurs, the final prospectus may have to be amended (rewritten) or supplemented (usually by "sticker" changes).

Section 10(a)(3) states that when a prospectus is used more than nine months after the effective date, it must contain no information older than 16 months. Furthermore, *at any time* occurrences render a prospectus materially misleading, the prospectus must be updated.

---

[16] Note that Rule 15c2–8(b) of the 1934 Act makes it a deceptive act for a broker or dealer participating in an issue of securities, the issuer of which has not previously been required to file reports under §§13(a) or 15(d) of the 1934 Act, not to deliver a preliminary prospectus at least 48 hours before a confirmation of sale.

S.E.C. v. MANOR NURSING CENTERS, INC.

458 F.2d 1082 (2d Cir. 1972)

An offering of 450,000 shares of Manor Nursing Centers was, according to the prospectus, to be offered and sold by the underwriter on an "all-or-nothing" basis; that is, unless all 450,000 shares were sold, the offering would terminate and all funds would be returned, with interest, to the subscribers. The funds were to be held in escrow, unavailable for other use, until the terms of the offering were met.

The SEC brought an action alleging violations of antifraud provisions of the 1933 and 1934 acts and violation of the prospectus delivery requirements of §5(b)(2) of the 1934 act. The district court found violations of both the antifraud rules and the prospectus-delivery requirements. Defendants appealed.

TIMBERS, CIRCUIT JUDGE:

[The appellate court first found defendants guilty of fraud because they had not amended the prospectus that had become misleading because of four posteffective developments: the public's funds were not returned even though the issue was not fully subscribed, an escrow account for the proceeds was not established, shares were issued for consideration other than cash, and certain individuals received extra compensation for agreeing to participate in the offering.]

In addition to concluding that appellants had violated the antifraud provisions of the federal securities laws, the district court also correctly held that they had violated the prospectus-delivery requirement of Section 5(b)(2) of the 1933 Act.

Section 5(b)(2) prohibits the delivery of a security for the purpose of sale unless the security is accompanied or preceded by a prospectus which meets the requirements of Section 10(a) of the 1933 Act. To meet the requirements of §10(a), a prospectus must contain, with specified exceptions, all "the information contained in the registration statement. . . ." In turn, the registration statement, pursuant to Section 7 of the 1933 Act, must set forth certain information specified in Schedule A of the 1933 Act. Among the items of information which Schedule A requires the registration statement, and therefore the prospectus, to contain are the use of proceeds (item 13), the estimated net proceeds (item 15), the price at which the security will be offered to the public and any variation therefrom (item 16), and all commissions or discounts paid to underwriters, directly or indirectly (item 17).

The Manor prospectus purported to disclose the information required by the above items of Schedule A. The evidence adduced at trial showed, however, that developments subsequent to the effective date of the registration statement made this information false and misleading. Moreover, Manor and its principals did not amend or supplement the prospectus to reflect the changes which had made inaccurate the information which §10(a) required the prospectus to disclose. We hold that implicit in the statutory provision that the prospectus contain certain information is the requirement that such information be true and correct. A prospectus does not meet the requirements of §10(a), therefore, if information required to be disclosed is materially false or misleading. Appellants violated §5(b)(2) by delivering Manor securities for sale accompanied by a prospectus which did not meet the requirements of §10(a) in that the prospectus contained materially false and misleading statements with respect to information required by §10(a) to be disclosed.

Manor contends, however, that §5(b)(2) does not require that a prospectus be amended to reflect material developments which occur subsequent to the effective date of the registration statement. This contention is premised on the assumptions that the prospectus spoke only as of the effective date of the registration statement and that the prospectus contained no false or misleading statements as of the effective date— December 8, 1969. Assuming the Manor prospectus was accurate as of December 8, 1969, appellants' claim is without merit.

In support of their argument that the prospectus need not be amended or supplemented to reflect post-effective developments, appellants cite an administrative decision in which the SEC held that it will not issue a stop order with respect to a registration statement which becomes misleading subsequent to its effective date because of material post-effective events— *Funeral Directors Manufacturing and Supply Co.*, 39 S.E.C. 33, 34 (1959). See also *Charles A. Howard*, 1 S.E.C. 6, 10 (1934). Under this

line of SEC decisions, a registration statement need not be amended after its effective date to reflect post-effective developments. These decisions, however, are not apposite here. Assuming that the registration statement does speak as of its effective date and that Manor did not have to amend its registration statement, appellants were obliged to reflect the post-effective developments referred to above in the prospectus. Even those SEC decisions holding that the registration statement need not be amended to reflect post-effective developments recognize that the prospectus must be amended or supplemented in some manner to reflect such changes. See *Charles A. Howard*, supra, at 10. In addition, as noted above, . . . the effect of the antifraud provisions of the 1933 and 1934 acts is to require that the prospectus reflect post-effective developments which make the prospectus misleading in any material respect. There is no authority for the proposition that a prospectus speaks always as of the effective date of the registration statement.

We hold that appellants were under a duty to amend or supplement the Manor prospectus to reflect post-effective developments; that their failure to do so stripped the Manor prospectus of compliance with §10(a); and that appellants therefore violated §5(b)(2).

Although some courts have disagreed with some of the legal conclusions in the *Manor Nursing Centers* case, it still behooves any issuer to update registration statements and prospectuses that have become inaccurate. At the very least, failure to update courts liability for fraud.

THE SEC REVIEW PROCESS

General Procedure

Unless the SEC takes some action, a registration statement will become effective, pursuant to §8(a), on the twentieth day after it is filed. It was originally contemplated that registration statements would be filed, remain in SEC files for 20 days while information about the issuer was disseminated, and then become effective so that sales could begin. This never became a reality, however, because of the Commission's approach to review. Unlike some states, the SEC does not engage in "merit" review; that is, it is supposedly concerned only with proper disclosure of information so the investing public will have a proper basis for an investment decision. Nonetheless, from the beginning the SEC staff discovered problems with most registration statements filed. In fact, formal stop order proceedings were recommended for many of the 80 registration statements filed on the first day such statements could be filed in 1933 when the act was brand new.[17]

Because the formal structure of the 1933 Act did not contemplate so many "deficient" registration statements, an informal procedure arose. The SEC staff issues what is officially known as a Letter of Comment (more popularly called a Deficiency Letter) to an issuer calling for corrections, clarifications, or additions. The letter might question accounting practices, indicate that financial statements are not in the proper form, require additional emphasis on an unfavorable earnings trend, or require substantiation of a positive claim.

As we shall see in the next chapter, the SEC has the power to block a registration statement from becoming effective or to suspend an already effective statement; therefore, most issuers are very eager to satisfy SEC objections. If substantial changes are needed, the SEC can require curative amendments that necessitate the recirculation of a revised preliminary prospectus. Minor changes can be made at the time of the pricing amendment, which is made after all major SEC objections have been satisfied and the statement is about to become effective.

Formerly, virtually every registration statement received a thorough review by SEC staff. However, from 1962 to 1982 the number of corporate filings (registration statements, annual reports, etc.) with the SEC jumped from 18,000 to 65,000 while the number of SEC personnel to review those filings dropped from 146 to 133.[18] Serious shortages of funds and staff led the SEC to scale back on its review of registration statements several times. The SEC's present policy concentrates the traditional thorough SEC review on the registration statements of companies filing for the first time, companies in financial trouble, and companies "going private." [19] Other registration statements are reviewed on a spot basis. Criteria for selecting stocks for spot review are continually changed.

An established company that files a registration statement will be quickly informed whether its filing will be reviewed. If not, the company will file a request for acceleration (why wait 20 days to sell if the SEC isn't going to review the statement?), which is treated by the Commission as a representation by the parties involved that they are aware of their statutory obligations under the 1933 Act.

Despite the newly limited review policy, swamped SEC employees still take

---

[17] Woodside, "Development of S.E.C. Practices in Processing Registration Statements and Proxy Statements," *Business Lawyer*, Vol. 24 (1969), p. 375.

[18] "As Stocks Climb, Short-Staffed SEC Tries to Cope with Flood of Securities Offerings," *The Wall Street Journal*, July 25, 1983, p. 11.

[19] Arieff, "New Stock Issues Glide Into the Market," *National Law Journal*, May 9, 1983, p. 1.

an average of 30 to 40 days to review a first-time filing. This delay can cause major upset to an issuer anxious to raise capital in a potentially volatile market. Theoretically, a registrant could force the SEC to "fish or cut bait," that is, to review and block quickly a statement, or to allow it to become effective because of the 20-day provision of §8(a). Most companies do not force the SEC's hand in this manner, however. Although the fact that the SEC allows a registration statement to become effective does not constitute a Commission finding that the registration statement is accurate or in a proper form, SEC approval is still a valuable insurance policy. It is very risky to begin to sell while the SEC is still reviewing the registration statement and may yet find reason to issue a stop order. Most companies do not allow their registration statements to become effective while the SEC is still engaged in review. Formerly such a company would slightly amend its registration statement, perhaps changing only a word, to extend the waiting period for another 20 days. Each amendment starts the 20-day waiting period running again. Today, Rule 473 allows an issuer to file what is effectively a permanent delaying amendment that prevents the registration statement from becoming effective until SEC approval is obtained. Companies that have chosen not to comply with this standard practice have met stiff SEC opposition, as will be seen in the next chapter.[20]

Acceleration

A company whose registration statement is reviewed will have to amend to mollify any SEC objection. Even a company that need make no correction has waited a substantial time for review and now must file a pricing amendment. The initial registration statement probably did not set the price of the issuance. Seldom would an underwriter commit itself to buy a new issuance at a certain price (contemplating resale at a higher price) knowing that it could not sell for at least 20 days during a volatile market. Underwriters do not like to be committed in such a manner for more than 48 hours or so before the effective date. After all other SEC objections have been satisfied, the company will file a pricing amendment establishing the price in light of the current market conditions. As noted before, any amendment, even a pricing amendment, restarts the 20-day waiting period. Therefore, the pricing amendment will be accompanied by a request for acceleration.

Since 1940 the SEC has had the authority to accelerate registration statements, allowing them to become effective before the expiration of the 20-day waiting period, even immediately. Although it has been strongly argued that the Commission should never deny acceleration for reasons unrelated to a disclosure deficiency, it has used the very attractive "carrot" of acceleration to impose on companies substantive requirements they would not otherwise have to meet.

For example, the SEC opposes indemnity agreements by which an issuer insures officers, directors, or underwriters from 1933 liability. The Commission believes that this improperly reduces the indemnified party's incentive to comply with the law. Therefore, any issuer seeking acceleration under Rules 460 and 461 is required [21] to include

---

[20] *Las Vegas Hawaiian Development Co.* v. *SEC*, 466 F.Supp. 928 (D. Hawaii 1979).
[21] Regulation S-K, Item 512(i).

in the registration statement a paragraph drafted by the SEC that states that the issuer has been informed by the SEC that it believes indemnity agreements are unenforceable as against public policy and that the issuer will not perform the agreement without first submitting to a court the question of whether the agreement is in fact against public policy.

As previously noted, Rule 460 states that the SEC, in exercising its discretion over requests for acceleration, will consider whether the issuer and underwriters have taken adequate steps to ensure distribution of the preliminary prospectus.

Rule 461 also provides that the SEC will consider the adequacy of information available to the public regarding the registrant and how easily that information is understood. Additionally, Rule 461 lists a number of grounds for denying acceleration, including that there has not been a *bona fide* effort to make the prospectus reasonably concise and readable, that deficient preliminary prospectuses have not been corrected and redistributed to the Commission's satisfaction, that the SEC is investigating the issuer or one of the underwriters, or that market manipulation is suspected.

Shelf Registration

When the SEC engages in review of a registration statement, the issuing process is time consuming and expensive. In an effort to streamline the process somewhat, in March 1982 the SEC issued Rule 415, which greatly expanded a concept called "shelf registration." Although shelf registration previously had been used in certain limited types of offerings, the SEC sought to expand its use to certain primary securities offerings. In essence, Rule 415 allows qualified issuers to file a registration statement which covers the amount of securities the issuer feels it may issue during the following two-year period. During that two years the issuer can pull securities off the shelf and sell them within a very short period of time. It need not file a new registration statement and go through the SEC review process every time it wishes to sell more securities. This speeds the process of issuing shares to allow corporations to take advantage of temporary market conditions.

Although Rule 415 was very controversial during its initial test period, in November 1983 it was permanently adopted in the following release.

SECURITIES ACT RELEASE No. 6499
EXCHANGE ACT RELEASE No. 20384
HOLDING COMPANY ACT RELEASE No. 23122

(November 17, 1983)

• • •

II. Background

Securities have been registered for continuous and delayed offerings for many years. Some of the instances in which shelf registration was allowed were set forth in Guide 4, which was promulgated in 1968. These included securities to be issued in continuing acquisition programs or those underlying exercisable options, warrants or rights. Administrative practice, however, accommodated traditional shelf offerings beyond those specified in the Guide. Shelf registration was permitted for such diverse offerings as limited partnership tax shelters, employee benefit plans, pools of mortgage backed pass through certificates offered from time to time, and customer purchase plans.

Rule 415 arose in connection with the development of the integrated disclosure system. As part of that effort, the Commission comprehensively reviewed all of the Guides for the Preparation and Filing of Registration Statements and Reports and reorganized them to separate the substantive disclosure and procedural provisions. The shelf rule was the procedural rule which resulted from the reevaluation of Guide 4 and reflected current administrative practice as well as the provisions of the Guide.

. . .

III. Experience

From March 1982 through September 1983, almost 4,600 shelf registration statements relating to $181 billion were filed. These shelf filings represent 52% of the over 8,800 registration statements and 52% of $345 billion of securities registered during this period.

Over 85% of the shelf registrations have been traditional shelf filings. Filings for employee benefit plans and dividend or interest reinvestment plans alone account for 55% of the shelf filings and represent 26% of the $181 billion in shelf registered securities.

Most of the balance have been filings for investment grade debt securities offered and sold from time to time on a delayed basis. These 369 debt filings (registering almost $70 billion) represent 53% of the $133 billion of total debt issues filed from March 1982 through September 1983. Approximately 94% of the 369 delayed debt filings were on Form S-3. Over 35% of the filings were made by companies in the financial industry and over 20% were made by utilities.

The remaining shelf filings related to 195 delayed equity filings (registering $12.5 billion). These filings amounted to about 3% of the over 7,700 equity registration statements and 6% of the $212 billion in equity securities registered. Over half were fixed price syndicated offerings which were filed under Rule 415 largely for the procedural convenience afforded by the Rule. Of the remaining delayed equity filings, 90% were on Form S-3. Approximately 70% were for common stock and 30% were for preferred stock. Fifteen percent listed an "at the market" distribution as one of the potential distribution methods described. Eleven of these filings were for so-called "dribble-outs" by utility companies, in which common stock is offered through an underwriter into an existing trading market on a regular basis.

IV. Discussion

A. *Benefits of Shelf Registration*

Virtually all commentators state that shelf registration provides substantial benefits for corporate financings. The principal benefit cited by commentators is that of cost savings. Empirical studies on shelf registration also suggest that securities sold under Rule 415 have lower issuance costs than securities not sold under the Rule.

Cost savings and other benefits are attributed to a number of factors. Flexibility is the Rule's most frequently cited benefit, because it is the source of the greatest cost savings and provides other advantages as well. Commentators stress that flexibility is important in today's volatile markets; that the procedural flexibility afforded by the Rule enables a registrant to time its offering to avail itself of the most advantageous market conditions: that by being able to meet "market windows," registrants are able to obtain lower interest rates on debt and lower dividend rates on preferred stock, thereby benefiting their existing shareholders. The flexibility provided by the Rule also permits variation in the structure and terms of securities on short notice, enabling registrants to match securities with the current demands of the marketplace.

Simplification of the securities registration process also is cited as reducing costs. Legal, accounting, printing and other costs are stated to have been reduced, because only a single registration statement need be filed for a series of offerings, rather than a separate registration statement each time an offering is made. Some commentators also state that simplification of the registration process has given them more flexibility in planning their financing schedules.

Finally, some commentators stress that increased competition among underwriters has resulted in lower underwriting spreads and offering yields, which produce cost savings for registrants and their shareholders. Empirical studies of debt and equity offerings under Rule 415 found lower issuance costs and attributed this primarily to increased competition among investment bankers. Some commentators note that increased competition has spurred the innovation of new financing products.

B. Concerns

1. *Adequacy of Disclosure*

A number of commentators, especially those from the securities industry, express concerns relating to the adequacy of disclosure. While Rule 415 has been the focal point of these concerns, these commentators question aspects of the Commission's integrated disclosure system, such as short form registration and incorporation by reference. They question the amount and quality of information available, as well as whether investors receive it in time to make investment decisions.

The Commission believes that the integrated disclosure system has enhanced the level of disclosure to investors. The basis for the system was the upgrading of the continuous reporting requirements under the Security Exchange Act of 1934 (the ''Exchange Act''). This upgrading was designed to ensure that complete and current information is available to all investors on a continuous basis, not only when a registrant makes a public offering of its securities, but for the trading markets as well. This focus recognized that the secondary trading market volume dwarfs the volume of Securities Act offerings.

For Securities Act registration, the integrated disclosure system builds upon the existence of timely and accurate corporate reporting. Thus, registrants that are widely followed in the marketplace may use Forms S-3 and F-3, which allow maximum use of incorporation by reference of Exchange Act reports and generally do not require information contained in those reports to be reiterated in the prospectus and delivered to investors. Forms S-3 and F-3 recognize the applicability of the efficient market theory to those companies which provide a steady stream of high quality corporate information to the marketplace and whose corporate information is broadly disseminated. Information about these companies is constantly digested and synthesized by financial analysts, who act as essential conduits in the continuous flow of information to investors, and is broadly disseminated on a timely basis by the financial press and other participants in the marketplace. Accordingly, at the time S-3/F-3 registrants determine to make an offering of securities, a large amount of information already has been disseminated to and digested by the marketplace.

2. Due Diligence

Concerns expressed about the quality of disclosure also relate to underwriters' ability to conduct due diligence investigations. Commentators attribute concerns about due diligence largely to fast time schedules.

The Commission recognizes that procedures for conducting due diligence investigations of large, widely followed registrants have changed and are continuing to change. Registrants and the other parties involved in their public offerings—attorneys, accountants, and underwriters—are developing procedures which allow due diligence obligations under Section 11(b) to be met in the most effective and efficient manner possible. The anticipatory and continuous due diligence programs being implemented combine a number of procedures designed both to protect investors by assuring timely and accurate disclosure of corporate information and to recognize the separate legal status of underwriters by providing them the opportunity to perform due diligence.

· · ·

3. Other Concerns

Securities industry commentators also raise concerns relating to institutionalization of the securities markets, the impact on retail distribution, increased concentration in the securities industry and effects on the secondary markets. Specifically, these commentators believe that Rule 415 is accelerating the trends toward institutionalization of the securities markets and concentration in the securities industry. In their view, the Rule is decreasing the number of syndicated offerings in which regional securities firms participate and excluding individual investors from the new issues market.

While the Commission recognizes the existence of these trends, it believes that they reflect economic and other factors apart from shelf registration. These factors include volatile interest rates and markets, the growth of mutual and pension funds which act as intermediaries for individual investors, and the homogenization of the financial services industry. These factors are not necessarily affected by Rule 415. Rule 415 is a procedural rule which presents an optional filing technique. It does not mandate any particular method of distribution. Indeed, many offerings of debt and equity securities registered under the Rule have been sold in traditional syndicated offerings. The Commission therefore believes that these concerns transcend Rule 415.

V. Commission Action

The Commission has considered all views and suggestions with respect to Rule 415. There are several reasons why it may be appropriate to adopt the shelf registration rule in substantially its present form. During the eighteen months the Rule has been in effect, it has worked well and has provided registrants with substantial benefits in their financings. Also, most of the concerns raised transcend shelf registration. On the other hand, the Commission believes that concerns raised about the quality and timing of disclosure and due diligence are important to address because they relate to the adequacy of disclosure investors receive in connection with public offerings. Having weighed all considerations, the Commission is modifying Rule 415 to strike an appropriate balance by making it available for offerings eligible to be registered on Form S-3 or F-3 and for traditional shelf offerings.

The Commission believes that shelf registration should continue to be available for registrants eligible to use short form registration. The integrated disclosure system addresses concerns about the quality and timeliness of disclosure by ensuring that the marketplace is provided with a continuous stream of high quality corporate information about registrants widely followed in the marketplace. Similarly, evolving continuous due diligence practices as described above address concerns about due diligence by enhancing the ability of underwriters to conduct due diligence investigations of widely followed registrants.

The Commission also believes that Rule 415 should continue to be available for traditional primary and secondary shelf offerings. Examples of traditional primary shelf offerings include those where securities are sold to employees, customers or existing shareholders; those involving interests in limited partnerships; those related to acquisitions and other business combinations; and those of securities underlying options, warrants, rights or conversions. The Commission is not aware of any disclosure, due diligence or other concerns having been raised about the registration of these securities on a continuous or delayed basis. Moreover, these types of shelf offerings may only be feasible on a traditional shelf basis.

For registrants not eligible to use short form registration, however, the Commission believes that concerns about disclosure and due diligence outweigh the benefits of Rule 415. The Commission also notes that shelf registration may not be as advantageous for such registrants because they cannot rely on subsequently filed Exchange Act reports for certain updating of the information in the shelf registration statement. Such updating requires the filing of post-effective amendments. Indeed, few non-S-3 or F-3 registrants have used Rule 415 for other than traditional shelf offerings.

VI. Operation of Revised Rule 415

For the reasons stated above, the Commission has determined to limit the availability of Rule 415 to continuous and delayed offerings of securities which may be registered on Form S-3 or F-3 and traditional shelf offerings.

INTEGRATED DISCLOSURE SYSTEM

Disclosure Requirements of the 1933 and 1934 Acts

The cornerstones of the 1933 Securities Act disclosure system are the registration statement, which is filed with the SEC, and the prospectus, which is distributed to potential and actual purchasers. The registration statement contains two main parts. Part I contains the prospectus. Part II contains certain supplemental information that is filed with the SEC and can be reviewed by interested parties.

The contents of the registration statement are specified by §7 of the 1933 Act, by reference to Schedule A of the Act (Schedule B for foreign issuers). Section 7 also authorizes the SEC to require that the registration statement contain such other information and documents as the SEC deems necessary for the protection of investors. Section 10(a)(1) delineates which portion of the material contained in the registration statement is to be included in the prospectus.

Unlike in the past, today any detailed discussion of the disclosure provisions of the 1933 Securities Act must be predicated on an understanding of the basic disclosure provisions of the 1934 Securities Exchange Act. For most of the existence of federal securities law, there was little coordination between the disclosure provisions of the two acts. On the one hand, the 1933 Act has a sporadic reporting system. Although it is potentially applicable to all issuers, it requires disclosure via registration statement and prospectus only when new securities are issued. On the other hand, the 1934 Act envisions continuous reporting by the companies to which it applies, whether they are presently issuing securities or not. A "reporting" company must file with the SEC annual statements (10-K's), quarterly statements (10-Q's), and supplemental statements (8-K's) whenever material changes in the company's status occur. Additionally, such companies are required by Section 14 of the 1934 Act to transmit to shareholders an annual statement that will keep them apprised of the company's progress.

Initially the 1934 Act conferred "reporting company" status on only those corporations with shares listed on the stock exchanges. However, the number of reporting companies was more than doubled in 1964 when the 1934 Act was amended. Today reporting companies, numbering about 10,000, include (1) all companies with a class of securities listed and traded on an exchange (§12(b)); (2) all issuers with total assets over $5 million and a class of securities held of record by 500 or more persons (§12(g)(1)); and (3) all issuers with outstanding securities sold pursuant to a 1933 Act registration statement (§15(d)), though they may end periodic reporting if they cease to have over 300 shareholders and need not provide annual reports because they are not covered by federal proxy rules.

Duplication

Much of the information contained in the 10-K's, 10-Q's, 8-K's, and annual reports to shareholders prepared by reporting companies under the 1934 Act was always similar to information the 1933 Act required of the registration statement and prospectus. Because there was no coordination between the two acts, it was not unusual for a reporting company to be required to report the same information (such as a description of its business or property) in a 1933 Act registration statement, a 10-K, and an annual report to shareholders. Worse still, the information might very well have to be in completely different form for 1933 Act disclosure than for 1934 Act disclosure. Even within the 1934 Act, there were differences. Certain financial statements that were required in annual reports to shareholders had only to be prepared in accordance with GAAP (generally accepted accounting procedures), while the same financial statements required in a 10-K had to comply with the more stringent accounting requirements of SEC Regulation S-X.

In its 1969 Wheat Commission Report, the SEC officially recognized this duplication that corporations had complained of for years. The Commission soon thereafter commenced a program of "integrated disclosure," largely completed by March 1982, aimed at reducing cost and duplication of effort for companies while at the same time preserving essential information for investors. The move toward a unitary disclosure system was made possible by the SEC's recognition that (1) the same basic information is pertinent to an investor's decision to buy, hold, or sell securities, whether a primary issuance under the 1933 Act or secondary trading regulated by the 1934 Act is involved; and (2) the efficient market hypothesis indicates that information filed with the SEC in the 1934 Act reports is analyzed by securities professionals and the financial press and then disseminated and absorbed by the market generally so that there is no need to duplicate the same information in a 1933 Act registration statement.[22]

---

[22] C. Johnson, "Preparation of Registration Statements Under the SEC's Integrated Disclosure System," *Mechanics of Underwriting* (Practising Law Institute, 1983), p. 53.

Critical to the integrated disclosure system was the decision to make Regulation S-K the complete compendium of disclosure requirements applicable to both 1933 and 1934 act filings. No longer must a corporation asked to describe its business operations in a 10-K and a registration statement give different details on different forms according to different instructions. Regulation S-K governs both acts.

Similarly, the disparity in financial reporting was eliminated by including in Regulation S-X the specific content provisions for financial statements required under both acts. For example, financial statements to be included in annual reports to shareholders must now comply with Regulation S-X, although many of the differences between the accounting requirements of Regulation S-X and GAAP have been eliminated.

Additionally, the SEC in 1982 streamlined Regulation C (Rules 400–497), which prescribes regulatory procedures and the general form of the registration statement and the prospectus. The Commission also eliminated a number of "guides" to preparation of registration statements and replaced them with fewer "industry guides" that give additional detail for certain industries (for example, oil and gas and real estate) requiring special attention.

A business wishing to file a registration statement today will select the appropriate form and then fill it out using the guidance of Regulation S-K, Regulation C, and the industry guides, including financial statements prepared in accordance with the prescriptions of Regulation S-X. These forms, which are more like guidelines rather than "fill-in-the-blank"–type forms, are perhaps the most important part of the registration statement preparation, and they were revamped in 1982 as part of the new integrated disclosure system.

Forms in the Integrated Disclosure System

There are now around 14 separate registration statement forms available for use by issuers of new securities under the 1933 Act. The heart of the new integrated disclosure system consists of Forms S-1, S-2, and S-3.

Form S-3

Form S-3 is the embodiment of the SEC's recognition of the efficient market hypothesis. Traditionally, a registration statement contained two basic types of information. First, it contained information about the registrant—its financial conditions, its management, its business and property, and so on. Second, it contained information about the specific transaction—type of securities being issued, amount, plan of distribution, contemplated use of proceeds, and so on.

Form S-3 allows reporting companies to limit their registration statement and prospectus to the transaction-related information about the issuance. The information about the registrant is already on file with the SEC in 10-K's, 10-Q's, 8-K's, and other 1934 Act filings. According to the efficient market hypothesis, that information has already been disseminated to the market by professional analysts and the financial press. Form S-3 allows the registrant to incorporate this information into the registration statement and prospectus by simply referring to the 1934 Act filings. Even documents filed pursuant to the 1934 Act *after* the registration statement was filed are deemed incorporated by reference into that statement and the prospectus (which is very handy for shelf registrants).

An issuer qualifies for use of Form S-3 if

1. It is organized in the United States with its principal place of business here.
2. It has a class of securities registered under §12(b) or §12(g)(1) of the 1934 Act or is required to file reports pursuant to §15(d).
3. It has been subject to these 1934 Act filing requirements for at least 36 months and has filed in a timely fashion during the last 12 months.
4. Neither the issuer nor any of its subsidiaries has failed to make a preferred dividend or sinking fund payment or defaulted on payment of any indebtedness or long-term rental agreement since the end of the fiscal year for which the last 10-K was filed.

These requirements are calculated to ensure that only major corporations that have continually filed substantial information with the SEC and that have undoubtedly received the attention of professional analysts and the financial press may use incorporation by reference.

A qualified issuer may use the Form S-3 for only specified types of transactions:

1. A primary or secondary offering of debt or equity securities, if
   a. The issuer has ''float'' (market value of the issuer's voting stock held by nonaffiliates) of at least $150 million, or
   b. The issuer has ''float'' of at least $100 million and a total trading volume of at least 3 million shares during a recent 12-month period.
2. A primary offering for cash of nonconvertible debt securities or preferred stock rated by one of four recognized rating agencies as being of ''investment grade.''
3. Any secondary offering (e.g., an offering of securities in the hands of major shareholders) of a security either listed on an exchange or quoted on NASDAQ.
4. Conversions, dividend reinvestment plans, rights offerings, or other types of distributions involving existing shareholders.

Only one S-3 registration statement in nine is reviewed by the SEC.

Form S-2

Form S-2 allows some incorporation by reference, but not as much as Form S-3. It allows an issuer to choose between using a full prospectus or furnishing business and financial information about itself by *delivering*, along with a limited prospectus containing transaction-related information, copies of the latest annual report to shareholders and any quarterly shareholder report or 10-Q subsequently filed. The issuer must also incorporate by reference its latest 10-K and subsequently filed SEC reports. In practice, most issuers have chosen to use a full prospectus rather than to deliver the shareholder reports because of the legal burden such delivery places on underwriters (who may then become liable for any inaccurate statements contained in those reports).

Form S-2 is available to issuers who meet the registrant requirements for Form

S-3 (domestic reporting company for 36 months), but who do not meet any of the transactional requirements. Thus, to the extent that Form S-2 is used for primary securities offerings, it is available for the smaller reporting companies that are not large enough to meet the "float" requirements of Form S-3.

Form S-1

Form S-1 is the full-blown registration form for companies that have not been reporting companies for at least 36 months. Incorporation by reference is not appropriate for such companies, which are frequently making their initial public offering. Because information about such entities has not permeated the market, Form S-1 requires a complete registration statement and prospectus in accordance with Regulations S-K and S-X.

Regulation S-K requires, inter alia, a description of the issuer's property (Item 102), legal proceedings pending against the issuer (Item 103), the market price and dividends of the issuer's common stock (Item 201), selected financial data for the past five years (Item 301), management's analysis of the issuer's financial condition and results of operations (Item 303), the issuer's directors and executive officers (Item 401), the issuer's compensation of and transactions with directors and officers (Item 402), major shareholders (Item 403), risk factors and ratios of earnings to fixed charges (Item 503), use of proceeds (Item 504), dilution of shareholder interest (Item 507), and the plan of distribution (Item 508).

Companies engaged in their initial public offering must explain how the offering price was determined (Item 505). This will usually involve consideration of such matters as the issuer's operating history, quality of management, competition in the industry, and general securities market conditions.

Other Forms

While Forms S-1, -2, -3 are the core of the present 1933 Act disclosure system, other forms exist for specific purposes. For example, Form S-4 was recently promulgated to allow integrated disclosure in certain corporate combinations where one company issues its shares to the shareholders of a target company in exchange for the shares of the target. Form S-8 is used for offering shares to an issuer's employees pursuant to an employee benefit plan, and Form S-11 is used for real estate venture offerings.

Form S-18, adopted in 1979,[23] encourages small companies to raise small amounts of capital and gradually blend into the 1934 Act reporting system without filing a full-blown S-1. The S-18 form is available to companies raising less than its $7.5 million limit. Small companies using it, frequently for their initial public offering, make similar but less detailed disclosures than those required by the S-1. Furthermore, the S-18 can be filed either at the SEC's Washington, D.C. office, where the other forms are filed, or in the appropriate SEC regional office where the processing time may be shorter.

---

[23] *Securities Act Release*, no. 6049 (April 3, 1979).

The S-18 quickly became very popular. In 1979 it was used to raise $45 million and largely displaced the S-1 as the primary registration statement form for small companies' initial public offerings. Part of the reason for its popularity was that the S-18 reduced the mean registration costs from $106,188 for the S-1 to $91,453.[24]

Special Disclosure Issues

Projections and Other Forward-Looking Information

For many years the SEC prohibited inclusion in 1933 and 1934 act disclosure documents of any "soft" information consisting of management projections of future economic performance. Eventually, however, it dawned on the Commission that such projections were among the most useful information that investors could have. Therefore, in Rule 175 of the 1933 Act, the SEC created a "safe harbor" for forward-looking statements. These projections will not be deemed fraudulent unless it is shown they were "made or reaffirmed without a reasonable basis or . . . disclosed other than in good faith."

The safe harbor applies to forward-looking statements in 1934 Act filings (allowed but not required) and to information relating to the effects of changing prices on the business enterprise and management's discussion of financial conditions and resulting operations pursuant to Items 302 and 303 of Regulation S-K. The rule defines "forward-looking statement" to include (1) projections of revenues, income, losses, earnings per share, capital expenditures, and dividends; (2) statements of management's plans and objectives for future operations; and (3) Item 303 management discussions of financial conditions and results of operations. Projections of specific future market prices for the issuer's shares are still forbidden.

Of course, an issuer will have a duty to correct any projection that it subsequently learns was materially erroneous.

Risk Factors

The prospectus has been termed a schizophrenic document. On the one hand, it is a selling document that should include the positive aspects of the issuer and its securities to encourage purchases. On the other hand, it is also an insurance policy in that it discloses the negative aspects so that the purchasers cannot later sue for fraud on grounds that they were misled by overly optimistic statements.

Many have argued that the SEC disclosure policy has caused issuers to be so cautious in limiting their positive statements and so thorough in disclosing their negative aspects that the prospectus is virtually worthless as a selling document. How can an investor choose between two investment opportunities when both sound equally dismal? Indeed, one lawyer the SEC sought to enjoin from filing too optimistic a registration statement later filed one containing these statements:

---

[24] Securities and Exchange Commission, *Form S-18: A Monitoring Report on Its Use in 1979* (1980).

"The present directors do not foresee the possibility of the corporation ever being in a position to pay any dividends or having any assets of determinable value. The continued existence of the corporation is questionable. Bankruptcy may result at any time."
"Anyone considering purchase of this security must be prepared for immediate and total loss."
"No representation is made that the possibility exists that the corporation can continue to exist."

The SEC refused to file the document on grounds that it was not a serious attempt to register securities, and a court later agreed.[25] Among the required disclosures that makes the prospectus so negative are the "risk factors." Item 503(c) of Regulation S-K requires disclosure on the first page after the cover page of the prospectus of the main factors that "make the offer speculative or one of high risk," including the absence of an operating history, recent unprofitability, precarious financial condition, lack of prior market for the issuer's shares, and so on.

Environmental and Other Legal Proceedings

In the 1970s environmental groups pressured the SEC to utilize disclosure rules under the 1933 and 1934 acts to preserve the environment. The SEC contemplated whether to require companies to disclose when their activities were not in compliance with any federal environmental standard. Instead, it decided to require disclosure only of material estimated capital expenditures for environmental control facilities.[26]

Today, Item 103 of Regulation S-K governs. Instructions to Item 103 state that a registrant need not disclose most lawsuits filed against it so long as the primary claim for damages does not exceed 10% of its current assets. Notwithstanding this, administrative or judicial proceedings brought against the issuer under federal, state, or local environmental laws must be described if (1) the proceeding is material to the business or financial condition of the registrant, (2) the proceeding involves potential damages or sanctions exceeding 10% of the current asset value of the registrant, or (3) a government authority is party to the suit that involves potential monetary sanctions, unless the registrant reasonably believes that the sanctions will amount to less than $100,000.

"Materiality"

The forms, regulations, rules, and industry guides of the 1933 Act are very helpful in the drafting of the registration statement and prospectus. However, they are only the starting point. Drafters of these rules cannot foresee every situation that might bear on creation of a document that truly informs the investing public. Therefore, the issuer must include not only all information specifically required by the law but also all "material" facts necessary to make the registration statement and prospectus not misleading.

---

[25] *Holmes* v. *Cary*, 234 F.Supp. 23 (N.D. Ga. 1964).
[26] *Securities Act Release*, no. 5704 (May 6, 1976).

A fact is "material" if "there is a substantial likelihood that a reasonable shareholder [or potential purchaser] would consider it important." [27] The following case illustrates a classic situation in which a registration statement and prospectus were deemed misleading.

IN THE MATTER OF DOMAN HELICOPTERS, INC.

41 S.E.C. 431 (1963)

Doman Helicopters, Inc. (registrant), was organized in 1945 to develop inventions in the field of helicopter rotor construction. Between 1945 and 1963, Doman engaged in no substantial manufacturing activity and never earned a profit. Except for one early experimental model sold in 1950, two prototype helicopter models delivered to the Army in 1956 and 1957 (both of which were subsequently repurchased by registrant), and one on loan to its Italian licensee, Doman had never made or sold any helicopters despite numerous unsuccessful attempts to sell to the military and to commercial users.

Doman frequently flirted on the edges of bankruptcy, and issued stock to pay employees and creditors. From its inception to September 30, 1961, registrant's sales amounted to only $2,044,417, of which $595,952 was derived from the sale of the two prototype helicopters to the Army. The remaining sales came from minor contracts to make such things as Navy missile containers, steel cabinets for the Army, and plastic-laminated bowling alley gutters. Doman's losses through September 30, 1961, amounted to $5,715,076. As of January 31, 1962, its current liabilities amounted to $392,446 as against current assets of only $13,178.

On April 19, 1962, Doman filed a registration statement with the SEC, proposing a public offering of 681,971 shares, some to be offered to existing shareholders, some to creditors, and some to the public. Doman's future plans were predicated on a proposed helicopter, the D-10B.

The SEC instituted a proceeding under §8(d) of the 1933 Act to determine whether a stop order should issue suspending the effectiveness of the registration statement.

FINDING AND OPINION OF THE COMMISSION:

Deficiencies in the Registration Statement

1. Status and Prospects of the Model D-10B

The prospectus describes the D-10B as though it were an existing and operational helicopter possessing superiority in specified respects over other helicopters offered on the market.

. . .

There is no adequate factual foundation for the foregoing statements, and they were false and misleading.

The D-10B has never been flown or tested

---

[27] *TSC Industries, Inc.* v. *Northway, Inc.*, 426 U.S. 438 (1976).

or even assembled in prototype form, crucial facts which are nowhere disclosed in the registration statement. Certain of the performance claims made for the D-10B were derived from tests on a model LZ-5 equipped with blades proposed for the D-10B, from engineering extrapolations and from data published in manufacturers' figures on engines. The unexplained reference to "test data" in the prospectus conveys the false impression that the tests were on the D-10B itself.

. . .

In view of the embryonic state of the D-10B there was clearly no justification for the claim of superior operating economy of registrant's "product" or for describing it as "the most attractive commercial machine being offered in the world today by considerable margins." Moreover, there is no evidence that the D-10B has ever been offered to customers, and at the oral argument Doman stated no such offers have been made. Under these circumstances inclusion in the prospectus of the statement that registrant "is quoting" at the $110,000 price was also highly deceptive, implying as it did that there was available for sale a fully developed helicopter possessing in fact the features attributed to it in the prospectus.

In light of the nascent and uncertificated status of the D-10B, registrant's past lack of success in obtaining military contracts, its limited resources and existing financial condition, and the presence of competitors who enjoy the benefits and strength derived from major government contracts, registrant's representation that it planned "to gear its sales and service activities to a goal of 10 percent of the United States market" conveyed a materially misleading impression of (i) the registrant's ability, financial and other, to establish a sales and service organization on such a scale and (ii) the prospects that the D-10B would be so favorably received by prospective purchasers.

The use of the specific market percentage goal implied that there was some sound and realistic basis for anticipating its attainability. That misleading implication was not negated, but was rather enhanced, by the selection of a percentage figure that perhaps was not patently excessive and the qualification that there was no assurance that the stated goal would be attainable.

2. The Doman Hingeless Rotor System

The prospectus makes the following claims for the so-called "Doman Hingeless Rotor System": "In comparison with other devices, this system provides greater inherent stability in forward flight, less vibration in any flight attitude or maneuver, long life for the rotor and blade assembly, relatively low initial and maintenance costs and exceptional permissible range of the center of gravity of the fuselage and its cargo." It then goes on to say that "The Doman system, as far as is known, is the only fully developed and proven helicopter design concept which does not involve the use of blade-hinges in any way. This system has been completely engineered and flight tested over 14 years for thousands of hours in the air. . . ." Under a separate subcaption entitled "Patents" the prospectus implies that this system is protected by an elaborate patent structure.

These representations present in their totality a misleading picture of uniqueness and substantiated superiority of the Doman rotor system. That system has been used only on a few converted or prototype models. No production model using the Doman rotor system has ever been subjected to normal day to day usage by a user or customer. In such circumstances the unqualified claims as to superior durability and lower maintenance costs were not warranted, and it was deceptive to describe the system as "fully developed and proven."

In addition, although the prospectus placed

great emphasis on the importance of the hinge-less feature of the Doman rotor system as resulting in superior helicopter performance, registrant has conceded in the stipulation that hingelessness is not in itself meaningful and that the discussion of that subject in the prospectus was incomplete. Nor was the hingeless feature exclusive with registrant's rotor system. Registrant's patents do not preclude others from developing hingeless rotor systems, and in fact, two other companies have such systems under development.

3. Efforts to Secure Defense Contracts

The prospectus makes only a passing reference to the fact that registrant unsuccessfully attempted to secure a military market for its helicopters. It does not disclose the nature of those attempts or of the action of the Department of Defense with respect to them. Registrant had from 1951 to 1962, made strenuous and persistent efforts to interest that Department in its proposals and devices. The Department made a number of tests with the two prototype helicopters that it purchased from the registrant and made an extensive study of the Doman rotor system. It found "no significant advantages in the Doman rotor system over other types," and those findings were reaffirmed upon successive reviews following objections raised by registrant.

· · ·

We need not and do not pass upon the merits of registrant's attempt to impeach the validity of the findings of the Department of Defense, although we do note that the record before us does not show that the Department's findings were the result of any bias or incompetence. Irrespective of the correctness of the Department's conclusions, they constitute a determination by the technical staff and responsible authorities of the largest single purchaser of helicopters that for their purposes registrant's rotor system

has no special merit. Such determination was a significant adverse factor, and the failure to disclose it rendered the prospectus misleading.

4. Application of Proceeds

The prospectus stated that the proceeds of the offering would be used to develop the D-10B, but failed to state the order of priority in which the proceeds would be applied as required by Instruction 2 to Item 3 of Form S-1. The prospectus did not adequately disclose that except to the extent that the creditors to whom part of the offering is to be made elected to take stock in exchange for their debt claims, $292,466 of the proceeds from the public offering would first have to be applied to the liquidation of registrant's outstanding indebtedness, thereby reducing and perhaps exhausting the funds that the prospectus stated would be allocated to the D-10B. It also failed to disclose that approximately $13,000 of the estimated proceeds would have to be used to pay the accrued salaries of certain officers and directors, and that a large portion of the proceeds would have to be used to meet current expenses, which were being incurred at the rate of $11,000 per month, and would be used for that purpose even if the proceeds of the offering were insufficient to permit registrant to go forward with its D-10B program.

5. Dilution Aspects of Offering

The prospectus fails to disclose the dilution aspects of the offering. As of January 31, 1962, registrant's shares had a book value of minus 30 cents per share. If all of the shares that the registrant proposes to offer to its existing stockholders and to its creditors were in fact sold at the proposed offering prices, that book value would increase to 55 cents per share. Purchasers paying $1.50 per share would therefore suffer an immediate dilution of 95 cents per share the benefit of which will inure entirely to the present stockholders. It was pertinent to an informed appraisal by the persons to whom the securities being offered may be sold that this dilution be described in the prospectus.

· · ·

6. Speculative Features of the Offering

The prospectus included, under a section headed "The Company," a summary of registrant's poor financial history, a statement that registrant is now insolvent, and a summary of the S.A.A.S. contract. However, no disclosure was made of the facts that there was no D-10B in existence and that the Department of Defense had found no special merit in registrant's rotor system, or of the dilution aspects of the offering.

We have repeatedly held that a registration statement with respect to an offering of speculative securities must make the risk characteristics of the securities plainly evident to the ordinary investor and that this can be done only when all of those characteristics are described in one place at an early point in the prospectus under an appropriate caption. The prospectus, by failing to refer to the highly important adverse factors we have noted, presented an incomplete and distorted portrayal of the complex of risk elements involved. In the circumstances it was essential that the speculative aspects of registrant's business and the dilution aspects of the offering be set forth and described concisely and lucidly at the very outset of the prospectus under an appropriate caption, directing attention to the fact that special risks are present. The heading "The Company" used in the prospectus did not serve that purpose.

· · ·

Other Matters

Registrant concedes that the registration statement is deficient but argues that no stop order is warranted because this was a mere "pre-liminary filing" which it always intended to amend, and because the deficiencies are not of sufficient gravity to warrant a stop order. Registrant also moved to dismiss the proceedings on the ground that they were prematurely brought because the Division did not send it a letter of comment or otherwise communicate its views with respect to the deficiencies and afford registrant an opportunity to submit a curative amendment. We find no merit in either contention.

The statutory scheme does not recognize the "preliminary filing" concept that registrant now asks us to sanction nor any right to receive a letter of comment. If registrants are to be permitted to disclose as much or as little as they see fit without regard to the statutory mandate of full disclosure in their initial filings, on the theory that deficiencies can always be cured by amendment, effective administration of the Act will become impossible. The letter of comment is an informal administrative aid developed by us for the purpose of assisting those registrants who have conscientiously attempted to comply with the Act. The burden of seeing to it that a registration statement filed with us neither includes any untrue statement of a material fact nor omits to state any material fact required to be stated therein or necessary to make the facts therein not misleading always rests on the registrant itself, and it never shifts to our staff. When the Division has reason to believe that a registrant has failed to make a proper effort to shoulder this burden, it is its duty to bring such information to our attention and to recommend that we proceed in accordance with Section 8(d) of the Act.

Registrant further asks us to deem its registration statement to have been superseded by an amended registration statement that it filed after the hearings had been begun. We have on occasion in the exercise of our discretion considered assertedly curative substantive amendments filed after the institution of a stop order proceeding. But we do so only where it appears that such consideration will be in the best interest of investors and of the public. This is not such a case. Here the deficiencies were serious, a large amount of registrant's stock is outstanding in the hands of approximately 8,000 public investors, and the misleading information in the registration statement has been a matter of public record on which investors may have relied. The registrant has not, so far as the record discloses, undertaken to disseminate to its stockholders or to public investors generally information which would adequately advise them of the misleading character of the information contained in the registration statement. In such circumstances the issuance of a stop order is essential for the protection of public investors in order to dispel the misleading information publicized by the filing of the registration statement.

. . .

A stop order will issue.

"Integrity of Management"

The rules and cases discussed to this point demonstrate that the concept of materiality is primarily an economic one. A fact is material if it relates to the economic value of the security being bought, sold, or held.

In the post-Watergate days of the 1970s, however, the SEC gave some indication that it would require corporations to disclose the illegal activities of their officers and directors even if those illegal acts did not have a quantitatively material impact on the companies' economic status. Some courts adopted this view, which was predicated on the notion that all shareholders had a right to know when there was reason to doubt the integrity of corporate management.

For example, in *SEC* v. *Joseph Schlitz Brewing Co.*,[28] the SEC sued Schlitz for failing to disclose (1) a kickback scheme wherein retailers of beer and malt beverages had been illegally paid $3 million to buy Schlitz products and (2) its participating in violations of Spanish tax and exchange laws in connection with transactions with certain Spanish corporations. Although the bribes amounted to only three-tenths of 1% of Schlitz' annual $1 billion in sales, the judge stated, "I believe that the question of the integrity of management gives materiality to the matters the Commission claims should have been disclosed." Thus, the judge rejected Schlitz' argument that it should prevail because no law specifically required a corporation to report its involvement in activities that at some future time might be adjudicated illegal.

Most courts, however, rejected the notion that the disclosure provisions of the securities laws should be used to force corporate management to police its own antisocial activities regardless of whether they had an economic impact on the corporation.[29] More recently, the SEC itself appears to have abandoned the "integrity of management"

---

[28] 452 F.Supp. 824 (E.D. Wis. 1978).

[29] For example, *Gaines* v. *Haughton*, 645 F.2d 761 (9th Cir. 1981); *Amalgamated Clothing Workers Union* v. *J. P. Stevens*, 475 F.Supp. 328 (S.D. N.Y. 1979).

standard of materiality. For example, in 1981 Citicorp failed to disclose that it had violated certain foreign banking laws. The payments involved were found to be only one-twentieth of 1% of Citicorp's earnings, certainly not material in any economic sense. Amid some public outcry, the Commission elected not to proceed against Citicorp, prompting one author to term the case "the definitive abandonment of the commission's post-Watergate adventure and [a] return to the principles that governed the SEC in the first 40 years of its existence." [30]

In an attempt to clarify SEC policy, the SEC's director of enforcement made the following statement: [31]

> Law enforcement action where there is a failure to disclose *illegal corporate or management behavior* is an important part of the effort against fraud by reporting companies. I will address five propositions in this area.
>
> First, the Commission should begin enforcement actions where failure to disclose unlawful conduct violates traditional quantitative standards of materiality. Illegal conduct may have material adverse economic consequences for a corporation that reasonable investors would consider important in making investment or voting decisions. Moreover, conduct that violates federal, state, or foreign law, may be, but is not necessarily material information affecting investors.
>
> *Second*, the Commission should initiate enforcement actions where there is a failure to disclose self-dealing or conflict-of-interest transactions. Shareholders have a special interest in information relating to the loyalty and honesty of directors and senior officers in their dealings with the corporation to which they owe a fiduciary duty.
>
> *Third*, the Commission should commence enforcement actions where there is a failure to disclose information mandated by the disclosure requirements of the Commission's rules for proxy materials, periodic reports, or registration statements—particularly facts about director or senior officer conduct. By its enforcement efforts, the Commission must preserve the integrity of the line item disclosure requirements.
>
> *Fourth*, the Commission should begin enforcement actions when untrue statements of material facts are made or statements are rendered misleading by the omission of material facts. Issuers must be held accountable for materially misleading statements in disclosure documents.
>
> *Fifth*, absent the foregoing circumstances, the Commission generally should not utilize the antifraud provisions of the securities laws for law enforcement where there is a failure to disclose conduct which may be considered qualitatively material. The antifraud provisions of the securities laws work well in the area of quantitative materiality because disclosure and enforcement decisions can be related to the benchmarks of earnings, assets, or liabilities. There also are guideposts in the other areas I have mentioned.
>
> In contrast, there are no benchmarks of general application in the area of qualitative materiality. The Commission has not promulgated line item disclosure requirements relating to all illegal conduct or, to the extent necessary, articulated a policy for law enforcement where information about such conduct has not been disclosed. Therefore, corporations do not have the procedural benefit of a rule specifying what type of unethical, antisocial, or illegal conduct may be deemed material by the Commission. Significant uncertainties and potential liabilities exist.

---

[30] M. V. Freeman, "The SEC and the Citicorp Case: The Legal Issue of Materiality," *National Law Journal*, November 15, 1982, p. 20.

[31] J. Fedders, "Fedders Explanation of Approach on Materiality," *Legal Times of Washington*, November 29, 1982, p. 17.

. . .

The Commission should exercise care and circumspection when determining whether failure to disclose qualitative information violates the antifraud provisions of the securities laws. Each action in this area should be consistent with prior disclosure standards articulated by the Commission or the courts. Each determination to initiate an enforcement action must be based on the facts of that case. The touchstone is whether there is a substantial likelihood that a reasonable investor would consider the information important enough to alter the total mix of information made available.

Criticisms of the Disclosure System

Although the move to an integrated disclosure system has been widely praised, many criticisms that challenge basic assumptions of this system remain. Congress and the SEC remain firmly committed to the 1933 and 1934 Act disclosure system in at least some form resembling its present one. Still, it is appropriate to conclude this section with excerpts from two thought-provoking criticisms of that system.

THE MYTH OF THE INFORMED LAYMAN *

Homer Kripke

Business Lawyer, Vol. 28 (1973), p. 631

[The SEC] has never admitted any hypothesis other than that the prospectus is intended for the man in the street, the unsophisticated lay investor. My theme is that the theory that the prospectus can be and is used by the lay investor is a myth. It is largely responsible for the fact that the securities prospectus is fairly close to worthless.

The Securities Act was sold to the Congress on the theory that securities are "intricate merchandise," and there is no doubt that this is so. They are becoming more intricate all the time.

We have novel packages of securities, like units of a bond or convertible debenture plus a stock or a warrant—"funny money," as we were saying a few years ago. We have particular companies with very sophisticated tax positions: now again the investment tax credit, percentage depletion, tax loss carry forwards, tax-sheltered distributions other than from earnings and profits.

We have the fact that many of the companies coming to market are very high technology companies. No layman could really understand either the products or their technical competitive positions; nor could even an expert get a solid understanding as long as disclosure is circumscribed by the push to make the prospectus short and readable for the layman.

Accounting, the basic mechanism of financial disclosure, is getting more complicated all the time. Professor Chambers, the Australian who lectured in the United States a few years ago, computed that a net income statement might represent one out of a million possible variations in the treatment of accounting items. While the Accounting Principles Board has limited the number of choices, a large number of choices do exist as to reporting the amount of the net income of a corporation.

Thus, securities have become increasingly intricate, just as other fields of knowledge have become intricate. In the law and medicine, we recognize the need for specialties.

Securities selection, too, has become a specialty, with two new professions, the profession of financial analyst and the profession of portfolio manager.

Yet the SEC goes on the theory that in the selection of investments from the numerous offerings of this very intricate merchandise, a simple readable prospectus on one company will enable the man in the street to make a wise choice between one company and the thousands of others about which no one may be telling him anything.

This myth that it is the layman to whom the prospectus is addressed permeates the SEC's concept of disclosure. It limits the usefulness of disclosure to those who should be its proper objective, the sophisticated investor and professional through whom information ought to filter down to the layman.

In the first place, the myth recognizes that the man in the street would not read a technical prospectus. Therefore it requires that the prospectus be made short and readable, no matter how much length might be realistically necessary in a prospectus to give a proper picture of a complex company.

Second, the myth forces the SEC into requiring emphasis on risk features of the offering with a simplicity that is sometimes less than a full picture. It requires a statement of the speculative aspects of a security, typically a statement that the management put in only a few dollars and is keeping a large percentage of the stock, while the public is asked to put in a large number of dollars and will get a small percentage of the stock. Because this kind of disclosure has never had its expected impact, the SEC now apparently assumes that the layman will not read or cannot read, and it has proposed that the prospectus draw pictures for him—bar charts or pie charts—so that the investor does not have to read but merely look.

· · ·

We find oversimplification for the layman working in many other fields of SEC law. The myth forces the Commission to forbid the disclosure in a prospectus of estimated values that might exist in excess of cost, e.g., in real estate, for fear that the lay investor could not be properly skeptical of an appraisal. The same myth induces the SEC to conceal potential mineral values, both oil and ore minerals, if they don't meet the Commission's concept of proven or probable minerals, for fear that the layman could not appraise, for instance, such information as the fact that oil has been discovered on the adjoining parcel of land. We read again and again in statements of Commission spokesmen that once the Commission permits something to be said in a document filed with the Commission, there is a danger that the investor will accept these assertions as gospel truth, despite all the disclaimers on the first page.

But this concern is only for the lay investor, not the professional who would be grateful for the opportunity to receive value estimates, and to consider them skeptically.

The same myth must be at least part of the motivation that has caused the Commission over many years to freeze accounting, the heart of financial disclosure, on the basis of historical cost instead of moving toward accounting recognition of values, as many accountants and economists are advocating.

These factors have pushed the SEC into a perpetually negativistic, pessimistic approach. The prospectuses of the real estate investment trusts, coming out today one after another in rapid succession, all read the same way. Each one has a list of 50 items, more or less, in the business of the company on which cold water is thrown. Each prospectus is such a tale of potential calamity that none of them does a proper job of disclosing the really serious risk that ought to be emphasized but is submerged in this tale of woe—the very substantial risk necessarily involved in construction financing, plus the risk that the take-out commitment might not be earned or might not eventuate.

We could parody all prospectuses of promotional companies in one sentence: "Our competition is too much for us, and no representation is made that we will stay out of bankruptcy after the closing date." A prospectus loses its effect if every prospectus cries "wolf" all the time.

THE SEC AND CORPORATE DISCLOSURE: A PROGRAM BY THE ABA COMMITTEE ON FEDERAL REGULATION OF SECURITIES *

A. A. Sommer, Jr.

36 Business Lawyer, Vol. 36 (1980), p. 119

Probably the first significant critic was George Stigler, who, in an article in 1964 which became the subject of fierce controversy among economists, suggested that the disclosures which had been mandated under the 1933 Act probably had very little impact, if any, in preventing fraud upon investors. He came to this conclusion via economic and statistical studies. He was immediately taken to task by a number of people who contended that his methodology and his conclusions were wrong.

Thereafter, George Benston at the University of Rochester began saying, in effect, "If you think the 1933 Act is bad, you ought to see what is happening under the 1934 Act." His principal contention was that the 1934 Act had not mandated any disclosures that really were useful to investors. Through a series of articles he elaborated that theme, again eliciting from others severe criticism and a considerable contest.

At the same time, a number of theories were being developed with regard to the markets, the economics of information and the manner in which stock prices reacted to various kinds of events. Let me summarize them.

The first one arose about 1959 and was really a revival of a theory that had been discussed back in the early part of the century in a somewhat different context: the so-called "random walk" theory. It is simple—the price of a security yesterday does not say anything about the price of the security today or tomorrow. Anyone who has followed the securities markets is readily willing to accept that and it appears to be fairly well accepted among economists today. Nonetheless, the chartists continue to make a lot of money selling charts that say if the Dow-Jones Averages are interpreted properly, "shoulders" and "heads" and various other things will appear; indeed, there are patterns, they say, in the movements of stock prices and money can be made from an awareness of them, despite all the statistical evidence to the contrary.

The random walk theory is generally regarded as the weak form of the "efficient market hypothesis." Most of the discussion about "portfolio" theory in recent years has at least started with the efficient market hypothesis. The medium-strong form of the efficient market hypothesis says simply that the market price of a security at any time has been affected by all of the publicly available information. The people who are making investments day to day, preeminently the analysts, take all available information and very quickly assimilate it in their judgment making process. That judgment eventuates in a buy, sell or hold decision. The price at any moment will reflect this myriad of judgments being made by informed investors; therefore, there is no way that the market can consistently be beaten by superior analysis of publicly available information and the exercise that analysts go through is essentially futile.

The strong form of the efficient market hypothesis says that not only is the price of a security affected by publicly available information, but also "inside" information, so that even insiders cannot make money with their inside information. I do not believe many people accept the strong form these days, although it is still discussed.

Out of all this there came other theories, e.g., the "capital asset pricing model" which Markowitz began to elaborate in the 1950s. The "modern portfolio" theory tried to distinguish between systematic and unsystematic risk and said that one area of risk could be eliminated simply by diversification. The information about a particular company was not as critical as the "betas" of securities. The "beta" of a security was the measure of it in relation to the market as a whole. A security with a beta over one generally moved up faster when the market was moving up than the market itself, and it also fell faster when the market was falling. If the beta was less than one, the opposite was the effect: the security moved up and down more slowly. This theory suggested that you decided the average beta (i.e., risk) you wanted in your portfolio; and then you simply selected securities that produced that average beta. It did not make any difference whether they were in the steel business, the automotive business, or the chemical business. What mattered was the beta.

These theories have become part and parcel of every analyst's equipment regardless of whether he intellectually accepts the consequences of the efficient market hypothesis.

This has led, I think, and quite rightly, as Homer [Kripke] points out in his book [*The SEC and Corporate Disclosure: Regulation in Search of a Purpose* (1979)] to a reevaluation of the importance of information about individual companies. Some analysts will contend that data regarding individual companies constitutes less than 20 percent of the data that they use in making investment decisions; they are more concerned with market movements as a whole and industry trends. Homer in his book, suggests that "firm specific" information may run as high as 40 percent of the data content of a manager's judgment. In any event, I believe it is generally accepted today that industry and macroeconomic data, such as newspaper reports about the President's antiinflation program, in the aggregate are probably more important in market decisions than firm specific information.

EDGAR

One innovation in disclosure that many applaud is EDGAR, or electronic data gathering and retrieval. The SEC is seeking to streamline its review and analytical process by having prospectuses, 10-K's, 10-Q's, and other such documents filed via computer over the phone lines. This system promises eventually to make almost instantaneous the flow of information from corporations to the SEC to the investing public. Ultimately, anyone with a home computer terminal should be able to gain easy access to the 110,000 reports (presently consisting of 4 million pages of paper) filed with the SEC each year.

STATE REGISTRATION PROVISIONS

Types of Regulation

The Uniform Securities Act gives three choices for registration. A state may choose any type or a combination.[32]

---

[32] *See, generally,* H. Sowards and N. Hirsch, *Blue Sky Regulation* (New York: Matthew Bender, 1982).

Notice Registration

Registration by notification is outlined in §302 of the Uniform Securities Act. Adopted by almost 30 states, this type of registration is available to companies that (1) have been in continuous operation for five years, (2) have not defaulted on interest or preferred dividend payments for at least three years, and (3) have average net earnings of 5% of the amount of outstanding securities during the previous five years.

Under this procedure, an issuer need only file certain basic information plus a copy of its prospectus or sales literature. Unless the state securities administrator takes action, the registration statement will become effective at 3:00 P.M. EST on the second full business day after filing.

Registration by notification is usually reserved for high-quality securities.

As with most Uniform Securities Act provisions, it must be remembered that the individual states frequently alter the language of the act.

Registration by Coordination

Section 303 of the U.S.A., adopted by a majority of states, is used when an issuer has also registered with the SEC. To avoid duplication, the issuer can simply file with the state the information already filed with the SEC. The state registration statement will become effective automatically when the federal registration statement does, if (1) no stop order is filed or is in effect, (2) it has been on file for at least ten days in the state, and (3) a statement of the maximum and minimum offering prices and maximum underwriter discount has been on file with the state for at least two days.

Registration by Qualification

Section 304 of the U.S.A., adopted in over 40 states, provides for registration by qualification. This is a complicated, demanding form of registration. Section 304 has 17 subsections (reduced in number by several states) specifying information and documents that must accompany each application for registration. Such a registration statement becomes effective when the state administrator so orders.

Merit Regulation

While the federal approach to securities regulation is content to require only disclosure so that investors can make up their own minds, over 30 states go farther. These states use "merit regulation," believing that it takes expertise, sophistication, and other elements, as well as disclosure, to protect the investor adequately.

Typically such state "merit regulation" statutes contain a number of criteria that can lead a state administrator to conclude that the offering is not "fair and equitable" so that registration should be denied or the offering withdrawn. These grounds include, inter alia (1) excessive sales commissions and offering expenses, (2) promoters holding substantial amounts of securities purchased at well below the public offering price, (3) unreasonable amounts of stock options and warrants held by insiders, (4) offering price unreasonable in relation to established market price, (5) diluted voting power for public investors, and (6) inadequate equity investment by insiders.

States also can deny registration on grounds of inadequate or misleading disclosures.

Recently there has been an assault on the concept of merit regulation in several states. Many believe that the policy of disclosure is adequate to protect investors and that merit regulation is costly, time consuming, and unnecessary. Others point out that a large percentage of offerings that states have refused to register were registered with the SEC and to studies that indicate that issuers that have been approved in merit regulation states have proved to be better investments than have those whose offerings were not approved.[33] At this writing, the debate continues.[34]

In fact, the merit regulation debate has been continued into the promulgation in 1985 of a revised Uniform Securities Act. The members of the National Conference of Commissioners on Uniform State Laws expressed their preference for elimination of merit review, but used brackets in the act to indicate that states could use merit regulation if they wished. The revised act contains other controversial features, including a new requirement that initial public offerings be registered with the states even if they are listed or approved for listing on national exchanges. It is too early to tell how widely the revised act will be accepted.

QUESTIONS AND PROBLEMS

1. A report concerning a registrant had been prepared by an engineering firm for use by prospective underwriters. The report contained a five-year projection of earnings. Copies were also made available, during the waiting period, to broker-dealers, to sales representatives who would be engaged in the offering and sale of the securities, and to certain investors. One broker-dealer firm had made available to sales reps excerpts from the report. Did distribution of this report go beyond acceptable pre-effective publicity? Discuss. See *Securities Act Release*, no. 3844 (October 8, 1957).

2. Should the SEC allow an issuer in a Rule 134 advertisement to include a logo, corporate symbol or trademark, or an attention-getting headline designed to direct the reader's attention to the textual material contained in the communication? Discuss. See *National Association of Securities Dealers, Inc., Federal Securities Law Reports* (CCH), ¶77,887 (Securities and Exchange Commission, May 23, 1984).

---

[33] C. Walker and B. Hadaway, "Merit Standards Revisited: An Empirical Analysis of the Efficacy of Texas Merit Standards," *Journal of Corporation Law*, Vol. 7 (1982), p. 651.

[34] *Compare* J. Mofsky and R. Tollison, "Demerit in Merit Regulation," *Marquette Law Review*, Vol. 60 (1977), p. 367, with J. Hueni, "Application of Merit Requirements in State Securities Regulation," *Wayne Law Review*, Vol. 15 (1969), p. 1417, and C. Goodkind, "Blue Sky Laws: Is There Merit in Merit Requirements?" *Wisconsin Law Review* (1976), p. 79.

3. Byrnes held White Shield Corp. shares that were not registered and could not be readily sold. However, Byrnes had acquired the right to include the stock in a later registration. White Shield filed a registration statement that became effective on June 7, 1971, which included Byrnes's shares. Byrnes arranged for Tobey & Kirk, a broker-dealer, to sell the shares when the registration statement became effective. On June 7, Tobey & Kirk arranged a sale to Faulkner, a market maker in White Shield stock. On that date, Tobey & Kirk sent a written confirmation of sale to Faulkner that was not accompanied or preceded by a prospectus and did not show that the stock was part of a registered distribution. On June 15, the certificates themselves were delivered, along with a prospectus. The prospectus disclosed that the shares were part of a registered secondary distribution. This information led Faulkner to reject the shares and cancel the deal. Faulkner's market maker status made the purchase illegal. When Byrnes finally sold the shares, it was for much less than Faulkner had agreed to pay. Byrnes sued Faulkner for breach of contract. Faulkner defended by arguing that its contract was unenforceable because it violated §5(b)(1). *Discuss.* See *Byrnes* v. *Faulkner, Dawkins & Sullivan*, 550 F.2d 1303 (2d Cir. 1977).

4. On February 10, 1955, Holly Uranium Corporation filed a registration statement that ultimately became effective on April 22, 1955. On March 30, 1955, Franklin, Meyer & Barnett ("registrant"), co-underwriter, mailed approximately 1,400 preliminary prospectuses with a cover letter. Costa, a salesman for registrant, enclosed his business card upon which he wrote: "Phone me as soon as possible as my allotment is almost complete on this issue." Six of his customers sold securities owned by them prior to the effective date to pay for the Holly stock. Five of his customers mailed checks to registrant prior to the effective date. Meyer, Barnett, and Zoref were supervisory personnel who deny any knowledge of the checks and had no procedures to detect the presence even of the checks that contained notations such as for "200 shs. of Holly Uranium." The SEC is considering whether registrant and its employees should be disciplined for a §5(a)(1) violation. Discuss. See *In re Franklin, Meyer & Barnett*, 37 S.E.C. 47 (1956).

5. In July 1971, Cartridge Television, Inc., went public. Plaintiff invested in Cartridge throughout 1971 at substantial profits as the stock price rose. In January 1972, plaintiff bought almost $2,000,000 worth of Cartridge shares. Unfortunately, the Cartridge product, a home video tape system, did not gain widespread consumer acceptance. The company took bankruptcy in June 1973, and plaintiff's entire investment was wiped out. Plaintiff sued under §11 of the 1933 Act alleging, inter alia, that defendants, including Cartridge's parent corporation and plaintiff's broker-dealer, had failed to disclose numerous facts, including a private report prepared for another party that reached a negative conclusion regarding consumer demand for Cartridge's product, and that no "state-of-the-art" patent search had been made to determine Cartridge's position. On the other hand, the prospectus contained no affirmative misrepresentations. It stated: "THESE SECURITIES INVOLVE A HIGH DEGREE OF RISK" and listed various "RISK FACTORS," including that Cartridge was a highly speculative venture, that it had never generated a dollar in revenue, and that it had debts of

$1,000,000. It also stated that a home video tape system was a novelty with unpredictable public demand, so that "no assurance can be given that the CARTRIVISION system will meet with general public acceptance." And the prospectus stated that the Company "does not expect to obtain fundamental patent protection for the basic concept or design of its system." Was plaintiff misled in a material fashion? *Parsons v. Hornblower & Weeks-Hemphill, Noyes*, 447 F.Supp. 482 (M.D. N.C. 1977).

6. Texas Glass Mfg. Co. intended to manufacture certain types of glass, though it had never engaged in any business and its only property was a plant site donated by the city of Bryan, Texas. It filed a registration statement on May 27, 1957, that stated, inter alia, that the company was incorporated in October 1952 as a new business and that until October 1955 was in a planning and development state, that it had offered its securities to residents of Texas "for a short period of time" during which 83,708 shares had been sold, that it had been assured that it would be able to build its plant for a specified estimated cost, and that a market survey indicated that its entire annual production would be consumed. An SEC investigation disclosed that the company was *still* in the planning and development stage and would be until it raised enough money to build its plant; that the "short period of time" was 17 months long, and Texas Glass had decided it would have to sell shares outside Texas; that Texas Glass had not yet entered into a contract for construction of the plant and therefore was not "assured" that costs would not exceed estimates; and that it obtained no professional market survey but had only made some inquiries by telephone and correspondence, reaching conclusions that ignored the potential effects of rising foreign competition. Should the SEC stop this registration statement from becoming effective because it is materially misleading? See *In re Texas Glass Mfg. Corp.*, 38 S.E.C. 630 (1958).

7. Plaintiff unions, which were also holders of a small number of J. P. Stevens & Co. shares, sued in invalidate election of Stevens' directors from 1972 through 1978 because the company's proxy solicitations falsely omitted to state that the nominees "either knowingly and willfully participated in a concerted effort to thwart the labor laws of this country" or failed to prevent management from so doing. Should the proxy statements have made such a disclosure? If J. P. Stevens filed a registration statement, should it contain such disclosures? Discuss. See *Amalgamated Clothing & Textile Workers Union* v. *J. P. Stevens & Co.*, 475 F.Supp. 328 (S.D. N.Y. 1979).

8. Following disclosures that it had made, with the approval of several senior executives, $30–38 million in questionable and off-the-books foreign payments ($22 million of which were bribes to foreign officials), Lockheed entered into a consent decree with the SEC. Plaintiff shareholder then sued, challenging Lockheed's proxy disclosures, which had not mentioned these illegal payments. Should they have been disclosed? Discuss. See *Gaines* v. *Haughton*, 645 F.2d 761 (9th Cir. 1981), *cert. denied*, 454 U.S. 1145.

16

CONSEQUENCES OF DEFECTIVE REGISTRATION

A party filing a defective registration statement faces both SEC proceedings and civil actions by individuals.

SEC AUTHORITY

Section 8

If the SEC deems a registration statement incomplete, misleading, or otherwise deficient, it can take a variety of avenues to prevent sale of the securities covered by the statement. In addition to denying acceleration, noted in Chapter 15, the SEC can use a variety of powers granted by §8 of the 1933 Act.

Refusal Orders

Subsection (b) of §8 authorizes the SEC to issue a "refusal order," under which the Commission refuses to allow a registration statement to become effective. However, such an order must be issued within ten days of the filing of the registration statement. The heavily understaffed SEC is seldom able to act so quickly. Furthermore, opportunity for a hearing must be afforded the registrant within ten days after issuance of the stop order, and it is arguable that only the most blatantly defective registration statements may be blocked because the statute refers only to a statement "on its face incomplete or inaccurate." Due to these procedural impediments, the SEC seldom issues refusal orders.

Stop Orders

Subsection (d) of §8 authorizes the SEC to issue a "stop order" suspending the effectiveness of a registration "at any time" such a statement contains a materially misleading statement or omission. Although it is reasonable to argue to the contrary, the SEC has successfully maintained that stop orders may be issued *before* as well as after a registration statement becomes effective.[1] Because a stop order is not hindered by a requirement that it be issued within ten days of the filing of the registration statement, it has become the SEC's favored tool for preventing sales under defective registration statements, whether or not they have become effective.[2] Once a stop order is issued, the SEC must afford the issuer an opportunity for a hearing within ten days.

Examinations

Subsection (e) of §8 specifically empowers the Commission to make an examination to determine whether a stop order should issue. The SEC may demand production of documents and testimony of the issuer, the underwriter or any other person. Failure of those investigated to cooperate constitutes a proper ground for issuance of a stop order.

Practice

In practice, the SEC has had to issue comparatively few stop orders. In 1970, for example, 4,314 registration statements were filed, yet only 28 examinations were commenced, and only 6 stop order proceedings were initiated.[3]

When utilized, the stop order proceeding is a powerful tool, and the courts have acted to ensure the SEC does not abuse it. For example, in *Las Vegas Hawaiian Development Co.* v. *SEC*,[4] the issuer filed a registration statement with a delaying amendment in May 1977. In July 1977, the SEC issued a deficiency letter. An amended registration statement, again with a delaying amendment, was filed in December 1977.

---

[1] *Red Bank Oil Co.*, 20 S.E.C. 863 (1945).

[2] Also, the SEC need not find "significant likelihood of public injury to issue a stop order"—*In the Matter of Advanced Chemical Corp.* [1983–84 Binder], *Federal Securities Law Reports* (CCH), ¶83,499 (Securities and Exchange Commission, February 9, 1984).

[3] 36 Securities and Exchange Commission, *Annual Report* (1970), p. 35.

[4] 466 F.Supp. 928 (D. Hawaii 1979).

A second deficiency letter was issued by the SEC in May 1978. Finally, on July 7, 1978, the registrant filed a second amended registration statement, this time with no delaying amendment. This prompted the SEC, on July 25, 1978, to decide to investigate the issuer more formally to determine whether to initiate a stop order proceeding. The issuer sued, but the SEC, which had not yet decided whether to issue a stop order, argued it had made no decision reviewable in court (although the registration statement had been on file for over a year).

Although the judge denied relief to the issuer because it had not exhausted its administrative remedies pursuant to the Administrative Procedure Act, he said that courts have the power to prevent the SEC from unreasonably delaying the registration process:

> [A] district court may, upon the petition of a registrant under the Securities Act of 1933, compel the SEC to make a determination within a reasonable time whether to notice a hearing on the issuance of a stop order under Section 8(d), where the Commission has ordered an examination under section 8(e) prior to the effective date of a registration statement and the determination whether a stop order has been unreasonably delayed.
>
> The court may not compel the Commission to institute a section 8(d) proceeding. But the clear import of 5 U.S.C. §706 [Administrative Procedure Act] is that the court may compel the SEC to either terminate a section 8(e) examination or institute a section 8(d) proceeding in a situation where the SEC's inaction has the effect of prohibiting the sale of registered securities, and when this determination has been unreasonably delayed.

Injunctions

If informal investigation leads the SEC to believe violations of *any* 1933 Act provisions are threatened or occurring, §20(a) authorizes the Commission to institute a formal investigation. That investigation may lead the SEC, pursuant to §20(b) to ask a federal district court to enjoin the alleged violation. Such courts, in their discretion, are empowered to enjoin violations or, under §20(c), to issue writs of mandamus compelling compliance with the act.

Criminal Proceedings

Section 20(b) also authorizes the SEC to transmit evidence regarding violations of the 1933 Act to the Attorney General who has discretion to institute criminal proceedings.

Willful violation of *any* provision of the 1933 Act, or of the SEC's rules issued thereunder, constitutes a criminal offense according to §24. The "willfulness" requirement means that only acts committed intentionally, though not necessarily with evil motive or knowledge that a law is being violated, are punishable criminally.[5]

This intent requirement was clarified in *U.S.* v. *Brown*,[6] where a defendant was charged with intentional violation of §17(a)'s ban on fraudulent offer or sale of

---

[5] *Van Duyse* v. *Israel*, 486 F.Supp. 1382 (E.D. Wis. 1980).
[6] 578 F.2d 1280 (9th Cir.), *cert. denied*, 439 U.S. 928 (1978).

securities. Defendant claimed that the government had not proved that he knew the forged land contracts he was selling were "securities" within the meaning of the 1933 Act. This was no defense, the court concluded:

> We think that the government is required to prove specific intent only as it relates to the action constituting the fraudulent, misleading or deceitful conduct, but not as to the knowledge that the instrument used is a security under the Securities Act. The government need only prove that the object sold or offered is a security; it need not be proved that the defendant had specific knowledge that the object sold or offered was a security.

Because of the federal "aiding and abetting" statute,[7] any person who knowingly assists a willful violation of the 1933 Act is guilty of a federal crime. Accountants and attorneys, for example, who knowingly assist in the filing of a false registration statement subject themselves to criminal liability. Violations may be punished by fines of up to $10,000 and/or imprisonment of not more than five years. Criminal actions under §24 are neither common nor unheard of.[8]

PRIVATE CAUSES OF ACTION

The Securities Act provides express remedies for parties injured by certain violations of the act. Those express remedies appear in §§11, 12(1), and 12(2). In addition, certain other remedies may be implied from the terms of the act.

Section 11

Prior to enactment of the 1933 Act, someone who purchased stock on the basis of false statements could successfully sue only by establishing the elements of common law fraud: that defendant made false statements, that the misstatements were as to material facts, that defendant knew the facts were false and intended plaintiff to rely on the misstatements, that plaintiff did rely and reasonably so, that plaintiff was in privity of contract with defendant, and that the injury was caused by the misrepresentations.[9] A plaintiff alleging common law fraud faced no easy task.

In §11, Congress granted an express right to sue on behalf of persons injured by false statements and misleading omissions in registration statements. In so doing, Congress eased the considerable burdens of an injured plaintiff so substantially that many feared "grass would grow on Wall Street." Surprisingly, though viewed as an

---

[7] 18 U.S.C. §2.

[8] For example, *Price* v. *U.S.*, 200 F.2d 652 (5th Cir. 1953) (13-month jail term and $1,000 fine given intentional violator of §5(a)(2)). Note, however, that most courts hold because §11 specifically lists potential defendants, there is no aiding and abetting civil liability. For example, *Ahern* v. *Gassoin*, 611 F.Supp. 1465 (D. Or. 1985). Some courts allow aiding and abetting civil liability under §12(2); others do not.

[9] See W. Prosser, *Law of Torts*, §105, 4th ed. (St. Paul, Minn.: West Publishing Co., 1971).

in terrorem remedy, §11 has led to comparatively little litigation [10] and remarkably few judgments. Perhaps the law has "terrorized" potential §11 defendants into compliance with the law. Or, on the other hand, perhaps limitations inherent in §11 have prevented it from being effectively used by potential plaintiffs.

Elements of a §11 Claim

Closer scrutiny of the elements of a §11 cause of action will illustrate where §11 has made it easier for a plaintiff to recover than was the case under the common law of fraud.

(1) False statements and omissions

Similar to common law fraud, §11 allows recovery for untrue statements of material fact *and omissions* of material fact necessary to make other statements not misleading. Keep in mind that §11 applies only to misrepresentations and omissions contained in the registration statement when it becomes effective. False statements in a prospectus are of course covered by §11, because the prospectus is part of the registration statement. Section 11 does not punish false statements made orally or in other written documents, though these may be the basis for a §12(2) claim. The same may be said for statements that are accurate when the registration statement becomes effective, but later become misleading due to changes in circumstances.

(2) Materiality

Section 11 does not afford a remedy for piddling misstatements or omissions. The misrepresentation must be "material." Rule 405 defines as material "those matters to which there is a substantial likelihood that a reasonable investor would attach importance in determining whether to purchase the security registered."

(3) Fault

The common law fraud defendant is liable only for misstatements and omissions made with intent to deceive. This stringent requirement was radically diluted for §11 purposes. For most §11 defendants, a negligence standard is applied. Even though §11 defendants did not intend to misstate or deceive, they are liable if false statements are made in the registration statement due to their mere negligence. Only if a §11 defendant can prove that he or she was not negligent—that "due diligence" was exercised—can liability be escaped. The "due diligence" defense will be discussed in detail presently.

The issuing company is the one §11 defendant that has *no* due diligence defense. Even if everyone involved exercised the utmost care, if a materially false statement finds its way into the registration statement, the issuer is subject to liability. In other words, under §11 the issuer has virtually absolute liability for errors in the registration statement. This fact, more than anything else, accounts for the *in terrorem* reputation of §11.

---

[10] The first major case litigated under §11 was not decided until 35 years after the law was enacted— *Escott* v. *BarChris Construction Co.*, 283 F.Supp. 643 (S.D. N.Y. 1968).

(4) Reliance

Generally speaking, a plaintiff who is injured after purchasing securities issued under a misleading registration statement can recover damages without proving reliance on the misstatement or omission. The plaintiff need not even allege that he or she read the registration statement, much less that he or she relied on the misstatements or omissions therein. There are two exceptions to this general rule.

First, if defendant can prove that plaintiff knew of the untruth or omission at the time of acquisition, recovery is barred. Second, an unusual provision in §11(a) states that if the plaintiff acquired the security after the issuer sent its shareholders an "earnings statement covering a period of at least 12 months beginning after the effective date of the registration statement," plaintiff must prove reliance. However, plaintiff may prove reliance without having read the registration statement, apparently by obtaining the information from other parties.

(5) Privity

A §11 plaintiff need not prove classic privity of contract as an element of recovery. Indeed, §11 liability potential extends far beyond the person who sold the securities to plaintiff. Section 11 specifically states that the following list of persons may be sued:

1. Every person who signed the registration statement; those required to sign the registration statement include
   a. The issuer.
   b. Principal executive officers of the issuer.
   c. Chief financial officer of the issuer.
   d. Principal accounting officer of the issuer.
   e. A majority of the board of directors.
2. Every person who was a director or partner in the issuer.
3. Every person consensually named as about to become a director.
4. Every accountant, engineer, appraiser, or other "expert" who has consensually been named as having prepared or certified any portion of the registration statement (liability is limited to that portion; for example, an accountant who certified financial statements contained in the registration statement would be liable for inaccuracies contained in those financial statements, but not for defects in other parts of the registration statement).
5. Every underwriter.[11]

Although plaintiffs need not prove that their securities were purchased from the defendants sued, they must show that the securities were issued pursuant to the defective registration statement. That plaintiffs are required to "trace" their securities

---

[11] Section 15 of the 1933 Act also provides that every person who "controls" a §11 or §12 defendant is jointly and severally liable with that controlled defendant "unless the controlling person had no knowledge or reasonable grounds to believe in the existence of the facts by reason of which the liability of the controlled person is alleged to exist." Thus, someone who by stock ownership owned a controlling interest in an underwriter could be liable for errors in a registration statement, but would be able to avoid liability by proving good faith—a defense not available to other §11 defendants.

to the defective registration statement is not burdensome if the issuer has had only one offering of this type of security. However, if other offerings have occurred under nondefective registration statements, plaintiffs who purchased in the secondary market may be unable to recover.

KIRKWOOD v. TAYLOR

590 F.Supp. 1375 (D. Minn. 1984)

A number of plaintiffs—including LaVictoire, Kahn, Neider, Graca, and Kirkwood (a class action)—bring §11 suits arising out of distribution of Minnetonka, Inc. stock. Defendants include Minnetonka; Shearson/American Express, Inc.; Piper, Jaffray & Hopwood (PJH); Taylor; and Community Investment Enterprises. Defendants move for dismissal and summary judgment on grounds that plaintiffs cannot trace the shares of Minnetonka stock that they purchased to the underwriting in question.

ALSOP, DISTRICT JUDGE:

Section 11(a) of the Securities Act of 1933, 15 U.S.C. §77k(a) (hereinafter the 1933 Act) provides in part that:

> In case any part of the registration statement, when such part became effective, contained an untrue statement of a material fact or omitted to state a material fact required to be stated therein or necessary to make the statements therein not misleading, *any person acquiring such security . . . may . . . sue . . .* (emphasis added)

Defendants contend that this section has been universally interpreted to require plaintiffs to prove that they acquired shares issued in the offering whose registration statement is claimed to be false or misleading. This tracing requirement, defendants argue, is strictly construed. It is not enough for plaintiffs to show that their

stock might be traceable to offering stock; plaintiffs bear the burden of proving that their shares were actually issued in the offering. Defendants concede that the results of a strict application of the tracing requirement can be harsh, but note that Congress has presumably been aware of this interpretation of the statute and has chosen not to eliminate the tracing requirement.

Furthermore, defendants note that a strict standing requirement is consistent with the general structure of §11. Section 11 imposes liability, without regard to a purchaser's reliance, for material misstatements or omissions in a registration statement covering a public offering. The section in effect presumes that those who purchased stock in the public offering relied upon the allegedly misleading documents. Section 11, in contrast to §10(b), does not require the plaintiffs to prove scienter. Plaintiffs in a §11 case then are relieved of the burden of proving reliance and scienter. In order to invoke these benefits, however, plaintiffs must meet some strict procedural requirements. Section 11 is very narrow in this sense. The statute of limitations, for example, is one year from the date of offering, not the date of discovery of the allegedly false or misleading statement or omission. Section 11 was intended only to apply to new offerings, not to subsequent sales. Strict application of the tracing requirement, defendants argue, is consistent with the statutory scheme.

Defendants claim that plaintiffs cannot meet their burden of proving that they hold shares either directly purchased in the offering or traceable to the offering. Thus, plaintiffs lack standing to bring their §11 claims and defendants are entitled to summary judgment on those claims.

Plaintiffs agree that §11 contains a tracing requirement, but read the section differently than do defendants. Plaintiffs claim that they have affirmatively traced their shares to the March 5, 1981 public offering. Plaintiffs rely on four methods of tracing. The court will discuss each method in turn.

The Direct Trace Method

The direct trace method is the easiest method to understand and prove. Under this method, stock is directly purchased in the underwritten public offering. A number of indicia will usually be present documenting the direct trace, including: an indication of interest by the broker on behalf of the customer, the customer's receipt of a preliminary prospectus with a legend in red ink (called a "red herring"), a notation on the purchase order ticket showing purchase in the offering, purchase at the offering price, lack of commission, language regarding the prospectus on the customer's confirmation slip, and special coding of the transaction by the brokerage firm.

Plaintiff Edward Graca purchased 200 shares of Minnetonka stock on the offering date through Craig-Hallum, Inc., one of the members of the investment syndicate that underwrote the public offering. Defendants admit that these 200 shares are traceable to the offering. Defendants move for partial summary judgment, however, on the grounds that Graca cannot trace the other 10,400 shares he alleges he purchased in the offering. Plaintiffs have not responded directly to this argument, but seem to imply that the tracing of the 200 shares is sufficient to deny defendants' motion.

The court agrees with defendants that plaintiff must trace all of the shares for which he claims damages to the offering. No efforts have been made to trace the 10,400 shares and discovery on the tracing issue has been closed. Therefore, insofar as count 1 of plaintiff Graca's complaint purports to raise a §11 claim regarding the 10,400 untraced shares, plaintiff lacks standing to bring that count and defendants' motion will be granted.

None of the other plaintiffs claims to have purchased his or her shares directly in the March 5, 1981 offering.

The Fungible Mass Method

Plaintiffs Eileen Kirkwood and Carl Kahn claim that they can trace their shares through a method the court has termed the "fungible mass" method. Before the March 5, 1981 offering, approximately 6.9 million shares of Minnetonka, Inc. from previous offerings were already outstanding. Plaintiffs refer to these shares as "old" shares. About 2.8 million of those shares were registered in the name of Cede & Co., the nominee name of the Depository Trust Company (DTC). The DTC is a stock clearing house, owned by a number of brokerage firms throughout the country. Participating brokers deposit the securities they hold in street name with DTC. Purchases and sales are accomplished by book entries crediting or debiting the brokerage firm's account, facilitating the transfer of securities without requiring physical movement of any certificates.

In the March 5 offering, 1.32 million shares of Minnetonka, Inc. were introduced into the market place. Plaintiffs refer to these shares as "new" shares. The DTC holds all certificates, both old and new, in its nominee name as pooled shares in a fungible mass for the benefit of all its members. Plaintiffs Eileen Kirkwood and Carl Kahn each purchased their stock after the offering date through brokerage firms that were members of the DTC. Plaintiffs claim that, since more than 25 percent of the shares of Minnetonka stock held by the DTC in a fungible mass were issued pursuant to the March 5, 1981 offering, plaintiffs own a proportionate interest in all of the DTC certificates, both old and new.

Defendants disagree with plaintiffs' fungible mass theory on several grounds. First, they say, the theory was rejected in *Lorber* v. *Beebe* 407 F.Supp. 279 (S.D. N.Y. 1975). In that case, plaintiff's broker, Lehman Brothers, Inc., bought the stock from defendant Blyth Eastman Dillon & Co. Inc. The purchase was completed in 1972 when Blyth delivered to a clearing house for Lehman's account a certificate directly traceable to one that had been issued before the effective date of the 1972 registration statement. Plaintiff did not take physical possession of his stock until a year later, when he received a certificate that came out of a Lehman house account holding both old and new shares on a fungible basis. The certificate thus could not be identified as either old or new. Plaintiff argued that the critical question was not the origin of the certificate delivered to his broker's clearing house account but instead the origin of the one delivered to him. Conceding his inability to identify conclusively the latter certificate as new, he contended the burden of identification should fall on defendants and that he should qualify for §11 relief by showing that the certificate *might* have been traceable to "new" stock. Id. at 286.

The court rejected both contentions saying, "[I]t is insufficient that stock "might" have been issued pursuant to a defective statement. A plaintiff must show that it actually was so issued." Id. at 287. The court also held that the transaction cleared when plaintiff acquired the rights and remedies in the shares, that is, when the old stock certificate was delivered to his broker's clearing house account. Thus, defendants in this case say, plaintiffs' fungible mass theory is not supported by the case law.

Defendants claim, common sense precludes

plaintiffs' interpretation of the tracing requirement. Suppose purchaser A decides to buy on January 3, 1981, 500 shares of stock and hold them in the street name of his broker. His broker on that day buys 500 shares for him and his broker's account at the DTC is credited for 500 shares. On March 5, the offering takes place and the new shares are issued. After some time, A's broker acquires new shares that are held on a fungible basis with the old. Under plaintiffs' theory, A would be the owner of a proportionate interest in the new shares even though A had no intent to purchase offering shares, did not see or rely on the registration statement and prospectus, and purchased prior to the offering. Even if the court somehow limited the class of plaintiffs to those who held shares on or after the offering date, all persons who held stock in street name on and after the offering date could claim a proportional interest in the shares. The issuer could find itself liable for far more than the number of shares issued in the challenged offering. For these reasons, defendants say, plaintiffs' fungible mass theory should be rejected.

The court agrees with defendants. The argument plaintiffs are making is merely a variation of one rejected years ago. Essentially, plaintiffs are showing only that their securities "might" have been issued in the offering and they are asking the court to presume that a pro rata portion of their shares are new shares. This approach is not too different from the argument that section 11 should extend to previously traded shares as well as to newly registered shares. In *Barnes* v. *Osofsky*, 373 F.2d 269 (2d Cir. 1967) plaintiffs claimed that section 11 should extend to previously traded shares. Plaintiffs argued that

[O]nce it is agreed that §11 is not limited to the original purchasers, to read that section as applying only to purchasers who can trace the lineage of their shares to the new offering makes the result turn on mere accident since most trading is done through brokers who neither know nor care whether they are getting newly registered or old shares. . . . [I]t is often impossible to determine whether previously traded shares are old or new, and tracing is further complicated when stock is held in margin accounts in street names since many brokerage houses do not identify specific shares with particular accounts but instead treat the account as having an undivided interest in the house's position.

The court rejected that argument, holding that plaintiffs' reading would be inconsistent with the over-all statutory scheme and contrary to the legislative history. Id. The court agreed that its construction gave §11 a rather accidental impact as between one open-market purchaser of stock already being traded and another, but nevertheless held that the agreement settling the §11 claim need not extend to those who purchased after the offering but could not trace their shares.

Finally, the court is persuaded that plaintiffs' construction of the statute violates common sense: the logical extension of plaintiff's fungible mass theory would, as defendants note, effectively circumvent the tracing requirement. Accordingly, plaintiffs Eileen Kirkwood and Carl Kahn do not have standing based on the "fungible mass" theory of tracing to bring their §11 claims.

The Contrabroker Method

Plaintiffs Arthur Sternberger and Arto Sales, Inc. (named plaintiffs in the Kirkwood class action) and plaintiff Carl Kahn in his individual action claim that they can trace their shares through a method the court has termed the "contrabroker" method. Plaintiff Kahn claims that he purchased his shares from his broker, Charles Schwab & Company, Inc. Charles Schwab purchased the 2,000 shares for Kahn's account from Dain Bosworth, Inc. (the contrabroker). In his transaction, Dain Bosworth was not acting for its own customer but was trading for its house

account (or "making a market" in the stock). Since Dain was an underwriter of the March 5 offering, plaintiff Kahn says that the stock purchased by Schwab from Dain is traceable to the offering. Plaintiffs Sternberger and Arto Sales, Inc. similarly claim to have purchased from Shearson, one of the co-managing underwriters of the offering.

The court finds that plaintiffs have not met the tracing requirements of §11. Plaintiff would have the court assume that Dain's house account inventory contained only new stock up through the date of Kahn's purchase. There is no evidence that Dain was not a market-maker in Minnetonka, Inc., stock either before or after the offering date. If Dain was a market-maker, its inventory could just as easily include old as well as new stock. Plaintiff Kahn has merely shown that he "might" have purchased offering shares.

Plaintiffs Sternberger and Arto Sales, Inc., have also not shown that just because they purchased from an underwriter that they necessarily bought only new offering stock. Obviously at some point plaintiffs' assumption must be false; otherwise anyone who ever purchased from a participant in the underwriting after the offering date could claim he or she bought "new" stock under this contrabroker theory.

. . .

The court concludes that plaintiffs Kahn, Sternberger and Arto Sales, Inc. do not have standing based on the "contrabroker" theory of tracing to bring their section 11 claims.

The "Heritage" Method

Plaintiffs N. M. Mittica, M.D., P.C.; Profit Sharing Plan and N. M. Mittica, M.D., P.C., Pension Plan (hereinafter the Plans) in the Kirkwood class action and plaintiffs LaVictoire and Neiders in their individual actions claim that they can trace their shares through what this court has termed the "heritage" method. This method is the most complex of the methods plaintiffs advance.

Plaintiffs contend that they purchased stock in the over-the-counter market and received stock certificates registered in their individual names. In the records of Minnetonka's stock transfer agent, plaintiffs identified by code number the certificates they had received. Then plaintiffs identified the particular certificates from which their individual certificates were issued. The process was continued until plaintiffs determined the ultimate origin of their certificates. Some of those certificates were expressly issued in the March 5, 1981 offering. Thus, plaintiffs maintain, they can trace their shares to the offering.

Defendants argue that this tracing only shows that the shares "might" have been issued in the offering. Defendants say, not all of the shares in certificates through which plaintiffs trace were offering shares. Plaintiffs cannot prove that the shares they received were traceable to the new versus old certificates. For example, defendants explain, the plaintiffs Neiders received three certificates for their stock, numbered MUO38,125 representing 1,000 shares, MUO38,126 representing 500 shares and MUO38,286 representing 500 shares. The first two certificates totalling 1500 shares were issued on the surrender of four different certificates, three of which could eventually trace part of their heritage to offering stock (MUO33,047, MUO37,214 and MUO37,106) and one which could not (MUO37,312). That latter certificate represented 2020 shares. Defendants explain that this one certificate with 2,020 shares could have produced plaintiffs' 1500 shares just as easily as the other three certificates totalling 7,490. Clearly all 9,510 shares (2,020 and 7,490) did not become part of plaintiffs' current certificates. It is just as likely that those certificates trace to "old" shares, then, as to "new." Plaintiffs' third certificate totalling 500 shares

was issued on the surrender of four certificates, three necessarily containing offering shares but one (MUO37,733) for 6,550 shares containing 5,500 old and 1,000 new shares. Since plaintiff received a certificate for only 500 shares, those shares could easily trace to the 5,500 old shares instead of to the new shares. Plaintiffs have merely shown that they "might" have received offering shares.

Defendants say, even if the court assumes that every possible offering share in the tracing histories became part of plaintiffs' certificates, most of the plaintiffs cannot prove that all of their shares would be new shares. Plaintiff LaVictoire, for example, could only prove that at most 1,200 to 1,300 of his 5,000 shares were offering shares.

The court agrees that plaintiffs have merely shown that they might have purchased offering stock. The court has followed the charts submitted by defendants and agrees that in no case is it clear that all or even any of plaintiffs' shares are *necessarily* offering shares. In some instances, it is true that plaintiffs can "trace" all of their shares to offering shares if the court presumes that at each surrender of a stock certificate the offering shares were preserved or converted first. On the equally likely assumption that at each surrender all old shares were preserved or converted into the more recent certificate first, however, the court in no instance finds that plaintiffs' certificates could not be comprised solely of old shares. (*See eg.*, plaintiffs Plans—two certificates for 830 shares and 1,000 shares were received on surrender of a certificate containing 9,450 shares, 6,200 of which were new but 3,250 of which were old).

Plaintiffs' position is similar to that of the plaintiff in *Lorber* v. *Beebe*, 407 F.Supp. 279 (S.D. N.Y. 1975) where the plaintiff conceded that the certificate he received from a house account which held both old and new shares could not be conclusively identified as new.

Id. at 286. Plaintiff in that case, like plaintiffs in this one, failed to show that his stock was *actually* issued in the offering. It was just as true in 1967 when *Barnes* v. *Osofsky*, 373 F.2d 269 (2d Cir.) was decided as it is today that reading section 11 to apply only to purchasers who can actually trace the lineage of their shares to the offering "makes the result turn on mere accident since most trading is done through brokers who neither know nor care whether they are getting newly registered or old shares." Id. at 271–72. It was and remains a fact that, "[I]t is often impossible to determine whether previ-ously traded shares are old or new," Id. at 272. Plaintiffs' assumption that all "new" shares should be deemed preserved or incorporated into the more recent stock certificates is but a more sophisticated version of the argument that, since plaintiffs cannot tell whether they have old or new shares, those shares should be treated as new and plaintiffs should be granted standing.

Accordingly, the court finds that plaintiffs Plans, LaVictoire and Neiders do not have standing based on the "heritage" theory of tracing to bring their section 11 claims.

(6) *Causation*

Section 11 eliminates the causation element of the common law fraud claim. Plaintiffs need not prove that the decline in the value of their securities was caused by the false statements or omissions of the registration statement. Rather, once the presence of a materially misleading statement or omission is proved, causation is presumed and the burden shifts to defendant to demonstrate other factors that caused the decline in value. The specifics of this affirmative defense will be discussed when we reach the matter of damages.

Defenses to a §11 Claim

Defendants can always defeat a §11 claim by negating plaintiffs' proof of the applicable elements of a cause of action. Defendants can prevail if they prevent plaintiffs from carrying their burden of proof as to falsity, materiality, or tracing. Defendants can also win by carrying their burden of proof to show plaintiffs that bought with knowledge of the falsity and can minimize recovery by proving alternative causation regarding the decline in the value of plaintiffs' securities.

Otherwise, defendants' §11 liability is nearly absolute, since plaintiffs need not prove scienter, reliance, or causation. Nonetheless, two important §11 defenses remain to be discussed.

(1) *Statute of Limitations*

Section 13 of the 1933 Act provides that generally plaintiffs can sue within one year of the discovery of an untrue statement or omission (or when discovery should have been made), but never later than three years after the security was first "bona fide offered to the public." This apparently means that if a plaintiff purchases securities under a registration statement more than three years after the first time the securities were delivered to the public, plaintiff's cause of action is extinguished by the statute of limitations before it even accrues.

(2) *Due Diligence*

Although the issuer is absolutely liable for material errors and omissions in the registration statement, the remaining defendants are judged by a negligence standard. They may escape liability by showing that they acted with "due diligence." A potential §11 defendant may not simply stand by inattentively while the registration statement is prepared. Passive ignorance is no defense. Rather, the defendant must demonstrate a reasonable belief that the registration statement was accurate and that this belief was based on a reasonable investigation. The "reasonableness" standard is based on what a prudent person would do in the management of his or her own property. However, one blanket standard cannot be applied to all defendants and all portions of the registration statement. Distinctions have been drawn between "expertised" and "nonexpertised" portions of the registration statement and among various categories of defendants.

"Expertised" portions of the registration statement are those portions prepared by so-called "experts"—people whose professions give authority to statements made by them. The certified financial statement of an accountant is expertised. So is the certified mineralogical report of a geologist or the title guarantee of an attorney. (Note that an accountant is not deemed an "expert" as to noncertified financial statements, nor is an attorney because he or she drafted most of the textual portions of a registration statement.)

As to the expertised portions of the registration statement, the experts who are responsible for them are held to a very high standard of care. They must reasonably believe the statements, and that belief must be based upon a reasonable investigation. The investigation must at least meet the standards of the profession, and some courts have held that an accountant could be liable even when he met the standards of the profession where the profession's standards were inadequate to provide full and fair disclosure.[12] Most courts are satisfied if the accountant meets the standards of the profession.[13]

If the only misstatements or omissions appear in the *expertised* portion of the registration statement, nonexpert §11 defendants usually avoid liability. All they must show is that they had no reasonable grounds to believe and did not believe the statements were false. No investigation is required, as they are allowed to rely on the experts. In this limited situation, passive ignorance is a defense so long as the nonexpert defendant had no grounds to suspect inaccuracy.

Nonexpertised portions of the registration statement, on the other hand, are judged by a stricter standard. Actual reasonable belief based upon reasonable investigation is required of every nonexpert defendant. The same standard is applied to statements made by other nonexperts as to those made by the particular defendant.

What constitutes a "reasonable" investigation—how much "diligence is due"—depends upon the particular defendant's position, responsibilities, and skills.

Inside directors, according to one leading case,[14] have an extremely high due

---

[12] For example, *U.S.* v. *Simon*, 425 F.2d 796 (2d Cir. 1969), *cert. denied*, 397 U.S. 1006 (1970) (a 1934 Act case).

[13] For example, *Escott* v. *BarChris Construct. Co.*, 283 F.Supp. 643 (S.D. N.Y. 1968).

[14] *Feit* v. *Leasco Data Processing Equipment Corp.*, 332 F.Supp. 544 (E.D.N.Y. 1971).

diligence threshhold. Because they have an intimate knowledge of corporate affairs and ready access to documents needed to verify independently the statements contained in the registration statement, inside directors are "virtual guarantors" of the accuracy of the registration statement.

Outside directors are held to a lower standard of due diligence than inside directors. They do not approach "guarantor" status, but they should still attend all board meetings while a registration statement is being prepared, read drafts of the registration statement, and ask at least a few general questions of the issuer's management, accountants, and lawyers.

Underwriters are held to a high standard because of their unique position. They have traditionally been considered the one potential §11 defendant that is independent and disinterested. Underwriters may not simply question management and be satisfied with facile answers. Rather, underwriters should probe, question, and independently investigate as though they are in an adversarial position in regard to the issuer, for that is exactly the position the SEC and the courts will expect them to take.

A major offering may involve many underwriters. It seems silly for each underwriter to undertake the same investigation to satisfy due diligence requirements. Therefore, normally the lead underwriter will "reasonably investigate" the registration statement, and the other underwriters will rely on that investigation. If the lead underwriter botches the job, it is clear that the remaining underwriters will also be liable under §11. They can appoint the lead underwriter as their "agent" to investigate, but they must suffer the consequences if the agent inadequately performs the task.

What is not clear is whether the other underwriters are absolved of §11 liability if the lead underwriter does reasonably investigate so as to satisfy the "due diligence" requirement, yet an erroneous statement appears in the registration statement. Most experts assume that reliance on the lead underwriter is adequate; nonetheless, extra "insurance" is usually added in the form of a "due diligence" meeting held just before the registration statement becomes effective. Theoretically, all the underwriters gather to question the issuer's management to satisfy the reasonable investigation component of the due diligence standard. Such meetings, in reality, tend to be mere formalities rather than useful investigations.

Substantial light is shed on the due diligence standard, and several other §11 issues, by the following case, which is the leading analysis of §11.

ESCOTT v. BARCHRIS CONSTRUCTION CO.

283 F.Supp. 643 (S.D.N.Y. 1968)

This §11 action was brought by more than 60 plaintiffs, purchasers of convertible subordinated debentures pursuant to a registration statement filed by BarChris Construction Co. that became effective in May 1961. Defendants included BarChris's auditors, Peat, Marwick, Mitchell & Co. and eight underwriters, including Drexel & Co., the lead underwriter. The remaining defendants were the signers of the registration statement, BarChris itself, its controller Trilling, and its nine directors. Of the nine directors, five—Vitolo (president), Russo (executive vice-president), Pugliese (vice-president), Kircher (treasurer), and Birnbaum (secretary)—were also officers of BarChris. The other four directors were Grant, a member of the law firm that served as Barchris's attorneys; Coleman, a partner in Drexel & Co.; and Auslander and Rose, who were not otherwise connected to BarChris.

BarChris originated in a partnership commenced in 1946 by Vitolo and Pugliese. They built bowling alleys, and the introduction of automatic pinsetters in 1952 created a boom in the industry. Vitolo and Pugliese incorporated BarChris, and sales rose from $800,000 in 1956 to $9,165,000 in 1960. Russo joined the organization and eventually became the executive vice-president.

BarChris had two methods of operation. One was to enter into a contract with a customer, who would make a small down payment, and then proceed to construct and equip the bowling alley. Upon completion, the customer would pay the balance of the contract price in notes, payable in installments over a period of years, which BarChris would discount with a factor, Talcott, receiving part of their face amount in cash. In event of default by the customer, Talcott had the right to demand that BarChris repurchase the notes. The other method was a sale and leaseback arrangement. Under either method, BarChris needed lots of cash because it spent considerable sums on construction before it was reimbursed.

In December 1959, BarChris sold 560,000 shares of common stock at $3.00 per share. But by early 1961, BarChris needed even more working capital. So, on March 30, 1961, BarChris filed a registration statement for convertible debentures. Amendments were filed on May 11 and May 16, and the statement became effec-

tive on May 16. On May 24, BarChris received the net proceeds of the financing, over $3 million.

By this time, BarChris was having difficulty collecting amounts due from its customers who were in arrears on payments due to factors on discounted notes. The industry was overbuilt, and alleys were starting to fail financially. On October 29, 1962, BarChris declared bankruptcy. On November 1, 1962, BarChris defaulted on the debentures sold under the May 1961 registration statement.

Plaintiffs base their §11 claim on several misstatements concentrated in 1960 financial statements and in the prospectus's description of BarChris's financial position in May 1961. In essence, plaintiffs complained that the December 31, 1960, balance sheet and earnings statements overstated 1960's earnings, net operating income, earnings per share, and current assets and understated contingent liabilities and direct liabilities. Plaintiffs further complained that the registration statement understated contingent liabilities as of April 30, 1961, and overstated sales and gross profit figures for the quarter ending March 31, 1961. Additionally, the registration statement allegedly overstated the backlog of unfilled orders, partly by indicating that contracts with entities such as T-Bowl were final and binding when they were not, in fact, executed. Finally, plaintiffs alleged that the textual portion of the registration statement failed to disclose that officers had loaned $386,615 to BarChris that had not been repaid as of the effective date of the registration statement; failed to disclose that over $1,160,000 of the proceeds of the offering would be used to pay off preexisting debts, including the loans to officers; failed to disclose defaults and impending defaults by customers and the liability BarChris would thereby incur to the factor; and failed to disclose that due to foreclosures BarChris was about to become engaged involuntarily in the business of operating bowling alleys.

MCLEAN, DISTRICT JUDGE:

[*After detailing the evidence arising out of 6,500 pages of transcript, the judge summarized his findings regarding plaintiffs' allegations of errors in the registration statement.*]

Summary

For convenience, the various falsities and omissions which I have discussed in the preceding pages are recapitulated here. They were as follows:

1. 1960 Earnings

    (a) Sales

As per prospectus	$9,165,320
Correct figure	8,511,420
Overstatement	$ 653,900

    (b) Net Operating Income

As per prospectus	$1,742,801
Correct figure	1,496,196
Overstatement	$ 246,605

    (c) Earnings per Share

As per prospectus	$.75
Correct figure	.65
Overstatement	$.10

2. 1960 Balance Sheet

    Current Assets

As per prospectus	$4,524,021
Correct figure	3,914,332
Overstatement	$ 609,689

3. Contingent Liabilities as of December 31, 1960 on Alternative Method of Financing

As per prospectus	$ 750,000
Correct figure	1,125,795
Understatement	$ 375,795
Capitol Lanes should have been shown as direct liability	$ 325,000

4. Contingent Liabilities as of April 30, 1961

As per prospectus	$ 825,000
Correct figure	1,443,853
Understatement	$ 618,853
Capitol Lanes should have been shown as a direct liability	$ 314,166

5. Earnings Figures for Quarter ending March 31, 1961

    (a) Sales

As per prospectus	$2,138,455
Correct figure	1,618,645
Overstatement	$ 519,810

    (b) Gross Profit

As per prospectus	$483,121
Correct figure	252,366
Overstatement	$230,755

6. Backlog as of March 31, 1961

As per prospectus	$6,905,000
Correct figure	2,415,000
Overstatement	$4,490,000

7. Failure to Disclose Officers' Loans Outstanding and Unpaid on May 16, 1961 $ 386,615

8. Failure to Disclose Use of Proceeds in Manner not Revealed in Prospectus
    Approximately $1,160,000

9. Failure to Disclose Customers' Delinquencies in May 1961 and BarChris's Potential
    Liability with Respect Thereto
    Over $1,350,000

10. Failure to Disclose the Fact that BarChris Was Already Engaged, and Was About
    to be More Heavily Engaged, in the Operation of Bowling Alleys

Materiality

[In essence, the judge found every error relating to the state of affairs in 1961 to be material. This included the overstatement of sales and gross profit for the first quarter, the understatement of contingent liabilities as of April 30, the overstatement of orders on hand and the failure to disclose the true facts with respect to officers' loans, customers' delinquencies, application of proceeds and the prospective operation of several allies.

Most of the errors regarding the state of affairs in 1960 were found not to be material, including the 1960 earnings figures, and the contingent liabilities as of December 31, 1960. The only errors relating to 1960 which were deemed material were the $609,689 overstatement of balance sheet current assets, and the failure to show Capitol Lanes as a direct liability.]

The "Due Diligence" Defenses

Every defendant, except BarChris itself, to whom, as the issuer, these defenses are not available, and except Peat, Marwick, whose position rests on a different statutory provision, has pleaded these affirmative defenses. Each

claims that (1) as to the part of the registration statement purporting to be made on the authority of an expert (which, for convenience, I shall refer to as the "expertised portion"), he had no reasonable ground to believe and did not believe that there were any untrue statements or material omissions, and (2) as to the other parts of the registration statement, he made a reasonable investigation, as a result of which he had reasonable ground to believe and did believe that the registration statement was true and that no material fact was omitted. As to each defendant, the question is whether he has sustained the burden of proving these defenses.

. . .

Before considering the evidence, a preliminary matter should be disposed of. The defendants do not agree among themselves as to who the "experts" were or as to the parts of the registration statement which were expertised. Some defendants say that Peat, Marwick was the expert, others say that BarChris's attorneys, Perkins, Daniels, McCormack & Collins, and the underwriters' attorneys, Drinker, Biddle & Reath, were also the experts. To say that the entire registration statement is expertised because some lawyer prepared it would be an unreasonable construction of the statute. Neither the lawyer for the company nor the lawyer for the underwriters is an expert within the meaning of Section 11. The only expert, in the statutory sense, was Peat, Marwick, and the only parts of the registration statement which purported to be made upon the authority of an expert were the portions which purported to be made on Peat, Marwick's authority.

· · ·

I turn now to the question of whether defendants have proved their due diligence defenses. The position of each defendant will be separately considered.

Russo

Russo was, to all intents and purposes, the chief executive officer of BarChris. He was a member of the executive committee. He was familiar with all aspects of the business. He was personally in charge of dealings with the factors. He talked with customers about their delinquencies.

Russo prepared the list of jobs which went into the backlog figure. He knew the status of those jobs.

· · ·

He had personally advanced large sums to BarChris of which $175,000 remained unpaid as of May 16.

In short, Russo knew all the relevant facts. He could not have believed that there were no untrue statements or material omissions in the prospectus. Russo has no due diligence defenses.

Vitolo and Pugliese

They were the founders of the business who stuck with it to the end. Vitolo was president and Pugliese was vice president. Despite their titles, their field of responsibility in the administration of BarChris's affairs during the period in question seems to have been less all embracing than Russo's. Pugliese in particular appears to have limited his activities to supervising the actual construction work.

Vitolo and Pugliese are each men of limited education. It is not hard to believe that for them the prospectus was difficult reading, if indeed they read it at all.

But whether it was or not is irrelevant. The liability of a director who signs a registration statement does not depend upon whether or not he read it or, if he did, whether or not he understood what he was reading.

And in any case, Vitolo and Pugliese were not as naive as they claim to be. They were members of BarChris's executive committee. At meetings of that committee BarChris's affairs were discussed at length. They must have known what was going on. Certainly they knew of the inadequacy of cash in 1961. They knew of their own large advances to the company which remained unpaid. They knew that they had agreed not to deposit their checks until the financing proceeds were received. They knew and intended that part of the proceeds were to be used to pay their own loans.

All in all, the position of Vitolo and Pugliese is not significantly different, for present purposes, from Russo's. They could not have believed that the registration statement was wholly true and that no material facts had been omitted. And in any case, there is nothing to show that they made any investigation of anything which they may not have known about or understood. They have not proved their due diligence defenses.

Kircher

Kircher was treasurer of BarChris and its chief financial officer. He is a certified public accountant and an intelligent man. He was thoroughly familiar with BarChris's financial affairs. He knew of the customers' delinquency problem. He participated actively with Russo in May 1961 in the successful effort to hold Talcott off until the financing proceeds came in. He knew how the financing proceeds were to be applied and he saw to it that they were so applied. He arranged the officers' loans and he knew all the facts concerning them.

Moreover, as a member of the executive committee, Kircher was kept informed as to those branches of the business of which he did not have direct charge.

. . .

Knowing the facts, Kircher had reason to believe that the expertised portion of the prospectus, the 1960 figures, was in part incorrect. He could not shut his eyes to the facts and rely on Peat, Marwick for that portion.

As to the rest of the prospectus, knowing the facts, he did not have a reasonable ground to believe it to be true. On the contrary, he must have known that in part it was untrue. Under these circumstances, he was not entitled to sit back and place the blame on the lawyers for not advising him about it.

Kircher has not proved his due diligence defenses.

. . .

Birnbaum

Birnbaum was a young lawyer employed by BarChris as house counsel and assistant secretary in October 1960. Unfortunately for him, he became secretary and a director of BarChris on April 17, 1961, after the first version of the registration statement had been filed with the Securities and Exchange Commission. He signed the later amendments, thereby becoming responsible for the accuracy of the prospectus in its final form.

He did not participate in the management of the company. As house counsel, he attended to legal matters of a routine nature. Among other things, he incorporated subsidiaries, with which BarChris was plentifully supplied.

. . .

Birnbaum examined contracts. In that connection he advised BarChris that the T-Bowl contracts were not legally enforceable. He was thus aware of that fact.

. . .

It seems probable that Birnbaum did not know of many of the inaccuracies in the prospectus. He must, however, have appreciated some of them. In any case, he made no investigation and relied on the others to get it right. He was entitled to rely upon Peat, Marwick for the 1960 figures, for as far as appears, he had no personal knowledge of the company's books of account or financial transactions. But he was not entitled to rely upon Kircher, Grant and Ballard for the other portions of the prospectus. As a lawyer, he should have known his obligations under the statute. He should have known that he was required to make a reasonable investigation of the truth of all the statements in the unexpertised portion of the document which he signed. Having failed to make such an investigation, he did not have reasonable ground to believe that all these statements were true. Birnbaum has not established his due diligence defenses except as to the audited 1960 figures.

Auslander

Auslander was an "outside" director, one who was not an officer of BarChris. He was chairman of the board of Valley Stream National Bank in Valley Stream, Long Island.

. . .

Auslander was elected a director on April 17, 1961. The registration statement in its original form had already been filed, of course without his signature. On May 10, 1961, he signed a signature page for the first amendment to the registration statement which was filed on May 11, 1961. This was a separate sheet without any document attached. Auslander did not know that it was a signature page for a registration statement. He vaguely understood that it was something "for the SEC."

Auslander attended a meeting of BarChris's directors on May 15, 1961. At that meeting he, along with the other directors, signed the signature sheet for the second amendment which constituted the registration statement in its final form. Again, this was only a separate sheet without any document attached. Auslander never saw a copy of the registration statement in its final form.

At the May 15 directors' meeting, however, Auslander did realize that what he was signing was a signature sheet to a registration statement. This was the first time that he had appreciated that fact. A copy of the registration statement in its earlier form as amended on May 11, 1961 was passed around at the meeting. Auslander glanced at it briefly. He did not read it thoroughly.

At the May 15 meeting, Russo and Vitolo stated that everything was in order and that the prospectus was correct. Auslander believed this statement.

In considering Auslander's due diligence defenses, a distinction is to be drawn between the expertised and non-expertised portions of the prospectus. As to the former, Auslander knew that Peat, Marwick had audited the 1960 figures. He believed them to be correct because he had confidence in Peat, Marwick. He had no reasonable ground to believe otherwise.

As to the non-expertised portions, however, Auslander is in a different position. Auslander made no investigation of the accuracy of the prospectus. He relied on the assurance of Vitolo and Russo, and upon the information he had received in answer to his inquiries back in February and early March. These inquiries were general ones, in the nature of a credit check. The information which he received in answer to them was also general, without specific reference to the statements in the prospectus, which was not prepared until some time thereafter.

It is true that Auslander became a director on the eve of the financing. He had little opportunity to familiarize himself with the company's affairs.

· · ·

Section 11 imposes liability in the first instance upon a director, no matter how new he is. He is presumed to know his responsibility when he becomes a director. He can escape liability only by using that reasonable care to investigate the facts which a prudent man would employ in the management of his own property. In my opinion, a prudent man would not act in an important matter without any knowledge of the relevant facts, in sole reliance upon representations of persons who are comparative strangers and upon general information which does not purport to cover the particular case. To say that such minimal conduct measures up to the statutory standard would, to all intents and purposes, absolve new directors from responsibility merely because they are new. This is not a sensible construction of §11, when one bears in mind its fundamental purpose of requiring full and truthful disclosure for the protection of investors.

I find and conclude that Auslander has not established his due diligence defense with respect to the misstatements and omissions in those portions of the prospectus other than the audited 1960 figures.

· · ·

Grant

Grant became a director of BarChris in October 1960. His law firm was counsel to BarChris in matters pertaining to the registration of securities. Grant drafted the registration statement for the stock issue in 1959 and for the warrants in January 1961. He also drafted the registration statement for the debentures. In the preliminary division of work between him and Ballard, the underwriters' counsel, Grant took initial responsibility for preparing the registration statement, while Ballard devoted his efforts in the first instance to preparing the indenture.

Grant is sued as a director and as a signer of the registration statement. This is not an action against him for malpractice in his capacity as a lawyer. Nevertheless, in considering Grant's due diligence defenses, the unique position which he occupied cannot be disregarded. As the director most directly concerned with writing the registration statement and assuring its accuracy, more was required of him in the way of reasonable investigation than could fairly be expected of a director who had no connection with this work.

There is no valid basis for plaintiffs' accusation that Grant knew that the prospectus was false in some respects and incomplete and misleading in others. Having seen him testify at length, I am satisfied as to his integrity. I find that Grant honestly believed that the registration statement was true and that no material facts had been omitted from it.

In this belief he was mistaken, and the fact is that for all his work, he never discovered any of the errors or omissions which have been recounted at length in this opinion, with the single exception of Capitol Lanes. He knew that BarChris had not sold this alley and intended to operate it, but he appears to have been under the erroneous impression that Peat, Marwick had knowingly sanctioned its inclusion in sales because of the allegedly temporary nature of the operation.

Grant contends that a finding that he did not make a reasonable investigation would be equivalent to a holding that a lawyer for an issuing company, in order to show due diligence, must make an independent audit of the figures supplied to him by his client. I do not consider this to be a realistic statement of the issue. There were errors and omissions here which could have been detected without an audit. The question is whether, despite his failure to detect them, Grant made a reasonable effort to that end.

Much of this registration statement is a scissors and paste-pot job. Grant lifted large portions from the earlier prospectuses, modifying them in some instances to the extent that he considered necessary. But BarChris's affairs had changed for the worse by May 1961. Statements that were accurate in January were no longer accurate in May. Grant never discovered this. He accepted the assurances of Kircher and Russo that any change which might have occurred had been for the better, rather than the contrary.

It is claimed that a lawyer is entitled to rely on the statements of his client and that to require him to verify their accuracy would set an unreasonably high standard. This is too broad a generalization. It is all a matter of degree. To require an audit would obviously be unreasonable. On the other hand, to require a check of matters easily verifiable is not unreasonable. Even honest clients can make mistakes. The statute imposes liability for untrue statements regardless of whether they are intentionally untrue. The way to prevent mistakes is to test oral information by examining the original written record.

There were things which Grant could readily have checked which he did not check.

. . .

I conclude that Grant has not established his due diligence defenses except as to the audited 1960 figures.

The Underwriters and Coleman

The underwriters other than Drexel made no investigation of the accuracy of the prospectus. One of them, Peter Morgan, had underwritten the 1959 stock issue and had been a director of BarChris. He thus had some general familiarity with its affairs, but he knew no more than the other underwriters about the debenture prospectus. They all relied upon Drexel as the "lead" underwriter.

Drexel did make an investigation. The work was in charge of Coleman, a partner of the firm, assisted by Casperson, an associate. Drexel's attorneys acted as attorneys for the entire group of underwriters. Ballard did the work, assisted by Stanton.

On April 17, 1961 Coleman became a director of BarChris. He signed the first amendment to the registration statement filed on May 11 and the second amendment, constituting the registration statement in its final form, filed on May 16. He thereby assumed a responsibility as a director and signer in addition to his responsibility as an underwriter.

The facts as to the extent of the investigation that Coleman made may be briefly summarized. He was first introduced to BarChris on September 15, 1960. Thereafter he familiarized himself with general conditions in the industry, primarily by reading reports and prospectuses of the two leading bowling alley builders, American Machine & Foundry Company and Brunswick. These indicated that the industry was still growing. He also acquired general information on BarChris by reading the 1959 stock prospectus, annual reports for prior years, and an unaudited statement for the first half of 1960. He inquired about BarChris of certain of its banks and of Talcott and received favorable replies.

The purpose of this preliminary investigation was to enable Coleman to decide whether Drexel would undertake the financing. It did not have direct reference to any specific registration statement for at that time, of course, none had been prepared. Coleman was sufficiently optimistic about BarChris's prospects to buy 1,000 shares of its stock, which he did in December 1960.

On January 24, 1961, Coleman held a meeting with Ballard, Grant and Kircher, among others. By that time Coleman had about decided to go ahead with the financing, although Drexel's formal letter of intent was not delivered until February 9, 1961 (subsequently revised on March 7, 1961). At this meeting Coleman asked Kircher how BarChris intended to use the proceeds of the financing. In reply to this inquiry, Kircher wrote a letter to Coleman dated January 30, 1961 outlining BarChris's plans. This eventually formed the basis of the application of proceeds section in the prospectus.

Coleman continued his general investigation. He obtained a Dun & Bradstreet report on BarChris on March 16, 1961. He read BarChris's annual report for 1960 which was available in March.

By mid-March, Coleman was in a position to make more specific inquiries. By that time Grant had prepared a first draft of the prospectus, consisting of a marked-up copy of the January 1961 warrant prospectus. Coleman attended three meetings to discuss the prospectus with BarChris's representatives.

At these discussions, which were extensive, successive proofs of the prospectus were considered and revised. At this point the 1961 figures were not available. They were put in the prospectus in May.

. . .

After Coleman was elected a director on April 17, 1961, he made no further independent investigation of the accuracy of the prospectus. He assumed that Ballard was taking care of this on his behalf as well as on behalf of the underwriters.

In April 1961 Ballard instructed Stanton to examine BarChris's minutes for the past five years and also to look at "the major contracts of the company." Stanton went to BarChris's office for that purpose on April 24. He asked Birnbaum for the minute books. He read the minutes of the board of directors and discovered interleaved in them a few minutes of executive committee meetings in 1960. He asked Kircher if there were any others. Kircher said that there had been other executive committee meetings but that the minutes had not been written up.

Stanton read the minutes of a few BarChris subsidiaries. His testimony was vague as to which ones.

As to the "major contracts," all that Stanton could remember seeing was an insurance policy. He did not examine the contracts with customers. He did not look to see what contracts comprised the backlog figure. Stanton examined no accounting records of BarChris. His visit, which lasted one day, was devoted primarily to reading the directors' minutes.

On April 25 Ballard wrote to Grant about certain matters which Stanton had noted on his visit to BarChris the day before, none of which Ballard considered "very earth shaking." As far as relevant here, these were (1) Russo's remark as recorded in the executive committee minutes of November 3, 1960 to the effect that because of customers' defaults, BarChris might find itself in the business of operating alleys; (2) the fact that the minutes of Sanpark Realty Corporation were incomplete; and (3) the fact that minutes of the executive committee were missing.

On May 9, 1961, Ballard came to New York and conferred with Grant and Kircher. They discussed the Securities and Exchange Commission's deficiency letter of May 4, 1961 which required the inclusion in the prospectus of certain additional information, notably net sales, gross profits and net earnings figures for the first quarter of 1961. They also discussed the points raised in Ballard's letter to Grant of April 25. As to the latter, most of the conversation related to what Russo had meant by his remark on November 3, 1960. Kircher said that the

delinquency problem was less severe now than it had been back in November 1960, that no alleys had been repossessed, and that although he was "worried about one alley in Harlem" (Dreyfuss), that was a "special situation." Grant reported that Russo had told him that his statement on November 3, 1960 was "merely hypothetical." On the strength of this conversation, Ballard was satisfied that the one-half of one per cent figure in the prospectus did not need qualification or elaboration.

As to the missing minutes, Kircher said that those of Sanpark were not significant and that the executive committee meetings for which there were no written minutes were concerned only with "routine matters."

It must be remembered that this conference took place only one week before the registration statement became effective. Ballard did nothing else in the way of checking during that intervening week.

Ballard did not insist that the executive committee minutes be written up so that he could inspect them, although he testified that he knew from experience that executive committee minutes may be extremely important. If he had insisted, he would have found the minutes highly informative, as has previously been pointed out. . . . Ballard did not ask to see BarChris's schedule of delinquencies or Talcott's notices of delinquencies, or BarChris's correspondence with Talcott.

Ballard did not examine BarChris's contracts with Talcott. He did not appreciate what Talcott's rights were under those financing agreements or how serious the effect would be upon BarChris of any exercise of those rights.

Ballard did not investigate the composition of the backlog figure to be sure that it was not "puffy." He made no inquiry after March about any new officers' loans, although he knew that Kircher had insisted on a provision in the indenture which gave loans from individuals priority over the debentures. He was unaware of the seriousness of BarChris's cash position and of how BarChris's officers intended to use a large part of the proceeds. He did not know that Bar-Chris was operating Capitol Lanes.

Like Grant, Ballard, without checking, relied on the information which he got from Kircher. He also relied on Grant who, as company counsel, presumably was familiar with its affairs.

. . .

I have already held that this procedure is not sufficient in Grant's case. Are underwriters in a different position, as far as due diligence is concerned?

The underwriters say that the prospectus is the company's prospectus, not theirs. Doubtless this is the way they customarily regard it. But the Securities Act makes no such distinction. The underwriters are just as responsible as the company if the prospectus is false. And prospective investors rely upon the reputation of the underwriters in deciding whether to purchase the securities.

The purpose of §11 is to protect investors. To that end the underwriters are made responsible for the truth of the prospectus. If they may escape that responsibility by taking at face value representations made to them by the company's management, then the inclusion of underwriters among those liable under §11 affords the investors no additional protection. To effectuate the statute's purpose, the phrase "reasonable investigation" must be construed to require more effort on the part of the underwriters than the mere accurate reporting in the prospectus of "date presented" to them by the company. It should make no difference that this data is elicited by questions addressed to the company officers by the underwriters, or that the underwriters at the time believe that the company's officers are truthful and reliable. In order to make the underwriters' participation in this enterprise of any value to the investors, the underwriters must make some reasonable attempt to verify the data submitted to them. They may

not rely solely on the company's officers or on the company's counsel. A prudent man in the management of his own property would not rely on them.

It is impossible to lay down a rigid rule suitable for every case defining the extent to which such verification must go. It is a question of degree, a matter of judgment in each case. In the present case, the underwriters' counsel made almost no attempt to verify management's representations. I hold that that was insufficient.

On the evidence in this case, I find that the underwriters' counsel did not make a reasonable investigation of the truth of those portions of the prospectus which were not made on the authority of Peat, Marwick as an expert. Drexel is bound by their failure. It is not a matter of relying upon counsel for legal advice. Here the attorneys were dealing with matters of fact. Drexel delegated to them, as its agent, the business of examining the corporate minutes and contracts. It must bear the consequences of their failure to make an adequate examination.

The other underwriters, who did nothing and relied solely on Drexel and on the lawyers, are also bound by it. It follows that although Drexel and the other underwriters believed that those portions of the prospectus were true, they had no reasonable ground for that belief, within the meaning of the statute. Hence, they have not established their due diligence defense, except as to the 1960 audited figures.

The same conclusions must apply to Coleman. Consequently, in his case also, he has not established his due diligence defense except as to the audited 1960 figures.

Peat, Marwick

Section 11(b) provides:

Notwithstanding the provisions of subsection (a) no person . . . shall be liable as provided therein who shall sustain the burden of proof—

. . .

(3) that . . . (B) as regards any part of the registration statement purporting to be made upon his authority as an expert . . . (i) he had, after reasonable investigation, reasonable ground to believe and did believe, at the time such part of the registration statement became effective, that the statements therein were true and that there was no omission to state a material fact required to be stated therein or necessary to make the statements therein not misleading.

• • •

This defines the due diligence defense for an expert. Peat, Marwick has pleaded it.

The part of the registration statement purporting to be made upon the authority of Peat, Marwick as an expert was, as we have seen, the 1960 figures. But because the statute requires the court to determine Peat, Marwick's belief, and the grounds thereof, "at the time such part of the registration statement became effective," for the purposes of this affirmative defense, the matter must be viewed as of May 16, 1961, and the question is whether at that time Peat, Marwick, after reasonable investigation, had reasonable ground to believe and did believe that the 1960 figures were true and that no material fact had been omitted from the registration statement which should have been included in order to make the 1960 figures not misleading. In deciding this issue, the court must consider not only what Peat, Marwick did in its 1960 audit, but also what it did in its subsequent "S-1 review." The proper scope of that review must also be determined.

• • •

The 1960 Audit

Peat, Marwick's work was in general charge of a member of the firm, Cummings, and more immediately in charge of Peat, Marwick's manager, Logan. Most of the actual work was performed by a senior accountant, Berardi, who had junior assistants, one of whom was Kennedy.

Berardi was then about thirty years old. He was not yet a C.P.A. He had had no previous experience with the bowling industry. This was his first job as a senior accountant. He could hardly have been given a more difficult assignment.

After obtaining a little background information on BarChris by talking to Logan and reviewing Peat, Marwick's work papers on its 1959 audit, Berardi examined the results of test checks of BarChris's accounting procedures which one of the junior accountants had made, and he prepared an "internal control questionnaire" and an "audit program." Thereafter, for a few days subsequent to December 30, 1960, he inspected BarChris's inventories and examined certain alley construction. Finally, on January 13, 1961, he began his auditing work which he carried on substantially continuously until it was completed on February 24, 1961. Toward the close of the work, Logan reviewed it and made various comments and suggestions to Berardi.

It is unnecessary to recount everything that Berardi did in the course of the audit. We are concerned only with the evidence relating to what Berardi did or did not do with respect to those items which I have found to have been incorrectly reported in the 1960 figures in the prospectus. More narrowly, we are directly concerned only with such of those items as I have found to be material.

Capitol Lanes

First and foremost is Berardi's failure to discover that Capitol Lanes had not been sold. This error affected both the sales figure and the liability side of the balance sheet. Fundamentally, the error stemmed from the fact that Berardi never realized that Heavenly Lanes and Capitol were two different names for the same alley.

• • •

Certain accounting records of BarChris, which Berardi testified he did not see, would have put him on inquiry.

The burden of proof on this issue is on Peat, Marwick. Although the question is a rather close one, I find that Peat, Marwick has not sustained that burden. Peat, Marwick has not proved that Berardi made a reasonable investigation as far as Capitol Lanes was concerned and that his ignorance of the true facts was justified.

The S-1 Review

The purpose of reviewing events subsequent to the date of a certified balance sheet (referred to as an S-1 review when made with reference to a registration statement) is to ascertain whether any material change has occurred in the company's financial position which should be disclosed in order to prevent the balance sheet figures from being misleading. The scope of such a review, under generally accepted auditing standards, is limited. It does not amount to a complete audit.

. . .

Berardi made the S-1 review in May 1961. He devoted a little over two days to it, a total of 20½ hours. He did not discover any of the errors or omissions pertaining to the state of affairs in 1961 which I have previously discussed at length, all of which were material. The question is whether, despite his failure to find out anything, his investigation was reasonable within the meaning of the statute.

What Berardi did was to look at a consolidating trial balance as of March 31, 1961 which had been prepared by BarChris, compare it with the audited December 31, 1960 figures, discuss with [director] Trilling certain unfavorable developments which the comparison disclosed, and read certain minutes. He did not examine any "important financial records" other than the trial balance. As to minutes, he read only

what minutes Birnbaum gave him, which consisted only of the board of directors' minutes of BarChris. He did not read such minutes as there were of the executive committee. He did not know that there was an executive committee, hence he did not discover that Kircher had notes of executive committee minutes which had not been written up. He did not read the minutes of any subsidiary.

In substance, what Berardi did is similar to what Grant and Ballard did. He asked questions, he got answers which he considered satisfactory, and he did nothing to verify them.

Accountants should not be held to a standard higher than that recognized in their profession. I do not do so here. Berardi's review did not come up to that standard. He did not take some of the steps which Peat, Marwick's written program prescribed. He did not spend an adequate amount of time on a task of this magnitude. Most important of all, he was too easily satisfied with glib answers to his inquiries.

This is not to say that he should have made a complete audit. But there were enough danger signals in the materials which he did examine to require some further investigation on his part. Generally accepted accounting standards required such further investigation under these circumstances. It is not always sufficient merely to ask questions.

Here again, the burden of proof is on Peat, Marwick. I find that that burden has not been satisfied. I conclude that Peat, Marwick has not established its due diligence defense.

The Causation Defense

Section 11(a) provides that when a registration statement contains an untrue statement of a material fact or omits to state a material fact, "any person acquiring such security . . . may . . . sue."

Section 11(e) sets forth a proviso reading as follows:

Provided, that if the defendant proves that any portion or all of such damages represents other than the depreciation in value of such security resulting from such part of the registration statement, with respect to which his liability is asserted, not being true or omitting to state a material fact required to be stated therein or necessary to make the statements therein not misleading, such portion of or all such damages shall not be recoverable.

Each defendant in one form or another has relied upon this proviso as a complete defense. Each maintains that the entire damage suffered by each and every plaintiff was caused by factors other than the material falsities and omissions of the registration statement. These factors, in brief, were the decline in the bowling industry which came about because of the fact that the industry was overbuilt and because popular enthusiasm for bowling diminished.

The position taken by defendants in their affirmative defenses is an extreme one which cannot be sustained. I cannot say that the entire damage suffered by every plaintiff was caused by factors other than the errors and omissions of the registration statement for which these defendants are responsible. As to some plaintiffs, or as to part of the damage sustained by others, that may be true. The only practicable course is to defer decision of this issue until the claim of each individual plaintiff is separately considered. As stated at the outset, this opinion is devoted only to matters common to all plaintiffs.

---

(3) *Due Diligence Under the Integrated Disclosure System*

Three major features of the integrated disclosure system developed in the early 1980s have raised concerns about the feasibility of actually achieving "due diligence" (especially by underwriters) and about the adequacy of investor protection under the new regime.

Increased use of *incorporation by reference* means that the focus of the issuing process is no longer on the preparation of the registration statement. During the month or so that it traditionally took to draft an S-1 registration statement, the underwriter could extensively investigate the issuer to fulfill its due diligence obligations. Today, under the S-2 and S-3 forms, the keystone is not preparation of a new registration statement but mere incorporation by reference of 10-K's, 10-Q's, and other documents as to which the underwriter probably had little input.

Elimination of staff review of most registration statements, except those of first-time issuers, also eliminates another opportunity that underwriters traditionally used to play "devil's advocate" regarding registration statement disclosures. Registration statements can now become effective in less than 48 hours, leaving underwriters and other §11 defendants little time to undertake a "reasonable investigation."

Shelf registration has also had a dramatic impact on due diligence practices. Not only can a registration statement become effective within hours after being pulled off the shelf thereby leaving the underwriter with little or no time for investigation, but also shelf registration has led to a very competitive situation. No longer is there a month or so in which to put together an underwriting syndicate. Today many underwriters will handle shelf registrations on a solo basis. An underwriter today will be reluctant to be the "naysayer" regarding the quality of registration statement disclosures for fear of losing the issuer's business to a competitor.

Although some have persuasively argued that due diligence practices sufficient to protect the investor are practically impossible under the integrated disclosure system,[15] the SEC has taken some steps, including the adoption of Rule 176, discussed in the following article, which may alleviate some of the problems.

"SPOTLIGHT SHINES ANEW ON STATUTORY DILIGENCE TASKS" *

John F. Olson

Legal Times of Washington, April 14, 1983, p. 14

When most registration statements were written on Form S-1, and most registrations even for longtime issuers were reviewed by the Securities and Exchange Commission staff, underwriters, and their counsel, as well as the issuer, its auditors, and counsel, all participated not only in the drafting of the disclosure documents but also in the relatively elaborate review and research process that supported the drafting effort. Beginning with forms S-7 and S-16, and continuing with new forms S-2 and S-3, much of the 1933 Act registration statement (in Form S-3, all except the description of the offering) is incorporated by reference from documents filed or prepared under the Securities Exchange Act of 1934. Such documents, prepared as periodic reports or as proxy solicitation materials, normally are prepared in the ordinary course of the issuer's business without participation by the underwriters or their counsel, indeed quite frequently at times when the issuer is not even contemplating an offering.

When it is later determined to proceed with an offering utilizing, for example, the very short Form S-3, neither issuers nor the underwriters competing for their business are prepared to pay—or to wait—for the elaborate de novo diligence procedures that once routinely accompanied the 1933 Act registration process.

When a Rule 415 registration statement is declared effective, neither the underwriters nor the offering date need be known. Since several underwriters may compete for each takedown from the issuer's registered shelf, each underwriter must be prepared to satisfy its diligence concerns as expeditiously and as economically as possible.

Limited Underwriter Defense

Why the concern with diligence anyway? Under §11(a) of the Securities Act of 1933, underwriters, like the issuer and its officers and directors, have essentially absolute liability for any material misstatement or omission in the disclosure documents. And, in the case of a short-form registration statement, that liability extends to material that is incorporated by reference from 1934 Act current reports and annual reports and proxy materials.

· · ·

---

[15] For example, L. Nicholas, "The Integrated Disclosure System and Its Impact upon Underwriters' Due Diligence: Will Investors Be Protected?" *Securities Regulation Law Journal* Vol. 11 (1983), p. 3; and A. Hovdesven and S. Wolfram, "Underwriter Liability In the Integrated Disclosure System," *National Law Journal*, July 5, 1982, p. 13.

New System Embraced

The commission adopted two new rules that directly addressed the diligence concerns that had increased for underwriters and their counsel with the growth of the integrated disclosure system.

First, Rule 412 provides that a document incorporated by reference in a 1933 Act registration statement is deemed to be modified or superseded by subsequent statements on the same subject in the statement itself or subsequently filed documents, and the changes are not to be deemed an admission that the first document was deficient. The purpose of this rule, of course, is to encourage updating and correction of previously filed reports where diligence reviews at the time of an offering indicate a change is appropriate.

Second, and more important, new Rule 176 . . . specifies eight relevant circumstances to which the commission believes courts should refer in determining when the conduct of underwriters (or others with potential §11 liability) has amounted to "reasonable investigation" and "reasonable ground for belief." These circumstances are:

1. The type of issuer;
2. The type of security;
3. The type of person whose liability is at issue (i.e., underwriter, officer, director, etc.);
4. The office held when the person is an officer;
5. The presence or absence of another relationship to the issuer (e.g., as regular outside counsel or as an officer) when the person is a director or proposed director;
6. Reasonable reliance on officers, employees, and others whose duties should have given them knowledge of particular facts (in light of the functions and responsibilities of the particular person with respect to the issuer and the filing);
7. When the person is an underwriter, the type of underwriting arrangement (e.g., whether firm or best efforts, whether the result of competitive bidding or not), the role of the particular person as an underwriter (e.g., whether a mere statutory or technical underwriter or a traditional, contractual underwriter), and the availability of information with respect to the registration (to the underwriter), and
8. Whether, with respect to a fact or document incorporated by reference, the particular person had any responsibility for the fact or document at the time of the filing from which it was incorporated (i.e., was the underwriter or its counsel in a position to perform diligence when the disclosure was prepared?).

· · ·

What, then, are the essential minimum contents of the underwriter diligence procedures that will meet the requirements of §11(b) of the 1933 Act (and preclude recklessness for purposes of the antifraud rules) while still permitting efficient utilization of the short-form registration and Rule 415 processes? The answer for most underwriters in most situations lies in two steps: First, the development of a continuous diligence program for issuers followed by the underwriter. Second, the development of special comfort procedures that can be implemented on short notice and completed quickly once the decision is made to proceed with an offering using a short-form registration statement, or with an already registered offering off of a Rule 415 shelf.

Continuous Diligence Program

The SEC itself has suggested the first foundation of a credible underwriter's diligence program in today's environment. In the proposing release for Rules 176 and 412, the commission specifically suggested that underwriting firms develop and maintain a "reservoir of information'' about issuers that are regular clients or likely candidates for the firms' distribution services. The ''reservoir'' for each issuer being followed by a prospective underwriter should include copies of annual reports, proxy statements, and 1934 Act periodic reports, as well as press releases and analysts' reports about the issuer.

Should the underwriter's diligence role include more than the passive collection and review of information about an issuer? Where the underwriter is named as a prospective managing underwriter in a shelf registration statement under Rule 415, the underwriter can and should do more. In such a case, the prospective managing underwriter can be expected to participate in the review of periodic disclosure documents before they are filed or used. This best can be accomplished by having the issuer and the entire group of prospective managing underwriters agree at the time the shelf registration statement is first filed on a single, experienced law firm to serve as underwriters' counsel, no matter which underwriting firms eventually are selected as managers for specific offerings off of the shelf. The law firm, representing all prospective underwriters, then can review the registration documents, all past filings to be incorporated by reference, and additional periodic filings to be made once the registration statement has become effective. It also can facilitate the eventual takedowns from the shelf by preparing master forms of underwriting agreements and, in the case of debt issues, preparing and qualifying master trust indenture forms in advance.

In addition, a reasonable program of continuous diligence will include meetings—at least annually—with senior officers of the issuer to review financial trends and business developments, attendance at meetings the issuer conducts for analysts, and early discussions with the issuer's financial officers about prospective offerings. In short, underwriters reasonably can be expected to ''follow'' those issuers who are regular or prospective clients as carefully, and in much the same manner, as analysts have traditionally followed companies and industries assigned to them.

Equally important to the performance of continuous diligence will be its documentation. Well-advised underwriters and their counsel will maintain diligence files for each issuer they follow, which will include not only copies of the annual reports, proxy statements, 1934 Act current reports, press releases, analysts' reports, and other materials that constitute the available reservoir of information about the issuer, but also memoranda of meetings with the issuer's officers and of each other diligence step taken.

Special Comfort Procedures

Once a short-form registration offering, or an offering off of the shelf, is set to proceed, what additional underwriter diligence steps are reasonable? The answer depends in part, of course, on what already has been done. If the underwriter has been following the issuer carefully, or in the shelf registration situation underwriter's counsel has been involved and performing diligence from the start, the burden of additional steps when the offering is set to proceed is less. Where the underwriter has not had substantial prior involvement, more can be expected—although, as Rule 176 makes clear, the extent and nature of what diligence is required may vary with the type and degree of underwriter involvement in the offering.

What seems most reasonable in either circumstance is something akin to the cold comfort review conducted by an issuer's outside auditing firm. In other words, at a minimum, the underwriter and its counsel can be expected to review with the issuer, its outside auditors and counsel the final prospectus that will be used and the most recent financial statements and other documents to be included or incorporated by reference in the prospectus. An auditor's comfort letter can and should be obtained. Most important the underwriter and its counsel should meet with senior officers, especially senior financial officers, of the issuer and review the present status of the issuer's business and financial position, including any recent or prospective material changes. The underwriters and their counsel also should meet separately and on a confidential basis with the issuer's outside auditors to review the same questions with particular attention to any variations from the norm or recent changes in accounting policies and to the quality of internal accounting controls.

Beyond these diligence steps to be taken in every case, additional procedures may be suggested by particular situations. The principal areas of risk for each issuer should be identified and reasonable steps taken to examine each of them. If, for example, the issuer's business is heavily dependent on a particular supplier or one customer or a small group of customers, prudence will dictate inquiry of those who are on the other side of these relationships. Where a patent is material, or a lawsuit may have a material impact, direct, confidential inquiry—supported in most cases by a written response—should be made of patent or litigation counsel.

Borrowing another technique from financial auditors, who review the adequacy of internal accounting controls in determining whether they need to take additional audit steps, underwriters should be able to satisfy an important part of their diligence obligations by satisfying themselves as to the integrity and adequacy of the process used by the issuer in preparing and reviewing the documents which are incorporated by reference in a registration statement. Where the underwriter is satisfied that an issuer has a thorough and effective review process, involving auditors and outside directors, for preparation of 1934 Act current reports, then the underwriter's own review of past filings justifiably can be more limited.

· · ·

There are, unfortunately, no exact standards as to when "enough" diligence has been done. There probably never will be. But underwriters need not be unduly disheartened. With the adoption of Rule 176 the commission has given clear support to the differential diligence standard. Underwriters who approach their responsibilities carefully, take prudent and reasonable steps to examine and verify material, information, and document what they have done, should be able to establish a diligence defense to Section 11 liability, and to obviate the basis for the recklessness element that is essential to an antifraud claim, in connection with offering disclosure documents, even in the new world of short-form registration statements and offerings off of the shelf.

Section 11 Damages

All defendants are jointly and severally liable under §11. Any single defendant can therefore be made to pay all of plaintiffs' losses, except that underwriter liability is expressly limited to the amount of securities individually underwritten. Thus, if a particular underwriter handled $5 million worth of securities in a $30 million offering, that underwriter could be liable for no more than $5 million in §11 damages, even if plaintiffs' total losses were much more.

Calculation of damages under §11 is a two-step process.[16] First, the "amount paid" for the securities must be determined. This will be the lesser of (1) the amount plaintiff actually paid or (2) the price at which the security was offered to the public.

---

[16] See, generally, Note, "Causation of Damages Under Section 11 of the Securities Act of 1933," *N.Y.U. Law Review*, Vol. 51 (1976), p. 217.

Assume that Company A issued common stock to the public at $5 per share and Mr. B purchased at that price and a week later sold his shares to Ms. C for $4 per share. The "amount paid" by Mr. B is $5 per share; the "amount paid" by Ms. C is $4 per share.

Once the "amount paid" is known, four possible situations must be considered.

Situation (1) If plaintiff sold the securities prior to filing suit, §11 damages equal the "amount paid" minus sale price. Thus, if Mr. B bought Primmer Corporation stock at $5 per share pursuant to a faulty registration statement, rode the market down to $2 per share and sold, and then filed suit when market value was $1 per share, Mr. B's damages would be $3 per share.

Situation (2) If plaintiff still holds the securities at time of judgment, damages equal "amount paid" minus value "at time of suit." Thus, if Ms. C purchased Primmer Corporation securities issued pursuant to a defective registration statement at $10 per share, filed suit when the market price was $8 per share, and won a judgment when the price was $6 per share, her damages would be $2 per share. (This assumes that market price equals "value," an assumption that will be examined shortly.)

Situation (3) If plaintiff sells during the pendency of the suit at a price *higher* than the price "at time of suit," damages under §11 equal "amount paid" minus sale price. Thus, if Mr. D purchased Primmer Corporation securities at $50 per share pursuant to a defective registration statement, filed suit when the price was $40 per share, and sold during pendency of the suit at $45 per share, his damages would be $5 per share.

Situation (4) Finally, if plaintiff sells during the pendency of the suit at a price *lower* than the price "at time of suit," damages equal "amount paid" minus value at time of suit. So, if Ms. E purchased Primmer Corporation stock at $80 per share pursuant to a defective registration statement, filed suit when the value was $60 per share, and sold during the pendency of the suit at $40 per share, Ms. E's damages would be $20 per share.

Note that a plaintiff holding the securities until judgment need not "mitigate" damages. For example, assume that investor X buys at $100 per share and files suit when the errors in the registration statement are disclosed. The price at time of suit is $50 per share, but during pendency of the suit the price rallies to $75 per share. By the time of judgment the price falls again to $40 per share. The investor will receive $50 per share in damages and will not be penalized because an opportunity to sell at only a $25 per share loss was forgone.

An overall ceiling on recovery is established by subsection (g) of §11, which provides that "in no case shall the amount recoverable exceed the price at which the security was offered to the public." Assume that Primmer Corporation stock is offered to the public pursuant to a defective registration statement at $3 per share, that plaintiff purchases such securities in the secondary market at $6 per share, and that the price later drops to $2 per share because of disclosed errors in the registration statement. If plaintiff files suit after selling at $2 per share, though plaintiff has lost $4 per share she cannot recover more than $3 per share.

Section 11's measure of damages is aimed at prevention rather than compensation, so a remedy is not always provided. Assume that stock is offered to the public at $4 per share and that Ms. F purchases in the secondary market at $7 per share. Errors in the registration statement come to light, and the price drops to $5 per share. Although Ms. F has sustained a loss of $2 per share, she cannot recover under §11 because the $4-per-share offering price established a ceiling for calculation of damages.

These relatively straightforward formulas for calculating damages are complicated somewhat by two rules that must be considered. *First*, the "value at time of suit" is not necessarily the market price at which the securities were selling that day, say, on the New York Stock Exchange. Rather, courts can take into account other factors to adjust the market price to reflect the supposed "true value" of the security.

For example, in *Beecher* v. *Able*,[17] Douglas Aircraft sold debentures on July 12, 1966. On October 14, 1966, investors who purchased between July 12 and September 29, 1969, sued under §11 claiming that the prospectus was materially erroneous. For purposes of determining the "value at time of suit," the court looked beyond the market price of 75½ that existed on October 14. The court concluded that the market price on the day suit was filed was heavily influenced by "panic selling" and that the long-term prospects of the issuer were good. Indeed, by the following February 1, the market price had risen to 100, and later peaked at 145. Adjusting for the "panic selling," the court established 85 as the "fair value" at time of suit, almost 10 points over the market price.

A *second* complicating factor is that defendants may affirmatively defend a §11 suit by proving that the decline in the value of plaintiffs' securities was caused by factors other than the false statements or omissions of the registration statement. For example, in *Feit* v. *Leasco Data Process Equipment Co.*,[18] the court took judicial notice of the fact that the entire stock market had taken a big plunge in 1969. Therefore, the court concluded, some of the downward movement in Leasco's securities must have been caused by general market factors operating on all securities and unrelated to the misstatements of Leasco's registration statement. The court chose Standard & Poor's Daily Stock Price Index as an appropriate guide to measure the impact of these general market forces.

A somewhat more obvious situation occurred in *Fox* v. *Glickman*,[19] where the offering price of $12.50 declined to $11.125 before errors in the registration statement were discovered and the price plunged even farther. The court concluded that the initial decline to $11.125 must have been caused by market factors unrelated to the then undiscovered misstatements in the registration statement and therefore established $11.125 as the ceiling value for calculating damages.[20]

---

[17] 435 F.Supp. 397 (S.D. N.Y. 1977).

[18] 332 F.Supp. 544 (E.D. N.Y. 1971).

[19] 253 F.Supp. 1005 (S.D. N.Y. 1966).

[20] Although investors prove that false statements in the registration statement caused them to purchase, they cannot succeed under §11 if those false statements did not cause the stock's decline. Section 11 focuses not on the causal relationship between the misstatements and the original price, but rather on the relationship between the misstatements and subsequent declines in value—*Akerman* v. *Oryx Communications, Inc.* [1984 Binder], *Federal Securities Law Reports* (CCH), ¶91,680 (S.D. N.Y. 1984).

Indemnity and Contribution

A defendant seeking *indemnity* is attempting to place the entire burden of plaintiffs' judgment onto another either because that other person was more at fault or because the defendant seeking indemnity was acting on behalf of the other person when liability was incurred. In the §11 setting, underwriters, officers, and directors would like to be indemnified from §11 liability by the issuer for whose benefit they are acting. However, the courts resist indemnity because it reduces the incentive for the party seeking indemnity to comply with the law. Why should an underwriter, for example, carry out its due diligence obligations if it can be indemnified by the issuer for any judgment it might sustain under §11? [21]

As noted in the previous chapter, the SEC is very much against agreements by which issuers indemnify their officers and directors from §11 liability. On the other hand, the Commission has allowed issuers to purchase liability insurance for these same officers and directors. The distinction is not easy to fathom, but undoubtedly relates to the very practical difficulty of inducing persons to serve as directors if such insurance were not available.

A defendant who has paid all a plaintiffs' judgment seeks *contribution* when he or she attempts to force other joint tortfeasors to pay their proportionate share of the judgment. For the same reason, §11 defendants are not entitled to indemnity; they are allowed contribution. Absent a right of contribution, wrongdoing defendants would be allowed to escape liability completely by letting a co-defendant pay the entire judgment. [22]

Section 12(1)

Section 12(1) of the 1933 Securities Act states that "any person who . . . offers or sells a security in violation of section 5 . . . shall be liable to the person purchasing such security." This is a very stringent liability provision that does not require proof of causation, reliance, scienter, or even negligence. There is no good faith, reasonable care, or due diligence defense.

Elements of a §12(1) Claim

(1) *Violation of Section 5*

Section 12(1) redresses only violations of §5 of the 1933 Act. Therefore, plaintiffs must demonstrate that defendants sold unregistered securities in violation of §5(a)(1),

---

[21] *Globus* v. *Law Research Service, Inc.*, 418 F.2d 1276 (2d Cir. 1969). Note that in *Goldstein* v. *Alodex Corp.*, 409 F.Supp. 1201 (E.D. Pa. 1976), two outside directors who established that they acted with due diligence did not have to contribute to a judgment paid by the issuer *and* were entitled to indemnity from the issuer for the $40,000 in attorney's fees they incurred in establishing their nonliability.

[22] *Globus* v. *Law Research Service, Inc.*, 318 F.Supp. 955 (S.D. N.Y. 1970), *aff'd*, 442 F.2d 1346 (2d Cir. 1971).

failed to deliver a prospectus in violation of §5(b)(2), delivered a prospectus that did not comply with §10 in violation of §5(b)(1), or made an illegal offer before a registration statement was filed ("gun jumping") or during a stop order or refusal order in violation of §5(c).

Numerically, most §12(1) cases involve sale of unregistered securities. Defendants normally claim that an exemption exists that permits the sale without registration, and the cases usually turn on the availability of the exemption.

As noted in Chapter 15, an illegal offer in violation of §5 will lead to §12(1) liability and is not cured by a subsequent legal sale.[23]

(2) Privity of Contract

Section 12(1) imposes a privity requirement by imposing liability only on the person who offered or sold the securities to plaintiffs. Courts have given varying meanings to the term "seller" in deciding how strictly to construe this privity requirement. Because most of the case law on privity has arisen under §12(2), which is similar to §12(1) respecting privity, these court interpretations will be discussed in relation to the §12(2) claim.

Statute of Limitations Defense

Just about the only defense available to a §12(1) defendant who has violated §5 is the statute of limitations. According to §13, no action may be brought more than one year after the §5 violation upon which the suit is based nor, in any event, more than three years after the security was first *bona fide* offered to the public.

Damages Under §12(1)

A successful §12(1) plaintiff who still holds the security is entitled to rescission damages—the amount paid for the security with interest (less the amount of any income received). A plaintiff who no longer has the security is entitled to recover general tort damages.

Section 12(2)

Section 12(2) is a very broad antifraud provision that complements, and even overlaps, the narrower §11. While §11 provides an express cause of action to remedy injuries caused by erroneous registration statements, §12(2) provides a remedy for misstatements and omissions in any written documents, including selling literature and even oral misrepresentations. It also applies whether or not the securities offered were or had to be registered. Additionally, it extends liability to persons not listed as potential defendants in §11.

---

[23] *Diskin v. Lomasney & Co.*, 452 F.2d 871 (2d Cir. 1971).

Elements of a §12(2) Cause of Action

Plaintiffs in a §12(2) suit need not prove reliance, causation,[24] or scienter. They must establish that they purchased securities, that a material omission or misstatement was made, and that it was made as to a material fact. In one leading case, it was deemed an implied material misrepresentation that defendant securities dealer recommended the securities of a financially troubled corporation to an institutional investor authorized by statute to purchase only prime grade securities.[25]

Additionally, the language of the section places at least three burdens on plaintiffs.

(1) Jurisdictional Means

Section 12(2) applies only to persons who sell securities "by the use of any means or instruments of transportation or communication in interstate commerce." Thus, defendants must have used the telephone, the mails, or some such means to offer the securities. Naturally, a defendant must work hard to avoid use of such facilities. Indeed, each separate use of the phone or mails constitutes a separate violation of §12(2). Thus, a single transaction may give rise to a multiple-count civil complaint or criminal indictment.

(2) Defendant's Knowledge

Plaintiff need not prove that defendant intentionally defrauded. In fact, a §12(2) plaintiff need only *allege* a defendant's knowledge to shift to defendant the burden of proof to establish "that he did not know, and in the exercise of reasonable care could not have known" of the misstatement or omission.

The §12(2) defendant's duty to prove "reasonable care" is obviously analogous to the §11 defendant's burden of establishing reasonable belief and reasonable investigation. In fact, the appellate court in *Sanders* v. *John Nuveen & Co., Inc.*,[26] found "no significance" in the difference between the "reasonable investigation" standard of §11 and the "reasonable care" language of §12(2). The Supreme Court refused to hear an appeal in *Sanders*, but Justice Powell dissented from the refusal, arguing that the "reasonable investigation" standard is more demanding than the "reasonable care" language contained in §12(2). Petitioner-underwriter Nuveen had relied on the certified financial statements of issuer W & H, Inc. Those statements had been rigged, with the complicity of W & H, Inc.'s auditor, to make the issuer appear profitable when in fact it had lost about $1 million. Justice Powell stated,

> The Court of Appeals' opinion may be read as holding that petitioner's duty of "reasonable care" under §12(2) required it independently to investigate the accuracy and complete-

---

[24] Although traditional causation is not required, there must be some connection between the alleged misstatement and the transaction. Erroneous but wholly unconnected statements do not lead to §12(2) liability— *Jackson* v. *Oppenheim*, 533 F.2d 826 (2d Cir. 1976).

[25] *Franklin Savings Bank of New York* v. *Levy*, 551 F.2d 521 (2d Cir. 1977).

[26] 619 F.2d 1222 (7th Cir. 1980), *cert. denied*, 450 U.S. 1005 (1980).

ness of the certified financial statements. It was customary, however—and in my view entirely reasonable—for petitioner to rely on these statements as accurately reflecting W & H's financial condition. Even under §11 of the act, an underwriter is explicitly absolved of the duty to investigate with respect to "any part of the registration statement purporting to be made on the authority of an expert" such as a certified accountant if "he had no reasonable ground to believe, and did not believe" that the information therein was misleading. . . . This provision is in the act because, almost by definition, it is reasonable to rely on financial statements certified by public accountants. Yet, in this case, the Court of Appeals nevertheless seems to have imposed the higher duty prescribed by §11 to investigate, but denied petitioner the right to rely on "the authority of an expert" that also is provided by §11.

. . . My concern is that the opinion of the Court of Appeals will be read as recognizing no distinction between the standards of care applicable under §§11 and 12(2), and particularly as casting doubt upon the reasonableness of relying upon the expertise of certified public accountants. Dealers may believe that they must undertake extensive independent financial investigations rather than rely on the accuracy of the certified financial statements. If this is so, the efficiency of the short-term financial markets will be impaired. I would grant certiorari.

(3) *Privity of Contract*

Section 12(2) states that *any* person who "offers or sells" via an untrue statement shall be liable to the purchaser. Many courts have viewed this as a strict privity requirement, allowing purchasers to sue only the actual seller of the security [27] or someone controlling that seller.[28]

Other courts have taken varying, broader views of who may be liable as a "seller" under §12(2). A middle view is that any person whose activities "proximately caused" plaintiffs' injuries may be liable. Thus, in *Junker* v. *Crory*,[29] an attorney who actively negotiated and implemented an allegedly fraudulent merger on behalf of his clients, the actual sellers, was held liable under §12(2).

The broadest view of privity is that a defrauded purchaser may sue any person who "participated" in or "aided and abetted" the sale. In *Sandusky Land, Ltd.* v. *Uniplan Groups, Inc.*,[30] the courts imposed §12(2) liability on an accounting firm that allegedly disseminated a misleading opinion letter concerning the sale of interests in a limited partnership.

The following case represents one court's resolution of a unique §12(2) privity problem.

---

[27] *Collins* v. *Signetics Corp.*, 605 F.2d 110 (3d Cir. 1979).

[28] Remember that §15 provides that anyone who "controls" a person liable under §11 or §12 is also liable, unless the controller had no knowledge or reasonable grounds to believe the facts alleged did not exist.

[29] 650 F.2d 1349 (5th Cir. 1981).

[30] 400 F.Supp. 440 (N.D. Ohio 1975).

KLEIN v. COMPUTER DEVICES, INC.

602 F.Supp. 837 (S.D. N.Y. 1985)

In 1983 Computer Devices, Inc., made a public offering of securities at $11.25 per share. Subsequently the price declined and the issuer took bankruptcy. Purchasers sued various principals of the issuer and Becker Paribas, Inc. (Becker), the lead underwriter of the public offering. Becker moved to dismiss plaintiffs' §12(2) claim on grounds of lack of privity. The trial court denied the motion. Becker moved for reconsideration.

GOETTEL, DISTRICT JUDGE:

Becker argues that the Court failed to consider the unique statutory status of an underwriter with respect to its liability under section 12(2). Becker argues that this section unambiguously requires privity between the buyer and the seller. Although it acknowledges that the courts have sidestepped the privity requirement by utilizing such theories as participation, aiding and abetting, and conspiracy, Becker contends that such theories are not applicable to an underwriter because of the statutory limitations that Congress articulated in sections 11 and 12.

In 1934, Congress amended section 11, adopting section 11(e), to provide that

> [i]n no event shall any underwriter (unless such underwriter shall have knowingly received from the issuer for acting as an underwriter some benefit, directly or indirectly, in which all other underwriters similarly situated did not share in proportion to their respective interests in the underwriting) be liable in any suit . . . for damages in excess of the total price at which the securities underwritten by him and distributed to the public were offered to the public.

Becker argues that section 12 must be read in conjunction with section 11. Such a reading, contends Becker, demonstrates Congress' intent to limit the liability of an underwriter to what that underwriter underwrote and sold as illustrated by the privity requirement of section 12 and the specific damage limitations for underwriters in section 11. Thus, argues Becker, Congress precluded judicial imposition of unlimited liability on underwriters which the Court's Opinion has expanded.

The plaintiffs agree that the two sections are to be read together. They argue, however, that Congress never intended to limit the liability of a managing underwriter, like Becker, as indicated by the parenthetical provision in section 11(e) which provides that an underwriter's liability is not limited if the underwriter received preferential treatment from the issuer. They contend that lead underwriters now evade the effect of section 11(e) by receiving their management fee from members of the underwriting syndicate rather than from the issuer.

As we held before, plaintiffs can sue not only their immediate sellers under section 12(2) but also those who substantially participated in the transaction. Participation can include active participation in the transaction or aiding and abetting or conspiring with the seller.

The Court agrees that sections 11 and 12 should be read together when construing the liability of an underwriter, such as Becker, under section 12(2). For this reason, an underwriter who is alleged to have violated section 12(2) merely by performing the functions of a typical lead underwriter cannot be liable as a participator under section 12(2), unless the plaintiff bought its stock from that underwriter. It is possible, however, that an underwriter can be liable as a participator if the underwriter participates in the sales transaction to a greater degree. Moreover, an underwriter, whether the lead underwriter or just a member of the syndicate, who aids and abets or conspires in the preparation of a false prospectus to be used in selling securities to purchasers, can be liable under section 12(2).

This will require proof of some sort of scienter. *See Lanza* v. *Drexel & Co.*, 479 F.2d 1277, 1298 (2d Cir. 1973) (*en banc*) ("[S]ection [12(2)] requires privity or, in the absence of privity, scienter."). . . . Requiring proof of scienter brings these theories of liability under section 12(2) close to liability under section 10(b) of the Securities Exchange Act of 1934 wherein the liability of an underwriter is not limited.

Next the Court must decide whether the complaints adequately allege causes of action against Becker under the exceptions to the privity requirement as clarified above.

The *Klein* complaint alleges that Becker participated in the sales transactions and aided and abetted or conspired with the other defendants to make or cause the misstatements and omissions in the prospectus. This complaint fails to adequately state a section 12(2) claim against Becker under the various exceptions to the privity requirement.

The substantial participation exception is not met because the allegations relating to Becker's participation in the sales transactions only allege the activities of the typical lead underwriter. The plaintiff alleges that

> Becker actively promoted the sale of shares to plaintiffs and all other members of the class through: a) its orchestration of the entire transaction, b) its placement of advertisements, c) its negotiation of compensation on behalf of the other underwriters, d) its processing of purchase orders received from members of the public by all other underwriters, e) its participation in preparing the Prospectus, and f) its administrative services to all other participating underwriters.

These allegations merely expand upon the definition of a managing underwriter contained in the regulations of the Securities and Exchange Commission. That regulation defines a managing underwriter as

> an underwriter . . . who, by contract or otherwise, deals with the registrant; organizes the selling effort; receives some benefit directly or indirectly in which all other underwriters similarly situated do not share in proportion to their respective interests in the underwriting; or represents any other underwriters in such matters as maintaining the records of the distribution, arranging the allotments of securities offered or arranging for appropriate stabilization activities, if any. 17 C.F.R. §240.12b-2 (1984)

Without more, Becker cannot be liable as a substantial participator.

The aiding and abetting and conspiracy exceptions are not met because the allegations are inexplicit and because scienter is not sufficiently set forth.

The §12(2) claims against Becker are dismissed.

Section 12(2) Defenses

A §12(2) defendant can prevail by carrying the burden of proof that he or she had exercised "reasonable care" or that plaintiff knew of the misstatements or omissions at the time of purchase. Beyond these defenses, the §12(2) defendant may also rely on the statute of limitations, which is the same as for §11: suit must be brought within one year of when the violation is or should be discovered, but never more than three years after the sale.

Section 12(2) Damages

Just as for §12(1), relief under §12(2) is rescission-like for the plaintiff still holding the securities and consists of regular tort damages for the plaintiff who has sold the securities. In *Randall* v. *Loftsgaarden*, 54 U.S.L.W. 5044 (1986), the Supreme Court held that the damages awarded a successful §12(2) plaintiff seeking rescission of an investment in a fraudulent tax shelter should not be reduced by any tax benefits received.

Section 17(a)

Section 17(a) of the 1933 Act outlaws the offer or sale of securities via jurisdictional means whenever defendants (1) employ any device to defraud, (2) obtain money or property by means of any material misstatement or omission, or (3) engage in any transaction or course of business that operates as a fraud upon the purchaser.

While §17(a) is generally considered an antifraud statute, in a §20(b) action by the SEC to enjoin a §17(a) violation, the Supreme Court held that only subsection (1) requires scienter by defendant. Subsections (2) and (3) may be violated by a defendant's mere negligence.[31]

A §17(a) that outlaws merely negligent conduct is a very attractive vehicle for a dissatisfied securities purchaser, especially because it applies to *any* defendants, not just those listed in §11 or within §12(2)'s privity rules. Additionally, §17(a) apparently protects parties other than regular investors, such as broker-dealers, as the Supreme Court held in a recent criminal action.[32] And §17(a) is unburdened by many of the procedural limitations of §§11 and 12.

However, unlike §§11 and 12, which expressly grant injured parties the right to bring a civil action to redress damages caused by their violation, §17(a) contains no such *express* cause of action. Therefore, according to Supreme Court precedent, a cause of action for a §17(a) violation may be implied from the section only if the wording or legislative history of the section reveal a congressional intent that such a cause of action exist.[33]

Lower federal courts scrutinizing the wording and history of §17(a) have reached different conclusions. Some have allowed a §17(a) suit;[34] others have refused.[35] The matter will remain unsettled until explicitly decided by the Supreme Court.

---

[31] *Aaron* v. *SEC*, 446 U.S. 680 (1980).

[32] *U.S.* v. *Naftalin*, 441 U.S. 768 (1979).

[33] *Transamerica Mortgage Advisors, Inc.* v. *Lewis*, 444 U.S. 11 (1979).

[34] *Kirshner* v. *United States*, 603 F.2d 234 (2d Cir. 1978), *cert. denied*, 444 U.S. 995 (1979); *Newman* v. *Prior*, 518 F.2d 97 (4th Cir. 1975).

[35] *Landry* v. *All American Assur. Co.*, 688 F.2d 381 (5th Cir. 1982); *Greater Iowa Corp.* v. *McLendon*, 378 F.2d 783 (3d Cir. 1967).

Section 10(b) of the 1934 Act

Although a cause of action under §10(b), the primary antifraud provision of the 1934 Act, requires a showing of scienter,[36] it is still a very appealing remedy for fraud in the issuance of securities under a registration statement. Section 10(b) is free of many of the procedural restraints of §§11 and 12 of the 1933 Act, and its requirements have been well established and liberally construed in a large body of case law.

Section 10(b), which will be explained in detail in a subsequent chapter, contains no express cause of action. Nonetheless, as shall be seen in that subsequent chapter, the Supreme Court has construed §10(b) to contain an implied cause of action and has held that a §10(b) claim may be brought to redress violations of the 1933 Act, even though an express remedy might also be available under §11 or §12.[37] That these remedies may overlap was not deemed to be a reason to hold §10(b) unavailable to remedy fraud in the offering of securities.

RICO

The many advantages of a Racketeer Influenced and Corrupt Organizations Act (RICO) claim were explained in Chapter 13. RICO has crept into virtually every phase of securities litigation, and most complaints containing claims under §§11, 12(1) and 12(2) of the 1934 Act will also include a RICO claim.

In *Kitchens* v. *U.S. Shelter Corp.*,[38] for example, the court held that a RICO claim was adequately pled alongside §§11 and 12(2) claims in a suit arising out of alleged material omissions and false representations contained in a prospectus and registration statement for an exchange offer. Naturally, the plaintiffs in *Kitchens* were seeking RICO's treble damages.

STATE REMEDIES

Issuers who violate state laws regarding registration of securities face liabilities and enforcement procedures analogous to those contained in the 1934 Act.

Section 306(2) of the Uniform Securities Act gives state securities administrators broad power to deny or revoke registration if a registration statement is fraudulent or otherwise violates a blue sky law.

Section 410 provides for civil liabilities roughly comparable to those of §12 of the 1934 Act. Several states have modified the Uniform Securities Act provisions, but the general thrust of most statutes is to loosen the burden plaintiffs had to bear under the common law of fraud, although all common law remedies remain available too.

---

[36] *Ernst & Ernst* v. *Hochfelder*, 425 U.S. 185 (1976).

[37] *Herman & MacLean* v. *Huddleston*, 459 U.S. 375 (1983).

[38] [1985 Binder] *Fed. Sec. L. Rep.* (CCH), ¶91, 838 (D.S.C. 1985).

QUESTIONS AND PROBLEMS

1. Advanced Chemical was a developing company with no operating history that was selling its stock in the speculative "penny stock" market. Its registration statement listed an encumbered certificate of deposit as a clear asset, improperly claimed income from it, and inflated the amount of its sales. Should the SEC issue a stop order? Discuss. See *In the Matter of Advanced Chemical Corp.*, *Federal Securities Law Reports* (CCH), ¶83,499 (Securities and Exchange Commission, 1984).

2. Aileen, Inc., had approximately 1,000,000 shares outstanding when it issued 200,000 more of the same class pursuant to a registration statement that misrepresented sales volume and earnings. When the figures were corrected, the price of the stock dropped by $9 a share, and several lawsuits were filed under §11. The judge approved a settlement of the suits that denied recovery to class members who could not prove that they purchased shares issued under the disputed registration rather than shares previously issued. Two investors, who could trace some of their stocks that they bought from underwriters to the defective registration but not others that they purchased on the open market during the same time frame, objected to the settlement. Should their objections be sustained? Discuss. See *Barnes* v. *Osofsky*, 373 F.2d 269 (2d Cir. 1967).

3. Tradex was originally a nonprofit corporation factoring the freight bills of its member freight carriers. In 1981 it began reorganizing into a for-profit corporation, filing an S-1 registration statement in December. Attorneys from the Schwabe, Williamson firm prepared the registration statement, which apparently contained numerous inaccuracies. This was the only role the attorneys played in the registration process. Discuss their potential §11 liability. See *Ahern* v. *Gaussoin*, 611 F.Supp. 1465 (D. Or. 1985).

4. Leasco gained control of Reliance Insurance by offering a package of its preferred shares and warrants to Reliance shareholders in exchange for their Reliance common shares. Reliance's management, especially Roberts, opposed the Leasco offer until about August 1, 1968, when Roberts was won over by a deal providing him considerable financial gain. A §11 suit was later filed by former Reliance shareholders who claimed that the registration statement for the Leasco preferred shares and warrants failed to disclose an approximate amount of "surplus surplus" (cash above the amount state insurance laws required Reliance to keep on hand to satisfy claims). Among the defendants was Hodes, a Leasco director who was intimately involved in the negotiations with Reliance. He argued that Leasco could not accurately calculate Reliance's "surplus surplus" because of the hostility of Reliance's management to the Leasco takeover. Roberts testified that he could have calculated the amount "damn quickly" if necessary. Evaluate Hodes's due diligence defense. See *Feit* v. *Leasco Data Processing Equipment Corp.*, 332 F.Supp. 544 (E.D. N.Y. 1971).

5. Consider the due diligence defense of White, Weld (WW), the underwriter in the previous case. WW carefully inquired of Leasco regarding "surplus surplus" and was told in July that Roberts was hostile to the take-over (which was true at that time) and that he would not cooperate by providing necessary information or an estimate of his own. WW concluded on July 5 that because Roberts would not

cooperate, "surplus surplus" could not be accurately calculated, so its omission was proper. Although WW remained in close contact with Leasco, it was not informed of Roberts's change of heart. Did WW exercise due diligence?

6. In 1976 and 1977, GTE paid bribes and kickbacks to officials of foreign companies, but did not disclose this activity. The SEC sued, as did plaintiff shareholders in this case, under §11. The court found the omission "material" though public disclosure did not have much impact on the price of GTE stock. The kickbacks came to light in part when the SEC sued on January 12, 1977. Plaintiffs filed this suit on January 18, 1977. Plaintiffs seek damages for a series of purchases they made between 1973 and January 1977 at an average price of $25.10, the last purchase in January 1977 being at the highest price, $31.75. Plaintiffs also seek damages for a series of purchases they made after the suit was filed until March 1978 at an average price of $31.28. Defendant points out that on the day plaintiffs filed suit, GTE's stock closed at $31⅛ and that plaintiffs could have sold all their shares in January 1977 at a profit, but chose not to do so. Discuss GTE's §11 damage exposure. See *Ross* v. *Warner*, Federal Securities Law Reports (CCH), ¶97,735 (S.D.N.Y. 1980).

7. On May 14, 1981, August 17, 1981, and October 6, 1982, plaintiff invested in Petro-Lewis (PL) oil income programs. On April 5, 1983, a *Wall Street Journal* article set forth in detail suspected PL financial problems. On April 8, 1983, PL issued a press release substantially denying the facts reported in the article. On February 6, 1984, PL finally revealed that it was experiencing extreme financial difficulties. On January 25, 1985, plaintiff filed a suit under §§11 and 12(2), alleging that PL's prospectuses had been misleading because they had omitted the details of PL's financial problems. PL raised a statute of limitations defense. Discuss the validity of this defense. See *Sanders* v. *Robinson Humphrey/American Express, Inc.*, Federal Securities Law Reports (CCH), ¶92,450 (N.D. Ga. 1985).

8. Plaintiffs bought shares in Smith's Pride Foods, Inc., over an eight-month period as Smith's was preparing to go public. The stock's price over the counter crashed before a registration statement was filed, and plaintiffs sued Smith's and Deltec under §§12(1) and 12(2). Deltec had previously had a lawsuit against Smith's which was settled, with Smith's owing Deltec $500,000. Smith's was making monthly payments on this sum to Deltec, quite likely from the proceeds of its sales of shares to plaintiffs. Is Deltec a "seller"? Discuss. See *Pharo* v. *Smith*, 621 F.2d 656 (5th Cir. 1980).

17

EXEMPT SECURITIES, EXEMPT TRANSACTIONS, AND RESALE OF SECURITIES

INTRODUCTION

It is obvious from what has been discussed in prior chapters that the registration process can be quite burdensome and expensive. Defects in registration also open the window to significant potential liability. In this chapter we will discuss a number of related but independent topics concerning possible exemptions from registration that Congress has provided and the SEC has clarified.

First, we will discuss exempt *securities*—investment interests that fit the standard definition of a ''security'' but that Congress has specifically exempted from coverage of the federal securities acts. Second, we will discuss a variety of *transactions* in securities that, due to their nonpublic nature, limited amount, or localized character, Congress has determined should be exempt from registration or at least not subject to full-blown registration procedures. Remember throughout that an exemption from the registration provisions of the 1933 Act does not exempt an issuer from the antifraud provisions of either the 1933 or the 1934 act. Any fraudulent act committed during the course of an exempt offering is punishable.[1]

---

[1] *For example*, *U.S.* v. *Tallant*, 547 F.2d 1291 (5th Cir.), *cert. denied*, 434 U.S. 889 (1977).

This chapter will also discuss certain special registration problems that arise in connection with corporate mergers and acquisitions. Finally, the application of 1933 Act registration provisions to resales of securities by nonissuers will be examined.

EXEMPT SECURITIES

Section 3(a) of the 1933 Act exempts a number of types of securities from coverage of the act. While these securities may be issued and resold without registration and not create a violation of §5, they may still be subject to the antifraud provisions of the act.

Congress exempted these securities either because regulation of them was deemed inappropriate or because they were already regulated by other federal laws. These exempted securities deserve listing though, fortunately, little substantive litigation has arisen in defining them.

Bank and Government Securities

Section 3(a)(2) exempts any securities issued by the United States, the 50 states, the District of Columbia, or any of their political subdivisions. When the section was recently amended to exempt certain types of industrial development bonds, some controversy arose because such bonds seem to constitute traditional corporate debt instruments that are within the scope of the act. Additionally, this section exempts securities issued by banks, which are heavily regulated by other federal and state laws.

Short-Term Notes

Section 3(a)(3) exempts debt instruments with maturity dates, exclusive of days of grace, not exceeding nine months from date of issuance.

Charitable Organizations

Section 3(a)(4) exempts from 1933 Act registration the issuance of securities by nonprofit religious, benevolent, fraternal, or charitable organizations.

Others

Sections 3(a)(5)–(8) exempt securities issued by regulated savings and loan associations,[2] federally regulated common carriers, receivers or trustees in bankruptcy (when issued with court approval), and insurance and annuity policies issued by state-regulated insurance companies.[3]

---

[2] Note that these exemptions are not coterminous with those of the 1934 Act, under which the Supreme Court has held that a savings and loan's withdrawable capital shares are "securities"—*Tcherepnin* v. *Knight*, 389 U.S. 332 (1957).

[3] Even under the 1933 Act, "variable annuities" whose return varies with the profitability of a portfolio of securities are "securities" that must be registered—*SEC* v. *United Benefit Life Ins. Co.*, 387 U.S. 202 (1967).

Exempt Transactions

Section 3(a) not only exempts some securities but also certain transactions in nonexempt securities. Substantial attention shall soon be given to the exemption in §3(a)(11) for exclusively intrastate offerings. Section 3(a)(9) also exempts an issuer's exchange of new securities for those securities already held by its shareholders. No new security holders can be involved and no commission can be paid, such as to an underwriter.

Section 3(a)(10) exempts an issuer's exchange of old for new securities in a recapitalization or reorganization when the fairness of the transaction is approved by a state court or administrative agency.

NONPUBLIC AND LIMITED OFFERING EXEMPTIONS

Section 5(a)'s prohibition of the sale of unregistered, nonexempt securities is very broadly worded. Nonetheless, Congress also built in some very substantial exemptions to registration and authorized the SEC to clarify and expand those exemptions.

Two of the most important exemptions provided by Congress are contained in §3(b) and §4(2). Section 3(b) provides a ''limited offering'' exemption, reflecting Congress' decision that full registration procedures may not be justified for small (dollarwise) offerings. Section 4(2) provides a ''private placement'' exemption that reflects Congress' view that registration protection is not needed in privately negotiated sales not involving public solicitation. Again it is important to keep in mind that these are only exemptions from registration, not from the antifraud provisions.

Section 3(b)

In §3(b) Congress authorized the SEC to establish rules and regulations to exempt offerings from registration where ''by reason of the small amount involved or the limited character of the public offering'' the Commission determines that registration ''is not necessary in the public interest and for the protection of investors.''

The SEC's authority is limited, however, by a ceiling on the exemption. The ceiling has been raised from time to time over the years and now stands at $5 million. The SEC does not have authority under this section to exempt offerings in excess of that amount.

The Commission has issued several rules to implement §3(b)'s exemption. One set of guidelines is in Rules 501–505 of Regulation D, which will soon be discussed in detail. Under proper circumstances, Rules 504 and 505 of Regulation D provide a complete exemption from registration for small offerings.

Also important and soon to be discussed is Regulation A (Rules 251–264), which eases the burden of registration for certain small offerings. Section 3(c) is similarly worthy of mention, as it authorizes the SEC to add to the traditional exemptions securities issued by small business investment companies under the Small Business Investment Act of 1958 if the SEC finds that registration of such securities is not necessary in the public interest.

Section 4(2)

By the terms of §4(2), the registration requirement of §5 does not apply to "transactions by an issuer not involving any public offering." Pursuant to this exemption, issuers can raise funds through "private placements"—usually sales to large institutional investors. The private placement exemption is also popular when securities are issued for the purpose of carrying out a corporate combination or acquiring corporate assets. The popularity of these private placements has been previously noted—in 1980, $11.5 billion of the total $78.1 billion in new offerings were private placements.

The leading §4(2) case is *SEC* v. *Ralston Purina*,[4] in which a company tried to use the exemption to offer treasury stock to its "key employees." Unfortunately for the company, the Court did not agree that the sale of $2 million in stock over a four-year period constituted a private placement when the 1,000 or so "key employees" to which the stock was offered included artists, bakeshop foremen, clerical assistants, electricians, mill office clerks, production trainees, and stenographers. The Court believed that the applicability of the exemption should turn on the employees' (or any offerees') need for the protection provided by the 1933 Act's registration process. Thus, only "[a]n offering to those who are able to fend for themselves is a transaction 'not involving a public offering.'"

Therefore, the Court held that

> The exemption, as we construe it, does not deprive corporate employees, as a class, of the safeguards of the Act. We agree that some employee offerings may come within [§4(2)], e.g., one made to executive personnel who because of their position have access to the same kind of information that the Act would make available in the form of a registration statement. Absent such a showing of special circumstances, employees are just as much members of the investing "public" as any of their neighbors in the community.

While *Ralston Purina* held the §4(2) exemption to turn on the offerees' access to information comparable to that contained in the registration statement, other courts have also required business experience or equivalent sophistication so that the offerees can effectively utilize the information to which they have access.

As with §3(b), the SEC has issued rules to clarify the application of §4(2). Presently, it is Rule 506 of Regulation D that provides a "safe harbor" for private placements. Any issuer meeting the terms of Rule 506 will be deemed to be within the §4(2) exemption. Rule 506 is not exclusive, and most corporate-type offerings (whether start-ups, venture capital, or small business offerings) are still handled as traditional private placements under §4(2).[5]

A recent §4(2) case, though decided under Rule 506's predecessor, Rule 146, should help to clarify application of the exemption.

---

[4] 346 U.S. 119 (1953).

[5] S. Keller, "Uniform Limited Offering Exemption," in *Blue Sky Laws* (New York: Practising Law Institute, 1984), p. 107.

S.E.C. v. INTERNATIONAL MINING EXCHANGE, INC.

515 F.Supp. 1062 (D. Colo. 1981)

Defendant Trenton H. Parker, individually, and several related corporate entities were engaged in two investment programs. For our purposes, the relevant program involved the organization and sale of limited partnership interests in four partnerships formed to renovate various mansions in the Denver area. Parker and his wholly owned corporation were the general partners in the limited partnerships. Parker retained complete control over all aspects of management. Investors in three of the mansions received no return on their investment, while investors in the fourth received a return of 80%. Parker failed to distribute proceeds of sales, refused to make books and records available to the limited partners, and was otherwise uncooperative.

Pursuant to §20(b), the SEC brought this action to enjoin violations by Parker of §§5(a) and (c), and other provisions of the securities laws. Regarding the limited partnership interests, defendants admitted these were securities, but claimed they were exempt from registration pursuant to §4(2)'s private offering exemption, as clarified in former Rule 146.

The trial judge granted the SEC's motion for summary judgment regarding the availability of the §4(2) exemption in the following opinion.

KANE, DISTRICT JUDGE:

The applicability of §4(2) turns on whether the particular class of persons affected needs the protection of the act. An offering to those who are shown to be able to fend for themselves is not a public offering—*Securities & Exchange Com. v. Ralston Purina Co.*, 346 U.S. at 125. . . . Other relevant factors include the number of offerees and their relationship to one another

and the issuer, the number of units offered, and the size and manner of the offering—*Doran v. Petroleum Management Corp.*, 545 F.2d 893, 900 (5th Cir. 1977).

An offering to a diverse and unrelated group would have the appearance of being public, *Securities & Exchange Com. v. Murphy*, 626 F.2d at 647, although a small number of shares issued does not cause the offering to be private—*Andrews v. Blue*, 489 F.2d at 367. Moreover each offeree in a private transaction must be afforded the same information that would have been afforded a prospective investor in a public offering, or the offeree must be shown to otherwise have had such information or ready access to it—*Securities & Exchange Com. v. Murphy*, 626 F.2d at 647. Finally evidence of a high degree of business or legal sophistication on the part of all offerees does not suffice to bring the offering within the private offering exemption. If the offerees do not possess the information required in a registration statement they cannot bring their sophisticated knowledge of business affairs to bear on deciding whether to invest. Thus sophistication is not a substitute for access to information that a registration statement would disclose.

The evidence shows that defendants did not supply sufficient information to investors on the first three mansions which were also the unregistered partnership interests. This is in marked contrast to the fourth mansion partnership which was registered and whose offering memo informed investors that the risk was high and that Parker's corporate entities would be hired to perform the work. No such information was furnished to investors in the first three mansions. Defendants, in their brief in opposition to summary judgment, cite testimony tending to show that some (but certainly not all) of the investors were rather sophisticated in their knowledge of investments and the inherent risks involved in such ventures. However, this is not a substitute for access to information that a registration statement would disclose.

Summary judgment motion granted.

Regulation D

In March 1982, the SEC promulgated Regulation D to provide a more cohesive and coherent system of exemptions that would ease the burdens of small companies seeking to raise capital.

Regulation D has three main exemptive provisions that are now the heart of the limited offering–private placement system of exemptions. Rules 504 and 505, promulgated pursuant to §3(b), provide two "safe harbors" for limited offering exemptions. Rule 506, issued under the authority of §4(2), constitutes the private placement safe harbor. Rules 501, 502, and 503 are definitional and procedural in nature. They are so important to an understanding of the Rule 504, 505, and 506 exemptions that they must be discussed first.

Rule 501

Rule 501 is the definitional section of Regulation D. Two particularly important terms (and several of lesser importance) are defined there.

The notion of a "sophisticated" investor—one with sufficient business acumen and experience to fend for himself or herself—has long been contained in the case law and SEC rules. Rule 501 refines this concept by defining an "accredited investor"—one who supposedly does not need the protections afforded by registration—as including any person who belongs, or which the issuer reasonably believes belongs, to the following categories:

1. Certain institutional investors, including banks, insurance companies, registered investment companies, investment advisers, small business investment companies licensed by the Small Business Administration, and qualified employee benefit plans.
2. Private business development companies as defined in the Investment Advisers Act of 1940.
3. Charitable, educational, or religious organizations with assets exceeding $5 million.
4. Any director, executive officer, or general partner of the issuer (or of a general partner of the issuer).
5. Any person who buys at least $150,000 of securities *if* the amount purchased does not exceed 20% of the purchaser's net worth (or joint net worth with spouse).
6. Any natural person whose individual or joint (with spouse) net worth exceeds $1,000,000.
7. Any natural person who has had an individual income exceeding $200,000 in each of the past two years and who reasonably expects to do the same in the current year (note the spouse's income has no relevance here).
8. Any entity such as a general partnership in which *all* of the owners are accredited investors within the meaning of the prior paragraphs.

The exact place of the "accredited investor" in the Regulation D scheme will become clear when we examine Rules 505 and 506.

The other very important definition in Rule 501 is that of a "purchaser representative." Investors who do not themselves meet the "accredited investor" definition may still receive the protection normally accorded by a registration statement so long as they act through a "purchaser representative" who is qualified and knowledgeable. Such a purchaser representative should have "such knowledge and experience in financial and business matters" that he or she is capable of evaluating "the merits and risks of the prospective investment." Of course, the purchaser representative should not be an affiliate of the issuer.

Rule 502

Regulation D's Rule 502 contains a number of important provisions critical to the operation of Rules 504–506.

Integration. The concept of integration is crucial to the 1933 Act's exemptive provisions. An issuer cannot take what is in essence a single offering that does not meet the requirements for an exemption and artificially divide that offering into two "separate" offerings that, standing alone, would each qualify for an exemption. For example, an issuer attempting to fit within the $5 million ceiling of §3(b) could not artificially divide a single $8 million offering into two $4 million offerings. The SEC and the courts must decide when to "integrate" offerings that issuers have tried to treat separately.

Rule 502 adopts the traditional criteria the SEC has suggested for determining whether offers and sales should be integrated:

1. Whether the sales are part of a single plan of financing.
2. Whether the sales involve issuance of the same class of securities.
3. Whether the sales have been made at or about the same time.
4. Whether the same type of consideration is received.
5. Whether the sales are made for the same general purpose.[6]

In addition, Rule 502 provides a "safe harbor" not present in earlier rules—a particular offering of securities will not be integrated with offers and sales made more than six months before it started or more than six months after it ended, so long as during those six-month periods the issuer offered or sold no similar securities, except under an employee benefit plan. If other offers and sales are made during these six-month periods, the decision whether to integrate will be controlled by the foregoing five criteria.

---

[6] *Securities Act Release*, no. 33–4552 (November 6, 1962).

Information Requirements. Issuers who sell securities either (1) exclusively under Rule 504 or (2) exclusively to accredited investors under Rules 505 and 506 need not disclose any information to their offerees and purchasers. That there is no disclosure requirement does not mean that information may not be furnished (though if it is it must be in writing). Indeed, issuers may wish to make nonrequired disclosures because the antifraud rules still apply, such disclosures may be required under blue sky laws anyway, and sales may be facilitated in the case of investors who under prior rules are accustomed to receiving private placement memoranda and offering circulars.

Issuers under Rules 505 and 506 who do sell to nonaccredited investors must meet information requirements established by Rule 502. These requirements will be discussed in the context of Rules 505 and 506.

Manner of Offering. Except under limited circumstances pursuant to Rule 504, no Regulation D offeror can engage in general solicitation or advertising. Thus, television and newspaper ads, or seminars to which the general public is invited are prohibited.

Limitations on Resale. The registration provisions of the 1933 Act would mean little if an issuer could sell to an affiliate, say, under the private placement exemption of §4(2), and the affiliate were then allowed immediately to turn around and resell to the public. The 1933 Act handles this problem by providing in §2(11) that the affiliate in this hypothetical situation would be an "underwriter." Remember, §4(1) provides a §5 exemption for "transactions by any person other than an issuer, underwriter, or dealer." The affiliate who bought with a view to resale, therefore, could not do so without finding its own exemption. Usually such securities would be held for at least two years and then resold under an exemption provided by Rule 144, which we shall discuss near the end of this chapter.

With a limited exception under Rule 504, Regulation D securities are "restricted securities" that must be purchased for investment, not with a view toward distribution. They may be resold only after the two-year holding period specified in Rule 144 is completed. To help enforce the restricted nature of Regulation D securities, Rule 502 requires issuers to take "reasonable care" to assure that purchasers of the securities are not §2(11) underwriters. "Reasonable care" includes, but is not limited to, (1) inquiries to determine if purchasers are buying for themselves or others, (2) written notice to all purchasers before the sale that the securities were not registered and therefore can be resold only if the purchasers can find their own exemption, and (3) placement of a legend on the securities stating that they have not been registered and referring to or describing the limitations on resale.

Rule 503

Rule 503 requires issuers to file with the SEC notices of sales on Form D. The Regulation D exemptions cannot be claimed unless Form D is filed within 15 days after the first sale of securities.

Rule 504

With procedural and definitional provisions behind us, we may now turn to the three exemptions contained in Regulation D. Rule 504 is the first of these, promulgated pursuant to §3(b). This rule manifests an SEC decision to cede to the states' blue sky laws all jurisdiction over small offerings by small issuers.

Rule 504 allows issuers to raise up to $500,000 in any 12-month period without registration. That ceiling must be diminished by the amount of any securities sold in the prior 12 months pursuant to §3(b) exemptions, such as Rule 505, or under Regulation A, or in violation of §5(a). Subsequent registered sales do not affect the $500,000 calculation. Regulation D gives this example of the aggregation principle:

> If an issuer sold $200,000 of its securities on June 1, 1982 under this Rule 504 and an additional $100,000 on September 1, 1982, the issuer would be permitted to sell only $200,000 more under this Rule 504 until June 1, 1983. Until that date the issuer must count both prior sales toward the $500,000 limit. However, if the issuer made its third sale on June 1, 1983, the issuer could then sell $400,000 of its securities because the June 1, 1982 sale would not be within the preceding 12 months.

The Rule 504 exemption is aimed at smaller issuers and is not available to 1934 Act reporting companies or to investment companies registered under the Investment Company Act of 1940.

Rule 504 contains no limit regarding the number or kind of purchasers. Offerees and purchasers need not be sophisticated or constitute "accredited investors." Nor need they be supplied with any specific information. Nothing need be filed with the SEC except the Form D notice of sale.

General advertising and solicitation are permitted under Rule 504 only if offers and sales are made exclusively in states that provide for registration of such securities and require delivery of a disclosure document prior to sale. If these conditions are met, Rule 504 similarly entails no resale requirement. The only exception would be if the particular state laws banned general solicitation or imposed resale restrictions.

Rule 505

Also issued pursuant to §3(b), Rule 505 is available to all issuers, including 1934 Act reporting companies, except (1) investment companies and (2) companies recently subject to proceedings arising out of federal securities act violations.

Qualified issuers can raise up to $5 million in a 12-month period. Like Rule 504, Rule 505's ceiling is diminished by the amount of all sales in the previous 12 months made under a §3(b) exemption (e.g., under Rule 504 or Regulation A) or in violation of §5(a).

Unlike Rule 504, Rule 505 places a limit on the number of purchasers. The $5 million in securities can be sold to no more than 35 nonaccredited investors, such as "WOGs" (widows, orphans, and grandmothers). The number of accredited investor purchasers is unlimited. General solicitation is not permitted.

Rule 505 also has disclosure requirements. If the issuer sells only to accredited investors, no information need be disclosed. However, if there are any sales to nonaccredited investors, the informational requirements of Rule 502 must be met. For *nonreporting companies*, that means furnishing information equivalent to that required by Part I of Form S-18, if the issuer would be qualified to use Form S-18. If not so qualified, the issuer must furnish the information required in Part I of a registration form the issuer would be entitled to use. Additionally, the issuer must furnish financial statements from the two previous years. Only the most recent year's statements must be audited. But if such an audited statement cannot be obtained without "unreasonable effort and expense," then only the issuer's balance sheet, dated within 120 days of the start of the offering, need be audited.

A *reporting company* that sells to nonaccredited investors must furnish a description of the securities and use of proceeds, its last proxy statement, and its last annual report to shareholders as supplemented by more recent filings such as 10-Q's. 10-K's must be furnished upon written request. Indeed, in lieu of the annual report and proxy statement, the issuer may provide a 10K, a Form S-1, or a Form 10 (registration under the 1934 Act), whichever is most recent.

Additionally, if accredited investors are given any further information, that same information must be given to the nonaccredited buyers. Also, the issuer must, at a reasonable time prior to purchase, give the opportunity to investors to ask questions and receive answers regarding the offering and to obtain any additional information the issuer possesses or can acquire "without unreasonable effort and expense" that is necessary to verify the information required by the other provisions.

A Form D must, of course, be filed.

Rule 506

The Rule 506 exemption, promulgated under §4(2), is available to most issuers, including 1934 Act reporting companies and investment companies. It has *no* ceiling amount. An unlimited dollar amount of securities may be sold without registration, but to no more than 35 nonaccredited investors plus an unlimited number of accredited investors. Additionally, the issuer must reasonably believe that each of the *non*accredited purchasers "alone or with his purchaser representative(s) has such knowledge and experience in financial and business matters that he is capable of evaluating the merits and risks of the prospective investment." This is a remnant of the "sophisticated" shareholder requirement of pre–Regulation D rules.

No general solicitation is allowed under Rule 506. Form D must be filed. The information requirements of Rule 506 are very similar to those of Rule 505. No information is required if sales are made only to accredited investors. If sales are made to nonaccredited investors, the rules for reporting companies and for nonreporting companies selling less than $5 million are identical to those described regarding Rule 505. However, a nonreporting company selling more than $5 million under the exemption, in addition to furnishing Part I of S-18 or another form it is entitled to use, must also furnish audited financial statements for the past three years and balance sheets for the preceding

Comparative Chart of Regulation D Exemptions

	AGGREGATE OFFERING PRICE LIMITATION	NUMBER OF INVESTORS	INVESTOR QUALIFICATION	COMMISSIONS	LIMITATIONS ON MANNER OF OFFERING	LIMITATIONS ON RESALE	NOTICE OF SALES	INFORMATION REQUIREMENTS
Rule 504	$500,000- 12 mos.	Unlimited	None required	Permitted	No general solicitations *unless* registered exclusively in states that require delivery of a disclosure document	Restricted *unless* exclusively registered in states that require delivery of a disclosure document	Form D required: 5 copies filed with commission 15 days after first sale, every 6 months after first sale, 30 days after last sale	No information specified

Rule 505	$5,000,000- 12 mos.	35 nonaccredited plus unlimited accredited	None required except to determine if accredited	Permitted	No general solicitation permitted	Restricted	Same as 504	1. If purchased solely by accredited, no information specified
								2. If purchased by nonaccredited investors (nonreporting companies)[1]
								3. Issuers must make available prior to sale:
								  a. exhibits
								  b. written information given to accredited investors must also be given to unaccredited investors
								  c. opportunity to ask questions and receive answers

Rule 506	Unlimited	35 nonaccredited plus unlimited accredited	Purchaser must be sophisticated	Permitted	No general solicitation permitted	Restricted	Same as 504	1. Same as 505 2. a. Same as 505[2] 3. Same as 505

[1] Offerings up to $5,000,000: Information in Part I of Form S-18 or available registration form, two-year financial statements, one-year audited—if undue effort or expense, issuers other than limited partnerships only balance sheet as of 120 days before offering must be audited—if limited partnership and undue effort or expense, financial statements may be tax basis.

[2] Offerings over $5,000,000: Information in Part I of available registration—if undue effort or expense, issuers other than limited partnerships only balance sheets as of 120 days before offering must be audited—if limited partnership and undue effort or expense, financials may be tax basis.

two. Again, where audited financial statements cannot be obtained without "unreasonable effort and expense," an audited balance sheet will suffice.

It is hoped that the chart on the preceding page will illustrate and clarify the operation of Regulation D's Rule 504, 505, and 506 exemptions.[7]

Section 4(6)

The Small Business Investment Incentive Act of 1980 added subsection (6) to the 1933 Act's §4. Today §4(6) is largely redundant of Rule 505. It allows an issuer to raise up to the maximum amount of §3(b) ($5 million) without registration so long as no general solicitation occurs, sales and offers are made only to "accredited investors," and a notice of sale is filed on Form D. Resales of §4(6) securities are also restricted.

Although its duplication of Rule 505 significantly reduces §4(6)'s importance, it does have these dissimilarities:

1. It is available to investment companies.
2. It contains no disqualification provision regarding past violations of securities laws.
3. Sales pursuant to other §3(b) exemptions during the prior 12 months do not reduce the ceiling amount *unless* the general requirements for integration are met.

On the other hand, an issuer under Regulation D who sells to a nonaccredited investor that was reasonably believed to be accredited does not lose the exemption. No such good faith defense exists under §4(6).

Regulation A

Like Rules 504 and 505, Regulation A (Rules 251–264) was issued pursuant to §3(b). Although frequently called an "exemption," Regulation A simply allows a relaxed form of registration. An issuer may raise up to $1.5 million in a 12-month period without filing a full registration statement. Of that amount, no more than $100,000 may be issued by any single affiliate of the issuer.

A Regulation A issuer files only a short-form offering statement rather than a full registration statement. It is filed with the regional offices of the SEC that have developed a review procedure similar to that the SEC uses in cases of full-blown registration. The issuer must circulate an "offering circular," which is a "miniprospectus" with information about the issuer and the securities offered, though attached financial statements generally need not be audited.

The filings, reviews, and offering circulars make Regulation A offerings perhaps only marginally less burdensome than full registration. Still, several features of Regulation A make it attractive. It is available to most issuers and their affiliates, though not to those that have recently been subject to judicial or administrative sanctions for securities

---

[7] The source of the chart is R. Newman and L. Goldenberg, "Venture Capital Formation Under the SEC's New Regulation D," *National Law Journal*, July 5, 1982, p. 16.

violations. A small company utilizing Regulation A will not become a 1934 Act reporting company until it meets the §12(g) requirements (500 shareholders and $5 million in assets). The exemption can be used to raise $1.5 million year after year. There are no resale restrictions, and general solicitation is allowed.

Despite these advantages and prior brisk use of Regulation A, undoubtedly the recent development of Form S-18 and Regulation D will limit its use.

INTRASTATE OFFERING EXEMPTION

Section 3(a)(11)

An exemption from registration for truly local offerings is provided by §3(a)(11), which exempts securities "offered and sold only to persons resident within a single State or Territory, where the issuer of such security is a person resident and doing business within, or, if a corporation, incorporated by and doing business within, such State or Territory."

Underlying this exemption is Congress' decision that state regulation and federal antifraud provisions are sufficient to protect the investing public in an intrastate offering. It is assumed that the states are close to the situation and that the investor will have a better opportunity to investigate a local issuer. Note, however, that availability of the exemption does not turn on the adequacy or even the existence of state registration and regulation. The exemption applies even in a state that has no registration requirement.

Section 3(a)(11) contains no dollar limitation and no ban on general solicitation. Nothing need be filed with the SEC, and there are no disclosure requirements. Still, the section "is designed to apply only to distributions genuinely local in character . . . exempt[ing] only issues which in reality represent local financing by local industries, carried out through local investment." [8] This point is effectively made in the following case.

S.E.C. v. McDONALD INVESTMENT CO.

343 F.Supp. 343 (D.Minn. 1972)

Defendants in this SEC suit are the McDonald Investment Co. (McDonald), a Minnesota corporation with its only business office and its records located in Rush City, Minnesota, *and certain corporate officers. Prior to October 19, 1971, defendants registered a $4 million offering of installment notes with the Minnesota Securities Division, but not with the SEC. Previ-*

---

[8] *Securities Act Release*, no. 4434 (November 6, 1961).

ously defendants had been enjoined from selling, without SEC registration, notes secured by lien land contracts and first mortgages on unimproved land located at various places in the United States, principally in Arizona. The subject offering, however, was to be made to Minnesota residents only. These notes were unsecured, and the proceeds were to be lent to land developers in Arizona and elsewhere. Although McDonald would take a mortgage and other liens, the Minnesota investors would have no direct ownership of or participation in the mortgages, liens, or businesses of the Arizona borrowers.

The SEC, claiming that the new issuance was not exempt from registration under §3(a)(11), filed suit under §20(b) seeking an injunction to prevent sale of the notes without registration.

NEVILLE, DISTRICT JUDGE:

The question presented to the court is whether the sale exclusively to Minnesota residents of securities, consisting of unsecured installment promissory notes of the defendant, a Minnesota corporation, whose only business office is situate in Minnesota, is exempt from the filing of a registration statement under §3(a)(11) of the 1933 Securities Act when the proceeds from the sale of such notes are to be used principally, if not entirely, to make loans to land developers outside of Minnesota. Though this is a close question, the court holds that such registration is required and the defendants have not satisfied their burden of proving the availability of an exemption under the Act; this despite the fact that the securities have heretofore been duly registered with the Securities Commissioner of the State of Minnesota for whom this court has proper respect.

The plaintiff predicates its claim for a permanent injunction on the ground that the defendants will be engaged in a business where the income

producing operations are located outside the state in which the securities are to be offered and sold and therefore not available for the 3(a)(11) exemption—*Securities and Exchange Commission* v. *Truckee Showboat*, 157 F.Supp. 824 (S.D. Cal. 1957); and *Chapman* v. *Dunn*, 414 F.2d 153 (6th Cir. 1969). While neither of these cases is precisely in point on their facts, the rationale of both is clear and apposite to the case at bar.

In *Truckee* the exemption was not allowed because the proceeds of the offering were to be used primarily for the purpose of a new unrelated business in another state, that is, a California corporation acquiring and refurbishing a hotel in Las Vegas, Nevada. Likewise, in *Dunn* the 3(a)(11) exemption was unavailable to an offering by a company in one state, Michigan, of undivided fractional oil and gas interests located in another state, Ohio. The *Dunn* court specifically stated at page 159:

> in order to qualify for the exemption of §3(a)(11), the issuer must offer and sell his securities only to persons resident within a single State and the issuer must be a resident of that same State. *In addition to this, the issuer must conduct a predominant amount of his business within this same State.* This business which the issuer must conduct within the same State refers to the income producing operations of the business in which the issuer is selling the securities. (Emphasis added)

This language would seem to fit the instant case where the income producing operations of the defendant, after completion of the offering, are to consist entirely of earning interest on its loans and receivables invested outside the state of Minnesota. While the defendant will not participate in any of the land developer's operations, nor will it own or control any of the operations, the fact is that the strength of the installment notes depends perhaps not legally, but practically, to a large degree on the success or failure of land developments located outside Minnesota, such land not being subject to the jurisdiction of the Minnesota court. The investor obtains no direct interest in any business activity outside of Minnesota, but legally holds only an interest as a creditor of a Minnesota corporation, which of course would be a prior claim on the defendant's assets over the shareholder's equity, now stated to be approximately a quarter of a million dollars.

This case does not evidence the deliberate attempt to evade the Act as in the example posed by plaintiff of a national organization or syndicate which incorporates in several or many states, opens an office in each and sells securities only to residents of the particular state, intending nevertheless to use all the proceeds whenever realized in a venture beyond the boundaries of all, or at best all but one of the states. . . . Defendant corporation on the contrary has been in business in Minnesota for some period of time, is not a "Johnny come lately" and is not part of any syndicate or similar enterprise; yet to relieve it of the federal registration requirements where none or very little of the money realized is to be invested in Minnesota, would seem to violate the spirit if not the letter of the Act.

Persuasive language is found in the Securities and Exchange Commission Release No. 4434, December 6, 1961, relating to exemptions for local offerings:

> The legislative history of the Securities Act clearly shows that this exemption was designed to apply only to local financing that may practicably be consummated in its entirety within the state or territory in which the issuer is both incorporated and doing business.
>
> In view of the local character of the section 3(a)(11) exemption, the requirement that the issuer be doing business in the state can only be satisfied by the performance of substantial operational activities in the state of incorporation. The doing business requirement is not met by functions in the particular state such as bookkeeping, stock

record and similar activities or by offering securities in the state. Thus, the exemptions would be unavailable to an offering by a company made in the state of its incorporation of undivided fractional oil and gas interests located in other states even though the company conducted other business in the state of its incorporation. . . . Similarly, an intrastate exemption would not be available to a "local" mortgage company offering interests in out-of-state mortgages which are sold under circumstances to constitute them investment contracts.

. . .

Exemptions under the Act are strictly construed, with the burden of proof on the one seeking to establish the same—*Securities and Exchange Commission* v. *Culpepper*, 270 F.2d 241, 246 (2d Cir. 1959).

. . .

Defendant notes that agreements with land developers will by their terms be construed under Minnesota law; that the income producing activities will be the earning of interest which occurs in Minnesota; that the Minnesota registration provides at close proximity all the information and protection that any investor might desire; that whether or not registered with the Securities and Exchange Commission, a securities purchaser has the protection of 15 U.S.C. §77e which attaches liability to the issuer whether or not registration of the securities are exempted for fraudulent or untrue statements in a prospectus or made by oral communications; that plaintiff blurs the distinction between sale of securities across state lines and the operation of an intrastate business; and that if injunction issues in this case it could issue in any case where a local corporation owns an investment out of the particular state in which it has its principal offices and does business such as accounts receivable from its customers out of state.

While these arguments are worthy and per-

haps somewhat more applicable to the facts of this case than to the facts of Truckee *and* Chapman, supra, *on balance and in carrying out*

the spirit and intent of the Securities Act of 1933, plaintiff's request for a permanent injunction should be granted.

Rule 147

The intricacies of the §3(a)(11) exemption are best understood by scrutinizing Rule 147, the SEC's clarification of the intrastate exemption. Although Rule 147 is theoretically not exclusive, it would be difficult for any issuer to take advantage of the §3(a)(11) exemption without meeting the requirements of Rule 147.

Residence of the Issuer

Rule 147 requires that the issuer's residence be in the state where all offers and sales occur. An individual, such as a promoter issuing preincorporation certificates, is deemed a resident of the state where his or her principal residence is located. Corporations, limited partnerships, trusts, and other businesses organized under state law are residents only of the state in which they were formed. A general partnership is a resident of the state where its principal office is located.

Business of the Issuer

An issuer cannot simply incorporate in a state to become a resident, yet do no business there and still utilize the §3(a)(11) exemption. To bring some mathematical certainty to the *Truckee-Dunn-McDonald* line of cases, Rule 147 requires that

1. The issuer's principal office be located in the state.
2. Eighty percent of its gross revenue come from business, property, or services rendered in the state (though an issuer need not meet this requirement if its gross revenues in its most recent 12-month period did not exceed $5,000).
3. Eighty percent of its assets, on a consolidated basis, be located in the state.
4. The issuer intends to and does use 80% of the net proceeds of the issue in the state.

Residence of Offerees and Purchasers

It is very important for an issuer seeking to utilize the §3(a)(11) exemption to investigate the residence of a potential offeree, because a single sale or *even a single offer* to a nonresident destroys the exemption for the entire offering.[9] Fortunately, if an

---

[9] *Hillsborough Inv. Corp. v. SEC*, 276 F.2d 665 (1st Cir. 1960).

offeree is a *bona fide* resident of the state at the time of the offer and sale, a later move to a different state will not destroy the exemption.

A corporation, partnership, or trust as offeree is deemed a resident of the state in which its principal office is located. An individual offeree resides in the state of his or her principal residence. Mere presence in the state, as with military personnel temporarily stationed in a state, is insufficient. To prevent nonresidents from circumventing the intent of the rule, any resident corporation or partnership that is formed solely to receive the issued securities is deemed a nonresident if any of its owners are nonresidents. Thus, if A and B, nonresidents, organize a corporation in the offering state for purposes of receiving the securities in a local offering, the corporation is deemed a nonresident.

Restrictions on Resale

Rule 147 must impose restrictions on resale. Otherwise, the registration requirements of §5(a) could be evaded by selling to a resident under the §3(a)(11) exemption with the intent that the resident would soon resell to nonresidents. In *Hillsborough Investment Corp.* v. *SEC*,[10] for example, a New Hampshire issuer listed securities in the name of New Hampshire residents for a period of 20 or 30 days and then transferred them to nonresidents. Naturally the court held the intrastate exemption unavailable. The residence of the purchasers must be determined as of the time the securities "come to rest." [11]

Rule 147 prohibits purchasers from reselling to nonresidents for a period of nine months after the date of the last sale of the offering by the issuer. These restrictions must be enforced by (1) appropriate legends on the certificates, (2) issuance of stop transfer orders to the issuer's transfer agents, and (3) receipt of written representations from all purchasers as to their residences.

Integration

Integration principles are important in the context of §3(a)(11). Absent such principles, an issuer could divide a $7 million offering into two parts, issuing $2 million solely to residents and the remaining $5 million under Rule 505. Rule 147 provides a safe harbor for all sales made more than six months before the start of the offering or more than six months after the end. These sales will not be integrated with the intrastate offering. However, other sales that occur during the offering period and the six months before and after may be integrated in accordance with the usual five integration factors listed previously: Are the offerings part of a single plan of financing? Do they involve the same class of security? Were they made at or about the same time? Was the same consideration received? Were they made for the same general purpose?

Of course, §3(a)(11) and Rule 147 provide no exemption from the antifraud provisions of the 1933 Act.

---

[10] 276 F.2d 665 (1st Cir. 1960).

[11] *Stadia Oil & Uranium Co.* v. *Wheelis*, 251 F.2d 269 (10th Cir. 1957).

BLUE-SKY EXEMPTIONS

Just as 1933 Act exemptions are important to issuers, so are exemptions from blue sky laws. "If the offering is being made on a national basis, blue sky compliance is a formidable task." [12] Issuers would like to avoid this burden if possible. Unfortunately, it is an equally formidable task to decipher the crazy quilt of state exemptions.

Survey of State Exemptions

It has been stated that state blue sky exemptions viewed individually are easy to understand, but when they are viewed "in combination . . . confusion arises." [13] The confusion comes from a gross lack of uniformity among the laws of the 50 states and District of Columbia and is compounded by the constant changes that seem to occur. No issuer can confidently plan a broad-based public offering without reviewing state laws for recent changes.

Most states have *exempt securities*, such as those issued by the federal government, states and their political subdivisions, foreign governments, banks, savings and loan associations, credit unions, and nonprofit corporations and charities. Many states have exemptions for shares listed on the New York or American stock exchanges, but the recently promulgated Revised Uniform Securities Act (RUSA) would eliminate that exemption if adopted. [14]

Naturally the states also have *transaction exemptions*. Although there are wide variations, many states base those exemptions on Section 402(b) of the Uniform Securities Act (USA). Some of the key exemptions are for issuers in a primary offering, some are for nonissuers in a secondary offering, and some are available to both. These include exemptions for small offerings in the state, for unsolicited offers to purchase made to nonissuers, for sales to sophisticated institutional investors, and for nonissuer distributions of well-recognized securities.

Many states have added exemptions to those listed in the USA. And specific limits as to numbers of investors and monetary size, rules of integration and advertising, and virtually every other aspect of the exemptions vary from state to state.

Federal-State Coordination

Congress and the SEC have recently reacted to the need for more uniformity among the states and more coordination between federal and state exemptions. Congressional passage in 1980 of §19(c) of the 1933 Act, which authorizes the SEC to work with the states to achieve uniformity, the response of the North American Securities Administrators

---

[12] H. Bloomenthal, *1982 Securities Law Handbook* (New York: Clark Boardman Co., Ltd., 1982) p. 75.

[13] H. Makens, "State Blue Sky Exemptions Before ULOE," *Blue Sky Laws* (New York: Practising Law Institute, 1984), p. 75.

[14] C. Braisted, "Regulation of Securities by States," *National Law Journal*, Mar. 25, 1985, p. 15.

Association (NASAA) to this initiative, and the promulgation of Regulation D, are three developments that have dramatically altered the picture regarding blue sky exemptions. Unfortunately, they have not yet produced the desired uniformity.

In 1978, the president of the NASAA requested the State Regulation of Securities Committee of the American Bar Association to draft a uniform limited offering exemption (ULOE). In September 1983, NASAA adopted a final draft of the ULOE, which features an attempt to coordinate state exemptions with Regulation D.

The ULOE exempts from state registration an offer or sale if it complies with Rule 505 of Regulation D and four additional requirements are met: (1) no commission is paid to broker-dealers or agents who are not registered with the state, (2) the issuer is not itself and is not affiliated with a ''bad boy'' (one involved in securities disciplinary proceedings), (3) a Form D is filed with the state securities administrator, and (4) the issuer reasonably believes either (a) that the investment is suitable for the unaccredited investors or (b) that the unaccredited investors who purchase are sophisticated.

A footnote to ULOE indicates NASAA's view that it is permissible to coordinate with Rule 506 on basically the same terms as Rule 505. Most states that have adopted ULOE have included both 505 and 506, but there has been little state effort to coordinate with Rule 504.

Because some states have tried to coordinate with Regulation D by altering their version of U.S.A. §402, others have simply added new exemptions comparable to Regulation D to supplement (and overlap) their old exemptions, and others have adopted but amended ULOE, consistency is still lacking in the blue sky exemption system. Widespread adoption of the recently promulgated RUSA could complicate or clarify—depending on how many states adopt and how much they alter the suggested provisions.

NONSALES AND RULE 145

Background

Certain types of corporate transactions—such as certain mergers, consolidations, reclassifications of securities, and transfers of assets—are approved by shareholder vote pursuant to state corporation laws. For example, if two-thirds of the shareholders of A Corporation approve a merger with B Corporation, they may all receive B Corporation shares in exchange for their A Corporation shares. The minority shareholders of A Corporation may receive B Corporation shares whether they want to or not. Because the element of choice is missing in this type of a transaction, the SEC originally took the position in Rule 133 that this transaction did not involve a ''sale'' of B Corporation stock and therefore did not have to be registered to satisfy §5.

Rule 133 permitted a number of serious abuses, however. For example, a small company about which little was known could transfer its shares to a public corporation in exchange for nominal consideration. The public corporation could then ''spin off'' those shares to its shareholders. All of a sudden, the unknown corporation's shares were being publicly traded, though no registration statement had ever been filed.[15] Frequently, these schemes involved substantial compensation to the persons controlling the public corporation.

A clear example of this type of abuse appears in the following case.

S.E.C. v. DATRONICS ENGINEERS, INC.

490 F.2d 250 (4th Cir. 1973), *cert. denied* 416 U.S. 937 (1974)

Datronics Engineering, Inc. ("Datronics"), a corporation engaged in construction of communication towers, had actively traded shares in the hands of about 1,000 shareholders. In a 13-month period in 1968 and 1969, it "spun off" the stock of nine corporations, three of which were wholly owned subsidiaries and six of which were independent corporations.

In each spinoff, Datronics would agree with the principals of a private company to merge that company into an existing Datronics subsidiary or into a new corporation Datronics would form. Under the agreement, the principals of the private corporation would receive the majority of the stock of the merged corporation with the rest received by Datronics for a nominal sum. Some of the stock would be retained by Datronics as compensation for its services, and the rest would be distributed to Datronics shareholders. Thus, under the scheme, the shares of a formerly private corporation would come into the hands of Datronics shareholders who could publicly trade them though no registration statement was ever filed in connection with the transaction.

The SEC ultimately brought an action under §20(b) seeking a court injunction to stop what it alleged was a violation of §5. The trial court granted summary judgment to defendants, Da-

tronics and certain of its officers and agents. The SEC appealed.

BRYAN, CIRCUIT JUDGE:

Primarily, in our judgment each of these spin-offs violated §5 of the Securities Act in that Datronics caused to be carried through the mails an unregistered security "for the purpose of sale or for delivery after sale." Datronics was actually an issuer, or at least a co-issuer, and not exempted from §5 by §4(1) of the Act, 15 U.S.C. §77d as "any person other than an issuer."

Datronics and the other appellees contend, and the District Court concluded, that this type of transaction was not a sale. The argument is that it was no more than a dividend parceled out to stockholders from its portfolio of investments. A noteworthy difference here, however, is that each distribution was an obligation. Their contention also loses sight of the definition of "sale" contained in §2 of the 1933 Act, 15 U.S.C. §77b. As pertinent here that definition is as follows:

> When used in this subchapter, unless the context otherwise requires—(3) The term "sale" or "sell" shall include every contract of sale or *dis-*

---

[15] *Securities Act Release*, no. 33–4982 (July 2, 1969).

position of a security or interest in a security, *for value*. The term ''offer to sell,'' ''offer for sale,'' or ''offer'' shall include every attempt or offer to dispose of, or solicitation of an offer to buy, a security or interest in a security, *for value*. (emphasis added)

As the term ''sale'' includes a ''disposition of a security,'' the dissemination of the new stock among Datronics' stockholders was a sale. However, the appellees urged, and the District Court held, that this disposition was not a statutory sale because it was not ''for value,'' as demanded by the definition. Here, again, we find error. Value accrued to Datronics in several ways. First, a market for the stock was created by its transfer to so many new assignees—at least 1,000, some of whom were stockbroker-dealers, residing in various States. Sales by them followed at once—the District Judge noting that ''[i]n each instance dealing promptly began in the spun-off shares.'' This result redounded to the benefit not only of Datronics but, as well, to its officers and agents who had received some of the spunoff stock as compensation for legal or other services to the spinoff corporations. Likewise, the stock retained by Datronics was thereby given an added increment of value. The record discloses that in fact the stock, both that disseminated and that kept by Datronics, did appreciate substantially after the distributions.

This spurious creation of a market whether intentional or incidental constituted a breach of the securities statutes. Each of the issuers by this wide spread of its stock became a publicly held corporation. In this process and in subsequent sales the investing public was not afforded the protection intended by the statutes. Further, the market and the public character of the spunoff stock were fired and fanned by the issuance of shareholder letters announcing future spinoffs, and by information statements sent out to the shareholders.

Moreover, we think that Datronics was an underwriter within the meaning of the 1933 Act. Hence its transactions were covered by the prohibitions, and were not within the exemptions, of the Act—§§3(a)(1) and 4(1) of the 1933 Act, 15 U.S.C. §§77c, 77d. By definition, the term underwriter ''means any person who has purchased from an issuer with a view to, or offers or sells for an issuer in connection with, the distribution of any security, or participates or has a direct or indirect participation in any such undertaking''—§2(11) of the 1933 Act, 15 U.S.C. §77b(11). Clearly, in these transactions the merger-corporation was an issuer; Datronics was a purchaser as well as a co-issuer; and the purchase was made with a view to the distribution of the stock, as commanded by Datronics' preacquisition agreements. By this underwriter distribution Datronics violated §5 of the 1933 Act—sale of unregistered securities.

· · ·

Finally, a summary of the activities of Datronics is conclusively convincing that they violated the statutes in question, and should now be restrained to prevent recurrences. To begin with, it is noteworthy that they were not isolated or minimal transgressions. There were, to repeat, nine sales and distributions of unregistered stocks in little more than a year. They were huge in volume, ranging from 75,000 to 900,000 shares. The distribution was not confined to a small number of recipients; nor was it incidental to Datronics' corporate functions. Concededly, none of the several distributions had a business purpose. In short, the spinoffs seemingly constituted the major operation of Datronics at the time.

The dismissal order of the District Court will be vacated. . . .

Rule 145

Abuses such as that of the *Datronics* case led the SEC to scrap Rule 133 in 1972 and replace it with Rule 145. The thrust of Rule 145

> is that an "offer," "offer to sell," "offer for sale," or "sale" occurs when there is submitted to security holders a plan or agreement pursuant to which such holders are required to elect, on the basis of what is in substance a new investment decision, whether to accept a new or different security in exchange for their existing security. Rule 145 embodies the Commission's determination that such transactions are subject to the registration requirements of the Act and that the previously existing "no-sale" theory of Rule 133 is no longer consistent with the statutory purposes of the Act.[16]

Rule 145 now specifically provides that "offers" and "sales" do occur when three types of transactions are submitted for shareholder approval:

1. Reclassifications, which involve the substitution of a security for another security (except for stock splits, reverse stock splits, or changes in par value).
2. Mergers or consolidations, or similar plans of acquisition where a shareholder will exchange securities for those of another issuer (except where the sole purpose of the transaction is to change an issuer's domicile).
3. Transfers of assets to another corporation in exchange for issuance of that corporation's securities *if*
   a. The voting security holders' corporation will be dissolved under the plan.
   b. The plan provides for a pro-rata distribution of issued securities to the voting security holders.
   c. Within a year of the vote the board of directors of the corporation accomplishes (a) or (b) by resolution.
   d. The transfer of assets is a part of a preexisting plan for distribution of the securities.

Rule 145 provides that these types of transactions must be registered,[17] requiring either the information for Form S-14 (which is less extensive than the S-1) or disclosure via proxy registration information (which is easier for a publicly traded corporation that has already compiled this information).

While these transactions requiring shareholder approval are now deemed "offers" and "sales" requiring registration, practicalities dictate some loosening of the prefiling publicity rules applicable to most registrations. For instance, state corporation laws normally require notice of shareholder meetings to approve such matters as a merger must be sent to the shareholders well in advance of the meeting. Therefore, bare-bones descriptions of the transactions to be voted on and proxy solicitation materials meeting the requirements of Rule 14a-12 of the 1934 Act are permitted.

To avoid abuses of Rule 145 by affiliates, there are some pertinent resale restrictions. Persons receiving securities in a Rule 145 transaction who are not control persons of either the acquired company or the acquiror may resell without restriction. However,

---

[16] Preliminary note to Rule 145.

[17] Registration can be avoided if the issuer can meet the requirements of the §3(a)(9) exemption for stock swaps or the §3(a)(11) intrastate offering exemption.

paragraph (c) of Rule 145 states that affiliates of the corporations can be deemed "underwriters" for §2(11) purposes if they resell.

To avoid the necessity of filing their own registration statement or finding their own exemption before they resell, these affiliates may turn to paragraph (d) of Rule 145. That paragraph allows affiliates to resell under two circumstances without being deemed involved in an offering requiring registration. First, if the party was an affiliate before the transaction but is not afterward, and has held the securities for at least two years, he or she can resell if the issuer has been a 1934 Act reporting company for the prior 12 months. Second, the affiliate may sell if the requirements of paragraphs (c), (e), (f), and (g) of Rule 144 are met. Rule 144 governs resales of restricted securities. It is a very important rule, and we shall now turn our attention to its provisions.

REGULATION OF RESALES

Introduction

The registration provisions of the 1933 Act could be circumvented if they applied only to "issuers," because those issuers could simply act through "affiliates" (persons who control or are controlled by the issuer). Similarly, the registration process could be circumvented if an issuer could sell securities to another party in a privately negotiated §4(2) transaction that is exempt from registration, but it was planned that the buying party would immediately resell the securities to the public.

To prevent such circumvention, the 1933 Act regulates offerings by affiliates and resales of "restricted securities" originally issued under exemptions. It does so by defining an "underwriter" to include "any person who has purchased from an issuer with a view to . . . the distribution of any security." [18] Thus, an affiliate seeking to "front" for an issuer and a purchaser of "restricted" securities are deemed "underwriters" and therefore cannot take advantage of §4(1)'s exemption for all persons other than issuers, *underwriters*, and broker-dealers. The §4(1) exemption, which allows secondary trading to occur freely among normal investors, is withheld from these statutory underwriters. Therefore, to resell they must either file a registration statement or find an independent exemption. [19]

Rule 144

Rule 144 is designed to provide a "safe harbor" for resales by affiliates and purchasers of restricted securities. Before Rule 144, such persons would usually have to hold the securities for three to five years, hoping that this passage of time would convince the

---

[18] Section 2(a)(11).

[19] A private placement pursuant to §4(2) is possible, of course, if the seller can find a sophisticated buyer with adequate information, as in a Regulation A offering. See *Securities Act Release*, no. 33–5223 (January 11, 1972).

courts that they had not originally acquired the securities "with a view to distribution." But the safe harbor of Rule 144 may be used only if certain requirements are met.

Current Public Information

The rule is designed to allow resale only when there is sufficient information generally available about the issuer to protect the investor. Therefore, the Rule 144 exemption is only available if the issuer has been a 1934 Act reporting company for at least 90 days *or* if not a reporting company there is nonetheless sufficient information about the issuer publicly available to meet the requirements of Rule 15c2–11(a)(4) of the 1934 Act.[20]

Note that recently the SEC created an exception to this information requirement by providing an exemption from it for resales by a *nonaffiliate* who has held the securities for at least three years.[21]

Holding Period

Restricted securities must be fully paid for and beneficially owned for at least two years before Rule 144 allows resale. Fungibility does not apply; that is, purchase of restricted securities will not restart the two-year period as to previously acquired securities. There are also complicated rules on tacking. For example, if Mr. A sells restricted securities to Ms. B under a private placement exemption, Ms. B must hold for two years to be able to resell under Rule 144. Ms. B cannot "tack on" the period of time Mr. A held the restricted securities to meet the two-year requirement sooner.

Limitation on Amount

Because §4(1)'s exemption was intended only for routine trading transactions between individual investors with respect to securities already issued, Rule 144 permits resale of securities only in limited quantities so as not to disrupt the market.

The maximum that an affiliate can sell in any three-month period is the *greater* of (1) 1% of the outstanding shares of that class or (2) the average weekly reported volume of trading in such shares on all national exchanges or reported through NASDAQ during four recent calendar weeks. This amount may be sold during successive three-month periods, but there is no accumulation allowed. For example, an affiliate could not skip one three-month period and then sell 2% of the outstanding shares of a class during the following three-month period.

However, there is no limitation on amount *if* the seller has not been an affiliate of the issuer for at least three months and has held the securities for at least three years. Similarly, such a person may ignore the manner of sale and notice requirements discussed in the paragraphs that follow.

---

[20] This is the substantial information that the 1934 Act requires be made public about an issuer before a broker may quote its over-the-counter securities.

[21] *Securities Act Release*, no. 6488 (September 23, 1983).

Manner of Sale

An affiliate can resell only through a customary, unsolicited "broker's transaction" in which the broker receives only the customary commission or in a transaction directly with a "market maker." The affiliate shall not solicit orders or make any payment in connection with the sale other than the usual commission to the broker who executes the sell order. Resale in this manner frees the securities of their restrictive characteristics.

Notice of Sale

If the amount of securities to be sold by an affiliate under Rule 144 is to exceed 500 shares or $10,000 in value during any three-month period, a notice of proposed sale must be filed with the SEC and on any exchange where the securities are traded. The person filing the notice (on Form 144) must have a *bona fide* intent to sell the securities within a reasonable time.

State Exemptions

The states also have exemptions for secondary transactions by nonissuers. Indeed, the Uniform Securities Act's nonissuer exemptions do not contain many of the stringent qualifications of Rule 144.[22]

QUESTIONS AND PROBLEMS

1. Defendant Petroleum Management Corp. organized oil and gas limited partnerships. Seven persons were offered "participant" interests: four accepted, including plaintiff Doran, a sophisticated investor who had adequate information. Later Doran sued to rescind his investment on grounds that the securities were unregistered but should have been because some of the other offerees were unsophisticated and/or lacked adequate information. Can Petroleum Management Corp. claim a §4(2) exemption? Discuss. See *Doran* v. *Petroleum Management Corp.*, 545 F.2d 893 (5th Cir. 1977).

2. Regulation D has some prohibitions against "general solicitations." Which of the following should be considered "general solicitations"?

   a. A solicitation by the general partner of a limited partnership to 330 sophisticated investors, all of whom are limited partners in other active programs sponsored by the general partner? See *Woodlands-Seattle, Ltd.* (Securities and Exchange Commission, July 8, 1982).

   b. Mailing brochures to members of a trade association, distributing brochures at a meeting attended primarily by the trade association's members, and advertising in its trade journal? See *Aspen Grove* (Securities and Exchange Commission, November 8, 1982).

---

[22] For example, Uniform Securities Act, §402(b).

   c. Engaging in product advertising through newspaper, television, and radio at the same time a Regulation D offering is being attempted? See *Printing Enterprises Management Science, Inc.* (Securities and Exchange Commission, March 23, 1983).

3. Assume that an issuer preparing to conduct an offering of equity securities under Rule 505 raised $2,000,000 from the sale of debt instruments under Rule 505 eight months earlier. How much may the issuer raise in the proposed equity offering?

4. On February 15, 1984, LaserFax, Inc., offered 437,500 shares of common stock at $2.00 to raise funds to organize the business, hire employees, buy furniture and office supplies, and generally establish the business. All shares were sold by April 1985. In August 1985, when it was preparing to receive orders, but had been unable to obtain bank loans, LaserFax proposed to sell up to $2.4 million of 10% convertible subordinated debentures due in 1990. LaserFax was also exploring the possibility of a public offering of registered shares that would raise approximately $16–20 million for the company. This offering, depending on market conditions, could occur sooner than six months after completion of the sale of the convertible debentures. LaserFax needs to know whether its sale of convertible debentures would be integrated with its prior offering or with the subsequent public offering under Regulation D. Discuss. See *LaserFax, Inc., Federal Securities Law Reports* (CCH), ¶78,136 (Securities and Exchange Commission, 1985).

5. Assume that X Corporation wishes to raise $450,000 through a nonpublic offering. Is Regulation D's Rule 506 available to X Corporation?

6. Levitt Corp. (Levitt) owns a subsidiary, Levitt Homes, that operates a home-building division in Puerto Rico. For tax reasons, Levitt decided to transfer its Puerto Rican operations to an inactive subsidiary, Levitt PR. Levitt finances its Puerto Rican operations by arranging for FHA- or VA-approved mortgages for homebuyers in Puerto Rico, accepting a small down payment, and pooling those mortgages into GNMA certificates. Due to financial conditions, Levitt would like to sell the GNMA certificates. Pursuant to an underwriter's advice, Levitt wishes to sell the GNMA certificates to Levitt PR that would in turn sell them to a newly formed subsidiary, Levitt Funding. Levitt Funding would then sell to Puerto Rican investors. The funds received from the sales would be used to finance operations in Puerto Rico; all Levitt Funding's assets are in Puerto Rico, as is its sole office; all proceeds would be used to repay short-term indebtedness incurred to fund Puerto Rican operations and to pay Puerto Rican income taxes. Can Levitt Funding utilize the §3(a)(11) exemption in offering the GNMA certificates? See *Levitt Corporation*, Federal Securities Law Reports (CCH), ¶77,886 (Securities and Exchange Commission, March 29, 1985).

7. The Lowry Market Timing Fund, Inc. (the Fund), was an open-end, diversified, management investment company, incorporated in Texas. To reduce operating expenses, the Fund wished to reorganize as a business trust in Massachusetts. The Fund would transfer all its assets to the Trust in exchange for a number of Trust shares and the assumption by the Trust of all liabilities and obligations. The Fund would then distribute the Trust shares to all Fund shareholders who would receive in exchange for cancellation of their Fund shares, full and fractional Trust shares in

an amount and having a net asset value equal to the amount and net asset value of the Fund shares. Must this reorganization be registered separately, or does Rule 145 provide an exemption? Discuss. See *Lowry Market Timing Fund, Inc.*, Federal Securities Law Reports (CCH), ¶77,896 (Securities and Exchange Commission, 1985).

8. In the ordinary course of its business as a broker-dealer, Morgan Stanley regularly extends credit to its customers on securities. Sometimes the customers pledge restricted or control securities as security for such credit. Assuming that Morgan Stanley has not been an affiliate of the issuer for at least three months, that the combined holding period of the customer and Morgan Stanley is at least three years, and that the pledge arrangement is *bona fide*, can Morgan Stanley sell the securities without compliance with the requirements of Rule 144? Discuss. See *Morgan Stanley & Co., Inc.*, Federal Securities Law Reports (CCH), ¶ 77,849 (Securities and Exchange Commission, 1984).

18

SECTION 10(b): CORPORATE DISCLOSURE

INTRODUCTION

The 1933 and 1934 Acts contain numerous antifraud provisions, but none is so important as the one discussed in this chapter and in Chapter 20—Section 10(b) of the 1934 Act. Section 10(b) makes it unlawful "[t]o use or employ, in connection with the purchase or sale of any security . . . any manipulative or deceptive device or contrivance" in violation of SEC rules. Pursuant to §10(b), the SEC has promulgated a number of rules, but none has spawned more litigation than Rule 10b-5, which is worth quoting in full:

> It shall be unlawful for any person, directly or indirectly, by the use of any means or instrumentality of interstate commerce, or of the mails or of any facility of any national securities exchange,
>
> (a) To employ any device, scheme, or artifice to defraud,
>
> (b) To make any untrue statement of a material fact or to omit to state a material fact necessary in order to make the statements made, in light of the circumstances under which they were made, not misleading, or
>
> (c) To engage in any act, practice, or course of business which operates or would operate as a fraud or deceit upon any person, in connection with the purchase or sale of any security.

This chapter will disclose why §10(b) and Rule 10b-5 have become the premier antifraud tools used by the SEC and private litigants to deter and punish a great variety of fraudulent activities touching the purchase and sale of securities.

Other Provisions

Many other antifraud provisions are scattered throughout the 1933 and 1934 acts. In Chapter 16, we discussed §§11, 12(2), and 17(a) of the 1933 Act.

Section 18

Section 18 of the 1934 Act prohibits false or misleading statements "in any application, report or document filed pursuant" to the 1934 Act. Furthermore, §18 expressly provides a cause of action for persons injured by its violation. This is a potentially important section, because so many documents (110,000 per year) must be filed with the Securities and Exchange Commission. Sections 12, 13(a), and 15(d) of the 1934 Act require many corporations (including those with shares listed on national exchanges and those with 500 shareholders of a single class and $5 million in assets) to register with the SEC and then to update the information annually with 10-K's, quarterly with 10-Q's, and whenever any significant change occurs with 8-K's. As we shall see in later chapters, the SEC also requires the filing of proxy solicitation materials in §14. These (except the 10-Q) and other documents filed with the SEC are the potential bases for a §18 cause of action if they contain any misstatements. Potential defendants are many, including all persons responsible for the reports. Major officers and a majority of the board of directors must sign a Form 10-K.

The utility of §18(a) as an antifraud weapon, however, has been greatly diminished by several factors. First, it applies only to "filed" documents and therefore is inapplicable to any fraudulent misstatements by "nonreporting" companies or to any misstatements of reporting companies made orally or in any document not filed with the SEC. Even annual reports that must be delivered to shareholders pursuant to §14 are not deemed "filed" documents for §18 purposes, even though seven copies must be filed with the SEC.[1]

Second, the section specifically provides a defense for all defendants who can prove that they "acted in good faith and had no knowledge" of the false statement. "Reckless" conduct by a defendant will not lead to liability as it apparently will under §10(b), and defendants need not prove due diligence.

A third drawback to §18 as a remedy for fraud is that it has a relatively short statute of limitations—suit must be filed within one year after discovery of the fraud but in no case more than three years after the claim accrued. Furthermore, the section allows the court, in its discretion, to require a plaintiff to post a bond to cover the defendants' costs and attorneys fees before the proceeding begins.

The most important limitation on §18's express cause of action is that it has

---

[1] Rule 14a–3(c).

been interpreted to require "eyeball" reliance by plaintiff. That is, a plaintiff who has not actually seen the filed document (or a copy of it) and relied on the false statement contained therein has no §18 claim.[2]

For all these reasons, there have been few successful suits by investors injured by violations of §18.

Section 9

Section 9(e) of the 1934 Act also provides an express private cause of action. It remedies violations of subsections (a) through (c) of §9, which prohibit various types of "manipulation" of securities prices.

As with §18, the usefulness of the express remedy of §9 is limited by several factors, including (1) it is limited to securities registered on the national exchanges; (2) it has a strong causation element (plaintiff must prove that defendant's manipulation *materially* affected the price of a security); (3) it has a stiff scienter requirement (plaintiff must prove defendant acted "willfully"—recklessness will not suffice); and (4) it also has a bond requirement and a short statute of limitations.

RICO

As noted in Chapter 13, because the Racketeering Influenced and Corrupt Organizations Act (RICO) is so broadly worded, contains such attractive remedies (including treble damages and attorney's fees), and lists "securities fraud" as a "racketeering act," it is becoming a very popular cause of action in securities litigation. Indeed, it has been said that RICO claims "could soon totally eliminate the use of traditional securities law remedies."[3] Though it is unlikely that §10(b) will be totally supplanted, RICO claims are becoming increasingly important.

Enforcement of Section 10(b)

SEC

The SEC can exert its full panoply of powers in enforcing §10(b) and Rule 10b-5. For example, the Commission can bring administrative actions against those who must register with it or practice before it, such as broker-dealers, underwriters, accountants, and attorneys. Furthermore, the SEC can go to federal district court to obtain injunctions to prohibit further violations of §10(b) and can even obtain orders of disgorgement to remedy past violations by forcing wrongdoers to forfeit their ill-gotten gains. In extreme cases, the SEC can use its authority in §20 of the 1934 Act to refer

---

[2] *Heit* v. *Weitzen*, 402 F.2d 909 (2d Cir. 1968).

[3] D. Lauter, "The Supreme Court Slows Its Conservative Shift," *National Law Journal*, July 15, 1985, p. 21 (quoting Stephen Shapiro).

cases to the Department of Justice for criminal prosecution. Section 32 makes it a crime intentionally to violate *any* provision of the 1934 Act.

Private Causes of Action

Nowhere in §10 did Congress expressly provide that persons injured by §10(b) violations would be entitled to sue those who caused their damages. Certainly §10(b) and Rule 10b-5 would never have achieved their present prominence if the courts had never *implied* a private cause of action under the section. But they did.

The first case allowing a private suit was a 1946 district court case, *Kardon* v. *National Gypsum Co.*[4] The other lower federal courts followed this decision for many years, building up a substantial body of precedent. However, in the 1970s, the viability of the implied §10(b) cause of action was questioned. The *Kardon* case had held that injured plaintiffs' right to sue for a §10(b) violation should be implied unless Congress' ''intention to withhold it should appear very clearly and plainly.'' This standard was directly in conflict with the Supreme Court's rulings in several 1970s cases that a private right of action should never be implied from a statute not expressly providing a right to sue unless the plaintiff provided clear evidence from the legislative history that Congress, notwithstanding its silence, intended a private cause of action to exist.[5] Because there is no clear evidence that Congress intended in 1934 that a private cause of action exist under §10(b), the matter was in some doubt until the Supreme Court's 1983 decision in the following case.

HERMAN & MacLEAN v. HUDDLESTON

459 U.S. 375 (1983)

In 1969 Texas International Speedway (TIS) filed a registration statement and prospectus with the SEC. Proceeds of the offering were to be used to build an automobile race track. The entire issue of $4,398,900 was sold on the offering date, October 30, 1969. Thirteen months later, TIS filed for bankruptcy.

Huddleston and other investors brought a class action claiming fraud by several defen-

dants, including the accounting firm, Herman & MacLean, which had certified the financial statements contained in the registration statement and prospectus.

After taking evidence, the trial court held for plaintiffs on their §10(b) and Rule 10b-5 claim. The circuit court of appeals held that this claim could be brought notwithstanding the availability of an express *cause of action under*

---

[4] 69 F.Supp. 512 (E.D. Pa. 1946).

[5] For example, *Touche Ross & Co.* v. *Redington*, 442 U.S. 560 (1979) (holding no private cause of action exists under §17(a) of the 1934 Act).

§11 of the 1933 Act, but reversed because it disagreed with the trial court's standard for the burden of proof. The appellate court believed a 10b-5 plaintiff should have to prove fraud by the common law standard of "clear and convincing" evidence.

The accounting firm appealed.

MARSHALL, JUSTICE:

· · ·

We granted certiorari to consider whether an implied cause of action under Section 10(b) of the 1934 Act will lie for conduct subject to an express civil remedy under the 1933 Act, . . . and to decide the standard of proof applicable to actions under Section 10(b). . . . We now affirm the court of appeals' holding that plaintiffs could maintain an action under Section 10(b) of the 1934 Act, but we reverse as to the applicable standard of proof.

II

The Securities Act of 1933 and the Securities Exchange Act of 1934 "constitute interrelated components of the federal regulatory scheme governing transactions in securities"—*Ernst & Ernst* v. *Hochfelder*, 425 U.S. 185 (1976). The Acts created several express private rights of action, one of which is contained in Section 11 of the 1933 Act. In addition to the private actions created explicitly by the 1933 and 1934 Acts, federal courts have implied private remedies under other provisions of the two laws. Most significantly for present purposes, a private right of action under Section 10(b) of the 1934 Act and Rule 10b-5 has been consistently recognized for more than 35 years. The existence of this implied remedy is simply beyond peradventure.

The issue in this case is whether a party should be barred from invoking this established remedy for fraud because the allegedly fraudulent conduct would apparently also provide the basis for a damage action under Section 11 of the 1933 Act. The resolution of this issue turns on the fact that the two provisions involve distinct causes of action and were intended to address different types of wrongdoing.

Section 11 of the 1933 Act allows purchasers of a registered security to sue certain enumerated parties in a registered offering when false or misleading information is included in a registration statement. The section was designed to assure compliance with the disclosure provisions of the Act by imposing a stringent standard of liability on the parties who play a direct role in a registered offering. If a plaintiff purchased a security issued pursuant to a registration statement, he need only show a material misstatement or omission to establish his *prima facie* case. Liability against the issuer of a security is virtually absolute, even for innocent misstatements. Other defendants bear the burden of demonstrating due diligence.

Although limited in scope, Section 11 places a relatively minimal burden on a plaintiff. In contrast, Section 10(b) is a "catchall" antifraud provision, but it requires a plaintiff to carry a heavier burden to establish a cause of action. While a Section 11 action must be brought by a purchaser of a registered security, must be based on misstatements or omissions in a registration statement, and can only be brought against certain parties, a Section 10(b) action can be brought by a purchaser or seller of "*any* security" against "*any* person" who has used "*any* manipulative or deceptive device or contrivance" in connection with the purchase or sale of a security (emphasis added). However, a Section 10(b) plaintiff carries a heavier burden than a Section 11 plaintiff. Most significantly, he must prove that the defendant acted with scienter, that is, with intent to deceive, manipulate, or defraud.

Since Section 11 and Section 10(b) address

different types of wrongdoing, we see no reason to carve out an exception to Section 10(b) for fraud occurring in a registration statement just because the same conduct may also be actionable under Section 11. Exempting such conduct from liability under Section 10(b) would conflict with the basic purpose of the 1933 Act: to provide greater protection to purchasers of registered securities. It would be anomalous indeed if the special protection afforded to purchasers in a registered offering by the 1933 Act were deemed to deprive such purchasers of the protections against manipulation and deception that Section 10(b) makes available to all persons who deal in securities.

. . .

A cumulative construction of the securities laws also furthers their broad remedial purposes. In enacting the 1934 Act, Congress stated that its purpose was ''to impose requirements necessary to make [securities] regulation and control reasonably complete and effective''—15 U.S.C. §78b. In furtherance of that objective, Section 10(b) makes it unlawful to use ''*any* manipulative or deceptive device or contrivance'' in connection with the purchase or sale of any security. The effectiveness of the broad proscription against fraud in Section 10(b) would be undermined if its scope were restricted by the existence of an express remedy under Section 11. Yet we have repeatedly recognized that securities laws combating fraud should be construed ''not technically and restrictively, but flexibly to effectuate [their] remedial purposes''—*SEC* v. *Capital Gains Research Bureau*, 375 U.S. 180 (1963).

. . .

Accordingly, we hold that the availability of an express remedy under Section 11 of the 1933 Act does not preclude defrauded purchasers of registered securities from maintaining an action under Section 10(b) of the 1934 Act. To this extent the judgment of the court of appeals is affirmed.

III

In a typical civil suit for money damages, plaintiffs must prove their case by a preponderance of the evidence. Similarly, in an action by the SEC to establish fraud under Section 17(a) of the Securities Act, 15 U.S.C. §77q(a), we have held that proof by a preponderance of the evidence suffices to establish liability— *SEC* v. *C. M. Joiner Leasing Corp.*, 320 U.S. 344, 355 (1943). ''Where . . . proof is offered in a civil action, as here, a preponderance of the evidence will establish the case.'' Ibid. The same standard applies in administrative proceedings before the SEC and has been consistently employed by the lower courts in private actions under the securities laws.

The Court of Appeals nonetheless held that plaintiffs in a Section 10(b) suit must establish their case by clear and convincing evidence. The Court of Appeals relied primarily on the traditional use of a higher burden of proof in civil fraud actions at common law. Reference to common law practices can be misleading, however, since the historical considerations underlying the imposition of a higher standard of proof have questionable pertinence here. See *Blue Chip Stamps* v. *Manor Drug Stores*, 421 U.S. 723, 744–745 (1975) (''[T]he typical fact situation in which the classic tort of misrepresentation and deceit evolved was light years from the world of commercial transactions to which Rule 10b-5 is applicable.''). Moreover, the antifraud provisions of the securities laws are not coextensive with common law doctrines of fraud. Indeed, an important purpose of the federal securities statutes was to rectify perceived deficiencies in the available common law protections by establishing higher standards of conduct in the securities industry. See *SEC* v. *Capital*

Gains Research Bureau, Inc., 375 U.S. 180, 186 (1963). We therefore find reference to the common law in this instance unavailing.

Where Congress has not prescribed the appropriate standard of proof and the Constitution does not dictate a particular standard, we must prescribe one.

. . .

A preponderance-of-the-evidence standard allows both parties to "share the risk of error in roughly equal fashion"—*Addington* v. *Texas*, 421 U.S., at 423. Any other standard expresses a preference for one side's interests. The balance of interests in this case warrants use of the preponderance standard. On the one hand, the defendants face the risk of opprobrium that may result from a finding of fraudulent conduct, but this risk is identical to that in an action under Section 17(a), which is governed by the prepon-

derance-of-the-evidence standard. The interests of defendants in a securities case do not differ qualitatively from the interests of defendants sued for violations of other federal statutes such as the antitrust or civil rights laws, for which proof by a preponderance of the evidence suffices. On the other hand, the interests of plaintiffs in such suits are significant. Defrauded investors are among the very individuals Congress sought to protect in the securities laws. If they prove that it is more likely than not that they were defrauded, they should recover.

We therefore decline to depart from the preponderance-of-the-evidence standard generally applicable in civil actions. Accordingly, the Court of Appeals' decision as to the appropriate standard of proof is reversed.

. . .

Affirmed in part and reversed in part.

The Supreme Court's decision in *Huddleston* was important on many levels. It established beyond a doubt the existence of an implied §10(b) cause of action. This decision was not surprising in light of the massive body of §10(b) precedent and previous Supreme Court rulings in such cases as *Blue Chip Stamps* v. *Manor Drug Stores*.[6] The decision also emphasized the broad nature of the §10(b) remedy, which applies to suits by purchasers or sellers of *any* security against *any* person who committed *any* fraud in connection with the sale or purchase of that security. It also established a relaxed burden of proof.

Perhaps most important, the Supreme Court also held that the implied §10(b) remedy was available to remedy injuries already covered by the express §11 cause of action in the 1933 Act. This holding lends support to lower court rulings that §10(b) is also available in situations where §18[7] and perhaps other sections of the 1934 Act expressly apply.

---

[6] 421 U.S. 723 (1975).

[7] For example, *Ross* v. *A. H. Robins Co.*, 607 F.2d 545 (2d Cir. 1979).

ELEMENTS OF A SECTION 10(b) CLAIM

Substantial litigation has arisen over the question of exactly what must be proved to establish a §10(b) cause of action. As with §§11 and 12(2) of the 1933 Act, much of that litigation has focused on how much the common law fraud elements of materiality, scienter, reliance, causation, and privity should be adjusted to suit the purposes of the federal securities laws.

Fraud

The first thing that any §10(b)/Rule 10b-5 plaintiff must establish is that the defendants engaged in some sort of fraudulent, deceptive, or manipulative conduct. These are general concepts that have been broadly applied. Because the 1934 Act is remedial in nature, most courts have striven to apply §10(b) to many of the countless varieties of deceptive practices that securities defrauders have invented. Still, most §10(b) cases fall into two major categories.

First, there is the "insider trading" case, which arises when corporate insiders take unfair advantage of their access to nonpublic information by trading securities for profit. This type of case is so important that Chapter 20 is entirely devoted to §10(b)'s application to insider trading.

Corporate Disclosure

This chapter is primarily concerned with the second main type of §10(b) claim— that arising out of corporate misstatements or omissions.[8] When corporations knowingly inflate their earnings projections, manipulate their financial records to show a paper profit rather than the real loss, or engage in numerous other ploys to deceive, a violation of §10(b) and Rule 10b-5 occurs. It is important to remember that deceptive omissions are just as misleading as affirmative misstatements. Section 10(b) and Rule 10b-5 make unlawful not only the making of an untrue statement of material fact, but also the omission of "a material fact necessary in order to make the statements made, in light of the circumstances under which they were made, not misleading." Liability can also arise from failing to correct a statement that was accurate when made, but has become misleading due to subsequent events.[9]

Most cases involve corporations charged with being too optimistic in their press releases, annual reports to shareholders, financial statements filed with the SEC, and so on. However, some cases arise out of the opposite situation. In *SEC* v. *Texas Gulf Sulphur*,[10] for example, TGS made a tremendous mineral find while drilling core samples

---

[8] There are additional types of §10(b) suits. For example, fraud and manipulation by brokers and dealers in the trading of stock is remediable under §10(b), as Chapter 23 will discuss.

[9] For example, *SEC* v. *Shattuck Denn Mining Corp.*, 297 F.Supp. 470 (S.D.N.Y. 1968).

[10] 401 F.2d 833 (2d Cir. 1968).

in Canada in November 1963. Although the drilling was merely preliminary, the results were astonishing, and those corporate insiders who knew of it purchased substantial amounts of TGS stock in their own behalf. The insider trading aspects of such a case are discussed in Chapter 20. For present purposes, the important point is that when in the following spring rumors of the ore strike began to circulate, the management of TGS issued an April 12 press release that, in essence, labeled the rumors as speculative and based on unreliable and inconclusive data. Finally, on April 16, the full magnitude of the ore strike was made known. Persons who sold their shares between April 12 and April 16, and therefore did not profit from the rapid rise in TGS stock prices following the announcement, sued. TGS and its officials were held liable by courts that held the April 12 press release to be misleadingly *pessimistic*.[11]

The defendants from Texas Gulf Sulphur argued that the results of their drilling were inconclusive and they faced a dilemma. If they announced a major strike, but further drilling revealed the earlier cores had been misleadingly favorable, they would face a lawsuit from all investors who purchased believing a great strike had occurred. However, choosing the more conservative path would lead to liability to those who sold TGS stock. The courts recognized the dilemma, but held that the facts showed sufficient basis for a conclusion that TGS knew as early as April 12 the information that was the basis of the April 16 announcement.

Another complication arises from the need for corporate secrecy. TGS had a legitimate reason to keep secret the information about the strike—so it could lease the surrounding areas without having to bid against competitors who might flock in if the information became public. Had the insiders of TGS not engaged in insider trading, this argument would have carried more weight. But the insider trading, coupled with the misleadingly pessimistic press release, doomed TGS's defense.

More successful was the defendant in *State Teachers Retirement Board* v. *Fluor Corporation*.[12] On February 28, 1975, Fluor Corporation received a signed contract to build a $1 billion coal gasification plant in South Africa. Its agreement mandated a publicity embargo until March 10 so that the South African company could complete negotiations for financing the project. Rumors soon began to circulate that Fluor had received the contract. Inquiries made to Fluor were answered with "no comment." Because of the rumors, volume in trading of Fluor stock boomed and the price rose. The plaintiff pension fund sold almost 300,000 shares of Fluor stock between March 3 and March 6. On March 7, the New York Stock Exchange halted trading in Fluor stock pending an announcement. On Monday, March 10, Fluor announced that it had the contract.

Plaintiff sued, claiming that Fluor should have disclosed the signing when the trading of its stock became so heavy. The court disagreed. Holding that "[a] company has no duty to correct or verify rumors in the marketplace unless those rumors can be attributed to the company," the court sustained Fluor Corporation's position that it had

---

[11] For example, *Mitchell* v. *Texas Gulf Sulphur Co.*, 446 F.2d 90 (10th Cir.), *cert. denied*, 404 U.S. 1004 (1971); and *SEC* v. *Texas Gulf Sulphur Co.*, 312 F.Supp. 77 (S.D.N.Y. 1970), *aff'd*, 446 F.2d 1301 (2d Cir. 1971).

[12] 654 F.2d 843 (2d Cir. 1981).

a good business reason not to disclose the information. Fluor's success at escaping liability may be attributed, in part, to the fact that unlike in *Texas Gulf Sulphur*, there was neither trading on inside information by corporate officials nor a misleading announcement. The "no comment" approach was successful.

Plaintiff also claimed that Fluor violated NYSE *Manual*, Section A2, which stated that a corporation should be prepared to make an immediate announcement of important corporate developments if unusual market activity occurred. The court held that even if this provision had been violated, it did not give rise to a private cause of action.

Although corporations have no duty to correct or confirm rumors not attributable to them, they can become so involved in preparation of, say, a newspaper article that they become responsible for its accuracy. This may occur, according to one court,

> when officials of the company have, by their activity, made an implied representation that the information they have reviewed is true or at least in accordance with the company's views. . . . A company which undertakes to correct errors in reports presented to it for review may find itself forced to choose between raising no objection to a statement which, because it is contradicted by internal information, may be misleading and making that information public at a time when corporate interests would best be served by confidentiality.[13]

Texas Gulf Sulphur and *Fluor* are both "good news" cases. Naturally, there is an even greater motivation to suppress disclosure or soften the blow when "bad news" is involved. The same general rules apply to a bad news case. A corporation may succeed with a "no comment" approach, so long as there is no insider trading, no market fluctuation due to rumors traceable to the corporation, and no prior SEC filings rendered misleading by the new negative developments.

However, the SEC's disclosure requirements and exchange and NASD rules all urge disclosure of negative information. A court will carefully scrutinize a corporation's "business reason" for not disclosing bad news. Certainly there can be business justifications for delaying disclosure of bad news—such as the need to verify potentially negative developments. But what if the bad news consists of imminent financial catastrophe that is being suppressed as the corporation desperately negotiates to refinance its debt? Does a good business reason for delaying disclosure arise from the fact that disclosure would cause a shareholder panic that would render refinancing impossible? The law is unclear, but if the first bad news that hits the press is an announcement of the corporation's filing for bankruptcy, a §10(b) violation is likely to be found.

Corporate Mismanagement

A recurrent §10(b) question is whether the section provides a remedy for mere corporate mismanagement; that is, can a shareholder whose main thrust is not "I have been deceived," but "I have been treated unfairly," claim the protection of §10(b)? Many early lower courts said "yes."

---

[13] *Elkind* v. *Liggett & Myers, Inc.*, 635 F.2d 156 (2d Cir. 1980).

The Supreme Court apparently, and only apparently, resolved the issue with a "no" answer in the following case.

SANTA FE INDUSTRIES, INC. v. GREEN

430 U.S. 462 (1977)

Santa Fe acquired 95% of the stock of Kirby Lumber Corporation between 1968 and 1973, paying from $65.00 to $92.50 per share. In 1974 Santa Fe decided that it wanted to own all of Kirby's stock, so it utilized Delaware's "short-form merger" statute, which permits the owner of 90% or more of a corporation's stock to buy out the other shareholders with or without their consent and even without advance notice. Santa Fe decided to pay $150 per share to the minority after Kirby's stock was valued at $125 per share by an investment banking firm.

Minority shareholders had the right to go to state court to exercise their right to a statutory appraisal setting the fair value of their stock. Instead, they initiated a §10(b) claim in federal court, claiming their shares were worth at least $772 each.

The district court dismissed the claim. The Second Circuit reversed, holding that a Rule 10b-5 claim was stated when a majority allegedly breached its fiduciary duty to the minority. Santa Fe appealed.

WHITE, JUSTICE:

. . .

The Court of Appeals' approach to the interpretation of Rule 10b-5 is inconsistent with that taken by the Court last Term in *Ernst & Ernst v. Hochfelder*, 425 U.S. 185 (1976).

Ernst & Ernst makes clear that in deciding whether a complaint states a cause of action for "fraud" under Rule 10b-5, "we turn first to the language of §10(b), for '[t]he starting point in every case involving construction of a statute is the language itself.'"

. . .

The language of §10(b) gives no indication that Congress meant to prohibit any conduct not involving manipulation or deception. Nor have we been cited to any evidence in the legislative history that would support a departure from the language of the statute. "When a statute speaks so specifically in terms of manipulation and deception, * * * and when its history reflects no more expansive intent, we are quite unwilling to extend the scope of the statute." Id., at 214. Thus the claim of fraud and fiduciary breach in this complaint states a cause of action under any part of Rule 10b-5 only if the conduct alleged can be fairly viewed as "manipulative or deceptive" within the meaning of the statute.

III

It is our judgment that the transaction, if carried out as alleged in the complaint, was neither deceptive nor manipulative and therefore did not violate either §10(b) of the Act or Rule 10b-5.

As we have indicated, the case comes to us on the premise that the complaint failed to allege a material misrepresentation or material failure to disclose. The finding of the District

Court, undisturbed by the Court of Appeals, was that there was no "omission" or "misstatement" in the Information Statement accompanying the notice of merger. On the basis of the information provided, minority shareholders could either accept the price offered or reject it and seek an appraisal in the Delaware Court of Chancery. Their choice was fairly presented, and they were furnished with all relevant information on which to base their decision.

We therefore find inapposite the cases relied upon by respondents and the court below, in which the breaches of fiduciary duty held violative of Rule 10b-5 included some element of deception. Those cases forcefully reflect the principle that "[s]ection 10(b) must be read flexibly, not technically and restrictively" and that the statute provides a cause of action for any plaintiff who "suffer[s] an injury as a result of deceptive practices touching its sale [or purchase] of securities." *Superintendent of Insurance* v. *Bankers Life & Casualty Co.*, 404 U.S. 6, 12–13 (1971). But the cases do not support the proposition, adopted by the Court of Appeals below and urged by respondents here, that a breach of fiduciary duty by majority stockholders, without any deception, misrepresentation, or nondisclosure, violates the statute and the Rule.

It is also readily apparent that the conduct alleged in the complaint was not "manipulative" within the meaning of the statute. Manipulation is "virtually a term of art when used in connection with securities markets." *Ernst & Ernst*, 425 U.S., at 199. The term refers generally to practices, such as wash sales, matched orders, or rigged prices, that are intended to mislead investors by artificially affecting market activity. Section 10(b)'s general prohibition of practices deemed by the SEC to be "manipulative"—in this technical sense of artificially affecting market activity in order to mislead investors—is fully consistent with the fundamental purpose of the 1934 Act "to substitute a philoso-

phy of full disclosure for the philosophy of *caveat emptor.*" *Affiliated Ute Citizens* v. *United States*, 406 U.S. 128, 151 (1972), quoting *SEC* v. *Capital Gains Research Bureau*, 375 U.S. 180, 186 (1963). Indeed, nondisclosure is usually essential to the success of a manipulative scheme. No doubt Congress meant to prohibit the full range of ingenious devices that might be used to manipulate securities prices. But we do not think it would have chosen this "term of art" if it had meant to bring within the scope of § 10(b) instances of corporate mismanagement such as this, in which the essence of the complaint is that shareholders were treated unfairly by a fiduciary.

IV

The language of the statute is, we think, "sufficiently clear in its context" to be dispositive here, *Ernst & Ernst*, 425 U.S., at 201; but even if it were not, there are additional considerations that weigh heavily against permitting a cause of action under Rule 10b-5 for the breach of corporate fiduciary duty alleged in this complaint. Congress did not expressly provide a private cause of action for violations of § 10(b). Although we have recognized an implied cause of action under that section in some circumstances, *Superintendent of Insurance* v. *Bankers Life & Cas. Co.*, supra, 404 U.S. at 13 n. 9, we have also recognized that a private cause of action under the anti-fraud provisions of the Securities Exchange Act should not be implied where it is "unnecessary to ensure the fulfillment of Congress' purposes" in adopting the *Act. Piper* v. *Chris-Craft Industries*, 430 U.S. at 41. As we noted earlier, the Court repeatedly has described the "fundamental purpose" of the Act as implementing a "philosophy of full disclosure"; once full and fair disclosure has occurred, the fairness of the terms of the transaction is at most a tangential concern of the statute. As in *Cort* v. *Ash*, 422 U.S. 66,

78, 80 (1975), we are reluctant to recognize a cause of action here to serve what is "at best a subsidiary purpose" of the federal legislation.

A second factor in determining whether Congress intended to create a federal cause of action in these circumstances is "whether 'the cause of action [is] one traditionally relegated to state law. * * *'" *Piper* v. *Chris-Craft Industries, Inc.*, 430 U.S., at 949. The Delaware Legislature has supplied minority shareholders with a cause of action in the Delaware Court of Chancery to recover the fair value of shares allegedly undervalued in a short-form merger. Of course, the existence of a particular state law remedy is not dispositive of the question whether Congress meant to provide a similar federal remedy, but as in *Piper* and *Cort*, we conclude that "it is entirely appropriate in this instance to relegate respondent and others in his situation to whatever remedy is created by state law." 430 U.S., at 962.

The reasoning behind a holding that the complaint in this case alleged fraud under Rule 10b-5 could not be easily contained. The result would be to bring within the Rule a wide variety of corporate conduct traditionally left to state regulation. In addition to posing a "danger of vexatious litigation which could result from a widely expanded class of plaintiffs under Rule 10b-5,"

Blue Chip Stamps v. *Manor Drug Stores*, 421 U.S. 723, 740 (1975), this extension of the federal securities laws would overlap and quite possibly interfere with state corporate law. Federal courts applying a "federal fiduciary principle" under Rule 10b-5 could be expected to depart from state fiduciary standards at least to the extent necessary to ensure uniformity within the federal system. Absent a clear indication of congressional intent, we are reluctant to federalize the substantial portion of the law of corporations that deals with transactions in securities, particularly where established state policies of corporate regulation would be overridden.

We thus adhere to the position that "Congress by §10(b) did not seek to regulate transactions which constitute no more than internal corporate mismanagement." *Superintendent of Insurance* v. *Bankers Life & Cas. Co.*, 404 U.S., at 12. There may well be a need for uniform federal fiduciary standards to govern mergers such as that challenged in this complaint. But those standards should not be supplied by judicial extension of §10(b) and Rule 10b-5 to "cover the corporate universe."

The judgment of the Court of Appeals is reversed, and the case is remanded for further proceedings consistent with this opinion.

That the *Green* case did not completely settle the issue soon became clear. In reprinting the opinion, for convenience and simplicity we omitted its many footnotes. But one footnote that has proved to be quite important is footnote 14, in which the Court stated that

> In addition to their principal argument that the complaint alleges a fraud under clauses (a) and (c) of Rule 10b-5, respondents also argue that the complaint alleges nondisclosure and misrepresentation in violation of clause (b) of the Rule. Their major contention in this respect is that the majority stockholder's failure to give the minority advance notice of the merger was a material nondisclosure, even though the Delaware short-form merger statute does not require such notice. Brief for Respondents 27. But respondents do not indicate how they might have acted differently had they had prior notice of the merger.

Indeed, they accept the conclusion of both courts below that under Delaware law they could not have enjoined the merger because an appraisal proceeding is their sole remedy in the Delaware courts for any alleged unfairness in the terms of the merger. Thus, the failure to give advance notice was not a material nondisclosure within the meaning of the statute or the Rule.

Subsequently the lower courts seized on this footnote to block at least partially the Supreme Court's apparent intent to relegate all claims of fiduciary breach to the state courts. The apparent thrust of *Green* is that breaches of fiduciary duty violate state laws and that claims arising out of such breaches should be brought in state court. But many lower federal courts have read footnote 14, which pointed out that even if the plaintiffs in *Green* had had legal notice before the merger, they had no state remedy they could have pursued, to imply that if such a state remedy does exist, a 10b-5 cause of action can arise. Arguably such cases eviscerate the holding of *Green*.

For example, like *Green*, *Goldberg* v. *Meridor* [14] involved a merger that minority shareholders claimed was unfair to them. Although their approval of the merger was not legally required, minority shareholders brought a 10b-5 action claiming that if the true purpose of the merger had been disclosed, they would have sued to enjoin it under state law. Focusing on footnote 14, the U.S. Court of Appeals for the Second Circuit held that a Rule 10b-5 claim was stated if the alleged deception prevented plaintiffs from pursuing their state court remedy. In essence, the court held that if a state court claim is *possible*, and some omission by defendants prevented plaintiffs from discovering they had a state court claim, a §10(b)/Rule 10b-5 claim arises.

In subsequent cases, other circuit courts agreed with *Meridor*, but required that a Rule 10b-5 plaintiff demonstrate that at least a *prima facie* case for relief existed regarding the state court claim, not just that a state court claim was possible. [15]

Materiality

Naturally, for a corporate misstatement or omission to constitute actionable fraud or deception, it must relate to a *material* fact. As we have seen in prior chapters, the test for materiality is whether there is a "substantial likelihood" that a misstated fact had or disclosure of an omitted fact would have "significantly altered the 'total mix' of information made available" in the eyes of a reasonable investor. [16]

Information regarding a giant mineral discovery, as in the *Texas Gulf Sulphur* case, is a classic example of information that is clearly material. Many cases have held false information about earnings, sales volumes, inventory value, and other financial

---

[14] 567 F.2d 209 (2d Cir. 1977).

[15] For example, *Alabama Farm Bureau Mutual Casualty Ins. Co., Inc.* v. *American Fidelity Life Ins. Co.*, 606 F.2d 602 (5th Cir. 1979), *cert. denied*, 446 U.S. 933 (1980). Plaintiffs may also have a good §10(b) claim if they are minority shareholders in a squeeze-out deprived of accurate information necessary to decide whether to accept the majority's offer or seek appraisal—*Lockspeiser* v. *Western Maryland Co.*, 768 F.2d 558 (4th Cir. 1985).

[16] *TSC Industries, Inc.* v. *Northway, Inc.*, 426 U.S. 438 (1976).

matters to be material. Even erroneous predictions have been held to be misleading "facts" leading to 10b-5 liability.[17]

One recent area of controversy involves disclosure of merger negotiations. In *Greenfield* v. *Heublein, Inc.*,[18] preliminary merger negotiations of a public corporation were held to be immaterial as a matter of law, because the need to protect shareholders from potentially misleading disclosure outweighed the right of the shareholders to have notice of the potentially important development. However, the SEC has not accepted this decision,[19] nor have certain other courts,[20] especially where the case involved a close corporation's merger talks.[21]

Many additional examples of materiality will be contained in the cases discussed in the remainder of this chapter.

Reliance

Traditional common law fraud theory requires plaintiff to prove reliance, that is, that he or she saw the misstatement and relied on its truthfulness in making an investment decision. Rule 10b-5 requires the same proof in a face-to-face transaction involving positive misstatements.

But is proof of reliance feasible in a case where the deceit arises not from a positive misstatement, but from an omission? The Supreme Court did not think so in *Affiliated Ute Citizens of Utah* v. *United States*.[22] In *Affiliated Ute*, assets of the Ute tribe had been placed in a corporation and the shares distributed to members of the tribe. Bank employees who were supposedly looking out for the best interests of the tribe purchased shares from the Indians and facilitated purchases by other whites, not disclosing that a much higher price for the shares existed in the non-Indian market. When tribal members discovered the true situation, they sued, claiming that the defendants should have told them of the active outside market.

Deeming it illogical that plaintiffs be forced to prove reliance on the very facts that were concealed from them, the Supreme Court held, "Under the circumstances of this case, involving primarily a failure to disclose, positive proof of reliance is not a prerequisite to recovery. All that is necessary is that the facts withheld be material."

The lower federal courts have concluded that materiality can also be a substitute for reliance even in certain cases of active misrepresentation. In developing a theory known as "fraud on the market," these courts have concluded that sometimes plaintiffs who did not directly see a false document should be able to sue because they relied on the integrity of the market that was undermined by the influence the false document had on other investors. A leading case follows.

---

[17] *Marx* v. *Computer Sciences Corp.*, 507 F.2d 485 (9th Cir. 1974).

[18] 742 F.2d 751 (3d Cir. 1984), *cert. denied*, 105 S. Ct. 1189 (1985).

[19] *In the Matter of Carnation Co.* [Current Binder], *Federal Securities Law Reports* (CCH), ¶83,801 (Securities and Exchange Commission, July 8, 1985).

[20] *Schlanger* v. *Four-Phase Systems, Inc.*, 582 F.Supp. 128 (S.D.N.Y. 1984).

[21] *Michaels* v. *Michaels*, 767 F.2d 1185 (7th Cir. 1985).

[22] 406 U.S. 128 (1972).

BLACKIE v. BARRACK

524 F.2d 891 (9th Cir. 1975),
cert. denied, 429 U.S. 816 (1976)

Ampex Corporation's May 1970 annual report described a $12 million annual profit. On August 3, 1972, Ampex reported a loss of $90 million for fiscal 1972, and the company's auditors withdrew their certification of Ampex's 1971 financial statements and refused to certify those of 1972 because they suspected the losses had been sustained earlier but concealed.

Several suits were filed by persons who purchased Ampex stock between May 1970 and August 1972. The §10(b) actions alleged that misrepresentations had been made in annual and interim reports, press releases, and SEC filings. The suits were consolidated and the plaintiffs moved for certification of a class action under the Federal Rules of Civil Procedure.

One requirement for a class action is that questions common to all plaintiffs must prevail over individual questions. Defendants claimed that class certification was inappropriate because, inter alia, each plaintiff would have to prove individually that he or she relied on the allegedly false statements and omissions. The trial judge certified a class anyway, and defendants appealed.

KOELSCH, CIRCUIT JUDGE:

· · ·

Defendants contend that any common questions which may exist do not predominate over individual questions of reliance and damages.

The amount of damages is invariably an individual question and does not defeat class action treatment.

· · ·

Individual questions of reliance are likewise not an impediment—subjective reliance is not a distinct element of proof of 10b-5 claims of the type involved in this case.

The class members' substantive claims either are, or can be, cast in omission or nondisclosure terms—the company's financial reporting failed to disclose the need for reserves, conditions reflecting on the value of the inventory, or other facts necessary to make the reported figures not misleading. The Court has recognized that under such circumstances

> involving primarily a failure to disclose, positive proof of reliance is not a prerequisite to recovery. All that is necessary is that the facts withheld be material in the sense that a reasonable investor might have considered them important in the making of this decision. This obligation to disclose and this withholding of a material fact establish the requisite element of causation in fact." (citations omitted) *Affiliated Ute Citizens of Utah* v. *United States*, 406 U.S. 128(1972).

· · ·

Moreover, proof of subjective reliance on particular misrepresentations is unnecessary to establish a 10b-5 claim for a deception inflating the price of stock traded in the open market. See *Chris-Craft Industries, Inc.* v. *Piper Aircraft Corp.*, 480 F.2d 341, 373–374 (2d Cir. 1973). . . . Proof of reliance is adduced to demonstrate the causal connection between the defendant's wrongdoing and the plaintiff's loss. We think causation is adequately established in the impersonal stock exchange context by proof of purchase and of the materiality of misrepresentations, without direct proof of reliance.

Materiality circumstantially establishes the reliance of some market traders and hence the inflation in the stock price—when the purchase is made the causational chain between defendant's conduct and plaintiff's loss is sufficiently established to make out a prima facie case.

Defendants argue that proof of causation solely by proof of materiality is inconsistent with the requirement of the traditional fraud action that a plaintiff prove directly both that the reasonable man would have acted on the misrepresentation (materiality), and that he himself acted on it, in order to establish the defendant's responsibility for his loss, which justifies the compensatory recovery.

We disagree. The 10b-5 action remains compensatory; it is not predicated solely on a showing of economic damage (loss causation). We merely recognize that individual "transactional causation" can in these circumstances be inferred from the materiality of the misrepresentation, and shift to defendant the burden of disproving a prima facie case of causation. Defendants may do so in at least two ways: (1) by disproving materiality or by proving that, despite materiality, an insufficient number of traders relied to inflate the price; and (2) by proving that an individual plaintiff purchased despite knowledge of the falsity of a representation, or that he would have, had he known of it.

That the prima facie case each class member must establish differs from the traditional fraud action, and may, unlike the fraud action, be established by common proof, is irrelevant; although derived from it, the 10b-5 action is not coterminous with a common law fraud action.

. . .

Here, we eliminate the requirement that plaintiffs prove reliance directly in this context because the requirement imposes an unreasonable and irrelevant evidentiary burden. A purchaser on the stock exchanges may be either unaware of a specific false representation, or may not directly rely on it; he may purchase because of a favorable price trend, price earnings ratio, or some other factor. Nevertheless, he relies generally on the supposition that the market price is validly set and that no unsuspected manipulation has artificially inflated the price, and thus indirectly on the truth of the representations underlying the stock price—whether he is aware of it or not, the price he pays reflects material misrepresentations. Requiring direct proof from each purchaser that he relied on a particular representation when purchasing would defeat recovery by those whose reliance was indirect, despite the fact that the causational chain is broken only if the purchaser would have purchased the stock even had he known of the misrepresentation. We decline to leave such open market purchasers unprotected. The statute and rule are designed to foster an expectation that securities markets are free from fraud—an expectation on which purchasers should be able to rely.

Thus, in this context we think proof of reliance means at most a requirement that plaintiff prove directly that he would have acted differently had he known the true facts. That is a requirement of proof of a speculative negative (I would not have bought had I known) precisely parallel to that held unnecessary in *Affiliated Ute* and *Mills* (I would not have sold had I known). We reject it here for the same reasons. Direct proof would inevitably be somewhat proforma, and impose a difficult evidentiary burden, because addressed to a speculative possibility in an area where motivations are complex and difficult to determine. That difficulty threatens to defeat valid claims—implicit in *Affiliated Ute* is a rejection of the burden because it leads to underinclusive recoveries and thereby threatens the enforcement of the securities laws. Here, the requirement is redundant—the same causal nexus can be adequately established indirectly, by proof of materiality coupled with the common sense that a stock purchaser does not ordinarily seek to purchase a loss in the form of artificially inflated stock. Under those circumstances we think it appropriate to eliminate the burden.

In a similar case, *Panzirer* v. *Wolf*,[23] plaintiff purchased stock of Allied Artists because of a favorable article about the company in a *Wall Street Journal* column. The authors of the column had interviewed stock analysts who had in turn based their opinion on Allied's annual report that allegedly contained misleading statements and omissions. Plaintiff was held to have met the reliance requirement, albeit indirectly, though she had never read or even seen the Allied annual report. That she had relied on the ''integrity of the market,'' which had been adulterated by Allied's false statements and omissions, was deemed sufficient.

Causation

As may be gathered from the discussions of materiality and reliance, the common law requirement of causation has been greatly watered down in the §10(b) fraud context. Because the very definition of materiality refers to facts that would influence the reasonable investor, the courts are frequently willing to assume that materiality plus reliance equals causation.

In *Affiliated Ute*, the Supreme Court stated that the ''obligation to disclose and this withholding of a material fact established the requisite element of causation in fact.'' However, in cases involving active misrepresentations in face-to-face transactions, the lower courts appear frequently to require proof of causation as well as reliance.

Actually, the law regarding causation is quite muddled. Courts frequently use the terms ''reliance'' and ''causation'' interchangeably. It appears courts will be more likely to require plaintiff to make a showing of each in an individual than in a class action, in an affirmative misrepresentation case than in an omissions case, and in a private transaction rather than a market transaction case.[24]

Scienter

Although many lower courts once held that negligence was a sufficient basis for a Rule 10b-5 claim, the Supreme Court disagreed and established scienter as the standard for liability.

---

[23] 663 F.2d 365 (2d Cir. 1981), *vacated Price Waterhouse* v. *Panzirer*, 103 S. Ct. 434 (1982).

[24] R. Jennings and H. Marsh, *Securities Regulation*, 5th ed. (Mineola, New York: The Foundation Press, Inc., 1982), p. 1047. What is clear is that courts will require more than ''but for'' causation—for example, but for defendant attorneys' assistance in raising funds, defendant corporate officers would not have have funds to steal—which they later did without the attorneys' knowledge or assistance—*Bloor* v. *Carro, Spanbock, Londin, Rodman & Fass*, 754 F.2d 57 (2nd Cir. 1985).

ERNST & ERNST v. HOCHFELDER

425 U.S. 185 (1976)

Ernst & Ernst was the accounting firm for First Securities Company of Chicago from 1946 through 1967. Nay, president of First Securities and owner of 92% of its stock, induced investors to put their funds in "escrow" accounts that he represented would yield a high rate of return. In fact, there were no such accounts, and Nay would convert the funds to his own use immediately upon receipt. The fraud was revealed in 1968 when Nay committed suicide, leaving a note describing the escrow accounts as "spurious."

Investors in these accounts sued Ernst & Ernst, claiming the accounting firm had aided and abetted Nay's violation of §10(b) and Rule 10b-5. Plaintiffs did not claim Ernst & Ernst knew of the scheme. Rather, they claimed that the accounting firm had been negligent *in failing to utilize appropriate auditing procedures. Specifically, plaintiffs pointed to the failure to discover Nay's "mail rule"—an internal practice that only Nay could open mail addressed to him or to First Securities for his attention, even if it arrived in his absence. Discovery of this rule, plaintiffs alleged, would have led to an investigation which would have exposed the fraud.*

The trial court held that no §10(b) or Rule 10b-5 liability could arise from mere negligence. The Seventh Circuit reversed. Ernst & Ernst appealed.

POWELL, JUSTICE:

. . .

Section 10(b) makes unlawful the use or employment of "any manipulative or deceptive device or contrivance" in contravention of Commission rules. The words "manipulative or deceptive" used in conjunction with "device or contrivance" strongly suggest that §10(b) was intended to proscribe knowing or intentional misconduct. See *SEC* v. *Texas Gulf Sulphur Co.*, 401 F.2d 833, 868 (CA2 1968) (Friendly, J., concurring), *cert. denied sub nom. Coates* v. *SEC*, 394 U.S. 976, 89 S.Ct. 1454, 22 L.Ed.2d 756 (1969).

In its *amicus curiae* brief, however, the Commission contends that nothing in the language "manipulative or deceptive device or contrivance" limits its operation to knowing or intentional practices. In support of its view, the Commission cites the overall congressional purpose in the 1933 and 1934 Acts to protect investors against false and deceptive practices that might injure them. . . . The Commission then reasons that since the "effect" upon investors of given conduct is the same regardless of whether the conduct is negligent or intentional, Congress must have intended to bar all such practices and not just those done knowingly or intentionally. The logic of this effect-oriented approach would impose liability for wholly faultless conduct where such conduct results in harm to investors, a result the Commission would be unlikely to support. But apart from where its logic might lead, the Commission would add a gloss to the operative language of the statute quite different from its commonly accepted meaning. The argument simply ignores the use of the words "manipulative," "device," and "contrivance"— terms that make unmistakable a congressional intent to proscribe a type of conduct quite different from negligence. Use of the word "manipulative" is especially significant. It is and was virtually a term of art when used in connection with securities markets. It connotes intentional or willful conduct designed to deceive or defraud investors by controlling or artificially affecting the price of securities.

In addition to relying upon the Commission's argument with respect to the operative language of the statute, respondents contend that since we are dealing with "remedial legislation," *Tcherepnin* v. *Knight*, 389 U.S. 332, 336 (1967), it must be construed " 'not technically and restrictively, but flexibly to effectuate its remedial purposes.' " See *Affiliated Ute Citizens* v. *United States*, 406 U.S., at 151. They argue that the "remedial purposes" of the acts demand a construction of §10(b) that embraces negligence as a standard of liability. But in seeking to accomplish its broad remedial goals, Congress did not adopt uniformly a negligence standard even as to express civil remedies. In some circumstances and with respect to certain classes of defendants, Congress did create express liability predicated upon a failure to exercise reasonable care. See, for example, 1933 Act §11(b)(3)(B) (liability of "experts," such as accountants for misleading statements in portions of registration statements for which they are responsible). But in other situations good faith is an absolute defense. See 1934 Act §18 (misleading statements in any document filed pursuant to the 1934 Act). And in still other circumstances Congress created express liability regardless of the defendant's fault, 1933 Act §11(a) (issuer liability for misleading statements in the registration statement).

It is thus evident that Congress fashioned standards of fault in the express civil remedies in the 1933 and 1934 Acts on a particularized basis. Ascertainment of congressional intent with respect to the standard of liability created by a particular section of the Acts must therefore rest primarily on the language of that section. Where, as here, we deal with a judicially implied liability, the statutory language certainly is no less important. In view of the language of §10(b), which so clearly connotes intentional misconduct, and mindful that the language of a statute controls when sufficiently clear in its context, further inquiry may be unnecessary. We turn now, nevertheless, to the legislative history of the 1934 Act to ascertain whether there is support for the meaning attributed to §10(b) by the Commission and respondents.

B

. . .

The extensive hearings that preceded passage of the 1934 Act touched only briefly on §10, and most of the discussion was devoted to the enumerated devices that the Commission is empowered to proscribe under §10(a). The most relevant exposition of the provision that was to become §10(b) was by Thomas G. Corcoran, a spokesman for the drafters. Corcoran indicated:

> Subsection (c) [§9(c) of H.R. 7852—later §10(b)] says, "Thou shalt not devise any other cunning devices."
> Of course subsection (c) is a catch-all clause to prevent manipulative devices. I do not think there is any objection to that kind of clause. The Commission should have the authority to deal with new manipulative devices.

This brief explanation of §10(b) by a spokesman for its drafters is significant. The section was described rightly as a "catchall" clause to enable the Commission "to deal with new manipulative [or cunning] devices." It is difficult to believe that any lawyer, legislative draftsman, or legislator would use these words if the intent was to create liability for merely negligent acts or omissions. Neither the legislative history nor the briefs supporting respondents identify any usage or authority for construing "manipulative [or cunning] devices" to include negligence.

. . .

The Commission argues that Congress has been explicit in requiring willful conduct when that was the standard of fault intended, citing §9 of the 1934 Act, which generally proscribes manipulation of securities prices. From this the Commission concludes that since §10(b) is not by its terms explicitly restricted to willful, knowing, or purposeful conduct, it should not be construed in all cases to require more than negligent action or inaction as a precondition for civil liability.

The structure of the Acts does not support the Commission's argument. In each instance that Congress created express civil liability in favor of purchasers or sellers of securities it clearly specified whether recovery was to be premised on knowing or intentional conduct, negligence, or entirely innocent mistake. See 1933 Act §§11, 12; 1934 Act §§9, 18, 20. For example, §11 of the 1933 Act unambiguously creates a private action for damages when a registration statement includes untrue statements of material facts or fails to state material facts necessary to make the statements therein not misleading. Within the limits specified by §11(e), the issuer of the securities is held absolutely liable for any damages resulting from such misstatement or omission. But experts such as accountants who have prepared portions of the registration statement are accorded a "due diligence" defense. In effect, this is a negligence standard. The express recognition of a cause of action premised on negligent behavior in §11 stands in sharp contrast to the language of §10(b), and significantly undercuts the Commission's argument.

We also consider it significant that each of the express civil remedies in the 1933 Act allowing recovery for negligent conduct, see §§11, 12(2), 15, is subject to significant procedural restrictions not applicable under §10(b).

. . .

The judgment of the Court of Appeals is reversed.

Following *Hochfelder*, which involved a private cause of action for damages, the Supreme Court decided that even the SEC would have to demonstrate that a defendant acted with "scienter" to obtain a court injunction. Although the case, *Aaron* v. *SEC*,[25] dealt with §17(a) of the 1934 Act, the Supreme Court stated that the language of §10(b) "strongly suggest[ed] that §10(b) was intended to proscribe knowing or intentional conduct."

Most lower courts addressing the issue have held that "recklessness"—usually defined as conduct so careless as to evince a total disregard for the welfare of others—will satisfy the scienter requirement. In *Rolf* v. *Blyth, Eastman Dillon & Co., Inc.*,[26] for example, a broker was held to have aided and abetted a §10(b) violation by an investment adviser to whose care he had entrusted plaintiff's account. Through a disastrous series of transactions motivated by self-dealing, the investment adviser had quickly reduced the value of plaintiff-investor's holdings by one-half. The finding that the broker-supervisor was guilty of recklessness was based on his knowledge of the low quality

---

[25] 446 U.S. 680 (1980).

[26] 570 F.2d 38 (2d Cir.), *cert. denied*, 439 U.S. 1039 (1978).

of securities selected by the investment adviser, his daily contact with the adviser that afforded him an opportunity to supervise, and the repeated, baseless reassurances he gave plaintiff whenever plaintiff expressed concern about what was happening to his investment.

Purchase or Sale

Because §10(b) outlaws fraud "in connection with a purchase or sale" of securities, a plaintiff must demonstrate that a purchase or sale occurred, that the alleged fraud occurred in connection with that purchase or sale, and that the plaintiff was a purchaser or a seller.

Purchase or Sale

The terms "purchase" and "sale" have been broadly interpreted in this context. Indeed, purchases and sales have been found where corporations issued their own securities, repurchased their own securities, entered into mergers, and engaged in many other types of transactions. Even the pledge of stock as collateral for a loan has been deemed a "sale" for §10(b) purposes. In *Rubin* v. *United States*,[27] the Supreme Court stated that "[o]btaining a loan secured by a pledge of shares of stock unmistakably involves a 'disposition of [an] interest in a security for value.' Although pledges transfer less than absolute title, the interest thus transferred nonetheless is an 'interest in a security.' "

In Connection with

The "in connection with" requirement has also been liberally construed . . . so liberally, in fact, that little attention has been paid to it.

The leading case is *Superintendent of Insurance of the State of New York* v. *Bankers Life and Casualty Co.*,[28] where a small group, through a series of fraudulent transactions, purchased a company with proceeds from the sale of the company's own portfolio of bonds. While the Supreme Court held that §10(b) did not provide a remedy for mere internal corporate mismanagement, foreshadowing its later decision in *Santa Fe Industries, Inc.* v. *Green*, it read §10(b) to protect creditors of the defrauded corporate buyer or seller. Because the defendants sold the corporation's securities without the corporation receiving any of their value, the Court said its injury resulted from "deceptive practices *touching* its sale of securities as an investor." A "touching" interpretation of the "in connection with" requirement is generous indeed.

A more recent application of this ruling appears in the following case.

---

[27] 449 U.S. 424 (1981).
[28] 404 U.S. 6 (1971).

BROWN v. IVIE

661 F.2d 62 (5th Cir. 1981), *cert. denied*, 455 U.S. 990

Plaintiff Brown and defendants Ivie and Lightsey were each an officer, director, and one-third shareholder in a closely held corporation. In 1976 they all entered into a "buy-sell agreement" that required shareholders no longer employed by the corporation to sell their stock back to the corporation at book value (which would almost certainly be less than fair market value.) Because the stock certificates were never endorsed with the restrictions as the agreement required, Brown claims the agreement was unenforceable.

In 1979, defendants decided to oust Brown and force him to sell his shares back to the corporation. Recognizing that the 1976 agreement was unenforceable, defendants drafted a similar agreement and presented it to Brown, telling him that it was necessary to effectuate a change in insurance companies and to increase the amount of insurance held by the corporation on each shareholder. Defendants did not tell Brown of their intent to oust him. Brown signed the agreement and was fired from his position as salesman by defendants seven days later. He was also removed as an officer and director. Defendants insisted that Brown sell his stock back to the corporation pursuant to the new 1979 agreement. Brown refused, and brought a §10(b) action.

The trial court dismissed the suit for failure to state a claim because Brown did not meet the "in connection with" requirement. Brown appealed.

JOHNSON, CIRCUIT JUDGE:

A necessary element of a Rule 10b-5 offense is that the fraud or deceit be "in connection with" the sale of a security—*Superintendent of Insurance* v. *Banker's Life & Cas. Co.*, 404 U.S. 6 (1971). In *Alley* v. *Miramon*, 614 F.2d 1372 (5th Cir. 1980), the Court determined that "in connection with" is to be flexibly applied but requires that there be a nexus between the defendant's fraud and the securities "sale." However, the "plaintiff in a Rule 10b-5 case need not establish a direct or close relationship between the fraudulent transaction and the purchase or sale, but only that the transaction [involving the sale] 'touch' the transaction involving the defendant's fraud." Whether fraudulent omissions or misrepresentations are too remote to be "in connection with" the sale of a security depends upon the individual facts of each case. Applying the "touch" test enunciated in *Alley*, we conclude that the alleged fraud by the defendants was made "in connection with" the sale of a security.

The district court determined that "[a]ny alleged misrepresentation by the [defendants] as to why they wanted [Brown] to sign the [1979] agreement, is too remote to be 'in connection with' a securities transaction," 490 F.Supp. at 411, and relied primarily upon *Ketchum* v. *Green*, 557 F.2d 1022 (3d Cir. 1977), *cert. denied*, 434 U.S. 940 (1978) to support the conclusion. *Ketchum* is, however, readily distinguishable from the present case. In *Ketchum* the plaintiffs alleged that they were ousted from the corporation as a result of defendants' misrepresentations and required by the terms of a "stock retirement agreement" to sell their stock back to the corporation at less than fair value. The *Ketchum* court concluded that the fraud was too remote to be "in connection with" the sale of a security.

The court stressed that the objective of defendants' alleged fraud was to expel plaintiffs from the corporation in order to gain control and that the resulting sale of securities was simply an "indirect" consequence of plaintiffs' expulsion. Significantly, the defendants in *Ketchum* did not as an integral part of their scheme induce the plaintiffs to enter into the stock-retirement agreement; the agreement had been executed over seven years prior to the alleged fraud. Thus, a nexus between the fraud and the securities transaction was clearly absent.

The facts, as alleged, in the instant case demonstrate a more direct causal connection between the fraud and the sale of securities than was present in *Ketchum*. Unlike the situation in *Ketchum*, Ivie and Lightsey collectively controlled two-thirds of the corporate stock and had the power to terminate Brown's employment at any time. It is alleged, however, that Ivie and Lightsey did not have an enforceable agreement that required Brown to sell his stock back to the corporation upon termination of employment. As a result, the plaintiff contends that the defendants fraudulently induced him to sign the 1979 agreement, thereby guaranteeing that they would obtain his stock at book value. Thus, accepting the fraud as alleged, there is a direct connection between it and the execution of the 1979 agreement obligating Brown to sell his stock for less than fair value. Since a contract for the sale or disposition of stock constitutes a sale of a security for purposes of the federal securities laws, the defendants' fraud, as alleged, is "in connection with" the sale of a security.

Reversed.

Purchaser or Seller

The "purchaser or seller" requirement has evolved into a doctrine of standing that the courts have used to limit the scope of §10(b)'s coverage. The first important case in the area was *Birnbaum* v. *Newport Steel Corporation*,[29] which involved the controlling shareholder of a corporation who sabotaged an opportunity to sell all the corporation's shares at a nice profit to one buyer so that he could sell just his own shares to another buyer at a greater profit. When the other shareholders discovered that their opportunity to sell had been blocked by the controlling shareholder's fraud, they sued under §10(b). The suit was dismissed because plaintiffs had neither purchased nor sold their shares in connection with the fraud. That plaintiffs had been deprived of an opportunity to sell their shares by the wrongdoing made no difference. Because they were not purchasers or sellers, they had no standing to sue.

The Supreme Court adopted the *Birnbaum* rationale in the following case. Justice Rehnquist's majority opinion should be scrutinized carefully, because it demonstrates a suspicious view of securities actions that has been prevalent in the Supreme Court's conservative approach to §10(b) since about 1975. A portion of a dissenting opinion is also reprinted to counterpoint the predominating conservative view.

---

[29] 193 F.2d 461 (2d Cir.), *cert. denied*, 343 U.S. 956 (1952).

BLUE CHIP STAMPS v. MANOR DRUG STORES

421 U.S. 723 (1975)

Blue Chip Stamp Co. entered into a consent decree with the United States to settle a civil antitrust action. The consent decree provided that "Old Blue Chip Stamp Co." would be merged into a newly formed corporation (New Blue Chip), the defendant in this action. The decree mandated that the holdings of the majority owners of the original corporation should be reduced. New Blue Chip was required to offer a substantial number of its shares at a bargain price to retailers who had used its services in the past and were injured by its antitrust violation. Approximately 50% of the offered securities were purchased.

Two years after the offering, a number of the retailers who had not purchased New Blue Chip securities sued claiming a violation of §10(b). Plaintiffs claimed they failed to purchase the securities because New Blue Chip's prospectus was overly pessimistic. Plaintiffs alleged that New Blue Chip intended to discourage sales to plaintiffs at the mandated bargain price so that it could later sell the securities to the public at a higher price.

The trial court dismissed the action for failure to state a claim. The Ninth Circuit reversed as to the Rule 10b-5 claim. New Blue Chip appealed.

REHNQUIST, JUSTICE:

. . .

Just as this Court had no occasion to consider the validity of the *Kardon* holding that there was a private cause of action under Rule 10b-5 until 20-odd years later, nearly the same period

of time has gone by between the *Birnbaum* decision and our consideration of the case now before us. As with *Kardon*, virtually all lower federal courts facing the issue in the hundreds of reported cases presenting this question over the past quarter century have reaffirmed *Birnbaum*'s conclusion that the plaintiff class for purposes of §10(b) and Rule 10b-5 private damage actions is limited to purchasers and sellers of securities.

In 1957 and again in 1959, the Securities and Exchange Commission sought from Congress amendment of §10(b) to change its wording from "in connection with the purchase or sale of any security" to "in connection with the purchase or sale of, *or any attempt to purchase or sell*, any security." In the words of a memorandum submitted by the Commission to a congressional committee, the purpose of the proposed change was "to make §10(b) also applicable to manipulative activities in connection with any attempt to purchase or sell any security." Opposition to the amendment was based on fears of the extension of civil liability under §10(b) that it would cause. Neither change was adopted by Congress.

The longstanding acceptance by the courts, coupled with Congress' failure to reject *Birnbaum*'s reasonable interpretation of the wording of §10(b), wording which is directed toward injury suffered "in connection with the purchase or sale" of securities, argues significantly in favor of acceptance of the *Birnbaum* rule by this Court.

Available evidence from the texts of the 1933 and 1934 acts as to the congressional scheme in this regard, though not conclusive, supports the result reached by the *Birnbaum* court. The wording of §10(b) directed at fraud "in connection with the purchase or sale" of securities stands in contrast with the parallel antifraud provision of the 1933 Act, §17(a), reaching fraud "in the offer or sale" of securities. Compare §5 of the 1933 Act. When Congress wished to provide a remedy to those who neither purchase nor sell securities, it had little trouble in doing so expressly. Compare §16(b) of the 1934 Act.

· · ·

Having said all this, we would by no means be understood as suggesting that we are able to divine from the language of §10(b) the express "intent of Congress" as to the contours of a private cause of action under Rule 10b-5. When we deal with private actions under Rule 10b-5, we deal with a judicial oak which has grown from little more than a legislative acorn. Such growth may be quite consistent with the congressional enactment and with the role of the federal judiciary in interpreting it, but it would be disingenuous to suggest that either Congress in 1934 or the Securities and Exchange Commission in 1942 foreordained the present state of the law with respect to Rule 10b-5. It is therefore proper that we consider, in addition to the factors already discussed, what may be described as policy considerations when we come to flesh out the portions of the law with respect to which neither the congressional enactment nor the administrative regulations offer conclusive guidance.

Three principal classes of potential plaintiffs are presently barred by the *Birnbaum* rule. First are potential purchasers of shares, either in a new offering or on the Nation's post-distribution trading markets, who allege that they decided not to purchase because of an unduly gloomy representation or the omission of favorable material which made the issuer appear to be a less favorable investment vehicle than it actually was. Second are actual shareholders in the issuer who allege that they decided not to sell their shares because of an unduly rosy representation or a failure to disclose unfavorable material. Third are shareholders, creditors, and perhaps others related to an issuer who suffered loss in the value of their investment due to corporate or insider activities in connection with the purchase or sale of securities which violate Rule 10b-5. It has been held that shareholder members of the second and third of these classes may frequently be able to circumvent the *Birnbaum* limitation through bringing a derivative action on behalf of the corporate issuer if the latter is itself a purchaser or seller of securities. See, for example, *Schoenbaum* v. *Firstbrook*, 405 F.2d 215, 219 (CA2 1968), *cert. denied sub nom. Manley* v. *Schoenbaum*, 395 U.S. 906 (1969). But the first of these classes, of which respondent is a member, cannot claim the benefit of such a rule.

A great majority of the many commentators on the issue before us have taken the view that the *Birnbaum* limitation on the plaintiff class in a Rule 10b-5 action for damages is an arbitrary restriction which unreasonably prevents some deserving plaintiffs from recovering damages which have in fact been caused by violations of Rule 10b-5.

· · ·

But we are of the opinion that there are countervailing advantages to the *Birnbaum* rule, purely as a matter of policy, although those advantages are more difficult to articulate than is the disadvantage.

There has been widespread recognition that litigation under Rule 10b-5 presents a danger of vexatiousness different in degree and in kind from that which accompanies litigation in general. . . .

We believe that the concern expressed for the danger of vexatious litigation which could result from a widely expanded class of plaintiffs under Rule 10b-5 is founded in something more substantial than the common complaint of the many defendants who would prefer avoiding lawsuits entirely to either settling them or trying them. These concerns have two largely separate grounds.

The first of these concerns is that in the field of federal securities laws governing disclosure of information even a complaint which by objective standards may have very little chance of success at trial has a settlement value to the plaintiff out of any proportion to its prospect of success at trial so long as he may prevent the suit from being resolved against him by dismissal or summary judgment. The very pendency of the lawsuit may frustrate or delay normal business activity of the defendant which is totally unrelated to the lawsuit.

. . .

The potential for possible abuse of the liberal discovery provisions of the Federal Rules of Civil Procedure may likewise exist in this type of case to a greater extent than they do in other litigation. The prospect of extensive deposition of the defendant's officers and associates and the concomitant opportunity for extensive discovery of business documents, is a common occurrence in this and similar types of litigation. To the extent that this process eventually produces relevant evidence which is useful in determining the merits of the claims asserted by the parties, it bears the imprimatur of those Rules and of the many cases liberally interpreting them. But to the extent that it permits a plaintiff with a largely groundless claim to simply take up the time of a number of other people, with the right to do so representing an *in terrorem* increment of the settlement value, rather than a reasonably founded hope that the process will reveal relevant evidence, it is a social cost rather than a benefit. Yet to broadly expand the class of plaintiffs who may sue under Rule 10b-5 would appear to encourage the least appealing aspect of the use of the discovery rules.

Without the *Birnbaum* rule, an action under Rule 10b-5 will turn largely on which oral version of a series of occurrences the jury may decide to credit, and therefore no matter how improbable the allegations of the plaintiff, the case will be virtually impossible to dispose of prior to trial other than by settlement. In the words of Judge Hufstedler's dissenting opinion in the Court of Appeals:

> The great ease with which plaintiffs can allege the requirements for the majority's standing rule and the greater difficulty that plaintiffs are going to have proving the allegations suggests that the majority's rule will allow a relatively high proportion of 'bad' cases into court. The risk of strike suits is particularly high in such cases; although they are difficult to prove at trial, they are even more difficult to dispose of before trial. 492 F.2d, at 147 n. 9.

The *Birnbaum* rule, on the other hand, permits exclusion prior to trial of those plaintiffs who were not themselves purchasers or sellers of the stock in question. The fact of purchase of stock and the fact of sale of stock are generally matters which are verifiable by documentation, and do not depend upon oral recollection, so that failure to qualify under the *Birnbaum* rule is a matter that can normally be established by the defendant either on a motion to dismiss or on a motion for summary judgment.

. . .

The second ground for fear of vexatious litigation is based on the concern that, given the generalized contours of liability, the abolition of the *Birnbaum* rule would throw open to the trier of fact many rather hazy issues of historical fact the proof of which depended almost entirely on oral testimony. We in no way disparage the worth and frequent high value of oral testimony when we say that dangers of its abuse appear to exist in this type of action to a peculiarly high degree. The Securities and Exchange Commission, while opposing the adoption of the *Birnbaum* rule by this Court, states that it agrees with petitioners "that the effect, if any, of a deceptive practice on someone who has neither purchased nor sold securities may be more difficult to demonstrate than is the effect on a purchaser or seller"—Brief for the Securities and Exchange Commission as *Amicus Curiae* 24–25. The brief also points out that frivolous suits can be brought whatever the rules of standing, and reminds us of this Court's recognition "in a different context" that "the expense and annoyance of litigation is 'part of the social burden of living under government.' " The Commission suggests that in particular cases additional requirements of corroboration of testimony and more limited measure of damages would correct the dangers of an expanded class of plaintiffs.

But the very necessity, or at least the desirability, of fashioning unique rules of corroboration and damages as a correlative to the abolition of the *Birnbaum* rule suggests that the rule itself may have something to be said for it.

. . .

In today's universe of transactions governed by the 1934 Act, privity of dealing or even personal contact between potential defendant and potential plaintiff is the exception and not the rule. The stock of issuers is listed on financial exchanges utilized by tens of millions of investors, and corporate representations reach a potential audience, encompassing not only the diligent few who peruse filed corporate reports or the sizable number of subscribers to financial journals, but the readership of the Nation's daily newspapers. Obviously neither the fact that issuers or other potential defendants under Rule 10b-5 reach a large number of potential investors, or the fact that they are required by law to make their disclosures conform to certain standards, should in any way absolve them from liability for misconduct which is proscribed by Rule 10b-5.

But in the absence of the *Birnbaum* rule, it would be sufficient for a plaintiff to prove that he had failed to purchase or sell stock by reason of a defendant's violation of Rule 10b-5. The manner in which the defendant's violation caused the plaintiff to fail to act could be as a result of the reading of a prospectus, as respondent claims here, but it could just as easily come as a result of a claimed reading of information contained in the financial pages of a local newspaper. Plaintiff's proof would not be that he purchased or sold stock, a fact which would be capable of documentary verification in most situations, but instead that he decided *not* to purchase or sell stock. Plaintiff's entire testimony could be dependent upon uncorroborated oral evidence of many of the crucial elements of his claim, and still be sufficient to go to the jury. The jury would not even have the benefit of weighing the plaintiff's version against the defendant's version, since the elements to which the plaintiff would testify would be in many cases totally unknown and unknowable to the defendant. The very real risk in permitting those in respondent's position to sue under Rule 10b-5 is that the door will be open to recovery of substantial damages on the part of one who offers only his own testimony to prove that he ever consulted a prospectus of the issuer, that he paid any attention to it, or that the representations contained in it damaged him.

. . .

The virtue of the *Birnbaum* rule, simply stated, in this situation, is that it limits the class of plaintiffs to those who have at least dealt in the security to which the prospectus, representation, or omission relates. And their dealing in the security, whether by way of purchase or sale, will generally be an objectively demonstrable fact in an area of the law otherwise very much dependent upon oral testimony. In the absence of the *Birnbaum* doctrine, bystanders to the securities marketing process could await developments on the sidelines without risk, claiming that inaccuracies in disclosure caused nonselling in a falling market and that unduly pessimistic predictions by the issuer followed by a rising market caused them to allow retrospectively golden opportunities to pass.

While much of the development of the law of deceit has been the elimination of artificial barriers to recovery on just claims, we are not the first court to express concern that the inexorable broadening of the class of plaintiff who may sue in this area of the law will ultimately result in more harm than good.

. . .

Thus we conclude that what may be called considerations of policy, which we are free to weigh in deciding this case, are by no means entirely on one side of the scale. Taken together with the precedential support for the *Birnbaum* rule over a period of more than 20 years, and the consistency of that rule with what we can glean from the intent of Congress, they lead us to conclude that it is a sound rule and should be followed.

IV

. . .

Even if we were to accept the notion that the *Birnbaum* rule could be circumvented on a case-by-case basis through particularized judicial inquiry into the facts surrounding a complaint, this respondent and the members of its alleged class would be unlikely candidates for such a judicially created exception. While the *Birnbaum* rule has been flexibly interpreted by lower federal courts, we have been unable to locate a single decided case from any court in the 20-odd years of litigation since the *Birnbaum* decision which would support the right of persons who were in the position of respondent here to bring a private suit under Rule 10b-5.

Respondent was not only not a buyer or seller of any security but it was not even a shareholder of the corporate petitioners.

. . .

Reversed.

MR. JUSTICE BLACKMUN, WITH WHOM MR. JUSTICE DOUGLAS AND MR. JUSTICE BRENNAN JOIN, DISSENTING:

Today the Court graves into stone *Birnbaum*'s arbitrary principle of standing. . . . In so doing, the Court exhibits a preternatural solicitousness for corporate well-being and a seeming callousness toward the investing public quite out of keeping, it seems to me, with our own traditions and the intent of the securities laws.

. . .

To support its decision to adopt the *Birnbaum* doctrine, the Court points to the "longstanding acceptance by the courts" and to "Congress' failure to reject *Birnbaum*'s reasonable interpretation of the wording of §10(b)." In addition, the Court purports to find support in "evidence from the texts of the 1933 and 1934 Acts," although it concedes this to be "not conclusive." But the greater portion of the Court's opinion is devoted to its discussion of the "danger of vexatiousness" that accompanies litigation under Rule 10b-5 and that is said to be "different in degree and in kind from that which accompanies litigation in general." It speaks of harm from the "very pendency of the lawsuit," something like the recognized dilemma of the physician sued for malpractice; of the "disruption of normal business activities which may accompany a lawsuit"; and of "proof . . . which depend[s] almost entirely on oral testimony," as if all these were unknown to lawsuits taking place in America's courthouses every day. In turning to, and being influenced by, these "policy considerations," or these "considerations of policy," the Court, in my view, unfortunately mires itself in speculation and conjecture not usually seen in its opinions. In order to support an interpretation that obviously narrows a provision of the securities laws designed to be a "catch-all," the Court takes alarm at the "practical difficulties" that would follow the removal of *Birnbaum*'s barrier.

Certainly, this Court must be aware of the realities of life, but it is unwarranted for the Court to take a form of attenuated judicial notice of the motivations that defense counsel may have in settling a case, or of the difficulties that a plaintiff may have in proving his claim.

Perhaps it is true that more cases that come within the *Birnbaum* doctrine can be properly proved than those that fall outside it. But this is no reason for denying standing to sue to plaintiffs, such as the one in this case, who allegedly are injured by novel forms of manipulation. We should be wary about heeding the seductive call of expediency and about substituting convenience and ease of processing for the more difficult task of separating the genuine claim from the unfounded one.

Instead of the artificiality of *Birnbaum*, the essential test of a valid Rule 10b-5 claim, it seems to me, must be the showing of a logical nexus between the alleged fraud and the sale or purchase of a security. It is inconceivable that Congress could have intended a broadranging antifraud provision, such as §10(b), and, at the same time, have intended to impose, or be deemed to welcome, a mechanical overtone and requirement such as the *Birnbaum* doctrine.

As with the plaintiffs who were allegedly defrauded into not buying in *Blue Chip Stamp*, so would an investor misled into not selling lack standing under §10(b).[30] On the other hand, a minority shareholder who is "cashed out" in a merger is deemed a "forced seller" who does have standing to bring a §10(b) claim.[31] Also, a person with an option to redeem shares is granted standing based on the contractual rights arising out of the option.[32]

The SEC benefits from an exception to the purchaser-seller requirement. It can institute administrative proceedings and seek injunctions without having purchased or sold securities. Similarly, some courts have held that a private plaintiff, who seeks only injunctive relief and not damages, need not be a purchaser or seller.[33] However, other courts do not recognize this exception for private plaintiffs.[34]

LIABILITY OF COLLATERAL PARTICIPANTS

Several avenues exist pursuant to §10(b) and Rule 10b-5 for imposing liability not just on those who directly committed the acts constituting a fraud, but upon collateral participants as well.

---

[30] *Gurley* v. *Documentation, Inc.*, 674 F.2d 253 (4th Cir. 1982).

[31] *Vine* v. *Beneficial Finance Co., Inc.*, 374 F.2d 627 (2d Cir.), *cert. denied*, 389 U.S. 970 (1967).

[32] *Aldrich* v. *McCulloch Properties, Inc.*, 627 F.2d 1036 (10th Cir. 1980).

[33] For example, *Mutual Shares Corp.* v. *Genesco, Inc.*, 384 F.2d 540 (2d Cir. 1967).

[34] For example, *Wright* v. *The Heizer Corp.*, 411 F.Supp. 23 (N.D.Ill. 1975), *modified* 560 F.2d 236 (7th Cir. 1977), *cert. denied* 434 U.S. 1066 (1978).

Controlling Persons

Section 20(a) of the 1934 Act provides that anyone "who, directly or indirectly, controls any person" who violates a 1934 Act provision shall be jointly and severally liable for the violation. Section 15 of the 1933 Act imposes similar liability for 1933 Act violations. The purpose of these provisions is to ensure that no one does indirectly that which the law prohibits from being done directly. Only a defendant who exercises control will be liable under §20(a). The "control relationship" usually arises out of an employer-employee or some other principal-agent arrangement. It can also arise out of stock ownership, interlocking directorates, and family ties.

Section 20(a) is frequently used to hold broker-dealer firms liable for 1934 Act violations of their employees. The firms are not automatically liable for employee violations, because §20(a) expressly provides a defense for the control person who "acted in good faith and did not directly or indirectly induce the act or acts constituting the violation." Most courts hold that an employer's failure to take measures to prevent injury from an employee's actions vitiates the good faith defense, although others find §20(a) liability only if the employer is actually culpable.[35]

Respondeat Superior

The common law doctrine of *respondeat superior*, which makes a principal liable for the wrongs of its agents acting within the scope of their authority, has been used by several courts to impose liability under §10(b). If available, the doctrine of *respondeat superior* is narrower than the "controlling person" provision in that liability arises only from an employer-employee or some other agency relationship. On the other hand, *respondeat superior* liability is broader than is controlling person liability in that the principal is automatically liable for wrongs of agents committed within the scope of their authority. Good faith and careful supervision are no defense for the principal.

A lively question has been whether common law *respondeat superior* liability is available under the 1934 Act, or whether §20(a) controlling person provisions are the sole means of imposing such secondary liability. Most courts hold that *respondeat superior* liability does exist under the 1934 Act.[36] But a few hold that *respondeat superior* is not available,[37] and others hold it is available only in certain circumstances.[38]

Aiding and Abetting

Yet another method of imposing secondary liability under the 1934 Act is the "aiding and abetting" theory that has been repeatedly used to ensnare accountants and attorneys in §10(b) litigation. Although the Supreme Court has not spoken, the lower courts are

---

[35] See R. Ferrara and D. Sanger, "Derivative Liability in Securities Law: Controlling Person Liability, Respondeat Superior and Aiding and Abetting," *Washington and Lee Law Review*, Vol. 40 (1983), p. 1007.

[36] For example, *SEC* v. *Geon Industries, Inc.*, 531 F.2d 39 (2d Cir. 1976).

[37] For example, *Zweig* v. *Hearst Corp.*, 521 F.2d 1129 (9th Cir.), *cert. denied*, 423 U.S. 1025 (1975).

[38] For example, *Sharp* v. *Coopers & Lybrand*, 649 F.2d 175 (3d Cir. 1981), *cert. denied*, 102 S. Ct. 1427 (1982).

virtually unanimous in holding that any person who aids and abets a §10(b) violation is jointly and severally liable with the primary violators.

The elements of aiding and abetting are (1) the existence of a securities law violation by the primary party, (2) knowledge of this violation by the aider and abettor, and (3) "substantial assistance" by the aider and abettor in the achievement of the primary violation.[39] The knowledge element is particularly important because of the *Hochfelder* scienter requirement, and because liability should not attach to parties such as bankers, brokers, stock transfer agents, or clearing agents who facilitate a fraudulent transaction but know nothing of the fraud.

Attorneys who draft misleading documents and accountants who prepare erroneous financial statements risk aiding and abetting liability if those false documents are used by the corporation to commit a fraud. Although aiding and abetting liability normally arises from some knowing act, one corporation was held to have aided and abetted by its mere silence when its officers knew of another's primary securities law violation but kept silent because that violation increased the value of the aider and abettor's stock, thereby benefiting it in a merger transaction.[40]

DEFENSES

Statute of Limitations

The primary affirmative defense in a §10(b)/Rule 10b-5 suit is the statute of limitations. Curiously, Congress has provided no such limitation period for §10(b) actions. Therefore, the federal courts, which have exclusive jurisdiction over §10(b) actions, have concluded that they should use the appropriate *state* statute of limitations. Unfortunately, the courts have not agreed on which state statute is appropriate.

Several courts have concluded that a federal securities action is most similar to a state blue-sky action; therefore, they borrow their state's blue-sky statute of limitations which is typically rather short.[41] Other courts apply the typically more liberal state statute of limitations for fraud actions, reasoning that the longer period is more consistent with the remedial purposes of the 1934 Act.[42] In applying a state's limitation period, courts will also use a "borrowing" statute if one exists. A borrowing statute provides that if a citizen from a state other than the forum state files suit in the forum, the court is to apply whichever statute of limitations is shorter—that of the forum state or that of plaintiff's home state.[43] The purpose of such a provision is to prevent plaintiffs

---

[39] *International Investment Trust* v. *Cornfeld*, 619 F.2d 909 (2d Cir. 1980).

[40] *Brennan* v. *Midwestern Life Ins. Co.*, 417 F.2d 147 (7th Cir. 1969), *cert. denied*, 397 U.S. 989 (1970).

[41] This approach has been adopted by the U.S. Courts of Appeal for the Fourth, Sixth, Seventh, Eighth, and District of Columbia Circuits.

[42] This approach has been adopted by the U.S. Courts of Appeal for the Second, Ninth, and Tenth Circuits. The Fifth Circuit acts on a state-by-state basis and has applied both.

[43] *Arneil* v. *Ramsey*, 550 F.2d 774 (2d Cir. 1977).

from across the country from delaying until their own statute of limitations has expired and then bringing suit in whichever state has the longest limitations period.

The lack of uniformity can become frighteningly complicated in a class action lawsuit where perhaps thousands of plaintiffs from all 50 states are governed by many differing statutes of limitation (if they file in a state with a borrowing statute). The obvious solution is for Congress to adopt one uniform federal statute of limitations for §10(b) actions, but Congress has shown no inclination to do so.

Due Diligence

Some courts hold that plaintiffs who do not look out for themselves—who do not exercise due diligence—should not be entitled to the protection of §10(b). For example, in *DuPuy* v. *DuPuy*,[44] plaintiff Milton DuPuy claimed that his brother Clarence defrauded him into selling to Clarence his 47% interest in a family corporation for an inadequate sum. Milton had taken an active role in the business and arguably should have known what a fair price was. The court held that Milton could recover only if he had not been reckless in entering into the transaction. A later case held that *justifiable* reliance by plaintiff "is a precondition to recovery and is frequently characterized as a requirement that the plaintiff show he acted with due diligence."[45]

Business Judgment Rule

The business judgment rule, which is discussed in detail in Chapter 11, has been used both as a shield to provide a defense and as a sword to terminate shareholder derivative litigation, even where the shareholder's claim was predicated on a §10(b) or some other federal securities law violation.

DAMAGES

Punitive damages cannot be recovered in a federal securities action. This is about the only thing that is clear about §10(b) damages. Although §28(a) limits 1934 Act recoveries to "actual damages," exactly how those actual damages are to be computed is not always clear. Indeed, the case law in this area is so disparate it has been said that "there is no law of damages under Rule 10b-5."[46]

Still, some conclusions can be drawn. First, in appropriate circumstances, a plaintiff is entitled to rescission. If plaintiff is a defrauded seller, he may return defendant's purchase price and be entitled to return of the securities together with any dividends or

---

[44] 551 F.2d 1005 (5th Cir. 1977).

[45] *Paul F. Newton & Co.* v. *Texas Commerce Bank*, 630 F.2d 1111 (5th Cir. 1980).

[46] Note, "Measurement of Damages in Private Actions Under Rule 10b-5," *Washington Univ. Law Quarterly* (1968), p. 165. See T. Sear, "Measure of Damages Crucial in Securities Fraud Actions," *National Law Journal*, January 27, 1986, p. 15.

interest defendant received. If plaintiff is a defrauded buyer, she is entitled to return of the purchase price upon tendering the securities.

But in many instances rescission is inappropriate. Perhaps plaintiff is a defrauded purchaser who no longer has the securities. Perhaps the defendant is a corporation whose false statements induced plaintiff to purchase its shares on the secondary market, but did not receive plaintiff's money. Another shortcoming of the rescission measure of damages is that it cannot account for factors other than the misrepresentation that might have affected the price of the securities.

Because of these shortcomings with the rescission measure, courts usually determine damages by the "out of pocket" measure familiar in common law fraud cases. A defrauded seller is generally entitled to the value of the securities sold minus sale price. Assume that Ms. B sold her stock in X Corporation for $50 a share because she believed X's press release that it had *not* made a major mineral strike in Canada. When it is announced that a strike did indeed occur (and the information circulates through the market), the value of X Corporation stock rises to $70 a share. Ms. B's damages would be $20 a share.[47]

A defrauded purchaser who still holds the securities at the time the fraud is uncovered is normally entitled to damages in the sum of the purchase price minus the true value. Assume that Mr. C buys Y Corporation stock at $50 a share because he believes its latest press release about its sales volume. It turns out that the press release is fraudulently overoptimistic, and when the true sales figures are released Y Corporation's stock falls to $40 a share. Assuming that no other factors impacted on the price of Y stock, Mr. C's damages are $10 a share.

Complications arise if a defrauded buyer sold prior to disclosure of the fraud. Assume that Ms. D purchased Z Corporation stock at $60 a share on the basis of a false representation that it was about to market a new computer, when in fact it had no such plans and therefore the true value of its shares was only $40 a share. Assume further that before the truth comes out the market for the type of computer Z Corporation is supposedly developing really booms. Z Corporation stock zooms to $80 a share, although it is still really worth only $40 a share. If Ms. D sells the shares to Mr. E at that point, she really has sustained no damage. She paid $20 a share more than the securities were worth, but she sold them for $40 a share more than they were worth. When the truth comes out and the market price drops to $40 a share, Mr. E can recover the difference between the $80 a share he paid and the $40 a share he will have to sell for.

What if before Ms. D sold and before the truth came out, the computer market started to falter and the price of Z Corporation's stock (still being traded on the false assumption that it was about to market a new computer) fell to $50 per share? If Ms. D sold then she would have sustained damages of $10 a share, which may be calculated by use of this formula:

---

[47] *Mitchell* v. *Texas Gulf Sulphur*, 446 F.2d 90 (10th Cir. 1971), emphasizes that the "true value" of the securities must be calculated after the misstatements or omissions have been corrected and the information has filtered through the marketplace.

$$\begin{array}{rcl}
\text{price} - \text{value (time of purchase)} & = (\$60 - 40) = & \$20/\text{share} \\
-\text{price} - \text{value (time of sale)} & = (\$50 - 40) = & \underline{\$10/\text{share}} \\
& & \$10/\text{share}
\end{array}$$

The out-of-pocket theory is helpful because its reliance on the true value of the securities allows the courts to take into account other factors (like the boom or bust in the computer market generally) that may have affected the price of the securities.[48] For example, in the *Huddleston* case, discussed earlier in this chapter, the trial court allowed plaintiff investors full return of the purchase price of their securities after the corporation went bankrupt and the value of the securities fell to zero. This rescission measure of damages was inappropriate, the appellate court decided,[49] because it did not take into account other factors such as weather, degree of spectator participation, and construction problems that contributed along with defendants' misstatements to the demise of the enterprise. According to the court,

> The use of the out-of-pocket rule will require that a "true" or "real" value, *i.e.*, the value the security would have had absent the misrepresentation, be established for each date on which the [plaintiff] class purchased. Once those values are obtained, possibly with the help of expert witnesses or a special master, then the determination of each individual plaintiff's recovery becomes a simple matter of subtraction of the "true" value of the securities on the date of plaintiff's purchase from the purchase price paid by plaintiff on that date.

The "out of pocket" measure will not be used where it is deemed inadequate. For example, if it produces a calculated sum of damages that is less than the sum defendant profited as a result of the fraud, the court may well order disgorgement on the theory that "it is more appropriate to give the defrauded party the benefit of windfalls than to let the fraudulent party keep them." [50]

In some instances, the courts will even grant "benefit of the bargain" damages. For example, in *Hackbart* v. *Holmes*,[51] Hackbart provided the money and Holmes the labor for a tire business. Holmes controlled the business; Hackbart held a 49% interest in the form of preferred stock. After almost six profitable years, Hackbart left the business by mutual agreement. Only then did Holmes tell Hackbart that his "preferred shares" did not entitle him to any share in the appreciated value of the business. Holmes was found to have defrauded Hackbart. Holmes argued on appeal that Hackbart's damages should be limited to "out of pocket," which he argued would mean Hackbart would receive back only his original contribution. Instead, the court gave Hackbart the benefit of his bargain by basing his recovery on 49% of the appreciated value of the business.

Finally, the Supreme Court held in 1986 that the rescissionary recovery of a

---

[48] *Green* v. *Occidental Petroleum Corp.*, 541 F.2d 1335 (9th Cir. 1976).

[49] *Huddleston* v. *Herman & MacLean*, 640 F.2d 534 (5th Cir. 1981), *rev'd on other grounds*, 459 U.S. 375 (1983). The Supreme Court did not address the matter of damages.

[50] *Janigan* v. *Taylor*, 344 F.2d 781 (1st Cir.), *cert. denied*, 382 U.S. 879 (1965).

[51] 675 F.2d 1114 (10th Cir. 1982).

successful §10(b) plaintiff who invested in a fraudulent tax shelter should not be reduced by the amount of tax benefits received.[52]

EXTRATERRITORIAL JURISDICTION

Because companies increasingly have crossed international borders both to do business and to seek capital,[53] the courts have often been faced with the difficult problem of delineating the scope of their jurisdiction under §10(b) to protect Americans from securities fraud perpetrated abroad and to protect foreign citizens from such fraud originating in the United States.

One leading case concluded that §10(b)'s provisions:

1. Apply to losses from sales of securities to Americans resident in the United States whether or not acts (or culpable failures to act) of material importance occurred in this country; and
2. Apply to losses from sales of securities to Americans resident abroad if, but only if, acts (or culpable failures to act) of material importance in the United States have significantly contributed thereto; but
3. Do not apply to losses from sales of securities to foreigners outside the United States unless acts (or culpable failures to act) within the United States directly caused such losses.[54]

So, generally speaking, U.S. courts base subject matter jurisdiction on either *conduct* that occurs in the United States or on *effects* felt in the United States from conduct that occurred abroad. The following case is illustrative.

GRUNENTHAL GmbH v. HOTZ

712 F.2d 421 (9th Cir. 1983)

This §10(b) action arises out of alleged misrepresentations made in connection with an agreement to sell all the common stock of defendant Productos to plaintiff Grunenthal. All defendants and plaintiff are either foreign corporations or foreign citizens. Plaintiff Grunenthal is a West German Corporation. Defendant Productos is a Mexican corporation controlled through a chain of Bahamian holding companies by a Bahamian trust whose beneficiary, Hotz, is a Swiss resident. Defendant Lowe, the managing director of Productos, is a citizen of Mexico.

---

[52] Randall v. Loftsgaarden, 54 U.S.L.W. 5044 (1986).

[53] Total transactions by foreign investors in U.S. equities were $134.3 billion in 1983. U.S. institutions hold $10–13 billion in foreign stocks, up from $1–2 billion in the late 1970s (SEC, *1934 Act Release*, no. 21958 April 18, 1985).

[54] *Bersch* v. *Drexel Firestone, Inc.*, 519 F.2d 974 (2d Cir.), *cert. denied*, 423 U.S. 1018 (1975).

The transaction was negotiated over the course of four meetings. The first occurred in Germany, when Lowe approached representatives of plaintiff and told them Hotz controlled Productos and was interested in selling it. Soon thereafter plaintiff's general counsel, Bernau, met with representatives of the Bahamian trust in the Bahamas. Further negotiations among Bernau, Lowe, and others occurred at a third meeting in Mexico. The fourth and final meeting took place in Los Angeles, at the law offices of plaintiff's American counsel. All the principals were present, including Hotz. At the meeting, Lowe stated in the presence of Hotz that Hotz controlled Productos. At the end of the meeting, Hotz and plaintiff's representatives signed the agreement.

The closing was to occur in the Bahamas, but the Bahamian trustees refused to approve the sale. Plaintiffs sued, alleging that defendants falsely represented that Hotz controlled Productos and falsely represented in Los Angeles that they had the present intention to perform the agreement.

The trial judge dismissed the complaint for lack of subject matter jurisdiction, reasoning that the parties and the securities were foreign and that the only contact in the United States occurred for convenience because Hotz was in Los Angeles on a temporary visa. Plaintiff appealed.

REINHARDT, CIRCUIT JUDGE:

While we [have] exercised jurisdiction in cases involving the extraterritorial application of the securities laws because the transactions produced "effects" within the United States, we have never held that the absence of such effects precludes the exercise of jurisdiction or that conduct alone is not enough. Indeed, consistent with the established objectives of the federal securities laws, we have recognized that "the jurisdictional hook need not be large to fish

for securities law violations"—*United Financial Group, Inc.*, 474 F.2d at 357 (quoting *Lawrence* v. *SEC*, 398 F.2d 276, 278 (1st Cir. 1968)). In our view, the test for subject matter jurisdiction formulated by the Eighth Circuit in *Continental Grain (Australia) Pty. Ltd.* v. *Pacific Oilseeds, Inc.*, 592 F.2d 409 (8th Cir. 1979), best satisfies those objectives.

In *Continental Grain*, plaintiff, an Australian corporation, purchased all of the stock of another Australian corporation from defendants. Defendants were an Australian corporation, a California corporation and a California resident. Plaintiff alleged that defendants defrauded it by failing to disclose certain facts about the principal assets of the acquired corporation. The transaction produced no effect in the United States. The conduct that occurred in this country consisted largely of the use of instrumentalities of interstate commerce to transmit communications that furthered the alleged fraud. After reviewing relevant case law from the Second, Third and Eighth Circuits, the court formulated a test for subject matter jurisdiction that considered

> whether defendant's conduct [that involved the use of instrumentalities of interstate commerce] in the United States was significant with respect to the alleged violation . . . and whether it furthered the fraudulent scheme . . . . The conduct in the United States cannot be merely preparatory . . . and must be material, that is, directly cause the losses.

Applying this test to the facts before it, the Eighth Circuit held that the defendants' conduct supported subject matter jurisdiction. The Third Circuit has adopted a similar view. See *SEC* v. *Kasser*, 548 F.2d 109, 114 (3d Cir.) ("The federal securities laws, in our view, do grant jurisdiction in transnational securities cases where at least some activity designed to further the fraudulent scheme occurs within this country."), *cert. denied*, 431 U.S. 938 (1977).

We believe that the test used by the Third

and Eighth Circuits advances the policies underlying federal securities laws. First, to deny jurisdiction in cases like *Continental Grain* might encourage "those who wish to defraud foreign securities purchasers or sellers to use the United States as a base of operations . . . [and,] in effect, create a haven for such defrauders and manipulators"—*Kasser*, 548 F.2d at 116. In addition, a "fundamental purpose, common to [the federal securities] statutes, was . . . to achieve a high standard of business ethics in the securities industry"—*SEC* v. *Capital Gains Research Bureau*, 375 U.S. 180, 186 (1963). Thus, the view adopted by the Third and Eighth Circuits is "consistent with the intent of Congress, as expressed in the antifraud provisions of the federal securities laws, to elevate the standard of conduct in securities transactions" within this country—*Continental Grain*, 592 F.2d at 421.

Assertion of jurisdiction may encourage Americans—such as lawyers, accountants, and underwriters—involved in transnational securities sales to behave responsibly and thus may prevent the development of relaxed standards that could "spill over into work on American securities transactions." Note, *American Adjudication of Transnational Securities Fraud*, 89 Harv.L.Rev. 553, 570–71 (1976).

We adopt the *Continental Grain* test and hold that defendants' conduct was sufficient to establish subject matter jurisdiction. The misrepresentations that took place in this country were "significant with respect to the alleged viola-

tion[s]," *Continental Grain*, 592 F.2d at 420, and "furthered the fraudulent scheme," *Kasser*, 548 F.2d at 114. Although Grunenthal had previously been told by Lowe that Hotz controlled Productos, the Los Angeles meeting furthered the fraudulent scheme because Hotz for the first time, through his silence, confirmed the claim that he owned Productos. Hotz' conduct in this country was not "merely preparatory"; rather, the conduct was "material" because immediately thereafter defendants signed and plaintiff was induced to execute the agreement. Moreover, the execution of the agreement in Los Angeles itself constituted an act that strongly supports our assertion of jurisdiction.

We disagree with the district court's view that the result in this case should be different because the allegedly fraudulent conduct occurred in this country by happenstance. We think it of little significance that the conduct in this country was "based on convenience." Indeed, to hold otherwise could make it convenient for foreign citizens and corporations to use this country and its lawyers, accountants and underwriters to further fraudulent securities schemes.

Because defendants utilizing instrumentalities of interstate commerce made misrepresentations in the United States that were significant with respect to the securities laws violations and furthered the fraudulent scheme, and because those misrepresentations were material and not merely preparatory, jurisdiction exists over plaintiff's cause of action.

Reversed.

STATE REMEDIES

In addition to the common law of fraud remedy that is available in each state to a plaintiff injured by securities fraud, each state's blue-sky law also prohibits such fraud. Section 101 of the Uniform Securities Act is an antifraud provision similar to §17(a) of the 1933 Act except that it outlaws fraud in the purchase as well as in the offer or sale of securities.

However, §10(b) has many advantages over these state remedies. Many of the advantages are substantive. We have already seen how requirements of privity, scienter, reliance, and causation have been relaxed in §10(b) litigation. There are also strong procedural advantages of the federal forum (which has exclusive jurisdiction over §10(b) litigation), including a wide choice of venue, worldwide service of process, and more liberal pleading, joinder, discovery, and class action provisions.

QUESTIONS AND PROBLEMS

1. Between early July and September 4, four executives of Carnation Co. discussed with The Nestlé Co. a sale of Carnation to Nestlé. During that time, various rumors of the possible sale of Carnation reached the marketplace, some of which identified Nestlé as the buyer. On August 7, Carnation's treasurer, who knew nothing of the discussions with Nestlé, issued a press release stating that there were no corporate developments that would account for the rumors and subsequent rise in Carnation stock. On August 20, the treasurer again responded to press questions saying he knew of no corporate developments and that "there is nothing to substantiate" the rumors. The potentially misleading effects of these statements disturbed both Nestlé and Carnation's investment bankers. After August 21, Carnation's CEO instructed the treasurer to respond to all questions with "no comment." Carnation made no further public comment until announcement of the sale on September 4. Discuss whether Carnation has met its §10(b) disclosure obligations. See *In re Carnation Co.*, Federal Securities Law Reports (CCH), ¶ 83,801 (1985).

2. The Hyman-Michaels Company was owned by Joseph (14%) and his uncles, Everett (50%) and Ralph (36%). Between 1966 and 1976, there had been approximately ten attempts to sell the company, all unsuccessful. On January 27, 1976, Joseph agreed to sell his shares to the company for $981,276. In July, Everett and Ralph sold the company for $13.4 million plus lifetime employment contracts. Joseph sued under §10(b), claiming that Everett and Ralph had purchased his interest without disclosing, among other things, that they had decided to retain a professional financial firm to obtain a purchaser and that Ralph had met with Angus Littlejohn in London and that Littlejohn had agreed to contact some prospective purchasers. Discuss the materiality of these omissions. See *Michaels* v. *Michaels*, 767 F.2d 1185 (7th Cir. 1985).

3. CSX owned 93% of Western Maryland, a timbering and mineral leasing concern. CSX decided to merge the two companies, eliminating the minority shareholders of Western Maryland. Western Maryland's proxy material, while indicating that its directors recommended the shareholders approve the plan that provided for them to receive $33 in cash or equivalent CSX stock for each Western Maryland share, did not disclose tonnage estimates of Western Maryland's coal reserves, its most valuable asset; timber holdings in board feet; book value per share; and the fact that the

purpose of the merger was to avoid paying substantial cash dividends to minority shareholders and to obtain the assets of Western Maryland for the benefit of CSX at the expense of the minority shareholders. The trial court held that these omissions did not constitute a violation of §10(b) under the rationale of *Santa Fe Industries* v. *Green*. Discuss. See *Lockspeiser* v. *Western Maryland Co.*, 768 F.2d 558 (4th Cir. 1985).

4. In early September 1979, Hamm bought 1,000 shares of Playboy stock at $17 a share. On April 13, 1981, Playboy disclosed that the operating licenses for its three London gambling casinos were being challenged for violations of British law. Soon thereafter, those licenses were suspended. During the 1978–1981 period, a substantial portion of Playboy's operating revenue was derived from these casinos. When the market price of Playboy stock dropped following these disclosures, Hamm sued under §10(b), indicating that Playboy had known as early as 1979 that its licenses were in danger but had not revealed this in its quarterly and annual reports. Playboy proved that Hamm had not read those reports anyway. Is this a good defense? Discuss. *HSL, Inc.* v. *Daniels*, Federal Securities Law Reports (CCH), ¶ 99,557 (N.D. Ill. 1983).

5. Plaintiff invested in a limited partnership tax shelter that later lost its favorable tax benefits due to an adverse IRS ruling. Plaintiff sued the tax shelter promoter's attorneys and accountants under §10(b) on the basis that certain tax returns and reports prepared after plaintiff invested were fraudulently prepared. Assuming that plaintiff proved misleading acts and scienter on the part of defendants, what about the ''in connection with'' requirement? Discuss. See *Hudson* v. *Capital Management Int'l, Inc.*, 565 F.Supp. 615 (N.D.Cal. 1983).

6. Cowin has long held certain shares of Bresler Company stock. He sued the company and its directors (who control 79% of the stock), alleging that they have recently manipulated the business for personal profit at the expense of minority shareholders in violation of §10(b). Should Cowin prevail if he can prove that defendant directors have depressed the stock of Bresler Co. shares by their self-dealing? Discuss. See *Cowin* v. *Bresler Co.*, 741 F.2d 410 (D.C.Cir. 1984).

7. Plaintiffs sold their business, which had an agreed-on value of $550,000, in exchange for 22,000 shares of defendant's stock. Several years later, defendant admitted that it had misstated its financial condition and earnings during the time of plaintiffs' sale. Plaintiffs sued under §10(b) and sought, by way of damages, rescission of the purchase agreement or, in the alternative, $550,000 plus interest. However, two years after suit was filed, the value of defendant's shares rose and plaintiffs sold their shares of defendant for $748,229. Should plaintiffs amend their complaint to seek a new measure of damages? See *Barrows* v. *Forest Laboratories, Inc.*, 742 F.2d 54 (2d Cir. 1984).

8. O'Driscoll, an Irish national, was living in Paris when he met a representative of Merrill Lynch (ML) who convinced him to place virtually his entire net worth in a discretionary cash and margin securities account in ML's London office. O'Driscoll, at ML's advice, simultaneously formed a Panamanian corporation to take title to

his holdings. Soon thereafter, O'Driscoll emigrated to Florida. In the ensuing 12 months, ML's trading generated $340,000 in commissions, but reduced O'Driscoll's net worth by $70,000. O'Driscoll and his corporation sued in the United States under §10(b). Discuss the availability of extraterritorial subject matter jurisdiction. See *O'Driscoll* v. *Merrill Lynch, Pierce, Fenner & Smith*, Federal Securities Law Reports (CCH), ¶ 99,486 (S.D.N.Y. 1983).

19

INSIDER TRADING: SECTION 16

INTRODUCTION

The keys to financial success in trading securities are knowledge, judgment, and luck. Unfortunately, if someone inside the corporate structure has access to specific, important information that outsiders do not know about, that insider has a big enough advantage to profit where outsiders with all the judgment and luck in the world will not. For example, if an insider learns that his company has just been granted a patent on a heretofore secret product, the insider may well be tempted to purchase stock in the company. As soon as the information becomes public, it is quite likely that the price of the company's stock will rise sharply.

Trading on inside information was for many years viewed almost as one of the "perks" that went with the job of being a corporate executive. There was terrible abuse of the practice, and few remedies existed. For example, in a 1933 case[1] a plaintiff sold his stock in a company after reading in a newspaper that the company had discontinued copper exploration in a certain area. At the same time plaintiff was selling, defendants, directors with the company, were buying stock because they knew, on the basis of

---

[1] *Goodwin* v. *Agassiz*, 283 Mass. 358, 186 N.E. 659 (1933).

inside information, that the company planned more exploration of the area based on a new geological theory. When the value of the stock later rose substantially, plaintiff sued. The Massachusetts Supreme Court denied recovery, holding that the directors did not breach their fiduciary duty to the shareholder. The court emphasized that there was no face-to-face transaction between plaintiff and defendants; rather, they acted through the "impersonal" stock exchange.

Because many believed that abuse of inside information contributed to the 1929 collapse of the stock market, Congress addressed the problem specifically when it passed the Securities Exchange Act of 1934. Section 16 of the 1934 Act is aimed specifically at the insider trading problem; it will be discussed in this chapter. Over the years, §10(b) of the 1934 Act and Rule 10b-5 have evolved into potent weapons against insider trading abuses; they will be discussed in the next chapter.

STATUTORY FRAMEWORK

Section 16 contains a direct, threefold attack on insider trading. Section 16(a) requires insiders to report their holdings and transactions in company stock to the SEC. Section 16(c) outlaws "short sales" by insiders in their company's stock; that is, insiders may not sell their company's equity securities (1) if they do not own the security sold or (2) if owning the security, they do not deliver it soon after the sale. If an insider contracts to sell company stock that he or she does not own at $20, there is obviously a sinister motive to do something to cause the company's performance to falter so that the market price of the stock will drop, to, say, $15 a share, so that a quick profit can be turned.

The most important provision is subsection (b), which provides that "short-swing" profits made by insiders are recoverable by the corporation. Subsections (d) and (e) provide limited exemptions for transactions by dealers and certain arbitrage transactions.

The SEC's role in §16 is unique. The subsection (a) reports are filed with and governed by the SEC. Also, the SEC has the express power to adopt exemptive rules for §16 for any transactions "not comprehended within the purpose" of §16(b). However, the SEC has no power to enforce the most important provision—§16(b). Insider trading, as defined in the section, is not unlawful; therefore, the SEC can neither enjoin it nor initiate criminal actions. Only private civil actions may be used to recover illicit short-swing profits.

"Objective" Approach

Section 16 takes a harsh—some would say too harsh—view of insider trading. If a person who is an "insider" within the meaning of the act engages in a purchase and sale, or a sale and purchase [2] within a six-month period and realizes a profit, that profit

---

[2] Obviously, if an insider buys 10 shares at $20 a share and three months later sells them at $30 a share, there has been a profit. Similarly, if an insider sells at $30 a share and repurchases three months later at $20 a share, there has been a profit. The insider owns the same number of shares and has $100 in pocket.

must be forfeited to the corporation. Section 16(b) liability exists regardless of whether the defendant controls the corporation and regardless of whether inside information was actually used. In fact, in the ordinary transaction, the insider can prove conclusively that inside information was *not* used and still have no defense. Congress decided that to require proof of actual use of inside information would make recovery too difficult. To require forfeiture of all such profits, on the other hand, would definitely discourage short-swing trading. This harsh, "objective" view of §16 is explained in the following landmark case.

SMOLOWE v. DELENDO CORP.

136 F.2d 231 (2d Cir. 1943)

A negotiated sale of assets of Delendo Corp. (then named Oldetyme Distillers Corporation) to Schenley Distillers Corporation fell through in 1936 because of Delendo's contingent tax liability for a claim by the United States, then in litigation. Later, negotiations were reopened and the sale was consummated on April 30, 1940. In the six months before the sale, defendants Seskis and Kaplan (both were officers, directors, and major shareholders of Delendo) bought Delendo stock which they then sold at substantial profits. Plaintiff shareholders of Delendo sued to recover those profits for the benefit of the corporation, apparently claiming that Seskis and Kaplan had inside information that the tax problem with the United States was being negotiated away, thus clearing the way for the profitable sale of assets.

Defendants claimed they did not use inside information in making their transactions, thus raising the issue of whether such use is a necessary element of recovery in a §16(b) claim. The trial court ruled for plaintiffs. Defendants appealed.

CLARK, CIRCUIT JUDGE:

The controversy as to . . . substantive liability . . . turns primarily upon the preamble, namely, "For the purpose of preventing the unfair use of information which may have been obtained by such beneficial owner, director, or officer by reason of his relationship to the issuer." Defendants would make it the controlling grant and limitation of authority for the entire section, and liability would result only for profits from a proved unfair use of inside information. We cannot agree with this interpretation.

We look first to the background of the statute. Prior to the passage of the Securities Exchange Act, speculation by insiders—directors, officers, and principal shareholders—in the securities of their corporation was a widely condemned evil. While some economic justification was claimed for this type of speculation in that it increased the ability of the market to discount future events or trends, the insiders' failure to disclose all pertinent information gave them an unfair advantage over the general body of stockholders which was not to be condoned. . . . By the majority rule, aggrieved stockholders had no right to recover from the insider in such a situation. And although some few courts enforced a fiduciary relationship and the U.S. Supreme Court in *Strong* v. *Repide*, 213 U.S. 419, announced a special circumstances doctrine whereby recovery would be permitted if all the circumstances indicated that the insider had taken an inequitable advantage of a stockholder, even these remedies were inadequate because of the heavy burden of proof imposed upon the stockholders.

The primary purpose of the Securities Exchange Act—as the declaration of policy in §2 makes plain—was to insure a fair and honest market, that is, one which would reflect an evaluation of securities in the light of all available and pertinent data. Furthermore, the Congressional hearings indicate that §16(b), specifically, was designed to protect the "outside" stockholders against at least short-swing speculation by insiders with advance information. It is apparent too, from the language of §16(b) itself, as well as from the Congressional hearings, that the only remedy which its framers deemed effective for this reform was the imposition of a liability based upon an objective measure of proof. This is graphically stated in the testimony of Mr. Corcoran, chief spokesman for the drafters and proponents of the Act, in Hearings before the Committee on Banking and Currency: "You hold the director, irrespective of any intention or expectation to sell the security within six months after, because it will be absolutely impossible to prove the existence of such intention or expectation, and you have to have this crude rule of thumb, because you cannot undertake the burden of having to prove that the director intended, at the time he bought, to get out on a short swing."

A subjective standard of proof, requiring a showing of an actual unfair use of inside information, would render senseless the provisions of the legislation limiting the liability period to six months, making an intention to profit during that period immaterial, and exempting transactions wherein there is a bona fide acquisition of stock in connection with a previously contracted debt. It would also torture the conditional "may" in the preamble into a conclusive "shall have" or "has." And its total effect would be to render the statute little more of an incentive to insiders to refrain from profiteering at the expense of the outside stockholders than are the common law rules of liability; it would impose a more stringent statute of limitation upon the party aggrieved at the same time that it allowed the wrongdoer to share in the spoils of recovery.

Had Congress intended that only profits from an actual misuse of inside information should be recoverable, it would have been simple enough to say so.

. . .

The present case would seem to be of the type which the statute was designed to include. Here it is conceded that the defendants did not make unfair use of information they possessed as officers at the time of the transactions. When these began they had no offer from Schenley. But they knew they were pressing the tax suit; and they, of course, knew of the corporate offer to settle it which reestablished the offer to purchase and led to the favorable sale. It is naive to suppose that their knowledge of their own plans as officers did not give them most valuable inside knowledge as to what would probably happen to the stock in which they were dealing. It is difficult to find this use "unfair" in the sense of illegal; it is certainly an advantage and a temptation within the general scope of the legislature's intended prohibition.

. . .

Affirmed.

This "crude rule of thumb" has been criticized as a "trap for the unwary." Indeed, in some instances its application in such a mechanical fashion does appear to produce unjust results. For example, in *Western Auto Supply Co.* v. *Gamble-Skogmo,*

Inc.,[3] Gamble-Skogmo purchased 26,000 shares of stock in its subsidiary, Western Auto, for $32.35 and immediately contributed them to its employees' profit-sharing trust. Within six months, it sold all its stock in Western Auto to Beneficial Finance Co. for $36 a share. Now Western Auto was Beneficial's subsidiary, and through Western Auto, Beneficial sued to recover over $94,000—the supposed profit from the sale of the 26,000 shares. The court allowed recovery, saying, "We . . . have noted the reference to the ethical position of Beneficial in seeking to recover, in effect, a part of the purchase price it willingly paid for the stock. The punctilios of the parties are not an issue here."

Although, as we shall see, there have been some moderations in this stern, objective approach to application of the statute, it remains §16's underlying philosophy. There remains, in ordinary cases, a conclusive presumption that insiders, as defined by the section, had access to and used inside information. There is no good faith defense for them.

SECTION 16(a) AND HOW IT WORKS

Section 16 contains no disclosure requirements other than the reporting requirements of §16(a). These requirements are twofold. First, any person who becomes an insider— an officer, director, or beneficial owner of 10%—must file an initial report on SEC Form 3. The report indicates the insider's holdings as of the date insider status is achieved. Then, changes in insider holdings are reported on SEC Form 4, which must be filed within ten days of the close of any month in which the insider bought or sold stock.

These are simple "fill-in-the-blank" forms, more than 100,000 of which are filed with the SEC each year.[4] SEC rules as to under what circumstances reports should be filed pursuant to §16(a) sometimes diverge from the courts' interpretation of terms in §16(b). More important, the SEC distributes summaries of these reports in the form of news releases on a regular basis. The forms even require a revelation of the prices of sales and purchases.

Because of the public nature of these forms, shareholders and lawyers interested in discovering §16(b) violations find them a very valuable resource.

SECTION 16(b)

Because of the objective approach underlying §16(b), its interpretation and application by the courts have been very mechanistic. Analysis of its individual components is the best way to understand §16(b)'s rule that any officer, director, or 10% beneficial owner

---

[3] 348 F.2d 736 (8th Cir. 1965), *cert. denied*, 382 U.S. 987 (1966).

[4] The SEC relaxed its monitoring of §16(a) in 1982. A year later, Ralph Nader informed the SEC that 50% of the board members he studied were not filing their §16(a) reports, and of those who were, 43% were filing late. Soon thereafter, the SEC filed several complaints against nonfiling directors: "SEC Alleges 12 Didn't Disclose Stock Dealings," *The Wall Street Journal* (Southwestern edition), March 14, 1984, p. 5.

who purchases and sells or sells and purchases equity securities in less than a six-month period is liable for the profit realized from the transaction.

"Registered Equity Security"

Not every officer, director, beneficial owner, and corporation is covered by §16(b). The act covers only "the beneficial owner of more than 10 per centum of any class of any equity security (other than an exempted security) which is *registered pursuant to section 12* of this title, or . . . a director or an officer of the issuer of *such security*."

If a corporation has not registered any of its equity securities under §12 of the 1934 Act, the officers and directors are not covered. Securities listed as "exempted securities" under §3(a)(12), such as securities issued by a corporation in which the United States has an interest, are not covered by §16. Even if a corporation has registered stock under §12, a beneficial owner is covered by §16 only if he or she owns more than 10% of that particular class of stock, or its equivalent. Owning 10% of an unregistered class of stock does not qualify one as an insider, *unless* that class is "sufficiently similar" to a registered class. For example, holding convertible preferred stock that is unregistered may qualify one as an insider if the stock is convertible to more than 10% of registered common stock.

If one qualifies as an insider of a corporation with registered stock, a violation occurs even if the trading is done in a class of stock that is unregistered.

Insiders

Because of their status, insiders—officers, directors, and beneficial owners of 10%—are conclusively presumed to have access to and to use illicit inside information in their short-swing trading. In the next section we shall begin a more detailed examination of the meaning of each of these three categories. But it should be noted that insiders cannot evade the proscriptions of §16(b) by trading through trusts, in the name of family members, or otherwise attempting to profit indirectly in a manner that cannot legally be accomplished directly. The next case illustrates the problem and one court's solution.

ALTAMIL v. PRYOR

405 F.Supp. 1222 (S.D. Ind. 1975)

Defendant Pryor was a director of Altamil for three years and during that time his wife profited from certain transactions in the sale of Altamil stock. These purchases and sales occurred within a period of less than six months and a total profit of over $8,000 was achieved. The evidence indicated that defendant had complete control over the transactions because he had the contacts and knowledge. His wife testified that she followed defendant's advice and *allowed him to execute the transactions. On the other hand, the evidence showed that the profits obtained from the transactions were maintained by the wife in her own separate accounts and were not used to support either herself or defendant. Defendant and his wife were married in 1931, and the wife brought no significant property into the marriage. Since that time she had received substantial gifts from her husband and had maintained such property in her own name.*

NOLAND, DISTRICT JUDGE:

. . .

Merely because the profits realized by the defendant's wife on the transaction in question have not directly benefited the defendant as to the support and maintenance of his household does not mean the defendant has not indirectly benefited from such profits or that he won't benefit in the future therefrom. . . . To the extent she can profit from favorable stock transactions made possible by reason of the defendant's close relationship with Altamil, the defendant may not feel the need to make taxable transfers to his wife. To this extent the defendant would directly benefit from such profits.

. . .

In the recent case of *Whiting* v. *Dow Chemical Company*, 386 F.Supp. 1130 (S.D. N.Y. 1974), *aff'd*, 523 F.2d 680 (3d Cir. 1975), the district court was faced with a situation closely analogous to the one herein. In that case the husband was a director of Dow Chemical and regularly gave his wife investment advice concerning the trading of Dow Chemical stock. While the Court recognized that the wife did not always follow her husband's advice, the Court found:

> The ability to exercise a controlling influence over sales and purchases of the spouse's shares, particularly when combined with a substantial common interest in mutual prosperity, indicates that the family situation is susceptible to the abuses which §16(b) was designed to prevent.

. . .

The defendant herein contends that the *Whiting* case is not controlling in this case because therein the profits of the sale were used by the insider and his wife jointly for purposes of household and family support, while no such situation exists herein. While the Court agrees the cases are distinguishable on that basis, it does not believe that such a distinction compels a judgment for the defendant herein. In the *Whiting* case the insider did not exercise complete control over his wife's investments as is the situation herein. Also, in *Whiting* the wife brought a significant estate into her marriage, whereas in this case the defendant made substantial transfers to his wife for the purposes of making better use of estate planning possibilities.

The Court believes that weighing all of the evidence leads it to the conclusion that the defendant has benefited from the profits realized by his wife on the transactions in question and, therefore, he is liable as a "beneficial owner" under §16(b). To the extent an insider can exercise complete control over transactions of corporate stock held in his wife's name and, thereby, increase his wife's individual estate, the Court believes such insider has acted as the "beneficial owner" of such stock and improperly benefited in violation of the policy and purposes of §16(b).

Judgment was entered for plaintiff in a sum exceeding $8,000.[5]

---

[5] There are cases that reject *Altamil's* view that a §16(b) defendant's "profit realized" can come through indirect benefits. These cases require a "direct pecuniary benefit" to defendant before imposing §16(b) liability. For example, *CBI Indus., Inc.* v. *Horton*, 682 F.2d 643 (7th Cir. 1982).

Who Is an "Officer"?

SEC Rule 3b-2 defines "officer" to include "president, vice-president, secretary, treasurer or principal financial officer, comptroller, or principal accounting officer, or any person routinely performing corresponding functions." These are the persons who will be considered "officers" for §16(b) purposes. The courts' general approach in defining an officer has been objective and mechanistic, sticking closely to this definition.

This approach has created a loophole in §16. The assistants of these officers, if they are truly supervised by their superiors, are not covered by the act even though they may have access to much or all of the same information their superiors see. These assistants may be liable under 10b-5 if they engage in insider trading, of course, but the more stringent requirements of §16(b) are inapplicable to them.

The courts have been sufficiently flexible to hold that the titles given persons are not controlling. For example, in *Colby* v. *Klune*,[6] defendant's title was "Production Manager." Although this title is not listed in the definition, the appellate court ordered a factual inquiry into whether defendant was nevertheless an officer, defining officer as "a corporate employee performing important executive duties of such character that he would be likely in discharging those duties, to obtain confidential information about the company's affairs that would aid him if he engaged in personal market transactions." This more subjective approach was approved in a case involving an opposite situation— in *Merrill Lynch, Pierce, Fenner & Smith, Inc.* v. *Livingston*.[7] Defendant had a title coming within the statute, but not the responsibilities. The court said the title "Vice-President" only raises an inference that the employee has executive duties and access to confidential information. The inference was overcome by evidence that Livingston was "simply a securities salesman who had none of the powers of an executive officer of Merrill Lynch." The trial court's judgment against defendant in the sum of almost $15,000 was reversed.

Who Is a "Director"?

The term "director" is not as elusive as that of "officer," and it is normally quite easy to tell who is a director and who is not. But suppose that a partnership trades in the stock of a corporation, netting short-swing profits, while one of its partners is on the board of directors of the corporation. Should the partnership be deemed to be a "director"? According to the Supreme Court in *Blau* v. *Lehman*,[8] the answer is "no" unless the partner has been "deputized" by the partnership to perform his director's duties for the partnership. The facts did not justify such a finding in that case, the Court concluded, so that although the partner who was also a director was forced to disgorge his proportionate share of the profits, his partners were allowed to keep almost $100,000 in profits they received.

---

[6] 178 F.2d 872 (2d Cir. 1949).
[7] 566 F.2d 1119 (9th Cir. 1978).
[8] 368 U.S. 403 (1962).

This ruling remains the law, although it was strongly criticized in dissent by Justice Douglas who noted that partners of this particular partnership, an investment banking and securities brokerage firm, were on the boards of directors of some 100 corporations, concluding that "What we do today allows all but one partner to share in the feast which the one places on the partnership table. They in turn can offer feasts to him in the 99 other companies of which they are directors."

In *Feder* v. *Martin Marietta Corp.*,[9] a virtually identical situation arose. Martin Marietta Corporation made a substantial short-swing profit by trading in Sperry Rand Corporation stock while its president, Bunker, was on Sperry Rand's board of directors. The evidence in the case convinced the court that Martin Marietta had "deputized" Bunker as its representative on the Sperry Rand board. Part of the evidence supporting this conclusion came in Bunker's letter of resignation from the Sperry Rand board in which he stated, "When I became a member of the Board in April, it appeared to your associates that the Martin Marietta ownership of a substantial number of shares of Sperry Rand should have representation on your Board." Because Bunker was held to have been acting on Martin Marietta's behalf while on the Sperry Rand board, Martin Marietta was deemed a "director" and forced to give up its short-swing profits.

One important point about both officers and directors is that they need to hold that status at only one end of a transaction to be held liable for short-swing profits. For example, if a person buys stock in a corporation before he becomes one of its directors, and sells the stock after he becomes a director, and the transactions occur within a six-month period, any profit realized must be disgorged.[10] Similarly, if a person buys stock while she is an officer in the corporation, resigns her position, and then sells the stock within six months of the purchase, the profits must be forfeited. So long as a person is an officer or a director during one of the transactions, the possibility of abuse exists.

On the other hand, if an officer learns of some inside information that is particularly startling, resigns, buys stock at a bargain price, and soon sells at a great profit after the inside information becomes public, there is no §16(b) liability.[11] The officer or director must have that status during at least one of the transactions. Although this is a loophole in §16(b), it would be a rare instance when a person would give up the salary and prestige of such a position in order to trade, especially when there would be the strong possibility of liability under Rule 10b-5, as we shall see in the next chapter.

Who Is a "Beneficial Owner of 10%?"

The SEC and the courts have taken a broad view of what constitutes beneficial ownership. For example, the SEC has stated that "[g]enerally a person is regarded as the beneficial owner of securities held in the name of his or her spouse and their minor children. Absent special circumstances such relationship ordinarily results in such person

---

[9] 406 F.2d 260 (2d Cir. 1969), *cert. denied*, 396 U.S. 1036 (1970).

[10] See *Adler* v. *Klawans*, 172 F.Supp. 502 (S.D.N.Y. 1958).

[11] See *Lewis* v. *Mellon Bank*, 513 F.2d 921 (3d Cir. 1971).

obtaining benefits substantially equivalent to ownership. . . . Accordingly, a person ordinarily should include in his reports filed pursuant to Section 16(a) securities held in the name of a spouse or minor children as being beneficially owned by him.'' [12] Although this SEC Rule applies only to §16(a), it is indicative of §16(b)'s policy that beneficial owners, like officers and directors, not be permitted to do indirectly that which is denied them directly. Similarly, a person cannot evade §16(b) by acting through a trust he controls,[13] or a corporation that is merely a conduit for individual investment activity.[14]

Calculation of the 10% figure can cause problems when convertible securities are involved. For example, in *Chemical Fund, Inc.*, v. *Xerox Corp.*,[15] a mutual fund purchased more than 10% of Xerox Corporation convertible debentures. However, if converted to common stock, the debentures would have produced only 2.72% of that class. When Chemical Fund sold common stock at a profit within six months of conversion, the court found no liability, holding that the debentures were not a class by themselves and were relevant only in that they could be converted into common stock. It is *equity* securities that give the holder voting power and therefore indirect control over the corporation's policies and access to its inside information. The SEC did not completely accept the ruling and continues to require the holder of 10% of a class of convertible securities to report under §16(a), even though once converted, the holder would not own 10% of the underlying equity security.[16]

Does a 10% beneficial owner, like an officer and director, have §16(b) liability even though he or she has insider status at only one end of the transaction? Early cases so held, but the Supreme Court disagreed when it addressed the issue.

FOREMOST-McKESSON, INC. v. PROVIDENT SECURITIES CO.

423 U.S. 232 (1976)

Provident Securities Co., a personal holding company, decided to liquidate and dissolve. Foremost-McKesson agreed to buy Provident's assets with $4.25 million in cash and $49.75 million in Foremost convertible subordinate debentures. Foremost agreed to register under the 1933 Act $25 million of the debentures and *to participate in an underwriting agreement by which the debentures would be sold to the public. On October 21, the underwriting agreement was signed; on October 24, Provident distributed $22 million in debentures to its shareholders. On October 28, the underwriter paid Provident for the $25 million underwriting. As of*

---

[12] *Securities Exchange Act Release*, no. 7793 (Securities and Exchange Commission, 1966).

[13] Rule 16a-8.

[14] *Securities Exchange Act Release*, no. 1965 (Securities and Exchange Commission, 1938).

[15] 377 F.2d 107 (2d Cir. 1967).

[16] *Securities Exchange Act Release*, no. 8325 (Securities and Exchange Commission, 1968).

October 20, Provident had all the debentures, which, when convertible, would have constituted more than 10% of Foremost's common stock. Foremost therefore brought a §16(b) action to recover the profit made on the sale which had followed a few days later.

POWELL, ASSOCIATE JUSTICE:

Section 16(b)'s last sentence . . . provides that it "shall not be construed to cover any transaction where such beneficial owner was not such both at the time of the purchase and sale, or the sale and purchase, of the security involved. . . ." The question presented here is whether a person purchasing securities that put his holdings above the 10% level is a beneficial owner "at the time of the purchase" so that he must account for profits realized on a sale of those securities within six months. The United States Court of Appeals for the Ninth Circuit answered this question in the negative. . . . We affirm.

. . .

The exemptive provision, which applies only to beneficial owners and not to other statutory insiders, must have been included in §16(b) for a purpose. Although the extensive legislative history of the act is bereft of any explicit explanation of Congress' intent, . . . the evolution of §16(b) from its initial proposal through passage does shed significant light on the purpose of the exemptive provision.

The original version of what would develop into the act was S.2693, 73rd Cong., 2d sess. (1934).

. . .

The structure of the clause imposing liability in the revised §16(b) did not unambiguously retain S.2693's requirement that beneficial ownership precede a purchase-sale sequence. But

we cannot assume easily that Congress intended to eliminate the requirement in the revised bill. The legislative history reveals that the requirement was made clear in the hearings, yet no complaint was made about it.

. . .

The legislative record thus reveals that the drafters focused directly on the fact that S.2693 covered a short-term purchase-sale sequence by a beneficial owner only if his status existed before the purchase, and no concern was expressed about the wisdom of this requirement. But the explicit requirement was omitted from the operative language of the section when it was restructured to cover sale-repurchase sequences. In the same draft, however, the exemptive provision was added to the section. On this record we are persuaded that the exemptive provision was intended to preserve the requirement of beneficial ownership before the purchase.

. . .

Foremost recognizes the ambiguity of the exemptive provisions, but argues that where "alternative constructions" of §16(b)'s terms are available, we should choose the construction that best serves the statute's purposes. . . . [N]othing suggests that the construction urged by Foremost would better serve to further congressional purposes. Indeed, the legislative history of §16(b) indicates that by adding the exemptive provision, Congress deliberately expressed a contrary choice. But even if the legislative record were more ambiguous, we would hesitate to adopt Foremost's construction. It is inappropriate to reach the harsh result of imposing §16(b)'s liability without fault on the basis of unclear language. If Congress wishes to impose such liability, we must assume it will do so expressly or by unmistakable inference.

It is not irrelevant that Congress itself limited

carefully the liability imposed by §16(b). . . . Even an insider may trade freely without incurring statutory liability if, for example, he spaces his transactions at intervals greater than six months. When Congress has so recognized the need to limit carefully the "arbitrary and sweeping" coverage of §16(b) . . . , courts should not be quick to determine that, despite an acknowledged ambiguity, Congress intended the section to cover a particular transaction.

Our construction of §16(b) also is supported by the distinction Congress recognized between short-term trading by mere stockholders and such trading by directors and officers. The legislative discourse revealed that Congress thought that all short-swing trading by directors and officers was vulnerable to abuse because of their intimate involvement in corporate affairs. But trading by mere stockholders was viewed as being subject to abuse only when the size of their holdings afforded the potential for access to corporate information. These different perceptions simply reflect the realities of corporate life.

It would not be consistent with this perceived distinction to impose liability on the basis of a purchase made when the percentage of stock ownership requisite to insider status had not been acquired. To be sure, the possibility does exist that one who becomes a beneficial owner by a purchase will sell on the basis of information attained by virtue of his newly acquired holdings. But the purchase itself was not one posing dangers that Congress considered intolerable, since it was made when the purchaser owned no shares or less than the percentage deemed necessary to make one an insider. Such a stockholder is more analogous to the stockholder who never owns more than 10% and thereby is excluded entirely from the operation of §16(b) than to a director or officer whose every purchase and sale is covered by the statute. While this reasoning might not compel our construction of the exemptive provision, it explains why Congress may have seen fit to draw the line it did.

. . .

Affirmed.

Note that the *Foremost* ruling was limited to the purchase-sale sequence. It clearly held that if a person buys 13% of a corporation's stock in one fell swoop, none of that 13% can be matched against a subsequent sale for purposes of computing a §16(b) profit. But what of the sale-repurchase sequence? The same reasoning would indicate that it is not covered either, but that creates a curious loophole. Theoretically, a person could buy 13%, sell down to 8%, repurchase back to 13%, sell down to 9%, and so on, without ever being covered by §16(b). The lower courts are split on how to handle this "yo-yo" effect. Some are inclined to plug the loophole by not applying the *Foremost* rationale to the sale-repurchase sequence; others believe the *Foremost* reasoning requires that the loophole be left unplugged.

Note also the language in *Foremost* in which the Supreme Court indicated that §16(b) should be read narrowly in light of its harsh results when it is applied. This is one of the major indications that the Supreme Court is not willing to follow the traditional mechanistic, objective approach in all applications of §16(b).

A similar expression of Supreme Court feelings in this regard appeared in the following case, which presented a problem related to the question of §16(b)'s coverage of beneficial owners.

RELIANCE ELECTRIC CO. v. EMERSON ELECTRIC CO.

404 U.S. 418 (1972)

*On June 16, 1967, Emerson Electric Co. bought 13.2% of the common stock of Dodge Manufacturing Co. in a tender offer. Emerson was attempting to gain control of Dodge, but recognized imminent failure when Dodge shareholders approved a merger with Reliance Electric Co. Faced with the prospect of being forced to exchange its shares in Dodge for Reliance shares in the merger, Emerson followed a plan to liquidate its holdings in Dodge. Because this was a pre-*Foremost *case, it was assumed that the one-time purchase of 13.2% of the stock of Dodge was covered under §16(b). Therefore, a two-step plan was devised. On August 28, Emerson sold to a brokerage house at $68 per share enough shares to reduce its holdings to 9.96% of Dodge common stock, realizing that it would probably have to forfeit its profit on those shares. The remaining 9.96% was sold to Dodge at $69 per share on September 11. The lower court held that the profits gained in the second sale were not recoverable under §16(b). Plaintiff Reliance appealed.*

STEWART, ASSOCIATE JUSTICE:

The history and purpose of §16(b) have been exhaustively reviewed by federal courts on several occasions since its enactment in 1934. Those courts have recognized that the only method Congress deemed effective to curb the evils of insider trading was a flat rule taking the profits out of a class of transactions in which the possibility of abuse was believed to be intolerably great. . . . Thus Congress did not reach every transaction in which an investor actually relies on inside information. A person avoids liability if he does not meet the statutory definition of an "insider," or if he sells more than six months after purchase. Liability cannot be imposed simply because the investor structured his transactions with the intent of avoiding liability under §16(b). The question is, rather, whether the method used to "avoid" liability is one permitted by the statute.

Among the "objective standards" contained in §16(b) is the requirement that a 10% owner be such "both at the time of the purchase and sale . . . of the security involved." Read literally, this language contemplates that a statutory insider might sell enough shares to bring his holdings below 10% and later—but still within six months—sell additional shares free from liability under the statute. Indeed, commentators on the securities laws have recommended this exact procedure for a 10% owner who, like Emerson, wishes to dispose of his holdings within six months of their purchase.

Under the approach urged by Reliance, . . . the apparent immunity of profits derived from Emerson's second sale is lost where the two sales, though independent in every other respect, are "interrelated parts of a single plan." But a "plan" to sell that is conceived within six months of purchase clearly would not fall within §16(b) if the sale were made after the six months had expired, and we see no basis in the statute for a different result where the 10% requirement is involved rather than the six-month limitation.

. . .

Affirmed.

Remember that the entire question that arose in *Reliance* would have been mooted had the case arisen after *Foremost*, because *Foremost* held that the purchase of 13.2% of the stock in a single transaction could not be matched against any subsequent sale for §16(b) purposes. Consider the combined effect of *Foremost* and *Reliance*. If a holder buys 11% one month in a single transaction, buys 4% more the next month, then sells 6% the next month, and the remaining 9% the next, insider liability would attach only for sale of the 4% that was purchased after the holder reached the 10% level.

The lower courts have been somewhat restrictive in their application of the *Reliance* ruling, and with good reason. For example, in *Reece Corp.* v. *Walco National Corp.*,[17] Walco made a series of open market purchases of Reece stock, including the purchase of 75,700 shares after it became a 10% holder. The average price paid for these shares was $10.38. Walco then decided to sell its entire holdings in Reece to Reece. Realizing that §16(b) problems existed for the 75,700 shares, Walco devised a plan to limit its liability. On April 29, Walco sold down to 9.5% at *$8.75 a share*, less than its purchase price. On April 30, Walco sold the remaining 9.5% at *$13.71 a share*, claiming that under *Reliance* the profit from this sale was exempt. Both sales were made to Reece. The claimed basis for the differential sales prices was that certain covenants were attached to the sales agreement of April 30, such as an agreement that Walco would not make another attempt to take over Reece for at least seven years.

When Reece sued Walco to recover short-swing profits, the court held that "the April 29 and April 30 'sales' constituted in fact a single sale at an agreed price of $12 per share" and assessed liability on the 75,700 shares on that basis.

What Is a "Purchase" or "Sale"?

Section 16(b) liability attaches only to a profit gained from a "sale and purchase" or "purchase and sale," and a number of interesting problems have arisen out of attempts to define and apply these terms.

Generally, it may be said that a gift of stock is not a "purchase" and may therefore be sold at a profit within six months of the giving. The same result exists for *stock dividends*—even insiders may sell them within six months of receiving them without fear of §16(b) liability.

Conversions of preferred stock or debt securities into common stock have caused many problems for the courts. Some courts have held that such a conversion is a sale of the convertible security and a purchase of common stock. Others have held that no "purchase" of common stock is involved in such a transaction. Still others have held that the conversion does not involve a "sale" of the convertible security. Fortunately, most of the problems caused by the courts' inability to agree on the issue have been averted by the SEC's promulgation of Rule 16b-9, which exempts most conversions of stock from the operation of Rule 16(b), except where there has been a purchase of the

---

[17] 565 F.Supp. 158 (S.D.N.Y. 1983).

convertible and a sale of the common or a sale of the convertible and a purchase of the common (other than the conversion transaction itself) within a period of six months.

Exercises of *stock appreciation rights* (SARs), a popular form of executive compensation, have also raised such questions. An SAR gives an executive the right to receive the increase in value of optioned shares over a period of time. The SAR is a form of incentive compensation—the better the corporation does, the greater the compensation. Plaintiffs in §16(b) actions have frequently argued that the exercise of an SAR is a simultaneous purchase and sale of stock.

In *Matas* v. *Siess*,[18] for example, seven defendants had SARs that gave them the option to receive either in cash or in stock, at their election, the increase in the value of certain optioned shares from the date of the grant of the option to the date of the exercise of the rights. Over the course of 18 months, the seven defendants received aggregate profits of some $400,000, mostly in cash. Defendants were found liable under §16(b), the court noting that "where stock appreciation rights are exercisable for cash, the possibility of speculative abuse clearly exists. The officer or director is in a position, by exercising stock appreciation rights for cash, to reap a profit which he speculates may or may not be realizable a few months hence, based on inside information."

The result in *Matas* v. *Siess* should be compared to contrary results in *Rosen* v. *Drisler*,[19] where the defendants had no control over the making of the offer or the date at which the option was to be appraised and in *Freedman* v. *Barrow*,[20] where defendant insiders were denied the right to receive cash when they exercised their SARs. In both these latter cases, the factual differences made it much less likely that insiders could profit from inside information.

The SEC clarified the SAR problem by exempting the exercise of SARs from 16(b) liability if the conditions of Rule 16b-3 are met. These requirements are quite complicated, but the most important provision is a requirement of shareholder approval for creation of the rights. Part of the rule, for example, exempts cash settlements of SARs if (1) the rights are not exercisable during the first six months of their existence, (2) the plan is administered by a disinterested board of directors empowered to decide the form (cash or stock) in which payment can be made, and (3) the election to exercise for cash is made only during a "window" period between the third and twelfth day following release of the corporation's quarterly and annual summary statements of sales and earnings when it is unlikely that insiders will have significant information not available generally.

Unsuccessful *takeover bids* have also been a very fertile source of §16(b) controversy. Several times in recent years corporations have attempted to take control of other corporations by the purchase of shares only to have the target corporation defeat the attempt by merging with a third corporation. The shares the first corporation purchased in the target are then exchanged for shares of the third corporation, frequently at a profit and usually within six months of the original purchase. If the objective approach

---

[18] 467 F.Supp. 217 (S.D.N.Y. 1979).

[19] 421 F.Supp. 1282 (S.D.N.Y. 1976).

[20] 427 F.Supp. 1129 (S.D.N.Y. 1976).

to §16(b) is applied, logically a "purchase and sale" has occurred and liability has attached.

However, the Supreme Court rejected application of the traditional approach to such situations in *Kern County Land Co.* v. *Occidental Petroleum Corp.*[21] Viewing the merger situation as "unorthodox," the Court spurned the traditional "objective" approach to §16(b) that conclusively presumes access to and use of inside information if an insider profits on transactions within six months. Instead, the Court applied a "subjective" approach, which recognizes that a defeated tender offeror in a hostile battle is unlikely to have had access to inside information of the target corporation (even if for a time it held more than 10% of the target's shares) and that a defeated tender offeror's sale of target shares is "involuntary."

Kern's rationale has recently been interpreted to mean that

> where (1) an atmosphere of suspicion, if not hostility, characterizes relations between the two corporations, (2) the exchange of shares is "involuntary" in that it is effectuated pursuant to a merger over which the investing corporation exercised no control or influence, and (3) there is no likelihood of access to material inside information, §16(b), the "paradigmatic strict liability statute," is inappropriate and will not apply.[22]

The "subjective" or "pragmatic" approach of *Kern* is discussed in the following case.

TEXAS INTERNATIONAL AIRLINES v. NATIONAL AIRLINES, INC.

714 F.2d 533 (5th Cir. 1983), *cert. denied*, 465 U.S. 1052 (1984)

On September 6, 1978, National Airlines and Pan American World Airways entered into a merger agreement, contingent upon approval by National's shareholders, under which Pan Am would pay not less than $50 in cash for each share of National's common stock. Texas International Airlines (TI) also sought control of National. On March 14, 1979, while already holding 10% of National's shares, TI purchased 121,000 more in open market brokerage transactions. However, on May 16, 1979, National shareholders did approve the merger with Pan Am.

TI stood to receive $50 for each share of National it held when the merger was closed. For whatever reason, TI decided not to wait until the merger went through to negotiate the sale of its shares to Pan Am. On July 28, 1979, TI sold its shares to Pan Am for $50 each. The Pan Am merger with National was not concluded until some time thereafter.

On August 2, 1979, TI filed this action seeking declaratory judgment that it was not liable to National under §16(b) for profits realized on the purchase and sale of National stock. National counterclaimed to seek recovery of

---

[21] 411 U.S. 582 (1973).

[22] *Heublein, Inc.* v. *General Cinema Corp.*, 722 F.2d 29 (2d Cir. 1983), *cert. denied*, 465 U.S. 1066 (1984).

those profits. The trial judge ruled in favor of National, allowing recovery of over $1,000,000 in profits realized from sale of the 121,000 shares. TI appealed.

JOHNSON, CIRCUIT JUDGE:

TI urges this Court to create an exception to automatic §16(b) liability in cases where a defendant can prove that, notwithstanding its ownership of over ten percent of the stock of the issuer, the defendant had no access to inside information concerning the issuer. According to TI, the classic example of such a case is a sale of stock in the hostile takeover context. Application of §16(b) in this type of case, argues TI, does not serve congressional goals— Congress intended short-swing profits to be disgorged only when the particular transaction serves as a vehicle for the realization of these profits based upon access to inside information.

TI's argument is unsupported by the legislative history of §16(b). Although the abuse Congress sought to curb was speculation by stockholders with inside information, "the only method Congress deemed effective to curb the evils of insider trading was a *flat rule* taking the profits out of a *class of transactions* in which the possibility of abuse was believed to be intolerably great"—*Kern County*, 93 S. Ct. at 1473 (emphasis added). In explaining the necessity for a "crude rule of thumb" to Congress, Thomas Corcoran, a principal draftsman of the act, stated: "You have to have a general rule. In particular transactions, it might work a hardship, but those transactions that are a hardship represent the sacrifice to the necessity of having a general rule." The Supreme Court explained the necessity for the flat rule or "objective approach" of the statute in *Reliance Electric Company* v. *Emerson Electric Company*, 404 U.S. 418 (1972), quoting *Bershad* v. *McDonough*, 428 F.2d 693, 696 (7th Cir. 1970):

In order to achieve its goals, Congress chose a relatively arbitrary rule capable of easy administration. The objective standard of Section 16(b) imposes strict liability upon substantially all transactions occurring within the statutory time period, regardless of the intent of the insider or the existence of actual speculation. This approach maximized the ability of the rule to eradicate speculative abuses by reducing difficulties in proof. Such arbitrary and sweeping coverage was deemed necessary to insure the optimum prophylatic effect.

In *Kern County* the Supreme Court approved an extremely narrow exception to the objective standard of §16(b). The Court held that when a transaction is "unorthodox" or "borderline," the courts should adopt a pragmatic approach in imposing §16(b) liability which considers the opportunity for speculative abuse, that is, whether the statutory "insider" had or was likely to have access to inside information.

TI engages in an analogy between the hostile and adversary relationship between the target company and the putative insider in *Kern County* and the adversary relationship between TI and National in the instant case. Even assuming the alleged parallelism between the adversary situations in the two cases and assuming that TI could prove that it neither had nor was likely to have access to inside information by virtue of its statutory "insider" status, no valid basis for an exception to §16(b) liability on these facts is perceived. The Supreme Court in Kern County inquired into whether the transaction had the potential for abuse of inside information only because the transaction fell under the rubric of "unorthodox" or "borderline." In *Kern County*, Occidental, a shareholder in Kern County Land Company (Old Kern), converted its shares in Old Kern into shares of the acquiring corporation pursuant to a merger. The Supreme Court clearly distinguished the unorthodox transaction—a conversion of securities—before it from the traditional cash-for-stock transaction in the instant case.

TI lays frontal attack on the unorthodox transaction test as fundamentally flawed, principally because the form of consideration received—cash or stock—has nothing to do with whether inside information was or might have been used. What this attack fails to consider, however, is the significance of the factor of voluntariness in the Supreme Court's decision. The Court's sole concern was not that cash-for-stock sales present a greater opportunity for abuse of inside information than do stock-for-stock sales. Rather, language in the Supreme Court's opinion indicates that traditional cash-for-stock sales were excluded from the concept of unorthodox transactions because of their voluntary nature:

> The critical fact is that the exchange took place and was required pursuant to a merger. . . . Occidental could, of course, have disposed of its shares of Old Kern for cash before the merger was closed. Such an act would have been a section 16(b) sale and would have left Occidental with a prima facie section 16(b) liability. . . . But the *involun-*

tary nature of Occidental's exchange, when coupled with the absence of the possibility of speculative abuse of inside information, convinces us that section 16(b) should not apply to transactions such as this one—Id. at 1747 (emphasis added).

In the instant case, TI voluntarily entered into the stock purchase agreement with Pan Am before the National–Pan Am merger was effectuated. Despite the alleged lack of access to inside information and therefore the possibility of speculative abuse, the volitional character of the exchange is sufficient reason to trigger applicability of the language of §16(b). For whatever reason, after the National–Pan Am merger had been approved, TI decided to take the initiative for the course of subsequent events into its own hands rather than wait for the merger to become accomplished. These circumstances do not warrant the creation of an exception to automatic §16(b) liability.

Affirmed.

Although dissenters in *Kern* criticized the "subjective" or "pragmatic" approach because it eliminates the objective approach's "bright-line" test for liability and substitutes a requirement that judges decide on an *ad hoc* basis whether there was access to information or voluntariness regarding the decision to sell, a dissenter in the *Texas International* case would have extended the *Kern* rationale to the latter case's facts. Many lower courts seem generally pleased with the opportunity to use the pragmatic approach.

The traditional approach simply asks whether someone meeting the statutory definition of an insider has engaged in short-swing transactions that resulted in a profit. If so, there is a conclusive presumption that inside information was used and abused. *Kern's* approach looks beyond the terminology to the reality of the situation and will not mechanistically apply the rules where they would produce an unfair result. However, as *Texas International* emphasizes, the pragmatic approach is strictly limited to unorthodox transactions. The forced merger remains the classic example of an unorthodox transaction.

A very liberal application of the pragmatic approach occurred in *Gold* v. *Sloan*.[23] The case involved a merger of Atlantic into Susquehanna, wherein the shareholders of Atlantic received Susquehanna stock in exchange for their Atlantic stock. Two directors of Atlantic also became directors of Susquehanna, and within six months of the merger sold their Susquehanna stock. The director who had negotiated the merger on behalf of Atlantic was found liable under §16(b). However, another director who was on bad

---

[23] 486 F.2d 340 (4th Cir. 1973), *cert. denied*, 419 U.S. 873 (1974).

terms with Atlantic's management, took no part in the negotiation of the merger, and had no access to inside information about the merger was held not liable because his acquisition of Susquehanna stock was deemed not to be a "purchase."

When Does a "Purchase" or "Sale" Take Place?

For purposes of determining whether six months have passed between two transactions, it is important to know when a purchase or sale takes place. If the parties are allowed to choose the time that will be the effective date of the purchase or sale, they will be able to frame their transactions so as to evade §16(b) altogether, as is indicated in the following case.

BERSHAD v. McDONOUGH

428 F.2d 693 (7th Cir. 1970), *cert. denied*, 400 U.S. 992 (1971).

On March 15 and 16, 1967, defendant McDonough and his wife each purchased 141,363 shares of Cudahy Company's common stock at $6.75 per share. Soon thereafter, McDonough and two of his business associates were elected to the Cudahy board. On July 20, 1967, the McDonoughs entered into an "option agreement" with Smelting Refining and Mining Co. that granted Smelting the right to purchase 272,000 shares of the McDonoughs' Cudahy stock. Upon execution of the agreement, Smelting paid $350,000. The option was exercisable on or before October 1, 1967. The $350,000 was to be applied to the purchase price of $2,448,000 ($9 per share) if the option was exercised, but was to belong to the McDonoughs if the option was not exercised. Under the agreement, the McDonoughs placed the shares in escrow, and granted Smelting an irrevocable proxy right to vote the shares until October 1. A few days after the option agreement was signed, McDonough and one of his associates resigned from the Cudahy board, and five Smelting representatives joined the board. On September 22, 1967, Smelting indicated that it was exercising the option, and the closing took place

on September 27. The McDonoughs realized a profit of $612,000.

Plaintiff, a Cudahy shareholder, sued under §16(b). Plaintiff prevailed at the trial court and the McDonoughs appealed.

CUMMINGS, CIRCUIT JUDGE:

Under §3(a)(14) of the act . . . , the "sales" covered by §16(b) are broadly defined to include "any contract to sell or otherwise dispose of" any security. [C]ourts have generally concluded that a transaction falls within the ambit of §16(b) if it can reasonably be characterized as a "purchase" or "sale" without doing violence to the language of the statute, and if the transaction is of a kind which can possibly lend itself to the speculation encompassed by §16(b).

The insider should not be permitted to speculate with impunity merely by varying the paper form of his transactions. The commercial substance of the transaction rather than its form must be considered, and courts should guard against sham transactions by which an insider disguises the effective transfer of stock.

The considerations thus guiding the application of §16(b) provide substantial support for coverage of an insider's sale of an option within six months of his purchase of the underlying security. The utility of various stock options as a tool of speculation is well recognized. As noted in *Booth* v. *Varian Association*, 334 F.2d 1, 4 (1st Cir. 1964), certiorari denied, 379 U.S. 961:

> Options, conversions and similar devices have lent themselves quite readily to the abuses uncovered in the Congressional investigation antedating the Act, and in order to give maximum support to the statute courts have attempted to include these transactions by characterizing them as purchases or sales.

The insider's sale of options in his stock is well adapted to speculation and abuse of inside information whether or not the option is subsequently exercised. The sale of the right to purchase the underlying security is itself a means of realizing a profit from that security. The right to purchase stock at a given price under specified circumstances although clearly not identical to the rights attendant upon ownership of the stock itself, derives from and is dependent upon the value of the underlying security. Sale of such purchase rights provides an easy vehicle for the use of inside information in extracting profits from the stock itself. Where the option is ultimately exercised, moreover, the exact date of exercise may be unimportant to the substance of the transaction from the point of view of the insider-vendor, since he can exploit his position in the corporation by setting the terms of sale in the option. In addition, parties frequently provide that the option price shall be considered a retroactive down payment of the purchase price of the stock sold upon exercise of the option. Under such circumstances, it may be reasonable to hold the parties to their own treatment of the transaction and date the "sale" of the stock at the purchase of the option rather than its exercise.

It is unnecessary, however, to rely solely upon these considerations to conclude that the McDonoughs' "sale" of the Cudahy stock to Smelting took place well in advance of the exercise of the option on September 22. The circumstances of the transactions clearly indicate that the stock was effectively transferred, for all practical purposes, long before the exercise of the option. The $350,000 "binder" ostensibly paid for the option represented over 14% of the total purchase price of the stock. Granting the magnitude of the sale contemplated, the size of the initial commitment strongly suggests that it "was not just a binder." The extent of that payment represented, if not the exercise of the option, a significant deterrent to the abandonment of the contemplated sale. In addition, the reverse side of the "Option Agreement" contained provisions for the transfer of the Cudahy stock, endorsed in blank, to an escrow agent pending completion of the transaction. At the same time, the McDonoughs delivered an irrevocable proxy to Smelting to vote the 272,000 shares at any regular or special shareholders' meetings. Within a few days, McDonough and one of his associate directors resigned and were replaced by representatives of Smelting's interests, including the chairman of the board of directors of Smelting, and the president and director of that corporation. Significantly, only a few days later after the expiration of the six-month period from the McDonoughs' purchase of the Cudahy stock, Smelting formally exercised its option, and, on the same day that Smelting mailed its notification, the McDonoughs executed the necessary stock powers.

We conclude that as a matter of law, the sale was effectively accomplished within the six-month period contemplated by §16(b).

Affirmed.

The time at which purchases or sales take place is another issue upon which the courts frequently disagree. Some hold that no purchase takes place until the buyer knows both the amount and the price of the stock. Others hold that the purchase occurs whenever the buyer becomes irrevocably committed to purchase the stock. However, the trend appears to be in the direction of the *McDonough* holding—that the purchase occurs whenever the purchaser agrees to a substantial economic forfeit if it does not take and pay for the stock. Had Smelting not exercised its option, it would have forfeited $350,000 dollars. Once that money was paid, it was a forgone conclusion that the option would be exercised.

"Less Than Six Months"

Section 16(b) requires an insider to forfeit profits realized on transactions occurring "within any period of *less* than six months." This is deemed an approximation of the maximum useful life of inside information that might be abused. Because the courts do not recognize fractions of days under §16(b), the very first minute of the day of the initial transaction must be counted, as must the very last minute of the day of the later transactions with which it is matched. Therefore, stock purchased by an insider on January 3 could safely be sold for a profit on July 2. Every minute of both days is counted, so a full six months has passed, no less. Therefore, the statute has been violated only if the second transaction takes place on or before the day two days prior to the corresponding date six months after the first transaction.

"Profit Realized"

The most striking and perhaps the harshest aspect of §16 is the calculation of the "profits realized" that must be forfeited by an insider in a short-swing transaction. Although there have been numerous suggestions for change, the usual method of calculating the "profit realized" is the "lowest-in, highest-out" method (LIHO). That is, in any six-month period, the court will match the purchase at the lowest price with the sale at the highest price. Then it will match the next lowest in with the next highest out, and so on. Furthermore, all matched transactions that result in a loss are disregarded. Therefore, an insider might sustain a real loss during a series of transactions, but still have to forfeit "profits realized" in accordance with the lowest-in, highest-out method.

For example, assume the following transactions by an insider:

DATE	TRANSACTION	NUMBER OF SHARES	PRICE
(1) Jan. 1	Purchase	100	$60/share
(2) Feb. 1	Sale	100	$50/share
(3) Mar. 1	Purchase	100	$40/share
(4) Apr. 1	Sale	100	$30/share

A quick glance reveals that the insider was engaged in two losing transactions. The "real" result of this series of transactions was a loss of $2,000. However, under the LIHO method, transaction 3 (the lowest in) is matched with transaction 2 (the highest out), to produce a $1,000 profit. The matching of transactions 1 and 4 produces a loss, but this is ignored.

To show how harsh this method of calculation can be, in *Gratz* v. *Claughton*,[24] an insider lost around $400,000 in a series of transactions. Yet, by using the LIHO method of calculating damages, the court ordered the defendant to forfeit an additional $300,000.

Use of the LIHO method is not always deemed appropriate. For example, in *Reece Corp.* v. *Walco National Corp.*,[25] mentioned earlier, Walco bought Reece stock in eight separate transactions after becoming a 10% holder. It then tried to sell its stock in two separate transactions, one day apart. The first transaction brought Walco's holdings to just under 10%, and the price was pegged at $8.75 per share, less than the $10.38 average Walco had paid for the shares. The second transaction that liquidated the remainder of Walco's holdings was at $13.71 per share. The court lumped the two transactions together, deeming them a single sale at an average of $12 per share. In calculating damages, the court said the LIHO method was "designed to deal with completely different problems from those in the present case." The court calculated liability by using the average prices of the purchases and sales, reaching a gross figure of $122,700.

The court in the *Walco* case went on to make other relevant points regarding calculation of damages. The courts are split as to whether dividends received on stock traded in short-swing transactions must be forfeited. No dividends were paid on the stock in *Walco*, so the point was moot. Most courts will allow defendants to deduct expenses, such as brokerage fees, incurred in making transactions. The court allowed Walco to deduct $5,342 in brokerage commissions, reducing the damages to a net profit of $117,358.

Courts also have discretion to award prejudgment interest. Most courts decline to do so, as did the court in *Walco*.

Procedure for Enforcement

Who can bring a §16(b) action to require insiders to return "profits realized"? The SEC cannot. Although the SEC sets the reporting requirements of §16(a) and has the power to exempt transactions from §16(b), it has no enforcement powers to force disgorgement of short-swing profits.

Management of the corporation has the power to bring such actions, but it frequently chooses not to do so. The very directors and officers who must make the decision to sue are the insiders who may well be defendants in such an action. They are understandably reluctant to authorize suit against themselves or their peers.

---

[24] 187 F.2d 46 (2d Cir.), cert. denied, 341 U.S. 920 (1951).
[25] 565 F.Supp. 158 (S.D.N.Y. 1983).

A shareholder has the right to demand that management bring a §16(b) suit. If management refuses or fails to act within 60 days of the demand, the shareholder can initiate the action. The 60-day waiting requirement is waived if the statute of limitations is about to run out or the defendant so dominates the corporate management that the request to sue would be futile. But the shareholder has little apparent incentive to sue because any recovery goes into the corporate treasury, and the individual shareholder's benefit will be indirect and probably minuscule.

The courts have remedied the apparent lack of incentive for bringing a §16(b) action by liberally awarding attorney fees. The precedent was set in *Smolowe* v. *Delendo Corp.*, where the court said

> The total recovery against defendants accruing to the corporation is $18,894.85, plus costs of $48.93. By this, plaintiffs will be benefited only to the extent of about $3, since they own but 150 shares of a total of 800,000. Upon their petition, however, the district court awarded them $3,000 for counsel fees, together with their expenses of $78.98, payable out of the funds accruing to the corporation.
>
> • • •
>
> And a stockholder who is successful in maintaining such an action is entitled to reimbursement for reasonable attorney's fees on the theory that the corporation which has received the benefit of the attorney's services should pay the reasonable value thereof. . . .
>
> While the allowance made here was quite substantial, we are not disposed to interfere with the district court's well-considered determination. Since in many cases such as this the possibility of recovering attorney's fees will provide the sole stimulus for the enforcement of §16(b), the allowance must not be too niggardly.

The courts have not been stingy in awarding attorneys' fees in §16(b) cases. Awards in six figures have been granted.[26]

Many attorneys have been encouraged to specialize in §16(b) actions. The fee awards are liberal. Furthermore, one need not be a shareholder of the corporation at the time of the violation. A person who learns of a violation can then purchase a single share of the corporation's stock and become entitled to make a demand that a §16(b) action be filed.

Investigation is easy; the §16(a) reports that are filed regularly with the SEC are public documents disclosing the dates of transactions, number of shares, and prices. Federal courts have exclusive jurisdiction over §16(b) actions. The 1934 Act provides for liberal venue and nationwide service of process. Suit can be brought in any federal district where a violation occurred, or where defendant is found or inhabits, or where an exchange is located if the violation occurred through an exchange transaction. Such suits are usually brought in the Southern District of New York, where most of the §16(b) bar resides.

---

[26] For example, *Newmark* v. *RKO General, Inc.*, 332 F.Supp. 161 (S.D.N.Y. 1971) ($750,000); *Lewis* v. *Chapman*, Federal Securities Law Report (CCH), ¶95,887 (S.D.N.Y. 1977) ($275,000).

QUESTIONS AND PROBLEMS

1. Between early 1981 and November 1982, Crane Co. gradually acquired 1,733,220 (22.4%) of the shares of Ferro Corporation at prices ranging from $22 to $27 per share. On November 3, 1982, Ferro started negotiating to repurchase the shares held by Crane; a tentative price of $30.30 per share was negotiated. However, Crane then decided that price was inadequate, because of its §16(b) liability on approximately 165,000 of the shares that had been acquired within the previous six months. Ferro then agreed to pay $31.03 per share, which resulted in an additional payment to Crane of $1,260,975, which matched Crane's §16(b) liability. The transaction was finalized on November 8, 1982, whereupon Ferro demanded a return of Crane's short-swing profits, and Crane delivered a check of $1,260,725. Some Ferro shareholders then brought a §16(b) suit alleging that the transaction constituted an illegal waiver of short-swing profits. Discuss. See *Sterman* v. *Ferro Corp.*, 785 F.2d 162 (6th Cir. 1986).

2. Assume that an insider exercised virtually complete control of his mother's business affairs due to a power of attorney. He felt free to utilize his mother's assets as his own. Discuss the insider's §16(b) liability when he trades shares owned by his mother, not himself, for a short-swing profit. See *Whittaker* v. *Whittaker Corp.*, 639 F.2d 516 (9th Cir.), *cert. denied*, 454 U.S. 1031 (1981).

3. Horton, a director of CBI, as trustee for his children, purchased shares of CBI stock within six months of a sale of his own CBI stock. A short-swing profit occurred if the sales are matched. While Horton controlled the trust, he did not benefit directly from it. His sons were college aged, living away from home. Should the sales be matched? Discuss. *CBI Industries* v. *Horton*, 682 F.2d 643 (7th Cir. 1982).

4. After General Cinema purchased 9.7% of Old Heublein, Old Heublein sued, claiming that General Cinema's Schedule 13D was defective because it did not disclose an intent to control. General Cinema continued to accumulate Old Heublein shares, and the corporations entered into negotiations in an attempt to settle their dispute without further litigation. Eventually General Cinema purchased 18.9% of Old Heublein before the latter's board approved a defensive merger with R. J. Reynolds Co. Old Heublein's shareholders approved the merger with Reynolds, though General Cinema voted its shares against it. Pursuant to the merger, General Cinema's holdings in Old Heublein were automatically swapped for Reynolds stock at an alleged profit of $74 million, $30 million of which was "short swing." Discuss the application of §16(b)'s "subjective" approach for unorthodox transactions to this case. See *Heublein, Inc.*, v. *General Cinema Corp.*, 722 F.2d 29 (2d Cir. 1983).

5. Assume that a director of a major corporation purchased 1,600 shares of the corporation's stock on December 22, 1970. On January 3, 1971, he retired as a director. On February 2, 1971 and March 26, 1971, he purchased 21,400 more shares. Finally, on July 6, 1971, he sold 6,300 shares at a much greater price than he had paid in the earlier transactions. Calculate the extent of his §16(b) liability. See *Lewis* v. *Vranes*, 505 F.2d 785 (2d Cir. 1974).

6. In 1972 and 1973, Gund, a director of First Florida Banks, Inc., purchased First Federal convertible debentures. He also owned First Federal common stock. In early 1974, the market for the debentures declined, and the market for common stock declined even further. From July 1976 until March 1977, Gund sold his entire bond holdings and used the proceeds to purchase 77,000 shares of First Federal common stock. Had he simply converted the debentures he would have received 49,895 shares of common. So, by selling as he did, he gained 50% more shares than he would have through simple conversion. In a subsequent §16(b) action, Gund argued that this was an "unorthodox" transaction calling for application of the "subjective" or "pragmatic" approach. It is conceded that Gund did not actually use inside information in making his trades. Discuss potential liability. See *Gund* v. *First Florida Banks, Inc.*, 726 F.2d 682 (11th Cir. 1984).

7. Reliance Corporation owned 3,198,233 shares of Walt Disney Productions Corporation in April 1984 when it instructed its broker to purchase an additional 1,000,000 shares of Disney. The broker purchased those shares for Reliance from several sources over several days, and then transferred formal title to the entire 1,000,000 shares on May 1, 1984. This transaction increased Reliance's share of Disney stock from 9.3% to 12.2%. On June 22, 1984, Reliance sold the 1,000,000 shares back to Disney at a profit of at least $5.20 per share. Plaintiff shareholders of Disney brought a §16(b) suit against Reliance, claiming that Reliance reached the 10% threshold as soon as the broker purchased 252,000 shares for its account, and therefore that Reliance is subject to §16(b) liability for the 748,000 shares purchased thereafter. Reliance argues, however, that its block purchase was a single transaction, and that it bought no shares after it became a 10% holder. Evaluate these positions. See *Piano Remittance Corp.* v. *Reliance Financial Services Corp.*, 618 F.Supp. 414 (S.D.N.Y. 1985).

8. Defendant Trueblood was president of Consolidated and a 61% owner of Petroleum Service (PS). On June 15, 1979, PS sold 3,000 shares of Consolidated for $41,706.06 ($13.90 per share). The net benefit to Trueblood's holdings was $25,440.70 (1,830 shares). On August 6 and August 10, 1979, Trueblood exercised nonqualified Consolidated stock options, buying 10,000 shares of Consolidated at $6.9375 per share. The aggregate difference between the price of 1,830 sold on June 15 and the 1,830 bought in August was $12,745.07. A Consolidated shareholder brought suit to recover that amount. Trueblood argued that this sum was not profit because he incurred "incentive income" within the meaning of §83 of the Internal Revenue Code of $13,953.75 that he was required to report as ordinary income and which raised his basis in the stock to $14.625 per share for income tax purposes. He claims he actually lost $.6626 per share. Discuss. See *Morales* v. *Consolidated Oil & Gas, Inc.*, Federal Securities Law Reports (CCH), ¶98,796 (S.D.N.Y. 1982).

20

INSIDER TRADING:
SECTION 10(b)
AND RULE 10b–5

INTRODUCTION

In Chapter 18, §10(b) and Rule 10b-5 were discussed as vehicles for preventing and punishing fraud in "corporate disclosure" cases. A second major type of 10b-5 case is the insider trading case. Section 16 is Congress' most obvious response to the perceived problem of insider trading. The legislative history of §10(b) is so sparse that it is impossible to conclude with any certainty that Congress intended it to be used as a tool against insider trading.

Nonetheless, Rule 10b-5 was written in response to a situation involving insider trading. Despite the sometimes strict nature of §16, its loopholes and limitations are significant. Flagrant insider trading abuses continue. Some statistical studies show that insiders do better in the trading of their company's stock than do outsiders, even where the outsiders are professional stock analysts. Therefore, over the past 20 years the SEC and the courts have molded Rule 10b-5 into an oft-used weapon against insider trading.

Because §10(b) and Rule 10b-5 were created with little fanfare and explanation, court decisions provide most of the guidelines in this legal area. Indeed, the study of Rule 10b-5 as a tool against insider trading must be based upon an analysis of important cases. Unfortunately the Supreme Court has seldom spoken on issues in this area. There-fore, there is still much conflict and uncertainty as the law of insider trading continues to develop. As this chapter is written, the SEC lists enforcement of insider trading restrictions as one of its top priorities. Over the years, some have challenged bans on insider trading. These critics argue not only that insider trading is very difficult to prevent, but also that it should not be discouraged because, in part, it provides an effective means of compensation for corporation executives. The SEC's view of the purposes and prospects of insider trading prohibitions is discussed in the following excerpt from an article written by an SEC Commissioner.

"SEC BATTLE AGAINST INSIDER TRADING IS WORTH THE EFFORT" *

Bevis Longstreth

Legal Times of Washington, May 10, 1982, at 16, col. 1.

Why Prohibit Insider Trading?

The prohibition against insider trading rests principally on the notion of fairness—both specifically in the operation of the marketplace and generally as an ethical concept. This notion is embedded in the preamble and findings of the Securities Exchange Act. The purpose of that act was to provide regulations to "prevent inequitable and unfair practices" in the marketplace for securities and "to insure the maintenance of fair and honest markets. . . ."

There are two aspects to a fair securities market in the economic sense. One is the egalitarian notion that to the maximum extent feasible, all investors should have equal access to material information. The other, based on pricing efficiency, is that a fair securities market should promptly and accurately value securities on the basis of all relevant information. Rules against insider trading clearly further the goal of equal access. However, these rules further the goal of efficiency only if they foster a larger amount of prompt disclosure than would occur if insider trading were permitted. Let's take a closer look at these two aspects of fairness.

Rules designed reasonably to assure equal access to information promote investor confidence. When insiders cannot derive special advantages from managing the flow of material information to the market, investors can participate with assurance that the game is fair and skills of analysis, applied to the information available, will have a fair chance of resulting in profits. The investing public does not demand profit guarantees before investing, just equal access to all relevant information to permit it to compete fairly in the marketplace. Obviously, if insiders are permitted to trade on undisclosed information, they can appropriate to themselves profits that otherwise potentially are available to all investors.

Promoting the goal of equal access redounds to the benefit of issuers as well. Investor confidence facilitates capital formation by encouraging greater participation in the primary securities markets. Moreover, if insiders were free to appropriate the value of inside information to themselves—in short, to take secret profits—the issuer would be forced to prove a higher overall rate of return on its securities to compensate investors for the profits siphoned off by insiders.

---

* Copyright 1982 by Legal Times of Washington, Inc. Reprinted with permission. This excerpt is drawn from a speech given by Mr. Longstreth in Washington, D.C. At the time, he was a Commissioner of the SEC.

Of course, no one really knows for sure what will be the magnitude of these consequences. Some believe that permitting insider trading would destroy public confidence in the fairness of the securities market, would impair substantially capital formation. These advocates carry the fairness argument beyond the limits of empirical evidence. One need not be able to establish the likelihood of such harmful consequences to feel strongly that the prohibition is warranted.

Some have argued that a prohibition against insider trading fosters prompt disclosure and thereby serves the goal of market efficiency. To trade effectively on inside information, the insider must delay disclosure of material corporate events until he has traded. The insider, then, has an incentive to withhold information needed by the marketplace to price the issuer's securities accurately. By prohibiting insider trading, the insider's incentive to avoid prompt disclosure is removed. . . .

The prohibition against insider trading also rests on powerful notions of fairness as a matter of ethics. We should not lose sight of one simple truth that transcends the technicalities of the lawyer and economist—insider trading offends the basic notions of fairness important to our society. There has grown up a general ethical consensus in the business community that insider trading is improper, and this notion is not peculiar only to dewy-eyed Americans. In virtually every free nation that has considered the issue in any formal way, the consensus is that insider trading is wrong. Judgments as to what to do about it may vary, but in no case is it generally considered that insider trading is an acceptable practice.

Arguments Against Prohibition

There persists a small body of opinion—largely economic—that holds our prohibitions against insider trading to be misconceived and counterproductive. In support of this view a number of points are often made:

• Insider trading hurts no one, at least in market transactions, because the innocent sellers and buyers who indirectly trade with the insider come to the transaction voluntarily. Since the price was right for them anyway, they have no reason to complain. And the market impact of inside trading is always in the direction of more accurate pricing.

• Insider trading is the only effective way of rewarding the entrepreneur whose unique talents are critically important to the success of modern business corporations.

• Even if insider trading is wrong, it is so pervasive and hard to detect that there is no way to control it without using methods so drastic and expensive that their costs will far exceed the benefits achieved.

After all, there is no evidence that insider trading harms the capital formation process or chills the willingness of investors to invest in securities.

Let us consider these arguments in detail.

Though it is true that people will make independent decisions to buy or sell securities while unaware of confidential information, this does not mean that they should be deprived of the fair value of their investments. Misappropriation of profits is no less wrong because the profits were not anticipated. Investors assume that they will be able to make investment decisions on the basis of all relevant information. To deny them this opportunity harms them.

Aside from security holders, other market participants may be harmed by insider trading. Issuers, for example, may find it more difficult—and therefore more expensive—to raise capital if insiders are siphoning off secret profits through informational advantages.

Perhaps the most dramatic example of harm is that done to market professionals.

The public securities markets are structured very much like an hourglass: masses of anonymous buyers and sellers at the top and bottom, with a small group of professional traders—specialists or market makers—occupying the narrow junction.

Under the rules of the commission and the self-regulatory organizations, specialists and market makers have a legal obligation to participate in—and thereby facilitate—everyday trading in securities. They constitute a cadre of ever-willing buyers and sellers who give the markets continuity, liquidity, and depth. If these professionals unknowingly trade with insiders armed with confidential information, they are exposed to severe losses because they cannot make rational pricing decisions. One good example of this type of harm is the plight of the options specialist who writes, for his own account, options to sell to public traders. In the recent Santa Fe take-over situation, several options specialists were bankrupted by having to honor commitments to insiders that would never have been made if the facts were known.

Some people feel that insider trading is an appropriate reward for entrepreneurs. However, the defects in this theory are numerous, including:

- the inability to identify the particular individual responsible for a given price rise in the stock of a large corporation and restrict the resulting benefit to him;
- the uncontrollable size of this reward, related as it is to the size of the company's float and to the entrepreneur's investment, rather than to the quality of his contribution;
- the irony of permitting the insider—through short selling and options trading—to benefit as much from bad as from good management.
- the inappropriateness of extracting a corporate manager's reward directly from the pockets of the shareholders rather than from the corporate treasury; and,
- the incongruity of permitting the blessings of good management or a friendly take-over to be captured chiefly by the insiders, limited only by their financial ability to make the necessary investment.

Few, if any, commentators have seriously endorsed this concept since it was espoused by Henry Manne in 1966.

Is Controlling Insider Trading Worth It?

Here is perhaps the most serious basis on which to question prohibitions against insider trading. As mentioned earlier, both the scholarly and popular press have suggested that the fight cannot be won at a reasonable cost. There is abundant evidence that insider trading exists, despite its illegality and the efforts of the commission to control it. What we do not know with accuracy is the extent of insider trading and the separate deterrent effects of its illegality, the likelihood of getting caught and the penalties to which one is likely to become subject if he is caught. It is equally possible, and not inconsistent with the first possibility, that enormous amounts of insider trading are occurring daily. Finally, it is possible that changes in the monitoring, enforcement and sanctioning process—either to strengthen or weaken it—could alter the commission's effectiveness dramatically one way or another.

Before trying to answer this question for the future, it is necessary to evaluate the commission's past effectiveness in the fight against insider trading. Viewed with some historical perspective, its past efforts to control insider trading have been a marked success.

Throughout the first half of the twentieth century whether trading for their own account or as fiduciaries, investors commonly used inside information in the investment process. Access to non-public information was a critically important tool to the investor—more important, in fact, than skill, industry and foresight. Fiduciaries and other money managers often were chosen precisely because of their multiple positions on the boards of corporations and the ready access to corporate developments that these positions allowed.

Since 1942, when Rule 10b-5 was issued, there has been a vast shift in the perception of the financial community as to what is right and what is wrong—what is legal and what is illegal—what is appropriate and what is inappropriate—in the use of material non-public information.

The evidence of this dramatic change is all around us. Boards of directors of public companies have adopted and enforced policies against insider trading. The stock exchanges and other self-regulatory organizations are on record with clear policies concerning the practice. Investment advisers, broker-dealers and banks have developed policies against insider trading and procedures for policing those policies, including Chinese walls where necessary to permit multi-purpose firms to continue their business. Investment companies and other institutional investors have likewise adopted formal policies prohibiting insider trading. And law firms and accounting firms have followed suit.

The breadth of these changes is cogent evidence of a basic shift in perception which places insider trading outside the bounds of lawful, or even ethical, behavior. These changes did not just happen. The commission made them happen. Through a combination of rule-making, monitoring, hectoring, lecturing and enforcing, the commission succeeded in bending the norms of business behavior toward the "disclose or refrain from trading" rule.

"DISCLOSE OR ABSTAIN"

It is impossible to ensure that every individual trades on an exactly equal basis. Some investors are more sophisticated than others. Some can react more quickly to important information. Some are more vigilant in tracking potential developments. Still, if the federal securities laws are to protect investor confidence in the market and advance the causes of equity and fairness, insiders must be prevented from trading on the basis of important information that no person outside the corporation could know about. Only an analysis of the development of the case law can illuminate the details and limitations of the law of insider trading.

An appropriate case with which to commence this analysis is the SEC proceeding in *Cady, Roberts & Co.*, which was the SEC's first major attempt to use Rule 10b-5 to stifle insider trading.

CADY, ROBERTS & CO.

40 S.E.C. 907 (1961)

On the morning of November 25, 1969, the board of directors of Curtiss-Wright met and voted to cut dividends substantially from what had been paid during the previous three quar- *ters. At approximately 11:00 A.M., the board authorized transmission of this information via telegram to the New York Stock Exchange. Because of certain transmission problems, this in-*

formation was not delivered to the Exchange until 12:29 P.M. The Wall Street Journal was not given the information until 11:45 A.M., and it did not appear on the Dow Jones ticker tape until 11:48 A.M.

After making the decision about dividends, the board recessed. During the recess, one of the directors, Cowdin, telephoned the offices of a brokerage firm registered with the SEC, Cady, Roberts & Co. (registrant) and left a message for one of its partners, Gintel, that the dividend had been cut. Cowdin was also a registered representative of Cady. As soon as he received this information, Gintel entered sell orders on behalf of Cady's clients. The sell orders were executed at 11:15 A.M. and 11:48 A.M. at 40¼ and 40⅜, respectively. When the dividend announcement appeared on the Dow Jones tape at 11:48 A.M., so many investors tried to sell that the Exchange had to suspend trading in Curtiss-Wright stock. Eventually trading was resumed, and Curtiss-Wright stock closed the day at 34⅞.

The SEC later brought administrative proceedings to determine whether the brokerage firm and Gintel, its selling broker, willfully violated §10(b) and Rule 10b-5, as well as §17(a) of the 1933 Act, by trading on inside information not generally available.

CARY, CHAIRMAN:

The crucial question is what are the duties of such a broker after receiving nonpublic information as to a company's dividend action from a director who is employed by the same brokerage firm.

. . .

Section 17 and Rule 10b-5 apply to securities transactions by "any person." Misrepresentations will lie within their ambit, no matter who the speaker may be. An affirmative duty to dis-close material information has been traditionally imposed on corporate "insiders," particularly officers, directors, or controlling stockholders. We, and the courts, have consistently held that insiders must disclose material facts which are known to them by virtue of their position but which are not known to persons with whom they deal and which, if known, would affect their investment judgment. Failure to make disclosure in these circumstances constitutes a violation of the antifraud provisions. If, on the other hand, disclosure prior to effecting a purchase or sale would be improper or unrealistic under the circumstances, we believe the alternative is to forgo the transaction.

The ingredients are here and we accordingly find that Gintel willfully violated §17(a) and 10(b) and Rule 10b-5. We also find a similar violation by the registrant, since the actions of Gintel, a member of registrant, in the course of his employment are to be regarded as actions of registrant itself. It was obvious that a reduction in the quarterly dividend by the Board of Directors was a material fact which could be expected to have an adverse impact on the market price of the company's stock. The rapidity with which Gintel acted upon receipt of the information confirms his own recognition of that conclusion.

We have already noted that the antifraud provisions are phrased in terms of "any person" and that a special obligation has been traditionally required of corporate insiders, for example, officers, directors, and controlling stockholders. These three groups, however, do not exhaust the classes of persons upon whom there is such an obligation. Analytically, the obligation rests on two principal elements: first, the existence of a relationship giving access, directly or indirectly, to information intended to be available only for a corporate purpose and not for the personal benefit of anyone, and, second, the inherent unfairness involved where a party takes advantage of such information knowing it is unavailable to those with whom he is dealing. In considering these elements under the broad language of the antifraud provisions, we are not to be circumscribed by fine distinctions and rigid classifications. Thus our task here is to identify those persons who are in a special relationship with a company and privy to its internal affairs, and thereby suffer correlative duties in trading in its securities. Intimacy demands restraint lest the uninformed be exploited.

The facts here impose on Gintel the responsibilities of those commonly referred to as "insiders." He received the information prior to its public release from a director of Curtiss-Wright, Cowdin, who was associated with the registrant. Cowdin's relationship to the company clearly prohibited him from selling the securities affected by the information about disclosure. By logical sequence, it should prohibit Gintel, a partner of the registrant. This prohibition extends not only over his own account, but to selling for discretionary accounts and soliciting and executing other orders. In somewhat analogous circumstances, we have charged a broker-dealer who effects securities transactions for an insider and knows that the insider possesses nonpublic material information with the affirmative duty to make appropriate disclosures or dissociate himself from the transaction.

· · ·

We cannot accept respondents' contention that an insider's responsibility is limited to existing stockholders and that he has no special duties when sales of securities are made to nonstockholders. This approach is too narrow. It ignores the plight of the buying public—wholly unprotected from the misuse of special information.

Neither the statutes nor Rule 10b-5 establish artificial walls of responsibility. Section 17 of the Securities Act explicitly states that it shall be unlawful for any person in the offer or sale of securities to do certain prescribed acts. Although the primary function of Rule 10b-5 was to extend a remedy to a defrauded seller, the courts and this Commission have held that it is also applicable to a defrauded buyer. There is no valid reason why persons who *purchase* stock from an officer, director, or other person having the responsibilities of an "insider" should not have the same protection afforded by disclosure of special information as persons who *sell* stock to them. Whatever distinctions may have existed at common law based on the view that an officer or director may stand in a fiduciary relationship to existing stockholders from whom he purchases but not to members of the public to whom he sells, it is clearly not appropriate to introduce these into the broader antifraud concepts embodied in the securities acts.

Respondents further assert that they made no express representations and did not in any way manipulate the market, and urge that in a transaction on an exchange there is no further duty such as may be required in a "face-to-face" transaction. We reject this suggestion. It would be anomalous indeed if the protection afforded by the antifraud provisions were withdrawn from transactions effected on exchanges, primary markets for securities transactions. If purchasers on an exchange had available material information known by a selling insider, we may assume that their investment judgment would be affected and their decision whether to buy might accordingly be modified. Consequently, any sales by the insider must await disclosure of the information.

· · ·

[I]t is further alleged that [Gintel] had a fiduciary duty to these accounts to continue the sales, which overrode any obligations to unsolicited purchasers on the Exchange. . . . [W]hile Gintel undoubtedly occupied a fiduciary relationship to his customers, this relationship could not justify any actions by him contrary to law. Even if we assume the existence of conflicting fiduciary obligations, there can be no doubt which is primary here. On these facts, clients may not expect of a broker the benefits of his inside information at the expense of the public generally.

[Because the Commission decided that Cowdin probably assumed when he called Gintel that the information was already public and Gintel then reacted spontaneously to the news intending primarily to benefit existing customers of Cady, Roberts & Co., Gintel was suspended from the New York Stock Exchange for only 20 days and the registrant received no sanction.]

Several very important points are made in the *Cady, Roberts* case. Foremost among these is promulgation of the "disclose or abstain" rule. If insiders possess material, nonpublic information that cannot feasibly be made public, they must refrain from trading. Furthermore, this duty extends not only to the traditional categories of insiders—officers, directors, and controlling stockholders—but also to "tippees" such as defendants in the case who were not insiders themselves but received valuable information from an insider. *Cady, Roberts* also held that this duty to disclose or abstain stems from two factors—existence of a relationship giving access to inside information and the inherent unfairness involved when a party takes advantage of such information in trading with a party who does not have access to it. As we shall see, the Supreme Court has not fully accepted this second factor.

It is also very important that *Cady, Roberts* held that Rule 10b-5 protected not just persons who dealt with defendants in face-to-face transactions, but also persons who traded at the same time on the impersonal securities exchanges. This involves somewhat of a legal fiction. The persons who bought Curtiss-Wright stock at the same time Gintel was selling would probably have made those same purchases, and thus been injured in the same manner, even if Gintel had not disclosed the information and simply refrained from trading. The actions of Gintel did not *cause* these persons to buy. Nonetheless, only by holding such persons injured by Gintel's conduct can Rule 10b-5 be effectively enforced in the extremely important exchange transactions.

The "disclose or abstain" rule was applied by the court in *SEC* v. *Texas Sulphur Co.*[1] In November 1963, Texas Gulf Sulphur Co. (TGS) drilled a core sample in a Canadian tract that was so rich in minerals none of the TGS experts had ever seen or heard of its like. The company attempted to keep information about the core sample quiet while it went about leasing adjoining tracts of land. However, between November 12, 1963, when the drilling of the core was completed, and March 31, 1964, when test drilling was resumed, several insiders of TGS and their tippees had purchased TGS shares or options to buy such shares. These insiders included mineral engineers, geologists, vice-presidents, and directors of TGS.

The additional drilling confirmed the discovery of an extraordinary body of ore. Even as the discovery was announced in a press release issued on April 16, 1964,

---

[1] 401 F.2d 833 (2d Cir. 1968).

insiders continued to buy. One ordered shares at midnight on April 15 and at 8:30 A.M. on April 16. Another ordered shares at 10:40 A.M. on April 16. The press release was made at 9:40 A.M. on April 16, but did not appear on Merrill Lynch's private wire until 10:29 A.M. or on the Dow Jones ticker tape until 10:54 A.M.

TGS stock, which had been selling at about 17 when the drilling began in November 1963, was selling at 29 on April 15, 1964, at 36 the next day, and at 58 by May 15, 1964.

Although TGS itself was not held liable, because it had a good business reason to keep the information secret, its insiders who traded on the information were held liable. The Second Circuit eagerly followed the rationale of *Cady, Roberts*, stating that:

> Rule 10b-5 was promulgated pursuant to the grant of authority given the SEC by Congress in Section 10(b) of the Securities Exchange Act of 1934. By that Act Congress purposed to prevent inequitable and unfair practices and to insure fairness in securities transactions generally, whether conducted face-to-face, over the counter, or on exchanges. . . . The Act and the Rule apply to the transactions here, all of which were consummated on exchanges.
>
> . . . The essence of the Rule is that anyone who, trading for his own account in the securities of a corporation has "access, directly or indirectly, to information intended to be available only for a corporate purpose and not for the personal benefit of anyone" may not take "advantage of such information knowing it is unavailable to those with whom he is dealing," i.e., the investing public—*Matter of Cady, Roberts & Co.*, 40 SEC 907, 912 (1961). Insiders, as directors or management officers are, of course, by this Rule, precluded from so unfairly dealing, but the Rule is also applicable to one possessing the information who may not be strictly termed an "insider" within the meaning of Sec. 16(b) of the Act—*Cady, Roberts*, supra. Thus, anyone in possession of inside information must either disclose it to the investing public, or, if he is disabled from disclosing it in order to protect a corporate confidence, or he chooses not to do so, must abstain from trading in or recommending the securities concerned while such inside information remains undisclosed. So, it is here no justification for insider activity that disclosure was forbidden by the legitimate corporate objective of acquiring options to purchase the land surrounding the exploration site; if the information was, as the SEC contends, material, its possessors should have kept out of the market until disclosure was accomplished.

To the extent that the *Texas Gulf Sulphur* opinion hints that mere access to or possession of inside information is sufficient to subject one to the duty to disclose or abstain, it is no longer good law. Nonetheless, this remains an important decision that presents a classic example of how insider trading problems can occur. "Disclose or abstain" is the basic 10b-5 rule on insider trading; we must now turn to how the rule is enforced, defined, and limited.

SEC ENFORCEMENT

Unlike with §16(b), under §10(b) and Rule 10b-5 the SEC can play an active role in enforcement of insider trading prohibitions. The Commission has three primary avenues of enforcement. First, several potential defendants, such as broker-dealers and underwriters, are registered with the SEC and must receive SEC permission to carry out their normal functions. The SEC has the power to take administrative actions against such defendants, as it did in the *Cady, Roberts* case.

Second, the SEC can go to court to enjoin illegal insider trading that it believes is occurring. The federal courts, which have exclusive jurisdiction over §10(b) cases, have the power to issue orders forcing disgorgement of profit and imposing penalties, as shall be explored later. In bringing such actions, the SEC benefits from an exception to the "purchaser or seller" requirement normally present in private 10b-5 suits.

Third, in egregious cases, the SEC can refer cases to the Department of Justice for criminal prosecution. Under §32 of the 1934 Act, any intentional violation of *any* provision of the 1934 Act is a criminal act. As insider trading has become an increasingly important priority for the SEC, it has sought more criminal prosecutions and stiffer penalties.

THE PRIVATE CAUSE OF ACTION

A private cause of action under Rule 10b-5 has both disadvantages and advantages when compared to the §16(b) remedy for insider trading. On the one hand, Rule 10b-5 has much broader application than does §16(b). It applies to trading in the stock of all companies, not just those registered under the 1934 Act. A cause of action can be brought by almost any injured party, without the requirement of the first making demand upon the subject corporation to bring suit. Damages, if recovered, go to the plaintiff not the corporation. The field of potential defendants, as shall be seen shortly, is much wider than the statutory "insiders" subject to §16(b).

On the other hand, the plaintiff in a Rule 10b-5 suit does not benefit from an automatic presumption that defendant used inside information. Rather, the plaintiff must carry the burden of proof to establish the elements of a 10b-5 claim. These elements are nearly identical to those discussed in the 10b-5 corporate disclosure cases in Chapter 18.

Misrepresentation or Omission of Facts

The element of deception needed for an insider trading claim comes from a breach of the duty to disclose or abstain. If a defendant with a duty to disclose or abstain engages in a transaction with someone who does not have access to the same important inside information that defendant has, the resulting unfairness satisfies the fraud element.

Material, Nonpublic Information

Not every bit of information that an insider has which an outsider does not will be deemed "material." The basic definition of materiality discussed in Chapter 18—that the information be of such a nature that there is a substantial likelihood that a reasonable investor would consider it important in making an investment decision—applies here. The Second Circuit in the *Texas Gulf Sulphur* case made this helpful comment:

> An insider is not, of course, always foreclosed from investing in his own company merely because he may be more familiar with company operations than are outside investors. An insider's duty to disclose information or his duty to abstain from dealing in his company's securities arises only in "those situations which are essentially extraordinary in nature and which are reasonably certain to have a substantial effect on the market price of the security if disclosed." [2]

This definition was recently applied to allow a former employee, a manufacturing engineer, to sell his stock in a computer corporation without suffering a §10(b) penalty. Although the employer had been seeking to develop a revolutionary flat-panel display screen for computers and the former employee had been involved in the work, the evidence showed that no technological breakthrough had occurred and the former employee knew nothing important that was not public knowledge. [3]

Material information may be "corporate inside information," such as changes in actual or projected earnings, changes in assets, proposed dividends, or proposed financings. It may also consist of what has been denominated "market information," which deals with the demand for a corporation's stock. For example, among the most valuable of all insider trading information is that relating to proposed mergers or tender offers, which can dramatically affect the value of a company's stock. What about market information that even insiders do not know about? What if, for example, a judge's law clerk knows that a judge is about to issue a decision in a major antitrust lawsuit that will greatly favor Company A. Even Company A's officers and directors have no knowledge of the information. Is this "inside information" for purposes of Rule 10b-5? The law is unclear, but it is certainly a possibility.

In addition to being material, the information must, of course, be nonpublic. The major question here is: When has the information been effectively disclosed? For example, in the *Texas Gulf Sulphur* case, a press release was issued at 9:20 A.M., and insiders placed orders at 10:40 A.M. The court found liability, although the purchases occurred after the making of the press release, holding that "at the minimum [the insider] should have waited until the news could reasonably have been expected to appear over the media of widest circulation, the Dow Jones broad tape."

Scienter

As in corporate disclosure cases, scienter is an element of a 10b-5 insider trading cause of action. For example, if a tippee has traded on material, nonpublic information, the

---

[2] *SEC* v. *Texas Gulf Sulphur Co.*, 401 F.2d 833 (2d Cir. 1968), quoting A. Fleischer, "Securities Trading and Corporate Information Practices," *Virginia Law Review*, Vol. 51 (1965), p. 1271.

[3] *Abatemarco* v. *Copytele, Inc.*, 608 F.Supp. 2 (E.D.N.Y. 1985).

court must be able to say that the tippee knew *or should have known* that he or she was trading on illicitly obtained inside information before imposing liability.

Reliance, Causation, Privity

The courts are split on the proper role of the elements of reliance, causation, and privity in 10b-5 insider trading cases. This will become clear when we discuss who can sue under 10b-5, who can be sued, and what damages can be awarded in the next three sections of this chapter. For now it is sufficient to note that many courts have dramatically altered these requirements to make it easier for private plaintiffs to recover.

WHO IS LIABLE?

A wide variety of persons have been held liable under Rule 10b-5 for violating insider trading proscriptions. In *Cady, Roberts*, the SEC pointed out that liability may extend beyond traditional ''insiders''—officers, directors, and controlling shareholders. *Cady, Roberts, Texas Gulf Sulphur*, and many other decisions have included tippees of insiders in the category of potential defendants. Tippees must be covered so that insiders do not accomplish indirectly that which they cannot accomplish directly. Furthermore, tippees of tippees (second-generation tippees) must also be covered; otherwise, a woman who received a tip from an insider could simply pass the tip on to her husband who could trade with impunity.

Persons whose ''special relationship'' to the issuer gives them unfair access to inside information, such as investment bankers, broker-dealers, and prospective merger partners, have also been held liable under Rule 10b-5. One study of 37 SEC insider trading actions listed among the defendants the trading issuer (1), officers and directors (6), and securities professionals, such as brokers and dealers (21).[4] This indicates the SEC pays particular attention to insider trading by those entities that it directly regulates. Another study, focusing primarily on private 10b-5 causes of actions, listed as defendants in its sample study: the issuing company (37), the issuer's parent company (8), officers and directors (36), employees of the issuer (4), and tippees (30).[5]

Insiders are liable whether they trade on their own account or simply tip someone else. A nontrading tipper who passes information to someone who is sure to trade clearly violates Rule 10b-5's prohibition on insider trading.

In cases involving ''outsiders,'' the reach of Rule 10b-5 has been clarified somewhat by the Supreme Court. Some lower courts had taken the view that simple possession of inside information, no matter who possesses it or how it was obtained, is sufficient to impose the duty to disclose or abstain. The Supreme Court disagreed the first time it addressed a Rule 10b-5 insider trading case.

---

[4] M. Dooley, ''Enforcement of Insider Trading Restrictions,'' *Virginia Law Review*, Vol. 66, (1980), p. 1.

[5] Scott, ''Insider Trading: Rule 10b-5, Disclosure and Corporate Policy,'' *Journal of Legal Studies*, Vol. 9 (1980), p. 801.

CHIARELLA v. UNITED STATES

445 U.S. 222 (1980)

Chiarella was a printer who worked as a "markup man" for Pandick Press, a financial printer in New York. He handled documents that announced tender offers. When one company was preparing to take control of another, it would deliver the documents to Pandick, concealing the identities of the corporations by using blank spaces or false names. The true names would be sent to the printer on the night of the final printing to preserve secrecy. Chiarella, however, was able to deduce the names of the companies involved. In at least five separate instances he bought stock in the proposed target company, and then sold after the price rose following announcement of the tender offer. He netted a profit of some $30,000.

The SEC then prompted the Department of Justice to bring a criminal action, alleging that Chiarella had intentionally violated §10(b). Chiarella was convicted by the trial court, and the Second Circuit affirmed the conviction. Chiarella appealed to the Supreme Court.

POWELL, JUSTICE:

The Commission [in *Cady, Roberts*] emphasized that the duty [to disclose or abstain] arose from (1) the existence of a relationship affording access to inside information intended to be available only for a corporate purpose and (2) the unfairness of allowing a corporate insider to take advantage of that information by trading without disclosure.

That the relationship between a corporate insider and the stockholders of his corporation gives rise to a disclosure obligation is not a novel twist of the law. At common law, misre-presentation made for the purpose of inducing reliance upon the false statement is fradulent. But one who fails to disclose material information prior to the consummation of a transaction commits fraud only when he is under a duty to do so. And the duty to disclose arises when one party has information "that the other [party] is entitled to know because of a fiduciary or other similar relation of trust and confidence between them." In its *Cady, Roberts* decision, the Commission recognized a relationship of trust and confidence between the shareholders of a corporation and those insiders who have obtained confidential information by reason of their position with that corporation. This relationship gives rise to a duty to disclose because of the "necessity of preventing a corporate insider from . . . tak[ing] unfair advantage of the uninformed minority stockholders"—*Speed v. Transamerica Corp.*, 99 F.Supp. 808, 829 (Del. 1951).

. . .

Administrative and judicial interpretations have established that silence in connection with the purchase or sale of securities may operate as a fraud actionable under §10(b) despite the absence of statutory language or legislative history specifically addressing the legality of non-disclosure. But such liability is premised upon a duty to disclose arising from a relationship of trust and confidence between parties to a transaction. Application of a duty to disclose prior to trading guarantees that corporate insiders, who have an obligation to place the shareholder's welfare before their own, will not benefit personally through fraudulent use of material nonpublic information.

In this case, the petitioner was convicted of violating §10(b), although he was not a corporate insider and he received no confidential information from the target company. Moreover, the "market information" upon which he relied did not concern the earning power or operations of the target company, but only the plans of the acquiring company. Petitioner's use of that information was not a fraud under §10(b) unless he was subject to an affirmative duty to disclose it before trading. In this case, the jury instructions failed to specify any such duty. In effect, the trial court instructed the jury that petitioner owed a duty to everyone; to all sellers, indeed, to the market as a whole. The jury simply was told to decide whether petitioner used material, nonpublic information at a time when "he knew other people trading in the securities market did not have access to the same information."

The Court of Appeals affirmed the conviction by holding that "[a]nyone— corporate insider or not—who regularly receives material nonpublic information may not use that information to trade in securities without incurring an affirmative duty to disclose." Although the court said that its test would include only persons who regularly receive material, nonpublic information, its rationale for that limitation is unrelated to the existence of a duty to disclose. The Court of Appeals, like the trial court, failed to identify a relationship between petitioner and the sellers that could give rise to a duty. Its decision thus rested solely upon its belief that the federal securities laws have "created a system providing equal access to information necessary for reasoned and intelligent investment decisions." The use by anyone of material information not generally available is fraudulent, this theory suggests, because such information gives certain buyers or sellers an unfair advantage over less informed buyers and sellers.

This reasoning suffers from two defects. First, not every instance of financial unfairness constitutes fraudulent activity under §10(b). See *Santa Fe Industries, Inc.* v. *Green*, 430 U.S. 462, 474–477 (1977). Second, the element required to make silence fraudulent—a duty to disclose—is absent in this case. No duty could arise from petitioner's relationship with the sellers of the target company's securities, for petitioner had no prior dealings with them. He was not their agent, he was not a fiduciary, he was not a person in whom the sellers had placed their trust and confidence. He was, in fact, a complete stranger who dealt with the sellers only through impersonal market transactions.

We cannot affirm petitioner's conviction without recognizing a general duty between all participants in market transactions to forgo actions based on material, nonpublic information. Formulation of such a broad duty, which departs radically from the established doctrine that duty arises from a specific relationship between two parties should not be undertaken absent some explicit evidence of congressional intent.

As we have seen, no such evidence emerges from the language or legislative history of §10(b). Moreover, neither the Congress nor the Commission ever has adopted a parity-of-information rule.

. . .

When an allegation of fraud is based upon nondisclosure, there can be no fraud absent a duty to speak. We hold that a duty to disclose under §10(b) does not arise from the mere possession of nonpublic market information.

. . .

The judgment of the Court of Appeals is reversed.

The Supreme Court's *Chiarella* opinion was a major decision limiting the scope of Rule 10b-5. Keying the duty to disclose or abstain to a prior fiduciary duty and refusing to adopt the parity of information approach, the Court limited liability much more than had prior lower court opinions. The ultimate effect of *Chiarella*, however, must be gauged in light of two developments. First, soon after *Chiarella*, the SEC issued Rule 14e-3, which although issued pursuant to §14 of the 1934 Act, had a direct impact on 10b-5 cases like *Chiarella*. The rule provides that if any person has taken substantial steps toward commencement of a tender offer, it shall constitute a deceptive or fraudulent practice for *any* other person who possesses such nonpublic information that he or she knows or has reason to know has come from the offeror, the target, or any of their insiders to trade on that information. Chiarella would certainly have violated this rule had it been in effect when he traded. Although there is some question as to the SEC's authority to issue such a rule that clearly is aimed at circumventing the *Chiarella* decision, the rule has been sustained by most courts.

Second, one theory that the Supreme Court refused to address in *Chiarella*, because it had not been submitted to the jury, was the notion that a duty to disclose or abstain could be imposed on Chiarella because he breached a *duty* to his employer and his employer's customer. Although the Supreme Court did not address this theory, the Second Circuit quickly adopted it in the following case.

UNITED STATES v. NEWMAN

664 F.2d 12 (2d Cir. 1981), *cert. denied*, 464 U.S. 193 (1983)

Morgan Stanley & Co., Inc., and Kuhn Loeb & Co. were investment banking firms that represented companies engaged in mergers, acquisitions, and tender offers. Courtois and Antoniu were employed by these firms and misappropriated confidential information about proposed takeovers, passing the information on to Newman, a securities trader of a New York brokerage firm. Newman passed the information along to co-conspirators Carniol, a resident of Belgium, and Spyropolous, who lived in Greece and France. Using secret foreign bank accounts and multiple brokers to avoid detection, Newman, Carniol, and Spyropolous purchased stock in proposed takeover targets and then sold at a profit after the takeovers were announced, splitting the profits with Courtois and Antoniu.

Newman was indicted and charged, inter alia, *with a criminal violation of §10(b). In light of the* Chiarella *decision, the trial court dismissed as defective the criminal indictment against Newman. The United States appealed.*

VAN GRAAFEILLAND, CIRCUIT JUDGE:

The thrust of the government's case in *Chiarella* was that the defendant violated §10(b) and Rule 10b-5 by failing to disclose material, nonpublic information to the shareholders of target companies from whom he purchased stock.

As the Court observed, "[t]he jury was not instructed on the nature or elements of a duty owed by petitioner to anyone other than the sellers." To remedy the deficiency in *Chiarella*, the government here has pointed its charge of wrongdoing in a different direction. The indictment charges that Courtois and Antoniu breached the trust and confidence placed in them and their employers by the employers' corporate clients and the clients' shareholders, and the trust and confidence placed in Courtois and Antoniu by their employers. The indictment charges further that Newman, Carniol, and Spyropoulos "aided, participated in and facilitated Courtois and Antoniu in violating the fiduciary duties of honesty, loyalty, and silence owed directly to Morgan Stanley, Kuhn Loeb, and clients of those investment banks." The indictment also charges that Courtois, Newman, and Carniol "did directly and indirectly, (a) employ devices, schemes and artifices to defraud and (b) engage in acts, practices, and courses of business which operated as a fraud and deceit on Morgan Stanley, Kuhn Loeb, and those corporations and shareholders on whose behalf Morgan Stanley or Kuhn Loeb was acting, and to whom Morgan Stanley or Kuhn Loeb owed fiduciary duties, in connection with the purchase of securities. . . ."

. . .

We hold that appellee's conduct as alleged in the indictment could be found to constitute a criminal violation of §10(b) and Rule 10b-5, despite the fact that neither Morgan Stanley, Kuhn Loeb nor their clients was at the time a purchaser or seller of the target company securities in any transaction with any of the defendants.

. . .

In determining whether the indictment in the instant case charges a violation of Rule 10b-5, we need spend little time on the issue of fraud and deceit. The wrongdoing charges against appellee and his cohorts was not simply internal corporate mismanagement. See *Superintendent of Insurance* v. *Bankers Life & Casualty Co.*, 404 U.S. 6, 12 (1971). In *United States* v. *Chiarella*, supra, 445 U.S. at 245, Chief Justice Burger, in dissenting, said that the defendant "misappropriated—stole to put it bluntly—valuable nonpublic information entrusted to him in the utmost confidence." That characterization aptly describes the conduct of the connivers in the instant case.

Had appellant used similar deceptive practices to mulct Morgan Stanley and Kuhn Loeb of cash or securities, it could hardly be argued that those companies had not been defrauded. . . . By sullying the reputations of Courtois's and Antoniu's employers as safe repositories of client confidences, appellee and his cohorts defrauded those employers as surely as if they took their money.

. . .

Appellee and his cohorts also wronged Morgan Stanley's and Kuhn Loeb's clients, whose take-over plans were keyed to target company stock prices fixed by market forces, not artificially inflated through purchases by purloiners of confidential information.

In a tender offer situation, the effect of increased activity in purchases of the target company's shares is, similarly, to drive up the price of the target company's shares; but this effect is damaging to the offering company because the tender offer will appear commensurately less attractive and the activity may cause it to abort.—B. Fox & E. Fox, *Business Organizations, Corporate Acquisitions and Mergers*, §27.05[4] (1981).

In other areas of the law, deceitful misappropriation of confidential information by a fiduciary, whether described as theft, conversion, or breach of trust, has consistently been held to be unlawful. Appellee would have had to be most ingenuous to believe that Congress intended to establish a less rigorous code of conduct under the Securities Acts.

· · ·

The order dismissing the indictment is reversed.

Thus, Rule 14e-3 and the *Newman* decision appear to "plug" to some extent the "gap" in Rule 10b-5 coverage left by the *Chiarella* decision. The exact impact of *Newman's* "misappropriation" theory cannot be known until the Supreme Court directly addresses the validity of this new basis for insider trading liability. Until that time, the lower courts will be busy fleshing out the details of its application, some of which—such as its impact in a civil lawsuit—shall be discussed later in the chapter.

The most recent Supreme Court decision on insider trading is *Dirks* v. *SEC*, which presents a very unusual factual situation. Although *Dirks* contains some specific language that could be read to indicate that the Supreme Court accepts the misappropriation theory, its overall tone is obviously restrictive.

DIRKS v. SEC

463 U.S. 646 (1983)

Dirks was an officer of a New York broker-dealer when he received a phone call from Ronald Secrist, a former officer of Equity Funding of America. Secrist told Dirks that Equity Funding, a very large and supposedly quite successful company, had vastly overstated its assets as the result of fraudulent corporate practices, including the writing of phony insurance policies. Secrist told Dirks that various regulatory agencies had failed to act on similar charges by Equity Funding employees, urging Dirks to verify and disclose the fraud publicly. Dirks investigated the claims, receiving denials of the charges by Equity Funding management, but receiving some verification from other employees. Dirks openly discussed the charges with a number of clients and investors, who sold some $16 million in Equity Funding stock, though neither Dirks nor his firm traded Equity Funding shares.

Dirks contacted a Wall Street Journal *bureau chief, but the latter declined to pursue the matter. During the two weeks in which Dirks investigated, Equity Funding stock fell from $26 per share to less than $15 per share. This caused the New York Stock Exchange to halt trading in Equity Funding stock. Soon thereafter, California insurance authorities impounded Equity Funding's records and discovered the fraud. Only later did the* Wall Street Journal *print an article on information assembled by Dirks.*

The SEC decided that Dirks, by disseminating information about the fraud to people who traded on the information, aided and abetted violations of §17(a) of the 1933 Act and Rule 10b-5. The SEC censured Dirks in its administrative hearings. Dirks appealed, and the District of Columbia Court of Appeals rendered judgment against him. Dirks appealed again.

POWELL, JUSTICE:

We were explicit in *Chiarella* in saying that there can be no duty to disclose where the person who has traded on inside information "was not [the corporation's] agent, ... was not a fiduciary, [or] was not a person in whom the sellers [of the securities] had placed their trust and confidence." Not to require such a fiduciary relationship, we recognized, would "depar[t] radically from the established doctrine that duty arises from a specific relationship between two parties" and would amount to "recognizing a general duty between all participants in market transactions to forgo actions based on material, nonpublic information." This requirement of a specific relationship between the shareholders and the individual trading on inside information has created analytical difficulties for the SEC and courts in policing tippees who trade on inside information. Unlike insiders who have independent fiduciary duties to both the corporation and its shareholders, the typical tippee has no such relationships. In view of this absence, it has been unclear how a tippee acquired the *Cady*, *Roberts* duty to refrain from trading on inside information.

The SEC's position, as stated in its opinion in this case is that a tippee "inherits" the *Cady*, *Roberts* obligation to shareholders whenever he receives inside information from an insider.

This view differs little from the view that we rejected as inconsistent with congressional intent in *Chiarella*. In that case, the Court of Appeals agreed with the SEC and affirmed Chiarella's conviction, holding that " '[a]nyone—corporate insider or not—who regularly receives material nonpublic information may not

use that information to trade in securities without incurring an affirmative duty to disclose' "— *United States* v. *Chiarella*, 588 F.2d 1358, 1365 (CA2 1978) (emphasis in original). Here the SEC maintains that anyone who knowingly receives nonpublic material information from an insider has a fiduciary duty to disclose before trading.

In effect, the SEC's theory of tippee liability in both cases appears rooted in the idea that the antifraud provisions require equal information among all traders. This conflicts with the principle set forth in *Chiarella* that only some persons, under some circumstances, will be barred from trading while in possession of material nonpublic information. Judge Wright correctly read our opinion in *Chiarella* as repudiating any notion that all traders must enjoy equal information before trading. "[T]he 'information' theory is rejected. Because the disclose-or-refrain duty is extraordinary, it attaches only when a party has legal obligations other than a mere duty to comply with the general antifraud proscriptions in the federal securities laws"— 681 F.2d at 837. We reaffirm today that "[a] duty [to disclose] arises from the relationship between parties . . . and not merely from one's ability to acquire information because of his position in the market"— 445 U.S., at 232–233, n. 14.

Imposing a duty to disclose or abstain solely because a person knowingly receives material nonpublic information from an insider and trades on it could have an inhibiting influence on the role of market analysts, which the SEC itself recognizes is necessary to the preservation of a healthy market. It is commonplace for analysts to "ferret out and analyze information," 21 S.E.C., at 1406, and this often is done by meeting with and questioning corporate officers and others who are insiders. And information that the analysts obtain normally may be the basis for judgments as to the market worth of a corporation's securities. The analyst's judgment in this respect is made available in market letters or otherwise to clients of the firm. It is the nature of this type of information, and indeed of the markets themselves, that such information cannot be made simultaneously available to all of the corporation's stockholders or the public generally.

The conclusion that recipients of inside information do not invariably acquire a duty to disclose or abstain does not mean that such tippees always are free to trade on the information. The need for a ban on some tippee trading is clear. Not only are insiders forbidden by their fiduciary relationship from personally using undisclosed corporate information to their advantage, but they may not give such information to an outsider for the same improper purpose of exploiting the information for their personal gain. Similarly, the transactions of those who knowingly participate with the fiduciary in such a breach are ''as forbidden'' as transactions ''on behalf of the trustee himself.'' [A] contrary rule ''would open up opportunities for devious dealings in the name of the others that the trustee could not conduct in his own.'' Thus, the tippee's duty to disclose or abstain is derivative from that of the insider's duty. . . . As we noted in *Chiarella*, ''[t]he tippee's obligation has been viewed as arising from his role as a participant after the fact in the insider's breach of a fiduciary duty''— 445 U.S., at 230, n. 12.

Thus, some tippees must assume an insider's duty to the shareholders not because they receive inside information, but rather because it has been made available to them *improperly*. And for Rule 10b-5 purposes, the insider's disclosure is improper only where it would violate his *Cady, Roberts* duty. Thus, a tippee assumes a fiduciary duty to the shareholders of a corporation not to trade on material nonpublic information only when the insider has breached his fiduciary duty to the shareholders by disclosing the information to the tippee and the tippee

knows or should know that there has been a breach. As Commissioner Smith perceptively observed in *Investors Management Co.*, ''[T]ippee responsibility must be related back to insider responsibility by a necessary finding that the tippee knew the information was given to him in breach of a duty by a person having a special relationship to the issuer not to disclose the information . . .''— 44 S.E.C., at 651 (concurring in the result). Tipping thus properly is viewed only as a means of indirectly violating the *Cady, Roberts* disclose-or-abstain rule.

In determining whether a tippee is under an obligation to disclose or abstain, it thus is necessary to determine whether the insider's ''tip'' constituted a breach of the insider's fiduciary duty. All disclosures of confidential corporate information are not inconsistent with the duty insiders owe to shareholders. In contrast to the extraordinary facts of this case, the more typical situation in which there will be a question whether disclosure violates the insider's *Cady, Roberts* duty is when insiders disclose information to analysts.

In some situations, the insider will act consistently with his fiduciary duty to shareholders, and yet release of the information may affect the market. For example, it may not be clear—either to the corporate insider or to the recipient analyst—whether the information will be viewed as material nonpublic information. Corporate officials may mistakenly think the information already has been disclosed or that it is not material enough to affect the market. Whether disclosure is a breach of duty therefore depends in large part on the purpose of the disclosure. This standard was identified by the SEC itself in *Cady, Roberts*: a purpose of the securities laws was to eliminate ''use of inside information for personal advantage''— 40 S.E.C., at 912, n. 15.

Thus, the test is whether the insider personally will benefit, directly or indirectly, from his disclosure. Absent some personal gain, there has been no breach of duty to stockholders. And absent a breach by the insider, there is no derivative breach. As Commissioner Smith stated in *Investors Management Co.*, ''It is important in this type of case to focus on policing insiders and what they do . . . rather than on policing information *per se* and its possession . . .''— 44 S.E.C., at 648 (concurring in the result).

The SEC argues that, if inside-trading liability does not exist when the information is transmitted for a proper purpose but is used for trading, it would be a rare situation when the parties could not fabricate some ostensibly legitimate business justification for transmitting the information. We think the SEC is unduly concerned.

. . .

Determining whether an insider personally benefits from a particular disclosure, a question of fact, will not always be easy for courts. But it is essential, we think, to have a guiding principle for those whose daily activities must be limited and instructed by the SEC's inside-trading rules, and we believe that there must be a breach of the insider's fiduciary duty before the tippee inherits the duty to disclose or abstain. In contrast, the rule adopted by the SEC in this case would have no limiting principle.

Under the inside-trading and tipping rules set forth above, we find that there was no actionable violation by Dirks. It is undisputed that Dirks himself was a stranger to Equity Funding, with no preexisting fiduciary duty to its shareholders. He took no action, directly or indirectly, that induced the shareholders or officers of Equity Funding to repose trust or confidence in him. There was no expectation by Dirk's sources that he would keep their information in confidence. Nor did Dirks misappropriate or illegally obtain the information about Equity Funding. Unless the insiders breached their *Cady, Roberts* duty to shareholders in disclosing the nonpublic information to Dirks, he breached no duty when he passed it on to investors as well as to *The Wall Street Journal*.

It is clear that neither Secrist nor the other Equity Funding employees violated their *Cady, Roberts* duty to shareholders by providing information to Dirks. The tippers received no monetary or personal benefit for revealing Equity Funding's secrets, nor was their purpose to make a gift of valuable information to Dirks. As the facts of this case clearly indicate, the tippers were motivated by a desire to expose the fraud. In the absence of a breach of duty to shareholders by the insiders, there was no derivative breach by Dirks. Dirks therefore could not have been ''a participant after the fact in [an] insider's breach of a fiduciary duty''— *Chiarella*, 445 U.S., at 230, n. 12.

We conclude that Dirks, in the circumstances of this case, had no duty to abstain from use of the inside information that he obtained. The judgment of the Court of Appeals therefore is *Reversed*.

Post-*Dirks* Developments

By holding in *Dirks* that a tippee's liability is derivative only and that therefore a tippee cannot be liable unless the tipper has breached a duty in disclosing, the Supreme Court took a restrictive view of §10(b) insider trading liability as it had done in *Chiarella*. The decision quickly had an impact. For example, in *SEC* v. *Switzer*,[6] the Commission

---

[6] 590 F.Supp. 756 (W.D.Okla. 1984).

sued University of Oklahoma football coach Barry Switzer and others who had profited to the tune of $591,000 by trading in the stock of a corporation, Phoenix, that had as a director Platt—who just happened to be CEO of a corporation that sponsored Switzer's coach's television show. The SEC could not disprove Switzer's story that he had simply overheard Platt talk to his wife about the proposed liquidation of Phoenix while they were all attending a track meet. Because Platt did not breach a duty to his corporation by simply carelessly speaking too loud, Switzer could not have the derivative liability of a tippee.

However, the *Dirks* decision did not mean the end of liability for "outsiders" (defendants other than directors, officers, controlling shareholders and other "traditional" insiders) who trade on inside information. Indeed, *Dirks* spawned a new theory of liability for "temporary insiders." To ensure that traditional defendants such as lawyers, accountants, and investment bankers hired by a corporation remained liable for insider trading, the *Dirks* opinion contained footnote 14, which stated that:

> Under certain circumstances, such as where corporate information is revealed legitimately to an underwriter, accountant, lawyer, or consultant working for the corporation, these outsiders may become fiduciaries of the shareholders. The basis for recognizing this fiduciary duty is not simply that such persons acquired nonpublic information, but rather that they have entered into a special confidential relationship in the conduct of the business of the enterprise and are given access to information solely for corporate purposes. . . . When such a person breaches his fiduciary relationship, he may be treated more properly as a tipper than a tippee. . . . For such a duty to be imposed, however, the corporation must expect the outsider to keep the disclosed information confidential, and the relationship at least must imply such a duty.

The "temporary insider" theory was soon applied in *SEC* v. *Lund*,[7] involving two friends, Lund and Horowitz. Horowitz was CEO of P&F Industries, Inc., and negotiated a casino deal on its behalf. He then approached Lund to determine whether his company, Verit Industries, might be interested in joining the venture. Lund declined the offer on his company's behalf, but bought some P&F stock in his own name, and profited by selling it after the casino deal became public knowledge. Because Lund received the nonpublic information from a corporate insider acting with a legitimate corporate purpose, and with an expectation that the information would be kept confidential, he was a temporary insider who assumed the duty of a traditional insider to disclose or abstain. The court held Lund had violated §10(b).

In addition to the "temporary insider" theory of 10b-5 liability, the *U.S.* v. *Newman* misappropriation theory seems to have survived *Dirks*. For example, in *U.S.* v. *Winans*,[8] criminal insider trading charges were brought against a *Wall Street Journal* columnist. The columnist, Winans, wrote columns that had a distinct impact on the market price of the corporations about which he wrote. Favorable columns would likely

---

[7] 570 F.Supp. 1397 (C.D.Cal. 1978).

[8] 612 F.Supp. 827 (S.D.N.Y. 1985), *aff'd in part, rev'd in part sub nom. U.S.* v. *Carpenter*, 791 F.2d 1024 (2d Cir. 1986).

lead to a price increase; unfavorable columns would likely lead to a price decrease. Winans tipped stockbrokers about articles that were about to appear in the *Journal*, though he knew this violated newspaper policy. The tippees traded for profits of some $690,000; Winans did not trade but received $31,000 in exchange for the tips, much paid indirectly through Winans's homosexual lover.

If *Dirks* provided the only authority, Winans would not have been guilty, because he was not a temporary insider, did not owe any duty to the corporations he wrote about, and was not a tippee. However, the judge held that *Dirks* did not invalidate the misappropriation theory. Because Winans had misappropriated information from his employer, he was held to have breached a duty that would support Rule 10b-5 liability.

As of this writing, the liability of an "outsider" who trades on inside information turns on how the information was obtained and from whom:

> An outsider, who trades on inside information obtained from an insider who breached a fiduciary duty in disclosing it, has tippee liability under *Dirks*. An outsider who trades on inside information obtained from an insider who disclosed the information for a legitimate commercial reason obtains *Lund* temporary insider status and its attendant liabilities, *if* the disclosure carried an expectation of confidentiality. An outsider who misappropriates or steals inside information, rather than receiving it from an insider, is also liable (at least criminally and in an SEC injunctive action) under *Newman*. Only the outsider who obtains the information by his own legitimate devices, such as an investment adviser who does his homework, is clearly not liable.[9]

WHO CAN SUE?

Because of the "purchaser or seller" requirement, the issuing company usually has no Rule 10b-5 insider trading cause of action. Rather, the private cause of action belongs to the person who trades without the information the insiders or tippees have. Certainly the person who buys or sells the insider's shares is allowed a 10b-5 cause of action. Furthermore, *Cady*, *Roberts*, *Texas Gulf Sulphur*, and other decisions extend liability beyond face-to-face transactions. These rulings effectively eliminate the privity requirement for insider trading cases as it has been eliminated for 10b-5 corporate disclosure cases. Elimination of privity is required in light of the anonymous, impersonal marketplace; few persons who trade can trace their shares to a particular buyer or seller.

Earlier mention was made of the fiction created in *Cady*, *Roberts* that by trading on inside information the defendant *causes* injury to those trading without the information even though had the defendant not disclosed and not traded, the plaintiff would probably have acted just the same. This fiction requires some tinkering with the reliance and causation requirements and leads to a potential for very great liability and also to controversy.

---

[9] Robert Prentice, "The Impact of *Dirks* on Outsider Trading," *Securities Regulation Law Journal*, Vol. 13 (1985), p. 38.

SHAPIRO v. MERRILL LYNCH, PIERCE, FENNER & SMITH

495 F.2d 228 (2d Cir. 1974)

Merrill Lynch was the prospective managing underwriter for a proposed offering of Douglas Aircraft Co. debentures under a registration statement filed with the SEC on June 7, 1966. Between June 17 and June 22, Douglas officials informed Merrill Lynch and certain of its officers, directors, and employees that its earnings for the first six months of the year and its projected earnings for the future would be much lower than had been previously indicated in public statements. Merrill Lynch was given this information solely in its capacity as underwriter for the debenture offering. However, several Merrill Lynch employees, in the period from June 20 to June 24, disclosed this confidential information to a number of institutional investors who were customers of Merrill Lynch's investment advising business. These defendants either sold from existing positions or made short sales of more than 165,000 shares of Douglas stock from June 20 through June 23. This was more than half the Douglas shares sold during that period of time. The information on the dive in Douglas' earnings was not made public until June 24.

Plaintiffs brought a class action on behalf of all persons who purchased Douglas stock during the period from June 21 through June 24. Defendants included Merrill Lynch, its individual employees who tipped the institutional investors, and the selling investors.

Defendants' motion to dismiss for failure to state a claim was denied by the trial judge. An appeal from that interlocutory order was taken.

TIMBERS, CIRCUIT JUDGE:

. . .

We also reject defendants' second asserted ground for distinguishing *Texas Gulf*—that our "disclose or abstain" rule is not applicable here because the only duty owed by defendants was to purchasers of the specific shares of Douglas stock sold by defendants and the transactions here involved were not face-to-face sales to plaintiffs. This argument totally misconstrues our *Texas Gulf* rule—401 F.2d at 848. It also ignores the fact that these transactions occurred on an anonymous national securities exchange where as a practical matter it would be impossible to identify a particular defendant's sale with a particular plaintiff's purchase. And it would make a mockery of the "disclose or abstain" rule if we were to permit the fortuitous matching of buy and sell orders to determine whether a duty to disclose had been violated. . . . To hold that Section 10(b) and Rule 10b-5 impose a duty to disclose on material inside information only in face-to-face transactions or to the actual purchasers or sellers on an anonymous public stock exchange, would be to frustrate a major purpose of the antifraud provisions of the securities laws: to ensure the integrity and efficiency of the securities markets. We hold that defendants owed a duty—for the breach of which they may be held liable in this private action for damages—not only to the purchasers of the actual shares sold by defendants (in the unlikely event they can be identified) but to all persons who during the same period purchased Douglas stock in the open market without knowledge of the material inside information which was in the possession of defendants.

. . .

We turn next to the remaining major legal question presented: assuming that defendants did violate the antifraud provisions of the securities laws by trading in or recommending trading in Douglas common stock (as we have held above), whether they are liable in a private action for damages to plaintiffs who during the same period purchased Douglas stock in the open market without knowledge of the material inside information which was in the possession of defendants.

The essential argument of defendants on this question is that, even if they did violate Section 10(b) and Rule 10b-5, their conduct did not "cause" damage to plaintiffs; that it was Douglas' precarious financial condition, not defendants' securities law violations, which precipitated the sudden, substantial drop in the market price of Douglas stock and hence the losses sustained by plaintiffs; that, since plaintiffs had no prior or contemporaneous knowledge of defendants' actions, they would have purchased Douglas stock regardless of defendants' securities law violations; and that, since defendants' sales were unrelated to plaintiffs' purchases and all transactions took place on anonymous public stock exchanges, there is lacking the requisite connection between defendants' alleged violations and the alleged losses sustained by plaintiffs.

The short, and we believe conclusive, answer to defendants' assertion that their conduct did not "cause" damage to plaintiffs is the "causation in fact" holding by the Supreme Court in *Affiliated Ute Citizens* v. *United States*, 406 U.S. 128, 153–54 (1972), upon the authority of which we conclude that the requisite element of causation in fact has been established here by the uncontroverted facts that defendants traded in or recommended trading in Douglas stock without disclosing material inside information which plaintiffs as reasonable investors might have considered important in making their decision to purchase Douglas stock.

. . .

As one branch of their absence of causation argument, defendants contend that there was no privity between themselves and plaintiffs. We hold here, as we have held before, that privity between plaintiffs and defendants is not a requisite element of a Rule 10b-5 cause of action for damages.

. . .

As further refinement of their absence of causation argument, defendants contend that, even if privity between plaintiffs and defendants is not required, it is still necessary to show a "connection" between defendants' nondisclosure conduct and plaintiffs' purchase of Douglas stock—in the sense that the former induced the latter—before a Rule 10b-5 claim can be established.

. . .

While the concepts of reliance and causation have been used interchangeably in the context of a Rule 10b-5 claim, the proper test to determine whether causation in fact has been established in a nondisclosure case is "whether the plaintiff would have been influenced to act differently than he did act if the defendant had disclosed to him the undisclosed fact"—*List* v. *Fashion Park, Inc.*, 340 F.2d at 463.

Even on the basis of the pre–*Affiliated Ute* decisions, therefore, we would reject defendants' essential causation argument, namely, that absent an allegation that plaintiffs' purchase of Douglas stock was induced by defendants' nondisclosure of material inside information, the requisite element of causation is lacking. On the contrary, the Rule 10b-5 causation in fact requirement is satisfied by plaintiffs' allegation that they would not have purchased Douglas stock if they had known of the information withheld by defendants.

. . .

In *Affiliated Ute*, members of a large class of holders of stock deposited in a bank alleged that two employees of the bank in arranging for sales of this stock had failed to disclose to plaintiffs facts regarding the bank's and the employee's positions as market makers and facts regarding the true value of the stock, in violation of Rule 10b-5. The Supreme Court, in reversing the Court of Appeals which had held that there could be no recovery under Section 10(b) and Rule 10b-5 without a showing of reliance, stated:

Under the circumstances of this case, involving primarily a failure to disclose, positive proof of reliance is not a prerequisite to recovery. All that is necessary is that the facts withheld be material

in the sense that a reasonable investor might have considered them important in the making of this decision. . . . This obligation to disclose and this withholding of a material fact establish the requisite element of causation in fact.

As applied to the instant case, this holding in *Affiliated Ute* surely warrants our conclusion that the requisite element of causation in fact has been established by the admitted withholding by defendants of material inside information which they were under an obligation to disclose, such information being clearly material in the sense that plaintiffs as reasonable investors might have considered it important in making their decision to purchase Douglas stock.

. . .

For the reasons set forth above, we hold that defendants are liable in this private action for damages to plaintiffs who, during the same period that defendants traded in or recommended trading in Douglas common stock, purchased Douglas stock in the open market without knowledge of the material inside information which was in the possession of defendants.

. . .

Affirmed.

Shapiro's holding that by trading on inside information a defendant *causes* an outside trader's injury has the potential to create vast liability. Although the Second Circuit did not address the damage issue in *Shapiro*, remanding the case to the trial court to determine that matter, it clearly hinted that the defendants were liable to *all* who bought during the brief period in which the tippees were selling, even though the tippees sold only about half the Douglas shares traded during that period of time. The result, it appears, would be the same if the selling defendants had sold only one-tenth the Douglas shares during that period—they would still be liable to *all* purchasers.

This liability extends to all who trade "contemporaneously" with the defendants. In some cases the class of plaintiffs has been indicated to be all those who traded without the inside information during the entire period from when defendants started trading until the information was disclosed—a period that could conceivably stretch over weeks or even months. In *Wilson* v. *Comtech Telecommunications, Inc.*,[10] the court interpreted the "contemporaneously" trading requirement to not allow suit by persons who traded one month after defendants had traded. In another case, a period of seven days between defendant's trading and plaintiff's was held to be too long.[11]

Despite the limitation on liability produced by allowing only contemporaneous traders to sue, staggering liability can still result from *Shapiro*'s logic. Its harshness was rejected by the Sixth Circuit in *Fridrich* v. *Bradford*,[12] wherein Bradford purchased stock of Old Line Life Insurance Company on inside information he had received from his father (an insider) who knew of an impending merger. Three months later, Bradford sold the stock for a $13,000 profit. The SEC investigated the transaction and required Bradford to disgorge this entire profit. Then a class action civil suit was brought against Bradford by persons who sold Old Line stock during the three months between Bradford's purchase and the announcement of the merger. Using the ruling of the *Shapiro* case, the trial judge held Bradford and some of his associates liable to all persons who sold Old Line stock during this period, even though plaintiffs didn't sell their stock to Bradford and perhaps did not even sell in the same month. Total liability was determined to be $361,186.75. Bradford appealed.

The Sixth Circuit held that Bradford was not liable at all, holding that:

> We conclude that upon the facts of this case defendants' conduct caused no injury to plaintiffs and the judgment of the district court must be reversed. It is undisputed that defendants did not purchase any shares of stock from plaintiffs, and that defendants' acts of trading in no way affected plaintiffs' decision to sell.
>
> We are unable to agree with the observation of the district judge in *Shapiro* that "it is the act of trading without disclosing material inside information which causes plaintiffs' injury." . . . The flaw in this logic, we conclude, is that it assumes the very injury which it then declares compensable.

Given the extreme divergence between the Second Circuit's approach in *Shapiro* and the Sixth Circuit's approach in *Fridrich*, most plaintiffs, who usually have a wide choice of where to file their lawsuits in terms of venue and jurisdiction, will choose to file in the district courts in the Second Circuit whenever possible. However, we shall soon see that even the Second Circuit has tightened up the *Shapiro* holding by putting a cap on liability.

Another limitation that must be mentioned arises from a companion to the *U.S.* v. *Newman* case, which announced the misappropriation theory. Newman was held to have violated §10(b) by aiding his confederates in misappropriating information from their employers (investment bankers) and their employers' clients (potential tender offerors). But the trading was not done in the stock of the tender offerors, but rather in

---

[10] 648 F.2d 88 (2d Cir. 1981).

[11] *Kreindler* v. *Sambo's Restaurants, Inc.*, *Federal Securities Law Reports* (CCH), ¶98,312 (S.D.N.Y., 1981).

[12] 542 F.2d 307 (6th Cir. 1976), *cert. denied*, 429 U.S. 1053 (1977).

the stock of the target corporations. When shareholders of a target corporation brought a civil action against Newman for damages, they were unable to recover because he did not owe or breach any duty *to them*. So, while Newman might be sued by the SEC for an injunction or convicted criminally, he could not be liable in damages to shareholders to whom he owed no duty. The Second Circuit said, ''Nothing in our opinion in *Newman* suggests that an employee's duty to 'abstain or disclose' with respect to his employer should be stretched to encompass an employee's 'duty of disclosure' to the general public.'' [13] However, classic ''insiders'' (officers, directors, controlling shareholders, etc.) apparently remain liable to such plaintiffs in a case such as this. [14]

DAMAGES AND PENALTIES

A number of different methods of calculating damages in Rule 10b-5 insider trading cases have been discussed over the years. A leading case that discusses some of these alternatives is *Elkind* v. *Liggett & Myers, Inc.*, in which even the Second Circuit sought to mitigate the extremely harsh results that the Sixth Circuit pointed out could flow from the *Shapiro* holding.

ELKIND v. LIGGETT & MYERS, INC.

635 F.2d 156 (2d Cir. 1980)

Liggett & Myers, Inc., began to receive information in June of 1972 that its earnings would not be as high as previous public projections. This inside information was tipped, at least by July 17. The information was made public on July 18. The trial court held Liggett liable to all persons who bought the company's stock from July 11 to July 18 without knowledge of the tipped information. In computing damages, the court attempted to award the plaintiffs the difference between the amount they paid for the stock ($60 a share average) and the value they received ($43 a share average). The latter figure was interpreted to be the price at which the stock would have sold had there been public

disclosure of the inside information. Plaintiff class members bought enough shares during the July 11–18 period that total damages were $740,000, to which $300,000 in prejudgment interest was added. It appears that the tippees in the case sold a total of about 1,900 shares of Liggett stock; yet Liggett was held liable to the purchasers of around 43,000 shares. Liggett appealed.

MANSFIELD, CIRCUIT JUDGE:

In determining what is the appropriate measure of damages to be awarded to the outside uninformed investor as the result of tippee trading

---
[13] *Moss* v. *Morgan Stanley, Inc.*, 719 F.2d 5 (2d Cir. 1983), *cert. denied*, 104 S. Ct. 1280 (1984).

[14] *O'Connor & Associates* v. *Dean Witter Reynolds, Inc.*, 600 F.Supp. 702 (S.D.N.Y. 1985).

through use of information that is not equally available to all investors, it must be remembered that investors who trade in a stock on the open market have no absolute right to know inside information. They are, however, entitled to an honest market in which those with whom they trade have no confidential corporate information.

Recognizing the foregoing, we in *Shapiro* suggested that the district court must be accorded flexibility in assessing damages, after considering

> the extent of the selling defendants' trading in Douglas stock, whether such trading effectively impaired the integrity of the market, . . . what profits or other benefits were realized by defendants [and] what expenses were incurred and what losses were sustained by plaintiffs. . . . Moreover, we do not foreclose the possibility that an analysis by the district court of the nature and character of the Rule 10b–5 violations committed may require limiting the extent of liability imposed on either class of defendants. We thus gave heed to the guidance provided by the Supreme Court in *Affiliated Ute Citizens* v. *United States*, 406 U.S. 128, 151 (1972), to the effect that "Congress intended securities legislation enacted for the purpose of avoiding frauds to be construed 'not technically and restrictively, but flexibly to effectuate its remedial purposes' "—Id.

Within the feasible framework thus authorized for determining what amounts should be recoverable by the uninformed trader from the tipper and tippee trader, several measures are possible. First, there is the traditional out-of-pocket measure used by the district court in this case. For several reasons, this measure appears to be inappropriate. In the first place, as we have noted, it is directed toward compensating a person for losses directly traceable to the defendant's fraud upon him. No such fraud or inducement may be attributed to a tipper or tippee trading on an impersonal market. Aside from this the measure poses serious proof problems that may often be insurmountable in a tippee-trading case. The "value" of the stock

traded during the period of nondisclosure of the tipped information (i.e., the price at which the market would have valued the stock if there had been a disclosure) is hypothetical. Expert testimony regarding that "value" may, as the district court found in the present case, be entirely speculative. This has led some courts to conclude that the drop in price of the stock after actual disclosure and after allowing a period of time to elapse for the market to absorb the news may sometimes approximate the drop which would have occurred earlier had the tip been disclosed. See *Harris* v. *American Investment Company*, 523 F.2d 220, 227 (8th Cir. 1975), *cert. denied*, 423 U.S. 1054 (1976). The court below adopted this approach of using post-public disclosure market price as *nunc pro tunc* evidence of the "value" of the stock during the period of nondisclosure.

Whatever may be the reasonableness of the *nunc pro tunc* "value" method of calculating damages in other contexts, it has serious vulnerabilities here. It rests on the fundamental assumptions (1) that the tipped information is substantially the same as that later disclosed publicly and (2) that one can determine how the market would have reacted to the public release of the tipped information at an earlier time by its reaction to that information at a later, proximate time. This theory depends on the parity of the "tip" and the "disclosure." When they differ, the basis of the damage calculation evaporates.

An equally compelling reason for rejecting the theory is its potential for imposition of Draconian, exorbitant damages, out of all proportion to the wrong committed, lining the pockets of all interim investors and their counsel at the expense of innocent corporate stockholders. Logic would compel application of the theory to a case where a tippee sells only 10 shares of a heavily traded stock (e.g., IBM), which then drops substantially when the tipped information is publicly disclosed. To hold the tipper and tippee liable for the losses suffered by every open market buyer of the stock as a result of the later decline in value of the stock after the news became public would be grossly unfair. While the securities laws do occasionally allow for potentially ruinous recovery, we will not readily adopt a measure mandating "large judgments, payable in the last instance by innocent investors [here, Liggett shareholders], for the benefit of speculators and their lawyers," *SEC* v. *Texas Gulf Sulphur Co.*, supra, 401 F.2d at 867 (Friendly, J. concurring); compare *Blue Chip Stamps* v. *Manor Drug Stores*, 421 U.S. 723, 739–40 (1975), unless the statute so requires.

An alternative measure would be to permit recovery of damages caused by erosion of the market price of the security that is traceable to the tippee's wrongful trading, that is, to compensate the uninformed investor for the loss in market value that he suffered as a direct result of the tippee's conduct. Under this measure an innocent trader who bought Liggett shares at or after a tippee sold on the basis of inside information would recover any decline in value of his shares caused by the tippee's trading. Assuming the impact of the tippee's trading on the market is measurable, this approach has the advantage of limiting the plaintiffs to the amount of damage actually caused in fact by the defendant's wrongdoing and avoiding windfall recoveries by investors at the expense of stockholders other than the tippee trader, which could happen in the present action against Liggett. The rationale is that if the market price is not affected by the tippee's trading, the uninformed investor is in the same position as he would have been had the insider abstained from trading. In such event the equilibrium of the market has not been disturbed and the outside investor has not been harmed by the informational imbalance. Only where the market has been contaminated by the wrongful conduct would damages be recoverable.

This causation-in-fact approach has some disadvantages. It allows no recovery for the tippee's violation of his duty to disclose the inside information before trading. Had he fulfilled this duty, others, including holders of the stock, could then have traded on an equal informational basis. Another disadvantage of such a measure lies in the difficult, if not impossible burden it would impose on the uninformed trader of proving the time when and extent to which the integrity of the market was affected by the tippee's conduct. In some cases, such as *Mitchell*, supra, and *Shapiro*, supra, the existence of very substantial trading by the tippee, coupled with a sharp change in market price over a short period, would provide the basis for measuring a market price movement attributable to the wrongful trading. On the other hand, in a case where there was only a modest amount of tippee trading in a heavy volume market in the stock, accompanied by other unrelated factors affecting the market price, it would be impossible as a practical matter to isolate such rise or decline in market price, if any, as was caused by the tippee's wrongful conduct.

· · ·

For these reasons, we reject this strict direct market-repercussion theory of damages.

A third alternative is (1) to allow any uninformed investor, where a reasonable investor would either have delayed his purchase or not purchased at all if he had the benefit of the tipped information, to recover any postpurchase decline in market value of his shares up to a reasonable time after he learns of the tipped information or after there is a public disclosure of it but (2) limit his recovery to the amount gained by the tippee as a result of his selling at the earlier date rather than delaying his sale until the parties could trade on an equal informational basis. Under this measure if the tippee sold 5,000 shares at $50 per share on the basis of inside information and the stock thereafter declined to $40 per share within a reasonable time after public disclosure, an uninformed purchaser, buying shares during the interim (e.g., at $45 per share) would recover the difference between his purchase price and the amount at which he could have sold the shares on an equal informational basis (i.e., the market price within a reasonable time after public disclosure of the tip), subject to a limit of $50,000, which is the amount gained by the tippee as a result of his trading on the inside information rather than on an equal basis. Should the intervening buyers, because of the volume and price of their purchases, claim more than the tippee's gain, their recovery (limited to that gain) would be shared *pro rata*.

This third alternative, which may be described as the disgorgement measure, has in substance been recommended by the American Law Institute in its 1978 Proposed Draft of a Federal Securities Code, §§1603, 1703(b), 1708(b), 1711(j). It offers several advantages. To the extent that it makes the tipper and the tippees liable up to the amount gained by their misconduct, it should deter tipping of inside information and tippee trading. On the other hand, by limiting the total recovery to the tippee's gain, the measure bars windfall recoveries of exorbitant amounts bearing no relation to the seriousness of the misconduct. It also avoids the extraordinary difficulties faced in trying to prove traditional out-of-pocket damages based on the true "value" of the shares purchased or damages claimed by reason of market erosion attributable to tippee trading. A plaintiff would simply be required to prove (1) the time, amount, and price per share of his purchase, (2) that a reasonable investor would not have paid as high a price or made the purchase at all if he had had the information in the tippee's possession, and (3) the price to which the security had declined by the time he learned the tipped information or at a reasonable time after

it became public, whichever event first occurred. He would then have a claim and, up to the limits of the tippee's gain, could recover the decline in market value of his shares before the information became public or known to him. In most cases the damages recoverable under the disgorgement measure would be roughly commensurate to the actual harm caused by the tippee's wrongful conduct. In a case where the tippee sold only a few shares, for instance, the likelihood of his conduct causing any substantial injury to intervening investors buying without benefit of his confidential information would be small. If, on the other hand, the tippee sold large amounts of stock, realizing substantial profits, the likelihood of injury to intervening uninformed purchasers would be greater and the amount of potential recovery thereby proportionately enlarged.

. . .

In the present case, the sole Rule 10b-5 violation was the tippee trading of 1,800 Liggett shares on the afternoon of July 17, 1972. Since the actual preliminary Liggett earnings were released publicly at 2:15 P.M. on July 18 and were effectively disseminated in a *Wall Street Journal* article published on the morning of July 19, the only outside purchasers who might conceivably have been damaged by the insider trading were those who bought Liggett shares between the afternoon of July 17 and the opening of the market on July 19. Thereafter all purchasers bought on an equal informational footing, and any outside purchaser who bought on July 17 and 18 was able to decide within a reasonable time after the July 18–19 publicity whether to hold or sell his shares in the light of the publicly-released news regarding Liggett's less favorable earnings.

The market price of Liggett stock opened on July 17, 1972, at $55 ⅝ and remained at substantially the same price on that date, closing at $55 ¼. By the close of the market on July

18 the price declined to $52 ½ per share. Applying the disgorgement measure, any member of the plaintiff class who bought Liggett shares during the period from the afternoon of July 17 to the close of the market on July 18 and met the reasonable investor requirement would be entitled to claim a *pro rata* portion of the tippee's gain, based on the difference between their purchase price and the price to which the market price declined within a reasonable time after the morning of July 19. By the close of the market on July 19 the market price had declined to $46 ⅜ per share. The total recovery thus would be limited to the gain realized by the tippee from the inside information, that is, 1,800 shares multiplied by approximately $9.35 per share.

Reversed and remanded.

Thus, although the Second Circuit is still firmly against the "trading causation" approach enunciated by the Sixth Circuit in *Fridrich*, it has deemed it necessary to adopt the "disgorgement" approach to calculating damages to avoid the almost unlimited liability that could flow from the reasoning of the *Shapiro* case.

A further refinement of the *Liggett* disgorgement approach occurred in *SEC* v. *MacDonald*,[15] an action where the SEC sought court-ordered disgorgement of insider profits. Somewhat simplified, the facts were that defendant purchased shares at $4 because he had nonpublic information about a lease that was being negotiated which would be of great benefit to the company. Soon after the information became public, the company's stock rose to about $5 per share. A little more than a year later, defendant sold the stock at $10 per share. The district court ordered the defendant to disgorge $6 per share, the difference between the selling price of $10 and the purchase price of $4, believing that it would be inequitable to allow defendant to keep any profit from shares he purchased with inside information. However, the appellate court reversed, holding that defendant need disgorge only the $1 difference between the price at which he purchased and the price to which the stock rose after disclosure of the inside information. The court said, "When a fraudulent buyer has reached the point of his full gain from the fraud, viz., the market price a reasonable time after the undisclosed information has become public, any consequences of a subsequent decision, be it to sell or to retain the stock, is *res inter alios*, not causally related to the fraud."

The disgorgement approach to damages, especially as refined in *MacDonald*, suffers from the problem of being too lenient. How much deterrence would a law against robbing banks have if the bank robber, when caught, faced a maximum punishment of having to give back the loot?

INSIDER TRADING SANCTIONS ACT

To put some deterrence back in the remedies for insider trading, Congress passed the Insider Trading Sanctions Act of 1984 (ITSA).[16] The act authorizes the SEC to seek

---

[15] 699 F.2d 47 (1st Cir. 1983) (en banc).
[16] Public Law 98–376 (98th Congress).

not only a court order of disgorgement of profits but also a penalty to be in the court's discretion but not to exceed three times the profit gained or the loss avoided. In one dramatic case, famous arbitrageur Ivan Boesky agreed to pay $50 million to the SEC as a penalty in addition to disgorging $50 million in profits derived through illegal trading on insider tips.[17] ITSA's penalty provision applies not only to persons who purchase or sell "while in possession of material nonpublic information" but also to persons "aiding and abetting" such a purchase or sale. The aiding and abetting provision was clearly aimed at punishing nontrading tippers, though it would not apply to a broker-dealer who merely executed a trade on a customer's behalf.

ITSA also increased criminal penalties by increasing the potential fine for a criminal violation of *any* provision of the 1934 Act from $10,000 to $100,000; the maximum potential jail term that may be added to such a fine was left at five years. In a recent case, an office manager of a law firm who had misappropriated inside information from his employer's files regarding proposed tender offers by the firm's clients was sentenced to 3½ years.[18] The main defendant in the *Winans* case, mentioned earlier, was given an 18-month prison term, fined $5,000, and ordered to perform 500 hours of community service.[19]

OTHER REMEDIES

RICO

Like a bad penny, the Racketeer Influenced and Corrupt Organizations Act (RICO) keeps turning up in all facets of securities litigation. Although RICO has not been often used in insider trading cases, due to its present broad interpretation there seems little doubt that its use will increase. Insider trading is securities fraud that constitutes one of the predicate acts of "racketeering" necessary for RICO liability.

State Remedies for Insider Trading

The states have taken a variety of approaches to insider trading. Some states, such as California, have passed legislation specifically addressing insider trading. In other states, the courts have taken an active role in creating remedies patterned after Rule 10b-5 to

---

[17] J. Stewart & D. Hertzberg, "Fall of Ivan Boesky Leads to Broader Probe of Insider Information," *The Wall Street Journal*, Nov. 13, 1986, p. 1.

[18] M. Siconolfi, "Law Firm Ex-Office Manager Receives 3-½-Year Prison Term for Insider Trades," *The Wall Street Journal* (midwest edition), June 17, 1985, p. 23.

[19] "Winans Gets 18-Month Term in Trading Case," *The Wall Street Journal* (midwest edition), August 7, 1985, p. 2.

punish insider trading.[20] On the other hand, in light of the vast expansion of Rule 10b-5 as a remedy for insider trading, other courts have refused to judicially create a similar remedy at the state level, holding such an expansion to be unnecessary judicial legislation.[21]

QUESTIONS AND PROBLEMS

1. A company failed to disclose a readjustment of its reported earnings from 85 cents per share for the first five months of the fiscal year to only 12 cents per share for the first six months. Is this the type of "material" information that might give rise to the duty to "disclose or abstain"? See *Financial Industrial Fund, Inc.* v. *McDonnell Corp.*, *Federal Securities Law Reports* (CCH), ¶93,004 (D. Colo. 1971).

2. Materia, a proofreader for a financial printer, deciphered tender offer targets from materials his employer was printing. He traded in the shares of the targets or passed the information to others. His employer had a policy, posted in writing, prohibiting employees from trading in securities on the basis of nonpublic information received in the course of their employment. The SEC brought an injunctive action based on §10(b) and §14(e). Discuss Materia's liability. See *SEC* v. *Materia*, 745 F.2d 197 (2d Cir. 1984), *cert. denied*, 105 S. Ct. 2112 (1985).

3. Assume that Materia was sued by shareholders of the tender offer targets who sold their shares in those targets at the same time Materia was buying, because they did not know of the impending tender offers. Discuss Materia's potential liability for civil damages under §10(b).

4. Rosenberg and Selzer had numerous business interests with Rothberg. Rosenberg and Selzer were also officers of Nytronics, Inc., and in that capacity learned that Nytronics was planning on purchasing all the shares of Gulton Industries, that a Dr. Gulton believed he controlled the Gulton board of directors and could persuade them to accept Nytronics' offer, and that the terms should be very favorable to holders of Gulton shares. While this information was nonpublic, Rosenberg and Selzer passed it along to Rothberg who formed a joint venture with Rosenberg's brother and Selzer's father to purchase Gulton shares. David Rosenbloom guaranteed Rothberg from loss. However, Dr. Gulton had overestimated his influence; Nytronics was unable to purchase Gulton Industries and the joint venture lost $443,000. Rothberg sued the Rosenblooms. An issue that arose was whether Rothberg's actions constituted illegal insider trading under §10(b). Discuss. See *Rothberg* v. *Rosenbloom*, 771 F.2d 818 (3d Cir. 1985).

5. O'Connor & Associates trades stocks and options for its own account. Between February 23, 1981 and March 6, 1981, O'Connor sold call options on Amax, Inc., stock. On March 10, 1981, O'Connor filed a §10(b) action against Dean Witter Reynolds, Inc., and A. G. Becker, alleging that they had purchased call options after having been tipped by insiders of Amax and Socal that Socal was going to make a tender offer for Amax. Announcement of the offer caused Amax stock to

---

[20] For example, *Diamond* v. *Oreaumuno*, 24 N.Y.2d 494 (1960).

[21] For example, *Freeman* v. *Decio*, 584 F.2d 186 (7th Cir. 1978) (applying Indiana law).

rise 18 points. Defendants claim they cannot be liable to O'Connor because they owed him no fiduciary duty. Is this defense viable? See *O'Connor & Associates* v. *Dean Witter Reynolds, Inc.*, 600 F.Supp. 702 (S.D.N.Y. 1985).

6. Assume that a director of Amax (in the previous question) related to his son certain nonpublic information about the impending Socal offer. The director fully expected his son to keep the information confidential, but the son instead traded in the shares of the target corporation and reaped a substantial profit. Discuss possible theories of liability which might apply in a §10(b) criminal action against the son. See *U.S.* v. *Reed*, 601 F.Supp. 685 (S.D.N.Y.), *rev'd in part on other grounds*, 773 F.2d 477 (2d Cir. 1985).

7. Gaspar worked for Baird, an investment banking firm that was assisting DKM Corporation in a potential acquisition of Clark Oil and Refining Corporation. Gaspar conveyed nonpublic information about the potential takeover to Schreck, a registered representative of a broker-dealer. Gaspar and Schreck had been close friends for over 20 years. Schreck and his associates bought lots of Clark stock on behalf of themselves and clients before the information received from Gaspar became public. Gaspar did not trade Clark shares. The SEC brought a §10(b) injunctive action against Gaspar. Discuss his potential liability. See *SEC* v. *Gaspar*, *Federal Securities Law Reports* (CCH), ¶92,004 (S.D.N.Y. 1985).

8. Moore was the psychiatrist of the spouse of an official of Posi-Seal. Posi-Seal was contemplating being acquired by another company. At a session with the spouse that the Posi-Seal official attended for purposes of facilitating Moore's treatment of the spouse, Moore learned of the details of the Posi-Seal acquisition. Before public announcement of those details, Moore bought 9,000 shares of Posi-Seal stock, ultimately profiting in the sum of $26,933.74. The SEC brought a civil injunctive action. Discuss Moore's liability. See *SEC* v. *Morgan F. Moore*, No. N-86–88-PCD (D. Conn. 1986).

21

PROXY
REGULATION

INTRODUCTION

In the corporate "democracy," the day-to-day business decisions are made by the officers who are selected, supervised, and guided by the board of directors. The shareholders in large corporations always have the "Wall Street option"; that is, they may sell their securities if they are unhappy with the business's progress. If they choose to hold their stock, however, they may exercise indirect control of the corporation they own by voting for the election and removal of directors, to adopt, amend, or repeal bylaws; to adopt resolutions; and to approve or reject certain extraordinary corporate matters such as mergers, dissolution, and charter amendments.[1]

The shareholders' right to vote and the substantive characteristics of the proxy (revocability, term of existence, etc.) are governed by state law. But state corporation laws do not regulate the proxy solicitation process, so the 1934 Act provides the fundamental rules for corporate suffrage. Congress believed that fair "corporate suffrage is an important right that should attach to every equity security bought on a public exchange."[2]

---

[1] H. Henn, *Law of Corporations*, (2d ed. St Paul, MN: West Publishing Co., 1970), §188.

[2] H. R. Rep. No. 1383, 73d Cong., 2d sess. 13 (1934).

To make meaningful and fair that right of corporate suffrage, Congress passed proxy laws that (1) promote full disclosure to shareholders of important corporate matters, (2) protect proxy contests from inaccurate or fraudulent statements and actions by participants, (3) provide means of enforcement of these rules, and (4) establish stockholder proposal mechanisms whereby shareholders can make their suggestions for corporate policy known to management.

This chapter will cover four main topics. First, it will examine the role of proxy regulation in the integrated disclosure system. Second, it will survey the regulation of proxy contests. Third, it will examine the substantial litigation that can arise from proxy battles. Finally, it will examine the shareholder proposal mechanism.

Scope

In reading this chapter, keep in mind that the term "proxy" is broadly defined to include attempts by management and others to solicit any sort of consent or authorization. For example, a document requesting debenture holders to consent to a waiver of a covenant in the indenture would probably constitute solicitation of a "proxy." [3]

Also remember that federal proxy rules apply only to corporations whose securities are registered under §12 of the 1934 Act, that is, generally corporations whose securities are traded on national securities exchanges and those having more than $5 million in assets and more than 500 shareholders.

PROXY DISCLOSURE

The Basic Rules

Section 14(a) of the 1934 Act outlaws the solicitation of proxies in violation of SEC rules. Congress has given substantial authority and discretion to the Commission in the proxy area. The SEC has promulgated many rules to ensure that the proxy solicitation process serves the public interest, but none is so important as Rule 14a-3. This rule prohibits the solicitation of proxies unless the persons solicited have been furnished with a written *proxy statement* containing the information specified in Schedule 14A. In addition, if the solicitation is by management relating to election of directors, each proxy statement must be accompanied or preceded by an *annual report*.

Rationale

Before passage of the 1933 and 1934 acts, it was often difficult for shareholders to learn much about the operation of their corporation. Most state corporation laws did not require a board of directors to disclose much information to shareholders. Some corporations' bylaws allowed the directors to refuse to divulge most all information

---

[3] P. Lochner, "Proxy Statements and Proxies Under the Securities Exchange Act of 1934," in *Securities Filings: Review and Update* (New York: Practising Law Institute, 1983), p. 114.

about corporate affairs unless a large majority of shareholders joined together to demand it.

Congress viewed regulation of the proxy solicitation process as a way to remedy this situation that prevented shareholders from making knowledgeable investment decisions. State laws require corporations to have an annual shareholders' meeting to elect directors, and a quorum is required for effective action. Most large corporations cannot obtain a quorum without use of the proxy solicitation process, because the thousands of shareholders needed for a quorum in many corporations could not and would not attend in person.

Because most 1934 Act reporting corporations must solicit proxies, a requirement that solicitation be preceded by a proxy statement and an annual report ensures that the shareholders will obtain the information that the Commission deems important. In addition, if a proxy contest develops, the rules ensure that the voting shareholder has adequate information as to both sides in order to make an informed choice. Many of the details of this disclosure will be covered in the section on proxy contests.

Nonelections

If the shareholders' proxies are sought not for election of a board of directors, but for some extraordinary corporate event, such as a merger, no annual report is required, but the proxy statement's requirements are tailored to disclose the information needed for the particular type of decision.

SEC Approval

Rule 14a-6(a) requires an issuer or an insurgent soliciting proxies to file copies of a preliminary proxy statement and any additional soliciting materials with the Commission at least ten days before the final version is sent out. The Commission has authority to shorten the period upon a showing of good cause. Although SEC approval is not legally required, the SEC has usually suggested that final proxy statements not be sent out until SEC staff comments are received. Due to shortages of personnel, the SEC recently discontinued its practice of reviewing all proxy statements.

Rule 14a-6(b) requires that any additional soliciting materials furnished after the proxy statement should be filed at least two days prior to being sent.

Copies of the definitive proxy statement must also be filed with the SEC, according to Rule 14a-6(c).

Unsolicited Shareholders

What if a reporting company's shares are so concentrated in the hands of a few shareholders that management need not solicit proxies from most shareholders to achieve a quorum? To prevent the shareholders whose proxies are not solicited from being fortuitously deprived of the information most shareholders receive, the Commission requires that each unsolicited shareholder be sent a copy of Schedule 14C, which contains essentially the same disclosures as Schedule 14A,[4] and an annual report similar to that required by Rule 14a-3.

Shares Held in Street Name

As often as securities are traded, it is expensive and cumbersome to pass the actual stock certificates continually from owner to owner. Large percentages of equity securities, therefore, are not physically transferred when sold. Rather, they are placed in the "street" or "nominee" name of a securities depository. The best known such depository is The Depository Trust Company, commonly known as "Cede & Co."

Such depositories keep physical possession of the certificates and maintain records as to their beneficial ownership. Thus, when a security is sold, the depository need only change its records as to beneficial ownership. The true buyer and seller do not exchange the certificate; rather, the depository transmits certificates as needed to transfer agents to reflect the overall change in holdings of the participants.[5]

Brokers also frequently hold their customers' securities in street name, as do banks and voting trustees.

To ensure that the proxy statement reaches the beneficial owners, the SEC requires in Rule 14a-13(a) that any issuer who knows that securities entitled to vote are held of record by brokers, dealers, depositories, banks, or voting trustees or their nominees shall, at least 20 days prior to the record date of the meeting (the date as of which the list of those entitled to vote shall be compiled), inquire of the record owner how many copies of the proxy statement and soliciting materials (and annual reports if it is an annual meeting for election of directors) are needed for the beneficial owners. When informed of the number of such owners, the issuer is required to supply the record holder with sufficient copies of the required documents and to pay the record owner's expenses in distributing them.

Rule 14b-1 requires brokers to reply within seven business days to an issuer's inquiry regarding the number of beneficial owners for whom it holds shares and to forward proxy materials to customers within five business days after they are received from the issuer.

To enhance direct communication between the issuer and the beneficial owners, Rule 17a-3 requires brokers to maintain a record of their customers who beneficially own securities held of record by the broker, who object to disclosing their names, addresses, and securities holdings to the issuer. The issuer is to be furnished this information regarding nonobjecting beneficial owners upon demand to the broker, according to Rule 14b-1.

---

[4] Rule 14c-2.

[5] See A. Tenney, "Preparing for the Annual Meeting of Stockholders," in *Preparation of Annual Disclosure Documents* (New York: Practising Law Institute, 1984), p. 86.

The Integrated Disclosure System

As part of its move to an integrated disclosure system, the SEC substantially amended proxy rules and the Form 10-K. Importantly, the Commission expanded the required disclosures of the annual report to shareholders, and then allowed much of the annual report to be incorporated by reference into Form 10-K to minimize duplication. In so doing the SEC predicted that the "annual report will become the principal resource for use in connection with most filings required" by the integrated disclosure system.[6]

It is therefore important to have at least a general idea of what must be disclosed in the annual report and the proxy statement.

Contents of the Annual Report

Rule 14a-3(b) dictates the contents of an annual report to shareholders.[7] The following are among the most important items that must be disclosed.

1. Consolidated, audited balance sheets as of the end of the two most recent fiscal years and audited statements of income and changes in financial position for each of the three most recent fiscal years. This provision refers to Item 301 of Regulation S-K.

2. Disagreements with accountants on accounting and financial disclosures as required by Item 304 of Regulation S-K. If the issuer recently changed accounting firms due to a disagreement with its original accountants, the annual report must set out the existence and nature of the disagreement and the effects on the financial statement if the method favored by the accountants were used.

3. Management's discussion and analysis (MDA) of financial condition and results of operations as required by Item 303 of Regulation S-K. This textual discussion of important features (e.g., liquidity, capital resources, impacts of inflation, material changes in cost/revenue ratio, etc.) and trends of the business plus a "realistic management assessment of corporate objectives and numerical results," coupled with the audited financial statements form the heart of the integrated disclosure system.

4. Selected financial data required by Item 301 of Regulation S-K, including a summary in comparative columnar form of net sales or operating revenues, aggregate and per share income, long-term debt, cash dividends per share, and perhaps other items for the past five years (or the life of company, whichever is shorter).

5. Data regarding the issuer's industry (Item 101 of Regulation S-K).

6. The identity, principal occupation, and employer of each of the company's directors and executive officers.

Contents of Proxy Statement

Schedule 14A lists 22 items that may have to be disclosed in a proxy statement, depending upon the nature of the election. Items to be disclosed when shareholder approval of a merger is sought are, in part, different than those required when directors are being

---

[6] *Securities Exchange Act Release*, no. 33–6231 (September 2, 1980).

[7] See, generally, J. Shulman, "Annual Reports to Security Holders and Financial Disclosure in Annual Reports to Security Holders and in Annual Reports on Form 10-K," in *Securities Filings: Review and Update* (New York: Practising Law Institute, 1983), p. 51.

elected. Many items are tailored for disclosure in case of specific proposed actions, including amending the corporate charter, disposing of corporate property, authorizing additional shares, modifying the rights of existing classes of shares, granting options or warrants, and instituting or altering pension and retirement plans.

If the solicitation is by management relating to an election of directors, several items must be disclosed, including the following.

1. A statement of whether the proxy is revocable.
2. An identification of the persons making the solicitation.
3. A statement of the classes of shares entitled to vote and the number of shares outstanding.
4. A table containing the information about directors and executive officers required by Item 401 of Regulation S-K. Among other things, Item 401 requires disclosure of names, ages, positions held, descriptions of arrangements or understandings between directors and any other person regarding the election, family relationships, business experience, involvement in legal proceedings, and amount of shares owned.

   Interestingly, Schedule 14A also requires disclosure of the total number of board meetings in the prior year and the names of directors who attended fewer than 75% of the meetings of the board and of board committees of which they were members.
5. Detailed disclosures of compensation and miscellaneous forms of remuneration paid to key officers and directors as required by Item 402 of Regulation S-K. These disclosures are still detailed and complicated, but the SEC created substantial controversy when it recently eased the requirements. For example, individual officer disclosure is required only for the five highest-paid executive officers who make over $60,000, and for officers as a group. Disclosure requirements for ''perks'' such as country club memberships and below-market interest rate loans were eliminated if the aggregate amount is less than the lesser of $25,000 or 10% of the officers' cash compensation.

Keep in mind that Schedule 14A's disclosure requirements represent the bare minimum permissible. Any other information that is ''material'' within the ''substantial likelihood that a reasonable shareholder would consider it important in deciding how to vote'' standard of *TSC Industries, Inc.* v. *Northway* [8] must also be disclosed. Otherwise, the discloser may run afoul of Rule 14a-9, which prohibits false or misleading statements or omissions in connection with any proxy solicitation. The impact of this materiality standard and Rule 14a-9 will become clear when viewed in light of the proxy contest rules discussed in the next section.

THE PROXY CONTEST

Introduction

Most proxy solicitations are done by management in connection with an election of directors at an annual meeting. Because the solicitation is unopposed, the main function of federal proxy regulation is to protect shareholder suffrage by ensuring the disclosures outlined in the previous section.

---

[8] 426 U.S. 438 (1976).

Occasionally a proxy solicitation will develop into a contest between management and one or more groups of insurgents. Traditionally, such contests occurred in only a minute percentage of solicitations. In recent years, however, the number of contests and the size of corporations they have involved have both increased.

Many of the contests have involved insurgent groups who proposed their own slate of candidates for the board of directors. Sometimes insurgents are not seeking control, but wish to force management to adopt a particular course of action. Frequently contests involve disputes over whether a merger should be approved.

The increased popularity of proxy fights is related to recent developments in tender offers, another method of gaining control (by buying a majority of shares), which is discussed in the next chapter. Many proxy fights have arisen over management attempts to deter tender offers. Also, management's success at making a tender offer more difficult to complete and the rising price of stocks that has made them more expensive have made the proxy fight a more attractive means of gaining control of a corporation.

Some of the recent developments are discussed in the following excerpt.

"CORPORATE CIVIL WARS" *

Time

May 9, 1983, p. 64.

TWA usually stands for Trans World Airlines. Last week it could have meant Tussle, Wrestle & Armtwist. At the annual meeting of TWA's parent, Trans World Corp., in Kansas City, a group of investors calling themselves Odyssey Partners attempted to break up the firm by splitting off the corporation's red-ink airline business from its four other subsidiaries, all moneymakers. With only 1% of Trans World's stock, they nonetheless persuaded shareholders who control perhaps a fourth of the company to vote their way. That fell short of the required 51% majority, but Trans World Chairman L. Edwin Smart must remain worried about another challenge. Said a pleased Leon Levy, leader of Odyssey: "The same forces are still at play. Our recommendation still stands."

A similar drama was unfolding, meanwhile, at the annual meeting of GAF in Charlotte, N.C. Stockholders witnessed a bruising battle between the company's current chairman, Jesse Werner, 66, and Samuel Heyman, 44, a Connecticut shopping-center magnate and owner of 5.7% of GAF's stock, over how to liquidate the moribund company. Factions on both sides have been attacking each other in a blitz of newspaper ads, questioning each other's competence and judgment. At one point, the Heyman group distributed a chart showing how Werner's salary and bonuses had gone from about $160,000 a year to nearly $525,000 at the same time that GAF's stock dropped from $42 to $10. Said GAF Stockholder Ben Alderson before the annual meeting started: "I'm glad to see someone like Heyman upset the canoe. I've had stock for ten years, and I'm not at all satisfied." After a chaotic, three-hour session that was interrupted by arguments over rules of order, Werner, fearful that he was losing to Heyman, postponed the deadline for voting to mid-May.

Many company directors must be longing for the good old days of annual meetings, when the chief distractions were usually corporate gadflies like Evelyn Y. Davis, Wilma Soss and the Gilbert brothers. Those "professional shareholders" just talked a lot, loudly, and annoyed company chairmen with demands for more "corporate democracy" through cumulative election of directors.

What is happening now is nothing short of corporate civil war in the form of proxy battles. Said Levy after the Trans World meeting: "No longer can management be certain it can get through any proposal. That is really what this was all about." In addition, proxy fights are growing in number—68 last year *vs.* 40 or so annually in the late '70s.

The normal way to amass a controlling majority of a company's stock is a tender offer or a proxy fight. But takeover by tender has become much more expensive because stock prices have risen more than 50% on the average since August in the ongoing bull market. The Dow Jones industrial average closed last week at a record 1226.20. Buying a controlling interest may have been possible a year ago for only a few million dollars; now the price could be much higher.

· · ·

Now that the shares of even troubled companies such as Trans World and GAF are up sharply, although nowhere near their historic highs, the threat to managements is likely to come mainly from people who already hold substantial blocks of stock. Says Joe Parella, a general partner at New York's First Boston Corp.: "Proxy battles are a cheap way to take over a company. All you do is hire a smart lawyer and run ads." That can often cost anywhere from $1 million to $10 million. Gaining outright control of large firms could run into the billions.

"Compared to proxy fights, takeover battles are downright gentlemanly," says a Wall Street veteran of many tussles. "This is where you get the real down and dirty, where the action can get bitter. Then they degenerate into slugfests." Says Kenneth Bialkin, a proxy expert with the New York City law firm Willkie Farr & Gallagher: "If management is doing a lousy job, you've still got to convince shareholders that a new team could do better."

Trans World's dissidents armed themselves heavily. They spent about $1 million on their campaign to get proxy statements explaining the breakup proposal into shareholders' hands and for a report from Booz, Allen & Hamilton, the powerful management consultant. The study showed that the sum of Trans World's parts was worth more than its whole. While TWA has not earned a profit domestically in almost a decade, Trans World subsidiaries such as Hilton International hotels, the Spartan Food Systems restaurant chain, Century 21 real estate and the Canteen Corp. vending-machine business were valuable and making money. The airline had a loss of $93 million during the first quarter of 1983, more than wiping out the $20 million earned before taxes by Trans World's nonflying parts. Levy and the other dissidents argued that all the parts of Trans World were worth as much as $70 a share, more than twice its current $31 stock price. "There is no synergism in Trans World," claimed Lester Pollack, a general partner in Odyssey. Trans World's defense to its shareholders, trumpeted in full-page newspaper ads, was that its diversification was a strength in *bad* economic times.

· · ·

Things are just as sticky in other major proxy battles, which sometimes sound like plots from next year's *Dallas* shows. In Houston, the future of Superior Oil (1982 sales: $2 billion) is being fought over by Howard B. Keck, 69, the founder's son, and Willametta Keck Day, 67, the founder's daughter. Day, who owns 4.5 million of Superior's 127.4 million outstanding shares, wants to set up a committee of outside directors to consider takeover offers for 45% or more of the company's stock, now selling at $35 but valued by analysts at $45 to $65. Keck, who controls 14.6 million shares, the

662

LAW OF SECURITIES REGULATION

largest single voting block, will have no part of that. Superior's management claims that Keck's sister is in effect putting a For Sale sign on the company and making it vulnerable to a takeover by a major oil company such as Exxon or Texaco. Day has filed suit seeking to stop Superior from holding its annual meeting in May. That would forestall the re-election of directors whom Day deems obstructionist.

One of Day's supporters in the struggle is T. Boone Pickens, chairman of Mesa Petroleum and a takeover artist. Mesa already owns a reported 3.2 million shares in Superior and plans to vote them for Day's proposals in May. Pickens sees the Superior fight as a sign of things to come. Says he: "We are entering an era of stockholder awareness."

. . .

Experts have mixed feelings about the proxy battles. Some believe that they are a good thing because they force managers who may have grown careless to face up to the wrath of stockholders. Says one proxy-battle lawyer: "This proliferation is part of the trend back to quality, hard work and the American way that is cropping up everywhere, from the auto industry to high tech."

But the positives seem to stop there. Martin Lipton, a Wall Street lawyer who is advising Trans World, thinks proxy battles are a draining waste of effort and energy. Says he: "This is the worst thing that could happen to the American economy. You might have a situation where every company is at the short-term mercy of institutional investors." Adds John Phillips, chairman of Louisiana Land: "I do not think proxy battles are a legitimate dialogue between shareholders and management."

Phillips has a point. Proxy battles frequently do little good for the companies involved or the economy as a whole. They seem mainly to distract investors and company officials from their real business and into nasty paper chases. But those who mount proxy battles also often have a legitimate grievance: corporate managers do sometimes get sloppy and deserve being called to task.

As noted in the article, by the time insurgents round up support from other shareholders, pick their slate of candidates; hire attorneys, public relations firms, proxy solicitors and vote counters, comply with SEC rules, and advertise—they will incur substantial expense. So will management as it answers in kind. In a 1982 proxy fight for control of Gulf Resources and Chemical Corporation, the combined expenses of management and insurgents was around $4.3 million in a proxy fight that lasted just over two weeks.[9] Most of the expenses are attorneys' fees. Most of these attorneys' fees are made necessary by the network of federal regulations that governs a proxy contest.

Definition of "Solicitation"

The proxy rules apply to every "solicitation" of proxies. That term has been broadly defined, and may catch an unwary insurgent unawares.

Rule 14a-1 defines "solicitation" to include (1) any request for a proxy, (2) any request to execute or not to execute, or to revoke, a proxy, or (3) the furnishing

---

[9] R. Vilkin, "Proxy Wars: 21 Battle Tales," *National Law Journal*, March 21, 1983, p. 26.

of proxy forms or other communications under circumstances "reasonably calculated" to result in the giving, withholding, or revocation of a proxy. Note that encouraging shareholders not to give proxies to someone else may be a "solicitation," though the persons do not solicit proxies for themselves.

The definition expressly excludes responses to unsolicited requests by shareholders for a form of proxy and ministerial acts performed on behalf of those soliciting. Also, Rule 14a-2 exempts from the rules, *inter alia*, solicitations of ten or fewer people made by persons not acting for the issuer, and the furnishing of proxy voting advice by financial advisers under certain conditions.

The courts have not been totally consistent in their application of the "solicitation" definition, but a leading case takes the very broad position that not just an actual request for a proxy, but any act that is part of a "continuous plan" leading to such a request is a "solicitation." [10] The rationale for such a liberal approach is explained in the following case.

STUDEBAKER CORPORATION v. GITTLIN

360 F.2d 692 (2d Cir. 1966)

This case arose on March 21, 1966, when Gittlin, a shareholder of Studebaker Corporation, filed suit in state court alleging that he was acting on behalf of himself and on written authorization of 42 other shareholders owning over 5% of Studebaker's stock [Gittlin did not himself own the 5% of stock requisite to the state law right to inspect a shareholder list]; that he and his associates had been negotiating with Studebaker's management for certain changes in its board of directors, but negotiations had broken down; that Gittlin's group intended to solicit proxies at the forthcoming annual meeting; and that he had requested access to a list of shareholders and had been refused.

Studebaker then filed this suit contending that Gittlin's gathering of the written authorizations of 42 shareholders constituted a "solicitation" and that Gittlin had violated Rules 14a-3 and 14a-6 by soliciting proxies without filing prelim-

inary and final proxy material with the SEC in timely fashion.

The trial judge granted an injunction preventing the Gittlin group from using the authorizations in the state court proceeding. Gittlin appealed.

FRIENDLY, CIRCUIT JUDGE:

The contention most heavily pressed is that §14(a) of the Securities Exchange Act does not include authorizations for the limited purpose of qualifying under a state statute permitting the holders of a given percentage of shares to obtain inspection of a stockholders list. The statute is worded about as broadly as possible, forbidding any person "to solicit any proxy or consent or authorization" in respect of any security therein specified "in contravention of such rules and regulations as the Commission may

---

[10] *SEC* v. *Okin*, 132 F.2d 784 (2d Cir. 1943).

prescribe as necessary or appropriate in the public interest or for the protection of investors''; the definitions in the Proxy Rules, 14a-1, exhaust the sweep of the power thus conferred. The assistant general counsel of the SEC, which responded to our request for its views with promptness and definitude, stated at the argument that the Commission believes §14(a) should be construed, in all its literal breadth, to include authorizations to inspect stockholders lists, even in cases where obtaining the authorizations was not a step in a planned solicitation of proxies.

We need not go that far to uphold the order of the district court. In *SEC* v. *Okin*, 132 F.2d 784 (2 Cir. 1943), this court ruled that a letter which did not request the giving of any authorization was subject to the Proxy Rules if it was part of "a continuous plan" intended to end in solicitation and to prepare the way for success.

This was the avowed purpose of Gittlin's demand for inspection of the stockholders list and, necessarily, for his soliciting authorizations sufficient to aggregate the 5% of the stock required by §1315 of New York's Business Corporation Law. Presumably the stockholders who gave authorizations were told something and, as Judge L. Hand said in *Okin*, "one need only spread the misinformation adequately before beginning to solicit, and the Commission would be powerless to protect shareholders''—132 F.2d at 786. Moreover, the very fact that a copy of the stockholders list is a valuable instrument to a person seeking to gain control is a good reason for insuring that shareholders have full information before they aid its procurement. We see no reason why, in such a case, the words of the Act should be denied their literal meaning.

Affirmed.

One case held that a mere organizational meeting by an insurgent's committee was not a solicitation triggering the filing requirements of the federal rules.[11] But solicitations were found in requests to shareholders for funds to finance litigation to oust the incumbent board [12] and in a newspaper ad urging conversion of a utility company to public ownership that appeared at a time when the company was engaged in a proxy fight with proponents of the conversion plan.[13]

Even management can be tripped up by a broad definition of "solicitation." In one unusual case, *Sargent* v. *Genesco, Inc.*,[14] a management guilty of serious misstatements in SEC filings and of not holding a required annual meeting wrote shareholders discussing a refinancing plan that would purportedly put the company back on its feet. In a lawsuit that followed, plaintiff shareholders claimed that the letter constituted a "solicitation" because its purpose was to obtain shareholder approval of the refinancing plan. Plaintiffs claimed that the defendant executives should have disclosed their personal

---

[11] *Calumet Ind., Inc.* v. *MacClure*, 464 F.Supp. 19 (N.D.Ill. 1974).

[12] *SEC* v. *York* [1981–82 Transfer Binder], *Federal Securities Law Reports* (CCH), ¶98,271 (S.D. Cal. 1981).

[13] *Long Island Lighting Co.* v. *Barbash*, *Federal Securities Law Reports* (CCH), ¶92,392 (2d Cir. 1985).

[14] 492 F.2d 750 (5th Cir. 1974).

interest in pushing the plan as a means to eliminate their personal liabilities and that they were trying to "lull" the shareholders into inaction.

Management argued that there was no solicitation because no shareholder vote on the plan was ever sought and shareholder approval was not required by state law. While the court agreed that "not every communication from management is a solicitation" and that the evidence might show the letter was purely informational, the "circumstances surrounding its transmittal" could not be ignored. The court apparently concluded that if the letter was more than merely informational, it could constitute a proxy solicitation.

Filing Requirements

If a proxy contest arises between management and insurgents concerning the election or removal of directors, all "participants" (except the issuer itself) in the solicitation must file a Schedule 14B to guarantee that voting shareholders are fully informed as to the background of the solicitors.

"Participants"

Rule 14a-11 defines "participants" to include

1. The issuer.
2. Any director or nominee for election to director of the issuer.
3. Any committee or group that solicits proxies and their members and organizers.
4. Any person who contributes more than $500 to finance a proxy contest.
5. Any person other than a bank or lending institution acting in the normal course of business who lends money or furnishes credit to finance a solicitation.
6. "[A]ny other person who solicits proxies."

The rule excludes, *inter alia*, professional proxy solicitors, attorneys, accountants, and other professionals hired by contestants, persons who perform merely clerical tasks in connection with a solicitation, and employees or officers of the issuer who are not involved in the solicitation.

Filing of Schedule 14B

All "participants" in an election contest must file a Schedule 14B. Nonmanagement participants must file them at least five business days *prior* to any solicitation by their group, and management participants must file them within five business days *after* any management solicitation. Where a solicitation is made or prepared before the opposition arises to create a contest, the Schedule 14B must be filed as soon as is reasonably practicable thereafter. Persons who become participants in the middle of a proxy fight must file the Schedule 14B within three business days of becoming a participant. Of course, if any material changes occur, the Schedule 14B must be promptly amended.

Contents of Schedule 14B

Schedule 14B requires disclosure of, *inter alia*, the following items:

1. The name and address of the issuer.
2. The identity and background of the filing participants (including criminal convictions and participation in other proxy fights in the past ten years).
3. The amount of securities owned both beneficially and of record on behalf of associates whose identity must be disclosed along with the source of funds for recent purchases.
4. The circumstances under which the participants became involved and the extent of his or her activities.
5. A description of any transactions or planned transactions between the participant and the issuer.
6. The nature of any arrangements or understandings with regard to future employment by the issuer of, or future transactions with the issuer, by the participant and his associates.
7. Any amounts over $500 contributed to the solicitation.

Most of the important information contained in Schedule 14B must be included in the proxy statement furnished to shareholders.

Tactics and Strategy

The following excerpt gives some flavor of the mechanics and strategy of a proxy fight. Written in part by Kenneth Bialkin, one of the nation's leading attorneys in the area, the essay focuses on tactics that can be used by insurgent groups. It also highlights how important legal constraints can be in shaping strategy.

"PROXY CONTESTS—LEGAL AND PRACTICAL ASPECTS: RECENT DEVELOPMENTS" *

Kenneth Bialkin, Clare Attura, Mike Donatelli, and Jonathan Gottlieb

Hostile Battles for Corporate Control (1984)

A. *Use of a Formal Stockholder Committee*

The formation of a stockholder committee to propose a slate of nominees in opposition to that of management is a procedure often utilized by insurgents in proxy contests. Such a committee seeks to achieve broadbased stockholder appeal, and solicitation efforts of a committee are better received by stockholders than are solicitations from a few ostensibly disgruntled stockholders. The committee represents a formal, organized effort with a semblance of seriousness that will aid in attracting members. A committee staffed by qualified and well chosen people can have much the same "clout" as management. All committee members, however, will be required to disclose certain information about themselves in a statement on Schedule 14B.

B. *Source of Funds and Manpower*

One of the first tasks of a committee will be to estimate the probable cost of undertaking a successful proxy contest. Expenses of the contest will include:

- professional fees paid to attorneys, accountants, proxy solicitors and public relations professionals;
- expenses of "street name" brokers and other nominees who forward materials to beneficial owners;
- litigation costs incurred in obtaining a stockholder list and in other matters;
- fees and expenses of proxy counters and tabulators;
- fees and expenses of inspectors of election;
- printing and mailing costs for several communications to stockholders;
- costs of newspaper advertisements;
- filing fees and related expenses;
- telephone, travel and entertainment expenses; and
- various other related personnel expenses.

Insurgents must often seek commitments of funds from supporters. Financial supporters will be deemed "participants" and must disclose certain information about themselves in . . . Schedule 14B . . . if they intend to contribute more than $500.

C. *Timetable*

Clearly, the target date which influences the scheduling of all aspects of the contest is the date of stockholder meeting. Working backwards from that date, time must be allotted to:

- organize the team of experts;
- prepare and file Schedule 13D if appropriate [insurgents own over 5% of shares];
- prepare Schedule 14B statements for each participant, which statements must be filed 5 business days prior to the undertaking of any solicitation; time must be allotted to prepare, circulate and complete a questionnaire which will provide the information required to be disclosed in Schedule 14B;
- demand a stockholder list well before any solicitation is scheduled to begin, since litigation may be required to secure the list;
- prepare the proxy statement in accordance with Schedule 14A which must be filed in preliminary form with the SEC at least 10 days before it is sent to security holders (although such period of time may be shortened);
- prepare additional soliciting materials which must be filed with the SEC at least 2 days before being sent to security holders (although such period of time may be shortened);
- print and mail soliciting materials; and
- personally contact stockholders, especially those with large positions.

Generally, the insurgents' proxy material will not be sent to stockholders until after management's statement has been sent. In order to prevent a substantial advantage from accruing to management, the insurgents must anticipate the timing of management's mailing and be prepared with their proxy statement as soon as possible. Thereafter, additional soliciting materials generally will be prepared and disseminated to stockholders specifically to address contentions of the opposition as set forth in their earlier materials. In so doing, sufficient time must be allowed for SEC review and clearance of all soliciting materials and advertisements.

Before deciding to undertake a contest, the time factors that will be called into play must be given serious consideration. Although generalities are dangerous since the actual timetable will depend upon the nature of the parties, issues and specific circumstances, a broad rule of thumb may be that a party will need at least two months' time prior to the meeting. Successful contests have been mounted, however, in substantially less time.

D. *Obtaining a Stockholder List*

Any security holder entitled to vote at a meeting for which the issuer is making or intends to make a solicitation may request the issuer to mail copies of any proxy statement and other soliciting materials which it prepares in certain circumstances. In lieu of such mailing, however, the issuer may furnish promptly to the shareholder (i) a reasonably current list of the names and addresses of the holders of record and (ii) a reasonably current list of the bankers, brokers or other persons holding securities in street or nominee name for beneficial owners, which list must be accompanied by a statement of the approximate number of such beneficial owners and a schedule of the handling and mailing costs of each such banker, broker or other person if available to the issuer— Rule 14a-7(c). The information required to be furnished pursuant to this rule, however, need not include data with respect to holdings by record or beneficial owners.

The shareholder also may elect to make a demand for a stockholder list pursuant to the provisions of the applicable state inspection statute. For example, where the securities of a Delaware corporation are the subject of a solicitation, section 220 of the Delaware General Corporation Law grants stockholders of record the right "during the usual hours for business to inspect for any proper purpose the corporation's stock ledger, a list of its stockholders, and its other books and records, and to make copies or extracts therefrom." To exercise this right, the stockholder must direct to the corporation a written demand under oath setting forth the purpose of the inspection. The statute defines "proper purpose" as any purpose "reasonably related" to a stockholder's interest. It is well established as a matter of Delaware law that seeking a list of stockholders in order to solicit proxies for the election of directors in opposition to management constitutes a proper purpose.

. . .

Other state statutes are more restrictive and permit stockholder lists to be obtained only by certain stockholders. For example, Section 624 of the New York Business Corporation Law grants to persons who have been stockholders of record for six months or who hold at least 5% of any class of outstanding shares, upon at least five days' written demand, the right to examine and make extracts from a list of stockholders. . . .

An insurgent committee usually will opt to make a demand for a list pursuant to state inspection statutes in order to obtain information concerning stock holdings, since such information is not required to be furnished pursuant to Rule 14a-7 if the issuer elects not to mail. In any event, management will be responsible for making any arrangements necessary to update continuously the information reflected in the list for the duration of the contest. Although the first reaction of management is to resist, since the trend of the courts is to find a "proper purpose" and to order issuers to make their lists able, management may be best advised to furnish a list to the stockholder unless it has substantial grounds for withholding the list.

. . .

E. *Purchase of Additional Shares of Stock*

To the extent that committee nominees and other participants are in a position to purchase additional shares and thereby increase the voting power of the committee, they should be encouraged to do so. Proxies must be demanded to be delivered with shares purchased after the record date in order to enable such shares to be voted. Outstanding stock options should be exercised, if possible. However, any officer, director or 10% stockholder participant who is trading in the issuer's securities should be cognizant of the 1934 Act's §16 requirements and limitations and the possibility of a direct corporate or derivative lawsuit brought to recover short-swing profits. In addition, the Schedule 13D and Hart-Scott-Rodino [antitrust law] filing requirements may be triggered by purchases of the issuer's stock.

. . .

F. *Stockholders' Derivative Suit*

Where it appears that management has breached its fiduciary duties to the stockholders, the committee may want to consider the efficacy of initiating a derivative suit. Such a suit will at least have the effect of casting management's contentions in doubt, although groundless or seemingly frivolous suits ultimately may adversely affect the committee's position.

G. *Conduct of the Meeting*

As a general matter, both management and insurgents are well advised to negotiate an agreement governing the conduct of the meeting and the tabulation of the proxies.

H. *Datagrams*

In order to facilitate last-minute voting by stockholders in the few remaining days before the meeting, management and insurgents alike in recent contests have arranged for "datagram" voting. The solicitation process begins with the exchange of proxy statements, and perhaps supplements thereto, in the mail. After the initial distribution of these materials, however, further stockholder communications usually take the form of newspaper advertisements. It is not uncommon to see an advertisement of management directed toward undermining the insurgents' position, only to be followed a day or so later by an advertisement run by the insurgents. Use of datagrams permits stockholders to vote immediately upon reading such an advertisement by including therein instructions for placing a toll-free call to a Western Union operator who will transmit a telegram form of proxy identical to the proxy card mailed to the stockholder and indicate the stockholder's vote thereon. The datagram is usually transmitted to the proxy solicitor. To facilitate last minute voting, it may be prudent to arrange for transmission to the hotel or, at least, to the city in which the meeting will be held.

. . .

I. *Consents*

An insurgent group may implement a stockholder proposal without the necessity of bringing the battle front to the annual meeting or requesting that a special meeting be called. The corporation laws of several states contain provisions which permit stockholder action without a meeting if written consents from stockholders representing the number of votes required to authorize such action at a meeting are obtained. See, for example, Del. Gen'l Corp. Law §228. . . . The consent approach is not viable, however, where the governing corporate law requires unanimous written consent in order for stockholders to take action without a meeting. See, for example, N.Y. Bus. Corp. Law §615.

The Commission responded to the adoption of consent provisions by the states by amending Regulation C (Rules 14c-1 to 14c-7) to provide that the taking of corporate action by written authorization or consent of stockholders solicited by the issuer could not be accomplished unless an "information statement" containing substantially all of the information required to be included in a proxy statement is sent by the issuer at least 20 days prior to the earliest date on which the corporate action may be taken to stockholders whose consent is *not* solicited. Rule 14c-2. The Rule requires an issuer who has not solicited a consent from all stockholders to make certain disclosures to those stockholders whose consent has not been solicited. Regulation 14C imposes disclosure obligations only upon issuers.

With respect to insurgents, however, the disclosure obligations attending the solicitation of consents are found in Regulation 14A, which applies, in substantial part, to every solicitation of a proxy with respect to securities registered pursuant to §12 of the 1934 Act. "Proxy" is defined in Rule 14a-1 to include a consent or authorization. Rule 14a-3 states that no solicitation shall be made unless each person solicited is furnished with a proxy statement containing the information specified in Schedule 14A. An insurgent soliciting consents, therefore, must prepare a "consent" statement which complies with Schedule 14A.

· · ·

J. *Litigation*

Insurgents must be financially and psychologically prepared to defend and initiate litigation during the course of the contest. The burden of litigation associated with a proxy contest is enormous, and will often have the effect of delaying the implementation of the results of the election.

In many cases management will refuse to provide insurgents with a stockholder list on the ground that the insurgents intend to use the list for an improper purpose. Management's position in such cases usually has the effect of merely delaying the insurgents' solicitation by forcing them to sue for the list, as the solicitation of proxies to elect an opposing slate of directors has been viewed by most courts as a proper stockholder purpose.

The insurgents' proxy statement and other soliciting materials in all likelihood will be the subject of a lawsuit by management alleging violations of §14(a) of the 1934 Act and Rule 14a-9 promulgated thereunder based upon alleged disclosure inaccuracies or omissions. Relief typically sought in such a lawsuit includes an injunction against voting any proxies solicited pursuant to such materials. The insurgents should consider commencing such a lawsuit with respect to management's soliciting materials, if a basis exists for such a lawsuit, with a view toward discrediting management's position on the issues.

The insurgents may also be sued for alleged violations of §13(d) of the 1934 Act if their respective Schedules 13D inaccurately describe their stockholdings, their status as a "group" or their intentions with respect to the issuer. Such a lawsuit can be effectively nullified, however, by filing a corrected Schedule 13D.

Where the insurgents have been actively involved in a stock purchase program in an attempt to increase their ownership of the issuer's stock, it may be alleged that they have engaged in a tender offer without complying with applicable state takeover statutes. The relief sought will typically include an order invalidating the proxies thus obtained.

Reimbursement of Expenses

Because a proxy contest is so expensive, availability of reimbursement for expenses is an important question. Win, lose, or draw, the expenses of management are almost always paid by the corporation. While there is some question as to whether reimbursement is proper when incumbent management is merely seeking to protect itself—for example, the contest is a matter of ''personality'' and not ''policy''—management nonetheless seems always to be reimbursed.[15]

If insurgents lose a battle for control of the corporation, they will not be reimbursed. If the insurgents are not seeking control, but merely to place some representatives on the board or to foil a proposed merger, they probably will not be reimbursed even if they succeed.

Only if the insurgents gain control and have approval by a majority of shareholders will they be reimbursed out of the corporate treasury for reasonable expenses.[16]

ENFORCEMENT AND LITIGATION

Both the SEC and private causes of action provide enforcement of the network of proxy regulations.

SEC Powers

Section 21 of the 1934 Act permits the SEC to investigate and bring federal court actions to enjoin violations of the proxy rules. Section 32(a), as we have seen before, provides a criminal penalty for any willful violation of the proxy (or any 1934 Act) rules. In practice, the SEC frequently negotiates a consent decree–type settlement in which the defendant promises to correct prior errors and ''go and sin no more.'' The SEC will require correction of erroneous disclosures and may demand recirculation of proxy materials or even a new shareholders' meeting to remedy the violation.

Implied Private Causes of Action

Existence

Like so many other provisions of the 1933 and 1934 Acts, §14(a), which prohibits violations of the SEC proxy rules, does not expressly say that an injured party has a private cause of action. Whether a cause of action would be implied under §14(a) if the question reached the Supreme Court today for the first time is questionable. However, like the §10(b) cause of action, the courts have recognized a §14(a) right to sue for so long that its continued existence seems assured.

The Supreme Court first recognized the §14(a) private cause of action in the following case.

---

[15] *Rosenfeld* v. *Fairchild Engine and Airplane Corp.*, 128 N.E.2d 291 (N.Y. 1955).

[16] *Steinberg* v. *Adams*, 50 F.Supp. 604 (S.D.N.Y. 1950) (Delaware law).

J. I. CASE CO. v. BORAK

377 U.S. 426 (1964)

Borak (respondent), a shareholder of the J. I. Case Co., brought suit in federal district court seeking to enjoin a proposed merger between Case and the American Tractor Corporation (ATC). Plaintiff alleged both a state law breach of fiduciary duty claim and a claim that the defendant company officials (petitioners) had circulated false and misleading proxy material in violation of §14(a) and Rule 14a-9. Plaintiff requested a ruling that the merger was void, damages for himself and other shareholders, and such further relief "as equity shall require."

The trial judge held that he had no power to redress violations of §14(a) but was limited solely to the granting of declaratory relief under §27 of the 1934 Act. Under a state derivative action statute, the judge required the posting of a $75,000 bond for expenses and dismissed the action when plaintiff refused to post it. The Court of Appeals reversed. Case petitioned for certiorari.

CLARK, JUSTICE:

. . .

II.

It appears clear that private parties have a right under §27 to bring suit for violation of §14(a) of the Act. Indeed, this section specifically grants the appropriate District Courts jurisdiction over "all suits in equity and actions at law brought to enforce any liability or duty created" under the Act. The petitioners make no concessions, however, emphasizing that Congress made no specific reference to a private right of action in §14(a); that, in any event, the right would not extend to derivative suits and should be limited to prospective relief only. In addition, some of the petitioners argue that the merger can be dissolved only if it was fraudulent or non-beneficial, issues upon which the proxy material would not bear. But the causal relationship of the proxy material and the merger are questions of fact to be resolved at trial, not here. We therefore do not discuss this point further.

III.

While the respondent contends that his Count 2 claim is not a derivative one, we need not embrace that view, for we believe that a right of action exists as to both derivative and direct causes.

The purpose of §14(a) is to prevent management or others from obtaining authorization for corporate action by means of deceptive or inadequate disclosure in proxy solicitation. The section stemmed from the congressional belief that "[f]air corporate suffrage is an important right that should attach to every equity security bought on a public exchange"—H.R. Rep. No. 1383, 73d Cong., 2d sess., 13. It was intended to "control the conditions under which proxies may be solicited with a view to preventing the recurrence of abuses which . . . [had] frustrated the free exercise of the voting rights of stockholders"—Id., at 14. "Too often proxies are solicited without explanation to the stockholder of the real nature of the questions for which authority to cast his vote is sought"—S. Rep. No. 792, 73d Cong., 2d sess., 12. These broad remedial purposes are evidenced in the language of the section which makes it "unlawful for any person . . . to solicit or to permit the use of his name to solicit any proxy or consent or authorization in respect of any security . . . registered on any national securities exchange in contravention of such rules and regulations as the Commission may prescribe as necessary or appropriate in the public interest *or for the protection of investors"* (italics supplied). While this language makes no specific reference to a private right of action, among its chief purposes is "the protection of investors," which certainly implies the availability of judicial relief where necessary to achieve that result.

The injury which a stockholder suffers from corporate action pursuant to a deceptive proxy solicitation ordinarily flows from the damage done the corporation, rather than from the damage inflicted directly upon the stockholder. The damage suffered results not from the deceit practiced on him alone but rather from the deceit practiced on the stockholders as a group. To hold that derivative actions are not within the sweep of the section would therefore be tantamount to a denial of private relief. Private enforcement of the proxy rules provides a necessary supplement to Commission action. As in antitrust treble damage litigation, the possibility of civil damages or injunctive relief serves as a most effective weapon in the enforcement of the proxy requirements. The Commission advises that it examines over 2,000 proxy statements annually and each of them must necessarily be expedited. Time does not permit an independent examination of the facts set out in the proxy material and this results in the Commission's acceptance of the representations contained therein at their face value, unless contrary to other material on file with it. Indeed, on the allegations of respondent's complaint, the proxy material failed to disclose alleged unlawful market manipulation of the stock of ATC, and this unlawful manipulation would not have been apparent to the Commission until after the merger.

We, therefore, believe that under the circumstances here it is the duty of the courts to be alert to provide such remedies as are necessary to make effective the congressional purpose. It is for the federal courts "to adjust their remedies so as to grant the necessary relief" where federally secured rights are invaded.

. . .

Nor do we find merit in the contention that such remedies are limited to prospective relief.

. . .

[W]e believe that the overriding federal law applicable here would, where the facts required, control the appropriateness of redress despite the provisions of state corporation law, for it "is not uncommon for federal courts to fashion federal law where federal rights are concerned"—*Textile Workers* v. *Lincoln Mills*, 353 U.S. 448, 457 (1957).

Moreover, if federal jurisdiction were limited to the granting of declaratory relief, victims of deceptive proxy statements would be obliged to go into state courts for remedial relief. And if the law of the State happened to attach no responsibility to the use of misleading proxy statements, the whole purpose of the section might be frustrated. Furthermore, the hurdles that the victim might face (such as separate suits, security for expenses statutes, bringing in all parties necessary for complete relief, etc.) might well prove insuperable to effective relief.

. . .

Affirmed.

Standing

The courts have been relatively liberal in granting standing in proxy litigation. Shareholders, of course, usually have standing to challenge proxy rule violations. The courts have even granted standing to parties who, though shareholders, were acting primarily in their capacity as tender offerors.

For example, in *FMC Corp. v. R. P. Scherer Corp.*,[17] tender offeror FMC was allowed to challenge an alleged violation of Rule 14a-9 by management of the target corporation. The alleged inaccuracies involved a failure to disclose that the target's controlling shareholders had an "ongoing scheme" to perpetuate their control at the expense of other shareholders. These allegedly misleading omissions appeared in target management's solicitation materials intended to induce the shareholders to adopt amendments to the corporate bylaws that would impede any tender offer attempt. Target shareholders who wished to sell their shares in the tender offer also intervened on plaintiff's side and were granted standing. It may be significant that FMC, as a shareholder, had actively entered the proxy contest, soliciting shareholders to defeat the proposed amendment.

The standing issue will arise again in the section on reliance.

Elements of a Cause of Action

Because most important litigation in the proxy area involves allegations of false and misleading statements and omissions in violation of Rule 14a-9,[18] that is the type of case we will concentrate on in exposition of the elements of a §14(a) cause of action.

(1) Material Misstatement

The first step in determining whether a §14(a)/Rule 14a-9 cause of action exists is to make what is usually a fairly straightforward determination of whether there was a misleading misstatement or omission in the proxy materials. The more difficult second step usually involves determining whether the misstatement or omission was material.

The following case illustrates one application of the concept of materiality that arose out of a very bitter proxy fight.

GAF CORPORATION v. HEYMAN

724 F.2d 727 (2d Cir. 1983)

In early 1983 Samuel Heyman reescalated his earlier efforts to oust the management of GAF Corporation. His insurgents' committee criticized the performance and competence of

---

[17] 545 F.Supp. 318 (D.Del. 1982).

[18] Rule 14a-9 has been called the "primary operative regulation" in the SEC's system of proxy regulation. See *GAF Corp. v. Heyman*, 724 F.2d 727 (2d Cir. 1983).

GAF's management, especially in light of the company's poor financial performance while executive salaries continued to rise. Heyman proposed a program to realize GAF's underlying values by liquidating certain divisions of the company.

As a highly publicized proxy contest was being fought between GAF's incumbent management and Heyman's slate of insurgents, GAF filed this action on March 22, 1983, alleging, inter alia, that Heyman's proxy materials had contained certain false and misleading statements.

The election was held on April 28. The insurgents won, it later turned out, rather handily. But on May 2, GAF returned to court and sought to have the election overturned because of the alleged misstatements and omissions. As the focus of its attack, GAF alleged that Heyman should have disclosed the existence of litigation in state court in Connecticut. In that suit, Heyman's sister Abigail had alleged that Heyman had, while acting as her partner, attorney-in-fact, and trustee, denied Abigail information about her assets and converted some of those assets to his own use. There were also allegations concerning an intrafamily loan.

From Heyman's side, evidence showed that he took charge of the family's considerable business affairs after his father died in 1968, that his mother and Abigail had prospered during the intervening years, and that Heyman and his mother were concerned with Abigail's judgment and therefore had arranged to have her assets transferred to Heyman's exclusive control until 1990. This concern arose from a number of facts, including that Abigail had divorced, had become pregnant while unmarried, had had an abortion that she photographed while the operation was in progress, had published the pictures in a nationally circulated book, had begun living with a married psychiatrist 20 years her senior, and had suffered periods of severe depression.

The trial judge ruled that Heyman had violated §14(a) and Rule 14a-9 by failing to disclose details of his sister's lawsuit in his proxy material. He therefore enjoined the entire insurgent slate from assuming the directorships to which they had been elected, and ordered a resolicitation and new election. Heyman appealed.

PRATT, CIRCUIT JUSTICE:

. . .

In *TSC Industries, Inc.* v. *Northway, Inc.*, 426 U.S. 438 (1976), the Supreme Court formulated the standard of materiality under Rule 14a-9(a) as follows:

> An omitted fact is material if there is a substantial likelihood that a reasonable shareholder would consider it important in deciding how to vote. . . . Put another way, there must be a substantial likelihood that the disclosure of the omitted fact would have been viewed by the reasonable investor as having significantly altered the "total mix" of information made available—Id. at 449.

The positions of the parties regarding the central issue on appeal are fairly straightforward. Heyman contends that the Committee had no obligation to disclose in a GAF proxy fight either the contested, unproven, and unpursued allegations of a complaint filed in an unrelated intra-family dispute or the circumstances surrounding a family loan transaction not even mentioned in that complaint. In any event, Heyman argues, GAF's dissemination of the "breach of trust" allegations in its March 13 press release cured these omissions, since the "total mix" of information available to GAF shareholders would not have been significantly altered by fuller disclosure. On the other hand, GAF argues that the fact that a candidate for a position as a corporate fiduciary is a defendant in a pending lawsuit, charging him with improper self-dealing and other fiduciary misconduct, is necessarily important to stockholders called upon to decide who should be entrusted with the stewardship of their collective investment.

In considering these competing arguments, we are guided not only by the principles outlined above, but also by SEC Regulation S-K. Regulation S-K, together with more general provisions such as Rule 14a-9, "states the requirements applicable to the content of . . . proxy and information statements under §14 of the Exchange Act." The regulation provides instructions regarding involvement in legal proceedings that must be disclosed.

Nothing in this detailed regulation, which has been relegated to a footnote in GAF's brief, required Heyman to make any disclosure about the unproven allegations in the Connecticut action, much less the disputed loan transaction. While this court and others have indicated that compliance with Schedule 14A does not necessarily guarantee that a proxy statement satisfies Rule 14a-9(a), . . . the regulation does provide us with the Commission's expert view of the types of involvement in legal proceedings that are most likely to be matters of concern to shareholders in a proxy contest.

· · ·

In our view, the regulation's emphasis on orders, judgments, decrees, and findings in civil proceedings, in stark contrast to its express coverage of all pending criminal proceedings, strongly suggests that regardless of how serious they may appear on their face, unadjudicated allegations in a pending civil action against a director-nominee should not automatically be deemed material. In a society as litigious as ours, where plaintiffs are permitted great latitude in their pleadings, a reasonable shareholder would not place much stock in the bald, untested allegations in a civil complaint not involving the subject corporation without first examining, among other relevant factors, the relationship between the parties, the nature of the allegations, the circumstances out of which they arose, and

the extent to which the action has been pursued. Whether that information would be considered important in deciding how to vote would then depend on the issues involved in the proxy contest itself.

Applying the first part of this approach to the unique circumstances present here, all of the relevant factual indicia militate against a finding of materiality. First, the Connecticut action was "pending" only in a technical sense. The action was stayed on consent only nine days after it was commenced, before Heyman even filed a responsive pleading. No formal discovery had been conducted.

· · ·

Second, the Connecticut action did not in any way involve GAF. . . . Nor did Abigail's complaint allege any violations of the securities laws of the type referred to in Regulation S-K. . . . While we do not mean to suggest that pending litigation against a director-nominee based on state law and involving a family or other non-public business can never be material, actions of that nature are less likely to be matters of importance to public shareholders.

Third, the circumstances surrounding Abigail's allegations negate their materiality. All available evidence suggests that the action was nothing more than the outgrowth of an intra-family feud between Abigail and her new husband on one side and her mother and brother on the other. . . . Once her mother and brother agreed to pursue an amicable settlement, she in effect voluntarily withdrew the action. Furthermore, she subsequently swore that she supported her brother's slate in the proxy contest.

Thus, viewed in context, the three specific allegations in Abigail's complaint seized upon by GAF raise no serious question about Heyman's fitness to serve as a corporate director. Of even less significance is the $1,425,000 loan transaction, which was never specifically referred to in Abigail's complaint, but was the cornerstone of GAF's presentation below. While it may be true, as the district judge observed, that Abigail's general allegation as to diversion of assets was "broad enough to pertain to the loan" there is no basis for assuming that Abigail had any intention of asserting such a claim. Given that the "proxy rules simply do not require management to accuse itself of antisocial or illegal policies"—*Amalgamated Clothing & Textile Workers Union* v. *J. P. Stevens & Co.*, 475 F.Supp. 328, 331–32 (S.D. N.Y. 1979), *vacated as moot*, 638 F.2d 7 (2d Cir. 1980) (per curiam)—it would be fundamentally unfair to require Heyman to have anticipated and then disclosed the interpretation that GAF would place on the open-ended language of Abigail's complaint once the proxy contest was over.

Moreover, it is hardly surprising that Abigail's 28-page complaint never mentioned the loan transaction complained of by GAF. The loan was permitted by the elder Heyman's will and, as the district judge found, was "typical of many transactions engaged in by Heyman on behalf of the Heyman family entities" "except possibly in magnitude and duration." It would seem the "reasonable investor" would not have been influenced to change his proxy vote had the loan been disclosed.

The significance of the Connecticut action fades even further when its dormant allegations are compared with the issues that were raised in the proxy contest. . . . The overwhelming weight of both sides' proxy literature and advertisements focused on fundamental economic issues of concern to shareholders: the record of management and the competing plans for realizing the asset values of GAF. Given the predominance of these economic issues, the district judge erred in holding that there was "a substantial likelihood" that a reasonable shareholder would have considered the Connecticut action "important in deciding how to vote"—*TSC*, 426 U.S. at 449.

The court further erred by holding there was

a "substantial likelihood" that disclosure of the action and its underlying facts "would have been viewed by the reasonable investor as having significantly altered the 'total mix' of information made available"—Id. The fact that Heyman had been sued by his sister for "breach of trust" was disseminated by GAF more than six weeks before the annual meeting in its March 13 press release.

While there can be no doubt that the allegations and underlying facts of the Connecticut action were not "thoroughly aired," . . . we are convinced that this information "is of such dubious significance" that its disclosure may have "accomplish[ed] more harm than good"—*TSC*, 426 U.S. at 448. . . . In the "hurly-burly" of this contest, . . . particularly in its last few weeks when GAF announced deal after deal after deal, the shareholders had their hands full sorting out the proposed transactions and evaluating them in light of the combatants' competing programs. While GAF's incumbent management obviously would have preferred to shift attention away from these core economic issues, "bury[ing] the shareholders in an avalanche of trivial information"—*TSC*, 426 U.S. at 448— would scarcely have served the interests of corporate democracy.

Moreover, the district court found that a reasonable person could conclude that Heyman had "acted with the best of motives, in good faith, in the best interests of Abigail, and for her benefit and protection." If resolicitation were required, Heyman would be free to characterize the facts underlying the Connecticut action in a similarly favorable fashion. In addition, he could state that Abigail, the supposed victim of his "breach of trust", supported his slate. It is therefore likely that the impact of GAF's press release would have been diminished rather than bolstered by any further disclosure.

Our conclusion that non-disclosure of the Connecticut action was not a material omission is reinforced by several additional factors. First, we consider it revealing that it was not until May 2, after the results of the election were apparent, that GAF asserted for the first time below that Heyman's failure to disclose the suit was material.

· · ·

Second, we cannot overlook that GAF is urging this court to hold Heyman to a stricter standard than GAF itself followed in deciding whether to disclose that a number of its incumbent directors had been defendants in various lawsuits alleging breach of fiduciary duty. . . .

Furthermore, under the decision below, both sides in a proxy contest would have every incentive and legal right to pursue massive discovery to unearth facts which, it can later be claimed, amount to a breach of fiduciary duty that should have been alleged in a prior action against an

opposing candidate. As the case graphically illustrates, the litigation ubiquitous in every proxy contest would thus become a forum for litigating, possibly relitigating, the issues in any pending or prior suit involving a director-nominee.

· · ·

This was a proxy contest fought on the issues of GAF's financial performance and future corporate policy. Presented with a clear choice, the shareholders voted decisively in favor of the insurgent slate. Given this resounding mandate, it is inconceivable that fuller disclosure of the dormant Connecticut action would have had "a significant *propensity* to affect the voting process."

The judgment of the district court is therefore reversed.

In other cases involving materiality, courts have held that misleading financial projections may be the basis for a §14(a) suit but that because such projections are necessarily speculative, they may be deleted without creating a misleading omission.[19] Several other cases have involved the distinction between "simple corporate mismanagement" (e.g., paying bribes or otherwise wasting corporate assets) and self-dealing by management (e.g., receiving kickbacks). Most courts have held that the latter must be disclosed as material, but not the former.[20] "No case [has] held that the proxy rules are violated because management has allegedly mismanaged the company, and the proxy statement does not say so."[21]

(2) *Causation*

The common law fraud notion of causation has been substantially liberalized in the proxy environment. In *Mills* v. *Electric Auto-Lite*,[22] the Supreme Court held that a plaintiff need not prove that a particular misstatement or omission *caused* the shareholders to vote the way they did. Rather, all a plaintiff need show is that the misstatement or omission was material and that the *solicitation* itself was "an essential link in the accom-

---

[19] *Caspary* v. *Louisiana Land & Exploration Co.*, 725 F.2d 189 (2d Cir. 1984).

[20] For example, *Gaines* v. *Haughton*, 645 F.2d 761 (9th Cir. 1981), *cert. denied*, 454 U.S. 1145 (1982).

[21] *Bank and Trust Co. of Old York Road* v. *Hankin*, 552 F.Supp. 1330 (E.D.Pa. 1982).

[22] 396 U.S. 375 (1970).

plishment of the transaction." The notion of "transaction causation" is discussed in the following case.

WEISBERG v. COASTAL STATES GAS CORP.

609 F.2d 650 (2d Cir. 1979), *cert. denied*, 445 U.S. 951 (1980)

On the basis of information that arose in part out of congressional hearings, plaintiff Weisberg, a shareholder of Coastal States Gas Corp., filed a §14(a) suit against Coastal and a number of other parties alleging that Coastal had paid $8 million in bribes in 1973 and 1974. Weisberg's first claim was that the proxy solicitation materials for the election of Coastal's board in the years 1974–1978 were materially misleading because the shareholders were not told of the bribes or of a subsequent alleged coverup by Coastal's Audit Committee.

Plaintiff sought only equitable relief—the setting aside of the old elections and ordering of new ones. The district judge dismissed the case because the claims did not satisfy the requirement of "transaction causation." Plaintiff appealed.

FEINBERG, CIRCUIT JUDGE:

In *Mills* v. *Electric Auto-Lite Co.*, 396 U.S. 375 (1970), the Court defined the elements of a §14(a) violation. Plaintiffs, who were shareholders of Auto-Lite, alleged that the corporation's directors had violated the statute by soliciting proxies for approval of a merger with Mergenthaler Linotype Co. without disclosing in the proxy materials that they were all nominees of, and controlled by, Mergenthaler. The Seventh Circuit Court of Appeals agreed that the proxy solicitation was misleading but nonetheless concluded that plaintiffs would not be entitled to relief under §14(a) if defendants could show on remand "that the merger would have received a sufficient vote even if the proxy statement had not been misleading"—403 F.2d 429, 436.

The Supreme Court reversed on this issue of causation, stressing that §14(a) embodied the legislative intention "to promote 'the full exercise of the voting rights of stockholders' by ensuring that proxies would be solicited 'with explanation to the stockholders of the real nature of the questions for which authority to cast his vote is sought' "—396 U.S. at 381, citing H.R. Rep. No. 1383, 73rd Cong., 2d sess. 14. The decision of the Court of Appeals, in contrast, allowed a bypassing of the stockholders

> on the basis of a finding that the merger was fair . . . at least where the only legal challenge to the merger is a suit for retrospective relief after the meeting has been held. A judicial appraisal of the merger's merits could be substituted for the actual and informed vote of the stockholders—396 U.S. at 381.

Concluding that it could not accept "[s]uch a frustration of the congressional policy," the Court set forth the following test of causation:

> Where the misstatement or omission in a proxy statement has been shown to be "material," as it was found to be here, that determination itself indubitably embodies a conclusion that the defect was of such a character that it might have been considered important by a reasonable shareholder

who was in the process of deciding how to vote. This requirement that the defect have a significant *propensity* to affect the voting process is found in the express terms of Rule 14a-9, and it adequately serves the purpose of ensuring that a cause of action cannot be established by proof of a defect so trivial, or so unrelated to the transaction for which approval is sought, that correction of the defect or imposition of liability would not further the interests protected by §14(a).

There is no need to supplement this requirement, as did the Court of Appeals, with a requirement of proof of whether the defect actually had a decisive effect on the voting. Where there has been a finding of materiality, a shareholder has made a sufficient showing of causal relationship between the violation and the injury for which he seeks redress if, as here, he proves that the proxy solicitation itself, rather than the particular defect in the solicitation materials, was an essential link in the accomplishment of the transaction. This objective test will avoid the impracticalities of determining how many votes were affected, and, by resolving doubts in favor of those the statute is designed to protect, will effectuate the congressional policy of ensuring that the shareholders are able to make an informed choice when they are consulted on corporate transactions.

· · ·

Appellant argues that the district court erred in holding in its first memorandum opinion that her complaint failed "to satisfy the transaction causation requirement of *Mills*. . . ." Appellees, in contrast, urge that we affirm the dismissal on this ground, asserting that "where the transaction authorized by the allegedly false or misleading proxy materials is the election of directors, previous improper corporate payments (as breaches of fiduciary duty) are not approved by shareholders voting for directors, and thus are not caused by the proxy statements." This argument, however, misconstrues plaintiff's claim. In the cases relied on by appellees, the plaintiff sought damages because of allegedly improper payments, which did not require shareholder approval. The causal link between the proxy solicitation for the election of directors and the injury complained of—the improper payments—was attenuated at best. In the instant case, however, the challenged "transaction" is the election of the directors, and we have no doubt that the "proxy solicitation itself . . . was an essential link in the accomplishment" of that transaction, within the meaning of *Mills*.

Indeed, the district judge's opinion after reargument apparently recognized the force of plaintiff's assertion that her complaint met the "transaction causation" requirement. In his second memorandum, the judge affirmed his dismissal of the first claim, but this time on the ground that plaintiff failed to assert that the alleged bribes resulted in kickbacks to the directors, citing our recent opinion in *United States* v. *Fields*, 592 F.2d 638 (2d Cir. 1978). This new rationale, by implying that an allegation of kickbacks would have changed the result, raises the much more difficult question of whether the alleged omissions were "material." As previously noted, the Supreme Court in *Mills* emphasized that a defect in the proxy statement would not violate §14(a) if it was "trivial" or lacked "a significant *propensity* to affect the voting process"—396 U.S. at 384. This requirement of materiality, as defined in *TSC Industries* v. *Northway*, supra, required the district court in the instant case to consider whether a reasonable shareholder would find information concerning the alleged bribes and cover-up to be important in deciding how to vote on the election of directors.

Utilizing this test of materiality, we believe that it was error to dismiss plaintiff's first claim for relief on a motion to dismiss without first providing plaintiff with some opportunity to demonstrate that the alleged omissions were material. . . . Plaintiff alleges that had she been provided with such an opportunity, she would have been able to establish the materiality of the alleged bribes by proving kickbacks. We cannot say as a matter of law that such an attempt would have been futile, particularly in light of the massive and unexplained overpayments by Coastal to Selman revealed in the hearings of the House Subcommittee on Oversight and Investigation.

. . .

Reversed and remanded.

---

(3) *Reliance*

Some courts have held that plaintiff shareholders who have not themselves granted a proxy have no individual standing to bring a §14(a) action because they did not act in reliance on the allegedly misleading solicitation materials. Instead, such shareholders are relegated to bringing a derivative action on behalf of the corporation and the courts may grant relief after taking into account equitable considerations based on the best interests of the shareholders as a whole.[23]

Courts will probably be quick to hold the reliance element met where a plaintiff who has given a proxy proves the elements of material misrepresentation and transaction causation.

(4) *Scienter*

The courts are split on how to handle the scienter element for §14(a) claims. The Second Circuit applied a negligence standard both to the soliciting corporation and apparently to outside directors and accountants in *Gerstle* v. *Gamble-Skogmo, Inc.*[24] Later, the Sixth Circuit in *Adams* v. *Standard Knitting Mills, Inc.*,[25] required that plaintiffs show scienter at least before recovering damages from outside accountants under Rule 14a-9.

The lower courts have struggled to reconcile the divergent Circuit Court holdings. Some courts require a showing of only negligence as to the corporation and its officials, but demand a showing of scienter for outside defendants such as accounting firms who do not directly benefit from the proxy vote.[26]

Where merely an injunction, and not damages, is sought, some courts do not even require a showing of negligence. They will enjoin a solicitation upon demonstration of the "objective [in]sufficiency of the disclosure." [27]

Other Federal Remedies

Sometimes §§10(b) and 18(a), discussed in earlier chapters, are pressed into duty by plaintiffs complaining of misleading proxy solicitation materials.

---

[23] For example, *Gaines* v. *Haughton*, 645 F.2d 761 (9th Cir. 1981).

[24] 478 F.2d 1281 (2d Cir. 1973).

[25] 623 F.2d 422 (6th Cir.), *cert. denied*, 449 U.S. 1067 (1980).

[26] *Fradkin* v. *Ernst*, 571 F.Supp. 829 (N.D. Ohio 1983).

[27] *Calumet Industries, Inc.* v. *MacClure*, 464 F.Supp. 19 (N.D.Ill. 1978).

Breach of Duty

State law remedies for breach of fiduciary duty may also apply in proxy contests. Sometimes such claims will be brought in state court; other times they will be in federal court on diversity grounds or pendent to a §14(a) suit. A typical case follows.

COALITION TO ADVOCATE PUBLIC UTILITY RESPONSIBILITY, INC. v. ENGELS

364 F.Supp. 1202 (D. Minn. 1973)

Plaintiffs in this case include the Coalition to Advocate Public Utility Responsibility (Coalition), a consumer interest group. Defendants include Northern States Power Co. (NSP) and its directors and officers. Alpha Smaby was a candidate for NSP's board who was supported by the Coalition. In the spring of 1973, when it began to look as if Smaby, with help from the considerable efforts of the Coalition and others, might control up to 9% of NSP's voting shares, the NSP directors voted to reduce the size of its board of directors from 14 to 12 and to classify the board into groups of four for election to staggered terms of one, two, and three years. Without this change, 7% of the shares, voted cumulatively, would have been sufficient to elect a member to the board; afterward, over 20% would be required.

NSP freely admitted it took this action for the specific purpose of hindering Smaby's candidacy. In addition, though it was in constant contact with the Coalition, NSP's board did not give plaintiffs the details of this change of structure until it received a court order to do so almost a month after the action was taken (which was less than a month before the scheduled shareholder meeting).

Plaintiffs brought this suit for an injunction to halt defendants' soliciting of proxies for the meeting on grounds that the last-minute secret

changes in the board's structure violated state fiduciary principles as well as §14.

LORD, DISTRICT JUDGE:

• • •

Plaintiffs concede that the actions of the defendants do not violate any state statutory law but argue that the manipulation of the corporate machinery by insiders for the sole purpose of frustrating the candidacy of a minority shareholder in this instance violates *both* the federal securities law and is a breach of the insiders' fiduciary duty to the minority shareholders. Plaintiffs rely heavily on two Delaware cases which basically stand for the proposition that actions by insiders, although otherwise lawful, may be enjoined if they act to injure the rights of minority shareholders—*Condec Corporation v. Lunkenheimer*, 230 A.2d 769 (Del. Ch. 1967), and *Schnell v. Chris-Craft Industries*, 285 A.2d 437 (Del. Supr. 1971). In *Schnell* the Delaware Supreme Court held that management's efforts to use the corporate machinery and Delaware law for the purpose of perpetuating itself in office and obstructing legitimate efforts of the dissident stockholders in the exercise of their rights to undertake a proxy contest against management was impermissible. The insiders had advanced the date of the stockholders' meeting in an effort to frustrate the efforts of minority shareholders who desired to wage a proxy contest. The actions of the insiders were enjoined despite the fact that they were in compliance with the company by-laws and applicable Delaware law. The basis for these opinions rests on the fiduciary duty imposed on directors and officers of a corporation to deal fairly and justly with the corporation and all of its shareholders including minority shareholders. The officers and directors of NSP are in a fiduciary relationship with the minority shareholders and as such owe them a duty to deal with them fairly and in good faith.

In the instant case, the actions of the insiders, if not unfair, were certainly questionable in light of their fiduciary obligation to the plaintiff shareholders. Not only did the defendants change the rules in the middle of the game, but they refused to disclose the existence of the changes when approached by the plaintiffs. Both of these actions served to frustrate the plaintiff shareholders' legitimate efforts to run for the Board of Directors and may well be a breach of fiduciary duty. From the evidence adduced at the hearing, it is the conclusion of the Court that plaintiffs have established a substantial likelihood that they will succeed on the merits.

Accordingly, based on the reasons as set forth above, it is ordered that the defendants shall cease all steps and activities in furtherance of the proposed changes in the number of directors and the procedure for electing members to the Board of Directors of NSP until further order of this Court.

The Business Judgment Rule

The courts are split on the question of whether shareholder proxy litigation should be terminated when, pursuant to the business judgment rule, an independent shareholder litigation committee (SLC) determines in good faith that the shareholder's suit is not in the best interests of the corporation.

Some courts have upheld the termination of such litigation pursuant to the business judgment of an SLC.[28] On the other hand, in *Galef* v. *Anderson*,[29] the court held that federal policies underlying the proxy rules should override the state law foundation of the business judgment rule.

SHAREHOLDER PROPOSALS

Introduction

To increase shareholder participation in corporate democracy, Rule 14a-8 provides a mechanism whereby shareholders can propose resolutions for the consideration of all shareholders at the annual or a special meeting. If proper requirements are met, manage-

---

[28] For example, *Lewis* v. *Anderson*, 615 F.2d 778 (9th Cir. 1979), *cert. denied*, 449 U.S. 869 (1980).

[29] 615 F.2d 51 (2d Cir. 1980).

ment must include the resolutions in its proxy statement, even though management opposes them.

Until recently, any shareholder could propose two resolutions per year. In 1983, the SEC reduced to one the number of resolutions a shareholder could introduce in a year. The Commission also instituted eligibility requirements—a proponent must have owned for one year prior to the meeting date the lesser of $1,000 (market value) worth of shares or 1% of the outstanding shares of a class. Several persons may aggregate their shares to meet the threshold.[30]

The proposed resolution, plus a supporting statement, may not cumulatively exceed 500 words. The proposal must be delivered to management at least 120 days prior to the date of the prior year's annual meeting or a "reasonable time" before solicitation is made if a special shareholder meeting is involved.

Management may choose not to oppose a particular proposal and simply include it in its proxy materials. However, if management opposes a resolution, it need not automatically include it. Rule 14a-8(c) lists 13 grounds on which management may omit a proposal. If management seeks to invoke one of those grounds for exclusion, it must submit the proposal, its position, and a supporting letter of legal counsel to the SEC at least 60 days prior to the date its preliminary proxy materials will be filed.

The staff of the SEC will then review the positions of the parties. The burden is on the corporation to convince the staff that omission is proper. If the corporation carries that burden, the staff will issue a letter indicating that it intends to take "no action" if the proposal is omitted. In fiscal year 1981, 991 proposals were submitted; management contested 303 of them of which the SEC agreed to exclude 193. Another 223 were voluntarily withdrawn by the proponent.[31] In 1982, AT&T had 21 proposals submitted; ultimately only 4 were included in its proxy statement.

The decisions of the staff are seldom reviewed by the courts or even by the Commission itself. If matters are challenged in court, the view of the staff is usually accepted by the judges.

Grounds for Omission

Rule 14a-8(c) lists 13 grounds for omission of a shareholder proposal. Frequently management will point to more than one as a basis for its decision to omit.

Not a Proper Subject for Shareholder Action

Rule 14a-8(c)(1) allows exclusion if a matter is not a proper subject for shareholder action under the law of the corporation's state of domicile. Because of the substantial discretion most state corporation laws give to the board of directors, the SEC has frequently allowed omission of resolutions that *mandated* certain action by the board, but has

---

[30] *Securities Exchange Act Release*, no. 34–20091 (August 16, 1983).

[31] American Society of Corporate Secretaries' Report on Shareholder Proposals (1981), quoted in W. L. Duffy, "Shareholder Initiatives," in *Proxy Contests* (New York: Practising Law Institute, 1982), p. 31.

held not excludable the same type of resolution framed merely to *advise or request* the board to act.

In one instance a shareholder proposal directing the board to dissolve the corporation was held excludable because state law required the board to place a resolution before the shareholders before they could consider dissolution. Therefore, the staff concluded that "unless the proposal is promptly revised by the proponent to the format of a recommendation or request that the board of directors take the steps necessary under Delaware law to effect a dissolution," no action would be taken if management omitted it.[32]

Violation of State, Federal, or Foreign Law

Rule 14a-8(c)(2) allows exclusion of any proposal that would violate state, federal, or foreign law. Thus, a resolution calling for the selection of a lesbian as the director of a bank could be omitted because it would constitute a violation of employment discrimination laws to mandate that a woman rather than a man would have to be chosen.[33]

Contrary to SEC Rules

Rule 14a-8(c)(3) allows exclusion of a proposal that violates an SEC rule. The most common ground for omission is that a proposal is false and misleading in violation of Rule 14a-9. One management was allowed to exclude a proposal that the company avoid business with communist countries and report to the shareholders within six months on its progress because the proposal did not disclose that the report would result in significant expense to the company and was therefore misleading.[34]

Personal Claim or Grievance

Rule 14a-8(c)(4) allows management to omit a proposal that merely represents a personal grievance of the proponent and is not of interest to shareholders generally. RCA's management successfully invoked this provision to omit a proposal by Synanon Foundation that RCA disclose the editorial policies of its subsidiary broadcasting stations. The staff concluded that the proposal constituted Synanon's attempt to retaliate against RCA's subsidiary, the National Broadcasting Company, for adverse publicity it had given Synanon.[35]

AT&T was allowed to exclude famous corporate "gadfly" Evelyn Y. Davis's

---

[32] *2B Systems, Inc.* [79–80 Transfer Binder], *Federal Securities Law Reports* (CCH), ¶82,402 (September 14, 1979).

[33] *North American Bank & Trust Co.*, *Securities Regulation & Law Reports* (BNA), Vol. 14 (February 17, 1982), p. 312.

[34] *Storage Technology*, March 10, 1980.

[35] *RCA Corporation* [1979 Transfer Binder], *Federal Securities Law Reports* (CCH), ¶82,024 (February 7, 1979).

proposal that the company report on its hiring and training of male employees for jobs traditionally held by females. The matter was deemed a personal grievance after the staff reviewed several of Ms. Davis's statements at annual meetings, including this one:

> I am opposed to women on the boards, because, as an attractive young woman I get a better deal from the worst men than the friendliest woman. You won't hear me nominating any women. . . .
>
> Well I think that directors like I told you that the secretaries wouldn't let me speak to their boss like Mr. Hewitt and Mr. Dillon if those women are too jealous to let their boss speak to another woman, someone who is glamorous and famous, they should definitely get a man as a secretary.[36]

Not Significantly Related to the Issuer's Business

Rule 14a-8(c)(5) allows management to exclude matters not significantly related to the issuer's business. Traditionally managements have tried to use this provision to omit proposals dealing with political, social, and religious issues. Their success has been mixed. One successful example involved IT&T, which was allowed to omit a proposal calling for corporate support of California's Proposition 13 because its call for a dramatic reduction in state taxes would not have a significant impact on the corporation.[37]

Some corporations have been allowed to omit proposals that they cease doing business with South Africa or with communist nations on grounds that they have done little or no business with those countries anyway. Other companies have not been so successful. Mobil, for example, was told it could not omit a proposal dealing with trade with communist nations on grounds that its sales to them represented less than 1% of total revenues because "there are many instances in which the matter involved in a proposal is significant in an issuer's business, even though such significance is not apparent from an economic standpoint." [38]

Recently the SEC has tried to clarify this area by instituting a percentage test. A proposal may now be omitted if it relates to operations accounting for less than 5% of the issuer's total assets and less than 5% of its net earnings and gross sales, *if* the matter is not otherwise "significantly related" to the issuer's business. This qualifying phrase preserves the SEC's view that a proposal related to just a small part of the issuer's business may raise important policy issues that could have a significant impact on the company's overall operations.

That the promulgation of a percentage test did not mean that the "significantly related" test became solely a matter of economic importance was illustrated in the following case.

---

[36] *American Telephone & Telegraph Co.* [1981 Transfer Binder], *Federal Securities Law Reports* (CCH), ¶76,805 (February 26, 1981).

[37] *International Telephone & Telegraph Co.* [1980 Transfer Binder], *Federal Securities Law Reports* (CCH), ¶76,375 (February 15, 1980).

[38] *Mobil Corp.* [1981 Transfer Binder], *Federal Securities Law Reports* (CCH), ¶76,832 (February 26, 1981), quoting *Securities Exchange Act Release*, no. 34–12999 (November 22, 1976).

LOVENHEIM v. IROQUOIS BRANDS, LTD.

618 F.Supp. 554 (D.D.C. 1985)

Plaintiff Lovenheim, who owned 200 shares of defendant Iroquois Brands, Ltd. (Iroquois/Delaware), submitted to defendant a shareholder proposal he intended to offer at the next annual meeting. The proposal dealt with the procedure used to force feed geese for production of pâté de foie gras in France, a type of pâté imported by defendant.

According to plaintiff, pâté de foie gras is made from the liver of geese, and the geese are frequently force fed to expand the liver and thereby produce a larger quantity of pâté. Force feeding usually begins when the geese are four months old. Where the farm is mechanized, the bird's body and wings are placed in a metal brace and its neck is stretched. Through a funnel inserted 10–12 inches down the throat of the goose, a machine pumps up to 400 grams of corn-based mash into its stomach. An elastic band around the goose's throat prevents regurgitation. When feeding is manual, the handler uses a funnel and a stick. Plaintiff has no evidence that force feeding is used by defendant's supplier, but his proposal calls for creation of a committee to investigate.

Defendant has refused to include plaintiff's proposal in its proxy material to shareholders, relying on the "not otherwise significantly related to the issuer's business" exception contained in Rule 14a-8(c)(5).

Plaintiff sued and moved for a preliminary injunction requiring defendant to insert his proposal into its proxy materials.

Gusch, District Judge:

The likelihood of plaintiff's prevailing in this litigation turns primarily on the applicability to plaintiff's proposal of the exception to the shareholder proposal rule contained in Rule 14a-8(c)(5).

Iroquois/Delaware's reliance on the argument that this exception applies is based on the following information contained in the affidavit of its president: Iroquois/Delaware has annual revenues of $141 million with $6 million in annual profits and $78 million in assets. In contrast, its pâté de foie gras sales were just $79,000 last year, representing a net loss on pâté sales of $3,121. Iroquois/Delaware has only $34,000 in assets related to pâté. Thus none of the company's net earnings and less than .05 percent of its assets are implicated by plaintiff's proposal. These levels are obviously far below the 5% threshold set forth in the first portion of the exception claimed by Iroquois/Delaware.

Plaintiff does not contest that his proposed resolution relates to a matter of little economic significance to Iroquois/Delaware. Nevertheless he contends that the Rule 14a-8(c)(5) exception is not applicable as it cannot be said that his proposal "is not otherwise significantly related to the issuer's business" as is required by the final portion of that exception. In other words, plaintiff's argument that Rule 14a-8 does not permit omission of his proposal rests on the assertion that the rule and statute on which it is based do not permit omission merely because a proposal is not economically significant where a proposal has "ethical or social significance."

Iroquois/Delaware challenges plaintiff's view that ethical and social proposals cannot be excluded even if they do meet the economic or 5% test. Instead, Iroquois/Delaware views the exception solely in economic terms as permitting omission for any proposals relating to a de minimis share of assets and profits. Iroquois/Delaware asserts that since corporations are economic entities, only an economic test is appropriate.

The Court would note that the applicability of the Rule 14a-8(c)(5) exception to Mr. Lovenheim's proposal represents a close question given the lack of clarity in the exception itself. In effect, plaintiff relies on the word "otherwise," suggesting that it indicates the drafters of the rule intended that other noneconomic tests of significance be used.

Prior to 1983, paragraph 14a-8(c)(5) excluded proposals "not significantly related to the issuer's business" but did not contain an objective economic significance test such as the 5% of sales, assets, and earnings specified in the first part of the current version. Although a series of SEC decisions through 1976 allowing issuers to exclude proposals challenging compliance with the Arab economic boycott of Israel allowed exclusion if the issuer did less than one percent of their business with Arab countries or Israel, the Commission stated later in 1976 that it did "not believe that subparagraph (c)(5) should be hinged solely on the economic relativity of a proposal"—Securities Exchange Act Release No. 12,999 (1976). Thus the Commission required inclusion "in many situations in which the related business comprised less than one percent" of the company's revenues, profits or assets "where the proposal has raised *policy questions* important enough to be considered 'significantly related' to the issuer's business."

As indicated above, the 1983 revision adopted the 5% test of economic significance in an effort to create a more objective standard. Nevertheless, in adopting this standard, the Commission stated that proposals will be includable notwithstanding their "failure to reach the specified economic thresholds if a significant relationship to the issuer's business is demonstrated on the face of the resolution or supporting

statement"—Securities Exchange Act Release No. 19,135 (1982). Thus it seems clear based on the history of the rule that "the meaning of 'significantly related' is not *limited* to economic significance."

The only decision in this Circuit cited by the parties relating to the scope of section 14 and the shareholder proposal rule is *Medical Committee for Human Rights* v. *SEC*, 432 F.2d 659 (D.C.Cir. 1970). That case concerned an effort by shareholders of Dow Chemical Company to advise other shareholders of their proposal directed at prohibiting Dow's production of napalm. Dow had relied on the counterpart of the 14a-8(c)(5) exemption then in effect to exclude the proposal from proxy materials and the SEC accepted Dow's position without elaborating on its basis for doing so. In remanding the matter back to the SEC for the Commission to provide the basis for its decision, id. at 682, the Court noted what it termed "substantial questions" as to whether an interpretation of the shareholder proposal rule "which permitted omission of [a] proposal as one motivated primarily by *general* political or social concerns would conflict with the congressional intent underlying §14(a) of the [Exchange] Act." 432 F.2d at 680 (emphasis in original).

Iroquois/Delaware attempts to distinguish *Medical Committee for Human Rights* as a case where a company sought to exclude a proposal that, unlike Mr. Lovenheim's proposal, was economically significant merely because the motivation of the proponents was political. The argument is not without appeal given the fact that the *Medical Committee* Court was confronted with a regulation that contained no reference to economic significance. Yet the *Medical Committee* decision contains language suggesting that the Court assumed napalm was not economically significant to Dow:

> The management of Dow Chemical Company is repeatedly quoted in sources which include the company's own publications as proclaiming that

the decision to continue manufacturing and marketing napalm was made not *because* of business considerations, but *in spite* of them; that management in essence decided to pursue a course of activity which generated little profit for the shareholders. . . . Id. at 681 (emphasis in original)

This Court need not consider, as the *Medical Committee* decision implied, whether a rule allowing exclusion of all proposals not meeting specified levels of economic significance violates the scope of §14(a) of the Exchange Act. See 432 F.2d at 680. Whether or not the Securities and Exchange Commission could properly adopt such a rule, the Court cannot ignore the history of the rule which reveals no decision by the Commission to limit the determination to the economic criteria relied on by Iroquois/Delaware. The Court therefore holds that in light of the ethical and social significance of plaintiff's proposal and the fact that it implicates significant levels of sales, plaintiff has shown a likelihood of prevailing on the merits with regard to the issue of whether his proposal is "otherwise significantly related" to Iroquois/Delaware's business.

Preliminary injunction granted.

Beyond the Issuer's Power to Effectuate

Rule 14a-8(c)(6) allows exclusion if a proposal is beyond the power of the issuer to accomplish. However, this exclusion has been narrowly construed. Bally Manufacturing Corp. was not allowed to omit a proposal that it terminate trading of standardized options relating to its common stock. The change was dramatic, but could be taken.[39]

Ordinary Business Operations

Although shareholders are entitled to select the board of directors and vote on major corporate changes, the day-to-day affairs of the corporation are within the purview of the officers supervised by the directors. Therefore, proposals relating to everyday business decisions may be omitted under Rule 14a-8(c)(7).

For example, Sears was allowed to omit a proposal asking management to describe the undesirable economic and ecological effects of relocating stores in shopping malls. Choosing store locations was deemed an ordinary business decision.[40] On the other hand, matters dealing with the structure or composition of management are a direct concern of the shareholders and, thus, a proposal that the executive committee be composed of a majority of outside directors could not be omitted.[41]

The staff has utilized this exception to exclude proposals it felt were too insignifi-

[39] *Bally Mfg. Co.* [1978 Transfer Binder], *Federal Securities Law Reports* (CCH), ¶81,550 (February 23, 1978).

[40] *Sears, Roebuck & Co.* [1980 Transfer Binder], *Federal Securities Law Reports* (CCH), ¶96,353 (March 6, 1980).

[41] *Minnesota Mining & Mfg. Co.* [1980 Transfer Binder], *Federal Securities Law Reports* (CCH), ¶76,390 (March 27, 1980).

cant or too complex for shareholders to deal with.[42] For example, management of Pennsylvania Power & Light Co. was allowed to omit a proposal regarding disposition of environmental litigation with the EPA.[43]

Companies have frequently attempted to characterize proposals relating to sales to communist countries, conversion from nuclear to solar power, smoking on airlines, and the like as matters of ordinary business operations. However, the staff has usually concluded that politically sensitive issues involve policy matters of legitimate concern to the shareholders and therefore may not be omitted on this basis.[44]

Elections to Office

Rule 14a-8(c)(8) allows exclusion of proposals relating to election of particular persons to office. Proposals concerning procedures or structures of the board, on the other hand, are not excludable.

Counterproposals

Rule 14a-8(c)(9) authorizes management to exclude a shareholder proposal that addresses the same subject as one of its own. One case allowed exclusion of a proposal to employ a particular accounting firm where management had proposed employment of another. Absent omission, both proposals might have received majority approval and then management would not know what the shareholders had authorized.[45]

Mootness

If management has already planned or instituted an action called for in a shareholder proposal, it may omit that proposal under Rule 14a-8(c)(10).

Duplication

Because there is no reason to submit two versions of the same proposal, Rule 14a-8(c)(11) establishes a first-come, first-served policy, allowing management to omit a proposal by one shareholder if it is already including a proposal by another shareholder that is substantially similar.

---

[42] P. Lochner, "Proxy Statements and Proxies Under the Securities Exchange Act of 1934," in *Securities Filings: Review and Update* (New York: Practising Law Institute, 1983).

[43] *Pennsylvania Power & Light Co.* [1980 Transfer Binder], *Federal Securities Law Reports* (CCH), ¶76,395 (January 29, 1980).

[44] K. Warwick, "Handling Shareholder Proposals," in *Proxy Statements, Annual Meetings and Disclosure Documents* (New York: Law & Business, Inc., 1983), p. 101.

[45] *B. F. Saul Real Estate Investment Trust* [1981–82 Transfer Binder], *Federal Securities Law Reports* (CCH), ¶77,097 (November 24, 1981).

Substantially the Same as Previously Unsuccessful Proposals

In order that management not be required to submit a proposal year after year that receives no significant shareholder support, Rule 14a-8(c)(12) allows omission of a proposal that deals with "substantially the same subject matter" as a previously submitted proposal that did not achieve established minimum levels of support. If a proposal has been submitted once in the past five years, it must have garnered at least 3% of the shareholder vote to be entitled to resubmission. If it has been submitted twice in that period, it must have received 6%, and if three times, 10% is the threshold for resubmission.

The difficulty is sometimes in deciding which proposals deal with substantially the same subject matter. For example, Emerson Electric Co. was not allowed to omit a proposal that would have required it to report on its foreign military sales despite Emerson's claim that this dealt with substantially the same subject matter as a previous unsuccessful proposal that Emerson establish certain "ethical criteria" for entering into Defense Department contracts. Although the proposals had a common motive, they asked the corporation to do different things.[46]

Specific Amounts of Dividends

To prevent a multitude of conflicting proposals that might bankrupt a company, management may, under Rule 14a-8(c)(13), exclude all proposals dealing with specific amounts of cash or stock dividends.

Evaluation of Shareholder Proposal Mechanism

The shareholder proposal mechanism is an established method of shareholder input into corporate control and policies. The number of proposals rose from 293 in fiscal 1970 to 991 in 1981 (though it has recently declined). Recently dissident shareholders have used the device in important battles in major corporations to facilitate take-overs. The device has been deemed a useful method of attempting to influence the board by changes of composition or structure because it is less burdensome than a full-fledged proxy fight for control.

Despite its popularity, the shareholder proposal mechanism is quite controversial. Critics point out that it is expensive and time consuming for corporations to include proper proposals and to gain the right to exclude improper ones.

Even shareholders' proposals that are properly included seldom gain significant shareholder support, usually achieving less than 5% of the vote. Furthermore, of the 991 proposals submitted in 1981, church groups and seven active individuals accounted for 66%.[47]

Former SEC Commissioner Barbara Thomas has said,

---

[46] Emerson Electric Co., *Securities Regulation & Law Report*, Vol. 49 (Washington, D.C.: Bureau of National Affairs, Inc., 1985), (SEC Nov. 1984).

[47] American Society of Corporate Secretaries Report on Shareholder Proposals (1981), quoted in Duffy, "Shareholder Initiatives," in *Proxy Contests* (New York: Practising Law Institute, 1982), p. 31.

Although this right of virtually unfettered access to the corporate voting process may represent an appropriate ideal, in real-world practice it has imposed burdens on both public companies and the commission staff that are simply not justified. . . .

The shareholder resolutions submitted for inclusion in proxy materials all too often may represent self-indulgent attempts to highlight issues of individual significance with little or no real connection to business of the corporation.[48]

On the other hand, proponents of the shareholder proposal view it as a valuable symbolic part of shareholder democracy. Additionally, they point out that even when a shareholder proposal elicits only a small percentage of the vote, it still forces management to at least justify its position on what may be important matters of corporate policy. Even more important, such proposals may generate enough publicity that management will voluntarily alter its conduct. Proponents say that shareholder proposals have induced many corporations to reduce their activities in South Africa, disclose their equal employment opportunity progress, and reconsider their policies on nuclear and environmental issues among others. Two such proponents have concluded that

Whether the shareholder proposal process is to be judged a success even if it only provides an opportunity to hold management accountable, or whether a judgment about the success of the process turns on whether it has resulted in changes in corporate behavior, there is abundant evidence that the process has succeeded.[49]

Annual Meetings

Shareholder proposals are part of the reason that the annual meetings of the big public corporations can be very interesting experiences. That their role is also controversial is illustrated in this chapter's concluding excerpt.

"The Annual Nightmare: Meeting with Shareholders" *

The Wall Street Journal

May 9, 1983, p. 28, col. 3

This is the season for one of the most spectacularly useless events in American business—the annual shareholder meeting. Thousands of these dreadful convocations have been held throughout the country in recent weeks.

The practice is considered the cornerstone of corporate democracy and is upheld by both tradition and law. State statutes of incorporation require an annual meeting of public companies, and the New York Stock Exchange informally demands it of every company whose shares it lists for trading. "Basically the exchange looks upon the annual meeting as a forum where shareholders can address their concerns to management,"

---

[48] Quoted in H. Einhorn, "SEC's Revisions and 'Non-Changes' in the Shareholder Proposal Rule," *National Law Journal*, December 12, 1983, p. 40.

[49] D. Schwartz and E. Weiss, "An Assessment of the SEC Shareholder Proposal Rule," *Georgetown Law Journal*, Vol. 65 (1977), pp. 635, 640.

says a Big Board official. A secondary purpose is to provide management the opportunity to explain in person its business mission to shareholders.

In practice, the meetings seldom live up to these ideals. Most fall into one of two categories: sleepers, where managers trundle out a few leftovers from the slagheap of information they've already released to the public; or circuses, where executives submit themselves to inane heckling from a handful of the attending shareholders. Sometimes, the meetings combine both.

Recently I attended the annual meeting of Merrill Lynch & Co., which, from my experience and the accounts of other reporters at this newspaper, is typical. The meeting was held in a vast ballroom at the Essex House Hotel in New York. In the anteroom, a spongy mass of Danish pastries and croissants was heaped on a long convention table. Another table bore stacks of proxy materials, annual reports and a sampling of investment brochures issued by the Wall Street giant.

Merrill Lynch Chairman Roger Birk and President William Shreyer, flanked by several other executives, reviewed an array of facts and figures showing the sources of the company's present and expected results. The information was a replay of data contained in the annual report and other materials put out in recent months. The only new information involved a stock split and the first-quarter earnings, both of which were released through normal channels several hours before the meeting.

Mr. Birk then opened the meeting up to the floor. He set out ground rules that questions or comments should relate to the business of Merrill Lynch, and that any shareholder be limited to two questions. These instructions went largely unheeded.

What followed was a bizarre ritual that precluded any intelligent colloquy between management and shareholders. It was instead a temporary reversal of roles, in which the usually powerful executives seemed to atone for their privileged position in life by allowing themselves to be pilloried by the most insignificant shareholders. Later, one Merrill Lynch official sighed, "It's one of the prices we have to pay to be a public company."

Dominating the meeting was the ubiquitous Evelyn Y. Davis, the itinerant heckler whose antics are well-known to dozens of American corporations. She quizzed Mr. Birk on the company's charitable contributions, which she suggested were excessive. She also took the occasion to insult Beverly Sills, whom Merrill Lynch had honored at a recent benefit.

Mrs. Davis has the manner of a demonic nursemaid, alternately coddling and scolding her subjects. She affectionately addressed the Merrill Lynch chief by his first name, then excoriated him for agreeing "to buy a small-time New Jersey bank run by a man with an Italian name" (the Raritan Savings & Loan Association, whose president is Joseph Paparetto). A weak titter arose among the thousand or so shareholders in the audience as she made a vulgar remark about New York Mayor Edward Koch.

An elderly man in a gray slicker questioned Mr. Birk about a stock dividend he imagined Merrill Lynch to have promised shareholders last August. After several minutes of invective over the matter, he was restrained by a young woman stationed by Merrill Lynch at the microphone where he spoke (the company remembered him from the previous year's meeting).

Some shareholders enjoy the sense that they can rescue a perspiring executive in the midst of these assaults. One man rose and embarked upon a confusing account about a misadventure with a discount broker—the natural enemy of Merrill Lynch and the other full-service brokers. Another suddenly called for a round of applause for Merrill Lynch and its management.

In the romper-room atmosphere that prevailed, it's unlikely that any shareholder would have found it productive to raise serious questions involving the content of Merrill Lynch's business. Nor was the forum suitable for airing social concerns that might involve Merrill Lynch. Yet Mr. Birk, like other chief executives, had to spend weeks preparing for the meeting. A phalanx of aides was asked to bone up on an array of trivial items annual meetings often focus on.

This is a waste of resources. Worse, the typical annual meeting probably serves to diminish shareholders' standing by creating the impression that they are an ill-informed, fractious lot who need to be tempered annually at a ritual meeting, then ignored.

In the early 1970s, Fuqua Industries tried to mail consent forms to its shareholders on business matters and dispense with the meeting. The Big Board scotched the plan. And last year, General Motors abandoned its plans for a brief meeting that would take up business matters, followed by a separate session to handle questions from the floor. Critics charged that GM was undercutting corporate democracy. Worse, Mrs. Davis swore that she would attend both meetings.

To some extent, annual meetings are an anachronistic throwback to a simpler age when companies were smaller, with a more containable community of shareholders. Moreover, shareholders no longer need the annual meetings as they once did to influence corporate policies. Prof. John C. Coffee of the Columbia Law School points out that regulatory actions and court decisions in the last decade have enhanced the ability of shareholders to propose and circulate resolutions, which he says "are a better tool than the annual meeting for raising a variety of issues."

But he and others say annual meetings have provided some definite benefits. The requirement to hold them has prevented certain entrenched managements from avoiding challenges indefinitely. Mr. Coffee believes that the Arab boycott of companies trading with Israel would have gained more support among U.S. business if managements hadn't been forced to explain their positions on this matter at open meetings.

Nevertheless, on a routine basis, the annual sessions seem to accomplish little beyond a ritual humbling of certain executives. A better way would be to conduct shareholder voting by mail, and require any public company to send, postage-paid, an inflatable doll of its chief executive to any shareholder requiring a corporate scapegoat or love object.

QUESTIONS AND PROBLEMS

1. Mendell owned common stock of Loehmann's, Inc., in 1981 when Loehmann's merged with an AEA Investors, Inc., subsidiary. Mendell claims in a §14(a) suit that approval of Loehmann's shareholders was improperly obtained. Among the defendants was Drexel, an investment banking firm that had provided an opinion with respect to the fairness of the merger price that was included in the proxy solicitation materials. Mendell claims that Drexel violated §14(a) by permitting the use of its name to solicit proxies in this manner. Was Drexel's act a "solicitation"? Discuss. See *Mendell* v. *Greenberg*, 612 F.Supp. 1543 (S.D.N.Y. 1985).

2. Gross brought a §14(a) action challenging the sufficiency of defendant officers' and directors' disclosures in a proxy statement. Among other complaints, Gross charged that the proxy statement did not disclose that defendants (a) knowingly made false statements, reports, entries in books, overvalued property, misapplied funds and committed other illegal acts in violation of federal law, and (b) enjoyed certain fringe benefits, including a rental free farm and purchase of land valuable enough to attract the corporation's interest. Were these matters "material"? Discuss. See *Bank and Trust Co. of Old York Road* v. *Hankin*, 552 F.Supp. 1330 (E.D.Pa. 1982).

3. Abbey, a shareholder of Control Data Corporation (CDC), sued several officers and directors of CDC seeking repayment of $1,131,800 in civil and criminal penalties levied on CDC as a result of the corporation's guilty plea to criminal charges stemming from illegal payments to certain foreign entities. Abbey contended that defendants violated various securities laws and fiduciary principles by making the payments *and* that they violated §14(a) by not disclosing the payments in proxy solicitation materials. Abbey argued that CDC would not have voted to elect certain officers or to grant certain stock options had the illegal payments been disclosed. Discuss. See *Abbey* v. *Control Data Corp.*, 603 F.2d 724 (8th Cir. 1979), *cert. denied*, 444 U.S. 1017 (1980).

4. Lerman headed an insurgent group that announced that it intended to wage a proxy contest for control of Diagnostic Data, Inc. (DDI), at its next annual meeting, then scheduled for the third Thursday in June. Soon thereafter, DDI's board of directors met, repealed its traditional June annual meeting date in favor of one left to the discretion of the board, and added a bylaw that required any insurgent group to submit information roughly equivalent to that required to be disclosed by the SEC's Schedule 14B "not less than seventy days prior to any meeting of stockholders called for the election of directors." Lerman's group challenged these changes, but before any resolution occurred, DDI's board scheduled the annual meeting for 63 days later. This action made compliance by Lerman's insurgent group with the board's information requirement an impossibility. Lerman challenged the action as inequitable. Discuss. See *Lerman* v. *Diagnostic Data, Inc.*, 421 A.2d 906 (Del. Ch. 1980).

5. All American sought to merge General United Group, Inc. (GUG), into a subsidiary All American specially created for that purpose. All American owned all GUG's Class B Common shares (10,623,150), but only a small portion (67,043 of 2,959,560) of its Common shares. The proxy statement sent to shareholders stated that the merger would be approved if at least two-thirds of the Common and Class B Common Stock, *voting as one class*, approved the merger. Only 41.8% of the Common shares were voted for the merger, but coupled with the Class B Common, a two-thirds majority was reached. Plaintiff, a shareholder of GUG who opposed the merger, challenged the transaction on several grounds. He argued, among other things, that Iowa law required the two-thirds approval of both classes of common shares when voted *separately*. The statute was unclear; the federal court where the suit was filed certified the question to the Iowa Supreme Court which concluded that the Iowa statute did in fact require separate class voting. Among plaintiff's claims was that the proxy statement violated §14(a) because of its inaccurate statement regarding Iowa law. The trial judge instructed the jury that defendants could be responsible for the erroneous statement if they acted *negligently*. The jury found no negligence and no liability, apparently because of the confused state of the law. Plaintiffs appeal, arguing that a strict liability standard should have been imposed. Discuss. See *Shidler* v. *All American Life & Financial Corp.*, *Federal Securities Law Reports* (CCH), ¶92,326 (8th Cir. 1985).

6. Hospital Corp. of America sought to omit a shareholder proposal that would prohibit the performance of induced abortions in the company's owned or managed facilities

other than those emergency procedures necessary to prevent the imminent death of a pregnant woman. Among other provisions, the company relies on Rule 14a-8(c) (7) permitting exclusion of proposals dealing with a matter relating to the conduct of ordinary business operations. Is exclusion proper? See *Hospital Corp. of America* (SEC, February 12, 1986).

7. A shareholder proposal sought to require General Electric Co.'s management to (a) set a target date after which no further generation of nuclear waste would be allowed by GE industrial processes, (b) terminate contracts for nuclear-related products, and (c) provide technical assistance to governmental agencies seeking a permanent solution to the problem of radioactive waste disposal. GE sought to omit the proposal under Rules 14a-8(c)(3) ("vague or misleading") and 14a-8(c)(6) ("beyond the power of the company to effectuate"). Evaluate GE's position. See *General Electric Co.* (SEC, January 7, 1986).

8. A shareholder proposal would require that any recommendation or decision by the CBS board of directors with respect to any offer to purchase 20% or more of the outstanding shares of common stock would have to be based upon the recommendation of the independent directors after obtaining a fairness opinion from an investment banking firm. CBS sought to omit the proposal on grounds that it violated federal law (14a-8(c)(1)) and that it violated SEC rules (14a-8(c)(2)) because it was false and misleading in violation of Rule 14a-9. Specifically, CBS argued that the supporting statement implied that the proposal was being put forward solely out of concern for the shareholders in general, when it was actually being sponsored for political reasons by the group Fairness in Media. Discuss. See *CBS, Inc.* (SEC, February 19, 1986).

22

TENDER OFFERS

INTRODUCTION

A proxy fight, discussed in the previous chapter, is one method of gaining control of a corporation. Another well-known method is the tender offer, which is an offer to purchase the shares of a corporation that is made directly to its shareholders, usually by a third party. The offer may well be to buy a majority of the "target" corporation's stock, though it need not be. The offeror (bidder) might offer the shareholders cash in exchange for their shares of target stock, but securities or a combination of cash and securities might also be the offered consideration. The tender offer may be "friendly," meaning the bidder has negotiated for and received the support of the target's management. It may also be "hostile," meaning that target management intends to oppose the tender offer by all means possible to maintain the target's independence.

Tender offers are a relatively new phenomenon. After World War II, large-scale corporate acquisitions gradually became popular. Huge conglomerates developed as corporations expanded not by developing new businesses, but by purchasing already existing enterprises. The tender offer gradually became an accepted form of making such acquisitions. From 1956 to 1960, there were a total of only 79 cash tender offers. Most of them added together would not have amounted to a billion dollars. In 1981 alone there were 124 tender offers, several involving acquisitions of multibillion-dollar corporations.

A large spurt in the growth of tender offers in the 1960s was largely due to a complete lack of state or federal regulation. In 1968, however, the Congress passed the Williams Act, which amended the 1934 Exchange Act to regulate tender offers. Most states followed suit by enacting even more restrictive tender offer regulations. Despite the increase in regulation, tender offers again rapidly increased in number, size, and scope in the early 1980s. As this chapter is written, there can be little doubt that tender offers are helping to restructure corporate America. No American corporation, no matter how large or small, is immune from being a target in a tender offer.

A tender offer battle is extremely exciting. It resembles nothing so much as a chess match. On the offense is the bidder, who must come up with the financing to make an attractive bid to the target's shareholders. On the defense is target management, which tends to believe that most bids are too low and therefore not in the best interests of the target's shareholders. Whether this belief is tied to the fact that the target's managers will frequently lose their jobs should the offer succeed and the offeror become the corporation's new owner is a matter of some speculation. Legal constraints imposed by the Williams Act are among the most limiting factors on offensive and defensive tactics. Some of the finest financial, managerial, and legal minds in the nation are constantly developing new offensive and defensive techniques that will help to advance or thwart hostile tender offers.

These exciting battles for control have even developed their own colorful terminology, much of which you will be exposed to during this chapter. For example, a hostile bidder or offeror is frequently referred to as a ''shark,'' a ''pirate,'' or a ''raider.'' The target is frequently referred to as a ''damsel in distress.'' One popular method of fighting off a hostile tender offer is to induce a third corporation to make a competing and, it is hoped, higher bid to the target's shareholders. This third corporation, because it has usually promised more favorable terms for the target's management, is frequently referred to as a ''white knight.''

The tender offer is extremely controversial. Some believe that we have too many successful tender offers. Many argue that tender offers are an inefficient way of allocating capital and that the constant fear of being the target in a tender offer leads many managers to emphasize short-term profits at the expense of long-term corporate goals. Others argue that tender offers *are* an efficient method of allocating capital and of punishing managers who have not been efficient. They maintain that the defensive tactics used in tender offers are not in the shareholders' best interests and should be severely limited.

The controversy over tender offers led the SEC to establish an ''Advisory Committee on Tender Offers.'' The Committee's 1984 report suggested approximately 50 changes in the legal regulation of tender offers. Although relatively few of those changes have been made as this chapter is written in the fall of 1986, the SEC and Congress have changed some rules and, it seems, are continually considering other changes. Many of the rules discussed in this chapter may be altered, at least to some extent, in the near future.

DEFINITION OF "TENDER OFFER"

The Williams Act contains no definition of a "tender offer." A helpful suggestion, though, is that a tender offer is:

> a public offer or solicitation by a company, an individual or a group of persons to purchase during a fixed period of time all or a portion of a class or classes of securities of a publicly held corporation at a specified price or upon specified terms for cash and/ or securities.[1]

Note again that a tender offer need not be "hostile," but it frequently is. It need not be for a majority or even a controlling block of stock, but it usually is.

The courts and the SEC have struggled to develop a more precise definition than that suggested, but many gray areas remain. The most prominent test for the presence of a tender offer was first explicated in *Wellman* v. *Dickinson*,[2] and has been applied to both third-party tenders and self-tenders. According to this test, eight factors must be weighed:

1. Was there an active and widespread solicitation of public shareholders for shares of an issuer?
2. Was the solicitation for a substantial percentage of the issuer's stock?
3. Was the offer to purchase made at a premium over the prevailing market price?
4. Was the offer firm and nonnegotiable?
5. Was the offer contingent on the tender of a fixed minimum number of shares, and perhaps subject to the ceiling of a fixed maximum number to be purchased?
6. Was the offer open for only a limited period of time?
7. Did the offer place pressure on the offerees to sell their stock?
8. Was there a public announcement of a purchasing program concerning the target company, preceded or accompanied by a rapid accumulation of large amounts of the target's securities?

The more "yes" answers are given to these questions, the more likely the purchases will be characterized as a tender offer.

Wellman involved Sun Company's making simultaneous secret offers to 28 large shareholders of Becton, Dickinson & Co. to purchase their shares (about 35% of all outstanding Becton shares) at $45 a share, well over the market price of $32 a share. The offerees were given anywhere from 30 minutes to overnight to accept the offer, were not told the identity of the purchaser, and were told in some cases that if

---

[1] E. Aranow and H. Einhorn, *Tender Offers for Corporate Control* (New York: Columbia University Press, 1973), p. 70.

[2] 475 F.Supp. 783 (S.D.N.Y. 1979), *aff'd*, 682 F.2d 355 (2d Cir. 1982), *cert. denied sub nom. Dickinson* v. *SEC*, 103 S. Ct. 1522 (1983).

they did not act quickly the purchasing program might be "oversubscribed" and they would be left out altogether. In this manner, Sun acquired 34% of Becton's stock. Virtually all eight factors were present, and the court found a tender offer had been made.

More recently, in *In re Paine Webber Jackson Curtis Co., Inc.*,[3] while a hostile tender offer for Diamond shares by a third party was pending, Simpson Paper Co. instructed Paine Webber, a broker-dealer, to (1) buy 9.9% of Diamond stock on an all-or-nothing basis; (2) offer $42.50 per share, a premium over the market price of $38.875; (3) not disclose the buyer's identity; (4) acquire the entire amount in a single transaction; and (5) do it all in one day. Paine Webber spent all day on the phone and just before the close of trading bought 1.28 million Diamond shares (9.96%) out of 2 million that had been tendered from 25 broker-dealers representing 256 Diamond shareholders. All eight of the elements, except perhaps a public announcement, were present. The administrative law judge concluded a tender offer had been made.

The result in *Wellman* and *Paine Webber* should be contrasted to that in *SEC v. Carter Hawley Hale Stores, Inc.*[4] In this case, Limited had made a hostile tender offer for Carter Hawley Hale (CHH). After announcing a stock repurchase program, CHH began purchasing its own shares to keep them out of the raider's hands. Within seven trading days, the company paid approximately $470 million for slightly more than 50% of its previously outstanding shares, all purchased over the stock exchanges. The SEC argued that the repurchases constituted a "self-tender offer," which had not complied with the Williams Act. The judge, however, concluded that only the final two elements of the eight-factor test were present. There was no widespread solicitation, because CHH's agents had followed instructions not to solicit shareholders and arbitrageurs (persons who specialize in purchasing stock which can be quickly resold elsewhere at a higher price). There was a substantial purchase, but not a *solicitation* to purchase a large amount. There was no premium, since CHH paid market price, though that price was somewhat inflated by the outstanding tender offer. Different prices were paid to different sellers, so the offer was not firm and nonnegotiable. The SEC conceded it was not contingent on a minimum tender, nor was the offer open for a limited period of time. The court rejected the SEC's argument.

The SEC lost another round in *Hanson Trust PLC v. SCM Corp.*,[5] wherein a shark terminated a tender offer and then immediately purchased 25% of the target's stock within 90 minutes from six sellers. The SEC argued that the purchase was functionally a tender offer that did not comply with the Williams Act. The court held that it was not a *de facto* tender offer because at least five of the six sellers were highly sophisticated sellers who were not pressured by any conduct the Williams Act was designed to alleviate and who received a price that could not be called a "premium" since it was only $1 over market.

---

[3] [1982–83 Transfer Binder], *Federal Securities Law Reports* (CCH), ¶83,310 (SEC 1983).

[4] 587 F.Supp. 1248 (C.D.Cal. 1984), *aff'd*, 760 F.2d 945 (9th Cir. 1985).

[5] 774 F.2d 47 (2d Cir. 1985). Unhappy with the results in *Carter Hawley Hale* and *Hanson Trust*, the SEC, as this chapter is written, is considering changes in its rules to alter these results.

THE WILLIAMS ACT

Introduction

Enacted in 1968 in response to perceived abuses in the tender offer process, the Williams Act amended the 1934 Act, which had previously left tender offers largely unregulated. Its basic purpose was twofold: first, to provide full disclosure by both the bidder and the target in a tender offer so that shareholders could make an informed decision, and, second, to create a "level playing field" so that neither the bidder nor the target could gain an upper hand that could manipulate or distort the shareholders' decision-making process.

The act's main provisions are found in §§13 and 14 of the 1934 Act. Section 13(d), as subsequently amended, provides disclosure and reporting requirements for any person or group purchasing more than 5% of the securities of a potential target. Section 13(e) provides for disclosure and regulation in an issuer's repurchases of its own shares. Section 14(d) provides the disclosure and reporting requirements for tender offerors and their opponents. It also provides the substantive regulation that shapes tender offers. Section 14(e) is an antifraud and antimanipulation provision that applies to all participants in a tender offer battle. Finally, §14(f) provides for disclosure to shareholders whenever a tender offeror intends to elect or designate a majority of target directors other than at a meeting of shareholders.

We shall now discuss the more important aspects of these Williams Act provisions.

Section 13(d)

According to §13(d), any person or group acquiring beneficial ownership of more than 5% of a class of voting equity securities registered under Section 12 of the 1934 Act must within ten calendar days file a Schedule 13D with the SEC and send copies to the issuer and each exchange where the issuer's shares are traded.

The purpose of this disclosure requirement is to alert shareholders of the issuer to the potential for a change in control. This portion of the Williams Act regulates the pre-tender offer proceedings and can serve as an "early warning device." Many persons contemplating a tender offer begin by accumulating through open market purchases a substantial portion of the issuer's stock. Of course, by not purchasing more than 4.99%, they can avoid tipping their hands.

The term "person" is broadly defined to include corporations, partnerships, and groups of individuals. Thus, if several shareholders agree to buy, sell, or vote together,[6] they must within ten calendar days of making that agreement file a Schedule 13D if cumulatively they own more than 5%, even if individually no member of the

---

[6] *Portsmouth Square, Inc.* v. *Shareholders Protective Comm.*, 770 F.2d 866 (9th Cir. 1985) (§13(d) did not apply to shareholders' committee that solicited dividends from other shareholders for a suit challenging validity of existing stock because the agreement to act together invoked neither voting nor investment power).

group owns that much. Some courts even require groups of the issuer's management who decide to act together, perhaps to fend off a tender offer, to file a Schedule 13D,[7] though other courts do not unless the management group is also intertwined with a third party.[8]

Disclosure

Schedule 13D requires disclosure of such matters as the title of the class of securities and the issuer, the identity and background of the filer, the source and amount of funds or other consideration used to purchase the shares including loans obtained, the purpose of the transaction, the nature and extent of the beneficial ownership, and any contracts, arrangements, understandings, or relationships (legal or otherwise) between the filer and any person with respect to securities of the issuer.

The most important of all the Schedule 13D requirements is that relating to the purpose of the acquisition. The filer is required to describe any plans or proposals that would relate to or result in (1) acquisitions or dispositions of shares of the issuer; (2) extraordinary corporate transactions such as mergers, reorganizations, or liquidations involving the issuer; (3) sales or transfers of substantial assets of the issuer; (4) changes in the issuer's board of directors; (5) changes in the issuer's capitalization or dividend policy; (6) material changes in the issuer's business or corporate structure; and (7) changes in the issuer's charter, bylaws, or other instruments that might impede acquisition of control of the issuer and additional similar changes.

In these disclosures, courts have required "fair accuracy, not perfection."[9] Problems have arisen for filers who reported only an intent to invest in the issuer, when in fact they had every intention of gaining control. Undisclosed intent or plans can constitute a §13(d) violation. On the other hand, increasingly courts are approving a "waffling disclosure" in which a filer lists a number of possible courses of action, but indicates no firm commitment to any one of them.[10]

Any "material" changes, including an increase in holdings of one percent or more, require that the Schedule 13D be "promptly" amended. An amendment within ten calendar days of the change is usually sufficient, though a shorter time might be required in the heat of a takeover battle.

Enforcement

The SEC is entitled to bring injunctive actions to stop violations of §13(d). Additionally, most (but far from all) courts allow the issuer to bring a court action seeking injunctive relief. Damage actions are not allowed. Further, the following Supreme Court case definitely limited the impact of an injunctive action.

---

[7] For example, *Podesta* v. *Calumet Industries, Inc.* [1978 Transfer Binder], *Federal Securities Law Reports* (CCH), ¶96,433 (N.D. Ill. 1978).

[8] For example, *Warner Communications, Inc.* v. *Murdoch*, 581 F.Supp. 1482 (D.Del. 1984).

[9] *Purolator, Inc.* v. *Tiger International Co.*, 510 F.Supp. 554 (D.D.C. 1981).

[10] For example, *Dan River, Inc.* v. *Icahn*, 701 F. 2d 278 (4th Cir. 1983).

RONDEAU v. MOSINEE PAPER CORP.

422 U.S. 49 (1975)

Plaintiff/respondent Mosinee Paper Corp. is a Wisconsin company whose common stock is registered under §12 of the 1934 Act. In April 1971, when Mosinee had 800,000 shares outstanding, Rondeau began making large purchases of Mosinee stock in the over-the-counter market. Some purchases were in Rondeau's name and others in the name of businesses and foundations controlled by him. By May 17, 1971, Rondeau owned 40,413 shares of Mosinee stock, more than 5%. Without filing a Schedule 13D, Rondeau continued to purchase Mosinee stock so that by July 30, 1971, he owned more than 60,000 shares. On that date Rondeau received a letter from Mosinee's chairman of the board that mentioned federal securities law problems.

Rondeau immediately stopped placing orders for stock and consulted an attorney. On August 25, 1971, Rondeau filed a Schedule 13D, which indicated that while his original purchases had been made with an investment intent, he was currently considering an attempt to obtain effective control of Mosinee, perhaps through a tender offer.

On August 27, Mosinee sent a letter to its shareholders informing them of Rondeau's tardiness in filing his Schedule 13D, which allegedly deprived them of information to which they had been entitled for more than two months. Six days later, Mosinee filed this lawsuit in federal district court alleging a §13(d) violation and seeking an injunction prohibiting Rondeau and certain associates from voting their stock or acquiring additional stock. An order of divestment and damages was also sought.

Defendant/petitioner Rondeau moved for summary judgment, conceding a violation of the Williams Act, but claiming that the violation had been unintentional due to unfamiliarity with the securities laws and that the shareholders had not been harmed in light of the corrective filing. The district court found no intentional violation of §13(d) and no irreparable injury to shareholders stemming from the violation. It therefore granted summary judgment to Rondeau. The court of appeals reversed, finding that no showing of irreparable injury was necessary to secure an injunction under §13(d). Rondeau appealed.*

BURGER, CHIEF JUSTICE:

As in the District Court and the Court of Appeals, it is conceded here that petitioner's delay in filing the Schedule 13D constituted a violation of the Williams Act. The narrow issue before us is whether this record supports the grant of injunctive relief, a remedy whose basis "in the federal courts has always been irreparable harm and inadequacy of legal remedies"—*Beacon Theatres, Inc.* v. *Westover*, 359 U.S. 500, 506 – 507 (1959).

The Court of Appeals' conclusion that respondent suffered "harm" sufficient to require sterilization of petitioner's stock need not long detain us. The purpose of the Williams Act is to insure that public shareholders who are confronted by a cash tender offer for their stock will not be required to respond without adequate information regarding the qualifications and intentions of the offering party. By requiring disclosure of information to the target corporation as well as the Securities and Exchange Commission, Congress intended to do no more than give incumbent management an opportunity to express and explain its position. The Congress expressly disclaimed an intention to provide a weapon for management to discourage takeover bids or prevent large accumulations of stock that would create the potential for such attempts. Indeed, the Act's draftsmen commented upon the ''extreme care'' which was taken ''to avoid tipping the balance of regulation either in favor of management or in favor of the person making the takeover bid''—S.Rep. No. 550, 90th Cong., 1st sess., 3 (1967); H.R. Rep. No. 1711, 90th Cong., 2d sess., 4 (1968).

The short of the matter is that none of the evils to which the Williams Act was directed has occurred or is threatened in this case. Petitioner has not attempted to obtain control of respondent, either by a cash tender offer or any other device. Moreover, he has now filed a proper Schedule 13D, and there has been no suggestion that he will fail to comply with the Act's requirement of reporting any material changes in the information contained therein. On this record there is no likelihood that respondent's shareholders will be disadvantaged should petitioner make a tender offer or that respondent will be unable to place its case adequately before them should a contest for control develop. Thus, the usual basis for injunctive relief, ''that there exists some cognizable danger of recurrent violation,'' is not present here— *United States* v. *W. T. Grant Co.*, 345 U.S. 629, 633 (1953).

Nor are we impressed by respondent's argument that an injunction is necessary to protect the interests of its shareholders who either sold their stock to petitioner at predisclosure prices or would not have invested had they known that a takeover bid was imminent. As observed, the principal object of the Williams Act is to solve the dilemma of shareholders desiring to respond to a cash tender offer, and it is not at all clear that the type of ''harm'' identified by respondent is redressable under its provisions.

In any event, those persons who allegedly sold at an unfairly depressed price have an adequate remedy by way of an action for damages, thus negating the basis for equitable remedy. Similarly, the fact that the second group of shareholders for whom respondent expresses concern have retained the benefits of their stock and the lack of an imminent contest for control make the possibility of damage to them remote at best.

We turn, therefore, to the Court of Appeals' conclusion that respondent's claim was not to be judged according to traditional equitable principles [requiring a showing of irreparable harm], and that the bare fact that petitioner violated the Williams Act justified entry of an injunction against him. This position would seem to be foreclosed by *Hecht Co.* v. *Bowles*, 321 U.S. 321 (1944). The District Judge's conclusions that petitioner acted in good faith and that he promptly filed a Schedule 13D when his attention was called to this obligation support the exercise of the court's sound discretion to deny an application for an injunction, relief which is historically ''designed to deter, not to punish'' and to permit the court ''to mould each decree to the necessities of the particular case''—Id. at 329. As Mr. Justice Douglas aptly pointed out in *Hecht Co.*, the grant of *jurisdiction* to issue compliance orders hardly suggests an absolute duty to do so under any and all circumstances.''

Respondent urges, however, that the ''public interest'' must be taken into account in considering its claim for relief and relies upon the Court of Appeals' conclusion that it is entitled to an injunction because it ''is in the best position'' to insure that the Williams Act is complied with by purchasers of its stock. This argument misconceives, we think, the nature of the litigation. Although neither the availability of a private suit under the Williams Act nor respondent's standing to bring it has been questioned here, this cause of action is not expressly authorized by the statute or its legislative history. Rather, respondent is asserting a so-called implied private right of action established by cases such as *J. I. Case Co.* v. *Borak*, 377 U.S. 426 (1964). Of course, we have not hesitated to recognize the power of federal courts to fashion private remedies for securities laws violations when to do so is consistent with the legislative scheme and necessary for the protection of investors as a supplement to enforcement by the [SEC]. However, it by no means follows that the plaintiff in such an action is relieved of the burden of establishing the traditional prerequisites of relief. Indeed, our cases hold that quite the contrary is true.

Reversed and remanded.

Since *Rondeau*, most courts will grant temporary injunctive relief until a Schedule 13D is filed or corrected, but then will dissolve the injunction. Only in particularly egregious circumstances involving intentional and prejudicial violations will the courts consider ordering harsher relief such as divestiture or termination of a tender offer.

The SEC is considering closing the §13(d) "ten-day window." Today, a purchaser of 5% may buy as many shares as possible during the ten calendar days following its reaching the 5% level before making any disclosure. It has been suggested that as soon as a purchaser reaches the 5% level it be prevented from purchasing any more shares until 48 hours after the filing of a Schedule 13D.

Section 14(d)—Bidder Disclosure

The disclosures to be made by a tender offeror are mandated by §14(d), which does for the postoffer period what §13(d) does for the pre-tender offer period. Indeed, the disclosures required under §14(d) are similar to those of §13(d). Section 14(d) does *not* apply to self-tenders by an issuer, which are governed by §13(e).

Rule 14d-3 requires the bidder to file with the SEC a Schedule 14D-1 as soon as possible on the date the offer is commenced. Copies are also to be delivered to the target company and any other company that has made a pending tender offer, and telephonic notice must be given to all exchanges where the target's shares are traded and to NASD, if appropriate. Copies of the Schedule 14D-1 must also be sent promptly.

The required contents of the Schedule 14D-1 are very similar to the contents required by Rule 14d-6 to be in the bidder's tender offer *materials*. These materials include the formal offer to purchase, the transmittal letter, and any press releases or advertisements sent to shareholders in direct or indirect solicitation. The common practice is for the bidder to disclose all the information in a printed offer to purchase and then to incorporate that information by reference in the Schedule 14D-1.

If the bidder is making an exchange offer, it will probably have to register its shares under the 1933 Act. It is required to file an S-1 registration form, even though it might be able to qualify for an S-2 or S-3 in a normal offering. This registration process guarantees that much valuable information will be disclosed about the bidder's securities, but it may delay the offer, putting it at a disadvantage when compared to cash offers.

Schedule 14D-1

Most tender offer litigation deals with the adequacy and accuracy of disclosures in the Schedule 14D-1. Therefore, it is quite important to prepare the disclosure document properly. Similar to the Schedule 13D, the Schedule 14D-1 requires disclosure of such matters as (1) the name and address of the subject company along with the title and number of shares being sought, the principal market on which the shares are traded, and quarterly high and low price information for the past two years; (2) the identity and background of the bidder; (3) contracts, transactions, and negotiations between the target and the bidder; (4) the source and amount of funds being used to make the bid, including summaries of plans for repaying any debt incurred; (5) the purpose of the tender offer and plans for changes in the target's management, business, financial structure, or share marketability; (6) the number of target shares owned by the bidder and transactions completed within the past 60 days; (7) contracts, arrangements, and understandings between the bidder and other persons relating to the target's shares; (8) persons retained by the bidder to assist in solicitation; (9) financial information about the bidder if it is not a natural person; and (10) information about regulatory compliance, pending litigation, and the applicability of antitrust rules.

Enforcement

Section 14(d) violations are remedied in much the same manner as are §13(d) violations. The SEC has the power to seek injunctions. Most courts grant private parties the right to seek injunctive relief, but upon correction of the Schedule 14D-1 will dissolve the temporary injunction except in egregious cases.

Litigation over the adequacy of §14(d) violations is a common feature of tender offer hostilities. Claims that §14(d) disclosure was inadequate or misleading are often accompanied by claims that this was intentional in violation of §10(b) and §14(e), which we shall soon examine.

Section 14(d)—Target Disclosure

Disclosure is a two-way street. If the bidder must disclose important information during the heat of the tender offer battle, so must management of the target corporation. Section 14(d) has spawned two rules that vitally affect target disclosure.

Rule 14d-9

This rule states that neither the target company nor its officers, directors, share-holders, employees, or affiliates shall make any solicitation or recommendation concerning a tender offer *unless* as soon as practicable on the day the solicitation or recommendation is disseminated, they file with the SEC a Schedule 14D-9. They must also give telephonic notice of key information to each exchange on which the target's shares are traded or to NASD and transmit copies of the Schedule 14D-9 to the bidder (and to the target if it is being filed by another person).

Schedule 14D-9 roughly mirrors Schedule 14D-1. Among other matters, it requires disclosure of the target's name and stock, the identity of the bidder, the identity and background of the filer, the solicitation or recommendation being made *and* the reasons therefor, whether the filer intends to tender his or her shares, and whether or not any negotiations are ongoing in response to the tender offer that might result in a merger, reorganization, tender offer by a third party, or other fundamental corporate change. The 14D-9 disclosure prevents target managers from telling the shareholders to reject a hostile tender offer while the managers hedge their bets by secretly tendering their own shares. It also requires disclosure of concrete negotiations with a "white knight" that might make a competing bid.

Rule 14e-2

This rule prevents target management from "stonewalling" a tender offer by requiring the target company, no later than ten business days from the commencement of the offer, to publish, send, or give its shareholders a statement disclosing that the company (1) recommends acceptance or rejection of the bidder's offer, (2) expresses no opinion and is remaining neutral, or (3) is unable to take a position with respect to the offer. Such statement must also include the *reasons* for the position being taken.

Compliance with Rule 14e-2 constitutes solicitation or recommendation under Rule 14d-9, which in turn requires the filing of a Schedule 14D-9.

Rule 14d-9(e) allows the target's managers to respond to a hostile bid *before* filing a Schedule 14D-9 by issuing what is denominated a "stop, look, and listen" communication in which it does no more than identify the tender offer by the bidder, state that the offer is under consideration by the target's management, state that on or before a specified date (no later than 20 calendar days after commencement of the offer) the subject company will advise the security holders as to its position toward the offer, and urge the shareholders to defer deciding whether to tender until after management's position is stated.

Self-tenders

The issuer may make a tender offer for its own shares. Sometimes this is done in response to a hostile tender offer, and the self-tender as a defensive tactic will be discussed in more detail later in this chapter. At this point we will only mention that self-tenders are not regulated by §14(e). Rather, they are governed by §13(e) and Rule 13e-4. Pursuant to Rule 13e-4, the issuer making a tender offer must file a Schedule 13E-4, which is similar to the Schedule 14D-1, as soon as possible on the date the tender offer is commenced.

Antifraud, Antimanipulation

An extremely important part of the Williams Act is the antifraud, antimanipulation provision of §14(e). It applies to virtually all tender offers, including self-tenders, except those for exempt securities as defined in §3(a)(12) of the 1934 Act.

Most tender offer litigation involves a claim of faulty disclosure that allegedly violated §14(e). This provision was patterned after the more general antifraud provision, §10(b) and is construed in a similar manner. The only significant difference is that §14(e) has no "purchaser or seller" requirement. Section 14(e) litigation frequently turns on whether a misstatement or omission was "material," and in the tender offer context financial capabilities and the intent to invest or control are frequently critical matters. An intentional misstatement or a material omission on a Schedule 13D, 13E-4, 14D-1, or 14D-9 or in any other oral or written statement made in a tender offer constitutes a §14(e) violation. Section 10(b) may also apply.

Section 14(e) also bans "manipulation" in the course of a tender offer. In recent years there has been much controversy as to what types of conduct, particularly inventive offensive and defensive tactics, are embraced by the concept of "manipulation." The following case sets forth the Supreme Court's view of the meaning of "manipulation."

SCHREIBER v. BURLINGTON NORTHERN, INC.

105 S. Ct. 2458 (1985)

In late 1982, respondent Burlington Northern, Inc., made a hostile tender offer for control of El Paso Gas Co. El Paso's management initially opposed the offer, but its shareholders responded favorably, fully subscribing the offer by its December 31 deadline. Burlington did not purchase the shares; rather it terminated the hostile offer and on January 10 announced that it had negotiated a friendly take-over with El Paso's management. Under the agreement, Burlington would purchase 4 million shares directly from El Paso itself and only 21 million (rather than the original 25) from El Paso's shareholders. It would also recognize "golden parachute" contracts of El Paso's officers.

By February 8, 1983, more than 40 million shares were tendered and the friendly take-over was complete. Because rescission of the first tender offer diminished payment to those shareholders who had tendered during the first offer (the second offer was greatly oversubscribed and subjected them to significant proration), petitioner Schreiber filed this suit on behalf of

herself and other shareholders who had tendered during the initial offer. She alleged that Burlington, El Paso, and members of El Paso's board violated §14(e)'s prohibition of "fraudulent, deceptive or manipulative acts or practices . . . in connection with any tender offer." She claimed that cancellation of the first offer and substitution of the second was a "manipulative" distortion of the market for El Paso stock.

The trial court dismissed the suit for failure to state a claim. The Third Circuit affirmed. Petitioner then brought the suit to the Supreme Court.

BURGER, CHIEF JUSTICE:

Petitioner relies on a construction of the phrase, "fraudulent, deceptive or manipulative acts or practices." Petitioner reads the phrase "fraudulent, deceptive or manipulative acts or practices" to include acts which, although fully disclosed, "artificially" affect the price of the take-over target's stock. Petitioner's interpretation relies on the belief that §14(e) is directed at purposes broader than providing full and true information to investors.

Petitioner's reading of the term "manipulative" conflicts with the normal meaning of the term. We have held in the context of an alleged violation of §10(b) of the Securities Exchange Act:

> Use of the word "manipulative" is especially significant. It is and was virtually a term of art when used in connection with the securities markets. It connotes intentional or willful conduct *designed to deceive or defraud* investors by controlling or artificially affecting the price of securities—*Ernst & Ernst* v. *Hochfelder*, 425 U.S. 185, 199 (1976). (emphasis added)

Other cases interpreting the term reflect its use as a general term comprising a range of misleading practices:

> The term refers generally to practices, such as wash sales, matched orders, or rigged prices, that are intended to mislead investors by artificially affecting market activity. . . . Section 10(b)'s general prohibition of practices deemed by the SEC to be "manipulative"—in this technical sense of artificially affecting market activity in order to mislead investors—is fully consistent with the fundamental purpose of the 1934 Act " 'to substitute a philosophy of full disclosure for the philosophy of *caveat emptor*. . . .' " . . . Indeed, nondisclosure is usually essential to the success of a manipulative scheme. . . . No doubt Congress meant to prohibit the full range of ingenious devices that might be used to manipulate securities prices. But we do not think it would have chosen this "term of art" if it had meant to bring within the scope of §10(b) instances of corporate mismanagement such as this, in which the essence of the complaint is that shareholders were treated unfairly by a fiduciary—*Santa Fe Industries, Inc.* v. *Green*, 430 U.S. 462, 476–477 (1977).

The meaning the Court has given the term "manipulative" is consistent with the use of the term at common law, and with its traditional dictionary definition.

She argues, however, that the term manipulative takes on a meaning in §14(e) that is different from the meaning it has in §10(b). Petitioner claims that the use of the disjunctive "or" in §14(e) implies that acts need not be deceptive or fraudulent to be manipulative. But Congress used the phrase "manipulative or deceptive" in §10(b) as well, and we have interpreted "manipulative" in that context to require misrepresentation. Moreover, it is a " 'familiar principle of statutory construction that words grouped in a list should be given related meaning.' "—*Securities Indus. Assn.* v. *Board of Governors*, 468 U.S. ——, —— (1984). All three species of misconduct, that is, "fraudulent, deceptive or manipulative," listed by Congress are directed at failures to disclose. The use of the term "manipulative" provides emphasis and guidance to those who must determine which types of acts are reached by the statute; it does not suggest a deviation from the section's facial and primary concern with disclosure or Congressional concern with disclosure which is the core of the Act.

Our conclusion that "manipulative" acts under §14(e) require misrepresentation or nondisclosure is buttressed by the purpose and legislative history of the provision. Section 14(e) was originally added to the Securities Exchange Act as part of the Williams Act, 82 Stat. 457. "The purpose of the Williams Act is to insure that public shareholders who are confronted by a cash tender offer for their stock will not be required to respond without adequate information"—*Rondeau* v. *Mosinee Paper Corp.*, 422 U.S. 49, 58 (1975).

It is clear that Congress relied primarily on disclosure to implement the purpose of the Williams Act. Senator Williams, the Bill's Senate sponsor, stated in the debate:

> Today, the public shareholder in deciding whether to accept or reject a tender offer possesses limited information. No matter what he does, he acts

without adequate knowledge to enable him to decide rationally what is the best course of action. This is precisely the dilemma which our securities laws are designed to prevent.—113 Cong. Rec. 24664 (1967) (Remarks of Sen. Williams).

The expressed legislative intent was to preserve a neutral setting in which the contenders could fully present their arguments. The Senate sponsor went on to say:

> We have taken extreme care to avoid tipping the scales either in favor of management or in favor of the person making the takeover bids. S. 510 is designed solely to require full and fair disclosure for the benefit of investors. The bill will at the same time provide the offeror and management equal opportunity to present their case—*Ibid.*

Nowhere in the legislative history is there the slightest suggestion that §14(e) serves any purpose other than disclosure, or that the term "manipulative" should be read as an invitation to the courts to oversee the substantive fairness of tender offers; the quality of any offer is a matter for the marketplace.

To adopt the reading of the term "manipulative" urged by petitioner would not only be unwarranted in light of the legislative purpose but would be at odds with it. Inviting judges to read the term "manipulative" with their own sense of what constitutes "unfair" or "artificial" conduct would inject uncertainty into the tender offer process. An essential piece of information—whether the court would deem the fully disclosed actions of one side or the other to be "manipulative"—would not be available un-

til after the tender offer had closed. This uncertainty would directly contradict the expressed Congressional desire to give investors full information.

Congress' consistent emphasis on disclosure persuades us that it intended takeover contests to be addressed to shareholders. In pursuit of this goal, Congress, consistent with the core mechanism of the Securities Exchange Act, created sweeping disclosure requirements and narrow substantive safeguards. The same Congress that placed such emphasis on shareholder choice would not at the same time have required judges to oversee tender offers for substantive fairness. It is even less likely that a Congress implementing that intention would express it only through the use of a single word placed in the middle of a provision otherwise devoted to disclosure.

We hold that the term "manipulative" as used in §14(e) requires misrepresentation or nondisclosure. It connotes "conduct designed to deceive or defraud investors by controlling or artificially affecting the price of securities"—*Ernst & Ernst* v. *Hochfelder*, 425 U.S., at 199. Without misrepresentation or nondisclosure, §14(e) has not been violated.

Applying that definition to this case, we hold that the actions of respondents were not manipulative. The amended complaint fails to allege that the cancellation of the first tender offer was accompanied by any misrepresentation, nondisclosure or deception. The District Court correctly found, "All activity of the defendants that could have conceivably affected the price of El Paso shares was done openly."

Affirmed.

This narrow definition of "manipulation" has led many litigants challenging the offensive and defensive tactics in tender offers to switch their focus from federal securities law claims to claims of breach of fiduciary duty and noncompliance with state corporate codes.

Enforcement

Most courts have allowed both bidders and targets to seek injunctive relief to block §14(e) violations by their opponents in a tender offer fight. Although the Williams Act was not passed to benefit the combatants, they have been allowed to seek injunctions to stop ongoing violations because such injunctions would inure to the benefit of the intended beneficiaries of the Act—the shareholders. However, defeated bidders and targets have not been allowed to sue for damages under §14(e) on the theory that the Williams Act was not meant to protect their interests.[11]

Substantive Provisions

The mechanics of a tender offer are substantially shaped by the substantive rules promulgated by the SEC pursuant to §14(d). Lawyers, managers, and investment bankers are constantly devising offensive and defensive schemes to maximize the effectiveness of techniques within these substantive rules. The SEC frequently tinkers with the rules in an attempt to ''level the playing field'' when a new innovation gives one side or the other an unfair advantage.

Commencement of the Tender Offer

To avoid undue manipulation of a target's shares, a tender offer must be "commenced" within five business days of a public announcement by the bidder of (1) the identity of a bidder, (2) the target company, (3) the number and class of shares sought, and (4) the price. If the tender offer is withdrawn within those five days, it is deemed to have never commenced. If it is not commenced, it is deemed withdrawn. Note that the "five-day rule" does not apply to self-tenders that are not subject to §14(d).

A *cash* tender offer or an exchange offer for exempt securities is deemed to have commenced at 12:01 A.M. on the earliest day one of the following occurs: (1) the long-form publication of the tender offer containing the information specified in Rule 14d-4(a)(1), (2) the summary advertisement of a tender offer pursuant to Rule 14d-4(a)(2), or (3) when the offer is otherwise first published or sent to shareholders.[12]

An exchange offer is deemed to have commenced at 12:01 A.M. on the day when the offer is first published or sent to shareholders *after* the registration statement becomes effective.

Note that Rule 14d-2(d) does contain a safe harbor allowing a bidder to publicly announce its identity and that of the target plus an intention to make a tender offer, so long as the statement does not specify the amount of securities sought or the consideration to be offered. The five-day "commence or withdraw" rule does not apply to such a statement.

Commencement of the offer must, naturally, include the filing of an appropriate schedule. Most hostile offerors begin by making the necessary filings and deliveries of the Schedule 14D-1, publishing a summary ad in *The Wall Street Journal*, and making

---

[11] *Piper v. Chris-Craft Industries*, 430 U.S. 1 (1977).

[12] Rules 14d-2(a) and 14d-6.

a demand on the target under Rule 14d-5 (which relates to the mechanics of delivering
the tender offer materials to the shareholders).

"Hold Open" Period

So that raiders cannot force shareholders into making a decision whether or
not to tender without the opportunity to study the merits of the offer, the Williams Act
requires that an offer must remain open for a minimum of 20 *business* days.[13]

If the bidder increases the offered consideration or the dealers' soliciting fee,
the SEC has long required the offer to remain open for at least 10 business days thereafter.[14]
In July 1986, the SEC amended the rules [15] to require a 10-day extension in the hold
open period upon the announcement of any increase or decrease in not only the consideration offered but also the percentage of securities being sought.

Twenty business days is a *minimum* hold open period. Normally it also functions
as somewhat of a maximum, because bidders usually attempt to speed the tender offer
along as much as possible. However, assume that a bidder was seeking to purchase
51% of the target's stock, and at the end of 20 business days only 49% had been
tendered. The bidder would then have the option of extending the length of the tender
offer by issuing a public announcement early on the first day following expiration of
the earlier period.

Withdrawal Rights

To protect shareholders fully who might change their minds upon deliberation,
the SEC has provided withdrawal rights. For a long time, the rules allowed a shareholder
to withdraw tendered shares at any time during the first 15 business days of a tender
offer, at any time during the first 10 business days following the announcement of a
competing tender offer, and at any time after 60 calendar days had passed following
the announcement of a tender offer. These rules were substantially simplified in July
1986 when the SEC extended withdrawal rights throughout the offering period.[16] At
the same time, the SEC eliminated the extension of withdrawal rights upon commencement
of a competing tender offer.

Proration Period

To ensure equal treatment of shareholders, SEC Rule 14d-8 imposes a proration
requirement on offers for less than all the target's shares. Assume, for example, that a
raider makes a tender offer for 50% of the target's stock. Assume further that the offer
is so attractive that 75% of the target's shares are tendered. Absent Rule 14d-8, the
target could purchase all the shares of Shareholder A, but none of Shareholder B. But

---

[13] Rule 14e-1(a).
[14] Rule 14e-1(b).
[15] *Securities Exchange Commission Release*, no. 33–6653 (July, 1986).
[16] *Securities Exchange Commission Release*, no. 33–6653 (July, 1986).

Rule 14d-8 requires that the shares be purchased on a pro rata basis. Under the assumed facts, the target would purchase two-thirds of the shares tendered by A and B and by all other shareholders.

Originally the proration period applied only to shares tendered within the first ten business days of an offer. Today, however, the proration period lasts the entire duration of an offer.

Best Price

In another attempt to ensure equal treatment, §14(d)(7) provides that if during the course of a tender offer a bidder raises the offering price, that new price must be paid to all who tender (including those who had tendered at the lower price).

This "best price" policy of the Williams Act was the foundation for a July 1986 amendment to the SEC's tender offer rules. Under the amended rules, a third party's (or issuer's) tender offer must be open to all holders of the class of securities subject to the tender offer. Furthermore, any security holder must be paid the highest consideration paid to any other security holder during the tender offer.

The impetus for this recent amendment came from a decision that we shall study later in the chapter—*Unocal Corp.* v. *Mesa Petroleum Co.* In that case, Unocal, the target of a hostile tender offer by Mesa, responded with a self-tender offer which offered to buy its shares from its shareholders at a premium, but excluded the shark (Mesa) from the offer. As we shall see, the court sustained this unequal treatment against Mesa's challenge that it violated *state* concepts of fiduciary responsibility. However, the SEC still believed that such an exclusion violated the equal treatment policies of the Williams Act.

Delivery of Tender Offer Materials

If the tender offeror does not possess a list of the target's shareholders, it will be forced to make a demand of target management under Rule 14d-5. If such a demand is made, target management has its choice of either promptly providing a shareholder list to the bidder so that it can disseminate the materials or mailing the bidder's materials itself after informing the bidder of the mailing costs. The target is entitled to reimbursement of these costs. Whichever alternative the target chooses must be maintained through the duration of the offer.

Most targets choose the second option because they can read the offeror's materials and promptly respond to them, and they can limit the offeror's access to target shareholders.

Exclusive Method of Purchase

During the pendency of a tender offer, the bidder may buy target shares only through that offer. It cannot, for example, go into the marketplace and purchase target shares at a price below that of the tender offer. This rule [17] ensures equal treatment of target shareholders.

---

[17] Rule 10b-13.

"Short Tendering"

One final regulation worth mentioning is Rule 10b-4, which brands "short tendering" a deceptive and manipulative act. Among other things, this rule prevents a shareholder from tendering his shares to both of two competing bidders. It also prevents a shareholder who owns 50 shares in a partial bid from tendering 75 shares upon the guess that his proration rights will entitle him to sell two-thirds of his shares tendered.

Under Rule 10b-4, a shareholder cannot tender unless he owns the securities tendered, or owns a security convertible into, or an option to purchase, the tendered security and, upon acceptance of his tender, he converts the security or exercises the option.

STATE REGULATION OF TENDER OFFERS

Almost 40 states followed the federal government's Williams Act example by enacting laws to regulate tender offers. Many of the laws were passed in response to tender offers of large corporations that would come into a state and "gobble up" a local company, much to the dismay of its employees and other local residents. Therefore, most of the state tender offer laws tended to have a pro-target tilt. For example, they frequently had more demanding disclosure requirements and longer hold open periods than did the Williams Act. They frequently required a long advance notice to the target before the tender offer could be commenced and sometimes allowed state officials to block completion of the tender offer on any of several grounds. The constitutionality of these acts, whereby one state could enjoin or seriously hamper a nationwide tender offer with provisions that were inconsistent with the Williams Act, was questioned many times.

The Supreme Court addressed the issue in *Edgar* v. *Mite Corp.*,[18] which involved the Illinois tender offer law. Among other provisions, the Illinois law required precommencement notice of the tender offer (which gave target corporations additional time to plan defenses) and allowed a hearing and merit review by state officials if the target management objected to the offer. The Court did seem to reject the notion that a single state can regulate a nationwide tender offer. However, the justices' votes were so split that it is difficult to understand fully their rationale.

Justice White's opinion was the key. It held the Illinois statute unconstitutional on three grounds. First, the Illinois law unduly favored target management and therefore violated the Supremacy Clause by contravening the "neutral" approach of the Williams Act. Second, the law imposed *direct* burdens on interstate commerce and was therefore violative of the Commerce Clause regardless of the state interests involved. Third, the law imposed *in*direct burdens on interstate commerce and violated the Commerce Clause because those burdens outweighed the Illinois interests served by the law. Only the

---

[18] 457 U.S. 624 (1982).

third rationale gained the support of a majority of the Justices of the Court, though the other two were not rejected.[19]

Since *Mite*, a number of state tender offer laws have been declared unconstitutional. However, hostile bidders cannot completely ignore state laws in light of *Cardiff Acquisition, Inc.* v. *Hatch*,[20] an Eighth Circuit decision. In *Hatch*, the court invalidated several portions of Minnesota's tender offer law, particularly disclosure requirements that went beyond factual matters. However, the court upheld a requirement that the bidder provide Minnesota shareholders with information concerning the impact of the proposed tender offer on Minnesota residents such as employees and suppliers ("community impact statement"). The court also held the Minnesota Commissioner of Commerce could review the adequacy of disclosures so long as he confined himself to purely factual matters. *Hatch* is arguably inconsistent with other cases that have not strained so hard to find portions of state take-over laws to uphold.[21]

Numerous states are continuing to amend their tender offer laws in an attempt to maintain regulation without crossing the somewhat vaguely drawn lines of the *Mite* decision. One popular type of statute, exemplified by Ohio's new law, gives substantial voice to shareholders, ostensibly under state corporation law, to approve or disapprove changes in control. Another popular approach, used by Maryland and other states that have followed its lead, regulates the price of the second half of a "two-tier" offer (an offer that seeks to purchase a controlling interest via a tender offer at a higher price, and then seeks to purchase the rest of the shares at a lower price in a subsequent merger). Both types of statutes are of questionable constitutionality.

OFFENSIVE APPROACHES

Introduction

Through this section, and the following one on defensive tactics, we will describe some of the strategic moves which make tender offers the high-stakes "chess matches" that they are. The tactics are, of course, influenced by corporate managerial and financial considerations. But to a very large extent, they are also shaped by legal requirements. For example, one of the earliest offensive tactics, in vogue before passage of the Williams Act, was known as the "Saturday night special." This tactic involved making a surprise hostile tender offer, perhaps late on a Friday afternoon so that target management could not effectively respond until at least the following Monday, and giving the shareholders only a week or ten days to consider the offer. This tactic forced many a shareholder to make the decision whether to tender without sufficient time to consider the offer's ramifications. This offensive tactic is now extinct, due to the Williams Act's hold open provision.

---

[19] See D. Goelzer, J. Huber, J. Connolly, and A. Cohen, "Recent Developments in Tender Offer Regulation," in *Hostile Battles for Corporate Control* (New York: Practising Law Institute, 1985), pp. 631–632.

[20] 751 F.2d 906 (8th Cir. 1984).

[21] For example, *L. P. Acquisition Co.* v. *Tyson*, 772 F.2d 201 (6th Cir. 1985); *Dynamics Corp. of America* v. *CTS Corp.*, 637 F.Supp. 389 (N.D. Ill. 1986), *aff'd* 794 F.2d 250 (7th Cir.), *cert. granted*, 55 SS U.S.L.W. 3198 (1986).

Both the shark's managers and those of the target want to develop tactics that will be as effective as possible in either facilitating or blocking a takeover. However, both must be concerned with the question of whether their tactic is "manipulative" within the meaning of Section 14(e). And target management, as it engages in defenses that may ward off an offer and thereby prevent shareholders from having the opportunity to sell their shares at a profit, must consider the fiduciary duty owed to shareholders. The decisions of corporate managers are usually protected by the "business judgment rule," but the courts have not been completely protective as we shall see.

"Any-and-All" Cash Offer

A tender offeror has many options in structuring its bid. It can offer cash to the target's shareholders, or it can offer its own securities. It can offer to buy "any and all" shares tendered, or all shares tendered up to a certain number, or a specified number if at least that many shares are tendered. For example, a shark already owning 4% of the target's shares accumulated through open market purchases might well make a tender offer for 47% of the target's shares if at least that many are tendered. The shark may want control and not just to be a minority shareholder, so the bid is conditioned on the minimum level of tendered shares necessary to assure control.

If the tender offeror is primarily concerned with the success of the bid, and if it has the wherewithal, an any-and-all cash offer is probably the most effective approach. Cash has several advantages. It is easy for a target shareholder to understand the difference between a $50 market price for his shares and a $70 cash tender offer price. An exchange offer may need some explaining, and the bidder must convince the target shareholders that the offered securities really are worth the amount stated. Also, with a cash tender offer, the bidder need not hassle with federal registration or blue-sky laws, and does not have to produce a whole new set of disclosure documents, such as the S-1, that would be subject to legal attack.

This does not mean that an exchange offer is without benefits. An offer of securities, or a combination offer of cash and securities may be the only alternative for a bidder that cannot come up with enough cash for a purely cash offer. Also, it is sometimes possible, at least in a friendly tender offer, to structure an exchange offer as a tax-free reorganization under §368 of the Internal Revenue Code.

The any-and-all offer, though not used too frequently in hostile tender offers, has tactical advantages in that it reduces the need for a major second-step transaction to "clean up" the deal, that is, to eliminate the minority shareholders so that the bidder can have complete ownership. These second-step transactions tend to be subject to serious legal challenges. Also, an any-and-all offer makes it more difficult for the target to line up a white knight.

Two-Tier, Front-End-Loaded Offer

A recently developed offensive tactic is the two-tier, front-end-loaded tender offer. It involves the complete takeover of a target in a two-step transaction. First, the bidder purchases a controlling interest in the target through a tender offer. The tender offer price is set at a very attractive premium over market price to ensure its success. Once control is purchased, the minority shareholders are eliminated through the second step, a merger into a newly created subsidiary of the bidder. The minority shareholders usually cannot block this merger, and they receive much less for their shares than the tender offer price. In one case, U.S. Steel, as a white knight, made a $125-per-share tender offer for a controlling interest in Marathon Oil Co., announcing at the same time that it would complete the transaction with a second-step merger wherein minority shareholders would receive U.S. Steel securities arguably worth only $76 per share.

The coercive nature of a two-tier bid is obvious. Each shareholder would prefer to receive $125 in cash instead of $76 in securities. To have a chance to have at least some of their shares purchased at $125, they must tender. Whatever shares are not purchased in the tender offer on a pro-rata basis will be relegated to the "back door" of the offer. To fail to tender is to receive the lower price for all shares.

This type of bid puts shareholders in the "prisoner's dilemma." Together they might be better off if they did not tender. Maybe $125 per share is too low. Maybe they should all hold out for a bid of $140 per share. But it is difficult for thousands of shareholders to act in concert. It is not in any individual shareholder's best interest to refrain from tendering if enough fellow shareholders tender to make the offer a success. To refrain ensures that the shareholder will not receive the highest tender offer price for any shares.

The two-tier offer is very controversial. It obviously places great pressure on shareholders to tender. For that reason, it has been argued to be "manipulative" and therefore in violation of §14(e). However, in *Radol* v. *Thomas*,[22] which involved a challenge to U.S. Steel's two-tier bid for Marathon Oil Co., this argument was rejected. Following the Supreme Court's decision in *Schreiber* v. *Burlington Northern, Inc.*, the court held that "manipulation" is a term of art requiring some sort of deception. Furthermore, the Marathon shareholders' eager response to the original shark's bid of $85 per share had convinced the trial court that the shareholders' willingness to tender to U.S. Steel was not a product of coercion.

Not only have the courts sustained the two-tier bid, the Office of the Chief Economist of the SEC undertook a study that concluded that "it is problematic whether target shareholders would benefit from regulatory inducements to use any-or-all instead of two-tier offers."[23]

Furthermore, many of the defensive tactics we shall study have been aimed at neutralizing the impact of the two-tier bid, reducing its popularity.

"Beachhead Acquisition"

Through stock accumulation programs, sharks seeking control can establish a "beachhead acquisition" to serve as a basis for further raids upon the target. It is presently a very

---

[22] 772 F.2d 244 (6th Cir. 1985).

[23] Office of the Chief Economist of SEC, "The Economics of Partial and Two-Tier Offers," reprinted in *Securities Regulation & Law Report*, Vol. 16 (Washington, D.C.: Bureau of National Affairs, Inc., June 29, 1984), p. 1123.

popular method of seeking control to accumulate gradually the target's stock on the open market and then, usually somewhere short of the 10% level, consider methods of seeking control.

Launching a proxy fight for control of the target is one takeover method available to the possessor of a beachhead acquisition. Of course, a proxy battle involves winning the other shareholders over by persuasion. Many shareholders are more easily persuaded by an opportunity to sell their shares at a profit. Therefore, beachhead acquisitions are often followed by various forms of tender offers.

"Bootstrap Offer"

A "bootstrap," also called a "toe-hold" offer, is a method by which a shark can finance a tender offer for a company many times its own size. Assume, for example, that a small shark has accumulated a small stake in a much larger target, but does not have the cash or credit to make an offer for control of the target. One strategy is to make a tender offer for a smaller percentage of stock, say, 15%, but to make the offer at such an attractive price that more than 50% of the target's shares are tendered by holders who wish to have at least some of their shares purchased on a pro-rata basis.

Once more than 50% of the target's shares are tendered, the shark can go to its bank and say, "Look, control of Target Corporation is mine for the taking. All I need is the money; a majority of shares have been tendered. Because control is there to be taken, I can use the assets of Target Corporation as collateral for the loan." The bootstrap offer gives many "Davids" a realistic chance to take control of some of America's "Goliath" corporations.

"Group Bids"

An increasingly used tactic is the "group bid." Many of America's most famous "sharks" have been very independent, individualistic people. However, recently many have learned that by working together, they can accomplish takeovers that they could not do alone. Assume, for example, that T Corporation is a very large company with major interests in both mining and timber. Assume further that A Company is a smaller corporation interested in T's mining business and that B company is a smaller corporation interested in T's timber business. Perhaps alone neither A nor B could mount a successful tender offer for T Corporation. But together they can pool their resources, mount a successful tender offer, and later split up T Corporation's assets with A receiving the mining portion and B the timber portion.

Frequently other members of the group will not be corporations, but will be speculators interested in receiving some of the high profits that frequently go to successful tender offerors.

"Junk" Bonds

A "junk" bond is a high-yield, high-risk bond that has recently come into vogue as a method of financing tender offers. More than ever before, investors are willing to purchase a relatively small shark's junk bonds to finance the shark's tender offer for a much larger target. Frequently, most of the collateral supporting the bonds is provided by the assets of the *target* company.

Following a fierce debate concerning the merits and demerits of junk bonds,[24] the Federal Reserve Board responded to fears that their use unduly benefited the shark and the investment bankers who market them at the expense of the financial security of investors. The Fed issued a ruling that extended the 50% margin requirement of Regulation G to the purchase of debt securities issued to finance the acquisition of a target company's margin stock by a shell corporation.[25] It is too early to determine the impact of this new rule.

"Bust-up" Take-over

To pay off the bootstrap loan or to pay the high rate of interest on junk bonds, frequently corporate raiders must "bust up" the target company, selling off assets and lines of business. The dismantling of the target in order to finance the purchase is called a bust-up take-over.

"Greenmail"

Sometimes the purchaser of a beachhead acquisition is not truly interested in buying control of the target. By merely buying a substantial block of target stock, and then "rattling the sabre" by threatening a proxy fight or a tender offer, the acquiror puts the target company "into play." At that point a number of things can happen, most of them good insofar as the acquiror is concerned.

Target management may decide to buy peace of mind by repurchasing the acquiror's shares at substantial profit to the acquiror if he will sign a "standstill" agreement wherein he promises to go away and not bother the target further for a specified period of time. Or target management may line up a white knight to make a tender offer to compete with the shark's. If the white knight succeeds, the shark is only momentarily disappointed, for he can tender his beachhead acquisition, usually purchased at market price, to the white knight at a substantial profit.

Buying a target's shares while threatening a takeover in an attempt to induce the target (or its white knight) to buy your shares out at a profit has been called "green-mail." It is a very profitable game that many sharks have been playing. In 1984, Saul Steinberg spent about three months attempting to gain control of Walt Disney Productions. In the end he failed, but the target repurchased his 12.2% interest for $325.3 million, which included "profit" of $31.7 million and "expenses" of $28 million.

Greenmail is a growing phenomenon. A recent study from the SEC indicated that from 1979 to 1984, raiders were paid $5.5 billion in greenmail by targets, some $1 billion of that sum being pure profit.[26]

---

[24] Compare F. Rohatyn, "Junk Bonds and Other Securities Swill," *The Wall Street Journal*, April 18, 1985, p. 30; with W. Carney, "Junk Bonds Don't Merit a Black-Hat Image," *The Wall Street Journal*, April 29, 1985, p. 22.

[25] Federal Reserve Board Docket No. R-0562 (January 10, 1986).

[26] Office of Chief Economist of SEC, "The Impact of Targeted Share Repurchases (Greenmail) on Stock Prices," reprinted in *Federal Securities Law Reports* (CCH), ¶83,713 (September 11, 1984).

Greenmail is very controversial, and most argue that it is not a practice that benefits the common shareholder. Still, the courts have generally upheld target repurchases where there appeared to be some hint of a proper business purpose.[27] The leading exception occurred in the Steinberg-Disney case where shareholders obtained a ruling from a state appellate court that target directors had probably breached their fiduciary duty by paying greenmail.[28] Congress has debated several bills aimed at limiting the practice, but as of this writing, the most it has done is diminish certain tax breaks the sharks gain from borrowing.[29]

DEFENSIVE TACTICS

Given the array of offensive weapons in the potential hostile bidder's arsenal, a target company that wishes to maintain its independence had best develop a few strategies of its own. This section discusses a few of the many strategies that have been developed over the years.

Advance Planning

Many experts believe that it is important for a potential target—and today most corporations regardless of size fit into that category—to plan for the day a hostile assault might occur. The advance planning will include development of a "team" of corporate officials and attorneys who will have primary authority to make a prompt response to any offer, formulation of criteria for an "acceptable" bid, development of many of the defensive tactics that are soon to be discussed, and perhaps even reincorporation in a jurisdiction where the corporate laws are particularly protective of such defensive moves. Sometimes all the material gathered is known as the "Pearl Harbor File," a file that is ready for use in case of a surprise attack.

Some courts have praised such preplanning by target managers as indicative of a well-planned concern for the best interests of shareholders. One judge noted that preplanning "removes management's decision-making from the pressures of an immediate takeover battle, thereby tending to reduce the possibility of irrational responses in a takeover bid." [30] On the other hand, there is always the possibility that a court might interpret too zealous a defensive system as indicating that target management is determined to reject any tender offer—no matter how favorable to the shareholders—to preserve the target's independence and their own jobs.

---

[27] For example, *Heine* v. *The Signal Companies, Inc.* [1976–77 Transfer Binder], *Federal Securities Law Reports* (CCH), ¶95,898 (S.D.N.Y. 1977).

[28] *Heckmann* v. *Ahmanson* [Current Binder], *Federal Securities Law Reports* (CCH), ¶92,346 (Cal. App. 1985).

[29] §51, Deficit Reduction Act of 1984, PL 98–369 (July 18, 1984).

[30] *Warner Communications* v. *Murdoch*, 581 F.Supp. 1482 (D.Del. 1984).

"Shark Repellents"

"Shark repellents" are amendments to the corporation's charter or bylaws that make takeovers more difficult or less attractive. There are countless variations, a few of which are discussed here.

Board Protection

Many charter changes are aimed at making it more difficult and time consuming for a shark to gain operating control of a target, even after purchasing a controlling interest. Most states allow removal of directors without cause, special elections, and other quick changes that would allow a successful bidder to remove a board quickly after buying control. But state laws do not *require* these provisions.

Therefore, a target company can take many steps to protect incumbent management. First, it can stagger the board. Instead of having all members of, say, a nine-member board elected each year, it could classify the board into three groups of three, each serving three-year terms. In that fashion, a shark, even after buying control, would have to wait through at least two annual meetings to control the board. Second, the target can eliminate shareholder ability to remove directors without cause, shareholder ability to call special meetings, and shareholder ability to act through written consents. Third, the target can institute cumulative voting, which would mean that a shark who had purchased 51% of the target's shares could in an election place a majority, but not necessarily all, of his candidates on the board. Fourth, the target can provide that only other directors have the power to replace directors who resign in the middle of their terms.

Supermajority Provisions

In many states, the law provides that a change of control such as a merger or consolidation needs only majority shareholder approval. Recently many corporations have changed their charters to require a much higher rate of approval, ranging from 67% to 95%. This would require a shark, plotting a two-stage takeover, to buy at least 67% to 95% of the target's shares to seek approval of the second-stage merger. Other times the supermajority provision will require that any merger be approved by the majority vote of the shareholders other than the shark and its affiliates.

One company recently obtained the same effect by following some British companies in providing that every share owned by a shareholder up to 10% of the company's stock is entitled to one vote, while every share above the 10% limitation is entitled to only 1/100th of a vote. To obtain a majority vote, a shark would have to buy a very high percentage of the target's stock.[31]

---

[31] M. Bancroft, "MCI Limits Shareholder Powers in British Fashion," *Legal Times of Washington*, February 28, 1983, p. 14. Compare *Baker* v. *Providence and Worcester Co.*, 378 A.2d 121 (Del. 1977) (upholding such a plan) with *Asarco, Inc.* v. *MRH Holmes A Court*, 611 F.Supp. 468 (D.N.J. 1985) (plan that gave different voting rights to shareholders of the same class ruled illegal under state corporate code).

Many supermajority provisions carry loopholes for mergers approved by target management.

"Fair Price" Provisions

Although the courts and legislatures have not eliminated the two-tier, front-end-loaded offer, many companies have attempted to do so by use of "fair price" amendments to their charter. These provisions typically require that the price paid in a merger equal or exceed by some percentage the price paid by the acquiror in the first-stage tender offer. Many similar pricing formulas have been used.

The "fair price" provision is frequently coupled with a "put" option that enables the shareholders to demand that the acquiror buy their shares at the formulated price.

Impact of Shark Repellents

Numerous studies have been done regarding the impact of shark repellents. Although no study has been conclusive, it does appear that shark repellents make a successful tender offer defense more likely. Perhaps because a good set of shark repellents may discourage bidders, there is also evidence that shark repellents reduce the market price of a corporation's stock and the premium of any tender offer that is made.[32]

Nonetheless, shareholders continue to approve shark repellents in record numbers. In 1984, 372 public companies asked their shareholders to approve amendments constituting shark repellents at annual meetings. Only 17 of the companies failed to gain approval. Furthermore, the courts have generally upheld shark repellents, at least if they were properly approved by the shareholders, *and* properly disclosed to the shareholders. In seeking shareholder approval at the annual meeting, target management's proxy material should fully disclose the impact of the repellents on potential bids.

A relatively rare instance of court disapproval of a shark repellent occurred in *Joseph E. Seagram & Sons, Inc.* v. *Conoco, Inc.*,[33] where in response to a tender offer by a Canadian corporation target management amended the bylaws to limit the percentage of shares that could be held by "aliens." The amendment was invalidated because it did not have the shareholder approval required by the law of Delaware (where the target was incorporated).

"Cyanide Capsules"

Similar to a charter or bylaw amendment, a "cyanide capsule" is exemplified by a provision in a long-term labor contract that makes the agreement immediately renegotiable upon a change of control or a provision in a long-term loan agreement that makes the

---

[32] J. Heard and J. Pound, "Shark Repellents May Fail to Benefit Shareholders," *Legal Times*, March 25, 1985, p. 12.

[33] 519 F.Supp. 506 (D.Del. 1981).

entire principal sum repayable immediately if control changes hands. A shark taking control of a target gets its liabilities as well as its assets, and a cyanide capsule can make those liabilities more imposing.

"Golden Parachutes"

A "golden parachute" is a long-term employment contract for a company's key executives that typically provides for compensation security in the event of a change of control. Some grant the executive lump-sum payments; some grant annual payments. Some are triggered if the executive is fired by the successful tender offeror; some are triggered by the executive's decision that he or she can no longer work effectively with the corporation following the change of control.

The most famous golden parachute was the $4 million severance payment given to William Agee of Bendix Corporation following Bendix's unsuccessful clash for control with Martin Marietta Corporation, which resulted in Bendix being taken over by a white knight, Allied Corporation. Some golden parachutes have been for much larger sums than Agee's.

The rationale behind the golden parachute is that it supposedly gives the executive peace of mind. In evaluating a proposed tender offer, the executive is free to consider the shareholders' best interests, as he or she is supposed to be doing anyway under fiduciary concepts, because whether the tender offer is approved or disapproved the executive will be financially secure. Furthermore, it is argued, a golden parachute allows a potential target to hire top-notch managers who otherwise might be hesitant to work for such a firm. These arguments have been sufficiently persuasive that a large number of the *Fortune* 500 companies have provided golden parachutes to their key executives.

It is not coincidental that a golden parachute also makes a tender offer more expensive for the shark. Nonetheless, payment of golden parachutes is generally only a small portion of the total takeover price, so they probably have little deterrent effect. That was the conclusion of the Advisory Committee on Tender Offers, and it draws support from a study that indicated adoption of golden parachutes has little negative impact on the stock prices of potential target companies.[34]

There are no definitive court decisions on the validity of golden parachutes as yet, but the SEC has acted to ensure that they are adequately disclosed to shareholders.[35]

In an attempt to limit golden parachutes, Congress inserted a provision in the Tax Reform Act of 1984 which provides that if the severance payment reaches 300% of a five-year pay average, an employer can't deduct the excess over 100% and an employee pays both income tax and a 20% excise tax on it.[36] In the fall of 1984,

---

[34] M. Jensen, "Takeovers: Folklore and Science," *Harvard Business Review*, November–December 1984, p. 118.

[35] *Securities Exchange Act Release*, no. 20220 (September 23, 1983) (amending Regulation S-K, Item 402(e)). At this writing, some lower courts have critically viewed golden parachutes. For example, *Weinberger* v. *Shumway*, No. 547586 (Super. Ct., San Diego Co., Calif., September 19, 1985).

[36] See R. Winter and B. Zins, "Tax Act Takes a Swipe at Golden Parachutes," *Legal Times of Washington*, November 19, 1984, p. 16.

Prentice-Hall, Inc., when faced with a potential tender offer by Gulf & Western, instituted golden parachutes that carefully limited payments to 299% of the average five-year salary of its executives to avoid these tax penalties. Other companies may be tempted simply to raise the sums to be paid even higher.

"Poison Pill"

"Poison pills" are one of the latest wrinkles in tender offer defenses. They can have a devastating impact. Most are very complicated, but a simplified version might work like this. A potential target company issues to its shareholders a "preferred" share for each common share they hold. The preferred share is relatively dormant unless a tender offer changes control and the acquiror attempts the usual second-stage merger. The change of control "triggers" the preferred shares' "springing warrant" that entitles each shareholder to buy $200 worth of stock in the proposed company (created by merger of the target with a wholly owned subsidiary of the acquiror) for $100. This has a devastating impact in terms of dilution of the value of the new company. The poison pills also usually carry exceptions that would allow friendly mergers approved by the target's board.

Poison pills have been strongly criticized as shifting power from the shareholders to the board, which may have the power to issue them without formal shareholder approval. Nonetheless, many decisions have upheld them.[37]

Antitrust

The antitrust laws can serve as a defensive shield for the target company. In general, it may be said that targets have had great success blocking tender offers in court when they were able to show that the shark's successful takeover would increase horizontal concentration in violation of §7 of the Clayton Act.[38] They have had some success where proving increased vertical integration,[39] but not much success in conglomerate-type takeovers.[40]

But what if there is no real antitrust problem to allege? Some target boards have remedied this problem by creating one. For example, when Ryder System, Inc., was plotting a tender offer for Frank B. Hall & Co., the latter company acquired Jartran, Inc., then in bankruptcy, knowing that Jartran was a competitor of Ryder. Although Ryder challenged the acquisition as "cynical business conduct," the court upheld the

---

[37] For example, *Gearhart Indus., Inc.* v. *Smith Int'l, Inc.*, 741 F.2d 707 (5th Cir. 1984); *Moran* v. *Household Int'l, Inc.*, 500 A.2d 1346 (Del. 1985).

[38] For example, *Grumman* v. *LTV Corp.*, 665 F.2d 10 (2d Cir. 1981).

[39] For example, *Gulf & Western Indus., Inc.* v. *Great Atlantic & Pacific Tea Co.*, 476 F.2d 687 (2d Cir. 1973).

[40] But see *Allis-Chalmers Mfg. Co.* v. *White Consolidated Indus., Inc.*, 414 F.2d 506 (3d Cir. 1969), *cert. denied*, 396 U.S. 1009 (1970).

acquisition because it had a potentially legitimate business purpose, and because "Hall's interest predated its knowledge of Ryder's interest in it." Nonetheless, the court acknowledged that the testimony of Hall's CEO regarding the defensive implications of the acquisition was "at best, disingenuous." [41]

Both sharks with potential antitrust problems and targets attempting to create antitrust problems must be cognizant of the requirements of the Hart-Scott-Rodino Antitrust Improvement Act, which imposes certain disclosure (to the FTC and the Antitrust Division of the Department of Justice) and waiting requirements in acquisitions presenting potential antitrust problems. Application of the Hart-Scott-Rodino Act can impede an expeditious conclusion of a tender offer.

Finally, a recent court ruling may dramatically reduce the utility of an antitrust defense for a target corporation. In *H.H. Robertson Co.* v. *Guardian Industries Corp.*,[42] the Third Circuit Court of Appeals held that a target corporation has no standing to challenge a takeover on antitrust grounds because it would suffer no anti-competitive injury.

Stock Repurchases

An open market stock repurchase program can serve as a defensive tactic for the target company. Repurchasing shares keeps them out of the hands of the shark and reduces the cash position (and probably increases the debt) of the target, thereby reducing its attractiveness. Such repurchases were given a boost as a defensive tactic by the court's decision in *SEC* v. *Carter Hawley Hale Stores, Inc.*,[43] discussed earlier in this chapter regarding the definition of a tender offer. In that case, Limited made a tender offer for CHH. CHH responded with a number of defensive tactics, including the issuance of shares convertible to 22% of its stock to a white knight, General Cinema. Under the agreement, the shares were to be voted by CHH's incumbent management. Then CHH engaged in a prolific stock repurchase program that had the effect of raising General Cinema's stake in the company from 22% to 37%, which presented a formidable obstacle to the takeover. Because the court characterized the action as a simple repurchase, subject only to the modest disclosure requirements of Rule 13e-1, the action could easily be upheld under the business judgment rule. Had the action been characterized as a self-tender offer, more demanding requirements would have applied as we shall soon see.

Of course, the most effective type of repurchase is to repurchase the shares from the shark. This, as we have seen earlier, usually constitutes "greenmail." It effectively ends the takeover threat. Although it may leave the target in a worse financial condition, such a repurchase will generally be upheld under the business judgment rule.[44]

---

[41] *Frank B. Hall & Co.* v. *Ryder System, Inc.*, No. 82 C0092 (N.D.Ill. July 1982).

[42] 50 A.T.R.R. (BNA) 166, *rehearing granted*, 50 A.T.R.R (BNA) 313 (3d Cir. 1986).

[43] 587 F.Supp. 1248 (C.D. Cal. 1984), *aff'd*, 760 F.2d 945 (9th Cir. 1985).

[44] For example, *Cheff* v. *Mathes*, 199 A.2d 548 (Del. Supr. 1964).

Self-tender Offer

If an attractively priced, well-structured tender offer has been made, a target might not be successful in initiating a repurchase program on the open market. Another tactic is to present the shareholders with an alternative offer in the form of a self-tender. To the extent that it is successful, a self-tender also takes shares out of the shark's hands and reduces the target's attractiveness by increasing its debt.

A self-tender is regulated by §13(e). Rule 13e-4 requires much more extensive disclosure than does Rule 13e-1 for simple repurchases. The issuer must file a Schedule 13E-4, which contains information roughly similar to Schedule 14D-1. The self-tender formerly had a tactical advantage over a third-party tender in that SEC rules imposed shorter hold open and withdrawal right periods. However, in January 1986, the SEC amended Rule 13e-4 to impose similar requirements.

Sometimes a target will use a "doomsday" or conditional self-tender offer. For example, when Coastal Corporation made a tender offer for 50% of the shares of Texas Gas Resources Corp., Texas Gas brought in CSX as a white knight. It also announced a self-tender offer for 50%, conditioned only on Coastal's acquisition of at least 40%. Thus, even if Coastal could outbid CSX, it would still be faced with the self-tender offer barrier. Coastal withdrew its bid.

Self-tenders have been generally upheld as proper defensive tactics protected by the business judgment rule. The following is a prominent case involving such a defensive tactic.

UNOCAL CORP. v. MESA PETROLEUM CO.

493 A.2d 946 (Del. 1985)

On April 8, 1985, Mesa (plaintiff), owner of approximately 13% of defendant Unocal's stock, launched a two-tier "front-loaded" cash tender offer for 37% (64 million shares) of Unocal's stock at $54 per share. The "back end" was designed to eliminate the remaining publicly held shares in exchange for securities purportedly worth $54 per share. However, these securities were admittedly highly subordinated "junk bonds."

Unocal's board of eight outside and six inside directors met on April 13 to consider the offer. In a nine and one-half hour meeting, the board heard detailed presentations by legal counsel

and Goldman Sachs & Co. and Dillon, Read & Co. Both Goldman Sachs and Dillon Read thought the Mesa proposal was inadequate. Goldman Sachs opined that $60 per share would be a minimum liquidation value.

Goldman Sachs also presented various defensive strategies available if the board determined to reject the offer. One such strategy was a self-tender by Unocal for its own stock with a price of $70 to $75 per share. While this would cost over $6 billion, thus saddling the corporation with substantial debt and reducing exploratory drilling, the company would remain a viable entity.

After the outside directors met independently with the financial advisors and attorneys, the board unanimously voted to reject Mesa's offer and pursue the self-tender. Another lengthy meeting on April 15 led to a decision to set the self-tender price at $72. The offer had two important provisions. First, the offer was contingent on Mesa's purchase of 64 million shares through its tender offer (Mesa purchase condition). Second, the offer to repurchase was not extended to Mesa (the Mesa exclusion).

The self-tender was begun on April 17, and Mesa promptly filed this suit. Soon the board partially waived the Mesa purchase condition. All directors tendered their shares on the advice of the financial advisors to show their support for the plan. The board did not alter the Mesa exclusion, and Mesa amended this suit to challenge that exclusion.

The Vice-Chancellor enjoined Unocal from pursuing the self-tender and Unocal appealed.

MOORE, JUSTICE:

. . .

II.

The issues we address involve these fundamental questions: Did the Unocal board have the power and duty to oppose a takeover threat it reasonably perceived to be harmful to the corporate enterprise, and if so, is its action here entitled to the protection of the business judgment rule?

Mesa contends that the discriminatory exchange offer violates the fiduciary duties Unocal owes it. Mesa argues that because of the Mesa exclusion the business judgment rule is inapplicable, because the directors by tendering their own shares will derive a financial benefit that is not available to *all* Unocal stockholders. Thus, it is Mesa's ultimate contention that Unocal can-

not establish that the exchange offer is fair to *all* shareholders. . . .

Unocal answers that it does not owe a duty of "fairness" to Mesa, given the facts here. Specifically, Unocal contends that its board of directors reasonably and in good faith concluded that Mesa's $54 two-tier tender offer was coercive and inadequate, and that Mesa sought selective treatment for itself. Furthermore, Unocal argues that the board's approval of the exchange offer was made in good faith, on an informed basis, and in the exercise of due care. Under these circumstances, Unocal contends that its directors properly employed this device to protect the company and its stockholders from Mesa's harmful tactics.

III.

We begin with the basic issue of the power of a board of directors of a Delaware corporation to adopt a defensive measure of this type. Absent such authority, all other questions are moot. Neither issues of fairness nor business judgment are pertinent without the basic underpinning of a board's legal power to act.

The board has a large reservoir of authority upon which to draw. Its duties and responsibilities proceed from the inherent powers conferred by 8 Del. C. §141(a), respecting management of the corporation's "business and affairs." Additionally, the powers here being exercised derive from 8 Del. C. §160(a), conferring broad authority upon a corporation to deal in its own stock. From this it is now well established that in the acquisition of its shares a Delaware corporation may deal selectively with its stockholders, provided the directors have not acted out of a sole or primary purpose to entrench themselves in office. *Cheff* v. *Mathes*, Del. Supr., 199 A.2d 548, 554 (1964); and *Bennett* v. *Propp*, Del. Supr., 187 A.2d 405, 408 (1962). . . .

Finally, the board's power to act derives from its fundamental duty and obligation to protect the corporate enterprise, which includes stockholders, from harm reasonably perceived, irrespective of its source. See for example, *Panter v. Marshall Field & Co.*, 646 F.2d 271, 297 (7th Cir. 1981). . . . Thus, we are satisfied that in the broad context of corporate governance, including issues of fundamental corporate change, a board of directors is not a passive instrumentality.

Given the foregoing principles, we turn to the standards by which director action is to be measured. In *Pogostin* v. *Rice*, Del. Supr., 480 A.2d 619 (1984), we held that the business judgment rule, including the standards by which director conduct is judged, is applicable in the context of a takeover. The business judgment rule is a "presumption that in making a business decision the directors of a corporation acted on an informed basis, in good faith and in the honest belief that the action taken was in the best interests of the company." *Aronson* v. *Lewis*, Del. Supr., 473 A.2d 805, 812 (1984). A hallmark of the business judgment rule is that a court will not substitute its judgment for that of the board if the latter's decision can be "attributed to any rational business purpose"— *Sinclair Oil Corp.* v. *Levien*, Del. Supr., 280 A.2d 717, 720 (1971).

When a board addresses a pending takeover bid it has an obligation to determine whether the offer is in the best interests of the corporation and its shareholders. In that respect a board's duty is no different from any other responsibility it shoulders, and its decisions should be no less entitled to the respect they otherwise would be accorded in the realm of business judgment. There are, however, certain caveats to a proper exercise of this function. Because of the omnipresent specter that a board may be acting primarily in its own interests, rather than those of the corporation and its shareholders, there is an enhanced duty which calls for judicial examination at the threshold before the protections of the business judgment rule may be conferred.

This Court has long recognized that:

> We must bear in mind the inherent danger in the purchase of shares with corporate funds to remove a threat to corporate policy when a threat to control is involved. The directors are of necessity confronted with a conflict of interest, and an objective decision is difficult. *Bennett* v. *Propp*, Del. Supr., 187 A.2d 405, 409 (1962).

In the face of this inherent conflict directors must show that they had reasonable grounds for believing that a danger to corporate policy and effectiveness existed because of another person's stock ownership — *Cheff* v. *Mathes*, 199 A.2d at 554–55. However, they satisfy that burden "by showing good faith and reasonable investigation. . . ." *Id.* at 555. Furthermore, such proof is materially enhanced, as here, by the approval of a board comprised of a majority of outside independent directors who have acted in accordance with the foregoing standards.

IV.

A.

In the board's exercise of corporate power to forestall a takeover bid our analysis begins with the basic principle that corporate directors have a fiduciary duty to act in the best interests of the corporation's stockholders. *Guth* v. *Loft, Inc.*, Del. Supr., 5 A.2d 503, 510 (1939). As we have noted, their duty of care extends to protecting the corporation and its owners from perceived harm whether a threat originates from third parties or other shareholders. But such powers are not absolute. A corporation does not have unbridled discretion to defeat any perceived threat by any Draconian means available.

. . .

B.

A further aspect is the element of balance. If a defensive measure is to come within the ambit of the business judgment rule, it must be reasonable in relation to the threat posed. This entails an analysis by the directors of the nature of the takeover bid and its effect on the corporate enterprise. Examples of such concerns may include: inadequacy of the price offered, nature and timing of the offer, questions of illegality, the impact on "constituencies" other than shareholders (i.e., creditors, customers, employees, and perhaps even the community generally), the risk of nonconsummation, and the quality of securities being offered in the exchange. . . . While not a controlling factor, it also seems to us that a board may reasonably consider the basic stockholder interests at stake, including those of short term speculators, whose actions may have fueled the coercive aspect of the offer at the expense of the long term investor. Here, the threat posed was viewed by the Unocal board as a grossly inadequate two-tier coercive tender offer coupled with the threat of greenmail.

Specifically, the Unocal directors had concluded that the value of Unocal was substantially above the $54 per share offered in cash at the front end. Furthermore, they determined that the subordinated securities to be exchanged in Mesa's announced squeeze out of the remaining shareholders in the "back-end" merger were "junk bonds" worth far less than $54. It is now well recognized that such offers are a classic coercive measure designed to stampede shareholders into tendering at the first tier, even if the price is inadequate, out of fear of what they will receive at the back end of the transaction. Wholly beyond the coercive aspect of an inadequate two-tier tender offer, the threat was posed by a corporate raider with a national reputation as a "greenmailer."

In adopting the selective exchange offer, the board stated that its objective was either to defeat the inadequate Mesa offer or, should the offer still succeed, provide the 49% of its stockholders, who would otherwise be forced to accept

"junk bonds," with $72 worth of senior debt. We find that both purposes are valid.

However, such efforts would have been thwarted by Mesa's participation in the exchange offer. First, if Mesa could tender its shares, Unocal would effectively be subsidizing the former's continuing effort to buy Unocal stock at $54 per share. Second, Mesa could not, by definition, fit within the class of shareholders being protected from its own coercive and inadequate tender offer.

Thus, we are satisfied that the selective exchange offer is reasonably related to the threats posed. Thus, the board's decision to offer what it determined to be the fair value of the corporation to the 49% of its shareholders, who would otherwise be forced to accept highly subordinated "junk bonds," is reasonable and consistent with the directors' duty to ensure that the minority stockholders receive equal value for their shares.

V.

Mesa contends that it is unlawful, and the trial court agreed, for a corporation to discriminate in this fashion against one shareholder. It argues correctly that no case has ever sanctioned a device that precludes a raider from sharing in a benefit available to all other stockholders. However, as we have noted earlier, the principle of selective stock repurchases by a Delaware corporation is neither unknown nor unauthorized. *Cheff* v. *Mathes*, 199 A.2d at 554; and *Bennett* v. *Propp*, 187 A.2d at 408. . . . The only difference is that heretofore the approved transaction was the payment of "greenmail" to a raider or dissident posing a threat to the corporate enterprise. All other stockholders were denied such favored treatment, and given Mesa's past history of greenmail, its claims here are rather ironic.

However, our corporate law is not static. It must grow and develop in response to, indeed in anticipation of, evolving concepts and needs. Merely because the General Corporation Law is silent as to a specific matter does not mean that it is prohibited. . . . As the sophistication of both raiders and targets has developed, a host of defensive measures to counter ever mounting threats has evolved and received judicial sanction. These include defensive charter amendments and other devices bearing some rather exotic, but apt, names: Crown Jewel, White Knight, Pac Man, and Golden Parachute. Each has highly selective features, the object of which is to deter or defeat the raider.

Thus, while the exchange offer is a form of selective treatment, given the nature of the threat posed here the response is neither unlawful nor unreasonable. If the board of directors is disinterested, has acted in good faith and with due care, its decision in the absence of an abuse of discretion will be upheld as a proper exercise of business judgment.

To this Mesa responds that the board is not disinterested, because the directors are receiving a benefit from the tender of their own shares, which because of the Mesa exclusion, does not devolve upon *all* stockholders equally. . . . However, Mesa concedes that if the exclusion is valid, then the directors and all other stockholders share the same benefit. The answer of course is that the exclusion is valid, and the directors' participation in the exchange offer does not rise to the level of a disqualifying interest.

Mesa also argues that the exclusion permits the director to abdicate the fiduciary duties they owe it. However, that is not so. The board continues to owe Mesa the duties of due care and loyalty. But in the face of the destructive threat Mesa's tender offer was perceived to pose, the board had a supervening duty to protect the corporate enterprise, which includes the other shareholders, from threatened harm.

Mesa contends that the basis of this action is punitive, and solely in response to the exercise of its rights of corporation democracy. Nothing precludes Mesa, as a stockholder, from acting in its own self-interest. However, Mesa, while pursuing its own interests, has acted in a manner which a board consisting of a majority of independent directors has reasonably determined to be contrary to the best interests of Unocal and its other shareholders. In this situation, there is no support in Delaware law for the proposition that, when responding to a perceived harm, a corporation must guarantee a benefit to a stockholder who is deliberately provoking the danger being addressed. There is no obligation of self-sacrifice by a corporation and its shareholders in the face of such a challenge.

Reversed.

A self-tender, such as Unocal's, has been denominated a "lollipop" because it tastes sweet to the company's long-time shareholders, but is a poison pill to the raider.[45] The *Unocal* opinion's application of the business judgment rule to the tender offer setting is representative of the traditional view. However, based on the Williams Act's policy of equal treatment, the SEC in July 1986 outlawed use of the "lollipop" self-tender offer.

---

[45] Leefeldt, "A Sweet Way to Foil Takeover Bids," *The Wall Street Journal*, September 4, 1985, p. 24.

Issuing Additional Shares

To make a tender offer more expensive for the bidder, the target can always issue additional shares. For example, assume that a shark makes a tender offer for 10 million of 20 million outstanding shares. By simply issuing 2 million more shares, the target has increased by one-tenth the number of shares that must be purchased to gain control. If the shares are issued to a friendly party ("white squire") that will not tender them, the defensive impact is even greater.

Generally speaking, such sales have been upheld under the business judgment rule, even where there was some question as to whether the consideration paid was adequate.[46]

ESOPs

An employee stock option plan (ESOP) is an excellent candidate to be a purchaser of target shares. The employees are normally loyal to management and fearful that their jobs will be jeopardized if a tender offer succeeds. Therefore, ESOPs, which are frequently managed by the officers and directors of the target, have often been recruited as allies in tender offer defenses.

For example, in 1981 LTV made a tender offer for a 70% interest in Grumman at $45 per share, a handsome premium over the $23-per-share market price. The Grumman board opposed the tender offer, and Grumman's pension plan's fiduciaries, consisting of Grumman's chairman and two other officers, decided not to tender any of the pension plan's 525,000 shares to LTV. Instead, they used the ESOP's funds to buy 1,158,000 additional shares on the open market at an average price of $38.34 to aid the defensive effort. The maneuver worked; LTV withdrew its bid.

The Grumman-LTV situation illustrates the decisive impact that defensive use of an ESOP can have. However, it also discloses the hazards. ESOPs and other pension plans are governed by the Employee Retirement Income Security Act of 1974 (ERISA), which is administered by the Department of Labor. The Department of Labor sued the directors of the Grumman pension plan for fiduciary breach, noting that when the LTV offer was withdrawn the market price of Grumman stock quickly dropped back down to its prebid level of around $23 per share, and the plan thereby experienced an unrealized loss of about $18 million.

The trial judge quickly issued a preliminary injunction prohibiting the fiduciaries operating the plan from buying, selling, or exercising any rights regarding the plan's stock without court approval. The Second Circuit affirmed in a decision that did not bar target managers from participating in tender offer decisions by such plans, but held that defendants should have sought independent advice regarding the best interests of the employees.[47]

Seventeen months after the tender offer battle, the ESOP sold its purchased

---

[46] *Treadway Companies, Inc.* v. *Care Corp.*, 638 F.2d 357 (2d Cir. 1980).

[47] *Donovan* v. *Bierwirth*, 680 F.2d 263 (2d Cir. 1982), *cert. denied*, 459 U.S. 1069 (1982).

shares for $47.55 per share, making a profit (including dividends) of some $13,217,780. Thereafter the case came to trial whereupon the trial judge dismissed the suit because the plan had a net profit on the transaction rather than a net loss. However, the Second Circuit reversed this opinion, holding the fiduciaries personally liable under ERISA for any ''loss'' caused by their breach of fiduciary duty. ''Loss,'' the court held, should be determined by comparing what the pension plan ''actually earned on the Grumman investment with what the Plan would have earned had the funds been available for other Plan purposes.'' [48]

Thus the plan fiduciaries were held personally liable for losses sustained by the plan due to their decision to act mainly on behalf of the target management's interests rather than on behalf of the interests of the plan. Had they sought independent advice or amended the plan to leave the decision to employee beneficiaries and counted on their loyalty, the fiduciaries might well have avoided liability.[49]

"White Knight"

A frequently used defensive technique, which we have already mentioned several times, is the recruiting of a ''white knight.'' This involves finding another potential suitor willing to make a tender offer that, it is hoped, will be more attractive to the shareholders and even to target management.

A classic example occurred in 1981 when Mobil Corporation made a tender offer for Marathon Oil Company. Marathon's market price had been about $75 per share, and Mobil's tender offer price was $86 per share. Mobil made it clear that if it succeeded, it intended to absorb Marathon fully and close Marathon's corporate headquarters in Findlay, Ohio. Marathon, among other defensive tactics, sought a white knight. It eventually found U.S. Steel willing to make a two-tier offer with a front door of $125 per share and to operate Marathon as an independent subsidiary with management largely unchanged and still located in Ohio.

U.S. Steel was not the first company that Marathon asked to become a white knight. It had disclosed its records to Gulf Oil, but Gulf declined to make a competing tender offer. This transaction is sometimes called ''sex without marriage'' because Marathon disclosed its intimate secrets to Gulf, but no permanent relationship resulted.

The attraction of a white knight is usually easily justified under the business judgment rule because it results in a higher offer for target shareholders than they would have received from the original hostile bid.

"Lock-up Options"

Sometimes a white knight requires an inducement to enter the fray. An increased chance for success is such an inducement. Consider again the Mobil–Marathon–U.S. Steel triangle. Mobil's main interest in taking over Marathon was in gaining possession of

---

[48] *Donovan* v. *Bierwirth*, 754 F.2d 1049 (2d Cir. 1985).

[49] See *Martin Marietta Corp.* v. *Bendix Corp.*, No. 82 Civ. 6134 (S.D.N.Y., September 16, 1982).

Marathon's 48% interest in the Yates Oil Field in Texas, the second richest oil field in the world. To ensure the success of the bid of U.S. Steel, its white knight, Marathon granted it two "lock-up" options. The first was an irrevocable option to purchase 17% of Marathon's common stock (authorized, but unissued) for $90 per share, a bargain price in light of the $125 tender offer. Second, Marathon granted U.S. Steel an option to purchase Marathon's Yates Oil Field interest, exercisable only in the event that U.S. Steel's bid failed and Marathon's control changed hands. Thus, even if Mobil outbid the white knight, the minute it gained control, U.S. Steel could purchase the one asset that Mobil truly wanted—the Yates Oil Field.

Lock-up options have been challenged as "manipulative" in violation of §14(e). However, in light of the Supreme Court's decision in *Schreiber* v. *Burlington Northern* this argument has little validity. On the other hand, some recent cases have invalidated lock-up options as constituting potential breaches of the target directors' fiduciary duty to shareholders.[50] Lock-ups appear to be on the way to extinction as defensive tools.

Sale of the "Crown Jewel"

Several defensive techniques are predicated on making the target less attractive to the shark. None is more extreme than the sale of the "crown jewel." Frequently a target will have one asset or one line of business that is its prize feature, its "crown jewel." Marathon's crown jewel was its interest in the Yates Oil Field. The option to sell that interest to U.S. Steel greatly reduced Mobil's interest in completing its tender offer.

Similarly, when Whittaker Corporation attempted a tender offer for control of Brunswick Corporation, Brunswick sold its crown jewel—a medical instruments subsidiary—to white knight American Home Products. Because this subsidiary was the portion of Brunswick that Whittaker most desired, it canceled its tender offer following the sale. The defensive tactic was later sustained in court.[51]

"Pac-Man"

The "Pac-Man" defense involves the target's making a tender offer for control of the shark that has made a tender offer for it. Martin Marietta's response to a tender offer by Bendix Corporation was to make a tender offer for control of Bendix. The battle was settled when Bendix was acquired by a white knight.

Cities Service went one step farther, initiating a preemptive strike by making a tender offer for Mesa Petroleum stock when it was clear Mesa was preparing a tender offer for Cities Service. Ultimately, neither acquired the other.

An interesting, and as yet untested, question is what would happen if both offers succeeded. Shark has bought control of target via a tender offer, but target has bought control of shark via a "Pac-Man" reverse tender offer. Which corporation would

[50] For example, *Hanson Trust PLC* v. *SCM Corp.*, 781 F.2d 264 (2d Cir. 1986); *Revlon, Inc.* v. *MacAndrews & Forbes, Inc.*, 506 A.2d 173 (Del. 1986).

[51] *Whittaker Corp.* v. *Edgar*, 535 F.Supp. 933 (N.D.Ill. 1982).

manage which might well depend on which could first gain control of the other's board of directors.[52]

When tested in court, the "Pac-Man" defense has generally been held a proper defensive tactic protected by the business judgment rule.[53]

"Corporate Suicide"

Perhaps the most drastic of all tender offer defenses is "corporate suicide," or liquidation in the face of a hostile tender offer. "Disaggregation," a partial restructuring of the corporation via partial liquidation, sale of the division, or a spinoff might be upheld under the business judgment rule, particularly if not solely in response to a tender offer.

Complete liquidation, on the other hand, is likely to be enjoined if challenged as simply too extreme a response.[54] Nonetheless, if the liquidation value of the corporation appears to be in excess of either the market price or the tender offer price, it certainly can be argued that the target board has a duty to consider liquidation as an alternative.

PROPRIETY OF TACTICS

Many of the offensive and defensive techniques discussed in this chapter seem fairly extreme. As long as there is full disclosure, it should not be too surprising that a shark is allowed to "play rough" in an attempted take-over. The Supreme Court's narrow reading of "manipulation" in *Schreiber* v. *Burlington Northern* indicates that sharks will continue to have much tactical leeway in the absence of legislative reforms. After all, sharks owe no fiduciary duty to the target's shareholders.

A greater controversy regards the propriety of virtually unfettered target management discretion to fend off tender offers that are made at a price that is attractive to target shareholders. In most cases, the defensive tactics we have discussed have been upheld. The reasoning of *Unocal* v. *Mesa* is representative. This has been the case even in some extreme situations.

For example, in *Panter* v. *Marshall Field & Co.*,[55] Field's stock was trading at $20 when Carter Hawley Hale (CHH) began planning a hostile tender offer. The contemplated offering price was $42, but the offer was withdrawn as a result of Field's defensive tactics, which included acquisitions for the purpose of creating antitrust problems for potential acquirors. After the offer collapsed, Field stock traded at below $16 per share. Not surprisingly, some Field shareholders, deprived of an opportunity to tender,

---

[52] See L. Herzel and J. Schmidt, "SEC Is Probing 'Double Pac-Man' Takeover Defense," *Legal Times of Washington*, April 18, 1983, p. 27.

[53] For example, *American General Co.* v. *NLT Corp.* [1982 Transfer Binder], *Federal Securities Law Reports* (CCH), ¶98,808 (S.D.Tex. 1982).

[54] For example, *Joseph E. Seagram & Sons, Inc.* v. *Abrams*, 510 F.Supp. 860 (S.D.N.Y. 1981).

[55] 646 F.2d 271, 301–04 (7th Cir.), *cert. denied*, 454 U.S. 1092 (1981).

were upset, but legal challenges by those shareholders failed. The business judgment rule was deemed to provide a shield for Field's management.

Blind application of the business judgment rule to the tender offer context has been criticized.[56] And in recent years there appears to be a trend to cast a slightly more critical eye upon defensive tactics. The following case contains an increasingly common conclusion.

NORLIN CORP. v. ROONEY, PACE INC.

744 F.2d 255 (2d Cir. 1984)

Norlin Corp. is an NYSE-listed company, incorporated in Panama, but with its principal place of business in New York. Piezo Electric Products, Inc., on two trading days, January 6 and 12, 1984, in conjunction with the investment banking firm of Rooney, Pace Inc., purchased 32% of Norlin's common stock in a series of separate market transactions. Fearful of an imminent takeover, Norlin filed suit on January 13, alleging various securities laws violations. Judge Edelstein quickly heard Norlin's motion for an injunction to stop further acquisition and to force divestiture, but denied the motion.

On January 20, Norlin transferred 28,295 shares of common stock to Andean Enterprises, Inc., a wholly owned subsidiary, incorporated in Panama, purportedly in consideration for Andean's cancellation of a Norlin promissory note of $965,454. On January 25, Norlin's board approved a transfer of 800,000 authorized but unissued shares of preferred stock to Andean in exchange for a $20 million promissory note. Also on January 25, Norlin created an ESOP and appointed three board members as trustees. The board immediately transferred 185,000 common shares to the ESOP in ex-

change for a promissory note of $6,824,945. In its SEC filings, Norlin admitted that its board was the beneficial owner of, and had voting control over, all transferred shares. As a result of these transactions, the Norlin board controlled 49% of the corporation's outstanding stock. Norlin's chairman, Stevens, and president, Simpkins, wrote the company's shareholders indicating that they were taking all necessary steps to oppose the Rooney, Pace–Piezo offer. The letter offered no justification for the transactions other than to defeat the potential takeover.

Norlin's attorneys warned Norlin that their actions might cause the New York Stock Exchange to delist Norlin stock, and on March 15, the NYSE suspended trading in Norlin stock and indicated an intent to delist because of issuance of stock to Andean and the ESOP resulted in a change of control of the company, which, under NYSE rules, requires shareholder approval.

On February 9, Piezo filed a counterclaim in this action alleging that Norlin's defensive transfer violated the laws of Panama and New York as well as federal securities laws. Piezo sought an order declaring the transfers void

[56] See sources cited in Robert Prentice, "Target Board Abuse of Defensive Tactics: Can Federal Law Be Mobilized to Overcome the Business Judgment Rule?" *Journal of Corporation Law*, Vol. 8 (1983), p. 227.

and barring Norlin from voting them. The trial judge, on April 16, granted Piezo's motion for a preliminary injunction. Norlin appealed.

KAUFMAN, JUDGE:

[The opinion first disposed of some procedural matters and then proposed to address the two key issues regarding the propriety of issuing a preliminary injunction—plaintiff's likelihood of success on the merits, and a showing of irreparable harm.]

Piezo asserts, and the district court appropriately found, that the illegality of voting the stock transferred to Andean and the ESOP had been demonstrated with sufficient certainty to warrant injunctive relief. As we will explain, the right of a wholly owned subsidiary to vote shares of a parent company's stock is controlled by statute. The propriety of an issuance of stock to an ESOP in the context of a contest for corporate control has not been legislatively resolved, and so must be assessed in relation to fiduciary principles governing the conduct of officers and directors. Thus, we must analyze the two issues separately.

[Regarding the transfers of stock to Andean, the court first addressed the "conflict of laws" issue by attempting to decide whether Panamanian or New York law should apply. Ultimately, it made no difference because "the relevant rules of law in New York and Panama are identical on this point: A wholly owned subsidiary may not vote shares of its parent's stock." The court then turned to the validity of the transfers to the ESOP.]

We now turn to the district court's conclusion that appellee had demonstrated probable illegality stemming from the voting of Norlin shares held by the ESOP. This is a somewhat more difficult problem, for we have little statutory authority to guide us in our quest. We must look instead to those fiduciary principles of state common law that constrained the actions of corporate officers and directors.

A board member's obligation to a corporation and its shareholders has two prongs, generally characterized as the duty of care and the duty of loyalty. The duty of care refers to the responsibility of a corporate fiduciary to exercise, in the performance of his tasks, the care that a reasonably prudent person in a similar position would use under similar circumstances. In evaluating a manager's compliance with the duty of care, New York courts adhere to the business judgment rule, which "bars judicial inquiry into actions of corporate directors taken in good faith and in the exercise of honest judgment in the lawful and legitimate furtherance of corporate purposes"—*Auerbach* v. *Bennett*, 419 N.Y.S.2d 920, 926, 393 N.E.2d 994 (1979).

The second restriction traditionally imposed, the duty of loyalty, derives from the prohibition against self-dealing that inheres in the fiduciary relationship. See *Pepper* v. *Litton*, 308 U.S. 295, 306–07 (1939). Once a prima facie showing is made that directors have a self-interest in a particular corporate transaction, the burden shifts to them to demonstrate that the transaction is fair and serves the best interests of the corporation and its shareholders.

In applying these principles in the context of battles for corporate control, we begin with the business judgment rule, which affords directors wide latitude in devising strategies to resist unfriendly advances. See, for example, *Treadway Companies, Inc.* v. *Care Corp.*, 638 F.2d 357, 380–84 (2d Cir. 1980); *Crouse-Hinds Co.* v. *Internorth, Inc.*, 634 F.2d 690, 701–04 (2d Cir. 1980). As Judge Kearse made clear in those cases, however, the business judgment rule governs only where the directors are not shown to have a self-interest in the transaction at issue—*Treadway*, 639 F.2d at 382. Once self-dealing or bad faith is demonstrated, the duty of loyalty supersedes the duty of care, and the burden shifts to the directors to "prove that the transaction was fair and reasonable to the corporation''—Id.

In this case, the evidence adduced was more than adequate to constitute a prima facie showing of self-interest on the board's part. All the stock transferred to Andean and the ESOP was to be voted by the directors; indeed, members of the board were appointed trustees of the ESOP. The precipitous timing of the share issuances, and the fact that the ESOP was created the very same day that stock was issued to it, give rise to a strong inference that the purpose of the transaction was not to benefit the employees but rather to solidify management's control of the company. This is buttressed by the fact that the board offered its shareholders no rationale for the transfers other than its determination to oppose, at all costs, the threat to the company that Piezo's acquisitions ostensibly represented. Where, as here, directors amass voting control of close to a majority of a corporation's shares in their own hands by complex, convoluted, and deliberate maneuvers, it strains credulity to suggest that the retention of control over corporate affairs played no part in their plans.

We reject the view, propounded by Norlin, that once it concludes that an actual or anticipated takeover attempt is not in the best interests of the company, a board of directors may take any action necessary to forestall acquisitive moves. The business judgment rule does indeed require the board to analyze carefully any perceived threat to the corporation and to act appropriately when it decides that the interests of the company and its shareholders might be jeopardized. As we have explained, however, the duty of loyalty requires the board to demonstrate that any actions it does take are fair and reasonable. We conclude that Norlin has failed to make that showing.

ESOPs, like other employee benefit plans, may serve a number of legitimate corporate purposes, and their creation is generally upheld in the courts when they do so. By establishing

an ESOP, corporate managers may seek to improve employee morale and loyalty, to raise capital for the corporation, or to supplement employee compensation or retirement benefits. When an ESOP is set up in the context of a contest for control, however, it devolves upon the board to show that the plan was in fact created to benefit the employees, and not simply to further the aim of managerial entrenchment. In applying that distinction, courts have looked to factors such as the timing of the ESOP's establishment, the financial impact on the company, the identity of the trustees, and the voting control of the ESOP shares.

In this case, an examination of each of these factors indicates that the ESOP was created solely as a tool of management self-perpetuation. It was created a mere five days after the district court refused to enjoin further stock purchases by Piezo, and at a time when Norlin's officers were clearly casting about for strategies to deter a challenge to their control. No real consideration was received from the ESOP for the shares. The three trustees appointed to oversee the ESOP were all members of Norlin's board, and voting control of all of the ESOP shares was retained by the directors. We therefore conclude that the record supports the finding that the transfer of stock to the ESOP was part of a management entrenchment effort.

Norlin, however, urges that even if the creation of the ESOP was not fair and reasonable in itself, it served other important corporate and shareholder interests, and hence should not be deemed unlawful. First, Norlin argues that a Piezo takeover would jeopardize a $25 million net operating loss carryforward currently on the company's books. This concern appears somewhat disingenuous in light of Norlin's own statement, in a letter to the NYSE, that ''[i]n Norlin's view, it is likely that Rooney, Pace and Piezo, if they achieve control, could have a public sale to safeguard the net operating loss carryforward.'' But even if Norlin's fears were legitimate, that would only help to justify the board's determination that an anticipated takeover attempt should be opposed as not in the corporation's best interest. It has no relevance to our evaluation whether the actions taken by the board in response to that decision were fair and reasonable. In a similar vein, the company contends that its actions were an appropriate response to reports of Rooney, Pace's "unsavory reputation" and to the possibility that Norlin's financial printing business might suffer if an investment house should acquire control. Again, this concern, however real it may be, does not help to establish the independent legitimacy of the actions taken by the board to counter a perceived threat.

Norlin's final justification, and one emphasized at oral argument, was that the board needed to consolidate control to "buy" time to explore financial alternatives to a Piezo takeover. The company asserts that the shareholders will benefit if the directors are insulated from challenges to their control, for an interim period of unspecified duration, so that all of Norlin's future operations can be considered with professional guidance. This argument stands our prior cases on their heads. It is true that in conformity with the duty of care, we have required corporate managers to examine carefully the merits of a proposed change in control. We have also urged consultation with investment specialists in undertaking such analysis. See, for example, *Treadway*, 638 F.2d at 384. The purpose of this exercise, however, is to insure a reasoned examination of the situation *before* action is taken, not afterwards. We have never given the slightest indication that we would sanction a board decision to lock up voting power by any means, for as long as the directors deem necessary, prior to making the decisions that will determine a corporation's destiny. Were we to countenance that, we would in effect be approving a wholesale wresting of corporate power from the hands of the shareholders, to

whom it is entrusted by statute, and into the hands of the officers and directors.

We thus find that Piezo has succeeded in demonstrating the likelihood of success on the merits, with regard to the share issuances to both Andean and the ESOP. We move on to the other requirement for the issuance of a preliminary injunction: a showing of irreparable harm.

[*The court then found that the potential delisting by the NYSE constituted irreparable harm. The court then concluded.*]

In analyzing the issues presented to us, we have been mindful of the preliminary stage at which this litigation stands. Developments in corporate control contests often proceed swiftly, and timing may have a crucial impact on the outcome. A more complete record will also be required to reach a final adjudication of the merits of Norlin's and Piezo's competing claims. We would therefore urge the district judge to proceed expeditiously to a trial on the important issues raised by the parties.

This case well illustrates the increasing complexity and bitterness of the tactics employed by contestants vying for corporate dominion. As here, each new offensive may be met with a counteroffensive intended, in turn, to weaken the aggressor. When these maneuvers fail, the courts themselves are too often drawn into the fray.

Although we are cognizant that takeover fights, potentially involving billions of dollars, profoundly affect our society and economy, it is not for us to make the policy choices that will determine whether this style of corporate warfare will escalate or diminish. Our holding here is not intended to reflect a more general view of the contests being played out on this and other corporate battlefields. We do, however, believe that a preliminary injunction was warranted in this case. Whatever denouement may flow from the events that have transpired, the rules of fairness we have outlined must govern the actions taken by both sides. Because Piezo has succeeded in demonstrating probable illegality in the issuance of shares to Andean and the ESOP, as well as irreparable harm there- from, we agree that the voting of those shares should, pending further proceedings, be en- joined. Accordingly, the order of the district court is affirmed.

The law regarding the validity of tender offer defenses is definitely in flux. However, several cases have now suggested that once target management decides to seek a white knight, thus putting the target company up for sale, target management becomes an "auctioneer" with a fiduciary duty to secure the highest price for target shareholders. Devices such as lock-up options, which can give one bidder an insurmounta- ble advantage thereby stultifying the bidding process, may be held invalid.[57]

QUESTIONS AND PROBLEMS

1. Gladstone, who owned 19.4% of University Bank's (the Bank) common stock, hired Cain to solicit options to purchase shares in the Bank. Cain, on Gladstone's behalf solicited 49 of the Bank's 650 shareholders, offering a $5.00 option price, exercisable at $18.00 per share on or before February 28, 1984. Through Cain, Gladstone acquired options on approximately another 4% of the Bank's shares. The Bank sued Gladstone, alleging several securities law violations. Among others, the Bank claimed that Glad- stone's solicitation through Cain had been a tender offer within the meaning of the Williams Act. The evidence showed that the 49 shareholders solicited held approxi- mately 22% of the Bank's shares, that some premium of an unclear amount had been offered, and that one offeree claimed Cain had called on him twice and "exerted pressure on him to accept the offer." Was this a tender offer? Discuss. See *University Bank and Trust Co.* v. *Gladstone*, 574 F.Supp. 1006 (D. Mass. 1983).

2. After acquiring 5% of the shares of Florida Commercial Banks, Inc. (the Bank), Culverhouse filed a Schedule 13D. He purchased more stock and eventually made a tender offer for control of the Bank. When he did so, the Bank filed suit alleging, among other things, that Culverhouse's Schedule 13D failed to disclose Culverhouse's intention systematically to purchase the Bank's stock for other than investment pur- poses, and his simultaneous negotiations with others for the sale of the Bank's stock. Culverhouse filed a motion to dismiss, arguing that the Bank had no standing to sue for corrective disclosures under §13(d), §14(d), and §14(e). Discuss. See *Florida Commercial Banks* v. *Culverhouse*, 772 F.2d 1513 (11th Cir. 1985).

3. Carl Icahn and a number of companies under his control acquired 5% of the shares of Dan River, Inc., filed a Schedule 13D, and commenced negotiations that Dan

---

[57] For example, *Edelman v. Fruehauf Corp.*, 798 F.2d 882 (6th Cir. 1986); *Revlon, Inc. v. MacAndrews & Forbes, Inc.*, 506 A.2d 173 (Del. 1986).

River characterized as of a "pay-me-greenmail-or-face-a-take-over" nature. Dan River sued Icahn on several grounds, including a challenge to his disclosures under §§13(d), 14(d), and 14(e). Specifically, Dan River seeks a court order "sterilizing" Icahn's shares (preventing him from voting them) because he failed to reveal that one of his controlled companies faced a contingent obligation of $5,000,000. Financial statements indicated that the Icahn group's equity was approximately $28,000,000. Was the omission material? Discuss. See *Dan River, Inc.* v. *Icahn*, 701 F.2d 278 (4th Cir. 1983).

4. When L. P. Acquisition Co. attempted a tender offer for control of ENA, a closely held company with no shares listed on any exchange or registered with the SEC, it deliberately ignored the Michigan take-over law. Instead, L. P. Acquisition challenged the constitutionality of the law, which had a 60-day hold open period, provision for a hearing by state officials and other matters not found in the Williams Act. The trial judge ruled that the Michigan law violated neither the Commerce Clause nor the Supremacy Clause because Congress had chosen to regulate only tender offers for registered securities. Discuss. See *L. P. Acquisition Co.* v. *Tyson*, 772 F.2d 201 (6th Cir. 1985).

5. Guardian Industries, with 22% of the market in high-performance architectural glass, began to purchase a substantial interest in H. H. Robertson, which had 10% of the market. Robertson sued to enjoin further purchases on antitrust grounds. The court found that the purchases would have an anticompetitive effect, but had to address the issue of whether Robertson had standing to complain of the antitrust injury that might flow from a combination of the two companies. Discuss. See *H. H. Robertson Co.* v. *Guardian Industries Corp.*, 50 A.T.R.R. (BNA) 166, rehearing granted en banc 50 A.T.R.R. (BNA) 313 (3d Cir. 1986).

6. On April 17, 1985, after significant negotiations, EAC purchased 51% of the shares of Frantz Manufacturing Co. The next day, EAC's president traveled to Frantz' headquarters to assert control through shareholder consents. The consents also made several changes in the bylaws, including requiring unanimous director approval for any board action. Notwithstanding the consents, the old board met on April 24 and authorized the funding of an ESOP with treasury shares, which diluted EAC's control to less than a majority interest. EAC sued. Discuss the validity of the Frantz directors' actions. See *Frantz Manufacturing Co.* v. *EAC Industries*, 501 A.2d 401 (Del. 1985).

7. Moran, a director of Household International, was considering a take-over of Household by another company he controlled. In the face of its vulnerability, the Household board issued a poison pill. Among other features, the pill had a "flip-over" provision that, if activated by a merger or consolidation, allowed Household shareholders to purchase $200 of the common stock of a tender offeror for $100. The resulting dilution would obviously discourage a would-be take-over hopeful. Moran challenged the validity of the poison pill. Discuss. See *Moran* v. *Household International, Inc.*, 500 A.2d 1346 (Del. 1985).

8. Pantry Pride made a hostile tender offer for Revlon at $47.50, even after Revlon had enacted a poison pill. Revlon then repurchased some shares and issued notes containing a cyanide capsule limiting Revlon's ability to incur additional debts and

sell assets (which would inhibit a shark's ability to sell parts of Revlon to pay for a tender offer). Pantry Pride then announced a new offer that was slowly raised to $53 on October 1. On October 3, Revlon approved a leveraged buyout by white knight Forstmann at $56 under which Revlon would cancel the pill. Pantry Pride raised its offer to $56.25. Forstmann responded by raising its bid to $57.25 contingent upon Revlon (a) giving it a lock-up option to buy two Revlon divisions for $100 – 175 million below value if another acquiror bought 40% of Revlon, (b) signing a "no-shop" provision (agreeing not to seek out a competing white knight), (c) removing the pill, and (d) paying a $25 million cancellation fee if another acquiror got more than 19.9% of Revlon's stock. Revlon's board consented. Pantry Pride raised its offer to $58, conditioned on nullification of the pill, waiver of the cyanide capsule, and injunction against the lock-up to Forstmann. Pantry Pride then went to court. Discuss the propriety of Revlon's defensive tactics. See *Revlon, Inc.* v. *MacAndrews & Forbes Holdings, Inc.*, 506 A.2d 173 (Del. 1986).

23

REGULATION
OF THE SECURITIES BUSINESS

INTRODUCTION

After the "Great Crash" of 1929, many persons believed that various activities of brokers, dealers, and investment advisers had contributed greatly to the crash and the subsequent onset of the Great Depression. Whether or not this was true, there remains substantial regulation of the activities of these market professionals. This chapter can only give a brief look at some of the key aspects of this regulation.

A *broker* is "any person engaged in the business of effecting transactions in securities for the account of others, but does not include a bank." [1] While a broker is merely an agent for another person, a *dealer* is "any person engaged in the business of buying and selling securities for his own account," again excluding banks. [2] An *investment adviser* is "any person who, for compensation, engages in the business of advising others, either directly or through publications or writings, as to the value of securities or as to the advisability of investing in, purchasing, or selling securities, or

---

[1] §3(a) (4) of the 1934 Act.

[2] §3(a) (5) of the 1934 Act.

. . . issues or promulgates analysis or reports concerning securities.''[3] Banks, broker-dealers, and a few others are excluded.

To act as a broker-dealer for any securities that are not exempt, one must register with the SEC under §15(a) of the 1934 Act. Similar registration of investment advisers is required by §203 of the Investment Advisers Act.

Naturally, the SEC is the most significant regulatory force in the world of these market professionals, but the national stock exchanges have comprehensive rules governing their member broker-dealers, and the National Association of Securities Dealers (NASD) has similar rules governing broker-dealers in the OTC market. Self-regulation by these industry organizations is an important supplement to SEC activity.

This chapter will begin by examining certain legal problems arising out of the conflicts of interest that frequently tempt broker-dealers. Then the recommending of securities without adequate basis will be discussed. Finally, the chapter will examine several related, miscellaneous regulatory matters.

CONFLICTS OF INTEREST

A broker is an agent of the investor. In that capacity the broker owes a fiduciary duty to look out for the investor's best interests. Unfortunately, there are a number of ways in which the broker's self-interest and the investor's best interests can conflict. Occasionally, the broker will give in to temptation and subordinate the client's interests.

Excessive Prices

One way in which a broker-dealer can sacrifice the client's interest is to charge prices on OTC stock which are well above the market price. The following classic case illustrates that even when purportedly acting on its own account as a dealer a securities professional cannot take unfair advantage.

CHARLES HUGHES & CO., INC. v. SEC

139 F.2d 434 (2d Cir. 1943), *cert. denied*, 321 U.S. 786 (1944)

This is an appeal from an SEC ruling revoking the registration of petitioner Charles Hughes Co., a broker-dealer. The Commission found that petitioner had violated the antifraud provisions of §17(a) of the 1933 Act and §15(c) (1) *of the 1934 Act by selling securities at prices substantially over the going market rate without disclosing the markup.*

Typical was the treatment of Mrs. Stella Furbeck. Petitioner's agent called Furbeck, who

---

[3] §202(a) (11) of the Investment Advisers Act of 1940.

knew little or nothing about investing, and told her of a "wonderful" stock she should buy. Although Furbeck said she was not interested, the agent kept calling until she relented. Petitioner's agents slowly worked their way into Furbeck's confidence until they completely controlled her portfolio. Every few days they would have a "marvelous" stock that was definitely "beyond the usual" for her to buy.

The price paid by Furbeck and others ranged from 16.1% to 40.9% over market value. Most of the transactions involved little or no risk to petitioner, because it would secure the customer's order before buying the securities to fill the order. Furbeck testified she was told the prices she paid were under current market value. Petitioner's agents deny this, but admit they never disclosed to her what the market value was.

CLARK, CIRCUIT JUDGE:

An over-the-counter firm which actively solicits customers and then sells them securities at prices as far above the market as were those which petitioner charged here must be deemed to commit a fraud. It holds itself out as competent to advise in the premises, and it should disclose the market price if sales are to be made substantially above that level. Even considering petitioner as a principal in a simple vendor-purchaser transaction (and there is doubt whether, in several instances at least, petitioner was actually not acting as broker-agent for the purchasers, in which case all undisclosed profits would be forfeited), it was still under a special duty, in view of its expert knowledge and proffered advice, not to take advantage of its customers' ignorance of market conditions. The key to the success of all of petitioner's dealings was the confidence in itself which it managed to instill in the customers. Once that confidence was established, the failure to reveal the mark-

up pocketed by the firm was both an omission to state a material fact and a fraudulent device. When nothing was said about market price, the natural implication in the untutored minds of the purchasers was that the price asked was close to the market. The law of fraud knows no difference between express representation on the one hand and implied misrepresentation or concealment on the other—*Strong v. Repide*, 213 U.S. 419, 430, 29 S.Ct. 521, 53 L.Ed. 853.

We need not stop to decide, however, how far common law fraud was shown. For the business of selling investment securities has been considered one peculiarly in need of regulation for the protection of the investor. "The business of trading in securities is one in which opportunities for dishonesty are of constant recurrence and ever present." *Archer v. Securities and Exchange Commission*, 8 Cir., 133 F.2d 795, 803, *certiorari* denied 319 U.S. 767. The well-known "blue sky laws" of 43 states have in fact proved inadequate, so that in 1933 Congress after the most extensive investigations started on a program of regulation, of which this is one of the fruits. In its interpretation of §17(a) of the Securities Act, the Commission has consistently held that a dealer cannot charge prices not reasonably related to the prevailing market price without disclosing that fact.

The essential objective of securities legislation is to protect those who do not know market conditions from the overreachings of those who do. Such protection will mean little if it stops short of the point of ultimate consequence, namely, the price charged for the securities. Indeed, it is the purpose of all legislation for the prevention of fraud in the sale of securities to preclude the sale of "securities which are in fact worthless, or worth substantially less than the asking price"—*People v. Federated Radio Corp.*, 244 N.Y. 33, 40, 154 N.E. 655, 658. If after several years of experience under this highly publicized legislation we should find that the public cannot rely upon a commission-licensed broker not to charge unsuspecting investors 25% more than a market price easily ascertainable by insiders, we should leave such legislation little more than a snare and a delusion. We think the Commission has correctly interpreted its responsibilities to stop such abusive practices in the sale of securities.

Petitioner's final contention is that the actual market price of the securities was never satisfactorily proved. We agree, however, with the Commission that the evidence of the quotations published in the National Daily Quotation Sheets, a recognized service giving "daily market indications," as petitioner itself stipulated, and the prices paid concurrently by petitioner sufficiently indicated prevailing market price in the absence of evidence to the contrary.

Order affirmed.

Over the years the SEC has generally attacked as excessive any markups exceeding 10%.[4]

The *Charles Hughes & Co.* case gave rise to what is known as the "shingle theory." The doctrine's "essence is that by engaging in business, the broker-dealer makes a broad basic representation to the public at large that he will deal fairly with his customers and handle transactions promptly, in the usual manner and in accordance with trade custom." [5]

Although the shingle theory arose out of excessive pricing cases such as *Charles Hughes & Co.*, it has been invoked to punish broker-dealers for executing unauthorized transactions, accepting payment for securities the broker-dealer could not deliver, diverting customers' funds to personal use, conducting business while insolvent, and failing to disclose any substantial long or short position of its own that might influence the broker-dealer's recommendations.

The shingle theory does not go so far as to make brokers guarantors of their recommendations. Faulty opinions or erroneous analyses are not condemned by the doctrine. What it does do is treat as fraud conduct that in the normal commercial world might be considered merely a breach of contract. It allows the establishment of statutory fraud where no intentional misstatements are present. We shall see more of the shingle theory later in the chapter.

Undisclosed Principal/Market Maker

A broker-dealer may very well act as a broker (acting as an agent in its customer's transaction with another) one minute and as a principal (selling to or buying from the customer on its own account) the next. The *Charles Hughes & Co.* opinion adverted to the problem the customer may have in knowing in which capacity the broker-dealer

---

[4] For example, *Alstead Dempsey & Co., Inc., Security Exchange Act Release*, no. 34–20825 (SEC, April 5, 1984).

[5] S. Jaffe, *Broker-Dealers and Securities Markets* (Colorado Springs, CO: Shepard's, Inc., 1977), §7.09.

is acting. A broker is expected to look out 100% for its principal's best interests. A dealer, on the other hand, can be expected to look out more for its own interests.

For a customer to know what to expect, the customer must know the broker-dealer's capacity. This is especially true when the broker-dealer is *making a market* in the particular stock. A market maker is a dealer holding itself out with respect to a particular security as being willing to buy or sell for its own account on a continuous basis.[6]

The following case involves a failure to disclose this information.

CHASINS v. SMITH, BARNEY & CO.

438 F.2d 1167 (2d Cir. 1970)

Appellee Chasins was the commentator on a musical radio show sponsored by appellant Smith, Barney & Co. Because of this relationship, Chasins retained Smith, Barney as his stock broker.

Appellant recommended purchases of Welch Scientific, Tex-Star Oil and Gas Corp., and Howard Johnson Company, among others. In at least four of these transactions, appellant was a market maker for the stock. Although appellant disclosed to appellee that it was acting as a principal in the transactions, it did not disclose that it was making a market or how much it had paid for the securities or that it had served as an underwriter for two of the stocks.

Appellee Chasins later sued. The trial court became the first court in the country to hold that failure to disclose market maker status was fraud in violation of Rule 10b-5, and a violation of Rule 15c1–4 (which has been replaced by Rule 10b-10, but at the time required a dealer to disclose when it was acting as a principal). The court, sitting without a jury, awarded Chasins $18,616.64—the difference between the price at which Chasins bought the securities

from appellant and the price at which he later sold them.

Smith, Barney appealed.

SMITH, CIRCUIT JUDGE:

Smith, Barney's major contention in attacking the district court's finding of a violation of Rules 10b-5 and 15c1–4 is that failure to disclose its "market-making" role in the securities exchanged over the counter was not failure to disclose a material fact. Appellant contends that the district court's holding went farther than any other decision in this area and that no court had ever found failure to disclose a "market-making" role by a stock brokerage firm to a client-purchaser to be a violation of Rule 10b-5. Smith, Barney also asserts that all brokerage firms had followed the same practice and had never thought such disclosure was required; moreover, the SEC had never prosecuted any firm for this violation. However, even where a defendant is successful in showing that it has followed a customary course in the industry, the first litigation of such a practice is a proper

---

[6] §3(a) (38) of the 1934 Act.

occasion for its outlawry if it is in fact in violation. See *Opper v. Hancock Securities Corp.*, 250 F.Supp. 668, 676 (2d Cir. 1966). In any event, it cannot fairly be said that no one in the trade had ever considered such nondisclosure to be significant. Appellant's own customers man (Delaney) testified that at the time (1961) he was disclosing to retail clients the firm's role as a market maker in a given security whenever he was aware of it.

Appellant also points to the fact that in over-the-counter trading, a market maker with an inventory in a stock is considered the best source of the security (the best available market); thus, the SEC has even punished a brokerage firm for not going directly to a firm with an inventory in a stock, that is, interposing another firm between them. However, the fact that dealing with a market maker should be considered by some desirable for some purposes does not mean that the failure to disclose Smith, Barney's market-making role is not under the circumstances of this case a failure to disclose a material fact. The question here is not whether Smith, Barney sold to Chasins at a fair price but whether disclosure of Smith, Barney's being a market maker in the Welch Scientific, Tex-Star Oil and Gas, and Howard Johnson securities might have influenced Chasins' decision to buy the stock. See *SEC v. Texas Gulf Sulphur Co.*, 401 F.2d 457 (2d Cir. 1965), *cert. denied*, 382 U.S. 811 (1965). The test of materiality "is whether a reasonable man would attach importance . . . in determining his choice of action in the transaction in question."

Knowledge of the additional fact of market making by Smith, Barney in the three securities recommended could well influence the decision of a client in Chasins' position, depending on the broker-dealer's undertaking to analyze and advise, whether to follow its recommendation to buy the securities; disclosure of the fact would indicate the possibility of adverse interests which might be reflected in Smith, Barney's recommendations. Smith, Barney could well be caught in either a "short" position or a "long" position in a security, because of erroneous judgment of supply and demand at given levels. If oversupplied, it may be to the interest of a market maker to attempt to unload the securities on his retail clients. Here, Smith, Barney's strong recommendations of the three securities Chasins purchased could have been motivated by its own market position rather than the intrinsic desirability of the securities for Chasins. An investor who is at least informed of the possibility of such adverse interests, due to his broker's market making in the securities recommended, can question the reasons for the recommendations.

In view of our agreement with the finding of violation of Rule 10b-5 we need not determine whether this failure to disclose market-making or dealer status also violated Rule 15c1-4.

[*The Court then affirmed the trial court's measure of damages (purchase price minus sale price), rejecting Smith, Barney's proffered alternative (purchase price minus fair market value on date purchased). The trial court's decision was affirmed.*

However, Smith, Barney then petitioned for a rehearing in banc (by the entire court). This petition was denied, but several judges disagreed with the denial. Judge Friendly wrote the following on their behalf.]

FRIENDLY, CIRCUIT JUDGE:

Although the narrowing of the opinion to the particular constellation of facts here presented substantially lessens its impact, we are nevertheless constrained to voice our dissent from the refusal to grant *in banc* reconsideration.

The district court initially found that the confirmations here, which disclosed that Smith, Barney was selling "as principal for our own account," were in full compliance with the rule.

It is conceded that in 1961 no rule of the SEC (other than, allegedly, the inevitable Rule 10b-5), the NASD or the New York Stock Exchange required disclosure of that fact to a customer.

The complaint nowhere asserted that Smith, Barney was under a duty to tell Mr. Chasins it was a "market maker" in the three over-the-counter stocks that he bought. It alleged rather that defendant did not disclose the "best price" at which these and other securities could have been bought or sold in the open market, or the prices it had paid or received, and that plaintiff was deceived by Smith, Barney's failure to disclose "the material fact of its adverse interest, the extent of which is today still unknown to and not determinable by plaintiff." Mr. Chasins had been plainly told of defendant's ownership by the confirmation slips. In addition, the Smith, Barney research report he had received on Tex-Star contained the legend in common use at the time:

> We point out that in the course of our regular business we may be long or short of any of the above securities at any time,

and the prospectus he received of Welch Scientific Company disclosed that Smith, Barney was one of the underwriters of that stock, which had only recently been placed on the market. All that the trial record contained about nondisclosure of market making was a statement by Delaney, a registered representative of Smith, Barney, that he normally would bring this fact to the attention of clients if he knew it; that he did know Smith, Barney was making a market in the three stocks; and that he couldn't recall whether or not he had brought this to Mr. Chasins' attention.

The issue of market making first assumed importance as a result of the opinion of the district judge. After finding against the plaintiff on all the contentions that had been advanced in the complaint and aired at the trial, he opined

that information with respect to market making "was material to the plaintiff in considering the price at which he purchased the securities, and to what extent the price was based on defendant's own market activities," and therefore plaintiff should recover his entire market loss. Smith, Barney then made a motion pointing out there was no basis for the "therefore," since on the judge's theory the only recoverable damage would be any excessive price obtained as a result of Smith Barney's being a market maker. On that issue it submitted proof by way of affidavit that the prices charged the plaintiff for the three stocks were entirely fair, indeed less than he would have paid if he had bought the stocks from a person acting solely as broker. It also submitted the opinion of the experienced manager of its trading department that

> From the point of view of the knowledgeable investor, disclosure to him that he would be purchasing from a market maker would only have encouraged him in his decision to buy.

Unwilling to hear evidence on the issue first raised by its opinion, the district court took a new tack. It held, in seeming contradiction of the initial opinion, that the confirmations, in a form widely used, did not comply with Rule 15c-1-4 since they conveyed "the impression that defendant had purchased a block of the securities and was selling part of it to plaintiff at the then prevailing market prices, when, in fact, defendant was acting as a dealer for its own account." We are unable to follow this, especially in light of the definition of "dealer" in §3(a) (5), and the court wisely does not base its decision upon it. Evidently lacking confidence in that holding, the judge then went on to conclude, without semblance of an evidentiary basis, that disclosure of market making might have led Mr. Chasins not to purchase the stocks at all.

The conclusions on the materiality of disclosure of market making by the district court and in this court's opinion are predicated on an essential misconception of the role of the market maker in over-the-counter transactions. When a reputable house like Smith, Barney acts as one of several market makers, as was the case here, it serves a highly desirable purpose in reducing the spreads characteristic of over-the-counter trading. It has been widely recognized that the "best price" can be obtained by dealing directly with market makers, for one reason because a commission to an intermediary is avoided. The district judge's fears concerning the ability of a market maker to set an arbitrary price are inapplicable when as here there were several market makers. Moreover Smith, Barney offered to prove that in fact Mr. Chasins bought at the lowest available price. So far as concerns the fears of ulterior motives voiced by the district judge and now by the court, the

market maker, who buys as well as sells, is *less* likely to be interested in palming off a stock than a dealer with only a long position. Yet the confirmation here would plainly have been adequate for such a dealer, and we held only recently, in a case curiously not cited, that a dealer need not make the additional disclosure that it had originally acquired the stock for investment and not with a view towards distribution, something considerably more material than being one of several market makers, *S.E.C.* v. *R. A. Holman & Co.*, 366 F.2d 456, 457 (2 Cir., 1966).

Although the opinion is now limited to the peculiar facts of this case, we fear it will encourage many suits by other speculators who have suffered losses. At minimum, Smith, Barney is entitled to a new trial where the issues of materiality and reliance raised by the district court's opinion can be fairly litigated.

Rule 10b-10

Rule 10b-10, which replaced Rule 15c1–4, has brought some clarity to this area. It requires a broker-dealer to disclose whether it is acting as an agent or as a principal and specifically requires disclosure of market maker status. It also requires disclosure by a broker-dealer acting in a principal capacity of such matters as the markup, markdown, or similar remuneration received.

The rule requires only that notice be given "at or before completion of the transaction." Disclosures in confirmation slips, even coming as long as a month after a trade, have been deemed sufficient.[7]

Manipulation

When broker-dealers act as underwriters, they may have an opportunity to manipulate the price of the issuer's shares. Such manipulation is condemned by several federal provisions, including Rules 10b-5 and 10b-6 which are applied in the following case.

---

[7] *Pross* v. *Baird Patrick & Co.*, 585 F.Supp. 1456 (S.D.N.Y. 1984).

IN THE MATTER OF PAGEL, INC.

Federal Securities Law Reports (CCH), ¶83,909 (Securities and Exchange Commission, 1985), *aff'd* ____ F.2d ____ (8th Cir. 1986).

In 1979, Pagel, Inc. (registrant), a registered broker-dealer, was principal underwriter in a firm underwriting agreement with FilmTec Corporation (FTC). FTC's initial public offering consisted of 320,000 shares offered at $3.25 per share under a Regulation A exemption. Registrant kept most of the share allotment for itself. The offering began on March 26, and was ostensibly completed on March 29. Aftermarket trading began on March 30.

On March 30, registrant arbitrarily raised FTC's stock price to 4 ³/₈ and 4 ⁵/₈ bid, increases of 35% and 42%, respectively, over the offering price. There was no demand to justify that increase. Indeed, over the next eight days registrant continued to raise the price—ultimately to 10 ¹/₂—though supply exceeded demand during the entire period. Registrant and its customers held over 90% of the FTC stock by the end of the eight-day period, and registrant purchased substantially more shares than it sold. Other dealers' retail customers sold 20,675 shares of FTC stock while purchasing only 6,850.

The SEC brought this action to revoke the license of registrant and its president, alleging that they had manipulated the price of FTC stock in violation of Rules 10b-5 and 10b-6. The administrative law judge found for the SEC. Pagel, Inc., and its president appealed.

THE COMMISSION:

[Regarding Rule 10b-5], [i]t seems clear that, when an underwriter such as registrant sells 90% of an offering to its own customers and the remainder is fragmented among a number of other dealers, trading in the aftermarket is necessarily contingent on the underwriter's customers furnishing the supply. Because the identity of those customers is known only to the underwriter, tapping that supply for resale lies uniquely within the underwriter's control. The fact that such an underwriter is in a position to dominate and control the trading market does not necessarily produce a manipulation, but it does enable the underwriter to control wholesale pricing to such an extent as to preclude an independent, competitive market from arising, notwithstanding the presence of other dealers who may be entering quotations. The price leadership resulting from its almost exclusive control of the source of supply empowers the underwriter to set prices arbitrarily. If that power is abused, the result is a manipulation.

In essence, a manipulation is intentional interference with the free forces of supply and demand. Proof of a manipulation almost always depends on inferences drawn from a mass of factual detail. Findings must be gleaned from patterns of behavior, from apparent irregularities, and from trading data. When all these are considered together, they can emerge as ingredients in a manipulative scheme designed to tamper with free market forces.

We think it clear that respondents abused their control of the market for FTC during the first eight days of trading. During that period, customer sales exceeded customer purchases by some 44,000 shares. But respondents did not allow the excess sales to depress FTC's market price, the result that would normally be expected in a free market. On the contrary, during the short span of eight trading days, the price of FTC rose sharply from the offering price of 3¼ to 10½. Respondents simply absorbed the excess stock into inventory so that, at the end of the period, the firm's inventory corresponded almost exactly to the excess of customer sales over purchases, while all other dealers had a short position of some 4,750 shares. At that point, registrant and its customers held 93.7% of the 352,000-share public offering. The inference is compelling that respondents used registrant's control position to cause a sharp and totally unwarranted rise in the price of FTC stock, and thereby engaged in unlawful conduct. As we have previously pointed out:

> [I]nvestors and prospective investors . . . are . . . entitled to assume that the prices they pay and receive are determined by the unimpeded interaction of real supply and real demand so that those prices are the collective marketplace judgments that they purport to be. Manipulations frustrate these expectations. They substitute fiction for fact. . . . The vice is that the market has been distorted and made into a ''stage-managed performance.''

[Regarding Rule 10b-6] As pertinent here, Rule 10b-6 under the Exchange Act provides that it is a manipulative or deceptive device for an underwriter participating in a distribution of securities to bid for or purchase such securities until it has completed its participation in the distribution. Pagel and Markus [officers of respondent], who were affiliates of the underwriter and therefore subject to the rule's prohibitions, purchased a total of 15,250 shares in the FTC offering through nominee accounts. Since respondents did not buy their stock for investment, their purchases had the effect of continuing the FTC distribution until the stock they had purchased was resold to the investing public. And, before that resale took place, Markus purchased additional FTC stock in the aftermarket, and registrant, whose trading activities were directed by Pagel and Markus, bid for and purchased shares of FTC stock.

We accordingly conclude that respondents willfully violated Section 10(b) of the Exchange Act and Rule 10b-6 thereunder.

Registration revoked.

Churning

The broker who handles OTC stock receives a relatively small commission—generally 2–4%, and under NASD guidelines rarely exceeding 5%. Thus, it requires a substantial volume of transactions to generate healthy commissions. This situation creates a conflict of interest, because it may be in the broker's interest to generate a series of transactions that are not in the customer's best interest. Such a practice is called *churning* the account.

Churning has been said to denote ''a course of excessive trading through which a broker advances his own interests (e.g., commissions based on volume) over those of his customer.'' [8]

Rules

Churning violates a host of statutes, rules, and common law principles. Courts have held that churning violates §10(b) and Rule 10b-5 as well as §15(c)(1) and Rule

---

[8] *Costello* v. *Oppenheimer & Co., Inc.*, 711 F.2d 1361 (7th Cir. 1983).

15c1-7(a) of the 1934 Act. Some courts have held churning within the scope of a RICO claim, and if the churning is of a commodities account, §46(A) of the Commodities Exchange Act is violated. Churning also clearly violates the shingle rule, §15 of the NASD's Rules of Fair Practice, and common law restrictions on fraud and breach of fiduciary duty.

"Controlling persons," such as a brokerage firm or its supervisors, might also be liable under §20(a) of the 1934 Act for churning done by subordinates.

Injured investors will have, at the very least, a private cause of action under §10(b) and under common law fraud and fiduciary rules. The SEC has pursued churners through injunctive, disciplinary, and even criminal channels.

Elements

The two main elements of churning that must be proved by a plaintiff are (1) that the broker controlled the account and (2) that excessive trading occurred. Some courts add a third element in §10(b) actions—that of intent. Most agree that reckless handling of an account is sufficient to satisfy this requirement; plaintiff need not always show a planned scheme to defraud. A few courts add a fourth element—that plaintiff lacked investor sophistication. The prototypical plaintiff in a churning case is a "WOG" (widow, orphan, or grandmother), not a seasoned investor with every opportunity to monitor his or her account to see the volume of transactions.

Control

As noted, the first critical element of a churning case is that the defendant broker controlled plaintiff's account. This element is automatically met if the account is a discretionary one that the broker can trade in without consulting the customer.

Even in a nondiscretionary account, control may be inferred from such facts as (1) the customer was inexperienced, (2) the customer had difficulty understanding the broker's advice and explanations, (3) there was a close personal relationship between the customer and broker, or (4) any other fact making it likely that the customer would blindly follow the broker's recommendations. In one case, control by the broker was found where the customer was continually intoxicated and unable to consent or object effectively to the broker's recommendations.[9] On the other hand, control *by the customers* was found in a case where the investors were a former U.S. ambassador and his wife, both with college educations, experience in investing, and a habit of closely following the market and frequently instructing the broker as to their desires.[10]

---

[9] *Knierieman* v. *Bache Halsey Stuart Shield, Inc., New York Law Journal*, March 1, 1982, p. 12 (Sup. Ct. N.Y. Co. 1982).

[10] *Smith* v. *Sade & Co.* [1982 Transfer Binder], *Federal Securities Law Report* (CCH), ¶98,846 (D. D.C. 1982).

Excessive Trading

The second key element of churning, that of excessive trading, is determined not by any precise mathematical formula but by "an overall, impressionistic view" of the dealings.[11] Still, there are some important specific factors to look for.

Turnover rate (total cost of purchases over a period divided by the account's average monthly investment) is a good guide to excessive trading. The average turnover rate in a common stock account, according to one study, is 21.3% per year.[12] As a rule of thumb, many courts say that when an account's turnover ratio exceeds six times per year, excessive trading is indicated.

In one case, a turnover of 70.77 times in nine and one-half months was held, obviously, to indicate excessive trading.[13] In another, an annual turnover rate of 1.87 was held not to be excessive.[14] In yet another a turnover of 1.13 in only 29 days was excessive.[15]

Another important factor is the ratio of commissions generated to the size of the account. Excessive trading was found in a case where a broker generated $189,000 in commissions on an initial account of $583,000,[16] but not where commissions were $9,000 on a $900,000 account.[17]

Of course mathematic ratios in isolation cannot alone decide the issue. Of critical importance is the investor's investment objective. If it was to speculate in the hopes of high profits, more trading will be permissible than if the main objective was merely to conserve the principal sum.

Other factors that courts have considered in determining whether excessive trading occurred include (1) existence of "in and out" trading (selling a particular security, then repurchasing it soon thereafter, maybe repeating the process several times); (2) total financial resources of the customer; (3) profits or losses in the account; (4) length of time securities were held; (5) quality of the securities; (6) frequency of departure from investment objectives; and (7) "cross trading" between accounts of different customers of the same broker.[18]

The following case illustrates some of the questions arising in a churning claim. It is particularly helpful in illustrating the potential liability of the churning broker's superiors and the firm itself.

---

[11] Note, "Churning by Securities Dealers," *Harvard Law Review*, Vol. 80 (1967), p. 869.

[12] Securities and Exchange Commission, *Institutional Investor Study Report*, H.R. Doc. No. 64, 92d Cong., 1st sess., pt.2, at 170 (1971).

[13] *Shearson, Hamill & Co., Securities Exchange Act Release*, no. 7743, p. 30.

[14] *Grove v. Shearson Loeb Rhoades, Inc.* [1983 Binder], *Federal Securities Law Reports*. (CCH) ¶99,229 (S.D. Fla. 1983).

[15] *Carras v. Burns*, 516 F.2d 251 (4th Cir. 1975).

[16] *Hecht v. Harris, Upham Co.*, 430 F.2d 1202 (9th Cir. 1970).

[17] *Carroll v. Bear, Stearns Co.*, 416 F.Supp. 998 (S.D. N.Y. 1976).

[18] *See* D. McCabe, "Churning," in *Broker-Dealers: New Legal, Business, and Compliance Developments* (New York: Practising Law Institute, 1983), p. 371.

KRAVITZ v. PRESSMAN, FROHLICH & FROST, INC.

447 F.Supp. 203 (D. Mass 1978)

Kravitz was 24 years old and had a B.S. degree in elementary education when she moved to Boston in June 1971. Her sole assets were $18,000 and a car. She had no investment experience. She soon met Contrado through a mutual friend. They became close friends and she gave Contrado, a broker at Bache, Halsey, Stuart, Inc., $300 to open a securities brokerage account for her. She told him she wanted to do something safe so that her money would last a long time. Contrado guaranteed that he would reimburse her if she suffered any losses. By November 30, 1972, Kravitz had deposited almost all her assets, $18,000, into the account. She received confirmation slips reflecting monthly trading activity, but she did not understand them and eventually ceased opening such mail.

During 1972, Contrado, acting solely on his own discretion, actively traded Kravitz's account. The number of transactions per month in 1972 was, respectively, 34, 47, 41, 30, 16, 3, 2, 31, 21, 0, 0, 0. In early May 1972 Kravitz received a letter from a Bache branch manager informing her that her account had generated commissions of $8,100, although there had been no substantial profit or loss to her. When she asked Contrado about the matter, he became angry and convinced her to trust his judgment. Trading did fall off for a while thereafter.

In December 1972, Contrado left Bache and joined defendant Pressman, Frohlich & Frost, Inc., taking plaintiff Kravitz's account with him. He filled out her new account form himself. As of February 1973, its net equity was $21,500. Again in 1973 there was frequent trading, monthly transactions totaling 24, 5, 21, 3, 20, 2, 6, 9, 69, 85, 42, and 6. Kravitz recognized

the great number of transactions, but when she again questioned Contrado he again became angry and again convinced her to trust him.

Pressman relied on Contrado for all its information about plaintiff's financial situation and her investment objectives. Neither Bond, Pressman's "titular head of compliance," nor any other Pressman supervisor noticed anything wrong with plaintiff's account for a long time. In the spring of 1973, Bond alerted a regional manager as to excessive trading by Contrado, but not until November of 1973 did he realize the Kravitz account was in bad shape. Contrado was fired in December, and plaintiff was told her account was worth only $500. Plaintiff had lost her entire investment except for the $500 and $1,800 she had received while the account was open.

Plaintiff sued Pressman and Contrado, alleging that her account was churned in violation of §17(a) of the 1933 Act, §§10(b) and 15(c) (1) of the 1934 Act, and of the NASD's Rules of Fair Practice. Pressman was alleged to be responsible for Contrado's actions under §20 of the 1934 Act as well as under common law notions of respondeat superior.

The following is the trial judge's opinion.

TAURO, DISTRICT JUDGE:

"Churning" occurs in a securities account when a dealer, acting in his own interests and against those of his customer, induces transactions in the customer's account that are excessive in size and frequency in light of the character of the account. See Note, *"Churning by Securities Dealers," Harvard Law Review*, Vol. 80 (1967), p. 869. A claim of churning has been held to state a cause of action under Section 10(b) and Rule 10b-5—*Landry* v. *Hemphill, Noyes & Co.*, 473 F.2d 365 (1st Cir.), *cert. denied*, 414 U.S. 1002 (1973); *Fey* v. *Walston & Co., Inc.*, 493 F.2d 1036 (7th Cir. 1974); and *Hecht* v. *Harris, Upham & Co.*, 430 F.2d 1202 (9th Cir. 1970).

Proof of churning requires the demonstration of two elements: (1) that the broker-dealer exercised control over the account and (2) that the broker engaged in excessive trading, considering the objectives and nature of the account—*Landry* v. *Hemphill, Noyes & Co.*, supra.

In determining the existence of control, various factors may be considered, such as whether all transactions are made at the dealer's discretion, the business and investment experience of the customer, and the relationship between the dealer and the customer.

Here, the transactions in plaintiff's account were made at Contrado's sole discretion. He not only made all investment decisions, but also refused to discuss with plaintiff her concerns about the trading in the account and demonstrated anger when plaintiff sought information about it.

Plaintiff had no prior experience in or knowledge of the securities market. She did not understand the monthly statements that she received and did not know the meaning of the basic terms associated with trading in the securities market.

In addition, the nature of the relationship between plaintiff and Contrado underscores his dominant position and her reliance on him. She met Contrado soon after she came to Boston from Ohio, and they became close friends, dating on a regular basis for a period of several months. She came to rely on him for advice on a wide variety of matters to the point of entrusting him with her blank, signed checks. She believed, on the basis of Contrado's reputation and her contacts with him, that he was a reliable broker, and someone she could trust.

Given their relationship, the fact that plaintiff received monthly statements and confirmation slips but never complained to others at Pressman about the volume of trading in her account does not undercut a finding that he exercised control over her account, or suggest that she ratified his actions.

Even express consent to churning does not raise the defense of waiver or estoppel if the consent is induced by undue influence over the customer, or results from the customer's trust and confidence in the broker—*Fey* v. *Walston & Co., Inc.*, supra, 493 F.2d at 1050. Similarly, even a customer with knowledge of trading transactions may not be estopped from claiming ignorance with respect to churning, because of the added experience and knowledge necessary to ascertain a pattern of churning—*Hecht* v. *Harris, Upham & Co.*, supra, 430 F.2d at 1209.

On all the evidence, this court concludes that Contrado exercised control over plaintiff's account.

The second element of churning is the existence of a pattern of trading, excessive in light of the size and objectives of the customer's account. Plaintiff's investment objectives were conservative and oriented to preservation of capital, throughout the entire period in question. The court accepts the opinion of plaintiff's expert witness that the pattern of trading in plaintiff's account was excessive in light of her objectives. He pointed in particular to the pattern of selling stocks only a few days after they were bought, and before there had been any real change in price. Such in-and-out trading is particularly characteristic of churning, as are disproportionate turnover and large brokerage commissions relative to the size of the account—*Carras* v. *Burns*, 516 F.2d 251 (4th Cir. 1975).

Commissions in plaintiff's account during 1973 almost equaled plaintiff's equity as of March 1973. The total volume of sales in her account in 1973 was 30 times her equity at the beginning of the year.

For the reasons stated, the court is persuaded by the evidence that Contrado churned plaintiff's account.

Having so determined, it is necessary to consider whether Pressman is liable for his actions, either under the controlling person doctrine of §20 of the Securities and Exchange Act of 1934 or under the doctrine of respondeat superior. Section 20 states in relevant part:

> Every person who, directly or indirectly, controls any person liable under any provision of this chapter or of any rule or regulation thereunder shall also be liable jointly and severally with and to the same extent as such controlled person to any person to whom such controlled person is liable, unless the controlling person acted in good faith and did not directly or indirectly induce the act or acts constituting the violation or cause of action.

In the context of this section, brokerage firms control their brokers and registered representatives.

Defendant Pressman asserts, however, that it was acting in good faith.

Authority is split on what actions on the part of a brokerage firm are sufficient to constitute a good faith defense to a claim of liability under §20, although authority is uniform that the defendant has the burden of proving good faith—*Carr* v. *New York Stock Exchange*, 414 F.Supp. 1292 (N.D. Cal. 1976).

Some courts have held that liability can be found under §20 only where there is culpable participation in the fraud by the brokerage house. Such culpability can be established by nonfeasance only if the failure to act was intended to further the fraud or prevent its discovery—*Rochez Brothers* v. *Rhoades*, 527 F.2d 880 (3d Cir. 1975).

There seems to be agreement, however, that a stricter standard is appropriate where the firm is being held accountable for the actions of its salesmen, rather than for the actions of its own officers or directors. Consequently, in cases concerning violations of 10b-5 by salesmen, in order to satisfy the good faith requirement of §20,

> it must be shown that the controlling person maintained and enforced a reasonable and proper system of supervision and internal control over controlled persons so as to prevent, as far as possible, violations of §10(b) and Rule 10b-5. *Zweig* v. *Hearst Corp.*, 521 F.2d 1129, 1134–35 (9th Cir. 1975)

The reason for the higher standard for supervision of the registered representative is the greater potential for abuse of that position. The representative and the broker-dealer earn their money, directly and indirectly, by sales activity. Customers often rely on their broker-representative for investment advice. "The opportunity and temptation to take advantage of the client is ever present"—*Zweig* v. *Hearst Corporation*, supra, 521 F.2d at 1135. This rule does not impose absolute liability on the broker-dealer, or make him an insurer for the acts of his salesmen, but it does impose a stringent duty of care—*SEC* v. *Lum's*, 365 F.Supp. 1046 (S.D. N.Y. 1973).

The controlling inquiry is whether or not sufficient precautionary measures were taken to prevent the type of loss that in fact occurred. Pressman argues that it had a sufficient set of supervisory procedures, as demonstrated by its compliance manuals, the visits of compliance officers to branch offices, and the periodic meetings between branch managers and salesmen. It argues further that the sales in plaintiff's account until September 1973 were reasonable, in light of her new account form that stated her investment objectives to be "short term trading profits."

This court is not persuaded by Pressman's protestations, and concludes that its supervisory role was inadequate under the circumstances of this case. Plaintiff's "new account form" was not signed by her. The information on it was neither verified by supervisory personnel nor discussed with her.

The trading in plaintiff's account should have attracted the attention of management or compliance personnel, given the number of trades, the low quality of the stocks, the pattern of in-and-out trading and the failure to buy dividend producing stocks.

Furthermore, in April 1973, the branch manager was alerted by a memo from supervisor Bond suggesting that he scrutinize Contrado's accounts for excessive trading, but there is no evidence of any follow-up, either by the branch manager or Bond. Had there been some review and follow-up even at that date, much of plaintiff's loss might have been averted.

Moreover, there is no evidence that the supervisory or compliance staff took any further notice of plaintiff's account until the fall. When Pressman did take action against Contrado, it was to discipline him for passing a bad check, not to punish his trading activity. His firing, therefore, is not persuasive evidence of active supervisory procedures.

The court concludes, therefore, that the defense of good faith is not available to Pressman, because of its failure to supervise Contrado's activities adequately. Pressman is liable as a controlling person under §20(a) for the churning by Contrado of plaintiff's account.

Even if Pressman had a valid good faith defense to liability under §20(a), it would, nonetheless, be liable under the common law doctrine of *respondeat superior*. Although there is a division of authority on this question, there appears to be a strong trend toward holding broker-dealers liable for the actions of their broker-representatives concurrently under §20 and under common law doctrines. See *SEC* v. *Geon Industries, Inc.*, 531 F.2d 39 (2d Cir. 1976).

Given the desirability and importance to the economy of protecting the investing public from predatory practices, it makes sense to consider §20 and the common law doctrine of *respondeat superior* as complementary rather than exclusive remedies.

Pressman, therefore, is liable for the actions of Contrado under the doctrine of *respondeat superior*, independent of its liability under §20.

[*The court entered a verdict for plaintiff in the sum of $21,308.00 plus interest.*]

Defenses

The primary churning defenses—waiver, ratification, estoppel, and laches—are all premised on a plaintiff's knowledge of high-volume transactions and failure to act to remedy the situation. As the *Kravitz* case demonstrates, if the plaintiff can establish the element of control, these defenses will rarely succeed.

As *Kravitz* also illustrates, a firm charged with being a "controlling person" under §20 of the 1934 Act also has a defense of good faith. However, that defense is not available if the firm's liability is premised on the common law doctrine of *respondeat superior*, or on a failure to establish, maintain, or diligently enforce a proper system of supervision and internal control over its employees.[19]

---

[19] *Del Porte* v. *Shearson, Hammill & Co., Inc.*, 548 F.2d 1149 (3d Cir. 1979). These principles of secondary liability apply in most of the areas discussed in this chapter, not just churning.

It is no defense that the plaintiff's account showed a profit. Churning liability has been found even where plaintiff's account avoided a loss, though this is rare.[20]

Damages

All courts agree that a successful plaintiff should receive as damages all the commissions paid on the account, plus interest. No deduction is allowed for commissions normal trading would have earned.

However, this quasi-contractual measure of damages by itself is frequently insufficient because the reckless trading that generated the commissions also depleted the plaintiff's account and deprived the plaintiff of the profits normal trading would have brought. Most courts refuse plaintiffs redress for these damages, however, on grounds that it would be impossible to determine the true losses with any certainty.

A few courts have attempted to compensate plaintiff for the loss in portfolio value. Some have simply focused on the out-of-pocket measure of damages, awarding plaintiff a sum to compensate for the decline of value in the account.

Because the out-of-pocket measure cannot compensate plaintiff for the loss of bargain—the profit normal trading would have generated—a few courts have devised elaborate tests to calculate this sum. *Rolf* v. *Blyth, Eastman Dillon & Co.*,[21] for example, suggested use of the average percentage performance in value of the Dow Jones Industrials or the Standard & Poor's Index to determine how plaintiff's portfolio might have performed given proper trading.

While punitive damages are not available under a federal law claim, they can be obtained pursuant to state common law fraud and breach of fiduciary duty claims.

MAKING RECOMMENDATIONS WITHOUT ADEQUATE BASIS

Boiler Room Operations

The SEC has long been concerned with *boiler room operations*, which typically involve "cold" calling of names compiled from "sucker" lists. The calls aggressively recommend large blocks of speculative securities using predictions of dramatic earnings and market price increases. Frequently the calls are long distance and push the stock of a single company.

A boiler room operation is described in the following SEC findings and opinion in a proceeding to determine whether to deny registration to a broker.

---

[20] *Zaretsky* v. *E. F. Hutton & Co., Inc.*, 509 F.Supp. 68 (S.D.N.Y. 1981).
[21] 637 F.2d 77 (2d Cir. 1980).

IN THE MATTER OF HAROLD GRILL

41 S.E.C. 321 (1963)

THE COMMISSION:

The record shows that between February and April 1959, applicant, while employed by Hannibal Associates, Inc. (Hannibal), then a registered broker-dealer, participated in an extensive long-distance telephone campaign to sell the stock of Alaska Dakota Development Company (Addco) at $3.50 or $4.00 per share. Six persons who purchased Addco stock from applicant during this period testified as to various representations made to them over the telephone.

According to the six purchasers, they were told that the stock of Addco, which company the record indicates was organized to acquire and develop mining and oil leases, was "quite safe," would be "one of the best investments going," would increase in price rapidly as soon as information about the company's recent purchases were made public, would go up to $7 or $8 per share within 6 months to a year, would double, triple, or increase tenfold, and would be listed on an exchange "very shortly"; that if the customer did not buy the stock immediately he could not get it at $4 per share because "it was already $4.25"; and that the company had excellent potential and was "sure" to make money.

These representations were false and misleading. No factual basis for them was shown, and applicant, who denies making the representations, admitted that he knew of none. He stated that Addco neither earned money nor had any producing oil wells, and that he considered the stock to be highly speculative. He testified that

he informed prospects of the speculative nature of the stock and that in reply to their questions would state that Addco had no balance sheet and was not a producing company. However, several of the purchasers testified that they were not informed of the speculative nature of the stock, and there is no suggestion that the purchaser-witnesses were cautioned as to the risks involved in purchasing the stock in the absence of adequate information.

As previously indicated, the fraudulent representations attributed to applicant by the customer witnesses had no factual basis. Applicant does not claim that the brochure supported those representations, and in fact the brochure did not provide such support. The brochure spoke glowingly of Addco's past achievements without specifying what these achievements were and touted the possibility of profits from the ownership of assertedly valuable gold deposits and oil leases near or adjacent to those of well-known oil operators. However, it did not furnish any basis in support of Addco's estimated ore reserves, it contained no financial information, and it lacked other disclosures necessary for an informed evaluation of the securities.

The record shows, and applicant has acknowledged, that Hannibal was conducting a boiler-room sales campaign with respect to Addco stock. Applicant was an active participant in this fraudulent, high-pressure operation for an extended period of time, selling only this admittedly promotional and speculative security over the long-distance telephone to persons whose financial condition he did not know or apparently consider relevant. The particularly high degree of inquiry required of a security salesman whose employer is engaged in such an operation was not satisfied by any reliance by applicant on the obviously inadequate information furnished by his employer. Nevertheless, he saw fit to make extravagant representations and predictions with respect to Addco's future prospects without any word of caution as to the risk involved in purchasing the securities in the absence of adequate information. Such fraudulent sales techniques rendered false his implied representation that he would deal fairly with his customers. Accordingly, we find, as did the hearing examiner, that applicant made false and misleading statements in the sale of Addco stock in willful violation of Section 17(a) of the Securities Act and Section 10(b) of the Exchange Act and Rule 10b-5 thereunder.

As we have found, applicant engaged in high-pressure boiler room activities in which highly colored and exaggerated representations and predictions were made of rapid and substantial market price rises, which were calculated not to inform but to mislead. We do not believe that the investing public should be exposed to further risk of such fraudulent conduct by one who has demonstrated his gross indifference to the basic duty of fair dealing required of those engaged in selling securities to the public.

Accordingly, we conclude that it is necessary and appropriate in the public interest to deny registration to applicant.

Most boiler room cases have involved SEC or NASD proceedings, though a private cause of action under §10(b) of the 1934 Act [22] is available to injured investors. The SEC has generally refrained from taking the position that boiler room operations are per se illegal, but that may well be the practical effect. The SEC has tried to expand the duty of salesmen to investigate by disciplining them when they merely rely on brochures they are handed.

The SEC is so concerned that representations made by securities salesmen have an adequate basis, it has punished persons for making representations without an adequate basis even when those representations ultimately turned out to be accurate and the investors profited. [23]

Developments in the duty to investigate and have an adequate basis for representations, discussed in the next section, have made it virtually impossible to legally conduct a boiler room operation.

Suitability and Know Your Customer Rules

The shingle theory and antifraud rules have been extended beyond the boiler room. *All brokers have a duty to avoid making representations not based on adequate information.* Beyond that, a broker's recommendations should be appropriate to the particular customer.

---

[22] And perhaps §§12(2) and 17(a) of the 1933 Act.

[23] See *Berko* v. *SEC*, 197 F.2d 116 (2d Cir. 1961), *on appeal from remand*, 316 F.2d 137 (2d Cir. 1963).

One key rule is the NASD's *suitability* provision. Article III, §2 of the NASD Rules of Fair Practice, provides:

> In recommending to a customer the purchase, sale or exchange of any security, a member shall have reasonable grounds for believing that the recommendation is suitable for such customer upon the basis of the facts, if any, disclosed by such customer as to his other security holdings and as to his financial situation and needs.

It seems that even when a broker is not asked for a recommendation by a customer—but only instructed to make a purchase—the broker should have a duty to speak up if it is obvious that the subject stock is not suitable for the customer.[24]

An important question is how great a duty to inquire as to the particular customer's situation should be placed on the broker. The suitability rule contains no explicit duty to investigate, but the SEC has imposed one by reading out the rule's "if any" language. The following case illustrates this point. The facts are summarized in the opinion.

ERDOS v. SEC

742 F.2d 507 (9th Cir. 1984)

BOOCHEVER, JUDGE:

Eugene Erdos petitions for review of a Securities and Exchange Commission (S.E.C.) order affirming disciplinary sanctions imposed on him by the National Association of Securities Dealers (NASD) for violating the Association's Rules of Fair Practice. We affirm.

The S.E.C.'s factual findings are conclusive if supported by substantial evidence. The evidence shows that in 1976 Mrs. Cole, a seventy-five year old retired widow with limited assets and a portfolio valued at approximately $115,000, opened an account with Erdos, a securities dealer. In 1977, Erdos engaged in more than 130 transactions for Mrs. Cole's account, totalling approximately $1.2 million. Those

transactions earned him about $25,000 in commissions. In the meantime Mrs. Cole's portfolio had decreased in value to $90,000, and yielded considerably less income than in prior years. The S.E.C. found that Erdos violated the NASD rules by making unsuitable recommendations for Mrs. Cole and engaging in excessive trading in her account. In light of Mrs. Cole's financial situation, we conclude that the S.E.C.'s findings were supported by substantial evidence.

The NASD rule against making unsuitable recommendations is governed by whether the dealer "fulfilled the obligation he assumed when he undertook to counsel the [customer], of making only such recommendations as would be consistent with the customer's financial situation and needs"—*Phillips & Co.*, 37 S.E.C. 66,

---

[24] R. Mundheim, "Professional Responsibilities of Broker-Dealers: The Suitability Doctrine," *Duke Law Journal* (1965), p. 445.

70 (1956). The record reveals that Erdos executed trades for Mrs. Cole that were highly risky in light of her particular financial situation.

Erdos maintains that he did not violate the NASD's suitability rule because Mrs. Cole did not disclose her age or her total financial situation to him. The argument lacks merit. The NASD's suitability rule is not limited to situations where comprehensive financial information about the customer is known to the dealer— *Gerald M. Greenberg*, 40 S.E.C. 133, 137–38 (1960). Erdos had a duty to act with caution and to make recommendations based on the concrete information that he did have rather than on his speculations about her situation. The record substantially supports the S.E.C.'s findings of unsuitable recommendations.

Similarly, the record supports the S.E.C.'s findings that Erdos also violated the NASD's rule against excessive trading.

Finally, Erdos claims the NASD regulatory rules are unconstitutional because: (1) regulating a customer's trading based on her needs infringes on the customer's constitutional right to exercise her free will; and (2) requiring a customer to disclose her financial situation to her securities dealer violates her constitutional right to privacy. Erdos lacks standing for the constitutional arguments he makes. See *Warth v. Seldin*, 422 U.S. 490 (1975); and *McMichael v. County of Napa*, 709 F.2d 1268, 1270 (9th Cir. 1983) (standing requires that a plaintiff assert his own rights, not those of a third party).

Accordingly, the S.E.C.'s order is affirmed.

The NASD's policy statement accompanying the suitability rule also requires a broker to investigate a customer's background before suggesting speculative, low-priced securities.[25]

The New York Stock Exchange also imposes on its member brokers a duty to investigate the customer's background. The NYSE's "Know Your Customer" rule, sometimes called the Eleventh Commandment of Wall Street, requires every member broker to use "due diligence" to learn "essential facts" relevant to every customer and order.[26] The American Stock Exchange has a similar rule.[27]

Furthermore, the SEC's Rule 15c2–5 imposes an affirmative duty on brokers to investigate the customer's needs and determine suitability before attempting to induce any purchase in connection with which the broker is to extend credit or arrange any loan.

Enforcement

The courts are split as to whether an injured investor can maintain a private cause of action against a broker who violated suitability or know your customer rules.[28] In recent years most courts, but not all, have held that no private right to sue should

---

[25] *NASD Manual* (CCH), ¶2152.

[26] New York Stock Exchange Rule 405.

[27] American Stock Exchange Rule 411.

[28] See *Zemaitis* v. *Merrill Lynch, Pierce, Fenner & Smith*, 583 F.Supp. 1552 (W.D.N.Y. 1984).

arise from violations of the self-regulating rules of NASD and the exchanges, because to recognize such suits would discourage these bodies from promulgating needed rules.[29] However, this point has become largely moot. The courts have completely blurred the line between a suitability violation and fraud and often allow recovery for suitability breaches under Rule 10b-5 and common law fraud theories.[30]

Quotations

Rule 15c2–11 represents another aspect of the SEC's attempt to ensure that broker-dealers' recommendations have an adequate basis following adequate investigation. The rule concerns fringe companies. It prohibits broker-dealers from quoting OTC the securities of companies that have not been continuously quoted unless the company has registered under the 1933 or 1934 acts and has kept current in its periodic reporting *or* basic financial data including names of directors, most recent balance sheet and profit and loss and retained earnings statements, and similar information for the two preceding fiscal years is available.

As this chapter is written in 1986, the SEC is studying whether to repeal Rule 15c2–11 because its costs might outweigh its benefits.

Negligence

As noted earlier, state common law fraud and breach of fiduciary duty claims often appear in the complaints alleging churning violations. The same may be said for suitability complaints. In addition to having a responsibility to refrain from acting fraudulently, as an agent a broker has a duty to act with reasonable care. If the broker negligently dispenses advice and information, liability may result, as the following case demonstrates.

ZURAD v. LEHMAN BROTHERS KUHN LOEB, INC.

757 F.2d 129 (7th Cir. 1985)

Plaintiff Zurad was a 54-year-old postal worker with a salary of $18,000 a year and some investment experience and understanding *of the complexities of stock market transactions. In January 1979, Zurad opened a cash account with defendant Lehman Brothers. She trans-*

---

[29] *Utah State University* v. *Bear, Stearns & Co.*, 549 F.2d 164 (10th Cir. 1977), *cert. denied*, 434 U.S. 890. A related question is whether an injured investor should be able to sue the self-regulating organization itself for failure to enforce its own rules. Most courts have said "no," unless the organization had actual knowledge of the violation. See *Hirsch* v. *du Pont*, 553 F.2d 750 (2d Cir. 1977); and *Parsons* v. *Hornblower & Weeks-Hemphill, Noyes*, 447 F.Supp. 482 (M.D.N.C. 1977), *aff'd*, 571 F.2d 203 (4th Cir. 1978).

[30] For example, *Clark* v. *John Lamula Investors, Inc.*, 583 F.2d 594 (2d Cir. 1978).

ferred into the account $26,803 in cash, 2,000 shares of Abbott Labs, and 45 shares both of Walt Disney Production and IBM. She told defendant's registered broker-dealer Curry that she had about $100,000 to invest and that her investment objectives included income production, financial growth, and recoupment of previous losses. Soon, on her own initiative, plaintiff also opened a margin account with defendant, and purchased 3,000 more shares of Abbott Labs.

In May and June of 1979 several articles appeared in newspapers in Chicago and New York, including The Wall Street Journal, *about a potential take-over of Walter E. Heller International Corporation (Heller). On June 29 there were reports of a $42.50 per share offer in the works from Midland Bank of London. Zurad had no knowledge of these stories.*

Curry called Zurad soon after this story, told her of the potential merger and that it was going through a federal approval process. Curry testified that he told Zurad she should sell her 2,000 shares of Abbott Labs and buy 2,000 shares of Heller, and that later she instructed him to raise both figures to 5,000. Zurad testified that Curry's recommendation was always 5,000, but the trial judge credited Curry's version.

Curry never told Zurad that there had been rumors in newspapers of the merger, that following the rumors Heller's market price had risen from $17 to $30 per share, that the flurry of trading had caused the NYSE to suspend trading, or that Heller was a dangerous investment.

On July 13 and 17, Curry bought 5,000 shares of Heller for Zurad's account at a price of $30 ⅞ per share for a total of $155,746.59, including commissions.

On October 22, when Heller stock was selling at $28 ¼, the merger was called off. When the market opened the next day, Heller stock had dropped to $18 ¼. On March 25 and April 4, 1980, Curry sold Zurad's Heller stock at

her instruction for $16 ⅛ to $17. Zurad's total loss was $75,891.49.

Zurad sued Lehman Brothers for violations of Rule 10b-5, NYSE "Know Your Customer" and NASD "suitability" rules, common law fraud, and negligent misrepresentation. The district judge dismissed the "Know Your Customer" and "suitability" claims on the ground that no implied right of action exists under NYSE or NASD rules. After a two-day bench trial, he entered judgment for defendant. Plaintiff appealed.

FAIRCHILD, SENIOR CIRCUIT JUDGE:

As already related, it is undisputed that Curry failed to tell Zurad of the recent Heller price per share of $17 just before the merger publicity, its rapid rise to $30, apparently because of the publicity, and that trading had been suspended while the rise was occurring.

These omissions were the basis of a Rule 10b-5 claim and a pendent state law negligent misrepresentation claim.

The district court found with respect to these omissions that Zurad had not established either intent or reckless conduct. We are not persuaded that the finding was clearly erroneous, and it disposed of the 10b-5 claim—*Ernst & Ernst v. Hochfelder*, 425 U.S. 185, 193 (1976).

We conclude, however, that plaintiff sustained her state law negligent misrepresentation claim.

Under Illinois law, to sustain a claim for negligent misrepresentation, the plaintiff must establish a duty owed by defendant to plaintiff, a breach of that duty, and injury proximately resulting from the breach.

Restatement (Second) of Torts defines negligent misrepresentation as follows:

Information Negligently Supplied for the Guidance of Others (1) One who, in the course of his business, profession or employment, or in any other transaction in which he has a pecuniary interest, supplies false information for the guidance of others in their business transactions, is subject to liability for pecuniary loss caused to them by their justifiable reliance upon the information, if he fails to exercise reasonable care or competence in obtaining or communicating the information. *Restatement (Second) of Torts* §552 (1965)

Therefore, to recover on a theory of negligent misrepresentation, Zurad had to demonstrate a breach of Curry's duty to exercise reasonable care or competence in obtaining or communicating information intended to guide her in her investment decisions.

The district court found that Zurad was not entitled to prevail on her claim of negligent misrepresentation because Curry—by advising Zurad against investing all her assets in Heller and indicating that the merger might not necessarily occur—exercised reasonable care in supplying information to Zurad. We are left, however, with the firm conclusion that the finding was clearly erroneous.

The district court did not discuss at this point the significance of the information Curry omitted concerning the recent market price, the quick rise due to merger speculation, and that trading had been twice suspended. We are satisfied that the failure to supply that highly significant information while advising Zurad to purchase the stock was a breach of Curry's duty to exercise reasonable care in obtaining and relaying information to guide Zurad in her investment decisions. The omission of this information, coupled with the information Curry did give Zurad, amounted to a misrepresentation of the material facts relating to the degree of speculation involved in the purchase of the Heller stock. Merely advising Zurad against investing all her funds in Heller, without more, did not fulfill his duty.

We know by hindsight that when the merger (at $42.50 according to reports) was abandoned, the price per share fell from approximately $30 to approximately $18. Of course no one could predict in July what would happen to the price if the merger plan were dropped, and it was Curry's opinion that the stock had been undervalued and was really worth the proposed merger price. But if defendants are to rely on plaintiff's awareness of the risk that the merger would not materialize, they cannot, it seems to us, escape responsibility for failing to inform Zurad of the market price of Heller just prior to rumors of the merger. Because that price might again be the market's judgment of worth in the absence of the rumored merger, that information would be most important in evaluating the risk. Even at 2,000 shares, Curry was advising plaintiff to invest almost 60% of her assets (there was a loan against the Abbott shares of about 30% of their value). Considering the difference in their positions and familiarity with the market, we cannot escape the conclusion that it was Curry's duty to give her this information. She was entitled to consider that fact in evaluating the risk undertaken, whether she decided only to follow his recommendation of 2,000 shares or to buy as much as she did. Although Curry was found not responsible for her decision to buy 5,000 shares, her decision to do so emphasized her need for full information. Curry's Office Manager admitted at trial that the purchase of 5,000 shares was not suitable for a person of Zurad's income and net worth.

Nothing in the facts suggests that Zurad should have known about or investigated any recent price inflation or suspension of trading of the Heller stock. In fact, Curry's assurances that the stock was a sound investment could have caused an investor to refrain from such inquiry. "In the absence of circumstances putting a reasonable person on inquiry, a person is justified in relying on a misrepresentation of a material fact without making further inquiry"—*Citizens Savings and Loan Association* v. *Fischer*, 214 N.E.2d at 616.

Accordingly, we reverse the judgment and remand for entry of judgment for Zurad on the negligent misrepresentation claim. The dam- *ages have been established at $75,891.49. We leave to the district court consideration of Zurad's claims to interest and attorney's fees.*

SCALPING

"Scalping," according to the Supreme Court in *SEC* v. *Capital Gains Research Bureau*,[31] is the practice by a broker-dealer "of purchasing shares of a security for his own account shortly before recommending that security for long-term investment and then immediately selling the shares at a profit upon the rise in the market price following the recommendation." Obviously scalping is a very agreeable way of making money for the scalper, and the more influence that the scalper's recommendations carry, the more money that can be made. However, the practice is obviously frowned upon because, among other things, it creates an inherent conflict of interest. After purchasing a particular security the scalper would have a strong motivation to recommend its purchase to customers regardless of developments in the market.

There have been two primary legal attacks on the practice of scalping, but both are in question as this chapter is written in 1986.

Investment Advisers Act of 1940

Investment advisers must register with the SEC under the Investment Advisers Act of 1940. In the *Capital Gains* case just mentioned, the Supreme Court was presented with respondent investment advisers who on six occasions had purchased shares of a particular security before recommending it in their investment newsletter that was mailed to 5,000 subscribers monthly. On each occasion the price of the security rose after publication and respondents sold at a profit.

The court held that scalping "operates as a fraud or deceit upon any client or prospective client" within the meaning of the Act, because respondents did not disclose their self-interest. Therefore, the Court allowed the SEC to seek an injunction to halt the practice.

The viability of the *Capital Gains* rationale is now in doubt, however, because of the Supreme Court's 1985 decision in *Lowe* v. *SEC*.[32] Lowe also published investment advisory newsletters. He was not scalping nor did the SEC have any particular objection to the accuracy of his recommendations. Nonetheless, the SEC sought permanently to enjoin Lowe from publishing such newsletters because he had not revealed in those publications that he had been guilty of misappropriating funds from an investment client, tampering with evidence to cover up fraud, and stealing from a bank.

A concurring opinion argued that the First Amendment principle prohibiting

---

[31] 375 U.S. 180 (1963).

[32] 105 S. Ct. 2557 (1985).

"prior restraints" applied. The opinion would have denied the SEC's request for a prepublication injunction, but would have allowed the Commission to punish Lowe after the fact for each publication.

However, the majority opinion was not so kind to the SEC. It held that publishers of advisory newsletters "do not offer individualized advice attuned to any specific portfolio or any client's particular needs" and therefore are within the Investment Adviser Act's express exemption from regulation for a "publisher of any bona fide newspaper, news magazine or business or financial publication of general and regular circulation." [33] This decision seems to eviscerate the usefulness of the *Capital Gains* holding. The newsletters that were part of the scalping scheme in that case also appear to be within the statutory exemption as now construed by the Supreme Court.

Rule 10b-5

The other main attack on scalping came in a case called *Zweig* v. *Hearst Corp.*,[34] which involved scalping by a newspaper columnist. In one instance, the columnist, Campbell, bought stock in a company known as ASI, recommended the stock to his readers, and then sold it at a nice profit after the recommendation caused the price to rise. This was particularly unfortunate for plaintiffs Zweig and Bruno who owned stock in a company merging with ASI. The merger agreement called for plaintiffs to receive a quantity of ASI stock based upon the market price as of a specified date. When that date came, plaintiffs received fewer ASI shares than they probably should have because Campbell's recommendation had temporarily inflated ASI's market price. Plaintiffs sued Campbell under §10(b) and Rule 10b-5.

The Ninth Circuit had no difficulty in holding that Campbell's failure to disclose his scalping plans was a "material" omission because clearly it could affect the quality of his advice. The stickier question was whether Campbell owed a duty to plaintiffs or any of his readers to disclose. The court found a duty to disclose to the readers based on a "flexible duty" standard encompassing such factors as the relationship of defendant to plaintiff, defendant's access to information as compared to plaintiff's, and defendant's benefit from the relationship. However, *Zweig's* flexible duty standard predated the Supreme Court's Rule 10b-5 insider trading decisions in *Chiarella* v. *U.S.*[35] and *Dirks* v. *SEC*,[36] both of which restricted the scope of the duty concept. *Chiarella* made it clear that failure to disclose a material fact, such as the existence of scalping, could only be fraud if a duty to speak existed. *Dirks* indicated that no such duty exists absent a fiduciary or some other close relationship or, perhaps, a "misappropriation." But *Lowe* holds that publishers of impersonal newsletters are not investment advisers, so it is arguable that neither they nor newspaper columnists owe a duty to their readers. Perhaps further developments will clarify the matter.

---

[33] See J. Olson, L. Spencer, and R. Heinke, "Court Creates Wide Exception to Advisers Act," *Legal Times of Washington*, July 1/8, 1985, p. 32.

[34] 594 F.2d 1261 (9th Cir. 1979).

[35] 445 U.S. 222 (1980).

[36] 463 U.S. 646 (1983).

OTHER REGULATIONS

Margin Rules

A margin transaction is the buying of securities on credit while the lender holds them as collateral. Obviously you can buy twice as many shares per dollar if you only have to put 50% down and may borrow the rest. As long as the price of securities goes up, this works fine. But if the price falls dramatically the lender is left holding collateral that is not worth enough to secure the debt. If the lender calls for more money and the investor does not have it, problems result.

Many persons believed that too much buying on margin by speculators helped to cause the Great Crash of 1929. Therefore, Congress decided the 1934 Act should regulate extension of credit for the purchase of securities to protect investors from buying on too thin a margin, to prevent excessive diversion of credit from productive sectors of the economy, and to minimize market fluctuation.

The key provision is §7 of the 1934 Act, which authorizes the Board of Governors of the Federal Reserve System to prescribe rules with respect to the amount of credit that may be initially extended and subsequently maintained on nonexempt securities. The Federal Reserve Board (FRB) has not issued rules governing subsequent maintenance of credit, but for initial purchases it has promulgated Regulation T for broker-dealer loans,[37] Regulation U for bank loans, and Regulation G for loans by others.

In general Regulation T prohibits sale of securities on credit, except for "margin securities." Margin securities are those traded on national exchanges or OTC securities on an approved list published by the FRB. When margin securities are sold on credit, the amount of the loan cannot exceed a percentage of the market value of the securities. That percentage can be adjusted by the FRB to reflect current conditions, but recently has usually been pegged at 50%.

Regulation T provides for a *margin account* and seven special accounts to record the transactions between broker-dealer and customer. If a transaction in a margin account creates a margin deficiency in the account, within seven business days that deficiency must be satisfied by a transfer from another account or a transfer of cash, margin securities, or exempt securities.

In a *cash account*, a creditor shall obtain full cash payment within seven business days. If the customer does not pay in time, the broker shall promptly cancel or otherwise liquidate the transaction. Although Regulation T concerns itself primarily with the initial purchase, the Exchanges and the NASD have their own rules governing *maintenance* of the margin account. These rules may require additional transfers by the investor when the value of the stock being used as collateral drops.

Overextensions of credit by broker-dealers have frequently led to SEC disciplinary actions. And §29(b) of the 1934 Act allows an investor to void a contract containing an illegal credit transaction.

---

[37] 12 C.F.R. §220 (1985).

Should an investor who is extended too much credit be able to sue the lending broker-dealer when large losses result? The courts have split on the issue but ever since Regulation X, which extends Regulation T to the *borrowers*, was promulgated in 1970, most courts have refused to recognize a private cause of action.[38]

Credit Disclosure

When broker-dealers do extend credit, Rule 10b-16 requires that certain disclosures be made to the customer regarding the conditions under which interest is to be charged, the rate of interest, the method of computing interest, other charges, conditions under which additional collateral will be required, and the like.

The SEC has its full arsenal of weapons including disciplinary sanctions to deal with Rule 10b-16 violations. Furthermore, most courts have recognized that the customer can sue under Rule 10b-16 for inadequate disclosure and under Rule 10b-5 if the omission is misleading.[39]

Financial Responsibility

Under authority granted in the 1934 Act, the SEC has issued a number of rules aimed at preserving the financial integrity of brokers and dealers.

Rule 15c3-1, the Net Capital Rule, requires broker-dealers to maintain a minimum of liquid assets in relation to their liabilities. The rule begins by stating that "[n]o broker or dealer shall permit his aggregate indebtedness to exceed 1500 percent of his net capital," but takes several additional pages to clarify and supplement the requirement.

Rule 15c3-3, the Customer Protection Rule, requires broker-dealers to establish special reserve bank accounts for the exclusive benefit of customers to eliminate conversion by the broker-dealer to its own use. It also requires the broker-dealer to obtain the customer's fully paid and excess margin securities and to maintain them in its own possession or in a control location.

Rules 17a-3 and 17a-4 contain detailed record keeping requirements regarding the background of important broker-dealer employees and all transactions with customers.[40]

Insider Trading

Brokers, when they have access to inside information, cannot trade or tip that information or they will violate Rule 10b-5. For example, in *In re Cady, Roberts & Co.*,[41] a broker, in his capacity as a director of a company, learned of the company's plan to cut its

---

[38] For example, *Utah State University* v. *Bear, Stearns & Co.*, 549 F.2d 164 (10th Cir. 1977), *cert. denied*, 434 U.S. 890.

[39] For example, *Angelastro* v. *Prudential-Bache Securities, Inc.*, 764 F.2d 939 (3d Cir. 1985).

[40] See M. Gregg and D. Malawsky, "SEC Enforcement," in *Broker-Dealers: New Legal, Business, and Compliance Developments* (New York: Practising Law Institute, 1983), p. 15.

[41] 40 S.E.C. 907 (1961).

dividends. Prior to public disclosure of the cut, the broker, in his capacity as a broker, sold his customers' shares in the company.

There is a natural conflict between the brokers' duty to those from whom they have received inside information and their duty to their customers. The SEC, in *Cady, Roberts* and several other cases, has held that the duty to observe insider trading rules must take precedence. The courts have agreed.

An interesting question frequently arises when a broker's tip of ''inside information'' turns out to be erroneous and causes the customer a loss. Should the customer be able to sue the broker for a false representation even though the customer thought he or she was participating in an insider trading violation?

The Supreme Court resolved the issue in *Bateman Eichler, Hill Richards, Inc. v. Berner*,[42] wherein plaintiff investors alleged that they bought TONM Corporation stock when the defendant broker's employee told them he had inside information about a gold strike and a joint mining venture in Surinam by TONM. Plaintiffs were allegedly told that TONM's market price would rise dramatically when the information became public. However, when the information turned out to be false, plaintiffs lost money. They sued the broker for false representations and material omissions in violation of §10(b) and Rule 10b-5.

The District Court dismissed the claim on grounds that plaintiffs themselves were violating Rule 10b-5 by trading on supposedly inside information. The doctrine *in pari delicto* provides that a court should not assist a plaintiff who is equally at fault in a wrong. The Circuit Court reversed, and the Supreme Court affirmed the reversal.

The Court denied the *in pari delicto* defense to stockbrokers in this circumstance, because (1) insiders and brokers who tip thereby commit a potentially broader range of violations than do the tippees, (2) such conduct is ''particularly egregious'' when done by a securities professional, and (3) the goals of the securities laws are better advanced if defrauded tippees are allowed to sue and thereby expose the wrongdoing.

STATE REGULATION

There is a wide variety of broker regulation at the state level. As noted, common law fraud, breach of fiduciary duty and negligence theories are frequently used in suits against brokers. Some states find a per se fiduciary relationship between broker and client; others apply a ''trust and confidence'' standard.[43] The shingle theory has also found its way into state jurisprudence.[44]

A prime incentive for use of state common law theories is the availability of punitive damages for intentional torts. Such damages are not available under federal securities law claims.

---

[42] 105 S. Ct. 2622 (1985).

[43] *Adams* v. *Paine, Webber, Jackson & Curtis, Inc.*, 686 P.2d 797 (Colo. App. 1983).

[44] For example, *Merrill Lynch, Pierce, Fenner & Smith v. Cole*, 189 Conn. 518, 457 A.2d 656 (1983).

Like the SEC, most states register brokers and regulate their activities. An increasing number of states have even added statutory suitability requirements.

QUESTIONS AND PROBLEMS

1. Alstead Dempsey, a brokerage firm, was the principal market maker in Flight Transportation Corp. stock, accounting for 86% of the volume of trading. SEC investigation disclosed that on the basis of the prices Alstead Dempsey paid other dealers for Flight stock it purchased from them just before making sales to customers, it had charged the customers markups in some 80 transactions that ranged from 11.1% to more than 20%. Should Alstead Dempsey be punished for charging "excessive" markups? See *Alstead Dempsey & Co.*, *Security Exchange Act Release*, no. 34–20825 (Securities and Exchange Commission, April 5, 1984).

2. Dean Witter was a market maker in around 1,200 stocks that it marketed aggressively through an "Overnight Offering List" containing a listing of shares in which Dean Witter had substantial inventory. A Dean Witter account executive who sells securities on the Overnight Offering List receives special incentives. A Dean Witter representative recommended to plaintiffs that they purchase 400 shares of Keldon Oil, which plaintiffs did to their ultimate economic detriment. Plaintiffs now sue under Rule 10b-5, alleging that while Dean Witter disclosed that it was a market maker in Keldon shares (as it is required to do under Rule 10b-10), it did not disclose that the special incentives attached to the Overnight Offering List meant that the account executive would receive compensation of $400 on this sale, rather than the usual $46.41. Should this extra compensation have been disclosed? Discuss. See *Shivangi* v. *Dean Witter Reynolds, Inc.*, 107 F.R.D. 303 (S.D.Miss. 1985).

3. The Hatrocks, a young couple with little investment experience, talked to Daugherty, a broker working for Edward D. Jones & Co., which identified itself as a "country broker." By telling the Hatrocks that a "good friend" of his was telling him that a takeover of El Paso Co. was on, then off, then on again, then off again, Daugherty induced the Hatrocks to buy, then sell, then buy again, then sell again El Paso stock. In the final three months of trading, he turned the Hatrocks' account over 6 or 7 times. The Hatrocks lost $36,880 and sued, claiming "churning." Do they have a good claim? Discuss. See *Hatrock* v. *Edward D. Jones & Co.*, 750 F.2d 767 (9th Cir. 1984).

4. In his first six months as an account executive of Thomson McKinnon Securities, Inc., Serhal earned commissions of $2,289. In January 1981, Serhal took personal bankruptcy. Also in that month he was given the $410,000 account of Aldrich, who wished to increase her income through a conservative investment strategy. Serhal had Aldrich sign a blank option trading agreement, which he later completed to inflate her annual income and to characterize her investment objective as short-term trading. In the next ten months, Serhal executed 400 trades in Aldrich's account, with sales and purchases both topping $3,000,000, generating commissions of $143,854 before totally exhausting the account. Although Serhal was later fired,

Thomson McKinnon supervisors had not disciplined him despite his trading frequently in violation of internal guidelines. Aldrich sued Serhal and Thomson McKinnon for "churning." Does she have a good claim? Discuss. See *Aldrich v. Thomson McKinnon Securities, Inc.*, 756 F.2d 243 (2d Cir. 1985).

5. Blinder Robinson, a Colorado broker-dealer, sold penny stocks through a three-call cold-call system. "Cold calls" are calls to persons not known to the sales representatives. Names are frequently gathered from the phone book. In the Blinder system, the first call basically said, "In the past we have had very successful results from our investments, where some of our people have made a lot of money. Can I send you some information?" The second call was basically, "Did you get the information I sent? Nothing exciting has come up yet, but when it does, I'll call you. Our research department is working on something that looks very exciting and as soon as it is put together I will be back to you." The third call, according to the Blinder script, went like this: "I am calling you about a situation that I think is very exciting and would like to discuss it with you now (explanation about company). This stock is trading at _____ and in my opinion this is an excellent speculation. Can you handle 100,000 shares or can you handle more?" Noting that Blinder had no research department, the SEC instituted disciplinary proceedings to punish Blinder under various antifraud provisions, including Rule 10b-5. Discuss. *In the Matter of Blinder, Robinson & Co., Inc., Federal Securities Law Reports* (CCH), ¶83,911 (Securities and Exchange Commission 1985).

6. Woodland Oil & Gas Co. had developed a machine, known as Speed-O-Fax, designed to transmit a facsimile of documents over telephone lines. Woodland had never operated at a profit and had an accumulated deficit of $132,465 as of August 31, 1960 and a net loss of $7,200 for the preceding nine months. Nor had Woodland produced the Speed-O-Fax on a commercial basis. Registrant Alexander Reid & Co.'s salesmen sold 400,000 shares of Woodland in the year following August 31, 1960, making statements that Woodland stock presented a tremendous investment opportunity, that it could double in a short period, should triple in 90 days, and was expected to go "sky high" within a year. The SEC pressed antifraud proceedings, and registrant defended by arguing that its statements merely reflected honest opinions and were presented as such. Discuss. See *In the Matter of Alexander Reid & Co., Inc.*, 40 S.E.C. 986 (1962).

7. Hiller was president of a broker-dealer, Bruce & Co., and a director of Transition Systems, Inc. Bruce & Co. salesmen recommended Transition stock on the basis of extravagant reports of government contracts and active interest in Transition's prospective product by a variety of glamorous potential purchasers. The source of these reports was the brother of one of Transition's principals. Hiller admits that he considered the source unreliable and was totally unable to confirm any of them. However, because his investigation uncovered no facts that specifically negated any of the rumors, he disputes SEC fraud charges on grounds that he and his salesmen had no "reasonable grounds to believe" that the statements made were untrue or misleading. Discuss. See *Hiller v. SEC*, 429 F.2d 856 (2d Cir. 1970).

8. Rothberg entered into a series of joint ventures whereby he provided the financing for joint ventures to engage in illegal insider trading. The illicit information was to come from Sanford and David Rosenbloom. David was providing much of the illicit information, and the Rosenblooms agreed to indemnify Rothberg from loss. One of the deals David predicted on the basis of inside information did not occur, and the joint venture lost money. Rothberg sued on the agreements signed by the Rosenblooms to guarantee him from loss. The Rosenblooms refused to pay, arguing that Rothberg was *in pari delicto* in an illegal scheme. Is this a good defense in light of *Bateman Eichler*? Discuss. See *Rothberg* v. *Rosenbloom*, 628 F.Supp. 746 (E.D.Pa. 1986).

INDEX

774